SIXTH EDITION

Marketing *for* Hospitality *and* Tourism

Philip Kotler

John T. Bowen

James C. Makens

PEARSON

Boston   Columbus   Indianapolis   New York   San Francisco   Upper Saddle River
Amsterdam   Cape Town   Dubai   London   Madrid   Milan   Munich   Paris   Montreal   Toronto
Delhi   Mexico City   São Paulo   Sydney   Hong Kong   Seoul   Singapore   Taipei   Tokyo

Editorial Director: Vernon Anthony
Senior Acquisitions Editor: William Lawrensen
Developmental Editor: Alexis Duffy
Assistant Editor: Dan Trudden
Editorial Assistant: Lara Dimmick
Director of Marketing: David Gesell
Marketing Manager: Stacey Martinez
Marketing Assistant: Les Roberts
Associate Managing Editor: Alexandrina Benedicto Wolf
Project Manager: Kris Roach
Senior Operations Supervisor: Pat Tonneman

Operations Specialist: Deidra Schwartz
Senior Art Director: Diane Ernsberger
Text and Cover Designer: Jason Moore
Cover Art: © ImageState / Alamy
Media Director: Karen Bretz
Full-Service Project Management and Composition: Revathi Viswanathan/PreMediaGlobal
Printer/Binder: RRD/Jefferson City
Cover Printer: Lehigh-Phoenix Color/Hagerstown
Text Font: 9/11 Melior

Library of Congress Cataloging-in-Publication Data
Kotler, Philip.
 Marketing for hospitality and tourism / Philip Kotler John T. Bowen James C. Makens.—Sixth edition.
  pages cm.
 Includes bibliographical references and index.
 ISBN-13: 978-0-13-278402-3
 ISBN-10: 0-13-278402-5
 1. Hospitality industry—Marketing. 2. Tourism--Marketing. I. Bowen, John T. II. Makens, James C. III. Title.
TX911.3.M3K68 2012
338.4'791068—dc23

2012037955

10 9 8 7 6 5 4 3 2 1

ISBN 10:   0-13-278402-5
ISBN 13: 978-0-13-278402-3

This book is dedicated to Nancy, my wife and best friend, with love.

P. K.

With love to my wife, Toni, and children, Casey and Kelly.

J. T. B.

To my wife, Kay.

J. C. M.

Brief Contents

Contents

13 Promoting Products: Communication and Promotion Policy and Advertising   361

14 Promoting Products: Public Relations and Sales Promotion   403

15 Professional Sales   431

16 Direct and Online Marketing: Building Customer Relationships   471

To the Student

Welcome to the sixth edition!

Marketing for Hospitality and Tourism guides you down the intriguing, discovery-laden road to learning marketing. It is our goal to help you master the basic concepts and practices of modern hospitality marketing in an enjoyable and practical way. Achieving this goal involves a constant search for the best balance among the "three pillars" that support the book: theories and concepts, practices and applications, and pedagogy (the art and science of teaching).

The hospitality and travel industry are undergoing rapid changes. The applications you learn today may not apply five years from now. Thus, it is important that you have an understanding of the marketing theories and concepts. This will allow you to analyze future situations and make the proper decisions. Practices and applications are provided to give you examples of how we currently apply the concepts to industry situations. Finally, we have included marketing highlights, opening cases, marginal Internet links to Web pages (e) that illustrate how companies are using the marketing principles covered in the book, written cases, video cases, color illustrations, and other features to make learning about marketing interesting and enjoyable.

Marketing is both an art and science. The art adds some ambiguity to marketing, which makes it difficult for some students. We recommend reading each chapter quickly and then going back and reading it more slowly the second time. This will give you a good understanding of the material in the chapter.

This book has been written with you in mind. The development of each edition has involved students who tell us which illustrations to use, which examples they find interesting, and which ones we should replace when we are writing the newest edition. It is our goal to develop a book that is student friendly and clearly explains and illustrates the application of marketing concepts.

We hope you enjoy *Marketing for Hospitality and Tourism* and we wish you success.

Philip Kotler, John Bowen, and James Makens

■■■ An Indispensable Guide to Successful Marketing in the Hospitality Industry

This book has been written with you in mind—explaining the how and why of everyone's role in marketing. Because customer contact employees are part of our product in hospitality and tourism marketing, marketing is everyone's job. *Marketing for Hospitality and Tourism* gives you an innovative and practical introduction to marketing. Its style and extensive use of examples and illustrations make the book straightforward, easy to read.

■■■ Text Organization

PART I: Understanding the Hospitality and Tourism Marketing Process—Introduces you to the concept of hospitality marketing and its importance.

PART II: Developing Hospitality and Tourism Marketing Opportunities and Strategies—Helps you understand the role of consumer behavior and how it affects the marketing environment.

PART III: Developing the Hospitality and Tourism Marketing Mix—Identifies and explains strategies for promoting products and the various distribution channels.

PART IV: Managing Hospitality and Tourism Marketing—Highlights the latest trends in electronic marketing, destination marketing, and planning for the future.

■■■ Chapter 2 Service Characteristics of Hospitality and Tourism Marketing

Marketing was initially developed in connection with selling physical products, such as cars, steel, and equipment. In Chapter 2 we cover the essence of why hospitality and travel products, which are intangible, have marketing concepts that are different from goods-producing firms. The principles found in Chapter 2 become the foundation for the rest of the book.

Courtesy of TOSHIFUMI KITAMURA/Staff/AFP/Getty Images.

Managers do not control the quality of the product when the product is a service.... The quality of the service is in a precarious state—it is in the hands of the service workers who "produce" and deliver it.
—KARL ALBRECHT

Service Characteristics of Hospitality and Tourism Marketing

Ritz-Carlton: Taking Care of Those Who Take Care of Customers

Ritz-Carlton, a chain of eighty luxury hotels located around the world, is renowned for outstanding service. Ritz-Carlton caters to the top 5 percent of corporate and leisure travelers. The company's credo sets lofty customer service goals: "The Ritz-Carlton Hotel is a place where the genuine care and comfort of our guests is our highest mission. We pledge to provide the finest personal service and facilities for our guest, who will always enjoy a warm, relaxed, yet refined ambience. The Ritz-Carlton experience enlivens the senses, instills well-being, and fulfills even the unexpressed wishes and needs of our guests."[1]

Ritz-Carlton instills a sense of pride in its employees. "You serve," they are told, "but you are not servants." Its motto, "We are Ladies and Gentlemen serving Ladies and Gentlemen," communicates that employees should take pride in who they are and the jobs they perform.

The credo and motto are more than just words on paper. Ritz-Carlton delivers on its promises. In surveys of departing guests, some 95 percent report that they've had a truly memorable experience. In fact, at Ritz-Carlton, exceptional service encounters have become almost commonplace. Take the experiences of Nancy and Harvey Heffner of Manhattan, who stayed at the Ritz-Carlton in Naples, Florida. As reported in the *New York Times*, "The hotel is elegant and beautiful," Mrs. Heffner said, "but more important is the beauty expressed by the staff. They can't do enough to please you." When the couple's son became sick, the hotel staff brought him hot tea with honey at all hours of the night, she said. When Mr. Heffner had to fly home on business for a day and his return flight was delayed, a driver for the hotel waited in the lobby most of the night. Such personal, high-quality service has also made the Ritz-Carlton a favorite among conventioneers. Comments one convention planner, "They not only treat us like kings when we hold our top-level meetings in their hotels, but also we just never get any complaints."[2]

Since its incorporation in 1983, the Ritz-Carlton Hotel Company has received all the major industry awards the hospitality industry and leading consumer organizations can bestow.

Rewards are important, and at Ritz-Carlton, service quality has resulted in high customer retention: More than 90 percent of Ritz-Carlton customers return. Despite its hefty room rate, the chain enjoys a 70 percent occupancy rate, almost nine points above the industry average. Most of the responsibility for keeping guests satisfied falls to Ritz-Carlton's customer-contact employees. Thus the

Objectives

After reading this chapter, you should be able to:

1. Describe a service culture.
2. Identify four service characteristics that affect the marketing of a hospitality or travel product.
3. Explain seven marketing strategies for service businesses.

■■■ Special Features: Connecting to the Real World

Chapter Opening Cases

Each chapter opens with a mini case showing you how actual hospitality and travel companies have successfully applied marketing. The cases help you understand and remember the concepts presented in the chapter. For example, Chapter 1 illustrates how Chipotle created the "Chipotle Experience" to create a loyal following. Learn how Chipotle has used social networking and word of mouth to reduce its promotion cost to 1 percent of sales when the industry average is 4 percent.

Marketing is so basic that it cannot be considered a separate function. It is the whole business seen from the point of view of its final result, that is, from the customer's point of view. . . . Business success is not determined by the producer but by the customer.
—Peter Drucker

Introduction: Marketing for Hospitality and Tourism

Chipotle Mexican Grill

Chipotle opened in 1993 with the goal of serving fresh, gourmet-quality food at reasonable prices. Over 1,200 restaurants and several million burritos later, the goal remains the same.

Chipotle is the dream and creation of Steve Ells. A graduate of the Culinary Institute of America, Steve learned the philosophy and skills of classical French cooking. After graduation, Steve had no intention of opening a business but instead moved to San Francisco where he worked for the renowned Star Restaurant under the direction of Jeremiah Tower.

The many taquerias of San Francisco opened Steve's eyes to opportunity. He watched how the employees handled the lines of customers. Steve then started crunching the numbers napkin.[1] Realizing the profit potential of the restaurant, he decided to open a quick-service Mexican restaurant.

He found an old ice cream parlor near the University of Denver. With the support of his father who invested $85,000 and a real estate broker, he was able to open the first Chipotle, which opened in July 1993.[2]

The principles upon which Chipotle operates are discussed below.

Food with Integrity (FWI): The Cornerstone of Chipotle's Vision

Chipotle sources food that is sustainably raised, has great taste, great nutrition, and great value. When possible they use animals raised without antibiotics, and locally produced produce (ideally organic).[3]

Fresh Ingredients

True to the tradition of French cooking, Steve insists on fresh products—not canned, frozen, or freeze-dried.

Organic, Naturally Raised Foods

With an emphasis on great-tasting food, quality, and simplicity, Steve entered the natural food niche in restaurant operations. The aim was to review each ingredient used in Chipotle and explore the possibility of incorporating as many organic or naturally raised foods as possible.

Objectives

After reading this chapter, you should be able to:

1. Understand the relationships between the world's hospitality and travel industry.
2. Define marketing and outline the steps in the marketing process.
3. Explain the relationships between customer value and satisfaction.
4. Understand why the marketing concept calls for a customer orientation.
5. Understand the concept of the lifetime value of a customer and be able to relate it to customer loyalty and retention.

Boxed Marketing Highlights

The boxed segments introduce you to real people and real industry examples, connecting the chapter material to real life.

| Marketing Highlight | JetBlue Uses Customers as a Credible Source to Deliver Messages: http://www.jetblue.com/experience/ |

13–2 Trying to choose the right airline? There's no need to ask your friends, relatives, or neighbors about their airline experiences or about which airline provides the best service. JetBlue has already done that for you. And it's sharing their stories with you and other travelers in a promotional campaign called "Sincerely, JetBlue." The campaign features a series of offbeat commercials in which actual customers share their JetBlue experiences.

The goal of the campaign is to retain JetBlue's upstart, small airline personality in the face of ambitious expansion plans. JetBlue is now the United States' number-two discount airline, behind Southwest, and it's adding planes and routes at a rapid pace. As it grows, it wants to hang on to the underdog grassroots appeal that's made it successful in the dog-eat-dog airline industry.

Some airlines have built their images through lush, big-budget ad campaigns. Not so for JetBlue. "This brand was created almost entirely on an experience, then on word of mouth about that experience," says the chief creative director at JWT, the New York ad agency that created the "Sincerely, JetBlue" campaign. An executive of the ad agency said that when JetBlue founder and CEO, David Needleman came to us, he said the thing that keeps him up at night is how he can grow the airline and keep the JetBlue experience. The answer: Let the JetBlue faithful themselves give voice to that experience. "Allowing our customers to tell our story will help the airline keep a local, small feel as JetBlue becomes more national in scope," says JetBlue's chief marketing executive.

JetBlue has built a huge infrastructure for breeding and collecting customer stories to use in the "Sincerely" ads. It has erected futuristic JetBlue "story booths" in eighteen cities, where passersby can recount and record their experiences flying on JetBlue. According to one observer, the booths are less like circus tents and more like futuristic spaceships. They're made of high-tech honeycomb mesh

down every irritating detail." But, she continues, "two flights later, I was staring at the same blank piece of paper. You've done nothing wrong and everything more than right, if that's possible." After detailing all the right things the airline does, she mock-laments, "JetBlue, I wanted to not like you, but it can't be done—at all. Sincerely, Melissa McCall, Portland, Oregon."

David Needleman, JetBlue CEO, hands out snacks during a flight. Courtesy of Mark Peterson/Corbis.

In a similar fashion, in other ads: Brian relates how a JetBlue flight attendant dashed from the plane just before takeoff to retrieve a brand-new iPod he'd left in a rental car. Ann recounts that when her JetBlue flight was delayed by a snowstorm, the airline eased the long wait by providing pizza and even a live band. "My three-year-old son was dancing. I was dancing," she remembers. "It was a great time! It made a horrible experience really nice." And the Steins tell about the time they arrived late at night for a family vacation in Florida with their three very tired small children only to learn that their hotel wouldn't take them in. Jason Stein recalls, "Out of nowhere we heard a voice from behind us say, 'Go ahead, take my room.' " His wife Nancy continues: "A superhero in a JetBlue pilot's uniform, who sacrificed his room graciously, saved our night. And we slept like babies. Thank you, JetBlue. Sincerely, Nancy and Jason Stein, Darien, Connecticut."

The tone and crafting of the ads makes them appealing and believable. It's almost like talking to your next-door neighbor, but with colorful, intriguing animations that help bring their stories to life. (Check out all of these stories and others at the JetBlue Web site at http://jetblue.com/expe-

Full-Color Visuals

Color format with lively photographs, drawings, and tables will maintain your interest and provide visual aids to learning.

■■■ Important Memory Tools

Chapter Objectives

At the start of each chapter, the list will help you focus and organize your thoughts as you are reading. The learning objectives summarize what you need to know after studying the chapter and doing the exercises.

Key Terms

Key marketing and hospitality terms, highlighted and defined in each chapter, provide you with a convenient source for learning and reviewing the professional vocabulary needed for effective communication on the job. These terms are found at the end of each chapter, and a glossary of all the terms can be found at the end of the book.

Chapter Review

At the end of each chapter, a summary of chapter content in outline form helps you review and retain key information. The format for the chapter review was the suggestion of a student.

■■■ Applying Your Knowledge

Experiential Exercises

These exercises are designed to provide experiences that will illustrate the concepts presented in the chapter and provide experiences that you can draw on in the future.

Internet Exercises

The Internet has become both an important marketing tool and a source of marketing information. The Internet exercises introduce you to information sources on the Internet and show how others are using the Internet.

■■■ Applying Your Critical Thinking Skills

Case Studies

The case studies at the end of the book represent real situations that can be used to analyze actual business situations and come up with solutions to your organization's problem. Sometimes your instructor will use these cases as the basis of class discussions.

City Location

The southwestern city in which World View was located consisted of approximately 150,000 residents with approximately 30 percent classified as minority. The largest part of the minority population was Mexican Americans. Blacks represented approximately a fourth of the minority group.

The city was heavily represented by a middle class, and although there were lower-income areas, there were surprisingly few areas that could be regarded as slums. This was due to a combination of a good industrial base, good public administration, and a civic pride among the residents. There were four major employers in the area and many smaller ones. The city was corporate headquarters for a company listed on the New York Stock Exchange and one listed on the American Exchange. These were involved in electronics and pharmaceuticals.

The predominant industries in the city were banking-finance, insurance, pharmaceuticals, and electronics. The city also boasted a large medical complex that attracted many patients from outside the area and two universities. The city was located on a major interstate highway and was served by three major airlines and two commuter airlines. Two national hotel chains operated downtown properties, and several chains operated motels along the interstate highway.

Competition

Eleven travel agencies existed in the city. One of these was an in-house agency for the largest employer in town. Consequently, very little direct business was gener-

Discussion Questions

These end-of-chapter questions will challenge you to address real-world situations and consider appropriate methods of action.

Preface

We would like to thank the students and instructors who have used this text in the past. Their support has enabled us to publish the sixth edition of *Marketing for Hospitality and Tourism,* now available in eight languages.

This book is written with the hospitality and travel student in mind. The solicited and unsolicited comments we received from students and instructors have been incorporated into the sixth edition. Students have told us *Marketing for Hospitality and Tourism* is readable and interesting. One student wrote, "I enjoyed reading this book—it didn't seem like I was reading a textbook." In this newest edition we strive to maintain the same tone. We had a team of students read each of the chapters to make sure the concepts presented made sense to them. Additionally, students were involved in the final choice of illustrations for the text to make certain the illustrations were both useful and interesting. For instructors, we made the text flow more smoothly from a teaching perspective.

The authors have extensive experience working with hospitality and travel businesses around the globe. Our understanding of the hospitality and travel business ensures that the end result is a book that clearly explains marketing concepts and shows how they apply to real-life situations.

The book has an international focus, which is especially important in this era of increasing globalization. Business markets have become internationalized—domestic companies are expanding overseas as foreign companies seek to enter U.S. markets—therefore, it is crucial that today's students be exposed to business and cultural examples from other parts of the world. Rather than have one chapter devoted to international marketing, we have incorporated examples throughout the text.

This text has truly evolved as a team project. Without the support of our students and faculty at other universities and colleges, this book would not have developed into the leading book in its category. We thank you for your support and acknowledge below some of the people who have been involved in the development of the book.

■■■ We Welcome Your Comments and Questions

We would like to hear your comments on this edition and your suggestions for future editions. Please address comments to John Bowen, Conrad N. Hilton College of Hotel and Restaurant Management, University of Houston, jbowen@uh.edu.

■■■ Acknowledgments

We would like to thank the students and the instructors who have used earlier editions of this book and provided feedback that added value to the users of this edition. Camille E. Kapoor developed the instructor's materials for the sixth edition. Sarah Robinson, a student at the University of Houston, helped with the research and development of the sixth edition. The following people provided reviews of the fourth edition, which helped shape this edition: Robert J. Kwortnik, Ph.D., Ken McCleary, and Hailin Qu, The following people provided reviews of the sixth edition: Deepak Chhabra, Arizona State University; Dan Creed, Metropolitan State University, St. Paul; Geralyn Farley, Purdue University, Calumet; Jeffrey Ivory, St. Louis Community College, Forest Park; Dianne Jolovich, College of Southern Idaho; Ingrid Lin, University of Hawaii, Honolulu; Juline Mills, University of New Haven; Hailin Qu, Oklahoma State University, Stillwater; and Kisang Ryu, University of New Orleans.

We owe special thanks to a number of people who helped make the first edition possible: Michael Gallo, for his research efforts; Anna Graf Williams and Allen Reich who served as early reviewers; Ming (Michael) Liang for suggesting the chapter review format; and Christa Myers for her help as project manager of the first edition. Thanks also to Carrie Tyler for her research work and for serving as project manager for the second edition. Walter Huertas, Shiang-Lih Chen McCain, Michelle North, and Tracee Nowlak made up the student team for the third edition, and Jason Finehout assisted in the fourth edition.

Thank you to those who reviewed the first edition of the text: Jennifer A. Aldrich, James A. Bardi, Jonathan Barsky, David C. Bojanic, Tim H. Dodd, Rich Howey, C. Gus Katsigris, Ed Knudson, Allen Z. Reich, Howard F. Reichbart, and Anna Graf Williams.

The following reviewers were helpful in guiding us through the revisions in the second edition: Bonnie Canziani, Andy Feinstein, Marvel L. Maunder, Ph.D., H. G. Parsa, Ph.D., Edward B. Pomianoski, CFBE, Emily C. Richardson, CHA, Ralph Tellone, and Gregory R. Wood, Ph.D.

The following reviewers were helpful in guiding us through the revisions in the third edition: Kimberly M. Anderson, Mark Bonn, Harsha E. Chacko, Tim Dodd, Geralyn Farley, Richard M. Howey, Ken McCleary, Joan Remington, John Salazar, Jane Boyland, Juline Mills, and Muzzo Uysal, reviewed the third edition and gave suggestions for the fourth edition.

We appreciate the support and enthusiasm of the companies that provided advertisements and illustrations for this book. These organizations put forth a great deal of effort in finding and providing the materials we requested; working with them was one of the most rewarding parts of producing this book. We would also like to thank Bill Lawrensen, Alexis Duffy, Lara Dimmick, and Kris Roach. Finally, we would like to thank our families for their support and encouragement.

What's New in the Sixth Edition

The overall goal of the revision for the sixth edition of *Marketing for Hospitality and Tourism* is to create a comprehensive, current and engaging book. Where appropriate, new material was added; old material was updated and no longer relevant or necessary material deleted. *Marketing for Hospitality and Tourism* allows those instructors who have used the fifth edition to build on what they have learned and done while at the same time offering a text that is unsurpassed in readability, breadth, depth and relevance for students experiencing *Marketing for Hospitality and Tourism* for the first time. As in past editions we have used feedback from instructors to improve this edition. A student read a draft of this edition and went over material that was not clear to her or hard to understand in one-to-one sessions with a co-author. These sections were rewritten and then tested again with the student. The end result is a text that will engage students and hopefully create a life-long interest in marketing.

Significant Changes to the Sixth Edition Include:

- **Marketing 3.0** In Chapter 1 we introduced the concept of marketing 3.0. Marketing 3.0 holds that instead of treating people simply as consumers, marketers approach them as whole human beings with minds, hearts, and spirits. Increasingly, consumers are looking for solutions to their anxieties about making the world a better place.

- **New Chapter Opening Vignettes** We developed new vignettes and updated those that were still relevant. By covering topical brands or companies, the vignettes are great classroom discussion starters.

- **Marketing Highlights** We updated some marketing highlights and replaced others. The marketing highlights provide examples of applications of the concepts being discussed in the text, making the text more relevant to the student.

- **Cases Studies** We added five new cases, updated others, and removed seven we felt were less relevant in today's marketing environment.

- **Chapter Content** Each chapter was reviewed and updated to provide information that was both current and relevant. The discussion of themes that are important in today's marketing environment, such as sustainability was expanded.

- **New Illustrations** We replaced many illustrations throughout the text, with a focus on illustrating the growth of international tourism.

- **New Slides and Instructor's Manual** The PowerPoint slides and instructor's manual for this edition were created by a master instructor, Camille E. Kapoor. This resource will help instructors have a successful class.

Philip Kotler
John Bowen
James Makens

About the Authors

Philip Kotler is S. C. Johnson & Son Distinguished Professor of International Marketing at the Kellogg School of Management, Northwestern University. He received his master's degree at the University of Chicago and his Ph.D. at MIT, both in economics. Dr. Kotler is author of *Marketing Management* (Prentice Hall), now in its 13th edition and the world's most widely used marketing textbook in graduate schools of business worldwide. He has authored dozens of other successful books and has written more than a hundred articles in leading journals. He is the only three-time winner of the coveted Alpha Kappa Psi award for the best annual article in the *Journal of Marketing.*

Professor Kotler was named the first recipient of two major awards: the Distinguished Marketing Educator of the Year Award given by the American Marketing Association and the Philip Kotler Award for Excellence in Health Care Marketing presented by the Academy for Health Care Services Marketing. His numerous other major honors include the Sales and Marketing Executives International Marketing Educator of the Year Award; The European Association of Marketing Consultants and Trainers Marketing Excellence Award; the Charles Coolidge Parlin Marketing Research Award; and the Paul D. Converse Award, given by the American Marketing Association to honor "outstanding contributions to science in marketing." In a recent *Financial Times* poll of a 1,000 senior executives across the world, Professor Kotler was ranked as the fourth "most influential business writer/guru" of the twenty-first century.

Dr. Kotler has served as chairman of the College on Marketing of the Institute of Management Sciences, a director of the American Marketing Association, and a trustee of the Marketing Science Institute. He has consulted with many major U.S. and international companies in the areas of marketing strategy and planning, marketing organization, and international marketing. He has traveled extensively throughout Europe, Asia, and South America, advising companies and governments about global marketing practices and opportunities.

John T. Bowen is dean of the Conrad N. Hilton College of Hotel and Restaurant Management at the University of Houston and the Barron Hilton Distinguished Chair. Professor Bowen has presented marketing courses and seminars in Asia, Australia, Central America, Europe, and South America. Dr. Bowen is a consultant to both large and small hospitality corporations. Before becoming an academic, Professor Bowen held positions in restaurant management at both the unit and corporate level. Professor Bowen is on the editorial boards of the *Cornell Hotel and Restaurant Administration Quarterly, Journal of Services Marketing,* and *International Journal of Contemporary Hospitality Marketing.* He is coauthor of *Restaurant Marketing for Owners and Managers.* Professor Bowen has received numerous awards for his teaching and research, including the UNLV Foundation Teaching Award, the Sam and Mary Boyd Distinguished Professor Award for Teaching, Founder's Award for Lifetime Support of Hospitality Graduate Education, and the Board of Regents Outstanding Faculty Member. He has been a three-time recipient of the annual award from the International Council on Hotel, Restaurant and Institutional Education (CHRIE) for superior published research in the hospitality industry, and he received the John Wiley Award for Lifetime Research Achievement from CHRIE. Professor Bowen was recently cited as one of the five most influential hospitality management faculty in an article published in the *Journal of Hospitality and Tourism Education.* Dr. Bowen's formal education includes a B.S. in hotel administration from Cornell University, an M.B.A. and an M.S. from Corpus Christi State University, and a Ph.D. in marketing from Texas A&M University.

James C. Makens is actively involved with the travel industry. He has conducted executive training for the Sheraton Corporation, Regent International Hotels, Taiwan Hotel Association, and Travelodge of Australia. He has also conducted marketing seminars for tourism ministries or travel associations in Australia, New Zealand, Canada, Indonesia, Singapore, Malaysia, and many nations of Latin America. Dr. Makens serves as a consultant and has written marketing plans for travel industry companies and tourism promotion boards. Other books he has authored or coauthored include *The Travel Industry* and the *Hotel Sales and Marketing Planbook.* His professional articles have appeared in the *Cornell Hotel and Restaurant Administration Quarterly, Journal of Travel Research, Journal of Marketing, Journal of Marketing Research,* and *Journal of Applied Psychology.* Dr. Makens earned an M.S., an M.B.A., and a Ph.D. from Michigan State University. He holds a B.S. from Colorado State University. He served as associate dean in the School of Travel Industry Management of the University of Hawaii. He was also an associate dean of INCAE, an affiliate of the Harvard Business School in Central America. Dr. Makens recently retired from the faculty at The Babcock Graduate School of Management at Wake Forest University.

Understanding the Hospitality and Tourism Marketing Process

Chipotle

MEXICAN GRILL

Falls Church, VA, USA—August 19, 2011: Chipotle Mexican Grill sign. Chipotle Mexican Grill, Inc. (NYSE: CMG), is a chain of restaurants in the United States, United Kingdom, and Canada specializing in burritos and tacos. The name derives from chipotle, the Mexican Spanish name for a smoked, dried jalapeño chili pepper. The company currently has more than 1,000 locations. Courtesy of Marcnorman/Dreamstime.

Introduction: Marketing for Hospitality and Tourism

Chipotle Mexican Grill

Chipotle opened in 1993 with the goal of serving fresh, gourmet-quality food at reasonable prices. Over 1,200 restaurants and several million burritos later, the goal remains the same.

Chipotle is the dream and creation of Steve Ells. A graduate of the Culinary Institute of America, Steve learned the philosophy and skills of classical French cooking. After graduation, Steve had no intention of opening a business but instead moved to San Francisco where he worked for the renowned Star Restaurant under the direction of Jeremiah Tower.

The many tacquerias of San Francisco opened Steve's eyes to opportunity. He watched how the employees handled the lines of customers. Steve then started crunching the numbers napkin.[1] Realizing the profit potential of the restaurant, he decided to open a quick-service Mexican restaurant.

He found an old ice cream parlor near the University of Denver. With the support of his father who invested $85,000 and a real estate broker, he was able to open the first Chipotle, which opened in July 1993.[2]

The principles upon which Chipotle operates are discussed below.

Food with Integrity (FWI): The Cornerstone of Chipotle's Vision

Chipotle sources food that is sustainably raised, has great taste, great nutrition, and great value. When possible they use animals raised without antibiotics, and locally produced produce (ideally organice).[3]

Fresh Ingredients

True to the tradition of French cooking, Steve insists on fresh products—not canned, frozen, or freeze-dried.

Organic, Naturally Raised Foods

With an emphasis on great-tasting food, quality, and simplicity, Steve entered the natural food niche in restaurant operations. The aim was to review each ingredient used in Chipotle and explore the possibility of incorporating as many organic or naturally raised foods as possible.

In 2001, Chipotle teamed up with Niman Ranch to provide free-range pork for the carnitas used in each restaurant. An additional 200 family farms have since agreed to Chipotle's standards for raising hogs.

Chipotle posters describe how today's corporate agriculture has replaced the practices of family farmers with what Steve described as the "senseless exploitation" of farm animals.

Steve said that dining is about the senses so that when Chipotle makes an emotional appeal, it wins with customers. He believes that once customers know about the Niman Ranch association, some will buy Chipotle because of taste, others because Niman does not use antibiotics, and others to support the family farmers. It doesn't matter to those at Chipotle what the reason might be because all support the cause of providing food with integrity (FWI).

Chipotle requires the chickens it buys be fed an all-vegetarian diet, are not given antibiotics, and be raised in more humane cages than large producers use. Chipotle's size means that it also must buy food from large producers, as well as small ones. Tyson developed a farm just for Chipotle to supplement the smaller growers.[4]

Restaurant Environment

Many Mexican food restaurants look alike with photos of Pancho Villa or other decorations that the public has come to expect as normal. A Chipotle restaurant is different!

The kitchen and food preparation areas are right in front of the customers and were designed to appeal to the senses. Customers observe freshness, cleanliness, and variety at the same time they smell spices and hear the sizzle of meat on the grill. All of this stimulates the appetite and blends the ambience of food preparation with food consumption. The most crowded part of any home during a party always seems to be the kitchen. Steve put this knowledge to work when planning the restaurant.

Instead of settling for serapes on the wall, Steve asked sculptor friend Bruce Gueswel to design artwork appropriate to the environment. This led to a unique line of original artwork and furniture using a variety of materials, including welded steel, corrugated metal, and wood to depict what has been described as modern renditions of ancient Mayan hieroglyphics. Chipotle is the only quick-service restaurant that commissions original art for each location. It's an example of the attention to detail that defines Chipotle.

Chipotle restaurants have been given awards for design by the American Institute of Architects. The style, known as "cantina moderne," employs metals, plywood, concrete, and glass to provide a sophisticated postindustrial feel with exposed duct work and pipes.

Each piece of music played within a Chipotle restaurant was self-selected by a team from Chipotle management. Described as "Funky Cool Groovish," each CD is designed for self-destruction after a set period of time to ensure freshness in the music as well as the food.

Pricing

Unlike most quick-service restaurant chains, Chipotle offers no coupons or specials. At Chipotle all food all the time is either full price or free.

Prices are comparatively reasonable but do vary by the marketplace. A typical crowd in the Denver restaurant included two police officers, young career professionals, and a woman with a baby. Most were dressed in casual attire. Thousands of promotional "bucks" for one free burrito are given away during the year. These are numbered and bear the engraving of a Maya prince with the words "In Burritos We Trust" above the picture and "Vaya Con Tacos" below. Free burrito promotions have proven to be very popular and productive in new markets. From there, word of mouth supported by free publicity in newspapers and magazines serves as the principal means of promotion.

Loyalty

Repeat visits by customers have proven to be very high within Chipotle restaurants. So too has staff loyalty. Chipotle's restaurant and kitchen designs intentionally place crew members up front. Managers encourage restaurant employees to have genuine interactions with customers no matter their job, whether preparing food or serving customers during our busiest period. They focus on attracting and retaining people who can deliver a great experience for each customer. This requires employees give customers individual attention and make every effort to respond to customer suggestions and concerns in a hospitable way. Chipotle feels its focus on creating a positive and interactive experience helps build loyalty and enthusiasm for its brand among restaurant managers, crew members, and customers alike.[5]

Social Networking

Social networks such as youtube.com and myspace.com are a relatively new, yet powerful form of media that many companies are trying to incorporate into their marketing plans. Chipotle has mastered the use of social networks. Several years ago it launched a Facebook page that now has over 1½ million friends. Chipotle offered a $30,000 prize to the universities or college teams that could produce the best Chipotle advertisement. Chipotle received forty-five entries from eighteen colleges and universities. The winners received air time in regional television and movie theaters. But many of the advertisements ended up on youtube.com and myspace.com. Some have received over a million hits. The ads were created by the generation that uses this media and were both an effective and an efficient way for Chipotle to penetrate this media.

This is one of the reasons why Chipotle spends less than 1 percent on advertising, whereas other restaurant chains average 4 percent. Steve Ells states, "Advertising is not believable." Chipotle prefers to create satisfied customers who will go out and tell their friends great things about Chipotle.

Over 1½ million people have given Chipotle's Facebook page a thumbs-up, indicating they like it. One of the characteristics of social media is that the content is authentic. Not everything posted on Chipotle's wall is positive. However, a representative of Chipotle responds to both the positive and negative comments, usually within the hour. Chipotle uses social media to engage its customers.

Steve Ells realized that a successful restaurant had to have a great atmosphere, a good product, effective marketing communications, and talented people in addition to good food. Chipotle created an integrated marketing program that delivers superior value, building customer relationships and delight. Chipotle's customers responded by patronage and advocacy for Chipotle. This is the essence of marketing.[6]

■■■ Your Passport to Success

As a manager in a global economy, marketing will greatly assist your personal career and the success of the enterprise you manage. In today's hospitality/travel industry, the customer is global and is king or queen. This title is bestowed not because of hereditary rights but because customers have the ability to enhance or damage your career through the purchase choices they make and the positive or negative comments they make to others.

The travel industry is the world's largest industry and the most international in nature. International travel has receipts of over $1 trillion and over 1 billion travelers.[7] China's 1.3 billion people take over 2.1 billion domestic trips each year, spending US $237 billion. The rapid growth of domestic tourism in China, combined with over 135 million inbound tourists, has led to a rapid growth of hotels, resorts, airport facilities, and other facilities to support tourism.[8] Thirty years ago there was nothing in Dubai but a creek, a sheik's palace, and a reputation as a smuggling capital of the Arabian Gulf. Today Dubai boasts some of the world's best hotels. One of the tourism projects is DUBAILAND, a US $70 billion tourism complex covering almost 70,000 acres that will include theme parks, resorts, shopping, sports facilities, and cultural venues. Some of the project is complete and attracting visitors; when the entire project is complete, it will attract 15 million visitors a year.[9] When many people think of Dubai, they think of an economy driven by oil. Yet today 30 percent of Dubai's gross domestic product (GDP) comes from travel and tourism.[10] The neighboring city of Abu Dhabi wants to take a slower approach to tourism so it can preserve its Arab culture. It has been building world-class tourist attractions such as Ferrari World theme park and attracting sporting events such as the Volvo Ocean. Its planned approach to tourism growth also includes the Environmental Health and Safety Management System (EHSMS). The goals of this system include reducing landfill waste by 20 percent, water usage by 20 percent, and energy by 10 percent.[11]

The title "The World's Best Airport" is not held by an American or European airport but by Hong Kong, a city with such land scarcity that the new airport was built in the bay on a largely manufactured island. Hong Kong International Airport boasts the world's largest enclosed space, with a terminal eventually capable of handling 87 million visitors per year. The world's best hotel is Jack's Camp in Botswana. Countries that were locations of the top-rated hotels included the Maldives, Italy, Hong Kong, Australia, France, India, and the Seychelles. The best international airline is Qatar Airlines.[12]

The world's travel industry is alive, exciting, and challenging. Hospitality companies and tourism planning/promotion departments are filled with college graduates from across the globe. Competition is strong and getting tougher each day. Yet opportunities are greater than ever before.

Welcome to marketing! Your passport to success!

Today marketing isn't simply a business function: It's a philosophy, a way of thinking, and a way of structuring your business and your mind. Marketing is much more than a new ad campaign. The task of marketing is never to fool the customer or endanger the company's image. Marketing's task is to provide real value to targeted customers, motivate purchase, and fulfill consumer needs.

Marketing, more than any other business function, deals with customers. Creating customer value and satisfaction is at the heart of hospitality and travel industry marketing. Many factors contribute to making a business successful. However, today's successful companies at all levels have one thing in common: They are strongly customer focused and heavily committed to marketing. Accor has become one of the world's largest hotel chains by delivering L'esprit Accor, the ability to anticipate and meet the needs of its guests, with genuine attention to detail.[13] Ritz-Carlton promises and delivers truly "memorable experiences" for its hotels' guests. McDonald's grew into the world's largest restaurant chain by providing its guests with QSC&V (quality, service, cleanliness, and value). These and other successful hospitality companies know that if they take care of their customers, market share and profits will follow.

e **1.1** http://www. oberoihotels.com/ Go to the Udaivilas, by selecting it from the leisure hotels button at the top of the page. Notice how the quality and selection of the photographs establishes the image of a world-class hotel.

The Oberoi Udaivilas, in Udaipur, India, was chosen as the world's best hotel by *Travel and Leisure* magazine. Courtesy of Robert Harding Picture Library Ltd/Alamy.

As a manager, you will be motivating your employees to create superior value for your customers. You will want to make sure that you deliver customer satisfaction at a profit. This is the simplest definition of marketing. This book will start you on a journey that will cause your customers to embrace you and make marketing your management philosophy.

■■■ Customer Orientation

The **purpose of a business** is to create and maintain satisfied, profitable customers.[14] Customers are attracted and retained when their needs are met. Not only do they return to the same cruise line, hotel, rental car firm, and restaurant, but they also talk favorably to others about their satisfaction.

"What about profits?" Some hospitality managers act as if today's profits are primary and customer satisfaction is secondary. This attitude eventually sinks a firm as it finds fewer repeat customers and faces increasingly negative word of mouth. Successful managers understand that profits are best seen as the result of running a business well rather than as its sole purpose. When a business satisfies its customers, the customers will pay a fair price for the product. A fair price includes a profit for the firm.

Managers who forever try to maximize short-run profits are short-selling both the customer and the company. Consider the following episode:

> A customer arrived at a restaurant before closing time and was greeted with "What do you want?" Somewhat surprised, the customer replied that he would like to get a bite to eat. A surly voice informed the customer that the restaurant was closed. At this point, the customer pointed to a sign on the door stating that the restaurant was open until 9 P.M. "Yeah, but by the time I clean up and put the food away, it'll be nine, so we're closed." The customer left and went to another restaurant a block away and never returned to the first restaurant.

Let's speculate for a moment. Why was the customer treated in such a shabby manner? Perhaps,

- the employee wanted to leave early.
- the employee was suffering from a headache.
- the employee had personal or family problems.

What really happened in the restaurant episode is that this employee once served a customer immediately before closing time, resulting in the employee working until 10:30 P.M. Instead of the corporate office thanking her for serving the customer and staying late, it reprimanded her for putting in extra time. The corporate office wanted to keep down overtime expenses. The employee's response was to close the business by 9 P.M. whatever the cost. Now the corporate office is happy—they just don't realize they are losing customers and future business. Much of the behavior of employees toward their customers is the result of management philosophy.

The alternative management approach is to put the customer first and reward employees for serving the customer well. Marriott's vice president of sales and marketing services said, "We used to reward restaurant managers for things that were important to us, such as food costs. When have you heard a customer ask for the restaurant's food costs? You have to reward for what customers want from your business."[15]

It is wise to assess the customer's long-term value and take appropriate actions to ensure a customer's long-term support. Two studies document this. The Forum Company found that the cost of retaining a loyal customer is just 20 percent of the cost of attracting a new one.[16] Another study found that an increase of five

Cruise ships have traditionally been competition for resorts. The Disney Fantasy and other Disney ships, complement Disney's resorts drawing on the Disney brand to create additional value for their guests. Courtesy of Jonathan Atkin/Sipa USA/Newscom.

percentage points in customer retention rates yielded a profit increase of 25 to 125 percent.[17] Accordingly, a hotel that can increase its repeat customers from 35 to 40 percent should gain at least an additional 25 percent in profits.[18] The former president of Scandinavian Airlines summed up the importance of a satisfied customer:

> Look at our balance sheet. On the asset side, you can still see so-and-so many aircraft worth so-and-so many billions. But it's wrong; we are fooling ourselves. What we should put on the asset side is the last year SAS carried so-and-so many happy passengers. Because that's the only asset we've got—people who are happy with our service and willing to come back and pay for it once again.[19]

Without customers, assets have little value. Without customers, a new multi-million-dollar restaurant will close, and without customers, a $300 million hotel will go into receivership, with the receivers selling the hotel at a fraction of its book value.

Starbucks Coffee has created customer loyalty, allowing it to open shops around the world. In this photo, Starbucks customers sit in a café in Bucharest, Romania. Courtesy of Dudau/Dreamstime.

■■■ What Is Hospitality and Tourism Marketing?

In the hotel industry, marketing and sales are often thought to be the same, and no wonder: The sales department is one of the most visible in the hotel. Sales managers provide prospective clients with tours and entertain them in the hotel's food and beverage outlets. Thus the sales function is highly visible, whereas most of the nonpromotional areas of the marketing function take place behind closed doors. In the restaurant industry, many people confuse marketing with advertising and sales promotion. It is not uncommon to hear restaurant managers say that they "do not believe in marketing" when they actually mean that they are disappointed with the impact of their advertising. In reality, selling and advertising are only two marketing functions and often not the most important. Advertising and sales are components of the promotional element of the **marketing mix**. Other marketing mix elements include product, price, and distribution. Marketing also includes research, information systems, and planning.

The four-P framework calls on marketing professionals to decide on the product and its characteristics, set the price, decide how to distribute their product, and choose methods for promoting their product. For example, McDonald's has a fast-food product. It uses quality ingredients and developed products that it can sell at prices people expect to pay for fast food. Most people will not spend more than 15 minutes to travel to a McDonald's restaurant. As part of its distribution plan, McDonald's must have restaurants that are conveniently located to its target market. Finally, McDonald's appeals to different market segments and has many units throughout a city. This allows McDonald's to make effective use of mass media, such as television. The marketing mix must be just that—a mix of ingredients to create an effective product/service package for the target market. Some critics feel the four Ps omit or underemphasize certain important activities.

If marketers do a good job of identifying consumer needs, developing a good product, and pricing, distributing, and promoting it effectively, the result will be attractive products and satisfied customers. Marriott developed its Courtyard concept; Darden designed the Olive Garden Italian Restaurant. They designed differentiated products, offering new consumer benefits. Marketing means "hitting the mark." Peter Drucker, a leading management thinker, put it this way: "The aim of marketing is to make selling superfluous. The aim is to know and understand customers so well that the product or service fits them and sells itself."[20]

This does not mean that selling and promotion are unimportant, but rather that they are part of a larger marketing mix, a set of marketing tools that work together to produce satisfied customers. The only way selling and promoting will be effective is if we first define customer targets and needs and then prepare an easily accessible and available value package.

Companies such as Sonic have brought strong marketing skills to the restaurant industry. Courtesy of Andrew Woodley/ Alamy.

■■■ Marketing in the Hospitality Industry

Importance of Marketing

As we have seen, the **hospitality industry** is one of the world's major industries. In the United States, it is the second largest employer. In more than half of the fifty states, it is the largest industry. In this book we focus on the hospitality and travel industries.

Marketing has assumed an increasingly important role in the restaurant sector of the hospitality industry. The entrance of corporate giants into the hospitality market transformed it from a mom-and-pop industry, where individually owned restaurants and hotels were the norm, to an industry dominated by chains. These chains operate in a highly competitive environment where aggressive marketing skills are used to win customers. Twenty-four companies now account for over a third of all restaurants in the United States. McDonald's leads the restaurant group, with over 30,000 restaurants in 119 countries serving 52 million customers each day.

The hotel industry is undergoing a consolidation, with companies such as Accor, Blackstone, and Starwood buying hotel chains and operating different brands under one organization. The marketing expertise of these large firms has created a competitive marketing environment. In response to growing competitive pressures, hotel chains are relying more on the expertise of the marketing director. While the marketing director is a full-time marketer, everyone else must be a part-time marketer. All managers must understand marketing.

Tourism Marketing

Visitors to international destinations, such as these tourists on the Brazilian side of Iguacu Falls, often purchase packages that include international airfare, ground transportation, and hotel accommodations. Courtesy of Demetrio Carrasco © Dorling Kindersley.

The two main industries that comprise the activities we call tourism are the hospitality and travel industries. Thus, throughout this book we refer to the hospitality and travel industries. Successful hospitality marketing is highly dependent on the entire travel industry. Meeting planners choose destinations based on the cost of getting to the destination, the value of the hotels, the quality of restaurants, and evening activities for their attendees.

The success of cruise lines is really the result of coordinated marketing by many travel industry members. For example, the Port of Boston wanted to attract more cruise line business. Massport (the port authority) aggressively marketed Boston to cruise lines. Having convinced them to come, they then promoted Boston to key travel agents. This was critical because travel agents account for 95 percent of all cruise line business. The result was that Boston doubled the number of port calls by cruise lines and added $17.3 million to the local economy through this combined marketing effort.

That's only the beginning of travel industry marketing cooperation to promote cruise lines. Airlines, auto rental firms, and passenger railways cooperatively develop packages with cruise lines. This requires coordination in pricing, promotion, and delivery of those packages. Like Massport, government or quasi-government agencies play an important role through legislation aimed at enhancing the industry and through promotion of regions, states, and nations.[21]

Marketing Highlight

1–1 As the guest's taxi pulled away, Roy Dyment, a doorman at Toronto's Four Seasons, noticed the guest's briefcase still sitting near the entrance to the hotel. Dyment phoned the guest in Washington, D.C., to let him know that he had found the briefcase. He learned that the briefcase contained key documents for an important meeting in the morning. Dyment knew one sure way of getting the briefcase to Washington before the morning meeting—take it himself. He caught a plane and delivered the briefcase. His first concern was taking care of the guest. He didn't worry about getting his boss's approval. Upon his return, instead of getting reprimanded or terminated, he was made employee of the year. Four Seasons is one of the world's great hotel chains that practice the marketing concept. Isadore Sharp, founder and chairman of Four Seasons Hotels and Resorts, states that the company's top priority is a satisfied guest. Concern for the customer starts with top management and flows through the operation. Four Season's corporate culture encourages employees to go that extra mile and respond with concern and dedication to customer needs. Employees are never penalized for trying to serve the customer.

According to a study by Peat Marwick McClintock, Four Seasons is an oddity because many hotel firms place profitability or growth as their number one goal. This, in part, explains why this hotel company has won an international reputation for customer service. Four Seasons has also shown that putting the customer first leads to profits with above-average financial performance and profit percentages that many hotel chains only dream about.

Sources: Patricia Sellers, "Getting Customers to Love You," *Fortune* (March 3, 1989): 38–41; Isadore Sharp, "Quality for All Seasons," *Canadian Business Review,* 17, no. 1 (spring 1990): 21–23: Four Seasons Hotels and Resorts Web site, accessed July 11, 2011, from http://www.fourseasons.com/about_us/corporate_bios/isadore_sharp/.

Few industries are as interdependent as travel–hospitality. This interdependence will increase in complexity. The travel industry will require marketing professionals who understand the big picture and can respond to changing consumer needs through creative strategies based on solid marketing knowledge.

Definition of Marketing

Marketing must be understood in the sense of satisfying customer needs. If the marketer understands customer needs; develops products that provide superior customer value; and prices, distributes, and promotes them effectively, these products will sell easily. Here is our definition of **marketing**: Marketing is the process by which companies create value for customers and society, resulting in strong customer relationships that capture value from the customers in return.

Figure 1–1
A simple model of the marketing process.

The Marketing Process

Figure 1–1 presents a simple five-step model of the marketing process. In the first four steps, companies work to understand consumers, create customer value, and build strong customer relationships. In the final step, companies reap the rewards of creating superior customer value. By creating value for customers, they in turn capture value from customers in the form of sales, profits, and long-term customer equity.

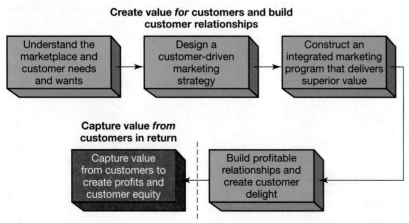

Create value *for* customers and build customer relationships

Understand the marketplace and customer needs and wants → Design a customer-driven marketing strategy → Construct an integrated marketing program that delivers superior value

Capture value *from* customers in return

Capture value from customers to create profits and customer equity ← Build profitable relationships and create customer delight

▪■■ Understanding the Marketplace and Customer Needs

As a first step, marketers need to understand customer needs and wants and the marketplace within which they operate. We now examine five core customer and marketplace concepts: (1) needs, wants, and demands; (2) marketing offerings (tangible products, services, and experiences); (3) value and satisfaction; (4) exchanges and relationships; and (5) markets.

Customer Needs, Wants, and Demands

Needs

The most basic concept underlying marketing is that of **human needs**. A human need is a state of felt deprivation. Included are the basic physical needs for food, clothing, warmth, and safety, as well as social needs for belonging, affection, fun, and relaxation. There are esteem needs for prestige, recognition, and fame, and individual needs for knowledge and self-expression. These needs were not invented by marketers, but they are part of the human makeup.

Wants

The second basic concept to marketing is that of **human wants**, the form human needs take as they are shaped by culture and individual personality. Wants are how people communicate their needs. A hungry person in Papua New Guinea needs food but wants taro, rice, yams, and pork. A hungry person in the United States needs food but wants a hamburger, french fries, and a Coke. Wants are described in terms of objectives that will satisfy needs. As a society evolves, the wants of its members expand. As people are exposed to more objectives that arouse their interest and desire, producers try to provide more want-satisfying products and services. Restaurants were once able to serve generic white wine by the glass. Today, customers are more sophisticated; restaurants now serve chardonnay, sauvignon blanc, and pinot grigio by the glass. Today's restaurant customers want and expect a good selection of wine.

The $625 billion U.S. restaurant industry is facing a dramatic shift in the way customers purchase meals. Many customers want the restaurant to prepare the meal, but they want to eat it in their own home. Well over half the meals purchased at the nation's 960,000 restaurants are "takeouts" to be eaten at home, the office, in the car, or other locations.[22]

This dramatic change in eating habits has caused some restaurants to change their delivery and even food preparation area. Most U.S. restaurants must be cognizant of this trend and plan for it. In 1955 about 25 percent of the money Americans spent for food was in restaurants, but in 2010 it was 49 percent.

Many sellers often confuse wants with needs. A manufacturer of drill bits may think that customers need a drill bit, but what the customer really needs is a hole. These sellers suffer from "marketing myopia."[23] They are so taken with their products that they focus only on existing wants and lose sight of underlying customer needs. They forget that a physical product is only a tool to solve a consumer problem. These sellers get into trouble if a new product comes along that serves the need better or cheaper. The customer will then have the same need but want a new product.

Demands

People have almost unlimited wants, but limited resources. They choose products that produce the most satisfaction for their money. When backed by buying power, wants become **demands**.

Outstanding marketing organizations go to great lengths to learn about and understand their customer's needs, wants and demands. They conduct customer research. Smart companies also have employees at all levels—including top management—stay close to customers. For example, at Southwest Airlines, all senior executives handle bags, check in passengers, and serve as flight attendants once a quarter. All Disney World managers spend one week per year on the front line—taking tickets, selling popcorn, or loading and unloading rides. Understanding customer needs, wants, and demands in detail provides important input for designing marketing strategies. The city of Santa Fe, New Mexico, has a beautiful and historic opera house, but only a small percentage of the population participated in operas. As Catherine Zacher, president of Sante Fe Economic Development, Inc., said, "Most Americans don't enjoy being yelled at in Italian." However, they did want other forms of entertainment. When the opera house was made available for a variety of musical concerts, the demand created for this contemporary entertainment sold all available seats.[24]

1.2 http://www.fourseasons.com/ Click on the Careers tab at the bottom of the page. If you desired a job with Four Seasons, how would the information in this section help you market yourself to Four Seasons?

Market Offerings: Tangible Products, Services, and Experiences

Consumer needs and wants are fulfilled through a market offering: a product that is some combination of tangible, services, information, or experiential product components. We often associate the word *product* with a tangible product or one that has physical properties (e.g., the hotel room or the steak we receive in a restaurant). In the hospitality industry, the intangible products including customer service and experiences are more important than the tangible products. Managers of resorts realize that their guests will be leaving with memories of their stay. They try to create experiences that will generate pleasant memories. At a Ritz-Carlton resort every evening at sunset managers set up chairs on the beach, hire a cellist to play relaxing music, and serve champagne to guests. They realize this event not only creates value for the guest, but it is also an experience that will create a lasting memory of their stay. Marriott provides Dolphin safaris at its Newport Beach property and a water rafting trip at its Utah property. Marriott uses the resources of the destination to create guest experiences that the guest remembers for a lifetime.

Non-U.S. airlines have created a new level of luxury market offering for first-class passengers. Both Lufthansa and Air France created a personalized first-class service above regular first class. Personalized first-class passengers at Frankfurt can arrive at the airport early and enjoy a gourmet meal and a private meeting with business associates in a separate facility. They can enjoy a bubble bath, smoke a cigar, and be driven directly to the airplane in a Mercedes or Porsche and board the plane through a separate staircase. This personalized service proved so popular that first-class ticket sales increased more than 40 percent.[25]

A market offering includes much more than just physical goods or services. Consumers decide which events to experience, which tourist destinations to visit, which hotels to stay in, and which restaurants to patronize. To the consumer these are all products.

The Gamboa Rainforest Resort offers an experience of a lifetime, allowing guests to explore Panama's rainforest and then relax at the resort enjoying a meal while watching ships traverse the Panama Canal. Courtesy of Bern Hotels and Resorts.

Customer Value and Satisfaction

Customer value is the difference between the benefits that the customer gains from owning and/or using a product and the costs of obtaining the product. Costs can be both monetary and nonmonetary. One of the biggest nonmonetary costs for hospitality customers is time. Luxury hotels in Hong Kong such as the Shangri-La do not expect "executive guests" to stand in line to register. Instead, they are escorted to their room where hot tea is waiting. The

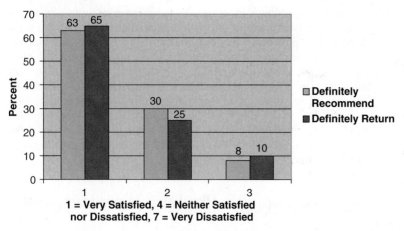

1 = Very Satisfied, 4 = Neither Satisfied
nor Dissatisfied, 7 = Very Dissatisfied

**Even though 3 is still a "positive" score on the above
7-point scale, few customers giving that rating will return.**

Figure 1–2
Scores of 1, 2, and 3 are all on the satisfaction side of the scale; that is, they are all better than a score of 4, which is "neither satisfied nor dissatisfied." You can see that satisfying the guest is not enough. Only when guests leave very satisfied are they likely to come back. As a manager, your goal is to have all guests leave very satisfied.

registration is completed for guests by the hostess. Domino's Pizza saves the customer time and provides convenience by delivering pizza. Limited-service hotels provide value to the overnight traveler by offering a free continental breakfast. One of the biggest challenges for management is to increase the value of its product for its target market. To do this, managers must know their customers and understand what creates value for them. This is an ongoing process, as customers and competition change over time.

Customer expectations are based on past buying experiences, the opinions of friends, and market information. If we meet customer expectations, they are satisfied. Marketers must be careful to set the right level of expectations. If they set expectations too low, they may satisfy those who buy but fail to attract new customers. If they raise expectations too high, buyers will be disappointed.

In the hospitality industry it is easy to set high expectations because guests will not be able to judge the product until after they have consumed it. For example, an owner can advertise that his or her restaurant serves the best seafood in the city. If this is not true, many customers will leave dissatisfied; the experience did not meet their expectations. However, if one sets expectations too low, there will be no customer demand. For example, we would not want to advertise that we are an average seafood restaurant. We must understand how we create value for our market and communicate that to our customers and potential customers. For example, we might specialize in fresh locally caught seafood. Customer satisfaction depends on a product's perceived performance in delivering value relative to a buyer's expectations. If the product's performance falls short of the customer's expectations, the buyer is dissatisfied. If performance matches expectations, the buyer is satisfied. If performance exceeds expectations, the buyer is delighted. Smart companies aim to delight customers by promising only what they can deliver and then delivering more than they promise.

Managers must realize the importance of creating highly satisfied customers, rather than just satisfied customers. On a 7-point scale, with 1 very satisfied and 7 very dissatisfied, most managers are happy to receive a 2. However, from Figure 1–2, which shows the results of a guest survey at a Boston hotel,[26] you can see the huge gap between a guest who rates a hotel a 1 and one who rates it a 2. Think of the last time you went to a restaurant and were just satisfied. Would you go back? Probably not. But when you walk out of a restaurant and say, "Wow, that was great!" you will probably return and tell others about your discovery.

Exchanges and Relationships

Marketing occurs when people decide to satisfy needs and wants through exchange. **Exchange** is the act of obtaining a desired object from someone by offering something in return. Marketing consists of actions taken to build and maintain desirable exchange relationships with target markets. Beyond simply attracting new customers and creating **transactions**, the goal is to retain customers and grow their business with the company. Marketers want to build strong relationships by consistently delivering superior customer value.

Markets

The concept of transactions leads to the concept of a market. A **market** is a set of actual and potential buyers of a product. These buyers share a particular need or want that can be satisfied through exchange relationships.

Marketing means managing markets to bring about profitable customer relationships. However, creating these relationships takes work. Sellers must search for buyers, identify their needs, design good market offerings, set prices for them, promote them, and deliver them. Activities such as product development, research, communication, distribution, pricing, and service are core marketing activities.

■■■ Designing Customer-Driven Marketing Strategy

Once it fully understands consumers and the marketplace, marketing management can design a customer-driven marketing strategy. We define **marketing management** as the art and science of choosing target markets and building profitable relationships with them. The **marketing manager**'s aim is to find, attract, keep, and grow target customers by creating, delivering, and communicating superior customer value. To design a winning marketing strategy, the marketing manager must answer two important questions: What customers will we serve (what's our target market)? and How can we serve these customers best (what's our value proposition)?

Selecting Customers to Serve

One way Olive Garden Italian Restaurants differentiates itself is by freshly grating cheese for the guest. Courtesy of Jeff Greenberg/Alamy Images.

The company must first decide who it will serve. It does this by dividing the market into segments of customers (market segmentation) and selecting which segments it will go after (target marketing). Some people think of marketing management as finding as many customers as possible and increasing demand. But marketing managers know that they cannot serve all customers in every way. By trying to serve all customers, they may not serve any customers well. Instead, the company wants to select only customers that it can serve well and profitably. For example, Ritz-Carlton Hotels profitably target affluent travelers; McDonald's restaurants profitably target families.

Choosing a Value Proposition

The company must also decide how it will serve targeted customers—how it will differentiate and position itself in the marketplace. A company's **value proposition** is the set of benefits or values it promises to deliver to consumers to satisfy their needs.

Such value propositions differentiate one brand from another. They answer the customer's question, "Why should I buy your brand rather than a competitor's?" Companies must design strong value propositions that give them the greatest advantage in their target markets.

Marketing Management Orientations

Marketing management wants to design strategies that will build profitable relationships with target consumers. But what philosophy should guide these marketing strategies? What weight should be given to the interests of customers, the organization, and society? Often, these interests conflict with each other. There are five alternative concepts under which organizations design and carry out their marketing strategies: production, product, selling, marketing, and marketing 3.0.

The Production Concept

The production concept is one of the oldest philosophies guiding sellers. The **production concept** holds that consumers will favor products that are available and highly affordable, and therefore management should focus on production and distribution efficiency. The problem with the production concept is that management may become so focused on production systems that they forget the customer.

A visitor was staying at a hotel in the Swiss Alps with a beautiful view of Lake Geneva. The dining room had an outdoor balcony to experience the beauty of the surroundings. Enjoying breakfast on the balcony was a perfect way to start a summer day. To the guest, the balcony was a great benefit; to the hotel, it was a nuisance. The balcony was at the edge of the dining room and thus the farthest spot from the kitchen. There were no service stations near the balcony, so all supplies had to come from the dining room. There was only one entrance to the balcony, making access difficult. Simply put, serving customers on the balcony was not efficient.

The hotel discouraged customers from eating on the balcony by not setting up the tables. If one asked to eat on the balcony, he or she received a pained expression from the service person. One then had to wait 15 minutes for the table to be set. Once the food was served, the service person disappeared, never to be seen again. This was the hotel's way of reminding the guest that no one should eat on the balcony. Yet the hotel should have viewed the balcony as providing a competitive advantage.

Every reader has surely experienced a common production-oriented restaurant after normal dining hours. The restaurant may be a third filled, yet all customers are forced to cluster in one section of the restaurant, thus creating unnecessary density and customer dissatisfaction. This is usually done to facilitate cleaning or to enable the wait staff to provide service with a minimum of walking.

Unionization of service staff is another reason for a production mentality. Hospitality workers who are unionized tend to work in accordance with union work rules, which often conflict with customer needs.

1.3 http://www. myswitzerland.com/ Switzerland attracts people who love the outdoors. Hospitality companies need to understand why tourists are visiting their destination, and then meet or exceed their expectations.

The Product Concept

The **product concept**, like the production concept, has an inward focus. The product concept holds that consumers will favor products that offer the most in quality, performance, and innovative features. Under this concept, marketing strategy focuses on making continuous product improvements.

Product quality and improvement are important parts of most marketing strategies. However, focusing only on the company's products can lead to marketing myopia. Consumers are trying to satisfy needs and might turn to entirely different products to better satisfy those needs, such as B&Bs instead of hotels or fast-food outlets in student centers instead of cafeterias.

Victoria Station was a restaurant chain that specialized in excellent prime rib. It was very successful and expanded quickly into a fifty-restaurant chain. Management focused on how to make its product better and at a lower cost. It came up with the right number of days to age its beef. The rib roasts were slow cooked to maintain the juices and avoid shrinkage. It had an excellent product and became a popular restaurant brand. Unfortunately, customer wants changed; red meat became less popular. Victoria Station did not keep up with these changes in the wants of its guests. It still produced great prime rib, but many of its customers no longer wanted prime rib. Victoria Station had a product orientation when it should have had a marketing orientation. Its customer counts declined, and it ended up filing for bankruptcy.

The Selling Concept

The **selling concept** holds that consumers will not buy enough of the organization's products unless the organization undertakes a large selling and promotion effort. The aim of a selling focus is to get every possible sale, not to worry about satisfaction after the sale or the revenue contribution of the sale.

The selling concept does not establish a long-term relationship with the customer because the focus is on getting rid of what one has rather than creating a product to meet the needs of the market. Restaurants often advertise when sales start to drop, without first analyzing why sales are dropping. They do not try to change their product to fit the changing market. They sell harder, pushing their products on the customer through increased advertising and couponing. Eventually, they go out of business because their product no longer satisfies the needs of the marketplace.

The selling concept exists within the hospitality industry. A major contributing factor is overcapacity. Virtually every major sector of this industry has suffered from overcapacity. When owners and top management face overcapacity, the tendency is to sell, sell, sell. Why do major sectors such as hotels, resorts, airlines, cruise lines, and even restaurants continuously face overcapacity?

- Pride in being the biggest, having the most capacity.

- A false belief that economies of scale will occur as size increases.

- Tax laws that encourage real estate developers to overbuild properties because of the generous tax write-offs.

- New technology, such as new products from aircraft manufacturers that offer higher productivity through larger seating capacity despite adequate existing capacity.

- Failure to merge revenue management with sales/marketing management.

- Economic incentives by governments to build a larger tourism/hospitality infrastructure to create economic growth.

- Poor or nonexistent forecasting and planning by owners, consultants, financial organizations, and governments.

The Marketing Concept

The **marketing concept** is a more recent business philosophy and one that has been adopted in the hospitality industry. The marketing concept holds that achieving organizational goals depends on determining the needs and wants of target markets and delivering the desired satisfaction more effectively and efficiently than competitors.

Amazingly, niche opportunities sometimes remain available long after suppliers recognize the need. This is probably due to difficulties in changing the behavior of those who supply the products, such as the wait staff in a restaurant. The American Association of Retired Persons (AARP) conducted a survey of readers of its magazine, *Modern Maturity*. Fifty-nine percent replied that they frequently ate in a restaurant alone; another 18 percent replied that they sometimes did. Eighty-four percent replied that the service they receive is worse than if they had other people at the table. Some restaurants have established special seating areas for singles with round tables that encourage single diners to sit together. This provides an opportunity for the diners to engage in conversation with other diners and allows the restaurant to conserve seating space. Other restaurants have deuces that face each other, again encouraging conversation if it is desired. These restaurants value the single diner and have built up a profitable segment. But many restaurants still continue to provide subpar service to people who dine alone.[27] The marketing concept starts with a well-defined market, focuses on customer needs, and integrates all the marketing activities that affect customers. It meets the organizational goals by creating long-term customer relationships based on customer value and satisfaction. As Herb Kelleher, former CEO of Southwest Airlines, stated, "We don't have a Marketing department: we have a Customer department" (Figure 1–3).

e **1.4**   http://www.swamedia.com/If you browse through the photos and videos on the Web site, you will get a sense of the importance of employees at Southwest Airlines.

Figure 1–3
The selling and marketing concepts contrasted.

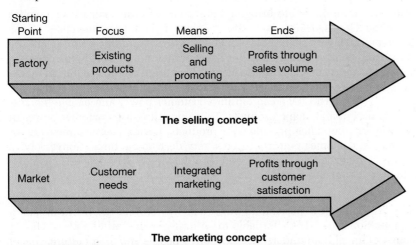

The selling concept

The marketing concept

Marketing 3.0

Marketing 3.0 is concept developed by Philip Kotler, Hermawan Kartajaya, and Iwan Setiawan.[28] Marketing 3.0 holds that instead of treating people simply as consumers, marketers approach them as whole human beings with minds, hearts, and spirits. Increasingly, consumers are looking for solutions to their anxieties about making the world a better place. Missionary tourism is growing, so are farmer markets to support local producers of food products. Sustainable hotel rooms sell at a premium price and hotel guests willingly reuse towels.

Customers are no longer passive or isolated from other customers. TripAdvisor is a powerful tool consumers use to choose hotels or restaurants based on reviews of other customers. A customer who has received poor service can go to TripAdvisor and release his or her frustration.

To understand marketing 3.0 better, let us examine three major forces that shape the business landscape toward marketing 3.0: the age of participation and collaboration, the age of globalization, and the age of creative society. These three major forces cause consumers to be more collaborative, cultural, and human spirit driven. These forces are both growing and enduring. We feel marketing concept will evolve into marketing 3.0. Smart managers will start making the transition to marketing 3.0.

PARTICIPATION AND COLLABORATION   Social media has enabled customers to participate and collaborate with each other and companies. JetBlue celebrated its 10th anniversary by traveling around the east coast and giving away hundreds of free round-trip tickets. In order to get a ticket, you had to show up a specific location with a specific gift for JetBlue. At one location it was a birthday card; at another location it was a piece of blue clothing. The locations were tweeted to people who followed a hashtag "10JB" with an abbreviation of the city, so New York was #JB10NY. JetBlue was able to mobilize thousands of fans through the dialogue the fans created with as a result of their excitement over the chance to get free airline tickets.[29] This was a brilliant campaign by JetBlue that created publicity and customer goodwill. JetBlue's loyal customers who followed it on social media made this promotion possible. What a fun and interactive way to celebrate JetBlue's 10th anniversary.

Social media is not always positive. Dave Carroll created a song, "United Breaks Guitars," after baggage handlers broke his guitar and no one at United Airlines seemed to be concerned. He posted his song on YouTube and within two years he had over 10 million hits. Two years later viewers who saw the video for the first time were commenting they would never fly United again. No one will ever know the amount of business United lost because some baggage handlers did not respect a customer's property. Today when a company fails to treat customers as whole human beings with minds and spirits, customers have the ability to make their case public, where it can go viral. This creates a greater need for marketers to make sure they treat customers with respect and work to resolve their problems.

Employee communities are bringing employees of multinational companies together. Hilton Hotels, H360, Web site connects Hilton team members across the globe. Team members share best practices and Hilton builds a strong culture amongst its team members. Team members also participate in worldwide contests, showing their outcomes through photos and videos posted on the site. Social media is changing how people communicate, participate, and collaborate. The customer has become very powerful. One can tap into customer power and enable the customer to help design and shape products. These practices use customer power in a positive way. If companies provide poor products, have no service recovery, or abuse customers, customer power will be a very destructive force. Conversely, if companies provide excellent products and treat customers with respect, customer power can be a very positive force.

GLOBALIZATION   Today it is possible to travel half way around the world for about $1,000. International travel is affordable to an ever-growing middle class. One of the outcomes of travel is an understanding of other people and their culture. One of the best experiences hospitality students can have is spending a term in a country where they do not know the language or culture. In this environment, they will often make embarrassing mistakes due to the inability to read directions and a lack of understanding of the local culture. They will also rely on locals to help them understand menus, directions, and other written and spoken forms of communication in the local language. Once they have gone through this experience, they will treat international customers in their own hotels or restaurants with more empathy, respect, and dignity.

Travelers have also experienced the paradoxes of travel. They may stay in a luxury hotel with its restaurants frequented by wealthy locals, while in a taxi only blocks from the hotel they are approached by a 10-year-old beggar. Or they may pass by brothels where teenage girls have been sold by their parents because the family was desperate for money. After seeing these situations first hand, many customers are more likely to deal with companies that have created and/or are involved in projects that support social, economic, or environmental issues in society.

Globalization also means that the world is connected. A call center may be located in India, creating cost advantages for the firm but displacing workers in other countries. As China becomes more industrialized and uses more resources, the price of raw materials around the globe increases. As gasoline prices increase in the United States, consumers spend what used to be discretionary income on gasoline, reducing the amount they have to spend on dining in restaurants.

CREATIVE SOCIETY Throughout the book we will discuss actions that businesses can take to help them follow the concepts of marketing 3.0. For example, fast-food restaurants will pursue more environmentally sound packaging and produce foods with more nutritional value. The National Restaurant Association, with the help of Ted Turner (founder of CNN), is developing an initiative to reduce waste and the carbon footprint of restaurants. A carbon footprint is a measure of the greenhouse gases produced by burning fossil fuels for heating, cooking, electricity, transportation, and so on. It is usually measured in tons or kilograms of carbon dioxide equivalent.[30] Restaurants are the retail world's largest energy user, and almost 80 percent of the energy a restaurant uses is lost due to inefficient food cooking, holding, and storage, according to one energy supplier. The average restaurant has a huge footprint, producing the equivalent of 490 tons of carbon dioxide per year.[31] Those companies that can reduce this footprint will make a better place to live for their customers, their employees, and their community. This is not about public relations; it is about weaving values into the corporate business. Profit will result from customers' appreciation of those companies that contribute to human well-being.

▪▪▪ Preparing an Integrated Marketing Plan

The company's marketing strategy outlines which customers the company will serve and how it will create value for these customers. Next, the marketer develops an integrated marketing program that will actually deliver the intended value to target customers. The marketing program builds customer relationships by transforming the marketing strategy into action. It consists of the firm's marketing mix, the set of marketing tools the firm uses to implement its marketing strategy.

The major marketing mix tools are classified into four broad groups, called the four Ps of marketing: product, price, place, and promotion. To deliver on its value proposition, the firm must first create a need-satisfying market offering (product). It must decide how much it will charge for the offer (price) and how it will make the offer available to target consumers (place). Finally, it must communicate with target customers about the offer and persuade them of its merits (promotion). The firm must blend all of these marketing mix tools into a comprehensive, integrated marketing program that communicates and delivers the intended value to chosen customers. We explore marketing programs and the marketing mix in much more detail in later chapters.

■■■ Building Profitable Customer Relationships

The first three steps in the marketing process—understanding the marketplace and customer needs, designing a customer-driven marketing strategy, and preparing an integrated marketing plan—all lead up to the fourth and most important step: building profitable customer relationships.

What specific marketing tools can a company use to develop stronger customer relationships? It can adopt any of three customer value-building tools.[32] The first relies primarily on adding financial benefits to the customer relationship. For example, airlines offer frequent-flyer programs, hotels give room upgrades to their frequent guests, and restaurants have frequent-diner programs. Although these reward programs and other financial incentives build customer preference, they can be imitated easily by competition and thus may fail to differentiate the company's offer permanently. Frequency programs often used tiered programs to encourage guests' preference for one brand. For example, Marriott has gold (15 nights), black (50 nights), and platinum (75 nights). Hilton has silver (10 nights), gold (36 nights), and diamond (60 nights). As guests move up in into higher tiers, they gain more benefits.[33]

The second approach is to add social as well as financial benefits. Here company personnel work to increase their social bonds with customers by learning individual customers' needs and wants and then individualizing and personalizing their products and services. They turn their customers into clients: Customers may be nameless to the institution; clients cannot be nameless. Customers are served as part of the mass or as part of larger segments; clients are served on an individual basis. Customers are served by anyone who happens to be available; clients are served by the professional assigned to them.[34] For example, a server recognizes repeat guests and greets them by name. A salesperson develops a good relationship with his or her clients. Both these people have developed social bonds with their clients. This keeps the client coming back, but it also often means clients will follow that person when he or she changes jobs. Managers of hospitality and travel organizations want to make sure that their key clients have social bonds with multiple people in the organization. The general manager, front-desk manager, food and beverage manager, convention services manager, banquet manager, and restaurant manager should all know key clients. In fact, general managers should go on sales calls to key clients. If this is done, when the salesperson leaves, clients feel like they still know key people in the hotel and are not dependent on the salesperson.

The third approach to building strong customer relationships is to add structural ties, as well as financial and social benefits. For example, airlines have developed lounges for their first-class customers, and some will send a limousine to deliver them to the airport. Airline customers who have elite status can choose their seat including exit rows, which are sold at a premium price to nonelite status customers. Sheraton developed flexible check-in and checkout times for their best customers. Hilton is using technology to provide a personalized welcome message on the guest's television. Structural changes are difficult to implement, but they are harder for competitors to match and create a competitive advantage until they are matched.

When it comes to relationship marketing, you don't want a relationship with every customer. In fact, there are some bad customers. A company should develop customer relationships selectively: Figure out which customers are worth cultivating because you can meet their needs more effectively than anyone else.[35] One of the purposes of customer frequency is to help companies track purchases so they know the characteristics of their customers and can classify them by their purchasing characteristics. Table 1–1 breaks customers into categories based on their frequency of purchase and their profitability. Those customers who are high on profitability and frequency deserve management attention. These are Marriott's Platinum members and Hilton's Diamond members. The customers high on profitability but low on frequency sometimes can be developed in higher frequency customers. Some of these customers are spreading their business across several different providers of the same service. If we can make our company the preferred provider for this type of customer, then we can turn them into our best customers. For

TABLE 1–1

Types of Customers

	Low Frequency	High Frequency
High Profitability	Try to get these customers to come more often.	These are your best customers; reward them.
Low Profitability	These customers will follow promotions. Make sure your promotions make money.	Some of these guests have the potential to become more profitable.

some of the high-frequency, low-profitability customers, there is a chance to motivate them to purchase by showing the value of additional purchases. For example, hotels can show a business traveler the advantage of staying on the concierge floor where there is a lounge to work in when he or she wants to take a break from working in his or her office. The concierge lounge also provides a quick and accessible breakfast, saving the guest time. Those guests who see the value in concierge floors are willing to pay the extra $40 a night. The guests who are in the low-frequency, low-profitability quadrant are often bargain hunters. They come when there is a promotion and avoid paying full price at all costs. It is very difficult to build a relationship with these price-sensitive customers. Knowing your customers helps you select the customers you want to develop a relationship with and to strengthen the relationship over time.

Customer Relationship Management

Customer relationship management (CRM) is perhaps the most important concept of modern marketing. Until recently, CRM has been defined narrowly as a customer data management activity. By this definition, it involves managing detailed information about individual customers and carefully managing customer "touch points" in order to maximize customer loyalty. A **customer touch point** is any occasion on which a customer encounters the brand and product—from actual experience to personal or mass communications to casual observation. For a hotel, the touch points include reservations, check-in and checkout, frequent-stay programs, room service, business services, exercise facilities, laundry service, restaurants, and bars. For instance, the Four Seasons relies on personal touches, such as a staff that always addresses guests by name, high-powered employees who understand the needs of sophisticated business travelers, and at least one best-in-region facility, such as a premier restaurant or spa.

Sometimes touch points are where you least expect, such as in customer billing. Meeting planners expect to have prompt and accurate billing. Reviewing the bill with the meeting planner during a multiday meeting can help build trust and a strong relationship.

CRM enables companies to provide excellent real-time customer service through the effective use of individualized information. Based on what they know about each valued customer, companies can customize market offerings, services, programs, messages, and amenities. CRM is important because a major driver of company profitability is the aggregate value of the company's customer base.

A pioneer in the application of CRM techniques is Harrah's Entertainment. In 1997 Harrah's Entertainment, Inc., in Las Vegas, launched a pioneering loyalty program that pulled all customer data into a centralized warehouse and provided sophisticated analysis to better understand the value of the investments the casino makes in its customers. Harrah's has fine-tuned its Total Rewards system to active near-real-time analysis: As customers interact with slot machines, check into casinos, or buy meals, they receive reward offers based on the predictive analyses. The company has now identified hundreds of customer segments among its more than 40 million slot players. By targeting offers to highly specific customer segments, the company was able to almost double its share of customers' gaming budgets in just eight years.[36]

More recently, however, CRM has taken on a broader meaning. In this broader sense, CRM is the overall process of building and maintaining profitable customer relationships by delivering superior customer value and satisfaction. It deals with all aspects of acquiring, keeping, and growing customers.

The Changing Nature of Customer Relationships

Significant changes are occurring in the ways in which companies are relating to their customers. Yesterday's big companies focused on mass marketing to all customers at arm's length. Today's companies are building deeper, more direct, and lasting relationships with more carefully selected customers. Here are some important trends in the way companies and customers are relating to one another.

Relating with More Carefully Selected Customers

Few firms today still practice true mass marketing—selling in a standardized way to any customer who comes along. Today, most marketers realize that they don't want relationships with every customer. Instead, they target fewer, more profitable customers. It is just as important to know which customers you do not want as well as those customers which you want. In Chapter 8 we will discuss the market segmentation, target marketing, and positioning. One of the most important lessons in marketing is that when you select customers you want to target, you also are selecting those you do not want to target. Chuck E. Cheese is an entertainment venue featuring pizza and games for young children. Even though Chuck E. Cheese might be slow on a Monday night, promoting a wine and pizza night for young couples would be ineffective, because by choosing to target families with young children it has chosen not to market to singles, couples, and families with older children.

Many companies now use customer profitability analysis to pass up or weed out losing customers and target winning ones for pampering. One approach is to preemptively screen out potentially unprofitable customers. For example, customers who have just a soup and salad in a busy restaurant on Saturday nights will be unprofitable because they take up seating capacity that could have been used to create a higher guest check. By requiring a minimum charge per person, the restaurant will lose these guests, but it will not lose the more profitable customers it is targeting. The trend is for companies to target fewer, more profitable customers, called selective relationship management. Many companies now use profitability analysis to weed out unprofitable customers and to target winning ones for pampering. Once they identify profitable customers, firms can create attractive offers and special handling to capture these customers and earn their loyalty.

Relating More Deeply and Interactively

Beyond choosing customers more selectively, companies are now relating with chosen customers in deeper, more meaningful ways. Rather than relying on one-way, mass-media messages only, today's marketers are incorporating new, more interactive approaches that help build targeted, two-way customer relationships. New technologies have profoundly changed the ways in which people relate to one another. New tools for relating include everything from e-mail, Web sites, blogs, cell phones, and video sharing to online communities and social networks, such as Facebook, LinkedIn, YouTube, and Twitter. This changing communications environment also affects how companies and brands relate to customers. The new communications approaches let marketers create deeper customer involvement and a sense of community surrounding a brand—to make the brand a meaningful part of consumers' conversations and lives. "Becoming part of the conversation between consumers is infinitely more powerful than handing down information via traditional advertising," says one marketing expert. Says another, "People today want a voice and a role in their brand experiences. They want co-creation."[37]

However, at the same time that the new technologies create relationship-building opportunities for marketers, they also create challenges. They give consumers greater power and control. Today's consumers have more information about brands than ever before, and they have a wealth of platforms for airing and sharing their brand views with other consumers. Thus, the marketing world is now embracing not only customer relationship management but also customer managed relationships.

Greater consumer control means that, in building customer relationships, companies can no longer rely on marketing by *intrusion*. Instead, marketers must practice marketing by *attraction*—creating market offerings and messages that involve consumers rather than interrupt them. Hence, most marketers now augment their mass-media marketing efforts with a rich mix of direct marketing approaches that promote brand–consumer interaction.

For example, many brands are creating dialogues with consumers via their own or existing *online social networks*. To supplement their marketing campaigns, companies now routinely post their latest ads and made-for-the-Web videos on video-sharing sites. They join social networks. Or they launch their own blogs, online communities, or consumer-generated review systems, all with the aim of engaging customers on a more personal, interactive level.

Take Twitter, for example. Organizations ranging from JetBlue Airways and Dunkin' Donuts to the Chicago Bulls and NASCAR have created Twitter pages and promotions. They use "tweets" to start conversations with Twitter's more than 150 million registered users, address customer service issues, research customer reactions, and drive traffic to relevant Web sites, contests, videos, and other brand activities. Similarly, almost every company has something going on Facebook these days. Starbucks has more than 7 million Facebook "fans."[38]

Most marketers are still learning how to use social media effectively. The problem is to find unobtrusive ways to enter consumers' social conversations with engaging and relevant brand messages. Simply posting a humorous video, creating a social network page, or hosting a blog isn't enough. Successful social network marketing means making relevant and genuine contributions to consumer conversations. "Nobody wants to be friends with a brand," says one online marketing executive. "Your job [as a brand] is to be part of other friends' conversations."[39]

Consumer-Generated Marketing

A growing part of the new customer dialogue is consumer-generated marketing, by which consumers themselves are playing a bigger role in shaping their own brand experiences and those of others. This might happen through uninvited consumer-to-consumer exchanges in blogs, video-sharing sites, and other digital forums. But increasingly, companies are inviting consumers to play a more active role in shaping products and brand messages.

Some companies ask consumers for new product ideas. For example, Coca-Cola's Vitaminwater brand recently set up a Facebook app to obtain consumer suggestions for a new flavor, promising to manufacture and sell the winner ("Vitaminwater was our idea; the next one will be yours."). The new flavor—Connect (black cherry-lime with vitamins and a kick of caffeine)—was a big hit. In the process, Vitaminwater doubled its Facebook fan base to more than 1 million.[40]

Other companies are inviting customers to play an active role in shaping ads. For example, PepsiCo and Southwest Airlines have run contests for consumer-generated commercials that have been aired on national television. However, harnessing consumer-generated content can be a time-consuming and costly process, and companies may find it difficult to glean even a little gold from all the garbage. For example, when Heinz invited consumers to submit homemade ads for its ketchup on its YouTube page, it ended up sifting through more than 8,000 entries, of which it posted nearly 4,000. Some of the amateur ads were very good—entertaining and potentially effective. Most, however, were so-so at best, and others were downright dreadful. In one ad, the would-be filmmaker brushed his teeth, washed his hair, and shaved his face with Heinz's product.[41]

Consumer-generated marketing, whether invited by marketers or not, has become a significant marketing force. Through a profusion of consumer-generated videos, blogs, and Web sites, consumers are playing an increasing role in shaping their own brand experiences. Beyond creating brand conversations, customers are having an increasing say about everything from product design, usage, and packaging to pricing and distribution.

Partner Relationship Management

When it comes to creating customer value and building strong customer relationships, today's marketers know that they can't go it alone. They must work closely with a variety of marketing partners. In addition to being good at customer relationship management, marketers must be good at partner relationship management. Major changes are occurring in how marketers partner with others inside and outside the company to jointly bring more value to customers.

Partners Inside the Company

Traditionally, marketers have been charged with understanding customers and representing customer needs to different company departments. The old thinking was that marketing is done only by marketing, sales, and customer-support people. However, in today's more connected world, every functional area can interact with customers, especially electronically. The new thinking is that—no matter what your job is in a company—you must understand marketing and be customer focused. One CEO said, "Marketing is far too important to be left only to the marketing department."[42]

Today, rather than letting each department go its own way, firms are linking all departments in the cause of creating customer value. Rather than assigning only sales and marketing people to customers, they are forming cross-functional customer teams. Necessary?

Marketing Partners Outside the Firm

Changes are also occurring in how marketers connect with their suppliers, channel partners, and even competitors. Most companies today are networked companies, relying heavily on partnerships with other firms. Their partners include food wholesalers, event planners, bakers, office supply companies, and others who supply products the company needs to carry out its business.

The supply chain describes a channel that stretches from raw materials to components to final products that are carried to final buyers. For example, the supply chain for a seafood diner consists of fishermen, the seafood processor, transporter of the seafood from southeast Asia to the distributor, the distributors, and the restaurant that prepares the meal.

Through supply chain management, many companies today are strengthening their connections with partners all along the supply chain. They know that their fortunes rest not just on how well they perform. Success at building customer relationships also rests on how well their entire supply chain performs against competitors' supply chains. These companies don't just treat suppliers as vendors. They treat both as partners in delivering customer value. It is also important for foodservice suppliers that they are viewed as partners and do their part to make the restaurant more profitable.

■■■ Capturing Value from Customers

The first four steps in the marketing process outlined in Figure 1–1 involve building customer relationships by creating and delivering superior customer value. The final step involves capturing value in return in the form of current and future sales, market share, and profits. By creating superior customer value, the firm creates highly satisfied customers who stay loyal and buy more. This, in turn, means greater long-run returns for the firm. Here, we discuss the outcomes of creating customer value: customer loyalty and retention, share of market and share of customer, and customer equity.

Customer Loyalty and Retention

Good customer relationship management creates customer delight. In turn, delighted customers remain loyal and talk favorably to others about the company and its products. Studies show big differences in the loyalty of customers who are less satisfied, somewhat satisfied, and completely satisfied. Even a slight drop from complete satisfaction can create an enormous drop in loyalty. Thus, the aim of customer relationship management is to create not only customer satisfaction but also customer delight.

Losing a customer means losing more than a single sale. It means losing the entire stream of purchases that the customer would make over a lifetime of patronage. For example, here is a dramatic illustration of customer **lifetime value (LTV)**.

Stew Leonard, who operates a highly profitable four-store supermarket in Connecticut and New York, says he sees $50,000 flying out of his store every time he sees a sulking customer. Why? Because his average customer spends about $100 a week, shops 50 weeks a year, and remains in the area for about 10 years. If this customer has an unhappy experience and switches to another supermarket, Stew Leonard's has lost $50,000 in revenue. The loss can be much greater if the disappointed customer shares the bad experience with other customers and causes them to defect. To keep customers coming back, Stew Leonard's has created what the *New York Times* has dubbed the "Disneyland of Dairy Stores," complete with costumed characters, scheduled entertainment, a petting zoo, and animatronics throughout the store. From its humble beginnings as a small dairy store in 1969, Stew Leonard's has grown at an amazing pace. It has built 29 additions onto the original store, which now serves more than 300,000 customers each week. This legion of loyal shoppers is largely a result of the store's passionate approach to customer service. "Rule #1: The customer is always right. Rule #2: If the customer is ever wrong, re-read rule #1."[43]

Stew Leonard is not alone in assessing customer LTV. Lexus, for example, estimates that a single satisfied and loyal customer is worth more than $600,000 in lifetime sales. Ritz-Carlton Hotels puts the LTV of a guest at more than $120,000. Domino's Pizza puts the LTV of a customer at more than $10,000.[44] A company can lose money on a specific transaction but still benefit greatly from a long-term relationship. This is one of the reasons successful companies empower employees to resolve customer complaints. The company wants to maintain the relationship with the customer. And that relationship keeps customers coming back.

Growing Share of Customer

Beyond simply retaining good customers to capture customer LTV, good customer relationship management can help marketers increase their share of customer—the share they get of the customer's purchasing in their product categories. Thus, restaurants want to get more "share of stomach" and airlines want greater "share of travel." To increase share of customer, firms can offer greater variety to current customers, for example, a coffee house can expand its selection of flavored teas and add smoothies. Or they can create to cross-sell pastries and other snacks and/or up-sell from brewed coffee to blended drinks to market more products and services to existing customers.

We can now see the importance of not only acquiring customers but also keeping and growing them. One marketing consultant puts it this way: "The only value your company will ever create is the value that comes from customers—the ones you have now and the ones you will have in the future. Without customers, you don't have a business."[45]

What Is Customer Equity?

The ultimate aim of customer relationship management is to produce high customer equity.[46] Customer equity is the total combined customer LTVs of all of the company's current and potential customers. Therefore, it's a measure of the future value of the company's customer base. Clearly, the more loyal the firm's profitable customers, the higher its customer equity. Customer equity may be a better measure of a firm's performance than current sales or market share. Whereas sales and market share reflect the past, customer equity suggests the future.

Building the Right Relationships with the Right Customers

Companies should manage customer equity carefully. They should view customers as assets that must be managed and maximized. But not all customers, not even all loyal customers, are good investments. Surprisingly, some loyal customers can be unprofitable, and some disloyal customers can be profitable. Which customers should the company acquire and retain?

The company can classify customers according to their potential profitability and manage its relationships with them accordingly. One classification scheme defines four relationship groups based on potential profitability and projected loyalty: strangers, butterflies, true friends, and barnacles.[47] Each group requires a different relationship management strategy. For example, "strangers" show low potential profitability and little projected loyalty. There is little fit between the company's offerings and their needs. The relationship management strategy for these customers is simple: Don't invest anything in them.

"Butterflies" are potentially profitable but not loyal. There is a good fit between the company's offerings and their needs. However, like real butterflies, we can enjoy them for only a short while and then they're gone. An example is stock market investors who trade shares often and in large amounts but who enjoy hunting out the best deals without building a regular relationship with any single brokerage company. Efforts to convert butterflies into loyal customers are rarely successful. Instead, the company should enjoy the butterflies for the moment. It should create satisfying and profitable transactions with them, capturing as much of their business as possible in the short time during which they buy from the company. Then it should cease investing in them until the next time around.

"True friends" are both profitable and loyal. There is a strong fit between their needs and the company's offerings. The firm wants to make continuous relationship investments to delight these customers and nurture, retain, and grow them. It wants to turn true friends into "true believers," those who come back regularly and tell others about their good experiences with the company.

"Barnacles" are highly loyal but not very profitable. There is a limited fit between their needs and the company's offerings. An example is smaller bank customers, who bank regularly but do not generate enough returns to cover the costs of maintaining their accounts. Like barnacles on the hull of a ship, they create drag. Barnacles are perhaps the most problematic customers. The company might be able to improve their profitability by selling them more, raising their fees, or reducing service to them. However, if they cannot be made profitable, they should be "fired."

The point here is an important one: Different types of customers require different relationship management strategies. The goal is to build the right relationships with the right customers.

Casino de Lac Leamy in Quebec is socially responsible. It is recognized as a leader in the fight against compulsive gambling. Courtesy of Alan Keohane © Dorling Kindersley.

Building Customer Equity

Customer equity is the discounted LTVs of all the company's current and potential customers. The best approach to customer retention is to deliver products that create high customer satisfaction and high perceived value, resulting in strong customer loyalty. Clearly, the more loyal the firm's profitable customers, the higher the firm's customer equity. Customer equity may be a better measure of a firm's performance than current sales or market share. Whereas sales and market share reflect the past, customer equity suggests the future.[48]

■■■ Marketing's Future

A technology executive stated, "The pace of change is so rapid that the ability to change has now become a competitive advantage." Rapid changes can quickly make yesterday's winning strategies out of date. As management thought leader Peter Drucker once observed, a company's winning formula for the last decade will probably be its undoing in the next decade. When we wrote the last edition, companies were trying to figure out how to use social media. Now social media has made an impact on marketing that has been a major driver of a new concept, marketing 3.0. Social media will forever change how we do marketing.

The worldwide growth of the travel industry has created a shortage of managers, as much so that in some regions projects are put on hold because the developer does not have and cannot acquire a management staff. These are truly great times for those entering the hospitality industry, but they are not without their challenges.

We are faced with rising oil prices, making travel more difficult to afford. Ethanol is seen by some as the answer to foreign oil; however, it is removing crops that are used to produce food, increasing food prices. The restaurant is faced with passing higher food costs on to the customers. In challenging times, good management is always sought.

This book is not just for students who desire a successful career in marketing; it is for students who desire a successful career. Marketing with its customer orientation has become the job of everyone and your passport to success.

■■■ KEY TERMS

Customer equity. The discounted lifetime values of all the company's current and potential customers.

Customer expectations. Expectations based on past buying experiences, the opinions of friends, and market information.

Customer relationship management (CRM). It involves managing detailed information about individual customers and carefully managing customer "touch points" in order to maximize customer loyalty.

Customer touch point. Any occasion on which a customer encounters the brand and product—from actual experience to personal or mass communications to casual observation.

Customer value. The difference between the benefits that the customer gains from owning and/or using a product and the costs of obtaining the product.

Demands. Human wants that are backed by buying power.

Exchange. The act of obtaining a desired object from someone by offering something in return.

Hospitality industry. Made up of those businesses that offer one or more of the following: accommodation, prepared food and beverage service, and/or entertainment.

Human need. A state of felt deprivation in a person.

Human want. The form that a human need takes when shaped by culture and individual personality.

Lifetime value (LTV). The lifetime value of a customer is the stream of profits a customer will create over the life of his or her relationship to a business.

Market. A set of actual and potential buyers of a product.

Marketing. The art and science of finding, retaining, and growing profitable customers.

Marketing concept. The marketing management philosophy that holds that achieving organizational goals depends on determining the needs and wants of target markets and delivering desired satisfactions more effectively and efficiently than competitors.

Marketing management. The art and science of choosing target markets and building profitable relationships with them.

Marketing manager. A person who is involved in marketing analysis, planning, implementation, and control activities.

Marketing mix. Elements include product, price, promotion, and distribution. Sometimes distribution is called place and the marketing situation facing a company.

Product concept. The idea that consumers will favor products that offer the most quality, performance, and features, and therefore the organization should devote its energy to making continuous product improvements.

Production concept. Holds that customers will favor products that are available and highly affordable, and therefore management should focus on production and distribution efficiency.

Purpose of a business. To create and maintain satisfied, profitable customers.

Relationship marketing. Involves creating, maintaining, and enhancing strong relationships with customers and other stakeholders.

Selling concept. The idea that consumers will not buy enough of an organization's products unless the organization undertakes a large selling and promotion effort.

Societal marketing concept. The idea that an organization should determine the needs, wants, and interests of target markets and deliver the desired satisfactions more effectively and efficiently than competitors in a way that maintains or improves the consumer's and society's well-being.

Transaction. Consists of a trade of values between two parties; marketing's unit of measurement.

Value proposition. The full positioning of a brand—the full mix of benefits upon which it is positioned.

■■■ CHAPTER REVIEW

I.   Introduction: Marketing in the Hospitality Industry

  A.   Customer orientation. The purpose of a business is to create and maintain profitable customers. Customer satisfaction leading to profit is the central goal of hospitality marketing.

II. What Is Hospitality Marketing? Marketing is the art and science of finding, retaining, and growing profitable customers.

III. Importance of Marketing

  A. The entrance of corporate giants into the hospitality market and the marketing skills these companies have brought to the industry have increased the importance of marketing within the industry.

  B. Analysts predict that the hotel industry will consolidate in much the same way as the airline industry has, with five or six major chains dominating the market. Such consolidation will create a market that is highly competitive. The firms that survive this consolidation will be the ones that understand their customers.

  C. In response to growing competitive pressures, hotel chains are relying on the expertise of the marketing director.

IV. Travel Industry Marketing

  A. Successful hospitality marketing is highly dependent on the entire travel industry.

  B. Government or quasi-government agencies play an important role in travel industry marketing through legislation aimed at enhancing the industry and through promotion of regions, states, and nations.

  C. Few industries are as interdependent as the travel and hospitality industries.

V.   Marketing Process. The marketing process is a five-step model of the marketing process. In the first four steps, companies work to understand consumers, create customer value, and build strong customer relationships. In the final step, companies reap the rewards of creating superior customer value. By creating value for customers, they in turn capture value from customers in the form of sales, profits, and long-term customer equity.

  A.   Understand customers

    1.   Needs. Human beings have many complex needs. These include basic physical needs for food, clothing, warmth, and safety; social needs for belonging, affection, fun, and relaxation; esteem needs for prestige, recognition, and fame; and individual needs for knowledge and self-expression.

    2.   Wants. Wants are how people communicate their needs.

    3.   Demands. People have almost unlimited wants but limited resources. They choose products that produce the most satisfaction for their money. When backed by buying power, wants become demand.

    4.   Market offerings. Some combination of tangible products, services, information, or experiences that are offered to the market.

5. **Value, expectations, and satisfaction**
   a. **Customer value** is the difference between the benefits that the customer gains from owning and/or using a product and the costs of obtaining the product.
   b. **Customer expectations** are based on past buying experiences, the opinions of friends, and market information.
   c. **Satisfaction** with a product is determined by how well the product meets the customer's expectations for that product.
B. **Exchange and relationships**
   a. **Exchange.** Exchange is the act of obtaining a desired object from someone by offering something in return.
   b. **Relationship marketing.** Relationship marketing focuses on building a relationship with a company's profitable customers. Most companies are finding that they earn a higher return from resources invested in getting repeat sales from current customers than from money spent to attract new customers.
   c. **Designing customer-driven marketing strategy.** Marketing management is the art and science of choosing target markets and building profitable relationships with them.
      i. **Selecting customers to serve.** The company must select those market segments it wishes to serve.
      ii. **Choosing a value proposition.** The company must also decide how it will serve targeted customers—how it will differentiate and position itself in the marketplace. A company's value proposition is the set of benefits or values it promises to deliver to consumers to satisfy their needs.

VI. **Five Marketing Management Philosophies**
A. **Production concept.** The production concept holds that customers will favor products that are available and highly affordable, and therefore management should focus on production and distribution efficiency.
B. **Product concept.** The product concept holds that customers prefer existing products and product forms, and the job of management is to develop good versions of these products.
C. **Selling concept.** The selling concept holds that consumers will not buy enough of the organization's products unless the organization undertakes a large selling and promotion effort.
D. **Marketing concept.** The marketing concept holds that achieving organizational goals depends on determining the needs and wants of target markets and delivering the desired satisfaction more effectively and efficiently than competitors.

E. **Societal marketing concept.** The societal marketing concept holds that the organization should determine the needs, wants, and interests of target markets and deliver the desired satisfactions more effectively and efficiently than competitors in a way that maintains or improves the consumer's and society's well-being.

VII. **Prepare an Integrated Marketing Plan.** The company's marketing strategy outlines which customers the company will serve and how it will create value for these customers. Next, the marketer develops an integrated marketing program that will actually deliver the intended value to target customers. The marketing program builds customer relationships by transforming the marketing strategy into action. It consists of the firm's marketing mix, the set of marketing tools the firm uses to implement its marketing strategy. The major marketing mix tools are classified into four broad groups, called the four Ps of marketing: product, price, place, and promotion.

VIII. **Build Customer Relationships.** Customer relationship management (CRM) involves managing detailed information about individual customers and carefully managing customer "touch points" in order to maximize customer loyalty.

IX. **Capturing Value from Customers.** We try to capture value from our customers in the form of current and future sales, market share, and profits. By creating superior customer value, the firm creates highly satisfied customers who stay loyal and buy more.
A. **Customer loyalty and retention.** The benefits of customer loyalty come from continued patronage of loyal customers, reduced marketing costs, decreased price sensitivity of loyal customers, and partnership activities of loyal customers. Loyal customers purchase from the business they are loyal to more often than nonloyal customers. They also purchase a broader variety of items. A manager who is loyal to a hotel brand is more likely to place his or her company's meetings with that hotel chain. Reduced marketing costs are the result of requiring fewer marketing dollars to maintain a customer than to create one and the creation of new customers through the positive word of mouth of loyal customers.
B. **Growing share of customer.** Beyond simply retaining good customers to capture customer lifetime value, good customer relationship management can help marketers to increase their share of customer—the share they get of the customer's purchasing in their product categories.
C. **Building customer equity.** Customer equity is the discounted lifetime values of all the company's current and potential customers. One builds customer equity by delivering products that create high customer satisfaction and have high perceived value.

■■■ DISCUSSION QUESTIONS

1. Discuss why you should study marketing.

2. Marketing can be defined in many ways. In your own words, describe marketing to someone who has not read this chapter.

3. Many managers view the purpose of business as making a profit, whereas some view the purpose as being able to create and maintain a customer. Explain how these alternative viewpoints could affect a company's interactions with its customers. If a manager views the purpose as being able to create and maintain a customer, does this mean that the manager is not concerned with profits?

4. A guest in your hotel complains that the air conditioning in his room did not work and because of this he did not get a good night's sleep. What would you do?

5. Talk to two people and ask them to think about a hotel they stayed in that was a good value. Ask them what made the hotel a good value. Record a summary of their comments.

6. A restaurant has a great reputation as the result of providing consistent food for over 10 years. The restaurant is full every weekend and has above-average business during the week. The manager claims that the restaurant does not practice marketing because it does not need marketing; the restaurant has more than enough business now. Is it true that this restaurant does not practice marketing?

7. Look at Figure 1–2. Why do you think persons who give you 2 (a relatively high score) out of 7 are not likely to return?

8. What is customer equity? How can a company increase its customer equity?

9. Give several examples you have found of hospitality companies being socially responsible. Include in your discussion how being socially responsible helps the company.

■■■ EXPERIENTIAL EXERCISES

Do one of the following:

Restaurant

Visit two restaurants in the same class, such as two fast-food restaurants or two casual restaurants. Observe the cleanliness of the restaurants, in-house signage, and other physical features. Then order a menu item and observe the service and the quality of the food. Write up your observations, and then state which restaurant you feel is more customer oriented. Explain why.

Hotel

Call the central reservation number of two hotels. Request information on room availability, different room types, and price for a date one month from now. (Note: Do not make a reservation.) Write up your experience, including a description of how quickly the phone was answered, the customer orientation of information provided, and the friendliness of the employee. Based on your experiences, which hotels do you feel had the more customer-oriented reservation system?

Other Hospitality Companies

If you are interested in another area of the travel industry, you may compare two organizations in that area for their customer orientation using similar criteria, as mentioned earlier. For example, if you are interested in tourism, you may contact two tourism organizations regarding their destinations. This could be a city convention and tourist bureau or it could be a government tourist bureau.

■■■ INTERNET EXERCISES

Exercise 1

In only a few short years, *consumer-generated marketing* has increased exponentially. It's also known as *consumer-generated media* and *consumer-generated content*. More than 100 million Web sites contain user-generated content. You may be a contributor yourself if you've ever posted something on a blog; reviewed a product at Amazon.com; uploaded a video on YouTube; or sent a video from your mobile phone to a news Web site. This force has not gone unnoticed by marketers— and with good reason. Nielsen, the TV ratings giant, found that most consumers trust consumer opinions posted online. As a result, savvy marketers encourage consumers to generate content. For example, Moe's restaurants has created a creative dance contest. These are the instructions for the contest. "To enter, create a dance video no longer than 30 seconds and upload it to www.ilovequeso.com any time before July 24, 2011." Moe's panel of judges will consider originality, video quality, dance moves, and the dance-off ranking to determine who will win the $10,000 grand prize (http://moes.com/). However, consumer-generated marketing is not without problems—just search "I hate (insert company name)" in any search engine!

1. Find two examples (other than those discussed in this chapter) of marketer-supported, consumer-generated content and two examples of consumer-generated content that is not officially supported by the company whose product is involved. Provide the Web link to each and discuss how the information impacts your attitude toward the companies involved.

2. Discuss the advantages and disadvantages of consumer-generated marketing.

Exercise 2

Choose three restaurant or hotel companies you have found on the Internet.

Based on information provided in each company's Web site:

A. Describe how each of these companies tries to satisfy a customer's wants.

B. How does each of these companies create value for the customer?

C. Do companies segment the market by offering pages for a specific market segment? For example, a hotel may provide information for meeting planners, and a restaurant may provide information for customers who are concerned about nutrition or families.

D. Select the company you would purchase from and state why.

■■■ REFERENCES

1. Jessica Shampora, "Chipotle: Rise of a Fast-Food Empire," *CNNMoney.com* (October 7, 2010) accessed September 15, 2012, http://money.cnn.com/2010/10/06/smallbusiness/chipotle_started.fortune/index.htm.

2. Danielle Schlanger and Kim Bhasin, "How Chipotle Changed Fast Food Forever," *Business Insider*, June 26, 2012, accessed September 15, 2012 http://www.businessinsider.com/steve-ells-and-the-rise-of-chipotle-2012-6?op=1.

3. Chipotle Website, accessed September 15, 2012, http://www.chipotle.com/en-US/fwi/fwi.aspx

4. Anna Kuchment, "A Chain That Pigs Would Die For; Can Food Be Fast and Fastidious? Chipotle Mexican Grill Insists on Humanely Raised Meat," *Newsweek* (May 12, 2008): 19.

5. Chipotle Mexican Grill, Inc., 2010 Annual Report; www.chipotle.com.

6. See also Anonymous, "Chipotle Completes Chain's 'Natural' Chicken Rollouts," *Nation's Restaurant News* (May 19, 2008): 156; Michael Arndt, "Burrito Buzz," *Business Week* (March 12, 2007): 84; Chipotle' wall on their Facebook page http://www.facebook.com/chipotle?sk=app_2392950137#!/chipotle?sk=wall (accessed July 7, 2011): Dina Berta, "Chipotle Incentive Program Aims to Keep, Promote GMs," *Nation's Restaurant News* (November 5, 2007): 18; Gregg Cebrzynski, "They May Be Students, But Winners of Chipotle's Ad Contest Produce Professional-Looking TV Spots," *Nation's Restaurant News* (December 3, 2007): 12.

7. "World Tourism Exceeds Expectations in 2007," January 31, 2008, www.htrends.com/article30983.html (accessed May 4, 2008).

8. "China's Outbound Travelers Rise," English.news.cn, January 1, 2011, retrieved July 11, 2011, from http://news.xinhuanet.com/english2010/china/2011-01/18/c_13696297.htm.

9. DUBAILAND Web site, retrieved July 9, 2011, from http://dubailand.ae.

10. "A New Itinerary," Economist.com, May 15, 2008, http://www.economist.com/displaystory.cfm?storyid=11374574 (accessed June 7, 2008).

11. *Abu Dhabi Tourism Authority Yearbook 2010,* Abu Dhabi Tourism Authority, 2011.

12. *Airport of the year 2011,* retrieved July 9, 2011, from http://www.worldairportawards.com/: Skytrax world airport survey, http://www.worldairportawards.com/ (accessed May 4, 2008); "Readers' Travel Awards 2010: the top 25," Conde Nast Traveller, retrieved July 11, 2011, from http://www.cntraveller.com/awards: "The 2011 World Airline Awards," retrieved July 11, 2011, from http://www.worldairlineawards.com/.

13. Accor 2001–2002 Asia Pacific Hotel Directory, p. 1.

14. Theodore Levitt, *Marketing Imagination* (New York: Free Press, 1986).

15. Christian Gronroos, *Service Management and Marketing* (Lexington, MA: Lexington Books, 1990).

16. Patricia Sellers, "Getting Customers to Love You," *Fortune* (March 13, 1989): 38–49.

17. Frederick Reichheld, *The Loyalty Effect* (Boston, MA: Harvard Business School Press, 1996).

18. James L. Heskett, Jr., W. Earle Sasser, and W. L. Hart Chistopher, *Service Breakthroughs* (New York: Free Press, 1990).

19. Karl Albrecht, *At America's Service* (Homewood, IL: Dow Jones/Irwin, 1988), p. 23.

20. Peter F. Drucker, *Management: Tasks, Responsibility, Practices* (New York: Harper & Row, 1973), pp. 64–65.

21. "Cruise Forum," *Travel Agent* (May 2, 1994): B2.

22. Bruce Horovits, "Takeout Takes Off," *USA Today* (June 13, 2007): 1A, 2A; "Facts at a Glance," National Restaurant Association, retrieved July 10, 2011, from http://www.restaurant.org/research/facts/.

23. Theodore Levitt, "Marketing Myopia," *Harvard Business Review* (July/August 1960): 45–46.

24. "The Changing Look of Tourism," Arts & Cultural Tourism. Speech given at Economic Summit 2004, May 26–27, 2004, Steamboat Springs, CO.

25. Scott McCartney, "A Bubble Bath and a Glass of Bubbly at the Airport," *Wall Street Journal* (July 10, 2007): D1.

26. John T. Bowen and Shiang-Lih Chen, "The Relationship Between Customer Loyalty and Customer Feedback," *Modern Maturity*, 40, no. 4 (July/August 1997): 12.

27. See also Dan Lago and James Kipp Poffley, "The Aging Population and the Hospitality Industry in 2010: Important Trends and Probable Services," *Hospitality Research Journal*, 17, no. 1 (1993): 29–47.

28. Philip Kotler, Hermawan Kartajaya, and Iwan Seyiawan, *Marketing 3.0* (Hoboken, NJ: Wiley, 2010).

29. Caroline McCarthy, " JetBlue Twitter Promotion Is a Hit," CNET.com, March 11, 2010; http://www.eturbonews.com/14853/jetblue-twitter-promotion-hit (accessed June 28, 2011). "Jetblue's Twitter Scavenger Hunt to Celebrate Their 10 Year Anniversary," Composure Marketing, http://composuremarketing.com/2010/03/10/jetblues-twitter-scavenger-hunt-to-celebrate-their-10-year-anniversary/ (accessed June 28, 2011).

30. http://www.carbonfootprint.com/carbonfootprint.html (accessed July 13, 2008).

31. Bruce Horovitz, "Can Restaurants Go Green," *USA Today*, May 15, 2008, http://www.usatoday.com/money/industries/environment/2008-05-15-green-restaurants-eco-friendly_N.htm.

32. Leonard L. Berry and A. Parasuraman, *Marketing Services: Competing Through Quality* (New York: Free Press, 1991), pp. 136–142.

33. Colleen Dejong, "Loyalty Marketing at a Glance; Hotel Programs," Colloquy from http://www.colloquy.com/cont_matrix.asp?industry=Hotel (retrieved October 24, 2001).

34. James H. Donnelly, Jr., Leonard L. Berry, and Thomas W. Thompson, *Marketing Financial Services: A Strategic Vision* (Homewood, IL: Dow Jones/Irwin, 1985), p. 113.

35. Thomas E. Caruso, "Kotler: Future Marketers Will Focus on Customer Data Base to Compete Globally," *Marketing News* (June 8, 1992): 21; Jeffrey Compton, " Harrah's Total Rewards One Card, 30 + Casinos, Countless Benefits," *Casino Center*, retrieved July 12, 2011, from http://www.casinocenter.com/?p=395.

36. Louis Columbus, "Lessons Learned in Las Vegas: Loyalty Programs Pay," *CRM Buyer* (July 29, 2005); Mark Leon, "Catering to True-Blue Customers," *Computerworld* (August 11, 2003): 37; John R. Brandt, "Dare to Be Different," *Chief Executive* (May 2003): 34–38; Joe Ashbrook Nickell, "Welcome to Harrah's," Business 2.0 (April 2002): 49–54; Del Jones, "Client Data Means Little Without Good Analysis," *USA Today* (December 24, 2001).

37. Quotes from Andrew Walmsley, "The Year of Consumer Empowerment," *Marketing* (December 20, 2006): 9; and Jeff Heilman, "Rules of Engagement: During a Recession, Marketers Need to Have Their Keenest Listening-to-Customers Strategy in Place," *The Magazine of Branded Content* (Winter 2009): 7. Also see Frank's Striefler, "5 Marketing Principles Brands Should Embrace in 2010," *Adweek* (January 13, 2010), accessed at www.adweek.com.

38. See James Rainey, "On the Media: Twitter's Charms Sort of Grow on You," *Los Angeles Times* (February 18, 2009): A1; B. L. Ochman, "Debunking Six Social Media Myths," *BusinessWeek* (February 19, 2009), accessed www.businessweek.com; Brian Morrissey, "Brand Sweepstakes Get Twitterized," *Adweek* (November 22, 2009), accessed www.adweek.com; and Alicia Wallace, "Owing Social: Businesses Dial in to Facebook, Twitter to Build Business," *McClatchy-Tribune Business News* (April 26, 2010).

39. Elizabteh A. Sullivan, "We Were Right!," *Marketing News* (December 15, 2008): 17.

40. Joel Rubenstein, "Marketers, Researchers, and Your Ears," *Brandweek* (February 15, 2010): 34.

41. Gavin O'Malley, "Entries Pour in for Heinz Ketchup Commercial Contest" (August 13, 2007), accessed http://publications.mediapost.com.

42. Philip Kotler and Kevin Lane Keller, *Marketing Management* (14th ed.) (Upper Saddle River, NJ: Prentice Hall, 2012), p. 17.

43. "Stew Leonard's," Hoover's Company Records, July 15, 2010, pp. 104–226; and www.stew-leonards.com/html/about.cfm (accessed August 2010).

44. Brad Rosenthal, "LTV Lifetime Value of a Customer," Lincolnrose Blog, May 10, 2011, retrieved July 14, 2011, from http://www.lincolnrosetrust.com/Blog.html?entry=ltv-lifetime-value-of-a.

45. Don Peppers and Martha Rogers, "Customers Don't Grow on Trees," *Fast Company* (Iuly 2005): 26.

46. For more discussion on customer equity, see Roland T. Rust, Valerie A. Zeithaml, and Katherine A. Lemon, *Driving Customer Equity* (New York: Free Press, 2000); Rust, Lemon, and Zeithaml, "Return on Marketing: Using Customer Equity to Focus Marketing Strategy," *Journal of Marketing* (January 2004): 109–127; Dominique M. Hanssens, Daniel Thorpe, and Carl Finkbeiner, "Marketing When Customer Equity Matters," *Harvard Business Review* (May 2008):

117–124; Thorsten Wiesel, Bernd Skieram, and Julian Villanueva, "Customer Equity: An Integral Part of Financial Reporting," *Journal of Marketing* (March 8, 2008): 1–14; and V. Kumar and Denish Shaw, "Expanding the Role of Marketing: From Customer Equity to Market Capitalization," *Journal of Marketing* (November 2009): 119.

47. Werner Reinartz and V. Kumar, "The Mismanagement of Customer Loyalty," *Harvard Business Review* (July 2002): 86–94. Also see Stanley F. Slater, Iakki I. Mohr, and Sanjit Sengupta, "Know Your Customer," *Marketing Management* (February 2009): 37–44.

48. See Roland T. Rust, Valerie A. Zeithaml, and Katherine A. Lemon, *Driving Customer Equity* (New York: Free Press, 2000); Robert C. Blattberg, Gary Cetz, and Jacquelyn S. Thomas, *Customer Equity* (Boston, MA: Harvard Business School Press, 2001); Rust, Lemon, and Zeithaml, "Return on Marketing: Using Customer Equity to Focus Marketing Strategy," *Journal of Marketing* (January 2004): 109–127; James D. Lenskold, "Customer-Centered Marketing ROI," *Marketing Management* (January/February 2004): 26–32; Rust, Zeithaml, and Lemon, "Customer-Centered Brand Management," *Harvard Business Review* (September 2004): 110; Don Peppers and Martha Rogers, "Hail to the Customer," *Sales & Marketing Management* (October 2005): 49–51; and Alhson Enright, "Serve Them Right," *Marketing News* (May 1, 2006): 21–22.

Service Characteristics of Hospitality and Tourism Marketing

Objectives

After reading this chapter, you should be able to:

1. Describe a service culture.

2. Identify four service characteristics that affect the marketing of a hospitality or travel product.

3. Explain seven marketing strategies for service businesses.

Ritz-Carlton: Taking Care of Those Who Take Care of Customers

Ritz-Carlton, a chain of eighty luxury hotels located around the world, is renowned for outstanding service. Ritz-Carlton caters to the top 5 percent of corporate and leisure travelers. The company's credo sets lofty customer service goals: "The Ritz-Carlton Hotel is a place where the genuine care and comfort of our guests is our highest mission. We pledge to provide the finest personal service and facilities for our guest, who will always enjoy a warm, relaxed, yet refined ambience. The Ritz-Carlton experience enlivens the senses, instills well-being, and fulfills even the unexpressed wishes and needs of our guests."[1]

Ritz-Carlton instills a sense of pride in its employees. "You serve," they are told, "but you are not servants." Its motto, "We are Ladies and Gentlemen serving Ladies and Gentlemen," communicates that employees should take pride in who they are and the jobs they perform.

The credo and motto are more than just words on paper: Ritz-Carlton delivers on its promises. In surveys of departing guests, some 95 percent report that they've had a truly memorable experience. In fact, at Ritz-Carlton, exceptional service encounters have become almost commonplace. Take the experiences of Nancy and Harvey Heffner of Manhattan, who stayed at the Ritz-Carlton in Naples, Florida. As reported in the *New York Times,* "The hotel is elegant and beautiful," Mrs. Heffner said, "but more important is the beauty expressed by the staff. They can't do enough to please you." When the couple's son became sick, the hotel staff brought him hot tea with honey at all hours of the night, she said. When Mr. Heffner had to fly home on business for a day and his return flight was delayed, a driver for the hotel waited in the lobby most of the night. Such personal, high-quality service has also made the Ritz-Carlton a favorite among conventioneers. Comments one convention planner, "They not only treat us like kings when we hold our top-level meetings in their hotels, but also we just never get any complaints."[2]

Since its incorporation in 1983, the Ritz-Carlton Hotel Company has received all the major industry awards the hospitality industry and leading consumer organizations can bestow.

Rewards are important, and at Ritz-Carlton, service quality has resulted in high customer retention: More than 90 percent of Ritz-Carlton customers return. Despite its hefty room rate, the chain enjoys a 70 percent occupancy rate, almost nine points above the industry average. Most of the responsibility for keeping guests satisfied falls to Ritz-Carlton's customer-contact employees. Thus the hotel chain takes great care in selecting its personnel. "We want only people who care about people," noted the company's vice president of quality.[3] Once selected, employees are given intensive training in the art of coddling customers. New employees attend a two-day orientation in which top management drums into them the "20 Ritz-Carlton Basics." Basic number one: "The Credo will be known, owned, and energized by all employees."

The 38,000 worldwide employees are taught to do everything they can to never lose a guest. "There's no negotiating at Ritz-Carlton when it comes to solving customer problems," says the vice president of quality. The staff learn that anyone who receives a customer complaint owns that complaint until it's resolved. They are trained to drop whatever they're doing to help a customer—no matter what they're doing or what their department. Ritz-Carlton employees are empowered to handle problems on the spot, without consulting higher-ups. Each employee can spend up to $2,000 to redress a guest grievance, and each is allowed to break from his or her routine for as long as needed to make a guest happy. "We master customer satisfaction at the individual level." "This is our most sensitive listening post . . . our early warning system."[4] Thus while competitors are still reading guest comment cards to learn about customer problems, Ritz-Carlton has already resolved them.

And so they do. When it comes to customer satisfaction, no detail is too small. Customer-contact people are taught to greet guests warmly and sincerely, using guests' names when possible. They learn to use proper language when speaking to guests— "Good morning," "Certainly," "I'll be happy to," and "My pleasure," never "Hi" or "How's it going?" The Ritz-Carlton Basics urge employees to escort the guest to another area of the hotel rather than pointing out directions, to answer the phone within three rings and with a "smile," and to take pride and care in personal appearance.

Ritz-Carlton recognizes and rewards employees who perform feats of outstanding service. Under its Five-Star Awards program, outstanding performers are nominated by peers and managers, and winners receive plaques at dinners celebrating their achievements. For on-the-spot recognition, managers award Gold Standard Coupons, redeemable for items in the gift shop and free weekend stays at the hotel. Ritz-Carlton further rewards and motivates its employees with events such as Super Sports Day, an employee talent show, luncheons celebrating employee anniversaries, a family picnic, and special themes in employee dining rooms. As a result, Ritz-Carlton's employees appear to be just as satisfied as its customers. Employee turnover is less than 30 percent a year, compared with 45 percent at other luxury hotels. Ritz-Carlton's success is based on a simple philosophy: To take care of customers, you must take care of those who take care of customers. Satisfied customers, in turn, create sales and profits for the company.

Ritz-Carlton is an example of a great service company. In this chapter, we discuss some of the elements that are required to build a great service organization.[5]

Marketing initially developed in connection with selling physical products, such as toothpaste, cars, steel, and equipment. But today, one of the major trends in many parts of the world is the phenomenal growth of services, or products, with little or no physical content. In most developed countries, services account for a majority of the gross domestic product (GDP). Service economies are not limited to developed countries; in developing countries the majority of the nonagricultural workforce is often employed in the hospitality and travel industries. These industries are part of this growing service sector. The growth of service industries has created a demand for research into their operation and marketing. Throughout the book we include the results of recent research into services and marketing issues. In this chapter, as well as in the remainder of the book, we examine the service characteristics of firms in the hospitality industry.

■■■ The Service Culture

Some managers think of their operations only in terms of tangible goods. Thus managers of fast-food restaurants who think they sell only hamburgers often have "slow, surly service personnel, dirty unattractive facilities, and few return customers."[6] One of the most important tasks of a hospitality business is to develop the service side of the business, specifically, a strong service culture.

The **service culture** focuses on serving and satisfying the customer. Creation of a service culture has to start with top management and flow down. The business mission discussed in Chapter 3 should contain a service vision. An organization should hire employees with a customer service attitude, and then it works with employees to instill the concept of service. The outcome of these efforts is employees who provide service to the customers. The Ritz-Carlton vignette at the opening of this chapter provides a good example of a company that has a service culture. In Ritz-Carlton, employees are taught to own the customer's request. A guest requesting towels from the front desk is not just transferred to housekeeping. The request is taken by the employee at the front desk. She will then call housekeeping. But that is not the end of her involvement. She will check back with housekeeping in 10 minutes to make sure the towels were delivered. If they were, she will call the guest to make sure the guest got the towels and ask if there is anything else she can do for the guest. The culture of Ritz-Carlton lets the employees know they are expected to deliver service to the guest and provides employees with the tools and support they need to deliver good service. Thus the managers serve as role models for the customers.

■■■ Characteristics of Service Marketing

Service marketers must understand the four characteristics of services: **intangibility**, **inseparability**, **variability**, and **perishability** (see Figure 2–1).

Intangibility

Unlike physical products, intangible products cannot be seen, tasted, felt, heard, or smelled before they are purchased. Hospitality and travel industry products are experiential only, and we do not know the quality of the product until after we have experienced it. A restaurant customer will not know how good the meal is until after he or she has consumed it. Likewise, a family planning a vacation will not know if the destination for their vacation and the choice of their resort was a good one until they have had their vacation experience.

One implication of experiential products is that we take away only the memories of our experiences. Marriott Vacation Clubs International realizes this and has made a deliberate effort to create memorable guest experiences. Marriott realizes that a white-water rafting trip can create memories that a family visiting their Mountainside Resort in Utah will talk about for years. The fun the family experienced while white-water rafting, along with their other experiences at the resort, will make them want to return. As a result, the staff at the Mountainside Resort know they must promote the activities of the destination as well as the resort. Other resorts create memories. It might be champagne and music on the beach at sunset or the special and unexpected attention that an employee provides for a guest, such as the one that is used for the opening of Chapter 10.

Because guests will not know the service they will receive until after they receive it, service marketers should take steps to provide their prospective customers

Figure 2–1
Four service characteristics.

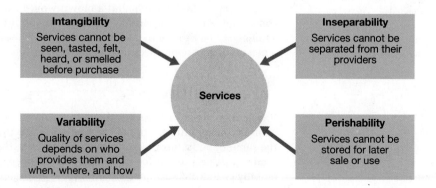

The awning, bright colors, and outside seating of this café in Perth, Australia, create an environment that attracts attention and is inviting to those who want informal dining. Courtesy of rick strange/world pictures/photoshot/Newscom.

with evidence that will help them evaluate the service.[7] This process is called providing tangible evidence. Promotional material, employees' appearance, and the service firm's physical environment all help tangibilize service. A hotel's promotional material will include photographs of the hotel's public area, guest rooms, and meeting space. It will also contain floor plans of the meeting space, including room capacities for the different types of setups, to help the meeting planner visualize the meeting space. Today, extensive print packages have been replaced with Web sites that contain this information. These sites will also include videos of the meeting space.

A banquet salesperson for a fine restaurant can make the product tangible by taking pastry samples on morning sales calls. This creates goodwill and provides the prospective client with some knowledge about the restaurant's food quality. The salesperson might also bring a photo album showing photographs of banquet setups, plate presentations for different entrees, and testimonial letters from past clients. For persons having a dinner as part of their wedding reception, some hotels prepare the meal for the bride's family before the wedding day. Thus the bride actually gets to experience the food before the reception so there are no surprises.

The salesperson may be the prospective customer's first contact with the hotel or restaurant. A salesperson who is well groomed and dressed appropriately and who answers questions in a prompt, professional manner can do a great deal to help the customer develop a positive image of the hotel. Uniforms also provide tangible evidence of the experience. The uniforms worn by front-desk staff of the Hotel Nikko San Francisco are professional and provide tangible evidence that the guest is walking into a four-diamond hotel.

Everything about a hospitality company communicates something. The wrappers put on drinking glasses in the guest rooms serve the purpose of letting the guest know that the glasses have been cleaned. The fold in the toilet paper in the bathroom lets the guest know the bathroom has been tidied.

Physical Evidence

Physical evidence that is not managed properly can hurt a business. Negative messages communicated by poorly managed physical evidence include signs that continue to advertise a holiday special two weeks after the holiday has passed, signs with missing letters or burned-out lights, parking lots and grounds that are unkempt and full of trash, and employees in dirty uniforms at messy workstations. Such signs send negative messages to customers. Restaurant managers are trained to do a preopening inspection of the restaurant. One of the things they look for is that all light bulbs are working. A little thing like a burned-out bulb can give a guest sitting near it an impression that the restaurant does not pay attention to detail. Our customers notice details; this is why a consistent message from industry leaders is that managers must pay attention to detail.

A firm's communications should also reinforce its positioning. Ronald McDonald is great for McDonald's, but a clown would not be appropriate for a Four Seasons hotel. All said, a service organization should review every piece of tangible evidence to make sure that each delivers the desired **organization image**—the way a person or group views an organization—to target customers.[8]

Inseparability

Physical goods are produced, then stored, later sold, and still later consumed. In contrast, hospitality products are first sold and then produced and consumed at the same time. In most hospitality services, both the service provider and the customer must be present for the transaction to occur. Inseparability means both the employee and the customer are often part of the product. The food in a restaurant

e **2.1** http://www.tonyshouston.com/ Click on "Restaurant" and then click on detail to see the different shots of the restaurant. The restaurant's owner has used both attention to detail and excellent photography to tangibilize the elegance of his restaurant.

2.2 http://www .chipotle. com/ Click on "Restaurants" and then on the Chipotle Experience. The customer and the employee work together to produce a customized product for the employee.

Entertainment, like that provided by the high-concept Blue Man Group, exhibits the quality of inseparability. As the group expanded from 3 to 60 performers, the Blue Men created an intensive training program to ensure that the experience they provide their audiences would be consistent from cast to cast around the world. Courtesy of Kevin Kolczynski/Universal Orlando Resorts/AP Photo.

may be outstanding, but if the employee serving the food to the customer has a poor attitude or provides inattentive service, customers will not be satisfied with their experience.

A couple may have chosen a restaurant because it is quiet and romantic, but if other customers include a group of loud and boisterous conventioneers seated in the same room, these customers will spoil the couple's experience. Managers must manage their customers so they do not create dissatisfaction for others.

Another implication of inseparability is that customers and employees must understand the service delivery system because they are coproducing the service. Customers must understand the menu items in a restaurant so that they get the dish they expect. This means hospitality and travel organizations have to train customers just as they train employees. A hotel at the Newark Airport is popular with international tourists who have just arrived from overseas. Many of these guests pay in cash or with travelers' checks because they do not use credit cards. On more than one occasion, the front-desk clerk has been observed answering the phone of an upset guest who claims the movie system does not work. The clerk must explain that the guest did not establish credit because cash was paid for his or her room. She informs guests that they must come to the front desk and pay for the movie before it can be activated. Guests obviously become upset on receiving this information. The hotel could avoid this problem and improve customer relations by asking guests at arrival time if they would like to make a deposit for anything they might charge, such as in-room movies.

Casinos know they must train customers how to play certain table games such as blackjack or craps. Casinos provide booklets on how to play the games and also offer free lessons in the casino. This enables the guest to enjoy the casino resort and creates new customers for the casino.

Finally, we often ask customers to coproduce the service they are consuming. This means organizations must select, hire, and train customers.[9] Fast-food restaurants train customers to get their own drinks. This gives the customer something to do while waiting and reduces the need for employees to fill drink orders themselves. Hotels, restaurants, airlines, and rental car companies train customers to use the electronic check-in and the Internet to get information and to make reservations. The customer using these services is performing both the job of customer service agent and reservationist. The benefits provided to the guest by becoming an "employee" include increased value, customization, and reduced waiting time. For example, Chipotle requires guests to wait on themselves, which allows them to provide lower prices than a full-service restaurant. The characteristic of inseparability requires hospitality managers to manage both their employees and their customers.

Variability

Services are highly variable. Their quality depends on who provides them and when and where they are provided. There are several causes of service **variability**. Services are produced and consumed simultaneously, which limits quality control. Fluctuating demand makes it difficult to deliver consistent products during periods of peak demand. The high degree of contact between the service provider and the guest means that product consistency depends on the service provider's skills and performance at the time of the exchange. A guest can receive excellent service one day and mediocre service from the same person the next day. In the case of mediocre service, the service person may not have felt well or perhaps experienced an emotional problem. Lack of communication and heterogeneity of guest expectations also lead to service variability. A restaurant customer ordering a medium steak may expect it to be cooked all the way through, whereas the person working on the broiler may define medium as having a warm pink center. The guest will be disappointed when he or she cuts into the steak and sees pink meat. Restaurants have solved this by developing common definitions of steak doneness and communicating them to the employees and customers. Sometimes the communication to the customer is verbal, and sometimes it is printed on the menu. Customers usually return to a restaurant because they enjoyed their last experience. When the product they receive is different and does not meet their expectations on the next visit, they often do not return. Variability or lack of consistency in the product is a major cause of customer disappointment in the hospitality industry.

When variability is absent, we have consistency, which is one of the key factors in the success of a service business.[10] Consistency means that customers receive the expected product without unwanted surprises. In the hotel industry, this means that a wake-up call requested for 7 A.M. always occurs as planned and that a meeting planner can count on the hotel to deliver coffee ordered for a 3 P.M. meeting break, which will be ready and waiting when the group breaks at that time. In the restaurant business, consistency means that the shrimp scampi will taste the same way it tasted two weeks ago, towels will always be available in the bathrooms, and the brand of vodka specified last week will be in stock next month. Consistency is one of the major reasons for the worldwide success of McDonald's.

Here are three steps hospitality firms can take to reduce variability and create consistency:

1. **Invest in good hiring and training procedures.** Recruiting the right employees and providing them with excellent training is crucial, regardless of whether employees are highly skilled professionals or low-skilled workers. Better-trained personnel exhibit six characteristics: *Competence:* They possess the required skill and knowledge. *Courtesy:* They are friendly, respectful, and considerate. *Credibility:* They are trustworthy. *Reliability:* They perform the service consistently and accurately. *Responsiveness:* They respond quickly to customers' requests and problems. *Communication:* They make an effort to understand the customer and communicate clearly. Excellent hospitality and travel companies such as Marriott and Southwest Airlines spend a great deal of time and effort making sure they hire the right employees. But their attention to employees does not end there. They also invest in their employees by providing ongoing training.

2. **Standardize the service-performance process throughout the organization.** Diagramming the service delivery system in a service blueprint can simultaneously map out the service process, the points of customer contact, and the evidence of service from the customer's point of view. The guest's experience includes a series of steps he or she must enact before even getting to sleep. Behind the scenes, the hotel must skillfully help the guest move from one step to the next. By visually representing the service, a service blueprint can help one understand the process and see potential design flaws while the service delivery system is still in the design stage. Figure 2–2 shows the service blueprint for a guest spending a night at a hotel. The line of interaction represents the guest's contact with hotel employees. The line of visibility represents those areas that will be visible to the guest and provide tangible evidence of the hotel's quality. The line of internal interaction represents internal support systems that are required to service the guest.

3. **Monitor customer satisfaction.** Use suggestion and complaint systems, customer surveys, and comparison shopping. Hospitality companies have the advantage of knowing their customers. Companies also have the e-mail addresses of those who purchase from their Web sites. This makes it easy to send a customer satisfaction survey after a guest has stayed in a hotel or used its service. Travel intermediaries, such as Travelocity.com, contact guests to see how satisfied they were with a hotel they booked on their site. They realize if a customer

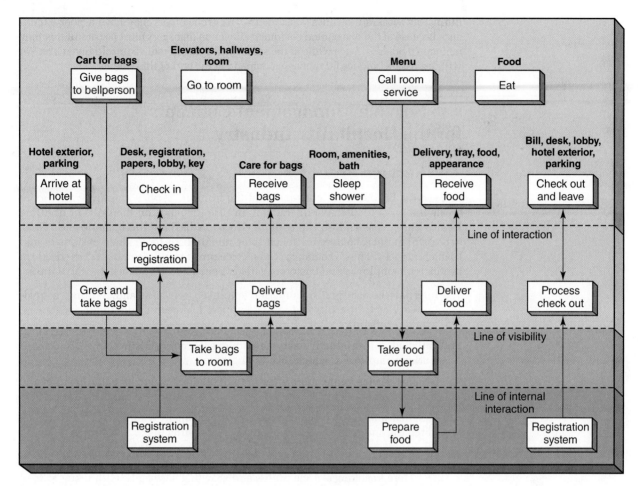

Figure 2–2
Blueprint for overnight hotel stay.
Source: Valarie Zeithaml, Mary Jo Bitner, and Dwayne D. Gremler, *Services Marketing: Integrating Customer Focus Across the Firm* (4th ed.) (New York: McGraw-Hill, 2006).

had a bad experience they may not use their service again, even though they cannot control the service and quality of the hotels they represent. They try to create a consistent experience and set customer expectations by using a star rating system and publishing customer comments. Firms can also develop customer information databases and systems to permit more personalized, customized service, especially online.

Perishability

Services cannot be stored. A 100-room hotel that sells only 60 rooms on a particular night cannot inventory the 40 unused rooms and then sell 140 rooms the next night. Revenue lost from not selling those 40 rooms is gone forever. Because of service **perishability**, airlines and some hotels charge guests holding guaranteed reservations when they fail to arrive. Restaurants are also starting to charge a fee to customers who do not show up for a reservation. They, too, realize that if someone does not show up for a reservation, the opportunity to sell that seat may be lost.

Some hotels will often sell hotel rooms at a very low rate rather let them go unsold. Because of inseparability, this can cause problems. Oftentimes, the discounted rate brings in a different type of customer that is not compatible with the hotel's normal customer. For example, one luxury hotel that normally sold rooms for $300 placed rooms on Priceline's (opaque channel) for $80.* The guest paying $80 a night may be a leisure customer, partying in his or her room at night while the regular hotel guests

2.3 http://www .mcdonalds.com/ In the food section click on burgers. Look how uniform all the sandwiches look. McDonald's has mastered the art of consistency.

_____
*An opaque channel is a one where the customer knows the general location and class of the hotel, but does not know the specific name of the hotel he or she is purchasing. These channels are used by hotels to prevent help loyal customers from purchasing discounted rates.

during the week are business customers. These customers may have a poor experience because of the discounted customers. Revenue managers must be careful that they maintain a brand's image while at the same time trying to reduce unsold inventory. We will discuss techniques for managing demand at the end of this chapter.

■■■ Service Management Concepts for the Hospitality Industry

The Service Profit Chain

In a service business, the customer and the frontline service employee *interact* to create the service. Effective interaction, in turn, depends on the skills of frontline service employees and on the support processes backing these employees. Thus, successful service companies focus their attention on *both* their customers and their employees. They understand the **service profit chain**, which links service firm profits with employee and customer satisfaction. This chain consists of five links:

1. **Internal service quality:** superior employee selection and training, a quality work environment, and strong support for those dealing with customers, which results in . . .

2. **Satisfied and productive service employees:** more satisfied, loyal, and hardworking employees, which results in . . .

3. **Greater service value:** more effective and efficient customer value creation and service delivery, which results in . . .

4. **Satisfied and loyal customers:** satisfied customers who remain loyal, repeat purchase, and refer other customers, which results in . . .

5. **Healthy service profits and growth:** superior service firm performance.

Therefore, reaching service profits and growth goals begins with taking care of those who take care of customers.[11]

The concept of the service profit chain is well illustrated by a story about how Bill Marriott, Jr., chairman of Marriott Hotels, interviews prospective managers:

> Bill Marriott tells job candidates that the hotel chain wants to satisfy three groups: customers, employees, and stockholders. Although all of the groups are important, he asks in which order the groups should be satisfied. Most candidates say satisfy the customer first. Marriott, however, reasons differently. First, employees must be satisfied. If employees love their jobs and feel a sense of pride in the hotel, they will serve customers well. Satisfied customers will return frequently to the Marriott. Moreover, dealing with happy customers will make employees even more satisfied, resulting in better service and still greater repeat business, all of which will yield a level of profits that will satisfy Marriott stockholders.[12]

Figure 2–3
Three types of marketing in service industries.

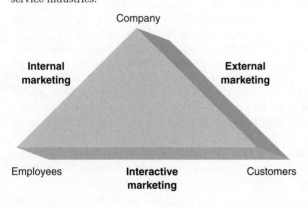

Three Types of Marketing

Service marketing requires more than just traditional external marketing using the four Ps. Figure 2–3 shows that service marketing also requires both internal marketing and interactive marketing.

Internal marketing means that the service firm must effectively train and motivate its customer-contact employees and all the supporting service people to work as a team to provide customer satisfaction. For the firm to deliver consistently high service quality, everyone must practice customer orientation. It is not enough to have a marketing department doing traditional marketing while the rest of the company goes its own way. Everyone else in the organization must also practice marketing. In fact, internal marketing must precede external marketing. Failure to practice internal marketing can be expensive. A study of thirty-three hotels showed that turnover costs averaged approximately $10,000 per employee for those with complex jobs.[13] In Chapter 10 we discuss internal marketing.

Interactive marketing means that perceived service quality depends heavily on the quality of the buyer–seller interaction during the service encounter. In product marketing, product quality often depends little on how the product is obtained. But in services of marketing, service quality depends on both the service deliverer and the quality of the delivery. The customer judges service quality not just on technical quality (the quality of the food) but also on its functional quality (the service provided in the restaurant). Service employees have to master interactive marketing skills or functions as well.[14]

Today as competition and costs increase and as productivity and quality decrease, more marketing sophistication is needed. Hospitality companies face the task of increasing three major marketing areas: their service differentiation, service quality, and service productivity.

■■■ Management Strategies for Service Businesses

Managing Service Differentiation

Service marketers often complain about the difficulty of differentiating their services from those of competitors. To the extent that customers view the services of different providers as similar, they care less about the provider than the price.

The solution to price competition is to develop a differentiated offering. The offer can include innovative features that set one company's offer apart from that of its competitors. For example, airlines have introduced such innovations as Internet access while in flight and seats that turn into flat beds. British Airways offers international travelers a sleeping compartment, hot showers, and cooked-to-order breakfasts. Unfortunately, most service innovations are copied easily. Still, the service company that innovates regularly usually gains a succession of temporary advantages and an innovative reputation that may help it keep customers who want to go with the best.

Service companies can differentiate their service delivery in three ways: through people, physical environment, and process. The company can distinguish itself by having more able and reliable customer-contact people than its competitors, or it can develop a superior physical environment in which the service product is delivered. It can design a superior delivery process. Finally, service companies can also differentiate their images through symbols and branding. For example, a familiar symbol would be McDonald's golden arches, and familiar brands include Hilton, Shangri-La, and Sofitel.

Managing Service Quality

One of the major ways that a service firm can differentiate itself is by delivering consistently higher quality than its competitors. One can have a number of objective criteria for evaluating a tangible product such as an automobile. For example, how long does it take it to go from zero to 60 miles per hour, how many miles to the gallon does it get, how much leg room does it have, and so on. With hospitality products, quality is measured by how well customer expectations are met. The key is to exceed the customers' service-quality expectations. As the chief executive at American Express puts it, "Promise only what you can deliver and deliver more than you promise!" These expectations are based on past experiences, word of mouth, and service firm advertising. If perceived service of a given firm exceeds expected service, customers are apt to use the provider again. Customer retention is perhaps the best measure of quality: A service firm's ability to retain its customers depends on how consistently it delivers value to them. A manufacturer's quality goal might be zero defects, but the service provider's goal is zero customer defections.

Marketing Highlight

2–1 In its 25-year history, Cirque du Soleil (French for "circus of the sun") has continually broken loose from circus convention. It takes traditional ingredients such as trapeze artists, clowns, muscle men, and contortionists and places them in a nontraditional setting with lavish costumes, new age music, and spectacular stage designs. And it eliminates other commonly observed circus elements—there are no animals. Each production is loosely fit together with a theme such as "a tribute to the nomadic soul" (Varekai) or "a phantasmagoria of" (Saltimbanco). The group has grown from its Quebec street-performance roots to become a dollar global enterprise, with 3,000 employees on four continents entertaining audiences millions annually.

Part of its success comes from a company culture that encourages artistic creativity and innovation and carefully safeguards the brand. One new production is created each year—always in-house—and is unique: There are no duplicate touring companies. In addition to Cirque's mix of media and local promotion, an extensive interactive e-mail program to its million-plus-member Cirque Club creates an online community of fans—20 to 30 percent of all ticket sales come from club members. Generating $800 million in revenue annually, the Cirque du Soleil brand has expanded to encompass a record label, a retail operation, and resident productions in Las Vegas (five in all), Tokyo, and other cities.

Source: Matt Krantz, "Tinseltown Gets Glitzy New Star," *USA Today* (August 24, 2009); Linda Tischier, "Join the Circus," *Fast Company* (July 2005): 53–58; "Cirque du Soleil," *America's Greatest Brands,* 3 (2004); Geoff Keighley, "The Factory," *Business 2.0* (February 2004): 102; Robin D. Rusch, "Cirque du Soleil Phantasmagoria Contorts," *Brandchannel.com,* (December 1, 2003).

Description: Sacramento, CA—May 11: The character Target at Cirque du Soleil's show "Quidam" on May 11, 2011, in Sacramento, California. Courtesy of Randy Miramontez/ Dreamstime

2.4 http://www .cirquedusoleil .com/ Look at some of Cirque du Soleil's shows to see how they have created a unique entertainment experience. The shows are very popular in Las Vegas in part because international visitors do not need to understand English to enjoy the show.

The service provider needs to identify the expectations of target customers concerning service quality. In Chapters 4, 5, and 6, we discuss how to obtain information on your customers and how to understand your customers. Knowing your customer is a requisite for delivering quality. Once customer expectations are determined, managers need to develop a service delivery system that will deliver a service that meets the guest's expectations. It is important that the service provider clearly define and communicate that level to its employees and customers what needs to be delivered to meet customer expectations. Investments in service usually pay off through increased customer retention and sales.

Studies of well-managed service companies show that they share a number of common virtues regarding service quality. First, top service companies are "customer obsessed." They have a philosophy of satisfying customer needs, which wins enduring customer loyalty. Second, well-managed service companies have a history of top management commitment to quality. Management at companies such as Marriott, Disney, and McDonald's look not only at financial performance but also at service performance. Third, the best service providers set high service-quality standards. A 98 percent accuracy standard may sound good, but using this standard, the MGM Grand Hotel would send fifty guests a day to rooms that are already occupied, the Outback Steak House chain would have hundreds of miscooked steaks, and Accor Hotels would make hundreds of errors in its central reservation office every week. This level of errors is unacceptable for customer-directed companies. Top service companies do not settle merely for "good" service; they aim for 100 percent defect-free service.

Fourth, the top service firms watch service performance closely, both their own and that of competitors. They use methods such as comparison shopping, customer surveys, suggestions, and complaint forms. Good service companies also communicate their concerns about service quality to employees and provide performance feedback. Ritz-Carlton has daily meetings with its employees to go over customer feedback and to review the guest history of arriving guests. Many quick-service restaurant chains offer customers a chance to win prizes by calling a toll-free number and answering several service-related questions.

Managing Service Productivity

With their costs rising rapidly, service firms are under great pressure to increase service productivity. They can do so in several ways. They can train current employees better or hire new ones who will work harder or more skillfully. Or they can increase the quantity of their service by giving up some quality. The provider can "industrialize the service" by adding equipment and standardizing production, as in McDonald's assembly-line approach to fast-food retailing. Finally, a service provider can harness the power of technology. Although we often think of technology's power to save time and costs in manufacturing companies, it also has great—and often untapped—potential to make service workers more productive.

However, companies must avoid pushing productivity so hard that doing so reduces quality. Attempts to industrialize a service or cut costs can make a service company more efficient in the short run. But that can also reduce its longer-run ability to innovate, maintain service quality, or respond to consumer needs and desires. For example, some airlines have learned this lesson the hard way as they attempt to economize in the face of rising costs. They stopped offering even the little things for free—such as in-flight snacks—and began charging extra for everything from curbside luggage check-in to aisle seats. The result is a plane full of resentful customers who avoid the airline whenever they can. In their attempts to improve productivity, these airlines mangled customer service.

Thus, in attempting to improve service productivity, companies must be mindful of how they create and deliver customer value. In short, they should be careful not to take the "service" out of service.

Resolving Customer Complaints

Many service companies have invested heavily to develop streamlined and efficient service-delivery systems. They want to ensure that customers will receive consistently high-quality service in every service encounter. Unlike product manufacturers, who can adjust their machinery and inputs until everything is perfect, service quality always varies, depending on the interactions between employees and customers. Problems inevitably occur. As hard as they try, even the best companies have an occasional late delivery, burned steak, or grumpy employee. A company cannot always s prevent service problems, but it can learn from them. Good service recovery can turn angry customers into loyal ones. In fact, good recovery can win more customer purchasing and loyalty than if things had gone well in the first place. Therefore, companies should take steps not only to provide good service every time but also to recover from service mistakes.

To have effective complaint resolution, managers must empower frontline service employees—to give them the authority, responsibility, and incentives they need to recognize, care about, and tend to customer needs. For example, Marriott places its employees in empowerment training, which encourages them to go beyond their normal jobs to solve customer problems. Empowered employees can act quickly and effectively to keep service problems from resulting in lost customers. The Marriott Desert Springs says the major goal for customer-contact employees is to ensure that "our guests experience excellent service and hospitality while staying at our resort." Well-trained employees are given the authority to do whatever

Marketing Highlight | Recommendations for Improving Service Quality

2–2 Berry, Parasuraman, and Zeithamil, pioneers in conducting academic service research, offer ten lessons that they maintain are essential for improving service quality across service industries.

1. **Listening.** Understand what customers really want through continuous learning about the expectations and perceptions of customers and noncustomers (e.g., by means of a service-quality information system).

2. **Reliability.** The single most important dimension of service quality, reliability must be a service priority.

3. **Basic service.** Service companies must deliver the basics and do what they are supposed to do: Keep promises, use common sense, listen to customers, keep customers informed, and be determined to deliver value to customers.

4. **Service design.** Develop a holistic view of the service while managing its many details.

5. **Recovery.** To satisfy customers who encounter a service problem, service companies should encourage customers to complain (and make it easy for them to do so), respond quickly and personally, and develop a problem-resolution system.

6. **Surprising customers.** Although reliability is the most important dimension in meeting customers' service expectations, process dimensions such as assurance, responsiveness, and empathy are most important in exceeding customer expectations (e.g., by surprising them with uncommon swiftness, grace, courtesy, competence, commitment, and understanding).

7. **Fair play.** Service companies must make special efforts to be fair, and to demonstrate fairness, to customers and employees.

8. **Teamwork.** Teamwork is what enables large organizations to deliver service with care and attentiveness by improving employee motivation and capabilities.

9. **Employee research.** Marketers should conduct research with employees to reveal why service problems occur and what companies must do to solve problems.

10. **Servant leadership.** Quality service comes from inspired leadership throughout the organization; from excellent service-system design; from the effective use of information and technology; and from a slow-to-change, invisible, all-powerful, internal force called corporate culture.

Source: Adapted from Leonard L. Berry, A. Parasuraman, and Valarie A. Zeithaml, "The Lessons for Improving Service Quality," *MSI Reports Working Paper Series, no. 03-Vol* (Cambridge, MA: Marketing Science Institute, 2003): 61–82. See also Leonard I. Berry's books, *On Great Service: A Framework for Action* (New York: Free Press, 2006), and *Discovering the Soul of Service* (New York: Free Press,1999), as well as his articles; Leonard L. Berry, Vankatesh Shankar, Janet Parish, Susan Cadwallader, and Thomas Dotzel, "Creating New Markets Through Service Innovation," *Sloan Management Review* (Winter 2006): 56–63; Leonard L. Berry, Stephen H. Haeckel, and Lewis P. Carbone, "How to Lead the Customer Experience," *Marketing Management* (January–February 2003): 18–23; and Leonard L. Berry, Kathleen Seiders, and Dhruv Grewal, "Understanding Service Convenience," *Journal of Marketing* (July 2002): 1–17.

---

it takes, on the spot, to keep guests happy. They are also expected to help management ferret out the cause of guests' problems, and to inform managers of ways to improve overall hotel service and guests' comfort.

Resolving customer complaints is a critical component of customer retention. One study by the Technical Research Programs Institute found that if a customer has a major complaint, 91 percent will not buy from you again, but if it was resolved quickly, 82 percent of those customers will return. The complaint resolution drops the customer defection from 91 out of 100 to 18 out of 100. With resolution of minor complaints, the defection rate can be reduced to less than 5 out of 100.[15] In complaint resolution there are two important factors. First, if you resolve a complaint, do it quickly—the longer it takes to resolve, the higher the defection rate— and second, seek out customer complaints.

For example, a businesswoman had just returned from an overseas trip. After a good night's sleep in a New York hotel, she was ready for an American breakfast. She dialed room service, and her breakfast was delivered promptly. A cheerful waiter wheeled the table into the room and positioned it so that the woman could look out the window. He opened the heating compartment and pulled out the breakfast that the woman had been waiting for: a full hot American breakfast. The waiter handed the woman the bill, and she promptly signed the bill and added a handsome tip. Now she was ready to start her breakfast.

The waiter said, "I'm sorry, you will have to pay cash." She explained that she did not have any money with her and pulled out her credit cards, offering the American Express gold card she had used to check into the hotel. The waiter called on the phone and after five minutes it was resolved that the woman could use her credit card. The woman, now upset, sat down to a cold breakfast.[16] If the waiter had been empowered to resolve complaints, he would have been able to leave the room, go down to the front desk, and resolve the problem at the front desk while the woman was enjoying her breakfast.

Complaints that come in by letter should be responded to quickly by a letter or phone call. If you respond by letter, customize part of the letter acknowledging the customer's specific complaint and what will be done to prevent it from happening again. A resolution to the complaint should be offered to the guest. A more effective way of resolving the complaint can be through the use of the telephone. Today it costs less to make a telephone call than it does to send out a letter. The telephone call allows personal contact with the guest and allows the manager to probe, finding out exactly what happened to the guest. The worst thing a company can do is send out a form letter or e-mail that shows no empathy to the guest's problem or not respond at all. *Restaurant Business* had an employee contact twenty-five customer service representatives of restaurant chains, stating she had received poor service. Of the twenty-five companies contacted, only fifteen responded to her complaint. One customer service representative told her, "I'm busy right now, can you call back in a half an hour?" When she called back, the customer service rep said, "Okay, I have a minute now. What's your problem—slow service, is that all? Okay, I can write up a report if you want." Of those restaurants that did respond, only ten did a good or excellent job of resolving the complaint. The customer service representatives at these restaurants did a nice job of showing concern on the initial phone call and followed up with a letter and coupons. In one case, a regional vice president called the customer back to find out what went wrong.[17]

Another critical area in complaint resolution is that most customers do not complain. They do not give managers a chance to resolve their problem. They just leave and never come back. When a customer does complain, management should be grateful because it gives them a chance to resolve the complaint and gain the customer's repeat business. Most complaints come from loyal customers who want to return, but they also want management to fix the problem so it will not occur on their next visit. Managers must develop ways to encourage customers to complain. Methods to seek complaints include customer hotlines that encourage customers to call about problems they are having. Customer comment cards encourage customers to discuss problems that they had with the product. Managers can train employees to look out for guests who look dissatisfied and try to determine their problems. A service guarantee is another way of getting customers to complain; to invoke the guarantee, they have to complain. If we shift our perspective to see complaints as gifts, we can more readily use the information the complaints generate to grow our own business. Customer complaints are one of the most available yet underutilized sources of customer and market information.[18]

A club manager told us about a surprise the club had from a truly excellent Christmas party. The staff was proud of the way the evening went because everything went as planned. The manager was truly surprised when a member of many years said he wanted to set up a conference call with the food and beverage manager, chef, and the manager to discuss the shortcomings of the event. The call lasted an hour and a half, with many of the complaints considered frivolous by the management team. Through careful listening, the manager was able to separate the symptoms from the real problem. The manager asked his staff to reflect on the call and set a meeting for the next day. He also asked the food and beverage manager to develop a profile of who came to the event. What they discovered is that most of the people attending the event were older retired members who did not have family in the area and were alone during the holidays. Normally the club's party attracted 45-year-old members and the party was planned for this group, not the 65 and older group who attended the party. This was the essence of the member's complaint: The menu and theme of the party were developed for a much younger group. By listening to what the member was saying and being open to the member's comments, the club's managers discovered the party was developed for the wrong target market. If the member had not complained or the club's managers were not open to the member's complaint, the holiday party would have continued to be developed for the wrong target audience.

A clean stylish uniform puts the server into the role of serving the guests and also the customers perceive him to be a professional server. Courtesy of Paul Kenward © Dorling Kindersley.

Managing Employees as Part of the Product

In the hospitality industry employees are a critical part of the product and marketing mix. This means that the human resources and marketing departments must work closely together. In restaurants without a human resources department, the restaurant manager serves as the human resource manager. The manager must hire friendly and capable employees and formulate policies that support positive relations between employees and guests. Even minor details related to personnel policy can have a significant effect on the product's quality.[19]

In a well-run hospitality organization, there are two customers, the paying customers and the employees.[20] The task of training and motivating employees to provide good customer service is called internal marketing. In the hospitality industry, it is not enough to have a marketing department focused on traditional marketing to a targeted external market. The job of the marketing department includes encouraging everyone in the organization to practice customer-oriented thinking[21] (see Chapter 10). The following excerpt from *In Search of Excellence* illustrates the importance of well-trained employees in a hospitality operation:

Canyon Ranch is known for its excellence. By providing a consitently high-quality product, Canyon Ranch has produced positive word of mouth that reduces the perceived risk of new customers. Courtesy of Canyon Ranch.

> We had decided, after dinner, to spend a second night in Washington. Our business day had taken us beyond the last convention flight out. We had no reservations but were near the new Four Seasons, had stayed there once before, and liked it. As we walked through the lobby wondering how best to plead our case for a room, we brace for the usual chilly shoulder accorded to latecomers. To our astonishment, the concierge looked up, smiled, called us by name, and asked how we were. She remembered our names! We knew in a flash why in the space of a brief year the Four Seasons had become the "place to stay" in the District and was a rare first-year holder of the venerated four-star rating.[22]

Managing Perceived Risk

Customers who buy hospitality products experience some anxiety because they cannot experience the product beforehand.[23] Consider a salesperson whose sales manager asks him or her to set up a regional sales meeting. Suppose that the salesperson had never set up a meeting or worked with hotels. The salesperson is obviously nervous. If the meeting goes well, the sales manager will be favorably impressed; if it goes badly, the salesperson may be blamed.

In arranging for the meeting place, the salesperson has to trust the hotel's salesperson. Good hotel salespeople alleviate client fears by letting them know that they have arranged hundreds of successful meetings. The salesperson's claims to professionalism can be affirmed through letters of praise from former clients and a tour of the hotel's facilities. A salesperson must reduce the client's fear and gain the client's confidence.

One way of combating concern is to encourage the client to try the hotel or restaurant in a low-risk situation. Hotels and resorts offer familiarization (or fam) trips to meeting planners and travel agents. Airlines often offer complimentary flight tickets because they are also interested in creating business. Hotels provide rooms, food, beverage, and entertainment at no cost to the prospective client in the hope that this exposure will encourage him or her to recommend the hotel. Fam trips reduce a product's intangibility by letting the intermediary customer experience the hotel beforehand.

The high risk that people perceive when purchasing hospitality products increases loyalty to companies that have provided them with a consistent product in the past. Crowne Plaza attracted its competitor's loyal customers by using the following tactic: Guests were billed at the regular room rate. However, they were free to pay less if they felt the accommodations and service were not worth the price. The promotion was highly successful, attracting a number of new guests, almost all of whom paid the full rate.

Meeting planners sometimes select the hotel for a client's meeting or are quite influential in the decision. It is not surprising that many select four or five-star-rated hotels even though other, equally suitable hotels may be available at lower costs. Meeting planners feel there is less personal risk in selecting a highly rated hotel, particularly in the event of unforeseen problems.

Managing Capacity and Demand

Managers have two major options for matching capacity with demand: change capacity or change demand. For example, airlines use dynamic capacity management to adjust capacity to match demand. The airlines swap small aircraft for larger aircraft on flights that are selling out faster than normal. The smaller aircraft are assigned to flights that are expected to have low load factors.[24] If a larger plane is not available, they can reduce demand by eliminating discounted fares and charging a higher fare. The higher fare means that some passengers, often pleasure travelers visiting friends and relatives, will decide not to make the trip or switch to another flight, thus reducing the overall demand. In this section we discuss capacity management, and in the next section we focus on demand management.

Capacity Management

Corporate management is responsible for matching capacity with demand on a long-term basis; unit managers are responsible for matching capacity with fluctuations in short-term demand. The techniques presented in this section assist in managing short-term demand.

INVOLVE THE CUSTOMER IN THE SERVICE DELIVERY SYSTEM   Getting the customer involved in service operations expands the number of people that one employee can serve, thus increasing the capacity of the operation. The concept has wide acceptance in food and beverage operations, but modern technology is responsible for its increasing use in the accommodation sector.

Self-service technologies (SSTs) allow the customer to serve as the company's employee. The adoption of SSTs that increase customer satisfaction represents one of the biggest opportunities for the travel and hospitality industry. A common example is a self-service soft drink dispenser in a fast-food restaurant. A more sophisticated SST is an online ordering site for a restaurant where the customer's order is placed automatically in the cooking queue at the proper time so it will be ready when the customer requested the item. For example, a customer places an order at 10 A.M. to pick up at 12:30 P.M. The system is integrated with the point of sale system in the restaurant; thus it can determine the time from placing the order to serving the food to the customer. Based on this knowledge of production, it can determine when to place the order so it will be freshly prepared and ready at 12:30 P.M. We can also design the service delivery system to allow the customer to become an employee. For example, many convention hotels have self-service food and beverage operations. They feature premade sandwiches and salads, enabling the operator to build a buffer inventory. When a meeting breaks and a number of the participants want a meal or snack, these operations have the capacity to serve many people quickly.

CROSS-TRAIN EMPLOYEES   In a hotel, the demand for all services does not rise and fall in unison. One outlet may experience sudden strong demand while other areas enjoy normal levels. When managers cross-train their employees, they can shift employees to increase the capacity. A hotel restaurant that does only thirty to forty covers a night cannot justify more than two service people, even though it may have eighty seats. However, such low staffing levels mean that the restaurant may have a difficult time serving more than sixty guests, especially if they arrive at about the same time. Having front-desk staff and banquet staff trained in à la carte service means the restaurant manager has a group of employees that can be called on if demand for the restaurant on any particular night exceeds the capacity of two service people.

USE PART-TIME EMPLOYEES   Managers can use part-time employees to expand capacity during an unusually busy day or meal period or during the busy months of the year for seasonal businesses. Summer resorts hire part-time staff to work during the summer period. They reduce their staff during the slower seasons and either reduce staff further or close during the low season. Part-time employees allow a hotel or restaurant to increase or decrease its capacity efficiently. Part-time employees can also be used on an on-call basis. Hotels usually have a list of banquet waiters to call for large events. Part-time employees give an organization the flexibility to adjust the number of employees to the level required to meet demand.

RENT OR SHARE EXTRA FACILITIES AND EQUIPMENT   Businesses do not have to be constrained by space limitations or equipment limitations. A hotel with an opportunity to book a three-day meeting from Tuesday to Thursday may have to turn down the business because all the function space is booked Wednesday evening, and there is no space for the group's Wednesday evening dinner. Rather than lose the group, a creative solution would be to suggest the group go outside the hotel for a unique dinner experience. In Paris, the alternative might be a dinner cruise on the Seine. In Arizona, it might be an outdoor steak fry, and in Hong Kong, it could be a dinner at Jumbo, the famous floating restaurant.

Catering firms often purchase only the amount of equipment they use regularly. When they have a busy period, they rent equipment. Renting, sharing, or moving groups to outside facilities can increase capacity to accommodate short-term demand.

SCHEDULE DOWNTIME DURING PERIODS OF LOW DEMAND   Businesses in seasonal resorts have periods of high and low demand. The actions we have discussed so far enable a business to increase capacity to meet peak demand. One way to decrease capacity to match the lower demand is to schedule repairs and maintenance during the low season.

CHANGE THE SERVICE DELIVERY SYSTEM   Because services are perishable, managing capacity and demand is a key function of hospitality marketing. For example, Mother's Day is traditionally a restaurant's busiest day of the year, with the peak time at lunch from 11 A.M. to 2 P.M. This three-hour period presents restaurateurs with one of their greatest sales opportunities. To take full advantage of this opportunity, restaurant managers must accomplish two things: First, they must adjust their operating systems to enable the business to operate at maximum capacity. Second, they must remember that their goal is to create satisfied customers.

Many restaurants feature buffets on Mother's Day to increase capacity. An attractive buffet creates a festive atmosphere, provides an impression of variety and value, and expedites service by eliminating the need to prepare food to order. Customers provide their own service, with the service staff providing the beverage and check, which frees the staff to wait on more customers. Buffets eliminate the time required for order taking and preparing the order. Food is available when customers arrive, allowing them to start eating almost immediately. This increases turnover of tables, further increasing the restaurant's capacity. The buffet also allows the restaurant to create a buffer inventory. Although three hours' worth of food cannot be kept on a steam table without a reduction in quality and attractiveness, the food can be cooked in batches that will last 20 to 30 minutes.

Restaurants and entertainment facilities can increase capacity by extending their hours. A hotel coffee shop that is full by 7:30 A.M. may find it useful to open at 6:30 A.M. instead of 7 A.M. If five tables arrive in the first half hour, these should be free in about a half hour, allowing the restaurant to have more tables available during the peak period. Leaps and Bounds, a children's entertainment center that is normally closed at night, offers all-night parties for groups of twenty or more. When the demand exists, the center supplies the capacity by opening at night. Many businesses can increase their capacity by expanding their hours of operation.

Demand Management

In an ideal situation, managers simply expand capacity to meet demand. However, during a citywide convention, a hotel may receive requests for rooms that exceed its capacity. The Saturday before Christmas, a restaurant could book more banquets if it had space, and during a summer holiday a resort could sell more rooms if it had them. All successful hospitality businesses become capacity constrained. Capacity management allows a business to increase its capacity, but it does not prevent situations where demand exceeds capacity. The following are some ways to manage demand.

http://www
.mgmgrand.com/
Click on check
rates in the reservation box;
then click on it in the second
window to open up a two-
month calendar with rates for
each day. On days when the
hotel is closed to full, the rates
may be four times as much as
when the hotel needs business.

USE PRICE TO CREATE OR REDUCE DEMAND Pricing is one method used to manage demand. To create demand, restaurants offer specials on slow days. For example, some Subway restaurants, a submarine sandwich shop, offer two-for-one specials on Tuesdays. Port of Subs (a competitor) offers special discounts after 5 P.M., because most people do not eat sandwiches for the evening meal. Resorts lower prices during the off-season, and city hotels offer weekend specials. Managers must make sure that the market segments attracted by the lower price are their desired targets.

When demand exceeds capacity, managers raise prices to lower demand. On New Year's Eve, many restaurants and nightclubs offer set menus and packages that exceed the normal average check. They realize that even with higher prices, demand remains sufficient to fill to capacity.

USE RESERVATIONS Hotels and restaurants often use reservations to monitor demand. When it appears they will have more demand than capacity, managers can save capacity for the more profitable segments. Reservations can also limit demand by allowing managers to refuse any further reservations when capacity meets demand.

Although reservations in restaurants can help manage demand, they can also decrease capacity. This is the reason that high-volume mid-priced restaurants do not usually take reservations. A group may arrive 10 minutes late, or one couple of a two-couple party may arrive on time and wait 20 minutes at the table until the other couple shows up. The estimated times of customer arrival and departure may not fit precisely, resulting in tables remaining empty for 20 minutes or more. In high-priced restaurants, guests expect to reserve a table and have it ready when they arrive. Customers of mid-priced restaurants have different expectations, allowing popular restaurants to increase their capacity by having customers queue and wait for the next available table. Queues allow managers to inventory demand for short periods of time and fill every table immediately when it becomes available, eliminating dead time.

To maximize capacity, some restaurants accept reservations for seating at designated times. For example, they may have seating at 6, 8, and 10 o'clock. When customers call to make a reservation, the receptionist makes them aware of the seating times and lets them know that the table is theirs for up to two hours. After two hours, another party will be waiting to use the table. The use of seatings increases capacity by ensuring that the restaurant will have three turns and by shifting demand. As the 8 o'clock seating fills, managers can shift demand to either 6 or 10 o'clock, depending on the customer's preference.

In cases where demand is greater than capacity, guests can be asked to prepay or make a deposit. For example, some New Year's Eve parties at hotels and restaurants require that guests purchase their tickets in advance. Resorts often require

Disney's FASTPASS helps manage demand. Courtesy of AP Photo/John Raoux.

a nonrefundable deposit with a reservation. By requiring an advance payment, managers help ensure that revenue matches capacity. If a customer fails to arrive, the resort does not lose revenue.

Disneyland has come up with its own form of reservations, Fastpass. Guests may go up to one of the rides offering the Fastpass service and obtain a reservation to come at a certain time. When the guests come back, they bypass the waiting line and move to the Fastpass line, often saving an hour or more in waiting. Guests are limited to one Fastpass every four hours to ensure that the rides are able to accommodate both Fastpass and regular guests. The beauty of Fastpass is that rather than waiting in line, guests can now spend money in the restaurants and shops. By handling demand with Fastpass, Disney has created a more satisfying customer experience and also created the opportunity for more sales.

Reservation systems can be very complex. It is not within the scope of this book to explore the variations of reservations for hotels, restaurants, and other hospitality organizations.

OVERBOOK   Not everyone who reserves a table or books a room shows up. Plans change and people with reservations become no-shows. Overbooking is another method that hotels, restaurants, trains, and airlines use to match demand with capacity. Hotel managers who limit reservations to the number of available rooms frequently find themselves with empty rooms. For example, at one hotel, 20 percent of guests holding nonguaranteed reservations and 5 percent of those holding guaranteed reservations typically do not honor those reservations. If this hotel has 80 guaranteed reservations and 40 nonguaranteed reservations, it will, on average, be left with 12 empty rooms. For a hotel with an average room rate of $150, this can mean a potential annual loss of more than $750,000 in room, food, and beverage revenue.

Overbooking must be managed carefully. Knowing the hotel's customers, past history of the event, availability of rooms at other hotels, and weather conditions are important factors to consider when overbooking. When a hotel fails to honor its reservations, it risks losing the future business of guests whose reservations are not honored and possibly the business of their companies and travel agents. Usually, it is better to leave a room unoccupied than to fail to honor a reservation.

Developing a good overbooking policy minimizes the chance of walking a guest. This requires knowing the no-show rate of different types of reservations. Groups who reserve rooms should be investigated to see what percentage of their room block they have filled in the past. One study found that reservations made one day before arrival and on the day of arrival had a higher no-show rate than reservations made much earlier.[25] Today with the help of well-designed software systems we can develop an accurate overbooking policy.

Some hotels do nothing for the traveler whose reservation is not honored. Well-managed hotels find alternative accommodations, pay for one night's stay at the new hotel, and provide transportation to the hotel. They may also give the guest a free phone to inform those back home of the new arrangements and keep the guest's name on their information rack so they can refer any phone calls the guest may receive to the hotel where the guest is staying. Smart managers try to get turned-away guests back by offering a free night's stay at their hotel the next day. Hotels that are careless in handling their reservations can be held liable. In one case a travel agent, Rainbow Travel Service, reserved forty-five rooms with the Fontainebleau Hilton for clients going to a Miami–Oklahoma football game. The Fontainebleau walked a number of Rainbow's clients, and Rainbow sued for damage to its reputation. A jury awarded the travel agency $250,000. The jury believed that the Fontainebleau should have altered its policy of overbooking by 15 percent because of the demand created by the football weekend.[26]

REVENUE MANAGEMENT   Overbooking is often part of a comprehensive **revenue management** system. Price is inversely related to demand for most products. Managers can create more demand for a product by lowering its price and lower demand by raising its price. With the help of computer programs, managers are using price, reservation history, and overbooking practices to develop a sophisticated approach to demand management called revenue management, a methodological approach to allocating a perishable and fixed inventory to the most profitable customers. Revenue management grew out of yield management, which was introduced in the 1980s. During the last 10 years many large business-class and luxury hotels added full-time revenue managers to their staff. For graduates of hospitality programs that enjoy numbers and marketing strategy, revenue management can be an interesting career. The ability to maximize revenue has become such an important management tool that today the position of corporate revenue manager has become a path to the position of corporate vice president of marketing. Well-designed revenue management bases pricing decisions on data and can increase revenue by 8 percent or more. A 200-room hotel was able to add $600,000 to its top line after implementing revenue management. Its system was designed to maximize RevPAR (revenue per available room). Revenue management techniques have also been designed for restaurants, where they are designed to maximize revenue per available seat (RevPASH). In restaurants, seat utilization along with off-peak pricing is among the tools used to maximize RevPASH.

Properly designed revenue management systems value the business or repeat customers. Thus a customer who stays at a hotel eleven times a year for two nights per stay is treated differently than a one-time convention guest. The frequent loyal guest's business is valued, and some hotel companies have developed corporate rates for these guests that do not fluctuate with the demand for business. They protect these guests. As one can see, the practice of revenue management for a hotel can be very complex. It takes an understanding of forecasting models and the hotel's customer base.[27]

USE QUEUING   When capacity exceeds demand and guests are willing to wait, queues form. Sometimes guests make the decision to wait; in other cases they have no choice. For example, a guest is told a restaurant has a 20-minute wait and he decides to wait. However, on occasion, hotel guests may find themselves waiting to check in to a hotel where they have made a reservation.

Voluntary queues, such as waits at restaurants, are a common and effective way of managing demand. Good management of the queue can make the wait more tolerable for the guest. Always overestimate the wait. When the estimated wait is 30 minutes, it is better to tell guests that it will be a 35-minute wait than to tell them they will have a 20-minute wait. Some managers fear that if the wait is too long they will lose guests, so they "shorten" the wait time. Once customers have accepted the wait time, they may sit down and have a drink, but they tend to keep their eyes on their watches. When their names have not been called after the allotted time, they run up to the host and ask where they are on the list. When guests wait longer than they were told they would, they go to their dining table upset and in a mood that makes them tend to look for other service failures. It can be difficult for the restaurant to recover from this initial failure, and many guests leave with memories of an unsatisfactory experience.

If the host tells guests it will be a 35-minute wait and then seats them in 30 minutes, the guests will be delighted. If a guest decides not to accept the wait, the host can suggest a time when the wait will be shorter.

In general, the higher the level of service, the longer the guest is willing to wait. Twenty minutes for sit-down service might be acceptable, whereas a five-minute wait at a fast-food restaurant will be unacceptable. Fast-food restaurants must raise their capacity to meet demand or lose customers.[28]

David Maister, a service expert, provides the following tips for the management of a waiting line:[29]

1. **Unoccupied time feels longer than occupied time.** Entertainment parks have characters who talk to kids in waiting lines, occupying time and making the wait pass faster. Restaurants send customers waiting for a dinner table into their cocktail lounge, where a cocktail and conversation make the time pass more quickly. The Rio Hotel places television monitors over the line for their buffet. The monitors promote different products that the resort has to offer, such as its entertainment and other food and beverage outlets. These are a few examples of how managers can occupy guests' time and make their wait more enjoyable.

2. **Unfair waits are longer than equitable waits.** Guests can become upset and pre-occupied with a wait if they feel they are being treated unfairly. Restaurants with a limited number of large tables try to maximize the capacity of these tables. For example, rather than put a party of four at a table for six, the restaurant seats a party of six at the table, even if there are several parties of four in front of them. This sometimes leads to anger on the part of the guests in the passed-over party of four. Because they were next, they feel the host should seat them next. In such cases the host should explain what is going on to the next party in line. Another example of an unfair wait is when a guest who has been waiting for 20 minutes to check in finally reaches the front of the line. Just as he is starting to give the details of his reservation to the front-desk clerk, the phone rings. The phone is answered promptly by the clerk, who gets involved in a 10-minute conversation with the caller. Marriott has started a policy of removing phones from the front desk to avoid this distraction and eliminate unfair waits.

3. **Uncertain waits are longer than known, finite waits.** Most travelers have experienced a flight delay. If the agent states the flight will be delayed an hour, the traveler can get something to eat, shop in the stores, or find other activities to fill his or her time. However, if the traveler is just told there will be a delay and when he or she asks how long the agent says, I am not sure it's a mechanical problem, the person often becomes anxious. The anxiety is caused by the uncertain delay. He or she does not want to leave the gate for fear the plane will be promptly fixed and depart. He or she is too anxious to relax. The 30-minute delay will seem like an eternity. When possible we should tell guests the reason for the delay and the expected amount of time of the delay. The reason airlines sometimes do not give delays is because they do not know how long it will take to fix the plane and they do not want people leaving the area. However, they should keep people updated on the progress to reduce the uncertainty.

Maister states that the customer's sense of equity is not always obvious and needs to be managed. Whatever priority rules apply, the service provider must make vigorous efforts to ensure that these rules match with the customer's sense of equity, either by adjusting the rules or by convincing the client that the rules are appropriate.

SHIFT DEMAND   It is often possible to shift the demand for banquets and meetings. A sales manager may want to set up a sales meeting for the end of October or the beginning of November and knows that when the hotel is called to check availability, a date must be given. Suppose that October 31 is picked, although it could have been October 24 or November 7 just as easily. Twenty rooms will be needed the night before and a meeting room the day of the event. The hotel is forecast to sell out on October 31 but presently has rooms available. The smart manager asks whether October 31 is a firm date. If the date is flexible, the manager shifts the date to a period when the hotel is not projected to sell out and needs the business.

CREATE PROMOTIONAL EVENTS   An object of promotion is to increase demand or, as we will learn later, to shift the demand curve to the left. During slow periods, creative promotions can be an effective way of building business. We discuss promotions later in the book.

The four characteristics of services intangibility, inseparability, variability, and perishability create the need for marketing strategies and tactics that are different from goods-producing companies. In the rest of the book we will discuss those strategies and tactics and the principles that support them.

■■■ KEY TERMS

Inseparability. A major characteristic of services - they are produced and consumed at the same time and cannot be separated from their providers.

Intangibility. A major characteristic of services; they cannot be seen, tasted, felt, heard, or smelled before they are bought.

Interactive marketing. Marketing by a service firm that recognizes perceived service quality depends heavily on the quality of the buyer–seller interaction.

Internal marketing. Marketing by a service firm to train effectively and motivate its customer-contact employees and all the supporting service people to work as a team to provide customer satisfaction.

Organization image. The way a person or group views an organization.

Perishability. A major characteristic of services; they cannot be stored for later use.

Physical evidence. Tangible clues such as promotional material, employees of the firm, and the physical environment of the firm. Physical evidence is used by a service firm to make its product more tangible to customers.

Revenue management. A pricing method using price as a means of matching demand with capacity.

Service culture. A system of values and beliefs in an organization that reinforces the idea that providing the customer with quality service is the principal concern of the business.

Service profit chain. A model that shows the relationships between employee satisfaction, customer satisfaction, customer retention, value creation, and profitability.

Variability. A major characteristic of services; their quality may vary greatly, depending on who provides them and when, where, and how they are provided.

■■■ CHAPTER REVIEW

I. **The Service Culture.** The service culture focuses on serving and satisfying the customer. The service culture has to start with top management and flow down.

II. **Five Characteristics of Services**
   A. **Intangibility.** Unlike physical products, services cannot be seen, tasted, felt, heard, or smelled before they are purchased. To reduce uncertainty caused by intangibility, buyers look for tangible evidence that will provide information and confidence about the service.
   B. **Physical evidence**
   C. **Inseparability.** In most hospitality services, both the service provider and the customer must be present for the transaction to occur. Customer-contact employees are part of the product. Inseparability also means that customers are part of the product. The third implication of inseparability is that customers and employees must understand the service delivery system.
   D. **Variability.** Service quality depends on who provides the services and when and where they are provided. Services are produced and consumed simultaneously. Fluctuating demand makes it difficult to deliver consistent products during periods of peak demand. The high degree of contact between the service provider and the guest means that product consistency depends on the service provider's skills and performance at the time of the exchange.
   E. **Perishability.** Services cannot be stored. If service providers are to maximize revenue, they must manage capacity and demand because they cannot carry forward unsold inventory.

III. **Service Management Concepts**
   A. **Service profit chain**
   B. **Types of marketing**

   1. Internal marketing
   2. External marketing
   3. Interactive marketing

IV. **Management Strategies for Service Businesses**
   A. **Managing differentiation.** The solution to price competition is to develop a differentiated offering. The offer can include innovative features that set one company's offer apart from that of its competitors.
   B. **Managing service quality.** With hospitality products, quality is measured by how well customer expectations are met.
   C. **Manage service productivity**
   D. **Resolving customer complaints.** Resolving customer complaints is a critical component of customer retention.
   E. **Managing employees as part of the product.** In the hospitality industry, employees are a critical part of the product and marketing mix. The human resource and marketing department must work closely together. The task of internal marketing to employees involves the effective training and motivation of customer-contact employees and supporting service personnel.
   F. **Managing perceived risk.** The high risk that people perceive when purchasing hospitality products increases loyalty to companies that have provided them with a consistent product in the past.
   G. **Managing capacity and demand.** Because services are perishable, managing capacity and demand is a key function of hospitality marketing. First, services must adjust their operating systems to enable the business to operate at maximum capacity. Second, they must remember that their goal is to create satisfied customers. Research has shown that customer complaints increase when service firms operate above 80 percent of their capacity.

■■■ DISCUSSION QUESTIONS

1. Illustrate how a hotel, restaurant, or theater can deal with the intangibility, inseparability, variability, and perishability of the service it provides. Give specific examples.

2. Ask three people the following: Think of hotel that you stayed in and would want to return to the next time you were in the area where the hotel was located. Why would you want to return to this hotel? Record what each person said. This will give you an idea of the things that make the difference of whether someone returns or tries a competitor.

3. Discuss how the service person in a restaurant is part of the product the customer receives when purchasing a meal.

4. What are some common management practices that restaurants use to provide a consistent product?

5. What are internal and interactive marketing? Give an example of how a specific firm or organization might use these concepts to increase the effectiveness of its services. How might these concepts be linked to services differentiation?

■■■ EXPERIENTIAL EXERCISES

Do one of the following:

1. Perishability is very important in the airline industry; unsold seats are gone forever, and too many unsold seats mean large losses. With computerized ticketing, airlines can easily use pricing to deal with perishability and variations in demand.
   a. Go to the Web site of an airline and get a fare for an eight-day stay between two cities it serves. Get prices on the same route for sixty days in advance, two weeks, one week, and tomorrow. Is there a clear pattern to the fares?
   b. When a store is overstocked on ripe fruit, it may lower the price to sell out quickly. What are airlines doing to their prices as the seats get close to "perishing"? Why are tomorrow's fares often higher?

2. Visit a restaurant or a hotel. Observe and record how they manage their customers. This could include how they get them to move through the hotel, stand in line, or throw their trash away in a hotel. Write what you think the business does well and what it does poorly. Explain your answer.

3. Visit a restaurant or hotel and give an example of how they use tangible evidence to tell the customer what type of business they are and how they are run. Things to look at include the exterior of the business, the inside of the business, signage, and employee uniforms. Write what you think the business does well and what it does poorly. Explain your answer.

■■■ INTERNET EXERCISES

A. Visit the Web site of a hotel chain. What does the Web site do to make the product tangible for the customer? Does anything in the site deal with the characteristic of perishables, for example, specials at some of the properties?

B. Visit the Web site of a tourism destination; it can either be a city or be a country. Explain how the site provides tangible evidence relating to the experiences a visitor to the destination can expect.

■■■ REFERENCES

1. Ritz Carlton website, accessed September 16, http://corporate.ritzcarlton.com/en/About/GoldStandards.htm.

2. Edwin McDowell, "Ritz-Carlton's Keys to Good Service," New York Times , March 31, 1993, accessed September 16, 2012, http://www.nytimes.com/1993/03/31/business/ritz-carlton-s-keys-to-good-service.html?pagewanted=all&src=pm.

3. Howard Schlossberg, "Measuring Customer Satisfaction Is Easy to Do—Until You Try," Marketing News (April 26, 1993): 27, 9.

4. Howard Schlossberg, "Measuring Customer Satisfaction Is Easy to Do—Until You Try," Marketing News (April 26, 1993): 5, 8.

5. Ritz Carlton website, accessed September 16, http://corporate.ritzcarlton.com/en/About/GoldStandards.htm; Quotes from Edwin McDowell, "Ritz-Carlton's Keys to Good Service," *New York Times* (March 31, 1993): D1; and Howard Schlossberg, "Measuring Customer Satisfaction Is Easy to Do—Until You Try," *Marketing News* (April 26, 1993): 5, 8. See also Rahul Jacob, "Why Some Customers Are Most Equal Than Others," *Fortune* (September 19, 1994): 215–224; Don Peppers, "Digitizing Desire," *Forbes* (April 10, 1995): 76; "About Us, Fact Sheet," www.ritzcarlton.com (accessed August 10, 2011).

6. Earl W. Sasser, R. Paul Olsen, and Daryl Wycoff, *Management of Service Operations* (Boston, MA: Allyn & Bacon, 1978).

7. G. Lynn Shostack, "Breaking Free from Product Marketing," *Journal of Marketing* (April 1977): 73–80.

8. Bernard H. Booms and Mary J. Bitner, "Marketing Services by Managing the Environment," *Cornell Hotel and Restaurant Administration Quarterly,* 23, no. 1 (1982): 35–39.

9. Robert C. Ford and Cherrill P. Heaton, "Managing Your Guest as a Quasi-Employee," *Cornell Hotel and Restaurant Administration Quarterly,* 42, no. 2 (2001): 46–61.

10. Diane Schanlensee, Kenneth L. Bernhardt, and Nancy Gust, "Keys to Successful Services Marketing: Customer Orientation, Creed, Consistency," in *Services Marketing in a Changing Environment,* ed. Thomas Bloch et al. (Chicago, IL: American Marketing Association, 1985), pp. 15–18.

11. See James L. Heskett, W. Earl Sasser, Jr., and Leonard A. Schlesinger, *The Service Profit Chain: How Leading Companies Link Profit and Growth to Loyalty, Satisfaction, and Value* (New York: Free Press, 1997); Heskett, Sasser, and Schlesinger, *The Value Profit Chain: Treat Employees Like Customers and Customers Like Employees* (New York: Free Press, 2003); Christian Homburg, Jan Wieseke, and Wayne D. Hoyer, "Social Identity and the Service-Profit Chain," *Journal of Marketing* (March 2009): 38–54; and Rachael W. Y. Yee and others, "The Service-Profit Chain: A Review and Extension," *Total Quality Management & Business Excellence* (2009): 617–632.

12. James L. Heskett, W. Earl Sasser, Jr., and Leonard A. Schlesinger, The Service Profit Chain: *How Leading Companies Link Profit and Growth to Loyalty, Satisfaction, and Value* (New York: Free Press, 1997).

13. Tracey J. Bruce and Timothy R. Hinkin, "The Costs of Employee Turnover: Where the Devil Is the Details?" *Cornell Hospitality Report,* 6, no. 15 (2006): 9.

14. For more reading on internal and interactive marketing, see Christian Gronroos, "A Service Quality Model and Its Marketing Implications," *European Journal of Marketing,* 18, no. 4 (1984): 36–44; and Leonard Barry, Edwin F. Lefkowith, and Terry Clark, "In Services, What's in a Name?" *Harvard Business Review* (September/October 1988): 28–30.

15. *Feelings Consultant Marketing Manual* (Bloomington, MN: Better Than Money Corporation, n.d.). The Technical Research Programs Institute does studies on customer complaints and the success of complaint resolution.

16. Linda M. Lash, *The Complete Guide to Customer Service* (New York: Wiley, 1989), pp. 68–69.

17. Majorie Coeyman, "You Call This Service?" *Restaurant Business* (May 15, 1997): 93–104.

18. Janelle Barlow and Claus Moller, *A Complaint Is a Gift* (San Francisco, CA: Berrett-Koehler, 1996).

19. Richard Norman, *Service Management: Strategy and Leadership in Service Businesses,* New York: Wiley, 1984.

20. See Karl Albrecht, *At America's Service* (Homewood, IL: Dow Jones/Irwin, 1988).

21. See Leonard Berry, "Big Ideas in Services Marketing," in *Creativity in Services Marketing,* ed. M. Venkatesan et al. (Chicago, IL: American Marketing Association, 1986), pp. 6–8.

22. Thomas J. Peters and Robert H. Waterman, *In Search of Excellence* (New York: Warner Books, 1982), p. xv.

23. See Valarie A. Zeithaml, "How Consumer Evaluation Processes Differ Between Goods and Services," in *Marketing of Services,* ed. James H. Donnelly and William George (Chicago, IL: American Marketing Association, 1981), pp. 186–190.

24. Sanne de Boer, "The Impact of Dynamic Capacity Management on Airline Seat Inventory Control," *Journal of Revenue and Pricing Management,* 2, no. 4 (2004): 315–320.

25. Carolyn U. Lambert, Joseph M. Lambert, and Thomas P. Cullen, "The Overbooking Question: A Simulation," *Cornell Hotel and Restaurant Administration Quarterly,* 30, no. 2 (1989): 15–20.

26. Mark Pestronk, "Finding Hotels Liable for Walking Guests," *Travel Weekly,* 49, no. 37 (1990): 371.

27. Sunmee Choi and Anna S. Mattila, "Hotel Revenue and Its Impact on Customer's Perceptions of Fairness," *Journal of Revenue and Pricing,* 2, no. 4 (2004): 303–314; Karyn Strauss and Jeff Weinstein, "Lesson in Revenue Management," *Hotels* (July 2003): 22; R. G. Cross, *Revenue Management: Hardcore Tactics for Market Domination* (New York: Broadway Books, 1997).

28. Carolyn U. Lambert and Thomas P. Cullen, "Balancing Service and Costs Through Queuing Analysis," *Cornell Hotel and Restaurant Administration Quarterly,* 28, no. 2 (1987): 69–72.

29. David H. Maister, "The Psychology of Waiting Lines," in *Service Encounter,* ed. John A. Czepiel, Michael R. Solomon, and Carol F. Surprenant (Lexington, MA: D.C. Heath, 1985).

The Landing in St. Lucia, RockResorts, are known for their spectacular settings.
Courtesy of Red Robin International, Inc.

The Role of Marketing in Strategic Planning

3

Objectives

After reading this chapter, you should be able to:

1. Explain company-wide strategic planning.

2. Understand the concepts of stakeholders, processes, resources, and organization as they relate to a high-performing business.

3. Explain the four planning activities of corporate strategic planning.

4. Understand the processes involved in defining a company's mission and setting goals and objectives.

5. Discuss how to design business portfolios and growth strategies.

6. Explain the steps involved in the business strategy planning process.

Red Robin

The origin of Red Robin® restaurants dates back 70 years to Sam's Tavern in Seattle. The tavern owner sang in a barbershop quartet, and one of his favorite songs was "When the Red, Red Robin Comes Bob, Bob, Bobbin' Along." He changed the name of the tavern to Sam's Red Robin. When the tavern was sold in 1969, "Sam's" was dropped from the name. The Red Robin® restaurant was born and began the transformation from a tavern to a family restaurant. In 1979, two regulars of the Seattle Red Robin, Mike and Steve Snyder, opened the company's first franchise in Yakima, Washington.

By 1985, Red Robin had expanded to seven company-owned restaurants and fifteen franchised restaurants. Around this time, the chain was sold to Skylark, a Japanese company operating family restaurants. Under Skylark, cash was infused into the company, and the chain saw rapid unit growth. However, revenues at company-owned stores declined because the company was unable to establish a focused and consistent concept or profitable operating results at its restaurants.

Meanwhile, the Red Robin® restaurants owned and operated by the Snyder Group Company thrived, indicating that the concept was viable. After 10 years of poor results at company-owned restaurants, Skylark appointed Mike Snyder president of the company. Snyder moved quickly to implement across the chain the systems he had installed in his franchised restaurants. He applied cost controls, improved service delivery, created a bonus system for managers, and provided recognition for line managers. He closed ten restaurants that were unprofitable. During his first five years as president, Snyder turned the company around and the profitability of Red Robin® restaurants improved.

Encouraged by its renewed success, Red Robin entered a new expansion stage. The company purchased Snyder's 14 restaurants and its ownership structure evolved through a series of business transactions until the company went public in 2002 as Red Robin Gourmet Burgers, Inc., its present name. By that time, the number of Red Robin® restaurants had expanded to nearly 200.

However, in August 2005, Red Robin leadership changed hands after an internal investigation identified various expenses by Snyder that were inconsistent with company policies or that lacked sufficient documentation. Snyder retired from Red Robin and the company's board of directors appointed Dennis Mullen as chairman of the board and chief executive officer. Mullen had been serving as a director on the company's board and chair of its audit committee, and had many years of experience as a corporate executive in the restaurant industry, including the role of chief executive officer for several restaurant chains. During his five years as Red Robin's chief executive, Mullen led the company through a period of continued growth and expansion across the United States and Canada to more than 445 restaurants, including the acquisition of more than 40 Red Robin® restaurants from several franchisees. Under Mullen's leadership, Red Robin company-owned and franchised restaurants achieved more than $1 billion in sales system-wide and achieved recognition by consumers and the industry as the gourmet burger leader. Despite this success, Red Robin's financial performance began to decline late in his tenure as chief executive, during a period of severe macroeconomic challenges, intense competitive pressure, and significant increases in commodity and other operating costs, all of which contributed to declining restaurant margins and profits.

In September 2010, Red Robin appointed a new CEO, Steve Carley. Carley had extensive experience in the restaurant industry, hospitality industry, and brand management. Red Robin's board felt he was the right person to return the chain to profitable and sustainable growth. When Carley arrived, the company's stock was trading at low multiples, and its valuation was depressed. This made the company a target for a takeover by another restaurant company or private equity firm. Carley needed to move quickly to improve Red Robin's business performance and increase shareholder value. His actions were deliberate, as he realized the importance of creating value for shareholders, but he did not want to do this at the expense of employees, which the company refers to as "Team Members," or customers, known at Red Robin as "guests." Carley had joined the company with a great deal of respect for Red Robin's previous four decades of success building a highly recognized restaurant brand. He also admired the strong Team Member culture at Red Robin and believed that there was considerable untapped potential within the company in terms of both talent and ideas. He knew that listening to his fellow Team Members would be an essential part of developing a plan that would improve business performance and create a "best-in-class" restaurant company that preserved the strong internal culture, served quality food and a great dining experience to guests, and delivered strong and consistent returns to shareholders.

Working with his management team and the company's board of directors, Carley led the development of Red Robin's long-term strategic plan, which the company named "Project RED." As Carley explained the plan's chosen shorthand, "RED, in addition to being a color that is almost universally associated with a sense of urgency, stands for Revenue growth, Expense management, and optimum Deployment of capital."

By way of example, prior to Carley's arrival, Red Robin teams developed an initiative to increase revenue called Red Royalty™, a loyalty program designed to not only increase frequency of guest visits but also establish true customer loyalty by understanding guest purchase behavior and preferences to tailor incentives for repeat visits. A trademark of any successful loyalty program is changing consumer behavior. For example, a guest who comes several times a year to a Red Robin might be offered only a free burger if he or she comes three times during the next month. A customer who comes in once a week might be offered a special on an appetizer or a signature drink. The program also features surprise offers that are designed to entice customers to try menu items they would not ordinarily order, such as appetizers or desserts. This creates an interesting and fun dining experience. Red Royalty™ had already been in a successful test phase in 45 restaurants. One of Carley's early moves to increase revenues was to accelerate rollout of the program to all company restaurants and begin a rollout to Red Robin's franchise system.

To address the "E" of Project RED, expense reduction, Carley directed his team's focus on three main areas of controllable costs: reducing administrative and restaurant-level expenses, reducing supply chain costs, and improving day-to-day business efficiencies and productivity. In addition to implementing a reduction in force at the company's home office, Carley challenged the company's operations teams to identify opportunities to improve restaurant operating margins by about 200 basis points, representing several million in annualized cost savings. Within the first year of the cost management directive, Red Robin's operations teams had identified more than 200 potential cost-saving opportunities, big and small and all across the business.

Finally, Carley's management team took a fresh look at how the company deploys capital, the "D" in Project RED. The goal was to establish capital deployment strategies that allow Red Robin to both grow the brand and maximize long-term shareholder value. Initiatives included continued efforts to improve the performance of new company-owned Red

Robin® restaurants to maximize cash-on-cash returns for new restaurant development, and increased investment to overhaul systems and infrastructure to not only better serve the existing restaurant base but also support future growth.

While Carley and his team moved quickly to implement Project RED initiatives, it was also important to make sure that the company continued to live its core values, which included taking care of Team Members. For Carley, an important part of respecting and taking care of Team Members was open and consistent internal communication—making sure that he and his senior team created a culture that encouraged honest assessment and sharing facts about how the company is performing—"telling our people the score," Carley explained.

Instead of hiding bad news from employees, Carley held meetings with key employees to discuss precisely the financial and market share problems facing Red Robin. When asked about this, Carley said, "Employees in any company know the company's problems and how serious they may be. They appreciate straight talk and honest answers to their questions. When employees are told the facts and are given an opportunity to assist in correcting problems, they will respond in a positive way."

Carley also said that it is counterproductive to blame poor financial performance on external factors, circumstances beyond the company's control or bad decisions from former leadership, or to make Team Members feel they somehow failed. Instead, he said it is much better to start by recognizing the many years of dedication and hard work by Team Members in the past that led to Red Robin's many years of growth and prosperity. Carley needed to make sure Team Members were now focusing on making Red Robin the truly great company that everyone in the organization knew it could become.

If the company's goal was to become great, it was important for Team Members to understand what greatness looks like, Carley said. The management of Red Robin selected several restaurants they considered to be great performers, many of which performed considerably better than Red Robin, even when faced with the same macroeconomic challenges in recent years, and used them as "best-in-class" benchmarks. Carley said that without such external benchmarks, companies revert to measuring performance against their own prior results.

Carley also employed the balanced scorecard. This concept was originally developed by Professors Kaplan and Norton of Harvard University. It is used by management to cover the following:

1. **The Financial Perspective.** The financial objectives of an organization are viewed and managers can track financial success and shareholder value.

2. **The Customer Perspective.** Customer objectives such as customer satisfaction are covered. Market share goals are also considered.

3. **Internal Process Perspective.** Internal operational goals are covered, as well as key processes necessary to deliver customer objectives.

4. **Learning and Growth Perspectives.** Intangible drivers of success such as human capital and information capital including skills, training, leadership, systems, and databases are covered.

About half of the companies in the United States, Europe, and Asia use a Balanced Scorecard system.[1] In the absence of a measurable management tool such as Balanced Scorecard, Carley said that his experience has shown that companies would slowly develop internal silos and that Team Member discontent would follow.

Carley feels that Team Members perform best when they and management receive feedback from critical sources such as the customer. He also said that he wanted to prevent "churn" in which Team Members are moved from location to location to the detriment of the company. He gave an example of top managers from a restaurant being moved to a poorly performing one with a result of Team Member dissatisfaction and unsatisfactory financial results.

Instead of churn, Carley believes that greater return on investment (ROI) in Team Members is achieved by enhancing tenure with a property. Carley feels this is particularly important in the case of restaurant general managers. He believes in hiring talented people that are passionate about working for Red Robin and providing them with the direction and support that will enable them to perform well. If you do this employees are self-motivating and will do their best to provide good serve to the customers, other employees, and the company.

As Carley talked about Red Robin Team Members, he continuously mentioned the importance of measurement metrics. Red Robin cannot be just a "feel-good" place, he said. It must be a company that continuously grows toward greatness. With that in mind, Carley said he wanted to ensure that transparency on all elements of the key operating metrics was available for Team Members. "Our people appreciate and deserve honesty," said Carley.[2]

■■■ Nature of High-Performance Business

The major challenge facing today's hospitality companies is knowing how to build and maintain healthy businesses in the face of a rapidly changing marketplace and environment. The consulting firm of Arthur D. Little proposed a model of the characteristics of a high-performance business.[3] It pointed to four factors: stakeholders, processes, resources, and organization. A review of these factors will help set the foundation for our study of strategic marketing.

Stakeholders

The starting point for any business is to define the stakeholders and their needs. Traditionally, most businesses focused on their stockholders. Today businesses increasingly recognize that they must nurture other stakeholders, including customers, employees, suppliers, and the communities where their businesses are located. A business must at least strive to satisfy the minimum expectations of each stakeholder group just mentioned.

A dynamic relationship connects the stakeholder groups. The progressive company creates a high level of employee satisfaction, which leads employees to work on continuous improvements as well as breakthrough innovations. The result is higher-quality products and services, which create high customer and stakeholder satisfaction. Growth creates opportunities for employee advancement. Profits from satisfied customers mean we can pay our employees a fair wage. There is always a synergistic loop between satisfied customers and satisfied employees. Satisfied employees create satisfied customers. Employees like dealing with customers who are happy and they know from previous visits. This creates more customer satisfaction, which in turn creates more employer satisfaction.

A critical and sometimes overlooked stakeholder group is that of owners of hotels managed by a hotel management company. Such a company may be one of the well-known flag companies or one that is unknown to the public. Many hotel owners are actually investors and do not wish to manage a property actively, so they contract with an experienced hotel management company.

Processes

Company work is traditionally carried on by departments. However, departmental organization poses some problems. Departments typically operate to maximize their own objectives, not necessarily the company's. Walls go up between departments creating silos, and there is usually less-than ideal cooperation. Work is slowed down and plans often are altered as they pass through departments.

Companies are increasingly refocusing their attention on the need to manage processes even more than departments. They are studying how tasks pass from department to department as well as the impediments to creative output. They are now building cross-functional teams that manage core business processes.

The Las Vegas Hilton was concerned with the profit contribution from various market segments and how to deal with this issue. The result was a radically different approach to hotel accounting called market segment accounting. This new approach incorporated marketing and strategic planning into accounting rather than viewing them as separate stand-alone areas and philosophies.[4]

The Las Vegas Hilton decided that "it is important to determine the optimal mix of the major market segments before deciding the strategic direction of the property." This required an interdepartmental analysis because different guests may have widely varying impacts on the profit implications for various departments.

This hotel wanted answers to the following questions:

1. What is the relative profitability of the gaming guest? The premium-gaming guest? The tour and travel guest?

2. How many room nights can each segment fill a year?

3. How much money should be spent to attract each segment?

4. How should rooms be priced for each segment?

5. How should these rooms be allocated to the segments during critical periods of the year?

Interdepartmental teams were formed representing finance, marketing, and information services. Eventually, the heads of all the hotel's major departments contributed to the new market segment accounting model.

Resources

To carry out processes, a company needs such resources as personnel, materials, machines, and information. Traditionally, companies sought to own and control most of the resources that entered the business. Now that is changing. Companies are finding that some resources under their control are not performing as well as those that they could obtain from outside. More companies today have decided to outsource less critical sources. However, they appreciate the need to own and nurture those core resources and competencies that make up the essence of their business. Smart companies are identifying their core competencies and using them as the basis for their strategic planning.

Table 3–1 provides a quick reference concerning organizational resources for use in strategic planning.

TABLE 3–1

Strategic Analysis: Questions That Generate Creative Ideas

1. How can this firm take advantage of changes that are expected to occur in society?
2. How can this firm use its relationships with customers to maximize its position in existing or future businesses?
3. Are there any stakeholders that should be seriously considered for partnerships?
4. Does the firm possess any resources or capabilities that are likely to lead to competitive advantage?
5. Are there any resources or capabilities the firm should consider developing to achieve competitive advantage?
6. Can the firm form joint ventures or other alliances with competitors or other stakeholders to acquire valuable knowledge, skills, or other resources?
7. Are there any resources or capabilities the firm does not possess, the absence of which might put it at a competitive disadvantage?
8. Are there any looming threats in the broad environment that the firm should consider in developing its strategy?

Source: Jeffrey S. Harrison, "Strategic Analysis for the Hospitality Industry," *Cornell Hotel and Restaurant Administration Quarterly,* 44, no. 2, April 2003, 152.

Cold Stone's Creamery's mission is to make people happy around the world by selling the highest quality, most creative experience with passion, excellence, and innovation. Courtesy of Jim West/Alamy.

Organization

The organizational side of a company consists of its structure, policies, and culture, all of which tend to become dysfunctional in a rapidly changing company. Although structure and policies can be changed, the company is the hardest to change. Companies must work hard to align their organization's structure, policies, and culture to the changing requirements of business strategy.

The corporate culture of RockResorts worked for 30 years, but in the late 1980s, it became an obstacle to meeting customer needs. RockResorts was founded by Laurence A. Rockefeller in the 1950s. The original market for RockResorts was the CEO, who could delegate business so that his vacation wouldn't be disturbed. At that time, decisions could wait until the CEO returned, and most CEOs were men.

Policies at RockResorts were sacrosanct and involved no phones in guest rooms, no television, adherence to a mandatory meal plan (the modified American plan), and small, unostentatious guest rooms. The corporate culture had been product driven. A change in corporate culture occurred at RockResorts under Michael Glennie, president and CEO, who said, "We have to listen to what the customer wants and cater to that without compromising the philosophy and ideals of our founder." This meant, among other changes, pampering guests with more amenities, larger bathrooms, and placing telephones in the room. "I believe that the mission for RockResorts is to take a company with a wonderful tradition, and build on that to meet the expectations of today's guests," said Glennie.[5]

Indeed RockResorts did build and change. In 2005 the company became fully owned by Vail Resorts and positioned itself as the best turnkey resort operator. By turnkey, RockResorts meant that it had the expertise and resources to develop and manage a luxury resort from initial planning, through all aspects of management, including sales/marketing, revenue management strategies and analysis, and other critical areas. The number of RockResorts grew with selected locations in spectacular natural settings such as those in Colorado and the Caribbean.

e **3.1** http:// rockresorts. com/ Look how RockResorts all have the feel of casual elegance in a spectacular natural setting.

■■■ Corporate Strategic Planning: Defining Marketing's Role

At the corporate level, the company starts the strategic-planning process by defining its overall purpose and mission (see Figure 3–1). This mission then is turned into detailed supporting objectives that guide the whole company. Next, headquarters

Figure 3–1
Steps in strategic planning.

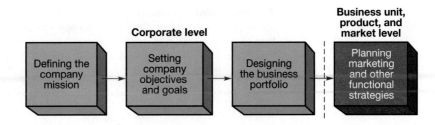

decides what portfolio of business and products is best for the company and how much support to give each one. In turn, each business and product develops detailed marketing and other departmental plans that support the company-wide plan. This marketing planning occurs at the business-unit, product, and market levels. It supports company strategic planning with more detailed plans for specific marketing opportunities.

Each company must find the game plan for long-run survival and growth that makes the most sense given its specific situation, opportunities, objectives, and resources. This is the focus of **strategic planning**, the process of developing and maintaining a strategic fit between the organization's goals and capabilities and its changing marketing opportunities.

Strategic planning sets the stage for the rest of the planning in the firm. Companies usually prepare annual plans, long-range plans, and strategic plans. The annual and long-range plans deal with the company's current businesses and how to keep them going. In contrast, the strategic plan involves adapting the firm to take advantage of opportunities in its constantly changing environment.

Corporate headquarters has the responsibility for setting into motion the whole planning process. Some corporations give a lot of freedom to their business units but let them develop their own strategies. Others set the goals and get heavily involved in the individual strategies.

The hospitality industry faces the need for greater empowerment of employees, particularly at middle-management levels. It has been suggested that many of the traditions within the hospitality industry have experienced little change. "Most of its managers, for instance, were trained in the classical management style." This system ensured that "formal rules and regulations guide decision making and ensure organizational stability. Work is done by the book ... one's rank in the hierarchy structure determines authority and decision making tends to be centralized, coming primarily from the top."[6] Increasingly, hospitality industry executives and researchers view this traditional approach as needing change.

The hospitality and tourism industries are international and multicultural. Attitudes and culture sometimes create sharp differences in management style and in the perceived importance of strategic planning, empowerment, and other concepts discussed in this chapter. A study of hospitality managers in Poland, France, and Austria demonstrated differences in risk taking and international vision. Interestingly, Polish managers were shown to have a greater international vision than those in France. The authors concluded that different attitudes of managers in the nations affected the degree of autonomy of the manager. The authors also believed that the strategy of a hospitality firm and its level of performance were affected by the differing attitudes of managers within the three nations.[7]

Defining the Corporate Mission

A hospitality organization exists to accomplish something: to provide a night's lodging, a day of adventure and entertainment for a family, a great dining experience for a couple, and so on. At first, it has a clear mission or purpose, but over time, its mission may become unclear as the organization grows, adds new products and markets, or faces new conditions in the environment. When management senses that the organization is drifting, it must renew its search for purpose. According to Peter Drucker, it is time to ask some fundamental questions.[8] What is our business? Who is the customer? What do customers value? What should our business be? These simple-sounding questions are among the most difficult the company will ever have to answer. Successful companies raise these questions continuously and answer them carefully and completely.

Many organizations develop formal mission statements that answer these questions. A mission statement is a statement of the organization's purpose—what it wants to accomplish in the larger environment. A clear mission statement acts like an "invisible hand" that guides people in the organization. Studies have shown that firms with well-crafted mission statements have better organizational and financial performance.[9]

Some companies define their missions myopically in product or technology terms ("We provide lodging" or "We are a hotel Internet reservations company"). However, a market-oriented mission statement defines the business in terms of satisfying customer needs. The following examples illustrate the difference between a product orientation and a market orientation. A product orientation for Disney would be "We run theme parks." A market orientation would be "We create fantasies—that enable the family to have a great time together and produce memories that will last a lifetime." A product-oriented mission statement for Ritz-Carlton would be "We rent luxury hotel rooms and have fine restaurants." A market-oriented mission statement would be "We create the Ritz-Carlton experience—one that enlivens the senses, instills well-being, and fulfills even the unexpressed wishes and needs of our guests."[10, 11]

Management should avoid making a mission too narrow or too broad. In many cases hospitality companies have gone into businesses that would not fit a marketing-oriented business statement. For example, a fast-food hamburger chain in Texas went into the cattle ranching business because their restaurants used thousands of pounds of beef. They felt they should cut out the middleman and produce their own beef. They soon found out that raising cattle and serving hamburgers took two different sets of business expertise. Mission statements should be realistic. Thai Airlines would be deluding itself if it adopted the mission to become the world's largest airline. However, it could provide excellent service and hospitality for persons flying from the cities that are Thailand's top source of business and/or tourist travelers.

Finally, the organization should base its mission on its distinctive competencies. McDonald's could probably enter the solar energy business, but that would not use its core competence.

The company's mission statement should be motivating. Employees need to feel that their work is significant and contributes to people's lives. Missions are at their best when they are guided by a vision, an almost impossible dream. Thomas Monaghan wanted to deliver hot pizza to any home within 30 minutes, and he created Domino's Pizza. Ruth Fertel wanted to provide customers with the finest steak dinners available, and she created Ruth's Chris Steakhouses. Phil Roberts wanted to bring back the warmth and passion of the immigrant southern Italian family-style neighborhood restaurant, so he created Bucca di Beppo.[12] James Thomson wanted to create a truly unique and memorable dining experience and created the Witchery by the Castle in Edinburgh, Scotland, one of the United Kingdom's finest. Following that success, James and his team, who were experienced in renovating old buildings, conducted an extensive renovation of a seventeenth-century estate called Prestonfield. Within a short time Prestonfield had gained a reputation as Edinburgh's most opulent retreat, Scotland's most romantic hotel, and one of the top 100 hotels in the world. The restaurant "Rhubarb" within Prestonfield gained an equal reputation.[13] The **corporate mission statement** should stress major policies that the company wants to honor. Policies define how employees should deal with customers, suppliers, competitors, and other important groups.

The company's mission statement should provide a vision and direction for the company for the next 10 to 20 years. Missions are not revised every few years in response to every new turn in the economy. But a company must redefine its mission if that mission no longer defines an optimal course.[14]

Culver's is a quick-service restaurant (QSR) chain with over 430 restaurants in the United States. Culver's has a simple, yet powerful, mission: "Every guest who chooses Culver's leaves happy."[15] Mandarin Oriental manages over 40 hotels across the globe in 26 countries. It is known for operating some of the finest hotels in the world. It describes its vision: "Our mission is to completely delight and satisfy our guests. We are committed to making a difference every day; continually getting better to keep us the best."[16]

Setting Company Objectives and Goals

The company needs to turn its mission into detailed supporting objectives for each level of management. Each manager should have objectives and be responsible for reaching them. "The Ritz-Carlton experience enlivens the senses, instills well-being, and fulfills even the unexpressed wishes and needs of our guests." This broad mission leads to a hierarchy of objectives, including business objectives and marketing objectives. Ritz-Carlton's overall objective is to build profitable customer relationships by providing genuine care and comfort for its guests. It does this by understanding what its guests want. This is done by observing guests, seeing how they use the room, and getting employees to provide feedback on what the guests say about Ritz-Carlton and its competitors. Profits can be improved by increasing sales or reducing costs. Sales can be increased by improving the company's share of leisure, group, and transient business markets. These goals then become the company's current marketing objectives.[17]

Marketing strategies and programs must be developed to support these marketing objectives. To increase its market share, Ritz-Carlton may add salespeople to attract the incentive travel market. It may expand its presence in international markets. Ritz-Carlton also realizes that condominiums as part of a Ritz-Carlton hotel project increase the value by 35 percent over an unbranded condominium. Therefore, this becomes an option to provide the cash flow and thus gain financing for new properties.

Each broad marketing strategy must then be defined in greater detail. For example, increasing the incentive travel business may require more salespeople, advertising, and public relations efforts; if so, both requirements will need to be spelled out. In this way, the firm's mission is translated into a set of objectives for the current period.

Designing the Business Portfolio

Most companies operate several businesses. However, they often fail to define them carefully. Businesses are too often defined in terms of products. Companies are in the "hotel business" or the "cruise line business."[18] However, market definitions of a business are superior to product definitions. A business must be viewed as a customer-satisfying process, not a product-producing process. Companies should define their business in terms of customer needs, not products.

Ski resorts are no longer content to sell only ski tickets. Major ski resorts today offer children's programs, summer mountain biking, and rock concerts. Country clubs are no longer just for golfing and occasional dining. Today they are a lifestyle that includes health clubs, spas, and summer camps for children.

3.2   www.culvers.com, Culver's has this statement on its Web site: "The goal is always the same: that every time you step into a Culver's, you'll always enjoy a fresh, handcrafted meal served with a smile and genuine pride. Welcome to delicious." This vision enables it to differentiate itself from other fast-food restaurants.

Prestonfield in Edinburgh is listed as one of the world's top hotels. Courtesy of Helena Smith/Rough Guides.

Chipotle was once an SBU of McDonald's. McDonald's then sold it to raise cash. Courtesy of Marcnorman/Dreamstime.

Management, of course, should avoid a market definition that is too narrow or too broad. Holiday Inns, Inc., the world's largest hotel chain, fell into this trap. There was a time when Holiday Inns broadened its business definition from the "hotel business" to the "travel industry." It acquired Trailways, Inc., then the nation's second largest bus company, and Delta Steamship, Inc., but it did not manage these companies well and later divested the properties.[19] Today Holiday Inns is part of the Intercontinental Hotel Group and has refocused on the lodging industry.

Companies have to identify those of its businesses that they must manage strategically. These businesses are called **strategic business units (SBUs)**. An SBU has three characteristics:

1. It is a single business or a collection of related businesses that can be planned for separately from the rest of the company.

2. It has its own set of competitors.

3. It has a manager who is responsible for strategic planning and profit performance and who controls most of the factors affecting profits.

The purpose of identifying the company's SBUs is to assign to these units strategic-planning goals and appropriate funding. These units send their plans to company headquarters, which approves them or sends them back for revision. Headquarters reviews these plans to decide which of its SBUs to build, maintain, harvest, and divest. Management cannot rely just on impressions. Analytical tools are needed for classifying businesses by profit potential.

Developing Growth Strategies

Companies need growth if they are to compete and attract top talent. "Growth is pure oxygen," states one executive. "It creates a vital, enthusiastic corporation where people see genuine opportunity…. In that way growth is more than our single most important financial driver; it's an essential part of our corporate culture." At the same time, a firm must be careful not to make growth itself an objective. The company's objective must be "profitable growth." Many would add that growth must be environmentally responsible. This is not unilaterally accepted, however.

Marketing has a responsibility to achieve profitable growth for the company. Marketing must identify, evaluate, and select opportunities and lay down strategies for capturing them. The **Ansoff product–market expansion grid** (Figure 3–2) offers a useful framework for examining growth.[20] Management first considers whether it could gain more market share with its current products in its current markets (market concentration strategy). Next it considers whether it can find or develop new markets for its current products (**market development strategy**).

Next, management should consider **product development**: offering modified or new products to current markets. By examining these three intensive growth strategies, management ideally will discover several ways to grow. Still, that may not be enough, in which case management must also examine diversification and integrative growth opportunities. For example, Starbucks developed packaged products that can be sold in supermarkets.

Figure 3–2
The product–market expansion grid is useful in helping managers visualize and identify market opportunities.

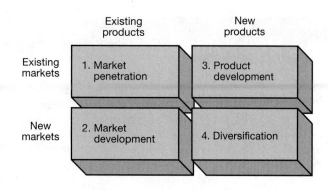

The Hunter's Head Tavern in the Virginia foothills of the Blue Ridge Mountains gained national publicity when it became the first restaurant in the United States to get an animal rights stamp of approval for the humane treatment of animals used in the restaurant. All animals are raised on the nearby Ayrshire Farms by the owner, Sandy Lerner, cofounder of Cisco Systems. Meat products with this stamp of approval thus become a new product and a means of differentiating the restaurant.[21]

Diversification Growth

Diversification growth makes sense when good opportunities can be found outside the present businesses. A good opportunity is one where the industry is highly attractive and the company has the mix of business strengths to be successful. Three types of diversification can be considered. First, the company could seek new products that have technological or marketing synergies with existing product lines, even though the products may appeal to a new class of customers (**concentric diversification strategy**). Second, the company might search for new products that could appeal to its current customers, although technologically unrelated to its current product line (**horizontal diversification strategy**). Hotels, restaurants, cruise lines, and airlines all pursue this strategy when they sell gift items such as T-shirts, perfume, and luggage. Many restaurants, such as the Hard Rock Café franchise, have found that the sale of restaurant logo clothing in their restaurants is highly profitable and the clothing serves as an excellent advertising medium.

Diversification opportunities sometimes arise as a result of new technology. A new class of lightweight aluminum ferries can cruise at 55 miles per hour and carry hundreds of passengers. This new technology allows ferries to serve new routes: Opportunities for on-board food and beverage service as well as the ferry service itself will be available to the hospitality/tourism industries.[22]

Finally, the company might seek new businesses that have no relationship to the company's current technology, products, or markets (**conglomerate diversification strategy**). The restaurant we mentioned earlier in this chapter that went into the cattle ranching business is an example of conglomerate diversification.

The company Sodexho of Marseille, France, was experienced and successful in providing hospitality services on ocean liners and cruise ships.[23] The company's founder, Pierre Bellon, decided to expand into other industries with similar needs, such as health-care facilities and schools, and to seek international expansion. Within five years, the company was successful in Belgium, and then expanded to North and South America and went public on the Paris Bourse. In 2008 Sodexho's global expansion led to a name change to Sodexo because in some countries a "xh" is difficult to pronounce.

Companies that diversify too broadly into unfamiliar products or industries can lose their market focus. Thus we see that a company can systematically identify new business opportunities by using a marketing systems framework.

Despite the risk, companies that started in one market often desire to enter others considered complimentary. The hospitality industry is witness to this

Marketing Highlight | Starbucks Coffee: Where Growth Is Really Perking

3−1 More than 25 years ago, Howard Schultz hit on the idea of bringing a European-style coffeehouse to America. He believed that people needed to slow down, to "smell the coffee" and enjoy life a little more. The result is Starbucks. This coffeehouse doesn't sell just coffee, it sells *The Starbucks Experience*—the comfy velvety chairs, the hissing steam, the rich aromas. Its coffee shops "provide an uplifting experience that enriches people's lives one moment, one human being, one extraordinary cup of coffee at a time." Starbucks gives customers what it calls a "third place"—away from home and away from work.

Starbucks is now a powerhouse premium brand in a category in which only cheaper commodity products once existed. Some 40 million customers a week flock to its nearly 13,500 shops in 40 countries. Growth is the engine that keeps Starbucks perking, and over the past two decades, the company's sales and profits have risen like steam off a mug of hot java. Starbucks targets (and regularly achieves) amazing revenue growth exceeding 20 percent each year.

Starbucks's success, however, has drawn a full litter of copycats, ranging from direct competitors such as Caribou Coffee to fast-food merchants (such as McDonald's) and even discounters (Kicks Coffee Café at a Wal-Mart). These days it seems that everyone is peddling his or her *own* brand of premium coffee. In the early 1990s, there were only 200 coffeehouses in the United States. Today there are more than 21,400. To maintain its phenomenal growth in an increasingly overcaffeinated marketplace, Starbucks has brewed up an ambitious, multipronged growth strategy. Let's examine the key elements of this strategy.

More Store Growth

Some 85 percent of Starbucks's sales come from its own stores. So, not surprisingly, Starbucks is opening new stores at a breakneck pace. Eleven years ago, Starbucks had just 1,015 stores, total—that's about 1,400 fewer than it plans to build in the coming year alone. Starbucks's strategy is to put stores *everywhere*. In Seattle, there's a Starbucks for every 9,400 people; in Manhattan, there's one for every 12,000. One three-block stretch in Chicago contains six of the trendy coffee bars. In New York City, there are two Starbucks in one Macy's store. In fact, cramming so many stores close together caused one satirical publication to run

this headline: "A New Starbucks Opens in the Restroom of Existing Starbucks." The company's ultimate goal is 40,000 stores worldwide.

Enhanced Starbucks Experience

Beyond opening new shops, Starbucks is adding in-store products and features that get customers to stop in more often, stay longer, and buy more. Its beefed-up menu added hot breakfast sandwiches plus lunch and dinner items, increasing the average customer purchase. To get customers to linger, Starbucks offers wireless Internet access in most of its stores. The chain also offers in-store music downloads, letting customers burn their own CDs while sipping their lattes. Out of cash? No problem—just swipe your prepaid Starbucks card on the way out ("a Starbucks store in your wallet"). Or use your Starbucks Card Duetto Visa (a credit card that also serves as a gift, stored-value, and rewards card).

New Retail Channels

The vast majority of coffee in America is bought in retail stores and brewed at home. To capture this demand, Starbucks has also pushed into America's supermarket aisles. It has a cobranding deal with Kraft, under which Starbucks roasts and packages its coffee and Kraft markets and distributes it. Beyond supermarkets, Starbucks has forged an impressive set of new ways to bring its brand to market. Some examples: Host Marriott operates Starbucks kiosks in America's airports, and several airlines serve Starbucks coffee to their passengers. Starbucks has installed coffee shops in most Barnes & Noble bookstores and many grocery stores. Starbucks also sells gourmet coffee, tea, gifts, and related goods through business and consumer catalogs. And its Web site, StarbucksStore.com, has become a kind of "lifestyle portal" on which it sells coffee, tea, coffee-making equipment, CDs, gifts, and collectibles.

New Products and Store Concepts

Starbucks has partnered over the years with several firms to extend its brand into new categories. For example, it joined with PepsiCo to stamp the Starbucks brand on bottled Frappuccino drinks and its DoubleShot espresso drink. Starbucks ice cream, marketed in a joint venture with Dreyer's, is now the leading brand of coffee ice cream. Starbucks has also

phenomenon. This is by no means a secure strategy because different businesses often require different management style and practices. Nestle Corp. may have found a model to avoid these risks successfully.

Nestle Corp. of Switzerland is a huge global consumer packaged food and beverage company. Nestle is also the world's largest coffee company. Nestle moved from selling unprepared coffee in various forms to selling its own brand and style of coffee machines that brew coffee from Nestle "grand cru pods." Based on this success, Nestle moved into Nespresso boutiques where customers can purchase diversified into the entertainment business. Starbucks Entertainment "selects the best in music, books, and film to offer Starbucks customers the opportunity to discover quality entertainment in a fun and convenient way as a part of their daily coffee experience." The entertainment initiative includes Hear Music (the Sound of Starbucks), which selects and sells music in Starbucks shops and also produces music CDs under its own label. Hear Music now runs its own XM satellite radio station, and Starbucks is opening new Starbucks Hear Music Coffeehouses in a number of major U.S. cities. The company has also teamed with Apple to create a Starbucks Entertainment area on the Apple Tunes store.

International Growth

Finally, Starbucks has taken its American-brewed concept global. In 1996 the company had only 11 coffeehouses outside North America. Today Starbucks has more than 5,000 stores in 46 international markets, from Paris to Osaka to Oman to Beijing. Starbucks continues to open new international stores at a rate of close to 400 per year.

Although Starbucks's growth strategy so far has met with amazing success, many analysts are now expressing strong concerns. What's wrong with Starbucks's rapid expansion? Critics worry that the company may be overextending the Starbucks brand name and diluting the Starbucks experience. People pay $4.50 for a cafe latte, say the critics, because of the brand's coffee-brewing expertise, cozy ambiance, and exclusivity. When you see the Starbucks name plastered on everything from airport coffee cups to supermarket packages, you wonder.

When gasoline hit $4 a gallon in the United States in 2008, it had appeared that Starbucks had grown too fast. At least too fast for the deteriorating economic environment in the United States. The increase in gasoline process meant that consumers were paying $50 or more a month for gasoline. This cut into their morning coffee budget. Part of strategic planning is trying to predict the economic environment. In this case Starbucks's market penetration strategy was fine for a strong economy, but when the economy worsened, it closed 600 sites in 2008, mostly stores that were close together and fighting each other for customers. Starbucks's problems led to the ouster of CEO Jim McDonald, and its founder, Howard Schultz, came back as CEO. Schultz felt that Starbucks had developed too many products and had

gotten away from creating a sense of community and the Starbucks experience. He eliminated the breakfast sandwiches whose smell interfered with the aroma of freshly brewing coffee. Starbucks's mission statement is, "Establish Starbucks as the premier purveyor of the finest coffee in the world while maintaining our uncompromising principles as we grow." Schultz also closed all the 7,100 stores for three hours to train the employees. He felt too many employees were no longer making the finest cup of coffee. Later in 2008, he realized a breakfast sandwich was drawing customers who wanted more than coffee and pastry for breakfast. Schultz added back breakfast sandwiches, but this time he developed ones that did not have an aroma that would interfere with the smell of fresh coffee. The moves that Howard Schultz in 2008 made were driven by his quest to move the company back to implementing its mission statement. The quest for growth moved Starbucks away from its mission. Starbucks provides a good example of the need to strategically plan growth and stay close to your mission.

Starbucks in a Barnes & Noble bookstore. Courtesy of Michael Newman/PhotoEdit.

Only time will tell whether Starbucks turns out to be the next McDonald's—it all depends on how well the company manages future growth. Says Schultz, "We are in the second inning of a nine-inning game."

Sources: Quotes and other information from "U.S. Coffee Shops Still Simply Too Hot to Handle," www.marketresearchworld.net (retrieved August 8, 2007); "Company Profile," May 2007, vnw. starbucks.com/aboutus/company, Profile.pdf; Burt Helm, "Saving Starbucks' Soul," *Business Week* (April 9, 2007): 56–62; Curt Woodward, "Weak Coffee: Some Question If Starbucks Expansion May Dilute the Brand," *Marketing News* (May 15, 2007): 1; Land Starbucks annual reports and other information accessed at www. starbucks.com, July 2008; Mellisa Allison, "Starbucks Closing 5 Percent of U.S. Stores," *The Seattle Times* (July 2, 2008): 1–3, http://seattletimes.nwsource.com; Brian White, "Starbucks to Close Stores and Discontinue Breakfast Sandwiches," *Blogging-Stocks* (January 31, 2008): 1, www.bloggingstocks.com; Sarah Gilbert, "Starbucks Nationwide to Close for Emergency Re-training Feb. 26," *BloggingStocks* (February 13, 2008); 1.

brewed coffee in a modern and shiny European boutique setting and also purchase machines and Nestle pods.

Three years ago we posed the question, Will Nespresso boutiques pose strong competition for Starbucks and McCafes? We now know the answer is no. However, boutiques have developed a niche in the high-end coffee market. Today there are over 225 Nespresso boutiques. Nestle formed Nespresso Club; in the last four years the club has grown from 3 million members to over 12 million members. These members and other customers consume 12,500 cups of Nespresso coffee every minute. By diversifying into the retail coffeehouse business, Nespresso developed a way for customer to try its product and build in-home use of its coffee.[24]

Integrative Growth

Opportunities in diversification, market development, and product development can be seized through integrating backward, forward, or horizontally within that business's industry. A hotel company could select **backward integration** by acquiring one of its suppliers, such as a food distributor, or it could acquire tour wholesalers or travel agents (**forward integration**). Finally, the hotel company might acquire one or more competitors, provided that the government does not bar the move (**horizontal integration**).

Marriott developed a restaurant supply distribution system known as Marriott Distribution Service. This grew out of Marriott's Fairfield Farms Commissary operation. The commissary operation was shut down and the business was refocused on distribution. Marriott opened six of these distribution centers to service concentrations of Marriott Hotels. With this guaranteed core business, each distribution center then aggressively sells to other restaurants in the area.[25] However with increased competition from food distributors such as Sysco, Marriott sold Marriott Distribution Services in 2004.

Through investigating possible integration moves, a company may discover additional sources of sales volume. These new sources may still not deliver the desired sales volume. In this case, the company may consider diversification moves. Integrative growth offers opportunities in related businesses, but a company must have or acquire the expertise to succeed in the new business. It then must make sure it can keep up with the industry leaders.

Thus we see that a company can systematically identify new business opportunities by using a marketing systems framework, looking at ways to intensify its position in current product markets, searching for profitable opportunities outside its current businesses, and considering ways to integrate backward, forward, or horizontally in relation to its current businesses.

■■■ Marketing Strategy and the Marketing Mix

The strategic plan defines the company's overall mission and objectives. Figure 3–3 shows marketing's role and activities and summarizes the major activities involved in managing a customer-driven marketing strategy and the marketing mix.

Consumers stand in the center. The goal is to create value for customers and build profitable customer relationships. Next comes **marketing strategy**, the marketing logic by which the company hopes to create this customer value and achieve these profitable relationships. The company decides which customers it will serve (segmentation and targeting) and how (differentiation and positioning). It identifies the total market and then divides it into caller segments, selects the most promising segments, and focuses on serving and satisfying customers in these segments.

Guided by marketing strategy, the company designs an integrated *marketing mix* made up of factors under its control—product, price, place, and promotion (the four Ps). To find the best marketing strategy and mix, the company engages in marketing analysis, planning, implementation, and control. Through these activities, the company watches and adapts to the actors and forces in the marketing environment. We now look briefly at each activity. Then, in later chapters, we discuss each one in more depth.

Customer-Driven Marketing Strategy

As we emphasized throughout Chapter 1, to succeed in today's competitive marketplace, companies need to be customer centered. They must *win* customers from competitors and then keep and grow them by delivering greater value. But before it can satisfy consumers, a company must first understand their needs and wants. Thus sound marketing requires a careful customer analysis.

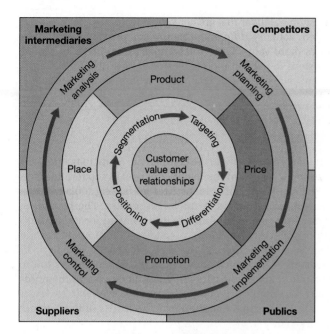

Figure 3–3
Managing marketing strategy
and the marketing mix.
Source: Kotler and Armstrong, *Principles of Marketing*, 12th ed., p. 47.

Companies know that they cannot profitably serve all consumers in a given market—at least not all consumers in the same way. There are too many different kinds of consumers with too many different kinds of needs. And most companies are in a position to serve some segments better than others. Thus each company must divide up the total market, choose the best segments, and design strategies for profitably serving chosen segments. This process involves *market segmentation, market targeting, differentiation,* and *positioning.*

Market Segmentation

The market consists of many types of customers, products, and needs. The marketer must determine which segments offer the best opportunities. Consumers can be grouped and served in various ways based on geographic, demographic, psychographic, and behavioral factors. The process of dividing a market into distinct groups of buyers who have different needs, characteristics, or behavior and who might require separate products or marketing programs is called **market segmentation**.

Every market has segments, but not all ways of segmenting a market are equally useful. It would be difficult to make one car model that was the first choice of consumers in both segments. Companies are wise to focus their efforts on meeting the distinct needs of individual market segments.

Market Targeting

After a company has defined market segments, it can enter one or many of these segments. Market targeting involves evaluating each market segment's attractiveness and selecting one or more segments to enter. A company should target segments in which it can profitably generate the greatest customer value and sustain it over time. A company with limited resources might decide to serve only one or a few special segments or "market niches."

Alternatively, a company might choose to serve several related segments— perhaps those with different kinds of customers but with the same basic wants. Most companies enter a new market by serving a single segment, and if this proves successful, they add segments. Large companies eventually seek full market coverage.

Market Differentiation and Positioning

After a company has decided which market segments to enter, it must decide how it will differentiate its market offering for each targeted segment and what positions it wants to occupy in those segments. A product's *position* is the place the product occupies, relative to competitors' products, in consumers' minds. Marketers want to develop unique market positions for their products. If a product is perceived to be exactly like others on the market, consumers would have no reason to buy it.

Positioning is arranging for a product to occupy a clear, distinctive, and desirable place relative to competing products in the minds of target consumers. As one positioning expert puts it, positioning is "why a shopper will pay a little more for your brand."[26] Thus marketers plan positions that distinguish their products from competing brands and give them the greatest advantage in their target markets.

In positioning its product, the company first identifies possible customer value differences that provide competitive advantages on which to build the position. The company can offer greater customer value either by charging lower prices than competitors do or by offering more benefits to justify higher prices. But if the company *promises* greater value, it must then deliver that greater value. Thus effective positioning begins with differentiation, actually *differentiating* the company's market offering so that it gives consumers more value. Once the company has chosen a desired position, it must take strong steps to deliver and communicate that position to target consumers. The company's entire marketing program should support the chosen positioning strategy.

Developing an Integrated Marketing Mix

After deciding on its overall marketing strategy, the company is ready to begin planning the details of the marketing mix, one of the major concepts in modern marketing. The marketing mix is the set of controllable, tactical marketing tools that the firm blends to produce the response it wants in the target market. The marketing mix consists of everything the firm can do to influence the demand for its product. The many possibilities can be collected into four groups of variables known as the four Ps: *product, price, place,* and *promotion.*

Product means the goods-and-services combination the company offers to the target market. *Price* is the amount of money customers must pay to obtain the product. *Place* includes company activities that make the product available to target customers. *Promotion* means activities that communicate the merits of the product and persuade target customers to buy it.

An effective marketing program blends all of the marketing mix elements into an integrated marketing program designed to achieve the company's marketing objectives by delivering value to consumers. The marketing mix constitutes the company's tactical tool kit for establishing strong positioning in target markets.

Some critics think that the four Ps may omit or underemphasize certain important activities. For example, they ask, "Where are services?" Just because they don't start with a *P* doesn't justify omitting them. The answer is that services, such as banking, airline, and retailing services, are products too. We might call them *service products.*

"Where is packaging?" the critics might ask. Marketers would answer that they include packaging as just one of many product decisions. All said, as Figure 3–3 suggests, many marketing activities that might appear to be left out of the marketing mix are subsumed under one of the four Ps. The issue is not whether there should be 4, 6, or 10Ps so much as what framework is most helpful in designing integrated marketing programs.

There is another concern, however, that is valid. It holds that the four Ps concept takes the seller's view of the market, not the buyer's view. From the buyer's viewpoint, in this age of customer value and relationships, the four Ps might be better described as the four Cs:[27]

4Ps	*4Cs*
Product	Customer solution
Price	Customer cost
Place	Convenience
Promotion	Communication

Thus whereas marketers see themselves as selling products, customers see themselves as buying value or solutions to their problems. And customers are interested in more than just the price; they are interested in the total costs of obtaining, using, and disposing of a product. Customers want the product and service to be as conveniently available as possible. Finally, they want two-way communication. Marketers would do well to think through the four Cs first and then build the four Ps on that platform.

Figure 3–4
The relationship between
analysis, planning,
implementation, and control.

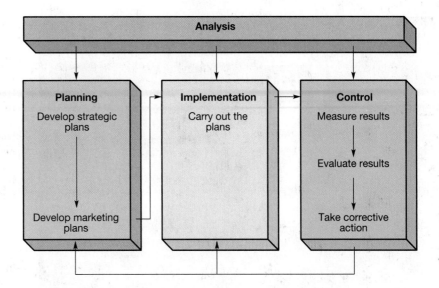

■■■ Managing the Marketing Effort

In addition to being good at the *marketing* in marketing management, companies need to pay attention to the *management.* Managing the marketing process requires the four marketing management functions shown in Figure 3–4: *analysis, planning, implementation,* and *control.* The company first develops company-wide strategic plans and then translates them into marketing and other plans for each division, product, and brand. Through implementation, the company turns the plans into actions. Control consists of measuring and evaluating the results of marketing activities and taking corrective action where needed. Finally, marketing analysis provides information and evaluations needed for all of the other marketing activities.

Marketing Analysis

Managing the marketing function begins with a complete analysis of the company's situation. The marketer should conduct a **SWOT analysis**, by which it evaluates the company's overall strengths (S), weaknesses (W), opportunities (O), and threats (T) (see Figure 3–5). Strengths include internal capabilities, resources, and positive situational factors that may help the company serve its customers and achieve its objectives. Weaknesses include internal limitations and negative situational factors that may interfere with the company's performance. Opportunities are favorable factors or trends in the external environment that the company may be able to exploit to its advantage. And threats are unfavorable external factors or trends that may present challenges to performance.

Figure 3–5
SWOT analysis.

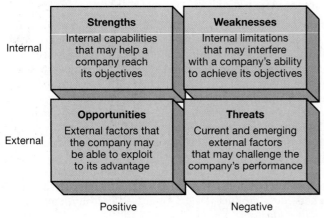

The company should analyze its markets and marketing environment to find attractive opportunities and identify environmental threats. It should analyze company strengths and weaknesses as well as current and possible marketing actions to determine which opportunities it can best pursue. The goal is to match the company's strengths to attractive opportunities in the environment while eliminating or overcoming the weaknesses and minimizing the threats.

The strengths of the Westin St. Francis are summarized on its Web site. "As the only lodging destination located on Union Square, ... our hotel literally places you in the middle of the action. Simply step outside, hop aboard one of the trolley cars pulling in, and enjoy a breathtaking ride to China Town, Alcatraz, or Fisherman's Wharf. Or set off on foot for the Financial District or the steep avenues of Nob Hill." Courtesy of Jerryway/Dreamstime.

Internal Environmental Analysis (Strengths and Weaknesses Analysis)

It is one thing to discern attractive opportunities in the environment and another to have the necessary competencies to succeed with these opportunities. Each business needs to evaluate its strengths and weaknesses periodically. Management or an outside consultant reviews the business's marketing, financial, manufacturing, and organizational competencies. Each factor is rated as to whether it is a major strength, minor strength, neutral factor, minor weakness, or major weakness. A company with strong marketing capability would probably show up with the ten marketing factors all rated as major strengths.

In examining its pattern of strengths and weaknesses, clearly the business does not have to correct all its weaknesses or gloat about all its strengths. The big question is whether the business should limit itself to those opportunities for which it now possesses the required strengths or should consider better opportunities.

Many hospitality industry specialists believe that to compete effectively, companies such as hotels, resorts, and cruise lines need seamless connectivity within their computer reservation systems (CRS), including a global distribution system (GDS). If a hotel company wishes to increase its international business and its reservations through travel agents, the existence or development of such a system would surely be viewed as a strength.[28] Sometimes a business does poorly not because its department lacks the required strengths, but because employees do not work together as a team. In some hospitality companies, salespeople are viewed as overpaid playboys and playgirls who produce business by practically giving it away to customers. In turn, salespeople often view those in operations as incompetent dolts who consistently foul up their orders and provide poor customer service. It is therefore critically important to assess interdepartmental working relationships as part of the internal environmental audit.

Every company must manage some basic processes, such as new product development, raw materials to finished products, sales leads to orders, customer orders to cash payments, and so on. Each process creates value and each process requires interdepartmental teamwork.

External Environmental Analysis (Opportunity and Threat Analysis)

The business manager now knows the parts of the environment to monitor if the business is to achieve its goals. In general, a business unit has to monitor key **macroenvironmental forces** (demographic-economic, technological, political-legal, and social-cultural) and significant **microenvironmental forces** (customers, competitors, distribution channels, and supplies) that will affect its ability to earn profits in the marketplace. The business unit should set up a marketing intelligence system to track trends and important developments. For each trend or development, management needs to identify the implied opportunities and threats.

The terrorist attacks on September 11, 2001, brought a sudden awareness to the worldwide hospitality/tourism industry of the dramatic impact such events can have on business and pleasure travel. This has caused tourism promotion agencies, convention centers, transportation firms, and lodging companies to seriously consider alternative markets, new product design, increased security, emergency energy sources, and many other factors.

The emergence of China, India, and Eastern Europe as new industrial and political powers is seriously affecting hospitality/tourism in ways that were unforeseen. For example, the high quality of health care combined with the low cost in countries such as India has created a new segment of tourism known as medical tourism. At the same time, the Texas Medical Center, one of the world's largest medical centers, has seen its medical tourism from the Middle East decline. In today's rapidly changing environment, external environmental threats and opportunities have taken on new importance in strategic planning.

OPPORTUNITIES   A major purpose of environmental scanning is to discern new opportunities. We define a **marketing opportunity** as follows: an area of need that a company can perform profitably.

Opportunities can be listed and classified according to their attractiveness and the success probability. Success probability depends on whether its business strengths match the key success requirements for operating in the target market and exceed those of competitors. The best performing company will be the one that can generate the greatest customer value and sustain it over time.

The concept of incorporating health and recreation clubs into resorts has been an opportunity for some resorts. Programs are aimed at local markets, allowing members to enjoy the resort facilities and sometimes even stay in the rooms. Membership programs offer opportunities for increased revenue, but there is a negative side if they are not well managed. Resort guests who are paying to stay in the resort and use its facilities will not appreciate the competition for tennis or golf times from local residents.[29] The franchising of B&Bs (bed and breakfasts) might offer an opportunity for a franchise company that is able to overcome considerable obstacles. The B&B industry today is comparable to the hotel/motel industry in the 1950s. B&B owners do not view franchising favorably, yet they have specific needs that could be met through franchising under a well-planned strategic franchise program.[30]

OPPORTUNITIES AS UNMET NEEDS   In North America and Europe, goods are increasingly transported by trucks. In the United States, truckers may not legally drive more than 11 hours at a stretch. Unless a truck has two drivers it must stop somewhere that is safe, clean, and offers services needed by truckers. Today, many trucks are forced to park along highways, near abandoned buildings, or other undesirable places due to a shortage of places to stop—even with 1,100 truck stops across the nation.

Most truck stops don't charge for stopovers but instead realize revenues from food, showers, merchandise, and vending machines. The average truck stop has sales of nearly $10 million per year. Zoning regulations, lack of vacant land near highways, and community resistance have created a need for more truck stops. Chains of truck stops exist, such as Petro Stopping Centers, Travel Centers of America, Flying J, and Pilot Travel Centers. Hospitality entrepreneurs need to develop new forms of truck stops to meet this huge, growing, and profitable market segment.[31]

Threats

Some developments in the external environment represent marketing threats. We define an environmental threat as follows: A challenge posed by unfavorable trends or developments that would lead, in the absence of defensive marketing action, to sales or profit deterioration. Threats should be classified according to their seriousness and probability of occurrence. After assembling a picture of major threats and opportunities, four outcomes are possible:

1.   An ideal business is high in major opportunities and low in major threats.

2.   A speculative business is high in both major opportunities and threats.

3.   A major business is low in major opportunities and threats.

4.   A troubled business is low in opportunities and high in threats.

Traditional institutional food-service providers to hospitals, schools, government offices, and office buildings face the threat of competition from QSRs. Many QSRs such as Pizza Hut, Dunkin' Donuts, and Burger King have entered this market. Traditional institutional food-service firms such as ARAMARK cannot ignore this threat.[32]

Today, the impact of threats is so critical that all hospitality companies must study possible threats and build risk management systems. We have previously spoken of the effects of 9/11, but risks such as mad cow disease and microbial contamination are of vital concern to hospitality companies. Several years ago, "The Jack-in-the-Box quick service restaurant chain was linked to 400 illnesses and deaths of three children due to an outbreak of *Escherichia coli* in their hamburgers. The chain was accused of serious deception, irresponsibility and poor communications."[33] Jack-in-the-Box suffered heavy financial loss for four years and nearly went out of business as a result of the problem.

Because microbial outbreaks are possible in any food establishment, they must be considered as risks with prescribed procedures to follow after an outbreak.

Goal Formulation

After the business unit has defined its mission and conducted a SWOT analysis, it can proceed to develop specific objectives and goals.

Very few businesses pursue only one objective. Most business units pursue a mix of objectives, including profitability, sales growth, market share improvement, and cost containment. The business unit sets these objectives and manages by objectives. The business unit should strive to arrange its objectives from most to least important. Where possible, objectives should be stated quantitatively. The objective "increase the return on investment" is not as satisfactory as "increase ROI [return on investment] to 15 percent" or even better, "increase ROI to 15 percent within two years." Objectives support measurable goals. A business should set realistic goals. The levels should arise from an analysis of the business unit's opportunities and strengths, not from wishful thinking.

Finally, the company's objectives need to be consistent. Objectives are sometimes in a tradeoff relationship. Here are some important tradeoffs:

- High profit margins versus high market share
- Deep penetration of existing markets versus developing new markets
- Profit goals versus nonprofit goals
- High growth versus low risk

The hotel industry is faced with unique challenges concerning goal formulation and performance measurement due to management agreements between hotel owners and hotel operating companies. Most industries such as manufacturing, construction, or retailing hire their own management staff rather than contracting with an independent operations management company. "Of all the issues addressed in the negotiation of a hotel management agreement, among the most difficult to resolve is establishing an appropriate performance test that is acceptable to both parties."[34]

Here are three examples of performance measures used in the hotel industry:[35]

1. **A hotel's return.** Returns-based performance tests measure income before fixed costs (IBFC) or net operating income (NOI). Owners and management companies can usually find agreement in the use of these measures.

2. **Operating margins.** Owners also often insist on performance measures based on increases in operating margins, such as increasing IBFC from 20 percent of revenue to 28 percent. Operating margin tests focus management's attention on an initial area but sometimes cause managers to think and act "short term," which may discourage management from using revenue management programs that accept some low-margin business during periods of weak occupancy.

Southwest Airlines designed a low-cost delivery system that includes using all of the same type of aircraft (Boeing 737s), eliminating meals, having its pilots fly more hours, and hedging fuel. Courtesy of Frank Ordonez/Syracuse Newspapers/The Image Works.

3. **Revenue per available room (RevPAR).** RevPAR tests assume that room revenue is a good indicator of a hotel's overall performance. These performance tests do not measure other revenue such as laundry, food and beverage, rents, and telephone. As a result, some hotel managers pay little attention to the marketing of these product lines. RevPAR tests also ignore the expense side. A hotel may achieve a high RevPAR through exceptional service by overstaffing but be less profitable than hotels with lower RevPAR and lower expenses. Those who use RevPAR often compare their results with other hotels, but the accuracy of comparative data may be questioned.

Goals indicate what a business unit wants to achieve; strategy answers how to get there. Every business must tailor a strategy for achieving its goals. Although we can list many types of strategies, Michael Porter has condensed them into three generic types that provide a good starting point for strategic thinking.[36]

1. **Overall cost leadership.** Here the business works hard to achieve the lowest costs. The problem with this strategy is that other firms usually emerge with still lower costs. The real key is for the firm to achieve the lowest costs among those competitors adopting a similar differentiation or focus strategy.

2. **Differentiation.** Here the business concentrates on achieving superior performance in an important customer benefit area valued by a large part of the market. The relative importance of customer benefits shifts as demographic and psychographic characteristics of market populations change. Younger, active hotel guests may value a swimming pool, a sauna, or an exercise room at a hotel, whereas older guests place high value in reliability and assurance of consistent hotel service.[37]

3. **Focus.** Here the business focuses on one or more narrow market segments rather than going after a large market. The firm gets to know the needs of these segments and pursues either cost leadership or a form of differentiation within the target segments.

Marketing Planning

Marketing planning involves deciding on marketing strategies that will help the company attain its overall strategic objectives. A detailed marketing plan is needed for each business, product, or brand. The plan begins with an executive summary, which quickly overviews major assessments, goals, and recommendations. The main section of the plan presents a detailed SWOT analysis of the current marketing situation as well as potential threats and opportunities. The plan next states major objectives for the brand and outlines the specifics of a marketing strategy for achieving them.

A *marketing strategy* consists of specific strategies for target markets, positioning, the marketing mix, and marketing expenditure levels. It outlines how the company intends to create value for target customers in order to capture value in return. In this section, the planner explains how each strategy responds to the threats, opportunities, and critical issues spelled out earlier in the plan. Additional sections of the marketing plan lay out an action program for implementing the marketing strategy along with the details of a supporting *marketing budget.* The last section outlines the controls that will be used to monitor progress, measure return on marketing investment, and take corrective action. As a manager or a director of sales of a hospitality business, you will be required to develop a marketing plan every year. A well-developed marketing plan is critical to the success of a business. This is why we have devoted the last chapter of this book to developing a marketing plan.

Implementation

Even a clear strategy and well-thought-out supporting program may not be enough. The firm may fail at implementation. Employees in a company share a common way of behaving and thinking. They must understand and believe in the company's strategy. The company must communicate its strategy to its employees and make them understand their part in carrying it out. To implement a strategy, the firm must have the required resources, including employees with the necessary skills to carry out that strategy.

Feedback and Control

All companies need to track results and monitor new developments in the environment. The environment will change. When it does, the company will need to review its strategies or objectives. Peter Drucker pointed out that it is more important to do the right thing (being effective) than to do things right (being efficient). Excellent companies excel at both.

Once an organization starts losing its market position through failure to respond to a changed environment, it becomes increasingly harder to retrieve market leadership. Organizations, especially large ones, have much inertia. Yet organizations can be changed through leadership, ideally in advance of a crisis.

The Emperor Hotel, a three-star property in Singapore, caters primarily to independent and corporate travelers, many in the oil industry. Because of a recession in Singapore, corporate income fell from $2.2 million to $1.9 million, a loss of $300,000. Problem areas were the following:

- A 45 percent drop in food and beverage revenue
- Declining hotel occupancy from 92 to 57 percent
- Intensive competition
- Rising fixed costs
- Shrinking market niche (fewer people in the oil industry)
- Autocratic management style

The owner conducted a strategic analysis of the hotel and determined strengths and weaknesses. As a result of the strategic analysis, the Emperor Hotel decided to "shrink selectively," particularly in the food and beverage area. Food and beverage operations were contracted out. This strategy was selected because it was felt that if a hotel boom occurred, the hotel would be in a good position to take advantage of the good times. If not, the hotel would be attractive to a prospective buyer and could be sold on short notice.[38]

The hotel-resort industry faces unique challenges in strategic planning. Most other members of the hospitality industry, such as airlines, cruise lines, and major restaurant chains, may approach strategic planning in much the same manner as a manufacturing company. These organizations have highly centralized management operations in which strategic decisions are made.

Measuring and Managing Return on Marketing Investment

Marketing managers must ensure that their marketing dollars are being well spent. In the past, many marketers spent freely on big, expensive marketing programs, often without thinking carefully about the financial returns on their spending. They believed that marketing produces intangible creative outcomes, which do not lend themselves readily to measures of productivity or return. But in today's more constrained economy, all that is changing.[39]

According to a recent study, as finances have tightened, marketers see return on marketing investment as the second biggest issue after the economy. "Increasingly, it is important for marketers to be able to justify their expenses," says one marketer. For a marketing program, says another, marketers need to ask themselves, "Do I have the right combination of strategy and tactics that will generate the most return in terms of share, revenue, and/or profit objectives from my investment?"[40]

In response, marketers are developing better measures of *marketing ROI*. **Return on marketing investment** or marketing ROI is the net return from a marketing investment divided by the costs of the marketing investment. It measures the profits generated by investments in marketing activities.

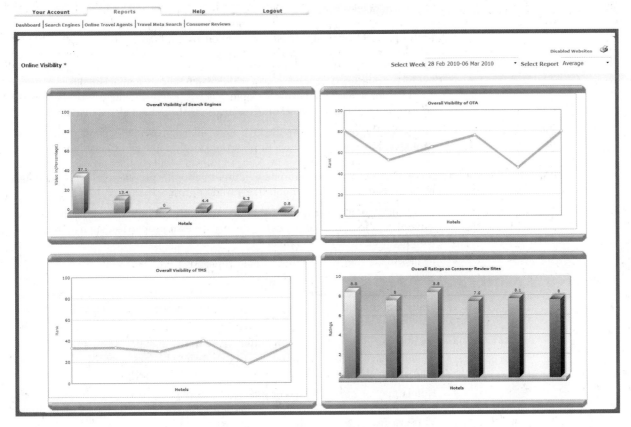

This dashboard from SearchView provides an overview of how a hotel is doing compared to its competitive set by providing information on (clockwise from top left); the visibility of a hotel on search engines, the visibility of the hotel on online travel agencies (OTAs), the visibility on travel meta search sites (such as Kayak) and the ratings on consumer review sites. Courtesy of TravelClick.

A recent survey found that although two-thirds of companies have implemented return on marketing investment programs in recent years, only 22 percent of companies report making good progress in measuring marketing ROI. Another survey of chief financial officers reported that 93 percent of those surveyed are dissatisfied with their ability to measure marketing ROI. The major problem is figuring out what specific measures to use and obtaining good data on these measures.[41]

A company can assess marketing ROI in terms of standard marketing performance measures, such as brand awareness, sales, or market share. Many companies are assembling such measures into *marketing dashboards*—meaningful sets of marketing performance measures in a single display used to monitor strategic marketing performance. Just as automobile dashboards present drivers with details on how their cars are performing, the marketing dashboard gives marketers the detailed measures they need to assess and adjust their marketing strategies.

There is commercial software that produces dashboards for both lodging and food-service operations. Searchview by TravelClickHotels is designed to give an instant update of one's online presence, including production by OTAs, page presence of these agencies, your star ratings on the OTA, performance of pay-per-click (PPC) activities, and the individual customer ratings and comments. A company can also compare its site with its ratings with its competitors on sites such as travel click. Restaurant dashboards can include sales mix reports, reports on promotions, coupon redemption, information on each comp, payroll costs, and costs of goods sold. Up until a few years ago intelligence would have been cost prohibitive for the individual property to collect.

■■■ Unique Challenges of the Hotel Industry

The hotel-resort industry is characterized by a unique management and ownership structure that complicates the process of strategic planning.

- Major chains commonly do not own all the properties they manage. Some hotel chains may, in fact, own no individual properties.

- Owners of hotel-resorts often show surprisingly little interest or knowledge of their properties. Hotels throughout the world have commonly been acquired because of tax benefits, perceived real estate appreciation, or as an ego-fulfilling device, particularly in the case of upscale showcase properties. A study of hotel investment returns in Southeast Asia demonstrated that "ego capital," or prestige associated with hotels, was a dominant reason for ownership. "Such non-economic benefits may drive up prices for hotels and make it possible to accept relatively low yields in comparison to other real-estate opportunities or investments in other global markets."[42]

- Occasionally, owners complain that hotel management companies are nonresponsive, have little expertise in planning, and do not work closely with owners or their representatives. In Asia, there reportedly exists an association of hotel owners who have grouped together in an effort to place pressure on hotel management companies, much like a trade union.

- Hotel management companies that are generally unknown or invisible to the general public may own or manage many diverse properties, such as Ramada, Holiday Inn, or Days Inn hotels.

- Professional managers of individual properties have commonly been educated and trained to manage properties with concern for areas such as maintenance and front-desk operations but with little or no training in strategic planning. Many feel that this is the responsibility of the owner, yet if the owner has little interest in this function, strategic planning at the property level is overlooked.

- Hotel management companies often have little real power to force owners to make necessary investments or the strategic changes deemed essential. In many cases, the only alternative has been to drop the property from the chain.

- Hotels may or may not own or manage secondary properties within the hotel, such as restaurants, retail stores, health and business centers, and nightclubs. This creates added complexity in strategic planning.

- **Strategic alliances** between hotel chains on a global basis may further complicate the planning process.

Marketing has a definite role to play in strategic planning. This department must maintain close and continuous ties with customers. Marketing is responsible for identifying and studying consumer needs and, as such, has a level of expertise in this area that is invaluable in strategic planning.

■■■ KEY TERMS

Ansoff product–market expansion grid. A matrix developed by cell, plotting new products and existing products with new products and existing products. The grid provides strategic insights into growth opportunities.

Backward integration. A growth strategy by which companies acquire businesses supplying them with products or services (e.g., a restaurant chain purchasing a bakery).

Concentric diversification strategy. A growth strategy whereby a company seeks new products that have technological or marketing synergies with existing product lines.

Conglomerate diversification strategy. A product growth strategy in which a company seeks new businesses that have no relationship to the company's current product line or markets.

Corporate mission statement. A guide to provide all the publics of a company with a shared sense of purpose, direction, and opportunity, allowing all to work independently, yet collectively, toward the organization's goals.

Forward integration. A growth strategy by which companies acquire businesses that are closer to the ultimate consumer, such as a hotel acquiring a chain of travel agents.

Horizontal diversification strategy. A product growth strategy whereby a company looks for new products that could appeal to current customers, which are technologically unrelated to its current line.

Horizontal integration. A growth strategy by which companies acquire competitors.

Macroenvironmental forces. Demographic, economic, technological, political, legal, social, and cultural factors.

Market development strategy. Finding and developing new markets for your current products.

Market segmentation. The process of dividing a market into distinct groups of buyers who have different needs, characteristics, or behavior and who might require separate products or marketing programs.

Marketing opportunity. An area of need in which a company can perform profitably.

Marketing strategy. The marketing logic by which the company hopes to create this customer value and achieve these profitable relationships.

Microenvironmental forces. Customers, competitors, distribution channels, and suppliers.

Product development. Offering modified or new products to current markets.

Return on marketing investment (or marketing ROI). The net return from a marketing investment divided by the costs of the marketing investment. It measures the profits generated by investments in marketing activities.

Strategic alliances. Relationships between independent parties that agree to cooperate but still retain separate identities.

Strategic business units (SBUs). A single business or collection of related businesses that can be planned separately from the rest of the company.

Strategic planning. The process of developing and maintaining a strategic fit between the organization's goals and capabilities and its changing marketing opportunities.

SWOT analysis. Evaluates the company's overall strengths (S), weaknesses (W), opportunities (O), and threats (T).

■■■ CHAPTER REVIEW

I.   Nature of High-Performance Business

   A. Stakeholder. The principle that a business must at least strive to satisfy the minimum expectations of each stakeholder group.

   B. Processes. Companies build cross-functional teams that manage core business processes in order to be superior competitors.

   C. Resources. Companies decide to outsource less critical resources. They identify their core competencies and use them as the basis for their strategic planning.

   D. Organization. Companies align their organization's structure, policies, and culture to the changing requirements of business strategy.

II.   Corporate Strategic Planning: Defining Marketing's Role

   A. Defining the corporate mission. A mission statement is a statement of the organization's purpose—what it wants to accomplish in the larger environment.

   B. Setting company objectives and goals. The company needs to turn its mission into detailed supporting objectives for each level of management. Marketing strategies and programs must be developed to support these marketing objectives.

   C. Designing the business portfolio. Market definitions of a business are superior to product definitions. A business must be viewed as a customer-satisfying process, not a product-producing process. Companies should define their business in terms of customer needs, not products.

     1. Developing growth strategies. Companies need growth if they are to compete and attract top talent.

       a. Ansoff product–market expansion grid offers a useful framework for examining growth.

     2. Diversification growth. Makes sense when good opportunities can be found outside the present businesses

       a. Concentric diversification strategy. The company could seek new products that have technological or marketing synergies with existing product lines, even though the products may appeal to a new class of customers.

       b. Horizontal diversification strategy. The company might search for new products that could appeal to its current customers, although technologically unrelated to its current product line.

       c. Conglomerate diversification strategy. The company might seek new businesses that have no relationship to the company's current technology, products, or markets.

     3. Integrative growth. Opportunities in diversification, market development, and product development can be seized through integrating backward, forward, or horizontally within that business's industry.

       a. Backward integration. Acquiring a supplier.

       b. Forward integration. For example, a hotel might acquire tour wholesalers or travel agents.

       c. Horizontal integration. Acquiring one or more competitors.

III.   Marketing Strategy and the Marketing Mix

   A. Customer-driven marketing strategy. Before it can satisfy consumers, a company must first understand their needs and wants. Thus sound marketing requires a careful customer analysis. Each company must divide up the total market, choose the best segments, and design strategies for profitably serving chosen segments.

     1. Market segmentation. The market consists of many types of customers, products, and needs. The marketer must determine which segments offer the best opportunities. Consumers can be grouped and served in various ways based on geographic, demographic, psychographic, and behavioral factors.

     2. Market targeting. Market targeting involves evaluating each market segment's attractiveness and selecting one or more segments to enter. A company should target segments in which it can profitably generate the greatest customer value and sustain it over time.

3. **Market differentiation and positioning.** After a company has decided which market segments to enter, it must decide how it will differentiate its market offering for each targeted segment and what positions it wants to occupy in those segments.

B. **Developing an integrated marketing mix.** The marketing mix is the set of controllable, tactical marketing tools that the firm blends to produce the response it wants in the target market. The marketing mix consists of everything the firm can do to influence the demand for its product.

   1. **Product.** The goods-and-services combination the company offers to the target market.
   2. **Price.** The amount of money customers must pay to obtain the product.
   3. **Place.** Company activities that make the product available to target customers.
   4. **Promotion.** Activities that communicate the merits of the product and persuade target customers to buy it.

IV. **Managing the Marketing Effort**

A. **Marketing analysis.** Managing the marketing function begins with a complete analysis of the company's situation. The marketer should conduct a SWOT analysis, by which it evaluates the company's overall strengths (S), weaknesses (W), opportunities (O), and threats (T).

   1. **Internal environmental analysis** (strengths and weaknesses analysis)
      a. **Strengths.** Internal capabilities, resources, and positive situational factors that may help the company to serve its customers and achieve its objectives.
      b. **Weaknesses.** Internal limitations and negative situational factors that may interfere with the company's performance.
   2. **External environmental analysis** (opportunity and threat analysis)
      a. **Opportunities.** Favorable factors or trends in the external environment that the company may be able to exploit to its advantage.
      b. **Threats.** Unfavorable external factors or trends that may present challenges to performance.
   3. **Goal formulation.** After the business unit has defined its mission and conducted a SWOT analysis, it can proceed to develop specific objectives and goals.
      1. **Overall cost leadership.** The real key is for the firm to achieve the lowest costs among those competitors adopting a similar differentiation or focus strategy.

2. **Differentiation.** The business concentrates on achieving superior performance in an important customer benefit area valued by a large part of the market.
3. **Focus.** The business focuses on one or more narrow market segments rather than going after a large market.
4. **Marketing planning.** Marketing planning involves deciding on marketing strategies that will help the company attain its overall strategic objectives. A detailed marketing plan is needed for each business, product, or brand.
5. **Implementation.** To implement a strategy, the firm must have the required resources, including employees with the necessary skills to carry out that strategy.
6. **Feedback and control.** All companies need to track results and monitor new developments in the environment. The environment will change. When it does, the company will need to review its strategies or objectives.
      1. **Measuring and managing return on marketing investment.** Marketing managers must ensure that their marketing dollars are being well spent.

V. **Unique Challenges of the Hotel Industry**

A. Major chains commonly do not own all the properties they manage.
B. Owners of hotels and resorts often show surprisingly little interest or knowledge of their properties.
C. Occasionally, owners complain that hotel management companies are nonresponsive, have little expertise in planning, and do not work closely with owners or their representatives.
D. Hotel management companies that are generally unknown or invisible to the general public may own or manage many diverse properties, such as Hilton Garden Inn, Holiday Inn, or Marriott Hotels.
E. Professional managers of individual properties have commonly been educated and trained to manage properties with concern for areas such as maintenance and front-desk operations but with little or no training in strategic planning.
F. Hotel management companies often have little real power to force owners to make necessary investments or the strategic changes deemed essential.
G. Hotels may or may not own or manage secondary properties within the hotel, such as restaurants, retail stores, health and business centers, and nightclubs.
H. Strategic alliances between hotel chains on a global basis may further complicate the planning process.

■■■ **DISCUSSION QUESTIONS**

1. Is strategic planning the same thing as marketing planning, sales planning, and restructuring?

2. In a series of job interviews, you ask three recruiters to describe the missions of their companies. One says, "To make profits." Another says, "To create customers." The third says,

"To fight world hunger." Analyze and discuss what these mission statements tell you about each of the companies.

3. What is the significance of an SBU?

4. What forms of vertical integration do you feel are likely to occur in the travel industry during the next 10 years?

5. Think about the shopping area near your campus. Assume that you wish to start a business here and are looking for a promising opportunity for a restaurant.
   a. Is there an opportunity to open a distinctive and promising business? Describe your target market and how you would serve it differently than current businesses do.
   b. What sort of marketing mix would you use for your business?

■■■ EXPERIENTIAL EXERCISES

Do one of the following:

1. Visit two hotels, restaurants, or other hospitality businesses. From your observations write down what you think are the strengths and weaknesses of the businesses. You will be able to observe elements such as location, physical facilities, employee attitude, quality of products, reputation of the brand (if it is a brand), and other factors.

2. Find a strategic alliance between a hotel company and another company (this can be for another hospitality organization or a company outside the hospitality industry). State what you think the benefits of the alliance are for each partner.

■■■ INTERNET EXERCISES

A. Find the mission statement of a hospitality or travel company on the Internet. Critique the mission statement against the guidelines for a mission statement, as stated in the text. If you have difficulty finding a mission statement, you can check the Web site under this exercise and you will find the URL to some mission statements.

B. Visit the annual report of a hospitality organization (these can usually be accessed through the company's home page). What does the annual report tell you about the organization's strategy?

■■■ REFERENCES

1. What is a Balanced Scorecard? Advanced Performance Institute, Buckinghamshire, MK12STS, United Kingdom.

2. Steve Coomes, *Nation's Restaurant News* (June 13, 2011): 32–33.

3. See Tamara J. Erickson and Everett Shorey, "Business Strategy: New Thinking for the 90s," *Prism* (4th Quarter 1992): 19–35.

4. Christopher W. Nordling and Sharon K. Wheeler, "Building a Market-Segment Accounting Model to Improve Profits," *Cornell Hotel and Restaurant Administration Quarterly,* 33, no. 3 (1992): 29–36.

5. Al Glonzberg and Glenn Withiam, "Culture at the Crossroads: Boca Raton and RockResort," *Cornell Hotel and Restaurant Administration Quarterly,* 32, no. 1 (1991): 39.

6. Bruce J. Tracey and Timothy R. Hinkin, "Transformational Leaders in the Hospitality Industry," *Cornell Hotel and Restaurant Administration Quarterly,* 35, no. 2 (1994): 18.

7. Patrick Legoherel, Philippe Callot, Karine Gallopel, and Mike Peters, "Personality Characteristics, Attitude Toward Risk and Decisional Orientation of the Small Business Entrepreneur: A Study of Hospitality Managers," *Journal of Hospitality and Tourism Research,* 28, no. 1 (2004): 117–118.

8. See Peter Drucker, *Management Tasks, Responsibilities and Practices* (New York: Harper & Row, 1973), Chapter 7.

9. For more on mission statements, see Frank Buytendijk, "Five Keys to Building a High-Performance Organization," *Business Performance Management* (February 2006): 24–29; Joseph Peyrefitte and Forest R. David, "A Content Analysis of Mission Statements of United States Firms in Four Industries," *International Journal of Management* (June 2006): 296–301; and Jeffrey Abrahams, *101 Mission Statements from Top Companies* (Berkeley, CA: Ten Speed Press, 2007).

10. Nike and eBay mission statements from www.nike. com/nikebiz/nikebiz.jhnnl?page=4 and http:/lpages. ebay.comlaboutebayllthecompany/companyoverview. html, respectively (accessed November 2007).

11. Ritz Carlton Website accessed September 16, 2012, http://corporate.ritzcarlton.com/en/About/GoldStandards.htm.

12. "Mission Statements for the Next Millennium," *Restaurant Hospitality* (December 1998): 46.

13. www.scotland-edinburgh.co.uh/hotel-home.asp, Prestonfield-Edinburgh's most indulgent retreat, 2008.

14. For more discussion, see Laura Nash, "Mission Statements: Mirrors and Windows," *Harvard Business Review* (March/April 1988): 155–156. See also Tom Feltenstein, "Strategic Planning for the 1990s: Exploiting the Inevitable," *Cornell Hotel and Restaurant Administration Quarterly,* 33, no. 3 (1994): 45.

15. Retrieved August 7, 2011, from http://www.mission-statements.com/restaurant_mission_statements.html.

16. Retrieved August 7, 2011, from http://www.mandarinoriental.com/.

17. See the BASF Innovations Web page, www.corporate.basi.comJenJinnovationenl7idZj-HA6MObcp4PX (accessed November 2007).

18. Theodore Levitt, "Marketing Myopia," *Harvard Business Review* (July/August 1960): 45–46.

19. See "Holiday Inns: Refining Its Focus to Food, Lodging, and More Casinos," *Business Week* (July 21, 1980): 100–104.

20. Igor H. Ansoff, "Strategies for Diversification," *Harvard Business Review* (September/October 1957): 113–124.

21. Matthew Barakat, "Animal Group: No Beef with Pub," *Denver Post* (May 14, 2004): 3A.

22. John Ritter, "Full Speed Ahead for New Ferries," *USA Today* (April 12, 2004): 3A.

23. Dennis Reynolds, "Managed Services Companies," *Cornell Hotel and Restaurant Administration Quarterly,* 38, no. 3 (1997): 90.

24. John Gapper, "Lessons from Nestle's Coffee Break," *Financial Times* (January 3, 2008): 7.

25. Gregory Norkus and Elliott Merberg, "Food Distribution in the 1990's," *Cornell Hotel and Restaurant Administration Quarterly,* 35, no. 3 (1994): 60–61.

26. Jack Trout, "Branding Can't Exist Without Positioning," *Advertising Age* (March 14, 2005): 28.

27. The four Ps classification was first suggested by B. Jerome McCarthy, *Basic Marketing: A Managerial Approach* (Homewood, IL: Irwin, 1960). For the 4Cs, other proposed classifications, and more discussion, see Robert Lauterborn, "New Marketing Litany: 4Ps Passé C-Words Take Over," *Advertising Age* (October 1, 1990): 26; Don F. Schulti, "New Definition of Marketing Reinforces Idea of Integration," *Marketing News* (January 15, 2005): 8; and Phillip Kotler, "Alphabet Soup," *Marketing Management* (March–April 2006): 51.

28. Rita M. Emmer, Chuck Tauck, Scott Wilkinson, and Richard G. Moore, "Marketing Hotels Using Global Distribution Systems," *Cornell Hotel and Restaurant Administration Quarterly,* 34, no. 6 (1993): 80–89.

29. Michael P. Sim and Chase M. Burritt, "Enhancing Resort Profitability with Membership Programs," *Cornell Hotel and Restaurant Administration Quarterly,* 34, no. 4 (1993): 59–63.

30. Ali Poorani and David R. Smith, "Franchising as a Business Expansion Strategy in the Bed & Breakfast Industry: Creating a Marketing and Development Advantage," *Hospitality Research Journal,* 18, no. 2 (1994): 32–33.

31. Robert Guy Matthews, "Rigs Keep on Trucking Searching for Parking," *Wall Street Journal* (May 1, 2007): B1, B8.

32. H. G. Parsa and Mahmood A. Khan, "Quick Service Restaurants of the 21st Century: An Analytical Review of Macro Factors," *Hospitality Research Journal,* 17, no. 1 (1993): 164.

33. Dennis Reynolds and William M. Balinbin, "Mad Cow Disease: An Empirical Investigation of Restaurant Strategies and Consumer Response," *Journal of Hospitality and Tourism Research,* 27, no. 3 (2003): 361.

34. Jonathan Berger, "Applying Performance Tests in Hotel Management Agreements," *Cornell Hotel and Restaurant Administration Quarterly,* 38, no. 2 (1997): 25.

35. Ibid.

36. See Michael E. Porter, *Competitive Strategy: Techniques for Analyzing Industries and Competitors* (New York: Free Press, 1980), Chapter 2.

37. Beth E. A.Wuest, Richard F. Tax, and Daniel A. Emenheiser, "What Do Mature Travelers Perceive as Important Hotel/Motel Customer Service?" *Hospitality Research Journal,* 20, no. 2 (1996): 90.

38. Kee Lee Weng and B. C. Ghosh, "Strategies for Hotels in Singapore," *Cornell Hotel and Restaurant Administration Quarterly,* 31, no. 1 (1990): 78–79.

39. Adapted from information found in Diane Brady, "Making Marketing Measure Up," *BusinessWeek* (December 13, 2004): 112–113; Gray Hammond, "You Gotta Be Accountable," *Strategy* (December 2008): 48; and Kate Maddox, "Optimism, Accountability, Social Media Top Trends," *BtoB* (January 18, 2010): 1.

40. See Kenneth Hein, "CMOs Pressured to Show ROI," *Brandweek* (December 12, 2008): 6; Lance Richard, "The Paradox of ROI and Decreased Spending in the Ad Industry," *American Journal of Business* (Fall 2009), www.bsu.edu/mcobwin/majb/?p=599; and Kevin J. Clancy and Peter C. Krieg, "Getting a Grip," *Marketing Management* (Spring 2010): 18–23.

41. See Hein, "CMOs Pressured to Show ROI": 6; Hammond, "You Gotta Be Accountable": 48; and Lawrence A. Crosby, "Getting Serious about Marketing ROI," *Marketing Management* (May/June 2009): 10–11.

42. Anna Mattila, "Investment Returns and Opportunities for Hotels in Asia," *Cornell Hotel and Restaurant Administration Quarterly,* 38, no. 1 (1997): 78.

Developing Hospitality and Tourism Marketing Opportunities and Strategies

Courtesy of Demetrio Carrasco/
Dorling Kindersley.

The Marketing Environment

Objectives

1. List and discuss the importance of the elements of the company's microenvironment, including the company, suppliers, marketing intermediaries, customers, and public.

2. Describe the macroenvironmental forces that affect the company's ability to serve its customers.

3. Explain how changes in the demographic and economic environments affect marketing, and describe the levels of competition.

4. Identify the major trends in the firm's natural and technological environments.

5. Explain the key changes that occur in the political and cultural environments.

6. Discuss how companies can be proactive rather than reactive when responding to environmental trends.

In 1955, Ray Kroc, a 52-year-old salesman of milkshake-mixing machines, discovered a string of seven restaurants owned by Richard and Maurice McDonald. Kroc saw the McDonald brothers' fast-food concept as a perfect fit for America's increasingly on-the-go, time-squeezed, family-oriented lifestyles. Kroc bought the small chain for $2.7 million and the rest is history.

McDonald's grew quickly to become the world's largest fast-feeder. Its more than 31,000 restaurants worldwide now serve 52 million customers each day, racking up system-wide sales of almost $60 billion annually. The Golden Arches are one of the world's most familiar symbols, and other than Santa Claus, no character in the world is more recognizable than Ronald McDonald. "By making fast food respectable for middle-class families," says one industry analyst, "the Golden Arches did for greasy spoons what Holiday Inn did for roadside motels in the 1950s and what Sam Walton later did for the discount retail store."[1] Says another, "McDonald's is much more than an ordinary fast-food chain. It is a cultural mirror [that] reflects the evolution of American eating habits."[2]

But just as the changing marketplace has provided opportunities for McDonald's, it has also presented challenges. In fact, the once-shiny Golden Arches had lost some of their luster as the company struggled to address shifting consumer lifestyles. Although McDonald's remained the nation's most visited fast-food chain, its sales growth slumped, and its market share fell by more than 3 percent between 1997 and 2003. In 2002 the company posted its first-ever quarterly loss.

What happened? In this age of obesity lawsuits and $5 lattes, McDonald's seemed a bit out of step with the times. Consumers were looking for fresher, better tasting food and more upscale atmospheres. As a result, McDonald's was losing share to what the industry calls "fast-casual" restaurants. New competitors such as Panera Bread, Baja Fresh, Pret A Manger, and Cosi were offering more imaginative meals in more fashionable surroundings. And for busy consumers who'd rather "eat-out-in," even the local supermarket offered a full selection of prepared, ready-to-serve gourmet meals to go.

Americans were also seeking healthier eating options. Fast-food patrons complained about too few healthy menu choices. Worried about their health, many customers were eating less at fast-food restaurants. As the market leader, McDonald's bore the brunt of much of this criticism. In one lawsuit, the parents of two teenage girls even charged that McDonald's was responsible for their children's obesity and related health problems, including diabetes.

Reacting to these challenges, in early 2003 McDonald's announced a turnaround plan—the "Plan to Win"—to better *align* the company with the new marketplace realities. Under the Plan to Win, McDonald's got back to the basic business of taking care of customers. The goal was to get "better, not just bigger." The company halted rapid expansion and instead poured money back into improving the food, the service, the atmosphere, and marketing at existing outlets. McDonald's redecorated its restaurants with clean, simple, more-modern interiors such as live plants, wireless Internet access, and flat-screen TVs showing cable news. Play areas in some new restaurants now feature video games and even stationary bicycles with video screens. To make the customer experience more convenient, McDonald's stores now open earlier to extend breakfast hours and stay open longer to serve late-night diners—more than one-third of McDonald's restaurants are now open 24 hours a day.

A reworked menu, crafted by Chef Daniel Coudreaut, a Culinary Institute of America graduate and former chef at the Four Seasons in Dallas, now provides more choice and variety, including healthier options, such as Chicken McNuggets made with white meat, a line of Snack Wraps, low-fat "milk jugs," apple slices, Premium Salads, and the Angus burger. Within only a year of introducing its Premium Salads, McDonald's became the world's largest salad seller. The company also launched a major multifaceted education campaign—themed "it's what i **eat** and what i **do** ... I'm lovin' it"—that underscores the important interplay between eating right and staying active.

McDonald's rediscovered dedication to customer value sparked a remarkable turnaround. Since announcing its Plan to Win, McDonald's sales have increased by more than 50 percent, and profits have more than quadrupled. In 2008, when the stock market lost one-third of its value—the worst loss since the Great Depression—McDonald's stock gained nearly 6 percent, making it one of only two companies in the Dow Jones Industrial Average whose share price rose during that year (the other was Walmart). Through 2010, as the economy and the restaurant industry as a whole continued to struggle, McDonald's outperformed its competitors by a notable margin. Despite the tough times, McDonald's achieved a lofty 15.5 percent three-year compound annual total return to investors versus the S&P 500 average of –5.6 percent.

Thus, McDonald's now appears to have the right mission for the times. Now, once again, when you think McDonald's, you think value—whether it's a college student buying a sandwich for a buck or a working mother at the drive-through grabbing a breakfast latte that's a dollar cheaper than Starbucks. And that has customers and the company alike humming the chain's catchy jingle, "I'm lovin' it."

McDonald's knows that as the marketing environment changes, the company must change with it. "We've learned. We've evolved. We think we've cracked the code," says McDonald's CEO James Skinner. "We're always evolving to meet the changing needs of our customers."[3]

A company's marketing environment consists of the actors and forces outside marketing that affect a company's ability to build and maintain successful relationships with its target customers. The marketing environment offers both opportunities and threats. Successful companies know the vital importance of constantly watching and adapting to the changing environment.

Managers who practice marketing will be the trend trackers and opportunity seekers. Good marketers have two special aptitudes. They have disciplined methods—marketing intelligence and marketing research—for collecting information about the marketing environment. They also spend more time in the customer and competitor environments. By carefully studying the environment, marketers can adapt marketing strategies to meet new marketplace challenges and opportunities.

The marketing environment is made up of a microenvironment and a macroenvironment. The **microenvironment** consists of factors close to the company that affect its ability to serve its customers, the company itself, marketing channel firms, customer markets, and a broad range of publics. The **macroenvironment** consists of the larger societal forces that affect the entire microenvironment, that is, demographic, economic, natural, technological, political, competitor, and cultural forces. We first examine the company's microenvironment and then its macroenvironment.

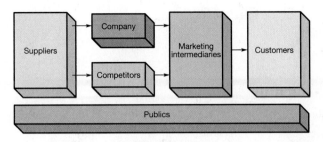

Figure 4–1
Major actors in
the company's
microenvironment.

∎∎∎ The Company's Microenvironment

Marketing management's job is to build relationships with customers by creating customer value and satisfaction. The success of marketing plans requires working closely with the company's microenvironment. These actors are shown in Figure 4–1. They include the company, suppliers, market intermediaries, customers, and publics that combine to make up the company's value delivery system.

The Company

Marketing managers do not operate in a vacuum. They must work closely with top management and the various company departments. The finance department is concerned with finding and using the funds required to carry out the marketing plan. The accounting department has to measure revenues and costs to help marketing know how well it is achieving its objectives. Housekeeping is responsible for delivering clean rooms sold by the sales department. Top management sets the company's mission, objectives, broad strategies, and policies. Marketing decisions must be made within the strategies and plans made by top management. For example, if top management positions our brand as a hotel for the business traveler, a general manager positioning his or her hotel as one for families will be following a policy that will weaken the brand.

Under the marketing concept, all managers, supervisors, and employees must "think consumer." They should work in harmony to provide superior customer value and satisfaction. Together, all departments have an impact on the marketing department's plans and actions.

Existing Competitors

We include competitors in both the microenvironment and macroenvironment. Existing customers are part of the microenvironment because we can identify and observe them closely. Every company faces a broad range of existing competitors. The marketing concept holds that a successful company must satisfy the needs and wants of consumers better than its competitors. Marketers must do more than adapt to the needs of target customers. They must also adapt to the strategies of other companies serving the same target markets. Companies must gain strategic advantage by strongly positioning their product in the minds of consumers.

No single competitive marketing strategy is best for all companies. Each firm must consider its size and industry position in relation to that of its competitors. Large firms with dominant positions in an industry can use certain strategies that smaller firms cannot afford. Small firms can also choose strategies that give them certain advantages. For example, a large restaurant chain can use its buying power to purchase national advertising, spreading the cost among hundreds or thousands of operations. But small individually owned restaurants are able to adjust quickly to local trends and can offer more menu variety because they do not have to worry about standardizing menu items across thousands of restaurants. Both large and small firms must find marketing strategies that give them specific advantages over competitors operating in their markets. In general a company should monitor three variables when analyzing each of its competitors:

1. **Share of market:** The competitor's share of the target market.

2. **Share of mind:** The percentage of customers who named the competitor in responding to the statement, "Name the first company that comes to mind in this industry."

Figure 4–2
Levels of competition.
Adapted from *Analysis for
Market Planning,* Donald
R. Lehmann and Russell
S. Winer, p. 22, © 1994,
by Richard D. Irwin.

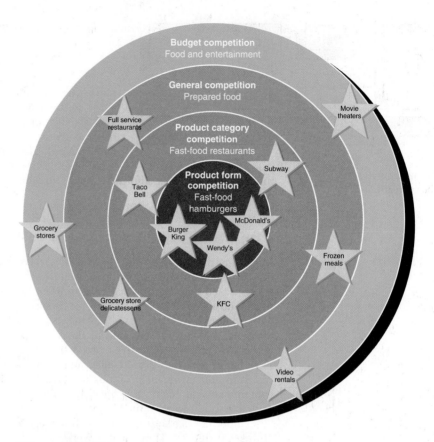

3. **Share of heart:** The percentage of customers who named the competitor in responding to the statement, "Name the company from whom you would prefer to buy the product."

Managers often fail to identify their competitors correctly. The manager of a Houston seafood restaurant said that his restaurant had no competition because there were no other seafood restaurants within several miles. Several months later the restaurant was out of business. Customers decided to spend their money at competitors, either by driving farther to other seafood restaurants or by dining at nearby non-seafood restaurants. Our research has shown that only about 40 percent of the customers that rate a hotel or restaurant as being good return, and the figure jumps to 90 percent when customers give a rating of excellent. Competitive forces are so strong in our industry that being good is no longer good enough. We must strive for excellence.

Professor Seyhmus Baloglu found that although 78 percent of the customers came to a casino regularly and were considered loyal customers, only 34 percent were considered truly loyal customers. The other 44 percent he called spurious loyals. In addition to having the behavioral loyalty of coming to the casino regularly, the true loyals exhibited attitudinal loyalty, and as a result they were more likely to recommend the casino to a friend. Although they exhibited the loyalty behavior of frequent visits, spurious loyals are not emotionally attached to the casino and are likely to leave if a new casino opens across town. It is important for managers to understand how many of their customers might be at risk if a new competitor opens in their market area.[4]

Every company faces four levels of competitors (see Figure 4–2):

1. A company can view its competitors as other companies that offer similar products and services to the same customers at a similar price. At this level, McDonald's views its competition as Burger King, Wendy's, and Hardee's.

2. A company can see its competitors as all companies making the same product or class of products. Here McDonald's may see its competition as all fast-food restaurants, including KFC, Taco Bell, Jamba Juice, and Arby's.

3. A company can see its competitors more broadly as all companies supplying the same service. Here McDonald's would see itself competing with all restaurants and other suppliers of prepared food, such as the deli section of a supermarket.

4. A company can see its competitors even more broadly as all companies that compete for the same consumer dollars. Here McDonald's would see itself competing with the self-provision of the meal by the consumer.[5]

Putting this framework into action, Subway sandwich shops came out with advertising targeting second-level competition. The ads stressed the nutritional value of their sandwiches compared with other types of fast food, such as hamburgers. The McDonald's "You deserve a break today" advertising campaign was aimed at the fourth level of competition, telling people to give themselves a break from cooking. Carnival Cruise Lines viewed its competition at the third level, that is, as other vacation destinations, such as Hawaii and Las Vegas.

Suppliers

Suppliers are firms and individuals that provide the resources needed by the company to produce its goods and services. Trends and developments affecting suppliers can, in turn, seriously affect a company's marketing plan. Suppose that a restaurant manager decides to run a live lobster special for the weekend. The seafood supplier is called, who promises to supply 200 lobsters for the weekend promotion. Friday morning the supplier calls and reports that lobsters were shorted on the shipment from Boston, and they will not be delivered until Saturday morning. The manager must now find an alternative source or disappoint guests who have reservations for Friday night.

In another case, a restaurant chain wanted to add a new scallop seafood dish to its menu. The corporate offices spent six months perfecting the scallop dish. During the development period, the price of scallops doubled. The restaurant would now have to charge a price higher than customers would pay. The project was scrapped. Management must pay attention to changes in supply availability (as affected by shortages and strikes) and supply costs.

Some hotels have contracted with restaurant companies to supply their food and beverage services. The W in Dallas brought in Craft, a famous restaurant in New York, to operate a restaurant in the W.[6] The New York, New York in Las Vegas has contracted with ARC restaurants to manage its restaurants. These and other hotels are bringing branded restaurants to their hotels to create value for their guests and expose restaurant guests to the hotel. The outsourcing of food and beverage operations allows the hotel to concentrate on lodging while letting a food and beverage specialist handle this area within the hotel. There are several ways to partner with a celebrity chef or branded restaurant. One is paying a licensing fee or management fee for a celebrity chef to oversee a restaurant and put his or her name on the restaurant. The fees generally run from 4 to 7 percent of the gross revenue. The second is a partnering deal where the chef is an equity partner, usually taking a 30 to 50 percent share of the equity. Additionally the chef gets a 3 to 6 percent management fee. This creates more of a commitment on the chef's part because the chef now shares directly in the profits of the restaurant.[7]

On paper this sounds like a great arrangement, and in real life it often works out well. However, the outsourcing is not as simple as it may seem. Focus groups of business travelers have told us that a coffee shop suitable for a business meeting is sometimes the deciding factor in the choice of a hotel. A problem for some hotels that have leased out their operations to upscale operators is that upscale restaurant operators often are not interested in the coffee shop and room service operations, and these operations often suffer as a result. Another problem is that the leasing of food-service operations ties up hotel space through lease agreements. This can be a problem if the hotel decides to renovate and change the design of the public spaces. When hotel guests complain about poor food service at the front desk, saying the hotel does not operate the restaurants is *not* an acceptable answer. Thus service recovery programs need to be worked out between the restaurant and the hotel. Like any supplier, suppliers of food and beverage for a hotel have to be chosen carefully. The concept works the best when the restaurant brought in for its brand name or brand name of its chef operates just the restaurant on an equity basis. The coffee shop, room service, and banquet operations are best left up to the hotel to run.

Tourist destinations need suppliers. Airline service, hotel, restaurants, ground operations, meeting facilities, and entertainment are some of the components of a tourist destination. One of the roles of a regional convention and visitors' bureau (CVB) is to make sure there is a good selection of suppliers of tourist products in their area. They must recruit organizations to provide visitors with a variety of tourist activities and options. CVBs must also work to represent the interests of these suppliers to make sure they do well after they are recruited.

Marketing Intermediaries

Marketing intermediaries help the company promote, sell, and distribute its goods to the final buyers. Intermediaries are business firms that help hospitality companies find customers or make sales. They include travel agents, wholesale tour operators, and hotel representatives, and online travel agencies (OTAs), such as Expedia, Travelocity, and Orbitz. The OTAs bundle airfare with hotel rooms, creating value for the customer.

The Internet has created both disintermediation and pricing transparency. **Disintermediation** is the elimination of intermediaries. Hotels have created their own Internet reservations systems, referred to as Brand.com (where the name of the company replaces "Brand," e.g., Hyatt.com). The brands are now less dependent on intermediaries, but still use them to provide extra demand. The demand cannot be filled through direct channels. Small hotels can now distribute their products worldwide over the Internet.

When hotels do sell to intermediaries who use the Internet, they have to be careful of price transparency. For example, group rates for associations often include free rooms for the association directors, which are factored into the hotel room rate. The association is also required to book a set number of rooms to take advantage of the complimentary services. If the group is given a rate of $229 per night for a hotel room and members of the organization can book directly on the hotel's Web site for $209, then members may choose to book directly rather than going through the associations block. Hotel sales managers should either set the prices of groups the same as group prices or give the group credit toward meeting their

Coca-Cola provides restaurants with more than just beverages. It also provides powerful marketing support. Courtesy of Xiaofeng12.../Dreamstime.

room block with people who have booked directly through the hotel. The Internet has created many distribution opportunities, but it has also made interactions with intermediaries and end users more complex.

Thus, today's marketers recognize the importance of working with their intermediaries as partners rather than simply as channels through which they sell their products. For example, restaurants serve as intermediaries for soft drink companies. When Coca-Cola signs on as the exclusive beverage provider for a fast-food chain, such as McDonald's, Wendy's, or Subway, it provides much more than just soft drinks. It also pledges powerful marketing support.[8]

Coca-Cola assigns cross-functional teams dedicated to understanding the finer points of each retail partner's business. It conducts a staggering amount of research on beverage consumers and shares these insights with its partners. It analyzes the demographics of U.S. zip code areas and helps partners determine which Coke brands are preferred in their areas. Coca-Cola has even studied the design of drive-through menu boards to better understand which layouts, fonts, letter sizes, colors, and visuals induce consumers to order more food and drink. Based on such insights, the Coca-Cola Food Service group develops marketing programs and merchandising tools that help its retail partners improve their beverage sales and profits. "We know that you're passionate about delighting guests and enhancing their real experiences on every level," says Coca-Cola to its retail partners. "As your partner, we want to help in any way we can." Such intense partnering efforts have made Coca-Cola a runaway leader in the U.S. fountain soft drink market.

Marketing services agencies are suppliers that help the firm formulate and implement its marketing strategy and tactics. These suppliers include public relations agencies, advertising agencies, and direct mail houses. They work directly with the company's marketing program and also include marketing research firms, media firms, and marketing consulting firms, which help companies target and promote their products to the right markets. These firms can vary in creativity, quality, service, and price. The company should regularly review its performance and replace those that no longer perform well.

Financial intermediaries include banks, credit companies, insurance companies, and other firms that help hospitality companies finance their transactions or insure the risks associated with the buying and selling of goods and services. Rising insurance costs, in particular liquor liability insurance, has forced some hospitality firms out of business. Because rising credit costs, limited credit, or both can seriously affect a company's marketing performance, the company has to develop strong relationships with important financial institutions. Small multiunit chains often feel the pressure to grow to keep their stock price up and their stockholders happy. This is what happened to Boston Market, Fuddrucker's, and Del Taco. These companies have all reorganized and recovered, but they went through some hard times. Companies must be careful that they do not succumb to the unmanageable growth expectations of their financial intermediaries.

4.1   www. CokeSolutions. com: Coca-Cola Food Service provides restaurateurs with a wealth of information, business solutions, and merchandising tips.

Customers

The hospitality company needs to study five types of general customer markets closely. Consumer markets consist of individuals and households that purchase hospitality services for leisure activities, medical needs, and gatherings such as reunions, weddings, or funerals. Business markets buy hospitality services to facilitate their business. This can be individual rooms for travelers representing the company or for group meetings the company or organization may conduct or produce. For example, companies have sales meetings, and associations have annual conventions. Resellers purchase a product and then resell it. For example, a tour operator may purchase airline seats, hotel rooms, ground transportation, and restaurant meals to package a tour, which will be resold to the consumer market. Government markets are made up of government agencies that, like businesses, purchase hospitality services for individual travelers and meetings. They often have room rates that are limited by government per diem rates. Finally, international markets consist of those buyers in other countries, including consumers, businesses, resellers, and governments. Each market type has special characteristics that call for careful study by the seller. We discuss these characteristics in Chapter 6 and 7.

Publics

The company's marketing environment also includes various publics. A **public** is any group that has an actual or potential interest in or impact on an organization's ability to achieve its objectives. We identify seven types of publics.

- Financial publics influence the company's ability to obtain funds. Banks, investment houses, and stockholders are the major financial publics.

- Media publics carry news, features, and editorial opinions. They include newspapers, magazines, and radio and television stations.

- Government publics. Management must take government developments into account. Marketers must often consult the company's lawyers on issues of product safety, truth in advertising, and other matters.

- Citizen-action publics. A company's marketing decisions may be questioned by consumer organizations, environmental groups, minority groups, and others. Its public relations department can help it stay in touch with consumer and citizen groups.

- Local publics include neighborhood residents and community organizations. Large companies usually appoint a community relations officer to deal with the community, attend meetings, answer questions, and contribute to worthwhile causes.

- General public. A company needs to be concerned about the general public's attitude toward its products and activities. The public's image of the company affects its buying.

- Internal publics include workers, managers, volunteers, and the board of directors. Large companies use newsletters and other means to inform and motivate their internal publics. When employees feel good about their company, this positive attitude spills over to external publics.

A company can prepare marketing plans for these major publics as well as for its customer markets. Suppose the company wants a specific response from a particular public, such as goodwill, favorable word of mouth, or donations of time or money. The company would need to design an offer to this public that is attractive enough to produce the desired response. For example, casino resorts in Las Vegas address how they are making efforts to conserve water when they announce plans for a new resort. They know the local residents and local government will be concerned about this issue.

■■■ The Company's Macroenvironment

The company and all of the other actors operate in a larger macroenvironment of forces that shape opportunities and pose threats to the company. Figure 4–3 shows the seven major forces in the company's macroenvironment. In the remaining sections of this chapter, we examine these forces and show how they affect marketing plans.

Competitors

We consider future competitors as part of the macroenvironment. The entrance of future competitors is often difficult to predict and can have a major effect on existing businesses.

Figure 4–3
Major forces in the company's macroenvironment.

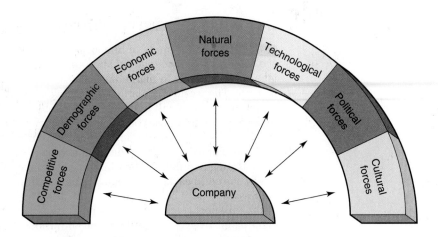

Barriers to Entry, Exit, and Competition

Two forces that affect the competition are the ability of companies to enter and exit markets.[9] Entry barriers prevent firms from getting into a business, and barriers to exit prevent them from leaving. Low barriers to entry characterize the restaurant industry. It takes a relatively small amount of capital to get started in the restaurant business. This makes it hard to predict future competition because a large pool of organizations and individuals are capable of opening restaurants. As a result, some restaurant managers open without direct competition and soon find themselves with four or five competitors in a year's time. This phenomenon points out the importance of anticipating competition and operating on the premise that one always has competition. Restaurant managers should always manage a business as if there is strong competition even if there is none. By taking this approach the manager will be prepared when competition does arrive.

Hotels have moderately high barriers of entry, due to the costs of building a hotel and the scarcity of good locations. High barriers to exit from the industry present a different set of competitive problems. The large capital investment required to build a hotel becomes a sunk cost. As a result, hotels that cannot meet all their debt payments, taxes, and other fixed costs, but can produce enough gross profit to partially offset these fixed costs, may operate at a loss rather than close their doors. Thus when hotel demand plummets, room supply remains the same. With fewer customers bidding for the same number of hotel rooms in a marketplace, competition becomes intensified.

The hotel's competitive environment is affected by another factor: Most hotels are planned during upswings in the business cycle when there is not enough supply to meet demand. But it can take four years or more from the planning stages to the opening of a hotel. By that time the economic cycle may have turned down. Sadly, new hotels often open their doors during a recessionary period.[10] So at a period when existing hotels are struggling to fill their rooms, it is not uncommon to have competitors enter the market.

It is easy to see after reading this section that the competitive environment in the hospitality industry is unpredictable. This is why we include it as part of the macroenvironment. A wealthy person will decide to open a restaurant in your market area that is completely unfeasible, but he or she does it for ego reasons. A hotel company wants to have a presence in your city. The hotel on its own is not feasible, but by giving the company a presence in your city it is able to justify the investment, even though it adds rooms to an already weak market. A wealthy international businessperson wants to invest in real estate and chooses the building of a hotel as a way to implement his or her investment. Although the project is not economically feasible in the short term, this investor is looking at long-term real estate gains. The projects just mentioned all bring capacity to markets that already have too much supply and not enough demand. If the projects were based on economic feasibility, they would not have been built. Investments in the hospitality industry are not always predictable. People must always operate as if they have strong competition.

Demographic Environment

Demography is the study of human populations in terms of size, density, location, age, gender, race, occupation, and other statistics. The demographic environment is of major interest to marketers because it involves people, and people make up markets. The world population is growing at an explosive rate. It now exceeds 6.6 billion people and will grow to 8.1 billion by 2030.[11] The world's large and highly diverse population poses both opportunities and challenges.

Changes in the world demographic environment have major implications for business. For example, consider China. More than a quarter century ago, to curb its skyrocketing population, the Chinese government passed regulations limiting families to one child each. As a result, Chinese children—known as "little emperors and empresses"—have been showered with attention and luxuries under what's known as the "six-pocket syndrome." As many as six adults—two parents and four doting grandparents—may be indulging the whims of each only child. The little emperors, now ranging in age from newborns to mid-twenties, are affecting markets for everything including restaurants and travel. Parents with only children at home now spend about 40 percent of their income on their cherished child.[12]

Starbucks is targeting China's older little emperors, positioning itself as a new kind of informal but indulgent meeting place.[13] Instead of believing in traditional Chinese collective goals, these young people embrace individuality. "Their view of this world is very different," says the president of Starbucks Greater China. "They have never gone through the hardships of our generation."[14] Starbucks is in sync with that, he says, given its customized drinks, personalized service, and original music compilations. In the United States about 80% of Starbucks business is takeout. In China Starbucks is a destination with about 90% of the consumption on premise. Mornings are a slow period with young people flocking to Starbucks in the afternoon to hangout with friends.[15] Source Janet Adamy, "Different Brew: Eyeing a Billion Tea Drinkers, Starbucks Pours It On in China," Wall Street Journal (November 29, 2006).

Starbucks knows that China will become its largest market and is preparing for that day. In 2011 they set up a coffee farm and processing facilities in China's southern Yunnan provence.[16] Laurie Burkitt, "Starbucks Menu Expands in China," Wall Street Journal, March 09, 2011: B.7

Marketers keep close track of demographic trends and developments in their markets, both at home and abroad. They track changing age and family structures, geographic population shifts, educational characteristics, and population diversity. Here, we discuss the most important demographic trends in the United States.

Changing Age Structure of the Population

The U.S. population is currently about 315 million and may reach almost 364 million by 2030.[17] The single most important demographic trend in the United States is the changing age structure of the population. The U.S. population contains several

In China Starbucks targets the "Me generation," positioning itself as a new kind of informal but indulgent meeting place. Courtesy of Xiaofeng12.../Dreamstime.

generational groups. Here, we discuss the three largest groups: the baby boomers, Generation X, and the Millennials—and their impact on today's marketing strategies.

The Baby Boomers

The post–World War II baby boom produced 78 million **baby boomers**, born between 1946 and 1964. Over the years, the baby boomers have been one of the most powerful forces shaping the marketing environment. Today's baby boomers account for nearly 25 percent of the population, spend about $2 trillion annually, and hold three-quarters of the nation's financial assets.[18] However, many baby boomers saw their retirement evaporate in the recession of 2008. As a result of the need for income and the desire to keep active, 70 percent of Americans between the ages of 45 and 74 plan on working in their retirement years.[19] This creates a new workforce for quick-service restaurants and hotels.

The youngest boomers are now in their mid-forties; the oldest are in their sixties. The maturing boomers are rethinking the purpose and value of their work, responsibilities, and relationships. As they reach their peak earning and spending years, the boomers constitute a lucrative market for travel and entertainment, eating out, spas, and other leisure activities. It would be a mistake to think of the boomers as aging and staid. Many boomers are rediscovering the excitement of life and have the means to play it out. For example, according to the Travel Industry Association of America, half of all U.S. adults took adventure vacations within the past five years. Some 56 percent of these travelers were boomers. Baby boomers do not feel old; one study found they feel 12 years younger than they actually are.[20] They will spend billions of dollars on travel, looking for active vacations where they can have adventure or explore, such as a polar bear sighting expedition in northern Canada or historical tours of Europe. Through their continuing education departments, universities have developed educational tours that target the baby boomers. Butterfield and Robinson, agents for upscale biking tours, market two-week bike tours with overnight stays in luxury accommodations to the boomers. Boomers look for value and research their vacations. One of the reasons cruises are popular with boomers is because of the value of the all-inclusive vacation.

Generation X

The baby boom was followed by a "birth dearth," creating another generation of 49 million people born between 1965 and 1976. Author Douglas Coupland calls them **Generation X** because they lie in the shadow of the boomers and lack obvious distinguishing characteristics. Others call them the "baby busters" or the "generation caught in the middle" (between the larger baby boomers and later Millennials).

The Generation Xers are defined as much by their shared experiences as by their age. Having grown up during times of recession and corporate downsizing, they developed a more cautious economic outlook. They care about the environment and respond favorably to socially responsible companies. Hotel and restaurant companies that are taking initiatives to be environmentally responsible are attractive to this group. Although they seek success, they are less materialistic; they prize experience, not acquisition. For many of the 30 million Gen Xers who are parents, family comes first, career second.[21]

The Gen Xers are a more skeptical bunch. "Marketing to Gen Xers is difficult," says one marketer, "and it's all about word of mouth. You can't tell them you're good, and they have zero interest in a slick brochure that says so. … They have a lot of 'filters' in place."[22] Another marketer agrees: "Sixty-three percent of this group will research products before they consider a purchase. [They are also] creating extensive communities to exchange information. Even though nary a handshake occurs, the information swap is trusted and thus is more powerful than any marketing pitch ever could be."[23]

The Gen Xers have brought us the quality movement. Food-service operations such as Starbucks, Chipotle's, and Panera Bread are favorites of Gen Xers. They like to be intrigued by menus more than Millennials or boomers. They enjoy menus that combine the familiar with the unique. When it comes to vacations, Gen Xers look for something different, which means they spend more than boomers. The Gen Xers have set a higher bar for casual dining, business travel, and midpriced hotels.[24]

Hyatt is positioning Andaz as an unpretentious upscale hotel catering to customers looking for fresh, uncomplicated luxury that is timeless and gimmick free. Andaz is squarely aimed at the maturing Generation X market. Gen Xers are now evolving from their grungy twentieth-century adolescence and rapidly becoming the major market segment for business travel. Like all great demographic segments, they demand alternative brands to those patronized by their parents, the baby boomers. Xers are notoriously uncomfortable with generic global brands and prefer to seek out local specialties and experiences instead. Whereas their parents might prefer hotels with identical bathrooms from Amsterdam to Zurich, Xers like to celebrate local differences. Andaz caters to this by allowing each of its hotels to celebrate its local autonomy through different designs and offerings. In fact, the word *Andaz* means personal style. Andaz will also cater to the Xer market by offering organic food and environmentally sound operating principles. Hyatt pitches the new hotel as a "luxury lifestyle brand" that "expresses individual style and personal independence in an environment of casual elegance. It offers local personality, innovative design, and a relaxed atmosphere, plus unpretentious, responsive, personalized service."[25]

The Virginia Tourism Corporation (VTC), the state's tourism destination marketing organization (DMO), is now targeting Gen X families:

Virginia's 40-year romance with the baby-boomer generation is waning. The VTC, best known for its enduring "Virginia is for Lovers" campaign, is now wooing a new audience: Generation X. They're younger and more adventuresome, and they spend more money on travel in Virginia. VTC research showed that Generation X households contribute about 45 percent of the $19.2 billion spent on travel in Virginia each year. Whereas most boomers are done or almost done with raising their children and lean toward more exotic travel locations farther from home, "the Generation Xers are new families who need new experiences close to home," says Alisa Bailey, CEO and president of VTC. "They want beaches, good places to relax, sun, and friendly people. They love amusement and theme parks, and they want places that are good for what we call soft adventure, like canoeing, and hiking." Don't worry; the slogan won't change. "What *will* change," explains Bailey, "is our strategy toward the younger market. We will be showing more Gen X families in our marketing. It will be a more family-oriented campaign." VTC plans to use Facebook, Twitter, and blogs to help reach Generation X households.[26]

Millennials

Both the baby boomers and Gen Xers will one day be passing the reins to the **Millennials** (also called **Generation Y** or the **echo boomers**). Born between 1977 and 2000, these children of the baby boomers number 83 million, dwarfing the Gen

Gen Xers and their familes are an important target market for Hospitality organizations. Courtesy of Rnonstx/ Dreamstime.

Xers and larger even than the baby-boomer segment. This group includes several age cohorts: *teens* (13 to 19) and *young adults* (20 to 35). With total purchasing power of more than $733 billion, Gen Y represents a huge and attractive market. One thing all of the Millennials have in common is their utter fluency and comfort with computer, digital, and Internet technology.[27]

Hotel concepts like Aloft and NYLO hope to attract the Millennials. NYLO developed a multiuse lobby, designed to encourage guests to socialize. It is fitted out with features like Wi-Fi, chairs that hang from the ceiling, and a Nintendo Wii. NYLO, like Aloft, also offers local entertainment such as bands, art shows, and movie nights, along with staff members who may be desk clerks by day but are dancers, writers, and artists by night.

Each Millennial segment constitutes a huge and attractive market. However, reaching these message-saturated segments effectively requires creative marketing approaches. An article in *Successful Meetings* states that Generation Y likes comfort food that is easy to eat while walking. This would include macaroni and cheese in ceramic dishes, dim sum in takeout containers, and burgers. Simple food that is creatively presented is the key for Generation Y. In future years, as they begin working and their buying power increases, this segment will more than rival the baby boomers in spending and market influence.[28]

Generational Marketing

One way marketers can segment is by forming precise age-specific segments within each group. More important, defining people by their birth date may be less effective than segmenting them by their lifestyle, life stage, or the common values they seek in the products they buy. We discuss many other ways to segment markets in Chapter 8.

Increasing Diversity

Countries vary in their ethnic and racial makeup. At one extreme is Japan, where almost everyone is Japanese. At the other extreme is the United States, with people from virtually all nations. The United States has often been called a melting pot: Diverse groups from many nations and cultures have melted into a single, more homogeneous whole. Instead, the United States seems to have become more of a "salad bowl" in which various groups have mixed together but have maintained their diversity by retaining and valuing important ethnic and cultural differences.

Marketers are facing increasingly diverse markets, both at home and abroad as their operations become more international in scope. The U.S. population is about 63 percent white, with Hispanics at 16 percent and African Americans at about 14 percent. The U.S. Asian American population now totals about 5 percent of the population. More than 12 percent of the population were born in another country. The nation's ethnic populations are expected to explode in coming decades. By 2050 Hispanics will comprise an estimated 24 percent of the U.S. population, with Asians at 9 percent.[29]

Diversity goes beyond ethnic heritage. For example, there are more than 60 million disabled people in the United States—a market larger than African Americans or Hispanics—representing almost $200 billion in annual spending power. This spending power is likely to increase even more in the years ahead as the wealthier, freer-spending baby boomers enter the "age of disabilities." Julie Perez sees the difference when she goes to the Divi Hotels resort at Flamingo Beach on the Caribbean island of Bonaire. "It is famous for being totally accessible," she says. "The hotel brochures show the wheelchair access. The dive staff are trained and aware, and they really want to take disabled people diving. They're not afraid." Perez, aged 35, of Ventura, California, is an experienced scuba diver, a travel agent, and a quadriplegic.[30] People with disabilities appreciate products that work for them. Explains Jim Tobias, president of Inclusive Technologies, a consultancy specializing in accessible products, "those with disabilities tend to be brand evangelists for products they love. Whereas consumers may typically tell 10 friends about a favorite product, people with disabilities might spread the word to 10 times that [many]."[31]

According to one estimate, 6 to 7 percent of the population who identify themselves as lesbian, gay, bisexual, and transgender (LGBT) have buying power of $712 billion.[32] The British Tourist Authority teamed up with British Airways and the London Tourist Board to target this market. The group worked with WinMark Concepts, a Washington marketing and advertising firm that specializes in advising mainstream companies on how to target the gay and lesbian market. "We wanted something that was gay-specific [and] fun, but also extremely tasteful," says WinMark's president. "These are educated, savvy consumers." One recent magazine ad shows five young- to early-middle-age men—the target age group is ages 35 to 50—posing in and around several of London's distinctive red phone booths. The headline reads: "One Call. A rainbow of choices."[33] The campaign has been successful. "The magazine ads got the word out that Britain is gay- and lesbian-friendly and also generated a database of 40,000 names across the country. Now, it's time for a more targeted direct-mail and e-mail campaign to people we know are interested in our offer."[34] Since BTA launched the campaign, both United Airlines and Virgin Airways have signed onto the program, as have the tourist boards of Manchester, Brighton, and Glasgow.[35]

As the population in the United States grows more diverse, successful marketers will continue to diversify their marketing programs to take advantage of opportunities in fast-growing segments.

The Changing American Family

The "traditional household" consists of a husband, wife, and children (and sometimes grandparents). Yet the once-American ideal of the two-child, two-car suburban family has lately been losing some of its luster.

In the United States today, married couples with children make up only 22 percent of the nation's 117 million households, married couples without children make up 29 percent, and single parents comprise another 11 percent. A full 38 percent are nonfamily households—single live-alones or adult live-togethers of one or both sexes.[36]

More people are divorcing or separating, choosing not to marry, marrying later, or marrying without intending to have children. Marketers must increasingly consider the special needs of nontraditional households because they are now growing more rapidly than traditional households. For example, people in their thirties who are marrying for the first time have gotten used to going out to eat frequently. When they do have children they continue to dine out, taking their children with them. Those in households without children do not have the expense of children and have more discretionary income for dining and travel.

The number of working women has also increased greatly, growing to 59 percent today. Both husband and wife work in 59 percent of all married-couple families.[37] As both heads of the household work, this has spawned the need for takeout food, prepared by someone else but eaten at the home dining table. Grocery stores are also preparing heat-and-serve entrees and side dishes. These grocery stores are now seeking graduates of culinary programs and hospitality programs as this business grows. Royal Caribbean targets time-crunched working mothers with budget-friendly family vacations that are easy to plan and certain to wow. Royal Caribbean estimates that, although vacations are a joint decision, 80 percent of all trips are planned and booked by women—moms who are pressed for time, whether they work or not. "We want to make sure that you're the hero, that when your family comes on our ship it's going to be a great experience for all of them," says a senior marketer at Royal Caribbean, "and that you, mom, who has done all the planning and scheduling, get to enjoy that vacation."[38]

Geographic Shifts in Population

This is a period of great migratory movements between and within countries. Americans, for example, are a mobile people, with about 15 percent of all U.S. residents moving each year. Over the past two decades, the U.S. population has shifted toward the Sunbelt states. The West and South have grown, whereas the Midwest and Northeast have lost population.[39] As companies look for new locations, they need to understand both national and local geographic trends relating to shifting populations.

A Better Educated, More White-Collar, More Professional Population

The U.S. population is becoming better educated. For example, in 2007, 87 percent of the U.S. population over age 25 had completed high school and 30 percent had completed college, compared with 69 and 17 percent in 1980. Moreover, nearly two thirds of high school graduates now enroll in college within 12 months of graduating.[40] The rising number of educated people will increase the demand for quality products, including luxury hotels, travel, wine, and dining at restaurants that have interesting menus.

Economic Environment

Markets require buying power as well as people. The **economic environment** consists of factors that affect consumer purchasing power and spending patterns. Nations vary greatly in their levels and distribution of income. Some countries have *subsistence economies:* They consume most of their own agricultural and industrial output. These countries offer few market opportunities. At the other extreme are *industrial economies,* which constitute rich markets for many different kinds of goods. Marketers must pay close attention to major trends and consumer spending patterns both across and within their world markets. Following are some of the major economic trends in the United States.

Changes in Income

Throughout the 1990s, American consumers fell into a consumption frenzy, fueled by income growth, a boom in the stock market, rapid increases in housing values, and other economic good fortune. They bought and bought, seemingly without caution, amassing record levels of debt. However, the free spending and high expectations of those days were dashed by the recession of the early 2000s. In fact, we are now facing the age of the "squeezed consumer." Along with rising incomes in some segments have come increased financial burdens. The collapse of the housing markets in 2008 eliminated the opportunity for many consumers to borrow home equity. This was combined with an increase in gasoline prices that created financial pressures for consumers. They now face repaying debts acquired during earlier spending splurges, increased household and family expenses, and saving ahead for children's college tuition payments and retirement. This reduction in discretionary income created hard times for the restaurant industry as customers cut back both on the number of times they dined out and on the amount they spent when they did dine out.

Over the past three decades, the rich have grown richer, the middle class has shrunk, and the poor have remained poor. The top 1 percent of American families now controls 33.4 percent of the nation's net worth, up 3.3 points from 1989. By contrast, the bottom 90 percent of families now control only 30.4 percent of the net worth, down 3.5 points.[41]

The Global Economy

Today the travel industry operates in a global environment. The growth of tourism in Croatia comes at the expense of other destinations. When the exchange rate between the Euro and the $US favors the Euro, fewer travelers from America go to Europe, and Americans diverted their vacations to locations in the United States and South America.

One of the positive outcomes of currency devaluations in Argentina is that it is gaining as a destination of conventions and meetings. In fact a room at a business-class hotel in Buenos Aires that once cost $280 today costs half that amount. But when international meeting planners move meetings to Santiago, São Paulo, Rio de Janeiro, Buenos Aires, and other cities of South America, that means the cities in Asia, Europe, and North America lose these conventions. Argentina, Chile, and Uruguay are all among tourist destinations, attracting over a million visitors. This is in part due to the economic consequences of currency exchange.

Favorable currency exchange has resulted in Argentina attracting more business meetings and tourists. Courtesy of Terry Vine/Corbis.

Marketers responsible for destinations must be aware of global travel trends and the development of new tourist destinations.

Natural Environment

The natural environment involves the natural resources that are needed as inputs by marketers or that are affected by marketing activities. Environmental concerns have grown steadily during the past three decades. In many cities around the world, air and water pollution have reached dangerous levels. World concern continues to mount about the possibilities of global warming, and many environmentalists fear that we soon will be buried in our own trash.

Marketers should be aware of several trends in the natural environment. The first involves growing *shortages of raw materials.* Air and water may seem to be infinite resources, but some groups see long-run dangers. Air pollution chokes many of the world's large cities, and water shortages are already a big problem in some parts of the United States and the world. By 2030 more than one in three of the world's human beings will not have enough water to drink.[42] Renewable resources, such as forests and food, also must be used wisely. Nonrenewable resources, such as oil, coal, and various minerals, pose a serious problem. These shortages have increased construction costs of new hotels, restaurants, and tourist attractions. A second environmental trend is *increased pollution.* Industry almost always damages the quality of the natural environment. Consider the disposal of garbage and sewage by resorts. In destinations where this is not managed, the groundwater has been polluted, damaging the water supply, and garbage can be seen on the beaches and back bays of the destination, dooming its sustainability. Hospitality companies must be good corporate citizens and embrace corporate responsibility.

The natural environment consists of many amenities that attract tourists, such as forests, clean beaches, pristine streams, wildlife, and clean air, may be lost. The Maldives, an island nation south of Sri Lanka, has seen its coral reefs bleached by warm water from El Niño. With 60 percent of their visitors doing some form of diving, the coral reefs are an important attraction. The global warming is causing the polar ice caps to melt. The Indian Ocean has risen by 25 cm in the last 20 years, and it could cover some of the Maldives by the end of the century.[43] Anyone involved in tourism has an obligation to protect the environment and develop sustainable tourism.

McDonald's is another company that has developed a recycling program. McDonald's eliminated polystyrene cartons years ago and now uses smaller recyclable paper wrappings and napkins. Beyond this, the company has a long-standing rainforest policy and a commitment to purchasing recycled products and energy-efficient restaurant construction techniques.[44] The concern for sustainability is increasing and has led to publications such as greenlodgingnews.com and organizations such as Green Restaurant Association.

A third trend is *increased government intervention* in natural resource management. The governments of different countries vary in their concern and efforts to promote a clean environment. Some, such as the German government, vigorously pursue environmental quality. Others, especially many poorer nations, do little about pollution, largely because they lack the needed funds or political will. Unfortunately, many of these countries often rely on tourism and suffer from the problems mentioned in the preceding paragraphs. The general hope is that companies around

Many tourist locations are dependent on the natural environment. Some scientists predict some of the Maldive Islands will be under water at the end of the century, a victim of global warming. Courtesy of Fraser Hall/Robert Harding World Imagery.

Dennis Tito was the first person to pay for a trip into space, thus becoming the world's first space tourist. He is seen here just before the launch of the Russian Soyuz spaceship. Advances in technology will make space travel a viable form of tourism in the future. Courtesy of AP Wide World Photos.

the world will accept more social responsibility, and less expensive devices can be found to control and reduce pollution.

Concern for the natural environment has spawned the so-called green movement. Today, enlightened companies go beyond what government regulations dictate. They are developing **environmentally sustainable** strategies and practices in an effort to create a world economy that the planet can support indefinitely. They are responding to consumer demands with more environmentally responsible products.

Technological Environment

The most dramatic force shaping our destiny is technology, which has given us wireless access to the Internet. This has made it possible for individuals to have interactions with others involving both audio and visual connections using programs such as Skype and FreeConference.com. Many organizations now accept a document that has been signed, scanned, and e-mailed instead of a hard copy of the original document. The end result is that speed at which business is occurring has increased dramatically. Sites like LinkedIn and Facebook allow us to keep track of both our business and personal networks. Technology has also released such horrors as nuclear missiles, chemical weapons, and products with mixed blessings, such as television and the automobile.

Technology has affected the hospitality industry in many ways. For example, Intelity has produced a product called ICE (Interactive Customer Experience) that can be accessed from a number of Web-enabled platforms, including smartphones and tablets. Guest services from the hotel such as room service, valet parking, dining room reservations, and spa services can be accessed from the tablet. External reservations at theaters, restaurants, golf courses, and airlines can also be accessed. Some of the advantages of ICE are that guests can multi-task (they can place a room service order while they are on a conference call); the information is available in multiple languages; it provides information that familiarizes the guest with the hotel and the local area. Hotels are providing this service to the guest through tablets such as iPads that are left in the rooms. To prevent theft the tables have tracking devices.[45]

The smartphone is a versatile tool for travelers. They can book and check on reservations, use it as a boarding pass for airlines, register at a hotel, and use it as a key access to the hotel room. These self-service technologies save the guest time and labor for the hospitality company. This also means that one's Web presence has to be formatted to work well on smartphones. Technology has also helped eliminate the theft of hotel products.[46]

Technology is also helping operations. Washable RFID (radio frequency identification) chips are being embedded in towels, bathrobes, banquet linen, and other washable linens. This allows management to determine the inventory of linen in storage closets on the hotel floors. Since it is becoming more common for full-service hotels to send their linen off premise to be cleaned, the RFID chips help the off-premise laundry keep track of where the linen came from and to locate any missing items.[47]

One of the most powerful changes is from social media. As we mentioned in Chapter 1, social media is changing how we market to customers, creating a powerful media for customers to interact with other customers and with organizations. We will discuss social media in Chapter 14.

Technological change faces opposition from those who see it as threatening nature, privacy, simplicity, and even the human race. Various groups have opposed the construction of restaurants in suburban and historical areas and high-rise hotels, airports, and recreational facilities in national parks. Marketers must understand and anticipate changes in the technological environment and use technologies that serve human needs. They must be sensitive to aspects of any innovation that might harm users and bring about opposition.

Political Environment

Marketing decisions are strongly affected by developments in the political environment. The **political environment** is made up of laws, government agencies, and pressure groups that influence and limit the activities of various organizations and individuals in society. We cite some current political trends and their implications for marketing management.

Increased Legislation and Regulation Affecting Business

As products become more complex, public concern about their safety increases. Governmental agencies have become involved in the investigation and regulation of everything from fire codes to food-handling practices. Employment and employee practices fall under government regulation, as do sales of alcohol, which vary from state to state and sometimes from precinct to precinct in the same county. Politicians also see travelers as good sources of revenue because nonresidents spend money but cannot vote against them. Hotel taxes and restaurant taxes have become popular sources of revenue for local governments. In many cases, hotel taxes are supposed to be used to support tourism; however, the spending of this money has been subject to liberal interpretation, such as for statues for suburban parks. Hotel managers must make sure that those taxes designated to promote tourism are used effectively. Managers must also work with hotel and restaurant associations to make sure that the taxes do not become oppressive. New York City hiked its hotel tax to over 21.25 percent for rooms costing over $100 in 1990. Many meeting and convention planners avoided New York because of the unfriendly tax; they simply took their business elsewhere. Convention business plunged by 37 percent during the next three years, and overall tax revenue declined despite the increase in the tax. The real loser was New York City's hospitality industry. New York has since reduced its hotel tax in line with other cities.[48]

Legislation and regulation affecting business have been enacted for three reasons. First, it protects companies from each other. Although most businesses praise competition, they try to neutralize it when it affects them. In the United States, it is the job of the Federal Trade Commission and the Antitrust Division of the Justice Department to define and prevent unfair competition. Cases often emerge in which one company lodges a complaint that another is guilty of an unfair practice, such as deceptive pricing or deceptive advertising, thereby injuring its business.

Second, government legislation and regulation also aim at protecting consumers from unfair business practices. If unregulated, firms might make unsafe or low-quality products, be untruthful in their advertising, or deceive through packaging and pricing. Various government units define unfair consumer practices and offer remedies. Businesses, of course, can minimize government intervention through active self-regulation. Such associations as the American Hotel and Motel Association and the National Restaurant Association (NRA) define and encourage good trade practices. These associations have developed guidelines for truth in menu presentation, alcoholic beverage service, and sanitation.

Third, government regulation also aims to protect society's interests against unrestrained business behavior. Profitable business activity does not always improve the quality of life. Thus regulations are passed to discourage smoking, littering, polluting, overcongestion of facilities, and the like, all in the name of protecting society's interests. Regulation aims to make firms responsible for the social as well as private costs of their production and distribution activities.

Marketing Highlight   Hostile Environment

4–1 Sometimes hospitality companies and products are boycotted or worse through no fault of their own because they are innocent victims of politics, misunderstandings, or actions of demagogues anxious to defray hostility from themselves.

McDonald's was the highly visible U.S. brand that has faced consumer boycotts in various nations. McDonald's was the target of a boycott in Egypt and other Arab countries due to U.S. support for Israel.

Here are some of the actions that targeted companies can take:

1. Emphasize the company's connections to the local community. In Indonesia, McDonald's launched television ads showing some of the staff of the local franchise owners wearing traditional Islam clothing. In Argentina where McDonald's entrances were blocked by protestors, the restaurant chain launched a campaign showing a Big Mac with the words "Made in Argentina" stamped on it.

2. Adopt a low profile. Avoid conflicts and even press interviews with reporters known to be against your product or company.

3. Counter lies and misinformation with professional public relations and advertising. Select a well-versed and believable spokesperson. Do not allow random staff members to be spokespeople.

4. Be patient. These kinds of things usually have a life of their own and fade away as protestors and the public lose interest.

Sources: Salah Al Shebil, Adbul A. Rasheed, and Hussam Al-Shammari, "Battling Bigots," *Wall Street Journal* (April, 28, 2007): R6, R11.

Government regulation and enforcement are likely to increase in the future. Business executives must know the major laws protecting competition, consumers, and society when planning their products and marketing programs.

Changing Government Agency Enforcement

To enforce laws, Congress has established several federal regulatory agencies: the Federal Trade Commission, the Food and Drug Administration, the Interstate Commerce Commission, the Federal Communications Commission, the Federal Power Commission, the Civil Aeronautics Board, the Consumer Products Safety Commission, the Environmental Protection Agency, and the Office of Consumer Affairs. These agencies can have a major impact on a company's marketing performance. Government agencies have some discretion in enforcing the laws, and from time to time, they appear to be overly eager. Lawyers and economists, who often lack a practical sense of marketing and other business principles, frequently dominate the agencies. In recent years, the Federal Trade Commission has added marketing experts to its staff to gain a better understanding of these complex issues.

The power of government is so great that the government can often dramatically affect a hospitality business without ever enforcing a law. An example is the case of a strike by American Airlines flight attendants in 1993. President Clinton intervened by calling Robert Crandal, CEO of American Airlines, and urging him to resolve the problem. The power and prestige of a head of state is so large that American Airlines settled in favor of the flight attendants. An airline is subject to many federal agencies, and the management at American Airlines obviously was intimidated.

Increased Emphasis on Socially Responsible Actions and Ethics

Written regulations cannot possibly cover all potential marketing abuses, and existing laws are often difficult to enforce. However, beyond written laws and regulations, business is also governed by social codes and rules of professional ethics.

SOCIALLY RESPONSIBLE BEHAVIOR   Enlightened companies encourage their managers to look beyond what the regulatory system allows and simply "do the right thing." These socially responsible firms actively seek out ways to protect the long-run interests of their consumers and the environment.

The recent rash of business scandals and increased concerns about the environment have created fresh interest in the issues of ethics and social responsibility. Almost every aspect of marketing involves such issues. Unfortunately, because these issues usually involve conflicting interests, well-meaning people can honestly disagree about the right course of action in a given situation. Thus, many industrial and professional trade associations have suggested codes of ethics. And more companies are now developing policies, guidelines, and other responses to complex social responsibility issues.

The boom in Internet marketing has created a new set of social and ethical issues. Critics worry most about online privacy issues. There has been an explosion in the amount of personal digital data available. Users, themselves, supply some of it. They voluntarily place highly private information on social-networking sites, such as Facebook or LinkedIn, or on genealogy sites that are easily searched by anyone with a computer or a smartphone.

However, much of the information is systematically developed by businesses seeking to learn more about their customers, often without consumers realizing that they are under the microscope. Legitimate businesses plant cookies on consumers' PCs and collect, analyze, and share digital data from every move consumers make at their Web sites. Critics are concerned that companies may now know *too* much and might use digital data to take unfair advantage of consumers. Although most companies fully disclose their Internet privacy policies and most work to use data to benefit their customers, abuses do occur. As a result, consumer advocates and policymakers are taking action to protect consumer privacy.

The number of public-interest groups has increased during the past two decades, as has their clout in the political arena. These groups take on issues of social responsibility. Cindi Lamb and her five-month-old daughter, Laura, were on their way home from a grocery store when a drunk driver slammed into their car. The accident left the baby paralyzed from the waist down. Cindi was outraged when she found out the drunk driver was a chronic offender. She set out to change the way judges, police officers, and politicians handled drunk driving. Joining together with her friends and other victims, she formed what is now known as MADD (Mothers Against Drunk Driving). MADD has had a major impact on the hospitality industry by demanding that restaurants be more responsible in their serving of alcohol and getting laws passed to require that those working with alcohol have training in the responsible serving of alcohol. MADD is helping push stronger legislation against drinking and driving.[49]

MADD is actively trying to stop drunk driving. It started as a public-interest group, but quickly influenced politicians to get tougher drunk-driving laws passed. Courtesy of Steve Skjoid/PhotoEdit.

People for the Ethical
Treatment of Animals (PETA)
is the world's largest animal
rights group. One of PETA's
tactics is to demonstrate in
favor of a non-meat diet.
In the photo two women
demonstrate in downtown
Seattle, attracting attention by
taking a "shower" in public.
Courtesy of Zyron/Dreamstime.

One expert who follows People for the Ethical Treatment of Animals (PETA) states that the organization would like to see all fast-food outlets that serve meat closed. PETA has campaigned against McDonald's, Burger King, Wendy's, and KFC. PETA does not focus just on chain restaurants. Nishiki Sushi in Sacramento used to serve "Dancing Shrimp," a popular menu item in Japan. The shrimp are served live, with customers instructed to squeeze lemon juice on the shrimp to make them "dance." PETA asked the restaurant to remove the shrimp from the menu, after receiving a number of complaints. The restaurant voluntarily removed the shrimp based on PETA's recommendation.[50] Certainly, the better treatment of animals would be good, but the complete elimination of animals from human diets is something that the majority of people would not embrace.[51]

CAUSE-RELATED MARKETING To exercise their social responsibility and build more positive images, many companies are now linking themselves to worthwhile causes. Cause-related marketing has become a primary form of corporate giving. It lets companies "do well by doing good" by linking purchases of the company's products or services with fund-raising for worthwhile causes or charitable organizations. Companies now sponsor dozens of cause-related marketing campaigns each year. Many are backed by large budgets and a full complement of marketing activities. For example, BJ's Restaurants, through its "Cookies for Kids" program, donates a portion of the sale of every signature "Pizookie" dessert to the Cystic Fibrosis Foundation. The Pizookie now raises up to $250,000 for the foundation every year.[52]

Cause-related marketing has stirred some controversy. Critics worry that cause-related marketing is more a strategy for selling than a strategy for giving—that "cause-related" marketing is really "cause-exploitative" marketing. Thus, companies using cause-related marketing might find themselves walking a fine line between increased sales and an improved image and facing charges of exploitation. However, if handled well, cause-related marketing can greatly benefit both the company and the cause. The company gains an effective marketing tool while building a more positive public image. The charitable organization or cause gains greater visibility and important new sources of funding and support. Spending on cause-related marketing in the United States skyrocketed from only $120 million in 1990 to more than $1.6 billion in 2010.[53]

Cultural Environment

The cultural environment includes institutions and other forces that affect society's basic values, perceptions, preferences, and behaviors. As a collective entity, a society shapes the basic beliefs and values of its members. They absorb a worldview that defines their relationship with themselves and others. The following cultural characteristics can affect marketing decision making.

Persistence of Cultural Values

People in any society hold certain persisting core beliefs and values. For example, most Americans believe in working, getting married, giving to charity, and being honest; these beliefs shape the more specific attitudes and behaviors found in everyday life. Core beliefs and values are passed on from parents to children and are reinforced by schools, churches, business, and government. Secondary beliefs and values, however, are more open to change. Believing in marriage is a core belief; believing that people should get married early is a secondary belief. Family planning marketers, for instance, could argue more effectively that people should get married later rather than not getting married at all. Marketers have some chance of changing secondary values but little chance of changing core values.

The hospitality industry is worldwide. Chances are very good that many of you will find yourselves serving in a foreign setting sometime during your career. Cultural norms and cultural prohibitions may affect your managerial roles in ways quite different from those in the United States and Canada. For example, hoteliers in Israel are expected to understand and observe the rules of *kashruth,* or keeping kosher. These are complicated and require constant supervision. Hotels in Israel must have two kitchen setups, one for meat and one for dairy products. Because kosher meat is expensive in Israel, hotel food costs are higher.[54]

A practice widely followed in China, Hong Kong, and Singapore (and that has also spread to Japan, Vietnam, and Korea), *feng shui* means wind and water. Practitioners of feng shui, or geomancers, recommend the most favorable conditions for any venture, particularly the placement of office buildings and the arrangement of desks, doors, and other items within. To have good feng shui, a building should face the water and be flanked by the mountains. It should also not block the view of the mountain spirits. The Hyatt Hotel in Singapore was designed without feng shui in mind, and, as a result, it had to be redesigned to boost business. Originally, the front desk was parallel to the doors and road, which was thought to lead to wealth flowing out. Furthermore, the doors were facing northwest, which easily let undesirable spirits in. The geomancer recommended designed alterations so that wealth could be retained and undesirable spirits kept out.[55]

Subcultures

Each society contains subcultures, groups of people with shared value systems based on common life experiences or situations. Episcopalians, teenagers, and working women all represent separate subcultures whose members share common beliefs, preferences, and behaviors. To the extent that subcultural groups have specific wants and buying behavior, marketers can choose subcultures as their target markets.

■■■ Linked Environmental Factors

When the first Millennials became teenagers, the total expenditures on food in restaurants and food-service operations exceeded food expenditures in grocery stores for the first time. In 1996 people in the United States purchased more meals outside the home than they ate home-prepared meals. One of the forces behind this change is that both heads of the household are working in many families. The average time spent on preparing meals is currently 15 minutes and dropping. No longer is the woman expected to prepare home-cooked meals for the man. Families are purchasing meals at restaurants or taking prepared food home. Many people still prefer to eat at home; they just do not have time to cook. The "home-meal replacement" restaurant has developed as a result of these trends. Robert Del Grande's Café Express restaurants in Texas and Arizona and Foodies Kitchen in Metairie, Louisiana, are examples of restaurant concepts creating quality meals with the convenience of self-service. Patrons can eat the meals on the premises or take them home. Foodies Kitchen was developed to take advantage of this trend.

Grocery stores are starting to provide competition for restaurants. According to David Audrian, vice president of the Texas Restaurant Association, the number-one trend in the food-service industry today is the growth of food service in supermarkets and convenience stores.[56] Most grocery stores have a food display near the deli counter of microwavable freshly prepared meals. These entrees include pot roast, teriyaki chicken, and pasta dishes that range in price from $2.50 to $7. The Hy-Vee grocery store at 14th and Park Avenue in Des Moines, Iowa, even has a drive-through window. People on their way home from work can order prepared meals from the store's deli to take home.[57]

These examples show how the elements of the environment are linked. Economic forces result in families with both heads of the household working. This is a demographic statistic that can be tracked over time. Women are also able to build careers and take management positions once reserved for men. The working heads of the household no longer have time to cook. Culturally, 30 to 40 years ago women were expected to stay home and cook. That is no longer the case. Thus we have seen a cultural change where men now participate in home duties and no one member of the household is expected to prepare all meals. Technology has also made it easier to reconstitute food and to warm prepared meals at home. Finally, the competitive environment between grocery stores and quick-service restaurants is expected to heat up. Grocery stores are building more elaborate delicatessens with a variety of prepared meals; they have fresh microwavable meals to go, and the drive-through window on the Hy-Vee store may become commonplace in the future. The change in food consumption patterns relates to economic, demographic, technological, cultural, and competitive trends.

■■■ Responding to the Marketing Environment

Many companies view the **marketing environment** as an "uncontrollable" element to which they must adapt. They passively accept the marketing environment and do not try to change it. They analyze environmental forces and design strategies that will help the company avoid the threats and take advantage of the opportunities that the environment provides.

Other companies take an **environmental management perspective**.[58] Rather than simply watching and reacting, these firms take aggressive action to affect the publics and forces in their marketing environment. Lobbyists are hired to influence legislation affecting their industries and to stage media events to gain favorable press coverage. They run advertorials (ads expressing editorial points of view) to shape public opinion. They press lawsuits and file complaints with regulators to keep competitors in line. They form contractual agreements to control their distribution channels better.

One of the elements of the macroenvironment that can be influenced is the political environment. Large companies hire lobbyists to present their interests at the local, state, and federal levels of government. These companies, along with smaller companies, join trade organizations, such as the American Hotel and Lodging Association (AH & LA), the American Society of Travel Agents (ASTA), the Hotel and Catering International Management Association (HCIMA), and the National Restaurant Association (NRA). The trade associations also hire lobbyists and form political action committees (PACs) to represent and communicate their industry's concerns to government officials. By communicating the possible effects of proposed legislation on the industry and the community, PACs can sometimes influence pending legislation.

Marketing management cannot always affect environmental forces; in many cases, it must settle for simply watching and reacting to the environment. For example, a company would have little success trying to influence geographic population shifts, the economic environment, or major cultural values. But whenever possible, smart marketing managers take a proactive rather than a reactive approach to the publics and forces in their marketing environment.

4.3 National Restaurant Association (NRA) PAC, http://www.restaurant.org/advocacy/action/nrapac/
The site of the National Restaurant Association's PAC will give you an idea of how a PAC works.

Environmental Scanning

Use of an environmental scanning plan has proved beneficial to many hospitality companies. The following steps are involved: (1) Determine the environmental areas that need to be monitored; (2) determine how the information will be collected, including information sources, the information frequency, and who will be responsible; (3) implement the data collection plan; and (4) analyze the data and use them in the market planning process. Part of the analysis is weighing the importance of the trends so the organization can keep the trends in proper perspective.

Using Information About the Marketing Environment

It is never sufficient simply to collect data about the environment. Information must be reliable, timely, and used in decision making. William S. Watson, senior vice president of Best Western Worldwide Marketing, offered advice on this subject:

> As marketers, we are willing to make some intuitive leaps because of the creative aspects of our characters. Nevertheless, we need enough information to make reasonable decisions, enough good data so that we can let our judgment move beyond the obvious, traditional interpretations we have learned as professionals. Researchers must put less emphasis on data and more on the interpretation of those data. They must work toward turning data into useful information. Collecting data for its own value is like collecting stamps. It is a nice hobby but it does not deliver the mail.[59]

■■■ KEY TERMS

Baby boomers. The 78 million people born between 1946 and 1964.

Demography. The study of human populations in terms of size, density, location, age, sex, race, occupation, and other statistics.

Disintermediation. The elimination of intermediaries.

Echo boomers. *See* Millennials. Born between 1977 and 1994, these children of the baby boomers now number 72 million, dwarfing the Gen Xers and almost equal in size to the baby-boomer segment. Also known as Generation Y.

Economic environment. The economic environment consists of factors that affect consumer purchasing power and spending patterns. Markets require both power and people. Purchasing power depends on current income, price, saving, and credit; marketers must be aware of major economic trends in income and changing consumer spending patterns.

Environmental management perspective. A management perspective in which a firm takes aggressive actions to affect the publics and forces in its marketing environment rather than simply watching and reacting to it.

Environmental sustainability. A management approach that involves developing strategies that both sustain the environment and produce profits for the company.

Financial intermediaries. Banks, credit companies, insurance companies, and other businesses that help finance transactions or insure against the risks associated with the buying and selling of goods.

Generation X. A generation of 45 million people born between 1965 and 1976; named Generation X because they lie in the shadow of the boomers and lack obvious distinguishing characteristics; other names include "baby busters," "shadow generation," or "yiffies"—young, individualistic, freedom-minded few.

Generation Y. *See* Millennials.

Macroenvironment. The larger societal forces that affect the whole microenvironment: competitive, demographic, economic, natural, technological, political, and cultural forces.

Marketing environment. The actors and forces outside marketing that affect marketing management's ability to develop and maintain successful transactions with its target customers.

Marketing intermediaries. Firms that help the company to promote, sell, and distribute its goods to final buyers; they include middlemen, physical distribution firms, marketing service agencies, and financial intermediaries.

Marketing services agencies. Marketing research firms, advertising agencies, media firms, marketing consulting firms, and other service providers that help a company to target and promote its products to the right markets.

Microenvironment. The forces close to a company that affect its ability to serve its customers: the company, market channel firms, customer markets, competitors, and the public.

Millennials (also called Generation Y or the echo boomers). Born between 1977 and 2000, these children of the baby boomers number 83 million, dwarfing the Gen Xers and larger even than the baby-boomer segment. This group includes several age cohorts: tweens (ages 8 to 12), teens (13 to 18), and young adults (the twentysomethings).

Political environment. Laws, government agencies, and pressure groups that influence and limit the activities of various organizations and individuals in society.

Public. Any group that has an actual or potential interest in or impact on an organization's ability to achieve its objectives.

Suppliers. Firms and individuals that provide the resources needed by a company and its competitors to produce goods and services.

■■■ CHAPTER REVIEW

I. **Microenvironment.** The microenvironment consists of actors and forces close to the company that can affect its ability to serve its customers. The actors in the microenvironment include the company, suppliers, market intermediaries, customers, and publics.
   A. **The company.** Marketing managers work closely with top management and the various company departments.
   B. **Existing competitors.** They are part of the microenvironment and must be monitored closely.
   C. **Suppliers.** Firms and individuals that provide the resources needed by the company to produce its goods and services.
   D. **Marketing intermediaries.** Firms that help the company promote, sell, and distribute its goods to the final buyers.
   E. **Disintermediation.** The elimination of intermediaries.
   F. **Marketing services agencies.** Marketing research firms, advertising agencies, media firms, and marketing consulting firms help companies to target and promote their products to the right market.
   G. **Financial intermediaries.** Includes banks, credit companies, insurance companies, and other firms that help hospitality companies to finance their transactions or insure risks associated with the buying and selling of goods and services.
   H. **Customers.** Managers must understand the different types of customers: consumers, business markets, government markets, resellers, and international markets.
   I. **Publics.** A public is any group that has an actual or potential interest in or impact on an organization's ability to achieve its objectives.

II. **Macroenvironment.** The macroenvironment consists of the larger societal forces that affect the whole microenvironment: demographic, economic, natural, technological, political, competitor, and cultural forces. Following are the seven major forces in a company's macroenvironment.

   A. **Competitive environment.** Each firm must consider its size and industry position in relation to its competitors. A company must satisfy the needs and wants of consumers better than its competitors do in order to survive.
   B. **Demographic environment.** Demography is the study of human populations in terms of size, density, location, age, sex, race, occupation, and other statistics. The demographic environment is of major interest to marketers because markets are made up of people.
   C. **Economic environment.** The economic environment consists of factors that affect consumer purchasing power and spending patterns. Markets require both power and people. Purchasing power depends on current income, price, saving, and credit; marketers must be aware of major economic trends in income and changing consumer spending patterns.
   D. **Natural environment.** The natural environment consists of natural resources required by marketers or affected by marketing activities.
   E. **Technological environment.** The most dramatic force shaping our destiny today is technology.
   F. **Political environment.** The political environment is made up of laws, government agencies, and pressure groups that influence and limit various organizations and individuals in society.
   G. **Cultural environment.** The cultural environment includes institutions and other forces that affect society's basic values, perceptions, preferences, and behaviors.

III. **Linked Environmental Factors**

IV. **Responding to the Marketing Environment.** Many companies view the marketing environment as an "uncontrollable" element to which they must adapt. Other companies take an environmental management perspective. Rather than simply watching and reacting, these firms take aggressive actions to affect the publics and forces in their marketing environment. These companies use environmental scanning to monitor the environment.

■■■ DISCUSSION QUESTIONS

1. How has the McDonald's concept changed since the 1960s? What environmental forces were behind these changes? How will the McDonald's concept change in the next decade, given the new forces operating in the environment?

2. What environmental trends will affect the success of a first-class hotel chain, such as Hyatt or Sofitel, over the next 10 years? If you were corporate director of marketing for this type of hotel, what plans would you make to deal with these trends?

3. The 78 million members of the baby-boomer generation are aging, with the oldest members in their early sixties. List some marketing opportunities and threats associated with this demographic trend for the hospitality and travel industry.

4. How have environmental trends affected the design of hotels?

5. Mobile marketing involves any type of marketing message—voice, text, image, or video—delivered to a handheld device such as a cell phone, iPhone, or BlackBerry. Although still in its infancy in the United States, mobile marketing has grown rapidly in other countries. Learn more about mobile marketing and discuss the current applications and the potential for future applications in the travel and hospitality industries.

6. If we have little control over the macroenvironment, why should we be concerned with it?

7. What environmental trends will affect the success of the Walt Disney Company in the next five years? If you were in charge of marketing at Disney, what plans would you make to deal with these trends?

■■■ EXPERIENTIAL EXERCISES

Do one of the following:

1. View the annual reports of several hospitality companies. How did you find out about how they might be changing their business to fit the environment from their annual report? If you do not have access to an annual report, visit the book's Web site for electronic access to annual reports.

2. Choose and visit a restaurant, club, or hotel you feel is designed for one of the generations discussed in the book (e.g., baby boomers, Generation X, echo boomers). After doing some research on the generation, state what the business you chose has done to cater to its target generation.

■■■ INTERNET EXERCISES

Support for these exercises can be found on the Web site for Marketing for Hospitality and Tourism, www.prenhall .com/kotler.

A. On the Internet, find how ecotourism is being used to attract tourists by different organizations.

B. From information you can find on the Internet, when do you think space tourism will be a viable form of

tourism? What organizations are working to develop space tourism?

C. Go to Web sites of travel or hospitality companies and find examples of how they are taking measures to sustain and improve the natural environment. Which companies that you examined do you think have the best programs? Explain your answer.

■■■ REFERENCES

1. Sherri Day, "After Years at Top, McDonald's Strives to Regain Ground," *New York Times* (March 3, 2003).

2. Michael Arndt, "McDonald's 24/7," *Business Week* (February 5, 2007): 64–72.

3. Michael Arndt, "McDonald's 24/7," *Business Week* (February 5, 2007): 64–72.

4. Seyhmus Baloglu, "Dimensions of Customer Loyalty, Separating Friends from Well Wishers," *Cornell Hotel*

and Restaurant Administration Quarterly, 43, no. 1 (2002): 47–59.

5. Philip Kotler, *Marketing Management* (Upper Saddle River, NJ: Prentice Hall, 1988); Donald R. Lehmann and Russel S. Winer, *Analysis for Marketing Planning* (Plano, TX: Business Publications, 1988).

6. Craft Web site, www.craftrestaurant.com (accessed August 1, 2008).

7. Tejal Rao, "The New Hotel Cuisine: Don't Bite the Brand That Feeds You," Sta Chefs.com, May 2007 (accessed August 2, 2008).

8. Information from Robert J. Benes, Abbie Jarman, and Ashley Williams, "2007 NRA Sets Records," at www.chefmagazine.com (accessed September 2007); and www.thecoca-colacompany.com/presscenter/presskit_fs.html and www.cokesolutions.com (accessed November 2010).

9. Michael Porter, *Competitive Strategy* (New York: Free Press, 1980).

10. Melinda Bush, "The Critical Need to Know," *Cornell Hotel and Restaurant Administration Quarterly*, 26, no. 3 (1985): 1.

11. World POPClock, U.S. Census Bureau, www.census.gov (accessed September 2007). This Web site provides continuously updated projections of the U.S. and world populations.

12. See Clay Chandler, "Little Emperors," *Fortune* (October 4, 2004): 138–150; "China's 'Little Emperors,' " *Financial Times* (May 5, 2007): 1; "Me Generation Finally Focuses on US," *Chinadaily.com.cn* (August 27, 2008), www.chinadaily.com.cn/china/2008-08/27/content_6972930.htm; Melinda Varley, "China: Chasing the Dragon," *Brand Strategy* (October 6, 2008): 26; Clifford Coonan, "New Rules to Enforce Chain's One-Child Policy," *Irish Times* (January 14, 2009): 12; and David Pilling, "Reflections of Life in China's Fast Lane," *Financial Times* (April 19, 2010): 10.

13. Adapted from information in Janet Adamy, "Different Brew: Eyeing a Billion Tea Drinkers, Starbucks Pours It On in China," *Wall Street Journal* (November 29, 2006). Also see, "Where the Money Is," *Financial Times* (May 12, 2007): 5 and Laurie Burkitt, "Starbucks Menu Expands in China," *Wall Street Journal*, March 09, 2011: B.7.

14. Janet Adamy, "Different Brew: Eyeing a Billion Tea Drinkers, Starbucks Pours It On in China," *Wall Street Journal* (November 29, 2006).

15. Janet Adamy, "Different Brew: Eyeing a Billion Tea Drinkers, Starbucks Pours It On in China," *Wall Street Journal* (November 29, 2006).

16. Laurie Burkitt, "Starbucks Menu Expands in China," *Wall Street Journal* (March 09, 2011): B.7.

17. U.S. Census Bureau projections and POPClock Projection, U.S. Census Bureau, www.census.gov (accessed September 2007).

18. Louise Lee, "Love Those Boomers," *Business Week* (October 24, 2005): 94–102; Tom Ramstack, "The New Gray: Boomers Spark Retirement Revolution," *Washington Tones* (December 29, 2005); and "Baby Boomers in the United States Have an Estimated Annual Spending Power of over $2 Trillion," *Business Wire* (April 27, 2007).

19. Noreen O'Leary, "Squeeze Play," *Adweek* (January 12, 2009): 8–9; David Court, "The Downturn's New Rules for Marketers," *The McKinsey Quarterly* (December 2008), accessed at www.mckinseyquarterly.com/the_downturn_new_rules_for_marketers_2262; Emily Brandon, "Planning to Retire: 10 Things You Didn't Know About Baby Boomers," *USNezvs.com* (January 15, 2009), accessed at http://money.usnews.com; and Iris Taylor, "Impact of Baby Boomers Delaying Retirement Explored," *McClatchy-Tribune Business News* (April 5, 2010).

20. See Simon Hudson, "Wooing Zoomers: Marketing to the Mature Traveler," *Marketing Intelligence & Planning*, 28, no.4 (2010): 444–461.

21. Scott Schroder and Warren Zeller, "Get to Know Gen X and Its Segments," *Multichannel News* (March 21, 2005): 55; and Jim Shelton, "When Children of Divorce Grow Up," *Knight Ridder Tribune Business News* (March 4, 2007): 1.

22. "Mixed Success: One Who Targeted Gen X and Succeeded—Sort Of," *Journal of Financial Planning* (February 2004) 17, 2: 15.

23. Paul Greenberg, "Move Over, Baby Boomers; Gen Xers Want Far More Collaboration with Companies, Both as Consumers and Employees," CIO 70 (March 1, 2006): 1.

24. Scott Hume, "Consumer Insights: The Leading Edge, Give Generation X the Credit It Is Due for Revolutionizing the American Dining Experience," Restaurants and Institutions online (www.rimag.com/article/CA6556319.html), May 1, 2008 (accessed July 28, 2008).

25. Adapted from information found in Mark Ritson, "Have You Got the Gen X Factor?" *Marketing* (April 25, 2007): 25; and "75 Wall Street to Be a Hyatt Andaz Property" (April 25, 2007), www.hotelchattcr,con0taghkndaz%20Hotels.

26. Based on information found in Donna C. Gregory, "Virginia Tourism Corp. Marketing to Generation X" (December 29, 2009), www.virginiabusiness.com/index.php/news/article/romancing-generation-x. Also see www.virginia.org/home.asp (accessed November 2010).

27. Deirde van Dyk, "The Generation Y Hotel," Time online (www.time.com), June 12, 2008 (accessed August 3, 2008); R. K. Miller and Kelli Washington, *Consumer Behavior 2009*; and Piet Levy, "The Quest for Cool," *Marketing News* (February 28, 2009): 6.

28. Pauline Parry and Linda Naiman, "Minding Your X's and Y's," *Successful Meeting* (July 2003): 29; Ken Gronback, "Marketing to Generation Y," *Home Textiles Today* (September 11, 2000): 14.

29. See U.S. Census Bureau, "U.S. Population Projections," www.census.gov/population/www/projections/summarytables.html (accessed August 2010); and "Characteristics of the Foreign-Born Population by

Nativity and US Citizenship Status," www.census.gov/population/www/socdemo/foreign/cps2008.html.

30. Dan Fost, "The Fun Factor: Marketing Recreation to the Disabled," *American Demographics,* 20. 2 (February 1998): 54–58.

31. Joan Voight, "Accessibility of Disability," *Adweek* (March 27, 2006): 20.

32. For these and other statistics, see Witeck-Combs Communications, "Buying Power of Gay Men and Lesbians in 2008," www.rivendellmedia.com/ngng/executive_summary/NGNG PPT and www.gaymarket.com/ngng/ngng_reader.html (accessed April 2009); and Paul Morrissette, "Market to LGBT C," *American Agent & Broker* (July 2010): 50.

33. Robert Sharoff, "Diversity in the Mainstream," *Marketing News* (May 21, 2001): 1, 13.

34. Robert Sharoff, "Diversity in the Mainstream," *Marketing News* (May 21, 2001): 1, 13.

35. For these and other examples, see Laura Koss-Feder, "Out and About," *Marketing News* (May 25, 1998): 1, 20; Jennifer Gilbert, "Ad Spending Booming for Gay-Oriented Sites," *Advertising Age* (December 6, 1999): 58; John Fetto, "In Broad Daylight," *American Demographics* (February 2001): 16, 20; Robert Sharoff, "Diversity in the Mainstream," *Marketing News* (May 21, 2001): 1, 13; David Goetzl, "Showtime, MTV Gamble on Gay Net," *Advertising Age* (January 14, 2002): 4; and Kristi Nelson, "Canada's Gay TV Network Gets Ready for U.S.," *Electronic Media* (Chicago, May 6, 2002).

36. See U.S. Census Bureau, "Families and Living Arrangements:2009," at www.census.gov/population/www/socdemo/hh-fam.html (accessed May 2010).

37. U.S. Census Bureau, "Families and Living Arrangements: 2009"; "Census Bureau News—2009 America's Families and Living Arrangements," *PR Newswire* (January 15,2010); and U.S. Census Bureau, "Facts for Features" (March 2010), accessed at https://www.census.gov/newsroom/releases/archives/facts_for_features_ special_editions/cbl 0-ff03.html.

38. See Marissa Miley and Ann Mack, "The New Female Consumer: The Rise of the Real Mom," *Advertising Age* (November 16, 2009): AI.

39. U.S. Census Bureau, "Geographical Mobility/Migration," www.census.gov/population/www/socdemo/migrate.html (accessed April 2010).

40. U.S. Census Bureau, "Educational Attainment," www.census.gov/population/www/socdemo/educ-attn.html (accessed April 2010).

41. Bradley Johnson, "Recession's Long Gone, But America's Average Income Isn't Budging," *Advertising Age* (April 17, 2006): 22. See also, Jeremy Siegel, "Why the Rich Got Richer," *Kiplinger's Personal Finance* (July

2007): 532; and Frederic L. Pryor, "The Anatomy of Increasing Inequity of U.S. Family Incomes," *Journal of SocioEconomics* (August 2007): 595.

42. Andrew Zolli, "Business 3.0," *Fast Company* (March 2007): 64–70.

43. Mohammadi Kamin, "Calling Robinson Crusoe," *Geographical Magazine,* responsibletravel.com (October 18, 2004); "Maldive Islands Could Be Sinking" (October 5, 2004), http://news.bbc.co.uk/cbbcnews/hi/world/newsid_3715000/3715928.stm (accessed October 18, 2004).

44. For more discussion, see "Earth in the Balance," *American Demographics* (January 2001): 24; and Subhabrata Bobby Banerjee, "Corporate Environmentalism: The Construct and Its Measurement," *Journal of Business Research* (March 2002): 177–191.

45. See www.intelitycorp.com (accessed August 18, 2010).

46. "Mobile Phones Replace Room Keys in Stockholm Hotel, Check in and Check out without Ever Stopping by the Front Desk," November 2, 2010, http://news.discovery.com/tech/mobile-phones-replace-hotel-keys.html (accessed August 18, 2011).

47. Roger Yu, "Hotels Use RFID Chips to Keep Linens from Checking Out" (July 31, 2011), http://abcnews.go.com/Travel/hotels-rfid-chips-linens-checking/story?id=14179579 (accessed August 18, 2011).

48. Gene Sloan, "Restaurant Taxes Gain Weight in Cash-Strapped Cities," *USA Today,* International Edition (Asia) (September 28, 1994): B7.

49. Ira Carnaharn, "Sober Up," *Forbes* (July 26, 2004): 100+; Rick Berman, "Recalling Prohibition Best Way for Operators to Halt Progress of Anti-Alcohol Campaigns," *Nation's Restaurant News* (May 24, 2004): 38+.

50. Chris Macias, "Restaurant Bows to Peta, Takes Live Shrimp Off Menu," *Sacramento Bee* (September 3, 2010): B2.

51. Jay Nordlinger, "PETA vs KFC," *National Review* (December 22, 2003): 27+, http://www.kentuckyfriedcruelty.com/ (accessed October 9, 2004).

52. Start a Cause-related Marketing Program, Cause Marketing Success Story—BJ's Restaurants, February, 11, 2010, http://www.cff.org/GetInvolved/BecomeACorporatePartner/CauseRelatedMarketing/ (accessed August 18, 2011).

53. See "The Growth of Cause Marketing," www.causemarketingforum.com/page.asp?ID=188 (accessed November 2010).

54. Kenneth J. Gruber, "The Hotels of Israel: Pressure and Promise," *Cornell Hotel and Restaurant Administration Quarterly,* 28, no. 4 (1988): 42.

55. J. S. Perry Hobson, "Feng Shui: Its Impacts on the Asian Hospitality Industry," *International Journal*

of Contemporary Hospitality Management, 6, no. 6 (1994): 21–26; Bernd H. Schmitt and Yigang Pan, "In Asia, the Supernatural Means Sales," *New York Times* (February 19, 1995): sec. 3, 11.

56. Richard L. Papiernik, "Foodservice–Food-Market Lines Blur, But Focus Is on the Big $650 Billion Pie," *Nation's Restaurant News* (September 1, 1997): 57.

57. Matthew Schifrin and Bruce Upton, "Crab Rangoon to Go," *Forbes* (March 24, 1997): 124–128.

58. Carl P. Zeithaml and Valarie Zeithaml, "Environmental Management: Revising the Marketing Perspective," *Journal of Marketing* (Spring 1984): 46–53.

59. William S. Watson, "Letters, the New Research Responsibility," *Cornell Hotel and Restaurant Administration Quarterly*, 34, no. 5 (1993): 7.

Marketing Information Systems and Marketing Research

5

Objectives

After reading this chapter, you should be able to:

1. Explain the importance of information in gaining insights about the marketplace and customers.

2. Explain the concept of the marketing information system.

3. Outline the marketing research process, including defining the problem and research objectives, developing the research plan, implementing the research plan, and interpreting and reporting the findings.

4. Explain how companies analyze and use marketing information.

Joseph, a 30-something New Yorker, recently went on a weekend trip to Atlantic City, New Jersey, where he hoped to stay at one of his favorite Harrah's resorts and enjoy some gaming and entertainment. Unfortunately for Joseph, he picked a weekend when all hotels were booked solid. But after swiping his Harrah's Total Rewards card to play the tables, the pit boss came by and directed him to the front desk. He was told that a room had become available, and he could stay in it for a reduced rate of $100 a night. When he checked out two nights later, Joseph was told that all the room charges were on the house.

Was this sudden vacancy a case of lady luck smiling down on an Atlantic City visitor? Or was it a case of a company that knows what managing customer relationships truly means? If you ask any of Harrah's Total Rewards program members, they will tell you without hesitation that it's the latter. "They are very good at upgrading or in some cases finding a room in a full hotel," Joseph reported later. "And I always liked the fact that no matter where I gambled, Atlantic City, Vegas, Kansas City, or New Orleans, or which of their hotels I gambled in, I was always able to use my [Total Rewards card]."

Harrah's customers like Joseph aren't the only ones praising its customer-relationship management (CRM) capabilities. In fact, Harrah's program is considered by CRM experts to set the gold standard. With the Total Rewards program at the center of its business and marketing strategies, Harrah's Entertainment has the ability to gather data, convert that data into customer insights, and use those insights to serve up a customer experience like no other.

Gathering Data

One thing that makes Total Rewards so effective is that Harrah's has a customer relationship culture that starts at the top with president and CEO Gary Loveman. In 1998, Loveman joined the company and turned its existing loyalty program into Total Rewards. The program worked well from the start. But through smart investments and a continued focus, Harrah's has hit the CRM jackpot.

The mechanics of the program go something like this: Total Rewards members receive points based on the amount they spend at Harrah's facilities. They can then redeem the points for a variety of perks, such as cash, food, merchandise, rooms, and hotel show tickets. The simplicity of Total Rewards gains power in volume and flexibility. Through numerous acquisitions over the past decade, Harrah's has grown to more than fifty properties under several brands across the United States, including Harrah's, Caesars, Bally's, Planet Hollywood, the Flamingo, and Showboat. Total Rewards members swipe their card every time they spend a dime at one of these properties: checking into 1 of 40,000 hotel rooms, playing 1 of 60,000 slot machines, eating at 1 of 390 restaurants, picking up a gift at 1 of 240 retail shops, or playing golf at 1 of its 7 golf courses. Over 80 percent of Harrah's customers—40 million in all—use a Total Rewards card. That's roughly one out of six adults in the United States. That's a big pile of data points. Added to this, Harrah's regularly surveys samples of its customers to gain even more details.

Customer Insights

Analyzing all this information gives Harrah's detailed insights into its casino operations. For example, "visualization software" can generate a dynamic "heat map" of a casino floor, with machines glowing red when at peak activity and then turning blue and then white as the action moves elsewhere. More importantly, Harrah's uses every customer interaction to learn something new about individuals—their characteristics and behaviors, such as who they are, how often they visit, how long they stay, and how much they gamble and entertain. "We know if you like gold … chardonnay, down pillows; if you like your room close to the elevator, which properties you visit, what games you play, and which offers you redeemed," says David Norton, Harrah's chief marketing officer.

From its Total Rewards data, Harrah's has learned that 26 percent of its customers produce 82 percent of revenues. And these best customers aren't the "high-rollers" that have long been the focus of the industry. Rather, they are ordinary folks from all walks of life—middle-aged and retired teachers, assembly line workers, and even bankers and doctors who have discretionary income and time. Harrah's "low-roller" strategy is based on the discovery that these customers might just visit casinos for an evening rather than staying overnight at the hotel. And they are more likely to play the slots than the tables. What motivates them? It's mostly the intense anticipation and excitement of gambling itself.

Kris Hart, vice president of brand management for Harrah's, reports on a survey of 14,000 Total Rewards members. We did a lot of psychographic segmenting—looking at what were the drivers of people's behavior. Were they coming because of the location? Were they coming because there were incented to do so with a piece of direct mail? Were they coming because they have an affinity for a loyalty program? And that allowed us to look at segments that clumped around certain drivers … and it enabled us to construct our brands and messaging … in a way that would capitalize on those drivers.

Customer Experience

Using such insights, Harrah's focuses its marketing and service development strategies on the needs of its best customers. For example, the company's advertising reflects the feeling of exuberance that target customers seek. Harrah's sends out over 250 million pieces of direct mail and almost 100 million e-mails to its members every year. A good customer can receive as many as 150 pieces of mail in a given year from one or all of its properties. From the customer's perspective, that might sound like a nightmare. But Harrah's has tested customer sentiment on receiving multiple mailings from multiple locations, and they actually like it. The reason is that the information that any given customer receives is relevant to him or her, not annoying. That's why Harrah's has a higher-than-average direct mail response rate.

Harrah's is certainly concerned about metrics, such as response rates, click-through rates, revenue, and customer profitability. But Harrah's program is one of the best because it places emphasis on knowing how all the outcomes are linked. And because Harrah's CRM culture extends from the IT department to frontline employees, the gaming giant has an uncanny ability to translate all its data into an exceptional customer experience.

Marilyn Winn, the president of three Las Vegas resorts, lives and breathes Harrah's CRM culture. "My job is to make money for Harrah's Entertainment by creating a great climate for customers and employees." She focuses on what goes on inside the hotel properties. She spot-checks details on casino floors and in gift shops. She attends weekly employee rallies that are not only a party but also a communications tool. Winn points out how Harrah's motivates its employees to do their best. "Every week, we survey our customers. Customer service is very specific at Harrah's, systematic." Based on customer service scores, employees have their own system for accumulating points and redeeming them for a wide variety of rewards, from iPads to pool equipment. "Every property has the goal to improve service. This is just one way we do it. We also use mystery shoppers to verify we are getting the service we want and we train our employees to our standards."

Harrah's combines its service culture with the brain center of Total Rewards. After a day's gaming, Harrah's knows which customers should be rewarded with free show tickets, dinner vouchers, or room upgrades. In fact, Harrah's processes customer information in real time, from the moment customers swipe their rewards cards, creating the ideal link between data and the customer experience. Harrah's chief information officer calls this "operational CRM." Based on up-to-the-minute customer information, "the hotel clerk can see your history and determine whether you should get a room upgrade, based on booking levels in the hotel at that time and on your past level of play. A person might walk up to you while you're playing and offer you $5 to play more slots, or a free meal, or perhaps wish you a happy birthday."

Harrah's is constantly improving its technology so that it can better understand its customers and deliver a more fine-tuned experience. Most recently, Total Rewards gained the ability to track and reward nongaming spending. This is good for people who don't view themselves as big gamblers. "We wanted to make it relevant to them as well because they could spend a couple of hundred dollars on a room, the spa, food, and shows and not be treated any better than a $50-a-day customer," Norton said. This demonstrates the "total" part of Total Rewards. It isn't a program about getting people into casinos. It's a program designed to maximize the customer experience, regardless of what that experience includes.

Hitting Twenty-One

Harrah's CRM efforts have paid off in spades. The company has found that happy customers are much more loyal. Whereas customer spending decreases by 10 percent based on an unhappy casino experience, it increases by 24 percent with a happy experience. And Harrah's Total Rewards customers appear to be a happier bunch. Compared with non-members, member customers visit the company's casinos more frequently, stay longer, and spend more of their gambling and entertainment dollars in Harrah's rather than in rival casinos. Since setting up Total Rewards, Harrah's has seen its share of customers' average annual gambling budgets rise 20 percent, and revenue from customers gambling at Harrah's rather than their "home casino" has risen 8 percent.

Although Harrah's and the entire gaming industry were hit hard by the Great Recession, things are turning back around; through its acquisitions and the success of its Total Rewards pro-ram, Harrah's is the biggest in its industry, with over $10 billion revenue in 2010. Loveman calls Total Rewards "the vertebrae of our business," and says "it touches, in some form or fashion, 85 percent of our revenue."[1] Dave Norton, David Norton, senior VP-relationship marketing say, "We know if you like golf ... chardonnay, down pillows, if you like your room close to the elevator which properties you visit, what games you play and which offers you redeemed," Mr. Norton said. "We not only use these things on the front end of marketing but for the service experience." Mr. Norton said it's a mixture of good customized messaging and a strong loyalty program that sets Harrah's program apart."[2]

Caesars Entertainment shows us how marketers can use information to gain powerful market insights.

■■■ Marketing Information and Customer Insights

To create value for customers and to build meaningful relationships with them, marketers must first gain fresh, deep insights into what customers need and want. Companies use such customer insights to develop competitive advantage. Such insights come from the good marketing information.[3]

But although customer and market insights are important for building customer value and relationships, these insights can be very difficult to obtain. Customer needs and buying motives are often anything but obvious—consumers themselves usually can't tell you exactly what they need and why they buy. To gain good customer insights, marketers must effectively manage marketing information from a wide range of sources.

Today's marketers have ready access to plenty of marketing information. With the recent explosion of information technologies, companies can now generate information in great quantities. In fact, most marketing managers are overloaded with data and often overwhelmed by it. Still, despite this data glut, marketers frequently complain that they lack enough information of the right kind. They don't need more information—they need better information. And they need to make better use of the information they already have. Says another marketing information expert, "transforming today's vast, ever-increasing volume of consumer information into actionable marketing insights ... is the number-one challenge for digital-age marketers."[4]

Thus, a company's marketing research and information system must do more than simply generate lots of information. The real value of marketing research and marketing information lies in how it is used—in the customer insights that it provides. "The value of the market research department is not determined by the number of studies that it does," says the marketing expert, "but by the business value of the insights that it produces and the decisions that it influences."[5]

Based on such thinking, many companies are now restructuring and renaming their marketing research and information functions. They are creating "customer insights teams," headed by a vice president of customer insights and made up of representatives from all of the firm's functional areas. For example, the head of marketing research at Kraft Foods is called the director of consumer insights and strategy.

Customer insight groups collect customer and market information from a wide variety of sources—ranging from traditional marketing research studies to mingling with and observing consumers to monitoring consumer online conversations about the company and its products. Then they use the marketing information to develop important customer insights from which the company can create more value for its customers. For example, one customer insights group states its mission simply as "getting better at understanding our consumers and meeting their needs."

■■■ The Marketing Information System

A **marketing information system (MIS)** consists of people, equipment, and procedures to gather, sort, analyze, evaluate, and distribute needed, timely, and accurate information to marketing decision makers. Figure 5–1 illustrates the MIS concept. The MIS begins and ends with marketing managers, but managers throughout the organization should be involved in the MIS. First, it interacts with managers to assess their information needs. Next, it develops needed information from internal

Figure 5–1
Marketing information system.

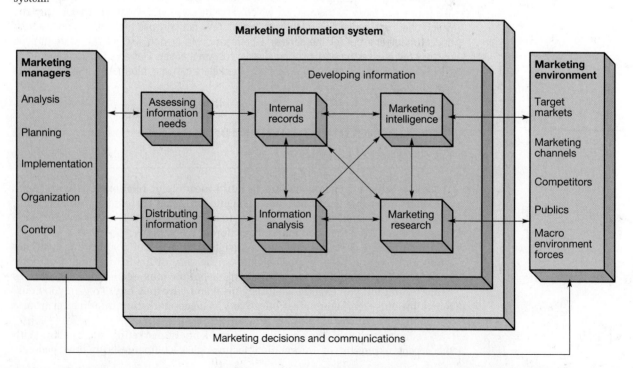

company records, marketing intelligence activities, and the marketing research process. Information analysts process information to make it more useful. Finally, the MIS distributes information to managers in the right form and at the right time to help in marketing planning, implementation, and control.

We now take a closer look at the functions of a company's MIS.

Assessing Information Needs

A good MIS balances information that managers would like to have against that which they really need and is feasible to obtain. A company begins by interviewing managers to determine their information needs. For example, Mrs. Field's Cookies provides its managers with sales forecasts with updates each hour. When sales are falling behind, the computer suggests merchandising techniques such as sampling in the mall to pick up sales.[6]

Some managers ask for whatever information they can get without thinking carefully about its cost or usefulness. Too much information can be as harmful as too little. Other busy managers may fail to ask for things they need to know, or managers may not ask for some types of information that they should have.

For example, managers need to anticipate new competitive product offerings. However, competitors withhold information to prevent their competition from knowing about the product. During KFC's development of one of its sandwiches, only a few corporate managers knew of the project. KFC had developed ingredient specifications for the making of the sandwich, and its suppliers had to sign secrecy agreements. KFC did not want competitors to learn about the new product offering before its test marketing. Yet competitors with a good MIS system might have picked up clues in advance about KFC's plans. They may have heard a bread supplier commenting about KFC's orders for small hamburger-style buns. They may have heard an executive stating how KFC would be strengthening its lunch business. Even with secret agreements, news inadvertently leaks out. Managers who keep their eyes and ears open can pick up on competitive moves using legal and ethical sources of information such as speeches by company executives and trade publications.

The company must estimate the value of having an item of information against the costs of obtaining it. The value depends on how it will be used, and this judgment is highly subjective. Similarly, estimating the cost of obtaining a specific item of information may be difficult.

The costs of obtaining, processing, storing, and delivering information can add up quickly. Sometimes additional information contributes little to improving a manager's decision. Its cost may exceed its benefit. Suppose that a restaurant manager estimates that launching a new menu item without further information will yield a lifetime profit of $500,000. The manager believes that additional information will improve the marketing mix and increase the company's profit to $525,000. It would be foolish to pay $30,000 or more to obtain the additional information. A good MIS balances the information users would like to have against what they really need and what is feasible to offer.

Developing Marketing Information

Information needed by marketing managers can be obtained from **internal data**, **marketing intelligence**, and **marketing research**.

Internal Data

Many companies build extensive internal databases, electronic collections of consumer and market information obtained from data sources within the company network. Marketing managers can readily access and work with information in the database to identify marketing opportunities and problems, plan programs, and evaluate performance. The answers to the questions in Table 5–1 will help managers assess their marketing information needs.

Information in the database can come from many sources. The marketing department furnishes information on customer transactions, demographics,

TABLE 5–1

Questions for Assessing Marketing Information Needs

1. What types of decisions do you make regularly?
2. What types of information do you need to make these decisions?
3. What types of useful information do you get regularly?
4. What social media sites can provide useful information?
5. What types of information would you like to get that you are not getting now?
6. What types of information do you get now that you don't really need?
7. What information would you want daily? weekly? monthly? yearly?
8. What topics would you like to be kept informed about?
9. What databases would be useful to you?
10. What types of information analysis programs would you like to have?
11. What would be the four most helpful improvements that could be made in the present information system?

psychographics, and buying behavior. The customer service department keeps records of customer satisfaction or service problems. The accounting department prepares financial statements and keeps detailed records of sales, costs, and cash flows. Operations reports on production schedules, shipments, and inventories. The sales force reports on reseller reactions and competitor activities, and marketing channel partners provide data on point-of-sale (POS) transactions Harnessing such information can provide powerful customer insights and competitive advantage.

Here is an example of how one company uses its internal database to make better marketing decisions:

> Pizza Hut's database contains detailed customer data on 40 million U.S. households, gleaned from phone orders, online orders, and POS transactions at its more than 6,600 restaurants around the nation. Pizza Hut also uses Facebook to get customers to register for deals, collecting their e-mail, phone number, zip code, and other information. The company can slice and dice the data by favorite toppings, what you ordered last, and whether you buy a salad with your cheese and pepperoni pizza. It then uses all this data to enhance customer relationships, sending customers deals that will create another order. Says one blogger, "So who is always on my mind when I feel like pizza? Who is sending me coupons and free things that make me want to get pizza rather than make dinner? You got it, Pizza Hut. They had me buy in and now they'll have my loyalty. They make it so easy that I wouldn't want to bother getting it anywhere else."[7]

e

5.1 www. pizzahut.com: Notice the different ways Pizza Hut can capture your information and how the use mobile apps.

Internal databases usually can be accessed more quickly and cheaply than other information sources, but they also present some problems. Because internal information was often collected for other purposes, it may be incomplete or in the wrong form for marketing decisions. For example, sales and cost data used by the accounting department for preparing financial statements must be adapted for use in evaluating the value of specific customer segment, sales force, or channel performance. Data also age quickly; keeping the database current requires a major effort. In addition, a large company produces mountains of information, which must be well integrated and readily accessible so managers can find it easily and use it effectively. Managing that much data requires highly sophisticated equipment and techniques.

Every company contains more information than any manager can possibly know or analyze. The information is scattered in countless databases, plans, and records, and in the heads of many longtime managers. The company must somehow bring order to its information gold mine, so that its managers can more easily find answers to questions and make informed decisions. Increasingly, companies are creating **data warehouses** to house their customer data in a single, more accessible location. Then, using powerful data mining techniques, they search for meaningful patterns in the data and communicate them to managers.

Useful marketing information is contained in kitchen production schedules and sales reports, front-desk reports, sales call reports, and functions. Managers can use information gathered from these and other sources to evaluate performance and detect problems and opportunities. Here are some examples of how companies use internal records to make marketing decisions:[8]

- Hotel managers use reservations records and registration information to aid in timing their advertising and sales calls. If most vacationers book February reservations in November, advertising in December will be too late.

- Reservation records also provide information concerning the hotel's top-producing travel agents. Hotel representatives can phone, fax, or visit travel agents to inform them of hotel-sponsored promotional activities in an effort to generate a higher volume of room sales.

- Louisiana found through visitors' studies that most families plan for their summer vacations in the spring. They now advertise to the family market January through May, so their message will be in front of prospective visitors while they are making the vacation decision.

GUEST HISTORY INFORMATION The single most important element in any hospitality MIS is to have a process for capturing and using information concerning guests. Guest information is vital to improving service, creating effective advertising and sales promotion programs, developing new products, improving existing products, and developing marketing and sales plans and to the development and use of an effective revenue management program. Unfortunately, far too many hospitality firms have only a vague idea of who their guests are.

Specific guest information needs may include any or all of the information shown in Table 5–2. At first appearance this list undoubtedly seems overbearing and unduly inquisitive. The fact is that hospitality companies increasingly collect and use this type of information. Obviously, a hotel, resort, cruise line, or other hospitality company must be very careful not to infringe on the privacy rights of guests or to disturb them. An amazing amount of this information is available from internal records. This requires interfacing with other departments, such as reservations and accounting.

GUEST INFORMATION TRENDS Information concerning guest trends is vital to planning and revenue/yield management. Types of guest trend information used by hotels, airlines, cruise lines, and auto rental companies include the following:

- Booking patterns
- Cancellations
- Conversion percentages (percentage of inquiries to reservations)
- Overbooking patterns
- Historical trends on occupancy for prime, shoulder, and low seasons
- Yield patterns by season

Gathering this vital information requires careful planning by a management information system. It is seldom, if ever, sufficient to try to retrieve and use data from a company's files if prior consideration was not given to the form in which it would be needed.

Guest history records enable hotel marketers to identify repeat guests and their individual needs and preferences. If a guest requests a particular newspaper delivered during one stay, a notation entered into the guest's file will ensure that the newspaper is received during all future visits. If a luxury hotel upgrades its guests to a better room on their fifth visit, its managers are increasing guest satisfaction. Frequent guests appreciate the free upgrade, and many request the higher-priced room on the next visit.

TABLE 5–2

Specific Guest Information That Might Be Collected

Personal guest information	Type of primary product/service purchased
Name	Examples for a hotel:
Address	Regular sleeping room
Postal code	Suite
E-mail address	Deluxe suite
Phone numbers	*Other purchases (cross-purchases)*
Home	Examples for a hotel:
Work	Long-distance phone
Cell	Laundry
E-mail	Room service
Number in party	Minibar
Reason for trip	Hotel restaurants
Business	Health club
Pleasure	Recreational facilities
Emergency	Retail products charged to bill
Person who made reservation	Length of stay
Self-days stayed	Specific dates as guest
Employer	Method of arrival
Source of reservation	Personal auto
Name of employer	Rental auto
Address of employer	Tour bus
Title/position	Train
Method of payment	Taxi or limo
Credit card	*Member of frequent guest programs*
Which?	This hotel (number)
Cash	Others presented for credit
Check	Airline (number)
Bill to company	Company (number)

Guest Information Management

Acquisition of this critical information cannot be left to chance or the whims of department managers. A system for obtaining guest information may include any or all of the techniques discussed next.

GUEST COMMENT CARDS   Guest comment cards are often found on dining room tables and in guest rooms or are handed to departing customers. They provide useful information and can provide insights into problem areas. For example, several negative comments on food would indicate a potential problem for a restaurant. If corrective action is taken and fewer negative comments are registered, the correction has been successful.[9] A problem with guest comment cards is that they may not reflect the opinions of the majority of guests. Commonly, only about 1 to 2 percent of the people who are very angry or very pleased take the time to complete a card.[10] Thus comment cards can be useful in spotting problem areas, but they are not a good indication of overall guest satisfaction. Also, if the distribution and control of comment cards is not well thought out, employees may selectively distribute comment cards to guests they feel will give a positive response. Employees may also discard negative comment cards if they have the opportunity to do so. Many companies have the card mailed to a corporate office to avoid this problem.

LISTENING TO AND SPEAKING WITH GUESTS   Many organizations have developed formal ways of interacting with guests. Hotels offer free receptions in the afternoon for their frequent guests. This not only is a way of saying thank you to the guests but also provides an opportunity for managers to speak with guests. Sea World in Australia requires that managers take several customer surveys every week. This is an excellent way to find out what guests think, and it lets management hear it firsthand. Wyndham hotels now call all guests five minutes before their room service order will arrive. This procedure was developed as a result of a guest's comment. The female business traveler said she often orders room service, takes a shower, gets dressed, and then eats breakfast. The call lets her know when the service person will arrive so she does not get caught in the shower. Wyndham found that all business travelers appreciated this thoughtfulness, and they were able to create a better service based on talking with their customers. Gaining information from your guests lets them know you are interested in them and can help create trust and customer loyalty.[11]

If employees are trained to listen to guest comments and feed them back to management, this can be a powerful source of information. Your employees can be like microphones recording guest comments. For this listening to work, management has to feed back to the employees how it is using the information, and there must be trust between the employees and management. Ritz-Carlton makes excellent use of the "listening posts" concept. Horst Schulze, former president of Ritz-Carlton, said, "Keep on listening to customers because they change. And if you want to have 100% satisfied customers then you have to make sure that you listen and change—just in case they change their expectations that you change with them."[12]

AUTOMATED SYSTEMS   The decreasing cost and increasing capacity of automated guest history systems will allow hotels to create close relationships with their customers once again.[13]

Obviously, any hotel property or hospitality company, such as a large cruise line, must use automated systems. A variety of systems are available and should be examined carefully and tested before purchasing. Remember that an automated guest information system is part of broader systems such as database marketing and yield/revenue management.

An automated guest history system can be of great benefit to the sales force. Salespeople can pull guest histories by a specific geographic area, such as a city. This information can greatly assist in a sales blitz by identifying frequent guests who can receive top priority in the blitz. The guest history can also identify former frequent guests who are no longer using the hotel. Salespeople will want to call on these former clients to see if they can regain their business.

An automated guest history system offers a real competitive advantage to a chain, particularly a smaller chain. "By means of a centralized system or network, a group of hotels could share guest information. Imagine how impressed a guest would be if he or she requested a suite, champagne, and a hypoallergenic pillow when staying at a hotel in Boston, then received the same services at a chain affiliate in Maui without even having to ask."[14]

This Cheesecake factory restaurant manager learns about his customers' likes and dislikes by talking to guests while they are in the restaurant. Courtesy of Spencer Grant/PhotoEdit.

MYSTERY SHOPPERS   Mystery shopping is a $1.5-billion industry. Hospitality companies often hire disguised or **mystery shoppers** to pose as customers and report back on their experience. Mystery shoppers are used in all types of operations. McDonald's uses a mystery shopping program to make sure their stores are performing to their standards. They post the results on the Web, making them accessible to local managers and corporate managers.[15]

A mystery shopper works best if there is a possibility for recognition and reward for good job performance. This is the concept of positive reinforcement. The most effective mystery shopping systems provide the employees with a list of the items the mystery shoppers will be checking. If employees feel that the only purpose of a disguised shopper program is to report poor service and reprimand them, the program will not fulfill its full potential.

COMPANY RECORDS   One of the most misused sources of information is company records. Marketing managers should take advantage of the information that is currently being generated by various departments. Guest history and client history on potential corporate clients is also useful information.

POINT-OF-SALE INFORMATION   For restaurants, the POS register will undoubtedly offer opportunities to compile and distribute, through a computer, information that is currently entered into reports manually. A POS system could collect information about individual restaurant patrons where credit cards are used.

Some observers of the fast-food industry believe that future POS systems will use expert systems that employ computers using artificial intelligence. One possible scenario is the "computaburger." Data concerning customer preference, order size, and volume will be taken from a POS machine and provided to an expert system. The expert system will then predict and possibly even order a volume of hamburger and the accompanying condiments for specific times in each day.[16]

The casino industry has displayed a high interest in POS systems and their increasing sophistication. Some slot machines are now capable of recording the numbers of play and the win–loss record of frequent players who activate the machines through use of a magnetic card. The player receives points based on the amount of play, and the casino is able to track the playing habits of players using the slot club cards.

Systems are also in place in most casinos to track players who are brought to the casino by junket reps. Tracking of these players is the responsibility of the pit boss in each gaming area, such as blackjack.

The Las Vegas Hilton provides an example of an internal system that can provide needed marketing information,[17] which includes the following:

- A front-desk tracking system that can classify each room night sold into the proper market segment

- A casino player tracking system that can identify players by market segments, that is, gaming rate versus slot tournament

- A database of all customers staying at the Hilton to identify their spending patterns by market segment

- Market research detailing guests demographic characteristics, visitor frequency, and spending habits by customer segment

The need to develop and use reliable guest information, particularly guest satisfaction data, has been examined by researchers within the restaurant industry, who observed that "restaurant failures are partly a result of management's lack of strategic orientation in measuring and focusing on customer satisfaction."[18]

Corporate Customer and Marketing Intermediary Information

A database of customers/prospects is of great value to a professional sales force. The sales force of Benchmark Hospitality Conference Resorts is trained to go beyond demographic studies and to target prospects by geography and industry segment. Benchmark's salespeople monitor the health of specific industries and qualify prospects. Before arranging a sales meeting with any corporate meeting planner, the salesperson obtains marketing information concerning the prospect, such as the following:

- The industry standing and strategic outlook for growth

- Profit and loss statements from annual reports

- Debt-to-equity ratios

- Corporate culture information

- Data concerning how this company uses meetings

5.2 Benchmark Hospitality International, www.benchmarkhospitality .com: Benchmark hospitality focuses on the conference center and resort business. This focus allows it to gather information to help it understand these markets.

This information can be obtained from annual reports, financial analyses of public companies, and articles on the company, and by talking with company employees. In addition to detailed information concerning prospects, Benchmark expects sales force members to be regular readers of the business press, such as the *Wall Street Journal* and the *New York Times*.[19]

Marketing Intelligence

Marketing intelligence includes everyday information about developments in the marketing environment that helps managers prepare and adjust marketing plans and short-run tactics. Marketing intelligence systems determine the needed intelligence, and they collect and deliver it in a useful format to marketing managers.

Internal Sources of Marketing Intelligence

Marketing intelligence can be gathered by a company's executives, front-desk staff, service staff, purchasing agents, and sales force. Employees, unfortunately, are often too busy to pass on important information. The company must sell them on their role as intelligence gatherers and train them to spot and report new developments. Managers should debrief contact personnel regularly.

Hotel owners and managers are essential parts of a marketing intelligence system. John F. Power, the general manager of the New York Hilton and Towers, served in this role on a trip to Japan. "I realized how different a Japanese breakfast is from our own," said Power, "and while most people like to sample the cuisine of the country they are visiting, everyone prefers to eat familiar food for breakfast."

As a result of marketing intelligence gathered on Power's trip, the New York Hilton now serves miso soup, nori (dried seaweed), yakizanaka (grilled fish), raw eggs, natto (fermented beans), oshiako (pickled vegetables), and rice as an authentic Japanese breakfast buffet.[20]

External Sources of Marketing Intelligence

A hospitality company must encourage suppliers, convention and tourist bureaus, and travel agencies to pass along important intelligence. It is worthwhile for a hospitality company to encourage the gathering of this information by treating vendors, salespeople, and potential employees in a friendly and receptive manner. Members of management should be encouraged to join community and professional organizations where they are likely to obtain essential marketing information.

Hotel and restaurant managers are in a particularly good position to acquire excellent information by entertaining key information sources in their properties. Sales force members are excellent conduits of information.

Sometimes rival companies offer you the information. For example, Bob Ayling, ex-chief executive of British Airways, accomplished such a mission when he visited the offices of the recently launched EasyJet. Ayling approached the company's founder, Stelios Haji-Ioannou, to ask whether he could visit, claiming to be fascinated as to how the Greek entrepreneur had made the budget airline formula work. Haji-Ioannou not only agreed, but allegedly he showed Ayling his business plan. A year later, British Air announced the launch of Go. "It was a carbon copy of EasyJet," says EasyGroup's director of corporate affairs. "Same planes, same direct ticket sales, same use of a secondary airport, and same idea to sell on-board refreshments. They succeeded in stealing our business model—it was a highly effective spying job."[21]

Sources of Competitive Competition

Competitive intelligence is available from competitors' annual reports, trade magazine articles, speeches, press releases, brochures, and advertisements. Hotel and restaurant managers should also visit their competitors' premises periodically. As mentioned in Chapter 4, a major consideration in any competitive information system is clearly defining the competition.

"In today's information age, companies are leaving a paper trail of information online," says an online intelligence expert. Today's managers "don't have to simply

Monthly Performance at a Glance – My Property vs. Competitive Set

Upscale Hotel Large City, USA

STR #   ChainID   MgtCo   Owner

For the Month of: August 2011   Date Created: September 28, 2011   Monthly Competitive Set Data Excludes Subject Property

August 2011

	Occupancy (%)			ADR			RevPAR		
	My Prop	Comp Set	Index	My Prop	Comp Set	Index	My Prop	Comp Set	Index
Current Month	86.1	67.5	127.8	159.54	139.97	113.1	137.94	94.43	144.5
Year To Date	80.7	78.2	101.8	185.78	163.60	113.9	149.46	127.93	116.0
Running 3 Month	84.0	79.8	105.3	173.17	152.10	113.9	145.43	121.35	119.8
Running 12 Month	75.8	74.1	102.2	188.40	165.35	113.9	142.83	122.61	116.5

August 2011 vs. 2010 Percent Change (%)

	Occupancy (%)			ADR			RevPAR		
	My Prop	Comp Set	Index	My Prop	Comp Set	Index	My Prop	Comp Set	Index
Current Month	3.9	-0.6	4.6	2.5	2.9	-1.2	6.8	2.3	3.3
Year To Date	-0.4	-0.2	-1.5	-0.6	-1.4	1.1	-1.3	-1.6	-0.4
Running 3 Month	0.1	2.7	-2.5	2.7	2.0	0.6	2.8	4.8	-1.9
Running 12 Month	-2.5	-1.8	-0.7	-1.4	-1.9	0.5	-3.9	-3.6	-0.3

SMITH TRAVEL RESEARCH, Inc

The Star report allows a hotel to compare how it is doing compared to a competitive set the management selects. The competitive set statistics are always shown as group data so the hotel is never able to determine the actual statistics for the different members of the competitive set. The Star report is a commonly used tool to provide competitive intelligence in the hotel industry. Provided with permission for Smith Travel Research Monthly Performance at a Glance—My Property vs. Competitive Set. Courtesy of Smith Travel Research.

rely on old news or intuition when making investment and business decisions."[22] Using Internet search engines, marketers can search specific competitor names, events, or trends and see what turns up. Intelligence seekers can also pore through any of thousands of online databases. Some are free. For example, the U.S. Security and Exchange Commission's database provides a huge stockpile of financial information on public competitors. And for a fee, companies can subscribe to more than 3,000 online databases and information search services such as Dialog, DataStar, LEXIS-NEXIS, Dow Jones News Retrieval, UMI ProQuest, and Dun & Bradstreet's Online Access. Hospitality managers can also subscribe to newsletters such as HotelMarketing.com, National Restaurant Association Smart Brief, and HotelOnline.net. One news service, HotelOnline.com, has editions by country, including Brazil, Germany, China, Poland, and Romania. To get your country's edition, add your country's Internet abbreviation to the URL, for example, www.HotelOnline.com.br for Brazil.

Associations sometimes collect data from member companies, compile it, and make it available to members for a reasonable fee. Information of this nature can often be misleading because member companies frequently provide incorrect data or may refuse to contribute any statistics if they have a dominant market share.

5.3   STR Global www.strglobal.com: STR Global provides a variety of competitive intelligence products for the hotel industry. A description of these products can be found on STR's Web site.

■■■ Marketing Research

Managers cannot always wait for information to arrive in bits and pieces from the marketing intelligence system. They often require formal studies of specific situations. When McDonald's decided to add salads to its menu, its planners needed to research customers' preferences for types of vegetables and dressings.

Ben's Steakhouse in Palm Beach, Florida, would like to know what percentage of its target market has heard of Ben's, how they heard about Ben's, what they know, and how they feel about the steakhouse. This would enable Ben's Steakhouse to know how effective their marketing communications have been. Casual marketing intelligence cannot answer these questions. Managers sometimes need to commission formal marketing research.

Marketing research is a process that identifies and defines marketing opportunities and problems, monitors and evaluates marketing actions and performance, and communicates the findings and implications to management.[23] Marketing researchers engage in a wide variety of activities. Their ten most common activities are measurement of market potentials, market-share analysis, the determination of market characteristics, sales analysis, studies of business trends, short-range forecasting, competitive product studies, long-range forecasting, MIS studies, and testing of existing products.

A company can conduct marketing research by employing its own researchers or hiring outside researchers. Most large companies—in fact, more than 73 percent—have their own marketing research departments. But even companies with their own departments hire outside firms to do fieldwork and special tasks.

Frank Camacho, a former vice president of corporate marketing services for Marriott, listed Marriott's research priorities as follows:[24]

- Market segmentation and sizing

- Concept development and product testing

- Price-sensitivity assessment

- Advertising and promotions assessment

- Market tracking

- Customer satisfaction

Small hotels or restaurants can obtain research help from nearby universities or colleges with business or hospitality programs. College marketing classes can be used to do exploratory research, find information about prospective customers, and conduct customer surveys. Instructors often arrange for their classes to gain marketing research experience in this way.

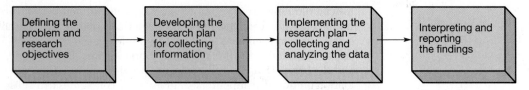

Figure 5–2
Marketing research process.

The marketing research process consists of four steps (see Figure 5–2): defining the problem and research objectives, developing the research plan, implementing the research plan, and interpreting and reporting the findings.

Defining the Problem and Research Objectives

Managers must work closely with marketing researchers to define the problem and the research objectives. The manager best understands the problem or decision for which information is needed, and the researcher best understands marketing research and how to obtain information.

Managers must know enough about marketing research to interpret the findings carefully. If they know little about marketing research, they may accept the wrong information, draw the wrong conclusions, or request much more information than they need. Marketing researchers can help the manager define the problem and use the findings correctly.

In one case a restaurant manager hired a researcher to determine the restaurant's level of awareness among the target market. The manager felt that lack of awareness explained low patronage. The researcher found, to the contrary, that many people were aware of the restaurant but thought of it as a special-occasion rather than an everyday restaurant. The manager had misdefined the problem and the research objective.

Assuming the problem is well defined, the manager and researcher must set research objectives. A marketing research project can have one of three types of objectives: **exploratory research**, to gather preliminary information that will help define the problem and suggest hypotheses; **descriptive research**, to describe the size and composition of the market; and **causal research**, to test hypotheses about cause-and-effect relationships. Managers often start with exploratory research and later follow with descriptive and/or causal research.

A sad example of the need for marketing research was a self-help project initiated on U.S. Indian reservations. A total of fifty-two hotels were built as a result of promoting and anticipating tourism. Only two survived because of poorly conceived plans. In several cases, hotels were built in seldom-visited

A cruise in Victoria Harbor is a popular tourist activity in Hong Kong. Tourist authorities such as the Hong Kong Tourist Association use research to determine who comes to their cities and what tourist attractions create value for them. Courtesy of Norman Chan/Shutterstock.

remote areas. Marketing research could have provided valuable information, such as visitor trends to the areas, identification of possible market segments, plus their size and travel preferences.[25]

Developing the Research Plan

The second marketing research step calls for determining the needed information and developing a data collection plan.

Determining Specific Information Needs

Research objectives must be translated into specific information needs. When Marriott decided to research a new lower-priced hotel system, it had two goals: to pull travelers away from competitors and to minimize cannibalization of its own existing hotels. This research might call for the following specific information:[26]

- What features should the hotel offer?

- How should the new hotels be priced?

- Where should the hotels be located? Can they safely be located near existing Marriott hotels without incurring cannibalization?

- What are the probable sales and profits?

Gathering Secondary Information

To meet a manager's information needs, researchers can gather secondary data, primary data, or both. **Secondary data** consist of information already in existence somewhere, having been collected for another purpose. **Primary data** consist of information collected for the specific purpose at hand.

Researchers usually start by gathering secondary data. Secondary data are usually obtained more quickly and at a lower cost than primary data. For example, Restaurants USA, published by the National Restaurant Association, provides a yearly projection of sales for food-service establishments, presenting the projections by state and by industry segment. A company has the options of paying a research firm to develop this information or of joining the National Restaurant Association and receiving this information through its publication. The latter is more cost effective. Groups on social media sites can also be good sources of secondary information. LinkedIn, for example, has groups that include hotel sales, revenue management, event management, and lodging, food, and beverage trends.

Basing decisions on secondary data, however, can also present problems. The required information may not exist. Even when it exists, it might not be very relevant, accurate, current, and impartial. For example, a trade magazine wanted to identify the best hotel chains in the minds of corporate travel managers and travel agents. It distributed its survey as inserts in its magazine. The response rate was less than 0.05 percent. Yet the magazine issued a ranking based on this unreliable response rate.[27] Additionally, if research of this type is not properly designed, it can favor the companies with the most hotels or restaurants because they will be more familiar to the respondent.

eCONNECT   The Hospitality Sales and Marketing Association International (HSMAI) provides a wealth of secondary information in the eConnect Web site. HSMAI has done a great job of cataloging information from a variety of sources. This portal, which delivers global information and resources on hospitality marketing topics, is a great resource for marketing professionals and students of hospitality marketing.

The site is divided into seven sections: industry news and resources, hotel sales and marketing, Internet marketing and social media, revenue management, resort marketing, destination marketing and hospitality sales, and marketing education. Each section contains information from a variety of sources, press releases, articles, suppliers, books, whitepapers, webinars and blogs. eConnect can be accessed through www.hsmai.org. HSMAI offers special memberships rates for students and faculty members.

5.4   HSMAI
eCONNECT,
http://www.
hsmaieconnect.org/index.html:
Look at the types of information
provided by eConnect.

TABLE 5–3
Planning Primary Data Collection

Research Approaches	Contact Methods	Sampling Plan	Research Instruments
Observation	Mail	Sampling unit	Questionnaire
Survey	Telephone	Sample size	Mechanical instruments
Experiment	Personal	Sampling procedure	
	Online		

Secondary data provide a good starting point for marketing research. However, when secondary sources cannot provide all the needed information, the company must collect primary data.

Planning Primary Data Collection

Some managers collect primary data by developing a few questions and finding people to interview. But data collected casually can be useless or, even worse, misleading. Table 5–3 shows that designing a plan for primary data collection calls for decisions about research approaches, contact methods, a sampling plan, and research instruments.

RESEARCH APPROACHES   Three basic research approaches are observations, surveys, and experiments. **Observational research** is the gathering of primary data by observing relevant people, actions, and situations. For example, a multiunit food-service operator sends researchers into competing restaurants to learn menu item prices, check portion sizes and consistency, and observe point-of-purchase merchandising. Another restaurant evaluates possible new locations by checking the locations of competing restaurants, traffic patterns, and neighborhood conditions. A hotel chain sends observers posing as guests into its coffee shops to check on cleanliness and customer service.

Observational research can yield information that people are normally unwilling or unable to provide. Observing numerous plates containing uneaten portions of the same menu item indicates that the food is not satisfactory. But feelings, beliefs, and attitudes that motivate buying behavior cannot be observed. Long-run or infrequent behavior is also difficult to observe. Because of these limitations, researchers often supplement observation with survey research.

A wide range of companies now use **ethnographic research**, which involves sending trained observers to watch and interact with consumers in their "natural habitat."

> Hotel companies will send researchers into hotel rooms after the guest has checked out to see how the guest has changed the furniture and accessories in the room to fit their wants. For example, did the guest move the TV around so they could see it while working at the desk? Did she move furniture next to the desk to create additional work space, to put materials on while they were working? By observing how the customer uses the room, ethnographers can help designers create rooms and furniture that meet the needs of the guest. Ethnographers have also helped in the design of hotel lobbies to make them more social. Rather than working, reading, watching television or spending time on social media in the confines of her room, the guest can now come to the lobby and engage in these activities in an inviting and open environment.

Ethnographic research often yields the kinds of details that just don't emerge from traditional research questionnaires or focus groups. Whereas traditional quantitative research approaches seek to test known hypotheses and obtain answers to well-defined product or strategy questions, observational research can generate fresh customer and market insights. The beauty of ethnography is that it provides a richer

Marketing Highlight   Ethnographic Research: Watching What Consumers Really Do

5–1 A girl walks into a bar and says to the bartender, "Give me a Diet Coke and a clear sight line to those guys drinking Miller Lite in the corner." If you're waiting for a punch line, this is no joke. The "girl" in this situation is Emma Gilding, corporate ethnographer at ad agency Ogilvy & Mather. In this case, her job is to hang out in bars around the country and watch groups of guys knocking back beers with their friends. No kidding. This is honest-to-goodness, cutting-edge marketing research—ethnography style.

As a videographer filmed the action, Gilding kept tabs on how close the guys stood to one another. She eavesdropped on stories and observed how the mantle was passed from one speaker to another, as in a tribe around a campfire. Back at the office, a team of trained anthropologists and psychologists pored over more than 70 hours of footage from five similar nights in bars from San Diego to Philadelphia. One key insight: Miller is favored by groups of drinkers, while its main competitor, Bud Lite, is a beer that sells to individuals. The result was a hilarious series of ads that cut from a Miller Lite drinker's weird experiences in the world—getting caught in the subway taking money from a blind musician's guitar case or hitching a ride in the desert with a deranged trucker—to shots of him regaling friends with tales over a brew. The Miller Lite ads got high marks from audiences for their entertainment value and emotional resonance.

Today's marketers face many difficult questions: What do customers *really* think about a product and what do they say about it to their friends? How do they *really* use it? Will they tell you? *Can* they tell you? All too often, traditional research simply can't provide accurate answers. To get deeper insights, many companies use ethnographic research, watching and interacting with consumers in their "natural environments."

Ethnographers are looking for "consumer truth." In surveys and interviews, customers may state (and fully believe) certain preferences and behaviors, when the reality is actually quite different. Ethnography provides an insider's tour of the customer's world, helping marketers get at what consumers *really* do rather than what they *say* they do. "That might mean catching a heart-disease patient scarfing down a meatball sub and a cream soup while extolling the virtues of healthy eating," observes one ethnographer, "or a diabetic vigorously salting his sausage and eggs after explaining how he refuses jelly for his toast."[28]

By entering the customer's world, ethnographers can scrutinize how customers think and feel as it relates to their products. Ethnographic research often yields the kinds of intimate details that just don't emerge from traditional focus groups and surveys. For example, focus groups told the Best Western hotel chain that it's men who decide when to stop for the night and where to stay. But videotapes of couples on cross-country journey showed it was usually the women. And observation can often uncover problems that customers don't even know they have. By videotaping consumers in the shower, plumbing fixture maker Moen uncovered safety risks that consumers didn't recognize—such as the habit some women have of shaving their legs while holding on to one unit's temperature control. Moen would find it almost impossible to discover such design flaws simply by asking questions.

Experiencing firsthand what customers experience can also provide powerful insights. Thus more and more marketing researchers are getting up close and personal with consumers—watching them closely as they act and interact in natural settings or stepping in to observe firsthand how they behave.

Source: Adapted excerpts and other information from Brooks Barnes, "Disney Expert Uses Science to Draw Boy Viewers," *New York Times* (April 14, 2009): A1; Linda Tischler, "Every Move You Make," *Fast Company* (April 2004): 73–75; and Ellen Byron, "Seeing Store Shelves Through Senior Eyes," *Wall Street Journal* (September 14, 2009): B1; Spencer E. Ante, with Cliff Edwards, "The Science of Desire," *Bloomberg Businessweek* (June 5, 2006), accessed August 25, 2011, http://www.businessweek.com/magazine/content/06_23/b3987083.htm

understanding of consumers than traditional research.[29] This is especially important in hotels and restaurants and all hospitality products where there is social interaction between the customers. One problem with customer research is consumers cannot always tell you what they want, especially if the product has not been developed. Ethnography gives us insight into how consumers use a product that they may not be able to articulate.

Beyond conducting ethnographic research in physical consumer environments, many companies now routinely conduct "Webnography" research—observing consumers in a natural context on the Internet. Observing people as they interact online can provide useful insights into both online and off-line buying motives and behavior.[30]

Observational and ethnographic research often yields the kinds of details that just don't emerge from traditional research questionnaires or focus groups. Yes, companies are still using focus groups, surveys, and demographic data to glean insights into the consumer's mind. But closely observing people where they live and work allows companies to zero in on their customers' unarticulated desires.[31] Agrees another researcher, "Classic market research doesn't go far enough. It can't grasp what people can't imagine or articulate. Think of the Henry Ford quote: 'If I had asked people what they wanted, they would have said faster horses.' "[32]

Survey research is the approach best suited to gathering descriptive information. Survey research can be structured or unstructured. Structured surveys use formal lists of questions asked of all respondents in the same way. Unstructured surveys let the interviewer probe respondents and guide the interview according to their answers.

Survey research may be direct or indirect. In the direct approach, the researcher asks direct questions about behavior or thoughts, for example, "Why don't you eat at Arby's?" Using the indirect approach, the researcher might ask: "What kinds of people eat at Arby's?" From the response, the researcher may be able to discover why the consumer avoids Arby's. In fact, it may suggest factors the consumer is not consciously aware of.

The major advantage of survey research is its flexibility. It can be used to obtain many different kinds of information in many different marketing situations. Depending on the survey design, it may also provide information more quickly and at lower cost than can be obtained by observational or experimental research.

Survey research also has some limitations. Sometimes people are unable to answer survey questions because they cannot remember or never thought about what they do and why. Or they may be reluctant to answer questions asked by unknown interviewers about things that they consider private. Busy people may not want to take the time. Respondents may answer survey questions even when they do not know the answer in order to appear smart or well informed. Or they may try to help the interviewer by giving pleasing answers. Careful survey design can help minimize these problems.

Experimental Research

The most scientifically valid research is experimental research, designed to capture cause-and-effect relationships by eliminating competing explanations of the observed findings. If the experiment is well designed and executed, research and marketing managers can have confidence in the conclusions.

Experiments call for selecting matched groups of subjects, subjecting them to different treatments, controlling extraneous variables, and checking whether observed response differences are statistically significant. If we can eliminate or control extraneous factors, we can relate the observed effects to the variations in the treatments or stimuli. American Airlines might introduce in-flight Internet service on one of its regular flights from Chicago to Tokyo and charge $15 one week and $10 the next week. If the plane carried approximately the same number of first-class passengers each week and the particular weeks made no difference, the airline could relate any significant difference in the number of passengers using the service to the different prices charged. Marketers using direct mail often will test different pricing levels when they send out an offer.

Experimental research is best suited for gathering causal information. Researchers at Arby's might use experiments before adding a new sandwich to the menu to answer such questions as the following:

- By how much will the new sandwich increase Arby's sales?

- How will the new sandwich affect the sales of other menu items?

- Which advertising approach would have the greatest effect on sales of the sandwich?

- How would different prices affect the sales of the product?

- Should the new item be targeted toward adults, children, or both?

For example, to test the effects of two different prices, Arby's might set up the following simple experiment. The company could introduce the new sandwich at one price in its restaurants in one city and at another price in restaurants in a similar city. If the cities are very similar and if all other marketing efforts for the sandwich are identical, differences in sales volume between the two cities should be related to the price charged. More complex experiments can be designed to include other variables and other locations.

Contact Methods

Information can be collected by mail, telephone, or personal interview.

Mail questionnaires have many advantages. They can be used to collect large amounts of information at a low cost per respondent. Respondents may give more honest answers to personal questions on a mail questionnaire than they would to an unknown interviewer in person or over the phone. No interviewer is involved to bias respondents' answers. Mail questionnaires are convenient for respondents, who can answer the survey when they have time. It is also a good way to reach people who often travel, such as meeting planners.

Mail questionnaires also have some disadvantages. They are not very flexible, they require simple and clearly worded questions, all respondents answer the same questions in a fixed order, and the researcher cannot adapt the questionnaire based on earlier answers. Mail surveys usually take longer to complete than telephone or personal surveys, and the response rate (the number of people returning completed questionnaires) is often very low. When the response rate is low, respondents may not be typical of the population being sampled. Also, the researcher has little control over who answers the questionnaire in the household or office.

Telephone interviewing provides a method for gathering information quickly. It also offers greater flexibility than mail questionnaires. Interviewers can explain questions that are not understood; they can skip some questions and probe more on others, depending on respondents' answers. Telephone interviewing allows greater sample control. Interviewers can ask to speak to respondents who have the desired characteristics or can even request someone by name, and response rates tend to be higher than with mail questionnaires.

Customer intercept surveys collected from people in a shopping mall can be a good way to access respondents for a survey. The survey often begins with screening questions to eliminate people who are not part of the target market of the hospitality firm conducting the research. Courtesy of Pearson Learning Photo Studio.

Telephone interviewing also has drawbacks. The cost per respondent is higher than with mail questionnaires, and some people may not want to discuss personal questions with an interviewer. Using an interviewer increases flexibility but also introduces interviewer bias. The interviewer's manner of speaking, small differences in the way interviewers ask questions, and other personal factors may affect respondents' answers. Different interviewers may interpret and record responses in a variety of ways, and under time pressures, there is the possibility that some interviewers may record answers without actually asking the questions.

One growing use of telephone surveys is when the customer volunteers to take the survey and calls into a toll-free number. The customer is told at the time of purchase that he or she has been selected to take part in a survey and will receive an incentive for taking part in it. Usually these incentives range from $3 to $5 off on their next visit. Some of these surveys are automated, which reduces the cost of the survey. Phil Friedman, CEO of McAlister's Deli, states that McAlister's uses a customer call-in system, which works well. McAlister's has over 150 restaurants, mainly in the midwestern and southwestern regions of the United States. The results of the survey are posted every day on the Web. They can be searched by location, date of survey, and survey question. McAlister's shows how companies are taking advantage of technology to develop low-cost customer feedback systems that provide easy access to information.[33]

Unfortunately, the general public has become increasingly reluctant to participate in telephone surveys. Many unethical companies have misled respondents into believing that legitimate research is being conducted when in fact this was a ruse for a sales call. Thieves have also used this approach to find out when homeowners are likely to be away and even to determine the contents of the house.

Personal interviewing takes two forms: individual (intercept) and group interviewing. The later methods are called qualitative methods. Intercept interviewing involves talking with people in their homes, offices, on the street, or in shopping malls. The interviewer must gain the interviewee's cooperation, and the time involved can range from a few minutes to several hours. For longer surveys, a small payment is sometimes offered to respondents in return for their time.

Intercept interviews are widely used in tourism research. For instance, Steamboat Springs, Colorado, used this technique to interview 600 summer visitors to the city. Intercept interviews allow the research sponsor to reach known visitors in a short period of time. There may be few or no alternative methods of reaching visitors whose names and addresses are unknown. Intercept interviews generally involve the use of judgmental sampling. The interviewer may be given guidelines as to whom to "intercept," such as 20 percent under age 20 and 40 percent over age 60. This always leaves room for error and bias on the part of the interviewer, who may not be able to correctly judge age, race, and even sex from appearances. Interviewers may also be uncomfortable talking to certain ethnic or age groups.

The main drawbacks to personal interviews are cost and sampling. Personal interviews may cost three to four times as much as telephone interviews. Because group interview studies generally use small sample sizes to keep time and costs down, it may be difficult to generalize from the results. In addition, because interviewers have more freedom in personal interviews, however, interview bias is a greater problem.

A common type of group interviewing is a focus group. Focus group interviewing is usually conducted by inviting six to ten people to gather for a few hours with a trained moderator to talk about a product, service, or organization. The moderator needs objectivity, knowledge of the subject and industry, and some understanding of group and consumer behavior. Participants normally receive a small sum or gift certificates for attending. The meeting is held in a pleasant place, and refreshments are served to create a relaxed environment. The moderator starts with broad questions before moving to more specific issues, encouraging open and easy discussion to foster group dynamics that will bring out true feelings and thoughts. At the same time, the interviewer focuses the discussion, hence the name "focus group" interviewing. Comments are recorded through note taking or on videotape and studied later to understand consumers' buying process. In many cases, a two-way mirror separates respondents from observers, who commonly include personnel from the ad agency and the client.

Focus group interviewing is rapidly becoming one of the major marketing research tools for gaining insight into consumers' thoughts and feelings. This method is especially suited for use by managers of hotels and restaurants, who have easy access to their customers. For example, some hotel managers often invite a group of hotel guests from a particular market segment to have a free breakfast with them. During the breakfast the manager gets a chance to meet the guests and discuss what they like about the hotel and what the hotel could do to make their stay more enjoyable and comfortable. The guests appreciate this recognition, and the manager gains valuable information. Restaurant managers use the same approach by holding discussion meetings with guests at lunch or dinner.

Here are examples of how restaurants have used group interviews:

- A steakhouse suffering from declining sales went to its customers to gain insight into the causes of its problem. Two focus groups were conducted, one composed of customers who indicated they would return and another composed of those who said they would not. From these sessions, the owners learned that patrons considered the restaurant a fun place but thought the food was boring. The problem was solved by expanding and upgrading the menu.[34]

- Focus groups provided critical information to Andy Reis of Café Provincial in Evanston, Illinois. He found that his clientele wanted valet parking. Reis had assumed because on-street parking and a nearby parking garage were available that parking was not a problem. He also found that his diners felt uncomfortable in the restaurant's Terrace Room. This was a casual dining room with glass tables and porch furniture. Apparently, it was too casual for his diners. The Terrace Room was remodeled, and valet parking was added. Now people request to sit in the Terrace Room. Reis states that focus groups are worthwhile if you listen carefully.[35]

In-depth interviews are another form of qualitative personal interviewing. As the name states, these are individual interviews using open-ended questions. They allow the researcher to probe and gain insight into consumer behavior. For example, if someone recalls one of his or her more memorable hotel stays involved a luxurious hotel suite, the researcher can probe to see what made the hotel suite luxurious. In-depth surveys can be used instead of focus groups when it is difficult to put together a focus group. For example, we wanted to probe a number of concepts with luxury hotel guests. It was impossible to get six or more travelers to participate in a focus group at a specific time. We were able to gain interviews of individuals during breakfast.[36]

Qualitative research is useful to gain insight into definitions and concepts. A good understanding of concepts is critical to designing a survey instrument; thus, focus groups and in-depth surveys are often done as part of the survey development process. Qualitative research is also useful to gain insight into survey results. For example, quick-service restaurant customers may tell us that speed of service is important. As managers, we need to know how customers measure and define speed of service. This information can be gained through qualitative research.

Online Interview

There are so many ways to use the Internet to do research. A company can embed a questionnaire on its Web site in different ways and offer an incentive to answer it, or it can place a banner on a frequently visited site such as Yahoo!, inviting people to answer some questions and possibly win a prize. One theme park management company has developed a survey panel of 11,000 guests. It surveys the members of the panel on a regular bias through the Internet. The company's research director claims Internet surveying saves him at least $30,000 over telephone surveying and provides good information.[37]

Online research is estimated to make up over 35 percent of all survey-based research, and Internet-based questionnaires also accounted for a third of U.S. spending on market research surveys.[38] Yet, as popular as online research methods are, smart companies are choosing to use them to augment rather than replace more traditional methods. A director of marketing states, "Online is not a solution in and of itself to all of our business challenges," he said, "but it does expand our toolkit."

Internet surveying is growing in popularity. It offers quick and inexpensive access to many samples. The data are also automatically tabulated, eliminating errors and time. Courtesy of Ruth Jenkinson © Dorling Kindersley.

Jacob Brown, a marketing researcher specializing in Internet-based surveys, has these suggestions. As with other surveys, always do a pretest. If you have a limited number of names in your database and don't want to waste them on a pretest, buy a list with similar characteristics and use this list for your pretest. This is a much better alternative to not pretesting. Look at the number of people who drop out after each question. If there is a high dropout rate after one question, this could indicate problems with that question. If the completion rate is low, but no one question has a high dropout rate, this could indicate the survey is too long. Using simple technology for a consumer market is critical. Don't expect respondents to wait for graphics to load or to reset their monitor's resolution. Internet surveys are quick and can be inexpensive. The response rate can be a problem if they are not properly designed and targeted.[39]

Marketing Highlight 5–2, "Pros and Cons of Online Research," outlines some of the advantages and disadvantages of online research thus far. Online researchers

Marketing Highlight   Pros and Cons of Online Research

5–2

Advantages

- *Online research is inexpensive.* A typical e-mail survey can cost between 20 and 50 percent less than what a conventional survey costs, and return rates can be as high as 50 percent.

- *Online research is fast.* Online surveys are fast because the survey can automatically direct respondents to applicable questions and transmit results immediately. One estimate says that 75 to 80 percent of a survey's targeted response can be generated in 40 hours using online methods compared to a telephone survey that can take 70 days to obtain 150 interviews.

- *People tend to be honest online.* Britain's online polling company YouGov.com surveyed 250 people via intercom in a booth and the other half online asking questions such as "Should there be more aid to Africa?" Online answers were deemed much more honest. People may be more open about their opinions when they can respond privately and not to another person whom they feel might be judging them, especially on sensitive topics.

- *Online research is versatile.* Increased broadband penetration offers online research even more flexibility and capabilities. For instance, virtual reality software lets visitors inspect 3D models of products such as cameras, cars, and medical equipment and manipulate product characteristics. Even at the basic tactile level, online surveys can make answering a questionnaire easier and more fun than paper-and-pencil versions.

- *Data are more accurate.* Online interviewing programs enable the survey responses to be tabulated as the respondent is entering them. As in any form of computer-aided interviewing, the next question automatically comes up in branching questions or skip sequences. For example, if a business traveler is to answer one set of questions and a pleasure traveler another set, when asked if you were traveling for business or pleasure, the proper set will come up.

Disadvantages

- *Samples can be small and skewed.* Some 33 percent of households are without Internet access in the United States; the percentage is even higher among lower-income groups, in rural areas, and in most parts of Asia, Latin America, and Central and Eastern Europe, where socioeconomic and education levels also differ. Although people older than 65 are one of the fastest growing segments of Internet users, they have been light users. Thus, one could expect to get a younger sample through an Internet survey. Tourism research has found significant differences in responses received from pen-and-paper surveys and Internet surveys, including demographic differences.[40] Although it's certain that more and more people will go online, online market researchers must find creative ways to reach population segments on the other side of the "digital divide." One option is to combine off-line sources with online findings. Providing temporary Internet access at locations such as malls and recreation centers is another strategy.

- *Online market research is prone to technological problems and inconsistencies.* Because online research is relatively new, many market researchers have not gotten survey designs right. Others overuse technology, concentrating on the bells and whistles and graphics while ignoring basic survey design guidelines. Problems also arise because browser software varies. The Web designer's final product may look very different on the research subject's screen.

Sources: "Survey: Internet Should Remain Open to All," www.consumeraffairs.com, January 25, 2006; "Highlights from the National Consumers League's Survey on Consumers and Communications Technologies: Current and Future Use," www.nclnet.org/, July 21, 2005; Catherine Arnold, "Not Done Net; New Opportunities Still Exist in Online Research," *Marketing News* (April 1, 2004): 17; Louella Miles, "Online, on Tap," *Marketing* (June 16, 2004): 39–40; Suzy Bashford, "The Opinion Formers," *Revolution* (May 2004): 42–46; Nima M. Ray and Sharon W. Tabor, "Contributing Factors; Several Issues Affect e-Research Validity," *Marketing News* (September 15, 2003): 50; Bob Lamons, "Eureka! Future of B to B Research Is Online," *Marketing News* (September 24, 2001): 9–10.

have also begun to use instant messaging (IM) in various ways—to conduct a chat with a respondent, to probe more deeply with a member of an online focus group, or to direct respondents to a Web site.[41] IM is also a useful way to get teenagers to open up on topics.

A primary qualitative Web-based research approach is **online focus groups.** Such focus groups offer many advantages over traditional focus groups. Participants can log in from anywhere; all they need is a laptop and a Web connection. Thus, the Internet works well for bringing together people from different parts of the country or world, especially those in higher-income groups who can't spare the time to travel to a central site. Also, researchers can conduct and monitor online focus groups from just about anywhere, eliminating travel, lodging, and facility costs. Finally, although online focus groups require some advance scheduling, results are almost immediate.

Online focus groups can take any of several formats. Most occur in real time, in the form of online chat room discussions in which participants and a moderator sit around a virtual table exchanging comments. Alternatively, researchers might set up an online message board on which respondents interact over the course of several days or a few weeks. Participants log in daily and comment on focus group topics.

Although low in cost and easy to administer, online focus groups can lack the real-world dynamics of more personal approaches. To overcome these shortcomings, some researchers are now adding real-time audio and video to their online focus groups. For example, online research firm Channel M2 "puts the human touch back into online research" by assembling focus group participants in people-friendly "virtual interview rooms."[42] Participants are recruited using traditional methods and then sent a Web camera so that both their verbal and nonverbal reactions can be recorded. Participants receive instructions via e-mail, including a link to the Channel M2 online interviewing room and a toll-free teleconference number to call. At the appointed time, when they click on the link and phone in, participants sign on and see the Channel M2 interview room, complete with live video of the other participants, text chat, screen or slide sharing, and a whiteboard. Once the focus group is under way, questions and answers occur in "real time" in a remarkably lively setting. Participants comment spontaneously—verbally, via text messaging, or both. Researchers can "sit in" on the focus group from anywhere, seeing and hearing every respondent. Or they can review a recorded version at a later date.

The Internet has become an important new tool for conducting research and developing customer insights. But today's marketing researchers are going even further on the Web—well beyond structured online surveys, focus groups, and Web communities. Increasingly, they are listening to and watching consumers by actively mining the rich veins of unsolicited, unstructured, "bottom-up" customer information already coursing around the Web. This might be as simple as scanning customer reviews and comments on the company's brand site or shopping sites such as zagat.com or tripadvisor.com. Or it might mean using sophisticated Web-analysis tools to deeply analyze mountains of consumer comments and messages found in blogs or on social networking sites, such as Facebook or Twitter. Listening to and watching consumers online can provide valuable insights into what consumers are saying or feeling about brands. As one information expert puts it, "The Web knows what you want."[43]

Perhaps the most explosive issue facing online researchers concerns consumer privacy. Some critics fear that unethical researchers will use the e-mail addresses and confidential responses gathered through surveys to sell products after the research is completed. They are concerned about the use of technologies that collect personal information online without the respondents' consent. Failure to address such privacy issues could result in angry, less-cooperative consumers and increased government intervention. Despite these concerns, most industry insiders predict continued healthy growth for online marketing research.[44]

Sampling Plan

Marketing researchers usually draw conclusions about large consumer groups by taking a sample. A **sample** is a segment of the population selected to represent the population as a whole. Ideally, the sample should be representative and allow the

TABLE 5–4

Types of Samples

Probability samples	
Simple random sample	Every member of the population has a known and equal chance of selection.
Stratified random sample	The population is divided into mutually exclusive groups (e.g., age groups), and random samples are drawn from each group.
Cluster (area) sample	The population is divided into mutually exclusive groups (e.g., blocks), and the researcher draws a sample of the groups to interview.
Nonprobability samples	
Convenience sample	The researcher selects the easiest population members from which to obtain information.
Judgment sample	The researcher uses his or her judgment to select population members who are good prospects for accurate information.
Quota sample	The researcher finds and interviews a prescribed number of people in each of several categories.

researcher to make accurate estimates of the thoughts and behaviors of the larger population.

Designing the sample calls for four decisions. First, who will be surveyed? This is not always obvious. For example, to study the decision-making process for a family vacation, should the researcher interview the husband, wife, other family members, the travel agent, or all of these? The researcher must determine what type of information is needed and who is most likely to have it.

Second, how many people should be surveyed? Large samples give more reliable results than small samples. However, it is not necessary to sample the entire target market or even a large portion to obtain reliable results. If well chosen, samples of less than 1 percent of a population can give good reliability.

Third, how should the sample be chosen? Sample members might be chosen at random from the entire population (a probability sample), or the researcher might select people who are easiest to obtain information from (a convenience sample). The researcher might also choose a specified number of participants from each of several demographic groups (a quota sample). These and other ways of drawing samples have different costs and time limitations and varying accuracy and statistical properties. The needs of the research project will determine which method is most effective. Table 5–4 lists the various kinds of samples.

A fourth decision—when will the survey be given?—is important in personal surveys. The days and hours should be representative of the flow of traffic. For example if 70 percent of the customers come after 7 P.M., then the data collection needs to be heavier in the evening. The type of guest may change depending on the day or time. People working in the area may visit a restaurant at lunch, whereas people living in the area visit the restaurant for dinner. Businesspersons stay at a hotel Sunday through Thursday, and pleasure travelers are heavier users on weekends. Thus, if the population of interest is business travelers, there should be heavier sampling during the week. Failure to match the time the data is collected with business patterns can result in invalid survey results.

RESEARCH INSTRUMENTS   In collecting primary data, marketing researchers have a choice of two main research instruments: the questionnaire and mechanical devices.

You can usually spot several errors in a carelessly prepared questionnaire (see Marketing Highlight 5–3).

Marketing Highlight   A "Questionable" Questionnaire

5–3 Suppose that the following questionnaire has been prepared by a restaurant manager to build a profile of his potential market. How do you as a consumer feel about each question?

1. What is your income to the nearest hundred dollars?

   People don't necessarily know their income to the nearest hundred dollars, nor do they want to reveal their income that closely. Furthermore, a questionnaire should never open with such a personal question. Personal questions should be placed at the end of the survey.

2. How often do you go out to eat?

   The question is ambiguous. To provide useful information one would need to know, at a minimum, the meal period and type of restaurant.

3. During the business week, how often do you eat breakfast?

   1 _____ 2 _____ 3 _____ 4 _____ 5 _____

   The responses are not collectively exhaustive. That is, they do not provide all responses possible. What if a person never eats breakfast? The addition of a sixth response, 0 _____, would solve the problem.

4. On average, how much do you spend for lunch?

   _____ 0 to $2   _____ $2 to $4
   _____ $4 to $6   _____ $6 to $8

The choices are overlapping. If someone spent $2, $4, or $6, he or she could mark his or her response in one of two spots. Also, the response choices are not collectively exhaustive. If someone spends more than $8, there is nowhere to mark this response.

5. Would you like (name of restaurant) to have live bands on Friday and Saturday night?

   Yes ( ) No ( )

   The word *like* does not indicate purchase behavior. Many respondents would answer yes because it offers them an entertainment option, but they would not come out on a regular basis. Also, many times there is a cost to adding an extra feature. If the respondent is going to pay for the cost through a cover charge or higher drink prices, it should be addressed. Finally, the question does not specify the type of band. Someone who wants a country-and-western band may answer yes and then be disappointed when the manager puts in a heavy metal band.

6. Did you receive more restaurant coupons this April or last April?

   Who can remember this?

7. What are the most salient and determinant attributes in your evaluation of restaurants?

   What are "salient and determinant attributes"? Don't use big words that the respondent may not understand.

The questionnaire is by far the most common instrument, whether administered in person, by phone, by e-mail, or online. Questionnaires are very flexible—there are many ways to ask questions. Closed-end questions include all the possible answers, and subjects make choices among them. Examples include multiple-choice questions and scale questions. Open-end questions allow respondents to answer in their own words. In a survey of airline users, Southwest Airlines might simply ask, "What is your opinion of Southwest Airlines?" Or it might ask people to complete a sentence: "When I choose an airline, the most important consideration is ...." These and other kinds of open-end questions often reveal more than closed-end questions because they do not limit respondents' answers.

Open-end questions are especially useful in exploratory research, when the researcher is trying to find out *what* people think but is not measuring *how many* people think in a certain way. Closed-end questions, on the other hand, provide answers that are easier to interpret and tabulate.

Researchers should also use care in the *wording* and *ordering* of questions. They should use simple, direct, and unbiased wording. Questions should be arranged in a logical order. The first question should create interest if possible, and difficult or personal questions should be asked last so that respondents do not become defensive.

In preparing a questionnaire, the marketing researcher must decide what questions to ask, what form the questions should take, and how to word and sequence the questions. Questionnaires too often omit questions that should be answered and include questions that cannot, will not, or need not be answered. Each question should be examined to ensure that it contributes to the research objectives. Questions that are merely interesting should be dropped. You can usually spot several errors in a carelessly prepared questionnaire (see Marketing Highlight 5–3).

Researchers in the hospitality industry must be extremely careful in developing questions and selecting the sample not to offend respondents unwittingly. This problem is less pervasive with many products, such as building tile or brass fittings. A classic example of a marketing research mistake was made by a U.S. airline. This company offered a special companion price for business travelers with the idea that the companion would be the executive's spouse. Following the promotion, questionnaires were sent to the spouse, not the executive. These innocently asked, "How did you like the recent companion trip?" In several cases the answer was, "What trip? I didn't go!" The airline received angry calls and threats of suits for invasion of privacy or contribution to the breakup of a marriage (Table 5–5).

MECHANICAL INSTRUMENTS   Researchers also use mechanical instruments to monitor consumer behavior. These methods are as simple as recording how much customers consume to measuring how brain activities change when exposed to different marketing stimuli. Restaurant managers use POS systems to track the sales of menu items. Managers can look for increases in sales of promotional items, to measure the success of a promotion. Customer loyalty programs track the purchasing habits of customers and use this information to offer loyalty rewards. If customers never buy an appetizer, they may be offered an appetizer as a loyalty bonus since this free item is not likely to reduce the customer's check average. Keeping track of what customers consume is a very simple yet very effective way of understanding customer behavior.

Researchers are applying "neuromarketing," measuring brain activity to learn how consumers feel and respond. Marketing scientists using MRI scans and EEC devices have learned that tracking brain electrical activity and blood flow can provide companies with insights into what turns consumers on and off regarding their brands and marketing. "Companies have always aimed for the customers heart, but the head may make a better target," suggests one neuromarketer. "Neuromarketing is reaching consumers where the action is: the brain."[45]

PepsiCo's Frito-Lay unit uses neuromarketing to test commercials, product designs, and packaging. Recent EEG tests showed that, compared with shiny packages showing pictures of potato chips, matte beige bags showing potatoes and other healthy ingredients trigger less activity in an area of the brain associated with feelings of guilt. Needless to say, Frito-Lay quickly switched away from the shiny packaging. Although neuromarketing techniques can measure consumer involvement and emotional responses second by second, such brain responses can be difficult to interpret. Thus, neuromarketing is usually used in combination with other research approaches to gain a more complete picture of what goes on inside consumers' heads.[46]

PRESENTING THE RESEARCH PLAN   The final stage of developing the research plan is to putting the plan in writing so the plan can be reviewed by those involved in the implementation of the plan and those involved in using the results of the research can review the plan. The plan should cover the management problems addressed, the research objectives, information to be obtained, sources of secondary information and/or methods for collecting primary data, and how the results will aid in management decision making. The plan should also include research costs and expected benefits. A written research plan helps ensure that management and researchers have considered all the important aspects of the research and they agree on why and how the research will be done. The manager should review the proposal carefully before approving the project.

TABLE 5–5
Types of Questions

A. Closed-End Questions

Name	Description	Example
Dichotomous	A question offering two answer choices.	"In arranging this trip, did you personally phone Delta?" Yes ☐ No ☐
Multiple choice	A question offering three or more answer choices.	"With whom are you traveling on this flight?" No one ☐ Spouse ☐ Spouse and children ☐ Children only ☐ Business associates/friends/relatives ☐ An organized tour group ☐
Likert scale	A statement with which the respondent shows the amount of agreement or disagreement.	"Small airlines generally give better service than large ones." Strongly disagree / Disagree / Neither agree nor disagree / Agree / Strongly agree 1 ☐ 2 ☐ 3 ☐ 4 ☐ 5 ☐
Semantic differential	A scale is inscribed between two bipolar words, and the respondent selects the point that represents the direction and intensity of his or her feelings.	*Delta Airlines* Large X : ___ : ___ : ___ : ___ : ___ : Small Experienced ___ : ___ : ___ : ___ : X : ___ : Inexperienced Modern ___ : ___ : ___ : X : ___ : ___ : Old-fashioned
Importance scale	A scale that rates the importance of some attribute from "not at all important" to "extremely important"	"Airline food service to me is" Extremely important / Very important / Somewhat important / Not very important / Not at all important 1 ___ 2 ___ 3 ___ 4 ___ 5 ___
Rating scale	A scale that rates some attribute from "poor" to "excellent."	"Delta's food service is" Excellent / Very good / Good / Fair / Poor 1 ___ 2 ___ 3 ___ 4 ___ 5 ___
Intention-to-buy scale	A scale that describes the respondent's intentions to buy.	"If in-flight telephone service were available on a long flight, I would" Definitely Buy / Probably buy / Not certain / Probably not buy / Definitely not buy 1 ___ 2 ___ 3 ___ 4 ___ 5 ___

(continued)

145

TABLE 5–5 (*continued*)
Types of Questions

A. Closed-End Questions		
Name	**Description**	**Example**
B. Open-End Questions		
Completely unstructured	A question that respondents can answer in an almost unlimited number of ways.	"What is your opinion of Delta Airlines?"
Word association	Words are presented, one at a time, and respondents mention the first word that comes to mind.	"What is the first word that comes to your mind when you hear the following?" Airline _____ Delta _____ Travel _____
Sentence completion	Incomplete sentences are presented, one at a time, and respondents complete the sentence.	"When I choose an airline, the most important consideration in my decision is _____"
Story completion	An incomplete story is presented, and respondents are asked to complete it.	"I flew Delta a few days ago. I noticed that the exterior and interior of the plane had very bright colors. This aroused in me the following thoughts and feelings." *Now complete the story.*
Picture completion	A picture of two characters is presented, with one making a statement. Respondents are asked to identify with the other and fill in the empty balloon.	 *Fill in the empty balloon.*
Thematic apperception tests (TATs)	A picture is presented, and respondents are asked to make up a story about what they think is happening or may happen in the picture.	 *Make up a story about what you see.*

Implementing the Research Plan

The researcher puts the marketing research plan into action by collecting, processing, and analyzing the information. Data collection can be done by the company's marketing research staff, which affords the company greater control of the collection process and data quality or by outside firms. Outside firms that specialize in data collection can often do the job more quickly at lower cost.

The data-collection phase of the marketing research process is generally the most expensive and the most subject to error. The researcher should watch the fieldwork closely to ensure that the plan is implemented correctly and to guard against problems with contacting respondents who refuse to cooperate or who give biased or dishonest answers, and interviewers who make mistakes or take shortcuts.

The collected data must be processed and analyzed to pull out important information and findings. Data from questionnaires are checked for accuracy and completeness and coded for computer analysis. The researcher applies standard computer programs to prepare tabulations of results and to compute averages and other measures for the major variables.

Interpreting and Reporting the Findings

The researcher must now interpret the findings, draw conclusions, and report the conclusions to management. The researcher should avoid overwhelming managers with numbers, complex statistical techniques, and focus. Instead, management desires major findings that will be useful in decision making.

Interpretation should not be left entirely to the researcher. Findings can be interpreted in different ways, and discussions between researchers and managers will help point to the best interpretations. The manager should also confirm that the research project was executed properly. After reviewing the findings, the manager may raise additional questions that can be answered with research data. Researchers should make the data available to marketing managers, so that they can perform new analyses and test relationships on their own.

Interpretation is an important phase of the marketing process. The best research is meaningless if a manager blindly accepts wrong interpretations. Similarly, managers may have biased interpretations. They sometimes accept research results that show what they expected and reject those that did not provide expected or hoped-for answers. Thus, managers and researchers must work closely together when interpreting research results. Both share responsibility for the research process and resulting decisions.

Interpreting and reporting findings is the last step of the four-step research process. It is important for managers to remember that research is a process and that the researcher must proceed through all steps of the process. Marketing Highlight 5–4 explains some of the problems that can occur during a research project.

Information gathered by the company's marketing intelligence and marketing research systems can often benefit from additional analysis to help interpret the findings. This might include advanced statistical analysis to learn more about the relationships within a set of data. Such analysis allows managers to go beyond means and standard deviations in the data and answer such questions as the following:

- What are the major variables affecting sales, and how important is each?

- If the price is raised 10 percent and advertising is increased 20 percent, what will happen to sales?

- What are the best predictors of who are likely to come to my hotel versus my competitor's hotel?

- What are the best variables for segmenting my market, and how many segments exist?

Marketing Highlight   Research Problem Areas

5–4

1. **Making assumptions.** A restaurant was considering adding a piano bar. Researchers developed a customer survey. One question asked customers if they would like entertainment in the lounge, without mentioning the type of entertainment. The customers could answer this question positively, thinking of a dance band. The manager, seeing the positive responses, would put in the piano bar and then wonder why so many customers did not respond to the piano bar. Luckily, this question was modified during a pretest of the survey.

   A country club asked its members if they felt the club needed a renovation. Most members said "yes." The club then paid consultants to draw up designs for the renovations. When these, along with the proposed dues increase, were presented, the members expressed outrage at the higher dues. If the original survey had addressed the costs associated with the renovation, it could have saved thousands of dollars in consulting fees.

2. **Lack of qualitative information.** Most surveys reported in trade magazines provide descriptive information. For example, a study done by Procter & Gamble found that the most important attribute in the decision of frequent travelers to return to a hotel was a clean appearance. To use this information, management needs to know how its guests judge clean appearance. Through focus groups, managers can learn what guests look for to determine whether the room is clean, what irritants there are concerning cleanliness, and other more specific information.

3. **Failing to look at segments within a sample.** Survey results should be analyzed to determine difference between customer groups. Often, the arithmetic means (averages) for each question are calculated, and the survey is analyzed based on this information, which can mask important differences between segments. For example, a club surveyed its membership on how satisfied the members were with the lunches purchased in the dining room. The average of all responses was 2, with 1 being very satisfied, 3 being satisfied, and 5 being not satisfied. However, when the total sample was divided into membership classes, it was found that one category of members had a high level of satisfaction 1.5, whereas another class gave an average rating of 2.7. This informa-

tion is more useful to management than the overall mean of 2. Management now had to decide whether to invest additional money to build satisfaction for the members who gave the dining room a lower rating or promote its food and beverage room to the satisfied segment.

4. **Improper use of sophisticated statistical analysis.** One researcher reported that faculty size explained a remarkable 96 percent of the enrollment in hospitality management programs housed in business schools. He then presented a formula for projecting student enrollment based on the number of faculty, implying that if a school had three faculty members it would have 251 students, but if two more faculty were hired, it would have 426 students. Schools that base decisions on this formula might be disappointed.

   The researcher claimed that adding a professor would increase enrollment. What happens at most universities is professors are added to meet an increase in student enrollment. The number of faculty and students are positively correlated; however, students create faculty positions, not the other way around.

5. **Failure to have the sample representative of the population.** A sample is a segment of the population selected to represent the population as a whole. Ideally, the sample should be representative so that the researcher can make accurate estimates of the thoughts and behaviors of the larger population. It is common for hotel managers to receive a bonus based on a customer satisfaction score. Sometimes segments of the population give ratings that are lower than other segments, even though they seem satisfied with the service. For example, in one customer satisfaction survey, respondents between 26 and 35 years of age rated the service attributes of the company lower than other segments. However, they also rated the competition lower, making the company's relative satisfaction compared with the competition the same as other segments. This segment did not appear to be displeased with the service; they just tended to rate lower on the scale. When segments like this are present in the population, they can skew the results of the survey if they are overrepresented or underrepresented. If they are underrepresented, the overall satisfaction will increase; if they are overrepresented, the overall satisfaction score will decrease.

Marriott's Kauai Beach Club, A Marriott Vacation Club Resort. Marriott Vacation Club uses marketing research to make certain it provides maximum value for its guests. This is one of the reasons for Marriott Vacation Club's success in the timeshare business. Courtesy of David L. Moore - HIK/Alamy.

Mathematical models might also help marketers to make better decisions. Each model represents a real system, process, or outcome. These models can help answer the questions "what if" and "which is best." In the past 20 years, marketing scientists have developed a great number of models to help marketing managers make better marketing mix decisions, design sales territories and sales call plans, select sites for retail outlets, develop optimal advertising mixes, and forecast new-product sales.[47]

Marketing information has no value until managers use it to make better decisions. The information gathered must reach the appropriate marketing managers at the right time. Large companies have centralized MISs that provide managers with regular performance reports, intelligence updates, and reports on the results of studies. Managers need these routine reports for making regular planning, implementation, and control decisions. But marketing managers also need nonroutine information for special situations and on-the-spot decisions. For example, a sales manager having trouble with an important customer needs a summary of the account's sales during the past year. Or a restaurant manager whose restaurant has stocked out of a best-selling menu item needs to know the current inventory levels in the chain's other restaurants. In companies with centralized information systems, these managers must request the information from the MIS staff and wait. Often, the information arrives too late to be useful.

Recent developments in information handling have led to a revolution in information distribution. With recent advances in microcomputers, software, and communications, many companies are decentralizing their MISs and giving managers direct access to information stored in the systems. In some companies, marketing managers can use a desk terminal to tie into the company's information network. Without leaving their desks, they can obtain information from internal records or outside information services, analyze the information, prepare reports on a word processor, and communicate with others in the network through telecommunications. The Internet is an excellent source of marketing information (see Marketing Highlight 5–5).

Marketing Highlight   HSMAI's eConnect: A Great Source of Marketing Information

5–5 The Hospitality Sales and Marketing Association—International (HSMAI) has refined its eConnect Web site over the last eight years. HSMAI has done a great job of cataloging hospitality marketing information from a variety of sources.

This portal, which delivers global information and resources on a variety of hospitality marketing topics, is a great resource for marketing professionals and students of hospitality marketing. The Industry News and Events section contains current news from a variety of sources.

The Hotel Sales and Marketing section contains information everything from job descriptions to marketing plans. It also contains links to the major regional business newspapers in the United States. The site also features sections on revenue management and internet marketing and social media. Like the other sections, these sections feature a blog, allowing members to have a dialogue with each other. Hotels are now hiring managers in the areas of revenue management and social media marketing at the individual property level. Students wishing to obtain a position in this area can keep up-to-date by reading the information and postings on eConnect. Two other sections are resort marketing and destination marketing. The final section focuses on hospitality marketing education.

A wealth of marketing information has been gathered into one searchable site. eConnect can be accessed through www.hsmai.org. HSMAI offers special membership rates for students and faculty members. Students interested in hospitality marketing should become familiar with the eConnect Web site and take advantage of the resources it offers.

Such systems offer exciting prospects. They allow managers to obtain needed information directly and quickly, and tailor it to their needs. As more managers become skilled in using these systems and as improvements in technology make them more economical, hospitality companies will increasingly use decentralized MISs.

▪▩▩ International Marketing Research

International marketing researchers follow the same steps as domestic researchers, from defining the research problem and developing a research plan to interpreting and reporting the results. However, these researchers often face more and different problems. Whereas domestic researchers deal with fairly homogeneous markets within a single country, international researchers deal with markets in many different countries. These different markets often vary dramatically in their levels of economic development, cultures and customs, and buying patterns.

In many foreign markets, the international researcher has a difficult time finding good secondary data. Whereas U.S. marketing researchers can obtain reliable secondary data from dozens of domestic research services, many countries have almost no research services at all. Even the largest international research services operate in only a relative handful of countries. For example, A. C. Nielsen, the world's largest marketing research company, has offices in many countries outside the United States.[48] Thus, even when secondary information is available, it usually must be obtained from many different sources on a country-by-country basis, making the information difficult to combine or compare.

Because of the scarcity of good secondary data, international researchers often must collect their own primary data. Here researchers face problems not encountered domestically. For example, they may find it difficult simply to develop appropriate samples. Whereas U.S. researchers can use current telephone directories, census tract data, and any of several sources of socioeconomic data to construct samples, such information is largely lacking in many countries. Once the sample is drawn, the U.S. researcher usually can reach most respondents easily by telephone or mail or in person. Reaching respondents is often not so easy in other parts of the world. In some countries, few people have phones—there are only 4 phones per 1,000 people in Egypt, 6 in Turkey, and 32 in Argentina. In other countries, the postal system is notoriously unreliable. In Brazil, for instance, an estimated 30 percent of the mail is never delivered. In many developing countries, poor roads and transportation systems make certain areas hard to reach, making personal interviews difficult and expensive.[49]

Differences in cultures from country to country cause additional problems for international researchers. Language is the most obvious culprit. For example, questionnaires must be prepared in one language and then translated into the languages of each country researched. Responses then must be translated back into the original language for analysis and interpretation. This adds to research costs and increases the risks for error.

Translating a questionnaire from one language to another is far from easy. Many points are "lost" because idioms, phrases, and statements mean different things in different cultures. A Danish executive observed, "Check this out by having a different translator put back into English what you've translated from the English. You'll get the shock of your life. I remember [an example in which] 'out of sight, out of mind' had become 'invisible things are insane.'"[50]

Buying roles and consumer decision processes vary greatly from country to country, further complicating international marketing research. Consumers in different countries also vary in their attitudes toward marketing research. People in one country may be very willing to respond; in other countries, nonresponse can be a major problem. For example, customs in some Islamic countries prohibit people from talking with strangers—a researcher simply may not be allowed to speak by phone with women about brand attitudes or buying behavior. High functional illiteracy rates in many countries make it impossible to use a written survey for some segments. In addition, middle-class people in developing countries often make false claims in order to appear well off. For example, in a study of tea consumption in India, over 70 percent of middle-income respondents claimed that they used one of several national brands. However, the researchers had good reason to doubt these results; more than 60 percent of the tea sold in India is unbranded generic tea.

Despite these problems, the recent growth of international marketing has resulted in a rapid increase in the use of international marketing research. Global companies have little choice but to conduct such research. Although the costs and problems associated with international research may be high, the costs of not doing it—in terms of missed opportunities and mistakes—might be even higher. Once recognized, many of the problems associated with international marketing research can be overcome or avoided.

■■■ Marketing Research in Smaller Organizations

Managers of small businesses often believe that marketing research can be done only by experts in large companies with large research budgets. But many marketing research techniques can be used by smaller organizations and at little or no expense.

Managers of small businesses can obtain good marketing information by observing what occurs around them. Thus, restaurateurs can evaluate their customer mix by recording the number and type of customers in the restaurant at different times during the day. Competitor advertising can be monitored by collecting advertisements from local media.

Managers can conduct informal surveys using small convenience samples. The manager of a travel agency can learn what customers like and dislike about travel agencies by conducting informal focus groups, such as inviting small groups to lunch. Restaurant managers can talk with customers; hospital food-service managers can interview patients. Restaurant managers can make random phone calls during slack hours to interview consumers about where they eat out and what they think of various restaurants in the area. Managers can also conduct simple experiments. By changing the design in regular direct mailings and watching results, a manager can learn which marketing tactics work best. By varying newspaper advertisements, a manager can observe the effects of ad size and position, price coupons, and media used.

Small organizations can obtain secondary data. Many associations, local media, chambers of commerce, and government agencies provide special help to small organizations. The U.S. Small Business Administration offers dozens of free publications giving advice on topics ranging from planning advertising to ordering business signs. Local newspapers often provide information on local shoppers and their buying patterns.

Sometimes volunteers and colleges carry out research. Many colleges are seeking small businesses to serve as cases for projects in marketing research classes. Sales management classes are eager to do sales blitzes for hotels.

Thus, secondary data collection, observation, surveys, and experiments can be used effectively by small organizations with small budgets. Although informal research is less complex and costly, it must still be done carefully. Managers must think through the objectives of the research, formulate questions in advance, and recognize the biases systematically. If planned and implemented meticulously, low-cost research can provide reliable information for improving marketing decision making.

■■■ KEY TERMS

Causal research. Marketing research to test hypotheses about cause-and-effect relationships.

Data warehouses. Collect data from a variety of sources and store it in an accessible location.

Descriptive research. Marketing research to better describe marketing problems, situations, or markets, such as the market potential for a product or the demographics and attitudes of consumers.

Ethnographic research. Trained observers interact with and/or observe consumers in their natural habitat.

Experimental research. The gathering of primary data by selecting matched groups of subjects, giving them different treatments, controlling related factors, and checking for differences in group responses.

Exploratory research. Marketing research to gather preliminary information that will help to better define problems and suggest hypotheses.

Internal data. Internal data consist of electronic databases and nonelectronic information and records of consumer and market information obtained from within the company.

Marketing dashboards. Are like the instrument panel in a car or plane, visually displaying real-time indicators to ensure proper functioning.

Marketing information system (MIS). A structure of people, equipment, and procedures to gather, sort, analyze, evaluate, and distribute needed, timely, and accurate information to marketing decision makers. The MIS begins and ends with marketing managers, but managers throughout the organization should be involved in the MIS. First, the MIS interacts with managers to assess their information needs. Next, it develops needed information from internal company records, marketing intelligence activities, and the marketing research process. Information analysts process information to make it more useful. Finally, the MIS distributes information to managers in the right form and at the right time to help in marketing planning, implementation, and control.

Marketing intelligence. Everyday information about developments in the marketing environment that help managers prepare and adjust marketing plans.

Marketing research. The systematic design, collection, analysis, and reporting of data and findings relevant to a specific marketing situation facing a company.

Mystery shoppers. Hospitality companies often hire disguised or mystery shoppers to pose as customers and report back on their experience.

Observational research. The gathering of primary data by observing relevant people, actions, and situations.

Primary data. Information collected for the specific purpose at hand.

Sample. (1) A segment of a population selected for marketing research to represent the population as a whole; (2) offer of a trial amount of a product to consumers.

Secondary data. Information that already exists somewhere, having been collected for another purpose.

Survey research. The gathering of primary data by asking people questions about their knowledge, attitudes, preferences, and buying behavior.

■■■ CHAPTER REVIEW

I. **Marketing Information and Customer Insights.** To create value for customers and to build meaningful relationships with them, marketers must first gain fresh, deep insights into what customers need and want.

II. **The Marketing Information System.** A marketing information system consists of people, equipment, and procedures to gather, sort, analyze, evaluate, and distribute needed, timely, and accurate information to marketing decision makers.
   A. **Assessing information needs.** A good marketing information system balances information that managers would like to have against that which they really need and is feasible to obtain.
   B. **Developing information.** Information needed by marketing managers can be obtained from internal company records, marketing intelligence, and marketing research. The information analysis system processes this information and presents it in a form that is useful to managers.
      1. **Internal data.** Internal data consists of information gathered from sources within the company to evaluate marketing performance and to detect marketing problems and opportunities.
      2. **Guest information management**
   C. **Marketing intelligence.** Marketing intelligence includes everyday information about developments in the marketing environment that help managers prepare and adjust marketing plans and short-run tactics. Marketing intelligence can come from internal sources or external sources.

   1. **Internal sources.** Internal sources include the company's executives, owners, and employees.
   2. **External sources.** External sources include competitors, government agencies, suppliers, trade magazines, newspapers, business magazines, trade association newsletters and meetings, and databases available on the Internet.
   3. **Sources of competitive information**

III. **Marketing Research.** Marketing research is a process that identifies and defines marketing opportunities and problems, monitors and evaluates marketing actions and performance, and communicates the findings and implication to management. Marketing research is project oriented and has a beginning and an ending. It feeds information into the marketing information system that is ongoing. The marketing research process consists of four steps: defining the problem and research objectives, developing the research plan, implementing the research plan, and interpreting and presenting the findings.
   A. **Defining the problem and research objectives.** There are three types of objectives for a marketing research project:
      1. **Exploratory.** To gather preliminary information that will help define the problem and suggest hypotheses.
      2. **Descriptive.** To describe the size and composition of the market.
      3. **Causal.** To test hypotheses about cause-and-effect relationships.
   B. **Developing the research plan for collecting information**

1. **Determining specific information needs.** Research objectives must be translated into specific information needs. To meet a manager's information needs, researchers can gather secondary data, primary data, or both. Secondary data consist of information already in existence somewhere, having been collected for another purpose. Primary data consist of information collected for the specific purpose at hand.

2. **Gather secondary information**

3. **Research approaches.** Three basic research approaches are observations, surveys, and experiments.

   a. **Observational research.** Gathering of primary data by observing relevant people, action, and situations.

   b. **Survey research (structured/unstructured, direct/indirect).** Best suited to gathering descriptive information.

   c. **Experimental research.** Best suited to gathering causal information.

4. **Contact methods.** Information can be collected by mail, telephone, or personal interview.

   a. **Sampling plan.** Marketing researchers usually draw conclusions about large consumer groups by taking a sample. A sample is a segment of the population selected to represent the population as a whole. Designing the sample calls for four decisions: (1) Who will be surveyed? (2) How many people should be surveyed? (3) How should the sample be chosen? and (4) When will the survey be given?

   b. **Ethnographic research**

   c. **Research instruments.** In collecting primary data, marketing researchers have a choice of primary research instruments: the interview (structured and unstructured), mechanical devices, and structured models such as a test market. Structured interviews employ the use of a questionnaire.

   d. **Presenting the research plan.** At this stage the marketing researcher should summarize the plan in a written proposal.

C. **Implementing the research plan.** The researcher puts the marketing research plan into action by collecting, processing, and analyzing the information.

D. **Interpreting and reporting the findings.** The researcher must now interpret the findings, draw conclusions, and report them to management.

   1. **Information analysis.** Information gathered by the company's marketing intelligence and marketing research systems can often benefit from additional analysis. This analysis helps to answer the questions related to "what if" and "which is best."

   2. **Distributing information.** Marketing information has no value until managers use it to make better decisions. The information that is gathered must reach the appropriate marketing managers at the right time.

IV. **International Marketing Research.** International marketing researchers follow the same steps as domestic researchers, from defining the research problem and developing a research plan to interpreting and reporting the results. However, these researchers often face more and different problems.

V. **Marketing Research in Smaller Organizations.** Managers of small businesses can obtain good marketing information by observing what occurs around them.

■■■ DISCUSSION QUESTIONS

1. What role should marketing research play in helping a firm to implement the marketing concept?

2. You own an elegant, high-priced restaurant in your area and want to improve the level of service offered by your thirty-person staff. How could observational research help you accomplish this goal?

3. Compare and contrast internal databases, marketing intelligence, and marketing research as a means for developing marketing information.

4. Researchers usually start the data-gathering process by examining secondary data. What secondary data sources would be available to the manager of a full-service restaurant that wanted to research consumer trends?

5. Discuss the advantages and disadvantages of using guest comment cards in a restaurant.

6. Which type of research would be most appropriate in the following situations, and why?

   a. A fast-food restaurant wants to investigate the effect that children have on the purchase of its products.

   b. A business hotel wants to gather some preliminary information on how business travelers feel about the menu variety, food, and service in its restaurants.

   c. A casual restaurant is considering locating a new outlet in a fast-growing suburb.

   d. A fast-food restaurant wants to test the effect of two new advertising themes for its roast beef sandwich sales in two cities.

   e. The director of tourism for your state wants to know how to use his or her promotion dollars effectively.

7. Focus group interviewing is both a widely used and a widely criticized research technique in marketing. What are the advantages and disadvantages of focus groups? What are some kinds of questions that are appropriate for focus groups to investigate?

■■■ EXPERIENTIAL EXERCISES

Do one of the following:

1. You have been asked to find out how the campus community feels about the food service on campus.
   a. Who is the population for this study?
   b. Develop a sampling plan, including times and places that will provide you with a sample that is representative of the population of interest.

2. Get a customer comment card from a local hospitality company. What, if any, design changes would you make to the form? If you were the manager, how would you use the information collected from the comment cards?

■■■ INTERNET EXERCISES

A. You are asked to develop a loyalty program for a hotel or restaurant. Go on the Internet and find out what information you can find out about loyalty programs, including existing hotel or restaurant loyalty programs. Write up a summary of your findings. The book's Web site has some suggestions on how to set up your search.

B. Perform an Internet search on "social media marketing" to find companies that specialize in monitoring social media. Discuss two of these companies. Then find two more sites that allow free monitoring and discuss how marketers can use these to monitor their brands. Write a brief report of your findings.

■■■ REFERENCES

1. Neil A. Martin, "A Tempting Wager," *Barron's* 86. 15 (April 10, 2006): 28, 30.

2. Michael Bush, "Why Harrah's Loyalty Effort Is Industry's Gold Standard," *Advertising Age* (October 5, 2009).

3. Unless otherwise noted, quotes in this section are from the excellent discussion of customer insights found in Mohanbir Sawhney, "Insights into Customer Insights," www.mohansawhney.com/registered/content/TradeArticle/Insights%20into%20Customer%20Insights.pdf (accessed March 15, 2007). The Apple iPod example is also adapted from this article.

4. Michael Fassnacht, "Beyond Spreadsheets," *Advertising Age* (February 19, 2007): 15.

5. Mohanhir Sawhney, "Insights into Customer Insights," p. 3.

6. Tom Richman, "Mrs. Field's Secret Ingredient" (October 1987), as cited in *Managing Services* by Christopher Lovelock (Upper Saddle River, NJ: Prentice Hall, 1992), pp. 365–372.

7. See "Pizza Hut and Its Local Agency Win Direct Marketing Association Award," *Pegasus Newswire* (November 18, 2006), www.pegasusnews.com; Jennifer Brown, "Pizza Hut Delivers Hot Results Using Data Warehousing," *Computing Canada* (October 17, 2003): 24; http://newspapergrl.wordpress.com/2006103/22lpizza-hut%E2%80%99s-vip-elub/; and www.yum.com/investors/fact/asp (accessed March 2007).

8. John Bowen, "Computerized Guest History: A Valuable Marketing Tool," in *The Practice of Hospitality Management II,* ed. Robert C. Lewis et al. (Westport, CT: AVI, 1990).

9. David Menzies, "Comment Cards," *Foodservice and Hospitality* 21, no. 5 (July/August 1988): 14; Robert C. Lewis and Abraham Pizam, "Guest Surveys: A Missed Opportunity," in *Strategic Marketing and Planning in the Hospitality Industry,* ed. Robert L. Bloomstrom (East Lansing, MI: Educational Institute of the AH&MA, 1988).

10. Mark Lynn, "Making Customer Feedback a Priority—A Key to Inducing Demand and Maximizing Value," *Hospitality Net,* http://hospitalitynet.org; June 28, 2004.

11. Rick Hendrie, "Hear Me Out: Talking, Listening to Current Guests May Be the Best Way to Get More Through the Door," *Nation's Restaurant News* (January 20, 2003): 28+; Cary Jehl Broussard, "Inside the Customer-Focused Company," *Harvard Business Review* (May 2000): S20.

12. James L. Heskett, W. Earl Sasser, Jr., and Leonard A. Schlesinger, *The Service Profit Chain* (New York: Free Press, 1997), p. 67.

13. Chekitan S. Dev and Bernard O. Ellis, "Guest Histories: An Untapped Service Resource," *Cornell Hotel and Restaurant Administration Quarterly,* 32, no. 2 (1991): 31.

14. Tammy P. Bieber, "Guest History Systems: Maximizing the Benefits," *Cornell Hotel and Restaurant Administration Quarterly,* 30, no. 3 (1989): 22.

15. Carolyn Taschner, "Commentary: Mystery Shopping Is Booming Business," *The Daily Record* (Baltimore) (May 15, 2004); Allison Perlik, "If They're Happy, Do You Know It," *Restaurants and Institutions* (October 15, 2002): 65–70.

16. Joseph F. Durocher and Neil B. Neiman, "Technology: Antidote to the Shakeout," *Cornell Hotel and Restaurant Administration Quarterly,* 31, no. 1 (1990): 35.

17. Christopher W. Nordling and Sharon K. Wheeler, "Building a Market-Segment Accounting Model to Improve Profits," *Cornell Hotel and Restaurant Administration Quarterly,* 33, no. 3 (1992): 32.

18. Laurette Dubé, Leo M. Renaghan, and Jane M. Miller, "Measuring Customer Satisfaction for Strategic Management," *Cornell Hotel and Restaurant Administration Quarterly,* 35, no. 1 (1994): 39.

19. Burt Cabanas, "A Marketing Strategy for Resort Conference Centers," *Cornell Hotel and Restaurant Administration Quarterly,* 33, no. 3 (1992): 47.

20 "Making Them Feel at Home," *Cornell Hotel and Restaurant Administration Quarterly,* 30, no. 3 (1989): 4.

21. James Curtis, "Behind Enemy Lines," *Marketing* (May 24, 2001): 28–29.

22. "Company Sleuth Uncovers Business Info for Free," *Link-Up* (January–February 1999): 1, 8.

23. *American Marketing Association,* officially adopted definition (1987).

24. Frank E. Camacho and D. Matthew Knain, "Listening to Customers: The Market Research Function at Marriott Corporation," *Marketing Research* (March 1989): 5–14.

25. "The Entrepreneurial Approach to Indian Affairs," *Cornell Hotel and Restaurant Administration Quarterly,* 29, no. 2 (1988): 5.

26. Jerry Wind, Paul E. Green, Douglas Shifflet, and Marsha Scarbrough, "Courtyard by Marriott: Designing a Hotel Facility with Consumer-Based Marketing," *Interfaces,* 19, no. 1 (1989): 25–47.

27. Robert C. Lewis and Richard E. Chambers, *Marketing Leadership in Hospitality: Foundations and Practices* (New York: Van Nostrand Reinhold, 1989), p. 518.

28. Linda Tischler, "Every Move You Make," *Fast Company* (April 2004): 73–75.

29. Spencer E. Ante, "The Science of Desire," *Business Week* (June 5, 2006): 99–106.

30. See Pradeep K. Tyagi, "Webnography: A New Tool to Conduct Marketing Research," *Journal of American Academy of Business* (March 2010): 262–268.

31. Spencer E. Ante, "The Science of Desire," *Business Week* (June 5, 2006): 100. Also see Jan Fulton and Suzanne Gibbs Howard, "Going Deeper, Seeing Further: Enhancing Ethnographic Interpretations to Reveal More Meaningful Opportunities to Design," *Journal of Advertising Research* (September 2006): 246–250.

32. Spencer E. Ante, "The Science of Desire," *BusinessWeek* (June 5, 2006): 100; Rhys Blakely, "You Know When It Feels Like Somebody's Watching You …," *Times* (May 14, 2007): 46; and Jack Neff, "Marketing Execs: Researchers Could Use a Softer Touch," *Advertising Age* (January 27, 2009), http://adage.com/article7article_id=134144.

33. Allison Perlik, "If You Are Happy, Do You Know It," *Restaurants and Institutions* (October 15, 2002): 65–70.

34. Joe L. Welch, "Focus Groups for Restaurant Research," *Cornell Hotel and Restaurant Administration Quarterly,* 26, no. 2 (1985): 78–85.

35. Dorothy Dee, "Focus Groups," *Restaurants USA,* 10, no. 7 (1990): 30–34.

36. Robert J. Kwortnik, "Clarifying 'Fuzzy' Hospitality-Management Problems with Depth Interviews and Qualitative Analysis: Properly Conducted Depth Interviews Can Dig to the Sometimes-Confusing Heart of Consumers' Motivation for Hospitality Purchases," *Cornell and Hotel Restaurant Administration Quarterly* (April 2003): 117–129.

37. Anne Chen, "Customer Feedback Key for Theme-Park," *eWeek* (December 15, 2003): 58.

38. Kate Maddox, "The ROI of Research," *B to B* (April 5, 2004): 25, 28.

39. Jacob Brown, "Survey Metrics Ward Off Problems," *Marketing News* (November 11, 2003) accessed online viaBusiness Source Premier, October 12, 2004.

40. Deborah L. Vence, "In an Instant: More Researchers Use IM for Fast, Reliable Results," *Marketing News* (March 1, 2006): 21.

41. Stephen W. Litvin and Goh Hwai Kar, "E-Surveying for Tourism Research: Legitimate Tool or a Researcher's Fantasy?" *Journal of Travel Research* (2001): 308–314.

42. Based on information found at www.channelm2.com/HowOnlineQualitativeResearch.html (accessed December 2010).

43. Stephen Baker, "The Web Knows What You Want," *BusinessWeek* (July 27, 2009): 48.

44. For more on Internet privacy, see "What Would You Reveal on the Internet?" *Privacy Journal* (January 2009): 1; Jayne O'Donnell, "Cookies Sound Sweet, But They Can Be Risky," *USA Today* (October 26, 2009), www.usatoday.com; and James Temple, "All Eyes on Online Privacy," *San Francisco Chronicle* (January 29, 2010): Dl.

45. Jessica Tsai, "Are You Smarter Than a Neuromarketer?" *Customer Relationship Management* (January 2010): 19–20.

46. This and the other neuromarketing examples are adapted from Laurie Burkitt, "Neuromarketing: Companies Use Neuroscience for Consumer Insights," *Forbes* (November 16, 2009), www.forbes.com/forbes/2009/1116/marketing-hyundai-neurofocus-brain-waves-battle-for-the-brain.html.

47. For further reading, see Gary L. Lilien, Philip Kotler, and K. Sridhar Moorthy, *Marketing Models* (Upper Saddle River, NJ: Prentice Hall, 1992).

48. Jack Honomichl, "Top Marketing/Ad/Opinion Research Firms Profiled," *Marketing News* (June 2, 1992): H2.

49. Many of the examples in this section, along with others, are found in Subhash C. Jain, *International Marketing Management* (3rd ed.) (Boston: PWS-Kent, 1990), pp. 334–339. See also Vern Terpstra and Ravi Sarathy, *International Marketing* (Chicago: Dryden Press, 1991), pp. 208–213.

50. Jain, *International Marketing Management,* p. 338.

Consumer Markets and Consumer Buying Behavior

A look at how the hotel industry reacted to the growing number of women business travelers provides some insight into why it is important to understand consumer behavior. It also illustrates understanding consumers is not easy. In 1970 women accounted for less than 1 percent of all business travelers. By 1991 women accounted for 25 percent of all business travelers. This rapid growth attracted the attention of hotel managers. However, the male general managers were not sure how to attract them. Should they develop special floors for women only? Should they designate certain rooms for women travelers, placing extra lights around the mirrors, hair dryers, and skirt hangers in these rooms? Should they develop a special program for women travelers and put "Lady" in front of their brand name as the name for this program? Hotel chains did all this and more. Some conducted research, asking women how they wanted to be treated differently from their male counterparts. This provided little insight because most women had not traveled as men, so they did not know how their male counterparts were treated. Second, they wanted to be treated as business travelers; they didn't want to be differentiated as a unique type of business traveler. These early programs aimed at the woman business traveler were unsuccessful.

Kimpton Hotels, whose president is a woman, has developed a Web site for women, "Women in Touch." The site includes profiles of women in key positions with the hotel company, travel tips, a blog for women travelers, and nutrition and exercise information. Kimpton is an example of a company that understands the woman traveler's wants. It has created a marketing mix that fulfills these wants. Kimpton will gain more than its fair share of this market.

Kimpton realizes that attracting the woman traveler is just more than adding amenities. It is a holistic approach that evokes the positive emotional feelings in the traveler. In a recent Cornell Research report, Judi Brownell states that "hospitality companies seeking to achieve a competitive advantage increasingly strive to create a guest experience that elicits positive emotional responses; attending the affective components of the customer's experience has repeatedly proven to be good for both the guest and experience."[1] Brownell claims rather than focus on specific amenities, hotels should focus on a bundle of services, amenities, and facilities that create a desired emotional response from the guest.

Security is consistently mentioned as one of the most important concerns for the women traveler. Security is not just dead bolts and key-accessed floors. Although these are important, it also includes well-lighted parking areas with intercoms, a valet parking option, well-lit hallways, nonconnecting rooms, offer of a hotel staff member escorting the women to her room, and the desk clerk not mentioning the room number at check-in. The combination of these items creates

Objectives

After reading this chapter, you should be able to:

1. Explain the model of buyer behavior.

2. Outline the major characteristics affecting consumer behavior, and list some of the specific cultural, social, personal, and psychological factors that influence consumers.

3. Explain the buyer decision process and discuss need recognition, information search, evaluation of alternatives, the purchase decision, and postpurchase behavior.

a feeling that the hotel is concerned about the guest's safety, creating an atmosphere where the guest feels safe.

In her article Judi Brownwell grouped services, amenities, and facilities desired by women travelers into three themes: feelings of security, feelings of comfort, and feelings of empowerment. The feelings of the comfort theme include the ability to get a good night's rest and attributes of the hotel room. Specific items include the comfort of the mattress; the availability of a selection of pillows; lighting; in-room climate controls; sufficient storage space for jewelry, clothes, shoes, and work materials; a makeup vanity table; and fresh flowers. According to Brownwell, the feelings of empowerment theme include items that provide the ability for both professional and personal advancement and the ability to provide a break from professional routine. Specific items in this group include sports centers that are well-lit, clean, have towels, exercise balls, floor mats, lighter weights, water and anti-bacterial spray; professional treatment by the hotel staff, excellent room service menu; spa services and in-room technology.

Over time, hotel managers have gained a better understanding of the consumer behavior of the woman business traveler. During this time the wants of this traveler changed and the tools marketers developed to understand consumer behavior also changed. This illustrates that the study of consumer behavior is a dynamic and never-ending journey. In this chapter we discuss how to understand consumer markets so managers can develop a marketing mix to attract the markets they wish to target.[2]

Marketers must exercise care in analyzing consumer behavior. Consumers often turn down what appears to be a winning offer. As soon as managers believe they understand their customers, buyer decisions are made that appear to be irrational. But what looks like irrational behavior to a manager is completely rational to the consumer. Buying behavior is never simple. It is affected by many different factors, yet understanding it is the essential task of marketing management.

In this chapter we explore the dynamics of consumer buying behavior and the consumer market. Consumer buying behavior refers to the buying behavior of final customers—individuals and households who buy goods and services for personal consumption. The consumer market consists of all these individuals and households. The U.S. consumer market includes more than 300 million persons who consume more than $12 trillion worth of goods and services, almost $10,000 worth for every man, woman, and child. Each year this market grows by several million persons and by more than $100 billion, making it one of the most attractive consumer markets in the world.[3]

Consumers vary tremendously in age, income, education level, and tastes, and they buy an incredible variety of goods and services. We now look at how consumers make their choices among these products.

∎▮▮ A Model of Consumer Behavior

Today's marketplace has become very competitive with thousands of hotels and restaurants. In addition, during recent years the hospitality and travel industries have undergone globalization. Hotel companies headquartered in nations as diverse as Germany, the United States, and Hong Kong compete aggressively in markets such as Singapore and Japan. The result is a fiercely competitive international market with companies fighting for their share of consumers. To win this battle, they invest in research that will reveal what customers want to buy, which locations they prefer, which amenities are important to them, how they buy, and why they buy.

This is the central question: How do consumers respond to the various marketing stimuli that a company might use? The company that really understands how consumers will respond to different product features, prices, and advertising appeals has a great advantage over its competitors. As a result, researchers from companies and universities are constantly studying the relationship between marketing stimuli and consumer response. Their starting point is the model of buyer behavior shown in Figure 6–1. This figure shows that marketing and other stimuli enter the

Figure 6–1
Model of buyer behavior.

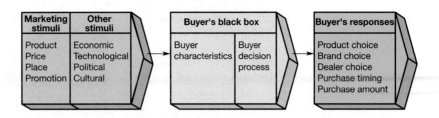

consumer's "black box" and produce certain responses. Marketers must determine what is in the buyer's black box.

On the left side of Figure 6–1, the marketing stimuli consist of the four Ps: product, price, place, and promotion. Other stimuli include major forces and events in the buyer's environment: economic, technological, political, and cultural. All these stimuli enter the buyer's black box, where they are turned into the set of observable buyer responses shown on the right: product choice, brand choice, dealer choice, purchase timing, and purchase amount.

Marketers must understand how the stimuli are changed into responses inside the consumer's black box. The black box has two parts. First, a buyer's characteristics influence how he or she perceives and reacts to the stimuli. Second, the buyer's decision process itself affects outcomes. In this chapter we look first at buyer characteristics that affect buying behavior and then examine the buyer decision process.

■■■ Personal Characteristics Affecting Consumer Behavior

Consumer purchases are strongly influenced by cultural, social, personal, and psychological characteristics. These factors are shown in Figure 6–2. For the most part, they cannot be controlled by the marketer, but they must be taken into account.

Cultural Factors

Cultural factors exert the broadest and deepest influence on consumer behavior. We examine the role played by the buyer's culture, subculture, and social class.

Culture is the most basic determinant of a person's wants and behavior. It comprises the basic values, perceptions, wants, and behaviors that a person learns continuously in a society. Today, most societies are in a state of flux. Determinants of culture learned as a child are changing in societies from Chile to California. Culture is expressed through tangible items such as food, architecture, clothing, and art. Culture is an integral part of the hospitality and travel business. It determines what we eat, how we travel, where we travel, and where we stay. Culture is dynamic, adapting to the environment.

Marketers try continuously to identify cultural shifts in order to devise new products and services that might find a receptive market. For example, the cultural

Figure 6–2
Factors influencing behavior.

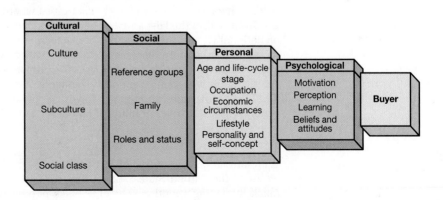

shift toward greater concern about health and fitness has resulted in many hotels adding exercise rooms or health clubs or developing an agreement with a local health club so that their guests can have access to it. The shift toward lighter and more natural food has resulted in menu changes in restaurants. The shift toward lighter-colored and simpler home furnishings is reflected in new restaurant designs.

At the same time, a significant number of consumers seem to be rebelling against foods that are good for them, preferring good taste. Restaurants face a consumer who orders broiled flounder and a light salad only to top it off with high-butterfat ice cream for dessert.

Subculture

Each culture contains smaller **subcultures,** or groups of people with shared value systems based on common life experiences and situations. Subcultures include nationalities, religions, racial groups, and geographic regions. Many subcultures make up important market segments, and marketers often design products and marketing programs tailored to their needs. Examples of three such important subculture groups are Hispanic, African American, and Asian consumers. As we discuss them, it is important to note that each major subculture is, in turn, made of many smaller subcultures, each with its own preferences and behavior.

Hispanic Consumers

The U.S. Hispanic market consists of Americans of Cuban, Mexican, Central American, South American, and Puerto Rican descent. The population of Hispanics is over 50 million. Hispanic consumers have a buying power of more than 950 billion, a figure that will grow to an estimated 1.4 trillion by 2013. Many Hispanics may be reached through the growing selection of Spanish-language broadcast and print media that cater to them.[4]

Although Hispanic consumers share many characteristics and behaviors with the mainstream buying pubic, there are also distinct differences. They tend to be deeply family oriented and make shopping a family affair; children have a big say in what brands they buy. Perhaps more important, Hispanic consumers, particularly first-generation immigrants, are very brand loyal, and they favor brands and sellers who show special interest in them.

Companies such as McDonald's and Burger King have developed special targeting efforts for this large consumer group. For example, Burger King sponsors an annual FUTBOL KINGDOM national soccer tour in eight major Hispanic markets across the United States. The family-oriented tour treats visitors to innovative street-level soccer events for all ages and skill levels, including skills challenges such as Domina como Rey (ball control), Los Reyes del Balon (speed), and Mata Penales (blocking ability). It's a "one-of-a-kind experience that has been incredibly successful with Hispanics around the United States," says Burger King's director of multicultural marketing.[5]

To make people aware of their purchasing power, as well as provide continuing education opportunities, the Hispanic meeting planners have formed the International Association of Hispanic Meeting Planners (IAHMP). Its membership includes meeting planners from the United States, Puerto Rico, Mexico, Portugal, Costa Rica, Panama, Guatemala, and Spain. In the United States, IAHMP is establishing chapters in the states and major cities where Hispanics are in the majority.[6]

Even within the Hispanic market, there exist many distinct subsegments based on nationality, age, income, and other factors. For example, a company's product or message may be more relevant to one nationality over another, such as Mexicans, Costa Ricans, Argentineans, or Cubans. Companies must also vary their pitches across different Hispanic economic segments.

Thus, companies often target specific subsegments within the larger Hispanic community with different kinds of marketing effort.

African American Consumers

With annual buying power of $913 billion, estimated to reach 1.2 trillion billion by 2013, the United States' 42 million African American consumers also attract much marketing attention. The U.S. black population is growing in affluence and

e **6.1** International Association of Hispanic Meeting Planners http://iahmp.org: How would a Hispanic meeting planner benefit from joining IHAMP?

With American markets becoming more diverse, companies are seeking managers who are members of a subculture that is a target market of their business. Courtesy of Andresr/Shutterstock.

e

6.2   www. myinspirasian.com: Go to this site to see how McDonald's is trying to serve and attract the Asian community.

sophistication. Although more price conscious than other segments, blacks are also strongly motivated by quality and selection. Brands are important. So is shopping. Black consumers seem to enjoy shopping more than other groups, even for something as mundane as groceries. Black consumers are also the most fashion conscious of the ethnic groups.[7]

One of the objectives of the National Coalition of Black Meeting Planners (NCBMP) is to develop a "network in the hospitality industry for African American association executives, meeting planners and suppliers. The network is set up to facilitate job referrals, exchange lists of consultants and vendors, and share other resources."[8] The NCBMP realizes that African American meeting planners are an important force in the hospitality industry.

Asian American Consumers

Asian Americans are the most affluent U.S. demographic segment. They now number more than 15 million and wield more than $500 billion in annual spending power, expected to reach $750 billion in 2013. They are the second fastest-growing population subsegment after Hispanics. Chinese Americans constitute the largest group, followed by Filipinos, Asian Indians, Vietnamese, Korean Americans, and Japanese Americans. The U.S. Asian American population is expected to double by 2050 when it will make up more than 9 percent of the U.S. population. Asian consumers may be the most tech-savvy segment; more than 90 percent of Asian Americans go online regularly and are most comfortable with Internet technologies such as online banking.[9]

As a group, Asian consumers shop frequently and are the most brand conscious of all the ethnic groups. They can be fiercely brand loyal. As a result, many firms are now targeting the Asian American market. For example, among its many other Asian American targeting efforts, McDonald's has built a special Web site for this segment (www.myinspirasian.com), offered in both English and Asian languages. The community-oriented site highlights how McDonald's is working with and serving the Asian American community.

Consumer Behavior Across International Cultures

Understanding consumer behavior is difficult enough for companies marketing within the borders of a single country. For companies operating in many countries, however, understanding and serving the needs of consumers can be daunting. Although consumers in different countries may have some things in common, their values, attitudes, and behaviors often vary dramatically. International marketers must understand such differences and adjust their products and marketing programs accordingly. Consider the following examples:[10]

- *Germany.* Be especially punctual. A U.S. businessperson invited to someone's home should present flowers, preferably unwrapped, to the hostess. During introductions, greet women first and wait until, or if, they extend their hands before extending yours.

- *United Kingdom.* Toasts are often given at formal dinners. If the host honors you with a toast, be prepared to reciprocate. Business entertaining is done more often at lunch than at dinner.

- *Saudi Arabia.* Although men kiss each other in greeting, they never kiss a woman in public. An American woman should wait for a man to extend his hand before offering hers. If a Saudi offers refreshment, accept—it is an insult to decline it.

- *Japan.* Friendliness from service providers is viewed as being disrespectful and formality is unequally preferred. Japanese expect promptness and prefer quick, unfriendly service over having a conversation with the service provider.

Failing to understand such differences in customs and behaviors from one country to another can spell disaster for a company's international products and programs. However, those companies that adapt can be winners. Restaurants in Israel learned to modify their products during the seven days of Passover. Many restaurants close during Passover, a time when many people travel and there is a high demand for restaurant products. KFC, Pizza Hut, Burger King, and McDonald's have adapted their menus to make them kosher for Passover. Burger King made rolls from corn flour and soy flour, McDonald's rolled its Chicken McNuggets in matzo meal, Pizza Hut used unleavened dough for its pizza crusts, and KFC replaced its breaded fried chicken with barbecued chicken.[11]

Through understanding international markets, particularly the Chinese market, Yum! Brands (KFC, Pizza Hut, and Taco Bell) are opening over a thousand restaurants a year outside the United States. Yum! tailors its menus to suit its overseas customers. In China, KFC developed a dark-meat chicken sandwich because Chinese customers prefer dark meat. It replaced its coleslaw with Chinese-style vegetables. One of its more innovative ventures is Taco Bell Grande, a sit-down service Taco Bell that looks more like a T.G.I. Friday's than it does a Taco Bell. There are no refried beans or hard tacos served at the restaurant because these items are not popular with the Chinese.[12]

Marketers must decide on the degree to which they will adapt their products and marketing programs to meet the unique needs of consumers in various markets. They want to standardize their offerings in order to simplify operations and take advantage of cost economies. However, adapting marketing efforts within each country results in products and programs that better satisfy the needs of local consumers. The question of whether to adapt or standardize the marketing mix across international markets has created a lively debate as more companies expand globally.

Social Class

Almost every society has some form of social class structure. **Social classes** are relatively permanent and ordered divisions in a society whose members share similar values, interests, and behaviors. Social scientists have identified the seven American social classes: upper uppers (1 percent), lower uppers (2 percent), upper middles (12 percent), middle (32 percent), working (38 percent), upper lowers (9 percent), and lower lowers (7 percent).[13]

Social class in newer nations such as the United States, Canada, Australia, and New Zealand is not indicated by a single factor such as income but is measured as a combination of occupation, source of income, education, wealth, and other variables. In many older nations, social class is something into which one is born. Bloodlines often mean more than income or education in such societies. Marketers are interested in social class because people within a given class tend to exhibit similar behavior, including buying behavior. Social classes show distinct product and brand preferences in such areas as food, travel, and leisure activity. Some marketers focus on only one social class. The Four Seasons restaurant in upper Manhattan targets upper-class patrons; Joe's Coffee Shop in lower Manhattan focuses on lower-class patrons. Social classes differ in media preferences, with upper-class consumers preferring magazines and books and lower-class consumers preferring television. Even within a media category such as television, upper-class consumers prefer news and drama, whereas lower-class consumers prefer soap operas and sports programs. There are also language differences between social classes, which means advertisers must compose copy and dialogue that ring true to the social class being targeted.

Social Factors

Consumer behavior is also influenced by social factors, including the consumers' groups, family, social roles, and status.

Groups

Many small **groups** influence a person's behavior. Groups that have a direct influence and to which a person belongs are called membership groups. In contrast, reference groups serve as direct (face-to-face) or indirect points of comparison or reference in forming a person's attitudes or behavior. People often are influenced by reference groups to which they do not belong. For example, an aspirational group is one to which the individual wishes to belong, as when a young basketball player hopes to someday emulate basketball star Lebron James and play professionally.

Marketers try to identify the reference groups of their target markets. Reference groups influence consumers in at least three ways: (1) They expose the person to new behaviors and lifestyles; (2) they influence the person's attitudes and self-concept; and (3) they create pressures to conform that may affect the person's product, brand, and vendor choices.

Groups to which the person belongs that have a direct influence are called **membership groups.** They include primary groups, such as family, friends, neighbors, and coworkers—specifically, those with whom there is regular but informal interaction. Secondary groups are more formal and have less regular interaction; they include religious groups, professional associations, and trade unions. In some societies, secondary groups may be membership groups. Members of the Mormon faith, for example, are greatly influenced by their religious affiliation. Mormons do not drink alcoholic beverages; therefore, they are a less attractive group for fine restaurants serving wine and other alcoholic beverages.

People can also be influenced by **aspirational groups** to which they do not belong but would like to. For example, a college freshman may aspire to be part of Hyatt's management team and may identify with this group even though not a member.

The importance of group influence varies by product and brand. It tends to be strongest when the product is visible to others whom the buyer respects. Purchases of products that are used privately are not greatly affected by group influence. Certain nightclubs can be associated with reference groups, attracting people who belong or wish to belong to the groups who frequent the nightclubs. Country clubs and city clubs tend to attract members who want to affiliate with their type of members.

Word-of-Mouth Influence and Buzz Marketing

Word-of-mouth influence can have a powerful impact on consumer buying behavior. The personal words and recommendations of trusted friends, associates, and other consumers tend to be more credible than those coming from commercial sources, such as advertisements or salespeople. Most word-of-mouth influence happens naturally: Consumers start chatting about a brand they use or feel strongly about one way or the other. Often, however, rather than leaving it to chance, marketers can help create positive conversations about their brands.

Marketers of brands subjected to strong group influence must figure out how to reach **opinion leaders**—people within a reference group who, because of special skills, knowledge, personality, or other characteristics, exert social influence on others. Some experts call this group *the influentials* or *leading adopters.* When these influentials talk, consumers listen. Marketers try to identify opinion leaders for their products and direct marketing efforts toward them. For example, the guest list for the grand opening of a restaurant or the first anniversary of a hotel should include opinion leaders.

NOP, a marketing research firm, has developed a profile of opinion leaders. It found that people are about four times as likely to contact an influencer as they are an average person. It also found that baby boomers are seeking information on restaurants and vacations from influentials at an increasingly higher rate. This is why companies like Heineken provide parties for influentials. They want these opinion leaders to order a Heineken instead of a wine or spirit when they go out with friends, influencing their friends to do the same. Companies try to influence scores of customers by influencing opinion leaders.[14]

Buzz marketing involves enlisting or even creating opinion leaders to serve as "brand ambassadors," who spread the word about a company's products. Many companies now create brand ambassador programs in an attempt to turn influential but everyday customers into brand evangelists. A recent study found that such programs can increase the effectiveness of word-of-mouth marketing efforts by as much as 50 percent.[15] For example, JetBlue's CrewBlue program employs real customers to create buzz on college campuses.[16]

Over the past few years, the JetBlue CrewBlue program has recruited a small army of college student ambassadors—all loyal JetBlue lovers. CrewBlue representatives advise JetBlue on its campus marketing efforts, talk up the brand to other students, and help organize campus events, such as JetBlue's BlueDay. Held each fall on twenty-one campuses, the highly successful event urges students to wear outlandish blue costumes (and, on occasion, blue skin and hair). Students with the best costumes are each given a pair of free airline tickets.

The CrewBlue ambassadors are crucial to the success of JetBlue's campus marketing efforts: "Students know what kinds of activities are important to other kids, what we should say to them in our marketing, and how we should say it," says a JetBlue marketing executive. You might think that such brand ambassadors would be perceived as best avoided. Not so, says the executive. "Our brand ambassadors are seen by their college friends as entrepreneurial, creative people." What they aren't, he adds, are the supercool people on campus who are typically thought of as influentials. The best ambassadors, says the executive, are "friendly, everyday brand loyalists who love to talk to people."[17]

Online Social Networks

Over the past few years, a new type of social interaction has exploded onto the scene—online social networking. **Online social networks** are online communities where people socialize or exchange information and opinions. Social networking media range from blogs (Gizmodo) and message boards (Craigslist) to social networking Web sites (Facebook and Twitter) and virtual worlds (Second Life). This new form of consumer-to-consumer and business-to-consumer dialog has big implications for marketers.

Marketers are working to harness the power of these new social networks and other "word-of-Web" opportunities to promote their products and build closer customer relationships. Instead of throwing more one-way commercial messages at consumers, they hope to use the Internet and social networks to *interact* with consumers and become a part of their conversations and lives.

For example, brands ranging from Burger King to the Chicago Bulls are tweeting on Twitter. Southwest Airlines employees share stories with each other and customers on the company's "Nuts about Southwest" blog. And Hilton developed H360 to connect Hilton employees from across the globe, allowing them to connect and share best practices.[18] Other companies, including Marriott, McDonald's, and Chipotle, regularly post ads or custom videos on video-sharing sites such as YouTube. McDonald's ad featuring former NBA basketball players Larry Bird and Michael Jordan has recorded over 1.5 million visits.

But marketers must be careful when tapping into online social networks. Results are difficult to measure and control. Ultimately, the users control the content, so social network marketing attempts can easily backfire. We will dig deeper into online social networks as a marketing tool in Chapter 15.

Family

Family members have a strong influence on buyer behavior. The family remains the most important consumer buying organization in American society and has been researched extensively. Marketers are interested in the roles and influence of the husband, wife, and children on the purchase of different products and services. Husband–wife involvement varies widely by product category and by stage in the buying process. Buying roles change with evolving consumer lifestyles. In the United States, the wife traditionally has been the main purchasing agent for the family, especially in the areas of food, household products, and clothing. But with 70 percent of women holding jobs outside the home and the willingness of husbands to do more of the family's purchasing, all this is changing. For example, women now make or influence up to 80 percent of car-buying decisions and men account for about 40 percent of food-shopping dollars.[19]

Children may also have a strong influence on family buying decisions. The United States' 36 million children aged 8 to 12 influence the spending of $30 billion in disposable income. They also influence an additional $150 billion that their families spend on them, such as food, clothing, entertainment, and personal items. One study found that kids significantly influence family decisions about everything from where they take vacation and what cars and cell phones they buy.[20]

For example, to encourage families to take their child out to eat again following the recent recession, casual restaurants reached out to children with everything from sophisticated children's menus and special deals to a wealth of kid-focused activities. At Applebee's, children eat free on Mondays with purchase of an adult entree. Carrabba's Italian Grill gives children a ball of dough, pepperoni slices, and cheese so they can make their own pizzas at the table, which are then cooked in the kitchen. And at Roy's Restaurants, as soon as children are seated, the Roy's server learns their names. "We want them to get excited and happy immediately," says a Roy's executive. Other kids' perks at Roy's include portable DVD players with movies and headphones on request and sundaes with kids' names written in chocolate. "They love seeing their name in chocolate," says a Roy's executive. Roy's big-hearted commitment to children's happiness is a no-brainer. Happy children equal happy parents.[21]

In Asia children are also becoming more influential. A recent study found that 66 percent of Asia's teens were influenced by television advertising and 20 percent by the Internet. This is significant because research conducted in Taiwan found that 98 percent of the children have a say in what programs they watch on television. Children all over the world are having an influence on where the family dines when they go out to eat. In the United States the food industry spends $14 billion advertising to children. A study by Mintel found that before the age of 12, children's eating habits are influenced primarily by their parents, but after 12 there is a shift to peer influence.[22]

Roles and Status

A person belongs to many groups: family, clubs, and organizations. An individual's position in each group can be defined in terms of role and status. A **role** consists of the activities that a person is expected to perform according to the persons around him or her. Common roles include son or daughter, wife or husband, and manager or worker.

Each role influences buying behavior. For example, college students dining with their parents may act differently than when they are dining with peers. A person purchasing a banquet for his church's men's club may be more price conscious than usual if he believes church activities call for frugality. The same person might be more interested in detail and quality than in price when purchasing a banquet for his company. Thus, a person's role at that time significantly affects his or her purchasing behavior.

Our roles are also influenced by our surroundings. People dining at an elegant restaurant behave differently than when they dine at a fast-food restaurant. They also have expectations about the roles that employees in different establishments should play. Failure to meet these role expectations creates dissatisfaction.[23] For example, diners at an elegant restaurant might expect waiters to hold their chairs during seating. The same diners would be surprised and possibly offended if a person cleaning tables at a White Castle hamburger restaurant assisted with seating.

Businesspeople will behave according to the role they are in and act differently than when they are enjoying a casual dining experience with friends. Courtesy of Ryan McVay/Getty Images, Inc./Photodisc.

Each role carries a status reflecting the general esteem given to it by society. People often choose products that show their status in society. For example, a business traveler became upset when all first-class seats were sold on a desired flight. The traveler was forced to fly economy class. When questioned about his concern over flying economy class, the traveler's main concern was what people he knew might think if they saw him sitting in the economy section. He did not seem to be concerned over the lower level of service or the smaller seating space provided by the economy section. These illustrations show that role and status are not constant social variables. Many marketing and sales professionals have made serious judgmental errors relative to the role and status of prospective customers.

Personal Factors

A buyer's decisions are also influenced by personal characteristics, such as age and life-cycle stage, occupation, economic situation, lifestyle, personality, and self-concept.

Age and Life-Cycle Stage

The types of goods and services people buy change during their lifetimes. Preferences for leisure activities, travel destinations, food, and entertainment are often age related. Important age-related factors are often overlooked by marketers. This is probably due to wide differences in age between those who determine marketing strategies and those who purchase the product/service. A study of mature travelers showed that this segment places great importance on grab bars in bathrooms, night lights, legible visible signs in hallways, extra blankets, and large printing on menus. Despite the logical importance of the factors, researchers found that this information "is not usually included in advertising and information listings."[24]

Successful marketing to various age segments may require specialized and targeted strategies. This will almost certainly require segmented target publications and database marketing. It may also require a marketing staff and advertising agency with people of varying ages and cultural backgrounds.

Buying behavior is also shaped by the **family life-cycle** stages. Young unmarried persons usually have few financial burdens, and they spend a good portion of their discretionary income on entertainment. Young married people without children have high discretionary incomes and dine out frequently. In fact, they have a higher frequency of dining out than any other group. Once they have children, their purchases from restaurants can change to more delivery and carryout. When the children leave home, the discretionary income can jump, and expenses on dining out can increase. Marketers often define their target markets in life-cycle terms and develop appropriate products and marketing plans.[25]

A National Restaurant Association study found that empty nesters spend 65 percent more on dining than couples with children at home. Buca di Beppo, known for its family-style platters of food, is now offering Buca for Two. They hope to attract couples without children and empty nesters with these smaller portions.[26]

6.3 The National Restaurant Association, http://www.restaurant.org/research/: This Web site provides a wealth of secondary information on consumer behavior of restaurant customers.

The Seychelles Islands are a unique and beautiful tourist destination. The Seychelles appeal to baby boomers who want to enjoy a unique destination and who have the discretionary income and desire to stay at a luxurious destination. Courtesy of Mirafilm/Dreamstime.

Occupation

A person's occupation affects the goods and services bought. For example, construction workers often buy their lunches from industrial catering trucks that come out to the job site. Business executives purchase meals from a full-service restaurant, whereas clerical employees may bring their lunch or purchase lunch from a nearby quick-service restaurant. Employees of some consulting firms are not allowed to eat in fast-food restaurants. The managers of these companies do not think it creates a proper image to have their clients see $300-an-hour consultants eating in a fast-food restaurant. Marketers try to identify occupational groups that have an above-average interest in their products.

Economic Situation

A person's economic situation greatly affects product choice and the decision to purchase a particular product. Consumers cut back on restaurant meals, entertainment, and vacations during recessions. They trade down in their choice of restaurants and/or menu items and eat out less frequently, looking for a coupon or deal when they do go out. Marketers need to watch trends in personal income, savings, and interest rates. If economic indicators point to a recession, they can redesign, reposition, and reprice their products. Restaurants may need to add lower-priced menu items that will still appeal to their target markets.

Many aging baby boomers still have active lifestyles and choose to stay at resorts offering outdoor activities. Courtesy of spotmatik/Shutterstock.com.

Conversely, periods of economic prosperity create opportunities. Consumers are more inclined to buy expensive wines and imported beers, menus can be upgraded, and air travel and leisure expenditures can be increased. Companies must take advantage of opportunities caused by economic upturns and take defensive steps when facing an economic downturn. Managers sometimes react too slowly to changing economic conditions. It pays to remain continuously aware of the macroenvironment facing customers. Regular reading of publications such as the *Wall Street Journal,* the business section of the local press, and regional economic reports by local and regional banks help to keep managers informed.

Lifestyle

People coming from the same subculture, social class, and occupation may have quite different lifestyles. A **lifestyle** is a person's pattern of living as expressed in his or her activities, interests, and opinions (Table 6–1). Lifestyle portrays the "whole person" interacting with his or her environment. Marketers search for relationships between their products and people who are achievement oriented. A chef may then target his or her restaurants more clearly at the achiever lifestyle. A study of tourists who purchase all-inclusive travel packages versus those who make travel arrangements independently revealed that lifestyle characteristics varied. All-inclusive travel purchasers were "more socially interactive, solicitous, and take their vacations mainly to relax." Tourists who preferred independent travel arrangements were more self-confident and often sought solitude.[27]

One of the most popular classifications based on psychographic measurements is the Values and Lifestyles (VALS) framework. The VALS framework has been the only commercially available psychographic segmentation system to gain widespread acceptance. The VALS classifies all U.S. adults into eight groups based on psychological attributes. The segmentation system is based on responses to a questionnaire featuring five demographics and forty-two attitudinal questions, as well as questions about use of online services and Web sites.

TABLE 6–1
Lifestyle Dimensions

Activities	Interests	Opinions	Demographics
Work	Family	Themselves	Age
Hobbies	Home	Social issues	Education
Social events	Job	Politics	Income
Vacation	Community	Business	Occupation
Entertainment	Recreation	Economics	Family size
Club membership	Fashion	Education	Dwelling
Community	Food	Products	Geography
Shopping	Media	Future	City size
Sports	Achievements	Culture	Stage in life cycle

Source: Joseph T. Plummer, "The Concept and Application of Life-Style Segmentation," *Journal of Marketing* (January 1974): 34.

The VALS questionnaire asks respondents to agree or disagree with statements such as, "I like my life to be pretty much the same from week to week," "I often crave excitement," and "I would rather make something than buy it."[28]

Here are two of the eight American lifestyles:

- *Believers:* Principle-oriented consumers with more modest incomes. They are conservative and predictable consumers who favor American products and established brands. Their lives are centered on family, church, community, and nation.

- *Achievers:* Successful work-oriented people who get their satisfaction from their jobs and their families. They are politically conservative and respect authority and the status quo. They favor established products and services that show off their success.

Prizm, developed by Jonathan Robbin, is another commonly used lifestyle classification scheme. Nielsen Claritas Prizm is a geodemographic system that allows researchers to know the mix or density of lifestyle groups in each of the United States' 36,000 zip code areas. A profile of one of these Prizm clusters is provided here. Blue-Chip Blues comprises about 6 percent of the U.S. population and are one of the largest users of fast-food restaurants.

> **Blue-Chip Blues** (2 percent of U.S. households): The nation's most affluent blue-collar households are concentrated in Blue-Chip Blues, composed of postwar suburban subdivisions in major metropolitan areas. Here lives a blue-collar version of the American dream: The majority of adults have high-school educations and own comfortable, middle-class homes. Boasting one of the highest concentrations of married couples with children, Blue-Chip Blues is the type of neighborhood with fast-food restaurants attached to every shopping center, baseball diamonds in the parks, and motorboats in the driveways.[29]

One of the criticisms of geodemographic systems is they assume everyone is like their neighbors. Although certain neighborhoods may contain more of a certain profile of person, not everyone in the neighborhood is the same. For example, most neighborhoods contain families and people without children. Jock Bickert developed a classification called Cohorts. Cohorts is built from a wealth of actual self-reported household-level data, rather than the inferred or geographic-level data used in other segmentation systems. The Cohorts are identified by twenty-seven highly cohesive groups of households. Cohorts results in a classification that is unique to the household. Marketing Highlight 6–1 provides an example of a successful application of Cohorts.

Lifestyle classifications are by no means universal. Advertising agency McCann-Erikson London, for example, found the following British lifestyles: Avant Guardians (interested in change); Pontificators (traditionalists, very British); Chameleons (follow the crowd); and Sleepwalkers (contented underachievers). The D'Arcy, Masius, Benton, & Bowles agency identified five categories of Russian consumers: Kuptsi (merchants), Cossacks, Students, Business Executives, and Russian Souls. Cossacks are characterized as ambitious, independent, and status seeking; Russian Souls as passive, fearful of choices, and hopeful.[30]

Personality and Self-Concept

Each person's personality influences his or her buying behavior. By **personality** we mean distinguishing psychological characteristics that lead to relatively consistent and enduring responses to the environment.

Personality can be useful in analyzing consumer behavior for some product or brand choices. For example, a beer company may discover that heavy beer drinkers tend to rank high in sociability and aggressiveness. This information can be used to establish a brand image for the beer and to suggest the type of people to show in an advertisement.

Stanley Paskie, the 72-year-old head bartender at the Drake Hotel in Chicago's Gold Coast, said, "It's imperative that a bartender possess the human touch.

Marketing Highlight   The San Diego Padres Baseball Club

6–1 The San Diego Padres selected Looking Glass to help it achieve its objectives. Looking Glass, now part of IXI Corporation, developed Cohorts. Most widely used segmentation systems are based on area-level U.S. Census data. They take the average income and spending patterns for a census tract and assume everybody in the census track is the same. Cohorts is based on the specific demographic and lifestyle makeup of each individual household. This information is gathered by obtaining information from public and private sources on each household. For example, from public real appraisal records, one can find out about the value and type of the dwelling, auto registration records give information about the type of car they drive, private companies will append data we have on individuals by adding information about travel expenditures, dining out expenditures, and so on. The information then allows Cohorts to put individuals into one of thirty cohort groups. Thus Cohorts does not assume that neighbors are in all cases similar. Cohorts understands that consumers will be more responsive to messages and offers that are relevant to their specific lives and lifestyles, rather than the average characteristics of their neighborhood.

The first step for the San Diego Padres was to find out about its customers. It built a database by running a questionnaire in the *San Diego Union-Tribune.* This questionnaire carried a number of questions regarding baseball behavior, as well as the demographics and lifestyle questions needed to Cohort-encode the respondents. Nearly 6,500 individuals responded. A similar questionnaire was also sent to season ticket holders. Looking Glass identified eleven Cohort segments that made up the baseball fan base in San Diego. Three segments accounted for more than half of the season ticket holders. Each segment had distinctive baseball behavior, whether it was price sensitivity or participation in numerous other sporting events. The Jules & Roz Cohort group, for example, displayed no price sensitivity—despite the presence of hot-dog-snarfing teenagers—but their attendance at Padres games was attenuated by their attendance at competing sports events.

The ability to marry actual baseball behavior with Cohort segment membership gave the Padres unusual sales and promotional insights, translatable into finely targeted promotions, both for single game and season tickets. For example, the Padres learned that a major fan segment of retirees—the Elwood & Willamae Cohort group—was intensely loyal to the team, regardless of win–loss record. However, they shunned night games. Knowing this gave the Padres the opportunity to package day games with less attractive opponents and target the 62,000 Elwood & Willamaes in the San Diego area. The Padres initiated a membership program called the Compadres Club. Members were encouraged to complete an application form that asked for name, address, and the demographic and lifestyle questions necessary to Cohort-encode each member. On completion of the application, fans were given a bar-coded membership card. By "swiping" that card at any game attended, the member earned points, redeemable for team merchandise and privileges in the ballpark. This also provided the Padres with valuable information about its fans and the behavior of the different cohort groups.

During its first season, the Padres estimates the increased ticket sales by over $2.5 million, and nearly that same amount in additional concessions and merchandise sales, solely attributable to the Compadres Club. The frequent fan club of the San Diego Padres has evolved into the Padres Frequent Friar Rewards Club. This marketing highlight shows how understanding our customers can modify consumer behavior so it fits the needs of the consumer and the organization. In this case, retired price-sensitive fans who wanted to go to day games were given packages that discounted day games when the Padres needed to fill seats. These were games during weekdays or when it was playing weak opponents.

Cohort Descriptions

Elwood & Willamae: Retired couples with modest incomes who dote on their grandchildren and when not touring the United States engage primarily in domestic pursuits. Median Age = 63; Median Income = $23,336.

Jules & Roz: Urban families who, despite having children at home, have sufficient financial resources to own the latest high-tech products and lead very active recreational and cultural lifestyles. Median Age = 43; Median Income more than $100,000.

Unfortunately, human relations isn't a required course at the nation's bartending schools where most bartenders now learn the craft. I've had conversations with customers in which I never said a word. I remember one customer who, as he was leaving, said 'thanks for listening to me, fella.' "[31] Paskie believed that a good bartender is part father, part philosopher, part confessor, and part devil's advocate. These traits are undoubtedly important in many areas of hospitality and travel marketing.

Many marketers use a concept related to personality: a person's **self-concept** (also called self-image). Each of us has a complex mental self-picture, and our behavior tends to be consistent with that self-image.[32] People who perceive themselves as outgoing and active will be unlikely to purchase a cruise vacation if their perception of cruises is one of elderly persons lying on lounge chairs. They would be more likely to select a scuba-diving or skiing vacation. The cruise line industry has been quite successful in changing its "geriatric" image and now attracts outgoing and active consumers.

The role of self-concept obviously has a strong bearing on the selection of recreational pursuits, including golf, sailing, dirt bike riding, fishing, and hunting. Anyone who enjoys boating will testify to the difference between boaters who use sails and those who use engines. Yachters/sail boaters refer to those who use engines as "stink potters." Stink potters think of the sailing crowd as stuffy, pretentious, and generally not much fun.

Psychological Factors

A person's buying choices are also influenced by four major psychological factors: motivation, perception, learning, and beliefs and attitudes.

Motivation

A person has many needs at any given time. Some are biological, arising from hunger, thirst, and discomfort. Others are psychological, arising from states of tension, such as the need for recognition, esteem, or belonging. Most of these needs are not strong enough to motivate a person to act at a given point in time. A need becomes a **motive** when it is aroused to a sufficient level of intensity. Creating a tension state causes the person to act to release the tension. Psychologists have developed theories of human motivation. Two of the most popular, the theories of Maslow and Herzberg, have quite different meanings for consumer analysis and marketing.

MASLOW'S THEORY OF MOTIVATION   Abraham Maslow sought to explain why people are driven by particular needs at particular times.[33] Why does one person spend much time and energy on personal safety and another on gaining the esteem of others? Maslow's answer is that human needs are arranged in a hierarchy, from the most pressing to the least pressing. Maslow's hierarchy of needs in order of importance are physiological needs, safety needs, social needs, esteem needs, and self-actualization needs. A person tries to satisfy the most important need first. When that important need is satisfied, it will stop being a motivator, and the person will then try to satisfy the next most important need. For example, a starving man (need 1) will not take an interest in the latest happenings in the art world (need 5), or in how he is seen or esteemed by others (need 3 or 4), or even in whether he is breathing clean air (need 2). But as each important need is satisfied, the next most important need will come into play.

Normally, needs are prioritized. For example, a college student with $500 to pay for incidental and recreational expenses during the term is unlikely to spend $400 on a trip to Florida over spring break. Instead, the money will probably be spent on smaller purchases of entertainment throughout the semester. If the student unexpectedly receives $2,000, there might be a strong temptation to satisfy a higher-order need.

HERZBERG'S THEORY   Frederick Herzberg developed a *two-factor theory* that distinguishes dissatisfiers (factors that cause dissatisfaction) and satisfiers (factors that cause satisfaction). The absence of dissatisfiers is not enough; satisfiers must be actively present to motivate a purchase. For example, a computer that does not come with a warranty would be a dissatisfier. Yet the presence of a product warranty would not act as a satisfier or motivator of a purchase because it is not a source of intrinsic satisfaction with the computer. Ease of use would be a satisfier.

Herzberg's theory has two implications. First, sellers should do their best to avoid dissatisfiers (e.g., a poor training manual or a poor service policy). Although these things will not sell a product, they might easily unsell it. Second, the manufacturer should identify the major satisfiers or motivators of purchase in the market and then supply them. These satisfiers will make the major difference as to which brand the customer buys.

Perception

A motivated person is ready to act. How that person acts is influenced by his or her perception of the situation. In the same situation, two people with the same motivation may act quite differently based on how they perceive conditions. One person may perceive the waiters at T.G.I. Friday's as casual and unsophisticated, whereas another person may view them as spontaneous with cheerful personalities. Friday's is targeting those in the second group.

Why do people have different perceptions of the same situation? All of us experience a stimulus by the flow of information through our five senses: sight, hearing, smell, touch, and taste. However, each of us receives, organizes, and interprets this sensory information in an individual way. Perception is the process by which an individual selects, organizes, and interprets information to create a meaningful picture of the world.[34]

The key word in the definition of perception is *individual*. One person might perceive a fast-talking salesperson as aggressive and insincere; another, as intelligent and helpful. People can emerge with different perceptions of the same object because of three perceptual processes: selective attention, selective distortion, and selective retention.

Most guests walking into the Palace, San Francisco, will perceive they are in a luxury hotel, based on what they see. Starwood has included this hotel in its Luxury Collection. The other hotel is comfortable, but does not convey a feeling of luxury. Both hotels have done a good job of creating a perception that will be consistent with how they would like to be positioned. Courtesy of Orionna/Dreamstime and tadija/Shutterstock.

SELECTIVE ATTENTION People are exposed to a tremendous amount of daily stimuli: The average person may be exposed to over 1,500 ads a day. Because a person cannot possibly attend to all of these, most stimuli is screened out—a process called selective attention. Selective attention means that marketers have to work hard to attract consumers' notice. The real challenge is to explain which stimuli people will notice. Here are some findings:

- People are more likely to notice stimuli that relate to a current need. A person who is motivated to buy a computer will notice computer ads; he or she will probably not notice stereo-equipment ads.

- People are more likely to notice stimuli that they anticipate. You are more likely to notice computers than radios in a computer store because you do not expect the store to carry radios.

- People are more likely to notice stimuli whose deviations are large in relation to the normal size of the stimuli. You are more likely to notice an ad offering $100 off the list price of a computer than one offering $5 off.

SELECTIVE DISTORTION Ever notice stimuli do not always come across in the way the senders intended? Selective distortion is the tendency to twist information into personal meanings and interpret information in a way that will fit our preconceptions. Unfortunately, marketers can't do much about selective distortion.

SELECTIVE RETENTION People forget much of what they learn but tend to retain information that supports their attitudes and beliefs. Because of selective retention, we are likely to remember good points mentioned about competing products. Selective retention explains why marketers use drama and repetition in sending messages to their target market.

Learning

When people act, they learn. **Learning** describes changes in an individual's behavior arising from experience. Most human behavior is learned. Learning theorists say that learning occurs through the interplay of drives, stimuli, cues, responses, and reinforcement.

When consumers experience a product, they learn about it. Members of the site-selection committee for a convention often sample the services of competing hotels. They eat in the restaurants, note the friendliness and professionalism of the staff, and examine the hotel's features. Based on what they have learned, a hotel is selected to host the convention. During the convention, they experience the hotel once again. Based on their experience and those of the attending conventioneers, they will either be satisfied or dissatisfied.

Hotels should help guests learn about the quality of their facilities and services. Luxury hotels give tours to first-time guests and inform them of the services offered. Repeat guests should be updated on the hotel's services by employees and by letters and literature.

Beliefs and Attitudes

Through acting and learning, people acquire beliefs and attitudes, which, in turn, influence their buying behavior. A **belief** is a descriptive thought that a person holds about something. A customer may believe that Adam's Mark Hotels have the best facilities and most professional staff of any hotel in the price range. These beliefs may be based on real knowledge, opinion, or faith. They may or may not carry an emotional charge.

Marketers are interested in the beliefs that people have about specific products and services. Beliefs reinforce product and brand images. People act on beliefs. If unfounded consumer beliefs deter purchases, marketers will want to launch a campaign to change them.

Unfounded consumer beliefs can severely affect the revenue and even the life of hospitality and travel companies. Among these beliefs might be the following:

- A particular hamburger chain served ground kangaroo meat.

- A particular hotel served as Mafia headquarters.

- A particular airline has poor maintenance.

- A particular country has unhealthy food-handling standards.

People have attitudes about almost everything: religion, politics, clothes, music, and food. An **attitude** describes a person's relatively consistent evaluations, feelings, and tendencies toward an object or an idea. Attitudes put people into a frame of mind for liking or disliking things and moving toward or away from them. For example, many people who have developed the attitude that eating healthy food is important perceive chicken as a healthy alternative to beef and pork. As a result, the per capita consumption of chicken has increased during recent years, leading the American Beef Council and National Pork Producers Council to try to change consumer attitudes that beef and pork are unhealthy. The National Pork Producers Council promotes pork as "the other white meat," trying to associate pork with chicken. Companies can benefit by researching attitudes toward their products. Understanding attitudes and beliefs is the first step toward changing or reinforcing them.

Attitudes are very difficult to change. A person's attitudes fit into a pattern, and changing one attitude may require making many difficult adjustments. It is easier for a company to create products that are compatible with existing attitudes than to change the attitudes toward its products. There are exceptions, of course, where the high cost of trying to change attitudes may pay off.

There is a saying among restaurateurs that a restaurant is only as good as the last meal served. Attitudes explain in part why this is true. A customer who has returned to a restaurant several times and on one visit receives a bad meal may begin to believe it is impossible to count on having a good meal at that restaurant. The customer's attitudes toward the restaurant begin to change. If this customer again receives a bad meal, negative attitudes may be permanently fixed and prevent a future return. Serving a poor meal to first-time customers can be disastrous. Customers develop an immediate negative attitude that prevents them from returning.

Attitudes developed as children often influence purchases as adults. Children may retain negative attitudes toward certain vegetables, people, and possibly places. Chances are equally good that they may retain very positive images toward McDonald's and Disneyland. Hospitality and travel companies are particularly subject to lifelong consumer attitudes that result from positive or negative childhood experiences. Harsh words from the manager of a miniature golf course or air sickness on a commercial flight in which the flight attendant showed little sympathy are negative attitude-building experiences.

Disney and McDonald's both view children as lifelong customers. They want children to return as teenagers, parents, and grandparents and treat them in a manner to ensure future business. Many hospitality and travel companies have still not learned from McDonald's and Disney.

Ski, golf, and ocean resorts have taken heed and have developed special programs, menus, and activities for kids. In many cases, hospitality and travel companies have discovered that there is good profit potential in kids' programs, as well as future patron-building potential. Steamboat Springs Ski Resort offers a professionally run children's program for kids from six months to fifteen years of age. Emphasis is on safety and fun at Steamboat. Other examples of top-notch kids' programs may be found at Smuggler's Notch in Vermont and the Omni Sagamore in New York. Hyatt Hotels is a leader in the field with its Camp Hyatt. Hyatt has proved that a hotel can be upscale and child directed.

Once negative attitudes are developed, they are hard to change. New restaurant owners often want quick cash flow and sometimes start without excellent quality. A new restaurateur complained that customers are fickle. When his restaurant first opened, there were lines of people waiting for a seat. A few months later, he had plenty of empty seats every night. Obviously, he had not satisfied his first guests. Even though he may have subsequently corrected his early mistakes, his original customers had been disappointed, were not returning, and probably were reporting negative comments to their friends.

We can now appreciate the many individual characteristics and forces influencing consumer behavior. Consumer choice is the result of a complex interplay of cultural, social, personal, and psychological factors. Many of these cannot be influenced by the marketer; however, they help the marketer to better understand customers' reactions and behavior.

◼▪▪ The Buyer Decision Process

We are now ready to look at how consumers make buying decisions. Figure 6–3 shows that the buyer decision process consists of five stages: need recognition, information search, evaluation of alternatives, purchase decision, and postpurchase behavior. This model emphasizes that the buying process starts long before and continues long after the actual purchase. It encourages the marketer to focus on the entire buying process rather than just the purchase decision.

The model appears to imply that consumers pass through all five stages with every purchase they make. But in more routine purchases, consumers skip or reverse some of these stages. A customer in a bar purchasing a glass of beer may go right to the purchase decision, skipping information search and evaluation. This is referred to as an *automatic response loop*.[35] The dream of every marketer is to have customers develop an automatic response to purchase its products. However, this does not typically happen. The model in Figure 6–4 shows the considerations that arise when a consumer faces a new and complex purchase situation.

To illustrate this model, we follow Rosemary Martinez, a college student. She has just remembered that next Saturday is her boyfriend's birthday.

Need Recognition

The buying process starts when the buyer recognizes a problem or need. The buyer senses a difference between his or her actual state and a desired state. The need can be triggered by internal stimuli. From previous experience, the person has learned how to cope with this need and is motivated toward objects that he or she knows will satisfy it.

Needs can also be triggered by external stimuli. Rosemary passes a restaurant, and the aroma of freshly baked bread stimulates her hunger; she has lunch with a friend who just came back from Bali and raves about her trip; or she watches a television commercial for a Hyatt resort. All these stimuli can lead her to recognize a problem or need.

At this stage, marketers must determine the factors and situations that trigger consumer problem recognition. They should research consumers to find out what kinds of needs or problems led them to purchase an item, what brought these needs about, and how they led consumers to choose this particular product.

Rosemary might have mentioned that she passed a card shop and noticed birthday cards, which reminded her that her boyfriend's birthday was approaching. She knew he liked German food, so she decided to take him to a German restaurant.

By gathering such information, marketers can identify stimuli that most often trigger interest in the product and develop marketing programs that involve these stimuli. Marketers can also show how their product is a solution to a problem. For example, T.G.I. Friday's advertised its gift certificates as a solution to Christmas shopping. Friday's food and atmosphere attracts a broad range of people; the gift certificates are easy to buy, avoiding the need to go to crowded shopping centers; and they can be bought in denominations that fit with planned expenditures. Friday's promoted gift certificates as a solution to a common problem experienced before Christmas.

Figure 6–3
Buyer decision process.

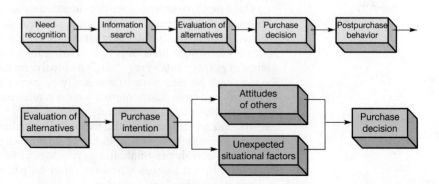

Figure 6–4
Steps between evaluation of alternatives and a purchase decision.

When looking for a hotel, "business travelers want a hotel to give them the tools to get their work done efficiently, which includes having competent staff members on duty, more than they want personalized services and fancy surroundings." Unfortunately, some hotels seem to confuse product opulence with providing features that will be benefits for the business market because they meet the needs of the business traveler. They provide great lobbies and restaurants but give businesspersons rooms that are not equipped as an office away from home, failing to meet the needs of this important market.[36]

The Travel Industry Association of America found that families with both heads of the household employed were finding it difficult to find a week when everyone was free. As a result, this segment needed three- and four-day getaways that could be booked at the last minute because 42 percent of this group makes plans within two weeks of the actual vacation.[37] These examples show that businesses must understand the needs of their customers and how these needs are translated into wants.

Information Search

An aroused consumer may or may not search for more information. If the consumer's drive is strong and a satisfying product is near at hand, the consumer is likely to buy it at that moment. If not, the consumer may simply store the need in memory and search for relevant information.

How much searching a consumer does will depend on the strength of the drive, the amount of initial information, the ease of obtaining more information, the value placed on additional information, and the satisfaction one gets from searching.

Rosemary asked several of her friends if they knew of a good German restaurant. Then she scanned a city magazine's restaurant listings. Finally, she looked in the Yellow Pages to see if she could find additional German restaurants. As a result of her search, Rosemary identified three German restaurants. She then tried to find friends and acquaintances who had been to one or more of the restaurants to get their impressions. She also looked in the *Zagat Restaurant Guide* for her city to see how the restaurants were rated.

The consumer can obtain information from several sources. These include the following:

- *Personal sources:* Family, friends, neighbors, acquaintances

- *Commercial sources:* Advertising, salespeople, dealers, packaging, displays

- *Public sources:* Restaurant reviews, editorials in the travel section, consumer-rating organizations

- *The Internet:* the company's Web site and comments from previous guests

With hospitality and travel products, personal and public sources of information are more important than advertisements. This is because customers do not know what they are going to receive until they have received it. People often ask others—friends, relatives, acquaintances, professionals—for recommendations concerning a product or service. Thus, companies have a strong interest in building such *word-of-mouth sources*. These sources have two chief advantages. First, they are convincing: Word of mouth is the only promotion method that is *of* consumers, *by* consumers, and *for* consumers.[38] Having loyal, satisfied customers who brag about doing business with you is the dream of every business owner. Not only are satisfied customers repeat buyers, but they are also walking, talking billboards for your business. Second, the costs are low. Keeping in touch with satisfied customers and turning them into word-of-mouth advocates cost the business relatively little. A customer cannot try out an intangible product before he or she purchases it. For example, people may hear of a restaurant through advertising but ask their friends about the restaurant before they try it. Responses from personal sources have more impact than advertising because they are perceived to be more credible. Christopher Lovelock lists these sources of information as ways customers can reduce the risk of purchasing a service:

- Seeking information from respected personal sources (family, friends, peers)

- Relying on a firm that has a good reputation

- Looking for guarantees and warranties
- Visiting service facilities or trying aspects of the service before purchasing
- Asking knowledgeable employees about competing services
- Examining tangible cues or other physical evidence
- Using the Internet to compare service offerings

By gathering information, consumers increase their awareness and knowledge of available choices and product features. A company must design its marketing mix to make prospects aware of and knowledgeable about the features and benefits of its products or brands. If it fails to do this, it has lost its opportunity to sell the customer. A company must also gather information about competitors and plan a differentiated appeal.

Marketers should carefully identify consumers' sources of information and the importance of each source. Consumers should be asked how they first heard about the brand, what information they received, and the importance they place on different information sources. This information is helpful in preparing effective communication.

Evaluation of Alternatives

We have seen how the consumer uses information to arrive at a set of final brand choices. But how does the consumer choose among the alternatives? How does the consumer mentally sort and process information to arrive at brand choices? Unfortunately, there is no simple and single evaluation process used by all consumers or even by one consumer in all buying situations. There are several evaluation processes.

Rosemary Martinez preferred a restaurant with good food and service. However, she believed that all the restaurants under consideration offered these attributes. She also wanted to patronize a restaurant with entertainment and a romantic atmosphere. Finally, she had a limited amount of money, so price was important. If several restaurants met her criteria, she would choose the one with the most convenient location.

Certain basic concepts help explain consumer evaluation processes. First, we assume that each consumer sees a product as a bundle of product attributes. For restaurants, these attributes include food quality, menu selection, quality of service, atmosphere, location, and price. Consumers vary as to which of these attributes they consider relevant. The most attention is paid to attributes connected with their needs. Second, the consumer attaches different degrees of importance to each attribute. That is, each consumer attaches importance to each attribute according to his or her unique needs and wants. Third, the consumer is likely to develop a set of beliefs about where each brand stands on each attribute. The set of beliefs held about a particular brand is known as the **brand image.** The consumer's beliefs may vary from true attributes because of the consumer's experience and the effects of selective perception, selective distortion, and selective retention. Fourth, the consumer is assumed to have a utility function for each attribute. A utility function shows how the consumer expects total product satisfaction to vary with different levels of different attributes. Fifth, the consumer arrives at attitudes toward the different brands through some evaluation procedure. One or more of several evaluation procedures are used, depending on the consumer and the buying decision.

When it was evaluated against its competitors Domnio's was known by many customers for the speed of its delivery, but not as the best-tasting pizza. Domino's decided to address negative perceptions about its taste head on. A major communication program featured documentary-style TV ads that opened with Domino's employees at corporate headquarters reviewing written and videotaped focus group feedback from customers. The feedback contained biting and vicious comments, such as, "Domino's pizza crust to me is like cardboard" and "The sauce tastes like ketchup." After President Patrick Doyle is shown on camera stating these results were unacceptable, the ads proceeded to show Domino's chefs and executives in their test kitchens proclaiming that its pizza was new and improved with a bolder, richer sauce; a more robust cheese combination; and an herb- and garlic-flavored crust. Many critics were stunned by the admission of the company that their number 2 ranked pizza, in effect, had been inferior for years. Others countered by noting that the new product formulation and unconventional ads were addressing a widely held, difficult-to-change negative belief that was dragging the brand down and required decisive action. Doyle summed up consumer reaction as "Most really like it, some don't. And that's OK."[39]

Purchase Decision

In the evaluation stage, the consumer ranks brands in the choice set and forms purchase intentions. Generally, the consumer buys the most preferred brand, but two factors can come between the purchase intention and the purchase decision. These factors are shown in Figure 6–4.

Attitudes of others represent the first. Rosemary Martinez selected a German restaurant because her boyfriend likes German food. Rosemary's choice depended on the strength of another person's attitudes toward her buying decision and on her motivation to comply with those wishes. The more intense the other person's attitude and the closer that person is to the decision maker, the more influence the other person will have. Nowhere is this better identified than in the case of children. Children do not hide their desires and parents and grandparents are affected intensely.

Purchase intention is also influenced by unexpected situations. The consumer forms a purchase intention based on factors such as expected family income, expected price, and expected benefits from the product. When the consumer is about to act, unexpected situations may arise to change the purchase intention. Rosemary Martinez may have an unexpected car problem that will cost $200 for repairs. This may cause her to cancel dinner reservations and select a less expensive gift.

Because customers do not know what the experience will be until after the purchase, managers must remember that first-time customers are really trying the product. While customers are in the purchase act, employees must do everything possible to ensure that they will have a good experience and the postpurchase evaluation will be favorable.

Postpurchase Behavior

The marketer's job does not end when the customer buys a product. Following a purchase, the consumer will be satisfied or dissatisfied and will engage in postpurchase actions of significant interest to the marketer. What determines postpurchase satisfaction or dissatisfaction with a purchase? The answer lies in the relationship between consumer expectations and perceived product performance.[40] If the product matches expectations, the consumer will be satisfied. If it falls short, the consumer will experience dissatisfaction.

Consumers base expectations on past experiences and on messages they receive from sellers, friends, and other information sources. If a seller exaggerates the product's likely performance, the consumer will be disappointed. The larger the gap between expectations and performance, the greater the consumer's dissatisfaction. This suggests that sellers must faithfully represent the product's performance so that buyers are satisfied. For example, Bermuda enticed tourists to enjoy the island during the off season at a lower price. It called this period "Rendezvous Time" and advertised that all the island's amenities would be available. When tourists arrived, they found that many facilities and attractions were closed. Hotels had shut down many of their food and beverage facilities, leaving tourists disappointed. Advertising claims initially brought tourists, but the truth got out and hotel occupancy dropped by almost 50 percent over a period of six years.[41]

Almost all major purchases result in **cognitive dissonance,** or discomfort caused by postpurchase conflict. Every purchase involves compromise. Consumers feel un-

Marketing Highlight — Unique Aspects of Hospitality and Travel Consumers

6–2 Valarie Zeithaml, a marketing consultant, published a classic article describing how the consumer evaluation process differs between goods and services. Persons purchasing hospitality and travel services rely more on information from personal sources. When looking for a good restaurant, people ask friends or people familiar with the town, such as front-desk employees or the concierge. Restaurants should attempt to affect positively those persons whom potential customers may contact. In larger cities there is a concierge association. Smart restaurateurs seek to host this club, letting their members experience the restaurants.

Postpurchase evaluation of services is important. The intangibility of services makes it difficult to judge the service beforehand. Consumers may seek advice from friends but use the information they receive from actually purchasing service to evaluate it. The first-time customer is on a trial basis. If the hotel or restaurant satisfies the customers, they will come back.

When purchasing hospitality and travel products, customers often use price as an indication of quality. A business executive who has been under a lot of pressure decides to take a three-day vacation now that the project is complete. She wants luxury accommodations and good food service. She is prepared to pay $175 a night for the room. She calls a hotel that offers a special rate of $85. This hotel may be able to satisfy her needs and has simply dropped its rate to encourage business. In this case, the hotel has dropped its rate too low to attract this customer. Because she has never visited the hotel, she will perceive that the hotel is below her standard. Similarly, a person who enjoys fresh seafood and sees grilled red snapper on the menu for $7.99 will assume that it must be a low-quality frozen product because fresh domestic fish usually costs at least twice as much. When using price to create demand, care must be taken to ensure that one does not create the wrong consumer perceptions about the product's quality.

When customers purchase hospitality and travel products, they often perceive some risk in the purchase. If customers want to impress friends or business associates, they usually take them to a restaurant they have visited previously. Customers tend to be loyal to restaurants and hotels that have met their needs. A meeting planner is reluctant to change hotels if the hotel has been doing a good job.

Customers of hospitality and travel products often blame themselves when dissatisfied. A man who orders scampi may be disappointed with the dish but not complain because he blames himself for the bad choice. He loves the way his favorite restaurant fixes scampi, but he should have known that this restaurant would not be able to prepare it the same way. When the waiter asks how everything is, he replies that it was okay. Employees must be aware that dissatisfied customers may not complain. They should try to seek out sources of guest dissatisfaction and resolve them. A waiter noticing someone not eating his or her food may ask if he or she could replace it with an alternative dish and suggest some items that could be brought out very quickly.

Source: Valarie Zeithaml, "How Consumer Evaluation Processes Differ between Goods and Services," in *Marketing of Services,* ed. James Donnelly and William R. George (Chicago: American Marketing Association, 1981), pp. 186–190.

easy about acquiring the drawbacks of the chosen brand and losing the benefits of the rejected brands. Thus consumers feel some postpurchase dissonance with many purchases, and they often take steps after the purchase to reduce dissonance.[42]

Dissatisfied consumers may take any of several actions. They may return the product or complain to the company and ask for a refund or exchange. They may initiate a lawsuit or complain to an organization or group that can help them get satisfaction. Buyers may also simply stop purchasing the product and discourage purchases by family and friends. In each of these cases, the seller loses.

Marketers can take steps to reduce consumer postpurchase dissatisfaction and help customers to feel good about their purchases. Hotels can send a letter to meeting planners congratulating them on having selected their hotel for their next meeting. They can place adds featuring testimonials of satisfied meeting planners in trade magazines. They can encourage customers to suggest improvements.

Understanding the consumer's needs and buying process is the foundation of successful marketing. By understanding how buyers proceed through problem recognition, information search, evaluation of alternatives, the purchase decision, and postpurchase behavior, marketers can acquire many clues as to how to better meet buyer needs. By understanding the various participants in the buying process and major influences on buying behavior, marketers can develop a more effective marketing program.

■■■ KEY TERMS

Aspirational group. A group to which a person wishes to belong.

Attitude. A person's enduring favorable or unfavorable cognitive evaluations, emotional feelings, and action tendencies toward some object or idea.

Belief. A descriptive thought that a person holds about something.

Brand image. The set of beliefs consumers hold about a particular brand.

Buzz marketing. Cultivating opinion leaders and getting them to spread information about a product to others in their community.

Cognitive dissonance. Buyer discomfort caused by postpurchase conflict.

Culture. The set of basic values, perceptions, wants, and behaviors learned by a member of society from family and other important institutions.

Family life cycle. The stages through which families might pass as they mature.

Group. Two or more people who interact to accomplish individual or mutual goals.

Learning. Changes in a person's behavior arising from experience.

Lifestyle. A person's pattern of living as expressed in his or her activities, interests, and opinions.

Membership groups. Groups that have a direct influence on a person's behavior and to which a person belongs.

Motive. A need that is sufficiently pressing to direct a person to seek satisfaction of that need.

Online social networks Online social communities – blogs, social networking, Web sites, or even virtual worlds- where people socialize or exchange information and opinions.

Opinion leaders. People within a reference group who, because of special skills, knowledge, personality, or other characteristics, exert influence on others.

Personality. A person's distinguishing psychological characteristics that lead to relatively consistent and lasting responses to his or her environment.

Reference groups. Groups that have a direct (face-to-face) or indirect influence on a person's attitude or behavior.

Role. The activities that a person is expected to perform according to the persons around him or her.

Self-concept. Self-image, the complex mental pictures people have of themselves.

Social classes. Relatively permanent and order divisions in a society whose members share similar values, interests, and behaviors.

Subculture. A group of people with shared value systems based on common life experiences and situations.

■■■ CHAPTER REVIEW

I. **Model of Consumer Behavior.** The company that really understands how consumers will respond to different product features, prices, and advertising appeals has a great advantage over its competitors. As a result, researchers from companies and universities have heavily studied the relationship between marketing stimuli and consumer response. The marketing stimuli consist of the four Ps: product, price, place, and promotion. Other stimuli include major forces and events in the buyer's environment: economic, technological, political, and cultural. All these stimuli enter the buyer's black box, where they are turned into a set of observable buyer responses: product choice, brand choice, dealer choice, purchase timing, and purchase amount.

II. **Personal Characteristics Affecting Consumer Behavior**
  A. **Cultural factors**
    1. **Culture.** Culture is the most basic determinant of a person's wants and behavior. It compromises the basic values, perceptions, wants, and behaviors that a person learns continuously in a society.
    2. **Subculture.** Each culture contains smaller subcultures, groups of people with shared value systems based on common experiences and situations.
    3. **Social classes.** These are relatively permanent and ordered divisions in a society whose

members share similar values, interests, and behaviors. Social class in newer nations such as the United States, Canada, Australia, and New Zealand is not indicated by a single factor such as income but is measured as a combination of occupation, source of income, education, wealth, and other variables.
  B. **Social factors**
    1. **Groups.** Groups that have a direct influence and to which a person belongs are called membership groups. In contrast, reference groups serve as direct (face-to-face) or indirect points of comparison or reference in forming a person's attitudes or behavior.
    2. **Word-of-Mouth Influence and Buzz Marketing.** The personal words and recommendations of trusted friends, associates, and other consumers tend to be more credible than those coming from commercial sources. Buzz marketing involves enlisting or creating opinion leaders to serve as "brand ambassadors," who spread the word about a company's products.
    3. **Online social networks.** These networks are online communities where people socialize or exchange information and opinions. Social networking media range from blogs to social

networking Web sites, such as MySpace.com and YouTube, to entire virtual worlds, such as Second Life.

4. **Family.** Family members have a strong influence on buyer behavior. The family remains the most important consumer buying organization in American society.

5. **Role and status.** A role consists of the activities that a person is expected to perform according to the persons around him or her. Each role carries a status reflecting the general esteem given to it by society. People often choose products that show their status in society.

C. **Personal factors**
1. **Age and life-cycle stage.** The types of goods and services people buy change during their lifetimes. As people grow older and mature, the products they desire change. The makeup of the family also affects purchasing behavior. For example, families with young children dine out at fast-food restaurants.

2. **Occupation.** A person's occupation affects the goods and services bought.

3. **Economic situation.** A person's economic situation greatly affects product choice and the decision to purchase a particular product.

4. **Lifestyle.** Lifestyles profile a person's whole pattern of acting and interacting in the world. When used carefully, the lifestyle concept can help the marketer understand changing consumer values and how they affect buying behavior.

5. **Personality and self-concept.** Each person's personality influences his or her buying behavior. By personality we mean distinguishing psychological characteristics that disclose a person's relatively individualized, consistent, and enduring responses to the environment. Many marketers use a concept related to personality: a person's self-concept (also called self-image). Each of us has a complex mental self-picture, and our behavior tends to be consistent with that self-image.

D. **Psychological factors**
1. **Motivation.** A need becomes a motive when it is aroused to a sufficient level of intensity. Creating a tension state causes a person to act to release the tension.

2. **Perception.** Perception is the process by which a person selects, organizes, and interprets information to create a meaningful picture of the world.

3. **Learning.** Learning describes changes in a person's behavior arising from experience.

4. **Beliefs and attitudes.** A belief is a descriptive thought that a person holds about something. An attitude describes a person's relatively consistent evaluations, feelings, and tendencies toward an object or an idea.

III. **Buyer Decision Process**
A. **Need recognition.** The buying process starts when the buyer recognizes a problem or need.

B. **Information search.** An aroused consumer may or may not search for more information. How much searching a consumer does will depend on the strength of the drive, the amount of initial information, the ease of obtaining more information, the value placed on additional information, and the satisfaction one gets from searching.

C. **Evaluation of alternatives.** Unfortunately, there is no simple and single evaluation process used by all consumers or even by one consumer in all buying situations. There are several evaluation processes.

D. **Purchase decision.** In the evaluation stage, the consumer ranks brands in the choice set and forms purchase intentions. Generally, the consumer buys the most preferred brand.

E. **Postpurchase behavior.** The marketer's job does not end when the customer buys a product. Following a purchase, the consumer will be satisfied or dissatisfied and will engage in postpurchase actions of significant interest to the marketer.

■■■ DISCUSSION QUESTIONS

1. Explain why marketers study buyer behavior and discuss characteristics affecting consumer behavior. Which characteristics do you think would have the greatest impact on your decision to select a restaurant to celebrate a special occasion, such as a birthday or anniversary?

2. Choose a restaurant concept that you would like to take overseas. How will the factors shown in Figure 6–2 work for or against the success of this restaurant?

3. Discuss when the family can be a strong influence on buying behavior regarding the choice of restaurants.

4. Apply the five stages in the decision process to your selection of a destination for your next vacation.

5. An advertising agency president says, "Perception is reality." What does he mean by this? How is perception important to marketers?

■■■ EXPERIENTIAL EXERCISE

Do one of the following:

1. Choose a hospitality or travel organization. You are in charge of designing a consumer advertisement for that organization. How would you determine the message of the advertisement?

2. Talk to several people about how they would choose a hotel in a city they have never been to before, a restaurant for a special occasion, or a place to vacation. What did you learn about the buyer decision process from these discussions?

■■■ INTERNET EXERCISES

Go to the Strategic Business Insights Web site and complete the VALS survey: http://www.strategicbusinessinsights.com/vals/presurvey.shtml.

What does VALS measure, and what is your VALS type? Does it adequately describe you? On what dimensions are the VALS types based? How can marketers use this tool to better understand consumers?

■■■ REFERENCES

www.strategicbusinessinsights.com/valspresurvey.shtml

1. Judi Brownell, "Creating Value for Women Traveler: Focusing on Emotional Outcomes," *The Center for Hospitality Research*, Cornell University, 2011.

2. See http://www.kimptonhotels.com/programs/women-intouch.aspx (accessed September 5, 2011); Jane-Michele Clark, "What Women Business Travellers Expect As Hotel Guests," *2010*, http://EzineArticles.com/?expert=Jane-Michele_Clark (accessed September 5, 2011); Judi Brownell, "Creating Value for Women Traveler: Focusing on Emotional Outcomes," *The Center for Hospitality Research,* Cornell University, 2011; Corinna Kretschimar-Joehnk, "What Women Want from Hotel Design," June 2010, from http://hospitalitystyle.com/content/what-women-want-from-hotel-design (accessed September 5, 2011); Paul Burnham Finney, "Women-Friendly Hotel Floors Return, with Modern Twists," *New York Times* (August 5, 2008); Pauline Loong, "What Women Want and Why," *Asiamoney* (March 2004): 39+; "Safety Is Preferred, Security Is Preferred," *Business Travel News* (January 2004): 12; Molly Cahill (February 2000), "Expecting Nearly Half of Business Travelers to Be Women, the Pan Pacific San Francisco Is Fine Tuning Amenities," http://www.hotelonline.com/Neo/News/Pressreleases2000_1st/feb00_womensurvey.html (accessed October 1, 2001); Christine Calloway-Holt (2001), "The Nob Hill Lambourne Creates 'Rebalancing Services' for Professional Women Travelers," http://www.hotel-online.com/Neo/News/PR2001_2nd/Jun01_Lambourne.html (accessed October 1, 2001); Suzanne Crampton and Jitendra Mishra, "Women in Management," *Public Personnel Management,* 28, 87–106, http://proquest.umi.com/pqdweb?TS=...=1&Did=000000039998327&Mtd=1&Fmt=4 (accessed April 6, 2000); Ruth Hill, "Women Road Warriors," *HSMAI Marketing Review* (Winter 2000/2001); Salina Khan, "Aiming to Please Women Business Travel Industry Introduces More Services for Female Customers,"http://www.usatoday.com (accessed October 24, 2001); Regina McGee, "What Do Women Travelers Really Want?" *Successful Meetings,* 37, no.

9 (1988): 54–56; Harry Nobles and Cheryl Thompson, "Female Business Travelers' Expectations," http://www.hotel-online.com/Neo/News/PR2001/Jun01_femaletravelers.html (accessed October 24, 2001).

3. GDP figures from *The World Facts Book* (March 12, 2007), www.cia.gov/cia/publications/factbook/. Population figures are from the World POPClock, U.S. Census Bureau, www.census.gov (accessed October 2007). This Web site provides continuously updated projections of the U.S. and world populations.

4. See U.S. "Hispanic Spending Growth Dwarfs the General Market," *PRNewswire* (January 5, 2010); and Noreen O'Leary, "Latin Flavor," *Next* (November 2, 2009): 10–11. For detailed information on the buying power of the subcultures discussed in this section, see Jeffrey M. Humphreys, *The Multicultural Economy 2008* (Athens, GA: Selig Center for Economic Growth, 2008), www.terry.uga.edu/selig/buying_power.html.

5. Jonathan Birchall, "Walmart Focuses on Smaller Format," *Financial Times* (October 19, 2009): 18; and "Burger King Wraps Up Its Annual FUTBOL KINGDOM National Tour with Scores of Success," *BusinessWire* (December 10, 2009).

6. http://www.iahmp.org/ (accessed August 29, 2011).

7. See Todd Wasserman, "Report Shows Shifting American Population," *Brandweek* (January 11, 2000): 6: R. Thomas Umstead, "BET: African-Americans Grow in Numbers, Buying Power" (January 26, 2010), www.multichannel.com/article/446028-BET_African_Americans_Grow_in_Numbers_Buying_Power.php and Mark Dolliver, "How to Reach Affluent African Americans," *Adweek* (February 2, 2010), www.adweek.com/aw/content_display/news/strategy/e3i8decb5ca03594f-57dadfad445ed35524; and U.S. Census Bureau reports, www.census.gov (accessed February 2010).

8. http://www.ncbmp.com/about/ (accessed August 29, 2010).

9. See Lynn Russo Whylly, "Marketing to Asian Americans," advertising supplement to *Brandweek* (May 26,

2008): S1–S3; Jeffrey M. Humphreys, *The Multicultural Economy 2008*; and U.S. Census Bureau reports, www.census.gov (accessed October 2010).

10. Susan Harte, "When in Rome, You Should Learn to Do What the Romans Do," *Atlanta Journal-Constitution* (January 22, 1990): D1, D6. See also Lufthansa's *Business Travel Guide/Europe*; Sergey Frank, "Global Negotiating," *Sales and Marketing Management* (May 1992), 64–69; Valarie Zeithaml and Mary Jo Bitner, *Services Marketing* (New York: McGraw-Hill, 2000); and Kathryn Frazer Winsted, "The Service Experience in Two Cultures," *Journal of Retailing,* 73, no. 3 (1997): 337–360.

11. "Briefcase—It's Fast and It's Kosher," *Houston Chronicle* (April 25, 1997): 4C.

12. "Yum! Brands, Inc in China," *China Business Review* (July–August 2004): 19; "Yum! Brands: Tasty Profits," Business Custom Wire, October 8, 2004, EBSCOhost, Accession Number CX2004282X7447.

13. See Richard P. Coleman, "The Continuing Significance of Social Class to Marketing," *Journal of Consumer Research* (December 1983): 264–280; Leon G. Shiffman and Leslie Lazar Kanuk, *Consumer Behavior* (6th ed.) (Upper Saddle River, NJ: Prentice Hall, 1997), p. 388.

14. Arun Sudhaman, "Heineken Takes Pulse to Win HK Consumers," *Media Asia* (June 18, 2004): 12; Becky Ebenkamp, "Under the Influence," *Brandweek* (August 9, 2004): 18; Becky Ebenkamp, "Keeping Up with the Joneses," *Brandweek* (May 19, 2004): 20+.

15. "Research Reveals Word-of-Mouth Campaigns on Customer Networks Double Marketing Results," *Business Wire* (October 27, 2009).

16. See "JetBlue Lovers Unite to Share Brand Perks with Peers," WOOMA Case, www.womma.org/casestudy/examples/create-an-evangelism-program/jetblue-lovers-unite-to-share/ (accessed March 2010); Joan Voigt, "The New Brand Ambassadors," *Adweek* (December 31, 2007): 18–19, 26; Rebecca Nelson, "A Citizen Marketer Talks," *Adweek* (December 31, 2007): 19; Holly Shaw, "Buzzing Influencers, *National Post* (March 13, 2009): FP 12; and information from www.repnation.com (accessed October 2010).

17. Joan Voigt, "The New Brand Ambassadors," *Adweek* (December 31, 2007): 18–19.

18. See Brian Morrissey, "Social Rings," *Brandweek* (January 18, 2010): 20.

19. See Darla Dernovsek, "Marketing to Women," *Credit Union Magazine* (October 2000): 90–96; and Sharon Goldman Edry, "No Longer Just Fun and Games," *American Demographics* (May 2001): 36–38.

20. R. K. Miller and Kelli Washington, *Consumer Behavior* (Atlanta, GA: Richard K. Miller and Associates, 2009), Chapter 27. Also see Michael K. Sullivan, *Consumer Behavior: Buying, Having and Being* (Upper Saddle River, NJ: Prentice Hall, 2011), pp. 439–445.

21. Ron Ruggless, "Casual Chains Cater to Kids as Way to Lure *Back* Families," *Nation's Restaurant News* (July 13, 2009): 1, 29–30.

22. Linda Abu-Shalback Zid, "What's for Dinner," *Marketing Management* (September/October 2004): 6; David Evans and Olivia Toth, "Parents Buy, But Kids Rule," *Media Asia* (November 14, 2003): 22+.

23. John E. G. Bateson, *Managing Services Marketing* (New York: Dryden, 1989), pp. 291–300.

24. Richard M. Howey, Ananth Mangala, Frederick J. De Micco, and Patrick J. Moreo, "Marketplace Needs of Mature Travelers," *Cornell Hotel and Restaurant Administration Quarterly,* 33, no. 4 (1992): 19–20.

25. Nanci Hellmich, "We Dine Out a Lot, But There's no Plate Like...," *USA Today* (October 13, 2004): 5D.

26. "Buca's Small Menu Signals Big Changes," *Restaurant Business* (March 1, 2004): 12; Joan Raymond, "The Joy of Empty Nesting," *American Demographics* (May 2000).

27. Jihwan Yoon and Elwood L. Shafer, "An Analysis of Sun-Spot Destination Resort Market Segments: All Inclusive Package Versus Independent Travel Arrangements," *Journal of Hospitality and Tourism Research,* 21, no. 1 (1997): 157–158.

28. Arnold Mitchell, *The Nine American Lifestyles* (New York: Warner Books), pp. viii–x, 25–31; Personal communication from the VALS Program, Business Intelligence Center, SRI Consulting (Menlo Park, CA, February 1, 1996). See also Wagner A. Kamakura and Michel Wedel, "Lifestyle Segmentation with Tailored Interviewing," *Journal of Marketing Research,* 32, no. 3 (1995): 308–317.

29. *Source: © 1988 by Michael J. Weiss. The Clustering of America* (New York: Harper & Row). Reprinted by permission of HarperCollins Publishers, Inc.

30. Stuart Elliot, "Sampling Tastes of a Changing Russia," *New York Times* (April 1, 1992): D1, D19; and Miller, "Global Segments from 'Strivers' to 'Creatives,' " p. 11. For an excellent discussion of cross-cultural lifestyle systems, see Phillip Kotler, Gary Armstrong, John Saunders, and Veronica Wong, *Principles of Marketing* (2nd ed.) (London: Prentice Hall Europe, 1999), pp. 240–242.

31. Edmund O. Lawler, "50 Years Behind the Bar," *F&B Magazine,* 2, no. 1 (1994): 44.

32. James U. McNeal, *Consumer Behavior: An Integrative Approach* (Boston, MA: Little, Brown, 1982), pp. 83–90.

33. Abraham H. Maslow, *Motivation and Personality* (2nd ed.) (New York: Harper & Row, 1970), pp. 80–106.

34. M. Joseph Sirgy, "Self-Concept in Consumer Behavior: A Critical Review," *Journal of Consumer Research* (December 1982): 287–300.

35. McNeal, *Consumer Behavior,* p. 77.

36. Anna Mattila, "Consumers' Value Judgments," *Cornell Hotel and Restaurant Administration Quarterly,* 40, no 1 (1999): 40.

37. "TIA Study: Weekend Trips Increasing in Popularity," *Travel Weekly* (July 2, 2001): 4.

38. For more on word-of-mouth sources, see Philip Kotler, *Marketing Management* (11th ed.) (Upper Saddle River, NJ: Prentice Hall, 2003), pp. 574–575.

39. Seth Stevenson, "Like Cardboard," *Slate* (January 1, 2010); Ashley M. Heher, "Domino's Comes Clean Wit! New Pizza Ads," *Associated Press* (January 11, 2010); Bob Garfield, "Domino's Does Itself a Disservice by Coming Clean About Its Pizza," *Advertising Age* (January 11, 2010); *Domino's Pizza,* www.pizzaturnaround.com.

40. Priscilla A. LaBarbara and David Mazursky, "A Longitudinal Assessment of Consumer Satisfaction/Dissatisfaction: The Dynamic Aspect of the Cognitive Process," *Journal of Marketing Research* (November 1983): 393–404.

41. Thomas Beggs and Robert C. Lewis, "Selling Bermuda in the Off Season," in *The Complete Travel Marketing Handbook* (Lincolnwood, IL: NTC Business Books, 1988).

42. Leon Festinger, *A Theory of Cognitive Dissonance* (Stanford, CA: Stanford University Press, 1957); Leon G. Schiffman and Leslie Lazar Kanuk, *Consumer Behavior* (Upper Saddle River, NJ: Prentice Hall, 1991), pp. 304–305.

The ideal salesperson in the company meetings segment isn't a salesperson in the traditional sense, but rather the problem-solver.

—ROBERT C. MACKEY

Organizational Buyer Behavior of Group Market

Objectives

After reading this chapter, you should be able to:

1. Understand the organizational buying process.
2. Identify and discuss the importance of the participants in the organizational buying process.
3. Identify the major influences on organizational buyers.
4. List the eight stages of the organizational buying process.
5. Identify and describe the group markets in the hospitality industry.

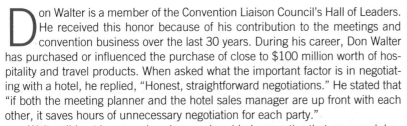

D on Walter is a member of the Convention Liaison Council's Hall of Leaders. He received this honor because of his contribution to the meetings and convention business over the last 30 years. During his career, Don Walter has purchased or influenced the purchase of close to $100 million worth of hospitality and travel products. When asked what the important factor is in negotiating with a hotel, he replied, "Honest, straightforward negotiations." He stated that "if both the meeting planner and the hotel sales manager are up front with each other, it saves hours of unnecessary negotiation for each party."

Walter did not buy on price alone and avoided properties that appeared desperate for his business. He claims that often these hotels have financial problems, which result in staff turnover and understaffing. In this type of hotel, you may have to deal with several people because of the turnover problem. When the meeting is held, the service is poor, meals that should take an hour end up taking an hour and a half because of understaffing, and changes in setups are difficult to accomplish. When people do show up to change the meeting room for you, they are often irritated and let the meeting planner know it. Walter went on to say that this type of poor service can ruin a meeting. If the meeting does not go off well, the savings in cost seems trivial in comparison to the damage done to the sponsoring association's reputation. Thus, when negotiating, Walter looks for a fair deal. He expects the hotel to make money, but he also expects good service and overall value. He observes the employees during a site visit to get a good idea of the type of service he can expect for his meeting. When he sees an employee bend over and pick up a gum wrapper, this is an indication to him that the employees have pride in their hotel. He likes to go back to a hotel where he sees the same faces he saw last year. Low turnover and promotion from within give him a good feeling about a hotel. Similarly, when an employee greets him by name as he enters the hotel, this shows that the hotel has gone to the effort of getting the employees to recognize him—a sign of attention to detail and caring.

After signing a contract with a hotel, Walter likes to deal with one person. By the way, Walter brings his own contract; he does not use the hotel's contract. Sometimes it is necessary to make changes to the room layouts he provides to the hotel. When he needed to make changes, he expected them to be done promptly and cheerfully.

When discussing things that have affected the meeting business, Walter said that requirements because of the Americans with Disabilities Act (ADA) should be a concern to both hotels and meeting planners. First, compliance ensures that everyone wanting to attend the meeting has access to the meeting. Second, failure to comply could result in lawsuits from attendees against both the meeting sponsor and the hotel.

Don Walter is an example of the tremendous purchasing power of an organizational buyer. He also provided some insights into what is important to meeting planners and association executives. They want good service at a fair price. They do not want any surprises, and when they need to make some changes during the event, they expect the hotel or convention hall to be supportive.

In most hotels and many food-service operations, organizations account for a large percentage of sales. In some ways, business markets are similar to consumer markets. For example, both involve people who assume buying roles and make purchase decisions to satisfy needs. However, business markets differ in many ways from consumer markets. The differences are in market structure and demand, the nature of the buying unit, the types of decisions, and the decision process involved.

In this chapter we discuss group markets that generate business for the hospitality and travel industry, including facilities like the Hong Kong Convention and Exhibition Centre, shown in the chapter-opening photo.

■■■ The Organizational Buying Process

Market Structure and Demand

The American Marketing Association (AMA) holds more than twenty conferences annually. Hyatt and Marriott share the majority of the AMA's conference business, with Marriott's share close to 3,000 room nights a year. When food and beverage sales are included, the value of this account is over $1 million. In addition to expenditures in the hotel, a delegate spends about $850 on transportation and $425 on entertainment, plus expenditures in local restaurants.[1] There are thousands of organizations like the AMA. Each of these organizations can deliver hundreds of thousands of dollars' worth of business to the hotel, airlines, and the destination's economy.

Organizational demand is **derived demand**; it comes ultimately from the demand for consumer goods or services. It is derived or a function of the businesses that supply the hospitality and travel industry with meetings, special events, and other functions. Las Vegas hosts two conventions for products people add to their cars, during the same week. These products include audio systems, special tires, navigation systems, and similar products. These shows attract a combined attendance of over 100,000 people. If car sales fall, the demand for these products will fail. The companies that sell and install the products will cut their spending on travel. Attendance at the conventions will fall, causing a loss of revenue to the hotels, casinos, restaurants, and shows in Las Vegas.

Through good environmental scanning, marketers can identify emerging industries, companies, and associations. They screen these organizations to find good business partners. Hotel managers need to understand the financial health of the corporations and associations they serve. If clients fall on hard times, managers need to look for industries that are healthy to replace the lost business, before it affects the revenue per available room (RevPAR).

Compared with consumer purchases, a business purchase usually involves more buyers and a more professional purchasing effort. Corporations that frequently use hotels for meetings may hire their own meeting planners. Professional meeting planners receive training in negotiating skills. They belong to associations such as Meeting Planners International (MPI), which educates its members in the latest negotiating techniques. A corporate travel agent's job is to find the best airfares, rental car rates, and hotel rates. Therefore, hotels must have well-trained salespeople to deal with well-trained buyers, creating thousands of jobs for salespeople. Additionally, once the meeting is sold, the account is turned over to a convention service manager who works with the meeting planner to make sure the event is produced according to the meeting planner's expectations. Outside the hotel, jobs relating to meetings include corporate meeting planners, association meeting planners, independent meeting planners, and convention and visitor bureau salespersons.

Types of Decisions and the Decision Process

Organizational buyers usually face more complex buying decisions than consumer buyers. Their purchases often involve large sums of money, complex technical features (room sizes, room setups, breakout rooms, audiovisual (AV) equipment, and the like), economic considerations, and interactions among many people at all levels of the organization. The **organizational buying process** tends to be more formalized than the consumer process and a more professional purchasing effort. The more complex the purchase, the more likely it is that several people will participate in the decision-making process. The total bill for a one-day sales meeting for twenty people can be several thousands of dollars. If a company is having a series of sales meetings around the country, it will be worthwhile for the company to get quotes from several hotel chains and spend time analyzing the bids.

Finally, in the organizational buying process, buyer and seller are often very dependent on each other. Sales is a consultative process. The hospitality organization's staff develops interesting and creative menus, theme parties, and coffee breaks. The staff works with meeting planners to solve problems. In short, the staff members roll up their sleeves and work closely with their corporate and association customers to find customized solutions to customer needs. Hotels and catering firms retain customers by meeting their current needs and thinking ahead to meet the customer's future needs.

Meetings and group functions are held at hotels, banquet halls, restaurants, museums, and other venues that meet the needs of an organization. Some graduates of hospitality and tourism programs will become meeting planners; others will serve the meeting planners as caterers, convention service managers in hotels, banquet managers in hotels and restaurants or as a salesperson who sells meeting space and banquets.

■■■ Participants in the Organizational Buying Process

The decision-making unit of a buying organization, sometimes called the **buying center**, is defined as "all those individuals and groups who participate in the purchasing decision-making process, who share common goals and the risks arising from the decisions."[2]

The *buying center* includes all members of the organization who play any of six roles in the purchase-decision process:[3]

1. **Users.** Users are those who use the product or service. They often initiate the buying proposal and help define product specifications. If attendees of a sales meeting have a poor experience, they are usually able to influence the company against using that hotel in the future.

2. **Influencers.** Influencers directly influence the buying decision but do not make the final decision themselves. They often help define specifications and provide information for evaluating alternatives. Past presidents of trade associations may exert influence in the choice of a meeting location. Executive secretaries, a spouse, regional managers, and many others can and do exert considerable influence in the selection of sites for meetings, seminars, conferences, and other group gatherings.

3. **Deciders.** Deciders select product requirements and suppliers. For example, a company's sales manager for the Denver area selects the hotel and negotiates the arrangements when the regional sales meeting is held in that area.

4. **Approvers.** Approvers authorize the proposed actions of deciders or buyers. Although the Denver sales manager arranges the meeting, the contracts may need to be submitted to the corporate vice president of marketing for formal approval.

5. **Buyers.** Buyers have formal authority for selecting suppliers and arranging the terms of purchase. Buyers may help shape product specifications and play a major role in selecting vendors and negotiating.

6. **Gatekeepers.** Gatekeepers have the power to prevent sellers or information from reaching members of the buying center. For example, a hotel salesperson calling on a meeting planner may have to go through a secretary. This secretary can easily block the salesperson from seeing the meeting planner. This can be accomplished by failing to forward messages, telling the salesperson the meeting planner is not available, or simply telling the meeting planner not to deal with the salesperson.

Buying centers vary by number and type of participants. Salespersons calling on organizational customers must determine the following:

*   Who are the major decision participants?

*   What decisions do they influence?

*   What is their level of influence?

*   What evaluation criteria does each participant use?

When a buying center includes multiple participants, the seller may not have the time or resources to reach all of them. Smaller sellers concentrate on reaching the key buying influencers and deciders. It is important not to go over the decider's head. Most deciders like to feel in control of the purchasing decision; going over a decider's head and working with the boss will be resented. In most cases the boss will leave the decision up to the decider, and the ill will created by not dealing with the decider directly will result in him or her choosing another company. Larger sellers use multilevel, in-depth selling to reach as many buying participants as possible. Their salespeople virtually "live" with their high-volume customers.

▪▪▪ Major Influences on Organizational Buyers

Organizational buyers are subject to many influences as they make their buying decisions. Some vendors assume that the most important influences are economic. They see buyers as favoring the supplier who offers the lowest price, best product, or most service. This view suggests that hospitality marketers should concentrate on price and cost variables.

Others believe that buyers respond to personal factors such as favors, attention, or risk avoidance. A study of buyers in ten large companies concluded that emotions and feelings play a part in the decision process of corporate decision makers. They respond to "image," buy from known companies, and favor suppliers who show them respect and personal consideration. They "overreact" to real or imagined slights, tending to reject companies that fail to respond or delay in submitting bids.[4]

In reality, organizational buyers commonly respond to both economic and personal factors. Where there is substantial similarity in supplier offers, price becomes an important determinant. When competing products differ substantially, buyers are faced with many decision variables other than price comparisons.

The various influences on organizational buyers may be classified into four main groups: environmental, organizational, interpersonal, and individual.[5] Figure 7–1 illustrates these groups.

Figure 7–1
Major influences on business buying behavior.

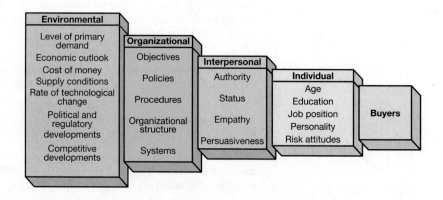

Environmental Factors

Organizational buyers are heavily influenced by the current and expected economic environment. Factors such as the level of primary demand, the economic outlook, and the cost are important. In a recession, companies cut their travel budgets, whereas in good times, travel budgets are usually increased.

Organizational Factors

Each organization has specific objectives, policies, procedures, organizational structures, and systems related to buying. The hospitality marketer has to be familiar with them and must know the following: How many people are involved in the buying decision? Who are they? What are the evaluation criteria? What are the company's policies and constraints on the buyers?

Interpersonal Factors

The buying center usually includes several participants, with differing levels of interest, authority, and persuasiveness. Hospitality marketers are unlikely to know the group dynamics that take place during the buying decision process. However, salespeople commonly learn the personalities and interpersonal factors that shape the organizational environment and provide useful insight into group dynamics.

Individual Factors

Each participant in the buying decision process has personal motivations, perceptions, and preferences. The participant's age, income, education, professional identification, personality, and attitudes toward risk all influence the participant in the buying process. Buyers definitely exhibit different buying styles. Hospitality marketers must know their customers and adapt their tactics to known environmental, organizational, interpersonal, and individual influences.

■■■ Organizational Buying Decisions

Organizational buyers do not buy goods and services for personal consumption. They buy hospitality products to provide training, to reward employees and distributors, and to provide lodging for their employees. Eight stages of the organizational buying process have been identified and are called *buyphases*.[6] This model is called the *buygrid framework*. The eight steps for the typical new-task buying situation follow.

1. Problem Recognition

The buying process begins when someone in the company recognizes a problem or need that can be met by acquiring a good or a service. **Problem recognition** can occur because of internal or external stimuli. Internally, a new product may create the need for a series of meetings to explain the product to the sales force. A human resource manager may notice a need for employee training and set up a training meeting. A CEO may feel that the executive team would benefit from a weekend retreat to reformulate the firm's strategy. Externally, the buyer sees an ad or receives a call from a hotel sales representative who offers a favorable corporate program. Marketers can stimulate problem recognition by developing ads and calling on prospects.

2. General Need Description

Having recognized a need, the buyer goes on to determine the requirements of the product and to formulate a **general need description**. For a training meeting, this would include food and beverage, meeting space, AV equipment, coffee break, and sleeping room requirements. The corporate meeting planner works with others—the director of human resources, the training manager, and potential participants—to gain insight into the requirements of the meeting. Together, they determine the importance of the price, meeting space, sleeping rooms, food and beverage, and other factors.

The hotel marketer can render assistance to the buyer in this phase. Often, the buyer is unaware of the benefits of various product features. Alert marketers can help buyers define their companies' needs and show how their hotel can satisfy them.

3. Product Specification

Once the general requirements have been determined, the specific requirements for the meeting can be developed. For example, a meeting might require twenty sleeping rooms, a meeting room for twenty-five set up classroom style with a whiteboard and overhead projector, and a separate room for lunch. For larger meetings with an exhibit area, the information need becomes more complex. Information often requested includes availability of water, ceiling heights, door widths, security, and procedures for receiving and storing materials prior to the event. Salespersons must be prepared to answer their prospective client's questions about their hotel's capabilities to fulfill the **product specification**.

4. Supplier Search

The buyer now conducts a **supplier search** to identify the most appropriate hotels. The buyer can examine trade directories, do a computer search, or phone familiar hotels. Hotels that qualify may receive a site visit from the meeting planner, who eventually develops a short list of qualified suppliers.

5. Proposal Solicitations

Once the meeting planner has drawn up a short list of suppliers, qualified hotels are invited to submit proposals. Thus hotel marketers must be skilled in researching, writing, and presenting proposals. These should be marketing oriented, not simply technical documents. They should position their company's capabilities and resources so that they stand out from the competition. Many hotels have developed videos for this purpose.

6. Supplier Selection

In this stage, members of the buying center review the proposals and move toward **supplier selection**. They conduct an analysis of the hotel, considering physical facilities, the hotel's ability to deliver service, and the professionalism of its employees. Frequently, the buying center specifies desired supplier attributes and suggests their relative importance. In general, meeting planners consider the following attributes in making their selection of a location:

- Sleeping rooms
- Meeting rooms
- Food and beverage
- Audio visual staff and equipment
- Billing procedures
- Check-in/checkout
- Staff
- Availability of online information

e

7.1 Meeting Matrix, www. meetingmatrix. com: Visit this site to see how it can help communicate your meeting space to the client.

Technology has made it possible for meeting planners to take a visual tour of the meeting space. Companies such as emarketing360.com specialize in capturing video images of meeting space and making it accessible to buyers on the Web. Meeting Matrix provides a Web site with meeting information, including room diagrams, and videos of meeting space. This helps meeting planners narrow their selection or even make their selection without visiting the site. The later would likely be made up of buyers who have a lot of faith in the brand.

The organization may attempt to negotiate with preferred suppliers for better prices and terms before making the final selection. There are several ways the hotel marketer can counter the request for a lower price. For example, the dates can be moved from a high-demand period to a need period for the hotel, or menus can be changed. The marketer can cite the value of the services the buyer now receives, especially where services are superior to competitors.

7. Order-Routine Specification

The buyer now writes the final order with the chosen hotels, listing the technical **order-routine specifications** of the meeting. The hotel responds by offering the buyer a formal contract. The contract specifies cutoff dates for room blocks, the date when the hotel will release the room block for sale to other guests, and minimum guarantees for food and beverage functions. Many hotels and restaurants have turned what should have been a profitable banquet into a loss by not having or enforcing minimum guarantees.

8. Performance Review

The buyer does a postpurchase **performance review** of the product. During this phase the buyer determines if the product meets the buyer's specifications and if the buyer will purchase from the company again. It is important for hotels to have at least daily meetings with a meeting planner to make sure everything is going well and to correct those things that did not go well. This manages the buyer's perceived service and helps to avoid a negative postpurchase evaluation by the buyer.

■■■ Group Business Markets

One of the most important types of organizational business is group business. It is important for marketing managers to understand the differences between a group market and a consumer market. The group business market is often more sophisticated and requires more technical information than the consumer market. Many group markets book more than a year in advance. During this time, cognitive dissonance can develop; thus, marketers must keep in contact with buyers to assure them that they made the right decision in choosing the seller's hotel.

The four main categories of group business are conventions, association meetings, corporate meetings, and SMERF (social, military, educational, religious, and fraternal organizations) groups. Conventions attract large numbers, but meetings occur much more frequently than conventions. Over 1.25 million corporate or business meetings are held in the United States annually. Associations generate a quarter of a million conventions, conferences, with the majority of these being conferences. Four thousand four hundred people attend the average convention, while eighty-four people attend the average corporate meeting.[7] When choosing a hotel, an important consideration for a meeting planner is whether the hotel can house the participants. Most hotels have the potential of attracting hundreds of small meetings, whereas larger hotels can attract conventions. Group business is a very important segment for most hotels. Successful hotels know which groups to attract, how to use group business to fill need dates, and how to sell groups on the hotel's benefits rather than just price.

The Convention Industry Council (CIC) is made up of thirty member organizations that represent both buyers and suppliers to the meetings industry. They

Preparation for a holiday (click image to zoom). Courtesy: © Bashta/Dreamstime.com

e

7.2 Convention Industry Council, http://www. conventionindustry.org/: Take a look at all of the associations that make up the CIC.

recently developed the Accepted Practices Exchange (APEX), which brings a set of standards and best practices to all parties involved in the creation and implementation of a meeting. APEX's event specifications provide a template of a checklist for planning an event, and its glossary brings a common meaning to terms used in the meetings industry. APEX is a great tool for those involved in selling or planning meetings.[8]

Conventions

Conventions are a specialty market requiring extensive meeting facilities. They are usually the annual meeting of an association and include general sessions, committee meetings, and special-interest sessions. Hotels with convention facilities, such as the Chicago Hyatt or the Atlanta Marriott Marquis, can house small and midsized conventions. Conventions that use a major facility, such as the Jacob Javitts Convention Center in New York, often have tens of thousands of delegates. They are called citywide conventions because hotels throughout the city house their delegates. There are almost 14,000 conventions held each year in the United States. Convention delegates stay an average of 3.6 days and spend an average of just over $1,500 per event. Of this amount about $350 is spent on lodging.[9]

Associations usually select convention sites two to five years in advance, with some large conventions planned 10 to 15 years before the event. October is the most popular month for conventions, followed by November, September, and April.[10] Some associations prefer to have their conventions in the same city year after year, whereas others prefer to move to a different area of the country each year.

A convention can be a major source of income for the sponsoring organization. Registration fees from attendees and sales of exhibition space in the trade show are major sources of revenue. A trade show gives suppliers a chance to show and sell their products to the association's members. Companies such as GES Exposition Services work with the association and conference center to provide electrical hookups, booth setup, and other services to make sure the trade show exhibitors have the resources they need to set up their exhibits. The price that can be charged for exhibition space is related to the number of attendees. When choosing a convention location, an association looks for sites that will be both accessible and attractive to members. Balancing the annual budget depends on a good turnout.

Convention planners listed the following as the most important factors in choosing a destination:

- Availability of hotels and facilities
- Ease of transportation
- Transportation costs
- Distance from attendees
- Climate
- Recreation
- Sights and cultural activities

Here are the most important attributes of the hotel:[11]

- Meeting rooms
- Negotiable rates
- Food and beverage quality
- Sleeping rooms

The Vancouver Convention and Exhibition Centre draws many visitors. Conventions and visitor bureaus can be a good source of business for hotels and restaurants. Courtesy of Peter Gridley/Getty Images, Inc.—Taxi.

- Support services
- Billing procedures
- Check-in/checkout
- Staff assignment
- Exhibit space
- Previous experience

Note that food quality is very important to the convention planner. Exceptional banquets, out-of-the-ordinary receptions, and unique coffee breaks can be a point of differentiation at a convention, something the attendees will discuss with colleagues. In contrast, poor food and poor service can generate negative feelings about the convention among the participants. Support services must be available when needed. A nonfunctioning DVD player must be repaired or replaced quickly to ensure that the presenter's flow is not interrupted.

Many hotels contract with independent AV companies to supply and maintain this equipment. The AV company can pool its equipment and staff within the city. So, when a group has special AV requirement the company can bring in the equipment and staff needed to produce the event. In large hotels, AV companies have an office in the hotel to store equipment and house technicians. For large meetings, AV companies have on-site technicians to remain with the group during the meeting to correct problems as they occur, thus ensuring that speaker presentations proceed as planned. Under this arrangement, the hotel bills the client for the AV and then pays the AV company an agreed-upon percentage of the charges, for example, 60 percent often goes to the AV company, with the hotel keeping 40 percent.

Having your meeting facilities online for meeting planners to access is important because more than 30 percent of meeting planners use meeting-specific software. Almost all meeting planners (99 percent) use the Web for information with convention and visitor bureau, hotel, and local city sites the top ones visited.[12]

Billing procedures are also important to convention planners. Billing can create problems for hotels that take it for granted and do not have a customer-oriented accounting department. Professional meeting planners want a bill that is understandable, accurate, and delivered in a timely manner. Without these characteristics, the bill can be a nightmare. Important attributes for a convention planner other than facilities and rates are food quality, billing procedures, and the professionalism and attention of the hotel's staff.

Convention Bureaus

Convention bureaus are nonprofit marketing organizations that help hotels sign conventions and meetings. These organizations are often supported by a hotel or sales tax and are run by chambers of commerce, visitor bureaus, or city and county governments. They are often one of the first sources of information for a convention or meeting planner. A hotel relying on meeting business for a significant portion of its occupancy should have a good working relationship with the convention bureau, which includes active membership in the organization.

Association Meetings

Associations sponsor many types of meetings, including regional, special-interest, educational, and board meetings. There are over 71,000 associations; 92 percent of them hold meetings. These associations create 227,000 association meetings annually, generating meeting business valued at $70 billion.[13] For example, the AMA has chapters in many large cities. These chapters gather once a month, usually at a luncheon or dinner meeting. The AMA sponsors or cosponsors educational meetings. It also has special-interest meetings, such as the marketing educators meeting held every August and February. Every major association schedules scores of meetings held throughout the year in various locations.

The most important attributes of a destination for an association meeting planner are availability of hotel and facilities, ease of transportation, distance from attendees, and transportation costs. Climate, recreation, and cultural activities are not as important as they are to the convention market because the meeting itself is the major draw. In selecting a hotel, the association meeting planner looks for food quality, rates, meeting rooms, billing procedures, and attributes similar to the convention planner except for exhibition space.[14] Notice that for the association meeting planner, food and beverage are the most important attributes.

Membership in the American Society of Association Executives (ASAE) is beneficial for hotels actively pursuing association business. It provides an opportunity to network with association executives and is a source of information on national and local associations. Many of the hotel's corporate clients are also members of trade associations. These customers can become ambassadors for the hotel at their trade association meetings.

Members attend association meetings voluntarily. The hotel should work with meeting planners to make the destination seem as attractive as possible. Making sure that the meeting planner is aware of local attractions, offering suggestions for spousal activities, and assisting in the development of after-convention activities can be useful to the hotel and the meeting planner. It is important to market both the destination and the hotel.

Corporate Meetings

For employees of a company, a **corporate meeting** is a command performance. They are directed to attend the meeting without choice. One implication of required attendance is a short lead time. Because corporations do not have to develop and implement a marketing plan to gain attendees, they often plan meetings with a few weeks' lead time. Corporate meetings can range in size from a board meeting for ten to twelve people to a sales meeting for several hundred people. Overall, 35 percent of corporate meeting are for ten to twenty-four people, 39 percent have twenty-five to forty-nine attendees, 18 percent have fifty to ninety-nine people, and 18 percent are for over a hundred attendees.[15]

Many corporate meetings are set up by mega agencies, such as American Express, Carlson Wagonlit, and Consortia. These agencies provide travel management services for companies, and the meeting planning area is a growing portion of their business. Thus, when seeking business from corporations, a hotel manager must understand who has the responsibility for booking meetings.[16]

The corporation's major concern is that the meeting be productive and accomplish the company's objectives. Types of corporate meetings include training, management, and planning. Another type of corporate meeting is the incentive meeting, which will be discussed later.

To a corporate meeting planner, the most important attributes in the choice of a destination are the availability of hotels, ease of transportation, transportation costs, and distance from the location of the attendees. The most important factors in the choice of a hotel are as follows:

- Food quality
- Meeting rooms
- Rates
- Sleeping rooms
- Wireless Internet access
- Two-line phones
- Fitness center
- Support service
- Billing procedures

Corporate meeting planners want to ensure that meetings are productive and the corporation gets good value for the money it spends. Their success depends on planning smooth-running meetings. Hotels interested in capturing and retaining corporate meeting business must make sure that meeting rooms are adequate and set up properly. Because meeting planners want attendees to be comfortable, sleeping rooms are important to them. They are also concerned about the quality of food. Recreation facilities may also be important. In a multiday technical meeting, the interaction of the participants outside the formal meetings is valuable. Golf or tennis can be used to encourage participants to interact socially and break up the monotony of the classroom sessions. Similarly, an evening outing to an area restaurant, sporting, or cultural event can serve as an enjoyable break for participants.

Corporate culture also plays an important part in the choice of a hotel. Hotel salespeople must develop an understanding of the client's corporate culture to gain insight into benefits the hotel can offer. Some companies feel meetings should be austere, rather than lavish. Such companies may feel they are setting an example for their employees, encouraging them by example to spend money wisely. Others view meetings as a time for employees to relax and enjoy themselves, a well-deserved break. Companies that believe meetings should both educate and rejuvenate employees and build their enthusiasm toward the company are willing to spend more money on food and beverage, entertainment, and deluxe hotel facilities.

Small Groups

The small corporate meeting, less than fifty rooms, is gaining the attention of hotel chains. Although small in terms of number of participants, thousands of small meetings are held every month. Hotels and hotel chains have developed special packages for small meetings, a segment often overlooked by large hotels. Upscale hotels such as the L'Ermitage and The Peninsula, both in Beverly Hills, go after executive meetings where expense is not a problem.[17]

Sheraton has also developed executive conference centers. These centers are designed for board meetings, strategic-planning sessions, and training sessions. The amenities in the centers were developed as the result of focus groups with clients to find out what they wanted in small meetings; these amenities were included in the executive conference centers and their smart meeting rooms. Select Sheraton hotels in Europe offer "Sheraton Smart Meetings," a program designed to provide small meeting planners with the technology needed for today's meeting. The smart meeting offers rooms equipped with ISDN lines, data port entries in the floor, built-in projection, and landline videoconferencing. Small meetings often have a 30-day or less lead time; thus, Sheraton has also expedited the reservation process by targeting meetings of fifteen to forty people that book on short notice.[18] The Holiday Inn Oceanfront in Ocean City, Maryland, near Washington, D.C., has developed a small meeting plan targeted at the many government agencies located in the area. Their "government package" provides a double occupancy room, continental breakfast, meeting room with AV equipment, and morning and afternoon beverage breaks for a set price per person. The set price makes it easy for meeting planners to understand their costs. Simplifying small meeting arrangements is critical because those who plan small meetings are often not meeting planners. The meeting package is available Sunday through Thursday, reserving the weekends for leisure travelers who want to come to the beach.[19]

Incentive Travel

Incentive travel, a unique subset of corporate group business, is a reward participants receive for achieving or exceeding a goal. Companies give awards for both individual and team performance. For instance, the employees of the best-performing region might be recognized. Michael Kennedy, manager of retail development at Isuzu Commercial Truck of America, kept his Winners' Circle program going through the recent economic turndown. He states, "If you polled our salespeople, the Winners' Circle would be right up there as one of the reasons they want to work for us." This shows the power of a well-planned incentive program. The top-tier

Winners' Circle members go to a lavish international destination; the silver winners go to an exciting domestic destination. Kennedy demonstrates the value of an incentive trip by recapping the percentage of sales that come from the winners, which is always high. A hotel salesperson selling incentives must be able to help his or her client justify the expenditure. Percentage of sales of the attendees is an excellent way to do this.[20]

Because travel serves as the reward, participants must perceive the destination and the hotel as something special. Climate, recreational facilities, and sightseeing opportunities are high on an incentive meeting planners' list of desired attributes.[21] The Caribbean, Hawaii, Europe, and resort destinations within the continental United States are common incentive travel destinations. The right location and excellent facilities are important. Brian Jones, senior vice president sales, at Morgans Hotel Group, states "it is also about creating unique experiences that motivate, celebrate, or educate. The more we speak to these issues the more successful we will be."[22]

Incentive trips used to last from three to seven days; however, the current trend is to keep the trips short and get the participants back to their jobs. Scott Walker, director of incentive and promotion certificates for Hyatt Hotels, states, "I am hearing, 'Let's change it from five nights to four, but add extras.' These extras include meals, spa treatments, a round on the golf course, or Hyatt Cheque certificates that they can spend any way they want."[23] The average expenditure per room is high. Winners of incentive trips sometimes receive a cash deposit to their account that can be used for charges to their account or services provided through the hotel, such as rental cars. For example, participants in an incentive trip sponsored by Revlon for the best regional sales performance received a $500 credit on their hotel bill that could be spent as they wished. In such cases the participants spend freely in the hotel's restaurants and bars, often supplementing the credit with their own money. Thus, incentive travel can be very profitable for a hotel.

During the 2008 recession there was considerable backlash against incentive travel after news of companies, particularly those companies that received government bailouts or laid off employees. One event that created a lot of negative publicity for incentive meetings was a $400,000 incentive meeting at the St. Regis in Monarch Beach, California, that was held one week after $85 billion of tax-payers money was given to AIG to keep it from going bankrupt. Branded luxury hotels such as St. Regis, Four Seasons, and Ritz-Carlton saw their occupancies decline as many companies did not want to say they were having a meeting at a luxury property because of the perception it would create.[25] Gradually normalcy returned to the luxury market and the luxury market was the fastest growing in 2010.[26]

The Hilton Hotel Villa Igiea Palermo is a five-star hotel in Sicily, which is an attractive destination for incentive groups. © Sabrina Dvihally/Dreamstime.com

Marketing Highlight | Green Meetings: The Right Thing to Do for the Environment and Business

7–1 The Convention Industry Council (CIC) provides this definition of a green meeting. A green meeting or event incorporates environmental considerations to minimize its negative impact on the environment. Green or environmental considerations are one aspect of sustainability. Sustainability takes a "triple bottom line" approach that seeks to balance the social, environmental, and economic concerns against business needs."[24]

The APEX, an initiative of the CIC, is creating standards for environmentally sustainable meetings. It has developed standards for nine sectors of a meeting; accommodations, audio/visual, communications and marketing, destinations, exhibits, food and beverage, meeting venue, on-site offices, and transportation.

New meeting facilities can be built to meet green standards. The Leadership in Energy and Environmental Design (LEED) Green Building Rating System provides design guidelines for environment-friendly buildings. A good environmental plan begins with the construction of the building.

A second area of sustainability is general facility management. Even for buildings that were not built with sustainability in mind, there are still ways to make the building greener. These include changing incandescent light bulbs to light-emitting diodes (LEDs) or compact fluorescent light bulbs, recycling programs, and the efficient management of room temperatures, which are just a few ways one can minimize the negative effect of the meeting venue on the environment.

The third component relates to the meeting. For example, boxed lunches using a disposable cardboard box with packaged chips and cookies have been an industry standard. Often the chips and cookies are thrown away by those on a diet. A green way to do boxed lunches is set up a sandwich buffet, with chips, salads, and desserts. This eliminates the package material and waste, since people are likely to take what they will eat. It also saves labor, as packing box lunches is labor intensive. Some hotels and restaurants have installed water purification systems, so they can serve bottled water quality from pitchers or carafes, eliminating the need to use water in disposable plastic or glass bottles and the shipping of water to the hotel

from faraway places. The St. Regis Houston Hotel puts this water in elegant carafes and charges banquet customers for the water, similar to a charge for imported bottled water. Using china instead of plastic plates and utensils can save tons of landfill waste. Recycling name badges reduces solid waste and can save the planner seventy-five cents per recycled badge. Serving bulk sugar and cream for coffee and tea breaks reduces solid waste from sugar wrappers and cream containers, while cutting the food cost by over 50 percent on those items.

A researcher found that 90 percent of the 140 largest companies in the United States believe that adapting environmentally responsible practices is important for their reputation. This group also feels that the importance of environmental sustainability will continue to grow. The Travel Industry Association of America found that over 80 percent of the customers surveyed were willing to spend 6.5 percent more on products and services provided by environmentally friendly companies. Green meeting practices can enhance reputation, save money, increase revenue, and are the right thing to do for the planet.

For more information on green meetings, see

Coalition for Environmentally Responsible Economies	www.ceres.org
Environmental Protection Agency– Green Meetings Initiative	www.epa.gov/oppt/greenmeetings
The Green Meeting Industry Council (GMIC)	www.greenmeetings.info
Council International Association of Conference Centers	www.iacconline.org
Meeting Professionals International Corporate Social Responsibility	http://www.mpiweb.org/Portal/CSR

Sources: "Green Meetings," Convention Industry Council, http://www.conventionindustry.org/StandardsPractices/GreenMeetings.aspx (accessed September 8, 2011); Green Meetings, www.mpiweb.com (accessed September 9, 2011); www.greenmeetings.info/goodforbusiness.htm (accessed August 23, 2008); "Green Meetings Policy," The National Recycling Coalition (accessed August 23, 2008); and www.ceres.org (accessed August 23, 2008).

Incentive travel is handled in-house or by incentive houses, travel agencies, consultants, and travel fulfillment firms that handle only the travel arrangements. The trend is moving away from in-house planners to incentive houses, fulfillment houses, and travel agencies.[27] One reason for the shift is that outside organizations specializing in incentive travel often buy blocks of airline seats and hotel rooms. As a result, they can put together packages more efficiently than in-house planners. Incentive houses usually provide a choice of several locations to the company, so the ultimate choice of location is made by the company, even when it uses an incentive house. The hotel must work with both the incentive house and the decision makers within the company.

SMERFs

SMERF stands for social, military, educational, religious, and fraternal organizations. On a broader scale, this meeting classification includes smaller specialty organizations that are price sensitive. The individual pays for the majority of the functions sponsored by these organizations, and sometimes the expenses are not tax deductible. As a result, participants are usually price conscious. They want a low room rate and often find the food and beverage within the hotel too expensive, preferring to eat elsewhere or purchase food and eat in their rooms. Because attendees are price sensitive, one of the biggest challenges is to get the attendees to book within the room block.[28] Hotels often provide concessions, such as free rooms or a free or reduced food and beverage function based on the number of room nights in the group's block. If the block does not materialize, the meeting planner is responsible for extra charges.

On the positive side, SMERFs are willing to be flexible to ensure a lower room rate. They are willing to meet during the off season or on weekends. Weekends are often preferred because most participants attend meetings during their free time. Also, the size of these segments should not be overlooked. In the United States, over 50,000 religious organizations have group travel programs.[29] Thus, SMERFs provide good filler business during off-peak times. If you decide to go into hotel sales upon graduation, there is a good chance you will be assigned to the SMERF market, as it is usually assigned to the most junior sales person.

Segmentation of Group Markets by Purpose of the Meeting

Besides dividing group markets into convention, association, corporate, and SMERF, they also can be broken into the purpose of the meeting. Four major purposes are conventions, conferences, seminars, and meetings. Table 7–1 shows a matrix describing some of the critical sales decision variables for these types of gatherings. This matrix reflects the general nature of sales decision variables within the group market. Exceptions can and do exist. A discussion of major sale segments of the group market follows.

TABLE 7–1

Decision Variable Matrix: Group Markets

Sales Decision Variables	Conventions	Conferences	Seminars	Meetings
Decision makers	Many: committees, chapter presidents, high-ranking officers	Conference organizer, meeting planner	Seminar organizer, boss, secretary	Boss, secretary, regional manager, meeting planner
Decision influencers	Many	Limited	Limited	Few
Degree of politicalization	Highly political	Somewhat political	Personal	Highly personal
Decision time	Years	One year or less	Months	Short time; sometimes one day
Customer price sensitivity	Very	Somewhat	Somewhat	Not highly sensitive
Personal service sensitivity	Low	Moderate	High	Extreme
Opportunity for upsell	Low	Moderate	Moderate	High
Team selling opportunity	Definitely	Sometimes	Probably not	No
Special advertising promotion	Definitely	Usually no	No	No
International	Definitely	Possible	Probably not	Usually not, but opportunities exist (board of directors)
Repeat sales opportunity	Long time, poor	Moderate time	Yes	Definitely
Need for personal sales call (travel)	Probably yes	Probably no	Probably no	Depends on the situation

Restaurants with banquet space can work with their local convention and tourist bureau to sell banquets and to promote their restaurant to visitors. Courtesy of Starush/Dreamstime.

7.3 Maggianos Little Italy, www. maggianos. com: Go to Maggianos Little Italy's Private Events section to see how this restaurant has developed a product to attract meetings and events.

Restaurants as a Meeting Venue

Restaurants are designing their space so they can take advantage of meetings, a room off of the main room that can be closed off for meetings, giving the restaurant the option of using it as part of the public dining space on Saturday night or a meeting room during a weekday. According to a meeting research firm, meetings held in space of 700 square feet or less (20 feet by 35 feet) increased by over 25 percent in the past two years. Meetings of fifty people or less can be a great source of business for a restaurant. Many times they are held at off-peak times, such as during a weekday. Restaurant Dante in Boston does a great private events business, with 70 percent of its business coming from small corporate meetings, and it has its own marketing and events manager. Many restaurants are adding private rooms and hiring salespeople to gain their share of the meetings market.[30]

∎∎∎ Dealing with Meeting Planners

When negotiating with meeting planners, it is important to try to develop a win–win relationship. Meeting planners like to return to the same property. Jim Jones, president of James E. Jones Associates, states, "For me, prior successful experience is the number one factor in choosing a site. Knowing the property takes away most of the anxiety. I know what the hotel can and cannot do, and I know that they're familiar with the idiosyncrasies of my client. I never book a hotel if I plan to use it once."[31]

Discussions over price can drive the meeting planner and the hotel sales executive apart or they can bring them together. One successful technique for negotiating with a meeting planner is to determine the group's requirements in detail and work out a package based on needs and budget. Some meeting planners try to negotiate every item separately, starting with the room rate. Then they choose a $65 banquet and try to negotiate the price to $45. In this scenario, every line item becomes a point of contention between the meeting planner and the hotel salesperson.

Taking a consultative approach is much more effective. If the hotel knows that the meeting planner wants to spend $50 for dinner, the chef can develop alternatives within this price range, suggesting something the attendees will enjoy, and the hotel can produce the meal at a profit and sell it for $50. The hotel gains a profitable meeting, and the meeting stays within the planner's budget. Debra Kaufman, an association meeting planner, states that if attendees are able to get work done while they are at the conference they will stay longer.[32] If space is available, the hotel can offer a small meeting room set up with business services, including Internet access, computers, and printers. Given the space is available; this can be a low-cost item to the hotel, which has a high value to the meeting planner.

The hotel salesperson must remember that most group rates are noncommissionable. Meeting planners sometimes turn meetings over to travel agents, who book about 5 percent of all corporate meetings. If the meeting planner does so without understanding that the rate is noncommissionable, problems can arise when the travel agent tries to collect a commission. If the rates are to be commissionable, it should be determined during the negotiation process. It is also common for hotels to give one complimentary room night for every fifty room nights that the group produces—another point of negotiation. Suites are usually counted as two rooms. Thus, a suite for three nights would be the equivalent of six room nights. When a hotel has a smaller meeting room that it will not be able to sell during a proposed meeting, it can be used in the negotiation process as a board-room or a space for the meeting manager to work. The hotel salesperson must look for items that will create value for the meeting planner without creating costs or sacrificing revenue for the hotel.

Many associations have a president, elected from the membership, and a professional executive, often called the executive vice president. In such case, the executive vice president usually sets up the meeting or supervises a meeting planner. In larger associations there may be a paid executive director, a convention manager, and one or more meeting managers who handle the association's meetings. In some associations the elected officers also like to get involved in the selection of sites and hotels for meetings or conventions. To further complicate matters, the previous year's president usually becomes the chairman of the association's board of directors and, therefore, can hold great power in the association, as can other past presidents. It is important for the salesperson to find out who is involved in the decision-making process, both officially and unofficially. Gatekeepers can give useful insights into the decision-making process within the organization.

When the vice president of sales asks a junior salesperson to organize a sales meeting, the salesperson is usually unsure of how to proceed with newly assigned and unfamiliar tasks. However, meeting administrators often know the business as well as the hotel salesperson. Salespeople should listen to the meeting administrator to understand his or her requirements. Sometimes meeting administrators know exactly what they want and simply desire a quote for the meeting according to their specifications. If this is the case, a salesperson trying to alter their specifications arbitrarily can appear unprofessional and lose the meeting administrator's business. For example, a hotel salesperson altered the meeting administrator's menu and developed a quotation based on the altered menus. The meeting administrator was planning a series of training sessions to be presented at various locations throughout the United States and had developed menus to meet group needs. This uninvited intrusion by the hotel salesperson infuriated the meeting administrator, who then proceeded to a competitive hotel.

Most meeting planners maintain a history of the group for the purpose of planning future meetings. This includes past dates, locations, and attendance figures. They also have evaluations of past meetings. A salesperson can gain valuable information by asking questions about past conferences. These questions can provide insight into room pickups, attendance at banquets, past problems with a hotel, and what their members have enjoyed. In addition to information volunteered by the meeting planner, the salesperson should interview hotels that hosted the conference in past years.

Consider the following expectations of meeting planners.[33] Meeting planners want their calls or e-mails returned the same day they are received. When they ask about the availability of meeting space, they expect a response the same day and a complete proposal in five days. They want check-in and checkout to last no more than four minutes. Most meeting planners want their bill within one week of the event, and 25 percent want it within two days. Planners feel that hotel management should empower the convention service manager to solve their problems. They do not want to wait while the convention service manager checks with a superior. Ultimately, when dealing with group business, the hotel has to please both the meeting planner and the meeting planner's clients. These clients include those attending the conference, association executives, and the president or senior officer of a corporation. Jonathan Tisch, president and CEO of Loews Hotels, states, "What we're looking to do is to create a win-win situation. If the senior officer is happy, then the planner's happy, and if the planner's happy, we've done our job."[34]

Not all meetings are large. There are thousands of meetings held with less than twenty attendees. © Weixin Shen | Dreamstime.com

One of the most important aspects creating a successful function is a prefunction meeting between the hotel staff and the meeting planner before the function. Accounting should be at the meeting so they can get acquainted with the function to make sure the bill meets both of their expectations. The bell captain should know if a gratuity for his or her staff is included in the package. If it is, Renee Goetz, a meeting planner, states that the staff should be instructed to say, "Thank you, that's been taken care of," when a guest offers a tip. The concierge needs to know the meeting has open nights with no banquets because this will allow the concierge to set aside tables at local restaurants. If garage space is limited, arrangements need to take place to make sure there is adequate space for the group. The hotel staff who will be receiving questions about the event and the event schedule, such as the front desk and operators, should be briefed. The reservations agents should know the names of the group's VIPs and who should get early check-in privileges. Those responsible for receiving packages for the meeting should know who will be sending packages and how they will be addressed so they can store them properly. A prefunction meeting going over the logistics of the meeting can go a long way to creating a successful event.[35]

■■■ The Corporate Account and Corporate Travel Manager

A nongroup form of organizational business is the individual business traveler. Most hotels offer a corporate rate, which is intended to provide an incentive for corporations to use the hotel. Because of competitive pressures, most hotels have dropped the qualification requirements for their basic corporate rate, offering it now to any businessperson who requests the corporate rate. To provide an incentive system for heavy users, hotels developed a second set of corporate rates. The basic corporate rate is about 10 to 15 percent below the hotel's rack rate;[36] the contract rate is a negotiated rate, usually 10 to 40 percent below the hotel's rack rate. It often includes other benefits besides a discounted rate. Common benefits include morning newspapers, upgrades when available, use of the hotel's fitness center, early check-ins, and late checkouts.[37] When negotiating a corporate contract, it is important to understand what creates value for the company.

The corporate business traveler is a sought-after segment. Although the corporate contract rate is a discounted rate, it is higher than the group rate. In addition to paying a good rate, the business traveler is on an expense account and makes use of the hotel's restaurants, health club, laundry, and business center facilities.

The competition for business travelers, once limited to mid-class and luxury hotels, has spread to limited-service hotels. Limited-service hotels now have a 34.5 percent market share of rooms generated by the business traveler. The strong showing of limited-service hotels can be attributed to the upgrading of amenities found in these hotels and businesses needing to cut costs to remain competitive. Companies that would have not considered putting their people in a limited-service hotel a few years ago are now using them. These companies realize that they can save thousands of dollars by purchasing less expensive accommodations and yet meet quality standards of guests.

Larger companies have corporate traveler management programs run by the company or in-house branches of a travel agency. These managers negotiate the corporate hotel contracts. These are the most important attributes to the travel managers when negotiating a hotel contract:

- A favorable image of the hotel's brand by the company's travelers

- Guaranteed availability of negotiated rate (focus groups have told us that a quick way to lose their business is to charge them a higher rate during citywide conventions or tell them rooms are not available during these conventions)

- Location

- Reputation of the hotel's brand

- Negotiated rate

- Flexibility on charges for late cancellation of room reservations[38]

In addition to developing corporate hotel contracts, the travel managers set per diem rates, specifying the amount a company traveler can spend on food and beverage. Often, these rates are set at different levels, with the per diem amount increasing as one moves up in the corporation. It is important to find out what a company's per diem rates are to determine whether the hotel is in the company's price range and what level of manager the hotel can expect to attract. The hotel can use this information to determine the volume the company will give them. For example, if the per diem for a company's salespeople is in the hotel's rate range, the hotel can expect more volume than it could expect if only the executive management falls within the price range.

Some corporations use in-house travel agencies, or in-plants, that also represent other corporations, providing the advantage of negotiating leverage. A business represented through an in-plant may have only one hundred room nights a year in New York, but the travel agency represented by the in-plant may service ten companies with a total of 1,500 room nights in New York. The travel agency can negotiate a rate based on the 1,500 room nights and pass this rate along to the individual companies. The hotel compensates in-plants by straight commissions, monthly fees, or a combination of a fee and commission.[39]

■■■ KEY TERMS

Buying center. All those individuals and groups who participate in the purchasing and decision-making process and who share common goals and the risks arising from the decisions.

Convention. A specialty market requiring extensive meeting facilities. It is usually the annual meeting of an association and includes general sessions, committee meetings, and special-interest sessions.

Corporate meeting. A meeting held by a corporation for its employees.

Derived demand. Organizational demand that ultimately comes from (derives from) the demand for consumer goods.

General need description. The stage in the industrial buying process in which a company describes the general characteristics and quantity of a needed item.

Incentive travel. A reward that participants receive for achieving or exceeding a goal.

Order-routine specification. The stage of the industrial buying process in which a buyer writes the final order with the chosen supplier(s), listing the technical specifications, quantity needed, expected time of delivery, return policies, warranties, and so on.

Organizational buying process. The decision-making process by which formal organizations establish the need for purchased products and services and identify, evaluate, and choose among alternative brands and suppliers.

Performance review. The stage of an industrial buying process in which a buyer rates its satisfaction with suppliers, deciding whether to continue, modify, or drop the relationship.

Problem recognition. The stage of the industrial buying process in which someone in a company recognizes a problem or need that can be met by acquiring a good or a service.

Product specification. The stage of an industrial buying process in which the buying organization decides on and specifies the best technical product characteristics for a needed item.

SMERF. SMERF stands for social, military, educational, religious, and fraternal organizations. This group of specialty markets has a common price-sensitive thread.

Supplier search. The stage of the industrial buying process in which a buyer tries to find the best vendor.

Supplier selection. The stage of the industrial buying process in which a buyer receives proposals and selects a supplier or suppliers.

■■■ CHAPTER REVIEW

I. The Organizational Buying Process. Their purchases often involve large sums of money; complex technical, economic considerations; and interactions among many people at all levels of the organization. Buyer and seller are often very dependent on each other.
  A. Market structure and demand
  B. Types of decisions and the decision process

II. Participants in the Organizational Buying Process
  A. Users. Users are those who use the product or service.

  B. Influencers. Influencers directly influence the buying decision but do not themselves make the final decision.
  C. Deciders. Deciders select product requirements and suppliers.
  D. Approvers. Approvers authorize the proposed actions of deciders or buyers.
  E. Buyers. Buyers have formal authority for selecting suppliers and arranging the terms of purchase.
  F. Gatekeepers. Gatekeepers have the power to prevent sellers or information from reaching members of the buying center.

III. Major Influences on Organizational Buyers

A. Environmental factors. Organizational buyers are heavily influenced by the current and expected economic environment.

B. Organizational factors. Each organization has specific objectives, policies, procedures, organizational structures, and systems related to buying.

C. Interpersonal factors. The buying center usually includes several participants with differing levels of interest, authority, and persuasiveness.

D. Individual factors. Each participant in the buying decision process has personal motivations, perceptions, and preferences. The participant's age, income, education, professional identification, personality, and attitudes toward risk all influence the participants in the buying process.

IV. The Organizational Buying Decisions

A. Problem recognition. The buying process begins when someone in the company recognizes a problem or need that can be met by acquiring a good or a service.

B. General needs description. The buyer goes on to determine the requirements of the product.

C. Product specifications. Once the general requirements have been determined, the specific requirements for the product can be developed.

D. Supplier search. The buyer now tries to identify the most appropriate suppliers.

E. Proposal solicitation. Qualified suppliers are invited to submit proposals. Skilled research, writing, and presentation are required.

F. Supplier selection. Once the meeting planner has drawn up a short list of suppliers, qualified hotels are invited to submit proposals.

G. Order-routine specification. The buyer writes the final order, listing the technical specification. The supplier responds by offering the buyer a formal contract.

H. Performance review. The buyer does postpurchase evaluation of the product. During this phase the buyer determines if the product meets the buyer's specifications and if the buyer will purchase from the company again.

V. The Group Business Markets

A. Conventions. Conventions are usually the annual meeting of an association and include general sessions, committee meetings, and special-interest sessions. A trade show is often an important part of an annual convention.

B. Association meetings. Associations sponsor many types of meetings, including regional, special-interest, educational, and board meetings.

C. Corporate meetings. A corporate meeting is a command performance for employees of a company. The corporation's major concern is that the meeting be productive and accomplish the company's objectives.

D. Small groups. Meetings of less than fifty rooms are gaining the attention of hotels and hotel chains.

E. Incentive travel. Incentive travel, a unique subset of corporate group business, is a reward participants receive for achieving or exceeding a goal.

F. SMERF groups. SMERF stands for social, military, educational, religious, and fraternal organizations. This group of specialty markets has a common price-sensitive thread.

G. Segmentation of Group Markets by Purpose of Meeting

H. Restaurants as a Meeting Venue

VI. Dealing with Meeting Planners.
When negotiating with meeting planners, it is important to try to develop a win-win relationship. Meeting planners like to return to the same property.

VII. The Corporate Account and Travel Manager.
A nongroup form of organizational business is the individual business traveler. Most hotels offer a corporate rate, which is intended to provide an incentive for corporations to use the hotel.

■■■ DISCUSSION QUESTIONS

1. What is derived demand? Give an example of derived demand for a hotel in your town.

2. The buying center consists of six roles. Why is it important for marketers to understand these roles?

3. Discuss the major environmental influences that affect the purchase meeting space by IBM (or another corporation of your choice) for its sales meetings.

4. How would a catering sales manager handle a mother and daughter making arrangements for the daughter's wedding differently from a meeting planner from a major corporation wishing to get a quote on a regional sales meeting, which he or she has already done in five other cities?

5. How can a hotel sales representative identify who is responsible for purchasing meeting space, banquets, and rooms for corporate travelers in the corporate headquarters of an insurance company?

■■■ EXPERIENTIAL EXERCISE

Do the following:

Talk with persons who travel for business. Ask them if they can choose their own hotel and airline when they travel for their company. If they can choose their own hotels and airlines, ask if they have any restrictions or guidelines. If they are not able to choose their own hotels and airlines, ask if they have any input into where they stay. How would this information help you market travel products to their organization?

■■■ INTERNET EXERCISE

Go to the Internet site of a travel organization (e.g., a hotel, cruise line, travel agency, large restaurant). Does it have a separate section for group or organizational purchases? If so, how does the information in this section differ from the organization's consumer site? If it does not have a separate site, go to another organization until you find one that has a separate site for group or organizational purchases.

■■■ REFERENCES

1. Julie Barker, "The State of the Industry Report," *Successful Meetings* (January 1999): 35–47.

2. Frederick E. Webster, Jr., and Yoram Wind, *Organizational Buying Behavior* (Upper Saddle River, NJ: Prentice Hall, 1972), pp. 33–37.

3. Ibid., pp. 78–80.

4. See Edward G. Brierty, Robert W. Eckles, and Robert R. Reeder, *Business Marketing* (3rd ed.) (Upper Saddle River, NJ: Prentice Hall, 1998), chap. 3; Murray Harding, "Who Really Makes the Purchasing Decision?" *Industrial Marketing* (September 1966): 76. This point of view is further developed in Ernest Dichter, "Industrial Buying Is Based on Same 'Only Human' Emotional Factors That Motivate Consumer Market's Housewife," *Industrial Marketing* (February 1973): 14–16.

5. Webster and Wind, *Organizational Buying Behavior.*

6. See Tom Reilly, "All Sales Decisions Are Emotional for the Buyer," *Selling* (July 2003): 13; Patrick J. Robinson, Charles W. Faris, and Yoram Wind, *Industrial Buying Behavior and Creative Marketing* (Needham Heights, MA: Allyn & Bacon, 1967), p. 14.

7. See Michelle Russell, "The 19th Annual Meetings Market Survey," *PCMA Convene* (March 2010): 31–40, www.pcma.ord (accessed September 8, 2011); Dave Kovaleski, "The Big News About Meetings," *Association Meeting* (April 2011): 14–21, pcma.com (accessed September 8, 2011).

8. See conventionindustry.org/apex, Lynn McCullough, "APEX: A Playbook for the Meetings Industry," Hotel Business Review (September 19, 2007), www.acomonline.org/APEXHotelExec91907.pdf (accessed August 23, 2008).

9. See Sarah J. F. Braley, *Meetings and Convention Magazine,* "2008 Meetings Market Report–Association" (August 2008).

10. Sarah J. F. Braley, "The Big Picture," *Meetings & Conventions* (October 1998): 2–35; and Sarah J. F. Braley, "Meetings Market Report 2008–Associations," *Meetings and Convention Magazine,* "2008 Meetings Report" (August 2008), www.ncmag.com (accessed August 17, 2008).

11. International Association of Convention and Visitor Bureaus, www.iacvb.org (accessed October 24, 2004); Larry Letich, "Let's Make a Deal," *Meeting and Conventions Meeting Market Report* (March 1, 1992): 123.

12. Sarah J. F. Braley, "Meetings Market Report 2008–Associations," *Meetings and Convention Magazine,* 2008 Meetings Report (August 2008), www.ncmag.com (accessed August 17, 2008).

13. American Society of Association Executives, www.asaenet.org (accessed October 24, 2004).

14. Julie Barker, "The State of the Industry Report," *Successful Meetings* (January 1999): 35–47.

15. Sarah J. F. Bailey, "Corporate Meetings Market Report," *Meetings and Conventions* (December 1, 2010), http://www.meetings-conventions.com/articles/corporate-meetings-market-report/a37846.aspx?page=3 (accessed September 9, 2011).

16. HSMAI econnect, www.hsami.org (accessed October 24, 2004).

17. Amy Drew Teitler, "Getting Personal," http://www.meetings-conventions.com/issues/0100/features/feature3.html (accessed November 12, 2001).

18. The World of Sheraton, "Meeting Services, Smart Meetings," http://www.starwood.com/sheraton/meetings/smart_meetings.html (accessed November 12, 2001); see also Braley, "The Big Picture," pp. 2–35.

19. Holiday Inn, "Government Package," http://www.ocmdhotels.com/holidayinn/meetings.html (accessed November 12, 2001).

20. Lisa Grimaldi, "Essential Rewards," *Meetings and Conventions Magazine* (June 2008), www.mcmag.com (accessed August 17, 2008).

21. Braley, "The Big Picture," pp. 2–35.

22. "Incentive Sales Revisited," *Hotels* (April 2004): 10–11.

23. Andrea Graham, "Companies Add Perks to Individual Travel Awards," *Corporate Meetings & Incentives* (October 1, 2004), www.cmi.meetingsnet.com (accessed October 24, 2004).

24. "Green Meetings," Convention Industry Council (accessed September 8, 2011), http://www.conventionindustry.org/StandardsPractices/GreenMeetings.aspx.

25. "Businesses Are Reviving Incentive Travel Programs," *ehotelier,* September 8, 2011, (accessed September 8, 2011), http://ehotelier.com/hospitality-news/item.php?id=21668.

26. STR: Luxury Segments Tops 2010 Performance, HotelNewsNow.com (January 21, 2011), http://www.hotelnewsnow.com/articles.aspx/4793/STR-Luxury-segment-tops-2010-performance (accessed September 8, 2011).

27. Penny C. Dotson, *Introduction to Meeting Management* (Birmingham, AL: Professional Convention Management Association), p. 17.

28. Regina McGee, "Getting a Fix on SMERF," *Association Meetings* (April 1, 2004), www.meetingsnet.com (accessed June 18, 2004).

29. "Special Report on the Religious Group Travel Market," http://www.premiertourismmarketing.com/fyi/religious .html (accessed October 24, 2004).

30. Naomi Kooker, "Small Meetings Driving Big Hotel, Restaurant Business," *Boston Business Journal* (November 9, 2007).

31. Letich, "Let's Make a Deal," p. 127.

32. Barker, "The State of the Industry Report," pp. 35–47.

33. Howard Feiertag, "New Survey Reveals Meeting Planners' Priorities," *Hotel and Motel Management* (November 23, 1992): 11.

34. James P. Abbey, *Hospitality Sales and Advertising* (East Lansing, MI: Educational Institute of the American Hotel and Motel Association, 1993), p. 569.

35. See Jonathan Vatner, "Inside Track,' *Meetings and Conventions,* www.meetings-conventions.co/printarticle.aspx? pageid=4366 (accessed June 7, 2004).

36. Lisa Casey Weiss, "How Different Hotel Rate Programs Stack Up," *Business Travel News* (July 26, 1993): 9–16.

37. Days Inn, http://www.daysins.com/ctg/cgi-bin/DaysInn/ incentives/AAAksrACwAAAANxAAO (accessed April 20, 2000).

38. Weiss, "How Different Hotel Rate Programs Stack Up," pp. 9–16.

39. Robert Lewis and Richard E. Chambers, *Marketing Leadership in Hospitality: Foundations and Practices* (New York: Wiley, 2000).

Courtesy of Bumper DeJesus/Star Ledger/Corbis.

Market Segmentation, Targeting, and Positioning

8

Objectives

After reading this chapter, you should be able to:

1. Define the major steps in designing a customer-driven marketing strategy: market segmentation, targeting, and positioning.
2. List and distinguish among the requirements for effective segmentation: measurability, accessibility, substantiality, and actionability.
3. Explain how companies identify attractive market segments and choose a market-targeting strategy.
4. Illustrate the concept of positioning for competitive advantage by offering specific examples.

A few years ago, Dunkin' Donuts paid dozens of faithful customers in Phoenix, Chicago, and Charlotte, North Carolina, $100 a week to buy coffee at Starbucks instead. At the same time, the no-frills coffee chain paid Starbucks customers to make the opposite switch. When it later debriefed the two groups, Dunkin' says it found them so polarized that company researchers dubbed them "tribes," each of whom loathed the very things that made the other tribe loyal to its coffee shop. Dunkin' fans viewed Starbucks as pretentious and trendy, whereas Starbucks loyalists saw Dunkin' as plain and unoriginal. "I don't get it," one Dunkin' regular told researchers after visiting Starbucks. "If I want to sit on a couch, I stay at home."

Dunkin' Donuts has ambitious plans to expand into a national coffee powerhouse, on par with Starbucks, the United States' largest coffee chain. But the research confirmed a simple fact: Dunkin' is not Starbucks. In fact, it doesn't want to be. To succeed, Dunkin' must have its own clear vision of just which customers it wants to serve (what segments and targeting strategy) and how (what positioning or value proposition). Dunkin' and Starbucks target very different customers, who want very different things from their favorite coffee shops. Starbucks is strongly positioned as a sort of high-brow "third place"—outside the home and office—featuring couches, eclectic music, wireless Internet access, and art-splashed walls. Dunkin' has a decidedly more low-brow, "everyman" kind of positioning.

Dunkin' Donuts built itself on serving simple fare at a reasonable price to working-class customers. But recently, to broaden its appeal and fuel expansion, the chain has been moving upscale—a bit but not too far. It's spiffing up its more than 6,500 stores in 34 states and adding new menu items, such as lattes and flatbread sandwiches. Dunkin' has made dozens of store-redesign decisions, big and small, ranging from where to put the espresso machines to how much of its signature pink and orange color scheme to retain and where to display its fresh baked goods. However, as it inches upscale, it's being careful not to alienate its traditional customer base. There are no couches in the remodeled stores. And Dunkin' renamed a new hot sandwich a "stuffed melt" after customers complained that calling it a "panini" was too fancy; it then dropped it altogether when faithful customers thought it was too messy. "We're walking [a fine] line," says the chain's vice president of consumer insights. "The thing about the Dunkin' tribe is, they see through the hype."

Dunkin' Donuts' research showed that although loyal customers want nicer stores, they were bewildered and turned off by the atmosphere at Starbucks. They groused that crowds of laptop users made it difficult to find a seat. They didn't like Starbucks' "tall," "grande," and "venti" lingo for small, medium, and large coffees. And they couldn't understand why anyone would pay so much for a cup of coffee. "It was almost as though they were a group of Martians talking about a group of Earthlings," says an executive from Dunkin's ad agency. The Starbucks customers that Dunkin' paid to switch were equally uneasy in Dunkin' shops. "The Starbucks people couldn't bear that they weren't special anymore," says the ad executive.

Such opposing opinions aren't surprising, given the differences in the two stores' customers. Dunkin' customers include more middle-income blue- and white-collar workers across all age, race, and income demographics. By contrast, Starbucks targets a higher-income, more professional group. But Dunkin' researchers concluded that it was more the ideal, rather than income, that set the two tribes apart: Dunkin' tribe members want to be part of a crowd, whereas members of the Starbucks tribe want to stand out as individuals.[1] "You could open a Dunkin' Donuts right next to Starbucks and get two completely different types of consumers," says one retailing expert.

Over the past several years, each targeting its own tribe of customers, both Dunkin' Donuts and Starbucks have grown rapidly, riding the wave of America's growing thirst for coffee. However, the recent recession has highlighted differences in the positioning strategies of the two chains. Dunkin' Donuts has found itself well positioned for tougher economic times; Starbucks not so much so. Paying a premium price for the "Starbucks Experience" doesn't sell as well in bad times as in good. When the economy drooped, many cash-strapped Starbucks customers cut back or switched to less expensive brands. After years of sizzling growth, Starbucks sales fell for the first time ever in 2009, down 6 percent for the year.

In contrast, Dunkin' Donuts' positioning seemed to resonate strongly with customers during hard times. Even as competition grew in the superheated coffee category, with McDonald's to 7-Eleven offering their own premium blends, Dunkin's 2009 sales grew by 2.5 percent. While Starbucks was closing stores, Dunkin' opened 200 new ones. And the company is aggressively expanding menu options, adding everything from personal pizzas and flatbread sandwiches to smoothies and gourmet cookies. Befitting its positioning, Dunkin' now offers a ninety-nine-cent breakfast wrap, proclaiming "Breakfast NOT Brokefast."

In refreshing its positioning, whatever else happens, Dunkin' Donuts plans to stay true to the needs and preferences of the Dunkin' tribe. Dunkin' is "not going after the Starbucks coffee snob," says one analyst, it's "going after the average Joe." So far so good. For four years running, Dunkin' Donuts has ranked number one in the coffee category in a leading customer loyalty survey, ahead of number-two Starbucks. According to the survey, Dunkin' Donuts was the top brand for consistently meeting or exceeding customer expectations with respect to taste, quality, and customer service. And on BrandIndex's buzz rating, the overall buzz score of Dunkin' Donuts is double that of McDonald's and triple that of Starbucks.

Dunkin' Donuts' positioning and value proposition are pretty well summed up in its popular ad slogan "America Runs on Dunkin'," and its latest campaign iteration—"You Kin' Do It." Dunkin' Donuts ads show ordinary Americans relying on the chain to get them through their day, especially in a tighter economic environment:

> The "You Kin' Do It" campaign encapsulates the spirit of Dunkin' Donuts and the brands' understanding of what everyday folks need to keep themselves and the country running. "The 'You Kin' Do It' campaign shines the spotlight on the accomplishments of hard-working Americans," says a Dunkin' Donuts marketing executive, "while reinforcing that Dunkin' Donuts will continue to fuel their busy day and provide a bit of happiness without blowing the lid off their budget."[2] The campaign cheers on everyday people who keep America running by reminding them that they can take on any task, even during challenging times. With a big, steaming cup of Dunkin' Donuts coffee, you kin' make it through the workday, you kin' shovel the snow out of that driveway, you kin' finish that paperwork. America runs on Dunkin'—it's where everyday people get things done every day.[3]

Figure 8–1
Steps in segmentation,
targeting, and positioning.

Figure 8–1
Steps in segmentation,
targeting, and positioning.

■■■ Markets

Companies today recognize that they cannot appeal to all customers in the market-place, or at least not all customers the same way. Customers are too numerous, too widely scattered, and too varied in their needs and buying processes. Moreover, the companies themselves vary widely in their abilities to serve different segments of the market. Instead, like Dunkin' Donuts, a company must identify the parts of the market that it can serve best and most profitably. It must design customer-driven marketing strategies that build the right relationships with the right customers.

Most companies have moved away from mass marketing and toward target marketing—identifying market segments, selecting one or more of them, and developing products and market programs tailored to each. Instead of scattering their marketing efforts (the "shotgun" approach), firms are focusing on the buyers who have great interest in the values they create well (the "rifle" approach).

Figure 8–1 shows the three major steps in target marketing. The first is **market segmentation,** dividing a market into distinct groups that might require separate products and/or marketing mixes. The company identifies different ways to segment the market and develops profiles of the resulting market segments. The second step is **market targeting,** evaluating each segment's attractiveness and selecting one or more of the market segments. The third step is **market positioning,** developing competitive positioning for the product and an appropriate marketing mix.

■■■ Market Segmentation

Markets consist of buyers who differ in one or more ways. They may differ in their wants, resources, locations, buying attitudes, and buying practices. Because buyers have unique needs and wants, each is potentially a separate market. Ideally, a seller might design a separate marketing program for each buyer. For example, a caterer can customize the menu, entertainment, and the setting to meet the needs of a specific client.

However, most companies are unable to offer complete segmentation because of cost. Companies, therefore, look for broad classes of buyers who differ in their product needs or buying responses. For example, married adults who vacation with small children have different needs than young single adults. Club Med developed resorts for families and resorts for couples without children.

The restaurant industry offers many examples of segmentation by a variety of variables. Because each customer group in an eating-out market may want a different product, a restaurant cannot serve all customers with equal effectiveness. The restaurant must distinguish the easily accessible consumer groups from the unresponsive ones. To gain an edge over its competition, a restaurant must examine market segments by identifying one or more subsets of customers within the total market and concentrate its efforts on meeting their needs.[4]

There is no single way to segment a market. A marketer has to try different segmentation variables. Table 8–1 outlines major variables that might be used in segmenting consumer markets. Here we look at the geographic, demographic, psychographic, and behavioristic variables used in segmenting consumer markets.

Geographic Segmentation

Geographic segmentation calls for dividing the market into different geographic units, such as nations, states, regions, counties, cities, or neighborhoods. A company

TABLE 8–1
Major Segmentation Variables for Consumer Markets

Variable	Typical Breakdown
Geographic	
World region or country	North America, Western Europe, Eastern Europe, Middle East, Pacific Rim, China, India, Canada, Mexico
Country region	Pacific, Mountain, West North Central, West South Central, East North Central, East South Central, South Atlantic, Middle Atlantic, New England
City or metro size	Under 5,000; 5,000–20,000; 20,000–50,000; 50,000–100,000; 100,000–250,000; 250,000–500,000; 500,000–1,000,000; 1,000,000–4,000,000; 4,000,000 or over
Density	Urban, suburban, ex-urban, rural
Climate	Northern, southern
Demographic	
Age	Under 6, 6 to 11, 12 to 19, 20 to 34, 35 to 49, 50 to 64, 65+
Gender	Male, female
Family size	1–2, 3–4, 5+
Family life cycle	Young, single; young, married, no children; young, married, youngest child under 6; young, married, youngest child 6 or over; older, married, with children; older, married, no children under 18; older, single; other
Income	Under $20,000; $20,001–$30,000; $30,001–$50,000; $50,001–$100,000; $100,001–$250,000; $250,001+
Occupation	Professional and technical; managers, officials, and proprietors; clerical, sales; craftspeople, foremen; operatives; farmers; retired; students; housewives; unemployed
Education	Grade school or less; some high school; high school graduate; some college; college graduate
Religion	Catholic, Protestant, Jewish, Muslim, Hindu, other
Race	Asian, Hispanic, black, white
Generation	Baby boomer, Generation X, Millennial
Nationality	North American, South American, British, French, German, Italian, Japanese
Psychographic	
Social class	Lower-lower class, upper-lower class, working class, middle class, upper-middle class, lower-upper class, upper-upper class
Lifestyle	Straights, swingers, longhairs
Personality	Compulsive, gregarious, authoritarian, ambitious
Behavioral	
Occasions	Regular occasion, special occasion, holiday, seasonal
Benefits	Quality, service, economy, convenience, speed
User status	Nonuser, ex-user, potential user, first-time user, regular user
Usage rate	Light user, medium user, heavy user
Loyalty status	None, medium, strong, absolute
Readiness stage	Unaware, aware, informed, interested, desirous, intending to buy
Attitude toward product	Enthusiastic, positive, indifferent, negative, hostile

decides to operate in one or several geographic areas, paying attention to geographic differences in customer preferences. For example, within the Central American countries, beans are a dietary staple, yet in one nation consumers prefer red beans while in another black beans are preferred. Popeyes, a fast-food restaurant chain, was started by Al Copeland in 1972 when he opened Chicken on the Run. The food at Chicken on the Run was too bland for the taste of the locals. He closed the restaurant and reopened it as Popeyes, named after the character Popeye Doyle in the

Popeyes started as a regional chain and has gradually expanded to a national chain. Courtesy of Popeye's Chicken.

movie *The French Connection.* The spicier food fit the taste of the local market, and the chain expanded throughout Louisiana, Texas, and then the rest of the country. Popeyes provides a good example of how a restaurant fit the needs of the local market and then expanded outside the region as it found customers in other regions who enjoyed spicy food.[5]

Hospitality companies such as Starwood Hotels and Resorts make effective use of geographic information in their databases. This information can be used to develop highly targeted promotions, special packages, and regional foods to guests. The absence of effective use of a database forces companies to rely on mass marketing tactics that are often of no interest to the majority of recipients.

Knowledge of geographic customer preferences permits a company to modify or change its product offering. This is particularly important in North America and Europe where immigration has created pockets of customers with very different product/service preferences. As an example, the growth of Muslim markets has created a need for prayer rug areas within some hotels. Hyatt initiated a program to offer regional dishes. The Four Seasons Hotel in Washington, D.C., became so concerned about offering local cuisine that it contracted with nearby farmers to ensure a supply of local products that were not always available from wholesale vendors.[6]

As companies expand internationally, cultural differences across geographic regions often create the need to develop products for the local customers. For example, in China, KFC tailored its menu to local tastes with items such as the Dragon Twister, a sandwich stuffed with chicken strips, Peking duck sauce, cucumbers, and scallions. KFC even has a Chinese mascot—a kid-friendly character named Chicky, which the company boasts has become "the Ronald McDonald of China."

Restaurants use geographic data about their customers to determine the extent of their market reach, which could be 2 miles for a fast-food restaurant to 50 miles or more for a specialty restaurant. A customer origin study can be collected by simply asking customers for their zip code, or they can be more sophisticated studies that will create customer databases that will include other customer data in addition to the geographic information. The customer origin information can be used to show the decay of a customer base over distance, the effect of competition, and the placement of media.[7]

The success of local and regional tourism depends on creative geographic segmentation. Tourists must have a strong reason to travel hundreds or thousands of miles to visitor destinations. The complaint is often heard that all towns increasingly look alike with chain-based lodging, eating, shopping, and entertainment. Not many years ago, the isolated town of Sedan, Kansas, appeared ready to die. Then Bill Kurtis, a Kansas native, had a different vision for the town and the area. Kurtis had served as anchor of the *CBS Morning News* and producer of programs for the A&E Television Network such as *Investigative Reports* and *Cold Case Files* and anchor of *American Justice.* He initiated a program to redevelop the town as a center for original prairie art. Places like Santa Fe and Taos, New Mexico, served as examples of what could be. Today revitalization has begun in Sedan. Prairie artists have located there, and unique restaurants, quilt shops, antiques stores, and other specialty retailers now occupy Main Street. Sedan attracted 80,000 visitors and the town's renaissance is only beginning. "It is just mind-boggling to see what can happen," said Judy Tolbert, who grew up nearby and owns a bed and breakfast.[8]

Demographic Segmentation

Demographic segmentation consists of dividing the marketing into groups based on demographic variables such as age, life cycle, gender, income, occupation, education, religion, race, and nationality. Demographic variables are the most popular bases for

Children in Copenhagen enjoy a Happy Meal. Courtesy of Francis Dean/The Image Works.

8.1   Disney Cruise Line, http://disneycruise.disney.go.com/: Go to Disney Cruise Line; What are the segments this cruise would attract and which ones would it not attract?

Disney Cruise Lines targets primarily families with children, large and small. Most of its destinations and shipboard activities are designed with parents and their children in mind. Courtesy of Ypkim/Dreamstime.com.

segmenting customer groups. One reason is that consumer needs, wants, and usage rates often vary closely with demographic variables. Another is that demographic variables are easy to measure. Even when market segments are first defined using other bases, such as personality or behavior, demographic characteristics must be known to assess the size of the market and to reach it efficiently. Now we show you how certain demographic factors have been used in market segmentation.

Age and Life-Cycle Stage

Consumer preferences change with age. Some companies offer different products or marketing strategies to penetrate various age and life-cycle segments. Other companies focus on the specific age of life-stage groups. For example, although consumers in all age segments love Disney cruises, Disney Cruise Lines focuses primarily on families with children, large and small. Most of its destinations and shipboard activities are designed with parents and their children in mind. On board, Disney provides trained counselors who help younger kids join in hands-on activities, teen-only spaces for older children, and family-time or individual-time options for parents and other adults. It's difficult to find a Disney Cruise Lines ad or Web page that doesn't feature a family full of smiling faces. In contrast, Viking River Cruises, the deluxe smaller-boat cruise line that offers tours along the world's great rivers, primarily targets older-adult couples and singles. You won't find a single child in a Viking ad or Web page.

Marketers must be careful to guard against stereotypes when using age and life-cycle segmentation. Although some 80-year-olds fit the doddering stereotype, others play tennis. Similarly, whereas some 40-year-old couples are sending their children off to college, others are just beginning new families. Thus, age is often a poor predictor of a person's life cycle, health, work or family status, needs, and buying power. Companies marketing to mature consumers usually employ positive images and appeals. For example, one Carnival Cruise Lines ad for its Fun Ships features an older boomer and child riding waterslides, stating "fun has no age limit."

American Express Travel and Vacation Services focuses much of its marketing attention on the mature market because individuals in this age segment account for 70 percent of tour industry bookings. Historic restorations such as Williamsburg and Old Salem receive a large percentage of bus tours with elderly vacationers. The entire museum and historic sites industry depends heavily on this market segment. Heritage Tourism has become one of the fastest growing tourism markets in North America. The growth of this market is heavily tied to an aging population.

The U.S. baby-boomer generation, although aging, is not greatly interested in escorted tours. Globes and Cosmos, a U.S. travel company, developed a travel package called Monograms, aimed at baby boomers who want to travel and find their own experiences but also want the ease of a package instead of having to make their own arrangements. Like traditional packages, the tours visit certain destinations for a set time period but travelers are not herded around in packs.[9]

Gender

Gender segmentation for hotels was discussed in the chapter opening vignette for Chapter 7. Researchers at the University of Guelph reported single women living in the city are more likely than single men or married couples to increase their spending on restaurants when they receive a salary increase.[10] Gender marketing is by no means simplistic. A "typical" male or female does not exist, yet droves of companies have erred in trying to develop and market a product

Marketing Highlight | Targeting Families by Targeting Kids

8-1 Friendly's is a casual restaurant originally known for its ice cream. Scott Colwell, Friendly's vice president of marketing, said it was known for sandwiches and ice cream, but not somewhere where a family would go for dinner. He wanted to reposition the restaurant as a place where customers would go for lunch and dinner. Research had shown that when determining where a family will eat, kids have a major influence. In fact, children influenced over $125 billion in restaurant spending. Families with children account for 56 percent of all dollars spent on food away from home. Colwell also realized that parents are pressed for time, and they often feel bad about not spending more time with their children. If he could make a dining experience that the children would enjoy, the family would have fun together and everyone would be a winner.

To find out what would make a good dining experience for children, Colwell held focus groups with children. One of the things that came out of the focus groups was that children wanted "real" menus, like their parents' menus. They didn't want placemat menus. The kids also told them what kind of food they wanted, and how they wanted it presented. Besides talking to kids, it is also useful to talk to their parents. At the Kids' Marketing Conference, parents told restaurant managers that comfortable seating was important; kids squirm in hard seats. They also said they did not like play areas in sit-down-service restaurants; they want to be with their kids. They also expect more nutritious meals in a sit-down-service restaurant than they do in a fast-food restaurant.

Friendly's put a kids' coordinator on each shift to make sure the wants of the children were being met. Parents mentioned that having servers who can deal with kids is important. According to image research done before and after the program, Friendly's effort to reposition as a family restaurant was successful, and its image as a good place for kids jumped 50 percent. Notice how Friendly's used marketing research to find out about the market it wanted to target. The marketing information it gathered helped it understand the consumer behavior of the family market, namely that kids play a major role in where the family dines. Knowing this, Friendly's created a program to make Friendly's a place where children would want to come.

Friendly's is not the only organization targeting children and the family market. In the United States, traveling with family members and traveling to see family members has become more important since September 11, 2001. Colorado is a state catering to the adventure traveler, featuring itineraries for family vacations in the state. Novotel has a site for families and states, "Novotel does everything to make the child feel at home." For many tourist destinations and hospitality businesses, the family can be an important market segment.

Source: "Young Family Travelers," http://www.youngfamilytravelers.com/europe/novotel/novotel.htm (accessed October 31, 2004); "Family Adventure Traveler," http://www.colorado.com/family/default.asp; "Family Friendly" (accessed October 31, 2004); *Restaurant Hospitality* (June 1998): 48; and Katie Smith, "Kiddin' Around," *Restaurant Hospitality* (April 2001): 52–64.

---

or service for such an individual. It is natural for each of us to think of typical as someone in our respective age, income, and lifestyle. This is always wrong. Gender marketing is most effective when combined with lifestyle and demographic information. As an example, many women (and a few men) have developed an interest in quilting and knitting. Clubs and travel opportunities exist for meetings and demonstrations.

Income segmentation has long been used by marketers of products and services. The lodging industry is particularly effective in using income segmentation. Upper-income guests and corporations serve as targets for country clubs, boxes at sports stadiums, and upscale hotels and resorts. The Four Seasons Miami recently offered a Five Diamond package that included a two-carat Graff diamond eternity band (or another diamond piece designed to your specifications) and a stay in the presidential suite with a bottle of 1990 Dom Perignon Oenotheque champagne, caviar for two, and an 80-minute in-suite couples massage using a lotion infused with real ground diamonds. The price tag: "From $50,000."[11]

8.2 Seadream Yacht Club Video, http://www.seadream.com/the-yachts/video-gallery: watch the Seadream Yacht Club Video; how would you describe the segment(s) it is trying to attract?

Seadream Yacht Club, a small-ship luxury cruise line, calls select guests after every cruise and offers to have the CEO fly out to their home and host, at Seadream's expense, a brunch or reception for a dozen of the couple's best friends. The cruisers tell the story of their cruise. Seadream offers a great rate to its guests and sells several cruises at $1,000 per person per night—not to mention the friends of the couple telling their friends. This has been so successful for Seadream that it has abandoned most traditional advertising.[12] In designing and marketing by income, it is well to keep in mind an old proverb, "Whoever sells to kings may dine with peasants, but whoever sells to peasants, may dine with kings."

The middle-income consumer is by far the largest segment for the hospitality industry but can be difficult to attract and retain. The term *middle income* encompasses a wide range of incomes and lifestyles, thus complicating marketing strategy and tactics. An abundance of competitors serve this segment, and product/service offerings are numerous. Changing preferences, economic cycles, and an immediate reaction to terrorism and violence by this segment complicates any marketer's life.

Income does not always predict which customers will buy a given product or service. Some upscale urban restaurateurs opened branches in upper-middle-class suburbs. They were attracted by high suburban household incomes. But many had to close their doors. Why? Urban dwellers tend to be singles and couples without children. A large portion of their income is discretionary and their lifestyle includes dining out frequently. According to the National Restaurant Association, singles spend more than half of their food budget dining out, whereas married couples spend only 37 percent of their food budget eating out. On the other hand, families in the suburbs often have a high household income, but spend a heavy percentage of their money on housing, automobiles, and children. Singles represent a prime market segment for the restaurant industry.[13]

Fractional ownership is a product clearly designed for the upscale income market. Major hotel chains, including Hyatt, Ritz-Carlton, Four Seasons, and Starwood, offer fractional ownership of major resorts. Fractional ownership is partial ownership of a property. For instance, the average Aspen ski country house costs $4 million. An eighth share of the three-bedroom lodge in the Timber Company fractional ownership costs about $430,000 plus yearly dues of about $10,000. The marketing of fractional ownership (also called residence clubs) is essentially a high-end real estate function.

Some individuals have worried that fractional ownership will harm the upscale hotel market. That may yet happen as fractional ownership grows, but others view it as an important component of upscale hotels such as Ritz-Carlton because fractional owners want the services of a hotel. Indeed, many fractional ownerships associated with a hotel offer airport pickup, ski concierge, spas, grocery restocking, restaurant reservations, maintenance, and reservations of the property. Steve Dring, the original developer of the concept, believes that few fractional ownership ventures will open in resort locations without some kind of upscale-boutique/hotel combinations. The concept also spread to yacht and jet ownership.[14]

Psychographic Segmentation

Psychographic segmentation divides buyers into different segments based on social class, lifestyle, or personality characteristics. People in the same demographic group can have very different psychographic characteristics. In Chapter 6, we discussed how the products people buy reflect their lifestyles. As a result, marketers often segment their markets by consumer lifestyles and base their marketing strategies on lifestyle appeals. For example, car-sharing nicher Zipcar rents cars by the hour or the day. But it doesn't see itself as a car-rental company. Instead it sees itself as enhancing its customer's urban lifestyles and targets accordingly. "It's not about cars," says Zipcar's CEO, "it's about urban life." In New York, the rental of a parking place for a car can be as expensive as an apartment in other cities. New York also has good public transportation. Many people living in Manhattan do not have a car. Zipcar becomes their car.[15]

Marketers also use personality variables to segment markets. For example, cruise lines target adventure seekers. Royal Caribbean appeals to high-energy couples and families by providing hundreds of activities, such as rock wall climbing and ice skating. Its commercials urge travelers to "declare your independence and become a citizen of nation—Royal Caribbean, The Nation of Why Not." By contrast, the Regent Seven Seas Cruise Line targets more serene and cerebral adventurers, mature couples, seeking a more elegant ambiance and exotic destinations such as the Orient. Regent invites them to come along as "luxury goes exploring."[16]

The Claire Tappan Lodge near the Sugar Bowl ski area on the northern shore of Donner Lake was built by the Sierra Club in the 1930s. This lodge appeals to individuals within a common psychographic segment. Guests represent varying ages and income brackets, but all have a common interest in seminars hosted by this cozy lodge, on topics such as photography, orienteering, and nature.

Social Class

In Chapter 6 we described the six social classes and explained that social class has a strong effect on preferences for cars, clothes, home furnishings, leisure activities, reading habits, and retailers. Afternoon tea at the Ritz-Carlton is aimed at the upper-middle and upper classes. A neighborhood pub near a factory targets the working class. The customers of each of these establishments would probably feel uncomfortable in the other establishments.

Lifestyle

Chapter 6 also showed the influence of people's lifestyles on the goods and services that they buy. Marketers are increasingly segmenting the markets by consumer lifestyles. For example, many bars/watering holes are designed for young singles wanting to meet the opposite sex, singles wanting to meet the same sex, and couples wanting to avoid the entire singles scene and enjoy each other's company.

Personality

Marketers use personality variables to segment markets, endowing their products and personalities. For example, cruise lines target adventure seekers. Royal Caribbean appeals to high-energy couples and families with hundreds of activities such as rock climbing walls and ice skating. Commercials, set to the Iggy Pop's "Lust for Life," tell prospective customers that "this is more than a cruise" and orders them to "get out there." By contrast, the Regent Seven Seas Cruise Line targets more serene and cerebral adventurers, mature couples seeking a more elegant ambiance and exotic destinations, such as Asia. Regent invites them to come along as "luxury goes exploring."[17]

Wendy's had a great personality in the person of Dave Thomas, the founder. Unfortunately Dave passed away, and the company was left without a memorable personality. That is a major reason why companies like McDonald's and Jack in the Box use fictional characters that never age and can adopt a personality.

One of the most notable uses of a personality is Dollyworld in Pigeon Forge, Tennessee. This theme park is named for Dolly Parton, the popular country-western singer. One can only wonder what will happen once Dolly is gone. Sure, the current generation may remember her, but subsequent generations may not have ever heard of her.

Behavioral Segmentation

In **behavioral segmentation,** buyers are divided into groups based on their knowledge, attitude, and use or response to a product. Many marketers believe that behavioral variables are the best starting point for building market segments.

Occasion Segmentation

Buyers can be grouped according to occasions when they make a purchase or use a product. Occasion segmentation helps firms build product use. For example, air travel is triggered by occasions related to business, vacation, or family. Airline advertisements aimed at the business traveler often incorporate service, convenience, and on-time-departure benefits in the offer. Airline marketing aimed at the vacation traveler uses price, interesting destinations, and prepackaged vacations. Airline marketing aimed at the family market often shows children traveling alone to visit a relative, under the watchful eye of an airline employee. A message of this nature is particularly relevant to the single-parent segment.

Occasion segmentation can help firms build product use. For example, Mother's Day has been promoted as a time to take your mother or wife out to eat.

St. Patrick's Day has been promoted as a night of celebration. Monday holidays, such as Labor Day and Memorial Day, have been promoted as times to enjoy a mini vacation. These are examples of occasion marketing.

The honeymoon market represents an occasion with excellent potential for the hospitality industry. In many cultures, the honeymoon trip is paid for by parents or other family members. As a gift, the honeymoon package may contain upscale products and services such as a hotel suite and first-class airfare.

Some hotels, such as those in the Pocono Mountains of Pennsylvania, specialize in the honeymoon market. In some cases rooms are equipped with heart-shaped beds and champagne glass–shaped spas. The Japanese honeymoon market is particularly important to the hospitality industry of Guam, Hawaii, New Zealand, and Australia. Group honeymoon tours have proved to be successful, in which several Japanese newlyweds participate in a tour of one or more destinations.

The Witchery at the Castle in Edinburgh, Scotland, is an upscale restaurant with an unexpected bonus. Special-occasion guests such as honeymoon or anniversary couples book a candlelight dinner in the restaurant followed by a night in a hidden upper room reached by climbing a winding staircase. Upon entering the room, they are delighted by the beautiful antique furnishings, candlelight, a feather bed with the comforter pulled back, and a bottle of champagne on ice.

Another example of special-occasion segmentation is the "Room at the Inn" program offered by Doubletree Hotels of Canadian Pacific for travelers needing emergency lodging between Thanksgiving and Christmas. These are persons who travel to visit loved ones undergoing emergency medical treatment. Local hospitals, the Red Cross, and the United Way provide referrals of eligible guests.

Benefits Sought

Buyers can also be grouped according to the product benefits they seek. After studying patrons and nonpatrons of three types of restaurants—family popular, atmosphere, and gourmet—one researcher concluded that there are five major ap-

Marketing Highlight   The VFR Traveler Segment

8–2 One of the largest traveler segments for many visitor destinations, city, state, region, or nation, is the VFR (visiting friends and relatives) market. This market is sometimes overlooked in destination marketing because VFR travelers often stay in private homes and eat many of their meals in the home.

A U.S. study of this market showed that "VFR travelers were highly homogeneous in terms of their travel party composition, demographic characteristics, and decision-making mode." This was the largest segment to stop at a travel information center (TIC). The majority of VFR travelers preferred to obtain information from TICs about hotels and attractions.

Contrary to some opinions that rate the VFR segment low in terms of market appeal, the study showed, "This segment performed well on profitability measurements, having the highest number of travelers, the highest average expenditures per person, and the highest expenditure on shopping."[18]

The author recommended the following:

- Tourism/hospitality marketers should take advantage of advertising and promotion opportunities available through TICs.

- Public tourism promotion agencies should allocate a significant amount of space in their travel guides to special events and festivals because the VFR segment wants this information.

- Destination marketers should implement strategies to enhance local residents' knowledge about things of interest to the VFR traveler because local residents are a prime source of information for this travel segment.

Although friends and relatives often do not use hotel rooms, it is common for visitors to invite their hosts to dinner. The local host often suggests the restaurant. This group of friends is enjoying a restaurant in Leuven, Belgium. Courtesy of Paul Kenward Dorling Kindersley.

Source: Soo K. Kang, Cathy H. C. Hsu, and Kara Wolfe, "Family Traveler Segmentation by Vacation Decision-Making Patterns," *Journal of Hospitality and Tourism Research,* 27, no. 4 (2003): 464–465.

peal categories for restaurant customers.[19] The relative importance of food quality, menu variety, price, atmosphere, and convenience factors across each group was studied. It was found that patrons of family-service restaurants sought convenience and menu. Variety patrons of atmosphere restaurants ranked food quality and atmosphere as the top attributes. Patrons of gourmet restaurants valued quality.

Knowing the benefits sought by customers is useful in two ways. First, managers can develop products with features that provide the benefits their customers are seeking. Second, managers communicate more effectively with their customers if they know what benefits customers seek.

The French Trianon Palace Hotel, on the edge of the world-famous Louis XIV's Versailles, discovered that many customers, including rich Americans, will not travel without their best friend—their dog. This hotel developed a $400 per night "Heavenly Pets" package. For that price, the owner and the dog received a deluxe double room, including breakfast. A special round-the-clock room service for the dog is available at $17, whose menu includes a dog hamburger, a seafood omelet, or a Queen's omelet with poached chicken. Starwood Hotels has developed a Love That Dog program, targeting people who travel with pets. At their W hotels, guests who indicate they are traveling with a pet receive a pet toy and treat at check-in. In the room they will find pet food and water bowls and a bed for their pet. The pet even receives a special treat as part of their turndown service. Starwood also provides cleanup bags and a notice to hang on the door saying there is a pet in the room to alert hotel employees.[20]

Thus, a benefit is a positive outcome received from a product feature. Those product features that create positive outcomes for guests create value. Features that do not offer positive outcomes for the guest will have no value.

User Status

Many markets can be segmented into nonusers, former users, potential users, first-time users, and regular users of a product. High-market-share companies such as major airlines are particularly interested in keeping regular users and attracting potential users. Potential users and regular users often require different marketing appeals.

Usage Rate

Markets can also be segmented into light, medium, and heavy product users. Heavy users are often a small percentage of the market but account for a high percentage of total consumption. For example, Burger King targets what it calls "Super Fans," young (ages 18 to 34), Whopper-wolfing males and females who make up 18 percent of the chain's customers but account for almost half of all customer visits. They eat at Burger King an average of 13 times a month. Burger King targets these Super Fans openly with ads that exalt monster burgers containing meat, cheese, and more meat and cheese that can turn "innies into outies."[21]

One of the most controversial programs ever employed by the hospitality and travel industries to ensure heavy patronage by key customers is the frequent flyer or frequent guest program. Researchers discovered that 4.1 percent of airline travelers account for 70.4 percent of airline trips, and thus airlines were eager to capture this lucrative market.[22] Many professors, consultants, and industry executives seriously question the long-run value of these programs and question the competitive advantage they create because most airlines have similar programs. However, the results of one study of frequent guest programs concluded, "While it is expensive to maintain frequent guest programs, they seem to be effective in keeping a large lucrative portion of the business travel market coming back. Therefore, unless the industry as a whole drops these programs, it appears that individual hotel chains and airlines will be forced to maintain them."[23] Clearly marketers are eager to identify heavy users and build a marketing mix to attract them. Many hospitality firms spread their marketing resources evenly across all potential customers. Seasoned marketers identify heavy users and focus marketing strategies toward them.

Loyalty Status

A market can also be segmented on the basis of consumer loyalty. Consumers of hospitality products can be loyal to brands, such as Courtyard by Marriott, or to companies, such as Qantas Airlines. Others are only somewhat loyal. They may be

The Dallas BBQ Restaurant close to Times Square in New York is successful at drawing both tourists and a business crowd. © Radoslaw Drewek/Dreamstime.com

loyal to two or three brands or favor one brand but buy others. Still other buyers show no brand loyalty at all. They want variety or simply buy whichever brand is cheapest or most convenient. These people will stop at a Ramada Inn or Holiday Inn, depending on which they see first when looking for a motel.

A study of hotel brand extensions showed that brand extensions are helpful in increasing customer loyalty and in promoting repeat buying. Customers who like a main-line, name-brand hotel are likely to patronize other hotels owned by that hotel company. Customer loyalty among hotel extensions seems to involve three hotel tiers (three different names).

A major reason for increasing customer loyalty is that "loyal customers are price insensitive compared to brand-shifting patrons."[24] In the hospitality and travel industries, marketers attempt to build brand loyalty through relationship marketing. Whereas manufacturing companies often lack direct contact with their customers, most hospitality and travel marketers do have direct contact. They can develop a guest history database and use this information to customize offers and customer communications.

One restaurant keeps a file on its frequent customers, detailing their preferred captain, wines, table choice, last visit, and even their appearance (making it easier for restaurant employees to recognize them). VIP customers are given a special reservation phone number by this restaurant. People who call that number are immediately identified as key customers, allowing their files to be viewed. The host can use the information on file to deliver personalized service.

A review of marketing strategies for resorts suggested that the first and most basic strategy is "to keep and expand the current market base. To encourage vital repeat business, resorts should stay in contact with their former guests through direct mail that lets them know of special events, discount offers, and new programs and facilities."[25]

Using Multiple Segmentation Bases

Marketers rarely limit their segmentation analysis to only one or a few variables. Rather, they often use multiple segmentation bases in an effort to identify smaller, better-defined target groups. Thus, a bank may not only identify a group of wealthy, retired adults but also, within that group, distinguish several segments based on their current income, assets, savings and risk preferences, housing, and lifestyles.

Several business information services—such as Nielsen, Acxiom, and Experian—provide multivariate segmentation systems that merge geographic, demographic, lifestyle, and behavioral data to help companies segment their markets down to zip codes, neighborhoods, and even households. One of the leading segmentation systems is the PRIZM system by Nielsen. PRIZM classifies every American household based on a host of demographic factors—such as age, educational level, income, occupation, family composition, ethnicity, and housing—and behavioral and lifestyle factors—such as purchases, free-time activities, and media preferences.

PRIZM classifies U.S. households into sixty-six demographically and behaviorally distinct segments, organized into fourteen different social groups. PRIZM segments carry such exotic names as "Kids & Cul-de-Sacs," "Gray Power," "Bohemian Mix," "Mayberry-ville," "Shotguns & Pickups," "Old Glories," "Multi-Culti Mosaic," "Big City Blues," and "Bright Lites L'il City." The colorful names help bring the clusters to life.[26] PRIZM and other such systems can help marketers segment people and locations into marketable groups of like-minded consumers.

Requirements for Effective Segmentation

Although there are many ways to segment a market, all are not equally effective. For example, buyers of restaurant meals could be divided into blond and brunette customers. But hair color does not affect the purchase of restaurant meals. Furthermore, if all restaurant customers buy the same number of meals each month and believe all restaurant meals are of equal quality and are willing to pay the same price, the company would not benefit from segmenting this market.

To be useful, market segments must have the following characteristics:

- *Measurability:* The degree to which the segment's size and purchasing power can be measured. Certain segmentation variables are difficult to measure, such as the size of the segment of teenagers who drink beer primarily to rebel against their parents.

- *Accessibility:* The degree to which segments can be assessed and served. One of the authors found that 20 percent of a college restaurant's customers were frequent patrons. However, frequent patrons lacked any common characteristics. They included faculty, staff, and students. There was no usage difference among part-time, full-time, or class year of the students. Although the market segment had been identified, there was no way to access the heavy-user segment.

- *Substantiality:* The degree to which segments are large or profitable enough to serve as markets. A segment should be the largest possible homogeneous group economically feasible to support a tailored marketing program. For example, large metropolitan areas can support many different ethnic restaurants, but in a smaller town, Thai, Vietnamese, and Moroccan food restaurants might not survive.

- *Actionability:* The degree to which effective programs can be designed for attracting and serving segments. A small airline, for example, identified seven market segments, but its staff and budget were too small to develop separate marketing programs for each segment.

■■■ Market Targeting

Marketing segmentation reveals a company's market-segment opportunities. The firm has to evaluate the various segments and decide how many and which ones to target. We now look at how companies evaluate and select target markets.

Evaluating Market Segments

When evaluating different market segments, a firm must look at three factors: segment size and growth, segment structured attractiveness, and company objectives and resources.

Segment Size and Growth

A company must first collect and analyze data on current segment sales growth rates and expected profitability for various segments. It will be interested in segments that have the right size and growth characteristics, but "right size and growth" is a relative matter. Some companies want to target segments with large current sales, a high growth rate, and a high profit margin. However, the largest, fastest growing segments are not always the most attractive ones for every company. Smaller companies often find they lack the skills and resources needed to serve the larger segments or that these segments are too competitive. Such companies may select segments that are smaller but are potentially more profitable.

Segment Structural Attractiveness

A segment might have desirable size and growth and still not offer attractive profits. The company must examine several major structural factors that affect long-run segment attractiveness. For example, a segment is less attractive if it already contains many strong and aggressive competitors. The existence of many actual or potential substitute products may limit prices and profits. For example, super-markets have entered the take-away-meals market which has had an impact on the fast-food restaurant market. The relative power of buyers also affects segment at-tractiveness. If the buyers in a segment possess strong bargaining power relative to sellers, they will force prices down, demand more quality services, and set com-petitors against one another. Large buyers, such as an airline with a hub in Dallas that needs fifty rooms a night for flight crews, will be able to negotiate a low price. Finally, a segment may not be attractive if it contains powerful suppliers who con-trol prices or reduce the quality of ordered goods and services. Suppliers tend to be powerful when they are large and concentrated, when few substitutes exist, or when the supplied product is an important input. In certain areas, restaurants spe-cializing in fresh seafood are limited to a few suppliers.

Company Objectives and Resources

All companies must consider their own objectives and resources in relation to avail-able segments. Some attractive segments can be dismissed quickly because they do not mesh with the company's long-run objectives. Although such segments might be tempting in themselves, they might divert a company's attention and energies away from its main goal. Or they might be a poor choice from an environmental, political, or social responsibility viewpoint. For example, Landry's, a hospital-ity company that owns a number of upscale and mid-scale restaurant concepts, decided that its 143-unit Joe's Crab Shack restaurants did not fit the company's pro-file. Tilman Fertitta, the company's CEO, stated, "Joe's has been an important part of our growth over the years. We are now going in a different strategic direction, focused more on our higher end restaurants, hospitality and gaming assets. Joe's just does not fit well in our future plans."[27]

If a segment fits the company's objectives, it must then decide whether it pos-sesses the skills and resources to succeed in that segment. If the company lacks the strengths needed to compete successfully in a segment and cannot readily obtain them, it should not enter the segment. A company should enter segments only where it can gain sustainable advantages over competitors.

Selecting Market Segments

After evaluating different segments, the company must decide which and how many segments to serve. This is a problem of target-market selection. A target mar-ket consists of a set of buyers who share common needs or characteristics that the company decides to serve. Figure 8–2 shows that a firm can adopt one of three market-coverage strategies: undifferentiated marketing, differentiated marketing, and concentrated marketing.

Figure 8-2
Three alternative market-coverage strategies.

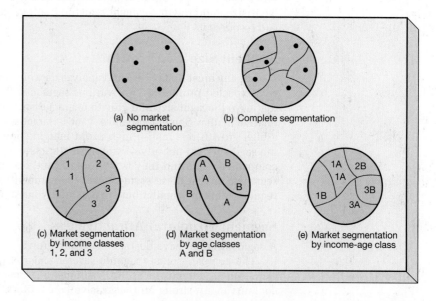

Undifferentiated Marketing

Using an undifferentiated marketing strategy, a company ignores market segmentation differences and goes after the entire market with one market offer. It focuses on what is common in the needs of consumers rather than on differences. It designs a marketing plan that will reach the greatest number of buyers. Mass distribution and mass advertising serve as the basic tools to create a superior image in consumers' minds.

Undifferentiated marketing provides cost economies. The narrow product line keeps down production, inventory, and transportation costs. An undifferentiated advertising program holds down advertising costs. The neglect of segmentation holds down marketing research costs and product development costs.

Public cafeterias sometimes believe they fit this model, but in fact, observation of their customer mix usually reveals a disproportionate number of middle-age and older customers.

Most contemporary marketers have strong doubts about the strategy in today's competitive environment. It is difficult to develop a product and brand that will satisfy all or even most consumers. When several competitors aim at the largest segments, the inevitable result is heavy competition. Small companies generally find it impossible to compete directly against giants and are forced to adopt market-niche strategies. Larger segments may become less profitable because of heavy marketing costs, including the possibility of price cutting and price wars.

Differentiated Marketing

Using a differentiated marketing strategy, a company targets several market segments and designs separate offers for each. Accor Hotels, a French company, operates under twelve trade names and manages several brands and types of hotels. Included in its brands are international luxury hotels (Sofitel), three-star hotels (Novotel), two-star hotels (Ibis), limited-service hotels (Formula One and Motel 6), and extended-stay hotels aimed at the elderly (Hotelia). This segmentation has allowed Accor to become one of the world's foremost hotel groups.

Starwood Hotels and Resorts owns Westin, Sheraton, Four Points, St. Regis, W Hotels, and Luxury Collection. Choice Hotels International owns Comfort Inn, Comfort Suites, Quality Inns, Sleep Inn, Clarion, and Main Stay Suites. Other hotel groups also own multiple brands.

Differentiated marketing typically produces more total sales than undifferentiated marketing. Accor gets a higher hotel room market share with three different brands in one city than if it only had one brand in a city. Sofitel attracts the upscale business traveler. Novotel attracts the mid-scale traveler, whereas Formula One attracts families and the budget traveler. Accor offers a different marketing mix to each target market. At the same time, it has to have marketing plans, marketing research, forecasting, sales analysis, promotion planning, and advertising for each brand.

Many hotel chains pursue a strategy of applying their trusted brand names in transient lodging to products that are quite different, such as time-shares. One of the riskiest may be the highly respected Ritz-Carlton luxury hotels' entrance into Ritz-Carlton brand condos and lavishly decorated homes. The logic behind this move was financial, not strategic marketing. Given the cost of land, construction, and operations, Ritz-Carlton felt that at $450 per night it could not realize desirable profits. "To build a luxury hotel today you have to look at some component that helps underwrite the cost," said Bill Marbus, vice president of development for Crescent Real Estates Equities.[28]

Concentrated Marketing

A fourth market-coverage strategy, concentrated marketing, is especially appealing to companies with limited resources. Instead of going for a small share of a large market, the firm pursues a large share of one or a few small markets.

There are many examples of concentrated marketing. Four Seasons Hotels and Rosewood Hotels concentrate on the high-priced hotel room market. Through concentrated marketing, hospitality companies achieve a strong market position in the segments that they serve, thanks to their greater knowledge of those segments' needs. The company also enjoys many operative economies. If the segment is well chosen, the company can earn a high rate of return on investment.

Kempinski, like Capella, Fairmont, Four Seasons, and Rosewood are some of the brands that focus on the customer who desires luxury accommodations. Courtesy of imagebroker/Alamy.

Chuck E. Cheese is a restaurant that targets families with young children. A writer for the publication *Real Money* said, "Parents are constantly scratching their heads to understand how to entertain kids. After a few trips to a stuffy restaurant with a couple young kids who end up crawling around the floor under your table or worse, running around the restaurant earning you dirty looks from other patrons, you won't be likely to return anytime soon. Likewise when you find a comfortable place where the kids are happy, the parents will be happy and will gladly spend their money. Kids love Chuck E. Cheese. It's like going to a state fair indoors and they serve pizza. What's not to like? You run around and you spend money on arcade games. The food is basic—pizza and wings—but sufficient to satisfy the kids."[29] For more on Chuck E. Cheese, see Case 21.

At the same time, concentrated marketing involves higher than normal risks. The particular market segment can turn sour. For this reason, many companies prefer to operate in two or more markets.

Choosing a Market-Coverage Strategy

Companies need to consider several factors in choosing a market-coverage strategy. One factor is the company's resources. When the company's resources are limited, concentrated marketing makes the most sense. Another factor is the **degree of product homogeneity.** Undifferentiated marketing is more suited for homogeneous products. Products that can vary in design, such as restaurants and hotels, are more suited to differentiation or concentration. The product's life-cycle stage must also be considered. When a firm introduces a new product, it may be practical to launch only one version, so undifferentiated or concentrated marketing makes the most sense. For example, the early McDonald's had a very limited selection compared with their present menu selection. In the mature stage of the product life cycle, differentiated marketing becomes more feasible. Another factor is **market homogeneity.** If buyers have the same tastes, buy a product in the same amounts, and react the same way to marketing efforts, undifferentiated marketing is appropriate. Finally, **competitors' strategies** are important. When competitors use segmentation, undifferentiated marketing can be suicidal. Conversely, when competitors use undifferentiated marketing, a firm can gain an advantage by using differentiated or concentrated marketing.

▪▪▪ Market Positioning

Once a company has chosen its target market segments, it must decide what positions to occupy in those segments. A product's position is the way the product is defined by consumers on important attributes—the place the product occupies in consumers' minds relative to competing products. Consumers are overloaded with information about products and services. They cannot reevaluate products every time they make a buying decision. To simplify buying decisions, consumers organize products into categories—they "position" products and companies in their minds.

Marketers do not want to leave their products' positions to chance. They plan positions that will give their products the greatest advantage in selected target markets and then design marketing mixes to create the planned positions. In the fast-food hamburger business, Wendy's promotes never-frozen meat, hot off the grill;

Burger King is known for its flame-broiled food; and Checkers and Rally's double drive-through restaurants use quality hamburgers at low prices to position itself in the marketplace.[30]

A hotel brand's position can be viewed from two perspectives—that of the brand's management and that of the guests. The brand's management must have a clear concept of the hotel's intended position. Its promotional efforts must articulate not only what the brand offers, but how its offerings are different from those of other brands. In the final analysis, a brand's position is determined by its customers.

Positioning Strategies

Marketers can follow several positioning strategies. They can position their products based on **specific product attributes.** Product attribute positioning can be dangerous. The attribute has to create a benefit for the consumer. Subway has been successful in positioning its sandwiches as a healthy alternative to fried foods and hamburgers. It features eight sandwiches that have six grams of fat or less. Its "Fresh Fit for Kids" program is aimed at parents. The following message is found on its Web site: "You no longer have to sacrifice nutrition or flavor when you're short on time. Choose a Mini sub (Black Forest Ham, Turkey Breast or Roast Beef) and pair it with a delicious side, like fresh apple slices. Then select from 1% low fat white milk or 100% juice for a tasty, better-for-them meal that kids will love."[31] Subway has been effective in promoting nutrition, without sacrificing flavor, as nutrition is an important food attribute to many people. Not all companies are successful in selecting meaningful product attributes. The Stamford Hotel in Singapore advertised that it is the world's tallest hotel (now the tallest in Southeast Asia). Most people are interested in service, location, and other attributes when choosing a hotel, but height is not a product attribute that is valued by many people. In fact hotel guests often to prefer to stay on lower floors as they perceive they will have a better chance of survival in case of emergency. If one promotes a product attribute that is not usually associated as a benefit, the benefits must be communicated. The Marina Bay Sands Singapore has done a good job at promoting the benefit of height for its swimming pool and SkyBar with these messages: "Imagine swimming in the clouds, overlooking Singapore's skyline. At 200m in the sky, the 150m swimming pool is the world's largest infinity & outdoor pool at that height. Hotel guests can indulge in this ultimate experience now." "Savour the view from Singapore's most iconic bar. The SkyBar is perched above the Marina Bay Sands SkyPark observation deck, the perfect hangout from which to survey the world below. Take in the vista of the city spread out before you and the panoramic view of the Singapore Strait as you sip on cocktail creations by KU DÉ TA mixologists."[32] Notice how the messages from the Marina Bay Sands have an emotional appeal, while simply stating you are the tallest hotel is an unemotional fact. In the hospitality industry, appealing to emotions is important.

Finally, products can be positioned against another product class. Cruise ships positioned themselves against other vacation alternatives such as destination resorts, and B&Bs are positioned as a home-like alternative to all other forms of lodging. Conference centers have consistently positioned themselves against hotels with conference facilities.

The Asian market such as Hong Kong or Singapore has consisted largely of deluxe, five-star, full-service hotels with world-class competitors such as the Peninsula, Mandarin, Shangri-La, Conrad, and Grand Hyatt Hotels. Less expensive hotel properties existed, but these appealed predominantly to nearby markets and to GIT (group-inclusive tour) segments. As rack rates increased in these markets and as customer familiarization with these destinations grew, niche products began to emerge.

The YMCA is a surprising niche competitor in Hong Kong. The YMCA enjoys a good location near the harbor and has been remodeled to meet the needs of American, European, and Australian guests. Occupancy and guest satisfaction in the YMCA remain high and serve as a warning to traditional five-star luxury properties that guests are willing to accept alternative lodging products.

e

8.3 Swissotel, The Stamford http:// www.swissotel.com/EN/ Destinations/Singapore/ Swissotel+The+Stamford/ Hotel+Home/Hotel+Description Go to Swissotel, the Stamford's Web site. How would you describe the hotel in terms of benefits that might attract a market segment or market segments?

When two or more firms pursue the same position, each must seek further differentiation, such as "a business hotel for a lower cost" or "a business hotel with a great location." Each firm must build a unique bundle of competitive advantages that appeal to a substantial group within the segment. This subpositioning is often called niche marketing.

Choosing and Implementing a Positioning Strategy

The positioning task consists of three steps:

1. Identifying a set of possible **competitive advantages** on which to build a position.

2. Selecting the right competitive advantages.

3. Effectively communicating and delivering the chosen position to a carefully selected target market.

A company can differentiate itself from competitors by bundling competitive advantages. It gains competitive advantage by offering consumers lower prices than competitors for similar products or by providing more benefits that justify higher prices.[33] Thus, a company must compare its prices and products to those of competitors and continuously look for possible improvements. To the extent that it can do better than its competitors, the company has achieved a competitive advantage.

Club Med used a successful bundling strategy of offering all services other than retail purchases to a young market segment that was unfamiliar with tipping, ordering from a menu, selecting wines, and asking a concierge for help in acquiring a tennis lesson. Club Med bundled all these products/services and eliminated the use of money at its resorts. Instead of dollars, pesos, or francs, Club Med's international guests could buy a round of drinks with beads given to them at check-in.

In some cases, unbundling of products has also worked as a positioning tactic. Until the early 1970s, many destination resorts sold only a bundled product known as the American Plan (AP), in which all or most of the resort's services such as food and beverage were included. Consumer preferences changed as many guests no longer wanted three daily meals, and a Friday evening formal dance was included in a package. Resort managers who observed this behavior began to differentiate their properties by offering a modified American plan (MAP), in which lunch was not included, or a European plan, which did not include meals.

Today, many resorts including four-star resorts in remote locations offer all-inclusive packages. Some include virtually everything except for shopping in retail stores on the property or gambling. Services not previously covered, such as golf, tennis, and scuba, are now included in some all-inclusive packages. It is unlikely that all-inclusive resorts today will force guests to eat at a prescribed time at a set table. Instead, many offer a choice of a buffet, a snack bar, a grill, or other type of restaurant, all included. Reservations may be needed for some of the most popular restaurants and activities. These resorts are often located in remote locations, providing guests with everything they need for their vacation. From a cultural standpoint, a negative aspect of all-inclusive resorts is that they isolate guests from the culture of the destination they are visiting.

Not every company faces an abundance of opportunities for gaining a competitive advantage. Some companies can identify only minor advantages, which are often easily copied and therefore highly perishable. These companies must continue to identify new potential advantages and introduce them one by one to keep competitors off balance. Few or perhaps no companies can achieve a major permanent advantage, but instead, they can gain smaller advantages that help them build their market share over time. Hotels, resorts, and restaurants sometimes believe that their locations on a beach, near an airport, next to a ski hill, or in the central business district provide them with a permanent advantage. History clearly depicts a different scenario. Beaches erode or become polluted, ski hills lose their popularity, airports move, and central business districts lose their appeal. In many cases the management of hospitality companies with perceived permanent advantages loses interest in customers and employees, thus further contributing to their inevitable demise.

Product Differentiation

A hospitality company or a visitor destination must differentiate its products/services from those of its competitors. Differentiation can occur by physical attributes, service, personnel, location, or image.

Physical Attribute Differentiation

Classic hotels such as the Waldorf-Astoria in New York, Palmer House in Chicago, Brown Palace in Denver, Raffles in Singapore, and Prestonfield House in Edinburgh differentiate themselves on past grandeur.

The five-star Casa Santo Domingo Hotel in Antigua, Guatemala, was built into the ruins of a sixteenth-century monastery partially destroyed in an earthquake. The architects and interior designers masterfully blended new construction with the remains of the old monastery, including a crypt. The roofless remains of the sanctuary, surrounded by thousands of blazing candles, serves as a popular site for evening weddings.

Unfortunately, many hotels, restaurants, and airlines lack physical differentiation. Motels in particular follow a standard architectural look that provides no differentiation. When this happens, price becomes the primary differentiating factor.

Restaurants such as Chez Panisse in Berkeley, Lidia's in Kansas City, and the chain Chipotle Mexican Grill use natural/organic foods to differentiate themselves. These restaurants have developed a network of farmers to provide fresh products produced to each restaurant's standards.[34]

Differentiation that excites the consumer and offers something new can lead to excellent public relations opportunities, customer loyalty, and greater profits.

Service Differentiation

Hospitality companies differentiate themselves on service. For example, Sheraton, Shangri-La, and other hotels provide an in-room check-in service. Red Lobster takes "call aheads." The customers call from home and give the number in the party and when they will arrive. They are not guaranteed a table when they arrive, but they

The Raffles Hotel is one of the most recognized buildings in Singapore. Courtesy of John Lamb/Getty Images, Inc.—Stone Allstock.

are given the next available table. Some restaurants offer home delivery as a point of differentiation. By providing services that benefit its target market, a company can achieve differentiation until the service is copied by competition.

Unwanted differentiation occurs when a company consistently provides a horrible level of guest service. Such a reputation often requires a change in management or ownership to correct. It is strange that so many members of service industries ignore good customer service. The basics of good customer service are comparable to the Golden Rule: "Do unto others as you would have them do unto you."

The results of customer service studies usually reveal common sense yet valuable insight. A study of the growing mature market (older than age 55) revealed that mature buyers place a high value on ease of use, comfort, efficiency, and practical features that help them overcome debilities of aging. Somewhere around 40, most people begin to experience problems reading small print. Restaurants that desire a candlelight atmosphere run the risk of offending guests who cannot read the menu. A simple lighting arrangement to illuminate menus is a valuable service offering.

Mature consumers place special value on friendly staff, guest name recognition by staff, assistance in making a product decision, opportunities to socialize, and no pressure to leave. These simple services can reap large rewards for members of the hospitality industry.[35] Because so many companies overlook the importance of good service, those who truly emphasize service will achieve positive differentiation.

Personnel Differentiation

Companies can gain a strong competitive advantage through hiring and retaining better people than their competitors. Thus, Singapore Airlines enjoys an excellent reputation largely because of the grade of its flight attendants. Southwest Airlines claimed that a competitor could replicate its low-cost system but would find it more difficult to create the spirit of Southwest's employees.

Personnel differentiation requires that a company select its customer-contact people carefully and train them well. These personnel must be competent and must possess the required skills and knowledge. They need to be courteous, friendly, and respectful. They must serve customers with consistency and accuracy, and they must make an effort to understand their customers, communicate clearly with them, and respond quickly to customer requests and problems. We will discuss how to create personnel differentiation in Chapter 10.

Location Differentiation

Location can provide a strong competitive advantage. For example, hotels facing Central Park in New York City have a competitive advantage over hotels a block away. Motels located right off a freeway exit can enjoy double-digit advantages in percentage of occupancy over hotels a block away. Hotels along the River Walk in San Antonio, Texas, have a strong advantage over hotels located off the river. International airlines often use their location as a point of differentiation in their home markets. For example, Qantas promotes itself as Australia's airline and has a strong following in its home market. Hospitality and travel firms should look for benefits created by their location, keeping in mind that this advantage is subject to chance. Factors such as a new highway bypass or criminal activity in a neighborhood can quickly turn an advantage into a problem.

Taco John's 425 quick-service restaurants are located in 25 states. However, their strength has been what the company calls "the Heartland of America." The company started in Cheyenne, Wyoming, and then expanded to places like Scottsbluff, Nebraska, and Rapid City, South Dakota. Most of its locations are still in small to midsized midwestern towns where it has obviously been successful. It is questionable if this success could be duplicated in towns such as San Antonio, Texas, or Los Angeles. Hospitality companies are well advised to seriously consider what geographic factors may have created their success before expanding too widely. Perhaps the sauces or something else in the product are perfect for people in Nebraska or Minnesota but might not be acceptable in other geographic regions.[36] Taco John did move to a nontraditional location by participating in several U.S. Armed Forces bases through the Army & Air Force Exchange Service after Taco Bell declined to participate.[37]

These restaurants along the River Walk in San Antonio have a competitive advantage over restaurants located a block away. Courtesy of Sandy Felsenthal/Corbis/Bettmann.

Image Differentiation

Even when competing offers look the same, buyers may perceive a difference based on company or brand image. Thus, hospitality companies need to work to establish images that differentiate them from competitors. A company or visitor destination image should convey a singular or distinctive message that communicates the product's major benefits and positioning. In the case of visitor destinations such as tropical locations, it is often impossible to distinguish the advertising of one from another. Most seem to employ beaches, clear water, and other environmental factors that do not differentiate any. Developing a strong and distinctive image calls for creativity and hard work. A positive image must be earned. Chili's developed an image as a casual and fun neighborhood restaurant. This image must be supported by everything that the company says and does.

The owners of the Telluride Ski and Golf Resort want to preserve the charm of Telluride. Courtesy of Mark Romanelli/ Getty Images, Inc./Image Bank.

A common mistake made by new owners/operators of a property is to implement a new image/positioning strategy before fully understanding the property, the community, and the market. In 2004 the new owners of the Telluride Ski and Golf Resort announced they would not make this mistake. Instead of announcing grand changes, the new owners said, "Our intentions are to honor unique characteristics that define Telluride. We want to preserve Telluride's authenticity, charm, and casual atmosphere." They further said that they would seek input from the community to develop a shared vision of what the resort should look like.[38]

One of the leading hotel and leisure companies in the world, Starwood Hotels & Resorts Worldwide, has 850 properties in more than 95 countries and 145,000 employees at its owned and managed properties. Starwood has differentiated its hotels, creating an image along emotional, experiential lines. Its hotel and call center operators convey different experiences for the firm's different chains, as does the firm's advertising. This strategy emerged from a major 18-month positioning project, started in 2006, to find positions for the portfolio of brands that would establish an emotional connection with consumers. Consumer research suggested these positions for some of the brands:

Sheraton. With the tagline "You don't stay here, you belong," Sheraton—the largest brand—is about warm, comforting, and casual. Its core value centers on "connections," an image aided by the hotel's alliance with Yahoo!, which cofounded the Yahoo! Link@Sheraton lobby kiosks and cyber cafes.

Four Points by Sheraton. For the self-sufficient traveler, Four Points strives to be honest, uncomplicated, and comfortable. The brand is all about providing a high level of comfort and little indulgences like free high-speed Internet access and bottled water. Its ads feature apple pies and talk about providing guests with "the comforts of home."

W. With a brand personality defined as flirty, for the insider, and an escape, W offers guests unique experiences around the warmth of cool.

Westin. Westin's emphasis on "personal, instinctive, and renewal" has led to a new sensory welcome featuring a white tea scent, signature music and lighting, and refreshing towels. Each room features Westin's own "Heavenly Beds," sold exclusively in the retail market through Nordstrom, further enhancing the brand's upscale image.[39]

Selecting the Right Competitive Advantages

Suppose that a company is fortunate enough to discover several potential competitive advantages. It now must choose the ones on which it will build its positioning strategy.

How Many Differences?

Many marketers think that companies should aggressively promote only one benefit to the target market. Adman Rosser Reeves, for example, said a company should develop a unique selling proposition (USP) for each brand and stick to it. Each brand should pick an attribute and tout itself as number one on that attribute. Buyers tend to remember number one better, especially in an overcommunicated society. Thus, Motel 6 consistently promotes itself as the lowest-priced national chain, and Ritz-Carlton promotes itself as a value leader. What are some number-one positions to promote? The major ones are best quality, best service, lowest price, best value, and best location. A company that hammers away at a position that is important to its target market and consistently delivers on it probably will become the best known and remembered.

Other marketers think that companies should position themselves on more than one differentiating factor. A restaurant may claim that it has the best steaks and service. A hotel may claim that it offers the best value and location. Today, in a time when the mass market is fragmenting into many small market segments, companies are trying to broaden their positioning strategies to appeal to more segments. For example, the Boulders in Arizona promotes itself as a top golf resort and as a luxury resort, giving guests a chance to experience the flora and fauna of the Sonoma Desert. By doing this, the Boulders can attract both golfers and nongolfers.

However, as companies increase the number of claims for their brands, they risk disbelief and a loss of clear positioning. In general, a company needs to avoid three major positioning errors. The first is **underpositioning,** or failing ever to position the company at all. Some companies discover that buyers have only a vague idea of the company or that they do not really know anything special about it. Many independent hotels trying to capture an international market are underpositioned. The Seoul Plaza Hotel, a luxury hotel in Seoul, Korea, is not well known in Europe or North America. To establish positions in distant markets, hotels like the Seoul Plaza are affiliating with marketing groups such as "Leading Hotels of the World" and "Preferred Hotels." The second positioning error is **overpositioning,** or giving buyers too narrow a picture of the company. Finally, companies must avoid **confused positioning,** leaving buyers with a confused image of a company. For example, Burger King has struggled for years to establish a profitable and consistent position. It has tried many advertising campaigns: "Herb the Nerd Doesn't Eat Here," "This is a Burger King Town," to "The Right Food for the Right Times," "Sometimes You've Gotta Break the Rules," "Get Your Burger's Worth," "It Just Tastes Better," "Got the Urge," "BK Tee Vee," "Back to Basics," and "It Just Tastes Better." The barrage of positioning statements left consumers confused and Burger King franchises with lower than expected sales. Their campaigns "Cookin' over an Open Fire," "The Fire Is Ready," and "Have It Your Way" focused on the advantages of flame broiling and preparing the burger to order.[40]

Good positioning helps build brand loyalty. In the case of hotels, it may not be enough to simply satisfy guests. Satisfied customers do not repurchase unless they are also attitudinally brand loyal.[41]

Which Differences?

Not all brand differences are meaningful or worthwhile. Not every difference makes a good differentiator. Each difference has the potential to create company costs as well as customer benefits. Therefore, a hospitality company or a visitor destination must carefully select the ways in which it will distinguish itself from competitors. A difference is worth establishing to the extent that it satisfies the following criteria:

- *Important.* The difference delivers a highly valued benefit to target buyers. In the case of a visitor destination, personal safety has become a top benefit.

- *Distinctive.* Competitors do not offer the difference, or the company can offer it in a more distinctive way.

- *Superior.* The difference is superior to other ways that customers might obtain the same benefit.

- *Communicable.* The difference is communicable and visible to buyers.

- *Preemptive.* Competitors cannot easily copy the difference.

- *Affordable.* Buyers can afford to pay for the difference.

- *Profitable.* The company can introduce the difference profitability.

Some competitive advantages may quickly be ruled out because they are too slight, too costly to develop, or too inconsistent with the company's profile. Suppose that a company is designing its positioning strategy and has narrowed its list of possible competitive advantages to four. The company needs a framework for selecting the one that makes the most sense to develop.

Customers of casinos exhibit two critical reasons for maintaining a long-term relationship and recommending a particular casino to others. These are trust and emotional ties.[42] A positioning statement that emphasizes game payout will not succeed if customers don't believe this statement. Likewise, a positioning statement that emphasizes the latest technology may not succeed if customers feel the casino is cold and mechanical rather than a place to which they can relate.

Communicating and Delivering the Chosen Position

Having chosen positioning characteristics and a positioning statement, companies must communicate their positions to targeted customers. All of a company's marketing mix efforts must support its positioning strategy. If a company decides to build service superiority, for example, it must hire service-oriented employees, provide training programs, reward employees for providing good service, and develop sales and advertising messages to broadcast its service superiority.

Building and maintaining a consistent positioning strategy is not easy; many counterforces are at work. Advertising agencies hired by the company may not like a selected position and may overtly or covertly work against it. New management may not understand the positioning strategy. Budgets may be cut for critical support programs such as employee training or sales promotion. The development of an effective position requires a consistent, long-run program with continuous support by management, employees, and vendors.

Companies normally develop a memorable statement to communicate their desired positions. Unfortunately, a new management team or new ad agency may discard a good statement.

In 2004 Kentucky Fried Chicken announced a new campaign to reposition KFC for the third time in a year. One industry observer said, "When you jump around a lot on a message, it just doesn't stick." A discarded positioning strategy used in 2003 suggested that eating fried chicken could help one stay slim and trim. KFC's commercials were derided as among the worst in 2003 and even caused an investigation by the Federal Trade Commission.

The latest strategy attempted to position KFC as "Kitchen Fresh Chicken." Critics said that KFC should instead return to its heritage and reposition itself on taste using the original slogan "Finger Lickin' Good."[43]

Avis, an auto rental company, originally positioned itself with a statement and strong supportive program to convince the customer, "We're only No. 2 so we try harder." This also positioned Avis with the number-one company, Hertz, and away from Budget, Dollar, National, and Thrifty.

Olive Garden opened a restaurant in Tuscany, Olive Garden Riserva di Fizzano, and developed the Culinary Institute of Tuscany. It added Tuscan dishes to its menu, sent its chefs to the Culinary Institute of Tuscany, and developed a Tuscan farmhouse design for its restaurants. It also included recipes and cooking tips on its Web site. The restaurant and Culinary Institute in Italy help communicate Olive Garden's position as an authentic Italian restaurant. Its advertisements enforced this by featuring Italian families dining at Olive Garden.[44]

A company's positioning decisions determine who its competitors will be. When selecting a positioning strategy, a company should review its competitive strengths and weaknesses and select a position that places it in a superior position against its competitors.

Positioning is enhanced and supported by creating memorable customer experiences. Hospitality companies provide many services throughout the day. Most of these become routine and are indistinguishable from competitors. The key to creating memorable and differentiating customer experiences is not simply to improve them but to layer an enjoyable/memorable experience on top.[45]

Positioning Measurement: Perceptual Mapping

Perceptual mapping, a research tool, is sometimes used to measure a brand's position. Figure 8–3 is an example of hotels plotted on the attributes of price and perceived service. On this map we see there is a correlation between service and price; as price goes up, so does service.

Figure 8–3
Positioning map of service level versus price.
From Christopher Lovelock, *Services Marketing* (Upper Saddle River, NJ: Prentice Hall, 1996), p. 178. Used with permission.

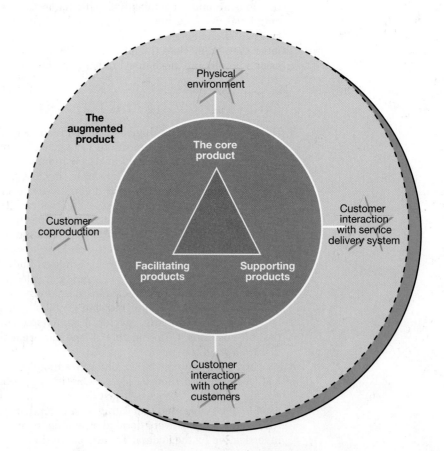

Some hotels appear to offer a better value than others. For example, Italia offers a little higher level of service than the Palace but is less expensive. Two-by-two perceptual maps provide an easy-to-read picture, but one often has to study multiple maps plotting different attributes to obtain a good feel of the marketplace. Perceptual maps can also be developed using consumers' perceptions of a number of product attributes. Increased competition or an ineffective positioning strategy can make repositioning necessary. Perceptual maps provide data supporting the need for repositioning.

Marriott International repositioned Fairfield Inn, which had expanded into urban markets with an upgraded product. The existing Fairfield Inns received upgraded furniture. The Fairfield Inn and Suites costs more to build than a regular Fairfield Inn, and it had higher average rates than a Fairfield Inn. Joe Lavin, senior vice president of franchising for Marriott International, said Fairfield's customers were becoming savvier. Thus, the upgrade was designed to allow Fairfield to keep up with its customers and also position itself apart from other limited-service competitors.[46]

■■■ KEY TERMS

Behavioral segmentation. Dividing a market into groups based on consumers' knowledge, attitude, use, or response to a product.

Competitive advantage. An advantage over competitors gained by offering consumers greater value either through lower prices or by providing more benefits that justify higher prices.

Competitors' strategies. When competitors use segmentation, undifferentiated marketing can be suicidal. Conversely, when competitors use undifferentiated marketing, a firm can gain an advantage by using differentiated or concentrated marketing.

Confused positioning. Leaving buyers with a confused image of a company.

Degree of product homogeneity. Undifferentiated marketing is more suited for homogeneous products. Products that can vary in design, such as restaurants and hotels, are more suited to differentiation or concentration.

Demographic segmentation. Dividing the market into groups based on demographic variables such as age, gender, family size, family life cycle, income, occupation, education, religion, race, and nationality.

Gender segmentation. Dividing a market on the basis of gender.

Geographic segmentation. Dividing a market into different geographic units such as nations, states, regions, counties, cities, or neighborhoods.

Income segmentation. Dividing a market into different income groups.

Market homogeneity. If buyers have the same tastes, buy a product in the same amounts, and react the same way to marketing efforts, undifferentiated marketing is appropriate.

Market positioning. Formulating competitive positioning for a product and a detailed marketing mix.

Market segmentation. Dividing a market into direct groups of buyers who might require separate products or marketing mixes.

Market targeting. Evaluating each market segment's attractiveness and selecting one or more segments to enter.

Overpositioning. Giving buyers a too-narrow picture of the company.

Psychographic segmentation. Dividing a market into different groups based on social class, lifestyle, or personality characteristics.

Specific product attributes. Price and product features can be used to position a product.

Underpositioning. Failing ever to position the company at all.

■■■ CHAPTER REVIEW

I.   **Market.** A market is the set of all actual and potential buyers of a product.

II. **Three Steps of the Target Marketing Process**

    A.   **Market segmentation** is the process of dividing a market into distinct groups of buyers who might require separate products and/or marketing mixes.

    B.   **Market targeting** is the process of evaluating each segment's attractiveness and selecting one or more of the market segments.

    C.   **Positioning** is the process of developing competitive positioning for the product and an appropriate marketing mix.

III. **Market Segmentation**

    A.   **Bases for segmenting a market.** There is no single way to segment a market. A marketer has to try different segmentation variables, alone and in combination, hoping to find the best way to view the market structure.

       1.   **Geographic segmentation** calls for dividing the market into different geographic units, such as nations, states, regions, counties, cities, or neighborhoods.

       2.   **Demographic segmentation** consists of dividing the market into groups based on demo-

graphic variables such as age, gender, family life cycle, income, occupation, education, religion, race, and nationality.

3. **Psychographic segmentation** divides buyers into different groups based on social class, lifestyle, and personality characteristics.

4. **Behavior segmentation** divides buyers into groups based on their knowledge, attitude, use, or response to a product.

B. **Requirements for Effective Segmentation**
1. **Measurability.** The degree to which the segment's size and purchasing power can be measured.

2. **Accessibility.** The degree to which segments can be accessed and served.

3. **Substantiality.** The degree to which segments are large or profitable enough to serve as markets.

4. **Actionability.** The degree to which effective programs can be designed for attracting and serving segments.

IV. **Evaluating Market Segments**
A. **Segment size and growth.** Companies analyze the segment size and growth and choose the segment that provides the best opportunity.

B. **Segment structural attractiveness.** A company must examine major structural factors that affect long-run segment attractiveness.

C. **Company objectives and resources.** The company must consider its own objectives and resources in relation to a market segment.

V. **Selecting Market Segments.** Segmentation reveals market opportunities available to a firm. The company then selects the most attractive segment or segments to serve as targets for marketing strategies to achieve desired objectives.

A. **Market-coverage alternatives**
1. **Undifferentiated marketing strategy.** An undifferentiated marketing strategy ignores market segmentation differences and goes after the whole market with one market offer.

2. **Differentiated marketing strategy.** The firm targets several market segments and designs separate offers for each.

3. **Concentrated marketing strategy.** Concentrated marketing strategy is especially appealing to companies with limited resources. Instead of going for a small share of a large market, the firm pursues a large share of one or more small markets.

B. **Choosing a market-coverage strategy.** Companies need to consider several factors in choosing a market-coverage strategy.

1. **Company resources.** When the company's resources are limited, concentrated marketing makes the most sense.

2. **Degree of product homogeneity.** Undifferentiated marketing is more suited for homogeneous products. Products that can vary in design, such as restaurants and hotels, are more suited to differentiation or concentration.

3. **Market homogeneity.** If buyers have the same tastes, buy a product in the same amounts, and react the same way to marketing efforts, undifferentiated marketing is appropriate.

4. **Competitors' strategies.** When competitors use segmentation, undifferentiated marketing can be suicidal. Conversely, when competitors use undifferentiated marketing, a firm can gain an advantage by using differentiated or concentrated marketing.

VI. **Market Positioning.** A product's position is the way the product is defined by consumers on important attributes—the place the product occupies in consumers' minds relative to competing products.

A. **Positioning strategies**
1. **Specific product attributes.** Price and product features can be used to position a product.

2. **Needs products fill or benefits products offer.** Marketers can position products by the needs that they fill or the benefits that they offer. For example, a restaurant can be positioned as a fun place.

3. **Certain classes of users.** Marketers can also position for certain classes of users, such as a hotel advertising itself as a women's hotel.

4. **Against an existing competitor.** A product can be positioned against an existing competitor. In the "Burger Wars," Burger King used its flame-broiled campaign against McDonald's, claiming that people prefer flame-broiled over fried burgers.

B. **Choosing and implementing a positioning strategy.** The positioning task consists of three steps: identifying a set of possible competitive advantages on which to build a position, selecting the right competitive advantages, and effectively communicating and delivering the chosen position to a carefully selected target market.

C. **Product differentiation**
1. **Physical Attributes**
2. **Service**
3. **Personnel**
4. **Location**
5. **Image**

D. Selecting the right competitive advantage
1. **How many differences?**
2. **Which differences?**

E. **Communicating and delivering the chosen position.** Once having chosen positioning characteristics and a positioning statement, a company must communicate its position to targeted customers. All of a company's marketing mix efforts must support its positioning strategy.

F. **Perceptual mapping**

▪▪▪ DISCUSSION QUESTIONS

1. Explain the process of market segmentation, market targeting, and market positioning.

2. Choose a hospitality business, for example, a hotel or restaurant. Explain some of the segments in its overall market (in this case, the hotel market or restaurant market), one of these markets that it targeted, and how it differentiated itself from its competitors to position itself in the market.

3. Identify a restaurant or hotel market segment in your community that you feel would be a good market segment to target. Explain the marketing mix you would put together to go after this market segment.

4. Some restaurateurs want to develop a restaurant with something for everyone. Why is this idea a dangerous policy?

5. Think about your classmates in this course. Can you classify them into different segments with specific names? What is your major segmentation variable? Could you effectively market products to these segments?

6. What roles do product attributes and perceptions of attributes play in the positioning of a product? Can an attribute common to several competing brands contribute to a successful positioning strategy?

▪▪▪ EXPERIENTIAL EXERCISE

Find an advertisement from a hospitality or travel company that targets a specific segment, such as children, young adults, seniors, or upper-income customers. Then visit a location of that company. What does the company do at the location with its marketing mix to attract the segment that it targeted in the advertisement? This can include sales promotions, signage, product mix, location of the company, and pricing of products.

▪▪▪ INTERNET EXERCISE

Go to the Web site of a major brand of hospitality or travel company. Explain how it appeals to different segments through the Web site. Give specific examples.

▪▪▪ REFERENCES

1. Janet Adamy, "Battle Brewing: Dunkin' Donuts Tries to Go Upscale, But Not Too Far," *Wall Street Journal* (April 8, 2006).

2. "Dunkin' Donuts New Advertising Offers a Rallying Cry for 2009: 'You Kin' Do It'," *PR Newswire* (January 5, 2009).

3. "Dunkin' Donuts New Advertising Offers a Rallying Cry for 2009: 'You Kin' Do It'," *PR Newswire* (January 5, 2009).

4. William R. Swinyard and Kenneth D. Struman, "Market Segmentation: Finding the Heart of Your Restaurant's Market," *Cornell Hotel and Restaurant Administration Quarterly,* 27, no. 1 (1986): 96.

5. www.Popeyes.com (accessed August 24, 2008).

6. John Jesitus, "The Regional Page: Diner's Search for That Down-Home Flavor," *Hotel and Motel Management,* 207, no. 1 (1992): 25–26.

7. Elisabeth A. Sullivan, "Customer Spotting," *Marketing News* (March 15, 2008): 10.

8. Stephen Kinzer, "Sowing Art on the Kansas Prairie," *New York Times* (January 22, 2004): B1, B5.

9. Janet Forgrieve, "Marketers Ignoring Reality of That Gray-Green, Author Says," *Rocky Mountain News* (February 19, 2004): 7B.

10. "Who's Dining Out?" *Cornell Hotel and Restaurant Administration Quarterly,* 26, no. 3 (1985): 4.

11. Peter Coy, "Why Price Is Rarely Right," *Bloomberg BusinessWeek* (February 1 and 8, 2010): 77–78.

12. Richard Baker, "Retail Trends—Luxury Marketing: The End of a Mega-Trend," *Retail* (June/July 2009): 8–12.

13. Chris Reynolds, "Me, Myself and I," *American Demographics* (November 2003): 1; Gary M. Stern, "Solo Diners," *Restaurants USA,* 10, no. 3 (1990): 15–16; www.unmarriedamerica.org (accessed August 23, 2008).

14. Les Christie, CNNMoney.com, June 23, 2006.

15. See Kunur Patel, "Zipcar: An America's Hottest Brands Case Study," *Advertising Age* (November 16, 2009): 16; Paul Keegan, "Zipcar: The Best New Idea in Business," *Fortune* (August 27, 2009), accessed at www.fortune .com; Elizabeth Olson, "Car Sharing Reinvents the Company Wheels," *New York Times* (May 7, 2009): F2; Stephanie Clifford, "How Fast Can This Thing Go, Anyway?" *Inc* (March 2008), accessed at www.inc.com; and www.zipcar.com, (accessed October 2010).

16. Information from www.rssc.com, and http://nationofwhynot.com (accessed November 2010).

17. www.smarttravel, www.rssc.com, and www.royalcaribbean.com (accessed November 2007).

18. Soo K. Kang, Cathy H. C. Hsu, and Kara Wolfe, "Family Traveler Segmentation by Vacation Decision-Making Patterns," *Journal of Hospitality and Tourism Research*, 27, no. 4 (2003): 464–465.

19. Robert C. Lewis, "Restaurant Advertising: Appeals and Consumers' Intensions," *Journal of Advertising Research*, 21, no. 5 (1981): 69–75.

20. From Starwood Hotel and Resorts, www.starwood.com/promotion/promo_landing.html?category=pets (accessed October 24, 2004): Elaine Sciolino, "Versailles Hotel Treats Dog Royally," *Denver Post* (December 4, 2003): 31A.

21. See J. Kate MacArthur, "BK Rebels Fall in Love with King," *Advertising Age* (May 1, 2006): 1, 86; and Kenneth Hem, "BK 'Lifestyle' Goods Aim for Young Males," *Adweek* (June 12, 2006): 8; Jennifer Ordonez, "Fast-Food Lovers, Unite!" *Newsweek* (May 24, 2004): 56. Jennifer Ordonez, "Cash Cows—Hamburger Joints Call Them Heavy Users But Not to Their Faces," *Wall Street Journal* (January 12, 2000): A1; Annette M. Budqisz, "QSR Foodservice: The International Market," press release from *Euromonitor International* (August 1, 2000).

22. Victor J. Cook, Jr., William Mindak, and Arch Woodside, "Profiling the Heavy Traveler Segment," *Journal of Travel Research*, 25, no. 4 (1987).

23. Ken W. McCleary and Pamela A. Weaver, "Are Frequent Guest Programs Effective?" *Cornell Hotel and Restaurant Administration Quarterly*, 32, no. 2 (1991): 45.

24. Jiang Weizhong, Chekitan S. Dev, and Vithala R. Rao, "Brand Extension and Customer Loyalty," *Cornell Hotel and Restaurant Administration Quarterly*, 43, no. 4 (2002): 15.

25. William P. Whelihan, III, and Kye-Sung Chon, "Resort Marketing Trends in the 90's," *Cornell Hotel and Restaurant Administration Quarterly*, 32, no. 2 (1991): 58.

26. See http://www.claritas.com/MyBestSegments/tutorials/Nielsen_PRIZM/engage.html (accessed July 21, 2012).

27. "Landry's to Sell 120 of Their Joe's Crab Shack Restaurants," *Restaurant News Resource* (October 10, 2006) accessed September 11, 2011, from http://www.restaurantnewsresource.com/article24523-Landry_s_to_Sell____of_Their_Joe_s_Crab_Shack_Restaurants.html.

28. Ryan Chittum, "Living Life Like Eloise: More Hotels and Condos," *Wall Street Journal* (July 25, 2007): B1.

29. Jackson, Eric, "Forget Kids, Investors Can Go for Chuck E. Cheese, *Breakout Performance* (Thursday, March 4, 2010), accessed November 22, 2011, http://breakoutperformance.blogspot.com/2010/03/forget-kids-investors-can-go-for-chuck.html.

30. C. S. Dev, M. S. Morgan, and S. Shoemaker, "A Positioning Analysis of Hotel Brands Based on Travel Manager Perceptions," *Cornell Hotel and Restaurant Administration Quarterly*, 36, no. 6 (1995): 49.

31. Accessed September 1, 2011, from http://www.subway.com/Menu/Product.aspx?CC=USA&LC=ENG&MenuTypeId=1&MenuId=41.

32. Accessed September 11, 2011, from http://www.marinabaysands.com/.

33. See Michael Porter, *Competitive Advantage* (New York: Free Press, 1980), chap. 2, for a good discussion of the concept of competitive advantage and methods for assessing it. See George A. Day and Robin Wensley, "Assessing Advantage: A Framework for Diagnosing Competitive Superiority," *Journal of Marketing* (April 1988): 1–20.

34. Dean Houghton, "Close to the Consumer," *The Furrow* (September/October 2003): 12, John Deer Agricultural Marketing Center, 1145 Thompson Avenue, Lenexa, KS 66219–2302.

35. George Moschis, Carolyn Folkman Curasi, and Danny Bellinger, "Restaurant Selection Preferences of Mature Consumers," *Cornell Hotel and Restaurant Administration Quarterly*, 44, no. 4 (2003): 59–60.

36. "Taco Johns—the Fresh Taste of West-Mex," www.TacoJohn.com.

37. Taco John's, Wikipedia, en.wikipedia.org (January 2008).

38. Chris Walsh, "New Partners to Preserve Old Charm of Telluride Ski," *Rocky Mountain News* (February 19, 2004): 7B.

39. Christopher Hosford, "A Transformative Experience," *Sales & Marketing Management*, 158 (June 2006): 32–36; Mike Beirne and Javier Benito, "Starwood Uses Personnel to Personalize Marketing," *Brandweek* (April 24, 2006): 9.

40. Advertising Fact Sheet, http://www.bk.com/CompanyInfo/bk_corporation/fact_sheets/ad_facts.aspx (accessed October 31, 2004); Schuster Enterprises, DBA Burger King, http://jobs.careerbuilder.com/JobSeeker/Companies/CompanyDetails.aspx?HHName=SchusterEnterprisesDBABurgerKing&cbRecursionCnt=1&cbsid=3a03617a8ba74188a526f53ac25eefe0–152535262-xe-2 (accessedOctober 31, 2004); Gail DeGeorge and Mark Landler, "Tempers Are Sizzling over Burger King's New Ads," *Business Week* (February 2, 1990): 33; Philip Stelly, Jr., "Burger King Rule Breaker," *Adweek* (November 9, 1990): 24, 26.

41. Back Ki-Joon and Sara C. Parks, "A Brand Loyalty Model Involving Cognitive, Affective and Cognitive Brand Loyalty and Customer Satisfaction," *Journal of Hospitality and Tourism Research*, 27, no. 4 (2003): 431.

42. Sui Jun Jian and Seyhmus Baloglu, "The Role of Emotional Commitment in Relationship Marketing: An Empirical Investigation of a Loyalty Model for Casinos," *Journal of Hospitality and Tourism Research*, 27, no. 4 (2003): 483.

43. Brian Steinberg, "KFC Cooks Up Yet Another Gambit," *Wall Street Journal* (March 16, 2004): B6.

44. Nancy Brumback, "Room at the Table," *Restaurant Business* (March 15, 2001): 71–82.

45. James H. Gilmore and B. Joseph Pine, II, "Differentiating Hospitality Operations vis Experiences," *Cornell Hotel and Restaurant Administration Quarterly*, 43, no. 3 (2002): 88.

46. Shannon McMullan, "Marriott International Repositions Fairfield Inn," *Hotel Business News* (February 21–March 6, 2000): 3.

Developing the Hospitality and Tourism Marketing Mix

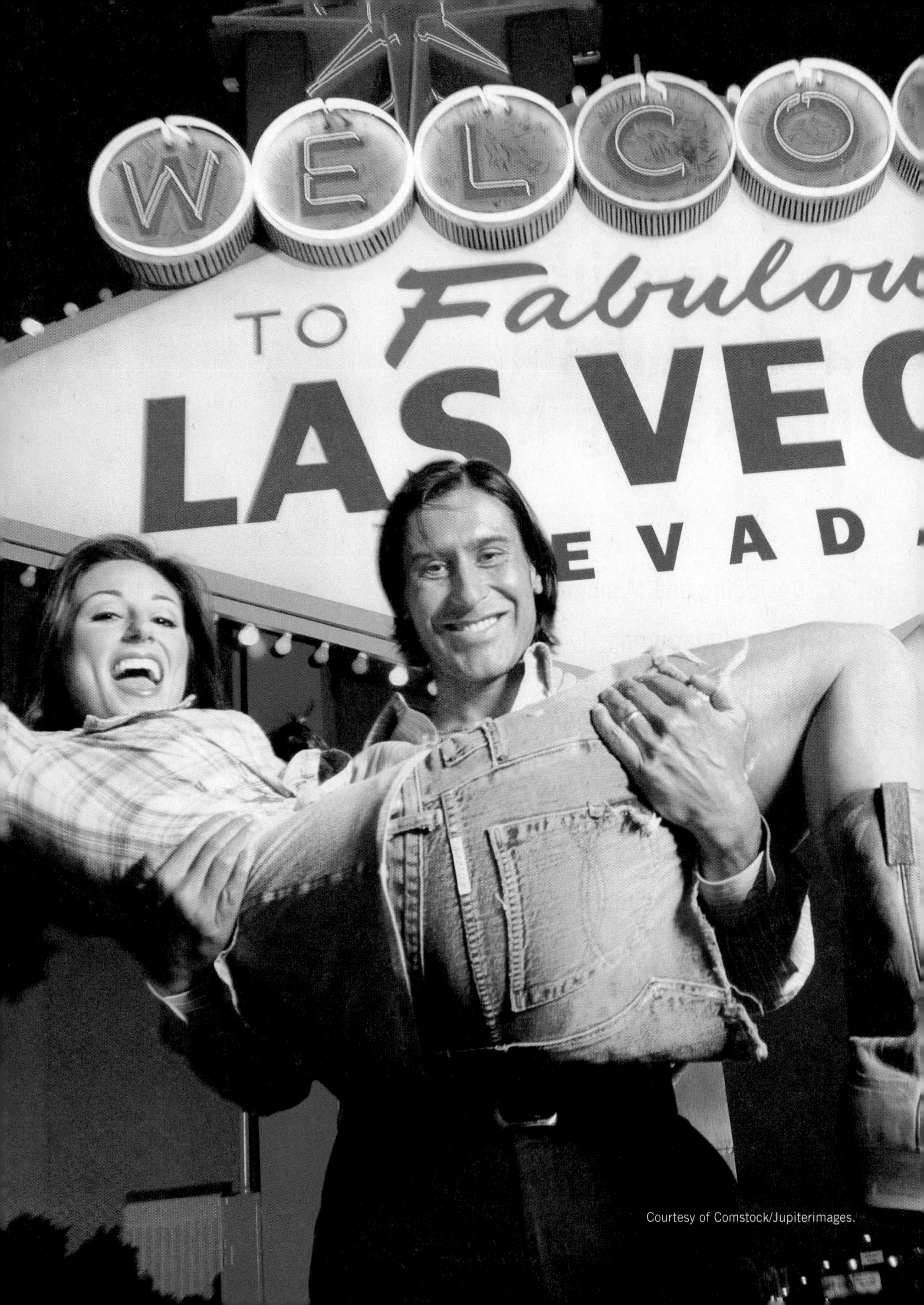

Courtesy of Comstock/Jupiterimages.

Profit is payment you get when you take advantage of change.

—Joseph Schumpeter

Being fed a decent meal in a casual environment is a commodity in far more supply than demand.

—Barry M. Cohen

Designing and Managing Products

Objectives

After reading this chapter, you should be able to:

1. Define the term *product*, including the core, facilitating, supporting, and augmented product.

2. Explain how accessibility, atmosphere, customer interaction with the service delivery system, customer interaction with other customers, and customer coproduction are all critical elements to keep in mind when designing a product.

3. Understand branding and the conditions that support branding.

4. Explain the new-product development process.

5. Understand how the product life cycle can be applied to the hospitality industry.

When you hear someone mention Las Vegas, what comes to mind? Sin City? Wholesome entertainment for the entire family? An indulgent luxury vacation? Or perhaps a value-oriented reward for hard-working Americans? If you answered "all of the above," you wouldn't necessarily be wrong. The truth: All of these have been characteristics associated with Las Vegas over the years. In recent times, the Las Vegas Convention and Visitors Authority (LVCVA) fielded several national ad campaigns. Tourism is Vegas's biggest industry, and the LVCVA is charged with maintaining the city's brand image and keeping visitors coming to one of the world's most famous cities.

Although the positioning of the Vegas brand has changed from time to time, the town will probably never entirely lose the "Sin City" label. That title was born when Las Vegas was young—an anything-goes gambling town full of smoke-filled casinos, bawdy all-girl revues, all-you-can-eat buffets, Elvis impersonators, and no-wait weddings on the Vegas Strip.

But as the 1990s rolled around, many Las Vegas officials felt that the town needed to broaden its target audience. So they set out to appeal to—of all things—families. Some of the biggest casinos on the Las Vegas Strip built roller coasters and other thrill rides, world-class water parks, and family-friendly shows like Treasure Island's live-action swashbuckler spectacle, visible to everyone passing by on the street. Although this strategy seemed effective for a brief time, marketers came to realize that the family image just didn't sync well with casino gambling—the high-profit product that built Las Vegas.

As the LVCVA started to consider its options, the terrorist attacks of September 11, 2001, dealt Las Vegas tourism one of its worst blows ever. Declining tourism led to 15,000 lost jobs. The LVCVA decided that it was time to unabashedly proclaim that Las Vegas was a destination for adults. That didn't just mean a return to the classic vices. The LVCVA engineered an image of Vegas as a luxury destination oozing with excess and indulgence. The theme parks were replaced by five-star resorts, high-rise condos, expansive shopping malls filled with the world's top luxury brands, and restaurants bearing the names of world-renowned chefs. A new breed of expensive stage shows for adult audiences replaced family-friendly entertainment. This change of strategy worked. Even as Las Vegas struggled through economic recovery in the post 9-11 world, visitors returned in record numbers.

However, to Rossi Ralenkotter, CEO of the LVCVA, it soon became apparent that the town was much more than just an assortment of facilities and amenities. "We talked to old customers and new customers to determine the essence of the brand of Las Vegas," he said.[1] The LVCVA found that to the nearly 40 million who flocked to the city each year, Vegas is an emotional connection—a total brand experience.

237

And just what is the "Las Vegas experience"? Research showed that when people come to Las Vegas, they're a little naughtier—a little less inhibited. They stay out longer, eat more, do some gambling, and spend more on shopping and dining. "We found that [the Las Vegas experience] centered on adult freedom," says Ralenkotter. "People could stay up all night and do things they wouldn't normally do in their own towns."[2]

Based on these customer insights, the LVCVA coined the now-familiar catchphrase—"Only Vegas: What happens here, stays here." The phrase captured the essence of the Las Vegas experience—that it's okay to be a little naughty in Vegas. That simple phrase became the centerpiece of what is now deemed one of the most successful tourism campaigns in history. The campaign transformed Las Vegas's image from the down-and-dirty "Sin City" to the enticing and luxurious "Only Vegas."

The $75 million ad campaign showed the naughty nature of people once they arrive in Las Vegas. In one ad, a woman spontaneously married a visibly younger man in a Las Vegas wedding chapel. Then, ignoring his ardent pleas, she kissed him goodbye and pulled herself away, insisting that she had to get back to her business convention. In another ad, an outgoing young woman is shown introducing herself to various men, each time giving a different name. In a third ad, a sexy woman hops into a limo, flirts with the driver, and emerges from the car at the airport for her trip home as a conservative business woman. At the end of each ad was the simple reminder, "What happens here, stays here."

The LVCVA continued investing heavily in the bold and provocative campaign and in a variation on the theme, "Your Vegas is showing." All the while, Las Vegas experienced its biggest growth boom in history. Hotel occupancy rates hovered at an incredible 90 percent, visitors came in ever-increasing numbers, and there was seemingly no end to the construction of lavish new luxury properties. To top it off, Las Vegas was dubbed the number two hottest brand by respected brand consultancy Landor Associates, right behind Google. It seemed that the LVCVA had found the magic formula and that Vegas had found its true identity. With everything going so well, what could possibly go wrong?

Then in 2008, Las Vegas suffered another one-two punch. First, the worst recession since the Great Depression had consumers scaling back on unnecessary expenses. Second, in the wake of government bailouts and a collapsing financial industry, company CEOs and executives everywhere came under scrutiny for lavish expenses. Suddenly, Las Vegas's carefully nurtured, naughty, indulgent image made even prudent, serious company conferences held there look bad. It didn't help matters when President Obama delivered a statement that Las Vegas's mayor, Oscar Goodman, perceived as the straw that broke the camel's back. Obama scolded Wall Street executives by saying, "You can't get corporate jets; you can't go take a trip to Las Vegas or go down to the Super Bowl on the taxpayer's dime." As a result of the new economic realities, both leisure travel and the convention industry—two staples in Las Vegas's success—took a big hit.

As a result, 2008 and 2009 were some of the worst years ever for Las Vegas. In 2009, the total number of visitors dropped to 36.4 million, 7 percent less than the 2007 peak of 39.1 million. This translated into a 24 percent decrease in convention attendance, a 22 percent drop in room occupancy, and a 10 percent decline in gambling revenues. "People aren't coming in the numbers they used to, and those that are bet on the cheaper tables" said Steven Kent, an analyst for Goldman Sachs. Nevada's unemployment rate climbed to one of the highest in the United States. The Las Vegas hospitality industry responded by chopping prices. Rooms on the Las Vegas Strip could be had as cheaply as $25 a night. Gourmet meals were touted for half price. The town was practically begging for visitors.

After years of successfully pedaling Vegas naughtiness as the primary selling point, the LVCVA realized it had to make a shift. So in the midst of the economic carnage, with so much to offer and great deals to be had, it focused on the value and affordability of a Vegas vacation. A new ad campaign, "Vegas Bound," urged hard-working Americans to take a well-deserved break in Las Vegas to recharge their batteries before returning return home to brave the tough economy. A series of Vegas Bound ads and online mini-documentaries showed average Americans in high-end nightclubs, spas, and restaurants. One grinning 81-year-old woman was even shown giving a thumbs-up after an indoor skydiving session.

"We had to think how we should address our customers during this financial crisis when they're reluctant to make big financial commitments," said Ralenkotter at the start of the campaign. "We're appealing to Americans saying, 'You're working hard. It's OK to take a break.'" The campaign didn't eliminate glamour and luxury. Rather, it repackaged these traits in an "affordable" and "well-deserved" wrapper.

But after so many years of hearing about Las Vegas as a guilt-free adult playground, no matter what the ad campaign said, consumers had a hard time seeing Vegas as prudent. Research showed that even in a painful recession, consumers still saw Vegas for what it was: a place they could go to for simple pleasures not available at home. It took the LVCVA only five months to pull the plug on "Vegas Bound" and resurrect "What happens here, stays here." In a near 180-degree flip, Ralenkotter said, "We feel it is time to get back to our brand messaging."

Although there is rarely a magic bullet in a situation like the one Las Vegas faced, the LVCVA's return to its core brand message seems to be working. As 2010 unfolded, the number of visitors was up. The LVCVA projected a 3 percent growth in visitors for the year to 37.5 million. "I think there's pent-up demand," said Cathy Tull, senior vice president of marketing for the authority. "People want to travel, they want to escape, and Vegas works very well for that."

Just as the needle started to budge, MGM Resorts International opened the most ambitious project Las Vegas had ever seen. In fact, its $8.5 billion CityCenter was said to be the largest privately funded construction project in U.S. history. A pedestrian-friendly resort, CityCenter, was designed as a small city in and of itself with four luxury hotels, two residential condo towers, and a 500,000-square-foot high-end shopping and dining center.

Adding 6,000 rooms and 12,000 jobs to the Las Vegas Strip has met with mixed reactions. Some speculate that this game-changing property will put an exclamation point on Las Vegas's image and provide additional oomph in a time of crisis. "History has shown that new properties increase visitation across the board," said Ralenkotter. But others see the introduction of such a large property as hazardous to recovery. "Will it cannibalize other properties?" asked Tony Henthorne, professor and chair of tourism and convention administration at the University of Nevada at Las Vegas. "Probably so, within a short-term period."

But even as such major signs of life are sprouting up along the Las Vegas Strip, there's an air of caution. Jim Murren, CEO for MGM, believes his company is not yet out of the woods. When asked if he thought CityCenter was in the clear, he responded emphatically. "Absolutely not. We're not declaring victory at all. We are a year or two away from even having a chance to consider that." That is probably the best attitude to take. After all, the Las Vegas Monorail filed for bankruptcy. Two other major projects that were expected to boost the Vegas economy have been shelved. Cheap (i.e., inexpensive) rooms are still available on the Las Vegas Strip. And although tourist visits are on the rise, the additional hotel room supply means it will be awhile, before 2007 occupancy rates are reached.

Las Vegas has certainly had its share of ups and downs. Times may be brightening now. But the city will face many challenges in the months and years to come. Goldman analyst Kent expresses confidence in the brand. "For the long-term, we believe in Vegas and its ability to transform itself and attract more customers." R&R Partners, the ad agency handling the Las Vegas marketing campaigns, made an important discovery that supports Kent's point of view. It found through its research that, especially during hard economic times, people wanted to know that the same Vegas they've known and loved is still there.[3]

As the Las Vegas example shows, in their quest to create customer relationships, marketers must build and manage products and brands that connect with customers. This change begins with a deceptively simple question: What is a product?

■■■ What Is a Product?

A room at the Four Seasons in Toronto, a Hawaiian vacation, McDonald's French fries, a vacation package in Bali, a catered luncheon, a bus tour of historic sites, and a convention in a modern convention center with group rates in a nearby hotel are all products. Consider the variety of products in a typical casino hotel.

We define the term *product* as follows: *A product is anything that can be offered to a market for attention, acquisition, use, or consumption that might satisfy a want or need. It includes physical objects, services, places, organizations, and ideas.*

This definition refers to the planned component of the product that the firm offers. Besides the planned component, the product also includes an unplanned component. This is particularly true in hospitality and travel products, which are often heterogeneous. For example, a consumer entered a restaurant in Dallas and was greeted by the hostess, who presented him with a menu. When he opened his menu, he saw a dead roach stuck to the inside on the menu. After receiving this unexpected bonus, the consumer decided to leave the restaurant. The restaurant certainly did not plan on having a dead roach in the menu. The product the customer receives is not always as management plans. Managers of service organizations need to work hard to eliminate unexpected negative surprises and make sure guests get what they expect.

■■■ Product Levels

Hospitality managers need to think about the product on four levels: the core product, the facilitating product, the supporting product, and the augmented product (Figure 9–1).

Core Products

The most basic level is **core product,** which answers the following question: What is the buyer really buying?

A four-day holiday in Dublin, Ireland, isn't a plane ride, hotel room, taxis, and meals. Depending on the visitor, it might be cultural enrichment, a return to one's roots, safe adventure, or even romance.

As all good steakhouses know, "Don't sell the steak, sell the sizzle." Marketers must uncover the core benefit to the consumer of every product and sell these benefits rather than merely selling features.

Figure 9–1
Product levels.
Source: Adapted from C. Gonroos, "Developing the Service Offering—A Source of Competitive Advantage," in *Add Value to Your Service,* ed. C. Surprenant (Chicago, IL: American Marketing Association, 1987), p. 83.

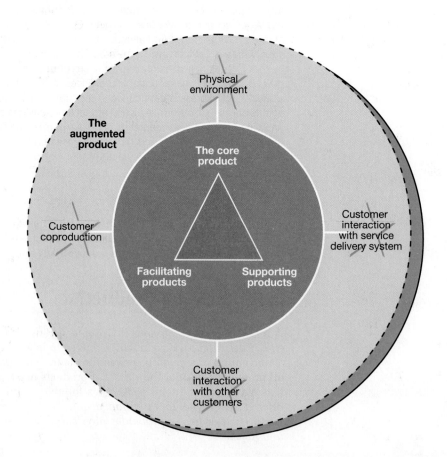

Facilitating Products

Facilitating products are services or goods that must be present for the guest to use the core product. A first-class corporate hotel must have check-in and checkout services, a business center, a restaurant, and valet service, for instance. In an economy hotel, facilitating services might be no more than check-in and checkout service. One important aspect of facilitating products is accessibility. Resort condominiums often close the office and registration desk in the evenings. They can get by with this if they notify guests and make arrangements for late-arriving guests to pick up keys. A business hotel could never get by with closing the front desk. Guests expect it to be accessible when they want to use it. Product design requires an understanding of the target markets and the facilitating services that they require.

A state park might not come to mind for customer service, but Chadron State Park in western Nebraska offers security for campers and cabin guests through a security station at the entrance. Late arrivals are welcomed by the security officer and given a key (cabins) as well as a map and instructions on how to find their location. Chadron State management knows that guests travel many miles to reach the park, and often arrive late at night.

Supporting Products

Core products require facilitating products but do not require supporting products. **Supporting products** are extra products offered to add value to the core product and help differentiate it from the competition. In a corporate hotel, an iPad in the room or a full-service health spa is a supporting product that exists to help draw and retain customers. The distinction between facilitating and supporting products is not always clear. Facilitating products for one market segment may be supporting products for another. For example, although families may not require restaurants and valet service when staying at a hotel, business travelers depend on them. Hyatt was among the first chains to offer a broad line of bathroom amenities, including shampoo, conditioners, and several choices of soap. When hotels first introduced these amenities, they were supporting the core product. Today, amenities have become facilitating products. Hilton spent two years analyzing consumer trends before developing its amenity package.[4]

9.1 www .villafeltrinelli.com: Watch the movie about Villa Feltrinelli and see how it portrays the elegance of the Villa. Who do you think would want to stay here? Even though people might be able to afford to stay here, who do you think would not want to stay here?

Bob Burns, the founder of Regent International Hotels, personally selected products that would enhance the chain's luxury image and provide differentiation. Guests staying found full-size bottles of high-quality shampoo in the bathroom. Speaking of bathrooms, Bob gained a reputation for introducing oversized bathrooms to the hotel industry. Bob also insisted that all his hotels serve fresh-squeezed orange juice, also in keeping with his concept of luxury hotels. Burns had studied and worked in the hotel industry for years, including a position as general manager of the upscale Kahala Hilton Resort in Hawaii. He had talked with thousands of guests over the years and felt that he knew what they wanted.

The Regent Chain was sold to Four Seasons Hotels, but Bob continued in the luxury sector by purchasing and renovating Villa Feltrinelli, the former residence of Victor Mussolini, in northern Italy on Lake Garda. This hotel is now regarded as one of the top luxury hotels in the world.[5]

The following is a review from the *Sunday Times* of London:

> If I had to choose my favorite hotel in the world, it would be Villa Feltrinelli. It was renovated by the famous hotelier Bob Burns, of Regent Hotels, as his retirement home, but he couldn't stop himself restoring it. So, when the budget passed the $30m mark and there was still quite a way to go, he decided to turn it into a hotel. This level of luxury, with millions spent on every room, doesn't make financial sense, so it's a complete fluke for the guest. The rooms are huge—the bathrooms are the size of a normal hotel room—and so beautiful. The villa fulfils every cliché you've ever heard about Italy. There's the stunning natural landscaping that just keep adding to its beauty. Then there's the 80 ft custom-built mahogany speedboat to take you to this little place on the island for lunch or to Verona for the opera, followed by dinner on board.
>
> Yes, it's expensive, but two nights here are better than a month anywhere else.[6]

Obviously not all hospitality firms can appeal to a luxury segment or develop the opulence of Bob Burn's hotels, but all members should choose supporting products that are not easily matched by the competition. They should also be able to deliver supporting services in a professional manner. For example, some midscale hotels offer room service because they see it as a competitive advantage to attracting the business traveler. However, unprofessional delivery of supporting products can do more harm than good. Many midpriced hotels offering room service lack a designated area in the kitchen for room-service carts, a room-service coordinator to answer the phone and write up the tickets, and designated room-service waiters. Necessary equipment and personnel are assembled at the time of the order, and as one might imagine, the results are sometimes disastrous. The person answering the phone lacks the proper training to ask the right questions (e.g., how the steak is to be cooked, the type of salad dressing the customer would like, and the type of potatoes desired). After taking the order, the next step is to find someone to set up the cart and take the order to the room. Likely candidates are the bell person, bus person, or a service person from the dining room. Personnel in the first two categories are not properly trained but may jump at the opportunity to gain a tip. Because they are not trained, the bell person and bus person may forget such essential items as salt and pepper, sugar, forks, and napkins when setting up the cart. To damage the hotel's image further, the guest puts the tray in the hallway after finishing the meal where it will sit until housekeeping picks it up the next morning.

Jogging is a popular means of exercise. Hotels are now offering jogging maps as well as bottles of water in the lobby for joggers. The Swiss Hotel in Boston provides serve-yourself coffee for early-morning flight crews. Some hotels place cold bottles of water as well as a note thanking the guest for staying at the hotel in the guest's car as it is returned to them by the valet after they have checked out of the hotel. These are examples of low-cost supporting products that add value.[7]

The Royal Gorge Route Railroad offers tourists an opportunity to enjoy the beautiful Royal Gorge near Canon City, Colorado, passing below the Royal Gorge Bridge on tracks alongside the Arkansas River. The train ride is complemented by gourmet lunches and dinners. The train and the gourmet food fit together as hand and glove. Which is the supporting product? Most readers will undoubtedly say the gourmet meals, but for many travelers, the two are inseparable.[8]

In summary, supporting products offer a competitive advantage, only if they are properly planned and implemented. They must meet or exceed customer expectations to have a positive effect.

Augmented Product

The **augmented product** includes accessibility, atmosphere, customer interaction with the service organization, customer participation, and customers' interaction with each other. These elements combine with the core facilitating and supporting products to provide the augmented product.

From a managerial standpoint, the core product provides a focus for the business; it is the reason for being. Facilitating products are those that are essential for providing the core product to the target market. Supporting products can help position a product. According to Christian Gronroos, a services marketing expert, the core, facilitating, and supporting products determine what customers receive but not how they receive it.[9] The delivery of the service affects the customer's perception of the service, illustrated by the room-service example earlier. The augmented service offering combines what is offered with how it is delivered.

The augmented product is an important concept because hospitality and travel services require customer coproduction of the service. For most hospitality products, the customer comes to the service delivery system and has to interact with the service delivery system. For example, guests have to check in at the front desk, get to the room, and understand how to use the television and telephone systems. They also have to interact with other customers and employees. Because guests come to the service, atmosphere is an important part of the product. The augmented product captures the key elements that must be managed when the customer comes to the service factory (e.g., the hotel, restaurant, country club, conference center, amusement park). We now take a look at some of the elements of the augmented product.

Accessibility

If a product is not accessible, it has no value. Two barriers to accessibility are hours of operation and lack of knowledge. A hotel health club or a swimming pool that opens at 7 A.M. does not help the businessperson who wants to work out at 6 A.M., eat breakfast, and get to an 8 A.M. business appointment. A restaurant that opens at 7 A.M. becomes an irritant to a guest who has to leave at 6 A.M. for the airport. International hotels housing guests suffering from jet lag may find that opening the restaurant earlier in the morning would provide both a valued service and additional revenue. If there is a line of guests waiting for the restaurant to open in the morning, it may indicate that the hours need to be adjusted to make the restaurant more accessible.

A restaurant that the guest is not aware of creates no value for the guest. The front-desk clerk and bell person should make the guest aware of the hotel's services. There are often unique shopping and dining areas that only local residents know about, but a traveler to the city will not. Providing information about the attractions in the city makes the attributes of the city accessible to the guest. Products must be accessible when the guest wants to use them.

Atmosphere: The Physical Environment

Atmosphere is a critical element in services. It can be the customer's reason for choosing to do business with an establishment. Burgundy's restaurant in Houston lacked street appeal and went out of business. The restaurant was located in a strip shopping center with a glass panel exterior and wall, common in many strip centers. The owners carpeted the concrete floor, put in booths, installed a sign over the door, and opened the restaurant. Perhaps they felt that their food quality and service would attract customers. But few ever reached the restaurant. The restaurant's exterior lacked identity or character and was not inviting to potential customers. People who saw Burgundy's simply did not come into the restaurant. Conversely, BJs Restaurant and Brewhouse has used atmosphere effectively. It builds all of its restaurants, rather than move into existing locations, to give them a common look inside and out. This also ensures they operate efficiently. The exterior is modern and inviting; the interior is casual and promotes a relaxed and fun environment.

Atmosphere is appreciated through the senses. Sensory terms provide descriptions for the atmosphere of a particular set of surroundings.

- The main **visual** dimensions of atmosphere are color, brightness, size, and shape.
- The main **aural** dimensions of atmosphere are volume and pitch.
- The main **olfactory** dimensions of atmosphere are scent and freshness.
- The main **tactile** dimensions of atmosphere are softness, smoothness, and temperature.

When a strong atmosphere is created through the senses, it can set expectations for the fifth sense, taste. If loyal customers walk into a Starbucks, the atmospherics set the taste expectations for a cup of their favorite Starbucks beverage. As they taste their beverage, the consistency of the product does not disappoint them.

Atmosphere can affect purchase behavior in at least four ways. First, atmosphere may serve as an attention-creating medium. The Casa Bonita Mexican Restaurant in Denver, Colorado, features an 85-foot bell tower to attract one's attention to the building. It has expanded the Mexican theme to include artificial volcanoes and a replica of the diving cliffs of Acapulco from which divers perform for dinner patrons. It has used atmospherics to develop an experiential product. People come to Casa Bonita not only for the food but for an experience.

Second, atmosphere may serve as a message-creating medium to potential customers. The modern style of Aloft Hotels is evident from the exterior design of the hotel. When one enters the lobby, one gets the sense of an urban loft environment, consistent with the exterior. This is how the Aloft Web site describes its public space, "It is a place where walls have been knocked down to create a space that is open in design and open to possibilities. A place where energy flows, personalities mingle, and opportunities abound. A place where anything can happen."[10]

The Aureole restaurant features a four-story-tall wine tower, housing almost 10,000 bottles of wine. The enclosed structure holds the wine at 55°F and 70 percent humidity, an ideal climate for wine. The wine stewards fetch the wine by going up and down the sides of the tower on mechanical hoists. The wine tower and the wine stewards create a "wow" effect for the Aureole restaurant. Courtesy of Gail Mooney-Kelly/Alamy.

9.2 Le Méridien LM100, http://www.starwoodhotels.com/lemeridien/lm100/index.html: Go to the Web site after reviewing it; explain how Le Méridien is using atmosphere to differentiate itself from competitive hotels.

According to this Aloft guest, the atmosphere of Aloft achieves its desired effect, "When you come down to the lobby, you always see an activity. It's like a car wreck: You have to stop and watch the scene."[11]

Third, atmosphere may serve as an effect-creating medium. Colors, sounds, and textures directly arouse visceral reactions that stimulate the purchase of a product. In Harrah's casino in Las Vegas, an area on the slot floor was infused with a pleasant odor over several weekends. The revenue from the scented floor exceeded the non-scented area by 45 percent. Today most large casinos follow similar strategies. When things are slow, a popcorn attendant at Disney World turns on a machine that produces a popcorn smell and a line for popcorn quickly forms.[12]

Finally, environment can be a mood-creating medium. An environmental psychologist has described environments as high load and low load. High and low refer to the information that one receives from the environment. Bright colors, bright lights, loud noises, crowds, and movement are typical elements of a high-load environment, whereas their opposites are characteristic of a low-load environment.[13] A high-load environment creates a playful, adventurous mood, whereas low-load environments create a relaxing mood. Vacationers going to Las Vegas or Branson, Missouri, are likely to react positively to a high-load environment that offers the excitement they were expecting. The front desk of the Flamingo Hilton is adjacent to the hotel's casino. While waiting to check in, guests hear the sounds of the casino, watch the players, and feel the excitement. In contrast, Courtyard by Marriott creates a relaxing, home-like low-load environment for business travelers who wish to relax after a busy day.

Le Méridien created a group of cultural innovators and artists who define and enrich the guest experience at Le Méridien.[14] The group comprises a global array of visionaries, from artists to photographers, musicians to designers, chefs to architects. Some members of the group appointed to develop a unique atmosphere for Le Méridien include Andrea Illy, of Illy Coffee, chef Jean-Georges Vongerichten, and perfume creators Fabrice Penot and Eddie Roschi, of Le Labo. Penot commented, "When you read a book or enter a library, you have the feeling of comfort. It's a place where your mind can go away. [When you stay at a hotel] you want to feel at home, you want to feel safe, but you also want to feel like you are away." The scent, LM01™, created by Le Labo to capture this feeling is the first thing one notices when you walk into any of Le Méridien's 120 hotels.[15]

Atmosphere must be considered when creating hospitality products. As marketers, we should understand what the customer wants from the buying experience and what atmospheric variables will fortify the beliefs and emotional reaction the buyers are seeking or, in some cases, escaping. Will the proposed atmosphere compete effectively in a crowded market?[16]

Customer Interaction with the Service Delivery System

The customer participates in the delivery of most hospitality and travel products. There are three phases to this involvement: joining, consumption, and detachment.[17] In the **joining stage,** the customer makes the initial inquiry contact. When designing products we must make it easy for people to learn about the new product. This information must be delivered in a professional way.

The joining phase is often enhanced through sampling. Visitors to foreign countries are often reluctant to order a full meal of native foods. The Inter-Continental Hotel of Jakarta, Indonesia, took steps to introduce visitors to the local cuisine by selling sample plates of selected native foods from a typical native pushcart in the afternoon cocktail area of the hotel adjacent to the lobby. This innovation created excitement and enhanced the atmosphere, introduced guests to native foods served in the hotel's restaurant, and served as a profit-making product line.

Unfortunately, some hospitality companies attempt to manage service variability by standardizing service behavior. "Adopting systems to increase organizational efficiency by constraining or scripting employee behavior may lead to counterproductive service outcomes."[18] A well-trained and knowledgeable employee can greatly assist customers in the joining stage without following a script or acting like an android.

As a consideration during the joining phase organizations must make it easy for customers to purchase the product. Pei Wei restaurants, a popular limited-service Asian restaurant, have a separate cash register and entrance for take-out orders. This enables the person who has made an order online to by-pass the line of dine-in customers waiting to order.

The **consumption phase** takes place when the service is consumed. In a restaurant it occurs when the customer is dining; in a hotel when an individual is a guest. Designers of hospitality products must understand how guests will interact with the product. The employees, customers, and physical facilities are all part of the product. A business hotel that opens a concierge floor aimed at the luxury market must train its employees to meet the expectations of this new class of traveler. In addition to employee–customer interaction, hospitality firms have to consider how customers will interact with one another during the consumption stage. A business hotel near a large amusement park developed a package for the summer family market. The package proved to be so popular that some of the hotel's main market, business travelers, was driven away. The noise of the children in the hallways and the lobby changed the atmosphere. Gone was the comfortable atmosphere desired by the business traveler.

Physical features, layout, and signage can also be used to help customers interact with the product. In many hotels, finding your way to a meeting can be frustrating. This problem can be overcome by proper attention to directional signage. Signage can also be used to make customers aware of the existence of supporting products. Guests may leave a hotel not realizing that it had a health club or a business center. It does no good to invest in supporting products if guests aren't aware of their existence.

Occasionally, even the best-designed signage is not observed or understood. Guests who appear lost in the Orlando Peabody Hotel are very apt to discover an employee, including the general manager, who will personally escort them to their destination. This does not occur by accident. Training and positive reinforcement in hotels such as the Peabody ensure that this type of service is an integral part of the hotel's product.

The **detachment phase** is when the customer is through using a product and departs. For example, hotel guests may need a bell person to help with the bags. They will need to settle their account and acquire transportation to the airport. International travelers may need an airport departure tax stamp.

Guests in a roadside motel may need to know directions, road conditions, the hours of check services, and other information. The manager of a Super 8 motel in Benson, Arizona, prides himself on serving

Disney World has a high-load environment, designed to entertain families. Courtesy of Vika Sabo/Alamy.

guests with this information. Unfortunately, this is not the case at many motels as front-desk clerks are often part-time employees, feel harassed by a line of guests, and give abrupt answers such as "I don't know; why don't you check the Internet?"

Thinking through these three stages helps management understand how the customer will interact with the service delivery system, resulting in a product designed to fit the needs of the customer. For example, where it is legal, some hotels purchase and resell airport departure tax stamps. The guest does not have to wait in line at the airport and the hotel has eliminated one concern for the guests. Although the hotel does not receive income from reselling departure stamps, the guest leaves with a good impression. Similarly, well-managed international hotels ask guests if they have their passports and airline tickets and if they have cleared their safety deposit box when they are checking out. Managers should think through and then experience the joining, consumption, and detachment phases of their guests.

Destination marketers have a special responsibility to carefully plan and help manage each of these phases. Visitor marketing is commonly the responsibility of chambers of commerce, convention bureaus, government agencies/departments, and other public or quasi-public organizations. Funding is often provided by sales tax or special room tax receipts.

Tourism promotion organizations sometimes feel their responsibility is solely to bring "heads to beds," in other words, to increase the number of visitors. This simplistic thinking has resulted in a mix-match of attracting the wrong visitor to the community. It also ignores the organization's responsibility to use part of its funding for crime awareness and prevention programs, service-sector personnel training, signage, language instruction, beautification, and many other support activities to help ensure visitor satisfaction.

Unfortunately, visitors sometimes have serious problems, such as the death of one of the travelers, crimes committed against a visitor, or accidents. Tourism promotion should include training policies and procedures to assist visitors. Far too many tourism promotion organizations can tell visitors where to find Italian restaurants but have no idea how to assist a visitor in crisis.

Crime occurs. Tourists are easy victims, and many are unwilling to return to testify against an accused criminal if travel costs are involved. Recognizing this, the Hawaii Visitors Bureau established a victims' assistance program to provide airline, hotel, and restaurant services free of charge to ensure that victims return to testify against the accused.

The positive word of mouth that occurs when visitors are provided assistance in time of need cannot be replaced with slick brochures inviting others to come.

Customer Interaction with Other Customers

An area that is drawing the interest of hospitality researchers is the interaction of customers with one another. An airline flight on Friday afternoon from Dallas to Houston was sold out with a number of people on standby. Some on standby were construction workers returning home from their job sites. The airline's ground crew, in an effort to maximize revenue, put a construction worker in an empty first-class seat. The passenger paying a premium to sit in first class did not appreciate a worker in dirty construction clothes in the next seat. Hospitality organizations must manage the interaction of customers to ensure that some do not negatively affect the experience of others.

The issue of customer interaction is a serious problem for hotels and resorts. The independent nontour guest consistently objects to the presence of large group-inclusive tours (GITs). This problem is magnified if the GIT guests represent a different culture, speak a foreign language, or are from an age group years different from that of independent nontour guests.

The Shangri-La Hotel of Singapore dealt successfully with this problem by constructing three different hotel properties on the same grounds. The tower hotel serves GIT and lesser-revenue, independent nontour guests. The Bougainvillea section serves a more upscale guest and a third executive property is for the exclusive use of very upscale guests. Interaction among the three groups is limited to the common outdoor swimming pool.

Ski resorts are now faced with how to manage the interaction of skiers and snowboarders. Courtesy of Frits Solvang © Dorling Kindersley.

Ski resorts are facing a serious problem of guest interaction. Traditionally, skiers have been a fairly homogeneous group with common cultural norms, even though they arrive from widely separated geographic areas. German, French, Japanese, American, and Mexican skiers tended to have societal commonalities, despite differences in language.

The arrival of the snowboard changed this congenial mix of guests. Skiers began to complain that they must share the slopes with people dressed in counterculture clothing who often show blatant disregard for slope-side courtesy. The management of ski resorts was suddenly faced with a serious problem. Taos responded by refusing entry to snowboarders and positioned itself as "Skiing for Purists." Others turned part of the ski areas into terrain peaks with half pipes and other physical attractions popular with "riders."

Many hotels such as Embassy Suites provide free wine and cheese for guests during a set time period in the evening. These hotels commonly report that this act of hospitality has an added benefit of bringing guests together. Lasting friendships and business deals have resulted from the evening wine and cheese.

The now common free breakfast offered by roadside lodging was modeled after bed and breakfasts (B&Bs). However, unlike most B&Bs, there is often little reason to become acquainted with other guests. Roadside hotels/motels could benefit by inducing guest interaction by seating arrangements that encourage guest mixing rather than double tables at which a couple silently sits drinking a cup of coffee and eating cold cereal. A midwestern motel removed the tables and chairs, replacing them with overstuffed furniture and coffee tables. Although this presented some problems in eating, it did encourage guest mixing.

If a free breakfast is offered, it should be planned to enhance the guest experience because this is the last moment to ensure that guests leave having enjoyed their final time at the property.

Customers as Employees

Customers often help hospitality organizations coproduce the product. Involving the guest as an employee can increase capacity, improve customer satisfaction, and reduce costs. The breakfast just mentioned is an example. Wait staff are not needed when guests help themselves.

The Las Vegas Sports Club used to have an attendant handing out keys and towels to members. The attendants would ask each member which locker he or she would like, negotiate alternatives when the member's favorite locker was unavailable, collect the member's card, issue the key, and return his or her card when the member was finished with the locker. The club installed a device that releases the locker key when the membership card is placed in a slot. When this occurred, the towel attendant simply gave out towels. The members were happy because they could select a locker in an uncrowded area, and the club's management was pleased because it was able to reduce the number of attendants at the towel counter. Then someone observed that members could get their own towels if they were neatly stacked on shelves. The club no longer needed the space for the towel attendant in both the women's and men's locker rooms. It reconfigured the locker rooms and created a spa. The processes given to the customer resulted in considerable labor savings for the club and additional revenue for the spa. The members received a new amenity and gained control over their locker room experience.

Self-service technologies (SSTs) are a rapidly growing means for increasing customer coproduction in food-service experiences. For example, managers at Disney noticed guests at one of Walt Disney World's water parks standing in line at a snack bar just to get their refillable drink mug filled. This process cost the customer valuable time, added additional people to the queue, and required employees to take the drink order and refill mugs. The solution was an SST that saved time for the guest and labor. Management developed a drink-dispensing system that was activated by a bar code on the mug. The customer holds the mug in front of a scanner, which scans the bar code on the mug and activates the drink machine long enough for him or her to fill the mug. To prevent misuse of the system, Disney changes bar codes each day of the week.[19]

■■■ Branding Strategy

Building Strong Brands

A **brand** is a name, term, sign, symbol, design, or a combination of these elements that is intended to identify the goods or services of a seller and differentiate them from competitors. Some analysts see brands as the major enduring asset of a company, outlasting the company's specific products and facilities. A former CEO of McDonald's declared, "If every asset we own, every building, and every piece of equipment were destroyed in a terrible natural disaster, we would be able to borrow all the money to replace it very quickly because of the value of our brand. . . . The brand is more valuable than the totality of all these assets."[20]

Branding is the process of endowing products and services with the power of a brand. It's all about creating differences between products. This process must be carefully developed and managed. In this section, we examine the key strategies for building and managing brands (Table 9–1).

Brand Equity

Brands are more than just names and symbols. They are a key element in the company's relationships with consumers. Brands represent consumers' perceptions and feelings about a product and its performance—everything that the product means to consumers. In the final analysis, brands exist in the heads of consumers. Adds Jason Kilar, CEO of the online video service Hulu, "A brand is what people say about you when you're not in the room."[21]

A powerful brand has high brand equity. **Brand equity** is the added value endowed on products and services. It may be reflected in the way consumers think, feel, and act with respect to the brand, as well as in the prices, market share, and

TABLE 9–1
Marketing Advantages of Strong Brands

Improved perceptions of product performance
Greater loyalty
Less vulnerability to competitive marketing actions
Less vulnerability to marketing crises
Larger margins
More inelastic consumer response to price increases
More elastic consumer response to price decreases
Greater cooperation and support from suppliers
Greater support from marketing intermediaries
Increased marketing communications effectiveness
Brand extension opportunities

profitability the brand commands for the firm. It's a measure of the brand's ability to capture consumer preference and loyalty. A brand has positive brand equity when consumers react more favorably to it than to a generic or unbranded version of the same product. It has negative brand equity if consumers react less favorably than to an unbranded version.

Brands vary in the amount of power and value they hold in the marketplace. Some brands—such as Hilton and McDonald's—become larger-than-life icons that maintain their power in the market for years, even generations. Other brands create fresh consumer excitement and loyalty, such as NYLO, Aloft, Red Mango, YouTube, and Twitter. These brands win in the marketplace not simply because they deliver unique benefits or reliable service. Rather, they succeed because they forge deep connections with customers.

Ad agency Young & Rubicam's Brand Asset Valuator measures brand strength along four consumer perception dimensions: differentiation (what makes the brand stand out), relevance (how consumers feel it meets their needs), knowledge (how much consumers know about the brand), and esteem (how highly consumers regard and respect the brand). Brands with strong brand equity rate high on all four dimensions. The brand must be distinct, or consumers will have no reason to choose it over other brands. But the fact that a brand is highly differentiated doesn't necessarily mean that consumers will buy it. The brand must stand out in ways that are relevant to consumers' needs. But even a differentiated, relevant brand is far from a shoe-in. Before consumers will respond to the brand, they must first know about and understand it. And that familiarity must lead to a strong, positive consumer–brand connection.[22] Thus, positive brand equity derives from consumer feelings about and connections with a brand. Consumers sometimes bond very closely with specific brands.

High brand equity provides a company with many competitive advantages. A powerful brand enjoys a high level of consumer brand awareness and loyalty. Because consumers are loyal to strong brands, the brand has more leverage in bargaining with the consumer and the members of the distribution channel. Because a brand name carries high credibility, the company can more easily launch line and brand extensions. A powerful brand offers the company some defense against fierce price competition.

Above all, however, a powerful brand forms the basis for building strong and profitable customer relationships. The fundamental asset underlying brand equity is customer equity—the value of customer relationships that the brand creates.

Sir Richard Branson leans against one of his Virgin Pendolino tilting trains, capable of speeds in excess of 125 mph. He claims shareholder value is determined by how your employees and customers feel about your brand. Courtesy of AP Wide World Photos.

A powerful brand is important, but what it really represents is a profitable set of loyal customers. The proper focus of marketing is building customer equity, with brand management serving as a major marketing tool. Companies need to think of themselves not as portfolios of products but as portfolios of customers.

Brand Positioning

Marketers need to position their brands clearly in target customers' minds. They can position brands at any of three levels.[23] At the lowest level; they can position the brand on product attributes. For example, a hamburger restaurant can state that it uses only Angus beef. In general, however, attributes are the least desirable level for brand positioning. Competitors can easily copy attributes. More importantly, customers are not interested in attributes; they are interested in what the attributes will do for them.

A brand can be better positioned by associating its name with a desirable benefit. In the hospitality and travel industry, these benefits often relate to customer service or experience. Fleming's Prime Steakhouse and Wine Bar targets an upscale market that enjoys great wine, food, and service and has the resources to dine at a top restaurant. Fleming's positions the restaurant as a place where you can experience the celebration of exceptional food and wine.

The strongest brands go beyond attribute or benefit positioning. They are positioned on strong beliefs and values. Even a seemingly mundane brand such as Amtrak can be positioned this way. Recent Amtrak ads suggest that an Amtrak train ride does more than just get you from point A to point B. The moment you come on board Amtrak the journey begins. With more ways to relax on your journey, including plenty of legroom, spectacular views, and a unique dining experience, your state of mind will transform just like the land you're passing through.

Successful brands engage customers on a deep, emotional level. According to Stengel, "marketing inspires life, and life inspires marketing."[24] Fleming's knows that its core customer enjoys wine. In order for a guest to try all one-hundred wines it has on its wine list, known as the Fleming's 100, a term it has trademarked, Fleming's provided a tasting of twenty-five wines each starting Friday at 5:30 P.M. for five consecutive weeks. It charged a nominal $25 for the tasting and sold small plates of food for those who wanted a snack.

When positioning a brand, the marketer should establish a mission for the brand and a vision of what the brand must be and do. The **brand promise** is the marketer's vision of what the brand must be and do for consumers. The brand promise must be simple and honest. Motel 6, for example, offers clean rooms, low prices, and good service but does not promise expensive furnishings or large bathrooms. In contrast, The Ritz-Carlton offers luxurious rooms and a truly memorable experience but does not promise low prices.

Co-branding can take advantage of the complementary strengths of two brands. For example, the Tim Hortons coffee chain is establishing co-branded Tim Hortons-Cold Stone Creamery shops. Tim Hortons is strong in the morning and midday periods, with coffee and baked goods, soups, and sandwiches. By contrast, Cold Stone Creamery's ice cream snacks are strongest in the afternoon and evening, which are Tim Hortons's nonpeak periods. The co-branded locations offer customers a reason to visit morning, noon, and night.[25]

Brand Portfolios

A brand can only be stretched so far, and all the segments the firm would like to target may not view the same brand equally or favorably. Marketers often need multiple brands in order to pursue these multiple segments. Some other reasons for introducing multiple brands in a category include:[26]

1. attracting consumers seeking variety who may otherwise have switched to another brand;

2. increasing internal competition within the firm;

3. yielding economies of scale in advertising, sales, merchandising, and physical distribution.

The brand portfolio is the set of all brands and brand particular category or market segment.

One of the leading hotel and leisure companies in the world, Starwood Hotels & Resorts Worldwide, has 850 properties in more than 95 countries and 145,000 employees at its owned and managed properties. In its rebranding attempt to go "beyond beds," Starwood has differentiated its hotels along emotional, experiential lines. Its hotel and call center operators convey different experiences for the firm's different chains, as does the firm's advertising. This strategy emerged from a major 18-month positioning project, started in 2006, to find positions for the portfolio of brands that would establish an emotional connection with consumers. Consumer research suggested these positions for some of the brands:[27]

Sheraton With the tagline "You don't stay here, you belong," Sheraton—the largest brand—is about warm, comforting, and casual. Its core value centers on "connections," an image aided by the hotel's alliance with Yahoo!, which cofounded the Yahoo! Link@Sheraton lobby kiosks and cyber cafes.

Four Points by Sheraton For the self-sufficient traveler, Four Points strives to be honest, uncomplicated, and comfortable. The brand is all about providing a high level of comfort and little indulgences like free high-speed Internet access and bottled water. Its ads feature apple pies and talk about providing guests with "the comforts of home."

W With a brand personality defined as flirty, for the insider, and an escape, W offers guests unique experiences around the warmth of cool.

Westin Westin's emphasis on "personal, instinctive, and renewal" has led to a new sensory welcome, featuring a white tea scent, signature music and lighting, and refreshing towels. Each room features Westin's own "Heavenly Beds," sold exclusively in the retail market through Nordstrom, further enhancing the brand's upscale image.

The hallmark of an optimal brand portfolio is the ability of each brand in it to maximize equity in combination with all the other brands in it. Marketers generally need to trade off market coverage with costs and profitability. If they can increase profits by dropping brands, a portfolio is too big; if they can increase profits by adding brands, it's not big enough. The basic principle in designing a brand portfolio is to maximize market coverage so no potential customers are being ignored, but minimize brand overlap so brands are not competing for customer approval. Each brand should be clearly differentiated and appealing to a sizable-enough marketing segment to justify its marketing and production costs.[28]

Marketers carefully monitor brand portfolios over time to identify weak brands and kill unprofitable ones.[29] Brand lines with poorly differentiated brands are likely to be characterized by much cannibalization and require pruning.[30]

Managing Brands

Companies must manage their brands carefully. First, the brand's positioning must be continuously communicated to consumers. Major brand marketers often spend huge amounts on advertising to create brand awareness and build preference and loyalty.

Advertising campaigns can help create name recognition, brand knowledge, and perhaps even some brand preference. However, the fact is that brands are not maintained by advertising but by customers' brand experiences. Today, customers come to know a brand through a wide range of contacts and touch points. These include advertising but also personal experience with the brand, word of mouth, and company Web pages. The company must put as much care into managing these touch points as it does into producing its ads. "Managing each customer's

Marriott differentiates each of its brands and develops unique logos for each one so that one can easily be identified. Courtesy of Marriott International, Inc.

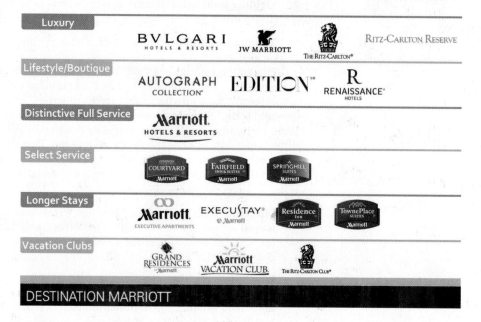

experience is perhaps the most important ingredient in building [brand] loyalty," states one branding expert. "Every memorable interaction ... must be completed with excellence and ... must reinforce your brand essence." A former Disney top executive agrees: "A brand is a living entity, and it is enriched or undermined cumulatively over time, the product of a thousand small gestures."[31] The brand's positioning will not take hold fully unless everyone in the company lives the brand. Therefore the company needs to train its people to be customer centered. Even better, the company should carry on internal brand building to help employees understand and be enthusiastic about the brand promise. Many companies go even further by training and encouraging their distributors and dealers to serve their customers well.

Finally, companies need to periodically audit their brands' strengths and weaknesses.[32] They should ask: Does our brand excel at delivering benefits that customers truly value? Is the brand properly positioned? Do all of our customer touch points support the brand's positioning? Do the brand's managers understand what the brand means to customers? Does the brand receive proper, sustained support? The brand audit may turn up brands that need more support, brands that need to be dropped, or brands that must be rebranded or repositioned because of changing customer preferences or new competitors.

■■■ The New-Product Development

Companies face a problem: They must develop new products, but the odds weigh heavily against success. To create successful new products, a company must understand its consumers, markets, and competitors and develop products that deliver superior value to customers. It must carry out strong new-product planning and set up a systematic, customer-driven *new-product development process* for finding and growing new products. Figure 9–2 shows the eight major steps in this process.

In 2004 Panda Restaurants developed a new retail line in partnership with Overall Farms of Texas, a supplier of frozen foods to the food-service industry. Panda placed two frozen entrees, beef with broccoli and mandarin chicken, into a test market within Costco and Sam's Clubs. "Consumers are ready to try our new

Figure 9–2
Major stages in new-product
development.

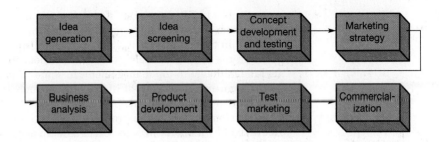

Figure 9–2
Major stages in new-product
development.

frozen products because they feel a familiarity with the entrees and our company,"
said David Landsberg, vice president of business planning.[33]

Perhaps so, but other restaurant chains such as El Chico have also tried
this form of product expansion and experienced severe problems. If consumers view the retail product the same as the restaurant one, they may question
why they need to visit the restaurant. In some cases, consumers believe that
the restaurant serves frozen rather than freshly prepared products. Two years
after launching its fast-food line, Panda announced that it was discontinuing the
line.[34]

Thus, companies face a problem: They must develop new products but the risk
of failure is high. The solution lies in strong new-product planning and in setting
up a systematic new-product development process for finding and nurturing new
products.

Idea Generation

New-product development starts with idea generation—the systematic search for
new-product ideas. A company typically generates hundreds of ideas, even thousands, to find a few good ones. Major sources of new-product ideas include internal
sources and external sources such as customers, competitors, and distributors and
suppliers.

Awareness of External Environment

All members of the hospitality industry are highly dependent on the external environment. Recession, inflation, economic growth, terrorists, an aging population,
and other external factors all directly affect this industry. Ideas for new products
should come from a familiarity with what is happening in the external world. As
an example, hotel security is of foremost importance, particularly to single women
and other segments. A study of 930 hotel guests revealed a high acceptance of certain security measures. Guests younger than forty said they would pay more for
added security, including a first-aid kit in the room.[35]

Internal Sources

Using internal sources, the company can find new ideas through formal R&D. However, in one survey, 750 global CEOs reported that only 14 percent of their innovation ideas came from traditional R&D. Instead, 41 percent came from employees,
and 36 percent came from customers.[36] Thus, beyond its internal R&D process,
companies can pick the brains of its employees—from executives to scientists,
engineers, and manufacturing staff to salespeople. Many companies have developed successful "intrapreneurial" programs that encourage employees to envision
and develop new-product ideas.

Increasingly, restaurant chains are creating formal research and development facilities at their corporate headquarters staffed by a chef or team of chefs.
For example T.G.I. Friday's and Whataburger have these centers with kitchens
replicating those found in their restaurants. The vice president of brand development for Whataburger states, "When it comes to menu development, having your
own facility offers convenience, accessibility, and confidentiality." Quick-service
chains such as Whataburger add around five items annually, whereas casual dining

restaurants add fifteen to sixty items. Usually new items are introduced as special promotions, with about 25 percent making it to the permanent menu.[37]

Within the hotel industry, new-product decisions are made at both the corporate and the property levels. New-product decision makers at the corporate level include midlevel to top management. In some cases, people not employed directly by the company but closely affiliated with it, such as bankers, lawyers, and consultants, become involved in this process.

Decision makers at the property level often include the owner if the hotel is not owned by a chain. In some cases, the owner is represented by someone, such as a president. Others involved in the process are the general manager, department managers, and directors of various areas. Often a corporate vice president from the chain may participate in the process. A danger with this source is that managers and employees may say "yes the idea is good" when in fact they believe it is abysmal.

External Idea Sources

Companies can also obtain good new-product ideas from any of a number of external sources. For example, distributors and suppliers can contribute ideas. Distributors are close to the market and can pass along information about consumer problems and new-product possibilities. Suppliers can tell the company about new concepts, techniques, and materials that can be used to develop new products. Competitors are another important source. Companies watch competitors' ads to get clues about their new products. They buy competing new products, take them apart to see how they work, analyze their sales, and decide whether they should bring out a new product of their own. Other idea sources include trade magazines, shows, and seminars; government agencies; advertising agencies; marketing research firms; university and commercial laboratories; and inventors.

Restaurant and hotel managers visit restaurants when they travel, looking for ideas they can bring back to their businesses. It is important from both a competitive standpoint and a product development standpoint to visit the competition.

Perhaps the most important source of new-product ideas is *customers* themselves. The company can analyze customer questions and complaints to find new products that better solve consumer problems. Or it can invite customers to share suggestions and ideas. For example, Starbucks sponsors My Starbucks Idea, a Web site that invites customers to share, discuss, and vote on new product and service ideas. "You know better than anyone else what you want from Starbucks," says the site. "So tell us. What's your Starbucks idea? Revolutionary or simple—we want to hear it."[38]

9.3 Starbucks My Idea http://mystarbucksidea.force.com/ is an example of crowdsourcing; Go to the Web site to look at the ideas that have been suggested and those that have been adopted.

Crowdsourcing

More broadly, many companies are now developing **crowdsourcing** or open-innovation new-product idea programs. Jeff Howe is credited with developing the term. He defines *crowdsourcing* as "the application of open source principles to fields outside of software."[39] Crowdsourcing throws the innovation doors wide open, inviting broad communities of people—customers, employees, independent scientists and researchers, and even the public at large—into the new-product innovation process. The idea, says one analyst, is that when it comes to helping to improve "your products, services, Web site, or marketing efforts ... two heads—or 2,000 or 20,000—are better than one."[40]

InterContinental Hotels Group's (IHG) partnered with Chase to develop a Priority Club Rewards Select Visa. This was targeted at members of its IHG's loyalty program. It hired Communispace, a provider of private online communities to gather 300 current Priority Club Visa cardholders willing to share their opinions on the proposed card benefits and current card features. Based on the comments of this group, benefits were expanded to provide points on products other than IHG hotels. 4Food, a restaurant in New York, is using crowdsourcing to develop menu items. The restaurant serves hamburgers with a hole in the middle that is filled with the customer's choice of forty different vegetarian dishes, including humus, salsa, and vegetarian chili. Customers can develop their own combination of these ingredients to create unique burgers and give them a name. If 4Food can get others to order "its" hamburger, it will get twenty cents for each burger sold. 4Food is using crowdsourcing to develop menu items and promote its restaurant.[41]

REO Eats in Lansing, Michigan, used crowdsourcing to gain ideas for its concepts. So, what does this mean? It means REO wants customers' input on everything, including its logo, interior design, exterior design of the building, menu ideas and pricing, and promotional strategy. It also used crowdsourcing to find investors and employees.[42] Crowdsourcing can produce a flood of innovative ideas. In fact, opening the floodgates to anyone and everyone can overwhelm the company with ideas—some good and some bad. "Even a small crowdsourcing event can generate a few hundred ideas. If I told you next year you're going to get 20,000 ideas from your customers, how would you process that?"[43]

Truly innovative companies don't rely only on one source or another for new-product ideas. Instead, according to one expert, they create "extensive networks for capturing inspiration from every possible source, from employees at every walk of the company to customers to other innovators and myriad points beyond."[44]

Idea Screening

The purpose of idea generation is to create a large number of ideas. The purpose of screening is to spot good ideas and drop poor ones as quickly as possible. Product development costs rise greatly in later stages, so the company wants to proceed only with ideas that will turn into profitable products. Most companies require their executives to write up new-product ideas on a standard form that can be reviewed by a new-product committee. The executives describe the product, the target market, and the competition. They make some rough estimates of market size, product price, development time and costs, manufacturing costs, and rate of return. They also answer the following questions: Is this idea good for our particular company? Does it mesh well with the company's objectives and strategies? Do we have the people, skills, equipment, and resources to make it succeed? Many companies have well-designed systems for rating and screening new-product ideas.

The idea or concept screening stage is the appropriate time to review carefully the question of product line compatibility. A common error in new-product development is to introduce products that are incompatible with the company. The following describes major compatibility issues. How will the product assist us to

- fulfill our mission?
- meet corporate objectives?
- meet property objectives?
- protect and promote our core business?
- protect and please our key customers?
- better use existing resources?
- support and enhance existing product lines?

Concept Development and Testing

Surviving ideas must now be developed into product concepts. It is important to distinguish between a product idea, a product concept, and a product image. A **product idea** envisions a possible product that company managers might offer to the market. A **product concept** is a detailed version of the idea stated in meaningful consumer terms. A **product image** is the way that consumers picture an actual or potential product.

Major restaurant chains cannot afford to place an untested menu in all their restaurants. Burger King, like others, uses test market restaurants in selected cities. The Piedmont area of North Carolina was used as a test market for American fries. Apparently, the product performed poorly because it disappeared from the menus. Hotels commonly introduce new-product ideas to selected floors and to selected properties. Guests are sometimes invited to an afternoon product screening.

Concept Development

In the late 1970s, Marriott recognized that the urban market for its current hotel products was becoming saturated. It needed a hotel concept that would work in secondary sites and suburban locations. Marriott decided to focus its assets on the company's core business, lodging, through the development of a new product.

This was a product idea. Customers, however, do not buy a product idea; they buy a product. The marketer's task is to develop this idea into alternative product concepts, determine how attractive each is to customers, and choose the best one.

The concept for the new product was called Courtyard by Marriott. Marriott selected persons from different areas of the company to manage the development of this new product. The company conducted extensive competitor and market analysis and, as a result of this research, developed the following conceptual framework for the project:[45]

1. It would be tightly focused for the transient market.

2. It would house fewer than 150 rooms.

3. It would project a residential image. (Through its research Marriott identified a major segment of hotel users who did not like hotels. These consumers preferred homelike settings.)

4. It would not have significant cannibalization of Marriott's other hotels.

5. It would have a limited-menu restaurant.

6. Public and meeting space would be limited.

7. It would be a standardized product with five to eight in a region.

8. The name Marriott would be attached for recognition and a halo effect. ("Halo" or "umbrella effect" refers to the carryover of a corporate or brand name to other products. The name Disney has a halo effect for many products, from movies to a cruise ship.)

Concept Testing

Concept testing occurs within a group of target consumers. New-product concepts may be presented through word or picture descriptions. Marriott tested its concept for the Courtyard Motel using a statistical technique called *conjoint analysis.* This involved showing potential target guests different motel configurations and having them rank the configurations from the most to the least desirable. The rankings were statistically analyzed to determine the optimal motel configuration.[46]

In most cases, however, simpler consumer attitude surveys are used. Suppose that 10 percent of the consumers said they "definitely" would buy and another 5 percent said "probably." The company would project these figures to the population size of this target group to estimate sales volume. But the estimate would be uncertain because people do not always carry out their stated intentions.

Unfortunately, the Marriott example is far too rare within the hospitality industry. The corporate headquarters of major hotel, resort, and restaurant chains do engage in professional concept testing, but smaller chains and individual properties often pass over this critical stage. They often move directly from product idea to full implementation.

In some cases, intuition or luck proves to be correct, and the new product is a winner, thus placing the company well ahead of competition. However, the history of the hospitality industry has proved that in many cases the idea needed concept testing because the product proved to be a disastrous mistake. In the case of a tactical product decision, such as a hotel room amenity or a new room service beverage, there may be relatively little damage from an incorrect new-product decision. This is not true of new-product decisions involving heavy capital expenditures, such as a new ship for a cruise line or a new destination resort. These decisions involve millions of dollars and have sometimes proved so disastrous that hospitality companies have been forced into bankruptcy. The expenditure of a few thousand dollars and a few extra months for concept testing might prove invaluable in the long run.

Marketing Strategy

The next step is marketing strategy development: designing an initial marketing strategy for introducing the product into the market. The marketing strategy statement consists of three parts. The first part describes the target market, the planned product positioning, and the sales, market share, and profit goals for the first few years. The target markets for Courtyard by Marriott were business travelers who wanted moderately priced, high-quality rooms and pleasure travelers who wanted a safe, comfortable room.

The second part of the marketing strategy statement outlines the product's planned price, distribution, and marketing budget for the first year. Statistical software enabled Marriott to build sophisticated models. These models provided information on pricing and expected market share based on these prices. The segmentation information gave Marriott the information it needed for marketing the hotels.

The third part of the marketing strategy statement describes the planned long-run sales, profit goals, and marketing mix strategy.

Business Analysis

Once management decides on the product concept and marketing strategy, it can evaluate the business attractiveness of the proposal. Business analysis involves a review of the sales, costs, and profit projections to determine whether they satisfy the company's objectives. If they do, the product can move to the product development stage.

To estimate sales, the company should look at the sales history, similar products, and should survey market opinion. It should estimate minimum and maximum sales to learn the range of risk.

After preparing the sales forecast, management can estimate the expected costs and profits for the product. The costs are estimated by R&D, operations, accounting, and finance departments. The analysis includes the estimated marketing costs. The company then uses the sales and cost figures to analyze the new product's financial attractiveness.

Many communities view arenas and conference centers as essential products to serve the needs of the local populace and to attract out-of-town visitors. Unfortunately, many have suffered from a lack of sound business analysis. Political and emotional pressures often prevail in the planning stage. "This town needs a baseball team and that means we must have a new multimillion-dollar arena." Sentiments such as these often prevail. In the movie *Field of Dreams,* it was "If you build it, they will come." Sadly this has proven to be untrue for many arenas and convention centers.

The Generals from Greensboro, North Carolina, play in the minor-league East Coast Hockey League. To keep the team from folding, thus further affecting the coliseum's revenue, the City of Greensboro took over the day-to-day operations of the Generals. The team's coach became a city employee. The coliseum's authority assumed responsibility for marketing ticket sales, resulting in a loss of about $300,000 from operating the team.[47] Sports arenas brand their product with the name of corporate sponsors, such as Coors Field in Denver. This does not guarantee a long life for the brand because sponsoring companies have declared bankruptcy, including some involved in great corporate scandals.

Visitor products supported by tax money such as coliseums, convention centers, museums, and zoos should be developed only after careful and unbiased business analysis, including a professional marketing plan.

Product Development

If the product concept passes the business test, it moves into product development and into a proto type. Up to now it existed only as a word description, a drawing, or mockup. The company develops one or more physical versions of the product concept. Restaurants can develop prototypes of menu items and run them as specials, hotels build guest room prototypes. It hopes to find a prototype that meets the following criteria:

1. Consumers perceive it as having the key features described in the product concept statement.

2. It performs safely under normal use.

3. It can be produced for the budgeted costs.

Developing a successful prototype can take days, weeks, months, or even years. Marriott built a Courtyard room prototype with portable walks. It developed three room types: a standard, a short, and a narrow configuration. The consumers liked the overall concept. They rejected the narrow version but not the short version, which Marriott estimated would result in substantial cost savings.

One problem with developing a prototype is that the prototype is often limited to the core product. Many of the intangible aspects of the product, such as the performance of the employees, cannot be included.

Test Marketing

If the product passes functional and consumer tests, the next step is market testing in which the product and marketing program are introduced into realistic market settings.

Market testing allows the marketer to gain experience in marketing the product, to find potential problems, and to learn where more information is needed before the company goes to the great expense of full introduction. Market testing evaluates the product and the entire marketing program in real market situations. The product and its positioning strategy, advertising, distribution, pricing, branding, packaging, and budget levels are evaluated during market testing. Market testing results can be used to make better sales and profit forecasts.

KFC test marketed its new Kentucky Grilled Chicken product for three years before rolling it out nationally. Says the chain's president, "We had to get it right." Courtesy of Dudau/Dreamstime.

Marketing Highlight

The National Food Laboratory Helps Restaurants Develop New Products and Improve Existing Products

9–1 Consider for a moment the enormous effort and expense it takes to put a new or improved restaurant item on the menu, or when producing and marketing a restaurant-branded product: R&D, purchasing, ramp-up, packaging, transport, advertising, even store product-slotting fees. After spending tens of thousands to millions, possibly, to develop and promote a new item, a restaurant chain cannot afford to have a product that is off-taste, off-color, off-odor, or worse, with features no one's willing to pay for.

Targeting Consumer Tastes with Accuracy

In a food-service environment, where even large restaurants and companies no longer have full-size R&D staffs, getting the product right the first time is more critical than ever. Often this means teaming up with the right partner, who can help ensure a product rollout is worth the effort. For decades, marketing professionals have turned to the National Food Laboratory (NFL), a leader in food and beverage-related consumer research, descriptive analysis, testing, and product development.

"The NFL understands our needs, our business, and is excellent at follow-through, which is what relationship building is all about," said Ed Yuhas, vice president of marketing for Aurora Food's breakfast division. "We look at them as a partner in bringing the right product to market in the right time frame." With the NFL as a partner, clients decide how wide or narrow the research focus is, and they often receive integrated advice that can solve small problems before they become big ones. Typically, the NFL custom-matches its research methods and protocol to suit each client's goals. For example, a custom roll-in, roll-out kitchen allows restaurant clients to test products on their own equipment, such as stoves and fryers, for practical, reality-based results.

"From no prep to high prep, the NFL can prepare and serve food the way our clients would in their own restaurants," says Kevin Buck, the NFL president. "Whether you're testing desserts or specialty pastas, we ensure product consistency and keep chefs on staff so we can start with raw ingredients."

The NFL can help guide marketing efforts with greatest accuracy in the concept stage using focus groups. In fact, consumer panels, which marketers often rely on to differentiate products from competitors and verify need, are one of NFL's specialties. Because knowing what consumers want can make the difference between promoting a successful product and one that fails, savvy marketers follow the adage, "It's better to measure twice and cut once."

Riding a Consumer Trend Through Product Development and Scale-Up

For smaller restaurant chains that do not have their own product development kitchen and chefs, the NFL provides trained chefs. Their chefs are cross-trained in food technology, and they work hand in hand with food scientists. This can be key in creating a hit that brings restaurant trends to the consumer level, and it can speed product development as well. Chefs are particularly good at brainstorming viable concepts at the early stages of product development in a short amount of time. Perhaps, more important, with a wide knowledge of food trends and ethnic dishes, chefs can help clients spot emerging consumer trends before spending further resources. Blending art and science, restaurants and food-service companies can develop better food and beverage products in less time, with more consumer panache.

"The NFL chef, working with food scientists, can help marketing departments zero in on the next consumer hot button," says Lohmeyer. "Our chef can immediately pull grocery store ingredients and put together a variety of concepts to jump-start product development." Because chefs draw on a broad knowledge of food techniques and styles, they can think up exciting new uses for existing products. For example, using a salad dressing as a marinade may significantly expand product use while opening new markets. From a chef's new product or line extension ideas, clients can quickly pick the most promising variations for further development.

An effective product development team requires a balance of skills and resources. The NFL has provided product development expertise for restaurant and food-service companies. It provides chefs to help develop new products and panelists to test finished products. Developing new products is a process, and gaining expert help along the way can increase the chances for success.

Source: Press release for the National Food Laboratory by Del Williams.

The amount of market testing needed varies with each new product. Market testing costs can be enormous, and market testing takes time, during which competitors may gain an advantage. When the costs of developing and introducing the product are low or when management is already confident that the new product will succeed, the company may do little or no market testing. Minor modifications of current products or copies of successful competitor products might not need testing.

The costs of market tests are high but are often small compared with the costs of making a major mistake. When the risks are high, or when management is not sure of the product or its marketing program, a company may do a lot of test marketing. For instance, KFC conducted more than three years of product and market testing before rolling out its major new Kentucky Grilled Chicken product. The fast-food chain built its legacy on serving crispy, seasoned fried chicken but hopes that the new product will lure back health-conscious consumers who dropped fried chicken from their diets. "This is transformational for our brand," says KFC's chief food innovation officer. Given the importance of the decision, "You might say, 'what took you so long,' " says the chain's president. "I've asked that question a couple of times myself. The answer is we had to get it right."[48]

Commercialization

Marketing testing gives management the information it needs to make a final decision about whether to launch a new product. If the company goes ahead with commercialization, it will face high costs. It may have to spend several million dollars for advertising and sales promotion alone in the first year. For example, McDonald's spent $100 million on an advertising blitz to introduce its McCafe coffee in the United States. The media spend included TV, print, radio, outdoor, the Internet, events, public relations, and sampling.[49]

When?

The first decision is whether it is the right time to introduce the new product. In Marriott's case the test market hotel experienced occupancy of 90 percent.

Where?

The company must decide whether to launch the new product in a single location, a region, several regions, the national market, or the international market. Few companies have the confidence, capital, and capacity to launch new products into full national distribution. Instead, they develop a planned market rollout over time. Small companies in particular tend to select an attractive city and put on a blitz campaign to enter the market. They may enter other cities one at a time. Large companies may decide to introduce their product into one region and then move to the next. Marriott decided to introduce the Courtyard in regional markets.

To Whom?

Within the rollout markets, the company must target its promotion to the best prospect groups. Management should have determined profiles of prime prospects during earlier market testing. It must now fine-tune its market identification, looking for early adopters, heavy users, and opinion leaders.

How?

The company must develop an action plan for introducing the new product into the selected markets and spend the marketing budget on the marketing mix.

■■■ Product Development Through Acquisition

Large companies such as McDonald's sometimes buy a small restaurant chain such as Chipotle rather than develop their own new concepts. They are able to watch the fledgling chain grow. They sit back and observe its customer base, volume of sales per unit, and how easy or difficult it is to open new stores. When they are convinced that the new chain looks like a winner and makes a good strategic fit with their organization, the large company simply buys the chain. This is what Brinker International did when it purchased Romano's Macaroni Grill and PepsiCo purchased California Pizza Kitchen. This method of product development reduces the risk considerably for large companies that have the assets to purchase and then develop the chain. This acquisition strategy has a new class of restaurant entrepreneurs, those who try to develop a chain with the specific purpose of selling it to a large chain.

Another technique is to purchase distressed chains. The mismanagement of a chain and resulting poor performance can drive the market value of the chain down. These chains become attractive targets for companies that believe they can turn them around.

▪▪▪ Product Life-Cycle Strategies

After launching a new product, management wants the product to enjoy a long and lucrative life. Although the product is not expected to sell forever, managers want to earn enough profit to compensate for the effort and risk. To maximize profits, a product's marketing strategy is normally reformulated several times. Strategy changes are often the result of changing market and environmental conditions as the product moves through the product life cycle (PLC).

The PLC (Figure 9–3) is marked by five distinct stages:

1. **Product development** begins when the company finds and develops a new-product idea. During product development, sales are zero and the company's investment costs add up.

2. **Introduction** is a period of slow sales growth as the product is being introduced into the market. Profits are nonexistent at this stage because of the heavy expenses of product introduction.

3. **Growth** is a period of rapid market acceptance and increasing profits.

4. **Maturity** is a period of slowdown in sales growth because the product has achieved acceptance by most of its potential buyers. Although sales are still high, profits level off or decline because of increased marketing outlays to defend the product against competition.

5. **Decline** is the period when sales fall off quickly and profits drop.

The product life-cycle concept can describe a product class (fast-food restaurants), a product form (fast-food hamburgers), or a brand (Popeyes). The PLC applies differently in each case. Product classes have the longest life cycles. The sales of many product classes stay in the mature stage for a long time. Product forms, in contrast, tend to have the standard PLC shape. Product forms such as the drive-in restaurant and roadside tourist court pass through a regular history of introduction, rapid growth, maturity, and decline. A specific brand's life cycle can change quickly because of changing competitive attacks and responses.

The PLC concept is a useful framework for describing how products and markets work. But using the PLC concept for forecasting product performance or for

Figure 9–3
Sales and profits over the product's line from inception to demise.

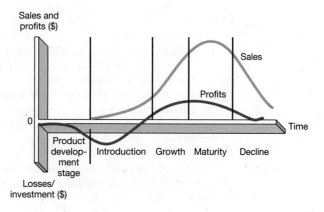

developing marketing strategies presents some practical problems. For example, managers may have trouble identifying a product's current life-cycle stage, determining when it has moved into the next stage, and enumerating the factors that affect how it will move through the stages. In practice, it is very hard to forecast the sales level at each PLC stage, the length of each stage, and the shape of the PLC curve.

Most marketing texts feature the PLC, yet very few managers claim that they use it in the development of marketing strategy. There are two explanations for this. First, managers make strategic decisions based on the characteristics of each stage of the PLC, without using the PLC itself as a tool. The second reason is that accurate prediction of the shape of the PLC is impossible. Many products do not follow the typical curve.

The PLC is not a predictive tool to determine the length of a product's useful life. It is, instead, a means of conceptualizing the effect of the market, the environment, and competition and understanding how that product may react to various stimuli.[50] Recognizing that products have life cycles with identifiable stages can provide insights into how to manage the cycle to extend its life. Unmanaged products travel along the life cycle with little resistance. Environmental and competitive changes move a product through its life cycle, and companies must react to keep their products salable. McDonald's has been able to extend by modifying the product concept. The McDonald's of today is a different concept than the McDonald's of the 1960s. The menu and the store design are different. McDonald's has evolved from stands with no seating into fast-food restaurants with attractive indoor seating areas and playgrounds for children. The company also changed its location strategy. In addition to its traditional suburban locations, McDonald's developed international, urban, and institutional locations such as hospitals and colleges. Often, when a product begins to peak in sales, management assumes that it has started its decline. The downturn could be attributable to many factors: ineffective marketing support, competition, economic conditions, or lack of market development. If managers wearing "PLC blinders" do not investigate these reasons, they risk seeing the PLCs as the cause of the slowdown.[51]

Using the PLC concept to develop marketing strategy can be difficult. Strategy is both a cause and a result of the product's life cycle. The product's current PLC position suggests the best marketing strategies, and the resulting marketing strategies affect product performance in later life-cycle stages. Yet when used carefully, the PLC concept can help in developing good marketing strategies for different stages of the product life cycle.

We looked at the product development stage of the PLC earlier. We now examine strategies for each of the other life-cycle stages.

Introduction Stage

The introduction stage starts when the new product is first made available for purchase. Introduction takes time, and sales growth is apt to be slow. Some products may linger in the introduction stage for many years before they enter a stage of rapid growth; suite hotels followed this pattern. Many companies watch others go into the market as pioneers. When suite hotels were introduced, many players sat on the sidelines until the product proved itself in the marketplace. Being a pioneer involves risk, but those who sit on the sidelines may watch others build market share quickly if the product is hot. The pioneers are then in an excellent position to defend their market share against attacks by late arrivals. Two new taco restaurant concepts, Taco Tote and Taco Palenque, may be examples. Time will tell. In the introductory stage, profits are negative or low because of low sales and high expenses. Promotion spending is high to inform consumers of the new product and encourage them to try it.

In the introductory stage, there are only a few competitors who produce basic versions of the product because the market is not ready for product refinements. Companies focus on selling to buyers who are ready to buy, usually the higher-income groups. Prices tend to be on the high side.

Growth Stage

If the new product satisfies the market, it enters the growth stage and sales start climbing quickly. The early adopters continue to buy, and later buyers start following their lead, especially if they hear favorable word of mouth. Competitors enter the market, attracted by the opportunity for profit. They introduce new product features, which expand the market.

Prices remain the same or fall only slightly. Companies keep their promotion spending at the same or at a slightly higher level to meet competition and continue educating the market. Profits increase during this growth stage, as costs are spread over a large volume and more efficient systems are developed.

Companies use several strategies to sustain rapid market growth as long as possible:

1. Product quality is improved and new product features and models are introduced.

2. New market segments are entered.

3. Advertising is shifted from building product awareness to building product conviction and purchase.

4. Prices are lowered to attract more buyers.

In the growth stage, a company faces a tradeoff between high market share and high current profit. By investing heavily in product improvement and promotion, it can capture and dominate a position. But it sacrifices maximum current profit in the hope of making it up in the next stage.

Maturity Stage

At some point a product's sales growth slows down, and the product enters the maturity stage. This stage normally lasts longer than the previous two stages, and it poses strong challenges to marketing management. Most producers are in the maturity stage of the life cycle, and therefore most marketing management deals with mature products.

The slowdown in sales growth causes supply to exceed demand. This overcapacity leads to greater competition. Competitors begin lowering prices, and they increase their advertising and sales promotion. "Burger wars" and "pizza wars" are the result of these products being in the mature stage. Real sales growth is about the same as population growth. The only way to increase sales significantly is to steal customers from the competition. Price battles and heavy advertising are often the means to do this. Both result in a drop in profits. Weaker competitors start dropping out. The industry eventually contains only well-established competitors in the main market segments, with smaller competitors pursuing the niche markets.

Applebee's restaurant chain has experienced product maturity. Things were not good when the founder, T. J. Palmer, said, "It doesn't have anything that would make me come back." In 2007 Applebee's found itself with falling profits, a lagging stock, and restless investors. According to the *Wall Street Journal,* "Applebee's didn't change quickly enough while a raft of competitors copied it. Applebee's stayed too long with a formula that had worked for it in the past."[52]

While Applebee's failed to change, U.S. customers were more exposed to ethnic cuisine and cooking shows. They also expressed concern about overprocessed foods and disliked the decor of high school sports paraphernalia and dark wood. In response, Applebee's made several product changes such as a high-low price strategy of offering a $14.95 New York strip steak on the front of the menu and a $5.99 soup and salad on the back. These did not stop the sales slide. In November 2007, Applebee's was bought by IHOP. The combination of IHOP and Applebee's resulted in the formation of DineEquity.

DineEquity was able to increase same store sales in 2010 for the first time since 2005, albeit the increase was only about .3 percent. DineEquity created new promotions such as "Sizzling Entrees," "Great Tasting Items Under 550 Calories," "2 for $20" (a shared appetizer and two entrees), and an advertising promotion called "There's No Place Like the Neighborhood." DineEquity through menu development, operating efficiencies, and effective advertising was able to create positive momentum. The Applebee's case shows how hard it is to create momentum in a mature product. It took DineEquity three years to change the direction of Applebee's. DineEquity's battle is not over; each year in a mature product is a battle to keep the product relevant and gain or maintain market share.[53]

In addition to old decor and an old menu, some blamed the lack of destination items. These are specialty items that diners seek out and are willing to go out of their way to purchase.

Market Modification

At this point the aggressive product manager tries to increase consumption of the product. The manager looks for new users and market segments and ways to increase use among present customers. McDonald's added breakfast, salads, desserts, and chicken sandwiches in its efforts to attract new users and increase use. Product managers may also reposition the brand to appeal to a larger or faster-growing segment. When anti-drunk-driving campaigns reduced alcoholic beverage consumption, Bennigan's emphasized its food.

Product Modification

The product manager can also change product characteristics, product quality, features, or style to attract new users and stimulate more usage. A strategy of quality improvement aims at increasing the performance of the product—its durability, reliability, speed, or taste. This strategy is effective when quality can be improved, when buyers believe the claim of improved quality, and when enough buyers want higher quality.

Marketing Mix Modification

The product manager can also try to improve sales by changing one or more marketing mix elements. Prices can be cut to attract new users and competitors' customers. A better advertising campaign can be developed. The company can also offer new or improved services to buyers.

Decline Stage

Sales of most product forms and brands eventually decline. The decline may be slow or rapid, as in the case of Minnie Pearl Chicken. Sales may plunge to zero, or they may drop to a low level and continue there for many years.

Sales decline for many reasons, such as technological advances, shifts in consumer tastes, and increased competition. Carrying a weak product can be very costly to the firm and not just in terms of reduced profit. There are also hidden costs. A weak product may take up too much of management's time. It often requires frequent price adjustments. The advertising and sales force attention consumed by the weak product could be used to make healthy ones more profitable. Its failing reputation can shake customer confidence in the company and its other products. But the biggest cost may well lie in the future. Keeping weak products delays the search for replacement, creates a lopsided product mix, hurts current profits, and weakens the company's foothold on the future.

Companies must pay close attention to their aging products. Regularly reviewing sales, market share, costs, and profit trends for each of its products will help identify products in the decline stage.

Management has to decide whether to maintain, harvest, or drop weak products. Management may decide to harvest the product, which means reducing various costs. Successful harvesting may increase a company's profits in the short run. Management may also decide to drop the product.

Destination and hospitality marketers must be aware of the product life cycle as it affects retailers. Hotels are often located near centers of shopping. In fact, the giant mall in Edmonton, Alberta, contains a hotel. Restaurants have found malls to be excellent locations, but the product life cycle is changing.

Shopping malls are in the decline stage in many parts of the United States.[54] Crime, teenagers hanging around, huge parking lots, confusing layouts, fear of terrorism, and expensive rents are among the reasons for this decline. Stores such as JC Penney, Sears, and the May Company served as anchors in malls but are now moving to free-standing locations.

Shopping remains one of the primary activities of travelers, particularly pleasure travelers. Additionally, thousands, if not millions, of travelers throughout the world plan overnight trips primarily for shopping. This includes international travelers. The motor coach industry in many nations derives a heavy percentage of income from shopping tours.

Hotels and restaurants should include motor coach operators as target markets in their marketing/sales plans. As one form of shopping declines, another gains ascendancy. Cabelas, Inc., a publicly traded hunting, fishing, and outdoor gear retailer, is an example of a retail product in ascendancy. In 2008 Cabelas had twenty-six stores, with seven more under construction. Many have become tourist attractions. Its stores in Kansas City, Kansas, and Owatonna, Minnesota, are among the top tourist destinations in their respective states.

Product Deletion

As we have seen, the product life cycle illustrates that most products will become obsolete and have to be replaced. One danger of the PLC is that a product may be replaced prematurely. Products take time, effort, and money to introduce. When a company has a winner, it wants to receive the maximum benefit from this product. Management will not want to delete it while profit potential exists. If a product is no longer profitable, it is important to terminate it rather than continue to pour time and resources into reviving it.

Thus, understanding the product deletion process is just as important as understanding product development. The Strawberry Patch, a successful restaurant in Houston, served a chicken breast topped with sautéed mushrooms. This dish enjoyed success for more than 10 years. When sales started to drop and the decline continued, it appeared that the product was no longer in favor with the restaurant's customers. Customers were asked about the dish, and they responded that it was too greasy. When the sautéed mushrooms were poured over the chicken breast, the butter collected at the bottom of the plate. When the product was first introduced, sauces were in vogue, but taste preferences changed. The restaurant removed the sautéed mushrooms and garnished the chicken with fresh sliced mushrooms. If management of the Strawberry Patch had been wearing life-cycle blinders, it would have deleted the product.

The deletion analysis (Figure 9–4) is a systematic review of a product's projected sales and estimated costs associated with those sales. If a product no longer appears to be profitable, the analysis looks at possible ways to make modifications and return it to profitability. If the analysis indicates that the product should be deleted, there are three choices: phase-out, run-out, or drop it immediately.[55]

Phase-out is the ideal method; it enables a product to be removed in an orderly fashion. For example, a menu item would be replaced on the next revision of the menu. A **run-out** would be used when sales for an item are low and costs exceed revenues, such as the case of a restaurant serving a crabmeat cocktail with sales of only one or two items per week. If the restaurant decides to delete the product, it may choose to deplete its existing stock of crabmeat rather than reorder. The last option is an immediate **drop.** This option is usually chosen when the product may cause harm or complaints; it is best to drop the item rather than continuing to create unhappy customers.

Figure 9–4
Product deletion process.
Source: From Martin J.
Bell, *Marketing: Concepts
and Strategy* (3rd ed.),
p. 267; ©1979, Houghton
Mifflin Company; used by
permission, Mrs. Marcellette
(Bell) Chapman.

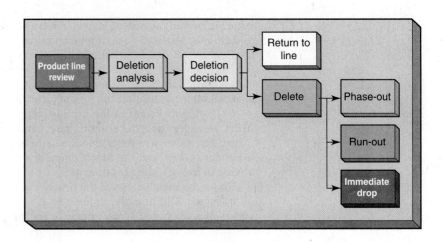

The political aspects of dropping a product often lead to a product being left on the menu longer than it should be. For example, if the bouillabaisse is the general manager's own recipe, the food and beverage manager may be reluctant to remove the dish from the menu.

The issue of dropping a product is particularly complex in the case of the properties of a hotel or restaurant chain. Management is usually quite aware of individual properties that should be dropped from the chain affiliation due to deterioration of the property or the neighborhood in which the property is located. In many cases it is impossible or impractical to close the property quickly or drop it from chain affiliation:

- Contracts may prohibit a quick close.

- The property may have sentimental attachments to the community and to management.

- Closure might have a negative effect on the community.

- A buyer may not be readily available.

- Special relationships may exist between the franchisee and the franchisor.

Despite difficulties in closing hotels or disassociating properties from a chain, eventually the inevitable must occur. As in the earlier example of menu items, it is best to make this difficult decision as quickly as possible.

■■■ KEY TERMS

Augmented products. Additional consumer services and benefits built around the core and actual products.

Aural. The dimension of atmosphere relating to volume and pitch.

Brand. A name, term, sign, symbol, design, or a combination of these elements that is intended to identify the goods or services of a seller and differentiate them from competitors.

Brand equity. The added value endowed on products and services. It may be reflected in the way consumers think, feel, and act with respect to the brand, as well as in the prices, market share, and profitability the brand commands for the firm.

Branding. The process of endowing products and services with the power of a brand. It's all about creating differences between products.

Brand promise. The marketer's vision of what the brand must be and do for consumers.

Consumption phase. Takes place when the customer consumes the service.

Core product. Answers the question of what the buyer is really buying. Every product is a package of problem-solving services.

Crowdsourcing. Is an open-innovation new-product idea program.

Decline. The period when sales fall off quickly and profits drop.

Detachment phase. When the customer is through using the product and departs.

Drop. The action taken toward a product that may cause harm or customer dissatisfaction.

Facilitating products. Those services or goods that must be present for the guest to use the core product.

Growth. The product life-cycle stage when a new product's sales start climbing quickly.

Introduction. The product life-cycle stage when a new product is first distributed and made available for purchase.

Joining stage. The product life-cycle stage when the customer makes the initial inquiry contact.

Maturity. The stage in a product life cycle when sales growth slows or levels off.

Olfactory. The dimension of atmosphere relating to scent and freshness.

Phase-out. The ideal method of removing an unpopular or unprofitable product; it enables a product to be removed in an orderly fashion.

Product concept. A detailed version of a product idea stated in meaningful consumer terms.

Product development. Developing the product concept into a physical product to ensure that the product idea can be turned into a workable product.

Product idea. Envisioning a possible product that company managers might offer to the market.

Product image. The way that consumers picture an actual or potential product.

Run-out. Removing a product after existing stock has been depleted; used when sales for an item are low and costs exceed revenues, such as the case of a restaurant serving a crabmeat cocktail with sales of only one or two items per week.

Supporting products. Extra products offered to add value to the core product and to help differentiate it from the competition.

Tactile. The dimension of atmosphere relating to softness, smoothness, and temperature.

Visual. The dimension of atmosphere relating to color, brightness, size, and shape.

■■■ CHAPTER REVIEW

I. **What Is a Product.** A product is anything that can be offered to a market for attention, acquisition, use, or consumption that might satisfy a want or need. It includes physical objects, service, places, organizations, and ideas.

II. **Product Levels**
    A. **Core product.** It answers the question of what the buyer is really buying. Every product is a package of problem-solving services.
    B. **Facilitating products.** These are services or goods that must be present for the guest to use the core product.
    C. **Supporting products.** These are extra products offered to add value to the core product and to help differentiate it from the competition.
    D. **Augmented products.** These include accessibility (geographic location and hours of operation), atmosphere (visual, aural, olfactory, and tactile dimensions), customer interaction with the service organization (joining, consumption, and detachment), customer participation, and customers' interactions with one another.
        1. **Accessibility.** This refers to how accessible the product is in terms of location and hours of operation.
        2. **Atmosphere.** Atmosphere is a critical element in services. It is appreciated through the senses. Sensory terms provide descriptions for the atmosphere as a particular set of surroundings. The main sensory channels for atmosphere are sight, sound, scent, and touch.
        3. **Customer interactions with the service system.** Managers must think about how the customers use the product in the three phases of

involvement: joining, consumption, and detachment.
        4. **Customer interactions with other customers.** Customers become part of the product you are offering.
        5. **Coproduction.** Involving the guest in service delivery can increase capacity, improve customer satisfaction, and reduce costs.

III. **Branding Strategy.** Brand is a name, term, sign, symbol, design, or a combination of these elements that is intended to identify the goods or services of a seller and differentiate them from those of competitors.
    A. **Building strong brands.** Brands are powerful assets that must be carefully developed and managed. In this section, we examine the key strategies for building and managing brands, see Table 9–1.
    B. **Brand equity.** It is the added value endowed on products and services. It may be reflected in the way consumers think, feel, and act with respect to the brand, as well as in the prices, market share, and profitability the brand commands for the firm.
    C. **Brand positioning.** Companies can position brands at any of three levels. At the lowest level, they can position the brand on product attributes. A brand can be better positioned by associating its name with a desirable benefit. The strongest brands go beyond attribute or benefit positioning. They are positioned on strong beliefs and values.
    D. **Brand portfolios.** The brand portfolio is the set of all brands and brand particular category or market segment. Marketers often need multiple brands in order to pursue these multiple segments.

E.   Managing brands. Companies must manage their brands carefully. First, the brand's positioning must be continuously communicated to consumers. The company should carry on internal brand building to help employees understand and be enthusiastic about the brand promise. Finally, companies need to periodically audit their brands' strengths and weaknesses.

IV.   New-Product Development

  A.   New-product development process

    1.   Idea generation. Ideas are gained from internal sources, customers, competitors, distributors, and suppliers.

    2.   Idea screening. The purpose of screening is to spot good ideas and drop poor ones as soon as possible.

    3.   Concept development and testing. Surviving ideas must now be developed into product concepts. These concepts are tested with target customers.

    4.   Marketing strategy development. There are three parts to the marketing strategy statement. The first part describes the target market, the planned product positioning, and the sales, market share, and profit goals for the first two years. The second part outlines the product's planned price, distribution, and marketing budget for the first year. The third part describes the planned long-run sales, profit, and the market mix strategy over time.

    5.   Business analysis. Business analysis involves a review of the sales, costs, and profit projections to determine whether they satisfy the company's objectives.

    6.   Product development. Product development turns the concept into a prototype of the product.

    7.   Market testing. Market testing is the stage in which the product and marketing program are introduced into more realistic market settings.

    8.   Commercialization. The product is brought into the marketplace.

V.   Product Development Through Acquisition. Large companies such as McDonald's sometimes buy a small restaurant chain such as Chipotle rather than develop their own new concepts. Another technique is to purchase distressed chains. The mismanagement of a chain and resulting poor performance can drive the market value of the chain down. These chains become attractive targets for companies that believe they can turn them around.

VI.   Product Life-Cycle Stages

  A.   Product development. It begins when the company finds and develops a new-product idea.

  B.   Introduction. It is a period of slow sales growth as the product is being introduced into the market. Profits are nonexistent at this stage.

  C.   Growth. It is a period of rapid market acceptance and increasing profits.

  D.   Maturity. It is a period of slowdown in sales growth because the product has achieved acceptance by most of its potential buyers.

  E.   Decline. It is the period when sales fall off quickly and profits drop.

■■■ DISCUSSION QUESTIONS

1. Given all the changes in the branding strategy for Las Vegas over the years, has the Vegas brand had a consistent meaning to consumers? Is this a benefit or a detriment to the city as it moves forward?

2. Use a product from the hospitality or travel industry to explain the following terms (provide an example in your explanation): (a) facilitating product, (b) supporting product, and (c) augmented product.

3. ARAMARK, a large-contract food-service company, is introducing branded food as part of its campus feeding. Why would ARAMARK pay a royalty to Burger King when it is capable of making its own hamburgers very efficiently?

4. As a hotel or restaurant manager, how would you gain new-product ideas?

5. Less than a third of new-product ideas come from the customer. Does this percentage conflict with the marketing concept's philosophy of "find a need and fill it"? Why or why not?

6. If you were the director of new-product development for a national fast-food chain, what factors would you consider in choosing cities for test marketing a new sandwich? Would the place where you live be a good test market? Why or why not?

7. Explain why many people are willing to pay more for branded products than for unbranded products. What does this tell you about the value of branding?

8. Apply the concept of the product life cycle to a hotel. How does a company keep its products from going into the decline stage?

■■■ EXPERIENTIAL EXERCISES

Do one of the following:

1. Visit a hospitality or travel company. Look around at the physical facilities and the atmosphere of the company. Things you should look at include the exterior appearance, cleanliness, employees, atmosphere, and signage. Does the physical atmosphere support the image of the company or communicate to prospective customers and existing customers? Explain your answer.

2. Visit two locations of the same brand, such as two restaurants or two hotels. Does each location portray the same brand image? Explain your answer. If the images are inconsistent, how could this affect prospective customers?

■■■ INTERNET EXERCISE

Go to the Internet site of a hospitality or travel company. Think about the company's target market and the brand image it should portray. Does the company's Web site reinforce this brand image? Why or why not? What suggestions do you have for enhancing the image that the site portrays?

■■■ REFERENCES

1. Damon Hodge, "Tourism Chief Aims to Continue Vegas' Hot Streak," *Travel Weekly* (February 12, 2007): 64.

2. Damon Hodge, "Tourism Chief Aims to Continue Vegas' Hot Streak," *Travel Weekly* (February 12, 2007): 64.

3. *Sources:* Jeff Delong, "After a Down Year, Vegas Hoping for a Rebound," *USA Today* (May 21, 2010): 2A; Nancy Trejos, "Las Vegas Bets the Future on a Game-Changing New Hotel Complex," *Washington Post* (January 31, 2010): F01; Tamara Audi, "Vegas Plans a New Push to Attract More People," *Wall Street Journal* (January 7, 2008): B2; John King, "Luck Running Low in Las Vegas—Will It Turn Around," *CNN.com* (May 22, 2009), accessed at www.cnn.com; Tamara Audi, "Vegas Tries Luck with Old Slogan," *Wall Street Journal* (May 13, 2009): B5; Damon Hodge, "Tourism Chief Aims to Continue Vegas' Hot Streak," *Travel Weekly* (February 12, 2007): 64; and Tamara Audi, "Las Vegas Touts Its Affordability," *Wall Street Journal* (February 4, 2009): B5.

4. Karl Albrecht and Lawrence J. Bradford, *The Service Advantage* (Homewood, IL: Dow Jones-Irwin, 1990), p. 69.

5. www.villafeltrinelli.com (accessed April 2008).

6. Herbert Ypma, "The Hip Italian Hotel Collection," *Times Online* (January 22, 2006): 1+.

7. Joseph A. Michelli, *The New Gold Standard* (New York: McGraw-Hill, 2008).

8. Lindsay Creative, "All Aboard," Royal Gorge Route Railroad, 401 Water Street, Canon City, CO 81212, 2004.

9. Christian Gronroos, *Service Management Marketing* (New York: Lexington Books, 1990), p. 69.

10. Accessed September 17, 2011, from http://www.starwoodhotels.com/alofthotels/about/index.html.

11. Andrea Sachs, "Aloft Hotels: A Hip Addition to the Inn Crowd," *Washington Post* (July 15, 2009), accessed September 24, 2011, from http://www.washingtonpost.com/wp-dyn/content/article/2009/07/14/AR2009071403194.html.

12. Martin Lindstrom, *Brand Sense* (New York: Free Press, 2005).

13. Bernard Booms and Mary J. Bitner, "Marketing Services by Managing the Environment," *Cornell Restaurant and Hotel Administration Quarterly* (May 1992): 35–39.

14. See Le Méridien LM 100 (accessed September 25, 2011), from http://www.starwoodhotels.com/lemeridien/lm100/index.html.

15. Britt Aboutaleb, "Le Labo's Scent for Le Meridien Smells of Libraries and The Little Prince, Elle (September 23, 2011), accessed September 24, 2011, from http://fashion.elle.com/life-and-love/.

16. Philip Kotler, "Atmospherics as a Marketing Tool," *Journal of Retailing,* 49, no. 4 (1973–1974): 48–64.

17. Gronroos, *Service Management and Marketing.*

18. Karthik Namasivayam and Timothy R. Hinkin, "The Customer's Role in the Service Encounter," *Cornell Hotel and Restaurant Administration Quarterly,* 44, no. 3 (2003): 34.

19. T. O'Brien, "Disney Looks to Fill Needs of Guests with Refill Soft Drink Mugs," *Amusement Business,* 114, no. 34 (2002): 7.

20. See "McAtlas Shrugged," *Foreign Policy* (May-June 2001): 26–37; and Philip Kotler and Kevin Lane Keller, *Marketing Management* (13th ed.) (Upper Saddle River, NJ: Prentice Hall, 2009), p. 254.

21. Quotes from Jack Trout, "'Branding' Simplified," *Forbes* (April 19, 2007), www.forbes.com; and a presentation by Jason Kilar at the Kenan-Flagler Business School, University of North Carolina at Chapel Hill, Fall 2009.

22. For more on Young & Rubicam's Brand Asset Valuator, see "Brand Asset Valuator," Value Based Management.net, www.valuebasedmanagement.net/methods_brand_asset_valuator.html (accessed May 2010); www.brandassetconsulting.com (accessed May 2010); and W. Ronald Lane, Karen Whitehill King, and Tom Reichert, *Kleppner's Advertising Procedure* (18th ed.) (Upper Saddle River, NJ: Pearson Prentice Hall, 2011), pp. 83–84.

23. See Scott Davis, *Brand Asset Management* (2nd ed.) (San Francisco, CA: Jossey-Bass, 2002). For more on brand positioning, see Philip Kotler and Kevin Lane Keller, *Marketing Management* (13th ed.), Chapter 10.

24. See www.jimstengel.com (accessed June 2010).

25. "Tim Hortons and Cold Stone: Co-Branding Strategies," *BusinessWeek* (July 10, 2009), www.businessweek.com/smallbiz/content/jul2009/sb20090710_574574.htm; and Steve McKee, "The Pros and Cons of Co-Branding," *BusinessWeek* (July 10, 2009), www.businessweek.com/smallbiz/content/jul2009/sb20090710_255169.htm.

26. David A. Aaker, *Brand Portfolio Strategy: Creating Relevance, Differentiation, Energy, Leverage, and Clarity* (New York: Free Press, 2004).

27. Christopher Hosford, "A Transformative Experience," *Sales and Marketing Management,* 158 (June 2006): 32–36; Mike Beirne and Javier Benito, "Starwood Uses Personnel to Personalize Marketing," *Brandweek* (April 24, 2006): 9.

28. Jack Trout, *Differentiate or Die: Survival in Our Era of Killer Competition* (New York: Wiley, 2000); Kamalini Ramdas and Mohanbir Sawhney, "A Cross-Functional Approach to Evaluating Multiple Line Extensions for Assembled Products," *Management Science,* 47 (January 2001): 22–36.

29. Nirmalya Kumar, "Kill a Brand, Keep a Customer," *Harvard Business Review* (December 2003): 87–95.

30. For a methodological approach for assessing the extent and nature of cannibalization, see Charlotte H. Mason and George R. Milne, "An Approach for Identifying Cannibalization Within Product Line Extensions and Multibrand Strategies," *Journal of Business Research,* 31 (October–November 1994): 163–170.

31. Stephen Cole, "Value of the Brand," *CA Magazine* (May 2005):. 39–40.

32. See Kevin Lane Keller, *Strategic Brand Management* (Upper Saddle River, NJ: Prentice Hall, 2008), Chapter 10.

33. "Panda Restaurants Goes into Retail," *American City Business Journal* (February 2004).

34. Howard Riell, "High Expectations," *Kahiki* (July 12, 2006), accessed September 19, 2011, from http://kahiki.blogspot.com/2006/09/frozen-food-age-article.html.

35. Julie Feickert, Rohit Verma, Gerhart Plaschka, and Cheikitan Dev, "Safeguarding Your Customers," *Cornell Hotel and Restaurant Administration Quarterly* (August 2006): 224.

36. John Peppers and Martha Rogers, "The Buzz on Customer-Driven Innovation," *Sales and Marketing Management* (June 2007): 13.

37. Kate Leahy, "Discovery Zone," *Restaurants and Institutions* (July 15, 2007): 49.

38. http://www.starbucks.com/coffeehouse/learn-more/my-starbucks-idea (accessed Juy 21, 2012).

39. Joseph Mackenzie, "Can hotels use crowdsourcing" (February 5, 2009), accessed September 19, 2011, from http://www.hotelmarketingstrategies.com/can-hotels-use-crowdsourcing/.

40. Elisabeth A. Sullivan, "A Group Effort: More Companies Are Turning to the Wisdom of the Crowd to Find Ways to Innovate," *Marketing News* (February 28, 2010): 22–29.

41. Lauren McKay, "300 current Priority Club Visa Cardholders Willing to Share Their Opinions on What Card Benefits and Services Are Important" (December 8, 2010), accessed September 17, 2011, from http://www.emarketer.com/blog/index.php/case-study-using-online-community-crowd-source-customer-loyalty-strategies/; Amanda Kludt, "4Food, the Bonkers Techie Resto Coming Soon to Midtown" (May 26, 2010), accessed September 17, 2010, from http://ny.eater.com/archives/2010/05/meet_4food_the_most_bonkers_restaurant_to_ever_hit_midtown.php.

42. "The REO Eats project, "accessed September 17, 2010, from http://www.reoeatsproject.com/about-the-project/.

43. Guido Jouret, "Inside Cisco's Search for the Next Big Idea," *Harvard Business Review* (September 2009): 43–45.

44. Kevin O'Donnell, "Where Do the Best Ideas Come From? The Un-likeliest Sources," *Advertising Age* (July 14, 2008): 15.

45. The Marriott example and this list were drawn from Christopher W. L. Hart, "Product Development: How Marriott Created Courtyard," *Cornell Hotel and Restaurant Administration Quarterly,* 27, no. 3 (1986): 68–69; and Jerry Wind, Paul E. Green, Douglas Shifflet, and Marsha Scarborough, "Courtyard by Marriott: Designing a Hotel Facility with Consumer Based Marketing," *Interfaces,* 19, no. 1 (1989): 25–47.

46. J. L. Heskett and R. Hallowell, "Courtyard by Marriott," *Harvard Case* 9-693-036 (Boston, MA: Harvard Business School Publishing, 1993).

47. Michael Lowrey, "Poor Attendance Plagues N. C. Arenas," *Carolina Journal,* 11, no. 3 (March 2004): 15.

48. Anonymous, "KFC Serves Up a Second Secret Recipe: Kentucky Grilled Chicken," *PR Newswire* (April 14, 2009).

49. See Emily Bryson York, "McD's Serves Up $100M McCafe Ad Blitz," *Cram's Chicago Business* (May 4, 2009), www.chicagobusiness.com; John Letzing, "Bing's Share Rises Again," *Wall Street Journal* (June 18, 2009), http://online.wsj.com; and Rita Chang, "With $100M Saturation Campaign, Droid Will Be Impossible to Avoid," *Advertising Age* (November 9, 2009): 3.

50. Levitt, Theodore, *The Marketing Imaginization* (New York: Free Press, 1986), p. 173.

51. Christopher W. Hart, Greg Casserly, and Mark J. Lawless, "The Product Life Cycle: How Useful?" *Cornell Hotel and Restaurant Administration Quarterly,* 25, no. 3 (November 1984): 54–63.

52. Janet Adamy, "A Shift in Dining Scene Nicks a Once-Hot Chain," *Wall Street Journal* (June 29, 2007): A1 and A3.

53. *Momentum!,* DineEquity Annual Report 2010.

54. Kortney Stringer, "Abandoning the Mall," *Wall Street Journal* (March 24, 2001): B1.

55. William Pride and O. C. Ferrell, *Marketing* (Boston, MA: Houghton-Mifflin Publishing, 1995), pp. 312–313.

In a service organization if you are not serving the customer, you had better be serving someone who is.
— JAN CARLZON

Hospitality is present when something happens for *you. It is absent when something happens* to *you. Those two simple prepositions—*for *and* to*—express it all.*
— DANNY MEYER

Internal Marketing

10

Objectives

After reading this chapter, you should be able to:

1. Understand why internal marketing is an important part of a marketing program.

2. Explain what a service culture is and why it is important to have a company where everyone is focused on serving the customer.

3. Describe the three-step process involved in implementing an internal marketing program.

4. Explain why the management of nonroutine transactions can create the image of being an excellent service provider.

Employees are the heart and soul of any hospitality organization. The guidance they receive from the organization's service culture can enable employees to carry out incredible moments of truth. Employees who are carefully selected, trained, and supported can be as great as or a greater asset than the physical structure of the hotels or restaurants companies create for our customers. We all have great examples of employee customer service; many of ours are found throughout the book. Below are a few of our favorites.

Exceptional employee customer service does have to come from once-in-a-lifetime opportunity to help a guest in an extraordinary situation. In fact it usually comes from employees who are empathetic to a guest's everyday circumstances. For example, one customer of Panera Bread, a chain of bakeries which also includes a restaurant, wanted a loaf of its Sweet Holiday Bread. The bread is made from egg dough mixed with a blend of honey, chocolate chips, raisins, and whole cranberries. The center contains a filling of chopped apples and cinnamon mixed with sugar. The bread is topped with a drizzle of icing.[1] This bread is so special that many people pre-order it from the bakery to ensure they have some for a family treat or a holiday party.

When a customer called the Panera Bread closest to her home, she was told that they had sold out of the product for the day. The employee said a store not too far away did have some left. Although disappointed, she replied that she did not want to drive that far and would just pick up some other bread at the store. When she arrived thirty minutes later, the Holiday Bread was waiting for her at the store. The employee had driven to the next other store and picked up the bread for her. This employee action is something the customer will never forget.[2]

One of our favorites is about Joshie, a teddy bear that belonged to an eight-year-old boy. His family had been vacationing at a Ritz Carlton and upon return realized they had forgotten to bring Joshie home with them. The little boy was devastated to think that his companion was lost and he might not ever see Joshie again. The parents contacted the hotel and were later told the stuffed bear had been located and would be sent to them by overnight express. Receiving the bear in an envelope the next day would have certainly pleased the little boy. However, the employees created a memory that will last in the minds of their guests forever. They took pictures of the bear around the resort and showed him enjoying his extra day at the resort. There were shots of him by the pool, driving a golf cart, hanging out with other teddy bears, and generally enjoying the resort. These souvenirs came packed in a card signed by the staff.[3]

These acts of customer service create pleasant memories, one of the most desired products a hospitality organization can produce. Today, favorable memories are often shared with hundreds if not thousands of other people over social media.

Figure 10–1
The relationship between the
marketing function and the
marketing department.
Source: From Christian
Gronroos, "Designing a Long
Range Marketing Strategy
for Services," *Long Range
Planning,* 40 (April 1980).

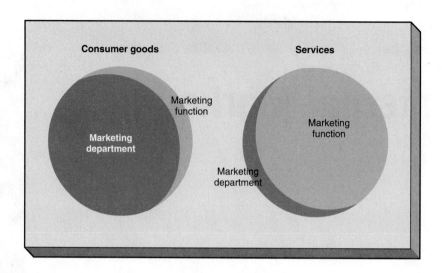

■■■ Internal Marketing

Marketing in the hospitality and travel industries must be embraced by all employees; it cannot be left to the marketing or sales department. Marketing must be part of the philosophy of the organization, and the marketing function should be carried out by all line employees. In manufacturing firms, the marketing function is often carried out by a marketing department because many employees do not interact with customers. In service industries, the line employees carry out a majority of the marketing function (see Figure 10–1). **Internal marketing** involves marketing to the firm's internal customers, its employees.

Danny Meyers stated in *Setting the Table,* "Virtually nothing else is important as how one is made to feel in any business transaction. . . . Hospitality is present when something happens *for* you. It is absent when something happens *to* you; these two propositions *for* and *to* express it all."[4]

A study by the American Society for Quality Control found that when consumers were asked what quality in services meant, the largest group of responses cited employee contact skills such as courtesy, attitude, and helpfulness.[5] In studies we have conducted in luxury hotels and/or large elaborate casinos, employees play a large role in whether the guests intend to return. No matter how much one spends on the physical environment, the human environment has to be warm, friendly, and caring for guests to return. Because employees are an important part of our product, we must make sure they are excited about our product and care about their customers. The importance of employees and internal marketing is supported by a study that found that internal marketing is one of the top three determinants of a company's financial performance.[6]

Richard Normann of the Service Management Group says that a key ingredient in almost all service companies is some innovative arrangement or formula for mobilizing and focusing human energy.[7] Normann developed the term *moments of truth.* A **moment of truth** occurs when employee and customer have contact. Normann states that when this occurs, what happens is no longer directly influenced by the company. It is the skill, motivation, and tools employed by the firm's representative and the expectations and behavior of the client together that create the service delivery process.[8] Normann borrowed the idea from bullfighters, who used the term to describe the moment when the bullfighter faces the bull in the ring. Despite all his training and preparation, a wrong move by the bullfighter or an unanticipated move by the bull can result in disaster. Similarly, when employees and customers interact, a careless mistake by an employee or an unanticipated request by a guest can result in a dissatisfied guest.

The hospitality industry is unique in that *employees are part of the product.* The hotel must have a staff that will perform well during moments of truth. When people think of marketing, they usually think of efforts directed externally toward

Marketing Highlight | Pinehurst Resort & Country Club "Do What's Right"

10-1 Pinehurst Resort & Country Club is known as the foremost golf resort and spa in the United States and shares international prominence with Saint Andrews of Scotland. Scott Bruton, general manager of Pinehurst, attributes much of this success to its loyal and motivated employees. "About half of our 1,200 employees were born near Pinehurst and many of the others moved here because of golf and Pinehurst. The parents and grandparents of many also worked here at Pinehurst so obviously there is tremendous employee loyalty and a love of golf."

Don Padgett, president of Pinehurst, has a simple philosophy of "Do What's Right." With 1,200 employees, many top executives would have chosen to introduce themselves in a huge meeting with a formal speech. Shortly after Don was appointed president, he held twenty-nine small meetings where he chatted with employees informally. Both Don and Scott believe it is important not to "hard sell" employees. They believe that employees are the face of Pinehurst to its customers. "Anybody can run a resort when things go well," said Scott, but "the moment of truth occurs when employees are confronted with unhappy guests or an emergency such as a sick guest."

Employees at Pinehurst are not allowed to hide behind corporate policy or the fact that they are not in top management. Employees are taught to fix a problem personally when it occurs. Employees must use ethical and moral behavior. They are guided by the knowledge that they will not be disciplined if they honestly tried to fix a customer problem but failed. Management may review the situation and coach the employee in better ways to handle customer problems, but they will not discipline the employee.

Pinehurst believes in rapid recognition of positive acts by employees. Instead of waiting for scheduled meetings, all managers carry "CHATSKYS," which are instant rewards such as gift certificates at Wal-Mart or Chick-fil-A or the local car wash. If a manager observes or is informed of a positive guest action, he or she thanks the employee and gives that person a Chatsky.

Employee news is changed every five to seven days and may be seen on e-mail in any of the 400 computers on the property. This prevents unfounded rumors and provides rapid employee peer recognition.

Pinehurst offers a unique employee assistance plan (EAP). This is administered by a board of employees, not management. Loans are made to employees who may have missed a mortgage payment, need to purchase an airplane ticket to attend a funeral, or have other unexpected financial needs. These are loans—not gifts.

Each year Pinehurst donates the use of its most famous course "No. 2" for one day to support the EAP. Players pay $200 per person to play the course, which can earn $20,000 for the EAP.

The employee cafeteria is another employee benefit with a small charge of only $2 per meal. Employees compare this price to a fast-food meal and know they receive a bargain. Members of management also eat in the cafeteria as well as the chef. This has an added benefit of encouraging management to mingle with employees.

Scott said that employee satisfaction depends on all managers. "Managers can't lead their staff if they can't motivate them. Managers can have great technical skills and a great education, but if they can't relate to their employees, they won't last long at Pinehurst."

Pinehurst believes strongly in the lifetime value of a customer. Guest records show that many guests first came to Pinehurst as kids with their parents or grandparents. Children are important guests at Pinehurst as witnessed by the summer golf schools for kids and the "Kids U.S. Open."

All of the employees know that Pinehurst respects kids as important guests. That sense of caring for the youngest guests is part of the culture of Pinehurst. Employees appreciate this because many are parents and grandparents and understand that an employee who cares for kids also cares for them.

the marketplace, but a hotel or restaurant's first marketing efforts should be directed internally to employees. Managers must make sure that employees know their products and believe they are a good value. The employees must be excited about the company they work for and the products they sell. Otherwise, it will be impossible for the guests to become excited. So all managers must understand marketing and its customer orientation. External marketing brings customers, but it does little good if the employees do not perform to the guest's expectations. It is often hard to differentiate the tangible part of the product of competing companies. Steak dinners and hotel rooms in the same price range tend to be similar. Product differentiation often derives from the people who deliver the service. It is the employees' delivery of the service that brings customers back. This explains why a study by the National Restaurant Association found the most important issue facing food-service managers was employees.[9] As Christine Andrews, vice president of human resources for Hostmark Hospitality, states, "If your people don't perform, your property won't perform."[10]

■■■ The Internal Marketing Process

Techniques and procedures must be developed to ensure that employees are able and willing to deliver high-quality service. The internal marketing concept evolved as marketers formalized procedures for marketing to employees. Internal marketing ensures that employees at all levels of the organization experience the business and understand its various activities and campaigns in an environment that supports customer consciousness.[11] The objective of internal marketing is to enable employees to deliver satisfying products to the guest. As Christian Gronroos notes, "The internal marketing concept states that the internal market of employees is best motivated for service-mindedness and customer-oriented performance by an active, marketing-like approach, where a variety of activities are used internally in an active, marketing-like and coordinated way."[12] Internal marketing uses a marketing perspective to manage the firm's employees.[13]

Internal marketing is aimed at the firm's employees. Internal marketing is a process that involves the following steps:

1. Establishment of a service culture

2. Development of a marketing approach to human resource management

3. Dissemination of marketing information to employees

Establishment of a Service Culture

An internal marketing program flows out of a service culture. A service marketing program is doomed to fail if its organizational culture does not support serving the customer. An article in *The Australian,* a national newspaper, reported that four firms had pumped $2 million into customer service programs with little result.[14] One reason these customer service efforts failed was that the companies' cultures were not service oriented. The companies carried out the customer service programs because they thought they would produce satisfied customers and make the firm more money. These firms soon discovered that a good customer service program involves much more than working with line employees. *An internal marketing program requires a strong commitment from management.*

A major barrier to most internal marketing programs is middle management. Managers have been trained to watch costs and increase profits. Their reward systems are usually based on achieving certain cost levels. Imagine a hotel's front-desk clerks returning from a training session, eager to help the guests. They may take a little extra time with the customers or perhaps give away a health club visit to help a dissatisfied guest recover from an unsatisfactory experience at the hotel. The front-office manager, who has not been through similar training, may see the extra time spent as unproductive and the services given away as wasteful.

If management expects employees' attitudes to be positive toward the customer, management must have a positive attitude toward the customer and the employees. Too often, organizations hire trainers to come in for a day to get their customer-contact employees excited about providing high-quality customer service. The effect of these sessions is usually short lived, however, because the organizations do little to support the customer-contact employees. Managers tell receptionists to be helpful and friendly, yet often the receptionists are understaffed. The greeting developed to make receptionists sound sincere and helpful—"Good morning, Plaza Hotel, Elizabeth speaking, how may I help you," becomes hollow when it is compressed into three seconds with a "Can you please hold?" added to the end. The net result from the guest's perspective is to wait fourteen rings for the phone to be answered and then receive a cold, rushed greeting. Management must develop a **service culture**: a culture that supports customer service through policies, procedures, reward systems, and actions.

An **organizational culture** is the pattern of shared values and beliefs that gives members of an organization meaning, providing them with the rules for behavior in the organization.[15] In well-managed companies, everyone in the organization embraces the culture. A strong culture helps organizations in two ways. First, it directs behavior. Culture is important to service organizations because every customer and each experience is different. The employee must have some degree of discretion over the creation and delivery of the experience to ensure the customer's differing needs and expectations are met.[16] Second, a strong culture gives employees a sense of purpose and makes them feel good about their company.[17] They know what their company is trying to achieve and how they are helping the company achieve that goal.

Here is how Kimpton hotels describes its culture.

> Our culture of care is setting us apart from those who strive to be like us. At Kimpton, we believe a culture of care will be established when every employee is on the alert, fully aware of all the opportunities to form an emotional connection with each guest. When we provide care, our guests experience comfort. Look for ways to create heartfelt moments with each guest and with each other. Kimpton Moments is our way of formalizing our unique culture of care and creating a shift that begins with everyone in our organization. Even though all our people don't come in contact with guests directly, they do work with each other. We encourage all our employees to support each other in the workplace. That will naturally translate into a culture of care for our guests. Every employee is empowered to represent all the services, amenities, and care that the hotel or restaurant has to offer. This is where you can shine, where your unique personality and enthusiasm can come through.[18]

Culture serves as the glue that holds an organization together. When an organization has a strong culture, the organization and its employees act as one. But a company that has a strong culture may not necessarily have a service culture. A strong service culture influences employees to act in customer-oriented ways and is the first step toward developing a customer-oriented organization.

Developing a customer-oriented organization requires a commitment from management of both time and financial resources. The change to a customer-oriented system may require changes in hiring, training, reward systems, and customer complaint resolution, as well as **empowerment** of employees. When a firm empowers employees, it moves the authority and responsibility to make decisions to the line employees from the supervisor.

It requires that managers spend time talking to both customers and customer-contact employees. Management must be committed to these changes. A service culture does not result from a memorandum sent by the chief executive officer (CEO). It is developed over time through the actions of management. For example, a hotel manager who spends time greeting guests and inquiring about their welfare during morning checkout and afternoon check-in demonstrates caring about guests.[19]

In some companies, including Hyatt, McDonald's, and Hertz, management spends time working alongside customer-contact employees serving customers. This action makes it clear to employees that management does not want to lose touch with operations and that managers care about both employees and customers. A service culture and internal marketing program cannot be developed without the support of management. Organizations cannot expect their employees to develop a customer-oriented attitude if it is not visibly supported by company management.

Weak Service Culture Compared to a Strong Service Culture

In firms that have weak corporate cultures, there are few or no common values and norms. Employees are often bound by policies and regulations, although these policies may make no sense from a customer service perspective. As a result, employees become insecure about making decisions outside the rules and regulations.[20] Because there are no established values, employees do not know how the company wants them to act, and they spend time trying to figure out how to behave. When they do come up with a solution, they must get their supervisor's permission before applying it to the problem. Supervisors, in turn, may feel the need to pass the responsibility upward. During the decision process, the guest is kept waiting minutes, hours, days, or even months to receive a reply. In a company with a strong

e

10.1 Kimpton Hotels, http://www. kimptonhotels. com/: Under human resources, go to internal philosophy. Notice on this page and in the related links at the bottom left of the page Kimpton communicates its service culture.

One of the ways restaurant creates a service culture is by hiring workers with a service attitude, training employees, creating a pleasant working atmosphere and regular communication between management and staff. Courtesy of Andres Rodriguez/ Fotolia.

service culture, employees know what to do, and they do it. Customers receive a quick response to their questions and quick solutions to their problems.

When you come into contact with an organization that has a strong service culture, you recognize it right away. There is a difference in the feeling a guest receives from an employee who has a genuine interest in guests and communicates this personally and an employee who does not care. Make sure your employees care about their guests.

Turning the Organizational Structure Upside Down

The conventional organizational structure is a triangular structure. For example, in a hotel the CEO (chief executive officer) and COO (chief operating officer) are at the peak of the triangle. The general manager is on the next level, followed by department heads, supervisors, line employees, and the customers (Figure 10–2). Ken Blanchard, author of *One Minute Manager,* states that the problem with a conventional organizational structure is that everyone is working for his or her boss. Employees want to do well in the organization. Thus, line employees are concerned with what their supervisors think of their performance, department heads are concerned with how the general manager views them, and the general managers want the corporate office to think highly of them. The problem with this type of organization is that everyone is concerned with satisfying people above them in the organization, and very little attention is paid to the customer.[21]

When a company has a service culture, the organizational chart is turned upside down. The customers are now at the top of the organization, and corporate management is at the bottom of the structure. In this type of organization, everyone is working to serve the customer. Corporate management is helping its general managers to serve the customer, general managers are supporting their departments in serving the customer, department heads are developing systems that will allow their supervisors to better serve the customer, and supervisors are helping line employees serve the customer.

A bell person at a Ritz-Carlton hotel delivered baggage to a guest about an hour after he had checked in due to an error. After he had delivered the luggage, he told his supervisor. The supervisor apologized to the guest and noted in the hotel's computer that this guest had experienced a problem and should receive exceptional service during the rest of his stay.[22] This seems like a rational way to handle the problem, but it is really an extraordinary event. In a hotel with a conventional organizational structure, if any employees make a mistake, they hope their supervisor

Figure 10–2
Turning the organizational structure upside down.

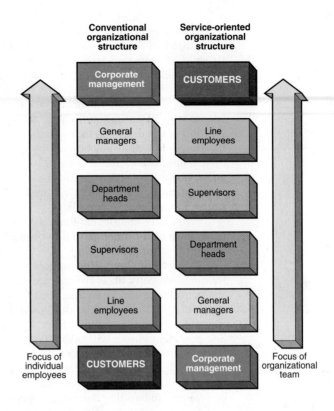

never finds out about it; they may even try to cover it up. They know that if their supervisor does find out about a mistake, they may be reprimanded. The Ritz-Carlton has a service culture; it has turned the organizational structure upside down. The bell person was concerned about the guest and knew his supervisor would take action that would enable the hotel to recover from his mistake. The supervisor was not afraid to communicate the department's mistake to other departments. When you turn the organization upside down, everyone works to serve the guest. When you have a conventional organizational structure, everyone works to please the boss.

Nonroutine Transactions

An advantage of a strong culture is that it prepares employees to handle nonroutine transactions. A nonroutine transaction is a guest transaction that is unique and usually experienced for the first time by employees. The number of possible nonroutine transactions is so great that they cannot be covered in a training manual or in training programs. One benefit of a service culture is that it provides employees with the right attitude, knowledge, communication skills, and authority to deal with nonroutine transactions. The ability to handle nonroutine transactions separates excellent hospitality companies from mediocre ones.

An example of a nonroutine transaction is a guest who requested a late checkout so he could hold a business meeting in his room. Unfortunately, the hotel was fully booked, and the room was needed for guests arriving that afternoon. The policy manual would have said to tell the guest that he could not be accommodated in this situation. A service culture creates a desire to service the guest. The manager made provisions for him to use a vacant conference room free of charge. The guest offered to pay, but the hotel refused. The room would have never been rented at the last minute, so there was no lost revenue. The future business the hotel received from the guest who was a business consultant and the positive word of mouth was many times the amount the hotel would have received from the guest if it charged him for the room.[23] Empowered and innovative employees can handle nonroutine transactions.

Management must be willing to give employees the authority to make decisions that will solve guests' problems. Management should exhibit confidence in its ability to hire and train employees by trusting the employees' ability to make decisions. Simon Cooper, former president of Delta Hotels and Resorts and now president of Ritz-Carlton, believes that having staff do nothing but control other staff reflects poorly on the organization. He states that the job of an assistant housekeeper is to go around and check that the maids are doing their job. Having that position is an admission that we can't hire the right people. Cooper says that Delta has only a few assistant housekeepers, who are now in training positions. When their housekeepers finish a room, they know that the next person in it will be a guest. Cooper states that the degree of trust makes them far better workers.[24] When we trust employees, they solve guest problems more effectively and create fewer causes for the guest to complain.

Hospitality companies that rely on rigid policies and procedures rather than motivated, well-trained, and empowered employees have little hope of achieving maximum guest satisfaction.

The issue of nonroutine transactions will become increasingly important in the future. Hospitality firms are now using technology to serve routine customer transactions. This use of technology will become even more pervasive. Computerized check-in, video checkout, and robotics will be adapted to the hospitality industry, so employees will find themselves dealing more frequently with nonroutine tasks. Self-confident guests will take advantage of technology designed to enhance and hasten guest service. The uncertain guest or guests with problems will wish to deal with an employee. As the workplace becomes more automated, employees will take a greater role in answering questions and solving guests' problems. They must also be prepared to handle nonroutine transactions.

As Parasuraman says, "Customer service earned through several satisfactorily performed routine transactions can be badly damaged by just one botched attempt at processing a non-routine transaction. No amount of written procedures, guidelines, or specifications can prevent the occurrence of such botched attempts; only true organizational dedication to customer satisfaction can."[25] A strong service culture enables employees to make decisions required to handle nonroutine transactions.

Development of a Marketing Approach to Human Resources Management

Creating Jobs That Attract Good People

Managers must use the principles of marketing to attract and retain employees. They must research and develop an understanding of their employees' needs, just as they examine the needs of customers. Not all employees are the same. Some employees seek money to supplement their incomes; others are looking for work that will be their sole source of income. Marketers can use marketing research techniques to segment the employee market, choosing the best segments for the firm and developing a marketing mix to attract those segments. For employees, the marketing mix is the job, pay, benefits, location, transportation, parking, hours, and intangible rewards, such as prestige and perceived advancement opportunities. Just as customers look for different attributes when they purchase a product, employees look for different benefits. Some may be attracted by flexible working hours, others are attracted by good health insurance benefits, and still others may be attracted by child-care facilities. Flexible working hours for office or housekeeping positions, cafeteria-style benefit programs in which employees design their own benefit package, and child care can all be used to attract a certain type of employee. Advertising should be developed with prospective employees in mind, building a positive image of the firm for present and future employees and customers. Employees choose employers and leave them the same way that guests select certain hotels and then decide to switch. It is expensive to lose both guests and employees.[26] Using a marketing approach to develop positions and company benefits helps to attract and maintain good employees. A reduction in turnover can result in hundreds of thousands of dollars in savings.[27]

10.2 Southwest Airlines—Careers, http://www .southwest.com/html/about-southwest/careers/culture. html: Notice how Southwest uses videos to give potential employees and ideas of what it is like for Southwest.

The Hiring Process

The service product, at least in part, is the attitude the employee displays as he or she delivers the service experience. It is unlikely that the service provider can teach the service attitude that all its customer-contact employees need. Service organizations need to hire for attitude and train for skills.[28] "Service characteristics like intangibility and customer contact require service employees to display more initiative, to cope more effectively with stress, to be more interpersonally flexible and sensitive, and to be more cooperative than their colleagues who work in manufacturing."[29] This idea means that service firms place more emphasis on personality, energy, and attitude than on education, training, and experience in their recruitment, selection, and training strategies. Finding employees who are good at creating a service experience is a vital goal and major hiring criterion of service organizations.

> Selecting people for customer service roles is similar to casting people for roles in a movie. First, both require artful performances aligned with the audience expectations. Creating an interpersonal experience that customers remember as satisfactory, pleasant, or dazzling is like an actor's mission of having audiences so caught up in the play or movie that they start believing the performer is the person portrayed. Second, both requirements need a casting choice based on personality.[30]

Swissair carefully screens its applicants, selects candidates for personal interviews, and puts them through a five- to six-hour selection process. The airline then puts successful applicants on probation for a three-month period. It invests a great deal in each candidate because it realizes it is better to spend money choosing the right employee than trying to repair mistakes caused by poor employees. Swissair understands the importance of hiring the right employees.[31]

Southwest Airlines strongly believes inherent attitudes cannot be changed in people. To test for behaviors such as a sense of humor, ability to work with others, and friendliness, Southwest's interview process includes group interviews where applicants tell jokes and role-play a variety of situations to demonstrate teamwork and the capacity to act spontaneously. Southwest can afford to be very selective because it receives an extremely large number of job applications with little active advertising, thanks to its reputation for being a unique and excellent place to work.

Southwest places special emphasis on preparing its people to perform and on teamwork. It considers employee training to be a continuous process rather than a single event. Throughout their careers, employees are cross-trained on multiple jobs to enrich every employee's work experience and to prepare them to perform flexibly in different positions as needed. In addition, employees are specifically assigned to work with a senior employee who serves as a mentor to provide a clear demonstration of Southwest's service quality and to be available to answer questions.[32] Colleen Barrett, president emeritus of Southwest Airlines, said, "We're in the customer service business; we happened to offer air transportation. We consider our employees to be our number one customer."[33]

Disney World allows its best employees, its star "**cast members**," to pick future employees. Disney gives cast members who will be used in the selection process three weeks of training. They are then turned loose in a 45-minute interview session to select potential new employees. James Poisant, a former manager at Disney World, explains that employees choose employees who mirror their own values. "In 45 minutes the cast members pick up on who is fooling and who's genuine."[34]

Careful selection can also have a positive effect on the employees who are hired because they feel special. Adam Hassan, a Ritz-Carlton boiler operator, explains, "When people take so much time to select you, you really want to prove they made the right choice. So if I see anything unusual I take care of it."[35]

Danny Meyer, New York restaurateur and author of *Setting the Table*, sums up the essence of hiring in the hospitality industry by stating that he looks for people who have good technical skills, but more importantly they must also have good emotional skills. The emotional skills include optimistic warmth, a curiosity to learn new things coupled with the intelligence that enables one to learn, a work ethic that includes attention to detail, empathy, and self-awareness and integrity.[36]

Disney allows its employees to help choose future cast members. Courtesy of Jiawangkun/Dreamstime.com.

Selection methods that identify customer-oriented candidates must be used as part of the hiring process. Employee's attitude, appearance, and willingness to handle the guest's requests help form a first impression of a hotel or a restaurant. Hiring and training, traditionally the responsibility of human resources management, are key areas in any internal marketing program. A marketing-like approach to human resources management starts with hiring the right employees.

Teamwork

If a company hires the right people, they will be team players. In companies that practice internal marketing, if one employee makes an error, other employees try to cover it before the guest notices. In these organizations, guests do not have to understand the hotel's organization and business to ensure that their needs are met. The front desk handles most requests, relaying the guest's desire to the appropriate department. In restaurants that have used internal marketing to create a service culture, staff members cover for each other. Employees who see that a guest needs something will serve the guest, even though it may not be their table.

Organizations that lack teamwork create an uncomfortable environment for the guest. For example, a guest called the front desk of a five-star resort, and asked for extra towels. The front-desk clerk answering the telephone acted puzzled. Surely a guest would know to call housekeeping for towels. The operator stated that this was the front desk, not housekeeping, told the guest to call housekeeping, and hung up. Many restaurant guests have asked for a drink while they are sitting at their tables looking over the dinner menu. The response to some of these guests is that they have mistaken the food-service person for a cocktail-service person. The food service then tells the customers to redirect their request to cocktail service and departs, leaving the guests' needs unfilled. In both of these incidents, the first employee contacted should have taken care of the customer's request and passed it along to the appropriate person. This is referred to as *ownership of the problem*. Customers should not have to learn the hotel or restaurant's organizational chart. They should not have to redirect their request for service to another employee. Hiring procedures need to identify those employees who are team players.

Older employees were one group that surprised some managers by their willingness to support other employees. Some managers believed the elderly might not be willing to cooperate with much younger workers or to accept direction from a youthful supervisor. KFC and McDonald's were among the first hospitality firms to prove the invalidity of these assumptions. A survey of National Restaurant Association members demonstrated that older workers were regarded to have better relations with guests and fellow employees than the "average employees."[37]

The Importance of Initial Training

A guest overheard a conversation between a guest and the dining-room hostess of a hotel. The guest asked for a recommendation concerning a good place to eat in the area. Managers would hope that the hostess first would suggest the hotel's restaurant and then mention other restaurants in the area. Instead, the hostess said she had just moved to the area and had not yet found a good place to eat. Too often, employees know nothing about the hotel they work for or its products and other items of interest to guests. If employees are not enthusiastic about the company they work for and the products they sell, it will be difficult to create enthusiastic customers.

At the other extreme, a guest checked into the Quality Suites Tech Center South in Denver, Colorado, on a Saturday night and asked the front-desk clerk if he knew where the closest Catholic Church was for Mass the next morning. The clerk replied that he was not of that faith and did not know but would find out. Five minutes after the guest was in his room, the phone rang. It was from the front-desk clerk who said he had found three Catholic churches and Mass times and had personally called a Catholic friend to see which of the three he would recommend. At the same time the desk clerk asked if the guest had eaten yet and when the answer was no, he proceeded to tell him of the great Mexican food in the hotel's restaurant and then offered to make a reservation. The guest enjoyed the Mexican food. If we hire right employees and provide good training, we will be well on the way to having enthusiastic employees create repeat guests.

When we spend a great deal of time and effort selecting employees, we want to keep them. Consultant Jeanne d'Orleans provides some suggestions on how to make employees feel welcome during their first week.

Day One

- Ask employees to arrive at a time when someone has time to greet them.
- Make the team aware they are coming so *everyone* can welcome them.
- Use bulletin boards or even marquees to say "Welcome Robert!"
- Give them a basic tour and introduce them to as many people as possible.

Within Week One

- Make sure employees participate in an organized orientation.
- Provide them with a partner/mentor during those first tenuous days.
- Have a skills training program for them to participate in.
- Tailor training to the level of expertise they bring.[38]

To be effective, employees must receive information regularly about their company. The company's history, current businesses, and its mission statement and vision are important for employees to know. They must be encouraged to feel proud of their new employer. Desire to contribute to the company's success must be instilled in them. At Disney all new employees take a course called "Traditions," in which they learn about the company, its founder, and its values and beliefs. Employees then receive specific training for their particular assignments. Disney trains its ticket takers for four days because the company wants them to be more than ticket takers; they want them to be cast members. The term *cast members* implies they are members of a team. Like other Disney cast members, they are putting on a performance. While they work in the ticket booths, guests will ask many questions. They must know the answers to these questions or be able to find them quickly. Disney understands the importance of these moments of truth. It provides its staff with extensive training before the first moment of truth is faced.[39] Disney has become so well known for its training and human resources management that it now conducts courses for other companies.

Opryland Hotel has developed a training program that begins with an orientation for new employees, designed to instill pride in the history, culture, and stature of the hotel. The purpose of the orientation process is to create an inspiring atmosphere and build a solid work commitment that helps reduce turnover. According to Marc Clark, the director of training at Opryland, "the new employee orientation program and all employee policies are built on a foundation of a sincere service attitude. If employees, particularly managers, are not serving guests directly, then they should be serving those who are."[40]

Continuous Training

Isadore Sharp, founder of Four Seasons Hotels and Resorts, told his managers, "Our competitive edge is service, service delivered by frontline employees we expect you to develop." "Your role then will be a leader, not a boss. Your job will be to bring out the best in all individuals and weld them into a winning team."[41]

Two principal characteristics have been identified in companies that lead their industries in customer service: They emphasize **cross-training**, and they insist that everybody share certain training experiences. Most hotel training programs for college graduates rotate new employees through all departments in the hotel. This gives the trainees an insight into the importance of each department and how they work together to provide customer service. James Coney Island, a fast-food restaurant chain, cross-trains its employees so that they understand all the positions in the restaurant. Some Embassy Suites Hotels goes a step further, providing employees an opportunity to increase their wages based on the number of positions they have mastered.

Companies must make sure that their employees are familiar with all the products they sell. For example, all restaurant employees should be prepared to tell guests about the restaurant's Sunday brunch. A restaurant service person in a hotel should be able to give directions to the hotel's health club. Often, employees do not have knowledge of products in their own areas because they have never been given the opportunity to sample them. When a service person does not know how an item tastes, it promotes the perception that the employee or management does not care about the customer.

A front-desk clerk in a large casino resort said she felt uneasy when guests asked her about the show in the casino's showroom. The hotel had stressed the importance of promoting it favorably but did not give the front-desk employees an opportunity to see the show. As a result, the front-desk clerk would tell the guest that it was a great show. Sometimes, the guest would start asking specific questions about the show. When this happened, her answers usually reflected her lack of firsthand knowledge about the show and made her feel foolish. It would have been wise for the hotel to provide an opportunity for front-desk employees to see the show. They could have enthusiastically promoted the show with firsthand knowledge instead of cringing when someone asked about it. They may even have promoted the show on their own rather than waiting for a guest to ask about it.

In well-managed restaurants, employees know the menu. They are trained to direct guests to the menu selections that will best suit their taste and instructed in how to sell the choices on the menu. Every restaurant should have tastings where employees sample the products they are selling. Product training is a continuous learning process; it should be part of every company's employee training.

The Olive Garden brand promise is "the idealized Italian family meal" characterized by "fresh, simple, delicious Italian food," "complemented by a great glass of wine," served by "people who treat you like family," "in a comfortable home-like setting." To live up to that brand promise, the Olive Garden has sent more than 1,100 restaurant general managers and team members on cultural immersion trips to Italy, launched the Culinary Institute of Tuscany in Italy to inspire new dishes and teach general managers and team members authentic Italian cooking techniques, conducts wine training workshops for team members and in-restaurant wine sampling for guests, and is remodeling restaurants to give them a Tuscan farmhouse look. Communications include in-store, employee, and mass media messages that all reinforce the brand promise and ad slogan, "When You're Here, You're Family."[42]

Product training sometimes must extend into the visual arts. The Grand Hyatt of Hong Kong is a magnificent hotel with caring and well-trained personnel. Yet even here there is room for additional training. The Grand Hyatt is truly an art museum within a hotel. The decor features sculpture, paintings, and other fine works of visual art. Unfortunately, none of the employees seems to have sufficient knowledge of these expensive and carefully selected art pieces to discuss them with inquiring guests. If exquisite art is part of the product, it should be part of the training. Guests will be impressed, and employees will gain pride in the hotel.

This results in the circular effect of creating satisfied and proud employees who in turn create satisfied guests. The results of a study of this circular effect clearly demonstrated that "as employees' job satisfaction, job involvement, and job security improve, their customer focus also improves."[43]

Insurance executives checking out of the Sheraton Boca Raton locked their keys in their car. The car was blocking traffic, and the executives had a plane to catch. The bellman telephoned the car's make and serial number to a nearby locksmith, and the hotel staff rolled the car out of traffic. Fifteen minutes after the bellman's call, the locksmith arrived with replacement keys.[44] The employees were successful in handling the problem because they were prepared for such an incident. They knew that a car blocking the entrance could cause problems, so they stored a car jack attached to a dolly nearby. The bell staff knew the phone numbers of nearby locksmiths. They also understood the importance of keeping guests informed to relieve anxiety. Throughout this event, they kept the insurance executives apprised of what was going on. Leaving the Sheraton Boca Raton could have been a disaster; instead, it provided an exciting incident that enabled the staff to show their professionalism and to further convince the guests that they had indeed chosen the right hotel.

The Hyatt Sanctuary Cove in Australia has adjusted its training programs. Training is now conducted by each department instead of by a trainer from the human resources department. Departments decide what their training needs are and develop programs to fill those needs. The hotel also allows any employee to attend any training session and posts all training sessions on the employee bulletin board so every employee can review the hotel's training program for the coming month. During a visit to the Hyatt, an accounting department employee was observed training a food-service waiter on the hotel's computerized food and beverage accounting system. It became obvious from their conversation that each was learning about the other's department and how the departments could better support each other.

The development of a good training program can start organizations on an upward spiral. A research study found that service quality is related inversely to staff turnover. Properly trained employees can deliver quality service, which helps the image of the firm, attracting more guests and employees to the organization.

Employee turnover rates of 100 percent or more are common in the hospitality industry. For example, limited-service restaurants have a turnover rate of 123 percent, whereas full-service restaurants have a turnover rate of 88 percent for hourly employees.[45] Firms with high turnover often ask why they should spend money training employees if they are just going to leave. This can turn into a self-fulfilling prophecy for firms that have this attitude. The employees are not properly trained and thus are not capable of delivering quality service. Not being able to deliver good service, they will feel uncomfortable in their jobs and quit. Unfortunately, this reinforces employers' beliefs that they should not spend money training their employees, but not investing in employee training programs leads to a cycle of high employee turnover and guest dissatisfaction.

Hospitality companies with a strong commitment to employee training are well advised to make this philosophy well known to all employees in action and in word. The Centennial Hotel Management Company of Canada has a written statement of a human resources philosophy that includes orientation and training. This statement is an excellent internal marketing tool:

Orientation

- The purpose of Centennial Hotel orientation is to assure the new employee that he or she has made the right decision and to build a strong sense of belonging to the company, the team, and the industry.

- Orientation assures the employees that the company provides the support they require to be successful. It is also a time to share the values of Centennial Hotel and to introduce the facilities of the hotel.

Training

- Centennial Hotel is committed to providing consistent basic training throughout the company, as well as continuous upgrading. Training is for everyone and must be planned, systematic, and comprehensive. The success of training must be measurable.[46]

Managing Emotional Labor

Just as we try to understand the needs of our customers, we need to understand the needs of our employees. One of these needs is the ability to manage their emotions. According to Zeithaml and Bitner, two services marketing experts, friendliness,

Training helps ensure product quality and consistency, while making employees more comfortable in their jobs. Courtesy of Bowie15/Dreamstime.

courtesy, empathy, and responsiveness directed toward customers all require huge amounts of emotional labor from frontline employees who shoulder this responsibility.[47] The term **emotional labor** was first used by Hochschild and has been defined as the necessary involvement of the service provider's emotions in the delivery of the service.[48] The display of emotions can strongly influence the customer's perception of service quality. To manage emotional labor, managers must hire employees who can cope with the stress caused by dealing with customers. Then emotional labor must be managed on a day-to-day basis. Some common techniques used to manage emotional labor include monitoring overtime and avoiding double shifts, encouraging work breaks, and support from fellow workers and managers. Managers are sometimes the cause of emotional stress, for example, by yelling at an employee before a shift and then sending the employee out to work with customers.

One of the biggest causes of emotional stress is long hours. Employees often find it hard to manage their emotions after working for 10 hours straight. At this point the employees are tired and often care little about the customer. We have all been in that position or observed service providers who were rude or uncaring after working a long shift. The cause of such behavior is that the employee is emotionally drained. The story is told of a waitress who was having a particularly hard day when a customer complained about the food. The customer shouted that his baked potato was bad. The waitress picked up the potato, slapped it a couple of times, yelling, "Bad potato, bad potato," put the potato back on the customer's plate, and walked away. Although this is a humorous story, the customer was not amused. When employees are overworked emotionally, service suffers.

Implementation of a Reward and Recognition System

To sustain a service culture, human resource policies must create a system that rewards and recognizes employees and managers that provide good customer service. Professors Sturman and Way state, "If you want to improve employee performance in the hospitality industry, ensure that the employees accurately perceive the practices, procedures, and behaviors that are rewarded, supported, and expected of them by your company."[49] Employees must receive feedback on how they are doing to perform effectively. Communication must be designed to give them feedback on their performance. An internal marketing program includes service standards and methods of measuring how well the organization is meeting these standards. The results of any service measurement should be communicated to employees. Major hotel companies survey their guests to determine their satisfaction level with individual attributes of the hotel. One researcher found that simply communicating information collected from customers changed employee attitudes and performance.[50] Customer service measurements have a positive effect on employee attitudes if results are communicated and recognition is given to those who serve the customer well. If you want customer-oriented employees, seek out ways to catch them serving the customer and reward and recognize them for making the effort.[51]

Reward systems in the hospitality and travel industry used to be based only on meeting financial objectives such as achieving a certain labor cost or food cost or increasing revenue. Now well-managed companies are giving rewards based on customer satisfaction. If companies want to have customer-oriented employees, they must reward them for servicing the customer. Reward systems and bonuses based on customer satisfaction scores are one method of rewarding employees based on serving the customer.

Dissemination of Marketing Information to Employees

Often, the most effective way of communicating with customers is through customer-contact employees. They can suggest additional products, such as the hotel's health club or business center, and they can upsell when it is to the guest's benefit. Employees often have opportunities to solve guest problems before these problems become irritants. To do this, they need information. Unfortunately, many companies leave customer-contact employees out of the communication cycle. The director of marketing may tell managers and supervisors about upcoming events, ad campaigns, and new promotions, but some managers may feel employees do not need to know this information.

Beth Lorenzini of *Restaurants and Institutions* states, "Promotions designed to generate excitement and sales can do just the opposite if employees aren't involved in planning and execution." Monica Kass, sales and marketing coordinator for Lawry's the Prime Rib, Chicago, says that employees and marketing people who develop promotions must communicate. Lawry's increased its Thanksgiving Day sales by 48 percent through employee involvement. Lawry's invited all the "wait staff" to a Thanksgiving dinner a week before Thanksgiving. This was the same meal it was serving to guests on Thanksgiving Day. The dinner not only was a festive affair to get everybody into the Thanksgiving holiday mood, but it also served as a training tool. Employees knew exactly what was going to be served on Thanksgiving Day, including wines that went well with the meal. The management of Lawry's also asked the staff for their input as to how to make the promotion run smoothly. On Thanksgiving Day, each wait person was given a corsage or a boutonniere. Like the employees at Lawry's, all staff should be informed about promotions. They should hear about promotions and new products from management, not from advertisements meant for external customers.[52]

The actions of management are one way that an organization communicates with its employees. Management at all levels must understand that employees are watching them for cues about expected behavior. If the general manager picks a piece of paper up off the floor, other employees will start doing the same. A manager who talks about the importance of employees working together as a team can reinforce the desire for teamwork through personal actions. Taking an interest in employees' work, lending a hand, knowing employees by name, and eating in the employee cafeteria are actions that will give credibility to the manager's words.

Hospitality organizations should use printed publications as part of their internal communication. Most multiunit companies have an employee newsletter, and larger hotels usually have their own in-house newsletters. Besides mass communication, personal communication is important to spread the word effectively about new products and promotional campaigns. Leonard Berry suggests having

Marketing Highlight | Internal Marketing in Action: Lewis Hotels

10–2 Burt and Andria Lewis of Boulder, Colorado, purchased second-rate failing hotels and turned them into award-winning properties with good rates and exceptionally high occupancy with strong guest and employee loyalty. The Golden Hotel in Golden, Colorado, was bought out of receivership. The hotel had reached such a depth of neglect that the front office was protected by bulletproof glass. The Lewises were able to turn the hotel around and within two and a half years the property's occupancy was so high that even friends of the owners had difficulty acquiring a room. This hotel received awards from Choice hotels, including the Platinum Award, Best in Brand, and a nomination for Inn of the Year.

Although Burt has been in the hotel business for over forty years, Andria joined the company eight years ago with no hotel experience. How was this accomplished by this husband/wife team who come from two very different backgrounds?

They use sound management practices and picked hotels in quality locations with limited potential for the development of new hotels. For example, they choose a city center hotel such as The Golden Hotel, where the availability and cost of a similar location would serve as a barrier to entry for other hotels. They also maintained their hotels.

One of the characteristics of their management was internal marketing. They created a quality product with amenities that created value for their guests. But they also wanted their employees to be able to say, "I am proud to work for this hotel." They also followed these internal marketing principles.

Hire Quality People Who Want to Succeed

Many employees are self-selected. They know about the Lewis Hotels and want to work there. Why?

- Each employee receives a thorough orientation in which the topic of personal and hotel success is foremost and accompanied by clear guidelines as to what is expected.

- Employees participate in analyzing costs and for all areas of their work such as the cost of silverware and glasses. Expense and profit information is shared with employees; thus they feel part of the management of the operation and continuously learn.

A Quality Management Team

Lewis Hotels calls this its SWAT Team. "Best investment in this hotel," Andria said of this team. In addition to assuming responsibility for critical areas such as food and beverage operations, the team is prepared to open new properties as Lewis Hotels expands.

Food and Beverage Director Connie Laslow is representative of the quality of the SWAT Team. Connie speaks five languages and has extensive experience working for a variety of hospitality companies, including upscale restaurants and hotels. Connie is so customer focused that she can often recall what customers ordered a year later. Connie said, "You are only as successful as your staff" and works closely with them while allowing them to be creative. "You can put your fingerprints on many exciting things in the Lewis Hotels," said Connie.

Employee Empowerment

They empower employees and encourage staff to think creatively and not be bound to standardized rules. The Lewises believe that this is probably not possible for a company like McDonald's, but it is highly possible and desirable for Lewis Hotels and has much to do with providing a quality guest experience.

Managers Create a Service Culture and Show They Care About Guest Satisfaction

If a guest is dissatisfied and has left the hotel, Andria personally calls the person. Guests are often stunned that the owner has contacted them to resolve a problem. This has led to repeat business by otherwise angry guests who would select another hotel.

Burt and Andria Lewis realize that physical facilities, guest amenities, and a sound business plan are important. But they also realize customer-oriented employees are responsible for their guests returning. They use their physical environment and the warmth created by their employees to cause both guests and employees to say "wow" on a continual basis. This is accomplished by striving to exceed guest expectations at all times.

Employees of The Golden Hotel are empowered and encouraged to think creatively when it comes to creating guest satisfaction and solving guest problems. Courtesy of The Golden Hotel.

two annual reports, one for stockholders and one for employees. Many firms are now implementing his suggestion.[53]

McDonald's initiated a "talking" annual report on videotape complete with commercials. This unusual and creative approach to presenting the required annual report proved to be an excellent means for reaching stockholders and employees. When introduced, it also produced a wealth of free publicity in major news media.

Snowshoe Mountain in Snowshoe, West Virginia, embarked on a marketing program to better brand the ski resort with a promise of an "authentic, rustic and engaging wilderness experience." In launching a branding initiative to define their goals and articulate what they wanted the Snowshoe Mountain brand to represent to visitors, the resort's marketers started inside. They incorporated the new brand promise in a forty-page brand book that contained the history of the resort and a list of seven attitude words that characterized how employees should interact with guests. On-mountain messaging and signs also reminded employees to deliver on the brand promise. All new hires received a brand presentation from the director of marketing to help them better understand the brand and become effective advocates.[54]

Ongoing communication between management and employees is essential—not just group meetings but regular individual meetings between the employee and management. Every customer-contact employee communicates with hundreds of customers. Managers should meet with these employees to gain customer need insights and determine how the company can make it easier for the employee to serve the customer.

Front-desk clerks are the communication center of the hotel, yet they frequently do not know the names of entertainers or the type of entertainment featured in the hotel's lounges. They may also be unaware of special marketing promotions. Hotels can use technology and training to provide employees with product knowledge. Technology can be used to develop a database. Information can be readily accessible to employees, who should then be trained in the hotel's products and services. Finally, employees can be encouraged to try the company's products. They can eat in the restaurants, stay overnight in the hotel, and receive special previews of lounge entertainment. It is much more convincing if the front-desk employee can give a potential guest firsthand information rather than reading a description.

Employees should receive information on new products and product changes, marketing campaigns, and changes in the service delivery process. All action steps in the marketing plan should include internal marketing. For example, when a company introduces a new mass media campaign, the implementation plan should include actions to inform employees about the campaign. The first time that most employees see company advertisements is in the media in which the advertisement is placed. Before the advertisements appear in the media, the company should share the ad with its employees. Managers should also explain the objective of the campaign and the implications.

One of the authors once worked in a restaurant whose owner decided to install a computer system without discussing it with the staff. The system was first used during a busy lunch period, and the restaurant had given the staff almost no prior training. The system did not perform well, and the staff grew determined to get rid of it. They found that the system was sensitive to grease spots on the check. If a service person got butter on a check, the guest would be charged for all sorts of extra items. Some staff would deliberately put grease spots on their checks to develop false charges for the customer. When the customer complained about the bill, the server would explain to the guest the problems they were having with the new system. Customers quickly sided with the service personnel, and within three months the owner was forced to eliminate the new system. If management had consulted the employees before installation, the employees might have supported the computer. Management could have shown the employees how the system would help them better serve the guest by adding their tickets automatically and keeping them current. This would have created employee support. Instead, without the proper information and training, employees were determined from the beginning to get rid of the computer.

Managers should involve employees in the choice of their uniforms. This waitress at the Officers Circle restaurant, Petrodvorets, St. Petersburg, Russia, proudly wears her uniform. Courtesy of Sylvain Grandadam/Age Fotostock.

Employee Involvement in Uniform Selection

Employees should be informed of and involved in the selection of the uniforms they wear every day. Selecting uniforms is often left to designers and managers, with little input from the service worker. Uniforms are important because employee dress contributes greatly to the guest's encounter with customer-contact employees. Uniforms also become part of the atmospherics of a hospitality operation or travel operation; they have the ability to create aesthetic, stylish, and colorful impressions of the property.[55] They distinguish employees from the general public, making employees accessible and easily identified. In cases where uniforms are lacking, guests may become frustrated because they have difficulty identifying employees when they need help. Uniforms have the ability to create attitudes about an employee's job. Employees dressing in formal wear state that they feel and behave differently once they put on their uniform. This anecdotal evidence has been supported by research. Clothing has been found to be a contributing factor in role playing, acting as a vivid cue that can encourage employees to engage in the behaviors associated with the role of the employee.[56] Putting on the costume can mean putting on a role and shedding other roles. Employees' dress can direct employees' behavior to be more consistent with the goals and standards of behavior established by the organization. A study of resort employees found a significant relationship between employees' perceptions of their uniforms and their overall job attitude. The higher the employee's perception of the uniform, the more positive was their rating of their overall attitude toward their job.[57]

Uniforms should be functional and accepted by the employees. Management often looks for uniforms that represent the property, acting as a marketing tool—enhancing the image of the organization. It is paramount to allow employees to be involved in uniform choices regarding both function and projected image. For example, food servers at a pirate-themed restaurant complained about the loose-fitting sleeves on their shirts and blouses. The uniforms looked great until the servers began working. The sleeves dragged across plates when they were being cleared or when trays were being unloaded at the dishwasher. In a few hours the sleeves were stained with food. The employees stated that the problem embarrassed them when they approached a guest, and they became less outgoing in their dealings with guests. Other problems with functionality include uniforms that are designed without pockets and uniforms that are uncomfortable. The selection of uniforms can have an impact on both the employees' attitude and their ability to serve the customer well. Managers need to consider the employees and involve them in uniform decisions.

Isadore Sharp claims that customer service provided by employees of Four Seasons could be a point of distinction for the brand. Some managers replied that all good hotels gave good service. They said, "look at their ads they all promoted smiling employees and great service." Sharp replied. "Your right they all do. By *their* standards. But we are going to do it differently. Do it so it is something we are known for." Creating an internal marketing program that produces distinctive service takes years to establish. Once one has created a competitive advantage based on employee service it creates a sustainable advantage. The competition may be aware of the advantage, but it will take them years to match the services levels—if they can.

Marketing Highlight | The Four Seasons: Taking Care of Those Who Take Care of Customers

10-3 At a Four Seasons hotel, every guest is a somebody. Other exclusive resorts pamper their guests, but the Four Seasons has perfected the art of high-touch, carefully crafted service. Guests paying $1,000 or more a night expect to have their minds read, and this luxury hotel doesn't disappoint. Its mission is to perfect the travel experience through the highest standards of hospitality. "From elegant surroundings of the finest quality, to caring, highly personalized 24-hour service," says the company, "Four Seasons embodies a true home away from home for those who know and appreciate the best."

As a result, the Four Seasons has a cultlike customer clientele. As one Four Seasons Maui guest recently told a manager, "If there's a heaven, I hope it's run by Four Seasons." But what makes the Four Seasons so special? It's really no secret. Just ask anyone who works there. From the CEO to the doorman, they'll tell you: It's the Four Seasons staff. "What you see from the public point of view is a reflection of our people—they are the heart and soul of what makes this company succeed," says Isadore Sharp, the founder and CEO of the Four Seasons. "When we say people are our most important asset—it's not just talk." Just as it does for customers, the Four Seasons respects and pampers its employees. It knows that happy, satisfied employees make for happy, satisfied customers.

The Four Seasons customer-service legacy is deeply rooted in the company's culture, which in turn is grounded in the Golden Rule. "In all of our interactions with our guests, customers, business associates, and colleagues, we seek to deal with others as we would have them deal with us," says Sharp. "Personal service is not something you can dictate as a policy," he adds. "How you treat your employees is a reflection of how you expect them to treat customers."

The Four Seasons brings this culture to life by hiring the best people, orienting them carefully, instilling in them a sense of pride, and motivating them by recognizing and rewarding outstanding service deeds. It all starts with hiring the right people—those who fit the Four Seasons culture. "Every job applicant, whether hoping to fold laundry or teach yoga, goes through at least four interviews," notes one reporter. "We look for employees who share that Golden Rule—people who, by nature, believe in treating others as they would have them treat us," says Sharp.

Once on board, all new employees receive three months of training, including improvisation exercises that help them fully understand customer needs and behavior. At the Four Seasons, the training never stops. But even more important are the people themselves and the culture under which they work. "I can teach anyone to be a waiter," says Sharp. "But you can't change an ingrained poor attitude. We look for people who say, 'I'd be proud to be a doorman.'" And the most important cultural guideline, restates Sharp, is "the Golden Rule: Do unto others.... That's not a gimmick." As a result, Four Seasons employees know what good service is and are highly motivated to give it.

Most importantly, once it has the right people in place, the Four Seasons treats them as it would its most important guests. According to the reporter:

Compared with the competition, Four Seasons salaries are in the 75th to 90th percentile, with generous retirement and profit sharing plans. All employees—for example, seamstresses, valets, the ski concierge, and the general manager—eat together regularly, free, in the hotel cafeteria. It may not have white linen or a wine list, but the food and camaraderie are good. Another killer perk for all employees: free rooms. After six months, any staffer can stay three nights free per year at any Four Seasons hotel or resort. That number increases to six nights after a year and steadily thereafter. Although the benefit may cost

Happy employees make for happy customers. At the Four Seasons, employees feel as important and pampered as the guests. Pictured above is the Four Seasons Hotel Chicago, next to the historic Water Tower. Courtesy of Thomas Barrat/Shutterstock.

a few thousand dollars a year per employee, the returns seem invaluable. The room stays make employees feel as important and pampered as the guests they serve. Says employee Kanoe Braun, a burly pool attendant at the Four Seasons Maui, "I've been to the one in Bali. That was by far my favorite. You walk in, and they say, 'How are you, Mr. Braun?' and you say, 'Yeah, I'm somebody!' " Adds another Four Season staffer, "You're never treated like just an employee. You're a guest. You come back from those trips on fire. You want to do so much for the guests."

As a result, the Four Seasons staff loves the hotel just as much as customers do. Although guests can check out anytime they like, employees never want to leave. The annual turnover for full-time employees is only 18 percent,

half the industry average. The Four Seasons has been included on *Fortune* magazine's list of 100 Best Companies to Work For every year since the list began in 1998. And that's the biggest secret to the Four Seasons' success. Just as the service profit chain suggests, taking good care of customers begins with taking good care of those who take care of customers.

Sources: Extract adapted from Jeffrey M. O'Brien, "A Perfect Season," *Fortune* (January 22, 2008): 62–66. Other quotes and information from Michael B. Baker, "Four Seasons Tops Ritz-Carlton in Deluxe Photo-Finish," *Business Travel News* (March 23, 2009): 10; Sean Drakes, "Keeping the Brand Sacred," *Black Enterprise* (April 2009): 47; "100 Best Companies to Work For," *Fortune* (February 8, 2010): 55; and http://jobs.fourseasons.com/Pages/Home.aspx and www.fourseasons.com/about_us/ (accessed November 2010).

■■■ KEY TERMS

Cast members. A term used for employees. It implies that employees are part of a team that is performing for their guests.

Cross-training. Training employees to do two or more jobs within the organization.

Emotional labor. The necessary involvement of the service provider's emotions in the delivery of the service.

Empowerment. When a firm empowers employees, it moves the authority and responsibility to make decisions to the line employees from the supervisor.

Internal marketing. Involves marketing to the firm's internal customers, its employees.

Moment of truth. Occurs when an employee and a customer have contact.

Organizational culture. The pattern of shared values and beliefs that gives members of an organization meaning and provides them with the rules for behavior in that organization.

Service culture. A system of values and beliefs in an organization that reinforces the idea that providing the customer with quality service is the principal concern of the business.

■■■ CHAPTER REVIEW

I. **Internal Marketing**
   A. The hospitality industry is unique in that employees are part of the product.
   B. Marketers must develop techniques and procedures to ensure that employees are able and willing to deliver quality service.
   C. Internal marketing is marketing aimed at the firm's employees.
   D. Employee satisfaction and customer satisfaction are correlated.

II. **The Internal Marketing Process**
   A. **Establishment of a service culture**
      1. A **service culture** is an organizational culture that supports customer service through policies, procedures, reward systems, and actions.
      2. An **organizational culture** is a pattern of shared values and beliefs that gives members of an organization meaning, providing them with the rules for behavior in the organization.
      3. Weak culture (not sure if this is a part of service/organization).

   4. **Turning the organizational chart upside down.** Service organizations should create an organization that supports those employees who serve the customers.
   5. Empower and train employees to handle nonroutine transactions.

   B. **Development of a marketing approach to human resources management**
      1. Create positions that attract good employees.
      2. Use a hiring process that identifies and results in hiring service-oriented employees.
      3. Use hiring procedures that identify those employees who are team players.
      4. Provide initial employee training designed to share the company's vision with the employee and supply the employee with product knowledge.
      5. Provide continuous employee training programs.
      6. Make sure employees maintain a positive attitude. Managing emotional labor helps maintain a good attitude.
      7. Reward and recognize customer service and satisfaction.

C. **Dissemination of marketing information to employees**
   1. Often, the most effective way of communicating with customers is through customer-contact employees.
   2. Employees should hear about promotions and new products from management, not from advertisements meant for external customers.
   3. Management at all levels must understand that employees are watching them for cues about expected behavior.

4. Hospitality organizations should use printed publications as part of their internal communication.
5. Hotels can use technology and training to provide employees with product knowledge.
6. Employees should receive information on new products and product changes, marketing campaigns, and changes in the service delivery process.

D. **Employee involvement in uniform selection**

■■■ DISCUSSION QUESTIONS

1. Why are employees called internal customers?
2. What is a service culture? Why is it a requirement for an internal marketing program?
3. Discuss the possible ways that marketing techniques can be used by human resources managers.
4. What are the benefits of explaining advertising campaigns to employees before they appear in the media?
5. The handling of nonroutine transactions separates excellent hospitality companies from mediocre ones. Discuss this statement.

■■■ EXPERIENTIAL EXERCISES

Do one of the following:

Visit a hospitality or travel company. Ask some questions about its products. For example, at a restaurant you may ask about the hours it is open and about menu items. You may state you are looking for a good steak restaurant and ask about its steaks. At a hotel you may ask about its rooms or restaurants. The idea is to have enough dialogue with its employees to be able to judge the customer orientation of the employees. Write your findings supporting how the employees demonstrated they had a customer orientation and ideas you have on how they could have been more customer oriented.

■■■ INTERNET EXERCISE

Explain the advantages and disadvantages of having a "live chat" option or other option to have a live dialogue with an employee on a Web site.

■■■ REFERENCES

1. Sweet Holiday Bread, accessed January 29, 2013, from http://mypanera.panerabread.com/articlestips/holidaybread/.
2. Panera Manager Really Wants Me to Have My Holiday Bread, accessed January 28, 2013, from http://consumerist.com/2012/12/31/8-above-and-beyond-customer-service-stories-from-consumerist-readers/.
3. The Best Customer Service Story Ever, August 10, 2012, 12:05 pm Kochie's Business Builders Yahoo! Accessed January 28, 2013, from http://au.smallbusiness.yahoo.com/inspiration/a/-/14516964/the-best-customer-service-story-ever/.
4. Danny Meyer, *Setting the Table* (New York: HarperCollins, 2006), p. 11.
5. Joseph W. Benoy, "Internal Marketing Builds Service Quality," *Journal of Health Care Marketing,* 16, no. 1 (1996): 54–64.
6. Julia Chang, "From the Inside Out," *Sales and Marketing Management* (August 2005): 14.
7. Richard Normann, *Service Management: Strategy and Leadership in Service Businesses* (New York: Wiley, 1984), p. 33.
8. Ibid., p. 9.
9. Bill Heatly, "Operators Who Make Staff Satisfaction a Top Priority Will Get Results on Bottom Line," *Nation Restaurant News* (May 17, 2004): 24.

10. John P. Walsh, "Employee Training Leads to Better Service, More Profits," *Hotel and Motel Management* (January 12, 2004): 14.

11. William R. George and Christian Gronroos, "Developing Customer-Conscious Employees at Every Level: Internal Marketing," in *The Handbook of Marketing for the Service Industries,* ed. Carole A. Congram (New York: American Management Association, 1991), pp. 85–100.

12. Christian Gronroos, *Strategic Management and Marketing in the Service Sector* (Cambridge, MA: Marketing Science Institute, 1983), as cited in C. Gronroos, *Service Management and Marketing* (Lexington, MA: Lexington Books, 1990), p. 223.

13. Ibid., p. 85.

14. *The Australian* (October 10, 1990).

15. S. M. Davis, *Managing Corporate Culture* (Cambridge, MA: Ballinger, 1985).

16. John Bowen and Robert Ford, "Service Organizations—'Does Having a Thing Make a Difference,' " *Journal of Management,* 28, no. 3 (2002): 447–469.

17. Terrence E. Deal and Allan A. Kennedy, *Corporate Cultures* (Reading, MA: Addison-Wesley, 1982), pp. 15–16.

18. Accessed September 21, 2011, from http://www.kimptonhotels.com/hr/cul_moments.aspx.

19. A. Parasuraman, "Customer-Oriented Corporate Cultures Are Crucial to Services Marketing Success," *Journal of Services Marketing,* 1, no. 1 (Summer 1987): 39–46.

20. Ibid.

21. Ibid., p. 107; Nathan Tyler, *Service Excellence,* Tap. 2 (videotape) (Boston, MA: Harvard Business School Management Productions, 1987).

22. James L. Heskett, W. Earl Sasser, and Leonard A. Schlesinger, *Saving Customers with Service Recovery* (videotape) (Boston, MA: Harvard Business School Management Productions, 1994).

23. Karl Albrecht and Ron Zemke, *Service America!: Doing Business in the New Economy* (Homewood, IL: Dow Jones-Irwin, 1985), pp. 127–128.

24. Carla B. Furlong, *Marketing for Keeps* (New York: Wiley, 1993), pp. 79–80.

25. A. Parasuraman, "Customer-Oriented Corporate Cultures," pp. 33–40.

26. Leonard L. Berry, "The Employee as Customer," *Journal of Retail Banking,* 3, no. 1 (1981): 33–40.

27. Hogan, "Turnover," p. 40.

28. Bowen and Ford, "Service Organizations."

29. B. Schneider and D. Bowen, *Winning the Service Game* (Boston, MA: HBS Press, 1995).

30. C. R. Bell and K. Anderson, "Selecting Super Service People," *HR Magazine,* 37, no. 2 (1992): 52–54.

31. Miliand Lele, *The Customer Is Key* (New York: Wiley, 1987), p. 252.

32. Andrew J. Czaplewski, Jeffery M. Ferguson, and John F. Milliman, "Southwest Airlines: How Internal Marketing Pilots Success," *Marketing Management* (September/October 2001): 14–17.

33. Steve Fisher, "Flying Off into the Sunset," *Costco Connection,* 22, no. 9 (2007): 17.

34. Tschohl, *Achieving Excellence,* p. 113.

35. Joseph A. Michelli, *The New Gold Standard* (New York: McGraw-Hill, 2008), p. 77.

36. Danny Meyer, *Setting the Table* (New York: Harper Collins, 2006), p. 143.

37. Ibid., p. 58.

38. Jeanne d'Orleans, "It's Basic Customer Service," *Hotel & Motel Management* (December 6, 2007), www.hotelmotel.com (accessed June 8, 2008).

39. N. W. Pope, "Mickey Mouse Marketing," *American Banker* (July 25, 1979), as included in W. Earl Sasser, Jr., Christopher W. L. Hart, and James L. Heskett, *The Service Management Course: Cases and Reading* (New York: Free Press, 1991), pp. 649–654.

40. Marc Clark, "Training for Tradition," *Cornell Hotel and Restaurant Administration Quarterly,* 31, no. 4 (1991): 51.

41. Isadore Sharp, *Four Seasons: The Story of a Business Philosophy* (Canada: Toronto, Penguin), p. 110.

42. Drew Madsen, "Olive Garden: Creating Value Through an Integrated Brand Experience," presentation at Marketing Science Institute Conference, *Brand Orchestration,* Orlando, Florida, December 4, 2003.

43. John R. Dienhart and Mary B. Gregoire, "Job Satisfaction, Job Involvement, Job Security and Customer Focus of Quick Service Restaurant Employees," *Hospitality Research Journal,* 16, no. 2 (1993): 41.

44. Christopher W. L. Hart, James L. Heskett, and W. Earl Sasser, Jr., *Service Breakthroughs* (New York: Free Press, 1990), p. 109.

45. Bruce Grindy, "The Restaurant Industry: An Economic Powerhouse," *Restaurants USA* (June/July 2000): 40–45.

46. Michael K. Haywood, "Effective Training: Toward a Strategic Approach," *Cornell Hotel and Restaurant Administration Quarterly,* 33, no. 6 (1992): 46.

47. Valarie A. Zeithaml and Mary Jo Bitner, *Services Marketing* (New York: McGraw-Hill, 1996).

48. A. R. Hochschild, *The Managed Heart* (Berkeley, CA: University of California Press, 1983); definition from Gunther Berghofer, "Emotional Labor," Working Paper (Bond University, Robina, Queensland, Australia, 1993).

49. Michael C. Sturman and Sean A. Way, "Questioning Conventional Wisdom: Is a Happy Employee a Good

Employee, or Do Attitudes Matter More?" The Center for Hospitality Research, Cornell University, March 2008.

50. Albrecht and Zemke, *Service America.*

51. Chip R. Bell and Ron Zemke, *Managing Knock Your Socks Off Service* (New York: American Management Association, 1992), p. 169.

52. Beth Lorenzini, "Promotion Success Depends on Employee's Enthusiasm," *Restaurants and Institutions* (February 12, 1992): 591.

53. Berry, "Employee as Customer," pp. 33–40.

54. Paula Andruss, "Employee Ambassadors," *Marketing News* (December 15, 2008): 26–27.

55. M. R. Solomon, "Dress for Effect," *Psychology Today,* 20, no. 4 (1986): 20–28.

56. A. Rafaeli and M. G. Pratt, "Tailored Meanings: On the Meaning and Impact of Organizational Dress," *Academy of Management Review,* 18, no. 1 (1993): 32–55.

57. Kathy Nelson and John Bowen, "The Effect of Employee Uniforms on Employee Satisfaction," *Cornell Hotel and Restaurant Administration Quarterly,* 41, no. 2 (2000): 86–95.

Courtesy of Peter Frank Edwards/Courtesy of Wild Dunes Resort.

The real issue is value, not price.

—ROBERT T. LINDGREN

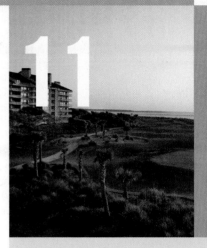

Pricing Products: Pricing Considerations, Approaches, and Strategy

Successful pricing at Wild Dunes® Resort requires coordinated planning and strategy. Located on the Isle of Palms near Charleston, South Carolina, Wild Dunes offers a mix of lodging, golf, tennis, dining, and family activities. This product mix combined with seasonal and special-occasion demand means that multiple factors must be considered in pricing decisions. Responsibility for planning and coordination of pricing is under the direction of Alex Gregory, Director of Sales and Marketing.

Lodging at Wild Dunes involves three distinct properties. The first is the Boardwalk Inn, a ninety-three-room hotel, with a private pool, billiards room, and the resort's fine dining restaurant option, the Sea Island Grill. The property is owned and operated by the resort.

The Village at Wild Dunes is the resort's newest offering, with 166 identically furnished rooms and suites and a family-style restaurant, fitness center, and day spa. Studios to three-bedroom suites and four-bedroom penthouses that were newly constructed were all sold to private owners who place their units into the property rental program, and share in the revenues.

Additional lodging is available in nearby private homes, which Wild Dunes also manages for absentee owners. Property owners are free to use other booking and property management firms. Alex and his staff must price these units to compete with them and also provide a good return to Wild Dunes and the property owners.

Wild Dunes also has other product lines—strategic business units (SBUs). These include two eighteen-hole golf courses, seventeen tennis courts ranked in the top ten by *Tennis Magazine,* and several tennis programs, including professional clinics and exhibitions. Island Adventures® offers recreational programs for preteen kids, teenagers, and adults. Each requires different pricing, such as the Pirate Adventure Pass and the VIP Club Pass for kids. Weekly entertainment events such as the Low Country Luau and the Blue Crabbing Expedition require price planning. Wellness programs such as group yoga, water aerobics, and spa services must also be price managed.

One of the major activities at any destination resort is dining, and Wild Dunes offers a variety in four restaurants, ranging from the Dunes Deli and Pizzeria to luxury dining at the Sea Island Grill. Dinner Delivered is another food and beverage (F&B) product that has become very popular with guests who rent condos or homes. Complete dinners such as southern fried chicken, Italian, and smoked BBQ are prepared and delivered to the guests' homes. Prices range from $145 to $220, but these also require careful price planning, particularly in times of increased competition and rising food costs.

Package pricing is a critical marketing responsibility. Golf is a major attraction for guests, and packages must be developed for commercial groups, groups such as a group of salespeople, and for individuals with varying abilities and interest in golf. Packages typically include accommodations, golf, and breakfast. Specialty packages also include additional items such as a 50-minute massage in the Ladies Golf Package. Packages must be priced to be competitive with other destination resorts, but success also depends on creativity in packaging. For instance, would guests prefer breakfast on the links or a lunch following golf? "Dudes on the Dunes" is a creative package designed for men that includes poker in a guest room with snacks and beer. The "Romance Package" was designed for those celebrating an anniversary or perhaps just reconnecting.

Packages offer excellent opportunities for cross-merchandising and upselling, both of which are important factors in revenue management. Participation by employees in building packages is important since these people "know the guests" better than management.

Wild Dunes employs three full-time revenue management professionals and a director of revenue optimization with responsibility for budgeting, forecasting, and help correctly position Wild Dunes and its product line.

Lodging revenue is the most important part of the product line and also the most variable. Golf and tennis lessons remain relatively stable, but the price of rooms is dependent on many variables. Therefore, the revenue optimization team, including the reservations manager, meets every Wednesday.

During the meeting, the team carefully examines room inventory at all price segments and also looks at the prices of two competitive sets, one in the Charleston area and another among a group of luxury destination resorts. According to the season and anticipated demand, Wild Dunes may decide to be the price leader and at other times to follow competitors.

Like most destination resorts, Wild Dunes faces prime, shoulder, and trough periods. Eight weeks during summer is prime and demand has been increasing 15 percent for this peak period. Rooms during this period were $295 per night but the same room sold for $495 earlier during Memorial Day in May.

The revenue optimization team is instructed to let the quality of the products drive price whenever they can. Sunday is traditionally a low-demand day. Package deals are often used to fill Sunday rooms.

The reservations sales team is also focused on increasing ancillary spending for products such as bike rentals, the spa, and excursions. This means cross-selling and creative packaging and promotions. Hotel guests are reminded of daily activities and items through a guest newsletter, the on-resort television channel, and the resort's magazine and vacation planner which is the comprehensive resource for events and activities.

Wild Dunes has found that guests crave the ability to plan their vacation their way. The Wild Dunes Web site allows guests to plan their experience through their online concierge. The concierge is a Web page that shows a calendar with all possible activities. Guests can select their itinerary and submit it through the Web site, where it will be received by the reservations call center. A pre-arrival concierge staff member from Wild Dunes responds to the inquiry and confirms the requests if available. Users of the online concierge indicate whether they prefer a response by telephone or e-mail. Guest satisfaction with this has been high and ancillary spending has increased.

Upselling has also improved as guests are encouraged to custom design their own packages. Alex said, "Everyone wants to create their ideal experience." When guests build their own package, they commonly upgrade much like buyers of a car who add more accessories or a kid in an ice cream store who orders a double scoop with "the works" on top.

Menu prices for each F&B outlet are also regularly examined against a competitive set.

Although Alex describes his position as complex, he is fortunate to have responsibility for three areas that absolutely must work together. They are the following:

1. Reservations

2. Group sales and catering

3. Marketing

Each department participates in the development of the marketing plan. All new associates under Alex are required to spend one and a half days in orientation and two weeks in training. During this time, concepts such as teamwork, cross-selling, upselling, and revenue optimization are stressed.

Alex feels that his breadth of managerial responsibility has allowed the area to understand the role and importance of revenue management and to work as a team to achieve revenue goals.

■■■ Price

Price is the only marketing mix element that produces revenue. All others represent cost. Some experts rate pricing and price competition as the number-one problem facing marketing executives. Pricing is the least understood of the marketing variables, yet pricing is controllable in an unregulated market. Pricing changes are often a quick fix made without proper analysis. The most common mistakes include pricing that is too cost oriented, prices that are not revised to reflect market changes, pricing that does not take the rest of the marketing mix into account, and prices that are not varied enough for different product items and market segments. A pricing mistake can lead to a business failure, even when all other elements of the business are sound. Every manager should understand the basics of pricing.

Simply defined, **price** is the amount of money charged for a good or service. More broadly, price is the sum of the values consumers exchange for the benefits of having or using the product or service. Price goes by many names:

> You pay rent for your apartment, a rate when you stay overnight in a hotel, tuition for your education, and a fee to your physician or dentist. Airlines, railways, taxis and bus companies charge you a fare. A hotel charges you a room rate. The bank charges interest for using their money. The price for driving your car on Florida's Sunshine State Parkway is a toll. The price of a front-desk clerk is a wage, while a bartender receives a wage and tips. A real estate agent who sells a restaurant charges a commission. Finally, income taxes are the price for the privilege of making money.[1]

Marketers and managers must have an understanding of price. Charging too much chases away potential customers. Charging too little can leave a company without enough revenue to maintain the operation properly. Equipment wears out, carpets get stained, and painted surfaces need to be repainted. A firm that does not produce enough revenue to maintain the operation eventually goes out of business. In this chapter we examine factors that hospitality marketers must consider when setting prices, general approaches, pricing strategies for new products, product mix pricing, initiating and responding to price changes, and adjusting prices to meet buyer and situational factors.

■■■ Factors to Consider When Setting Prices

Internal and external company factors affect a company's pricing decisions. Figure 11–1 illustrates these. Internal factors include the company's marketing objectives, marketing mix strategy, costs, and organizational considerations. External factors include the nature of the market, demand competition, and other environmental elements.

Figure 11–1
Factors affecting price
decisions.

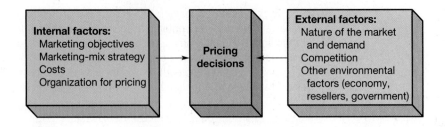

Internal Factors Affecting Pricing Decisions

Marketing Objectives

Before establishing price, a company must select a product strategy. If the company has selected a target market and positioned itself carefully, its marketing mix strategy, including price, will be more precise. For example, Four Seasons positions its hotels as luxury hotels and charges a room rate that is higher than most. Motel 6 and Formula One have positioned themselves as limited-service motels, providing rooms for budget-minded travelers. This market position requires charging a low price. Thus, the strategic decisions on market positioning have a major influence on price.

SURVIVAL Companies troubled by too much capacity, heavy compensation, or changing consumer wants set survival as their objective. In the short run, **survival** is more important than profit. Hotels often use this strategy when the economy slumps. A manufacturing firm can reduce production to match demand. During a recession a 300-room hotel still has 300 rooms to sell each night, although the demand has dropped to 140 a night. The hotel tries to ride out the slump in the best way possible by cutting rates and trying to create the best cash flow possible under the conditions. This strategy directly affects immediate competitors and sometimes the entire industry. Competitors in the hospitality industry are highly cognizant of price changes and usually respond if they feel threatened. This results in soft markets: Not only does occupancy fall, room rates and profits also fall.

Observers of the hospitality industry have sometimes suggested that competition using a survival pricing strategy should be monitored carefully but not necessarily emulated. If the hotel is one of two in a market such as a small town, the effect of price discounting could be considerable. In contrast, if the hotel is in Orlando, Florida, it is one of many and represents a fraction of the total room supply. In this case competitors with a strong marketing program may want to use their marketing skills to gain customers rather than cut their price. Also, for a hotel with good marketing it can make sense to allow a competitor to lower prices and skim off the budget-conscious customers, leaving more profitable business for them, particularly if the hotel using a survival strategy has a small market share.

CURRENT PROFIT MAXIMIZATION Many companies want to set a price that will maximize current profits. They estimate what demand and costs will be at different prices and choose the price that will produce the maximum current profit, cash flow, or return on investment (ROI), seeking current financial outcomes rather than long-run performance. For example, a company may purchase a distressed hotel at a low price. The objective becomes to turn the hotel around, show an operating profit, and then sell. If the hotel owners can achieve a successful turnaround, they may receive a good capital gain.

Some entrepreneurs develop a restaurant concept with the objective of selling the concept to a major chain. They realize that the concept's viability must be proved through a small chain that produces a high net profit. If they can do this, they may attract the attention of a major corporation. The pricing objective in this case is current profit maximization. The success of Steve Ells with Chipotle Mexican Grill and its sale to McDonald's is a prime example.

A study of Chevys Arrowhead Restaurant in Glendale, Arizona, demonstrated that gross revenue could be increased 5 percent by carefully analyzing revenue factors and making appropriate changes. This study showed it is important to establish a measure of baseline revenue performance known as RevPASH which is the revenue per available seat hour.

"By analyzing its service process and table mix, Chevys Arrowhead was able to increase revenue by approximately five percentage points more than two other Chevys that we examined. This performance boost came from its improved table mix, changes in the service delivery, and improved training. Seat occupancy and RevPASH increased, dining duration and variation in that duration increased, and revenue and profitability increased."[2]

MARKET-SHARE LEADERSHIP   Some companies want to obtain a dominant market-share position. They believe that a company with the largest market share will eventually enjoy low costs and high long-run profit. Thus prices are set as low as possible. Marriott strives to be the market-share leader in its class. When it opens a new hotel, Marriott builds market share as quickly as possible. For example, Marriott opened its resort on Australia's Gold Coast with $99 rates; six months later the hotel charged almost twice this rate. Low opening rates created demand. As the demand increased, low-revenue business was replaced with higher. Such a strategy uses price and other elements of the marketing mix to create the awareness of better value than the competition.

PRODUCT-QUALITY LEADERSHIP   The Ritz-Carlton chain has a construction or acquisition cost per room that often exceeds $500,000. Besides a high capital investment per room, luxury chains have a high cost of labor per room. Their hotels require well-qualified staff and a high employee-to-guest ratio to provide luxury service. They must charge a high price for their luxury hotel rooms' product.

Groen, a manufacturer of food-service equipment, is known for its high-quality steam-jacketed kettles. Kitchen designers specify Groen equipment because of its known quality, enabling the company to demand a high price for its equipment. To maintain its quality, Groen must have a well-engineered product comprised of high-quality materials. It also must have the budget to ensure that it maintains its position as a quality leader.

Quality leaders such as Ritz-Carlton and Groen charge more for their products, but they also have to reinvest in their operations continuously to maintain positions as quality leaders.

A bowl of chili and a beverage does not exceed $10 in most restaurants, but the Red Sage Restaurant in Washington, D.C., charges twice that amount for its southwestern cuisine. Patrons pay for more than just a bowl of chili. This two-story restaurant spent $5 million to re-create the wide-open spaces of the West. More than one hundred craftspeople and artists were employed to create stunning original designs, such as murals of horses and a cloud sculpture that flashes blue lightning.[3]

OTHER OBJECTIVES   A company also might use price to attain other, more specific objectives. A restaurant may set low prices to prevent competition from entering the market or set prices at the same level as its competition to stabilize the market. Fast-food restaurants may reduce prices temporarily to create excitement for a new product or draw more customers into a restaurant. Thus, pricing may play an important role in helping accomplish the company's objective at many levels.

The case of two upscale restaurants in New York, both owned by former major-league baseball players, offers an example of contrasting pricing strategies.[4] Mickey Mantle's restaurant purposely established a high price for alcoholic beverages. "A beer here isn't cheap," said John Lowy, co-owner. "We charge more than other bars to keep out the kids. This is a high-exposure place. If something bad happened, it would get out real quick."

An opposite pricing strategy is employed at Rusty Staub's Restaurant. Rusty's pricing philosophy for wine is unique for the industry. He believes that "the better the wine, the less the markup." "We work on a thin margin," said Staub. "A lot of people in the industry say that you should charge at least three times the cost of the wine. But we're way under that. I want people to know we're one of the great-value restaurants."

Which pricing philosophy is correct, Mantle's or Staub's? It all depends on the objectives an owner is attempting to meet. These objectives fit with the company's marketing strategy. There is never one pricing strategy that is right for all competitors in the hospitality industry.

Marketing Mix Strategy

Price is only one of many marketing mix tools that a company uses to achieve its marketing objectives. Price must be coordinated with product design, distribution, and promotion decisions to form a consistent and effective marketing program. Decisions made for other marketing mix variables may affect pricing decisions. For example, resorts that plan to distribute most of their rooms through wholesalers must build enough margins into their room price to allow them to offer a deep discount to the wholesaler. Owners usually refurbish their hotels every five to seven years to keep them in good condition. Prices must cover the costs of future renovations.

A firm's promotional mix also influences price. A restaurant catering to conventioneers receives less repeat business than a neighborhood restaurant and must advertise in city guides targeted to conventioneers. Managers of restaurants who do not consider promotional costs when setting prices experience revenue/cost problems.

Companies often make pricing decisions first. Other marketing mix decisions are based on the price a company chooses to charge. For example, Marriott saw an opportunity in the economy market and developed Fairfield Inns, using price to position the motel chain in the market. Fairfield Inns' target price defined the product's market, competition, design, and product features. Companies should consider all marketing mix decisions together when developing a marketing program.

Costs

Costs set the floor for the price a company can charge for its product. A company wants to charge a price that covers its costs for producing, distributing, and promoting the product. Beyond covering these costs, the price has to be high enough to deliver a fair rate of return to investors. Therefore, a company's costs can be an important element in its pricing strategy. Many companies work to become the low-cost producers in their industries. McDonald's has developed systems for producing fast food efficiently. A new hamburger franchise would have a hard time competing with McDonald's on cost. Effective low-cost producers achieve cost savings through efficiency rather than cutting quality. Companies with lower costs can set lower prices that result in greater market share. Lower costs do not always mean lower prices. Some companies with low costs keep their prices the same as competitors, providing a higher ROI.

Costs take two forms, fixed and variable. **Fixed costs** (also known as *overhead*) are costs that do not vary with production or sales level. Thus, whatever its output, a company must pay bills each month for rent, interest, and executive salaries. Fixed costs are not directly related to production level. **Variable costs** vary directly with the level of production. For example, a banquet produced by the Hyatt in San Francisco has many variable costs; each meal may include a salad, rolls and butter, the main course, a beverage, and a dessert. In addition to the food items, the hotel provides linen for each guest. These are called variable costs because their total varies with the number of units produced. **Total costs** are the sum of the fixed and variable costs for any given level of production. In the long run, management must charge a price that will at least cover total costs at a given level of sales.

Managers sometimes forget that customers are not concerned with a business's operating costs; they seek value. The company must watch its costs carefully. If it costs the company more than competitors to produce and sell its product, the company must either charge a higher price or make less profit.

Many hospitality companies are developing sophisticated models and software to better understand costs and their relations to price. Embassy Suites recognizes this relationship and believes the most valuable guest is not necessarily the one who pays the highest price for a suite. A contribution model developed by Embassy Suites now examines costs to acquire and service guests, such as room labor costs, advertising, special promotions, and associated costs.

Cost Subsidization

Destination ski resorts such as Steamboat Springs, Colorado, and Sun Valley, Idaho, depend upon air transportation to bring guests from distant markets. In many cases these ski resorts are served by only one commuter airline during the non-ski season. This is insufficient for the ski season when the resorts depend upon daily flights by major carriers.

Major carriers are unwilling to assume the entire financial risk of serving resort locations for only a few months each year. Therefore, the resorts and the nearby towns that profit from ski visitors are asked to help ensure that flights will be profitable by guaranteeing an agreed-to revenue base for the airlines. Steamboat Springs Ski Corporation guaranteed $3.35 million to five airlines for the 2011 ski season.[5]

Airlines point to the fact that visitors to ski resorts do not arrive in equal numbers each day. Instead, they want to arrive on Thursday and go home on Sunday. This means that Monday, Tuesday, and Wednesday may have fewer passengers for the airlines. Additionally, many skiers have school-age children and they try to schedule vacations accordingly, creating peaks and valleys for the airlines.

During the 2010 ski season, airlines serving Steamboat Springs witnessed this sample of load factors:

Saturday	January 15	84 percent
Monday	January 17	26 percent
Tuesday	January 18	22 percent
Saturday	February 26	96 percent[6]

Revenues guaranteed to airlines are commonly derived from a variety of sources such as sales tax revenue, membership dues, community fund-raisers, and contributions by local businesses.

Pricing decisions by the airlines are often influenced by spokesmen for the local ski industry who want seats filled with skiers while the airlines may be more concerned with overall yield factors. A process of negotiations may ensue between the ski resort and the airlines regarding periods of weaker demand.

Organizational Considerations

Management must decide who within the organization should set prices. Companies handle pricing in a variety of ways. In small companies, top management, rather than the marketing or sales department, often sets the prices. In large companies, pricing is typically handled by a corporate department or by regional or unit managers under guidelines established by corporate management. A hotel develops a marketing plan that contains monthly average rates and occupancies for the coming year. Regional or corporate management approves the plan. The hotel's general manager and sales manager are then responsible for achieving these "averages." In times of high demand, they can achieve rates significantly above their projected average, whereas in periods of low demand, they will be below their objective. Management may have some freedom in the prices it charges for different groups, but at the end of the financial period, it is responsible for achieving overall pricing and occupancy objectives.

Many corporations within the hospitality industry now have a **revenue management** department with responsibility for pricing and coordinating with other departments that influence price. Airlines, cruise lines, auto rental companies, and many hotel chains have developed revenue management departments. According to Brian Rice, the director of revenue planning and analysis for Royal Caribbean cruise line, the development of a revenue management department was an evolutionary process:

> To practice effective revenue management we needed to make sure that our pricing structures were supportive of what we were doing in inventory

management, and that sales were targeting the same market segments we needed to push. Now we have got to the point where we meet weekly with the sales group to set priorities, we also work with advertising, inventory management and reservations.[7]

The potential rewards are enormous from professional revenue management in a large hospitality company. According to Brian Rice, "If the average yield at Royal Caribbean goes up by $1 a day, it is worth $5.5 million and 100% of it goes to the bottom line." Brian conservatively estimated the monetary benefits of "baby-sitting" the revenue on a day-to-day basis at Royal Caribbean at over $20 million per day.[8]

External Factors Affecting Pricing Decisions

External factors that affect pricing decisions include the nature of the market and demand, competition, and other environmental elements.

Market and Demand

Although costs set the lower limits of prices, the market and demand set the upper limit. Both consumer and channel buyers such as tour wholesalers balance the product's price against the benefits it provides. Thus, before setting prices, a marketer must understand the relationship between price and demand for a product.

Rudy's was one of the finest restaurants in Houston. It prospered during Houston's boom, but later Houston moved into recession. The demand for fine dining fell and Rudy's suffered. Its lunches were just breaking even. Management considered a price increase as a way to push revenue above the break-even (BE) point. On the surface this may have seemed like a good idea: Just charge each customer $5 more, and the revenue would move above BE. This tactic assumed that the market was price inelastic.

Business dropped at Rudy's because people could no longer afford its prices. An increase in price would have further reduced the size of the market that could afford the restaurant's prices. Another restaurant in Houston, La Colombe d'Or, adapted its pricing tactics to fit the recession. The meal was a loss leader because most guests ordered wine with their meal. The restaurants frequently booked business luncheons, and the host of a business luncheon generally does not force guests to order the cheapest item on the menu. As a result, La Colombe d'Or sold many meals at regular prices and had healthy wine sales. Yet even with the loss leader the owner realized that other prices must offer value.

Royal Caribbean Cruises has developed a revenue management department with the responsibility for price and coordinating with other departments that influence price. Courtesy of Heeb Christian/Prisma Bildagentur AG/Alamy.

Cross-Selling and Upselling

The owner of La Colombe d'Or used **cross-selling**, one of the basics of effective revenue management. Cross-selling opportunities abound in the hospitality industry. A hotel can cross-sell F&B, exercise room services, and executive support services, and it can even sell retail products ranging from hand-dipped chocolates to terry-cloth bathrobes. A ski resort can cross-sell ski lessons and dinner sleigh rides.

Upselling, also part of effective revenue management, involves training sales and reservations employees to continuously offer a higher-priced product, rather than settling for the lowest price. One proponent of upselling believes that any hotel can increase its catering revenue by 15 percent through upselling.[9]

Hundreds of upselling opportunities exist. They must be recognized and the programs are implemented to ensure their success. The common practice of offering after-dinner coffee can be turned into an upselling opportunity by offering high-image upgraded presentations of coffee and tea rather than the standard pot of coffee. Gourmet coffee sales are expected to reach or exceed 30 percent of U.S. coffee sales.[10]

Price changes are easy to make and are often seen as a quick fix to a complex problem. Although it is easy to increase or decrease prices, it is hard to change a perception that your price is incorrect.

In this section we look at how the price–demand relationship varies for different types of markets and how buyer perceptions of price affect pricing decisions. We also discuss methods for measuring the price–demand relationship.

Consumer Perceptions of Price and Value

In the end, it is the consumer who decides whether a product's price is right. When setting prices, management must consider how consumers perceive price and the ways that these perceptions affect consumers' buying decisions. Like other marketing decisions, pricing decisions must be buyer oriented.

"We can't see the value of our product," explains Carlos Talosa, senior vice president of operations at Embassy Suites. "We can only set price. The market value is set by our customers and our ability to sell to it." According to Talosa, "Even in recessionary times, consumers aren't necessarily buying the cheapest options, but they are demanding value for their dollars and rightly so. If you aren't value-selling, then you are giving away precious assets."[11]

Pricing requires more than technical expertise. It requires creative judgments and awareness of buyers' motivations. Effective pricing opens doors. It requires a creative awareness of the target market, why they buy, and how they make their buying decisions. Recognition that buyers differ in these dimensions is as important for pricing as it is for effective promotion, distribution, or product policy.

Marketers must try to look at the consumer's reasons for choosing a product and set price according to consumer perceptions of its value. Because consumers vary in the values that they assign to products, marketers often vary their pricing strategies for different segments. They offer different sets of product features at different prices. For example, a quarter-pound hamburger might cost $4 at McDonald's, $9 at a sit-down service restaurant such as Chili's, and $15 in an exclusive city club.

Buyer-oriented pricing means that the marketer cannot design a marketing program and then set the price. Good pricing begins with analyzing consumer needs and price perceptions. Managers must consider other marketing mix variables before setting price. Most hotel and restaurant concepts are designed by identifying a need in the marketplace. The product concept usually contains a price range that the market is willing to pay. Limited-service hotels identified a market that did not value many amenities found in a full-service motel, the commercial traveler staying for one night. These guests did not use cocktail lounges, hotel restaurants, and banquet and meeting facilities. By eliminating these features, owners of limited-service hotels saved money in both construction and operating costs. They passed these savings along to the customer as lower prices, offering the same sleeping room at a lower price than that of midscale hotels.

Consumers tend to look at the final price and then decide whether they received a good value. For example, two people dining in a restaurant receive their bill and see that it is $80. The diners then decide whether they were satisfied during the post-purchase evaluation. Rather than going over each item on the menu individually and judging its value, they judge the entire dining experience against the cost of that experience. If a restaurant offers a good value on food but a poor value on wine—charging $9 a glass for house wine, for instance—a couple who consume six glasses of wine may feel the check total is too high when $54 for wine is added to the bill.

Melvyn Greene, a hotel marketing consultant, once interviewed guests immediately after they had paid their bills and were leaving the hotel. Only about a fifth could remember the room rate they had just paid. They could, however, state whether they had received good value. Most of the guests had stayed for more than one day, used the Internet, and dined in the hotel's F&B outlets. The room rate was only one part of the charges on their total bill. They tended to accept the charges and sign their charge card.[12] The guests based their perception of value on the total dollar amount of the bill, the products they had received, and their satisfaction with those products.

Different market segments evaluate products differently. Managers must provide their target markets with product attributes that the target market will value and eliminate those features that do not create value. Then they have to price the product so it will be perceived to be a good value by the desired target market. For some markets, this means modest accommodations at a low price; for other markets, this means excellent service at a high price. Perceived value is a function of brand image, product attributes, and price.

Analyzing the Price–Demand Relationship

Each price a company can charge leads to a different level of demand. The demand curve illustrates the relationship between price charged and the resulting demand. It shows the number of units the market will buy in a given period at different prices that might be charged. In the normal case, demand and price are inversely related; that is, the higher the price, the lower the demand (Figure 11–2). Thus, the company would sell less if it raised its price from P_1 to P_2. Consumers with limited budgets usually buy less of something if the price is too high.
Most demand curves slope downward in either a straight or a curved line. But for prestige goods, the demand curve sometimes slopes upward. For example, a luxury hotel may find that by raising its price from P_1 to P_2, it sells more rooms rather than fewer: Consumers do not perceive it as a luxury hotel at the lower price. However, if the hotel charges too high a price, (P_3), the level of demand will be lower than at P_2.

Most company managers understand the basics of a demand curve, but few are able to measure their demand curves. The type of market determines the type of demand curve. In a monopoly, the demand curve shows the total market demand resulting from different prices. But if the company faces competition, its demand at different prices will depend on whether competitors' prices remain constant or change with the company's own prices.

Estimating demand curves requires forecasting demand at different prices. For example, a study by the Economic Intelligence Unit (EIU) estimated the demand curve for holiday travel in Europe. Its findings suggested that a 20 percent reduction in the price of visiting a holiday destination increases demand by 35 percent, whereas a 5 percent decrease results in a 15 percent increase in demand.[13] The EIU study used vacation destinations in the Mediterranean and assumed that other variables were constant.

Figure 11–2
Two hypothetical demand schedules.

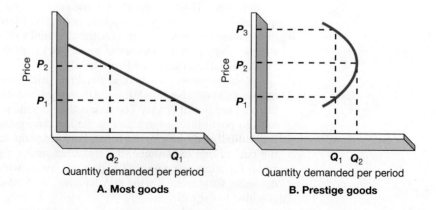

Quantity demanded per period

A. Most goods

Quantity demanded per period

B. Prestige goods

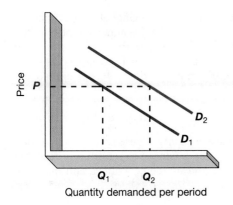

Figure 11–3
Effects of promotion and other nonprice variables on demand through shifts of the demand curve.

Researchers can develop models that assume other variables remain constant. For managers, it's not that simple. In normal business situations, other factors affect demand along with price. These factors include competition, the economy, advertising, and sales effort. If a resort cut its price and then advertised, it would be hard to tell what portion of the increased demand came from the price decrease and what portion came from the advertising. Price cannot be isolated from other factors.

Economists show the impact of nonprice factors on demand through shifts in the demand curve rather than movement along it. Suppose that the initial demand curve is D_1 (Figure 11–3), the seller is charging P and selling Q_1 units. Now suppose that the economy suddenly improves or the seller doubles in advertising budget. Higher demand is reflected through an upward shift of the demand curve from D_1 to D_2. Without changing the price, P, the demand has increased.

Price Elasticity of Demand

Marketers also need to understand the concept of price elasticity, how responsive demand will be to a change in price. Consider the two demand curves in Figure 11–4. In Figure 11–4A, a price increase from P_1 to P_2 leads to a small drop in demand from Q_1 to Q_2. In Figure 11–4B, however, the same price increase leads to a large drop in demand from Q_1 to Q_2. If demand hardly varies with a small change in price, we say that the demand is inelastic. If demand changes greatly, we say the demand is elastic.

$$\frac{\% \text{ Change in Quantity Demanded}}{\text{Price Elasticity of Demand}} = \% \text{ Change in Price}$$

Suppose that demand falls by 10 percent when a seller raises its price by 2 percent. Price elasticity of demand is therefore –5 (the minus sign confirms the inverse relation between price and demand) and demand is elastic. If demand falls by 2 percent with a 2 percent increase in price, elasticity is 1. In this case the seller's total revenue stays the same: The seller sells fewer items but at a higher price that preserves the same total revenue. If demand falls by 1 percent when the price is increased by 2 percent, elasticity is 0.5 and demand is inelastic. The less elastic the demand, the more it pays for the seller to raise price.

What determines the price elasticity of demand? Buyers are less price-sensitive when the product is unique or when it is high in quality, prestige, or exclusiveness. Chains try to differentiate their brand to create a perception of uniqueness. Consumers are also less price-sensitive when substitute products are hard to find. After the closure of the Neil House in downtown Columbus, Ohio, Stouffer's Hotel became one of the few places in the central business district to hold a major banquet

Figure 11–4
Inelastic and elastic demand.

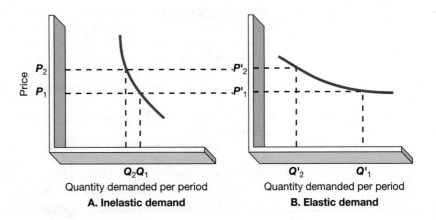

function. With supply down, it could charge more for its banquets. It maintained this advantage until new hotels were built and the market became competitive.

If demand is elastic rather than inelastic, sellers generally consider lowering their prices. A lower price produces more total revenue. This practice makes sense when the extra costs of producing and selling more products do not exceed the extra revenue.

Factors Affecting Price Sensitivity[14]

We now look at some factors that affect price sensitivity. These include the unique value effect, the substitute awareness effect, the business expenditure effect, the end-benefit effect, the total expenditure effect, the shared cost effect, and the price quality effect.

UNIQUE VALUE EFFECT In Houston the Pappas family has converted failed locations into successful restaurants, taking what had been dead restaurants and turning them into businesses with a one-hour wait on weeknights. The Pappas family did not have to use coupons or other price discounts to sell its food. It created a perception of value by giving large portions of food at a moderate price, which appealed to the upper lower class and the middle class.

Creating the perception that your offering is different from those of your competitors avoids price competition. In this way the firm lets the customer know it's providing more benefits and offering a value that is superior to that of competitors, one that will attract either a higher price or more customers at the same price.

SUBSTITUTE AWARENESS EFFECT The existence of alternatives of which buyers are unaware cannot affect their purchase behavior. Hotel restaurants often charge more for meals based on the substitute awareness effect. The guest who arrives in the evening, being unfamiliar with the city, usually has breakfast in the hotel. The guest knows that a better value probably exists elsewhere but is unfamiliar with other restaurants in the city. Although the breakfast in the hotel may cost twice as much as a meal in a nearby restaurant, the search costs, the time it would take to find the restaurant, and the travel time to it are greater than the dollar savings of the meal.

Restaurants that target the convention market or out-of-town guests use the substitute awareness effect to their advantage. These restaurants have large advertisements in the city's entertainment magazines that are distributed in the hotels. They are often not the choice of the local resident, who perceives them as overpriced, but they do attract hotel guests who are unaware of alternatives. There must be a continuous source of uninformed customers to use the substitute awareness effect as the rationale for charging premium prices.

When consumers discover products offering a better value, they switch to those products. Many hotel restaurants are empty in the evening. They are perceived as overpriced by the local market. Hotel guests have time during the day to find alternatives. These hotels often view F&B as a required amenity rather than an opportunity to compete for local business. A better philosophy is to use F&B as a means to attract customers.

BUSINESS EXPENDITURE EFFECT When someone else pays the bill, the customer is less price-sensitive. An executive fully reimbursed for all travel expenses is unlikely to be attracted to a discount rate offer for a hotel room and a restaurant offering a $9.99 dinner special. This person would probably prefer to stay in an upscale hotel, have a room-service breakfast, and eat lunch and dinner in a more expensive restaurant. When setting rates, management needs to know what the market is willing to pay. If a hotel can attract executives who have a generous travel allowance and are willing to pay high room rates, the hotel is leaving money on the table by offering discounts.

Airlines sometimes offer a second business-class ticket at a substantial discount when one is purchased at full price. Hotels offer bonus frequent-flyer miles. Both of these promotions are taking advantage of the business expenditure effect. The airline knows that the business will pick up the full-fare ticket, and the business traveler will be able to take a companion along at a discount. The hotel knows that because the traveler's company will pay for the hotel room, cutting prices by a few dollars might not bring in extra business travelers, but giving the business traveler bonus frequent-flyer miles that they can use for vacation trips will be effective. The business expenditure effect has numerous applications in the hospitality and travel industry.

Many hotels use information about corporate per diem rates to determine rate structures and identify target markets that are willing to pay the price. For example, when the Mandarin Oriental chain entered the U.S. market with a hotel in San Francisco, a survey of potential corporate clients was conducted to learn their per diem rates. From this information, target markets were identified.

END-BENEFIT EFFECT   Customers are more price-sensitive when the price of the product accounts for a large share of the total cost of the end benefit. For example, a Japanese couple paying $3,000 in airfare to travel to Australia will pay $350 a night for a luxury ocean-front hotel. The $350 is a small cost of the end benefit (their vacation). Many families driving to the Gold Coast from Sydney (a 500-mile trip) are looking for less expensive accommodations. These families are often on a limited budget and prefer a less expensive motel a few blocks from the ocean.

When the Japanese couple goes to Dreamworld (a theme entertainment park), they pay the full per-person entrance fee without hesitation. The admission fee is a small portion of the price of their vacation. However, the local family of four looking for weekend entertainment may view the charges as high. In this case, the entry fee amounts to a large portion of their entertainment expenses for the month. To attract the local customer, Dreamworld offers yearly passes for just twice the single admission charge. Dreamworld knows that if it were to raise its prices by 20 percent, it would lose more local customers than international travelers. Thus, it is important for Dreamworld to know its customer mix. If 75 percent of Dreamworld's customers are local residents, Dreamworld must be cautious about its price increases. It is common for tourist attractions to provide special rates for local residents.

Upscale hotels can use the end-benefit effect as a tool to convince potential customers to pay an additional amount for hotel rooms. A company holding a two-day sales meeting may spend $750 in airfare, pay $500 in salary per day, and spend $100 in speaker fees per participant. A smart hotel salesperson may convince the meeting planner to upgrade by pointing out that the hotel costs are a small portion of the total costs. The sales presentation might be structured like this:

> And the difference between our luxury accommodations and the hotel accommodations you're considering is only $75 per night or $150 per participant, which is a small portion of your total cost per participant. Don't you think it's worth $150 to instill pride in your employees and show them that you care enough about them to put them in one of the best hotels in the city? Surely, the attitude difference this will create in the participants will play a significant role in the total success of the conference. Let's get the contracts drawn up for your sales meeting right now while we still have the space.

When working with price, the end-benefit price is an important concept to consider. The end-benefit price identifies price-sensitive markets and provides opportunities to overcome pricing objections when the product being sold is a small cost of the end benefit. To take full advantage of this effect, remember that many purchases have nonmonetary costs. For example, a mother planning the wedding of her daughter wants everything to be perfect and to avoid embarrassing moments. High emotional involvement often makes the buyer less price-sensitive.

TOTAL EXPENDITURE EFFECT   The more someone spends on a product, the more sensitive he or she is to the product's price. For example, limited-service chains such as Hampton Inns, Red Roof Inns, and La Quinta have made a successful effort to appeal to salespersons. The travel expenses of a salesperson can be significant, especially for those who average two to three days a week away from home. A salesperson who saves just $20 a night can realize annual savings of more than $2,000. This savings adds to the profit of salespeople on straight commission. Companies that pay the expenses of their salespeople can save $2,000 times the number of salespeople that they employ. Thus, a company with twelve salespeople can save $24,000.

The total expenditure effect is useful in selling lower-price products or products that offer cost savings to volume users. The hotel concepts mentioned earlier provide salespeople with the benefits that they seek in a hotel: clean, comfortable rooms; security; free telephone calls; and a coffee shop nearby.

The total expenditure effect is a dominant decision-making force for thousands of travelers who are provided with a set figure per trip. Many truckers are given a predetermined amount of cash, such as $500 for a trip. Expenditures over that level are not reimbursed. Not all motels desire the business of truckers, but those who do are highly cognizant of the fixed expenditures of their guests. They realize that ample parking for a sixteen- or eighteen-wheeler, a clean room with two beds, and a reasonable price will attract business.

Hotels that cater to upscale travelers frequently feature one king-size bed in a room because few people on unlimited or high-expense accounts wish to share a room. Quite the opposite is true of truckers or pipeline construction teams with fixed-expenditure travel budgets. A $40 room shared by two extends a fixed budget.

Aspen Skiing Company is an example of a company that takes the total expenditure effect into account when it makes its pricing decision. It knows that most of its customers are from out of state. It knows these customers want well-maintained facilities and are willing to pay good money for them. Only 20 percent of their budget on a ski trip goes toward lift tickets.

e **11.1** Walt Disney World Resort, disneyworld. disney.go.com: Go to special offers and put in a Florida zip code, 33825, and see the special offers it gives to residents of Florida.

PRICE QUALITY EFFECT Consumers tend to equate price with quality, especially when they lack any prior experience with the product. For example, a friend may recommend that you stay at the Grand Hotel on your trip to Houston. If you call to make reservations and the reservationist offers you a $69 weekend rate, you may perceive this rate as too low for the class of hotel that you want and select another. The Grand Hotel may have met all your needs, but because of the low price, you assumed it would not.

A high price can also bring prestige to a product because it limits availability. Restaurants where the average check is more than $100 per person for dinner would lose many of their present customers if they lowered their prices. In cases where price is perceived to relate to quality or where price creates prestige, a positive association between price and demand may exist with some market segments. For example, the Gosforth Park Hotel, an upscale hotel in Newcastle, England, found that occupancy increased as its rates increased.[15]

Competitors' Prices and Offers

Competitors' prices and their possible reactions to a company's own pricing moves are other external factors affecting pricing decisions. A meeting planner scheduling a meeting in Chicago will check the price and value of competitive hotels.

Once a company is aware of its competitors' prices and offers, it can use this information as a starting point for deciding its own pricing. For example, if a customer perceives that the Sheraton in Singapore is similar to the Hilton, the Sheraton must set its prices close to those of the Hilton or lose that customer. This is called a competitive set. Additionally, the Sheraton would have to charge less than more luxurious hotels and more than those that are not as good. Sheraton uses price to position its offer relative to others in its sets.

Price-Rate Compression

During periods of weak demand very few competitors escape the effect of a weak market. Those with a strong and loyal customer base are best suited to "ride out" such a market. In many cases, competitors are inclined to lower prices as a response rather than seek other strategies. Under these conditions "price compression" may occur.

Price (rate) compression occurs when the difference between room rates for three to four and five-star properties is not significant. This occurs when higher-priced hotels lower these rates to maintain occupancy and become direct competitors to lower-rated hotels. This creates margin problems for economy sector hotels which may have less ability to lower rates.

Other External Elements

When setting prices, the company must also consider other factors in the external environment. Economic factors such as inflation, boom, or recession and interest rates affect pricing decisions. For example, when gasoline prices went from $2.40 a gallon to $3.80 a gallon many families were paying $50 to $100 more a month for gasoline. This money reduced their discretionary budget, reducing the money they had to spend on restaurants. Many restaurants had to reduce their prices to maintain customer counts. Most cannot offer the same product at a lower price and survive. The restaurants create new menus with lower-cost items that can be sold at a lower price.

▪▫▪ General Pricing Approaches

The price the company charges is somewhere between one that is too low to produce a profit and one that is too high to produce sufficient demand. Product costs set a floor for the price; consumer perceptions of the product's value set the ceiling. The company must consider competitors' prices and other external and internal factors to find the best price between these two extremes.

Companies set prices by selecting a general pricing approach that includes one or more of these sets of factors. We look at the following approaches: the cost-based approach (**cost-plus pricing**, break-even analysis, and target profit pricing), the value-based approach (perceived-value pricing), and the competition-based approach (going rate).

Cost-Based Pricing

The simplest pricing method is cost-plus pricing, adding a standard markup to the cost of the product. F&B managers often use the cost-plus method to decide wine prices. For example, a bottle of wine that costs $14 may sell for $42, or three times the cost.

Cost as a percentage of selling price is another commonly used pricing technique in the restaurant industry. Some restaurant managers target a certain food cost and then price their menu items accordingly. For example, a manager wanting a 40 percent food cost prices the items 2.5 times greater than their cost. The multiplicand is found by dividing the desired food cost percentage by 100. A manager desiring a 30 percent food cost would multiply the cost by 3.33. Managers using this type of pricing should realize that a restaurant is not 100 percent efficient. To make up for spoilage, shrinkage, and mistakes, managers usually have to price three or four percentage points below their desired food cost. Thus, a manager wanting a 40 percent food cost would need to price the menu at 36 to 37 percent. The adjustment figure varies depending on the volume and efficiency of the operation. In high-volume, limited-menu operations, it is lower.

For managers using this technique, it is advisable to use prime cost, the cost of labor and food, when determining menu prices. There is often a tradeoff between labor and food costs; thus prime cost is a truer reflection of the cost of producing a menu item. For example, if a restaurant makes its own desserts, the cost of the ingredients is usually cheaper than that of buying a similar product from a bakery; however, there are no labor costs for the preparation of the purchased product. It is better to look at both labor and food costs to determine prices.

Does using standard markups to set prices make logical sense? Generally, no. Any pricing method that ignores current demand and competition is not likely to lead to the best price. Some items with high costs such as steaks may have a lower markup, whereas signature desserts or appetizers have a high markup. Most managers who use cost as a percentage of selling price to determine menu prices use this technique to develop a target price. They adjust individual prices for menu items based on factors such as what the market will bear, psychological pricing, and other techniques discussed in this chapter.

Wine was typically sold in restaurants at about three times cost. A growing trend is to reduce the markup as the price increases. For example, at three times markup the sales price for bottles of wine costing $6, $25, and $50 would be $18, $75, and $150. A more rational approach is to sell less expense bottles for three to four times markup and gradually reduce the cost multiplier on higher-priced bottles to 1.5 times cost. Using this model the price of bottles that cost $6, $25, and $50 would be $22, $55, and $85. We increase the margin on the lower-price wines so the profit per bottle increases; reducing price on the higher cost wine, we receive a higher dollar profit per bottle. This type of pricing also attracts guests who enjoy finer wines and also tend to enjoy fine dining, increasing the overall check average.[16] In the case of exceptional wines, some establishments prefer to reserve them for a special gourmet dinner involving many courses and several wines. The price per person for such a dinner can easily exceed $100 per guest. The Steamboat Inn, situated 38 miles north of Roseburg, Oregon, on the Umpqua River, has built a strong reputation with such dinners.

Markup pricing remains popular for many reasons. First, sellers are more certain about costs than about demand. Tying the price to cost simplifies pricing, and managers do not have to adjust as demand changes. Second, because many F&B operations tend to use this method, prices are similar, and price competition is minimized.

Break-Even Analysis and Target Profit Pricing

Another cost-oriented pricing approach is BE pricing, in which the firm tries to determine the price at which it will break even. Some firms use a variation of BE pricing called *target profit pricing,* which targets a certain ROI.

Target profit pricing uses the concept of a BE chart (Figure 11–5). For example, a buffet restaurant may want to make a profit of $200,000. Its BE chart shows the total cost and total revenue at different levels of sales. Suppose that fixed costs are $300,000, and variable costs are $10 per meal. Variable costs are added to fixed costs to find total costs, which rise with volume. Total revenue starts at zero and rises with each unit sold. The slope of the total revenue reflects the price. If the restaurant sells 50,000 meals at a price of $20, for example, the company's revenue is $1 million.

Figure 11–5
Break-even chart for determining target price.

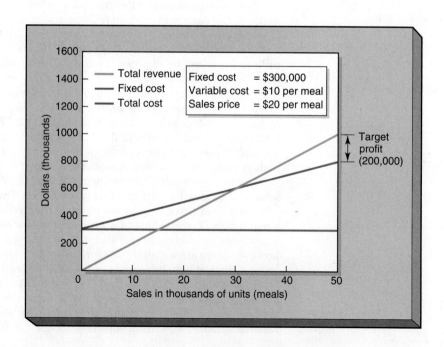

At the $20 price, the company must sell at least 30,000 units to break even; that is, at this sales level, total revenues will equal total costs of $600,000. If the company wants a target profit of $200,000, it must sell at least 50,000 meals, or 137 meals a day. This level of sales will provide $1 million of revenue to cover costs of $800,000, plus $200,000 in target profits. In contrast, if the company charges a higher price, say $25 per meal, it will need to sell only 33,334 meals, or 92 a day, to meet its target profit. The higher the price, the lower the company's BE point. The selling price less the variable cost represents the gross profit or contribution that the sale makes toward offsetting fixed costs. Here is the formula for the BE point:

$$BE = Fixed\ Costs/Contribution\ (Selling\ Price - Variable\ Cost)$$

In the previous example,

$$BE = \$300,000/\$10\ (\$20\ Selling\ Price - \$10\ Variable\ Cost) = 30,000\ meals$$

Hotels use this concept of contribution margin to set rates when demand drops. Hotels set low rates, rationalizing that at least they are covering their variable costs. This can be effective if it creates additional demand. However, some hotels try to steal business during good times by cutting rates. Figure 11–6 is a spreadsheet that shows the increase in occupancy needed to make up for a reduction in rate. This chart illustrates the difficulty of recuperating from any substantial cut in prices in an inelastic market. At 70 percent occupancy, a hotel that lowers its rate from $75 to $60 (20 percent) will need to increase its occupancy to 95.5 percent to offset the decrease in price.[17]

Much depends on the relationship between price and demand. For example, suppose a company calculates that given its current fixed and variable costs, it must charge a price of $30 for the product to earn its desired target profit. But marketing research shows that few customers will pay more than $25 for the product. In this case the company must trim its costs to lower the BE point so it can charge the lower price that consumers expect.

Figure 11–6
Price of rate-cutting.
Source: From *The Horwath Accountant,* 47(7): 8.

The price of rate-cutting

| Present occupancy | Reduction in present rate | | | | |
	5%	10%	15%	20%	25%
	Occupancy required to make up for reduction				
76%	81.4%	87.7%	95.0%	103.6%	114.0%
74	79.3	85.4	92.5	100.9	111.0
72	77.1	83.1	90.0	98.2	108.0
70	75.0	80.8	87.5	95.5	105.0
68	72.9	78.5	85.0	92.7	102.0
66	70.7	76.2	82.5	90.0	99.0
64	68.6	73.8	80.0	87.3	96.0
62	66.4	71.5	77.5	84.5	93.0
60	64.3	69.2	75.0	81.8	90.0
58	62.1	66.9	72.5	79.1	87.0
56	60.0	64.6	70.0	76.4	84.0
54	57.9	62.3	67.5	73.6	81.0
52	55.7	60.0	65.0	70.9	78.0
50	53.6	57.7	62.5	68.2	75.0

(Based on cost of operating additional occupied rooms equal to 25% of present rate)

Value-Based Pricing

An increasing number of companies are basing their prices on the products' perceived value. **Value-based pricing** uses the buyers' perceptions of value, not the seller's cost, as the key to pricing. Value-based pricing means that the marketer cannot design a product and marketing program and then set the price. Price is considered along with other marketing mix variables before the marketing program is set. The company uses the nonprice variables in the marketing mix to build perceived value in the buyers' minds, setting price to match the perceived value.

Consider the various prices different restaurants charge for the same items. A consumer who wants a cup of coffee and a slice of apple pie may pay $5 at a family restaurant, $6 at a hotel coffee shop, $10 for hotel room service, and $15 at an elegant restaurant. Each succeeding restaurant can charge more because of the value added by each type of service.

Any company using perceived-value pricing must learn the value in the buyers' minds for different competitive offers. Sometimes researchers ask consumers how much they would pay for each benefit added to the offer. One method of identifying how much customers are willing to pay involves using a technique called *tradeoff analysis*. Researchers ask buyers how much they would pay for a hotel room with and without certain amenities. This information provides an idea of which features add more value than the cost. If the seller charges more than the buyers' perceived value, its sales will suffer. Many companies overprice their products, resulting in poor sales. Other companies underprice. Underpriced products sell very well, but they produce less revenue than they would if the company raised its price to the perceived-value level.

Jack Welch, the former CEO of General Electric, stated, "The best way to hold your customers is to constantly figure out how to give them more for less."[18] More and more marketers have adopted value pricing strategies. They strive to offer just the right combination of quality and good service at a fair price. This can result in redesigning existing brands to provide more quality or offer the same amount of quality for a lower price. For example, Holiday Inn was developed for customers who just wanted a room without the restaurant facilities. They are able to offer express rooms at a lower price, creating value for this market.

Understanding the value a segment places on a product can help marketers allocate their supply among the different segments. A study of meeting planners provided evidence that meeting planners perceived a greater value in paying $200 for a room than $175. Apparently, planners, like many guests, associate quality with higher price.[19]

The price of a hotel room may vary according to the type of customer. The hotel may have a rate for individual business guests, a group rate for groups of ten or more, and a convention rate for associations that want to hold large functions at the hotel. If a hotel has the objective of maintaining 60 percent occupancy at an average rate of $180, it needs to determine its mix of customers and the average rate per segment. For example, it might develop the following mix to achieve a $180 rate:

	Percentage of Business	Average Rate ($)
Business	30	200
Corporate group	40	180
Association	30	160

To achieve its target rate of $180, the hotel would have to sell above the average rate in peak times to compensate for discounted prices during off-peak times. It is important to develop target rates and keep on track toward meeting these goals. If the hotel offers a group one hundred rooms for three nights at a rate of $150, it will need to make up $4,500 [(100 rooms × 3 nights × $90 target rate) − (300 × $75 actual rate)] in revenue. It must sell to other groups above the $90 target rate, sell more business rooms at the $100 rate, or increase the targeted occupancy rate and sell additional rooms.[20]

A successful guest price mix depends on careful study of the behavior profiles of major guest segments. For most hospitality companies, this begins with a separation of guests into leisure and business segments. Subsegmentation of each category may occur, providing greater information about these major guest categories. Undoubtedly, the most important distinguishing profile characteristics of these two major segments are their relative degree of price elasticity. In general, business travelers exhibit inelastic price behavior and leisure travelers an elastic price response.

Competition-Based Pricing

A strategy of **going-rate pricing** is the establishment of price based largely on those of competitors, with less attention paid to costs or demand. The firm might charge the same, more, or less than its major competitors. Some firms may charge a bit more or less, but they hold the amount of difference constant. For example, a limited-service hotel chain may charge $10 more than Motel 6 in markets where they compete. This form of pricing is quite popular. When elasticity is hard to measure, firms feel that the going price represents the collective wisdom of the industry concerning the price that will yield a fair return. They also feel that holding to the going price will avoid harmful price wars.

■■■ Pricing Strategies

New-Product Pricing Strategies

Pricing strategies usually change as a product passes through its life cycle. The introductory stage is especially challenging. Several options exist for pricing new products: prestige pricing, market-skimming pricing, and market-penetration pricing.

Prestige Pricing

Hotels or restaurants seeking to position themselves as luxurious and elegant enter the market with a high price to support this position. Nightclubs may charge a cover charge to attract a certain type of clientele and create an image of exclusiveness. In each of these cases, lowering the price would reposition the business, resulting in a failure to attract the target market.

Market-Skimming Pricing

Price skimming is setting a high price when the market is price-insensitive. Price skimming can make sense when lowering the price will create less revenue. For example, the owner of the only motel in a small town in South Dakota during pheasant hunting season can set high prices if there is more demand than rooms. Price skimming can be an effective short-term policy. However, one danger is that competition will notice the high prices that consumers are willing to pay and enter the market, creating more supply and eventually reducing prices. The hospitality industry is particularly affected by this because market entry by competitors is relatively easy.

Market-Penetration Pricing

Rather than setting a high initial price to skim off small but profitable market segments, other companies set a low initial price to penetrate the market quickly and deeply, attracting many buyers and winning a large market share. Theodore Zinck's, a cocktail lounge in downtown Dallas, opened with prices about 20 percent lower

The Hotel Vier Jahreszeiten Kempinski, built in 1858, is situated on Maximilianstrasse, regarded as Munich's most desirable street. Kempiniski operates a chain of luxury hotels. It has a prestigious name and is often the price leader in the markets in which it operates. Courtesy of Dorota and Mariusz Jarymowicz © Dorling Kindersley.

than the competition. Management had negotiated a low lease, giving Zinck's a competitive advantage. Competitors could not match Zinck's lower prices because of the higher overhead. The policy allowed Zinck's to attract many customers quickly.

Several conditions favor setting a low price: The market must be highly price-sensitive so that a low price produces more market growth, there should be economics that reduce costs as sales volume increases, and the low price must help keep out competition.

Existing-Product Pricing Strategies

The strategies just described are used primarily when introducing a new product. However, they can also be useful with existing products. The following strategies are ones that can be used with existing products.

Product-Bundle Pricing

Sellers who use product-bundle pricing combine several of their products and offer the bundle at a reduced price. For example, hotels sell specially priced weekend packages that include room, meals, and entertainment or offer commercial rates that include breakfast and a newspaper. Product bundling can promote the sales of products that consumers might not otherwise buy, but the combined price must be low enough to convince them to buy the bundle. The items added to the core service must hold more value to the customer than they cost to provide.

Product-bundle pricing is a strategy that has been well developed by cruise lines, tour wholesalers, and casinos. Cruise lines typically offer fly-cruise or fly-drive cruise packages in which the services of an auto rental company, airline, cruise line, and hotel are combined at a price well under the cost of purchasing each separately. The Internet has increased the use of product bundling by allowing companies to sell related products over their sites, such as airlines selling hotel rooms, rental cars, and vacation packages on their Web sites. Intermediaries (Orbitz.com and Expedia.com); tour operators (Carlsontravel.com); destinations (Lasvegas.com); travel-related search engines (Kayak.com); travel agency consortia (Vacation.com) and global distribution systems (Amadeus and Sabre) all sell packages. With the Internet as the distribution system, product bundles are expected to continue to grow in popularity.[21]

Price bundling has two major benefits to hospitality and travel organizations. First, customers have different maximum prices or reservation prices they will pay for a product. Thus, by packaging products we can transfer the surplus reservation price on one component to another component of the package. For example, customer "A" may be willing to pay $280 for two nights in a hotel room near Disneyland and $350 for two 3-day passes to Disneyland. Customer "B" is willing to pay $325 for two nights in a hotel room and $300 for two 3-day passes. If a hotel that wants to get $160 for a night for its rooms is able to get discounted three-day passes to Disneyland and offer a package that includes a room for two for two nights and two 3-day passes for $620, both customers will take advantage of the package. Even though the room price of $20 a night is above what the one customer wanted to pay, when the room and tickets are packaged together, the components are below the reservation price. In this case the three-day pass was $50 below customer A's reservation price for the pass and the hotel price was $20 a night above what customer A wanted to pay. When they were packed together, the passes and the room were $10 less than customer A's reservation price for the package. Customers have different reservation prices; by bundling we can transfer surpluses from one component to another to expand the market.

A second benefit of price bundling is that the price of the core product can be hidden to avoid price wars or the perception of having a low-quality product. For example, a Las Vegas hotel that normally has an average rate above $100 may sell rooms to airlines for $45 to help fill the hotel. The airline bundles the hotel with a round-trip air ticket. The airline's package includes two nights in the hotel and airfare from Los Angeles for $299. This creates a much better perception for the hotel than if it ran an advertisement pushing $45 room rates. The $45 rates give a message to some that the hotel is desperate for business, to others who do not know the hotel it will give a perception of a hotel of the $45 quality level, and guests who had paid $109 for a room may ask for a refund. By selling the rooms to an airline and creating a bundled product, the hotel avoided the image problems that can come with low rates. Hotels can also create their own bundles. For example, the Royal Palms Hotel and Spa in Phoenix offers a "Royal Romance Package." The package includes champagne, chocolate-covered strawberries, a rose-petal turndown, dinner for two, and a room for $456. The rack rate is $439 for a room for the same date. Rather than cut rates to try to attract guests, the exclusive resort bundled a number of products that have value to a couple wanting to get away.[22]

Price-Adjustment Strategies

Companies usually adjust their basic prices to account for various customer differences and changing situations. We look at the following adjustment strategies: discount pricing and allowances, and discriminatory pricing.

VOLUME DISCOUNTS   Most hotels have special rates to attract customers who are likely to purchase a large quantity of hotel rooms, either for a single period or throughout the year. Hotels usually offer special prices or provide free goods for association and corporate meeting planners. As an example, suppose that a convention held by an industry association is attended by people who pay their own room charges. The association may prefer to receive a free room night for every twenty room nights booked, rather than a lower room rate. It can use the free nights for its staff and invited speakers, reducing the association's total costs. Hotels offer corporate rates to companies that will guarantee their use of the hotel for an agreed-upon number of room nights per year.

DISCOUNTS BASED ON TIME OF PURCHASE   Seasonal discounts allow the hotel to keep demand steady during the year. Hotels, motels, and airlines offer seasonal discounts during selling periods that are traditionally slower. Airlines often offer off-peak prices, based on the time of day or the day of the week that the passenger flies. International flights adjust the price according to seasonal demand. Restaurants offer early-bird specials to attract customers before their normal rush. Unfortunately, the various discount rates offered by a company sometimes clash to negate the desired positive effects. For example, restaurants that offer seniors 10 percent discounts have more difficulty offering early-bird specials. Seniors often feel no reason to accept the early-bird special because they will qualify for a discount at peak hours.

DISCRIMINATORY PRICING   The term *discriminatory pricing* often invokes mental images of discrimination on the basis of race, religion, gender, or age. Sex-based price discrimination has historically served as a promotional tactic in nightclubs and bars that offer a ladies night or ladies-only coupon that heavily discounts prices of admission or drinks. In California, a suit was filed against an establishment that offered ladies-only discounts. The court ruled against the owner of the establishment under the Civil Rights Act.[23] **Discriminatory pricing** refers to segmentation of the market and pricing differences based on price elasticity characteristics of these segments. Price discrimination as used in this chapter is legal and viewed by many as highly beneficial to the consumer.

Companies often adjust basic prices to allow for differences in customers, products, and locations. In discriminatory pricing, the company sells a product or service at two or more prices, although the difference in price is not based on differences in cost.

Suppose, for example, that a steak dinner has a menu price of $20, and the demand is one hundred dinners at this price. If the restaurant lowers the price to $14, demand increases to 200 dinners. If the variable costs for preparing and serving the dinner are $8, the gross profit in each case will be $1,200. However, if we assume that of the 200 persons willing to pay $14 for the steak, 100 were part of the group willing to pay $20, $600 of potential income is lost from these 100 customers.

Price discrimination works to maximize the amount that each customer pays. In the case illustrated, we would charge $20 to customers willing to pay $20. Those who are willing to pay only $14 would be charged $14. How do we do this? We can't ask the customer, "Would you like to pay $20 or would you like to pay $14?" Obviously, everyone would say $14. Instead, we give different prices to different segments, offering the highest price to those segments that are less price-sensitive. For example, our standard price is $20 for the dinner. We offer an early-bird special of $14 to diners arriving before 6 P.M. A person who works until 5 P.M. probably is unwilling to rush home and rush to the restaurant to take advantage of the discount. This customer prefers to relax at home after work and arrive at the restaurant at 8 P.M. However, retired persons who may be more price-sensitive, but less time-sensitive, would be attracted by this special. The restaurant could also choose to send a coupon in a direct-mail package to prospective customers. The price-sensitive customers keep the coupon and use it the next time they go out to eat. Other people who receive the coupon throw it away. These customers do not want to be bothered with filing the coupon and then looking for it when they want to dine out. To these customers the $6 savings is not worth the hassle of using the coupon. Price discrimination discriminates in favor of the price-sensitive customer.

The supersaver fares on airlines usually require an advance purchase and a stay-over on a Saturday night. The weekend stay eliminates most business travelers, whereas the advance purchase eliminates business trips made on short notice. Airlines know that business travelers are less price-sensitive; that is, they exhibit inelastic price behavior. Airlines offer low fares with the leisure traveler in mind. The leisure traveler uses discretionary income to pay for travel and as a result is more price-sensitive than the business traveler. A reduction in price often results in additional demand from the leisure segment.

Table 11–1 shows the prices available on a typical flight. Notice that coach seats range from $629 to $129 for a senior who has purchased tickets in advance

11.2 Westin Hotels, www.Westin.com: Look at the rates of a Westin Hotel in the city of your choice; notice how it uses price discrimination to offer rates to seniors. Also look at the variety of rates available, including prepaid rates.

TABLE 11–1

Examples of Airfare Categories for a Flight from Detroit to Los Angeles

---

First class: 32 seats; 36 fares

Examples of first-class fares:

$944, normal first-class fare

$849, normal fare with 10 percent senior-citizen discount

$629, free upgrade with full coach fare for frequent-flyer Gold member

$305 or $239, free update on 14-day advance purchase excursion fare for frequent-flyer Gold member; limited number of seats at this fare

Free, frequent-flier award ticket

Coach class: 256 seats; 22 fares

Examples of coach fares:

$629, normal fare

$566, normal fare with 10 percent senior-citizen discount

$466 or $238, one-way military fare; limited number of seats at each fare

$309, bereavement fare

$239, excursion fare with 14-day advance purchase

$189, visit USA fare, good for foreign travelers

$179, excursion fare (sale currently in effect) with seven-day advance purchase

$129, senior-citizen travel based on coupon booklet

Special fares

Convention fares, usually 5 percent off lowest excursion fare or 40 percent off normal coach fares

Group fares, specially negotiated for group travel; generally close to lowest excursion fares

Bulk fares, special deals for tour operators

Tour fares, for travelers on a tour package, such as a cruise

Corporate fares, negotiated with certain corporations; can be from 10 to 35 percent off the full coach or first-class fare

---

Source: Reprinted with permission of *The Detroit News.*

through a multiple-coupon book. The lower fare is aimed at the price-sensitive leisure traveler. Like the airlines, many hotels discriminate between the leisure and business segments. Business hotels in central business districts often suffer low occupancy on weekends. Many of these hotels have developed lower-priced weekend packages to entice the leisure traveler.

Low variable costs combined with fluctuations in demand make price discrimination a useful tool for smoothing demand and bringing additional revenue and profits to most businesses. This form of pricing uses lower prices to attract additional customers, without lowering the price for everyone.

Major sectors of the hospitality industry, such as airlines, hotels, cruise lines, and railroads, are faced with enormous fixed costs. Companies in these sectors are faced with the need to fill seats or beds. Richard Hanks, vice president of revenue management for the Marriott Corporation, believes that "our greatest opportunity cost is an empty room." Marriott and other hotel chains employ a pricing system based on discriminatory pricing to fill rooms and maximize revenue opportunities using fencing to keep price-inelastic customers from using rates designed for price-elastic segments.[24]

Fencing at Marriott is accomplished by establishing restrictions that allow customers to self-select price discriminatory rates that are best for them. Such fences include advance reservations and nonrefundable advance purchases. These policies permit price-sensitive customers to enjoy lower rates and inelastic segments to pay full fare without restrictions.

To price-discriminate successfully, the following criteria must be met:[25]

1. Different groups of consumers must have different responses to price; that is, they must value the service differently.

2. The different segments must be identifiable and a mechanism must exist to price them differently.

3. There should be no opportunity for persons in one segment who have paid a lower price to sell their purchases to other segments.

4. The segment should be large enough to make the exercise worthwhile.

5. The cost of running the price discrimination strategy should not exceed the incremental revenues obtained. This is partly a function of criterion 4.

6. The customers should not become confused by the use of different prices.

Revenue Management

One application of discriminatory pricing is revenue management. Revenue management involves upselling, cross-selling, and analysis of profit margins and sales volume for each product line. Revenue management system is used to maximize a hospitality company's yield or contribution margin. In the case of hotels, this is done by the rates that a hotel will charge and the number of rooms available for each rate based on projected occupancies for a given period. These systems help hotels achieve the maximum contribution margin based on the demand for hotel rooms. The concept behind revenue management is to manage revenue and inventory effectively by pricing differences based on the elasticity of demand for selected customer segments.

Hotel companies are placing a great deal of emphasis on revenue management because the extra revenue it generates is pure profit that drops to the bottom line. However, at a meeting of revenue managers, half of the respondents indicated that their senior management did not understand revenue management.[26] If you are going into the hospitality industry, an understanding of revenue management will give you a competitive advantage today and will be a requisite 10 years from now.

An effective revenue management system establishes fences to prohibit customers from one segment receiving prices intended for another. For example, business travelers on an expense account exhibit somewhat inelastic price behavior. Leisure travelers are commonly more price-sensitive (price-elastic). A typical fencing strategy for leisure travelers would be to require a Friday and Saturday night stay with a 30-day advance reservation. This effectively fences out business travelers, who then pay higher rates to stay during a business week with little or no advance reservations.

e **11.3** MGM Grand Hotel, http://www .mgmgrand.com: On MGM's reservation site check rates and then go to the calendar (the option will be at the top right of the page). Notice how the rates may vary from $80 to $350 a night for the same room. The hotel is using revenue management to fill periods of low demand with low rates.

Marketing Highlight

Segmented Pricing: The Right Product to the Right Customer at the Right Time for the Right Price

11–1 Many companies would love to raise prices across the board—but fear losing business. When an opera company located in the nation's capital was considering increasing ticket prices after a difficult season, Ticket Services Manager Jimmy Legarreta decided there had to be a better way. He found one after carefully reviewing opera economics. Legarreta knew—and his computer system confirmed—that the company routinely turned away people for Friday and Saturday night performances, particularly for prime seats. Meanwhile, midweek tickets went begging.

Legarreta also knew that not all seats were equal, even in the sought-after orchestra section. So the ticket manager and his staff sat in every one of the opera house's 2,200 seats and gave each a value according to the view and the acoustics. With his revenue goal in mind, Legarreta played with ticket prices until he arrived at nine levels, up from five. In the end, the opera raised prices for its most coveted seats by as much as 50 percent but also dropped the prices by some 600 seats. The gamble paid off in a 9 percent revenue increase during the next season.

Legarreta didn't have a name for it, but he was practicing "segmented pricing," an approach that also has many other labels. Airlines, hotels, and restaurants call it revenue management and practice it religiously. Robert Cross, a longtime consultant to the airlines, argues that all companies should apply revenue management concepts, which emphasize an aggressive micromarket approach to maximizing sales. "Revenue management," Cross writes, "assures that companies will sell the right product to the right consumer at the right time for the right price."

Segmented pricing and yield management aren't really new ideas. For instance, Marriott Corporation used seat-of-the-pants yield-management approaches long before it installed its current sophisticated system. Back when J. W. "Bill" Marriott was a young man working at the family's first hotel, the Twin Bridges in Washington, D.C., he sold rooms from a drive-up window. As Bill tells it, the hotel charged a flat rate for a single occupant, with an extra charge for each additional person staying in the room. When room availability got tight on some nights, Bill would lean out the drive-up window and assess the cars waiting in line. If some of the cars were filled with passengers, Bill would turn away vehicles with just a single passenger to sell his last rooms to those farther back in line who would be paying for multiple occupants. He might have accomplished the same result by charging a higher rate at peak times, regardless of the number of room occupants.

Cross's underlying premise: No two customers value a product or service exactly the same way. Furthermore, the perceived value of a product results from many variables that change over time. Some of Cross's clients use sophisticated yield-management simulation models and high-powered computer systems to predict sales at different price levels, but the technique doesn't have to be rocket science. If you understand your customers' motivation for buying and you keep careful sales records, it's possible to adjust prices to remedy supply-and-demand imbalances. Legarreta, for example, ended his midweek slump by

The Galveston Opera House. Courtesy of Richard Cummins/ CORBIS.

making opera affordable for more people, yet he accurately predicted that the in-crowd would pay higher prices for the best weekend seats.

Probably the simplest form of segmented pricing is off-peak pricing, common in the entertainment and travel industries. Marc Epstein, owner of the Milk Street Cafe in Boston, discovered that technique more than 10 years ago when he noticed he had lines out the door at noon but a near-empty restaurant around his 3 P.M. closing time. After some experimentation, Epstein settled on a 20 percent discount for the hours just before noon and after 2 P.M.—and he's pleased with the results. "If we didn't offer this, our overall revenue would be less," he argues. Epstein did not feel he could simultaneously raise prices during the lunch rush; instead, he has expanded the corporate-catering side of his business, where he can charge more per sandwich because "the perceived value of a catered lunch is higher."

Many other companies could conceivably segment their prices to increase revenues and profits. Cross cites examples ranging from a one-chair barbershop to an accounting firm to a health center. But there are risks. When you establish a range of prices, customers who pay the higher ones may feel cheated. "It can't be a secret that you're charging different prices for the same service," Cross advises. "Customers must know, so they can choose when to use a service."

The moral of the story? You can never know too much about your customers and the different values they assign to your product or service. With that customer knowledge comes the power to make the best pricing decisions.

Sources: Portions adapted with permission from Susan Greco, "Are Your Prices Right?" *INC.* (January 1997): 88–89. Copyright 1997 by Goldhirsh Group, Inc., 38 Commercial Wharf, Boston, MA 02110. Other information from Robert G. Cross, *Revenue Management: Hard Core Tactics for Market Domination* (New York: Broadway Books, 1998); and William J. Quain, Michael Sansbury, and Dennis Quinn, "Revenue Enhancement, Part 3: Picking Low-Hanging Fruit—A Simple Approach to Yield Management," *Cornell Hotel and Restaurant Administration Quarterly* (April 1999): 76–83. Also see Plumrao Desiraju and Steven M. Shugan, "Strategic Service Pricing and Yield Management," *Journal of Marketing* (January 1999): 44–56.

The earlier discussion of a restaurant offering an "early-bird" steak special before 6 P.M. is another example of fencing.

Revenue management involves the development and use of different rate classes based on the projected demand for the service. These rates are used to maximize yield. This is the formula for yield:

$$\frac{\text{room} - \text{nights sold}}{\text{room} - \text{nights available}} \times \frac{\text{actual average room rate}}{\text{room rate potential}} = \text{yield}$$

A hotel with sufficient history can project occupancy based on current booking patterns. If low occupancy is projected, the hotel keeps lower rate classes open to increase occupancy. The lower rates typically use price discrimination techniques that favor the leisure traveler. Sheraton, for example, has 21-day advance supersaver rates. The idea is to create extra demand with low rates, attracting guests that the hotel would not have otherwise. If the projected occupancy is high, the lower rates will be closed, and only the higher rate classes will be accepted. Today, several computerized systems are available that automatically project occupancy levels for a given date and suggest pricing levels for each day. It is common for a yield-management system to increase revenues by at least 5 percent. Reservations for Hyatt's Regency Club concierge floors climbed 20 percent after Hyatt implemented yield management. One Hilton hotel increased its average transient rate by $7.50 with no reduction in occupancy the first month after installing a yield-management system.[27]

Two important concepts in revenue management are RevPAR and RevPASH. RevPAR is revenue per available room. It takes into consideration both occupancy and average rate, by determining the average rate per available room. A one hundred–room hotel that sold sixty rooms at an average rate of $200 would have a RevPAR of $120 (60/100 × $200). RevPASH is the revenue per available seat hour. It is tracked hourly because we do not sell a seat for a day, like we do hotel rooms. For example, it identifies peak periods and periods of less demand. It supplies data to track the effectiveness of the promotions to fill the low-demand periods. For many restaurants, increasing RevPASH can be as easy as getting the right table configurations. Seating a deuce at a four-top results in zero revenue for two seats. Thus, having two-tops that combined to seat a party of four is a nonprice method of increasing revenue. The County Inn and Suites uses RevPAR measurements to compare renovated hotels in the chain to those it views as stabilized.

An analysis of renovated rooms revealed a 5.7 percent favorable RevPAR which equated to an additional $140,000 in annual revenue for an average eighty-room hotel.[28]

This chain also uses a RevPAR index as a measurement to gauge nonperforming hotels. Terminated hotels had a RevPAR score that was far below others in the chain.

Another use of RevPAR by this chain is to compare its RevPAR improvement against that of competitive hotels. As an example, if RevPAR increased 10 percent for this chain but 13 percent for competitors, then the conclusion was that it was not performing as well as competitors. RevPASH can also provide data to help us with revenue management.[29]

Revenue management systems must be based on sound marketing. They should be developed with the long-term value of the customer in mind. One early yield-management system cut off reservations from travel agents when projected occupancy for a given date was high. This was done to eliminate travel agency commissions when the hotel could sell the rooms. This system saved money in the short term by saving travel agency commissions. However, in the long term the hotel could lose a significant portion of its travel agency business. Think of the person who wants to stay at the Regal Hotel in Orlando and fly to Orlando on Delta. The travel agent informs the client that the airline is confirmed, but no rooms are available at the Regal, so a reservation was made at the Gator Hotel. The client calls the Regal only to find that rooms are available. The client now thinks the travel agent is pushing the Gator Hotel and gets upset with the travel agent. The travel agent becomes upset with the Regal and refuses to book future business with them. The Regal gains short-run extra revenue but loses the travel agent's business in the long term. Revenue management programs should focus on long-term profitability, not just the maximization of one day's revenue.

With some revenue management systems, customers staying a longer period can be charged more than those staying only a few nights. Normally, one might expect a concession for longer stays. Sometimes the longer stay may take the guest into a period of high occupancy. These yield-management systems average the occupancy over the guest's stay. For example, based on the occupancy levels in the following table, a guest checking in May 8 and checking out May 10 would be quoted a $65 rate as the lowest available rate. A guest checking in May 8 and checking out May 12 would be quoted $85 as the lowest available rate because the hotel can sell more rooms for May 10 and 11 at a minimum of $105 a night. Under this system the staff must be well trained to explain rate differences to the guest.

	Projected Occupancy (%)
May 8	60
May 9	60
May 10	85
May 11	90

Revenue management systems can be useful in managing the number of rooms available for transient demand. Most hotels have a base of transient demand composed of individual guests who pay a high rate. Some of these transient guests are businesspersons who may stay in the hotel several times during the year. Groups make their reservations well in advance of the transients. When group business displaces transient business, the average rate drops, and some displaced transient guest may never return, deciding to stay at an alternative hotel. Revenue management systems help eliminate the problem of displaced transient guests by projecting the number of transient rooms that will be used on any given date.

If used properly, revenue management systems can provide extra revenue. A good revenue management system benefits both the hospitality company and the guest. It opens low-rated rooms for the leisure traveler during times of low occupancy and saves rooms during periods of peak demand for the business traveler willing to pay full rates. The company gains because revenue management focuses on maximizing revenue, not cutting costs.

A revenue management system requires the availability of good data. This has forced many hospitality companies to go back to the basics and develop sound information-retrieval systems for internal data, such as booking patterns, and to develop and use better forecasting methods. The end result is that without even using yield management, the company is in a far better position to make intelligent management decisions.

An effective revenue management system depends on several variables.[30] These are the ability to segment markets, perishable inventory, ability to sell product in advance, fluctuating demand, low-marginal sales costs, high-marginal production costs (can easily add another room), booking pattern data, information on demand pattern by market segment, an overbooking policy, knowledge of effect of price changes, a good information system for internal and external data, and ability to fence customer segments.

Use of revenue management within the hospitality industry is expanding to new sectors. The Dalmahoy Golf and Country Club Resort near Edinburgh, Scotland, implemented a yield-management program for its golf course operation. This tied the costs of an annual membership to the time and day that the purchaser used the golf course.[31]

Hotel guests commonly realize that different prices are charged for similar rooms for a specific night. To offset customer perceptions of this being unfair, one study showed that if customers were given information about how the system works, the feelings of unfair prices were reduced. Specifically, when customers were told that rates vary according to day of the week, length of stay, and how far in advance the reservation was made, perceptions of fairness improved.[32]

REVENUE MANAGEMENT SOFTWARE   While revenue management is possible through a manual system, the use of specially developed software offers substantial benefits. According to Isabelle Keiflin, Group Director of Revenue for Langham Hospitality

Group, it is vital today to effectively and quickly manage all distribution channels in order to drive incremental businesses. Isabelle went on to say that online business and social media have created a need for hoteliers to better analyze business in detail. She said, "The opportunity for incremental revenue lies in the detail."[33]

Distribution Channels

There are a variety of distribution channels that can be sued to create demand. If used effectively they can result in a higher RevPAR. In Chapter 12 we will discuss distribution channels. Successful revenue managers have mastered the science of determining the right mix of channel members.

DEFLAGGING   An example of a strategic decision that directly affects pricing and cost control is deflagging.

Private hotel groups throughout the world commonly have a variety of flag properties in their portfolios. Several of these groups are reconsidering this strategy and are building their own flag ship with the properties they own. Reasons for this include the following:

> Eliminate licensing cost—Typically franchisors charge 8 to 10 percent of revenue.

> Inflexibility of franchisors—Hotel owners sometimes complain that franchisors have outdated rules that prohibit changes that the owners feel are essential.

> Evolving brand standards—Market conditions change. A market that may have been value/price-sensitive before may now better support upscale hotels. Instead of changing flags the hotel owners may prefer to develop their own—an example is Apple Core Hotels that dropped Red Roof, Super Eight, and Wyndham Worldwide brands. Vijay Dandapani, president and COO, said that RevPAR increased 20 percent after deflagging.

> Ceiling for rates with flag properties—A brand such as Super 8 may be excellent for a value-conscious market but if that market changes temporarily (e.g., during peak demand periods) or permanently, hotels bearing that flag may not be able to dramatically increase prices due to preconceived guest concepts of the brand.[34]

> Managing customer segments—This basic responsibility of marketing/sales also has a direct bearing on price.

> National/international accounts—National accounts such as large companies, government agencies, and others have traditionally been high-volume/high-margin customers loyal to a particular brand and enticed to return through loyalty programs. During the recession beginning in 2008, many national accounts negotiated serious rate reductions with hotels. "So instead of being our highest margin customers, they end up being our lowest margin customers while consuming the greatest amount of our services," said Bruce White, chairman and CEO of White Lodging Services Corp.[35]

Bar Pricing

Best available rate (BAR) pricing is a relatively new pricing technique used for guests who stay several nights. Instead of charging a single rate for a multiple-night stay, such as $100 per night, BAR pricing charges different rates for each night. Thus, some nights might be priced below $100 and others above the rate. These daily rates are determined through yield management.

BAR pricing originated with the Internet intermediaries Hotels.com, Expedia, Priceline, and Orbitz. The practice then spread to hotel companies. To assure customers that they are receiving the BARs for any date, price guarantees are often given. These vary in terms between firms offering them.[36] BAR is sometimes referred to as nonblended pricing.

Nonuse of Revenue Management

Many members of the hospitality industry have chosen not to use a revenue management system. Observers of long waiting lines at restaurants often comment that a pricing system such as the early-bird steak example is needed. However, researchers on this subject concluded, "Waiting is part of life and particularly part of an experience with a restaurant. Having long waits for tables in a restaurant does not necessarily mean there is a problem. Demand in restaurants like Cheesecake Factory, Houston's, and Outback Steakhouse far exceeds supply on most days."[37]

Instead of using price discrimination and fencing, Outback Steakhouse sets a menu price but offers a streamline takeaway service to assist those who don't wish to wait for table service (uncaptured demand).

Psychological Pricing

Psychological pricing considers the psychology of prices, not simply the economics. Earlier in this chapter, we discussed the relationship between price and quality. Prestige can be created by selling products and services at a high price.

Another aspect of psychological pricing is reference prices; these are prices that buyers carry in their minds and refer to when they look at a given product. A buyer's reference price might be formed by noting current prices, remembering past prices, or assessing the buying situation. Popular products often have reference prices. For a given type of restaurant, most consumers have a preconceived idea about the price or price range of certain items, such as a cup of coffee, a strip steak, or a hamburger. For example, a pizza chain may advertise its medium pizza for a price it knows is $2 less than the competition to establish a reference price for pizza eaters. But its price for beverages and extra items will be the same as that of the competition. The reference item creates the perception of value; consequently, little would be gained by cutting the price of the other items.

Customers tend to simplify price information by ignoring end figures. For instance, there is greater perceived distance between $0.69 and $0.71 than there is between $0.67 and $0.69. Consumers also tend to round figures. One restaurant study found that consumers round prices ranging from $0.86 to $1.39 to a dollar, from $1.40 to $1.79 to a dollar and a half, and from $1.80 to $2.49 to two dollars. If this is the case, there may be little change in demand caused by a price increase of $0.30 from $1.45 to $1.75, but there may be a significant decrease in demand between $1.75 and $2.06.[38]

The length of the field is another consideration. The jump from $0.99 to $1.00 or the jump from $9.99 to $10.00 can be perceived as a significant increase, although it is only $0.01. Taco Bell's value prices were all under $1, and therefore only two digits. Some psychologists argue that each digit has symbolic and visual qualities that should be considered in pricing. For example, because the number 8 is round, it creates a soothing effect, whereas 7 is angular, creating a jarring effect.

Promotional Pricing

When companies use promotional pricing, they temporarily price their products below list price and sometimes even below cost. Promotional pricing takes several forms. Fast-food restaurants price a few products as loss leaders to attract customers to the store in the hope that they will buy other items at normal markups. Donut shops may offer coffee for 50 cents, knowing a customer will usually buy at least one donut. Jack-in-the-Box offers two tacos for a dollar because it often sells french fries and a soft drink with the order. During slow periods, hotels may offer special promotional rates to increase business. Rather than just lower prices, well-managed hotels create special events: a Valentine's weekend special including a room, champagne upon arrival, a dinner for two and a breakfast in the room; or a theater package including a room, tickets to a play, dinner for two, and breakfast for two. These promotions give the guest a reason to come; the bundle of products adds value for the customer. The promotion creates a positive image, whereas straight price discounting can create a negative image.

The gaming industry is particularly aware of the importance of product bundling and promotional pricing. A casino executive stated, "We are in the adult entertainment business; our main product offering is gambling and there are many components that support it, such as hotels, entertainment facilities, and restaurants." Casino managers view hotel rooms as a means to entice and enable customers to gamble. Casinos must ensure that rooms are readily available for the most profitable gaming customers.[39] Hotel pricing reflects the fact that the company's main product offering is gaming, and a hotel room is only a supporting product for gaming.

Value Pricing

The term *value pricing* is confusing. It could be argued that anytime a product/service is purchased, at any price, the buyer must have perceived value in that product. Value pricing has become synonymous with the term *everyday low prices* (*EDLP*). It has been used as a marketing strategy by some members of the hospitality industry, such as Taco Bell and Southwest Airlines.

"Value pricing can be extremely risky. Properly conceived and executed, it can earn positive results." It can also be disastrous.[40] In its simplest form, value pricing means offering a price below competitors permanently, which differs from promotional pricing, in which price may be temporarily lowered during a special promotion.

Value pricing is risky if a company does not have the ability to cut costs significantly. It is usually most appropriate for companies able to increase long-run market share through low prices (Taco Bell) or niche players with a lower-cost operating basis who use price to differentiate their product (Southwest Airlines). A study of value pricing in retail stores showed that "retailers can be profitable charging low prices but only when they have low costs."[41]

Prior to initiating a strategy of value pricing, managers must ask themselves these questions:

* What will happen if this starts a price war?

* Can our company significantly lower costs or increase productivity to compensate for lower prices?

* What is the price elasticity of our products?

* Can we gain significant market share or ensure a strong market niche position with this strategy?

* Can we reverse this strategy if it doesn't work, or will we create price levels that can't be sustained and can't easily be raised?

■▦▦ Price Changes

Initiating Price Changes

After developing their price structures and strategies, companies may face occasions when they want to cut or raise prices.

Initiating Price Cuts

Several situations may lead a company to cut prices. One is excess capacity. Unable to increase business through promotional efforts, product improvement, or other measures, a hotel may resort to price cutting. As the airline, hotel, rental car, and restaurant industries have learned, cutting prices in an industry loaded with excess capacity generally leads to price wars as competitors try to regain market share.

Companies may also cut prices in a drive to dominate the market or increase market share through lower costs. Either the company starts with lower costs than its competitors, or it cuts prices in the hope of gaining market share through larger volume. Price cutting to increase revenue must be carefully planned. Studies conducted across hotel sectors and in the United States and Asia have shown that in most mature markets, price cutting increases occupancy but the RevPAR decreases. Thus, the increased occupancy does not overcome the decrease in average rate. For an established hotel, the best tactic is to maintain prices slightly above the competitive rate.[42] Exceptions include hotels, such as casino hotels where high non-room expenditures, such as casino gaming or F&B, would offset the decrease in room revenue.

Initiating Price Increases

Inevitably many companies must eventually raise prices. They do this knowing that price increases may be resented by customers, dealers, and their own sales force. However, a successful price increase can greatly increase profits. For example, if the company's profit margin is 3 percent of sales, a 1 percent price increase increases profits by 33 percent if sales volume is unaffected.

A major factor in price increases is cost inflation. Increased costs squeeze profit margins and lead companies to regular rounds of price increases. Companies often raise their prices by more than the cost increase in anticipation of further inflation. Companies do not want to make long-run price agreements with customers. They fear that cost inflation will reduce profit margins. For example, hotels prefer not to quote a firm price for conventions booked three years in advance. Another factor leading to price increases is excess demand. When a company cannot supply all its customers' needs, it raises its prices, rations products to customers, or it does both. When a city hosts a major convention, hotels may charge rates that are twice the average room rate. They know that demand for hotel rooms will be great, and they can take advantage of this demand.

Raising prices in the hospitality industry can be dangerous even when caused by inflation. It must be remembered that with the exception of some travel such as business or to attend funerals, the demand for travel generally faces an elastic demand curve. A couple may plan to celebrate their wedding anniversary with friends and relatives at a restaurant or resort, but if prices dramatically increase they may switch to a gathering at home or even a nearby park shelter. The travel industry has learned that much business travel can be postponed or conducted through electronic means including the use of software such as GoToMeeting and Skype which allow two-way audio video using personal computers.

Cross substitutability of demand is a reality that always faces members of the hospitality industry, for example, the wedding anniversary or the use of electronic communication rather than an airline trip.

In passing price increases on to customers, the company should avoid the image of price gouger. It is best to increase prices when customers perceive the price increase to be justified. Restaurants had an easier time implementing increased menu prices after the price of beef jumped because their customers noticed this price increase in the supermarket. If food prices are going down while the other costs of operating a restaurant are going up, it is difficult to gain customer acceptance of the need for a price increase. Restaurant managers should try to time price increases so they will be perceived as justified by customers, such as when increases in the price of food receive media attention, after an increase in the minimum wage, or when inflation is in the news. Price increases should be supported with a company communication program informing customers and employees why prices are being increased.

Buyer Reaction to Price Changes

Whether the price is raised or lowered, the action affects buyers, competitors, distributors, and suppliers. Price changes may also interest the government. Customers do not always put a straightforward interpretation on price changes. They may perceive a price cut in several ways. For example, what would you think when you see a restaurant advertising a buy-one-meal-get-one-free special? If you know the restaurant and have a positive feeling, you might be attracted. Someone who doesn't know the restaurant may feel it is having trouble attracting customers or something is wrong with the food or service. Or you might wonder if portion size has been reduced or inferior-quality food was being served. Remember, buyers often associate price with quality when evaluating hospitality products they have not experienced directly.

Similarly, a price increase that would normally lower sales may have a positive meaning for buyers. A nightclub that increases its cover charge from $5 to $10 might be perceived as the "in place" to go.

Competitor Reactions to Price Changes

A firm considering a price change has to worry about competitors' reactions. Competitors are most likely to react when the number of firms involved is small, when the product is uniform, and when buyers are well informed.

One problem with trying to use price as a competitive advantage is that competitors can neutralize the price advantage by lowering their prices. In a competitive market where supply exceeds demand, this often sets off price wars in which the industry as a whole loses. In the United States, Burger King and McDonald's are locked in a battle for market share. When one of these fast-food giants cuts its price, the other usually follows.

Competitors may choose to retaliate in different markets. For example, when Southwest Airlines cut prices on its Houston-to-San Antonio flights, its competitors reacted by cutting prices on their Houston-to-Dallas flights. The Houston-to-Dallas flights were Southwest's bread and butter. By hitting here, the competition hurt Southwest more than they could have by matching prices on the Houston-to-San Antonio route. Competitors may also react to a price cut with nonprice tactics. When Continental Airlines offered a "chicken-feed" discount fare, the competition responded by not booking their connecting passengers on Continental's flights. Continental was forced to rescind its price cuts. Before cutting prices, it is essential to consider competitive reactions. As we mentioned at the beginning of this chapter, price is a very flexible element of the marketing mix. It can easily be matched by the competition. A firm that lowers its price and has it matched by competition loses both its competitive advantage and profit.[43]

Responding to Price Changes

Here we reverse the question and ask how a firm should respond to a price change by a competitor. The firm needs to consider several issues. Why did the competitor change the price? Was it to gain more market share, to use excess capacity, to meet changing cost conditions, or to lead an industry-wide program change? Does the competitor plan to make the price change temporary or permanent? What will happen to the company's market share and profits if it does not respond? Are other companies going to respond? What are the competitors' and other firms' responses likely to be to each possible reaction?

In addition to these issues, the company must make a broader analysis. It must consider its own product's stage in the life cycle, its importance in the company's product mix, the intentions and resources of the competitor, and possible consumer reactions to price changes.

When Marriott's Fairfield Inns was just getting started, it offered a special discounted rate that was 40 percent less than its average daily rate. Its competitors decided not to match the rate because Fairfield had only thirty hotels at the time. Joan Ganje-Fischer, vice president of Super 8, said that if a major chain such as Super 8, Econo Inns, or Days Inn matched the discount, it would catch the attention of the other organizations. A price war would be the likely result of such a cut by a major chain. But because Fairfield Inns consisted of only thirty units, major competitors were unwilling to reduce rates across their hundred-plus motel chains. Fairfield Inns used size to its advantage, recognizing that the larger chains would be unwilling to give up revenue from hundreds of hotels and thousands of rooms to match the price of a thirty-unit chain.[44]

These examples show how companies can avoid competitive reactions to price changes by planning those changes carefully.

■■■ KEY TERMS

Cost-plus pricing. Adding a standard markup to the cost of the product.

Cross-selling. The company's other products that are sold to the guest.

Discriminatory pricing. Refers to segmentation of the market and pricing differences based on price elasticity characteristics of the segments.

Fixed costs. Costs that do not vary with production or sales level.

Going-rate pricing. Setting price based largely on following competitors' prices rather than on company costs or demand.

Price. The amount of money charged for a product or service, or the sum of the values that consumers exchange for the benefits of having or using the product or service.

Revenue management. Forecasting demand to optimize profit. Demand is managed by adjusting price. Fences are often built to keep all customers from taking advantage of lower prices. For example, typical fences include making a reservation at least two weeks in advance or staying over a Saturday night.

Survival. A technique used when a company's or business unit's sales slump, creating a loss that threatens its existence. Because the capacity of a hotel or restaurant is fixed, survival often involves cutting prices to increase demand and cash flow. This can disrupt the market until the firm goes out of business or the economy improves.

Total costs. Costs that are the sum of the fixed and variable costs for any given level of production.

Upselling. Training sales and reservation employees to offer continuously a higher-priced product that will better meet the customers' needs, rather than settling for the lowest price.

Value-based pricing. Uses the buyer's perceptions of value, not the seller's cost, as the key to pricing.

Variable costs. Costs that vary directly with the level of production.

■■■ CHAPTER REVIEW

I. **Price.** Simply defined, price is the amount of money charged for a good or service. More broadly, price is the sum of the values consumers exchange for the benefits of having or using the product or service.

II. **Factors to Consider When Setting Price**
  A. **Internal factors**
   1. **Marketing objectives**
      a. **Survival.** It is used when the economy slumps or a recession is going on. A manufacturing firm can reduce production to match demand and a hotel can cut rates to create the best cash flow.
      b. **Current profit maximization.** Companies may choose the price that will produce the maximum current profit, cash flow, or ROI, seeking financial outcomes rather than long-run performance.
      c. **Market-share leadership.** When companies believe that a company with the largest market share will eventually enjoy low costs and high long-run profit, they set low opening rates and strive to be the market-share leader.
      d. **Product-quality leadership.** Hotels like the Ritz-Carlton chain charge a high price for their high-cost products to capture the luxury market.
      e. **Other objectives.** Stabilize market, create excitement for new product, and draw more attention.
   2. **Marketing mix strategy.** Price must be coordinated with product design, distribution, and promotion decision to form a consistent and effective marketing program.
   3. **Costs**
      a. **Fixed costs.** Costs that do not vary with production or sales level.
      b. **Variable costs.** Costs that vary directly with the level of production.
   4. **Cost subsidization**
   5. **Organization considerations.** Management must decide who within the organization should set prices. In small companies, this will be top management; in large companies, pricing is typically handled by a corporate department or by a regional or unit manager under guidelines established by corporate management.
  B. **External factors**
   1. **Nature of the market and demand**
      a. **Cross-selling.** The company's other products are sold to the guest.
      b. **Upselling.** Sales and reservation employees are trained to offer continuously a higher-priced product that will better meet the customer's needs, rather than settling for the lowest price.
   2. **Consumer perception of price and value.** It is the consumer who decides whether a product's price is right. The price must be buyer oriented. The price decision requires a creative awareness of the target market and recognition of the buyers' differences.
   3. **Analyzing the price–demand relationship.** Demand and price are inversely related; the higher the price, the lower the demand. Most demand curves slope downward in either a straight or a curved line. The prestige goods demand curve sometimes slopes upward.
   4. **Price elasticity of demand.** If demand hardly varies with a small change in price, the demand is inelastic; if demand changes greatly, the demand is elastic. Buyers are less price-sensitive when the product is unique or when it is high in quality, prestige, or exclusiveness. Consumers are also less price-sensitive when substitute products are hard to find. If demand is elastic, sellers generally consider lowering their prices to produce more total revenue. The following factors affect price sensitivity.
   5. **Factors Affecting Price–Demand Relations**
      a. **Unique value effect.** Creating the perception that your offering is different from those of your competitors avoids price competition.
      b. **Substitute awareness effect.** Lack of the awareness of the existence of alternatives reduces price sensitivity.
      c. **Business expenditure effect.** When someone else pays the bill, the customer is less price-sensitive.
      d. **End-benefit effect.** Consumers are more price-sensitive when the price of the product accounts for a large share of the total cost of the end benefit.

      e.   **Total expenditure effect.** The more someone spends on a product, the more sensitive he or she is to the product's price.

      f.   **Price quality effect.** Consumers tend to equate price with quality, especially when they lack any prior experience with the product.

   6.   **Competitors' price and offers.** When a company is aware of its competitors' price and offers, it can use this information as a starting point for deciding its own pricing.

      a.   **Price-rate compression.** This occurs when higher-priced hotels lower these rates to maintain occupancy and become direct competitors to lower-rated hotels.

   7.   **Other environmental factors.** Other factors include inflation, boom or recession, interest rates, government purchasing, and birth of new technology.

III. General Pricing Approaches

   A.   **Cost-based pricing.** Cost-plus pricing: a standard markup is added to the cost of the product.

   B.   **Break-even analysis and target profit pricing.** Price is set to break even on the costs of making and marketing a product, or to make a desired profit.

   C.   **Value-based pricing.** Companies based their prices on the product's perceived value. Perceived-value pricing uses the buyers' perceptions of value, not the seller's cost, as the key to pricing.

   D.   **Competition-based pricing.** Competition-based price is based on the establishment of price largely against those of competitors, with less attention paid to costs or demand.

IV. Pricing Strategies

   A.   **New product pricing strategies**. Pricing strategies usually change as a product passes through its life cycle. The introductory stage is especially challenging.

      1.   **Prestige pricing.** Hotels or restaurants seeking to position themselves as luxurious and elegant enter the market with a high price that supports this position.

      2.   **Market-skimming pricing.** Price skimming is setting a high price when the market is price-insensitive. It is common in industries with high research and development costs, such as pharmaceutical companies and computer firms.

      3.   **Marketing-penetration pricing.** Companies set a low initial price to penetrate the market quickly and deeply, attracting many buyers and winning a large market share.

      4.   **Product-bundle pricing.** Sellers using product-bundle pricing combine several of their products and offer the bundle at a reduced price. Most used by cruise lines.

   B.   **Existing-product pricing strategies.** The strategies just described are used primarily when introducing a new product. However, they can also

be useful with existing products. The following strategies are ones that can be used with existing products.

   1.   **Price-adjustment strategies.** Companies usually adjust their basic prices to account for various customer differences and changing situations.

      a.   **Volume discounts.** Hotels have special rates to attract customers who are likely to purchase a large quantity of hotel rooms, either for a single period or throughout the year.

      b.   **Discounts based on time of purchase.** A seasonal discount is a price reduction to buyers who purchase services out of season when the demand is lower. Seasonal discounts allow the hotel to keep demand steady during the year.

      c.   **Discriminatory pricing.** Segmentation of the market and pricing differences based on price elasticity characteristics of the segments. In discriminatory pricing, the company sells a product or service at two or more prices, although the difference in price is not based on differences in cost. It maximizes the amount that each customer pays.

   2.   **Revenue management.** A yield-management system is used to maximize a hotel's yield or contribution margin.

   3.   **Psychological pricing.** Psychological aspects such as prestige, reference prices, round figures, and ignoring end figures are used in pricing.

   4.   **Promotional pricing.** Hotels temporarily price their products below list price, and sometimes even below cost, for special occasions, such as introduction or festivities. Promotional pricing gives guests a reason to come and promotes a positive image for the hotel.

   5.   **Value pricing.** Value pricing means offering a price below competitors permanently, which differs from promotional pricing, in which price may be temporarily lowered during a special promotion.

V. Price Changes

   A.   **Initiating price cuts.** Reasons for a company to cut price are excess capacity, inability to increase business through promotional efforts, product improvement, follow-the-leader pricing, and desire to dominate the market.

   B.   **Initiating price increases.** Reasons for a company to increase price are cost inflation or excess demand.

   C.   **Buyer reactions to price changes.** Competitors, distributors, suppliers, and other buyers associate price with quality when evaluating hospitality products they have not experienced directly.

D. **Competitor reactions to price changes.** Competitors are most likely to react when the number of firms involved is small, when the product is uniform, and when buyers are well informed.

E. **Responding to price changes.** Issues to consider are reason, market share, excess capacity, meeting changing cost conditions, leading an industry-wide program change, temporary versus permanent.

■■■ DISCUSSION QUESTIONS

1. One way of increasing revenue is through upselling. Give examples from the hospitality or travel industries of when upselling can result in a more satisfied guest.

2. You have just been hired as the dining room manager at a local hotel. The manager asks you to evaluate the menu prices to see if they need to be adjusted. How would you go about this task?

3. A number of factors affecting price sensitivity are discussed in this chapter. Provide some examples of the application of these factors in the hospitality or travel businesses.

4. Many restaurants have unbundled their products to lower prices. For example, some restaurants that normally included a salad bar with all meals now offer a dinner price that includes the salad bar and a lower à la carte price that does not. Why do you think these restaurants are unbundling their products? When is product bundling effective?

5. Give an example of an effective use of price discrimination. Support your reasons for thinking that it is a good example.

6. Can a hotel or restaurant increase or maintain customer satisfaction after implementing its first revenue management program? Explain your answer.

7. Airlines and hotels give bonus frequent-flyer miles, gifts, and free companion tickets to attract the business traveler. These promotions are often provided in lieu of a price cut. The traveler benefits personally, although his or her company does not get the benefit of lower rates. Is this ethical?

■■■ EXPERIENTIAL EXERCISE

Do the following:

Conduct a price comparison of several hotels or restaurants in the same class. What price differences did you find? Do you feel the companies that had the higher prices could justify those higher prices by offering additional features or a higher-quality product?

■■■ INTERNET EXERCISE

Choose a large hotel in a city of your choice. Do an Internet search to see how many different prices you can find for the same type of room. Write up your findings.

■■■ REFERENCES

1. David J. Schwartz, *Marketing Today: A Basic Approach* (3rd ed.) (New York: Harcourt Brace Jovanovich, 1981), pp. 270–273.

2. Sheryl E. Kimes, "Restaurant Revenue Management at Chevys Arrowhead," *Cornell Hotel and Restaurant Administration Quarterly,* 45, no. 1 (2004): 52–56.

3. Janet Denefe, "Yearning for Learning," *F&B Magazine,* 2, no. 1 (1994): 13.

4. Jack Smith, "Of Fame and Fundamentals," *F&B Magazine,* 2, no. 1 (1994): 34–35.

5. Tom Ross, "A Complex Equation," *Steamboat Today* (Saturday, July 20, 2011): 1–2.

6. Ibid.

7. "Royal Caribbean Breaks Through," *Scorecard: The Revenue Management Quarterly* (Third Quarter, 1992), 3.

8. Ibid., p. 6.

9. Howard Feiertag, "Up Your Property's Profits by Upselling Catering," *Hotel and Motel Management,* 206, no. 14 (1991): 20.

10. Gail Bellamy, "Hot Stuff: Upselling Coffee and Tea," *Restaurant Hospitality,* 75, no. 2 (1991): 120–124.

11. "Embassy's Suite Deal," *Scorecard: The Revenue Management Quarterly* (Second Quarter, 1993), 3.

12. Melvyn Greene, *Marketing Hotels and Restaurants into the 90's* (New York: Van Nostrand Reinhold, 1987).

13. Anthony Edwards, "Changes in Real Air Fares and Their Impact on Travel," *EIU Travel and Tourism Analyst,* 2 (1990): 76–85.

14. This section draws on Thomas T. Nagle, *The Strategy and Tactics of Pricing* (Upper Saddle River, NJ: Prentice Hall, 1987).

15. Melvyn Greene, *Marketing Hotels and Restaurants into the 90's,* p. 47.

16. Juliet Chung, "Cracking the Code of Restaurant Wine Pricing," *Wall Street Journal,* online.wsj.com (accessed August 15, 2008): 1–4.

17. *The Horwath Accountant,* 47, no. 7 (1967): 8.

18. Philip Kotler and Gary Armstrong, *Principles of Marketing* (Upper Saddle River, NJ: Prentice Hall, 2001), p. 387.

19. Leo M. Renaghan and Michael Z. Kay, "What Meeting Planners Want: The Conjoint Analysis Approach," *Cornell Hotel and Restaurant Administration Quarterly,* 28, no. 1 (1987): 73.

20. Melvyn Greene, *Marketing Hotels and Restaurants in the 90's,* p. 42.

21. William J. Carroll, Robert J. Kwortnik, and Norman L. Rose, "Cornell Hospitality Report: Travel Packaging: An Internet Frontier,"*The Center for Hospitality Research,* 7, no. 17 (2007): 7.

22. Royal Palms Resort and Spa Web site, http://www.royalpalmshotel.com (accessed January 23, 2009).

23. John E. H. Sherry, "Sex-Based Price Discrimination: Does It Violate Civil Rights Laws?" *Cornell Hotel and Restaurant Administration Quarterly,* 35, no. 2 (1994): 16–17.

24. Richard O. Hanks, Robert G. Cross, and Paul R. Noland, "Discounting in the Hotel Industry: A New Approach," *Cornell Hotel and Restaurant Administration Quarterly,* 33, no. 1 (1992): 23.

25. John E. G. Bateson, *Managing Services Marketing* (Fort Worth, TX: Dryden Press, 1992), p. 339.

26. "Survey Findings on Hotel Revenue Management," Hotelmarketing.com, September 16, 2008 (accessed September 25, 2008).

27. Eric B. Orkin, "Boosting Your Bottom Line with Yield Management," *Cornell Hotel and Restaurant Administration Quarterly,* 28, no. 4 (1988): 52–56.

28. *Hotline: The Magazine of Carlson Hotels,* GBC, 2011, Vision in Action, pp. 38 and 41.

29. Gary M. Thompson and Heeju (Louise) Sohn, "Cornell Hospitality Report: Accurately Estimating Time-Based Restaurant Revenues Using Revenue per Available Seat-Hour," *The Center for Hospitality Research,* 8, no. 9 (2008).

30. Zvi Schwartz and Eli Cohen, "Hotel Revenue Management Forecasting: Evidence of Expert-Judgment Bias,"

Cornell Hotel and Restaurant Administration Quarterly, 45, no. 1 (2004): 49.

31. William H. Kaven and Myrtle Allardyce, "Dalmahoy's Strategy for Success," *Cornell Hotel and Restaurant Administration Quarterly,* 35, no. 6 (1994): 87–88.

32. Sunmee Choi and Anna S. Mattila, "Impact of Information on Customer Fairness Perceptions of Hotel Revenue Management," *Cornell Hotel and Restaurant Administration Quarterly,* 46, no 4 (2005): 444–445.

33. Toni McQuilken, "Revenue Management Software Makes the Grade," *Hotel Business* (April 2, 2011): 68.

34. Stefani C. O'Connor, "Apple Core Hotels Continues on Boutique Path," *Hotel Business* (June 21, 2011): 14 and 42.

35. "White Blames Reactionary Rate Sloshing for Some of Industry's Woes," *Hotel Business* (March 7, 2011): 26.

36. Kristin V. Rohlfs and Sheryl E. Kimes, "Customers' Perceptions of Best Available Hotel Rates," *Cornell Hotel and Restaurant Administration Quarterly,* 46, no. 2 (2007): 151.

37. Alex M. Susskind, Dennis Reynolds, and Eriko Tsuchiya, "An Evaluation of Guests' Preferred Incentives to Shift Time-Variable Demand in Restaurants," *Cornell Hotel and Restaurant Administration Quarterly,* 45, no. 1 (2004): 82.

38. JoAnn Carmin and Gregory X. Norkus, "Pricing Strategies for Menus: Magic or Myth," *Cornell Hotel and Restaurant Administration Quarterly,* 31, no. 3 (1990): 50.

39. "High Stakes at Harrah's," *Scorecard: The Revenue Management Quarterly* (First Quarter, 1993), 3.

40. David K. Hayes and Lynn M. Huffman, "Value Pricing: How Long Can You Go?" *Cornell Hotel and Restaurant Administration Quarterly* (February 1995): 51–56.

41. Stephan J. Hock, Xavier Drge, and Mary E. Park, "EDLP, Hi-Low, and Margin Arithmetic," *Journal of Marketing,* 58 (1994): 27.

42. Linda Canina and Cathy Enz, "Pricing for Revenue Enhancement in Asian Pacific Region Hotels: A Study of Relative Pricing Strategies," *Cornell Hospitality Report,* 8, no. 3 (February 2008).

43. Nagle, *The Strategy and Tactics of Pricing,* pp. 95–96.

44. "Fairchild Cuts Rates to Gain Stronger Presence," *Hotel and Motel Management* (June 19, 1989): 11.

Courtesy of Linda Whitwam/Dorling Kindersley.

Distribution Channels

12

Objectives

After reading this chapter, you should be able to:

1. Describe the nature of distribution channels, and tell why marketing intermediaries are used.

2. Understand the different marketing intermediaries available to the hospitality industry and the benefits each of these intermediaries offers.

3. Discuss channel behavior and organization, explaining corporate, contractual, and vertical marketing systems, including franchising.

4. Illustrate the channel management decisions of selecting, motivating, and evaluating channel alternatives.

5. Identify factors to consider when choosing a business location.

Sunflower Travel of Wichita, Kansas, and Belair/Empress Travel in Bowie, Maryland, typify the kind of business most threatened by the advent of new marketing channels, particularly the surge in Internet selling. Like other traditional travel agencies, they face some scary new-age competitors. In recent years, they have seen a flurry of online competitors, ranging from giant travel superstars such as Expedia, Travelocity, Priceline, and Orbitz to newcomers like Trip.com that let consumers surf the Web for rock-bottom travel deals. To make matters worse, the airlines themselves now sell more than half of their own tickets online and no longer pay travel agencies commissions on ticket sales. Hotels are also aggressively promoting booking on their Web sites to avoid paying 10 percent commissions to travel agents. Travel ranks as the number-one product sold over the Internet.

These new channels give customers more choices, and they threaten the very existence of many travel agencies. During the 1990s, the number of U.S. travel agents dropped by 18 percent, and some studies suggest that another 25 percent will go out of business during the next few years. This is a worldwide trend. In the United Kingdom, the number of leisure travelers booking through travel agents has dropped by 12 percent over the last three years and the number of travel agents who were members of the Association of British Travel Agents (ABTA) dropped by 14 percent.

There is a fancy word to describe this phenomenon: *disintermediation*. Strictly speaking, *disintermediation* means the elimination of a layer of intermediaries from a marketing channel. More broadly, disintermediation includes not only the elimination of channel levels through direct marketing but also the displacement of traditional sellers by radically new types of intermediaries. Disintermediation works only when a new channel form succeeds in bringing greater value to consumers. The success of Internet-based travel distributors suggests they are bringing value to the customer.

If travel agents are to survive, they will have to counter the lower prices offered by the Internet distribution of travel products with another form of value: personal service. Sunflower Travel has added a number of value-added products. These include adventure and active travel such as white-water rafting, safaris, houseboat rental, and trips to remote fishing lodges. Many consumers are likely to seek the advice of an expert when purchasing these travel products. Ciclismo Classico is a tourist agency specializing in bicycling tours of eight regions around the world, including the northeastern United States and Italy. The agency is located in Arlington, Massachusetts. It sells travel personally through its office, over the phone, and over the Internet. It targets adventure tourists by offering a unique product. It has selected the tour routes, arranged for rental bikes, and packaged the lodging and food and beverage. It has created value through its knowledge of the product and incorporating this knowledge into the products it sells. Travel agents that add personalized service and unique or customized products will be able to survive disintermediation.[1]

■■■ Supply Chains and the Value Delivery Network

Producing a product or service and making it available to buyers requires building relationships not just with customers but also with key suppliers and resellers in the company's **supply chain.** This supply chain consists of "upstream" and "downstream" partners. Upstream from the company is the set of firms that supply the raw materials, components, parts, information, finances, and expertise needed to create a product or service. Marketers, however, have traditionally focused on the "downstream" side of the supply chain—on the *marketing channels* (or *distribution channels*) that look toward the customer. Downstream marketing channel partners, such as wholesalers and retailers, form a vital connection between the firm and its customers.

Both upstream and downstream partners may also be part of other firms' supply chains. But it is the unique design of each company's supply chain that enables it to deliver superior value to customers. An individual firm's success depends not only on how well *it* performs but also on how well its entire supply chain and marketing channel compete with competitors' channels.

The term *supply chain* may be too limited: It takes a make-and-sell view of the business. A better approach is a value delivery network made up of the company, suppliers, distributors, and ultimately customers who "partner" with each other to improve the performance of the entire system. For example, Red Lobster does more than just serve seafood dinners. It manages a network of seafood producers, suppliers, and a transportation system. Red Lobster has a team that regularly inspects its seafood producers to make sure the product is safe and meets all its other quality standards. In this age of globalization, both seafood and other products are sourced from throughout the globe. Seafood may come from farms in Central America, furniture for a hotel comes from China with a six-month order to delivery time, and a company's call center may be in India. Managing the participants in an organization's supply chain is both an important and a complex task.

This chapter focuses on marketing channels, the downstream side of the value delivery network. However, remember that this is only part of the full-value network. In creating customer value, companies need upstream supplier partners just as they need downstream channel partners. Red Lobster working with seafood producers is an example of a company with upstream suppliers. Increasingly, marketers are participating in and influencing their company's upstream activities as well as their downstream activities. More than marketing channel managers, they are becoming full-value network managers.

e **12.1** Red Lobster, www.redlobster.com: Go to Red Lobster's commitment to quality page (located at the bottom of the home page). Notice how it manages its suppliers to make sure it gets a safe and quality product.

■■■ Nature and Importance of Distribution Systems

If we view properties as the heart of a hotel company, distribution systems can be viewed as the company's circulatory system.[2] Distribution systems provide a steady flow of customers. A well-managed distribution system can make the difference between a market-share leader and a company struggling for survival. Many hospitality companies are making greater use of the marketing channels available to them. For example, Ritz-Carlton receives a significant share of business from travel agents because of aggressive development of this channel. Marriott entered a marketing alliance with New Otani Hotels, giving Marriott exposure to Japanese travelers in North America. In return, New Otani gained Marriott's marketing expertise to help reach Americans traveling to Japan.[3] In today's competitive environment, it is not enough to count on a central reservation system (CRS) and your own sales force. Companies must develop increasingly complex distribution networks.

Competition, a global marketplace, electronic distribution techniques, and a perishable product have increased the importance of distribution. Innovative ways of approaching new and existing markets are needed. Globalization has meant that many hotel companies must choose foreign partners to help them market or distribute their products. Sheraton built an alliance with the Welcome Group in India, which manages Sheraton Hotels on the Indian subcontinent. New electronic distribution methods have resulted in the growth of international reservation systems such as Utell. Finally, the importance of distribution has increased because hospitality products are perishable. RCI, a time-share exchange company, uses its large membership base to negotiate special hotel rates for its members. The agreement works well for both parties: Hotels have a chance to sell rooms during a soft period, and RCI can offer its members a benefit.

■■■ Nature of Distribution Channels

A distribution channel is a set of independent organizations involved in the process of making a product or service available to the consumer or business user.[4] Development of a distribution system starts with the selection of channel members. Once members are selected, the focus shifts to managing the channel. Distribution networks in the hospitality industry consist of contractual agreements and loosely organized alliances between independent organizations.[5] In marketing, distribution systems are traditionally used to move goods (tangible products) from the manufacturer to the consumer. In the hospitality and travel industries, distribution systems are used to move the customer to the product: the hotel, restaurant, cruise ship, or airplane.

We first look briefly at traditional distribution systems. These systems provide the framework for the development of hospitality distribution networks. The products used by hospitality and travel companies come through distribution channels; thus, it is important to understand their structure. Graduates of hospitality and tourism programs often work for companies that distribute products. Graduates with restaurant experience may find themselves working for a company that distributes food or beverages to restaurants. They may sell food-service equipment or tabletop items to restaurants and hotels.

Some graduates have taken jobs as food brokers. The food **broker** works as an **agent** for the manufacturer, trying to create demand for a product. For example, if Mrs. Smith's pies develops a new no-bake pie for the food-service industry, brokers representing Mrs. Smith's pies would introduce the product to food-service managers they think will be interested in using it. The hospitality and travel industries use billions of dollars' worth of products, all moved through distribution channels. These distribution channels create thousands of jobs.

Why Are Marketing Intermediaries Used?

Why does Shenago China sell its chinaware to restaurants through an intermediary? Although doing so means giving up control over pricing the products, Shenago does gain advantages from selling through an intermediary. The company does not have to maintain several display rooms and a large sales force in every major city. Instead, a restaurant supply company displays, promotes, and makes personal sales calls. The restaurant supply house sells hundreds of other items. Its large assortment makes it a convenient supplier to the restaurant industry. The sales potential from its product assortment allows it to make personal sales calls, send catalogs, and provide other support for the products that it represents. Selling through wholesalers and retailers usually is much more efficient than direct sales.

A restaurant manager can make one call to a restaurant supply house and order a French knife, a dozen plates, a case of candles, a dozen oyster forks, a case of

Figure 12–1
How a distributor reduces
the number of channel
transactions.

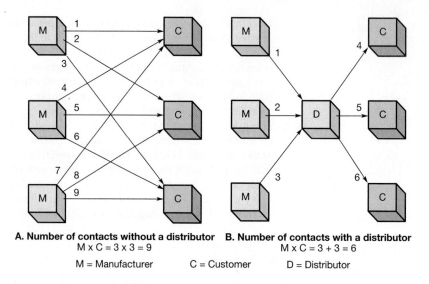

A. Number of contacts without a distributor
M x C = 3 x 3 = 9

B. Number of contacts with a distributor
M x C = 3 + 3 = 6

M = Manufacturer   C = Customer   D = Distributor

wine glasses, and a case of cocktail napkins. Each of these items is produced by a different manufacturer, but they are all available through one phone call. To the purchaser, this means access to small quantities of products because these become part of a large order. This reduces inventory requirements, number of deliveries, and number of processed invoices. Figure 12–1 shows one way that intermediaries can provide economies. Without distribution systems, the restaurateur would have to call individual manufacturers, such as a knife manufacturer, a china company, and a paper company. Each of these manufacturers would receive thousands of calls from individual restaurants. This would create unnecessary work and shipping costs for both the manufacturer and the customer, as represented in Figure 12–1A. Figure 12–1B shows the efficiencies created by a distribution system. The restaurants or customers call one distributor and get all of their supplies. The manufacturers can reach many restaurants through one distributor.

Distribution Channel Functions

A distribution channel moves goods from producers to consumers. It overcomes the major time, place, and possession gaps that separate goods and services from those who would use them. Members of the marketing channel perform many key functions:

1. **Information:** Gathering and distributing marketing research and intelligence information about the marketing environment

2. **Promotion:** Developing and spreading persuasive communications about an offer

3. **Contact:** Finding and communicating with prospective buyers

4. **Matching:** Shaping and fitting the offer to the buyer's needs, including such activities as manufacturing, grading, assembling, and packaging

5. **Negotiation:** Agreeing on price and other terms of the offer so that ownership or possession can be transferred

6. **Physical distribution:** Transporting and storing goods

7. **Financing:** Acquiring and using funds to cover the costs of channel work

8. **Risk taking:** Assuming financial risks such as the inability to sell inventory at full margin

The first five functions help complete transactions. The last three help fulfill the completed transactions.

All these functions have three things in common: They use scarce resources, they can often be performed better through specialization, and they can be shifted among channel members. Shifting functions to the intermediary may keep producer costs and prices low, but intermediaries must add a charge to cover the cost of their work. To keep costs low, functions should be assigned to channel members who can perform them most efficiently. For example, a cruise is an expensive purchase with many options for the traveler. Travel representing all the major cruise lines answers questions about cruise lines, itineraries, activities in the ports of call, and the many other questions a guest may have about the selection of a cruise. Online travel agents specializing in cruise products allow customers to browse through the different products and talk to an agent when they have questions or are ready to purchase. The online travel agencies (OTAs) as well as the agents with physical locations provide a broad distribution network for this infrequently purchased and complex product. This is why the majority of cruise ship bookings are made through travel agents. Frequently purchased products such as hotel rooms are less complex. Once people find a brand they like, they often prefer to book directly with the brand.

Number of Channel Levels

Distribution channels can be described by the number of **channel levels**. Each layer that performs some work in bringing the product and its ownership closer to the final buyer is a channel level. Because the producer and the final consumer both perform some work, they are part of every channel. We use the number of intermediary levels to show the length of a channel. Figure 12–2 shows several consumer distribution channels.

Channel 1, called a **direct marketing channel**, has no intermediary level. It consists of a manufacturer selling directly to consumers. For example, a restaurateur may buy produce directly from the grower at a farmers' market. Channel 2 contains one level. In consumer markets, this level is typically a **retailer**. The Fisherman's Pier restaurant in Geelong, near Melbourne, Australia, purchases its fish from a fisherman's cooperative. The cooperative markets the fish, allowing the fishers to specialize in fishing, not marketing.

Many of the agricultural products purchased by the hospitality industry come from cooperatives. In the United States, Sunkist, Diamond Walnuts, and Land O'Lakes butter are all producer cooperatives. New Zealand Milk Products Company is also a cooperative and sells dried milk and cheese throughout Southeast Asia and Latin America.

Figure 12–2
Business-to-consumer
and business-to-business
marketing channels.

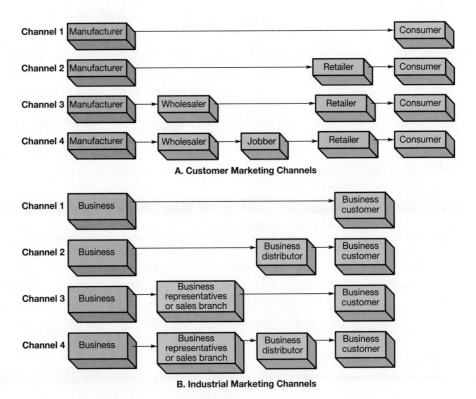

A. Customer Marketing Channels

B. Industrial Marketing Channels

Channel 3 contains two levels. In consumer markets, these are typically a **wholesaler** and a retailer. This type of channel is used by smaller manufacturers. Channel 4 contains three levels. The jobber buys from wholesalers and sells to smaller firms that are not served by larger wholesalers. From the producer's point of view, a greater number of intermediaries in the channel means less control, more complexity, and more cost.

All the institutions in the channel are connected by several types of flows. These include the physical flow of products, the flow of ownership, payment flow, information flow, and promotion flow. These flows can make channels with only one or a few channels very complex.

Many specialized channels are available to hospitality and travel organizations. We discuss the following components of a hospitality or travel distribution system: travel agents; tour wholesalers; specialists; hotel representatives; national, state, and local tourist agencies; consortia and reservation systems; global distribution systems (GDSs); the Internet; and concierges. A manager must choose the intermediaries that will make up the distribution system and the number of levels that the distribution system will have.

■■■ Hospitality Distribution Channels

Major Hospitality Distribution Channels

Most reservations are booked with the hotel directly. This includes the rooms booked by the sales force, those taken by the front desk, and by phone calls directly to the hotel. This is followed by brand.com, which is reservation booked through the brand's (Hilton, Hyatt, Marriott, Starwood, etc.) Web site. Other sources are voice (toll-free) calls to a central reservation office (CRO), GDSs, and OTA. The cost of these different channels varies greatly. The least expensive way is when the guest makes a reservation through the brand's Web site. However, when a hotel has rooms to fill, OTAs can help sell the rooms. A revenue manager has to manage the channels, knowing when to open and close different channels. See Table 12–1.

Direct Booking

On average, reservations received directly at the hotel account for 54.3 percent of a hotel's reservations, but only 46.5 percent of the revenue.[6] Managers often like to encourage direct booking because of the low transaction costs. However, front-desk personnel are usually not trained in revenue management. Front-desk staff also develop a personal relationship with repeat guests. Thus, a repeat guest who is making a future reservation and is quoted a $189 rate by a front-desk clerk quickly asks for the $139 rate he paid during his last stay. The front-desk clerk is unable to explain why there is such a price difference and quickly acquiesces to the lower

TABLE 12–1
Comparison of Channel Costs

	Rate ($)	Commission	Transaction Fee ($)	Total Cost ($)	Net Rate ($)
Brand.com	209	0	0	0	209.00
Brand.com*	209	$17.77 (8.5%)	$0	$17.77	$191.23
CRO—Phone	209	0%	$3.00	$3.00	$206.00
GDS	209	$20.90 (10%)	$0	$20.90	$188.10
OTA	209	$37.62 (18%)	$0	$37.62	$171.38

*Brand.com accessed through a search engine (Google, Bing, etc.).
Source: John Bowen based on charges for a branded property. The rate for OTAs will vary by the agency. Through negiotations large brands receive better pricing with some OTAs than independent hotels. The Brand.com and CRO rates will vary across brands; these are indicative rates.

rate. The Hilton University of Houston found that reservations booked through the front desk were approximately 15 percent less than reservations booked through the CRO or Hilton.com. Hotels are advised to refer nongroup customers to brand.com or the brand's toll-free number, rather than to take nongroup reservations at the hotel. Together the Web and the brand's 800# account for about 40 percent of a hotel's reservations.[7] It is important that the photos, wording, and packages on the brand.com Web site are accurate and do a good job of promoting the hotel. In addition to hotels, restaurants also receive most of their reservations through direct booking.

Online Travel Agency (OTA)

Online travel agenies (OTAs) conduct business through the Internet with no physical locations or stores. OTAs account only about 6.5 percent of a hotel's reservation. One way of dividing OTAs is into opaque and nonopaque. The nonopaque OTAs include merchant, retail, and referral models. The most popular nonopaque sites are merchant agencies that collect payment from the customer and include well-known names like Hotels.com, Travelocity, and Expedia. OTAs became popular after September 11, 2011. The travel industry suffered a big decline and hotels were looking for ways to sell rooms. During this period it was common for OTAs to sell rooms at a price that was less than a customer would pay on brand.com. This was the result of the hotels offering rooms to the OTAs at a heavy discount, hoping to create new customers through the OTAs. What happened was much of the business from OTAs was from brand.com customers attracted by the low rates, rather than new business. To correct error, hotel companies changed their agreements with the OTAs so they could not undersell them. The brand.com sites were soon guaranteeing the lowest price. Hotel companies also do not provide loyalty points to guests who purchase their rooms on an OTA, thus encouraging loyal customers to book through brand.com. Although they only produce 6.5 percent of a hotel's reservation, it is estimated that 75 percent of U.S. online hospitality shoppers are on OTA sites prior to booking.[8] One important feature of an OTA is people often search through hotel choices and then go to brand.com to book the reservation. Cindy Estess Green calls this the Billboard Effect. It is important that the hotel have a good presence in terms of photos and description on the OTA sites.

Opaque sites reduce cannibalization of brand.com by not disclosing the brand and specific hotel one is purchasing until it is purchased in a nonrefundable transaction with the consumer. For example, Hotwire will describe a hotel as a 3½ star hotel in the Ohio State University area for $99. Priceline also uses a general location within the city and stars to categorize its hotels. Priceline uses an auction system where the buyer "names" the price he or she will pay; if the buyer's price is high enough, he or she will get the room; if not, he or she may bid again after waiting 24 hours. People who are loyal to a certain brand or want to stay at a specific brand are not attracted to opaque agencies since they have no guarantee they will get the brand or hotel they want. Some hotels will give excess inventory to opaque merchants at deeply discounted prices to attract additional guests. When using opaque OTAs, one should consider that OTAs can reduce the perceived value for those who purchase through brand.com, if people in the same hotel discuss what they paid for the room. It can also bring in price-sensitive guests who will not spend money on food and beverage.

Another type of OTA is a retail agency, which is similar to a conventional travel agency; the hotel pays a commission to the agent and collects the room rental directly from the guest. OTAs also sell rental cars, airplane flights, ground transportation, cruises, and tours.

Persons who purchase from a third party on the Internet pay the third party. Thus, if hotels want to capture guests for their database, they need to collect the guests' names and addresses when they register. Hotels selling rooms through third-party vendors on the Internet should make their reservationists and desk staff aware they are doing this and that there may be a delay between the time the guest books the hotel room and when the distributor transfers the information to the hotel. Guests who are new to Internet booking are often anxious and call the hotel to confirm the booking after making the reservation. The hotel may have no record, and the reservationist has to spend valuable time trying to sort out the status of the reservation. By simply asking guests how they made the reservation, the hotel employee can identify those who book with a third party and inform them that the reservation has not been transferred yet, and advise them when to check back.

Global Distribution Systems

Global distribution systems (GDSs) are computerized reservation systems that serve as a product catalog for travel agents and other distributors of hospitality products. These reservation systems were originally developed by the airlines to promote sales. Before the Internet, GDSs offered a way for suppliers and end users to connect globally. As the Internet evolved, they developed Internet solutions for their customers. A distribution service provider provides the connection between a hotel's CRS and the GDS. Smaller hotel chains or independent hotels may link through a reservation service. There are four main GDSs: Amadeus, Galileo, Sabre, and Worldspan. Amadeus is the largest producer of travel bookings. It has a network that includes 75,000 travel agencies, 500 airlines, and 78,000 hotels. It also has an interest in vacations.com, the leading OTA for vacation travel. Travelport is a distribution system that owns Galileo and Worldspan. It produces 1.1 billion travel transactions per day. Additionally Travelport has an interest in four OTAs, including Gulliver's Travel Associates. Sabre is the other major GDS. It has also expanded into the OTA business and is the owner of Travelocity as well as a number of other brands.[9]

e

12.3 Amadeus, Amadeus.net: The consumer site of the GDS available in twelve languages.

Travel Agents

One way of reaching a geographically diverse marketplace is through travel agents.[10] The number of travel agents has been decreasing in recent years due to the growth of direct booking and customers self-booking travel on the Internet. Today the majority of airline reservations are booked directly on the airline's Web site. Almost all airlines have discontinued paying commissions to travel agents.[11] This has led agencies to charge a $25 to $50 fee for issuing tickets. In addition to selling airline tickets, travel agents book hotel sales, and nearly all cruise travel.[12] Hotels typically pay 10 percent commission to travel agents, and cruise lines can pay up to 15 percent. The combination of reduced commissions and growth of direct sales from hotels and airlines to the consumer has led to a steady decrease of travel agents in the United States.

Hotels interested in travel agency business are listed in airline reservation systems and hotel guides. Hotels also send information packages to travel agents that include collateral material and hotel news, including updates about hotel packages, promotions, and special events. Travel agents are also invited to visit hotel property on familiarization tours (fam trips). Airlines sometimes assist with these trips by providing free airfare. It is important that fam trips be well organized.[13] Finally, promotional campaigns can be directed at travel agents through travel agent publications such as *Travel Weekly, Travel Trade,* and *Travel Agent.* The use of promotional campaigns targeted at travel agents is discussed in Chapter 14.

Hotels seeking travel agent business must make it easy for agents to make reservations. Providing toll-free reservation numbers is essential. Hotels that generate many bookings from travel agents have a separate number dedicated to business travel. Travel agents like to be paid quickly. Hotels that want travel agent business process commissions rapidly. Hyatt guarantees payment within one week of the guest's departure.[14] Foreign chains are now paying commissions in the travel agent's local currency, eliminating the need for the agent to go through the costly process of converting a commission check. On a $50 commission foreign currency check, the travel agent stands to lose nearly the full amount because most banks charge a minimum of $30 to $40 per transaction for processing and converting checks drawn on a foreign bank.

Hospitality providers who serve travel agents must remember that agents entrust the hotel with their customers. In a travel agency market survey, travel agents rated reputation for honoring reservations, reputation for good service, ease of collecting commission, and room rates as the most important factors in choosing a hotel.[15] Hotels must do everything possible to make a favorable impression on guests booked through travel agents to ensure future business from that agent. When business is obtained through an intermediary, the hospitality provider, such as a hotel or cruise line, has two customers, the guest and the intermediary. The majority of cruise lines do not sell directly to the ultimate consumer but insist that bookings be made through travel agents or tour operators.

Corporate travel agents are one of the strongest areas of the travel agency business. Companies are a major source of travel bookings. U.S. corporations spend over $150 billion on travel. Each dollar of that amount represents a cost that corporations would like to reduce. Consequently, companies make arrangements with travel agents and in some cases set up their own travel agency. Many organizations sign an exclusive agreement with one travel agency, and employees are required to book through this firm. The travel agency assumes responsibility for locating the least expensive travel alternatives for the company.

Tour Wholesalers

Tour wholesalers assemble travel packages usually targeted at the leisure market. These generally include transportation and accommodations but may include meals, ground transportation, and entertainment. In developing a package, a tour wholesaler contracts with airlines and hotels for a specified number of seats and rooms, receiving a quantity discount. The wholesaler also arranges transportation between the hotel and the airport. Retail travel agents sell these packages. The tour wholesaler has to provide a commission for the travel agent and give consumers a package that is perceived to be a better value than what they could arrange on their own. Additionally, tour operators have to make a profit for themselves. The profit margin on each package is small. Generally, wholesalers must sell 85 percent of the packages available to break even.[16] This high break-even point leaves little room for error. As a result, it is not uncommon for a tour wholesaler to go broke. Thus, it is important that hospitality providers check the history of the tour operator, receive a deposit, and get paid promptly. Additional security is provided by dealing with tour operators who are members of the U.S. Tour Operators Association (USTOA). USTOA requires its members to post a $100,000 indemnity bond for its consumer payments protection program. This ensures refund of tour deposits and payments in the event of financial failure of any of its members.[17]

With the increased number of international resorts, tour wholesalers are becoming a powerful member of the distribution channel. It is impossible for travel agents to know every resort. Instead, they rely on catalogs provided by tour wholesalers. If a couple wants to holiday on Saipan, they are given the catalog of a tour operator covering Micronesia. The catalog contains a selection of several luxury hotels, four-star hotels, three-star hotels, and tourist hotels. The wholesaler writes a description of each. The hotel may provide information, but the tour operator decides on the description of the hotel that goes in the brochure.

If a couple wants to stay at a luxury hotel, the brochure may include only three luxury hotels. Others are eliminated from consideration and will not be part of the couple's awareness set. The couple chooses a resort that seems to offer the best value based on the information provided by the tour wholesaler. So the tour wholesaler exerts a powerful force over resorts, especially remote international markets.

The Caribbean resort industry is particularly dependent on tour wholesalers, who provide over half the business. One effect of the power of tour wholesalers in this area is the existence of substantial discounts to them regardless of seasonal demand. This seriously affects the ability of Caribbean hotel managers to control pricing through tools such as yield management (see Chapter 11). It also affects cash flow. Caribbean wholesalers collect payment from customers three to six months before they arrive at a hotel, but most hotels have to wait 60 days after guest arrival for payment from wholesalers.

Airlines may also serve as tour operators. Almost all major airlines have vacation packages promoted through brochures and their Web sites. An airline such as Air New Zealand offers farm/ranch or bed and breakfast packages for the FIT (foreign independent traveler) market. Visitors to New Zealand can book auto rentals or camper rentals and reservations with these specialized lodging providers through the tour desk of Air New Zealand.

Colonial Williamsburg and other historic tourist attractions often rely on bus tours as a source of guests. Courtesy of Cary Wolinsky/Aurora Photos.

Specialists: Tour Brokers, Motivational Houses, and Junket Reps

Tour brokers sell motor coach tours, which are attractive to a variety of markets. Tours through New England to view the fall foliage, trips to college and sporting events, tours built around Mardi Gras, and regularly scheduled tours of the Washington, D.C., area are examples of popular motor coach trips. Some motor coach tours are seasonal, some are based on one event, and others are year round. For hotels on their routes, motor coach tours can provide an important source of income.[18]

Motor coach tours are very important to museums and historic restorations such as historic Colonial Williamsburg in Virginia. Hospitality providers such as historic restorations, hotels, and destination cities usually participate in a travel conference sponsored by the American Bus Association. Booth space is rented, and salespeople representing these providers scramble to make appointments with bus tour companies that serve their area.

Motivational houses provide incentive travel offered to employees or distributors as a reward for their efforts. Companies often use incentive travel as a prize for employees who achieve sales goals or for the sales team achieving the highest sales. The incentive trip is usually to a resort area and includes first-class or luxury properties. For resorts or upmarket properties in destination cities, such as New York, San Francisco, Chicago, or Boston, motivational houses represent an effective distribution channel. Ways of reaching tour brokers and incentive houses include trade magazines and trade associations, such as the National Tour Association and the Society of Incentive Travel Executives.[19]

Junket reps serve the casino industry as intermediaries for premium players. Junket reps maintain lists of gamblers who like to visit certain gaming areas, such as Reno, Las Vegas, or Atlantic City, and they work with one or a few casinos rather than the entire industry. They are paid a commission on the amount the casino earns from the players or in some cases on a per-player basis. Members of a junket receive complimentary or low-cost hospitality services, including air transportation, ground transportation, hotel lodging, food and beverage, and entertainment. The amount of complimentary services received depends on the amount that players gamble in the casino.

Hotel Representatives

Hotel representatives sell hotel rooms and hotel services in a given market area. It is often more effective for hotels to hire a hotel representative than to use their own salesperson. This is true when the market is a distant one and when cultural differences may make it hard for an outsider to penetrate the market. For example, a corporate hotel in Houston may find it is more effective to hire a hotel representative in Mexico City than to send a sales manager there. Hotel sales representatives should represent noncompeting hotels. They receive a straight commission, a commission plus a salary, or a combination of both. It takes time for a hotel representative to learn a company's products and inform the market about them. The choice of a hotel representative should not be taken lightly. Frequent changes in hotel representatives are not cost efficient or cost effective.

National, State, and Local Tourist Agencies

National, state, and local tourist agencies are an excellent way to get information to the market and gain room bookings. National associations promote tourism within their own countries. Their impact can be important to hotel chains that have locations throughout the country. State agencies promote the state resources and

This photo of the Sydney Opera House and Bridge is an example of the type of images Convention and Tourist Bureaus supply to promote their destinations. Courtesy of Instinia/Dreamstime.

attractions overseas, nationally, and in the state itself. State tourist agencies usually have tourist information centers strategically located throughout the state, often at entrance points. Regional associations can also help the independent and chain operators.

The Sydney Convention and Visitors Bureau (SCVB) has offices in London, Melbourne, and New York, in addition to its main office in Sydney. The staff members in these offices work to bring meetings and conventions to Sydney by making them aware of the facilities and amenities the city has to offer. The SCVB also provides materials for organizations to help promote their meeting in Sydney. For example, It provides promotional videos of Sydney, postcards for teaser campaigns, slides for presentations, and brochure shells with images of Sydney that can be overprinted with the program, registration material, or other information. The SCVB also helps event planners match their needs with what the city has to offer, including venues for meeting, lodging accommodations, and ideas for unique activities. One suggestion is a private breakfast on Shark Island in the middle of Sydney Harbor, with the sunrise over the Opera House and the harbor bridge. Another is having an Australian bush theme party in a five-star hotel complete with live kangaroos, koalas, and sheep shearing. The SCVB, like other convention and visitors' bureaus, serves as a channel to bring business to its city or region.[20]

Consortia and Reservation Systems

Reservation systems such as Loews Representation International and Steigenberger Reservation Service are expanding their services. Reservation systems provide a CRS for hotels. They usually provide the system for small chains or provide an overseas reservation service, allowing international guests to call a local number to contact the hotel.

In ski areas, the ski resort may operate the hotel's reservation system. The resort books hotel reservations at independent hotels or motels for a commission such as 15 percent. Because the resort commonly has its own lodging, independent hotel and motel managers sometimes fear the power of this organization and may refuse to cooperate in joint promotional efforts because they do not wish to share their databases.

A consortium is a group of hospitality organizations that is allied for the mutual benefit of the members. Marketing is often the reason why consortia are formed. The consortium allows a property to be independent in ownership and management while gaining the advantages of group marketing. An example of a consortium is Leading Hotels of the World. The distinction between consortia and reservation services is becoming blurred, as reservation services such as SRS, Utell, and Supranational are now expanding into marketing activities. It is a natural evolution for reservation systems to add additional services once they have a critical number of hotels as subscribers.

e **12.4** Hong Kong Tourism Board, www .discoverhongkong.com: Go to the "Interactive Corner" and discover the different media that is available.

Five of the largest consortia, as measured by rooms represented, are Supranational, Logis de France, Leading Hotels of the World, Golden Tulip, and Utell. Logis de France is an association of more than 3,200 small one-, two-, and three-star hotels in France. Logis de France is a consortium, with hotels identifying themselves as members of the organization through signage on the hotel as well as road signs. Utell works with over 3,000 hotels through regional centers throughout the world. Utell generates reservations resulting in over 9.6 million room nights or $1.4 billion in sales.[21] The difference between a consortium and reservation company is that the consortium provides a more comprehensive range of marketing services and its members pay for these services with initial joining fees and annual fees. Reservation companies gain the majority of their revenue by charging for each reservation they book. As a representation company, Utell provides more marketing services than a reservation company but less than a consortium.[22]

Regions are also developing consortia to promote their area as a tourism attraction. For example, tourist attractions in the Bath area of the United Kingdom have formed the Association of Bath and District Leisure Enterprises (ABLE). This type of cooperative allows smaller hospitality organizations to develop and distribute promotional material. Travel agents have formed consortia to negotiate lower rates for hotel rooms, airlines, and other tourist products. One of the larger travel agent consortia is Woodside Management Systems. Consortia can also develop vertical marketing systems (VMSs) by negotiating special prices on supplies that members may use. Consortia and reservation systems combined with OTAs have allowed non-branded hotels to compete effectively with branded properties.[23]

Concierges

A concierge can be an excellent source of business for restaurants and tourist attractions. Courtesy of michaeljung/Fotolia LLC.

Concierges, bell staff, and front-desk employees can be good sources of business for local hospitality products and travel, such as restaurants, tours, and fishing guides. Concierges can be a major source of business for a restaurant that has a unique menu, atmosphere, or simply excellent food and service. These attributes are an attraction to travelers. Restaurants wishing to cultivate a relationship with concierges usually invite them for a complimentary meal so they can experience the restaurant firsthand. The restaurant's management may also volunteer the restaurant as a site for the local concierge association meetings if the restaurant has meeting space. The restaurant should also supply the hotel with menus they can show to guests asking about the restaurant. Finally, the restaurant instructs the staff on how to handle calls from a concierge. For example, even though concierges know there is no chance of getting a reservation at a popular restaurant on a Saturday night, they are still obliged to call because the guest has requested it and is standing at their side. Thus, when such requests do come, the person answering the phone at the restaurant should be courteous and understand the situation.

Restaurant Distribution Systems

There are a number of online reservation systems for restaurants. The largest one, OpenTable, serves 20,000 restaurants. OpenTable charges $1 for each reservation received from its Web site and $0.25 for every reservation that the customer books directly with the restaurant after linking through OpenTable. OpenTable is linked with a number of sites that provide restaurant reviews, such as TripAdvisor, allowing the customer review restaurant choices and then make a reservation through OpenTable.[24]

OpenTable's $1 fee per person for reservation over its site can be high for some restaurants. An independent restaurant may make only 5 to 10 percent profit; thus a $1 fee can be the profit from $20 in sales. Restaurants with low-check averages may want to look at other online options. Also, a restaurant that has meal periods with low-check averages, such as breakfast, may want to close this meal period off to reservations from OpenTable.

■■■ Channel Behavior and the Organization

Distribution channels are more than simple collections of firms tied together by various flows. They are complex behavioral systems in which people and companies interact to accomplish goals. Some channel systems consist of formal interactions among loosely organized firms. Others consist of formal interactions guided by strong organizational structures. Channel systems do not stand still. New types surface and new channel systems evolve. We now look at channel behavior and how members organize to do the work of the channel.

Channel Behavior

A distribution system consists of dissimilar firms that have banded together for their common good. Each channel member is dependent on the others, playing a role in the channel and specializing in performing one or more functions.

Ideally, because the success of individual channel members depends on general channel success, all channel firms should work together. They should understand and accept their roles, coordinate their goals and activities, and cooperate to attain overall channel goals. By cooperating they can understand and serve the target market more effectively.

But individual channel members rarely take such a broad view. They are usually more concerned with their own short-run goals and their dealings with the firms operating closest to them in the channel. Cooperating to achieve overall channel goals sometimes means giving up individual company goals. Although channel members depend on each other, they often act alone in their own short-run best interests. They frequently disagree on the roles each should play or who should do what for which rewards. Such disagreements over goals and roles generate **channel conflict**.

Horizontal conflict is conflict between firms at the same level of the channel. For example, some Pizza Inn franchisees may complain about other Pizza Inn franchisees cheating on ingredients and giving poor service, thereby hurting the overall Pizza Inn image.

Vertical conflict, conflicts between different levels of the same channel, is even more common. In recent years, for example, Burger King has had a steady stream of conflicts with its franchised dealers over everything from increased ad spending and offensive ads to the prices it charges for cheeseburgers. At issue is the chain's right to dictate policies to franchisees.

The price of a double cheeseburger has generated a lot of heat among Burger King franchisees. In an ongoing dispute, the burger chain insisted that the sandwich be sold for no more than $1—in line with other items on its "Value Menu." Burger King saw the value price as key to competing effectively in the current economic environment. But the company's franchisees claimed that they would lose money at that price. To resolve the dispute, angry franchisees filed a lawsuit (only one of several over the years) asserting that Burger King's franchise agreements don't allow it to dictate prices. (The company had won a separate case in 2008 requiring franchisees to offer the Value Menu, which is core to its efforts to attract price-conscious consumers.) After months of public wrangling, Burger King finally let franchisees have it their way. It introduced a $1 double-patty burger with just one slice of cheese, instead of two, cutting the cost of ingredients. The regular quarter-pound double cheeseburger with two pieces of cheese remained on the Value Menu but was priced at $1.19.[25]

Some conflict in the channel takes the form of healthy competition. Such competition can be good for the channel; without it, the channel could become passive

In past years Burger King has had a steady stream of conflicts with its franchised dealers over everything from advertising content to the price of its cheeseburgers. Courtesy of Scott Olson/Getty Images.

and noninnovative. For example, Burger King's conflict with its franchisees might represent normal give-and-take over the respective rights of the channel partners. But severe or prolonged conflict can disrupt channel effectiveness and cause lasting harm to channel relationships. Burger King should manage the channel conflict carefully to keep it from getting out of hand.

Vertical Marketing Systems

For the channel as a whole to perform well, each channel member's role must be specified, and channel conflict must be managed. The channel will perform better if it includes a firm, an agency, or a mechanism that provides leadership and has the power to assign roles and manage conflict.

Historically, *conventional distribution channels* have lacked such leadership and power, often resulting in damaging conflict and poor performance. One of the biggest channel developments over the years has been the emergence of **vertical marketing systems (VMS)** that provide channel leadership. Figure 12–3 contrasts the two types of channel arrangements.

A conventional distribution channel consists of one or more independent producers, wholesalers, and retailers. Each is a separate business seeking to maximize its own profits, perhaps even at the expense of the system as a whole. No channel member has much control over the other members, and no formal means exists for assigning roles and resolving channel conflict.

In contrast, a VMS consists of producers, wholesalers, and retailers acting as a unified system. One channel member owns the others, has contracts with them, or wields so much power that they must all cooperate. The VMS can be dominated by the producer, the wholesaler, or the retailer.

We now look at the three major types of VMSs. Each type uses a different means for setting up leadership and power in the channel. In a **corporate VMS**, coordination and conflict management are attained through common ownership at different levels in the channel. In an administered VMS, leadership is assumed by one or a few dominant channel members. In a contractual VMS, leadership and power are attained through contractual agreements among channel members.

A corporate VMS combines successive stages of production and distribution under single ownership. For example, Red Lobster has its own food-processing plants and distributes food products to its

Figure 12–3
Comparison of conventional distribution channel with VMS.

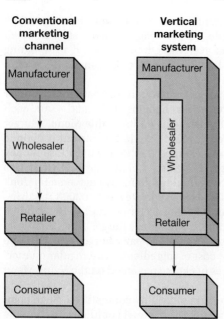

restaurants. Breweries in Great Britain own pubs, which serve only the beers from the owner's brewery.

An **administered VMS** coordinates successive stages of production and distribution not through common ownership or contractual ties but through the size and power of the parties. The world's airline industry has been affected by administered VMSs since the birth of the industry. Many nations continue to cling to a subsidized national carrier known as a flag carrier. These airlines often exert an inordinate amount of power over reservations systems, tour operators, and travel agencies within their respective nations.

The third type of VMS is contractual. A **contractual VMS** consists of independent firms at different levels of production and distribution who join through contracts to obtain economies or sales impact. A contract with a hotel representative would be an example of a contractual VMS. An important form of contractual VMS is franchising.

Franchising

"Franchising is a method of doing business by which a franchisee is granted the right to engage in offering, selling, or distributing goods or services under a marketing format which is designed by the franchisor. The franchisor permits the franchisee to use its trademark, name, and advertising."[26] Franchising has been the fastest-growing retailing form in recent years. Industry analyst Stephen Rushmore found that franchised hotels account for more than 65 percent of the existing U.S. hotel-room supply.[27] One of the reasons for the popularity of franchising is that it is the safest way to start a new business. Estimates of the success rate for different methods of starting a business are as follows:[28]

- *Starting a new business:* a 20 percent chance for survival

- *Buying an existing business:* a 70 percent chance for survival

- *Buying a franchise:* a 90 percent chance for survival

Franchises have been popular forms of distribution for both hotels and restaurants. Some popular hotel franchises include Hyatt Place, Holiday Inn Express, Hilton Garden Inn, and Fairfield Inn by Marriott. Restaurant franchises include McDonald's, Burger King, KFC, Pizza Hut, Subway, and T.G.I. Friday's. Franchises have been responsible for shifting the restaurant business from individual operators to multiunits. Franchised restaurant companies account for more than half of all restaurant sales.

For the right to use the name, methods of operation, and other benefits that come with a franchise, the franchisee pays an initial fee, a royalty, and a marketing fee to the franchise organization. In the case of hotels, a fee for use of the CRS is also charged. Radisson charges an initial fee that is a minimum of $50,000. The royalty is 4 percent of gross room revenue, the marketing fee is 1.75 percent of gross room revenue, and the reservation fee is 2 percent of gross room revenue.[29] Note that these percentages are gross percentages. The franchisor can verify gross receipts through tax reports.

The initial fee and the royalty depend on the brand equity of the franchise. For example, McDonald's is recognized as a fast-food restaurant around the world. People in London, Paris, Hong Kong, and New York recognize McDonald's. The stronger the market position, the more valuable is the brand name. Thus, a McDonald's franchise offers more value than a Mr. Quick franchise. These are the advantages of the franchise to the franchisee (person or organization buying the franchise):

- Recognition of brand

- Less chance of a business failure

- National advertising, premade advertisements, and marketing plans

- Faster business growth

- Help with site selection

- Architectural plans

- Operational systems, software, and manual to support the systems

- National contracts with suppliers

- Product development

- Consulting

- Help with financing

The disadvantages of purchasing a franchise are as follows:

- Fees and royalties are required.

- It limits the products sold and the recipes used.

- The franchisee is often required to be open a minimum number of hours and offer certain products.

- A poorly operated company can affect the reputation of the entire chain.

- The franchisor's performance affects the profitability of franchisees.

- Some franchisees may not benefit from national advertising as much as other franchisees—often a source of conflict.

One of the reasons that companies decide to franchise is that it allows for increased distribution of their products. The franchisee's money expands the business while the franchisor collects an initial fee and royalties. Table 12–2 provides an overview of franchisee fees. Franchising is not effective for all companies. The company must be able to offer the operational systems, management support, and a good business concept. For new businesses it requires time and money to provide a good franchisee package. Smaller chains often franchise to people who are close to the business. For example, franchising is used in smaller restaurant chains to help them retain managers. It is difficult for a small chain to compete with opportunities that a large chain offers its managers. Some small chains combat the career opportunities of the large chains by helping their best managers get their own store through franchising. This allows the chain to keep managers who might otherwise grow bored and unchallenged. The advantages of franchising for the franchisor are as follows:

- Receives a percentage of gross sales

- Expands brand

- Gets support for national advertising campaign

- Is able to negotiate support for national contracts with suppliers

TABLE 12–2
Restaurant Franchisees

Chain	Application Fee ($)	Royalty Fee	Marketing Fee	Total Investment
Applebee's Neighborhood Grill & Bar	40,000	4% initial 5% after two years	4.0%	600–1 million
Arby's	37,500	4%	4.2%	.35–2.5 million
KFC	45,000	5%	5%	.3–2.5 million
McDonald's	45,000	4%	4.5%	1.3–2.5 million
Pizza Hut	25,000	6%	4.25%	300,000–400,000
Subway Sandwiches & Salads	15,000	8.0%	4.5%	100,000–300,000
Taco Bell	45,000	5.5%	5.5%	1.3–2.5 million
T.G.I. Friday's	100,000	4.0%	$500/month	2–6 million

Sources: www.yum.com; www.subway.com; www.fridays.com; www.applebees.com; www.aboutmcdonalds.com; www.discoverarbys.com; www.world-franchising.com (accessed October 10, 2011).

The disadvantages of a franchise for a franchisor are as follows:

- There are limits on other options of expanding distribution; for example, the ability to develop alliances may be limited if the alliances violate the territorial agreements of the franchisees.

- Franchisees must be monitored to ensure product consistency.

- There is limited ability to require franchisees to change operations; for example, Pizza Hut had a difficult time getting franchisees to add delivery when Domino's was developing the delivery market.

- Franchisees want and need to have an active role in decision making.

A variation of the traditional form of franchising is subfranchising. In this form of franchising, the franchisor sells the right to distribute a franchise to a third party, and this agent then sells to the franchisees.[30] For example, a franchisor sells the right to distribute and manage franchises to a subfranchisor. The subfranchisor then receives payment from the franchises it has sold and passes a portion of these fees to the franchisor and retains the rest. The subfranchisor also provides management support for its franchisees. One researcher estimates that 31 percent of quick-service restaurants and 37 percent of family restaurants use subfranchise contracts.[31] This allows the franchisor to expand by taking advantage of an agent's management and marketing resources. Another example would be a company that would become a subfranchisor, selling franchises to its franchisees or business associates. For example, Uni-Mart, a gas and convenience store, is a subfranchisor for Blimpie Subs and Salads restaurants.[32]

Alliances, another form of contractual agreement, are developed to allow two organizations to benefit from each other's strengths. In the beginning of this chapter, we mentioned the alliance between the Welcome Group and Sheraton Hotels. It would be difficult, if not impossible, for Sheraton to go into India by itself because of India's regulation of foreign-owned businesses. The Welcome Group offered Sheraton an Indian partner. Additionally, the Welcome Group had a good reputation in India and understood how to do business there. Sheraton offered the Welcome Group a name that was known to the international business traveler. Sheraton offered training and management support systems. Thus, both partners benefited from the alliance.

Restaurants are expanding their locations through alliances with hotel chains. This provides the restaurant with a good location and access to the hotel's guests. The hotel gains the value of the brand name of the restaurant. For example, Trader Vic's, one of the first restaurants to align with hotels, has locations in several Hiltons, the Marriott Royal Garden Riverside (Bangkok), and the New Otani hotels in Tokyo and Singapore. Ruth's Chris Steak Houses has locations in hotels operated by Marriott, Holiday, and Westin. Good Eats, a casual, regional chain well known in Texas, has developed an alliance with Bristol Hotels.[33] The new resorts opening in Las Vegas are developing alliances with branded restaurants; names such as the Rainforest Café, California Pizza Kitchen, Benihana, Wolfgang Puck Café, Tony Roma's, and Gordon Biersch can be found in the resorts. Additionally, many resorts have food courts similar to those in the malls, featuring branded fast-food outlets. The use of branded restaurants is attracting the attention of hotel management and creating opportunities for restaurants to expand their distribution.

Alliances by two or more noncompeting firms are a popular and effective way of expanding markets. For example, restaurants are developing alliances with convenience stores and hotel properties to distribute their products. Convenience stores sell branded donuts such as Dunkin' Donuts or Winchell's. Chain fast-food operations located in convenience stores allow the store to offer brand-name products, and the chain gains additional high-traffic distribution points. Many consumers perceive hotel restaurants to be overpriced and of poor quality. The introduction of well-known chain restaurants into hotels overcomes this problem.

Airlines are developing alliances to access customers in other parts of the world and to provide their customers with new destination opportunities. For example, SAS developed an alliance with Continental Airlines to give it access to the U.S. market. Before the alliance, SAS served only a handful of U.S. cities. Since the alliance, Continental's U.S. flights can be used to feed into SAS's flights to Europe. Continental gained the SAS passengers flying into Newark and other U.S. gateways, who will now use Continental to reach their final destination in the United States.

The National Motor Coach Network, a marketing consortium of motor coach operators, has developed a partner program to bring charter business to preferred hotels. Now tour operators sometimes extend their trips to include an overnight stay. In the past, operators preferred a day trip to staying overnight in an unfamiliar hotel. A network representative visits all participating hotels before they are accepted. The alliance brings business to the hotels and provides motor coach operators with negotiated rates at hotels that meet their standards.[34]

Growth of Horizontal Marketing Systems

Another channel development is **horizontal marketing systems (HMSs)**, in which two or more companies at one level join to follow a new marketing opportunity.[35] By working together, companies can combine their capital, production capabilities, or marketing resources to accomplish more than what one company can accomplish working alone. For example, Seaworld offers tickets at a discount to an automobile club, which promotes these discount tickets as one benefit for its members. In return, Seaworld gains access to several hundred thousand automobile club members. Such symbiotic marketing arrangements have increased in number in recent years, and the end is nowhere in sight.

American Express, the Coeur d'Alene resort, and K2 Skis worked together to offer a free pair of skis at check-in if the guest booked an American Express "Ski Week Holiday."

Growth of Multichannel Marketing Systems

In the past, many companies used a single channel to sell to a single market or market segment. Today, with the proliferation of customer segments and channel possibilities, more companies have adopted **multichannel marketing distribution.** Such multichannel marketing occurs when a single firm sets up two or more marketing channels to reach one or more customer segments.[36] For example, McDonald's sells through a network of independent franchisees but owns more than a fourth of its outlets. Thus, the wholly owned restaurants compete to some extent with those owned by McDonald's franchisees.

The multichannel marketer gains sales with each new channel but also risks offending existing channels. Existing channels can cry "unfair competition" and threaten to drop the marketer unless it limits competition or repays them in some way. For example, franchisees have brought lawsuits against franchisors that have developed competing operations in their market area.

∎∎∎ Selecting Channel Members

Selecting channel members involves a number of factors, including customer needs, the company's ability to attract channel members, the economic feasibility of the channel member, and the control that might be given up to gain a channel member.

Food-service distributors used to be primarily confined to selling to all types of sit-down restaurants ranging from college cafeterias and fast-food places to exquisite dining establishments. Today, these companies serve a relatively new food-service outlet known as convenience stores.

At one time there was a feeling that convenience stores primarily served blue-collar customers. Blue-collar workers such as construction people remain important to convenience stores, as may be witnessed in the morning and lunchtime by those who purchase fast foods of all kinds. Today, 92,000 convenience stores exist in the United States, and the phenomenon is growing in many nations. Hundreds of millions of dollars are spent each year for prepared fast foods from convenience stores. These range from hot dogs to fried chicken, tacos, pizza, and many more. Fast-food chains such as American Favorite Chicken Company (Popeye's and Church's Chicken) have 30 fast-food outlets in convenience stores and have contracts for 200 more.[37]

Marketing Highlight — Restaurant Franchising

12–1 These days, it's nearly impossible to stroll down a city block or drive on a suburban street without seeing a Wendy's, a McDonald's, a Pizza Hut, or a Starbucks. One of the best-known and most successful franchisers, McDonald's, has more than 31,000 stores in more than a hundred countries. Gaining fast is Subway, one of the fastest-growing franchises, with more than 30,000 shops in eighty-seven countries.

How does a franchising system work? The individual franchises are a tightly knit group of enterprises whose systematic operations are planned, directed, and controlled by the operation's innovator, called a franchiser. The franchisee is required to pay for the right to be part of the system. Yet this initial fee is only a small part of the total amount that franchisees invest when they sign a franchising contract. Startup costs include rental and lease of equipment and fixtures and sometimes a regular license fee. McDonald's franchisees invest as much $1 to $2 million in initial startup costs. Subway's success is partly due to its low startup cost of $100,000 to $300,000, which is lower than most other franchises. However, Subway franchisees pay an 8 percent royalty on gross sales, one of the highest in the food franchise industry, plus a 4.5 percent advertising fee.

The franchiser provides its franchisees with a marketing and operations system for doing business. McDonald's requires franchises to attend its "Hamburger University" in Oak Brook, Illinois, for three weeks to learn how to manage the business; franchisees must also adhere to certain procedures in buying materials.

In the best cases, franchising is mutually beneficial to both franchiser and franchisee. Franchisers can cover new territory in little more than the time it takes the franchisee to sign a contract. They can achieve enormous purchasing power. Franchisers also benefit from the franchisees' familiarity with local communities and conditions and from the motivation and hard work of employees who are entrepreneurs rather than "hired hands." Similarly, franchisees benefit from buying into a proven business with a well-known and accepted brand name. And they receive ongoing support in areas ranging from marketing and advertising to site selection, staffing, and financing.

As a result of the franchise explosion in recent years, some fast-food franchisers are facing worrisome market saturation. One indication is the number of franchisee complaints filed with the Federal Trade Commission against parent companies, which has been growing by more than 50 percent annually since 1990. The most common complaint is that franchisers "encroach" on existing franchisees' territory by bringing in another store. For example, McDonald's franchisees in California and other states recently complained when the company decided to open new company-owned stores in their areas. Franchisees may object to parent company marketing programs that may adversely affect their operations. For instance, franchisees often strongly resist value promotions in which the company reduced prices on menu items in an effort to revive stagnant sales. Many franchisees believe that the value promotion cheapens the image of the chain and unnecessarily reduces their

In 2010 Subway surpassed McDonald's as the largest restaurant chain. This Subway restaurant is in Paris. Courtesy of Tupungato/Dreamstime.

profit margins. Another complaint is higher-than-advertised failure rates. Subway, in particular, has been criticized for misleading its franchisees by telling them that it has only a 2 percent failure rate when the reality is much different. In addition, some franchisees feel that they've been misled by exaggerated claims of support, only to feel abandoned after the contract is signed and money has been invested.

There will always be a conflict between the franchiser, who seeks systemwide growth, and the franchisees, who want to earn a good living from their individual franchises. One new direction that may deliver both franchiser growth and franchisee earnings is expansion abroad. Fast-food franchises have become very popular throughout the world. For example, Domino's has entered Japan with master franchisee Ernest Higa, who owns 106 stores in Japan with combined sales of $140 million. Part of Higa's success can be attributed to adapting Domino's product to the Japanese market, where food presentation is everything. Higa carefully charted the placement of pizza toppings and made cut-mark perforations in the boxes for perfectly uniform slices.

It appears franchise fever will not cool down soon. Experts estimate franchises capture 50 percent of all U.S. retail sales. Of the top twelve franchisees in worldwide sales, ten are related to the travel and hospitality industry. These franchises include McDonald's, Carlson Wagonlit Travel, Burger King, KFC, Pizza Hut, Wendy's, Marriott Hotels, Subway Restaurants, Sheraton, and Taco Bell.

Sources: www.mcdonalds.com (accessed December 5, 2004); www.subway.com (accessed December 5, 2004); "The Top 200," *Franchise Times* (October 2003); Norman D. Axelrad and Robert E. Weigand, *"Franchising—A Marriage of System Members,"* in *Marketing Managers Handbook* (3rd ed.), ed. Sidney Levy, George Frerichs, and Howard Gordon (Chicago, IL: Dartnell, 2004), pp. 919–934; Andrew E. Sewer, "McDonald's Conquers the World," *Fortune* (October 17, 1994): 103–116; Roberta Maynard, "The Decision to Franchise," *Nation's Business* (January 1997): 49–53; Cliff Edwards, "Campaign '55 Flop Shows Power of Franchisees," *Marketing News* (July 7, 1997): 9; Richard Behar, "Why Subway Is the Biggest Problem in Franchising," *Fortune* (March 16, 1998): 126–134, and Patrick J. Kaufman and Sevgin Eroglu, "Standardization and Adaptation in Business Format Franchising," *Journal of Business Venturing* (January 1999): 69–85.

Customer Needs

Selecting channel members starts with determining the services that consumers in various target segments want. The Victoria House in Belize caters to customers from the United States. Its customers do not want to call Central America to reserve a room but need an easy way to communicate with the hotel. In response, the Victoria House aligned with a Houston travel agent with a toll-free number. The travel agent receives reservations directly from guests and from other travel agents throughout the United States, relaying the information to the Victoria House.

A large resort such as the Fiesta Americana in Puerto Vallarta, Mexico, might consider aligning with a wholesaler. The wholesaler would put together a package that includes airfare, rooms, and ground transportation and distribute it through travel agents in the United States. In doing so, the wholesaler provides a package that gives guests everything they need to go on a vacation in Puerto Vallarta, eliminating the worry of finding their way around a foreign country. To design an effective channel, the company must understand the services its customers require and then balance the needs of those customers against the feasibility and costs of meeting them.

Attracting Channel Members

Companies vary in their ability to attract qualified intermediaries. Well-known hotel companies that have a reputation for paying commissions promptly and honoring the reservations of travel agents have no trouble gaining the support of intermediaries. A new hotel chain with only a few hotels will have difficulty getting most of the country's travel intermediaries firm to sell its chain. It would be wiser for the new chain to choose one to work with in key cities that are likely to generate business.

When contracting with a hotel sales representative, the hotel company should investigate the number and type of other hotels that the firm represents. It will also want to investigate the size and quality of its workforce. Just as a company carefully chooses its employees, it should carefully choose channel members. These firms will represent the company and will be partially responsible for the company's image.

Evaluating Major Channel Alternatives

Economic Feasibility of the Channel Member

Each channel produces different levels of sales and costs. The business that channel members bring must offset the cost of paying and supporting the channel member. These costs are measured in two ways: directly and by opportunity costs. For example, some casinos use bus operators to bring customers to them. The bus operator is paid a fee for each bus, plus the riders get an incentive, such as a free roll of quarters from the casino. Some casinos found that the cost of bringing a bus customer to the casino was greater than the casino's win from the bus customer. Previous management felt good because the buses brought hundreds of customers to the casino. However, when the buses were evaluated from an economic standpoint, they were found to be unprofitable because they did not cover their direct costs. Another direct cost of working with intermediaries is the support they will need from the company. Intermediaries require brochures and other collateral material, training, familiarization trips, and regular communication. A company should limit the size of its distribution system to one that it is able to support.

When the MGM Grand hotel opened, it used tour operators to fill many of its rooms. This business brought a low room rate, but the room rate more than covered the variable cost of the room, creating an operating profit. As demand for the MGM Grand's rooms grew, MGM could sell its rooms directly through travel agents and receive a higher room rate. At this point there was an opportunity cost associated with the tour operator, that is, the difference between the tour operator's rate and the higher rate that could be received through travel agents. An opportunity cost is created when we sell a product for a lower price than its market value. Opportunity costs are created when we discount products, only to find out that we could sell them for a higher price. In the example, the hotel decreased its allocation of rooms to tour operators and increased its allocation to travel agents to reduce the opportunity cost of selling rooms to tour operators.

A company must regularly evaluate the performance of its intermediaries. As business changes, the value of an intermediary may change, as was the case with MGM. The intermediary may not perform as expected. In this case the company must work with the intermediary to try to bring about the desired performance or eliminate the intermediary if it becomes unprofitable.

Checking on intermediaries is a delicate business. Sometimes problems may be due to improper support from the supplier. Companies need to evaluate the support they are giving their channel members and make the necessary adjustments. Underperforming intermediaries need to be counseled. They may need more training or motivation. If they do not shape up, it might be better to terminate them.

Control Criteria

An important consideration in the choice of channels is control. Using sales representatives offers less control than building your own sales force. Sales representatives may prefer to sell rooms in other hotels because it requires less effort. They may avoid smaller customers, preferring instead to call on larger companies who can use most of the hotels they represent.

In this example, it could be that the smaller customers are actually more profitable than the larger ones. This points out the importance of having data that show the degree of profit or loss from different customer groups and from all intermediaries. In the absence of the information, marketing/sales managers are forced to make decisions based on the assumptions or guesses or personal preferences. None of these is the basis for sound decision making.

Unfortunately the accounting departments of most hospitality companies do not offer this kind of assistance. Therefore, it may be necessary for the marketing department to hire its own analyst to provide this vital information.

Control is also an important consideration in franchising and choosing multiple channel members. One problem with franchising is that a company sacrifices some control to gain wider distribution. The company may have trouble getting franchisees to add new products or to participate in promotions. Some companies have problems getting their franchisees to meet quality control standards.

When a firm adds multiple channels, it must consider the rights of existing channel members. Often, existing channel members limit their activities with new channel members. For example, earlier in this chapter we talked about the promotion between Embassy Suites Hotel and Hertz. The promotion was modified because it went against the interests of another channel member, the travel agent.

Each channel involves a long-term commitment and loss of flexibility. A hotel firm using a sales representative in Mexico City may have to sign a five-year contract. During this five-year period, the hotel company may develop an alliance with an airline or hotel company based in Mexico. The sales representative in Mexico City may become unnecessary, but the company will be unable to end the relationship until the contract has ended. There is often a tradeoff between the benefits created by developing a long-term alliance and the loss of flexibility that often comes with such alliances. Understanding the tradeoffs and how the marketplace might change in the future can help a manager make decisions regarding the length of contractual agreements with channel members.

■■■ Responsibilities of Channel Members and Suppliers

The company and its intermediaries must agree on the terms and responsibilities of each channel member. For instance, hotels make it clear to travel agents which rates are commissionable and the amount of commission to be paid, and they often guarantee to pay the commission within a certain number of days. Wendy's and other companies provide franchisees with promotional support, a record-keeping system, training, and general management assistance. In turn, franchisees must meet company standards for physical facilities, cooperate with new promotional programs, provide requested information, and buy specified food products. To avoid disputes, it is important that companies have an explicit arrangement in writing with their channel members.

After the selection of the channel members, a company must continuously motivate its members. Just as a firm must market to its employees, it must also market to its intermediaries. Most firms use positive incentives during times of slow demand. For example, during slow periods, hotel or rental car companies often increase the percentage of commission that they pay. Keeping channel members informed about the company's products is another way to motivate channel members. Hotels with sales representatives must keep them informed about changes in facilities and new products. A company must provide communication and support for its channel members.

■■■ Business Location

One of the most important aspects of distribution for hospitality organizations is location. For businesses whose customers come to them, the business must be conveniently located. Many retailers say the three secrets of successful retailing are "location, location, and location." There is no single formula for location. A good location for a Ritz-Carlton Hotel is different from that of a Motel 6 or a Burger King. Restaurant sites tend to be evaluated on the ability of the local area to provide business. Hotel sites are evaluated on the attractiveness of their location to persons coming to that destination. In both cases, location depends on the firm's marketing strategy. Each firm has its own set of location evaluation characteristics.

The Waldorf-Astoria promotes its prime location. "At the heart of the world stands the Waldorf-Astoria, the flagship of Hilton Hotels, a marvelous and soothing environment where the quality and service of yesterday still exist today. Approach on Park Avenue and stand for a moment outside. You're at the center of it all, bounded by the theaters of Broadway, the country's most fashionable shopping district along Fifth Avenue, the United Nations, the commerce of the world." From a promotional brochure from the Waldorf-Astoria, a Hilton Hotel. Courtesy of Jon Arnold Images Ltd/Alamy.

In general, there are four steps in choosing a location. The first is understanding the marketing strategy and target market of the company. La Quinta motels cater to the traveling salesperson and other midclass hotel guests arriving primarily by automobile. Locations are typically along freeways outside major metropolitan areas. They are close enough to the central business district to offer convenient access, yet far enough away to allow economic purchase of the site. Hyatt, in contrast, caters to groups and the businessperson who often arrives by plane. Hyatt hotels are often located in the heart of the central business district. The location decision, like other marketing decisions, cannot be separated from the marketing strategy.

The second step of the selection is regional analysis, which involves the selection of geographic market areas.[38] A restaurant chain may plan to expand into a new metropolitan market. It may need to find a region that will support at least five new stores. A business hotel chain expanding into Southeast Asia may target key cities such as Singapore, Bangkok, Kuala Lumpur, and Jakarta. The chain wants to have a presence in major cities of the region so that business travelers can stay in the chain as they travel throughout the region.

A firm would want to make sure a region has sufficient and stable demand to support the hotel(s) or restaurant(s). A growing area with a diverse economic base is attractive. Areas based on one industry are often attractive when that industry is in favor but are highly vulnerable when that industry suffers.

This is equally true when tourism and hospitality are the primary industries. Miami Beach experienced industry problems when some European tourists were assaulted or killed. The ski industry and ski resort towns depend on the whims of nature. Too little or too much snow can create major economic problems.

Once the firm has chosen a geographic region, the next step is to select an area within that region. If a restaurant chain wants to open five restaurants in a metropolitan area, it must choose favorable sites. The chain will look at the demographic and psychographic characteristics of the area. Competition and growth potential of the different areas will be evaluated. The result will be a choice of five areas within the region that seem most promising.

Finally, the firm will choose individual sites. A key consideration in site analysis is compatible businesses. A restaurant or hotel will look for potential demand generators. For a hotel these can be major office complexes, airports, or integrated retail, residential, and business complexes. A restaurant may look for residential communities, shopping centers, or motels without food and beverage facilities. Demand generators vary depending on the target markets of the business. It is important for firms to have a good profile of their customers when they look for customer sources within a given area.

In addition to demand generators, a firm looks at competitors. If there is an adequate supply of similar restaurants or hotels, the site is usually rejected. Hotels have entered saturated markets just to gain a presence in that city. Competition is not always a negative factor. Restaurants often tend to be clustered, creating a restaurant row. This can be beneficial. Customers going to one restaurant are exposed to a selection of others.

Site evaluation includes accessibility. Is the site easily accessible by traffic going in different directions, or do uncrossable medians create a barrier? Is the site visible to allow drivers to turn? Speed of traffic is also a factor. The slower the traffic is, the longer the visibility. Restaurant sites at intersections with a stoplight have the benefit of exposure to waiting drivers. The desirability of the surroundings is another consideration. Is the area attractive? If the site is in a shopping center, is the center well maintained? Other considerations for the site include drainage, sewage, utilities, and size.

Often, companies develop a profile of preferred sites. For example, Carl's Jr. Restaurant, a fast-food hamburger restaurant, developed this profile:[39]

- Free-standing location in a shopping center

- Free-standing corner location (with a signal light at the intersection)

- Inside lot with 125-foot minimum frontage

- Enclosed shopping mall

- Population of 12,000 or more in a one-mile radius (growth areas preferred)

- Easy access of traffic to location

- Heavy vehicular/pedestrian traffic

- An area where home values and family income levels are average or above

- Close to offices and other demand generators

- A parcel size of 30,000 to 50,000 square feet

- No less than two or three miles from other existing company locations

The choice of a site is often determined by a checklist, statistical analysis, or a combination of both. A checklist usually contains items such as those listed in the profile and specific building requirements. Items such as building codes, signage restrictions, availability of utilities, parking, and drainage are also included in a checklist. A common type of statistical analysis used in site selection is regression analysis. The dependent variable in the equation is sales, and the independent variables are factors that contribute to sales. Typical independent variables might include population within the market area, household income of the market, competitors, and attributes of the location.

Restaurants have been downsizing to allow access to smaller markets and new types of locations. For example, Captain D's fast-food seafood restaurant developed a 1,800 square-foot location that seats thirty-three to forty-two diners. Its original design called for 128 seats and the design required 3,250 square feet. This makes the unit feasible in locations that do not have room for a full-size unit or cannot support the sales the larger unit would require. McDonald's was one of the first chains to develop smaller units that made it feasible for the franchise to go into smaller towns and inside retail outlets. Chili's, a casual service restaurant, has developed a smaller version with a reduced menu called Chili's Too for airport and other nontraditional locations. The Cheesecake Factory, a popular sit-down service restaurant, developed its Cheesecake Factory Café as an outlet for its signature desserts.[40] As good locations become more difficult to find, restaurants are looking for nontraditional locations and building units that will fit these sites. They are then using the strength of their brand name as a competitive advantage. Location is a key attribute for a hotel or restaurant. The location must not only be favorable at the present time but also continue to be good throughout the life of the business.

Chain operations generally have a real estate department that is responsible for selecting locations and negotiating leases or contracts to purchase successful properties. Commercial real estate agencies can be extremely helpful to hospitality companies desiring to locate in a new market. These firms should be expected to participate in multiphases from planning to acquisition of properties. They should offer services to assist in many or all of the tasks previously described that are associated with locating and acquiring new properties.

■■■ KEY TERMS

Administered VMS. A vertical marketing system that coordinates successive stages of production and distribution, not through common ownership or contractual ties, but through the size and power of one of the parties.

Agent. A wholesaler who represents buyers or sellers on a more permanent basis, performs only a few functions, and does not take title to goods.

Alliances. Alliances are developed to allow two organizations to benefit from each other's strengths.

Broker. A wholesaler who does not take title to goods and whose function is to bring buyers and sellers together and assist in negotiations.

Channel conflict. Disagreement among marketing channel members on goals and roles—who should do what and for what rewards.

Channel level. A level of middleman that performs some work in bringing the product and its ownership closer to the final buyer.

Contractual VMS. A vertical marketing system in which independent firms at different levels of production and distribution join together through contracts to obtain more economies or sales impact than they could achieve alone.

Corporate VMS. A vertical marketing system that combines successive stages of production and distribution under single ownership. Channel leadership is established through common ownership.

Direct marketing channel. A marketing channel that has no intermediary levels.

Franchise. A contractual vertical marketing system in which a channel member called a franchiser links several stages in the production distribution process.

Horizontal conflict. Conflict between firms at the same level.

Horizontal marketing system (HMS). Two or more companies at one level join to follow new marketing opportunities. Companies can combine their capital, production capabilities, or marketing resources to accomplish more than one company working alone.

Junket reps. Serve the casino industry as intermediaries for premium players.

Motivational houses. Provide incentive travel offered to employees or distributors as a reward for their efforts.

Multichannel marketing distribution. Multichannel distribution, as when a single firm sets up two or more marketing channels to reach one or more customer segments.

Online travel agency (OTA). A travel agency that conducts business through the Internet with no physical locations or stores.

Retailer. Business whose sales come primarily from retailing.

Supply Chain. Upstream and downstream partners. Upstream from the company is a set of firms that supply raw materials, components, parts, information, finances, and expertise needed to create a product. Downstream marketing channel partners, such as wholesalers and retailers, form a vital connection between the firm and its customers.

Vertical conflict. Conflict between different levels of the same channel.

Vertical marketing systems (VMS). Distribution channel structures in which producers, wholesalers, and retailers act as a unified system: Either one channel member owns the others, or has contracts with them, or has so much power that they all cooperate.

Wholesaler. Firms engaged primarily in wholesaling activity.

■■■ CHAPTER REVIEW

I. Supply Chains and the Value Delivery Network

II. Nature and Importance of Distribution Systems. A distribution channel is a set of independent organizations involved in the process of making a product or service available to the consumer or business user.

   A. Reasons that marketing intermediaries are used. The use of intermediaries depends on their greater efficiency in marketing the goods available to target markets. Through their contacts, experience, specialization, and scale of operation, intermediaries normally offer more than a firm can on its own.

   B. Distribution channel functions

      1. Information. Gathering and distributing marketing research and intelligence information about the marketing environment.

      2. Promotion. Developing and spreading persuasive communications about an offer.

      3. Contact. Finding and communicating with prospective buyers.

      4. Matching. Shaping and fitting the offer to the buyers' needs.

      5. Negotiation. Agreeing on price and other terms of the offer so that ownership or possession can be transferred.

      6. Physical distribution. Transporting and storing goods.

      7. Financing. Acquiring and using funds to cover the cost of channel work.

      8. Risk taking. Assuming financial risks, such as the inability to sell inventory at full margin.

   C. Number of channel levels. The number of channel levels can vary from direct marketing, through which the manufacturer sells directly to the consumer, to complex distribution systems involving four or more channel members.

III. Hospitality Distribution Channels

   A. Major hospitality distribution channels

      1. Direct booking

      2. Online travel agencies

      3. Global distribution systems

      4. Travel agents

      5. Tour wholesalers

   B. Specialists: tour brokers, motivational houses, and junket reps

   C. Hotel representatives

   D. National, state, and local tourist agencies

   E. Consortia and reservation systems

   F. Concierges

   G. Restaurant distribution systems

IV. Channel Behavior

   A. Channel conflict. Although channel members depend on each other, they often act alone in their own short-run best interests. They frequently disagree on the roles each should play on who should do what for which rewards.

      1. Horizontal conflict. Conflict between firms at the same level.

      2. Vertical conflict. Conflict between different levels of the same channel.

V. Channel Organization. Distribution channels are shifting from loose collections of independent companies to unified systems.

   A. Conventional marketing system. A conventional marketing system consists of one or more independent producers, wholesalers, and retailers. Each is a separate business seeking to maximize its own profits, even at the expense of profits for the system as a whole.

   B. Vertical marketing system. A vertical marketing system consists of producers, wholesalers, and retailers acting as a unified system. VMSs were developed to control channel behavior and manage channel conflict and its economies through size, bargaining power, and elimination of duplicated services. The three major types of VMSs are corporate, administered, and contractual.

      1. Corporate. A corporate VMS combines successive stages of production and distribution under single ownership.

      2. Administered. An administered VMS coordinates successive stages of production and distribution, not through common ownership or contractual ties, but through the size and power of the parties.

      3. Contractual. A contractual VMS consists of independent firms at different levels of production and distribution who join through contracts to obtain economies or sales impact.

         a. Franchising. Franchising is a method of doing business by which a franchisee is granted the right to engage in offering, selling, or distributing goods or services under a marketing format that is designed by the franchisor. The franchisor permits the franchisee to use its trademark, name, and advertising.

         b. Alliances. Alliances are developed to allow two organizations to benefit from each other's strengths.

   C. Horizontal marketing system. Two or more companies at one level join to follow new marketing opportunities. Companies can combine their capital, production capabilities, or marketing resources to accomplish more than one company working alone.

   D. Multichannel marketing system. A single firm sets up two or more marketing channels to reach one or more customer segments.

VI. Selecting Channel Members

   A. Customer needs

   B. Attracting channel members

   C. Evaluating major channel alternatives

      1. Economic feasibility of channel member

      2. Control criteria

VII. Responsibilities of Channel Members and Suppliers. The company and its intermediaries must agree on the terms and responsibilities of each channel member. According to the services and clientele at hand, the responsibilities are formulated after careful consideration.

VIII. Business Location. There are four steps in choosing a location:
  A. Understanding the marketing strategy. Know the target market of the company.
  B. Regional analysis. Select the geographic market areas.

  C. Choosing the area within the region. Demographic and psychographic characteristics and competition are factors to consider.
  D. Choosing the individual site. Compatible business, competitors, accessibility, drainage, sewage, utilities, and size are factors to consider.

■■■ DISCUSSION QUESTIONS

1. Discuss how you think technology will change distribution channels in the hospitality and travel industries over the next five years.
2. Explain how international travel changed distribution channels in the hospitality and travel industries.
3. What are the major differences between a distribution channel for a business making tangible products and a firm producing hospitality and travel products?
4. Can a business have too many channel members? Explain your answer.
5. Explain the difference between a tour wholesaler and a travel agent.

6. Why is franchising such a fast-growing form of retail organization?
7. According to the International Franchising Association, between 30 and 50 percent of all new franchise applicants are people who formerly worked in large corporations and who lost their jobs as a result of corporate downsizing. How do you think these midlevel, midcareer corporate executives will adapt to life as franchise owners? How will their previous corporate experience help them? How will it hurt them?

■■■ EXPERIENTIAL EXERCISES

Do one of the following:

1. Visit a restaurant that offers take-out service. What has it done to facilitate take-out service? For example, does it have a special order and pickup area; does it have paper menus to take home; does it accept phone, fax, or Internet orders; and does it have special packaging for take-out? Report on what you find and any suggestions that you might have.

2. Investigate franchises available in the hospitality or travel business. Select a franchise you feel would be a good business investment based on what the franchise offers and the fees the franchiser charges. Support your findings in a two- to three-page report.

■■■ INTERNET EXERCISE

Find a hospitality or travel company that allows customers to make reservations directly through its Web site. What customer segment do you think will make reservations through this site, and do you think the design of the site is effective? Explain your answer.

■■■ REFERENCES

1. "Not all Gloom and Doom," *Travel Weekly* (October 1, 2004): 12. Juliet Dennis, "Survey Finds Market Share Is Diminishing," *Travel Weekly* (October 1, 2004): 12; Alan Ching-biu Tse, "Disintermediation of Travel Agents in the Hotel Industry," *International Journal of Hospitality Management,* 22 (2003): 453–460; Bill Anckar, "Consumer Intentions in Terms of Electronic Travel Distribution, *eService Journal* (Winter 2003): 68–86; Paulette Thomas, "Case Study: Travel Agency Meets Technology's Threats," *Wall Street Journal* (May 21, 2002): B4.
2. E. Raymond Corey, Frank V. Cespedes, and V. Kasturi Rangan, *Going to Market* (Boston, MA: Harvard Business School Press, 1989), p. xxvii; Sunflowertravel.com, Ciclismoclassico.com.

3. Amy Ricciardi, "Marriott, Otani Enter Marketing Pact," *Travel Weekly,* 51, no. 12 (1992): 3.
4. Louis W. Stern and Adel I. El-Ansary, *Marketing Channels* (3rd ed.) (Upper Saddle River, NJ: Prentice Hall, 1988), p. 3.
5. Corey, Cespedes, and Rangan, *Going to Market.*
6. Stephanie Ricca, "Distribution Channel Analysis," *Hotel Management.net* (June 15, 2011), http://www.hotelmanagement.netaccessed on October 8, 2011).
7. "TravelClick: Direct Hotel Bookings Are Most Popular," *Hotel Management.net* (September 20, 2011), http://www.hotelmanagement.net (accessed on October 8, 2011).

8. Patrick Mayock, "Consumer booking behavior in the age of comparison shopping," *HotelNewsNow.Com* (January 15, 2011), accessed August 5, 2012, http://www.hotelnewsnow.com/Articles.aspx/4861/Consumer-booking-behavior-in-the-age-of-comparison-shopping; Stacey Mieyal Higgins, " Researchers: Distribution ROI closer to reality," *HotelNewsNow.Com* (June 15, 2011), accessed August 5, 2012, from http://www.hotelnewsnow.com/Articles.aspx/5760/Researchers-Distribution-ROI-closer-to-reality.

9. Stowe Shoemaker and Margaret Shaw, *Marketing Essentials in Hospitality and Tourism: Foundations and Practices* (Upper Saddle River, NJ: Pearson Education, 2008); www.sabre-holdings.com; www.Travelport.com; www.amadeus.com (accessed September 29, 2008).

10. *Frequently Asked Questions: Travel Agents by the Numbers,* http://www.astanet.com/about/faq.asp#many (accessed November 28, 2004).

11. *Airline Commissions,* http://www.traveltrade.com/generic_page.jsp?articleID=1335 (accessed November 28, 2004).

12. Robert C. Lewis, *Marketing Leadership in Hospitality: Foundations and Practices* (3rd ed.) (New York: Wiley, 2000).

13. For more information on familiarization trips, see *How to Plan and Program Travel Agent Familiarization Tours* (Washington, DC: Hotel Sales and Marketing Association, undated).

14. James R. Abbey, *Hospitality Sales and Advertising* (East Lansing, MI: Educational Institute of the American Hotel and Motel Association, 1989).

15. Fran Golden, "Room for Growth," *Travel Weekly,* 53, no. 65 (1994): 118.

16. Michael M. Coltman, *Tourism Marketing* (New York: Van Nostrand Reinhold, 1989).

17. Chuck Y. Gee, James C. Makens, and Dexter J. L. Choy, *The Travel Industry* (New York: Van Nostrand Reinhold, 1989).

18. For more information on tour brokers, see *HSMA/Group Tour Information Manual* (Washington, DC: Hotel Sales and Marketing Association, undated).

19. Coltman, *Tourism Marketing.*

20. *Sydney Convention and Visitors Bureau,* http://www.scvb.com.au (accessed November 28, 2004).

21. Utell's Web site, http://www.utell.com/ (accessed September 29, 2008).

22. France Martin, "Consortia Extend Hotels' Regional, Global Reach," *Hotels,* 25, no. 9 (1991): x; Chris Baum, "How Utell Reacts to the Market," *Hotel,* 25, no. 9 (1991): 73–74; James Carper, "The New Brand of SRS," *Steigenberger Hotels,* 25, no. 10 (1991): 72–74.

23. See J. C. Holloway and R. V. Plant, *Marketing for Tourism* (London: Pitman, 1992), pp. 124–126.

24. Matt Marshall, "OpenTable Seats 3M Diners a Month, Releases a Mobile Version," www.VentureBeat.com, June 29, 2008 (accessed September 25, 2008).

25. Example adapted from Richard Gibson, "Burger King Franchisees Can't Have It *Their* Own Way," *Wall Street Journal* (January 21, 2010): BI; with additional information from Emily Bryson York, "BK Swears Off Sex in Ads to Quell Franchisee Freak Out," *Advertising Age* (July 13, 2009): 1; and York, "Burger King, Franchisees Start Making Nice," *Advertising Age* (February 17, 2010), http://adage.com/article?article_id=142158.

26. Andy Kostecka, *Franchising in the Economy* (Washington, DC: U.S. Government Printing Office, 1987), p. 2.

27. Stephen Rushmore, "Hotel Franchising: How to Be a Successful Franchisee," *Real Estate Journal* (Summer 1997): 56; cited in James R. Brown and Chekitan S. Dev, "The Franchisor–Franchisee Relationship," *Cornell Hotel and Restaurant Administration Quarterly* (December 1997): 30–31.

28. Michael Levy and Barton A. Weitz, *Retailing Management* (Homewood, IL: Richard D. Irwin, 1995), pp. 29–35.

29. David Fraboutta, " The Price of Franchising," *Hotel and Motel Management* (May 21, 2001): 23–32.

30. See Yae Sock Roh and William P. Andrew, "Sub-franchising," *Cornell Hotel and Restaurant Administration Quarterly* (December 1997): 39–45.

31. R. Bond, *Source Book of Franchise Opportunity* (Homewood, IL: Dow Jones–Irwin, 1993): 216–301.

32. Roh and Andrew, "Sub-Franchising," p. 40.

33. Robert Strate and Clinton Rappole, "Strategic Alliances Between Hotels and Restaurants," *Cornell Hotel and Restaurant Administration Quarterly* (June 1997): 50–61.

34. Bill Poling, "Motor Coach Network Launches Partner Program for Hotels," *Travel Weekly,* 51, no. 83 (1992): 7.

35. See Lee Adler, "Symbiotic Marketing," *Harvard Business Review* (November/December 1966): 59–71; P. Varadarajan and Daniel Rajaratnam, "Symbiotic Marketing Revisited," *Journal of Marketing* (January 1986): 7–17.

36. See Robert Weigand, "Fit Products and Channels to Your Markets," *Harvard Business Review* (January/February 1977): 95–105.

37. Louise Kramer, *Nation's Restaurant News* (May 20, 1996).

38. See Avijit Gosh, *Retail Management* (Fort Worth, TX: Dryden Press, 1990), pp. 216–249.

39. Donald E. Lindberg, *The Restaurant from Concept to Operation* (New York: Wiley, 1985), p. 35.

40. Paul Frumkin, "Have Concept, Will Travel: Chains Find Smaller Units Have Legs," *Nation's Restaurant News* (February 19, 2001): 55–58.

Promoting Products: Communication and Promotion Policy and Advertising

13

The Internet has created a new marketing phenomenon called viral marketing. Some business experts claim viral marketing is electronic word of mouth. Others claim viral marketing differs from word of mouth because in viral marketing the originator of the communication and those who spread the message have a vested interest in recruiting others to spread the word. Viral marketing has two major features. The first is that people are pushing the message to others. The second is they are often pushing it to people they know and asking them to push it to people they know. The ease of use of the Internet combined with other sources for electronic communication such as text messaging makes these forms of media ideal for viral marketing. Many people delete e-mail advertisements without opening them, and often spam filters prevent some people from even receiving the advertisements. With viral marketing, the message is coming from a friend, so it is opened.

Companies such as Heinz Ketchup and Chipotle have been encouraging their customers to make advertisements for them. Chipotle used viral marketing to create over 17 million views on YouTube in just six weeks. It is estimated that just the placement of electronic media to reach this many views would cost $346,000. Additionally, the campaign created a media buzz that generated publicity valued at over $1 million. The cost to Chipotle was $50,000, which included prize money.

Chipotle invited university students to submit a 30-second ad in its "Chipotle Mexican Grill—30 Seconds of Fame" advertising contest. There were two tiers, one for the best creative and one for the most watched. The best creative award was $20,000, and the most viewed advertisement received $10,000. The money was split between the university and the students who created the advertisement. There were sixty-nine entries from twenty-one schools.

After six weeks, there were more than 17.3 million views of the submissions, with the top two creating over 15 million views. The "Dady," featuring a bald-headed father who criticizes his young son's drawing for making his head the wrong shape and not spelling his name correctly, featured the theme that Chipotle seeks perfection. Students from the university of Nebraska-Lincoln produced "Dady," which won the most viewed award, receiving over 8 million views by the end of the contest. Students from Southern Methodist University won the $20,000 award for the most creative. Their video, "The Wall," was also runner-up for the most viewed, with over 7.5 million views.

How did these videos create so many views? The answer is viral marketing. Students went out on their campus, asking other students to view their work. Students were encouraged to send the link to their friends. Parents sent links

Objectives

After reading this chapter, you should be able to:

1. Discuss the process and advantages of integrated marketing communications in communicating customer value.

2. Define the five promotion tools and discuss the factors that must be considered in shaping the overall promotion mix.

3. Outline the steps in developing effective marketing communications.

4. Explain the methods for setting the promotion budget and factors that affect the design of the promotion mix.

5. Define the roles of advertising in the promotion mix.

6. Describe the major decisions in advertising, including setting objectives and budget; creating the advertising message; selecting advertising media; choosing media types, vehicles, and timing; and evaluating advertising.

to their friends asking them to view their children's work. People were asked to view the videos multiple times to increase the number of "votes" for the video. Chipotle's contest motivated students to create scores of advertisements for them and mobilize thousands of people to look at the advertisements. Additionally, the uniqueness of the contest made it an ideal candidate for publicity in print and electronic media. There were a number of articles in university newspapers and newspapers in the towns that were home to the universities whose students submitted videos.

Chipotle achieved two main objectives. It created a promotion that would reach Millennials, one of its target markets. Typically, this age group does not read print media, but they do use Web 2.0. Second, they successfully applied viral marketing to spread word about Chipotle. This campaign shows how an effectively designed promotional program can receive your target market on a budget you can afford.[1]

Building good customer relationships calls for more than just developing a good product, pricing it attractively, and making it available to target customers. Companies must also *communicate* their value propositions to customers, and what they communicate should not be left to chance. All of their communications must be planned and blended into carefully integrated marketing communications (IMC) programs. Just as good communication is important in building and maintaining any kind of relationship, it is a crucial element in a company's efforts to build profitable customer relationships.

■▪▪ The Promotion Mix

A company's total **promotion mix**—also called its marketing communications mix—consists of the specific blend of advertising, public relations, personal selling, sales promotion, and direct-marketing tools that the company uses to communicate customer value and build customer relationships persuasively. Definitions of the five major promotion tools follow:[2]

Advertising: Any paid form of nonpersonal presentation and promotion of ideas, goods, or services by an identified sponsor

Sales promotion: Short-term incentives to encourage the purchase or sale of a product or service

Personal selling: Personal presentation by the firm's sales force for the purpose of making sales and building customer relationships

Public relations: Building good relations with the company's various publics by obtaining favorable publicity, building up a good corporate image, and handling or heading off unfavorable rumors, stories, and events

Direct marketing: Direct connections with carefully targeted individual consumers to both obtain an immediate response and cultivate lasting customer relationships—the use of direct mail, the telephone, direct-response television, e-mail, the Internet, and other tools to communicate directly with specific consumers

Each category involves specific promotional tools used to communicate with consumers. For example, advertising includes broadcast, print, Internet, outdoor, and other forms. Sales promotion includes discounts, coupons, displays, and demonstrations. **Personal selling** includes sales presentations, trade shows, and incentive programs. Public relations includes press releases, sponsorships, special events, and Web pages. And direct marketing includes catalogs, telephone marketing, kiosks, the Internet, and more.

At the same time, marketing communication goes beyond these specific promotion tools. The salesperson's manner and dress, the place's decor, the company's stationery—all communicate something to the buyers. Every brand contact delivers an impression that can strengthen or weaken a customer's view of the company. The whole marketing mix must be integrated to deliver a consistent message and strategic positioning.

■■■ Integrated Marketing Communications

In past decades, marketers perfected the art of mass marketing: selling highly stand-ardized products to masses of customers. In the process, they developed effective mass-media communications techniques to support these strategies. Large compa-nies now routinely invest millions or even billions of dollars in television, maga-zine, or other mass media advertising, reaching tens of millions of customers with a single ad. Today, however, marketing managers face some new marketing com-munications realities. Perhaps no other area of marketing is changing so profoundly as marketing communications, creating both exciting and scary times for marketing communications.

The New Marketing Communications Landscape

Several major factors are changing the face of today's marketing communications. First, consumers are changing. In this digital, wireless age, they are better informed and more connected. Rather than relying on marketer-supplied information, they can use the Internet and other technologies to seek out information on their own. More than that, they can more easily connect with other consumers to exchange brand-related information or even to create their own marketing messages.

Second, *marketing strategies* are changing. As mass markets have fragmented, marketers are shifting away from mass marketing. More and more, they are devel-oping focused marketing programs designed to build closer relationships with cus-tomers in more narrowly defined micromarkets.

Finally, sweeping advances in *communications technology* are causing re-markable changes in the ways in which companies and customers communicate with each other. The digital age has spawned a host of new information and com-munication tools—from smartphones and iPods to satellite and cable television systems to the many faces of the Internet (e-mail, social networks, blogs, brand Web sites, and much more). These explosive developments have had a dramatic impact on marketing communications. Just as mass marketing once gave rise to a new gen-eration of mass-media communications, the new digital media have given birth to a new marketing communications model.

Although television, magazines, newspapers, and other mass media remain very important, their dominance is declining. In their place, advertisers are now adding a broad selection of more specialized and highly targeted media to reach smaller customer segments with more personalized, interactive messages. The new media range from specialty cable television channels and made-for-the-Web videos to Internet catalogs, e-mail, blogs, cell phone content, and online social networks. In all, companies are doing less *broadcasting* and more *narrowcasting*.

Some advertising industry experts even predict that the old mass-media com-munications model will soon be obsolete. Mass media costs are rising, audiences are shrinking, ad clutter is increasing, and viewers are gaining control of message exposure through technologies such as video streaming or digital video recordings (DVRs) that let them skip past disruptive television commercials. As a result, they suggest, marketers are shifting ever-larger portions of their marketing budgets away from old-media mainstays such as 30-second TV commercials and glossy maga-zine ads to digital and other new-age media. For example, one study forecasts that whereas TV advertising spending will grow by only 4 percent per year over the next five years, ad spending on the Internet and other digital media will surge by 17 percent a year.[3]

The Shifting Marketing Communications Model

The shift toward segmented marketing and the explosive developments in informa-tion and communications technology have had a dramatic impact on marketing com-munications. Just as mass marketing once gave rise to a new generation of mass-media communications, the shift toward targeted marketing and the changing communica-tions environment are giving birth to a new marketing communications model.

Some advertising industry experts are predicting a doom-and-gloom "chaos scenario," in which the old mass-media communications model will collapse entirely. They believe that marketers will increasingly abandon traditional mass media in favor of "the glitzy promise of new technologies—from Web sites and e-mail to cell phone content and video on demand (VOD). Fragmentation, the bane of network TV and mass marketers everywhere, will become the Holy Grail, the opportunity to reach—and have a conversation with—small clusters of consumers who are consuming not what is force-fed them, but exactly what they want."[4]

Just think about what's happening to television viewing these days. "Adjust your set," says one reporter, "television is changing as quickly as the channels. It's on cell phones. It's on digital music players. It's on almost anything with a screen. Shows can be seen at their regular times or when you want [with or without the commercials]. Some 'TV' programs aren't even on cable or network or satellite; they're being created just for Internet viewing."[5]

Consumers, especially younger ones, appear to be turning away from the major television networks in favor of cable TV or altogether different media. According to one study,

> Only one in four 12-to-34 year olds can name all four major broadcast-ing networks: ABC, NBC, CBS, and Fox. Teens may not be able to name the big four, but they know MTV, Cartoon Network, and Comedy Central. The most popular activity? That would be surfing the Internet, which 84 percent said they did during their idle periods. Hanging out with friends came in second at 76 percent, watching movies third at 71 percent, and TV viewing fourth at 69 percent.[6]

As a result, marketers are losing confidence in television advertising. As mass media costs rise, audiences shrink, ad clutter increases, and viewers use VOD and DVR systems to skip past disruptive television commercials; many skeptics even predict the demise of the old mass-media mainstay: the 30-second television commercial. "Consider something barely imaginable," says a major "chaos scenario" proponent, "a media world substantially devoid of brand advertising as we have long known it. It's a world in which consumer engagement occurs without consumer interruption in which marketing—and even branding—are conducted without much reliance on the 30-second spot because nobody is much interested in seeing [it], and because soon [it] will be largely necessary."[7]

Thus, many large advertisers are shifting their advertising budgets away from network television in favor of more targeted, cost-effective, interactive, and engaging media. "The ad industry's plotline used to be a lot simpler: Audiences are splintering off in dozens of new directions, watching TV shows on iPods, watching movies on videogame players, and listening to radio on the Internet," observes one analyst. So marketers must "start planning how to reach consumers in new and unexpected ways."[8]

Rather than a "chaos scenario," however, other industry insiders see a more gradual shift to the new marketing communications model. They note that broadcast television and other mass media still capture a lion's share of the promotion budgets of most major marketing firms, a fact that isn't likely to change quickly. Although some may question the future of the 30-second spot, it's still very much in use today. TV ad spending actually rose last year by more than 7 percent (although online advertising grew 25 percent). Moreover, advertising experts advise, "Because TV is at the forefront of many technological advances [such as DVRs and video on demand]; its audience will continue to increase. So if you think that TV is an aging dinosaur, or you're a national advertiser who is thinking of moving ad dollars away from TV, maybe you should think again."[9]

Thus, it seems likely that the new marketing communications model will consist of a gradually shifting mix of both traditional mass media and a wide array of exciting new, more targeted, more personalized media. "We need to reinvent the way we market to consumers," says A. G. Lafley, chief executive of Procter & Gamble. "Mass marketing still has an important role, [but] we need new models to initially coexist with mass marketing, and eventually to succeed it."[10]

The Need for *Integrated* Marketing Communications

The shift toward a richer mix of media and communication approaches poses a problem for marketers. Consumers today are bombarded by commercial messages from a broad range of sources. But consumers don't distinguish between message sources the way marketers do. In the consumer's mind, messages from different media and promotional approaches all become part of a single message about the company. Conflicting messages from these different sources can result in confused company images, brand positions, and customer relationships.

All too often, companies fail to integrate their various communication channels. The result is a hodgepodge of communications to consumers. Mass-media advertisements say one thing while a price promotion sends a different signal, and a product label creates still another message. Company sales literature says something altogether different, and the company's Web site seems out of sync with everything else.

The problem is that these communications often come from different parts of the company. Advertising messages are planned and implemented by the advertising department or an advertising agency. Personal selling communications are developed by sales management. Other company specialists are responsible for public relations, sales promotion events, Internet marketing, and other forms of marketing communications. However, whereas these companies have separated their communications tools, customers won't. Mixed communications from these sources will result in blurred consumer brand perceptions.

Today, more companies are adopting the concept of **integrated marketing communications** (IMC). Under this concept, as illustrated in Figure 13–1, the company carefully integrates its many communications channels to deliver a clear, consistent, and compelling message about the organization and its brands.

Integrated marketing communications calls for recognizing all touchpoints where the customer may encounter the company and its brands. Each brand contact will deliver a message—whether good, bad, or indifferent. The company's goal should be to deliver a consistent and positive message to each contact. IMC leads

Figure 13–1
Integrated marketing communications.

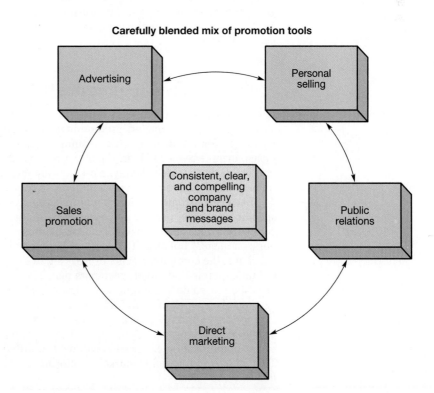

to a total marketing communications strategy aimed at building strong customer relationships by showing how the company and its products can help customers solve their problems.

Integrated marketing communications ties together all of the company's messages and images. Its television and print ads have the same message, look, and feel as its e-mail and personal selling communications. And its public relations materials project the same image as its Web site or social network presence. Often, different media play unique roles in attracting, informing, and persuading consumers; these roles must be carefully coordinated under the overall marketing communications plan.

A great example of the power of a well-integrated marketing communications effort is Burger King's now-classic, award-winning, Whopper Freakout campaign: To celebrate the 50th anniversary of the iconic Whopper, Burger King launched a campaign to show what would happen if it suddenly removed the sandwich from its menu forever. It dropped the Whopper in selected restaurants and used hidden cameras to capture the real-time reactions of stricken customers. It then shared the results in a carefully integrated, multipronged promotional campaign. The campaign began with coordinated TV, print, and radio spots announcing that "We stopped selling the Whopper for one day to see what would happen. What happened was, people freaked!" The ads drove consumers to a Web site which featured a video documentary outlining the entire experiment. The documentary was also uploaded to YouTube. At the Web site, visitors could view Freakout ads showing the disbelieving, often angry reactions of a dozen or more customers. Burger King also promoted the campaign through rich media ad banners on several other popular Web sites. Customers themselves extended the campaign with spoofs and parodies posted on YouTube. The richly integrated Whopper Freakout campaign was a smashing success. The ads became the most recalled campaign in Burger King's history, and the Web site received 4 million views in only the first three months. In all, the IMC campaign drove store traffic and sales of the Whopper up a whopping 29 percent.[11]

In the past, no one person or department was responsible for thinking through the communication roles of the various promotion tools and coordinating the promotion mix. To help implement IMC, some companies appoint a marketing communications director who has overall responsibility for the company's communications efforts. This helps to produce better communications consistency and greater sales impact. It places the responsibility in someone's hands—where none existed before—to unify the company's image as it is shaped by thousands of company activities.

A View of the Communication Process

Integrated marketing communications involves identifying the target audience and shaping a well-coordinated promotional program to obtain the desired audience response. Too often, marketing communications focus on immediate awareness, image, or preference goals in the target market. But this approach to communication is too shortsighted. Today, marketers are moving toward viewing communications as *managing the customer relationship over time.*

Because customers differ, communications programs need to be developed for specific segments, niches, and even individuals. And, given the new interactive communications technologies, companies must ask not only "How can we reach our customers?" but also "How can we let our customers reach us?"

Thus, the communications process should start with an audit of all the potential touchpoints that target customers may have with the company and its brands. For example, someone purchasing a new cell phone plan may talk to others; see television ads; read articles and ads in newspapers and magazines; visit various Web sites for prices and reviews; and check out plans at Best Buy, Walmart, or a wireless provider's kiosk or store at the mall. The marketer needs to assess what influence each communication experience will have at different stages of the buying process. This understanding helps marketers allocate their communication dollars more efficiently and effectively.

Figure 13–2
Elements in the
communication process.

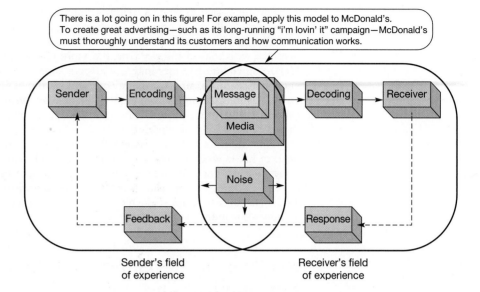

There is a lot going on in this figure! For example, apply this model to McDonald's. To create great advertising—such as its long-running "i'm lovin' it" campaign—McDonald's must thoroughly understand its customers and how communication works.

To communicate effectively, marketers need to understand how communication works. Communication involves the nine elements shown in Figure 13–2. Two of these elements are the major parties in a communication—the *sender* and the *receiver*. Another two are the major communication tools—the *message* and the *media*. Four more are major communication functions—*encoding, decoding, response,* and *feedback.* The last element is *noise* in the system. Definitions of these elements follow and are applied to a McDonald's "i'm lovin' it" television commercial.

- *Sender: The party sending the message to another party—here, McDonald's.*

- *Encoding:* The process of *putting thought into symbolic form*—for example, McDonald's ad agency assembles words, sounds, and illustrations into a TV advertisement that will convey the intended message.

- *Message:* The *set of symbols* that the sender transmits—the actual McDonald's ad.

- *Media:* The *communication channels* through which the message moves from the sender to the receiver—in this case, television and the specific television programs that McDonald's selects.

- *Decoding:* The process by which the receiver *assigns meaning to the symbols* encoded by the sender—a consumer watches the McDonald's commercial and interprets the words and images it contains.

- *Receiver:* The *party receiving the message* sent by another party—the customer who watches the McDonald's ad.

- *Response:* The *reactions of the receiver* after being exposed to the message—any of hundreds of possible responses, such as the consumer likes McDonald's better, is more likely to eat at McDonald's next time, hums the "i'm lovin' it" jingle, or does nothing.

- *Feedback:* The part of the *receiver's response communicated back to the sender*—McDonald's research shows that consumers are either struck by and remember the ad or they write or call McDonald's, praising or criticizing the ad or its products.

- *Noise:* The *unplanned static or distortion* during the communication process, which results in the receiver getting a different message than the one the sender sent—the consumer is distracted while watching the commercial and misses its key points.

For a message to be effective, the sender's encoding process must mesh with the receiver's decoding process. The best messages consist of words and other symbols that are familiar to the receiver. The more the sender's field of experience overlaps with that of the receiver, the more effective the message is likely to be. Marketing communicators may not always *share* their customer's field of experience. For example, an advertising copywriter from one socioeconomic level might create ads for customers from another level—say, wealthy business owners. However, to communicate effectively, the marketing communicator must *understand* the customer's field of experience.

This model points out several key factors in good communication. Senders need to know what audiences they wish to reach and what responses they want. They must be good at encoding messages that take into account how the target audience decodes them. They must send messages through media that reach target audiences, and they must develop feedback channels so that they can assess an audience's response to the message.

■■■ Steps in Developing Effective Communications

We now examine the steps in developing an effective integrated communications and promotion program. Marketers must do the following: Identify the target audience, determine the communication objectives, design the message, select the communication channels, select the message source, and collect feedback.

Identifying the Target Audience

A marketing communicator starts with a clear target audience in mind. The audience may be potential buyers or current users, those who make the buying decision, or those who influence it. The audience may be individuals, groups, special publics, or the general public. The target audience heavily affects the communicator's decision on what will be said, how it will be said, when it will be said, where it will be said, and who will say it. To create effective communication, a marketer must understand the target audience by creating a message that will be meaningful to them in a media they will understand. For example, a study of bed and breakfast (B&B) owners found that other than word of mouth, they felt the two most important communication channels were brochures and guidebooks. When guests of B&Bs were asked the channels they used most often, the two highest—other than word of mouth—were magazines and newspapers (one category) and signs.[12] Managers need to understand their target markets before they can communicate with them.

Determining the Communication Objective

Once a target audience has been defined, the marketing communicator must decide what response is sought. Of course, in most cases the final response is purchase. But purchase is the result of a long process of consumer decision making. The marketing communicator needs to know where the target audience stands in relation to the product and to what state it needs to be moved.

The Indian tribes of South Dakota wished to increase significantly tourist visitation to their reservations. These were their objectives:

- To provide guests for B&B operations.

- To increase the market for Indian products.

- To participate in other tourism-related incomes.

- To correct misconceptions about the American Indian. It was deemed important to show that the Lakota, Dakota, and Nakota people are living cultures.

This combination of economic and cultural education objectives led to the development of the Alliance of Tribal Tourism Advocates (ATTA) as a communication

Figure 13–3
Buyer readiness stages.

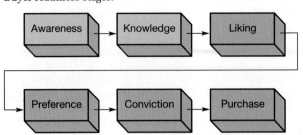

vehicle. Instead of depending on the South Dakota Department of Tourism or other organizations, Indians would promote themselves. "If you want to visit an Indian, the best person to talk with is a Native American," said Ronald L. Neiss, acting director of ATTA and a member of the Rosebud Sioux Tribal Council.[13]

The target audience may be in any of six buyer readiness states: awareness, knowledge, liking, preference, conviction, or purchase, which are shown in Figure 13–3.

Awareness

First, the communicator must be able to gauge the target audience's awareness of the product or organization. The audience may be totally unaware of it, know only its name, or know one or a few things about it. If most of the target audience is unaware, the communicator tries to build awareness, perhaps by building simple name recognition. This process can begin with simple messages repeating the name. Even then, building awareness takes time. Suppose that an independent restaurant named the Hungry Hunter opens in a northern suburb of Houston. There are 50,000 people within a three-mile radius of the restaurant. Initially, the restaurant has little name recognition. The Hungry Hunter may set an objective of making 40 percent of the people living within three miles of the restaurant aware of its name.

Red Roof Inns use the color of its roofs and locations with good visibility (near freeways) to create awareness. Another Red Roof strategy is to develop several properties in an area simultaneously. This has a "mushroom" effect, as motorists suddenly see Red Roof Inns everywhere. People forget names of other people, places, and products. Thus, awareness communication is a never-ending responsibility. A product must have top-of-mind awareness.

Knowledge

The target audience might be aware of the company or product but know little else. The Hungry Hunter specializes in wild game, but the market may not be aware of this. The restaurant may decide to select product knowledge as its first communication objective.

The chain of Ruth's Chris Steak House restaurants uses a simple slogan and advertises on a quarter page in airline in-flight magazines. The message is directed at frequent flyers who deserve a "sizzling reward." The advertisement features a color photo of a very thick steak, a list of restaurant addresses, and the slogan of Ruth's Chris Steak House, "Home of Serious Steaks." This simple message quickly gives the reader knowledge of restaurant location, size of the steak, and seriousness of the restaurant as a steakhouse.

Liking

If target audience members know the product, how do they feel about it? We can develop a range of preference, such as a Likert scale covering degrees of liking, for example, "dislike very much," "dislike somewhat," "indifferent," "like somewhat," and "like very much." If the market is unfavorable toward the Hungry Hunter, the communicator must learn why and then develop a communication campaign to create favorable feelings. If unfavorable feelings are based on real problems, such as slow service, communication alone cannot do the job. The Hungry Hunter has to fix its problems and then communicate its renewed quality.

Preference

A target audience might like the product but not prefer it to others. In this case the communicator must try to build consumer preference. The communicator promotes the product's quality, value, performance, and other features. The communicator can check on the campaign's success by measuring audience preferences after the campaign. If the Hungry Hunter finds that many area residents like the name and concept but choose other restaurants, it will have to identify those areas where its offerings are better than competing restaurants. It must then promote its advantages to build preference among possible customers.

Conviction

A target audience might prefer the product but not develop a conviction about buying the product. Marketers have a responsibility to turn favorable attitudes into conviction because conviction is closely linked with purchase. Communication from the Hungry Hunter will work toward making its target market believe it offers the best steaks at a fair value in its market area.

Purchase

Finally, some members of the target audience might have conviction but not quite get around to making the purchase. They may wait for more information or plan to act later. The communicator must lead these consumers to take the final step. Actions might include offering the product at a low price, offering a premium, or letting consumers try it on a limited basis. The Hungry Hunter may provide a "Tuesday Night Special," offering prime rib or its seafood of the day for $14.95 instead of the usual price of $19.95.

Designing the Message

Having defined the desired audience response, the communicator turns to developing an effective message. Ideally, the message should get attention, hold interest, arouse desire, and obtain action (a framework known as the AIDA model). In practice, few messages take the consumer all the way from awareness to purchase, but the AIDA framework does suggest the desirable qualities of a good message.

In putting the message together, the marketing communicator must solve three problems: what to say (message content), how to say it logically (message structure), and how to say it symbolically (message format).

It's a fair statement to say that Americans like Australia and everything Australian. Outback Steakhouse built on that positive image. The company says, "Outback Steakhouse is an Australian steakhouse" (actually it's a member of an American multi-restaurant chain, but who cares?).

Outback offers what it describes as a "no worry zone." This too is typical of Australia where people commonly say, "No worry, mate." Outback's commercial says, "Kick back for the moment. Toss all your worries in the air cause you'll forget them when you're here. Let's go outback tonight."

Message Content

The communicator has to figure out an appeal or theme that will produce a desired response. The three types of appeals are rational, emotional, and moral.

Rational appeals relate to audience self-interest. They show that the product will produce desired benefits. Occasionally, rational appeals are overlooked. This is the traditional problem of missing the forest because of the trees. The city of Denver received considerable negative feedback from large potential conventions because it did not have a 1,000-room convention hotel, yet development costs were too high to justify building such a structure.

The problem was solved when the existing 511-room Hyatt Regency and the 613-room Marriott Hotel, one block apart, joined forces to jointly market their properties as a 1,000-room hotel suitable for conventions. By marketing the two hotels as one, several customer benefits became apparent, such as elimination of duplicate planning meetings, a single bill combining charges at both hotels, free telephone calls between the two hotels, combined service staffs, and posting of events at both hotels.[14]

Emotional appeals attempt to provoke emotions that motivate purchase. These include fear, guilt, and shame appeals that entice people to do things that they should (brush their teeth, buy new tires) or stop doing things they shouldn't (smoke, drink too much, or overeat).

Emotional appeals are widely used by resorts and hotels to stimulate cross-purchases:

- Commercials on in-room television, posters, and desktop tents promote the health center and the need to reduce stress and work off "pounds gained from eating in the hotel."

- The "Think of the Spouse and Kids at Home" theme is widely used to promote a myriad of products available in the hotel, from hand-dipped chocolates to stuffed animals. This appeal is also used to convince business guests to purchase a vacation for the family at one of the chain's resort properties.

Moral appeals are directed to the audience's sense of what is right and proper. They are often used to urge people to support such social causes as a cleaner environment, better race relations, equal rights, and aid to the needy.

Message Structure

The communicator must also decide how to handle three message structure issues. The first is whether to draw a conclusion or leave it to the audience. Early research showed that drawing a conclusion was usually the most effective. More recent re-

Oberoi hotels have consistently been ranked among the best hotels in the world. In this ad, The Oberoi Udaivilas, ranking as the best resort in Asia, has been used to send a rational message, that the Oberoi Group operates excellent hotels and resorts. Courtesy of Oberoi Hotels and Resorts.

13.1 San
Alfonso del Mar,
http://www.
sanalfonso.cl/ingles/main.
html: Under project description
click on Salt Water Lagoon to
see description of the "World's
Largest Pool."

search, however, suggests that in many cases the advertiser is better off asking questions and letting buyers come to their own conclusions.

The second message structure issue is whether to present a one- or two-sided argument. Usually, a one-sided argument is more effective in sales presentations except when audiences are highly educated and negatively disposed.

The third message structure issue is whether to present the strongest arguments first or last. Presenting them first creates strong attention but may lead to an anticlimactic ending.[15]

"World's Largest Outdoor Swimming Pool" is the first message presented by the San Alfonso del Mar Resort in Chile. The accommodation and food actually take a second seat to the beauty and immensity of the 1-km-long salt water swimming pool, 115 feet deep and holding 66 million gallons of water.

Message Format

The communicator also needs a strong format for the message. In a print ad, the communicator has to decide on the headline, copy, illustration, and color. To attract attention, advertisers can use novelty and contrast, eye-catching pictures and headlines, distinctive formats, message size, position, color, shape, and movement. If the message is to be carried over the radio, the communicator has to choose words, sounds, and voices. The "sound" of Tom Bodett promoting Motel 6 is different from that of an announcer promoting Hyatt.

If the message is to be carried on television or in person, all these elements, plus body language, must be planned. Presenters plan their facial expressions, gestures, dress, posture, and hairstyle. If the message is carried on the product or its package, the communicator has to watch texture, scent, color, size, and shape. For example, color plays a major communication role in food preferences. When consumers sampled four cups of coffee that had been placed next to brown, blue, red, and yellow containers (all the coffee was identical, but the consumers did not know this), 75 percent felt that the coffee next to the brown container tasted too strong, nearly 85 percent judged the coffee next to the red container to be the richest, nearly everyone felt that the coffee next to the blue container was mild, and the coffee next to the yellow container was perceived as weak.

Selecting Communication Channels

The communicator must now select channels of communication. The two broad types of communication channels are personal and nonpersonal.

Personal Communication Channels

In personal communication channels, two or more people communicate directly with each other. They might communicate face to face, on the phone, via mail or e-mail, or even through an Internet "chat." Personal communication channels are effective because they allow for personal addressing and feedback.

Some personal communication channels are controlled directly by the company. For example, company salespeople contact business buyers. But other personal communications about the product may reach buyers through channels not directly controlled by the company. These channels might include independent experts—consumer advocates, online buying guides, and others—making statements to buyers. Or they might be neighbors, friends, family members, and associates talking to target buyers. This last channel, word-of-mouth influence, has considerable effect in many product areas.

Personal influence carries great weight for products that are expensive, risky, or highly visible. Hospitality products are often viewed as being risky because they cannot be tried out beforehand. Therefore, personal sources of information are often sought before someone purchases a travel package, selects a restaurant, or stays at a hotel.

Online recommendations have become a powerful influence on consumers. One author states, "It doesn't matter how loud or often you tell consumers your 'truth,' few today are buying a big-ticket item before they know what existing users have

Marketing Highlight   Thank You—A Great Personal Communication

13–1 Two of the most powerful words in any language are *thank you*. That's a sales manager for a limited service hotel in Indianapolis, Indiana, decided to initiate a special thank-you program for guests.

The manager's objectives were to increase corporate business and let guests know that the inn appreciated their patronage and wanted them to return. She felt that a handwritten note would be appreciated in this high-tech world of e-mail, Internet, and voice-mail communications.

Names and addresses were obtained from business cards left by guests in a fish bowl qualifying them for a monthly drawing. After the drawing was held, any one of the three desk clerks would write thank-you notes during slow times on the desk. Each desk clerk is provided with personalized business cards that are included with the handwritten note.

The manager has spoken with many guests who were amazed that the inns took time to write a personal note to them. One client mentioned that he really liked having the business card sent from a front-desk associate rather than a general manager or salesperson. Because the desk associates are usually the ones to make reservations, guests like having the name of someone to ask for when they call back for future reservations.

The thank-you notes help to build a relationship between the guests and the hotel. They let the guests know that the staff appreciates their business and cares about them as individuals. The manager's support of the program lets the employees know that creating positive guest relations are important to the hotel.

to say about the product. This is a low-trust world. That's why 'recommendation by a relative or friend' comes out on top in just about every survey of purchasing influences. One study found that 90 percent of customers trust recommendations from people they know, compared to advertisements where the trust level runs from 40% to under 10%."[16]

One study found that consumers trust negative reviews of hotels more than they do positive reviews. However, they did find that positive reviews did help develop their level of trust for the travel product, especially when the reviewers identified themselves by their name.[17] The power of online ratings means that it is important to provide great service, to help eliminate negative reviews. It also means that one must monitor and respond to both negative and positive reviews. For negative reviews, it is best to take the conversation off-line. This can be done by apologizing online and asking the reviewer that had a problem to contact the manager directly by email.

Companies can take steps to put personal communication channels to work for them. They can create *opinion leaders* for their brands—people whose opinions are sought by others—by supplying influencers with the product on attractive terms or by educating them so that they can inform others. **Buzz marketing** involves cultivating opinion leaders and getting them to spread information about a product or service to others in their communities.

Nonpersonal Communication Channels

Nonpersonal communication channels are media that carry messages without personal contact or feedback. They include media, atmospheres, and events. Major **media** consist of print media (newspapers, magazines, direct mail), broadcast media (radio and television), display media (billboards, signs, posters), and online media (e-mail, Web sites, and online social and sharing networks). **Atmospheres** are designed environments that create or reinforce the buyer's leanings toward purchasing a product. The lobby of a five-star hotel contains a floral display, original works of art, and luxurious furnishings to reinforce the buyer's perception that the hotel is a five-star hotel. **Events** are occurrences staged to communicate messages to target audiences. Public relations departments arrange press conferences, grand openings, public tours, and other events to communicate with specific audiences.

The Scanticon Princeton (a conference center) used its lobby as a gallery for original artworks by members of the Princeton Artists Alliance. This resulted in excellent publicity, including a full-page story with pictures and the address of Scanticon Princeton in the Sunday edition of a major Philadelphia newspaper.

Nonpersonal communication affects buyers directly. In addition, using mass media often affects buyers indirectly by causing more personal communication. Mass communications affect attitudes and behavior through a two-step flow of communication. In this process, communications first flow from television, magazines, and other mass media to opinion leaders and then from these opinion leaders to others. Thus, opinion leaders step between mass media and their audiences and carry messages to people who are less exposed to media.

Selecting the Message Source

The message's impact on the audience is also affected by how the audience views the sender. Messages delivered by highly credible sources are persuasive. What factors make a source credible? The three factors most often found are expertise, trustworthiness, and likability. Expertise is the degree to which the communicator appears to have the authority needed to back the claim. Doctors, scientists, and professors rank high on expertise in their fields. Trustworthiness is related to how objective and honest the source appears to be. Friends, for example, are trusted more than salespeople. Likability is how attractive the source is to the audience. People like sources who are open, humorous, and natural. Not surprisingly, the most highly credible source is a person who scores high on all three factors: expertise, trustworthiness, and likability.

Memphis used prominent people to promote that city as a convention and meeting site. A video was produced in which convention planners, tour wholesalers, and association officials endorsed the city as an ideal convention location. Messages delivered by attractive sources achieve higher attention and recall. Advertisers often use celebrities as spokespeople, such as Michael Jordan for McDonald's. Celebrities are likely to be effective when they personify a key product attribute. But what is equally important is that the spokesperson must have credibility.

The use of living personalities to serve as spokespeople for a company or product carries inherent problems:

• Celebrities are often difficult to work with and may refuse to participate in important media events or to pose under certain conditions.

• Living personalities are sometimes publicly embarrassed.

13.2 Grand Hotel Villa Feltrinelli, www. villafeltrinelli.com: This site has a simple elegance, which is attractive to an older upscale market.

Qantas Airlines has been successful using a kangaroo and a koala bear as symbols. For decades McDonald's has effectively used the imaginary Ronald McDonald. Cartoon characters and animals are dependable and unlikely to create negative publicity.

An increasingly popular Web site design for luxurious hotels, such as Grand Hotel Villa Feltrinelli (www.villafeltrinelli.com), is to use a minimum of written words but instead depend on mood music and beautiful scenes of the hotel, furnishings, and grounds to create the image of luxury. The Ritz-Carlton, Wolfsburg-Germany, uses this same tactic in its promotional CDs to targeted customers.

Collecting Feedback

After sending the message, the communicator must research its effect on the target audience. This involves asking the target audience whether they remember the message, how many times they saw it, what points they recall, how they felt about the message, and their past and present attitudes toward the product and company. The communicator would also like to measure behavior resulting from the message: How many people bought a product, talked to others about it, or visited the store.

After not using television advertising for seven years, Sheraton Hotels and Resorts started an aggressive mass media campaign that included television, radio, and print media. The objective of the ad was to tell travelers about Sheraton's upgraded

Marketing Highlight

JetBlue Uses Customers as a Credible Source to Deliver Messages:
http://www.jetblue.com/experience/

13-2 Trying to choose the right airline? There's no need to ask your friends, relatives, or neighbors about their airline experiences or about which airline provides the best service. JetBlue has already done that for you. And it's sharing their stories with you and other travelers in a promotional campaign called "Sincerely, JetBlue." The campaign features a series of offbeat commercials in which actual customers share their JetBlue experiences.

The goal of the campaign is to retain JetBlue's upstart, small airline personality in the face of ambitious expansion plans. JetBlue is now the United States' number-two discount airline, behind Southwest, and it's adding planes and routes at a rapid pace. As it grows, it wants to hang on to the underdog grassroots appeal that's made it successful in the dog-eat-dog airline industry.

Some airlines have built their images through lush, big-budget ad campaigns. Not so for JetBlue. "This brand was created almost entirely on an experience, then on word of mouth about that experience," says the chief creative director at JWT, the New York ad agency that created the "Sincerely, JetBlue" campaign. An executive of the ad agency said that when JetBlue founder and CEO, David Needleman came to us, he said the thing that keeps him up at night is how he can grow the airline and keep the JetBlue experience. The answer: Let the JetBlue faithful themselves give voice to that experience. "Allowing our customers to tell our story will help the airline keep a local, small feel as JetBlue becomes more national in scope," says JetBlue's chief marketing executive.

JetBlue has built a huge infrastructure for breeding and collecting customer stories to use in the "Sincerely" ads. It has erected futuristic JetBlue "story booths" in eighteen cities, where passersby can recount and record their experiences flying on JetBlue. According to one observer, the booths are less like circus tents and more like futuristic spaceships. They're made of high-tech honeycomb mesh and have LED screens underneath the shell, pressure-sensitive floors, and voice-activated walls. Inside the booths, a virtual crew member guides customer storytellers through their experiences. JetBlue also invites customers to submit stories at its Web site, and it places postcards in seat-back pockets, which passengers can use to keep and submit mini-journals on their JetBlue journeys.

Once collected, the stories are incorporated into simple but colorful, cleverly animated commercials in which customers themselves share their JetBlue experiences. "You take this little story and you give it to an animator and they turn it into something marvelous," says a JWT creative director. In one ad, customer Melissa confides, "Let me tell you, I wanted to not like you, if only because everyone seems to love you. I got on a flight with a pen and paper, waiting to take down every irritating detail." But, she continues, "two flights later, I was staring at the same blank piece of paper. You've done nothing wrong and everything more than right, if that's possible." After detailing all the right things the airline does, she mock-laments, "JetBlue, I wanted to not like you, but it can't be done—at all. Sincerely, Melissa McCall, Portland, Oregon."

David Needleman, JetBlue CEO, hands out snacks during a flight. Courtesy of Mark Peterson/Corbis.

In a similar fashion, in other ads: Brian relates how a JetBlue flight attendant dashed from the plane just before takeoff to retrieve a brand-new iPod he'd left in a rental car. Ann recounts that when her JetBlue flight was delayed by a snowstorm, the airline eased the long wait by providing pizza and even a live band. "My three-year-old son was dancing. I was dancing," she remembers. "It was a great time! It made a horrible experience really nice." And the Steins tell about the time they arrived late at night for a family vacation in Florida with their three very tired small children only to learn that their hotel wouldn't take them in. Jason Stein recalls, "Out of nowhere we heard a voice from behind us say, 'Go ahead, take my room.' " His wife Nancy continues: "A superhero in a JetBlue pilot's uniform, who sacrificed his room graciously, saved our night. And we slept like babies. Thank you, JetBlue. Sincerely, Nancy and Jason Stein, Darien, Connecticut."

The tone and crafting of the ads makes them appealing and believable. It's almost like talking to your next-door neighbor, but with colorful, intriguing animations that help bring their stories to life. (Check out all of these stories and others at the JetBlue Web site at http://jetblue.com/experience/.) "The various illustrations—including animation, paper cutouts, and miniature doll pieces—have a wonderful rhythm and flow," comments an advertising analyst, "and the stories have an on-the-fly populist quality, which fits the brand."

In all, the campaign just seems to work. It's the ultimate word of mouth. Says the JWT executive, "The best way to get people who haven't tried the airline to try it is for them to hear from people they know and trust."

Sources: Quotes and other information from Stuart Elliot, "JetBlue May Be Big, But It Wants Fliers to Think Small," *New York Times* (March 30, 2006): C3; and Barbara Lippert, "Voices Carry," *Adweek* (April, 2006): 32; and www.jetblue.com (accessed December 2006 and October 2008).

Figure 13–4
Feedback measurements for two brands.

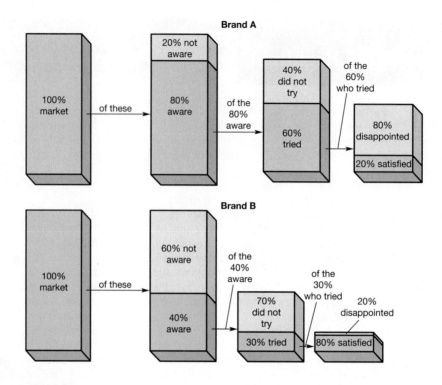

The Sheraton "S," shown in the sign here, was featured in a Sheraton advertising campaign to increase awareness of the Sheraton brand. Courtesy of Tupungato/Dreamstime.

services and amenities. Sheraton's iconic "S" was featured in its advertisements to reestablish the identity of the icon. A test found that the Sheraton "S" has an unaided recall of 93 percent. It is called unaided recall if there is no prompting with elements of the ads or commercials being examined. With prompting, the results are called aided recall.[18] After the campaign, Web bookings also increased by 20 percent.[19]

Figure 13–4 shows an example of feedback measurement. Looking at hotel brand A, we find that 80 percent of the total market was aware of it, 20 percent of those who were aware had tried it, but only 20 percent of those who tried it were satisfied. These results suggest that although the communication program created awareness, the product failed to give consumers the satisfaction expected. The company should therefore try to improve the product while continuing the successful communication program. With hotel brand B, the situation was different: Only 40 percent of the total market was aware of it. Only 10 percent of those had tried it, and 80 percent of those who tried it were satisfied. In this case, the communication program needed to be stronger to take advantage of the brand's power to create satisfaction.

■■■ Setting the Total Promotion Budget and Mix

We have looked at the steps in planning and sending communications to a target audience. But how does the company determine its total promotion budget and the division among the major promotional tools to create the promotion mix? By what process does it blend the tools to create IMC? We now look at these questions.

Setting the Total Promotional Budget

One of the hardest marketing decisions facing companies is how much to spend on promotions. John Wanamaker, the department store magnate, once said, "I know that half of my advertising is wasted, but I don't know which half. I spent $2 million for advertising, and I don't know if that is half enough or twice too much."

How do companies determine their promotion budget? Four common methods are used to set the total budget for advertising: (1) the affordable method, (2) the percentage of sales method, (3) the competitive parity method, and (4) the objective and task method.[20]

Affordable Method

Many companies use the affordable method: They set a promotion budget at what they think the company can afford. One executive explained this method as follows: "Why, it's simple. First, I go upstairs to the controller and ask how much they can afford to give this year. He says a million and a half. Later, the boss comes to me and asks how much should we spend and I say 'Oh, about a million and a half.' "[21]

Unfortunately, this method of setting budgets completely ignores the effect of promotion on sales volume. It leads to an uncertain annual promotion budget, which makes long-range marketing planning difficult. Although the affordable method can result in overspending on advertising, it more often results in underspending.

Percentage of Sales Method

Many companies use the percentage of sales method, setting their promotion budget at a certain percentage of current or forecasted sales, or they budget a percentage of the sales price. Some firms use this method because it is easy. For example, some restaurateurs know that the mean expenditure for promotion for restaurants is 4 percent; therefore, they set their promotion budget at 4 percent.

A number of advantages are claimed for the percentage of sales method. First, using this method means that promotion spending is likely to vary with what the company can "afford." It also helps management think about the relationship between promotion spending, selling price, and profit per unit. Finally, it supposedly creates competitive stability because competing firms tend to spend about the same percentage of their sales on promotion.

However, despite these claimed advantages, the percentage of sales method has little justification. It wrongly views sales as the cause of promotion rather than as the result. The budget is based on availability of funds rather than on opportunities. It may prevent increased spending, which is sometimes needed to turn around falling sales. Because the budget varies with year-to-year sales, long-range planning is difficult. Finally, the method does not provide a basis for choosing a specific percentage, except past actions or what competitors are doing.

Competitive Parity Method

Other companies use the competitive parity method, setting their promotion budgets to match competitors' outlays. They watch competitors' advertising or get industry promotion spending estimates from publications or trade associations and then set their budgets based on the industry average. For example, the advertising expenditures for the average hotel are 1 percent of sales, and the marketing budget is 5 percent. However, for limited-service hotels, the advertising expenditure is 2 percent of sales and the marketing budget.[22]

Two arguments are used to support this method. First, competitors' budgets represent the collective wisdom of the industry. Second, spending what competitors spend helps prevent promotion wars. Unfortunately, neither argument is valid. There are no grounds for believing that competition has a better idea of what a company should be spending on promotion. Companies differ greatly, and each has its own special promotion needs. Furthermore, no evidence indicates that budgets based on competitive parity prevent promotion wars.

Objective and Task Method

The most logical budget setting method is the objective and task method. Using this, marketers develop their promotion budgets by (1) defining specific objectives, (2) determining tasks that must be performed to achieve these objectives, and (3) estimating the costs of performing them. The sum of these costs is the proposed promotional budget.

The objective and task method forces management to spell out its assumptions about the relationship between dollars spent and promotional results. It is also the most difficult method to use because it can be hard to determine which tasks will achieve specific objectives. Management must consider such questions even though they are difficult to answer. With the objective and task method, the company sets its promotion budget based on what it wants to accomplish.

■■■ Managing and Coordinating Integrated Marketing Communications

The concept of IMC suggests that the company must blend the promotion tools carefully into a coordinated *promotion mix.* But how does it determine what mix of promotion tools to use? Companies within the same industry differ greatly in the design of their promotion mixes.

The Nature of Each Promotion Tool

Each promotion tool has unique characteristics and costs. Marketers must understand these characteristics in shaping the promotion mix. Often one promotional tool must be used to promote another. Thus, when McDonald's decides to run a million-dollar sweepstakes in its fast-food outlets (a sales promotion), it has to run ads to inform the public. Many factors influence the marketer's choice of promotion tools. Each promotional tool, advertising, personal selling, sales promotion, public relations, and direct marketing, has unique characteristics and costs. Marketers must understand these characteristics to select their tools correctly.

Advertising

Because of the many forms and uses of advertising, generalizing about its unique qualities as a part of the promotion mix is difficult. Yet several qualities can be noted. Advertising's public nature suggests that the advertised product is standard and legitimate. Because many people see ads for the product, buyers know that purchasing the product will be publicly understood and accepted. Advertising also allows the seller to repeat a message many times. Large-scale advertising by a seller says something positive about the seller's size, popularity, and success. Advertising can be used to build a long-term image for a product (e.g., Four Seasons or McDonald's ads) and also stimulate quick sales (as when Embassy Suites in Phoenix advertises a promotion for the Fourth of July holiday). Advertising can reach masses of geographically dispersed buyers at a low cost per exposure.

Advertising also has shortcomings. Although it reaches many people quickly, advertising is impersonal and cannot be as persuasive as a company salesperson. Advertising is able to carry on only a one-way communication with the audience, and the audience does not feel it has to pay attention or respond. In addition, advertising can be very costly. Although some forms, such as newspaper and radio advertising, can be done on small budgets, other forms, such as network TV advertising, require very large budgets.

For hotels, restaurants, and other hospitality companies that cater to traveling visitors in private vehicles, the use of advertising (billboards) represents the largest expenditure item in their advertising budgets.

The Little America group of hotels has used a theme that all parents recognize with their tired and bored children: "Are we there yet?" In some cases these hotels also advertise very inexpensive ice cream cones at the next exit, at Little America.

A critical challenge faced by hotel marketers is creating an immediate awareness of brand name to ensure that their properties are included in the traveler's evoked set of lodging choices. The evoked set of brand preferences and the relative impact of advertising and prior stay were investigated in a study of frequent travelers. It was found that chains whose names were well established in a traveler's evoked set most often won the traveler's business. There was little influence on chain name recall of prior stay without ad exposure or influence on ad exposure without prior stay. The combined effect of ad exposure and prior stay was an important influence on brand selection.[23]

Personal Selling

Personal selling is the most effective tool at certain stages of the buying process, particularly in building buyer preference, conviction, and purchase. Compared with advertising, personal selling has several unique qualities. It involves personal interaction between two or more people, allowing each to observe the other's needs and characteristics and make quick adjustments. Personal selling also lets all kinds of relationships spring up, ranging from a matter-of-fact selling relationship to a deep personal friendship. The effective salesperson keeps the customer's interests at heart to build a long-term relationship. Finally, with personal selling the buyer usually feels a greater need to listen and respond, even if the response is a polite "no thank you."

These unique qualities come at a cost. A sales force requires a longer-term company commitment than advertising; advertising can be turned on and off, but sales force size is harder to vary. Personal selling is the company's most expensive promotion tool, costing industrial companies an average of $225 per sales call.[24] American firms spend up to three times as much on personal selling as they do on advertising.

Personal selling by members of the hospitality industry is used primarily for large key customers, travel intermediaries, and meeting planners and others with responsibility for group sales.

Sales Promotion

Sales promotion includes an assortment of tools, coupons, contests, cents-off deals, premiums, and others, and these tools have many unique qualities. They attract consumer attention and provide information that may lead the consumer to buy the product. Sales promotions offer strong incentives to purchase by providing inducements or contributions that give additional value to consumers, and they invite and reward quick response. Advertising says "buy our product." Sales promotion says "buy it now."

Companies use sales promotion tools to create a stronger and quicker response. Sales promotion can be used to dramatize product offers and to boost sagging sales. Its effects are usually short lived, however, and are not effective in building long-run brand preference.

Public Relations

Public relations offers several advantages. One is believability. News stories, features, and events seem more real and believable to readers than do ads. Public relations can reach many prospects who avoid salespeople and advertisements. The message gets to the buyers as news rather than as a sales-directed communication. Like advertising, public relations can dramatize a company or product.

A relatively new addition to the promotion mix is the infomercial, a hybrid between advertising and public relations. Companies provide interesting stories on videotape for use on television during periods of light viewing, such as early morning. Infomercials provide enough information to keep the attention of viewers, combined with a "soft" approach to product or brand advertising.

Hospitality marketers tend to underuse public relations or use it only as an afterthought. Yet a well-thought-out public relations campaign used with other promotion mix elements can be very effective and economical.

Direct Marketing

Direct marketing connections carefully targeted individual consumers to both obtain an immediate response and cultivate lasting customer relationships: the use of direct mail, the telephone, direct-response television, e-mail, the Internet, and other tools to communicate directly with specific consumers. Although there are many forms of direct marketing they all share four distinctive characteristics. Direct marketing is *nonpublic:* The message is normally directed to a specific person. Direct marketing is *immediate* and *customized:* Messages can be prepared very quickly and can be tailored to appeal to specific consumers. Finally, direct marketing is *interactive:* It allows a dialogue between the marketing team and the consumer, and messages can be altered depending on the consumer's response. Thus, direct marketing is well suited to highly targeted marketing efforts and to building one-to-one customer relationships.

Promotion Mix Strategies

Companies consider many factors when developing their promotion mix, including the following: type of product and market, push versus pull strategy, buyer readiness state, and product life-cycle stage.

Type of Product and Market

The importance of different promotion tools varies among consumers and commercial markets. When hospitality firms market to consumer markets, they spend more on advertising and sales promotion and often very little on personal selling. Hospitality firms targeting commercial organizations spend more on personal selling. In general, personal selling is used more heavily with expensive and risky goods and in markets with fewer and larger sellers. A meeting or convention is customized for the organization putting on the event. It takes a skilled salesperson to put together a package that will give clients what they want at an appropriate price that will provide good revenue for the company.

Push Versus Pull Strategy

The promotional mix is heavily affected by whether a company chooses a push or pull strategy. The two strategies are contrasted in Figure 13–5. A push strategy involves "pushing" the product through distribution channels to final consumers. The manufacturer directs its marketing activities (primarily personal selling and trade promotion) at channel members to induce them to order and carry the product and to promote it to final consumers. For example, Dollar Rent-A-Car offered travel agents a 15 percent commission instead of 10 percent, to persuade them to order its brand for clients. Continental Plaza Hotels and Resorts developed a promotion that gave travel agents an extra $10 in addition to their normal commission for bookings. A push strategy provides an incentive for channel members to promote the product to their customers or push the product through the distribution channels.

Using a pull strategy, a company directs its marketing activities (primarily advertising and consumer promotion) toward final consumers to induce them to buy the product. For example, Sheraton placed an ad for its Hawaiian properties in the

Figure 13–5
Push versus pull promotion strategy.

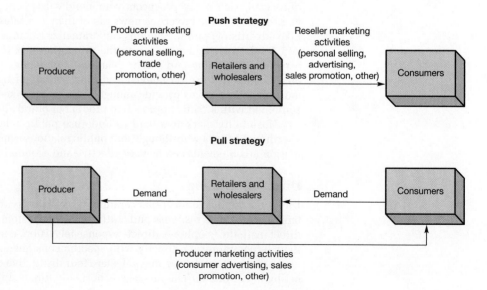

Marketing Highlight   How Does an Advertising Agency Work?

13-3
Madison Avenue is a familiar name to most Americans. It's a street in New York City where some major advertising agency headquarters are located. But most of the United States' 10,000 agencies are found outside New York, and almost every city has at least one agency, even if it's a one-person shop. Some ad agencies are huge. The largest U.S. agency, BBDO Worldwide, has annual worldwide revenue of more than $1.5 billion. In recent years, many agencies have grown by gobbling up other agencies, thus creating huge agency holding companies. The largest of the agency "mega groups," Omnicom Group, includes several large advertising agencies, public relations, and promotion agencies with combined worldwide revenues of over $11 billion.

Even companies with strong advertising departments use advertising agencies. Agencies employ specialists who can often perform advertising tasks better than the company's own staff. Agencies also bring an outside point of view to solving the company's problems, along with the experience of working with different clients and situations. Agencies are partly paid from media discounts and often cost the firm very little. Because a client can drop its agency at any time, most agencies work hard to do a good job. Smaller clients are generally charged a fee because they often do not use much commissionable media.

Advertising agencies usually have four departments: creative, which develops and produces ads; media, which selects media and places ads; research, which studies audience characteristics and wants; and business, which handles the agency's business activities. Each account is supervised by an account executive; staff members in each department are usually assigned to work on one or more accounts.

Agencies often attract new business through their reputation or size. Generally, however, a client invites a few agencies to make a presentation for its business and then selects one of them.

Ad agencies have traditionally been paid through commissions and some fees. Under this system, the agency receives 15 percent of the media cost as a rebate. Suppose that the agency buys $60,000 of magazine space for a client. The magazine bills the advertising agency for $51,000 ($60,000 less 15 percent), and the agency bills the client for $60,000, keeping the $9,000 commission. If the client bought space directly from the magazine, it would pay $60,000 because commissions are paid only to recognized advertising agencies. Both advertisers and agencies have become increasingly unhappy with the commission system. Larger advertisers complain that they pay more for the same services received by smaller ones simply because they place more advertising. Advertisers also believe that the commission system drives agencies away from low-cost media or noncommissionable media and short advertising campaigns. Agencies are unhappy because they perform extra services for an account without receiving additional revenue. As a result, the trend is now toward paying either a straight fee or a combination commission and fee. Some large advertisers are tying agency compensation to the performance of the agency's advertising campaigns.

Source: For agency revenues, see "Agency Report on Advertising Agency Revenues" from "Agency Report 2007," *Advertising Age* (April 25, 2007), www.adage.com; Walecia Konrad, "A Word from the Sponsor: Get Results or Else," *Business Week* (July 4, 1988): 66.

Phoenix, Arizona, paper. Interested readers were instructed to call their travel planner or Sheraton. If the strategy is effective, consumers will purchase the product from channel members, who will, in turn, order it from producers. Thus, under a pull strategy, consumer demand "pulls" the product through the channels.

Buyer Readiness State

Promotional tools vary in their effects at different stages of buyer readiness. Advertising, along with public relations, plays a major role in the awareness and knowledge stages, more important than that played by cold calls from salespeople. Customer liking, preferences, and conviction are more affected by personal selling, which is closely followed by advertising. Finally, closing the sale is accomplished primarily with sales calls and sales promotion. Only personal selling, given its high costs, should focus on the later stages of the customer buying process.

Product Life-Cycle Stage

The effects of different promotion tools also vary with stages of the product life cycle. In the introduction stage, advertising and public relations are good for producing high awareness, and sales promotion is useful in product early trial. Personal selling must be used to get the trade to carry the product in the growth stage; advertising and public relations continue to be powerful while promotion can be reduced because fewer incentives are needed. In the mature stage, sales promotion again becomes important relative to advertising. Buyers know the brands, and advertising is needed only to remind them of the product. In the decline stage, advertising is kept at a reminder level, public relations is dropped, and salespeople give the product only a little attention. Sales promotion, however, may continue to be strong.[25]

■■■ Advertising

The remainder of this chapter examines advertising in more detail. Subsequent chapters deal with personal selling and sales promotion. We define **advertising** as any paid form of nonpersonal presentation and promotion of ideas, goods, or services by an identified sponsor.

The fast-food industry in the United States has reached the mature stage, and fast-food companies are fighting for market share. McDonald's, Yum Brands, Burger King, and Wendy's are stepping up their campaigns and trying to take market share from each other. Marketing wars such as the burger wars and pizza wars are fought with advertising dollars. Marketing wars break out in mature markets where growth of the market is slow. To increase their sales, companies must try to steal market share from their competitors.

Advertising is a good way to inform and persuade, whether the purpose is to sell Hilton Hotels around the world or to get residents of Kuala Lumpur, the capital of Malaysia, to stay at a nearby resort on the island of Langkawi. Organizations have different ways of managing their advertising. The owner or the general manager of an independent restaurant usually handles the restaurant's advertising. Most hotel chains give responsibility for local advertising to the individual hotels, whereas corporate management is responsible for national and international advertising. In some corporate offices, the director of marketing handles advertising. Other firms might have advertising departments to set the advertising budget, work with an outside advertising agency, and handle direct-mail advertising and other advertising not done by the agency. Large companies commonly use an outside advertising agency because it offers several advantages.

■■■ Major Decisions in Advertising

Marketing management must make five important decisions in developing an advertising program. These decisions are listed in Figure 13–6 and discussed next.

Setting the Objectives

The first step in developing an advertising program is to set advertising objectives, which should be based on information about the target market, positioning, and marketing mix. Marketing positioning and mix strategies define the role that advertising must perform in the total marketing program.

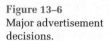
Figure 13–6
Major advertisement
decisions.

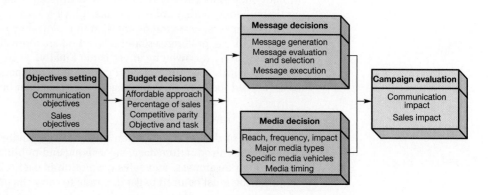

THE TRUTH IS OUT!
DUNKIN' BEAT STARBUCKS

In a recent national blind taste test, more Americans preferred
the taste of Dunkin' Donuts coffee over Starbucks.
It's just more proof it's all about the coffee (not the couches or music).

Courtesy of Dunkin' Brands,
Inc.

An advertising objective is a specific communication task to be accomplished with a specific target audience during a specific period of time. Advertising objectives can be classified by their aim: to *inform, persuade,* or *remind.* **Informative advertising** is used heavily when introducing a new product category and when the objective is to build primary demand. When an airline opens a new route, its management often runs full-page advertisements informing the market about the new service. Junior's Deli, in the Westwood section of Los Angeles, uses direct-mail campaigns to create new customers. New residents in the neighborhood receive a gift certificate for a Deli Survival Kit, which contains a chunk of beef salami, two types of cheese, a loaf of fresh rye bread, and a home-baked dessert. The kit is absolutely free, with no purchase required, but the certificate must be redeemed at the restaurant. More than a 1,000 new neighbors come in to claim their kits each year. Thus, the kit not only informs potential customers about the restaurant but also results in visits to the restaurant by customers who sample its products.[26]

Persuasive advertising becomes more important as competition increases and a company's objective becomes building selective demand. Some persuasive advertising has become comparison advertising, which compares one brand directly or indirectly with one or more other brands. For example, Dunkin' Donuts ran a TV and Web campaign comparing the chain's coffee to Starbucks's brews. "In a recent national blind taste test," proclaimed the ads, "more Americans preferred the taste of Dunkin' Donuts coffee over Starbucks. It's just more proof it's all about the coffee (not the couches or music)."Dunkin' Donuts ran a TV and Web campaign comparing the chain's coffee to Starbucks's brews. "Try the coffee that won," the ads concluded.

Advertisers should use comparative advertising with caution. All too often, such ads invite competitor responses, resulting in an advertising war that neither competitor can win. Upset competitors might take more drastic action, such as filing complaints with the self-regulatory National Advertising Division of the Council of Better Business Bureaus or even filing false-advertising lawsuits. An unwritten rule of using comparison ads is that the prestige brands and market-share leaders should never use this tactic because it draws attention to competitors and causes the customer to question the value of the market-share leader or prestige brand.

Reminder advertising is important for mature products because it keeps consumers thinking about the product. Expensive McDonald's ads on television are designed to remind people about McDonald's, not to inform or persuade them.

Advertising is not a substitute for poor products. For an advertising campaign to create long-term sales, the product advertised must create satisfied customers. One mistake frequently made by the owners of new restaurants is advertising before the operation has gone through a shakedown period. Eager to get a return on their investment, the owners advertise before the restaurant's staff is properly trained and the restaurant's systems are tested under high-demand situations.

Because most people look forward to trying a new restaurant, advertising campaigns are usually effective, resulting in waits during peak periods. However, success can be short lived when restaurateurs deliver poor-quality food, poor service, or poor value. Dissatisfied customers quickly spread negative word of mouth to potential customers, who are eager to find out about the new restaurant. Frequently, advertising a noncompetitive product quickens the product's death through negative word. The owner of a restaurant in Houston who went through this experience and ultimately went out of business blamed his loss on fickle customers. In his words, "The restaurant used to have waits every night of the week. Now, the restaurant is empty. I can't believe how fickle customers are." The customers weren't fickle; in fact, they knew exactly what they wanted: good food and good service. These were things the restaurant did not offer.

The president of a hospitality marketing, advertising, and public relations firm believes that the implementation of an effective advertising campaign is one of the fastest ways to jeopardize the performance of a mediocre property. You must first be sure the property can live up to the promises your advertising makes. If your property or service is inconsistent with the claims made, the money you spend to generate additional business will probably do little more than increase the number of dissatisfied guests.[27]

Even highly satisfied customers need frequent reminders. Ski and scuba-diving resorts share a common problem. Satisfied guests often fail to return because they wish to experience new slopes and new dive areas. Years may pass before the guest is ready to return. Reminder advertising may shorten that period of time.

Setting the Advertising Budget

After determining advertising objectives, a company can establish an advertising budget for each product. The role of advertising is to affect demand for a product. The company wants to spend the amount needed to achieve the sales goal. Four commonly used methods for setting the promotional budget were discussed earlier in this chapter. These methods—the affordable method, the percentage of sales method, the competitive parity method, and the objective and task method—are also often used when determining the advertising budget. The advertising budget also has some specific factors that should be considered when setting a budget:

- *Stage in the product life cycle.* New products typically need large advertising budgets to build awareness and gain consumer trial. Mature brands usually require lower budgets as a ratio to sales. For example, a casual neighborhood restaurant may want to budget heavily for advertising in its first year of operation and less per month after its first year. By the end of the first year, it should have established a clientele. After this point it will need to maintain its existing customers and gain new customers (albeit at a lower rate than the first year). Its loyal customers should be spreading positive word of mouth by the end of the first year.

- *Competition and clutter.* In a market with many competitors and heavy advertising support, a brand must be advertised more frequently to be heard above the noise of the market.

- *Market share.* High-market-share brands usually require greater advertising expenditures as a percentage of sales than do low-share brands. Building a market or taking share from competitors requires larger advertising budgets than maintaining current share. For example, McDonald's spends about 18 percent of its sales on advertising.

- *Advertising frequency.* Larger advertising budgets are essential when many repetitions are needed to present the brand's message.

- *Product differentiation.* A brand that closely resembles others in its product class (pizza, limited-service hotels, air travel) requires heavy advertising to set it apart. When a product differs greatly from those of competitors, advertising can be used to communicate differences to consumers.

How much impact does advertising really have on consumer purchases and brand loyalty? One study found that advertising increased purchases by loyal users but was less effective in winning new buyers. The study found that advertising appears unlikely to have a cumulative effect that leads to loyalty. Features, displays, and especially price have a stronger impact on response than advertising.[28]

These findings were not well received by the advertising community, and several advertising professionals attacked the study's data and methodology. They claimed that the study measured primarily short-run sales effects and thus favored pricing and sales promotion activities that tend to have a more immediate impact. Most advertising takes many months or even years to build strong brand positions and consumer loyalty. Long-run effects are difficult to measure. This debate underscores the fact that the measurement of sales results from advertising remains in its infancy.

Strategic Versus Tactical Budgets

The last three areas deal with strategic issues, building brand awareness, and brand image. Another budget decision is deciding how much will be spent for strategic advertising and how much will be spent on tactical advertising. Tactical advertising deals with sales promotions and often includes price discounts. Thomson, the United Kingdom's largest tour operator, divides its advertising budget equally between tactical and strategic advertising. It refers to its strategic advertising as advertising to build brand awareness for Thomson and holiday destinations.[29]

Overall Promotional Budget

Another factor in planning the advertising budget is the overall promotional budget. To gain synergy between the different elements of the promotional mix, money should be available for training employees about new promotions, in-house sales promotion materials, collateral material, and public relations.

Consistency

In his book *Guerrilla Advertising,* Jay Conrad Levinson states that the advertising budget should be viewed like rent, something that has to be paid each month.[30] When times are tough, there is often a tendency to cut the advertising budget. The rent, employees, utilities, and suppliers all have to be paid; the advertisements for the coming month are seen as discretionary. This view of advertising can lead to continued poor sales and the eventual decline of the business.

Opportunities to Stretch the Budget

Hospitality companies often have ways they can stretch their advertising dollars. Tradeouts are one of these ways. Tradeouts involve trading advertising for products the media company can use, such as rooms, food, or travel. A tradeout can be a good way of getting advertising without using cash. To be a good deal, the target market of the media gained through the trade must match the target market of the restaurant, hotel, or travel company. Second, the advertisements should be played when the market will be exposed to them. Another way of expanding the budget is through cooperative advertising, that is, two or more companies getting together to pay for an ad. For example, a credit card company may pay for a portion of an advertisement if it is mentioned in the ad, and cruise lines will provide cooperative advertising for their top agents. Travel agents can also use tagging, that is, placing their ad below a wholesaler's, resort's, or cruise line's advertisement, so that those reading the ad and interested in the product come to the travel agent's ad immediately after reading the main advertisement.

The Final Budget

The advertising budget is a subset of the marketing budget. It depends on the objectives of the marketing plan and the promotional plan. Setting an advertising budget becomes a complex process. It must consider the other uses of the marketing budget. It must balance the objectives of the advertising plan against the money available from the company. The method most effective for setting a budget is the objective and task method: determining what needs to be done and then developing a budget to accomplish the task, as long as the expense results in positive returns.

However, often the budget is dictated by the corporate office. In this case the marketing manager has to defend his or her case for a higher budget or make do with a lower budget. If a lower budget is required, the budget must be reviewed and prioritized, with the lower priority items being eliminated.

The final advertising budget makes effective use of the funds allocated to the budget. It takes into account funds needed for other areas of the promotional mix. Finally, it provides funds for promotional campaigns throughout the year.

Developing Advertising Strategy

Advertising strategy consists of two major elements: creating advertising messages and selecting advertising media. In the past, companies often viewed media planning as secondary to the message-creation process. The creative department first created good advertisements, and then the media department selected and purchased the best media for carrying those advertisements to desired target audiences. This often caused friction between creatives and media planners.

Today, however, soaring media costs, more-focused target marketing strategies, and the blizzard of new digital and interactive media have promoted the importance of the media-planning function. The decision about which media to use for an ad campaign—television, newspapers, magazines, cell phones, a Web site or an online network, or e-mail—is now sometimes more critical than the creative elements of the campaign. As a result, more and more advertisers are orchestrating a closer harmony between their messages and the media that deliver them. In fact, in a really good ad campaign, you often have to ask, "Is that a media idea or a creative idea?"

Creating the Advertising Message

No matter how big the budget, advertising can succeed only if advertisements gain attention and communicate well. Good advertising messages are especially important in today's costly and cluttered advertising environment. In 1950, the average U.S. household received only three network television channels and a handful of major national magazines. Today, the average household receives more than 118 channels, and consumers have more than 20,000 magazines from which to choose.[31] Add in the countless radio stations and a continuous barrage of catalogs, direct mail, e-mail and online ads, and out-of-home media, and consumers are being bombarded with ads at home, work, and all points in between. As a result, consumers are exposed to as many as 3,000 to 5,000 commercial messages every day.[32]

Breaking Through the Clutter

If all this advertising clutter bothers some consumers, it also causes huge headaches for advertisers. Take the situation facing network television advertisers. They pay an average of $302,000 to make a single 30-second commercial. Then, each time they show it, they pay an average of $122,000 for 30 seconds of advertising time during a popular prime-time program. They pay even more if it's an especially popular program, such as *American Idol* ($642,000), *Sunday Night Football* ($340,000), *Grey's Anatomy* ($240,000), *Two and a Half Men* ($227,000), or a mega-event such as the *Super Bowl* (nearly $3 million per 30 seconds!).[33]

Then their ads are sandwiched in with a clutter of other commercials, announcements, and network promotions, totaling nearly 20 minutes of nonprogram material per prime-time hour, with commercial breaks coming every six minutes on average. Such clutter in television and other ad media has created an increasingly hostile advertising environment. According to one recent study, more than 70 percent of Americans think there are too many ads on TV, and 62 percent of national advertisers believe that TV ads have become less effective, citing clutter as the main culprit.[34]

Until recently, television viewers were pretty much a captive audience for advertisers. But today's digital wizardry has given consumers a rich new set of information and entertainment choices. With the growth in cable and satellite TV, the Internet, VOD, video downloads, and DVD rentals, today's viewers have many more options. Digital technology has also armed consumers with an arsenal of weapons for choosing what they watch or don't watch. Increasingly, thanks to the growth of DVR systems, consumers are choosing not to watch ads. More than 33 percent of American TV households now have DVRs, and an estimated 44 percent will have them by 2014. One ad agency executive calls these DVR systems "electronic weed whackers." Research shows that DVR owners view only about 40 percent of the commercials aired. At the same time, VOD and video downloads are exploding, allowing viewers to watch programming on their own time terms—with or without commercials.[35]

Thus, advertisers can no longer force-feed the same old cookie-cutter ad messages to captive consumers through traditional media. Just to gain and hold attention, today's advertising messages must be better planned, more imaginative, more entertaining, and more emotionally engaging. Simply interrupting or disrupting consumers no longer works. Instead, unless ads provide information that is interesting, useful, or entertaining, many consumers will simply skip them.

Message Strategy

The first step in creating effective advertising messages is to plan a message strategy—the general message that will be communicated to consumers. The purpose of advertising is to get consumers to think about or react to the product or company in a certain way. People will react only if they believe they will benefit from doing so. Thus, developing an effective message strategy begins with identifying customer benefits that can be used as advertising appeals.

Ideally, the message strategy will follow directly from the company's broader positioning and customer value strategies. Message strategy statements tend to be plain, straightforward outlines of benefits and positioning points that the advertiser wants to stress. The advertiser must next develop a compelling creative concept—or "big idea"—that will bring the message strategy to life in a distinctive and memorable way. At this stage, simple message ideas become great ad campaigns. Usually, a copywriter and an art director will team up to generate many creative concepts, hoping that one of these concepts will turn out to be the big idea.

The creative concept may emerge as a visualization, a phrase, or a combination of the two. The creative concept will guide the choice of specific appeals to be used in an advertising campaign. Advertising appeals should have three characteristics. First, they should be meaningful, pointing out benefits that make the product more desirable or interesting to consumers. Second, appeals must be believable. Consumers must believe that the product or service will deliver the promised benefits. However, the most meaningful and believable benefits may not be the best ones to feature. Appeals should also be distinctive. They should tell how the product is better than competing brands.

Message Execution

The impact of the message depends on what is said and how it is said: message execution. The advertiser has to put the message across in a way that wins the target market's attention and interest. Advertisers usually begin with a statement of the objective and approach of the desired ad.

The advertising agency's creative staff must find a style, tone, words, and format for executing the message. Any message can be presented in different execution styles, such as the following:

1. **Slice of life** shows one or more people using the product in a normal setting. Bennigan's developed a television ad showing friends enjoying an evening at Bennigan's.

2. **Lifestyle** shows how a product fits with a lifestyle. For example, an airline advertising its business class featured a businessperson sitting in an upholstered chair in the living room, having a drink, and enjoying the paper. The other side of the ad featured the same person in the same relaxed position with a drink and a paper in one of the airline's business-class seats.

Yao Ming, a former professional basketball player from China, promotes McDonald's. Courtesy of Damian Dovarganes/AP Wide World Photos.

3. **Fantasy** creates a wonder world around the product or its use. For instance, Cunard's *Sea Goddess* featured a woman lying in a raft in the sea, with the luxury liner anchored in the background. A cocktail server in a tuxedo is walking through the ocean carrying a drink for the woman.

   The use of fantasy has also occurred in the development of resort hotels. Disney may have started the trend with hotels on the property of Disney World, but Hyatt Corporation, Westin Hotels and Resorts, and many others have adopted the concept. Such hotels are designed to surround the guests with a fantasy ambience, including costumed employees, entertainment, and dramatic physical structures such as waterfalls, a pyramid, or a miniature Amazon River. Fantasy hotels are very expensive to build and maintain. The human psyche is receptive to fantasy. Archaeologists often have difficulty discerning whether cave paintings represent fantasy or sights really observed. Many children's books, cartoons, and top-selling novels are fantasy. It is not surprising that fantasy advertising is effective within an industry that appeals to one's desire to escape.

4. **Mood or image** builds a mood or image around the product, such as beauty, love, or serenity. No claim is made about the product except through suggestion. Bally's resort in Las Vegas developed an advertisement designed to change its image after its renovation. The headlines in the ad were "To them a watch does more than tell time, a car is not merely transportation, and their resort is Bally's in Las Vegas."

5. **Musical** shows one or more people or cartoon characters singing a song about the product. Many cola ads have used this format. Delta Airlines used music effectively in its "We Love to Fly and It Shows" campaign. Certain cultures seem particularly receptive to the use of theme songs and sing-along melodies in advertisements. Australians often use simple but catchy melodies in their advertisements. Brazilians often use adaptations of samba music, particularly music that is popular during carnival.

6. **Personality** symbol creates a character that represents the product. The character might be created by the company, such as McDonald's Ronald McDonald, or real, such as Tom Bodett of Motel 6.

7. **Technical expertise** shows the company's expertise with the product. Hotels often use this style in advertisements directed toward meeting and convention planners, emphasizing that they have the technical expertise to support the meeting planner. American Airlines makes heavy and frequent use of expertise, particularly that of its pilots and mechanics.

8. **Scientific evidence** presents survey or scientific evidence that the brand is better or better liked than one or more other brands.

9. **Testimonial evidence** features a highly believable or likable source endorsing the product (e.g., sports personalities, such as Peyton Manning and Phil Mickelson, or other well-known figures, such as Bill Cosby). McDonald's chose Yao Ming because he was dynamic, fun, and caring. McDonald's also has over 700 restaurants in China, where he was described as the country's most popular celebrity.[36]

The advertiser must choose a tone for the ad. Hyatt always uses a positive tone, with ads that say something very positive about its own products. Hyatt ads avoid humor that might take attention away from the message or be misunderstood by its many international guests. By contrast, Taco Bell ads have used humor, in the form of an odd, but cute, talking Chihuahua. The hungry little dog became famous for his Spanish-language statement, "Yo quiero Taco Bell," meaning *I want Taco Bell.* The little dog pushed Taco Bell's sales up 4.3 percent during its run.[37]

Finally, format elements make a difference in an ad's impact and cost. A small change in design can make a big difference in an ad's effect. The illustration is the first thing the reader notices. It must be strong enough to draw attention. Then the headline must effectively entice the right people to read the copy. The copy, the main block of text in the ad, must be simple but strong and convincing. These three elements must effectively work together. Even then, a truly outstanding ad is noted

Emirates first-class features: your own cabin, a shower spa, and a lounge. It can cost up to eight times as much as an economy seat on the same flight. The first-class cabin fits the lifestyle of the wealthy, who are willing and capable of paying the fare. Courtesy of Emirates.

by less than 50 percent of the exposed audience. An even smaller percentage, about 30 percent, can recall the main point of the headline. Only 25 percent will remember the advertiser's name, and fewer than 10 percent read most of the body copy. Less-than-outstanding ads do not even achieve these results.

Consumer-Generated Messages

Taking advantage of today's interactive technologies, many companies are now tapping consumers for message ideas or actual ads. They are searching existing video sites, setting up their own sites, and sponsoring ad-creation contests and other promotions. Sometimes the results are outstanding; sometimes they are forgettable. If done well, however, user-generated content can incorporate the voice of the customer into brand messages and generate greater consumer brand involvement.

Many brands develop brand Web sites or hold contests that invite consumers to submit ad message ideas and videos. Not all consumer-generated advertising efforts, however, are successful. As many big companies have learned, ads made by amateurs can be well, pretty amateurish. Done well, however, consumer-generated advertising efforts can produce new creative ideas and fresh perspectives on the brand from consumers who actually experience it. Such campaigns can boost consumer involvement and get consumers talking and thinking about a brand and its value to them.[38]

Message Decisions

The message decision is a third decision in the advertising management process. A large advertising budget does not guarantee a successful advertising campaign. Two advertisers can spend the same amount on advertising with dramatically different results. Studies have shown that creative advertising messages can be more important than the number of dollars spent. No matter how big the budget, advertising can succeed only if its message gains attention and communicates well.

Good advertising messages are especially important in today's costly and cluttered advertising environment. All this advertising clutter bothers some consumers and causes big problems for advertisers. Take, for instance, the situation facing network television advertisers. They typically pay hundreds of thousands of dollars for 30 seconds of advertising time during a popular prime-time TV program and even more if it is an especially popular program or event such as the Super Bowl.[39]

Until recently, television viewers were an almost captive audience for advertisers. Viewers had only a few channels from which to choose. Those who found the energy to get up and change channels during unwelcome commercial breaks usually found only more of the same on other channels. With the growth in cable TV, DVDs, and remote controls, today's viewers have many more options. They can avoid ads altogether by watching commercial-free cable channels. They can "zap" commercials by pushing the fast-forward button during taped programs, instantly turn off the sound during a commercial, or "zip" around the channels. Advertisers take such "zipping" and "zapping" seriously. One author claims that 60 percent of all TV viewers may regularly be tuning out commercials.[40]

Thus, just to gain and hold attention, today's advertising messages must be better planned and more imaginative, entertaining, and rewarding to consumers. Creative strategy will play an increasingly important role in advertising success. Developing a creative strategy requires three message steps: generation, evaluation and selection, and execution.

Message Generation

Hotels, resorts, B&Bs, and cruise lines face an inherent barrier to effective communication with the customer: the intangibility of the product. A hotel's product is experienced only at or after the time of purchase. This characteristic of services in

The Red Mountain resort shows what people come to the resort for in its ad: relaxation and rejuvenation. Courtesy of Red Mountain Resort.

general poses genuine challenges for message creation. As the editor of the *Cornell Quarterly* pointed out, "An advertisement can depict a product—a food item, a desk, an exercise machine—but how does one illustrate a hotel stay?"[41]

Creative people have different ways of developing advertising messages. Many start by talking to consumers, dealers, experts, and competitors. Others imagine consumers using the product and determine the benefits that consumers seek. Although advertisers create many possible messages, only a few are used.

Marketing managers bear a responsibility to review critically the message, the media, and the illustration and creative concepts recommended by the advertising agency. A fine line sometimes exists between responsible review and unwarranted intrusion into the professional work of advertising agencies. Marketing managers for client companies such as a hotel or excursion train are expected to know their products, customers, and employees better than any ad agency. In the final analysis, they must assume responsibility for messages that fail to motivate customers or that offend employees. On the brighter side, they can also shine in the glory of creative, well-received advertising.

Message Evaluation and Selection

The advertiser must evaluate possible appeals on the basis of three characteristics. First, messages should be meaningful, pointing out benefits that make the product more desirable or interesting to consumers. Second, appeals should be distinctive. They should tell how the product is better than competing brands. Finally, they must be believable. Making message appeals believable is difficult because many consumers doubt the truth of advertising. One study found that, on average, consumers rate advertising messages as "somewhat unbelievable."

Choosing Among Major Media Steps

The major steps in media selection are (1) deciding on reach, frequency, and impact; (2) choosing among major media types; (3) selecting specific media vehicles; and (4) deciding on media timing.

Deciding on Reach, Frequency, and Impact

To select media, the advertiser must decide what reach and frequency are needed to achieve advertising objectives. Reach is a measure of the percentage of people in the target market who are exposed to the ad campaign during a given period of time. For example, the advertiser might try to reach 70 percent of the target market during the first year. Frequency is a measure of how many times the average person in the target market is exposed to the message. For example, the advertiser might want an average exposure frequency of three. The advertiser must also decide on desired media impact, the qualitative value of message exposure through a given medium. For products that must be demonstrated, television messages using sight and sound are more effective. The same message in one magazine (*Newsweek*) may be more believable than in another (*National Enquirer*).

Suppose that the advertiser's product has the potential to appeal to a market of 1 million consumers. The goal is to reach 700,000 consumers (70 percent of 1 million). Because the average consumer will receive three exposures, 2.1 million exposures (700,000 × 3) must be bought. If the advertiser wants exposures of 1.5 impact (assuming that 1.0 impact is the average), a rated number of exposures of 3.15 million (2.1 million × 1.5) must be bought. If 1,000 exposures with this impact cost $10, the advertising budget must be $31,500 (3,150 × $10). In general, the more reach, frequency, and impact that the advertiser seeks, the larger the advertising budget has to be.

Gross rating points (GRPs) show the gross coverage or duplicated coverage of an advertising campaign. GRPs are determined by multiplying reach times frequency. In the preceding example, an ad with a reach of 700,000 and frequency of three exposures would produce 210 GRPs if the market was 1 million. Each GRP is equal to 1 percent of the market.

Waste is the part of the medium's audience not in the firm's target market.[42] An entrepreneur owning a single restaurant in Worthington, Ohio (north of Columbus), will find that only about 20 percent of those reading the *Columbus Dispatch* will be in that entrepreneur's market area. Thus he or she will probably advertise in other media. A travel agency may advertise in a newspaper targeted at seniors knowing that only 50 percent of the readers will spend more than $1,000 on travel annually. The travel agency factored this in when they purchased the media. Despite the waste, the medium still offered a good value. In choosing media, the circulation aimed at your target market is the important factor, not the total circulation.

Choosing Among Major Media Types

The media planner has to know the reach, frequency, and impact of each major media type. Table 13–1 summarizes the major advertising media. The major media types, in order of advertising volume, are newspapers, television, direct mail, radio,

TABLE 13–1

Profiles of Major Media Types

Medium	Advantages	Limitations
Newspapers	Flexibility; timeliness; good local market coverage; broad acceptance; high believability	Short lift; poor reproduction quality; small pass-along audience
Television	Combines sight, sound, and motion; appealing to the senses; high attention; high reach; appeals to the senses	High absolute cost; high clutter; fleeting exposure; less audience selectivity
Direct mail	High audience selectivity; flexibility; no ad competition within the same medium; personalization	Relatively high cost; junk mail image
Radio	Good local acceptance; high geographic and demographic selectivity; low cost	Audio only; lower attention ("the half-heard medium) fragmented audiences
Magazines	High geographic and demographic selectivity; credibility and prestige; high-quality reproduction; long life; good pass-along readership	Long ad purchase lead time; some waste circulation; no guarantee of position
Outdoor	Flexibility; high repeat exposure; low cost; low message competition	Little audience selectivity; creative limitations
Internet	Audience selectivity; personalization; immediacy, interactive capabilities	Demographically skewed audience; relatively low impact; audience controls exposure

magazine, and outdoor. Each medium has advantages and limitations. For example, more than 75 percent of Holiday Inn Express guests arrive by car. Jennifer Ziegler, director of marketing for Holiday Inn Express said, "Billboards serve as a reinforcement. They create top-of-mind awareness that make a difference when last-minute decisions about lodging are being made."[43]

Media planners consider many factors when making their media choices, including the media habits of target consumers. Radio and television, for example, are the best media for reaching teenagers. The nature of the product also affects media choices. Resorts are best shown in color magazines. Fast-food ads targeted at young children are best on television. Different types of messages may require different media. A message announcing a Mother's Day buffet would be conveyed effectively on radio or in newspapers. A message that contains technical data, such as an ad explaining the details of a travel package, might be disseminated most effectively in magazines or through direct mail. Cost is also a major factor in media choice. Television is very expensive; newspaper advertising costs much less. The media planner looks at both the total cost of using a particular medium and at the cost per 1,000 exposures, that is, the cost of reaching a 1,000 people.

Ideas about media impact and cost must be reexamined regularly. For many years, television and magazines dominated the media mixes of national advertisers while other media were neglected. Recently, costs and clutter (competition from competing messages) have increased, and audiences have dropped. As a result, many marketers have adopted strategies targeted at narrower segments, and TV and magazine advertising revenues have leveled off or declined. Advertisers have increasingly turned to alternative media, including cable TV, outdoor advertising, specialty advertising, and Internet advertising. Given these and other media characteristics, the media planner must decide how much of each type of media to buy.

Selecting Specific Media Vehicles

The media planner must now choose the best specific media vehicles within each general media type. A comparison of the top television shows in the United States with younger (ages 18 to 34) and older audiences (age 35 to 54) found there were no shows that appeared on the top ten list for both groups. Each group had a unique set. Thus, advertising must know the favorite media of its target market. Magazine vehicles include *Newsweek, Travel and Leisure, The New Yorker,* and *Town and Country.* If advertising is placed in magazines, the media planner must look up circulation figures and the costs of different ad sizes, color options, ad positions, and frequencies for various specific magazines. The planner then evaluates each magazine on such factors as credibility, status, reproduction quality, editorial focus, and advertising submission deadlines. The media planner decides which vehicles give the best reach, frequency, and impact for the money.

Media planners also compute the cost per thousand persons reached by a vehicle. If a full-page, four-color advertisement in *Newsweek* costs $100,000 and *Newsweek*'s readership is 3.3 million people, the cost of reaching a 1,000 persons is $28. The same advertisement in *Business Week* may cost only $57,000 but reach only 775,000 persons, at a cost per 1,000 of about $74. The media planner would favor magazines with the lower cost per 1,000 for reaching target consumers.

The media planner must also consider the costs of producing ads for different media. Whereas newspaper ads can cost very little to produce, flashy television ads may cost millions. Some ads with special effects can cost over $1 million for a 30-second spot.[44]

The media planner must thus balance media cost measures against several media impact factors. First, costs should be balanced against the media vehicle's audience quality. For a corporate hotel advertisement, *Business Week* would have a high-exposure value; *People* would have a low-exposure value. Second, the media planner should consider audience attention. Readers of *Vogue,* for example, typically pay more attention to ads than do readers of *Newsweek.* Third, the planner assesses the vehicle's editorial quality; *Time* and the *Wall Street Journal* are more believable and prestigious than the *National Enquirer.*

Media planners are increasingly developing more sophisticated measures of effectiveness and using them in mathematical models to arrive at the best media mix. Many advertising agencies use computer programs to select the initial media and then make further media schedule improvements based on subjective factors not considered by the media section model.[45]

Deciding on Media Timing

The advertiser must also decide how to schedule advertising over the course of a year. For a hotel or resort, effective advertising requires knowledge of the origin of its guests and how far in advance they make their reservations. If guests living in Connecticut make their reservations in November to go to a Caribbean resort in January, it will not be effective for a resort to advertise in December after consumers have already made their vacation plans. Mauritius launched a major campaign in the United Kingdom in October to create demand for the December holiday season.[46] Restaurants with a strong local demand may decide to vary their advertising to follow the seasonal pattern, to oppose the seasonal pattern, or to be the same all year. Most firms do some seasonal advertising.

Finally, the advertiser must choose the pattern of the ads. **Continuity** means scheduling ads evenly within a given period. **Pulsing** means scheduling ads unevenly over a given period. Thus, fifty-two ads could either be scheduled at one per week during the year or pulsed in several bursts. Those who favor pulsing feel that the audience will learn the message more completely and that money can be saved. Once they have done a burst of ads, they remove themselves from the advertising market. A company could use a six-month burst of advertising, for example, to regain its past sales growth rate.[47]

Road Blocking

Advertisers can sometimes use a tactic known as *road blocking* to help ensure that an intended audience receives the advertising message. The tropical island resort Great Keppel in Queensland, Australia, knew that its audience in Brisbane, Sydney, and Melbourne listened to certain FM rock stations. Great Keppel purchased drive-time radio spots for exactly the same time on all rock stations in the three markets. This prevented listeners from switching stations to avoid the advertisement.

Evaluating Advertising Effectiveness and the Return on Advertising Investment

Managers of advertising programs should regularly evaluate the communication and sales effects of advertising.

Measuring the Communication Effect

Measuring the communication effect reveals whether an ad is communicating well. Called **copy testing,** this process can be performed before or after an ad is printed or broadcast. There are three major methods of advertising pretesting. The first is **direct rating,** in which the advertiser exposes a consumer panel to alternative ads and asks them to rate the ads. Direct ratings show how well the ads attract attention and how they affect consumers. Although it is an imperfect measure of an ad's actual impact, a high rating indicates a potentially effective ad. In **portfolio tests,** consumers view or listen to a portfolio of advertisements, taking as much time as they need. The interviewer then asks the respondent to recall all the ads and their contents. The recall can be either aided or unaided by the interviewer. Recall level indicates the extent to which an ad stands out and how well its message is understood and remembered. **Laboratory tests** use equipment to measure consumers' physiological reactions to an ad: heartbeat, blood pressure, pupil dilation, and perspiration. The tests measure an ad's attention-getting power but reveal little about its impact on beliefs, attitudes, or intentions.

There are two popular methods of post-testing ads. Using **recall tests,** the advertiser asks people who have been exposed to magazines or television programs to recall everything they can about the advertisers and products that they saw. Recall scores indicate the ad's power to be noticed and retained. In **recognition tests,** the researcher asks readers of, for instance, a given issue of a magazine to point out what they have seen. Recognition scores can be used to assess the ad's impact in different market segments and to compare the company's ads with those of competitors.

Measuring the Sales Effect

What quantity of sales is caused by an ad that increases brand awareness by 20 percent and brand preference by 10 percent? The sales effect of advertising is often harder to measure than the communication effect. Sales are affected by many factors besides advertising, such as product features, price, and availability. One way to measure sales effect is to compare past sales with past advertising expenditures. Another is through experiments.

Measuring the Awareness Effect

If the objective of the advertising is to inform, then conducting a pretest and a post-test of the target markets' awareness of the product or brand is often used as a method of measuring the effect of an advertising campaign. For example, in Figure 13–3, 60 percent of the market is not aware of the product of brand B. The objectives of brand B's advertising campaign are to increase awareness to 50 percent and increase trail from 30 to 50 percent of those who were aware of brand B. By replicating the research that produced the data for Figure 13–3, they could see if the campaign met its goals.

To spend a large advertising budget wisely, advertisers must define their advertising objectives, develop a sound budget, create a good message, make media decisions, and evaluate the results.

■■■ KEY TERMS

Advertising. Any paid form of nonpersonal presentation and promotion of ideas, goods, or services by an identified sponsor.

Atmosphere. Designed environments that create or reinforce a buyer's leanings toward consumption of a product.

Buzz marketing. Cultivating opinion leaders and getting them to spread information about a product to others in their community.

Continuity. Scheduling ads evenly within a given period.

Copy testing. A process performed before or after an ad is printed or broadcast.

Direct marketing. Connections carefully targeted individual consumers to both obtain an immediate response and cultivate lasting customer relationships: the use of direct mail, the telephone, direct-response television, e-mail, the Internet, and other tools to communicate directly with specific consumers.

Direct rating. The advertiser exposes a consumer panel to alternative ads and asks them to rate the ads.

Events. Occurrences staged to communicate messages to target audiences, such as news conferences or grand openings.

Informative advertising. Advertising used to inform consumers about a new product or feature to build primary demand.

Integrated marketing communications. Under this concept the company carefully integrates its many communications

channels to deliver a clear, consistent, and compelling message about the organization and its brands.

Laboratory test. This test uses equipment to measure consumers' physiological reactions to an ad: heartbeat, blood pressure, pupil dilation, and perspiration.

Media. Nonpersonal communications channels, including print media (newspapers, magazines, direct mail), broadcast media (radio, television), and display media (billboards, signs, posters).

Personal selling. Personal presentation by the firm's sales force to make sales and build customer relationships.

Portfolio tests. Consumers view or listen to a portfolio of advertisements, taking as much time as they need.

Promotion mix. The specific mix of advertising, personal selling, sales promotion, and public relations a company uses to pursue its advertising and marketing objectives.

Pulsing. Scheduling ads unevenly over a given period.

Recall tests. The advertiser asks people who have been exposed to magazines or television programs to recall everything they can about the advertisers and products that they saw.

Recognition tests. The researcher asks readers of, for instance, a given issue of a magazine to point out what they have seen.

Reminder advertising. Advertising used to keep consumers thinking about a product.

■■■ CHAPTER REVIEW

I. **Promotion Mix**
    A. **Advertising.** Any paid form of nonpersonal presentation and promotion of ideas, goods, or services by an identified sponsor.
    B. **Sales promotion.** Short-term incentives to encourage the purchase or sale of a product or service.
    C. **Personal selling.** Personal presentation by the firm's sales force for the purpose of making sales and building customer relationships.
    D. **Public relations.** Building good relations with the company's various publics by obtaining favorable publicity, building up a good corporate image, and handling or heading off unfavorable rumors, stories, and events.
    E. **Direct marketing.** Direct connections with carefully targeted individual consumers to both obtain an immediate response and cultivate lasting customer relationships: the use of direct mail, the telephone, direct-response television, e-mail, the Internet, and other tools to communicate directly with specific consumers.

II. **Integrated Marketing Communications.** The company carefully integrates its many communications channels

to deliver a clear, consistent, and compelling message about the organization and its brands.

A. **The new marketing communications landscape**
B. **Shifting marketing communications model**
C. **Factors changing the face of communication**
    1. Customers can use the Internet and other technologies to seek out information on their own.
    2. As mass markets have fragmented, marketers are shifting away from mass marketing to narrowly defined micromarkets.
    3. The digital age has spawned a host of new information and communication tools, from cell phones and iPods to the Internet and satellite and television systems.
D. **Characteristics of integrated marketing communications**
    1. IMC calls for recognizing all contact points where the customer may encounter the company and its brands. The company wants to deliver a consistent and positive message with each contact.
    2. IMC ties together all the company's messages and images. The company's television and

print advertisements have the same message, look, and feel as its e-mail and personal selling communications. And its public relations materials project the same image as its Web site.

III. Steps in Developing Effective Communications
A. **Identify the target audience**
B. **Determine the communication objective.** The six buyer readiness states are awareness, knowledge, liking, preference, conviction, and purchase.
C. **Design a message**
   1. **AIDA model.** The message should get attention, hold interest, arouse desire, and obtain action.
   2. **Three problems that the marketing communicator must solve:**
      (a) **Message content (what to say).** There are three types of appeals:
         (i) Rational appeals relate to audience self-interest. They show that the product will produce desired benefits.
         (ii) Emotional appeals attempt to provoke emotions that motivate purchase.
         (iii) Moral appeal is directed to the audience's sense of what is right and proper.
      (b) **Message structure (how to say it)**
         (i) Whether to draw a conclusion or leave it to the audience.
         (ii) Whether to present a one- or two-sided argument.
         (iii) Whether to present the strongest arguments first or last.
      (c) **Message format (how to say it symbolically)**
         (i) Visual ad: using novelty and contrast, eye-catching pictures and headlines, distinctive formats, message size and position, color, shape, and movement.
         (ii) Audio ad: using words, sounds, and voices.
D. **Select communication channels**
   1. **Personal communication channels.** Used for products that are expensive and complex. It can create opinion leaders to influence others to buy.
   2. **Nonpersonal communication channels.** Include media (print, broadcast, and display media), atmospheres, and events.
E. **Message source.** Using attractive sources to achieve higher attention and recall, such as using celebrities.
F. **Measure the results of the communication.** Evaluate the effects on the targeted audience.

IV. Setting the Total Promotion Budget and Mix
A. **Setting the total promotional budget**
   1. **Affordable method.** A budget is set based on what management thinks it can afford.
   2. **Percentage of sales method.** Companies set promotion budget at a certain percentage of current or forecasted sales or a percentage of the sales price.
   3. **Competitive parity method.** Companies set their promotion budgets to match competitors.
   4. **Objective and task method.** Companies develop their promotion budget by defining specific objectives, determining the tasks that must be performed to achieve these objectives, and estimating the costs of performing them.

V. Managing and Coordinating Integrated Marketing Communications
A. **The nature of each promotional tool**
   1. **Advertising** suggests that the advertised product is standard and legitimate; it is used to build a long-term image for a product and to stimulate quick sales. However, it is also considered impersonal one-way communication.
   2. **Personal selling** builds personal relationships, keeps the customers' interests at heart to build long-term relationships, and allows personal interactions with customers. It is also considered the most expensive promotion tool per contact.
   3. **Sales promotion** includes an assortment of tools: coupons, contests, cents-off deals, premiums, and others. It attracts consumer attention and provides information. It creates a stronger and quicker response. It dramatizes product offers and boosts sagging sales. It is also considered short lived.
   4. **Public relations** has believability. It reaches prospective buyers and dramatizes a company or product.
B. **Promotion mix strategies**
   1. **Type of product and market.** The importance of different promotional tools varies among consumers and commercial markets.
   2. **Push versus pull strategy**
      (a) **Push strategy.** The company directs its marketing activities at channel members to induce them to order, carry, and promote the product.
      (b) **Pull strategy.** A company directs its marketing activities toward final consumers to induce them to buy the product.
      (c) **Buyer readiness state.** Promotional tools vary in their effects at different stages of buyer readiness.
      (d) **Product life-cycle stage.** The effects of different promotion tools also vary with stages of the product life cycle.

VI. Advertising. We define advertising as any paid form of nonpersonal presentation and promotion of ideas, goods, or services by an identified sponsor.

VII. Major Decisions in Advertising

    A. Setting objectives. Objectives should be based on information about the target market, positioning, and market mix. Advertising objectives can be classified by their aim: to inform, persuade, or remind.

        1. Informative advertising. Used to introduce a new product category or when the objective is to build primary demand.

        2. Persuasive advertising. Used as competition increases and a company's objective becomes building selective demand.

        3. Reminder advertising. Used for mature products because it keeps the consumers thinking about the product.

    B. Setting the advertising budget. Factors to consider in setting a budget are the stage in the product life cycle, market share, competition and clutter, advertising frequency, and product differentiation.

        1. Strategic versus tactical budgets

        2. Overall promotional budget

        3. Consistency

        4. Opportunity to stretch the budget

        5. The final budget

    C. Developing the advertising strategy

    D. Creating the advertising message

        1. Breaking through the clutter

        2. Message strategy

        3. Message execution. The impact of the message depends on what is said and how it is said.

        4. Consumer-generated messages

        5. Message decisions. Advertising can succeed only if its message gains attention and communicates well.

        6. Message generation. Marketing managers must help the advertising agency create a message that will be effective with their target markets.

        7. Message evaluation and selection. Messages should be meaningful, distinctive, and believable.

    E. Choosing among major media steps

        1. Deciding on reach, frequency, and impact

        2. Choosing among major media types. Choose among newspapers, television, direct mail, radio, magazines, and outdoor.

        3. Selecting specific media vehicles. Costs should be balanced against the media vehicles: audience quality, ability to gain attention, and editorial quality.

        4. Deciding on media timing. The advertiser must decide on how to schedule advertising over the course of a year based on seasonal fluctuation in demand, lead time in making reservations, and if they want to use continuity in their scheduling or use a pulsing format.

        5. Road blocking

    F. Evaluating advertising effectiveness and the return on advertising investment. There are three major methods of advertising pretesting and two popular methods of post-testing ads.

        1. Measuring the communication effect—copy testing

            (a) Direct rating. The advertiser exposes a consumer panel to alternative ads and asks them to rate the ads.

            (b) Portfolio tests. The interviewer asks the respondent to recall all ads and their contests after letting the respondent listen to a portfolio of advertisements.

            (c) Laboratory tests. Equipment is used to measure consumers' physiological reactions to an ad.

        2. Post-testing

            (a) Recall tests. The advertiser asks people who have been exposed to magazines or television programs to recall everything that they can about the advertisers and products they saw.

            (b) Recognition tests. The researcher asks people exposed to media to point out the advertisements they have seen.

            (c) Measuring the sales effect. The sales effect can be measured by comparing past sales with past advertising expenditures and through experiments.

            (d) Measuring the awareness effect

■■■ DISCUSSION QUESTIONS

1. Explain the difference between promotion and advertising.

2. Explain the concept of integrated marketing communications.

3. Recently, a number of restaurants have shifted some of their promotional budget from advertising to public relations. What benefits does public relations offer that would make the restaurants spend more?

4. The percentage of sales method is one of the most common ways of setting a promotional budget. What are some advantages and disadvantages of this method?

5. Apply the five major tools in the marketing communication mix to a hospitality or travel company by showing how a company can use all these tools.

6. According to advertising expert Stuart Henderson Britt, good advertising objectives spell out the intended audience, the advertising message, the desired effects, and the criteria for determining whether the effects were achieved (e.g., not just "increase awareness" but "increase awareness 20 percent"). Why should these

components be part of the advertising objective? What are some effects that an advertiser wants a campaign to achieve?

7. What factors call for more frequency in an advertising media schedule? What factors call for more reach? How can you increase one without either sacrificing the other or increasing your advertising budget?

■■■ EXPERIENTIAL EXERCISES

Do one of the following:

1. Provide an example of a communication from a hospitality or travel company that does a good job of communicating with a specific market segment. The example can be any form of communication (e.g., an advertisement, a sales promotion, or publicity).

2. Find an example of a promotion for a hospitality company that uses the push promotion strategy. Explain how the company is using the strategy.

3. Provide evidence that a hospitality company is using integrated marketing communications, by finding two communications by the firm that have the same message, look, and feel.

■■■ INTERNET EXERCISE

Find several advertisements for a hospitality or travel industry organization. Then visit its Web site. Is the communication provided on the site congruent with and support

its print advertising and broadcast advertising? Explain your answer.

■■■ REFERENCES

1. Theresa Howard, " 'Viral' Advertising Spreads Through Marketing Plans," *USA Today* (October 4, 2008): 1–3; Ron Ruggles, "Students Low-Cost Chipotle Ads Draw 18 Million Online Viewers," *Nations Restaurant News* (December 4, 2006): 4+; Heather Leszczewicz, "Chipotle YouTube," www.onmilwaukee.com (accessed October 5, 2008); Chris Arnold, "Chipotle," www.chipotle.com (accessed October 4, 2008): 1–3; Fred Minnick, "Updated: Chipotle Contest Receives 17.3 Million YouTube Views," *Fast Casual* (November 22, 2006): 1–2; "Actually It Is a Popularity Contest" (October 4, 2008): 1–2; Joseph E. Phelps, Regina Lewis, Lynne Mobilio, David Perry, and Niranjan Raman, "Viral Marketing or Electronic Word-of-Mouth Advertising: Examining Consumer Responses and Motivations to Pass Along Email," *Journal of Advertising Research* (December 2004): 333–348.

2. These definitions, except for sales promotion, are from *Marketing Definitions: A Glossary of Marketing Terms* (Chicago, IL: American Marketing Association, 1995). Other definitions can be found on www.marketingpower.com/live/mg-dictionary.php.

3. Piet Levy, "Touching the Dial," *Marketing News* (March 3, 2010): pp. 16–18. Also see Bob Garfield, *The Chaos Scenario* (Franklin, TN: Stielstra Publishing, 2009); Garfield, "Future May Be Brighter But It's Apocalypse Now," *Advertising Age* (March 23, 2009): 1, 14; and James Othmer, "When I Knew Advertising Had Completely Changed," *Advertising Age* (January 4, 2010): 4, 23.

4. Bob Garfield, "The Chaos Scenario, "*Advertising Age* (April 4, 2005): 1, 57+; and "Readers Response to 'Chaos Scenario,' " *Advertising Age* (April 18, 2005): 1+.

5. Chase Squires and Dave Gussow, "The Ways in Which We Watch TV Are Changing Right Before Our Eyes," *St. Petersburg Times* (April 27, 2006); and Geoff Colvin, "TV Is Dying? Long Live TV!" *Fortune* (February 5, 2007): 43.

6. Abbey Klassen, "Study: Only One in Four Teens Can Name Broadcast Networks," *Advertising Age* (May 15, 2006).

7. Bob Garfield, "The Chaos Scenario 2.0: The Post-Advertising Age," *Advertising Age* (March 26, 2007): 1, 12–13.

8. Brian Steinberg and Suzanna Vranica, "As 30-Second Spot Fades, What Will Advertisers Do Next?" *Wall Street Journal* (January 3, 2006): A15.

9. Mike Shaw, "Direct Your Advertising Dollars Away from TV at Your Own Risk," *Advertising Age* (February 27, 2006): 29.

10. Jack Neff, "P&G Chief: We Need New Model Now," *Advertising Age* (November 15, 2004): 1, 53.

11. "Integrated Campaigns," Advertising Annual 2008, *Communication Arts*, pp. 72–73; Emily Bryson York, "'Whopper Freakout' Wins Grand Effie," *Advertising Age* (June 4, 2009), accessed at http://adage.com/article?article_id=137066; and www.bk.com/en/us/campaigns/whopper-freakout.html, accessed December 2010.

12. Marc Lubetkin, "Bed-and-Breakfast," *Cornell Hotel and Restaurant Administration Quarterly,* 40, no. 4 (1999): 84–90.

13. Konnie Le May, "South Dakota Tribes Beating Tomtoms to Drum Up Increased Tourist Trade," *Star-Ledger* (May 8, 1994): Sec. 8, 6.

14. Steve Raabe, "2 Hotels Link Up for Sales," *Denver Post* (May 4, 1994): C1.

15. For more on message content and structure, see Leon G. Schiffman and Leslie Lazar Kanuk, *Consumer Behavior* (4th ed.) (Upper Saddle River, NJ: Prentice Hall, 1991), Chapter 10; Frank R. Kardes, "Spontaneous Inference Processes in Advertising: The Effects of Conclusion Omission and Involvement on Persuasion," *Journal of Consumer Research* (September 1988): 225–233.

16. Jonah Bloom, "The Truth Is: Consumers Trust Fellow Buyers Before Marketers," *Advertising Age* (February 13, 2006): 25.

17. Sony Kusumasondjaja, Tekle Shanka, and Christopher Marchegiani, "Credibility of Online Reviews and Initial Trust: The Roles of Reviewer's Identity and Review Valence," *Journal of Vacation Marketing* (2012) 18: 185.

18. *Marketing Glossary Dictionary,* American Marketing Association, http://www.marketingpower.com/mgdictionary.php?Searched=1&SearchFor=recall%20test (accessed December 12, 2004).

19. "Sheraton Wakes Up," *Hotels* (January 2004): 20.

20. For a more comprehensive discussion on setting promotion budgets, see Michael L. Rothschild, *Advertising* (Lexington, MA: D.C. Heath, 1987), Chapter 20.

21. Quoted in Daniel Seligman, "How Much for Advertising?" *Fortune* (December 1956): 123.

22. The Hospitality Research Group of PKF Consulting, as cited in *Hotel and Motel Management* (May 15, 2000): 44.

23. Michael S. Morgan, "Traveler's Choice: The Effects of Advertising and Prior Stay," *Cornell Hotel and Restaurant Administration Quarterly,* 32, no. 4 (1991): 40–49.

24. "The Rise (and Fall) of Cost per Call," *Sales and Marketing Management* (April 1990): 26.

25. For more on advertising and the product life cycle, see John E. Swan and David R. Rink, "Fitting Market Strategy to Product Life Cycles," *Business Horizons* (January/February 1982): 60–67.

26. Leslie Ann Hogg, *50 More Promotions That Work for Restaurants* (New York: Walter Mathews Associates, 1989), p. 11.

27. Peter C. Yesawich, "Execution and Measurement of Programs," *Cornell Hotel and Restaurant Administration Quarterly,* 29, no. 4 (1989): 89.

28. Gerald J. Tellis, "Advertising Exposure, Loyalty, and Brand Purchase: A Two-Stage Model of Choice," *Journal of Marketing Research* (May 1988): 57–70.

29. Scheherazade Daneshkhu, "Media: A Trade in Dreams of Escape," *Financial Times* (February 10, 1997): 15.

30. Jay Conrad Levinson, *Guerrilla Advertising* (New York: Houghton Mifflin, 1994).

31. "Average U.S. Home Now Receives a Record 118.6 TV Channels, According to Nielsen" (June 6, 2008), http://en-us.nielsen.com/content/nielsen/en_us/news/news_releases/2008/June/average_u_s.home.html;

and "Number of Magazines by Category," http://www.magazine.org/asme/editorial%5Ftrends (accessed August 2010).

32. Louise Story, "Anywhere the Eye Can See, It's Likely to See an Ad," *New York Times* (January 15, 2007): A12; and James Othmer, "Persuasion Gives Way to Engagement," *Vancouver Sun* (August 20, 2009): A13.

33. See Bill Carter, "An 'Idol' Ratings Loss, But Not in Its Pocket-book," *New York Times* (April 6, 2010), www.nytimes.com; "Executive Summary of the 4A's Television Production Cost Survey" (December 15, 2009), www.aaaa.org/news/bulletins/Documents/2008TVPCSExecSumcosts.pdf; Bill Gorman, "Fox's Average Ad Price in Q4 2009: $122,000" (March 16, 2010), www.tvbytheNumbers.com; Brian Steinberg, " 'Sunday Night Football' Remains Costliest TV Show," *Advertising Age* (October 26, 2009): 8; and "Sluggish Economy Pinches Super Bowl Ad Prices," *Associated Press* (January 11, 2010).

34. "Advertising in the U.S.: Synovate Global Survey Shows Internet, Innovation and Online Privacy a Must" (December 3, 2009), accessed at http://www.synovate.com/news/article/2009/12/advertising-m-the-us-synovate-global-survey-shows-internet-innovation-and-online-privacy-a-must.html; and Katy Bachman, "Survey: Clutter Causing TV Ads to Lack Effectiveness," *MediaWeek* (February 8, 2010).

35. "Report: Ad Execs Stymied by DVR Ad Skipping," *Mediaweek* (June 29, 2009), accessed at http://www.adweek.com/aw/Content_display/news/e3i4f-e3d67e44c8b3aded206ae7b29cd20b; Nielsen, *How DVRs Are Changing the Television Landscape* (April 2009), http://blog.nielsen.com/nielsenwire/wp-content/uploads/2009/04/dvr_tvlandscape_043009.pdf; Bill Carter, "DVR, Once TVs Mortal Foe, Helps Ratings," *New York Times* (November 2, 2009), www.nytimes.com; and Andrew O'Connell, "Advertisers: Learn to Love the DVR," *Harvard Business Review* (April 2010): 22.

36. "Celebrity Sweepstakes: In Advertising, the Answers Don't Necessarily Lie in the Stars," *Nation's Restaurant News* (March 1, 2004): 24.

37. Philip Kotler, *Marketing Management* (Upper Saddle River, NJ: Prentice Hall, 2000), p. 580.

38. For more on consumer-generated advertising, see Emma Hall, "Most Winning Creative Work Involves Consumer Participation," *Advertising Age* (January 6, 2010), accessed at http://adage.com/print?article_id=141329; Stuart Elliott, "Do-It-Yourself Super Ads," *New York Times* (February 8, 2010), www.nytimes.com; Michael Learmonth, "Brands Team Up for User-Generated-Ad Contests," *Advertising Age* (March 23, 2009): 8; and Rich Thomaselli, "If Consumer Is Your Agency, It's Time for Review," *Advertising Age* (May 17, 2010): 2.

39. "Advertisers Quickly Buy Time on Super Bowl XXXVIII Broadcast," *Finance CustomWire* (December 2, 2004), item CX20044337X9209.

40. Christine Dugas, "And Now, a Wittier Word from Our Sponsors," *Business Week* (March 24, 1986): 90; see also Felix Kessler, "In Search of Zap-Proof Commercials," *Fortune* (January 21, 1985): 68–70; Dennis Kneale, "Zapping of TV Ads Appears Pervasive," *Wall Street Journal* (April 25, 1988): 29.

41. Withiam Glenn, "Hotel Advertising in the 80's: Surveying the Field," *Cornell Hotel and Restaurant Administration Quarterly,* 27, no. 1 (1986): 33–34.

42. Joel R. Evans and Barry Berman, *Principles of Marketing* (Upper Saddle River, NJ: Prentice Hall, 1995), p. 432.

43. Jeff Higley, "Hoteliers Emphasize Importance of Billboard Marketing," *Hotel and Motel Management* (November 3, 2003): 76.

44. Jane Meyers and Laurie Freeman, "Marketers Police TV Commercial Costs," *Advertising Age* (April 3, 1989): 51.

45. See Roland T. Rust, *Advertising Media Models: A Practical Guide* (Lexington, MA: Lexington Books, 1986).

46. "Mauritius launches 1 m ad Campaign," *Travel Trade Gazette* (October 29, 2004): 60.

47. Philip H. Dougherty, "Bud 'Pulses' the Market," *New York Times* (February 18, 1975): 40.

Promoting Products: Public Relations and Sales Promotion

Objectives

After reading this chapter, you should be able to:

1. Understand the different public relations activities: press relations, product publicity, corporate communications, lobbying, and counseling.

2. Understand the public relations process: research, establishing marketing objectives, defining the target audience, choosing the PR message and vehicles, and evaluating PR results.

3. Explain how companies use public relations to communicate and influence important publics.

4. Explain how sales promotion campaigns are developed and implemented.

5. Implement a crisis management program in a hospitality business.

The launch of Sputnik I in 1957 started a series of successes for the Soviet Union's space program. These achievements became propaganda vehicles promoting the achievements and advantages of communism. President Kennedy used the "space gap" between the United States and the Soviet Union to his advantage, claiming that the Republicans had let the Soviet Union pass the United States. He campaigned under the banner of a New Frontier.

After Kennedy's election in 1960, the American space program had some success. In May and July 1961, America's self-image was boosted by the suborbital flights of Shepard and Grissom. However, the pride these flights provided was short lived. In July 1961, Gherman Titov flew a seventeen-orbit mission for the Soviets, making the suborbital flights look like child's play.

NASA was eager to build America's pride. It canceled a third suborbital flight and announced that John Glenn would be America's first person to orbit the world. Glenn was well known to most Americans. He had served as a pilot in World War II and the Korean War and made headlines in 1957 for setting a new cross-continent flying speed record. As a result of this achievement, he was invited to participate on two television host shows and was the most publicized of the seven U.S. astronauts.

NASA's publicity machine set the stage for the event. It was America's first attempt at an orbital flight with America's most publicized astronaut. NASA needed to create as much hype as possible to give Americans a sense they were still in the space race. As a result of this hype, over 100 million people were expected to watch the televised launch of *Friendship 7*.

Bud Grice, a Marriott sales manager, thought about all those people who were expected to watch the launch. What a great way to expose Americans to a growing Marriott Corporation. Grice knew that Marriott could not afford television ads, but the idea of all those people watching the coverage of the launch intrigued him; if only Marriott could communicate with an audience of that size.

On February 20, 1962, 135 million Americans watched Glenn take off on his five-hour, three-orbit flight. Grice was one of them, and he was still thinking about the opportunities created by so many people watching a single event. Once the flight was off, cameras switched to the Glenn residence. There were scores of reporters at the residence and the area was a beehive of activity. The Glenns lived in the Washington, D.C., suburb of Arlington, Virginia, not too far from Marriott's corporate headquarters. Grice saw his opportunity. He would have lunch delivered to Mrs. Glenn by Marriott's Hot Shoppes. He put buckets of fried chicken with large Marriott labels in a station wagon and had it delivered to the Glenn residence. The real test would be getting through the police barricades. This proved to be too easy a challenge as the driver simply said that he was delivering Mrs. Glenn's lunch. The Marriott vehicle pulled up in front of the residence, and the Marriott containers were soon seen by an estimated 100 million Americans still watching television.

In a conversation with President Kennedy after the flight, Glenn stated that he was looking forward to spending some time with his family and that he would like to stay at a Marriott hotel because the staff were so good to his wife. Marriott again had another public relations opportunity. It invited Glenn to stay in a complimentary Marriott suite and received additional publicity when the press followed Glenn into the Marriott.

This story illustrates several uses of public relations. First, we are shown how governments use events to promote their ideologies. Second, we see how public relations can be planned to take advantage of opportunities. In this case, Grice created an event, serving lunch to Mrs. Glenn, to gain exposure of the Marriott name to millions of viewers. Finally, by being aware of Glenn's desire to stay in a Marriott hotel, Marriott gained additional publicity from the event.[1]

■■■ Public Relations

"Public relations, perhaps the most misunderstood part of marketing communications, can be the most effective tool."[2] Definitions for public relations differ widely. We think that this definition by Hilton best fits the hospitality industry: "The process by which we create a positive image and customer preference through third-party endorsement."[3]

Public relations (PR) is an important marketing tool that until recently was treated as a marketing stepchild. PR is moving into an explosive growth stage. Companies are realizing that mass marketing is no longer the answer to some of their communication needs. Advertising costs continue to rise while audience reach continues to decline. Advertising clutter reduces the impact of each ad. Sales promotion costs have also increased as channel intermediaries demand lower prices and better commissions and deals. Personal selling can cost over $500 a call. In this environment, PR holds the promise of a cost-effective promotional tool. The creative use of news events, publications, social events, community relations, and other PR techniques offers companies a way to distinguish themselves and their products from their competitors.[4]

The PR department of cruise lines, restaurant chains, airlines, and hotels is typically located at corporate headquarters. Often, its staff is so busy dealing with various publics—stockholders, employees, legislators, and community leaders—that PR support for product marketing objectives tends to be neglected. Many four- and five-star hotel chains have corrected this deficiency by hiring local PR managers.

In the past it was common for the marketing function and PR function to be handled by two different departments within the firm. Today these two functions are increasingly integrated. There are several reasons for this integration. First, companies are calling for more market-oriented PR. They want their PR departments to manage PR activities that contribute toward marketing the company and improving the bottom line. Second, companies are establishing marketing PR groups to support corporate/product promotion and image-making directly. Thus, marketing PR, like financial PR and community PR, serves a special constituency, the marketing department.

Social media has proven to be a great way to reach thousands of customers and potential customers. Today, most effective PR campaigns use Internet; Web sites, blogs, and social networks such as YouTube, Facebook, and Twitter are providing interesting new ways to reach more people. "The core strengths of public relations—the ability to tell a story and spark conversation—play well into the nature of such social media," says a PR expert. Consider the recent Papa John's "Camaro Search" PR campaign:[5]

During a road trip this summer to find his long-lost Camaro, John Schnatter, the "Papa John" of Papa John's pizza, set a record for the world's highest pizza delivery (at the Willis Tower's Skydeck in Chicago), rang the closing bell at the Nasdaq

Marketing Highlight | Taco Bell Provided Example of Creative Publicity

14–1 On April Fools' Day (April 1, 1996), Taco Bell placed a full-page ad in seven major papers, saying that it had purchased the Liberty Bell and would rename it the Taco Liberty Bell. Although this was a paid advertisement, it created a flood of publicity, and newspapers and television news programs picked up the story. Some readers were upset over Taco Bell's treatment of a national shrine. Overall the ad was a clever publicity ploy, creating what Taco Bell said was $22 million worth of free publicity. The ad became a news event and was mentioned across the country by both print and broadcast media. The ad marked the launching of Taco Bell's "Nothing Ordinary About It" $200 million advertising campaign.

One industry analyst said, "Taco Bell still understands a lot about the value of 'sizzle' in today's marketplace." The attention-grabbing ploy served not only to tout the new advertising campaign but also to reinforce Taco Bell's image as a hip, rebellious restaurant chain that is anything but staid. In this world of advertising clutter, where it is sometimes hard to tell the ads from the stories on the evening news and where itchy remote-control fingers can make the distinction obsolete, it takes creativity to stand out. To borrow from Taco Bell's former ad campaign, sometimes you've got to break the rules. The advertisement represents an innovative use of advertising to gain publicity.

Sources: Louise Kramer and Richard Martin, "Taco Bell Commits $200M to Reverse Sales Declines," *Nation's Restaurant News* (April 15, 1996): 1, 4; Rick Van Warner, "April Fools! Reaction to Taco Bell Prank Hits Nerves, Funny Bones," *Nation's Restaurant News* (April 15, 1996).

14.1 Papa John's Pizza, www. papajohns/com: Look at the different promotions featured on the site and the go to Papa John's Facebook page.

stock exchange, and visited a children's hospital. The road trip got solid pickup in the media, with stories in the *New York Times*, the *Wall Street Journal*, and *USA Today*. ABC World News Tonight, CNBC, and CNN also covered the story, which included a $250,000 reward for the person reuniting Schnatter with his beloved Camaro Z28. These were all traditional pre-Web kinds of PR moves.

But unlike the old days, online social media was a key to getting the word out about this Papa John's journey. A Web site dedicated to the trip drew 660,000 unique visitors. On the day of the media conference announcing Schnatter's reunion with his old Chevy classic—Kentuckian Jeff Robinson turned up with the car and took home the cash—there were more than 1,000 tweets about him finding his car, with links galore. In addition, hundreds of people posted photos of themselves on Facebook (in their own Camaros) picking up the free pizza Papa John offered to all Camaro owners as part of the celebration. In all, the Web was buzzing about the Camaro Search story. Pre-Web, "there were different techniques used for [PR]—speeches, publicity, awards," says a PR executive. "Now we're applying the same mindset to social media to build relationships that are critical to any corporate entity.

■■■ Major Activities of PR Departments

PR departments perform the five activities discussed next, not all of which feed into direct product support.

Press Relations

The aim of **press relations** is to place newsworthy information into the news media to attract attention to a person, product, or service. One reason for the growth of press relations in the hospitality industry is its credibility. Most types of publicity are viewed by the consumer as third-party information. A favorable write-up of a restaurant in the local newspaper by the food editor has more impact than an advertisement written by the restaurant's management.

Product Publicity

Product publicity involves various efforts to publicize specific products. New products; special events, such as food festivals; redesigned products, such as a newly renovated hotel; and products that are popular because of current trends, such as nonfat desserts, are all potential candidates for publicity.

Corporate Communication

Corporate communication covers internal and external communications and promotes understanding of the organization. One important marketing aspect of corporate communication is communication directed toward employees, such as company newsletters. Companies also need to manage their communication with their stockholders to make sure the stockholders understand the company's goals and objectives. Stockholders should be viewed as an excellent target market by hospitality firms in various forms of communication.

Lobbying

Lobbying involves dealing with legislators and government officials to promote or defeat legislation and regulation. Large companies employ their own lobbyists, whereas smaller companies lobby through their local trade associations.

Counseling

Counseling involves advising management about public issues and company positions and image.[6] Counseling is important when there may be sensitive issues associated with the business. For example, water is a scarce commodity in Las Vegas. Major resorts with water displays, such as the Mirage, counsel their managers on the resort's water conservation efforts, such as recycling the hotel's wastewater to be used in the hotel's fountains.

■■■ Publicity

Publicity is a direct function of PR. Publicity is the task of securing editorial and news space, as opposed to paid space, in print and broadcast media to promote a product or a service. Publicity is a popular PR tool used in the five activities just described. Some popular uses of publicity are described next.

One of the uses of publicity is to assist in the launch of new products. For example, when the Hard Rock Café announced it was going into the hotel business with the development of the first Hard Rock Hotel, the media covered the event during the initial announcement and the groundbreaking ceremonies. Later, when the hotel opened, a concert staged at the hotel featuring Sheryl Crow was broadcast on MTV. This concert, the uniqueness of the hotel, and a concert the following day by the Eagles and Sheryl Crow ensured that the opening of the hotel received worldwide publicity.

Publicity is also used with special events. To be successful, the **press release** developed to gain the publicity must be of interest to the target audience of the media the company is targeting. For example, a food editor is interested in recipes and food history. A travel editor is interested in unique aspects of the destination, not just the hotel's features. A business editor is interested in the financial success of the operation. A press release should be written for a target audience and have value for the media's audience. We now look at some ways publicity can be used to enhance an organization's image.

Companies can use publicity to build a positive image with specific target markets or stakeholders. For example, McDonald's sponsors special neighborhood events in Hispanic and black communities for good causes. The sponsorship of the events and the publicity generated from the sponsorship build a good company image.

Marketing Highlight A Creative Example of Publicity from Casino Mogul Steve Wynn

14–2 The implosion of the Dunes hotel was a publicity event to celebrate the opening of the Treasure Island Resort in Las Vegas. Mirage Resorts, the parent company of Treasure Island at the time of its opening, purchased the Dunes property for the development of Bellagio. Steve Wynn, CEO of Mirage Resorts, developed a plan to prematurely raze the ten-story sign and twenty-three-story north tower of the Dunes. The empty buildings were going to have to be razed at some point, so why not raze them as part of an opening celebration for Treasure Island? As many as 200,000 people watched the multimillion-dollar pyrotechnic show. Later that evening and the next morning, hundreds of millions of people would see glimpses of the same show on their television.

Building implosions are a common and cost-effective way of clearing land. Thus, if the Dunes implosion was to attract the media's attention, it would have to be extraordinary. Steve Wynn hired a pyrotechnics expert and developed a spectacular show. The show included six minutes of fireworks set from the building's roof. This was followed by explosions of fireballs, representing cannon shots from a replica of the HMS *Britannia* at Treasure Island. These cannon shots first hit the ten-story Dunes sign, bringing it to the ground. Then they hit the building, igniting 550 gallons of aviation fuel and sending flames shooting up the building. Finally, 365 pounds of dynamite were detonated, sending the building to the ground.

Besides this event, the resort placed an ad that appeared simultaneously on all three major television networks. As viewers changed channels, they saw the same message, hinting of the opening of a wonderfully mysterious place. This unique placement of the ads created its own publicity. The resort also placed one-page ads featuring a skull and crossbones in key cities throughout the country.[9]

Most hotels and restaurants do not have $4 million to spend on opening promotions. However, the techniques applied by Treasure Island apply to all operations. The opening promotion of the Mirage was well planned and creative. Maximum benefit was gained from every promotional dollar spent because of preplanning. The resort used several different media and integrated its publicity and advertising efforts. To be effective, promotional efforts must be well planned and well executed.

Clearly, PR can make a memorable impact on public awareness at a fraction of the cost of advertising. The company does not pay for the space or time obtained in the media. It pays for a staff to develop and circulate stories and manage certain events. If the company develops an interesting story, it could be picked up by all the news media and be worth millions of dollars in equivalent advertising. Furthermore, it would have more credibility than advertising. Some experts say that consumers are five times more likely to be influenced by editorial copy than by advertising.

Steve Wynn, a master of publicity, created a publicity event around the razing of the Dunes to make way for his new resort, the Bellagio. MGM Mirage now owns and operates Bellagio. Photo © Dorling Kindersley, Courtesy of the Hotel Bellagio, Las Vegas.

---

e **14.2** McDonald's—Explore the World of McDonald's, http://www.mcdonalds.com/us/en/websites.html: Notice how McDonald's gives back to its customers and groups important to them to create goodwill.

Publicity is used to defend products that have encountered public problems. After a series of hotel fires made national news, the Adam's Mark Hotel in Houston invited a television crew to come to the hotel and see the latest safety devices incorporated into the hotel. As a result, it received several minutes of coverage on the evening news, showing that the fire safety problem had been addressed.

Tourist destinations are particularly influenced by negative publicity. When disaster hits a region or city, tourists instantaneously learn of the problem and quickly find alternative destinations. In part, tourism recovery depends on the reintroduction of a tourism destination. The reintroduction must overcome the adverse publicity resulting from the natural disaster, and it may take several years to rebuild business to predisaster levels. The speed of recovery depends on these factors:[7]

1. The extent of damage caused by the disaster

2. The efficiency with which tourism partners bring their facilities back online

3. An effective marketing message that clearly states the destination is once again open (or still is) and ready for business

Publicity builds corporate image in a way that is congruent with the organization's communication strategy. Olive Garden restaurants developed a charity program that tied in its sponsorship of a team entering the "Olive Garden Rafanelli V-10" in the American Le Mans races. The company worked with America's Second Harvest to help fill its food banks in its "Drive Against Hunger" program. The "Drive Against Hunger" was linked to race-car "driving" by donating eight truckloads of food in the eight cities where the Le Mans races were held. By tying the two events together, Olive Garden was able to create synergy across the events in its PR efforts. This example illustrates the benefits of planning and integrating marketing communications.[8]

■■■ The Public Relations Process

Effective PR is the result of a process. This process must be integrated with the firm's marketing strategy. One common misconception about PR and publicity is that quantity is more important than quality. Some PR firms measure success by the number of articles placed in media. As in other marketing efforts, PR should be meaningful to the target market.

The PR process consists of the following steps: conducting research, establishing the market objectives, defining the target audience, choosing the PR messages and vehicles, implementing the PR plan, and evaluating the results.

Pamela Parseghian, executive editor of *Nation's Restaurant News,* provides a great example of the importance of using the PR process. She discusses a chef who proposed writing a column in a major newspaper. She states the chef had developed no previous relations with the newspaper and the newspaper had not even reviewed his restaurant. Thus, there was no chance that it was going to let a "stranger" to write a column in its paper. She says that if you want to get a story in a publication, first research and read the publication. She states she has people calling her asking if *Nation's Restaurant News* publishes articles on restaurants! Obviously these people have never seen the publication, but they are ready to send in an article. Once you know the media, you can match their objectives and target market with your objectives. Then choose some news stories they will likely publish, such as recipes for new dishes, unique backgrounds, and themed dinners. She also states that making the story exclusive adds value. Once you get some articles placed, then you can decide whether writing regular columns makes sense based on the results the other articles created for your business.[10]

Research

Before a company can develop a PR program, it must understand the company's mission, objectives, strategies, and culture. It should know the vehicles that will be effective in delivering messages to the target audience. Much of the information needed by a PR manager is contained in a well-written marketing plan. Ideally, the PR manager should be involved in the formation of the marketing plan.

The firm's environmental scanning system is another important source of information for the PR manager. Analysis of this information should identify trends and give the firm insights into how they it react to these trends. For example, many hotel and restaurant companies are now showing what they are doing to save and protect the natural environment and lessen global warming.

Establishing the Marketing Objectives

Once the PR manager has identified opportunities through product experiment and research, priorities can be established and objectives set. Marketing PR can contribute to the following objectives:

- *Build awareness.* PR can place stories in the media to bring attention to a product, service, person, organization, or idea.

THE BEST REVIEWS START WITH THE BEST STEAKS.
We're very picky. We only serve USDA Prime beef. Only .005% makes it into our kitchen and ultimately onto your plate. If you've never experienced a steak at III Forks, please come in. And see for yourself what everyone is talking about.

Original Great Steakhouse of North America.
-Independent Retail Cattlemen's Association

Rated Excellent.
-Zagat Survey

1201 Fannin Houston, Texas
77002 · (713) 658-9457
FOLLOW ON FACEBOOK & TWITTER 3FORKS.COM

MAKE YOUR VALENTINE'S DAY RESERVATION TODAY!

III Forks Restaurant uses the publicity it received in its advertising as a third-party testimonial to support the excellent quality of the restaurant. Courtesy of III Forks Restaurant.

- *Build credibility.* PR can add credibility by communicating the message in an editorial context. Credibility can be enhanced through positive associations with respected institutions, companies, and individuals. Cabela's is a highly respected outdoor sporting goods company with several stores in many states. Hunting, fishing, and boating enthusiasts in these areas are very familiar with Cabela's and have faith in the products and services that Cabela's offers.

Oak Tree Lodge in Clark, South Dakota, offers pheasant, duck, and goose hunting packages on 8,000 acres of hunting land at prices ranging from $750 to $1,000 per day per hunter. These packages include upscale lodging and meals as well as the actual hunting experience. Oak Tree is a Cabela's certified hunting lodge. This designation gave the lodge great publicity, enhanced its image, and served as another channel of distribution. To receive this designation, the owner and staff of Oak Tree Lodge had to work closely with Cabela's and demonstrate that the Lodge was indeed worthy of this designation and would maintain high standards.

III Forks restaurant has received favorable reviews from Independent Retail Cattlemen's Association and Zagat. III Forks integrated these reviews into an advertisement, and used to provide evidence that it is its selection of top-quality meat that helped earn the positive reviews.

- *Stimulate the sales force and channel intermediaries.* PR can help boost sales force and franchisee enthusiasm. Positive stories about a new menu item will make an impression on the customers, employees, and franchisees of a restaurant chain. The publicity Ritz-Carlton receives from winning the Baldrige Award provides its sales force with great ammunition when it makes a sales call.

- *Lower promotion costs.* PR costs less than direct mail and media advertising. The smaller the company's promotion budget is, the stronger the case for using PR to gain share of mind.

Specific objectives should be set for every PR campaign. The Wine Growers of California hired the PR firm of Daniel J. Edelman, Inc., to develop a publicity campaign to convince Americans that wine drinking is a pleasurable part of good living and to improve the image and market share of California wines. The following publicity objectives were established: (1) Develop magazine stories about wine and place them in top magazines (*Time, House Beautiful*) and in newspapers (food columns, feature sections); (2) develop stories about wine's many health values and direct them to the medical profession; and (3) develop specific publicity for the young adult market, college market, governmental bodies, and various ethnic communities. These objectives were refined into specific goals so that final results could be evaluated.

The Homestead of Hot Springs, Virginia, conducts special weekends that serve as a part of that hotel's promotion mix. These weekends bring members of the media to the resort and give them an event to write about in addition to the resort's amenities. The resort features events around long-weekend holidays such as Martin Luther King Jr. Day and President's Day weekend. It also has created events for women. For example, "Just for Women" features a number of classes and seminars, including nutrition, financial advice, and organizing your life. It also includes luxurious spa treatments and a Friday night fashion show. Another feature has wine experts giving wine seminars and offering a special gourmet dinner on Saturday evening.[11]

The restaurant association in many cities sponsors a Taste of the Town. This event features food from the city's restaurants. The restaurants have a chance for exposure to many potential customers in one evening. The association usually charges an admission fee, which helps ensure that those attending are interested in restaurant fare rather than obtaining a free dinner. The fee is then donated to a charity, providing additional publicity.

Defining the Target Audience

A relevant message delivered to a target audience by the appropriate vehicle is crucial to the success of any PR campaign. Effective PR practitioners carefully identify the publics they wish to reach. They study these publics and find media that can be used to deliver their message. They identify issues that will be important to the public and form the message so it will seem natural and logical to the target audience.

Choosing the PR Message and Vehicles

The PR practitioner is now ready to identify or develop interesting stories about the product or service. If the number of stories is insufficient, the PR practitioner should propose newsworthy events that the company can sponsor. Here the challenge is to create news rather than find it. PR ideas include hosting major academic conventions, inviting celebrity speakers, and developing news conferences. Each event is an opportunity to develop a multitude of stories directed at different audiences.

Publications

Companies rely extensively on communication materials to reach and influence their target markets. These include annual reports, brochures, cards, articles, audiovisual materials, and company newsletters and magazines. Brochures can play an important role in informing target customers about a product, how it works, and how it is to be assembled. McDonald's developed a series of brochures discussing the quality ingredients that it uses, the actions that it has taken to help protect the environment, and the nutritional content of its products. Thoughtful articles written by company executives can draw attention to the company and its products. Company newsletters and magazines can help build the company's image and convey important news to target markets. Audiovisual materials, such as DVDs, are very useful as promotion tools. The cost of audiovisual materials is usually greater than that of printed material, but so is the impact. Many resort destinations use DVDs to promote their properties. Disney World created a 20-minute DVD aimed at families considering it as a vacation site. Wet-N-Wild developed a four-minute one aimed at travel agents, tour agents, and other members of the distribution channel.

McDonald's developed a creative and trend-setting annual report for stockholders that contained statements by members of top management as well as commercials. Publicly traded hospitality corporations with thousands of stockholders should consider the annual report and other stockholder communication as opportunities to promote the company's products and services, not simply as information required by law.

Events

Hospitality companies can draw attention to new products or other company activities by arranging special events, such as the Homestead Wine and Food Festival mentioned earlier. Events include news conferences, seminars, outings, exhibits, contests and competitions, anniversaries, and sport and cultural sponsorships that will reach the target publics.

The Gaylord Palms Resort and Convention Center in Orlando created "Christmas at the Palms" to provide a demand for rooms in December. The festive event created a reason to stay at the Gaylord Palms, turning it into a destination. The result was articles in the media about the resort. The event gave the media a reason to discuss the resort. The outcome for the hotel was 135,000 visitors and increased room occupancy.[12]

Crowne Plaza Hotels and Resorts developed a "Marry Me 11.11.11." promotional event. Crowne Plaza gave away a complete wedding package in New York to eleven lucky couples, knowing there is only one 11.11.11 (November 11, xx11) every hundred years. It was also supposed to be a lucky day to be married. Numerologist Glynis McCants states, "I have dozens of people who have contacted me and want to get married on that day. They wanted to know if it's a good day, a lucky day." Two means love. You always want a two in your wedding day. And four is about couples and commitment. In short, said McCants, the numbers say yes.[13] The uniqueness of the event created both pre-event and post-event publicity for Crowne Plaza.

A less elaborate event is Little Woodrow's Turtle Race. The weekly event features turtles with numbers on their backs starting from an elevated spot in the center of the race circle. The event creates excitement for the customers and helps create word of mouth. If you go on YouTube, you are likely to see several videos of the event, with some having thousands of hits.

Trine Palace is a historical restoration of the original governor's mansion when North Carolina was a British colony. Located in New Bern, this attraction draws thousands of tourists annually. December used to be a poor month for attendance, with inclement weather and preparation for Christmas occupying the minds of potential visitors. Trine Palace developed a Christmas tour that included actors costumed as the original governor and wife, tables heaped with Christmas food (for display only), strolling bagpipe musicians, Christmas candles, holly, and a reception for guests following the tour at which punch and cookies are served. This relatively simple idea has become so successful that December is now among the top-attendance months.

New York's Vista Hotel decided to offer a Cajun dinner, but needed a "hook" to make the event authentic and newsworthy. That hook was Paul Prudhomme, the colorful Cajun chef. The Vista arranged to host a publication party for Paul's Cajun cookbook at the hotel during the Cajun dinner. This type of creative thinking creates a great PR event from an otherwise interesting but not particularly newsworthy event.[14]

News

A major task of PR professionals is to find or create favorable news about the company, its products, and its people. News generation requires skill in developing a story concept, researching it, and writing a press release. But the PR person's skill must go beyond preparing news stories: getting the media to accept press releases and attend press conferences calls for marketing and interpersonal skills. A good PR media director understands press needs for stories that are interesting and timely and for releases that are well written and attention getting. The media director needs to gain the favor of editors and reporters. As the press is cultivated, it is increasingly likely to provide better coverage to the company.

A proven technique for writing a good press release is to use the Hey-You-See-So technique. Imagine that a teenager saw a friend in front of the high school. The teenager might yell, "Hey (attention getter) Bill and Helen (you), look what I have, three tickets for Saturday's rock concert (see). Let's plan to go (so)." When this simple technique is followed in a press release, effectiveness is increased.

Another journalistic technique is to write a press release in an inverted pyramid form. Think of a pyramid standing on its point, and remember that editors can and do shorten a press release to serve space requirements. A press release should be written so that the bulk of the information the company wishes to transmit is contained in the first paragraph. Each additional paragraph simply adds to the original and is less and less damaging to the story if clipped by an editor.

Speeches are another tool for creating product and company publicity. Increasingly, company executives must field questions from the media or give talks at trade associations or sales meetings. These appearances can build or hurt the company's image. Companies are choosing their spokespersons carefully and using speech writers and coaches to help improve the speaking ability of those selected.

The creation of a high-quality speech is costly for any company. A considerable amount of staff and executive time must be devoted to the project. It therefore makes sense to obtain maximum PR mileage from each speech. This is accomplished by printing copies of the speech or excerpts for distribution to the press, stockholders, employees, and other publics. A speech that is given but not distributed represents a wasted PR opportunity.

Public Services Activities

Companies can improve public goodwill by contributing money and time to good causes. A large company typically asks executives to support community affairs where its offices and plants are located. In other instances, companies offer to donate a certain amount of money to a specified cause from consumer purchases. Called cause-related marketing, it is used by a growing number of companies to build public goodwill.[15] Restaurant and hotel chains donate so much of each sale to a charitable cause for a given amount of time. For example, a fast-food restaurant may donate five cents from every sandwich purchased on a certain day to the Muscular Dystrophy Association. Applebee's restaurant sponsors a special recognition program for the students of Lee School. Every month, each teacher nominates two students who have displayed one of the following six pillars of character: trustworthiness, respect, responsibility, fairness, caring, or citizenship. A drawing is held to pick three nominated students and one teacher who will go to Applebee's restaurant to eat lunch together. The restaurant receives free publicity on the school's Web site for this promotion.[16]

Identity Media

Normally, a company's PR material acquires separate looks, which creates confusion and misses an opportunity to create and reinforce corporate identity. In a society subject to overcommunication, companies must compete for attention. They should strive to create a visual identity that the public immediately recognizes. The visual identity is carried by the company's logos, stationery, brochures, signs, business forms, business cards, buildings, uniforms, dress codes, and rolling stock.

Implementing the Marketing PR Plan

Implementing publicity requires care. Consider the matter of placing information in the media. Exciting information is easy to place. However, most press releases are less than great and might not get the attention of busy editors. A chief asset of publicists is their personal relationship with media editors. PR practitioners are often former journalists who know many media editors and what they want. PR people look at media editors as a market to satisfy so they will continue to use the company's press releases.

Publicity requires extra care when it involves staging special events, such as testimonial dinners, news conferences, and national contests. PR practitioners need a good head for detail and for coming up with quick solutions when things go wrong. Most hotel corporations have a crisis plan included as part of their PR plan. In this plan they state who can talk to the media and who should not. These plans usually state that staff should not speak to media but instead direct inquiries to the director of PR.

Evaluating PR Results

The contribution of PR is difficult to measure because it is used along with other promotion tools. If it is used before other tools come into action, its contribution is easier to evaluate.

Exposures

The easiest measure of PR effectiveness is the number of exposures created in the media. Publicists supply the client with a clipping book showing all the media that carried news about the product and a summary statement, such as the following:

Media coverage included 3,500 column inches of news and photographs in 350 publications with a combined circulation of 79.4 million; 2,500 minutes of air time on 290 radio stations and an estimated audience of 65 million; and 660 minutes of air time on 160 television stations with an estimated audience of 91 million. If this time and space had been purchased at advertising rates, it would have amounted to $1,047,000.[17]

This exposure measure is not very satisfying. There is no indication of how many people actually read, heard, or recalled the message and what they thought afterward. There is no information on the net audience reached because publications overlap in readership. Because publicity's goal is reach, not frequency, it would be useful to know the number of unduplicated exposures. It is also important that publicity reach target markets. A common weakness of publicity is that the persons exposed to it are not part of the company's target market.

Awareness/Comprehension/Attitude Change

A better measure is the change in product awareness/comprehension/attitude resulting from the campaign (after allowing for the effect of other promotional tools). For example, how many people recall hearing the news item? How many told others about it (a measure of word of mouth)? How many changed their minds after hearing it? The Potato Board learned, for example, that the number of people who agreed with the statement "Potatoes are rich in vitamins and minerals" went from 36 percent before the campaign to 67 percent after the campaign, a significant improvement in product comprehension.

Sales-and-Profit Contribution

Sales-and-profit impact is the most satisfactory measure, if obtainable. A well-planned PR campaign is usually part of an integrated promotional campaign. This makes it very difficult to isolate the impact of the PR campaign.

■■■ PR Opportunities for the Hospitality Industry

Individual Properties

Public relations is by far the most important promotional tool available to entrepreneurs and individual properties, such as a single restaurant, tourist attraction, bed and breakfast (B&B), tour operator, or hotel. Seldom can these enterprises afford costly advertising or other promotional programs. Successful PR programs by individual operators have demonstrated winning strategies that can be emulated by others.

Employees should be trained to look for PR opportunities. For example, a convention service manager developed a story about 200 chinchilla breeders who were meeting at the hotel, a bell person heard that a famous person would be a speaker at a dinner in the ballroom, and a room clerk found out that one of the hotel guests was 104 years old. All these stories resulted in positive exposure for the employees' hotels.[18]

Build PR Around the Owner/Operator

The owner/operator and the enterprise itself often become one and the same in the minds of customers. Obviously, this strategy holds dangers, such as the death of the owners, but benefits usually exceed risks. The success of a restaurant operator named Joe is an example. The name of this restaurant—not surprisingly—was Joe's. Joe used to drive a Cadillac, with two magnetic signs advertising his restaurant. Everyone in the community knew Joe and watched for his car as it rolled about town. Joe built his own personal image by wearing white cook's pants, a starched white shirt, and big comfortable black shoes that squeaked. Joe wore this uniform everywhere. If people failed to see Joe coming, they knew by the aroma of his big cigar that he was near. Joe knew the power of visibility and built a gigantic window so that passersby could look directly into the kitchen. He had a team of "trained chefs" who knew the value of show biz. They stirred, flipped, and flamed dishes to the delight of all. Joe knew the value of show biz, but most of all he realized the value of "Joe." Joe's most powerful PR asset was that he was always at the restaurant. He called this personal goodwill. Customers came to see Joe. In turn, he knew them by name and greeted each with a firm handshake. Joe was a pro at "selling Joe."[19]

The owner/operator of a fishing lodge in Costa Rica had been a circus trapeze artist before retiring to the jungles of Costa Rica. Each year, U.S. and Canadian TV and radio talk shows featured this entrepreneur and his fishing lodge. This owner/operator knew that the media is always hungry for a good human interest story.

Individuals successful at promoting themselves often use theatrical costumery such as Joe's squeaky shoes or General MacArthur's corncob pipe. Ken Hamblin, an African American columnist and talk show host, is never seen without a hat. Obesity, a wart on the nose, a bony appearance, a limp, a mustache, and dozens of other personal characteristics have been used successfully to build memorable personalities. As increasing numbers of men wear ponytails and earrings, the blue suit and white shirt IBM-type appearance may become a differentiating "costume."

Build PR Around Location

Some restaurants and B&Bs are almost impossible to find. Normally, this would be viewed as the kiss of death for a hospitality firm. Hundreds of owners/operators of these enterprises have turned their lemon into lemonade. The isolation and obscurity of the enterprises is used as a PR tactic.

A restaurant in San Francisco lies directly under a freeway that collapsed during an earthquake. Sure enough, instead of discouraging patrons, interest increased as the restaurant was featured on national TV as the little restaurant that refused to succumb to an earthquake.

Build PR Around a Product or Service

14.3 Wall Drug Store, http://walldrug.com/: Visit Wall Drugs Web site to see how this drug store has transformed into a tourist attraction. An evolution that was started by offering

Placing signs, "Free Ice Water—Wall Drug," started a flow of travelers that has never stopped. Courtesy of Ffooter/ Dreamstime

Wall Drug Store is a major tourist stop and tourist attraction for the state of South Dakota. Located in a town of less than a 1,000 residents, Wall Drug attracts 15,000 or more visitors daily during tourist season. Wall Drug's reputation was built on free ice water. Before the days of air-conditioned cars, Mr. and Mrs. Ted Hustead, the owners, saw tourists passing by on their way to the Black Hills. These folks looked thirsty and indeed they were. Ted hand-painted a few signs reading "Free Ice Water—Wall Drug" and placed them along the highway. Before Ted returned from planting these signs, tourists had already found their way to Wall Drug. They have never stopped coming. Today, word of mouth and PR have replaced many of the road signs, but Wall Drug remains the free ice-water stop.

The Raffles Hotel in Singapore has a colorful and long history, but most visitors know it as the birthplace of the drink called the Singapore Sling. Today the renovated bar serves thousands of Singapore Slings. Even the empty glasses are sold and serve as a PR vehicle throughout the world. Hospitality enterprises everywhere have built a solid and long-lasting image around a drink, a dessert, a special entree, fireplaces in the guest rooms, and even ducks. The Peabody Hotel of Memphis became well known for a flock of ducks that waddled daily from the rooftop via the elevator to a fountain in the lobby. When the Peabody opened their Orlando property, the Peabody ducks became one of the features of the property, creating publicity for the new hotel.

Unique service also serves as a PR focal point. Usually, this means exceptionally fine service, but sometimes the reverse is true. Occasionally, a bar and grill or a restaurant gains a reputation for having the rudest and sometimes the ugliest wait staff anywhere in the country. A Dallas bar and grill popular with the lunchtime business crowd was notorious for its surly staff. Those familiar with the place loved to take unsuspecting newcomers to see how badly their companion could be insulted.

■■■ Crisis Management

An important area of PR is crisis management. Not all publicity is good. Hotels are open 24 hours a day, major airline companies have thousands of flights a day, and fast-food companies serve millions of customers each day. There are times when things go wrong; sometimes it is management's fault, and sometimes it is beyond management's control. Managers must realize that things do go wrong: Guests fall asleep while smoking, people are poisoned by tainted or spoiled restaurant food, thieves rob guests, planes crash, earthquakes destroy buildings, and flooding occurs somewhere every spring. A crisis management program will reduce the negative effects of these events.

The first step in crisis management is to take all precautions to prevent negative events from occurring. As a communications consultant, Eric Bergman states that in crisis management we should concentrate more on the management and communication and less on the crisis.[20] Robert Irvine divides crises into two main categories a sudden crisis and a smoldering crisis.[21] A sudden crisis is the one that comes without any warning. These can be natural disasters, such as earthquakes and floods, workplace or domestic violence, an outbreak of food poisoning, and fires. Smoldering crises can include sexual harassment by supervisors, safety violations that could result in fines or illegal actions, health code violations, and fire code violations.

The sudden crises need to be anticipated. Crisis management is a series of ongoing, interrelated assessments or audits of kinds of crises and forces that can pose a major problem to a company.[22] Companies and their management need to determine those crises that have a chance of occurring and develop plans in case they do occur. Hotels should have fire plans, and employees should know what to do in case of a fire. Hotels in areas where earthquakes are prevalent should have an earthquake plan. For example, Deborah Roker, PR director for Sonesta International Hotels, designed a crisis-communication program for each of the hotels in the eighteen-property chain. She conducts a half-day training session annually at each property, going over crisis management plans with department heads. Part of this training includes a session at which managers are asked challenging questions that may be asked by guests or the media.[23]

Smoldering crises can often be eliminated with good management. Smoldering crises give warning before they occur. It may be a drop in grades on a health report, an informal claim that a supervisor is practicing sexual harassment, grease dripping from exhaust ducts, or strangers walking the property. Good sanitation practices reduce the risk of serving poisoned food. Strict policies regarding sexual harassment create a climate where sexual harassment is not tolerated. Regular cleaning of kitchen ducts and employee training can eliminate grease fires in the kitchen. Hotels that train all their employees to look out for suspicious actions and report them to security can reduce the risk of crimes against guests. A well-managed property is the best form of crisis management.

The Internet is an area where major crises are being spawned. A damaging message about your organization (whether true or not) can be spread over the Internet to millions of people.[24] This has two important implications for management. First, the stakes of crisis management have been raised. It is very important to reduce the risk of a crisis occurring. Second, managers should monitor chat groups on the Internet to find out what they are saying about their organization. For example, a hotel in Miami should monitor the various chat groups for tourists to Miami.

Odwalla effectively used the Internet to help manage a crisis involving several bottles of Odwalla apple juice sold on the West Coast that were found to contain *E. coli* bacteria. Odwalla initiated a massive product recall. Within only three hours, it set up a Web site laden with information about the crisis and Odwalla's response. Company staffers also combed the Internet looking for newsgroups discussing Odwalla and posted links to the site. In this age where "it's easier to disseminate information through e-mail marketing, blogs, and online chat," notes an analyst, "public relations is becoming a valuable part of doing business in a digital world."[25] As with the other promotion tools, in considering when and how to use product PR, management should set PR objectives, choose the PR messages and vehicles, implement the PR plan, and evaluate the results. The firm's PR should be blended smoothly with other promotion activities within the company's overall integrated marketing communications effort.

When a crisis does occur, good communication with the press can reduce the impact of negative publicity. For example, a fire in a guest room resulting in no injuries could result in negative or positive publicity. If the hotel provides no information to the press, the headline might read "Regal Hotel Fire Forces Evacuation of 360 Guests." If the hotel contacts the press, the hotel has a chance to tell its story. In this case, the hotel could state that there was a hotel fire. "The smoke alarm went off at 12:33 A.M., setting the hotel's fire plan into action. The fire department was called and employees conducted an orderly evacuation of the hotel as a precautionary measure. No one was injured and all guests were able to return to their rooms within thirty minutes. Ms. Roberta Dominquez, the general manager of the Regal, praised the quick action of the employees. She stated that as a result of the hotel's monthly fire drills, all employees knew exactly what to do." The headline from this story might read: "Well-Trained Employees Quickly Move Guests to Safety."

To have good crisis management, the company should appoint a spokesperson. Other employees should be instructed to refer media to this person. This ensures that the company is giving a consistent story based on facts. Second, this person should gather the facts and speak only from facts. This person needs to make timely statements and keep the press updated.[26] If the press receives regular updates from the spokesperson, this will help get them from trying to gain information from other employees. The spokesperson should never use the term *no comment* because it raises suspicion. Using the term *I don't know at this time* is a better response. If the hotel has a PR agency, the agency should be contacted. In a major crisis, it is a good idea to seek the help of a PR firm. Finally, the company should notify the press when a crisis does occur and keep the press updated. The media will learn about the event, so it is best that they find out from the company. Every company should have a crisis management plan and instruct employees in crisis management as part of their initial training. "It is no longer a question of if a major crisis will strike an organization, but only when."[27]

■■■ Sales Promotion

Sales promotion consists of short-term incentives to encourage the purchase or sale of a product or service. Sales promotion includes a variety of promotional tools designed to stimulate earlier or stronger market response. It includes consumer promotion (samples, coupons, rebates, price-off, premiums, contests, demonstrations), trade promotion-buying allowances (free goods, cooperative advertising, and push money), and sales force promotion (bonuses and contests). Often a well-planned sales promotion can result in publicity. The Omni San Antonio Hotel offered a Teacher's Appreciation Special in recognition of their contribution as educators. This sales promotion created goodwill among the teachers and the community and generated publicity for the hotel. It also generated room sales during a soft period.[28] Applebee's gives a free child's meal to students who make an A. This rewards students who get good grades and provides the school with a no-cost way of recognizing students who have done well. In addition to the PR benefits, it brings the child's parents and siblings to Applebee's when the free meal is redeemed. Thus, Applebee's generates profitable sales from the promotion.

Sales promotion tools are used by most organizations. Estimates of annual sales promotion spending run as high as $100 billion. Spending has increased rapidly in recent years. Formerly, the ratio of advertising to sales promotion spending was about 60:40. Today, in many consumer packaged–goods companies, the picture is reversed, with sales promotion often accounting for 60 or 70 percent of all marketing expenditures. Sales promotions are most effective when they are used with advertising or personal selling. Consumer promotions must normally be advertised and can add excitement and pulling power to ads. Trade and sales force promotions support the firm's personal selling process. In using sales promotions, a company must *set objectives, select the right tools, develop the best program, pretest and implement it,* and *evaluate the results.* These steps are discussed next.

Setting Sales Promotion Objectives

Sales promotion objectives vary widely. Consumer promotions can increase short-term sales or they can be used to help build long-term market share. The objective may be to entice consumers to try a new product, lure consumers away from competitors, or hold and reward loyal customers. For the sales force, objectives include building stronger customer relations and obtaining new accounts.

Sales promotions should be consumer franchise building; that is, they should promote the product's positioning and include a sales message. Ideally, the objective is to build long-run consumer demand rather than to prompt temporary brand switching. If properly designed, every sales promotion tool has consumer franchise-building potential.

Selecting Sales Promotion Tools

Many tools can be used to accomplish sales promotion objectives. The promotion planner should consider the type of market, the sales promotion objectives, the competition, and the costs and effectiveness of each tool. The main consumer promotion tools are described next.

Consumer Promotion Tools

The main consumer promotion tools include samples, coupons, premiums, patronage rewards, point-of-purchase (POP) displays, contests, sweepstakes, and games.

Samples are offers of a trial amount of a product. Some samples are free. For others, the company charges a small amount to offset its cost. McDonald's offered a cup of coffee and an apple-bran muffin for $1. The promotion was designed to get customers to try the muffin. Some people do not eat bran muffins, and by charging a small price for the muffin, McDonald's avoided giving the muffin away to customers who would never buy one in the future.

The Inn on the Park in Houston invited potential customers and influential community members to stay in the luxury hotel at no charge. The promotion accomplished two objectives: (1) salespeople were aided in selling corporate contracts because many of their potential customers had experienced the hotel and (2) positive word of mouth about the hotel was created. Sampling is the most effective but also the most expensive way to introduce a new product.

Sampling by the staff who are employed by a hospitality firm such as a hotel, restaurant, or ski resort can be a very useful educational and promotional device. Thorough knowledge of the product is particularly beneficial to upselling. It is difficult for anyone to recommend a premium-priced Bordeaux or California merlot if he or she has no idea how the wine tastes. The sales and reservation staff of a hotel or resort can more convincingly sell a prospect on the idea of upgrading to a poolside cabaña or suite if they have a personal knowledge of the product.

How does the staff obtain personal knowledge of the product or services of a company? Several successful approaches have been used to accomplish staff product knowledge:

1. Provide continuous training programs and invite suppliers such as vintners, cheese producers, and gourmet coffee distributors to provide samples and assist with product training.

2. Offer sales and performance incentives that include prizes on the property, such as a five-course meal, a month's use of the health club, or a weekend in the deluxe suite.

3. Create an employee's day in which the staff has full use of the facility. Country clubs often provide a special day in which employees and sometimes their families are treated to exclusive use of the pool, the golf course, the restaurant, and even the ballroom for an evening dance.

4. Share product information with employees through newsletters or product brochures. Often, product information brochures remain only in the offices of the purchasing department, the food and beverage manager, or some other executive office.

5. Talk continuously about the company's products and services in a positive and upbeat manner. People have a tendency to forget the many positive attributes of the facilities and the services that surround us daily.

Preston L. Smith, the president and CEO of S-K-I Limited, regularly sends memos to company managers urging them to hit the slopes. Smith personally manages to ski over sixty times each season. "Everyone skis here. It's a way of sharing the customer's experience. It's also a way to achieve personal growth because skiing is exhilarating and exciting."[29]

Coupons are certificates that offer buyers savings when they purchase specified products. More than 280 billion coupons are distributed in the United States each year, with a total face value of more than $350 billion. Consumers redeemed 2.6 billion coupons, or a little less than 1 percent of those distributed.[30] Coupons can be mailed, included with other products, or placed in ads. Coupons are most popular in the restaurant industry; however, hotel, rental car companies, tourist attractions, and cruise lines also use coupons. American Express cardholders received coupon packs featuring mid- and upscale restaurants. The prestige of American Express allows these restaurants to use coupons without detracting from their image.

Some restaurants have suffered from overcouponing. In the "pizza wars," the major chains fought for market share by distributing coupons at least once a week. Some pizza restaurants posted signs saying that they would honor competitors' coupons to neutralize the impact of competitor advertising. During the pizza wars, the price of pizza dropped to the discounted coupon price for most customers. These customers felt they were getting poor value if they purchased a pizza without a coupon. Overcouponing should be avoided because it lowers the price so the coupon no longer offers a competitive advantage.

Besides stimulating sales of a mature product, coupons are also an effective way to promote the trial of a new product. For example, when a fast-food chain develops a new product, it often introduces the product in print advertisements featuring a coupon. The coupon provides an incentive and reduces the risk for customers trying the new product.

Marketers are also cultivating new outlets for distributing coupons, such as supermarket shelf dispensers, electronic point-of-sale coupon printers, e-mail and online media, or even mobile text-messaging systems. Mobile couponing is very popular in Europe, India, and Japan, and it's now gaining popularity in the United States. For example, consider Cellfire, a mobile couponing company in California.[31]

Cellfire (cellfire.com) distributes digital coupons to the cell phones of consumers nationwide who sign up for its free service. Cellfire's growing list of clients includes Domino's Pizza, TGI Friday, Hollywood Video, 1-800-flowers.com, and

Hardee's restaurants. Cellfire sends an ever-changing assortment of digital coupons to users' cell phones. To use the coupons, users simply call up the stored coupon list, navigate to the coupon they want, press the "Use Now" button, and show the digital coupon to the store cashier. Domino's even permits consumers holding the mobile coupons to simply click on a link to have their cell phones dial the nearest Domino's store to place an order.

Coupons distributed through Cellfire offer distinct advantages to both consumers and marketers. Consumers don't have to find and clip paper coupons or print out Web coupons and bring them along when they shop. They always have their cell phone coupons with them. For marketers, mobile coupons allow more careful targeting and eliminate the costs of printing and distributing paper coupons. "We don't pay for distribution of digital coupons," says one client. "We pay on redemptions." And the redemption rates can be dazzling. According to Cellfire's chief executive, Brent Dusing, "We're seeing redemption rates as high as 10 to 15 percent, while the industry average paper response is less than 1 percent."

Many professional marketing consultants and observers of marketing and sales practices feel that too much promotion creates a commodity out of a differentiated product. It is argued that companies spend millions of dollars and years of effort to develop a distinct image and a high level of product differentiation in the minds of consumers, only to have it destroyed by promotions.

In far too many cases, promotions have created an impression that margins were unreasonably high to begin with or the company could not have made this offer. They have also led to coupon wars and other forms of price discounting, all the while detracting from the intrinsic value of the company's product or service. Managers should be careful turning coupons into an entitlement. Because of the extensive couponing done by pizza restaurants, many pizza customers do not feel they are getting a good value unless they use a coupon. In the hospitality industry where demand varies greatly by time period, coupons should have blackout periods during those times when a person using a coupon may displace a regular guest. For example, restaurants are typically busy on Fridays and Saturdays, so a new restaurant that is using coupons to attract new customers should make the coupons good Sunday through Thursday. Coupons can employ an important part of a communications program, but like any promotion their use should be well thought out and be part of an effective integrated communications plan.

Promotions often involve packages of a number of the company's products. Packages are particularly popular with hotels and resorts that have a number of products to offer. The Ritz-Carlton in Tyson's Corner developed a Fine Art of Cuisine weekend. The weekend features gourmet meals matched with the appropriate wines. The hotel developed packages around the meals, tastings, and demonstrations. Guests receive a room, tickets to the Grand Wine Tasting, and the Chef's brunch.[32] Packages can also be developed around local events. The Best Western Palm Beach, Florida, created a three-night package that includes a room for three nights, tickets to two baseball games (several teams had spring training near the hotel), a continental breakfast, and an evening cruise on a casino ship.[33] Promotions such as these bring in business during a slow period and create a memorable experience for the guest.

Premiums are goods offered either free or at low cost as an incentive to buy a product. For example, fast-food restaurants often offer a free promotional glass instead of their normal paper cup. A self-liquidating premium is a premium sold to consumers who request it. For example, McDonald's in Australia offered Batman figures for 95 cents with the purchase of a burger.

Many restaurants, such as the Hard Rock Café, have discovered that promotional items such as caps, T-shirts, and sweatshirts can be sold at a good profit, thus creating another profit center for the company. Others offer a premium-priced drink or dessert that is served with a special glass or plate. Guests actually pay for the glass or plate in the price of the product, take the "gift" home with them, and are reminded of a pleasant restaurant experience each time it is later seen. Pat O'Brien's in the French Quarter of New Orleans serves a Hurricane cocktail in a commemorative glass. These glasses can be seen in homes throughout the world. The name recognition developed through its Hurricane glasses has helped make Pat O'Brien's a major tourist attraction in the French Quarter.

14.4 Pat O'Brien's www. patobriens. com: Go to Pat Obrien's Facebook page. How does its Facebook page create a positive image and customer preference through third-party endorsement?

Marco Polo cruises gave a free flight to Europe for passengers from Sydney taking one of its Mediterranean cruises. The booking had to be made in the previous year and was restricted to Sydney, an area where the cruise line was trying to build additional business.[34]

Patronage rewards are cash or other awards for regular use of a company's products or services. For example, most airlines offer frequent-flyer plans that award points for miles traveled. Most of the hotel chains have a frequent-stay program and many restaurants have frequent-diner programs. These programs reward local customers, gather guest information, and ideally create a positive change in the consumer behavior of the member. This change could be more frequent purchases, larger purchases, or spreading positive word of mouth.

Hotels or restaurants can also create events to show their appreciation of loyal customers. For example, a casino invited 25,000 of its best customers to come to "Free Hug Friday." Five thousand players showed up to get a mug of Hershey's chocolate kisses and a hug from the company's executives. The players thought it was great, and the casino brought 5,000 of its best players out in one night.[35]

Another type of patronage rewards are specials for repeat customers. The Elephant Walk restaurants in Massachusetts are constantly looking for fine wines. Often their finds are wines that have limited availability. From their search for fine wines, they feature six wines each month. These are usually wines that do not have enough availability to put on their regular wine list. Customers are e-mailed information about the wines and can reserve a bottle for lunch or dinner. The restaurants sell these wines at normal retail levels, about half what a restaurant would normally charge for the wine. This promotion creates goodwill with their frequent customers and gives them another reason to dine at the restaurants. The unique promotion has also generated publicity for the restaurants.[36]

Point-of-purchase (POP) promotions include displays and demonstrations that take place at the point of purchase or sale. For example, a representative of Richmond Estate Wines might offer a taste of the estate's wines in the Robina Tavern package store.

The value of POP has long been recognized by the retailing industry and is making rapid inroads in restaurants, hotels, auto rental companies, and other hospitality industry firms. Hospitality firms have discovered that POP may be used (1) to disseminate information about the company's products or services and (2) to sell additional products and services, thus adding to gross revenue.

Hotels use display racks in the lobby to promote other hotels in the chain and additional services, from valet parking to sleigh rides. Restaurants such as Perkins, the Village Inn, and Denny's use the space near the cash register to create eye-catching displays of bakery items and desserts to be taken home by the guests.

Several years ago, Farrell's Restaurants in Hawaii discovered a means to add over 10 percent to the bottom line without decreasing prices or adding new customers. Farrell's appealed heavily to families with preteen children. Keeping the customer profile in mind, a decision was made to design a new passageway out of the restaurant before reaching the cash register. This passageway involved walking through thousands of gift, candy, and gum items selected for child irresistibility. This unique and colorful passageway served as a giant POP that added revenue directly to the bottom line.

Contests, sweepstakes, and games give consumers a chance to win something, such as cash or a trip. A contest calls for consumers to submit an entry—a jingle, guess, or suggestion—to be judged by a panel. A sweepstakes calls for consumers to submit their names for a drawing. A game presents consumers with something every time they buy bingo numbers or missing letters that may or may not help them win a prize. A sales contest urges dealers or the sales force to increase their efforts, with prizes going to the top performers.

Dunkin' Donuts recently launched a new $10 million integrated campaign to remind people of its roots as a doughnut maker and not just a coffee brand. From TV to Internet to in-store displays, "you can't walk in the door without thinking about donuts," says Dunkin's vice president of consumer engagement. At the heart of the "donut domination" campaign is a "Create Dunkin's Next Donut" contest that urges people to visit the contest Web site and design their own doughnuts. "Put on your apron and get creative," the campaign urges. "You kin' do it." At the site, entrants

Courtesy of Dunkin' Brands, Inc.

Tourists staying at the Ritz-Carlton near the Powerscourt Mansion, shown in this illustration, have a package that provides relaxing activities to compliment walking through the famous Powerscourt gardens. Courtesy of Lukewschmi/Dreamstime.

selected from a list of approved ingredients to create the new doughnut, give it a name, and write a one hundred-word essay about why they think their doughnut creation is the best. Online voting selected from among twelve semifinalists, who cooked up their creations at a bake-off in the company's test kitchens at Dunkin' Donuts University in Braintree, Massachusetts. The grand winner received $12,000 and the winning doughnut—Toffee for Your Coffee—was added to the company's everyday value menu. In all, contestants submitted nearly 130,000 creations online. "We were absolutely amazed at the number of entries into our contest," says a Dunkin' marketing executive.[37]

Promotions can involve contests for employees along with guests. The general manager of the Holiday Inn in Youngstown, Ohio, developed a contest to encourage customer service. Whenever an employee helps out another employee, he or she receives a "thank you" from the employee he or she. At the end of the week, the "thank yous" are put into a drawing for $50.[38]

Tom Feltenstein, a restaurant marketing consultant, suggests a program where loyal customers are sent a $20 gift certificate. They can use $10 toward the purchase of their meal and the other $10 they give to an employee who provides them with the best service. Thus, the employee tries to pick up as much money as possible by providing exceptional service.[39]

Finding Creative Ideas

The Internet makes it possible to see what sales promotion activities other companies are doing. If they are outside your market area, it is a good chance you can adapt the ideas to fit your needs.

Ideas found on the Internet include these. Hilton is co-branding a promotion with the popular food network called the Food Network Travel Package. It includes a Food Network Travel tote packed with culinary travel ideas and specially prepared dishes representative of the local cuisines by

Hilton's chefs. For example, at the Hilton Gaithersburg, Maryland, near Washington, D.C., the chef prepares Maryland crab cake sliders presented on soft mini rolls to accentuate a perfect combination of spices and sauces. Accompanying this scrumptious local dish is a collection of to-go crab flavors, including Crab chips, Old Bay crab cake classic mix, Gordon's Chesapeake Classics Maryland-style red crab soup, and spicy Chesapeake peanuts.[40] This promotion allows foodies to try a local treat.

The Ritz-Carlton at Powerscourt in Ireland put together a package that includes its regular offerings. However, by packaging the items, it creates value for the guest and receives more per night from the guest. The package is called "Enliven the Senses," and the two-night getaway includes these enticements:

- Two nights of accommodation in a deluxe room
- Daily breakfast in the restaurant
- Dinner for two in Gordon Ramsay at Powerscourt for one night (excluding beverages)
- A one-hour aromatherapy massage

Four Seasons Hotel Cairo at Nile Plaza created a promotion called the Best of France. Its chef is from France and the promotion had the chef create dishes from his home country. The description of the promotion is as follows:

> From October 19, for two weeks, a French promotion replete with haute cuisine from the culture-rich nation will beguile gourmets in Aqua Restaurant at Four Seasons with French music, flowers and art, along with an oyster and champagne bar, to provide the perfect ambience.
>
> Gastronomes will experience this autumn highlight under the auspices of resident French chef Christophe Gillino, a native of Provence. Gillino has designed courses especially for the occasion that reveal all of the hallmarks of expertly crafted, modern French dégustation menus.

The two-week time period creates sense of urgency for those who want to take advantage of the promotion.[41]

Friday's in the United Kingdom offers a twist on restaurant birthday clubs. Instead of telling persons celebrating their birthday what they will get, they can sign up for their gift when they join the birthday club. They can choose from free cocktails, champagne, or desserts for their party. Many people celebrate their birthday by dining out; thus, a well-designed birthday club can provide a reason for the birthday celebration to be held at your restaurant.[42]

Another reason to celebrate is with a dining experience on Father's Day. Mother's Day is the busiest day of the year for restaurants in the United States. So why not encourage families to eat out on Father's Day as well? That is exactly what Outback did. For anyone bringing their husband or father to Outback on Father's Day, Outback gave a $10 certificate valid on their next visit. This type of certificate is called a bounce-back certificate because it encourages diners to return. However, Outback went one step further by collecting information about who came on Father's Day. Dads will need to activate the certificate online at http://outback.com/. The certificate was valid for five weeks and had to be used with a purchase of $25 or more. Thus, Outback was encouraging a quick return visit, and the minimum purchase of $25 ensured that Outback would at least break even on the bounce-back visit.[43]

Chick-fil-A is a master of promotions. One of its promotions is giving away fifty-two Chick-fil-A meal coupons to the first hundred people when it opens a new restaurant. Dan Cathy, president of Chick-fil-A, states that he could not believe it when fans showed up 18 hours in advance of the opening the first time it started the promotion.[44] The store opening creates local publicity as newspapers, radio stations, and television stations cover the unique event and interview people who sleep in the parking lot so they can claim their free meals. The cost of the meals is more than offset by the publicity created from the event.

Consulting companies also give some ideas online as a way to attract potential clients. One firm lists ten promotional tactics for restaurants. One of these is partnering with a business or social organization to expose the restaurant to potential customers. They state that if you select the right group to partner with, you can leverage their resources to promote your restaurant, and you can also target your core audience. Host socials where the food is center stage. Arrange photo opportunities that include your displays in the background and submit to local media. Partnering with a business or charitable organization works on many levels and can help you stretch your marketing budget while still delivering higher returns on investment than can be achieved with traditional advertising.[45] There is no end to the type of promotions one can do. But managers must remember to fit the promotion to the operation. Camping out in a parking lot works well for a fast-food restaurant but not for an upscale restaurant.

Developing the Sales Promotion Program

The third step in developing a sales promotion is to define the full sales promotion program. This step calls for marketers to make other decisions. First, they must decide on the size of the incentive. A certain minimum incentive is necessary if the promotion is to succeed. A larger incentive produces more sales response. The marketer must also set conditions for participation. Incentives might be offered to everyone or only to select groups. Sweepstakes might not be offered in certain states, to families of company personnel, or to persons under a certain age.

The marketer must then decide how to promote and distribute the promotion program. A restaurateur can distribute coupons at the restaurant, by mail, or in an advertisement. Each distribution method involves a different level of reach and cost. The length of the promotion is also important. If the sales promotion period is too short, prospects who would not buy during that time will be unable to take advantage of it. If the promotion runs too long, the deal will lose some of its "act now" force.

The question of how to distribute a promotional program has resulted in problems for companies. An example is a restaurant that decided to print 10,000 flyers announcing a promotion and have employees place them under the windshield wipers of cars in a shopping center. The following results occurred: Employees threw most in the dumpster; several auto owners threatened to sue, claiming their wipers had been broken; the owner of the shopping center demanded someone clean up the mess; and, finally, an employee and a car owner engaged in a fistfight. The employee won the fistfight, but the company paid an out-of-court settlement to the auto owner with a broken nose.[46]

Restaurant promotions often consist of cards, flyers, coupons, and other devices featuring two-for-one specials, 20 percent off, free drinks, or other "hooks." Normally, these bear a date at which the promotion becomes ineffective. In theory, this should work well, but in actuality, customers often present coupons months or even years old and become enraged when they are told the promotion is no longer in effect. A prospective new owner or buyer of any hospitality company should ask if there are outstanding promotions in the community. Many new owners have been shocked to witness a flood of promotional coupons that negatively affected cash flow.

Other problematic media used by hospitality companies include hot-air balloons bearing the company's logo that crashed on freeways or atop buildings, road signs that ended up in strange places such as the mayor's lawn, and sponsored bicycle races in which the restaurant rider crashed through a competitor's storefront. In today's "I'll sue you" environment, it is wise to discuss proposed promotions with an attorney and with the company's insurance agent prior to initiation.

Marketing managers need to set promotion dates that will be used by production, sales, and distribution. Some unplanned promotions may also be needed, requiring cooperation on short notice.

Finally, the marketer has to decide on the sales promotion budget. It can be developed in two ways. The marketer can choose the promotions and estimate total cost. However, the more common way is to use a percentage of the total budget for sales promotion. One study found three major problems in the way that companies budget for sales promotion. First, they do not consider cost effectiveness. Second, instead of spending to achieve objectives, they simply extend the previous year's spending, take a percentage of expected sales, or use the "affordable approach." Finally, advertising and sales promotion budgets are too often prepared separately.[47]

Partnerships can stretch a budget. The Palm, a national upscale steakhouse, developed a promotion with a Chicago car dealer to promote its Chicago restaurant. The car dealer offered a $20 gift certificate for the Palm to all who test-drove its luxury-model cars. The cost of the certificate was split equally between the partners. The dealership gained an incentive to attract customers with a certificate that was steeply discounted, and the restaurant gained additional customers for $10 per table.[48] Partnerships can also be used to acquire prizes in sweepstakes. Companies often discount or provide merchandise in exchange for advertising exposure.

Pretesting and Implementing the Plan

Whenever possible, sales promotion tools should be pretested to determine if they are appropriate and of the right incentive size. Consumer sales promotions can be pretested quickly and inexpensively, yet few promotions are ever tested ahead of time. Seventy percent of companies do not test sales promotions before initiating them. To test sales promotions, researchers can ask consumers to rate or rank different promotions. Promotions can also be tried on a limited basis in selected geographic test areas.

Companies should prepare implementation plans for each promotion, covering lead time and sell-off time. Lead time is the time necessary to prepare the program before launching it. Sell-off time begins with the launch and ends when the promotion ends.

Evaluating the Results

Even though result evaluation is important, many companies fail to evaluate their sales promotion programs. Others do so only superficially. Many evaluation methods are available, the most common of which is sales comparisons before, during, and after a promotion. Suppose that a company has a 6 percent market share before the promotion, which jumps to 10 percent during the promotion, falls to 5 percent immediately after, and rises to 7 percent later. The promotion appears to have attracted new customers and more purchases from current customers. After the promotion, sales fell as consumers used inventories or moved purchases forward. For example, a person planning on traveling to see relatives in New York in June may move the trip forward to April to take advantage of an airline promotion that expires on April 30. The long-run rise to 7 percent means that the airline gained some new users, but if the brand's share returned to the prepromotion level, the promotion changed only the timing of demand rather than total demand.

The results of consumer research demonstrate the kinds of people who responded to the promotion and their postpromotion buying behavior. Surveys can provide information on how many consumers recall the promotion, what they thought of it, how many accepted it, and how it affected their buying patterns. Sales promotions can also be evaluated through experiments that include variables such as incentive value, length, and distribution method.

Clearly, sales promotion plays an important role in the total promotion mix. To use it well, the marketer must define sales promotion objectives; select the best tools; design the sales promotion program; and pretest, implement, and evaluate the results.

■■■ Local Store Marketing

Local store marketing, also called local area marketing or neighborhood marketing, is defined as a low-cost, hands-on effort to take advantage of all opportunities within the immediate trading area to promote and market a business.[49] Although all areas of the promotional mix are used, PR is the heart of any local area marketing program. Local area marketing is used by both small and large companies;

Rock Bottom restaurants create cause-related promotions that help the community and provide publicity for their restaurants. Courtesy of Robert Christie Mill/ Rock Bottom Restaurants, Inc. Raymond Boyd/Michael Ochs Archives/Getty Images

however, it is an area in which small companies can compete just as effectively as large companies. Independently owned businesses, such as restaurants or travel agencies, have an advantage over large companies because the owners become permanent fixtures of the community, whereas the large companies tend to replace their store managers every two or three years. Research has shown that 75 percent of a restaurant's customers come from within a 10-minute drive. With fast-food restaurants, the radius shrinks to three to five minutes' drive time.[50]

Examples of PR activities included in local store marketing are providing tours of your facility. Primary schools look for places to take their students on field trips. A restaurant or hotel can be an exciting venue. A short tour, followed by a tasting and providing the students with a coupon (so that they can show their parents where they went), can be a good way to create business and goodwill. Many suburban areas have weekly papers; providing a weekly or monthly article on travel, food, or wine is a good way to gain exposure. If the articles are well written, the paper will appreciate the free articles, and the writer will gain exposure and credibility in the local market. Being a speaker at meetings of local social and service clubs is another way to gain exposure. During the holiday season, a business can become a depository for charities collecting toys for disadvantaged children. But don't accept this task passively. For example, if the local firefighters ask you to collect toys for their campaign, suggest that the campaign be started with a kickoff drive, including fire engines, sirens, and firefighters in uniform in your parking lot on a Saturday. If they agree, call the local news station and get some television coverage.[51]

Organizations such as the school band, girl scouts, and the local little league team are always looking for fund-raisers. Many restaurants will give a portion of their proceeds to these groups if they refer business. For example, at Sweet Tomatoes restaurants, the organization must hand out flyers and the flyers are redeemed at the restaurant on a specific night designated for that organization, resulting in a 15 percent donation to the organization. This promotion drives business to the restaurant and creates an easy way for the organization to raise money. Sweet Tomatoes also offers an alternative program that the organization sells script that can be used at face value at the restaurant. The group receives the script at a 10 percent discount and sells it at face value. Again, this drives business to the restaurant and provides funds for the organization. Sweet Tomatoes also makes donations of gift certificates and food; however, the script and organizational night programs allow it to reach more organizations and for the organizations to receive cash because it does not make cash donations except through these promotions.[52]

Cause-related promotions are another local area marketing tactic. These promotions bring business to the hotel or restaurant and help the community. Rock Bottom restaurants frequently create promotions that are cause related. For example, one of the beers the brew pub creates is Firechief Ale. The company developed a fiery line of appetizers and teamed them with its Firechief Ale to create a promotion that helped local firehouses. Dallas-based Canyon Café promotes a charitable cause at the grand opening of each of its restaurants. This has given the restaurant a reputation for being a responsible business and a good neighbor.[53]

El Torito restaurants, based in California, had a television campaign that was based almost exclusively in Los Angeles because the chain could not afford to advertise in multiple markets. As a result, restaurants outside of Los Angeles gained little benefit from the ads. Joe Herrera, the restaurant's manager, decided to scrap the television ads and build a local store marketing campaign. Its ad dollars went into local papers and community marketing. Now El Torito has a presence in all its markets, and Herrera stated the managers were happy to have the marketing help.[54]

A good local area marketing campaign creates goodwill in the community and exposure for the restaurant, which translates into increased business and customer loyalty. Successful local marketers do not give products or money away freely; they evaluate every opportunity and make sure the effort will be worthwhile. By being creative, managers can ensure that their local marketing efforts will be noticed.

■■■ KEY TERMS

Contests, sweepstakes, and games. Give consumers a chance to win something, such as cash or a trip.

Corporate communications. This activity covers internal and external communications and promotes understanding of an organization.

Counseling. Involves advising management about public issues and company positions and image.

Coupons. Certificates that offer buyers savings when they purchase specified products.

Lobbying. Dealing with legislators and government officials to promote or defeat legislation and regulation.

Patronage rewards. Cash or other awards for regular use of a company's products or services.

Point-of-purchase (POP) promotions. Includes displays and demonstrations that take place at the time of sale.

Premiums. Goods offered either free or at low cost as an incentive to buy a product.

Press relations. Placing newsworthy information into the news media to attract attention.

Press release. Information released to the media about certain new products or services.

Product publicity. Various efforts to publicize specific products.

Public relations. The process by which a positive image and customer preference are created through third-party endorsement.

Sales promotion. Consists of short-term incentives to encourage the purchase or sale of a product or service.

Samples. Offers of a trial amount of a product.

■■■ CHAPTER REVIEW

I. Public Relations. The process by which a positive image and customer preference are created through third-party endorsement.

II. Major Activities of PR Departments
   A. Press relations. The aim of press relations is to place newsworthy information into the news media to attract attention to a person, product, or service.
   B. Product publicity. Product publicity involves efforts to publicize specific products.
   C. Corporate communication. This activity covers internal and external communications and promotes understanding of the organization.
   D. Lobbying. Lobbying involves dealing with legislators and government officials to promote or defeat legislation and regulation.
   E. Counseling. Counseling involves advising management about public issues and company positions and image.

III. Publicity. Publicity is a direct function of PR. Publicity is the task of securing editorial and news space, as opposed to paid space, in print and broadcast media to promote a product or a service. Publicity is a popular PR tool used in the five activities described earlier. Three other popular uses of publicity are new product launches, special events, and crisis management.

IV. The Public Relations Process
   A. Researching to understand the firm's mission, culture, and target of the communication
   B. Establishing marketing objectives
      1. Build awareness
      2. Build credibility
      3. Stimulate the sales force and channel intermediaries
      4. Lower promotion costs
   C. Defining the target audience

D. **Choosing the PR message and vehicles**
   1. **Publications.** Companies can reach and influence their target market via annual reports, brochures, cards, articles, audiovisual materials, and company newsletters and magazines.
   2. **Events.** Companies can draw attention to new products or other company activities by arranging special events.
   3. **News.** PR professionals cultivate the press to increase better coverage to the company.
   4. **Speeches.** Speeches create product and company publicity. The possibility is accomplished by printing copies of the speech or excerpts for distribution to the press, stockholders, employees, and other publics.
   5. **Public service activities.** Companies can improve public goodwill by contributing money and time to good causes, such as supporting community affairs.
   6. **Identity media.** Companies can create a visual identity that the public immediately recognizes, such as with company's logos, stationery, signs, business forms, business cards, buildings, uniforms, dress code, and rolling stock.
E. **Implementing the marketing PR plan**
F. **Evaluating PR results**
   1. Exposures
   2. Awareness/comprehension/attitude change
   3. Sales-and-profit contribution

V. **PR Opportunities for the Hospitality Industry**
   A. **Individual properties.** Public relations is by far the most important promotional tool available to entrepreneurs and individual properties, such as a single restaurant, tourist attraction, bed and breakfast (B&B), tour operator, or hotel. Seldom can these enterprises afford costly advertising or other promotional programs.
   B. **Build PR around the owner/operator**
   C. **Build PR around the location.** For instance, the isolation and obscurity of an enterprise can be used as a PR tactic.
   D. Build PR around a product or service

VI. **Crisis Management**
   A. **Take all precautions to prevent negative events from occurring.**

B. **When a crisis does occur:**
   1. **Appoint a spokesperson. This ensures that the company is giving a consistent story based on facts.**
   2. **Contact the firm's public relations agency if it has one.**
   3. **The company should notify the press when a crisis happens.**

VII. **Sales Promotion**
   A. **Setting sales promotion objectives.** Sales promotion objectives vary widely and can include increasing short-term sales, increasing long-term sales, getting consumers to try a new product, luring customers away from competitors, or creating loyal customers.
   B. **Selecting sales promotion tools.** Many tools can be used to accomplish sales promotion objectives. The promotion planner should consider the type of market, the sales promotion objectives, the competition, and the costs and effectiveness of each tool. Common sales promotion tools include samples, coupons, premiums, patronage rewards, point-of-purchase (POP) displays, contests, sweepstakes, and games.
   C. **Finding creative ideas**
   D. **Developing the sales promotion program.** The following steps are involved in developing a sales promotion program:
      1. **Decide on the size of the incentive**
      2. **Set the conditions for participation**
      3. **Decide how to promote and distribute the promotion program**
      4. **Set promotion dates**
      5. **Decide on the sales promotion budget**
   E. **Pretesting and implementing the plan.** The marketer should pretest to determine if sales promotion tools are appropriate and the incentive size is efficient and effective.
   F. **Evaluating the results.** The company should evaluate the results against the objectives of the program.

VIII. **Local Store Marketing.** A good local store marketing campaign is an effective way for both a chain and an individually owned restaurant or hotel to gain goodwill and exposure in the community.

■■■ DISCUSSION QUESTIONS

1. What is meant by the term *public*? Can a company have more than one public?

2. Why might it make sense for a hotel chain to shift some of its advertising dollars to public relations?

3. Give some examples of how a hospitality organization might be able to gain publicity.

4. Is publicity free?

5. Compare and contrast publicity with advertising. What are the benefits and drawbacks of each?

6. Bring to class a sample of a hospitality or travel company's sales promotion. What do you think is the objective of the sales promotion? Do you think it will accomplish its objective? What do you think is the most interesting or intriguing part about the sales promotion? Should it be continued? Why or why not? What are some of the negatives associated with this sales promotion, and with sales promotions in general?

■■■ EXPERIENTIAL EXERCISE

Do the following:

Find a good example of publicity in a print medium that has been linked to a social medium such as Facebook.

Explain how the print and electronic media complement each other.

■■■ INTERNET EXERCISE

Find two Web sites of hospitality or travel organizations that offer PR support. This could be corporate announcements, a "press room section," or a gallery of photos that one can download for publicity purposes. Report on the sites you found and the support they offered for persons wanting to write a story about the organization.

■■■ REFERENCES

1. Dale Carter, *The Final Frontier: The Rise and Fall of the American Rocket State* (London: Verso, 1988); C. Dewitt Coffman, *Marketing for a Full House* (Ithaca, NY: School of Hotel Administration, Cornell University, 1975); Jon Trux, *The Space Race, from Sputnik to Shuttle: The Story of the Battle for the Heavens* (London: New English Library, 1985).

2. Jessica Miller, "Marketing Communications," *Cornell Hotel and Restaurant Administration Quarterly,* 34, no. 5 (1993): 49.

3. Ibid.

4. Philip Kotler, "Public Relations Versus Marketing: Dividing the Conceptual Domain and Operational Turf" (paper presented at the Public Relations Colloquium 1989, San Diego, CA, January 24, 1989).

5. Adapted from information in "PR in the Driver's Seat," *Advertising Age* (October 26, 2009): S6–S7.

6. Adapted from Scott M. Cutlip, Allen H. Center, and Glen M. Brown, *Effective Public Relations* (6th ed.) (Upper Saddle River, NJ: Prentice Hall, 1985), pp. 7–17.

7. Joe Durocher, "Recovery Marketing: What to Do After a Natural Disaster," *Cornell Hotel and Restaurant Administration Quarterly,* 35, no. 2 (1994): 66.

8. "Olive Garden's Drive Against Hunger Raises More Than $1M," *Nation's Restaurant News* (June 25, 2001): 30.

9. David Baines, "A Mogul and His Mirage Are a Reality Placing Their Bets," *Vancouver Sun* (March 3, 1994): A1; Scott Craven, "Dunes Hotel Brought Down in the Face of New Mega Resorts," *Phoenix Gazette* (October 28, 1993): B6; Jefferson Graham, "Vegas Casino Opens with a Blast," *USA Today* (October 27, 1993): D1; Jamie McKee, "New Resorts Spend Millions to Reach National Audience," *Las Vegas Business Press,* 10, no. 37 (1993): 1.

10. Pamela Parseghian, "Chefs Looking for New Recipe to Drum Up Publicity Should Serve Up Side of Smarts," *Nation's Restaurant News* (September 6, 2004): 42.

11. The Homestead Resort Web site, http://www.thehomestead.com/welcome/calendar.asp (accessed December 18, 2004); Karen Weiner Escalera, "How to Get News Out of Nothing," *Lodging* (March 1992): 25–26.

12. Christine Blank, "Driving Revenue," *Hotel and Motel Management* (October 4, 2004): 3.

13. Anne-Marie Dorning, "11-11-11 A Lucky Date," *ABC News* (February 14, 2011), retrieved October 24, 2011, from http://abcnews.go.com/US/11-11-11-lucky-date/story?id=12912104.

14. Arthur M. Merims, "Marketing's Stepchild: Product Publicity," *Harvard Business Review* (November/December 1972): 111–112; see also Katharine D. Paine, "There Is a Method for Measuring PR," *Marketing News* (November 7, 1987): 5.

15. For further reading on cause-related marketing, see P. Rajan Varadarajan and Anil Menon, "Cause-Related Marketing: A Co-alignment of Marketing Strategy and Corporate Philanthropy," *Journal of Marketing* (July 1988): 58–74.

16. Lee Elementary School Web site, http://lee.usd383.org/LeeSchool/leeschool.htm (accessed December 18, 2004).

17. Arthur M. Merims, "Marketing's Stepchild: Product Publicity," *Harvard Business Review* (November–December 1972): 111–112. For more on evaluating public relations effectiveness, see Katharine D. Paine, "There Is a Method for Measuring PR," *Marketing News* (November 6, 1987): 5; and Eric Stoltz and Jack Torobin, "Public Relations by the Numbers," *American Demographics* (January 1991): 42–46.

18. Tom McCarthy, "Add Publicity in the Mix," *Lodging Hospitality* (October 1999): 17.

19. Michael M. Lefever, "Restaurant Advertising: Coupons, Clauses and Cadillacs," *Cornell Hotel and Restaurant Administration Quarterly,* 29, no. 4 (1989): 94.

20. Eric Bergman, "Crisis? What Crisis?" *Communications World,* 11, no. 4 (1994): 19–23.

21. Robert B. Irvine, "What's a Crisis Anyway?" *Communications World,* 14, no. 7 (1997): 36–41.

22. Ian I. Mitroff, "Crisis Management and Environmentalism: A Natural Fit," *California Management Review,* 36, no. 2 (1994): 101–114.

23. Julie Miller, "Crisis to Calm," *Hotel and Motel Management* (August 11, 1997): 261.

24. Louise Kramer, "Food for Thought: Playing Sound Bites," *Nation's Restaurant News,* 29, no. 43 (1995): 54.

25. Paul Holmes, "Senior Marketers Are Sharply Divided About the Role of PR in the Overall Mix," *Advertising Age* (January 24, 2005): C1–C2.

26. Irvine, "What's a Crisis Anyway?"

27. Mitroff, *California Management Review,* p. 114.

28. "The Omni San Antonio Hotel," *San Antonio Business Journal* (July 20, 2001): 36.

29. David H. Freedman, "An Unusual Way to Run a Ski Business," *Forbes* (December 7, 1992): 28.

30. See Donna L. Montaldo, "2006 Coupon Usage Trends" (May 2007), http://couponing,about.com; and Jack Neff, "Package-Goods Players Just Can't Quit Coupons," *Advertising Age* (May 14, 2007): 8.

31. Quotes and other information from Alan J. Liddle, "Hardee's Connects with Mobile Device Users, Offer Discounts," *Nation's Restaurant News* (May 14, 2007): 16; and www.cellfire.com (accessed August 2007).

32. Jennifer Coleman, "The Fine Art of Fine Dining," *Travel Agent* (September 18, 2000): 96.

33. David Cogswell and Sara Perez Webber, "Spring Flings," *Travel Agent* (February 21, 2000): 108.

34. "Free-Fly Offer to Join Marco Polo Cruises," *Traveltrade* (October 20, 2004).

35. Tricia Campbell, "Cozying up to Customers," *Sales & Marketing Management* (December 1999): 15.

36. Mary Ewing-Mulligan and Ed McCarthy, "Wine Lists Used Creatively Are Vintage Opportunity to Attract New Customers," *Nation's Restaurant News* (July 23, 2001): 43–46.

37. Based on information found in "Dunkin' Donuts Returns to Its Roots—Doughnuts—in $10 Million Campaign," *Promo* (March 18, 2009), accessed at http://promomagazine.com/contests/dunkindonutscampaign/; "Time to Judge the Donuts," *PR Newswire* (May 18, 2009); Steve Adams, "Dunkin Donuts Contest Finalists Cooked Their Unique Creations in Bake-Off," *Patriot Ledger* (May 29, 2009), accessed at http://www.patriotledger.com/business/xl594716181/Doughnut-design-101; and www.dunkindonuts.com/donut/, August 2010.

38. Bridget Falbo, "Wow Customers with Service to Build Positive PR," *Hotel & Motel Management* (May 4, 1998): 45.

39. Tom Feltenstein, "Slay the Neighborhood Goliath," *Restaurant Hospitality* (October 1999): 38.

40. http://www.hilton.com/en/hi/promotions (accessed October 5, 2008).

41. http://www.ameinfo.com/169802.html (accessed October 5, 2008).

42. http://www.tgigreattimes.co.uk/ (accessed October 5, 2008).

43. http://outback.com/; http://www.thefashionablehousewife.com/?p=3907 (accessed October 5, 2008).

44. http://www.reuters.com/article/pressRelease/idUS80974+06-Aug-2008+MW20080806 (accessed October 5, 2008).

45. http://www.quantifiedmarketing.com/learning_center/restaurant-promotions.php (accessed October 5, 2008).

46. Michael M. Zefener, "Restaurant Advertising, Coupon Claims and Cadillacs," *Cornell Hotel and Restaurant Administration Quarterly,* 29, no. 4 (1989): 98.

47. Roger A. Strang, "Sales Promotion Fast Growth, Faulty Management," *Harvard Business Review* (July/August 1976): 98.

48. Steve Weiss, "Promotions Trend: Get Yourself a Partner," *Restaurants and Institutions,* 103, no. 26 (1993): 78–93.

49. National Restaurant Association, *Promoting the Neighborhood Restaurant: A Local Store Marketing Manual* (Chicago, IL: National Restaurant Association, 1988).

50. Tom Feltenstein, "Wily Underdogs with Fewer Resources Still Have Bite in Competitive Foodservice Industry," *Nation's Restaurant News* (May 7, 2001): 40.

51. Tom Feltenstein, *Restaurant Profits Through Advertising and Promotion* (New York: Van Nostrand Reinhold, 1983).

52. http://www.souplantation.com/communityspirit/donations.asp (accessed October 5, 2008).

53. Theresa Howard, "Chartible Promos Can Be Profitable Market Strategy," *Nation's Restaurant News* (June 9, 1997): 18.

54. Scott Hume, "Taking It to the Streets," *Restaurants and Institutions* (October 15, 1999): 101–108.

Professional Sales

15

T he city of Grapevine, Texas, became an important tourism destination without the benefit of beaches or mountains or a Grand Canyon. Sales planning and team sales work brought this about. What Grapevine had was available land for development and access to seven major highways, the Dallas-Fort Worth (DFW) Airport, and a team of salespeople consisting of a mayor, city council, and the city manager's office "Go Team" who sold Grapevine to prospective hospitality companies.

Situated just north of the DFW metroplex and the DFW airport, Grapevine decided that tourism and hospitality were the industries it wanted. While many Texas communities continued to seek manufacturing industries, Grapevine decided that tourism, hospitality, and shopping would create thousands of jobs and would attract out-of-area visitors as well as day shoppers and restaurant patrons from the DFW metroplex. It was felt that these were complementary to the historic nature of the community and would assist in preserving the culture of a small town.

The mayor, city council, and the city manager's office believed in the value of tourism and the hospitality industry. Tommy Hardy, assistant city manager, was charged to promote the destination and tourism economic development of Grapevine. Tommy decided that to be successful, he would need to fully understand tourism and the hospitality industry. This meant knowing the major players in the hospitality industry and understanding their language, such as ADR and RevPAR. It also meant that Grapevine would need to develop a marketing plan with desired target hospitality companies to become members of the Grapevine community and then pursue them with professional marketing/sales strategies.

Tommy and staff members attended hospitality industry conventions as well as the huge ICSC (International Council of Shopping Centers) show in Las Vegas. This permitted them to build a database, determine new trends, and establish contacts with executives who might bring a new hospitality company to Grapevine.

The city of Grapevine worked closely with developers, architects, and the financial community. Tommy Hardy and staff made sales calls on targeted companies. They conducted tours, hosted receptions for prospects to meet members of the community, and, most important, provided continuous follow-up to "close the sale." Tommy said that he and staff were never afraid to go to the private sector for assistance in planning and marketing. "We always took big steps," he said, and "the private community supported us. Our responsibility is to bring prospect companies together with brokers and developers. Once that has been accomplished, we walk out of the room."

Objectives

After reading this chapter, you should be able to:

1. Explain the role and nature of personal selling and the role of the sales force.

2. Describe the basics of managing the sales force, and explain how to set sales force strategy, how to pick a structure—territorial, product, customer, or complex—and how to ensure that sales force size is appropriate.

3. Identify the key issues in recruiting, selecting, training, and compensating salespeople.

4. Discuss supervising salespeople, including directing, motivation, and evaluating performance.

5. Apply the principles of the personal selling process, and outline the steps in the selling process: qualifying, preapproach and approach, presentation and demonstration, handling objections, closing, and follow-up.

The mayor of Grapevine was born and raised in the community and has great civic pride in Grapevine. Unlike some desk-bound mayors, he worked aggressively with Tommy and staff to bring desired hospitality and retailing companies to the community. He also has a reputation as a great "closer" and personally clinched many deals.

Developing and building a visitor infrastructure is critical, but all this must be supported by advertising and promotion. Sales and bed taxes generated by the complex support the Grapevine Convention and Visitors Bureau, which organizes visitor events such as GrapeFest, one of the top one hundred festivals in the United States, provides promotional materials, conducts familiarization tours, and helps coordinate and promote activities with other organizations. Events have proven very popular with the local community and with day visitors from the metroplex, adding to tourism revenue.

Results

An area in northeast Grapevine was targeted for commercial tourism/hospitality development. One of the earliest companies was the Gaylord Texan mega-resort, which opened in 2004 with 1,511 hotel rooms and a 400,000-square-foot convention center. Nine additional hotels were located in the development area, and in 2006 Great Wolf Resorts began construction of a $60 million, 402 all-suite hotel and a 50,000-square-foot indoor water park and a conference center. Great Wolf then decided to add 203 more rooms and more meeting space.

Despite the growth in Grapevine hotel rooms, performance comparisons with other metroplex areas are excellent, as seen in the following table. Restaurant sales also increased during this time period by $3 to $5 million per year.

Tourism development planners know the importance of retail shopping, and a huge retail shopping area was developed, including Grapevine Mills Mall, an indoor mall of over 2 million square feet that annually attracts 15 million shoppers from a five-state region. The spectacular Bass Pro Shops Outdoor World with 200,000 square feet of space was built in proximity and by itself attracts 2 million visitors per year.

Success attracts others, including the Glass Cactus, a 26,000-square-foot entertainment center and Lone Star Crossing, a 120,000-square-foot shopping center.

Tourism development also occurred outside the destination corridor within the historic downtown Grapevine area and other areas of Grapevine. The Grapevine Vintage Railroad connects Grapevine with the renovated Fort Worth Stockyards. A complex of upscale restaurants known as the Epicenter was developed on South Main Street in Grapevine. This complex complemented other downtown retailers, restaurants, and art galleries.

Attraction	Annual Visitors
Grapevine Mills Mall	13 million
Bass Pro Shops Outdoor World	2 million
Lake Grapevine	1.5 million
Festivals/events/historic district	1.15 million
Hotel guests	532,000
Grapevine Winery visitors	235,000
Heritage/information centers	150,000
Grapevine Vintage Railroad	80,000

Source: Grapevine Convention and Visitors Bureau.

Tourism in Grapevine means 13 million visitors annually. Thousands of individuals are directly employed in the industry, providing a healthy economy. Tourism has allowed downtown Grapevine to flourish as contrasted to the dying centers of many Texas towns. It has also encouraged historical preservation and cultural growth in the arts. Grapevine also saw over a 22 percent increase in its RevPAR, over twice the rate of its competitors.

None of this would have been possible without the teamwork between the private sector and the public. Nor would it have been possible without sales planning and strategy by a dedicated team of the mayor, city council, and city staff who wanted to see Grapevine grow in a desired and beneficial manner.

e **15.1** The Grapevine Convention and Visitors Bureau promotes "Urban" winery tours, https://www.grapevinetexasusa.com/.

■■■ Management of Professional Sales

Success or failure within the hospitality industry ultimately rests on the ability to sell. A roadside motel at an intersection of major highways or a popular restaurant with waiting lines is sometimes viewed as being above the need "to sell." No member of the hospitality industry can accept this as a long-run viewpoint.

Discourteous front-desk clerks and cashiers who would impress Grumpy of the Seven Dwarfs are part of one's sales force. These and all others who face the public can drive away or attract business. In the best cases, they can upsell through suggestive desserts, special drinks, and even a gift certificate for a friend. Higher-margin suites can be sold instead of the lowest priced room.

Successful owners and managers know that they must sell continuously. County commissioners, tax evaluation officials, planning boards, the press, bankers, and the local visitor center must all be sold on one's hospitality business. The city of Grapevine, Texas, in the opening vignette clearly demonstrates the need to sell and the research that follows.

Libraries could be filled with tales of lost sales or needlessly fractured guest relationships because of a curt response or an unsavory attitude on the part of support staff who mistakenly believe that sales is not their responsibility.

Everyone must sell, but a few individuals have the specific responsibility for ensuring that payrolls can be met, invoices can be paid, and a fair return on investment (ROI) can be achieved. These are the professional salespeople.

In this chapter we focus on seven major areas:

1. Nature of hospitality sales

2. Sales force objectives

3. Sales force structure and size

4. Organizing the sales department

5. Recruiting and training a professional sales force

6. Managing the sales force

7. Managing strategic client relationships

■■■ Nature of Hospitality Sales

Sales personnel serve as the company's personal link to customers. The sales representative *is* the company to many customers and in turn brings back much-needed customer intelligence. Personal selling is the most expensive contact and communication tool used by the company.

Cost estimates for making a personal sales call vary depending on the industry and the company, but one conclusion remains constant. However measured, the cost is high!

Add to this the fact that sales orders are seldom written on the first call and often require five or more calls, particularly for larger orders. The cost of obtaining a new client thus becomes enormously high, as depicted in Table 15–1. Despite the high cost, personal selling is often the most effective tool available to a hospitality company. Sales representatives perform one or more of the following tasks for their companies:

- *Prospecting*. Sales representatives find and cultivate new customers.

- *Targeting*. Sales representatives decide how to allocate their scarce time among prospects and customers.

- *Communicating*. Sales representatives communicate information about the company's products and services.

- *Selling*. Sales representatives know the art of salesmanship: approaching, presenting, answering objections, and closing sales.

TABLE 15–1
Cost of Obtaining a New Client

Number of Calls Needed to Close a Sale	Total Cost to Obtain a New Client at Various Estimates of Cost of Sales Call ($)		
	AT 250	AT 500	AT 700
1	250	500	700
2	500	1,000	1,400
3	750	1,500	2,100
4	1,000	2,000	2,800
5[a]	1,250	2,500	3,500
6	1,500	3,000	4,200
7	1,750	3,500	4,900
8	2,000	4,000	5,600
9	2,250	4,500	6,300
10	2,500	5,000	7,000

[a]Five sales calls seem to be the estimate commonly given to obtain a new client.

- **Servicing.** Sales representatives provide various services to the customers—consulting on their problems, rendering technical assistance, arranging financing, and expediting delivery.

- **Information gathering.** Sales representatives conduct market research and intelligence work and fill in call reports.

- **Allocating.** Sales representatives decide which customers to allocate scarce products to during product shortages.

- **Maintaining strategic partnerships.** Senior salespeople, including the sales manager, provide valuable planning assistance to clients.

The sales representative's mix of tasks varies with the state of the economy. During product shortages, such as a temporary shortage of hotel rooms during a major convention, sales representatives find themselves with nothing to sell. Some companies jump to the conclusion that fewer sales representatives are then needed. But this thinking overlooks the salesperson's other roles: allocating the product, counseling unhappy customers, and selling the company's other products that are not in short supply. It also ignores the long-run nature of hospitality sales.

Many conventions and conferences are planned years in advance, and hospitality salespeople must often work with meeting and convention planners two to four years in advance of the actual event. Resorts in the United States have concentrated much of their selling efforts on meetings and conferences, which by now represent 35 percent or more of their customers.[1] This was not achieved by viewing professional sales as a short-run tactic. A senior analyst with Tourism Canada demonstrated that Canadian resort salespeople are effective in reaching foreign markets. Guests in Canadian resorts are 60 percent Canadian and 40 percent foreign. By comparison, U.S. resorts have a mix of 91 percent American and 9 percent foreign.[2] Again, penetrating foreign markets is not accomplished in the short run.

As companies move toward a stronger market orientation, their sales forces need to become more market focused and customer oriented. The traditional view is that salespeople should worry about volume and sell, sell, sell, and the marketing department should worry about marketing strategy and profitability. The newer view is that salespeople should know how to produce customer satisfaction and company profit. They should know how to analyze sales data, measure market potential, gather market intelligence, develop marketing strategies and plans, and become proficient at the use of sales tactics.

Days Inn of America recognizes that the general manager (GM) is responsible for a property's sales efforts. "It is immensely important that the GM be equipped with the necessary sales and marketing tools," said John Russell, the president of Days Inn.[3] Chains such as Days Inn, Super 8 Motel, and Travelodge of Australia must view the GM as the head of sales. Larger hotels and resorts, such as Sheraton, Hilton, Shangri-La, and Four Seasons, employ professional sales managers. In these cases, the GM may be considerably less involved with details of the sales function.

Sales representatives need analytical skills. This becomes especially critical at the higher levels of sales management. Marketers believe that a sales force will be more effective in the long run if members understand marketing as well as selling. The newer concept is basic to the successful use of yield management in the hospitality industry.

This has become very clear as micro marketing, including database marketing, has gained importance within the hospitality industry. Group sales have been particularly affected. After viewing the importance of marketing information to sales, a hospitality industry writer with *Hotel and Motel Management* magazine concluded the following:[4]

- Closing sales has more to do with professionalism than anything else.

- Understanding the identity of real prospects increases sales productivity.

- Sales force members can save hours of time by having information about prospect group clients.

- It is critical to know what groups have a history of booking rooms in your type of hotel.

Competitive Analysis and Competitive Sets

Sales managers within the hospitality industry are often held accountable for the performance of their properties against members of a competitive set. The selection of a comparable competitive set is, therefore, critical to meaningful comparative sales analysis.

Small bed and breakfasts (B&Bs) usually have no difficulty defining their competitive set. However, restaurants may not find this task an easy one. As an example, should a family-owned-and-run catfish restaurant be grouped with seafood restaurants such as Red Lobster? Perhaps it should be grouped with family-owned restaurants, but does this make sense to place it with Italian and Greek restaurants?

In the case of hotels three common approaches are used to determine which competitive set or cluster is most appropriate.

ADR: The basis for ADR (average daily rate) clusters is that properties which are similar tend to sell for similar prices in a competitive market.

Product type: Properties may be grouped as luxury, resort, or in other ways such as the AAA diamond rating system or Mobil-star system. Whatever factors are selected to form a competitive set, there are certain to be inequalities.[5]

Management company set: Professional management companies may have contracts with a variety of hotels operating under different flags. It is tempting to use these hotels as a competitive set, but this practice is subject to criticism.

Hotels operating under the direction of an independent management company may have few competitive characteristics. Therefore, comparisons between these properties can be highly misleading.

Sales managers who focus on the actions and results of competitors may be focusing on the wrong variables. A study of customer orientation versus competitor orientation by management showed that "a customer orientation has a greater effect on a hotel's performance than does a competitor orientation." "A customer orientation that concentrates on acquisition, satisfaction and retention of customers is superior to a competitor orientation focused on monitoring, managing and outflanking competitors."[6]

∎∎∎ Sales Force Objectives

Hospitality companies typically establish objectives for the sales force. Sales objectives are essential for two reasons:

1. Objectives ensure that corporate goals are met. Goals may include revenue, market share, and improved corporate image.

2. Objectives assist sales force members to plan and execute their personal sales programs. Objectives also help ensure that a salesperson's time and company-support resources such as personal computers are used efficiently.

Sales force objectives must be customer designed annually for each company. Individual sales objectives are established to support corporate goals and marketing and sales objectives. Annual marketing and sales objectives are normally broken into quarterly and monthly objectives. Sales force members break them down further into personal objectives by day and week.

It is the responsibility of the sales manager to establish and assign objectives to individual salespeople. These are often developed after consultation with the salesperson. An experienced salesperson is in the best position to understand what is happening in the marketplace and to assist the sales manager in formulating realistic objectives.

Occasionally, annual objectives must be changed before year end. This is generally due to a dramatic occurrence, such as the outbreak of war or a natural disaster.

Although sales objectives are custom designed, there are general objectives commonly employed by members of the hospitality industry.

Sales Volume

Occupancy, passenger miles, and total covers are common measures of sales volume within the hospitality industry. They all mean the same thing: Bring in as many customers as possible. An emphasis on volume alone inevitably leads to price discounting, attracting undesirable market segments, and cost cutting.

Sales Volume by Selected Segments

Exclusive resorts, charter flight services, and upper-end cruises tend to operate with the philosophy that if one establishes volume objectives but restricts prospecting to highly selective segments, price and profits will take care of themselves. Although appropriate for a few niche players, this thinking cannot be applied to the majority of the hospitality industry. Nevertheless, the concept of establishing sales objectives by specific market segment is feasible and basic to effective sales. Sales strategies must be analyzed and reviewed continuously in view of quantitative sales results.

Canadian resort operators targeted the meeting and convention market, with the result that this segment made up 25 percent of their customer mix, compared with 35 percent for U.S. resorts. This led to questions of whether the differences were the result of the sales techniques employed in the two nations.[7]

Sales Volume and Price/Margin Mix

Establish sales volume objectives by product lines to ensure a desired gross profit. This system is the basis for revenue management. Salespeople often criticize the system as restrictive and unrealistic. The fact is, it works. British Airways, Hertz, Sheraton Hotels, and Royal Caribbean Cruises are representative of the firms that use this system. Whether a revenue management system is in place, establishing objectives by volume and by price/margin segments leads to improved revenue.

Upselling and Second-Chance Selling

Excellent profit opportunities exist for hospitality companies, particularly hotels and resorts, to upgrade price and profit margins by selling higher-priced products such as suites through upselling. A related concept is second-chance selling, in

British Airways is using technology and training to develop a sophisticated revenue management system. It trains its sales staff and intermediaries so they understand their pricing policies. Courtesy of citypix/ Alamy.

which the sales department contacts a client who has already booked an event such as a two-day meeting. Opportunities exist to sell additional services, such as airport limousine pickup and delivery or to upgrade rooms or food and beverage (F&B) from chicken to prime rib.

Second-chance selling encourages cooperation and teamwork between departments, such as catering, F&B, and sales. Hospitality researchers who have studied second-chance selling concluded, "Hoteliers [who do not employ second-chance selling] may be overlooking an opportunity to increase revenues substantially with little additional cost. By establishing specific values for business that has already been booked, hotel managers can encourage salespeople to increase the productivity of existing resources. If salespeople have clearly established goals and objectives for a second chance to increase their rewards, they may work harder to achieve goals."[8]

Market Share or Market Penetration

Airlines, cruise lines, major fast-food chains, and rental car companies are highly concerned with market share and market penetration. These concepts have considerably less meaning to many restaurants, hotels, resorts, and other members of the hospitality industry.

Entertainment venues like Gameworks use a sales staff to sell their venues to organizations for parties. This type of venue is a popular spot for corporate parties and team building exercises. Courtesy of ZUMA Press/ Newscom.

e

15.2 Maggiano's Little Italy is a restaurant that has extensive banquet facilities and uses a salesperson to sell these facilities. Go to http://www.maggianos.com/.

The management of most hotels is concerned primarily with measures such as occupancy, average room rate, yield, and customer mix. The corporate marketing department of a chain, however, is likely to be concerned about market share, particularly if it is a dominant chain in a market such as Hawaii. Hilton, Sheraton, Aston, Outrigger Hotels, Marriott, and others actively compete for market share in that market.

Evidence indicates that hotel management companies are increasingly held accountable for clearly defined performance standards. Among these is the level of market penetration. This is a clear departure from the past when contracts between owners and hotel management companies contained vague references to standards of performance.[9]

As a result, it is very possible that the sales department of hotels and resorts will increasingly be required to measure market potential and will be held accountable for a predetermined level of market penetration. Independent measures of market penetration such as STAR will undoubtedly assume increased importance in the measurement of hotel sales. STAR is a joint project of Smith Travel Research and PricewaterhouseCoopers. It provides information on average rate, occupancy, and RevPAR for Asia/Pacific, the Americas, Europe, the Middle East, and Africa.

Product-Specific Objectives

Occasionally, a sales force is charged with the specific responsibility to improve sales volume for specific product lines. This objective may be associated with up-selling and second-chance selling but may also be part of the regular sales duties of the sales force. A sales force may be asked to sell more suites, higher-margin coffee breaks, holiday packages, honeymoon packages, and other product lines.

Excellent opportunities for enhanced revenues exist within many hotels and resorts from nonroom sales. Recreation club memberships, including children's programs, are sometimes sold to local residents. A properly designed club membership can generate substantial income from membership fees, dues, and F&B revenues. The Boca Raton Resort initiated a Premier Club Membership program that produced membership sales in excess of $40 million the first three years. The club gave residents access to its beach, spa, golf course, tennis course, children's activities, and concierge services. Additionally, special events were planned for career club members.[10]

■■■ Sales Force Structure and Size

The diverse nature of the hospitality industry means that different sales force structures and sizes have evolved. The structure of a sales force within the airline industry is different from that of a hotel or cruise line. In general, most restaurants do not use a sales force but depend on other parts of the marketing mix, such as advertising and sales promotion.

The hotel/resort industry traditionally uses a functional, hierarchical structure. Within this structure, hotel departments are organized around particular functions, such as housekeeping or sales. Department managers, including the sales manager, report to a GM. In smaller hotels such as roadside motels, the GM usually serves as sales manager because the organization is not large enough to support functional departments. Within large hotels and resorts, the sales department may have directors of specialized sales such as a convention and meetings sales director or a corporate accounts sales director.

The structure of a hotel sales department depends on the culture of the organization, size of the property, nature of the market, and type of hotel. A casino hotel might contain the same number of rooms as a ski resort hotel yet have a somewhat different organizational structure. Some casino hotels have sales directors who are responsible for working with junket reps and premium players. A resort hotel might have a sales director responsible for working with travel agents and tour wholesalers, or with nationwide ski clubs.

The sales force structures commonly used in the hospitality industry today are described next.

Territorial-Structured Sales Force

In the simplest sales organization, each sales representative is assigned an exclusive territory to represent the company's full line. This sales structure has a number of advantages. First, it results in a clear definition of the salesperson's responsibilities. As the only salesperson working the territory, he or she bears the credit or blame for area sales to the extent that personal selling effort makes a difference. Second, territorial responsibility increases the sales representative's incentive to cultivate local business and personal ties. These ties contribute to the sales representative's selling effectiveness and personal life. Third, travel expenses are relatively small because each sales representative travels within a small geographic area.

A territorial sales organization is often supported by many levels of sales management positions. Each higher-level sales manager takes on increasing marketing and administration work. Sales managers are paid for their management skills rather than their selling skills. The new sales trainee, in looking ahead, can expect to become a sales representative, then a district manager, and then a regional manager, and, depending on his or her ability and motivation, may move to still higher levels of sales or general management.

Territory Size

Territories can be designed to attempt to provide either equal sales potential or equal workload. Each principle offers certain advantages. Territories of equal potential provide each sales representative with the same income opportunities and provide the company with a means to evaluate performance. Persistent differences in sales yield by territory are assumed to reflect differences in ability or effort of individual sales representatives. Customer density varies by territory, and territories with equal potential can vary widely in size. The potential for selling cruises in Chicago is larger than in several Rocky Mountain states. A sales representative assigned to Chicago can cover the same sales potential with much less effort than the sales representative who sells in the Rocky Mountain West. The sales representative assigned to the larger and sparser territory is going to end up with either fewer sales and less income for equal effort or equal sales through extraordinary effort. A common solution is to acknowledge that territories differ in attractiveness and assign the better or more senior sales representatives to the better territories.

Alternatively, territories might be designed to equalize the sales workload. Each sales representative could then cover his or her territory adequately. This principle results in some variation in territory sales potential. This does not concern a sales force on straight salary, but when sales representatives are compensated partly on commission, territories vary in their attractiveness.

Territory Shape

Territories are formed by combining smaller units, such as counties or states, until they add up to a territory of a given sales potential or workload. Territorial design must take into account the location of natural barriers, the adequacy of transportation, and so on. Many companies prefer a certain territory shape because the shape can influence the cost and ease of coverage and the sales representatives' job satisfaction.

The territorial structure is most commonly used by airlines, cruise lines, and rental car companies, and at the corporate level by hotel chains. It is not frequently used by individual hotel/resort properties that instead seem to organize their sales departments by function or type of customer.

Market-Segment-Structured Sales Force

Companies often specialize their sales forces along market segment lines. Separate sales forces can be set up by different industries for the convention/meeting segment, the incentive travel market, and other major segments. This is the most common type of structure within the hotel industry. For example, associations have different needs than corporations; thus one salesperson may be assigned to the association market, while another is assigned to the corporate market.

Market-Channel-Structured Sales Force

The importance of marketing intermediaries, such as wholesalers, tour operators, travel agencies, and junket reps, to the hospitality industry has created sales force structures to serve different marketing channels.

The cruise line industry has historically depended on travel agents for the bulk of its sales. A study by Claritas, the marketing support company, showed that 96 percent of cruise line passengers purchased tickets through a travel agency. This company developed thematic maps targeting the areas in which the best prospects for a cruise line were concentrated. The cruise line then used these maps in presentations by its sales force to travel agents.[11]

A segment of the cruise line industry, cargo freighters are ships that carry freight everywhere in the world and offer a few berths to travelers. They lack the glamour and service of cruise ships but appeal to travelers with time. Highly specialized travel agents sell this product. Information is also available at www.freightword. com or www.traveltips.com.

Some hotels such as those near historical sites receive substantial bookings through motor coach tour brokers. The location, size, and type of hospitality companies greatly affect the relative importance of travel intermediaries. This in turn affects whether a company designs its sales force structure by travel intermediary.[12]

15.3 Companies such as US Foods, which service restaurants, and other foodservice organizations often use a territory-based sales force as one of the ways they use to organize their sales force. Go to http://usfoods.com/.

Customer-Structured Sales Force

A customer-structured sales force recognizes that specific customers who are critical to the success of the organization exist. The sales force is usually organized to serve these accounts through a key or national account structure.

Key Accounts

Large accounts (called key accounts, major accounts, or national accounts) are often singled out for special attention and handling. If the account is a large company with divisions operating in many parts of the country, it is likely to be handled as a national account and assigned to a specific individual or sales team. If the company has several such accounts, it is likely to organize a national account management (NAM) division.

NAM is growing for a number of reasons. As buyer concentration increases through mergers and acquisitions, fewer buyers account for a larger share of a company's sales. Another factor is that many buyers are centralizing their purchases instead of leaving them to the local units. This gives buyers more bargaining power. Still another factor is that as products become more complex, more groups in the buyer's organization become involved in the purchase process, and the typical salesperson might not have the skill, authority, or coverage to be effective in selling to the large buyer.

Sheraton Hotels noted that business travelers were not shifting from one hotel chain to another as much as in the past. In response, Sheraton developed a reservations system that allowed the establishment of national accounts.

In organizing a national account program, a company faces a number of issues, including how to select national accounts; how to manage them; how to develop, manage, and evaluate a national account manager; how to organize a structure for national accounts; and where to locate NAM in the organization.

Combination-Structured Sales Force

Some hotels and resorts have a sales force structured by product, market segment, market channel, and customer. A large hotel might have a catering/banquet sales force (product), a convention/meeting sales force (market segment), a tour wholesale sales force (marketing intermediary), and a national accounts sales force (customer). Proponents of such a sales force believe it encourages the sales force

This photo of Doha, Qatar, shows the pyramid-shaped Sheraton Doha Resort and Convention Hotel. Sheraton developed a database which includes an account system that allows hotels worldwide to quote the correct rate for organizations with negotiated accounts. Courtesy of Paulcowan/Dreamstime.

to reach most available customers. They also contend it is impossible for a single salesperson to understand and effectively sell all the hotel's products to all available customer segments through all marketing channels. Sales specialists can become familiar with major customers, understand trends that affect them, and plan appropriate sales strategies and tactics.

Opponents of this system feel that in many cases this sales force structure indicates the hotel is trying to be all things to all people in the absence of long-run goals and strategies. They contend that such a structure is difficult to manage and can be confusing to the sales force and the customer because the same customer may be classified in different areas and thus be handled by more than one salesperson.

Regardless of which structure is used by a hotel or resort, a particular market segment neglected by many North American hoteliers is local markets. Many local markets offer potential for F&B and function room sales. Although a resort such as the Greenbriar in a rural area of West Virginia might not have a large local market, it is scarcely the case for most hotels. The Japanese seem to be particularly adept at penetrating local markets; 40 to 50 percent of Japanese hotel sales are accounted for by parties and other events from local companies.[13] Sales managers must be aware of the local market and develop a sales force structure appropriate for penetrating this market.

Seven months after opening, the Dalmahoy Golf and Country Club Resort near Edinburgh, Scotland, recognized the need for a strong sales effort in the local market and for a combination-structured sales force. Dalmahoy was experiencing low occupancy and less than desirable membership growth. Many factors were involved, such as a poor economy and almost no awareness by Edinburgh area golfers. As a member of the U.K.-based Country Club Hotel Group, Dalmahoy had the assistance of this company's national sales force. The management of Dalmahoy knew that a strong property-level sales effort was also needed and employed two salespersons to serve the local market, plus a travel trade manager to work with intermediaries to attract overseas business.[14]

Sales Force Size

Once the company clarifies its sales force strategy and structure, it is ready to consider sales force size. After determining the type and number of desired customers, a workload approach can be used to establish sales force size. This method consists of the following steps:

1. Customers are grouped into size classes according to their annual sales volume.

2. The desirable call frequencies (number of sales calls on an account per year) are established for each class.

3. The number of accounts in each size class is multiplied by the corresponding call frequency to arrive at the total workload for the country in sales calls per year.

4. The average number of calls a sales representative can make per year is determined.

5. The number of sales representatives needed is determined by dividing the total annual calls required by the average calls made by a sales representative.

Suppose that the company estimates its national market consists of 1,000 A accounts and 2,000 B accounts. A accounts require nine calls a year, whereas B accounts require six calls a year. This means that the company needs a sales force that can make 21,000 sales calls a year. Suppose that the average sales representative can make 1,000 calls a year. The company would need twenty-one full-time sales representatives.

The size of a sales force is determined by changes in the market, competition, and corporate strategies and policies. The sales process also directly affects decisions concerning sales force size. The following describes several of the factors that influence the size of a hotel's sales force:

- *Corporate/chain sales support.* Several major hotel chains have employed a corporate sales force to reach the meeting/convention/conference market. The concept behind this sales force is that individual hotel properties may not be in a position to search out and track this important market and that a sales force representing the chain can recommend and sell all appropriate hotels within the chain, not simply a single property. In recent years, some chains have begun to question the value of this sales force and may drop this area of sales support. If this occurs, individual properties may find it necessary to employ one or more additional sales force members to ensure coverage of this important segment.

- *Use of overseas independent sales reps.* Sales reps have traditionally been used by hotels and resorts to serve foreign countries. With the growing importance of many foreign markets, several companies are rethinking the use of independent reps and may substitute salaried sales staff in these markets.

- *Team selling.* Team selling has proved to be an effective and powerful tactic to reach and retain key customers. Its opportunities and limitations are only beginning to be realized in the hospitality industry.

- *Electronic and telephone sales.* Electronic sales are now firmly entrenched as an important sales tool for the hospitality industry. Even local restaurants use a Web site as an informational and sales tool. This tool is particularly effective in international sales where customers and providers such as B&Bs can quickly interface. The majority of hospitality firms do not depend solely on this tool but have instead found that electronic sales is most effective when used as part of a marketing/sales mix, including database marketing, telephone (800 numbers), personal sales, and a carefully selected blend of media.

- *Search engine marketing sales—SEM.* "Search Engine Marketing (SEM) is a form of online marketing whereby marketers and webmasters use a range of techniques to ensure that their webpage history appears in a favorable location in search engine results pages (e.g. Google, Bing, Alltheweb, Altavista). The key strategy is to optimize webpages for the search engines by ensuring that the company's webpages contain appropriate keywords and that the websites' page hierarchy is logically arranged. An appropriate website design encourages the search engines' web crawlers or spiders to index a particular set of pages and proper keywords promote an optimism ranking in search engines."[15]

- *Proprietary Web sites* —Effective SEM requires careful planning, including the development of a Web site.

A few strategies to create effective sales results from proprietary Web sites include the following:

A. Conduct data mining of potential guest profiles through information collected from frequent guest program databases or from guests at check-in.

B. Complement and support Web sites through direct mail sent to past guests inviting them to return and to use the company's Web site.

C. Provide Best Rate Guarantees that prices available on the Web site will match any price offered by an online travel agency (OTA).

D. Advertise on Google by "pay by click" to entice Google or another search engine to encourage the company's Web site to appear higher on the search.

Acquire the services of a Web page consultant to optimize key words which help to locate a Web page higher on the search.

E. Entice customers to use a company's call center or on-site toll-free telephone number by offering "freebies," such as parking, breakfast, movies, and WiFi.

Experts in the field recognize that the use of toll free and call centers is labor intensive, but they say that the cost is less than paying commissions to OTAs.

Telephone Sales

A related area of importance to hospitality sales managers is the management of sales from telephone distribution systems, such as the 800-number reservation system of a chain or an independent group such as Preferred Hotels. Some hotel chains, such as Omni Hotels, have signed exclusive agreements with a single reservation service to manage worldwide reservations. Omni appointed Intel International to handle worldwide reservations for its U.S., Mexico, Singapore, and Hong Kong properties. "With such a spread of destinations, it was important for us to select a reservation facility that could provide international marketing support," said the senior vice president of sales and marketing for Omni.[16] He went on to say that Omni is integrating the sales and marketing function worldwide and therefore had to have a system that facilitated rather than complicate the sales/marketing process.

- *Seamless Reservation Systems.* Many hotel chains have experienced the need for an integrated and seamless reservation system. A customer reservation system (CRS) is increasingly required to offer travel agents direct links to a hotel company's entire inventory so agents can be assured that booking rates won't change when their clients arrive at the hotel. Radisson Hotels, in cooperation with Apollo, developed seamless reservation availability, giving agents the ability to enter Radisson's reservations system, view the entire inventory, and make a reservation electronically. Many hotel chains and hotel sales managers have realized they must be equally adept at managing technology as they are at managing people.

- *Travel intermediary dependency.* Hospitality industry members historically viewed travel intermediaries with mixed emotions. Some hotels may have allowed wholesalers to assume too great a degree of sales power. A study of Caribbean hotels found that "wholesalers play a valuable role in the Caribbean resort hotel industry by helping hotels market and sell their rooms. But in recent years, wholesalers' power has increased, causing operational and financial problems for some Caribbean resort-hotel operators."[17] In some cases, it may be advisable to increase the size of the sales force and aggressively seek ways to lessen wholesaler dependence.

The size of a sales force may need to increase to support new marketing strategies. The sales manager then has the responsibility to "sell" top management because a budgetary increase will almost certainly be necessary. Similarly, a professional sales manager must be aware of changing trends and new technology. Rather than tenaciously support a larger-than-necessary sales force, the sales manager must be prepared to downsize and substitute technology when appropriate.

■■■ Organizing the Sales Department

As discussed previously, hospitality companies traditionally design departments along functional lines. It is common to find hotels with several marketing-related departments, such as a sales department, a guest relations department, and an advertising and public relations department, but not a "marketing" department. In recent years, some hotels have given the title "sales and marketing" to the previously named sales department but with limited training in marketing for the sales manager.

Today's sales managers may have two types of salespeople within their departments: an inside sales force and a field sales force. The term *inside sales* can be misleading because many field salespeople spend a great deal of their time inside the hotel calling clients and prospects, meeting with them, making arrangements with other departments, answering mail, and performing many other duties, such as completing sales reports.

Inside Sales Force

Inside salespeople include three types. There are technical-support persons, who provide technical information and answers to customers' questions. There are sales assistants, who provide clerical backup for the field salespersons. They call ahead and confirm appointments, carry out credit checks, follow up on deliveries, and answer customers' questions when they cannot reach the outside sales rep. There are also telemarketers, who use the phone to find new leads, qualify them, and sell to them. Telemarketers can call up to fifty customers per day compared with the four or five that an outside salesperson can contact. They can be effective in the following ways: cross-selling the company's other products, upgrading orders, introducing new company products, opening new accounts and reactivating former accounts, giving more attention to neglected accounts, and following up and qualifying leads.

Telemarketing has found a role in the hospitality industry. Some members of the cruise industry use a telemarketing sales force to reach individual guest prospects. Telemarketing has found disfavor among many recipients of these calls. Within the hospitality industry, meeting planners are besieged by hotel sales reps who have done no research concerning the planner. Instead, they commonly begin a conversation with the question, "Do you plan meetings?" Busy meeting planners find this disruptive and frustrating, particularly if frequently called by the same hotel but different sales reps.[18]

Because of the high turnover among hotel salespeople and lack of an updated prospect database, a meeting planner may be called two to three times within a year by a hotel's sales rep asking the same questions. Telemarketing can be much more productive if the salesperson has basic information concerning the prospect. Telemarketing failed in one hotel company because members of the sales force were required to perform this function one day a week. The hotel's salespeople felt forced into an unpleasant task. The supervisor resigned, management gave up, and the sales force rejoiced.[19]

A more successful outcome has occurred in hospitality enterprises that employ a specialist in telemarketing to generate leads. This does not relieve sales force members from calling clients. High-volume salespeople in all fields have found that "working their customer list" is a surefire tactic for success. The best-paid salespeople rely on calls to previous clients and prospects to sell new products and ask for repeat business.

Information Needed by the Sales Force

At the least, salespeople need a database of their customers/clients. This helps them prepare for sales calls and also to answer questions while taking with customers.

Basic Database Needs

- List of clients alphabetically and by key client listing
- Sales history of client
- Volume of sales by client
- Seasonality of sales by client
- Products/services purchased by client

- Profitability of client (many companies will not release this to the sales force)
- Buyer contact information
  - Name
  - Title
  - Address (both mailing, courier and post office)
  - E-mail
- Special needs of client
- Past problems of/with client

This is a partial list of the type of information that may be provided to sales force members. The purpose is not to overwhelm the sales force with data but instead to assist them to better serve the client and in turn realize sales success.

Reservations Department

The reservations department is a very important inside sales area for many hospitality companies because reservationists may speak with 80 percent of a company's customers. This department is sometimes not viewed as part of the sales team. It is sometimes a separate department, and unfortunately, the reservations and sales departments may have little communication. In worst-case scenarios, they may actually find themselves at odds. This is not the case at Hyatt Hotels, where reservations are under sales/marketing.

A study of reservations departments at a hotel company, airline, and cruise line revealed that much can be done to improve the effectiveness of this critical inside sales force.[20] The results of this study showed that reservations training is critical. The training program prescribed was remarkably similar to that for any sales position. Hyatt focuses on technical aspects, including how to sell. Hyatt's philosophy is that the skills necessary to be an effective salesperson can be taught.

Reservationist candidates at American Airlines are interviewed and hired for their sales ability. Days Inns has a program to hire the elderly and the physically challenged and through training turn them into reservation salespeople. Training your reservationists to be good company representatives and teaching them how to sell will pay big dividends in the long run.[21]

Field Sales Force

Today, sales managers face an increasingly complex marketplace, which has created the need to review the organizational design of the field sales force. We next discuss different types of field sales forces currently used by hospitality companies.

Commissioned Reps

Hotels and resorts commonly use commissioned sales representatives in distant markets where the market potential does not justify employing a salaried salesperson. A Los Angeles hotel may contract with commissioned sales reps in New York or Miami to reach companies and associations that are known to the local sales reps. Commissioned sales reps normally represent several different properties or chains but attempt not to represent competing clients. This is sometimes difficult in the case of chains, which have competing properties.

It is important to follow a few simple rules when working with commissioned sales reps.

1. **Select markets with care.** Distant markets should be selected to match corporate goals and marketing/sales objectives, not simply to have someone represent the company in a location.

2. **Visit the market personally.** Meet with prospective sales reps, examine their offices, check out references, note their personal appearance, ask for a list of current clients, ask for a credit report, and clear the rep through the police and the Better Business Bureau or the equivalent. In general, it is important

to be as careful or even more careful in hiring a sales rep to cover distant markets as in hiring salaried sales force members. In some developing nations, a commissioned sales rep is considered to be a member of the client company's workforce and is dependent on that company for livelihood. Local courts often decide in favor of the rep and may award the rep large financial settlements in cases such as dismissal for failure to meet performance standards.

3. **Include the sales rep as part of the hotel's sales force.**   It is important to visit the offices of distant sales reps occasionally. This requires an adequate budget for travel and may entail considerable effort to convince the GM that such an expenditure of time and money is worthwhile.

Salaried Sales Force

Most hospitality industry sales force members are paid a salary plus benefits. Additional compensation is sometimes available through commissions, bonuses, profit sharing, or other financial remuneration. In some nations, a sales force, by law, is paid an additional month's salary at Christmas or New Year's and may qualify for benefits unknown to North American companies, such as a month of paid vacation each year.

Team Sales

Team sales have become a necessity in many industries. The hospitality industry is no exception. The concept of a sales team is two or more persons working in concert toward a common sales objective. These persons are not necessarily from the same company. The purpose for a team sales approach is to accomplish objectives through the synergism of two or more people that would be impossible or unduly costly through individual sales efforts.

In addition to traditional objectives, such as to increase occupancy in a hotel, other nonquantifiable objectives are sometimes established for teams. These generally deal with enhancing image and goodwill. People from various disciplines and departments are sometimes brought together to improve morale, teach teamwork, and cross-educate.

Teams within the hospitality industry have traditionally been used for specific tasks, which include but are not limited to the following:

*   Sales blitz

*   Travel mission

*   Charity promotions

*   Community improvement programs

Although teams are used for many purposes, the primary purpose for team sales should be to improve sales competitive position. Teams are best used when the needs of the customer or prospect are complex and require the input of specialists. An example might be a large conference that requires the expertise and cooperation of an airline, a golf resort, and a ground transportation company.

Today the concept of team sales is moving beyond occasional use, such as during a sales blitz, to the allied concepts of relationship marketing and strategic alliances.

■■■ Relationship Marketing and Strategic Alliances

The goal of personal selling traditionally was viewed as a specific contract with a customer. But in many cases the company is not seeking simply a one-time sale. It has targeted a major customer account that it would like to serve for a long period of time. The company would like to demonstrate that it has the capabilities to serve the account's needs in a superior way. The type of selling to establish a long-term collaborative relationship is more complex than a short-run, one-time sales approach. Obtaining long-run commitment involves many more agreements than simply closing the sale.[22]

More companies today are moving their emphasis from transaction marketing to relationship marketing. Today's customers are large and often global. They prefer suppliers who can sell and deliver a set of products and services to many locations, and who can work closely with customer teams to improve products and processes.

Companies recognize that sales teamwork increasingly is the key to winning and maintaining accounts. They recognize that asking their people for teamwork doesn't provide it. They need to revise their compensation system to give credit for work on shared accounts; they must set up better goals and measures for their sales forces; and they must emphasize the importance of teamwork in their training programs while honoring the importance of individual initiative.

Relationship marketing is based on the premise that important accounts need focused and continuous attention. Salespeople working with customers under relationship marketing must do more than call when they think customers might be ready to place orders. They should monitor key accounts, know their problems, be ready to serve them in a number of ways, and strive to become part of the client's team.

When a relationship management program is implemented properly, the organization begins to focus as much on managing its customers as on managing its products. At the same time, companies should realize that although there is a strong move toward relationship marketing, it is not effective in all situations. Hospitality companies must determine which customers will respond profitably to relationship marketing.

The Boca Raton Resort and Club provides an example of the benefits that can accrue from relationship marketing. "To keep a national association coming back amidst a sea of competitors, our resort cannot merely serve as a site for their conference," explained David Feder, the Boca's senior vice president of sales and marketing. "We look to ourselves as much more than that: We can actually help associations fulfill their goals and shape their futures."[23]

Strategic alliances are a highly developed form of relationship marketing that are common between vendor and buyer or between noncompeting vendors and a common buyer. "Alliances are relationships between interdependent parties that agree to cooperate but still retain separate identities."[24] A strategic alliance may involve sharing a combination of any of the following: confidences, database, market knowledge, planning resources, risks, security, and technology.

Examples of strategic alliances within the hospitality industry include the following:

- An agreement between Carlson Hospitality Group, a division of Carlson Company, Inc., and Hospitality Franchise Systems (HFS), whereby HFS would operate existing F&B systems on a franchise or lease basis in Carlson's hotel properties. This agreement included cooperative buying in which hotel companies could purchase supplies, services, and equipment at reduced prices.[25]

- An agreement was made between Hostmark International (Denver) and the Management Group (Chicago) to form a partnership to manage hotels. This alliance enabled the two companies to approach major financial institutions as a national company rather than as two regional companies.[26]

Strategic alliances have become a necessity due to a variety of factors: globalization, complicated customer needs, large customers with multiple locations, the need for technology, highly interdependent vendor/buyer relationships, intensified competition, and low profitability within the hospitality industry.

Strategic alliances directly affect the nature of the professional sales function within hospitality companies. The need for professional sales is dramatically enhanced.

Large customers may require services, such as assistance with planning, extended financing, and equity participation. In turn, these needs affect the policies and procedures of suppliers. A buyer who demands that all invoices be sent and settled through electronic data interchange (EDI) may create a need for new investment in hardware and software on the part of the suppliers.

Salespeople must be able to understand increasingly sophisticated buyer needs and communicate them to management. In many cases, the real test of a salesperson's skills comes in the ability of that person to convince his or her own management of the need to change policies and procedures.

The remainder of this chapter discusses the process of sales management. The topics selected are basic to sales managers of virtually all hospitality companies. Although these concepts have application to the management of an inside sales force, a commission sales force, and team selling, they were developed primarily for the management of a traditional sales force composed of individual salaried salespeople. The majority of the remaining examples in this chapter refer to this traditional form of sales force.

■■■ Recruiting and Training a Professional Sales Force

Importance of Careful Selection

At the heart of a successful sales force operation is the selection of effective sales people. The performance difference between an average and a top sales person can be considerable. One survey revealed that the top 27 percent of the sales force brought in over 52 percent of the sales. Beyond the differences in sales productivity are the great wastes entailed in hiring the wrong person. When a salesperson quits, the cost of finding and training a new salesperson plus the cost of lost sales can be substantial. Additionally, a sales force with many new people is generally less productive.[27]

What Makes a Good Sales Person?

Selecting sales people would be simple if we knew what traits to look for. Most customers say they want sales representatives to be honest, reliable, knowledgeable, and helpful.

Look for traits common to the most successful salespeople in the company. A study of superachievers found that super sales performers exhibit the following traits: risk taking, powerful sense of mission, problem-solving bent, care for the customer, and careful planning.[28] Effective salespeople have two basic qualities: empathy, the ability to feel as the customer does; and ego drive, a strong personal need to make the sale.[29]

Establishing a Profile of Desired Characteristics Matching the Corporate Culture

The management of each hospitality company has a responsibility to determine a desired sales force profile. The GM, vice president marketing/sales, and others may help determine the preferred characteristics for a sales force.

The person who should first exemplify these is the sales manager. Management selects this person and then empowers him or her with the primary responsibility for recruiting, training, motivating, and controlling the sales force.

The rhetoric of most hospitality companies regarding a desired sales force is much the same, but actually putting words into action varies. This is due to the fact that managers sometimes overlook the importance of their unique corporate culture and simply adopt a generic profile description. All hotels are not alike, nor are all cruise lines, nor are the members of any hospitality company.

The corporate culture within some organizations is formal and authoritarian. In others, such as Southwest Airlines, fun is encouraged. Substantial differences exist among hospitality firms. Both the employer and the salesperson need to fully recognize that success cannot be realized if the two parties are incompatible. A salesperson might be very successful with InterContinental or Four Seasons Hotels but unable to adapt to the culture of Ramada or Novotel Hotels.

The Ritz-Carlton Hotel Corporation embraces a corporate philosophy that both the guests it serves and its employees are cultured individuals who should be treated with respect and should be referred to as ladies and gentlemen. This message is transmitted in advertisements, such as the one in the *South China Morning Post* that read as follows: "The Ritz-Carlton Hong Kong, situated in the heart of Central, with 216 guest rooms, offering the finest tradition in hospitality, is now offering committed, energetic, and enthusiastic Ladies and Gentlemen opportunities to fill the following positions...."[30]

In service encounters, customers perform roles and employees perform roles. Satisfaction of both parties is likely when the customer and service provider engage in behaviors that are consistent with each other's role expectations. Ritz-Carlton realizes that its customers expect to be treated professionally and with a degree of formality. It communicates to its employees that they are ladies and gentlemen to prepare them for the role of providing professional service to their customers, who are also ladies and gentlemen.[31]

Matching Career Acquisitions with Corporate Objectives

The aspirations of a salesperson must first be clearly understood by that person and clearly communicated to the potential employer. The hospitality industry does not generally offer sales positions that allow a person to become wealthy from commissions or bonuses. Salespeople seeking great wealth are advised to seek careers in commercial real estate or securities. Despite this, the hospitality industry does offer many advantages to a salesperson:

- The industry is fun. Unlike selling funeral plots or cancer insurance, the product is by nature fun and even exciting.

- Clients are generally personable and willing to listen, unlike industries in which the client has little time to talk and exhibits an aggressive knock-you-over attitude.

Marketing Highlight   Code of Ethics and Business Conduct

15–1 Members of a company's sales force sometimes find themselves confronted with opportunities to act in ways that may have ethical repercussions. The California Pizza Kitchen Company published a seven-page guide for employees concerning a Code of Ethics and Business Conduct. The following is the conclusion.

In the final analysis you are the guardian of CPK's ethics. While there are no universal rules, when in doubt ask yourself:

- Will my actions be ethical in every respect and fully comply with the law and with CPK policies?

- Will my actions have the appearance of impropriety?

- Will my actions be questioned by my supervisors, fellow employees, family, or the general public?

If you are uncomfortable with your answer to any of the above, you should not take the contemplated actions without first discussing them with your supervisor, general man-

ager, or regional director or the Ethics Officer. If you are still uncomfortable, follow the steps outlined in the sections on "Compliance Resources" and "Reporting Procedures."

Any employee, director, or officer who ignores or violates any of CPK's ethical standards, and any supervisor who penalizes a subordinate for trying to follow these ethical standards, will be subject to corrective action, including immediate dismissal. However, it is not the threat of discipline that should govern your actions. CPK expects you to share its belief that a dedicated commitment to ethical behavior is the right thing to do and is good business, as well as being the surest way for CPK to remain a world-class organization.

Source: California Pizza Kitchen, Inc., *Code of Ethics and Business Conduct for Employees, Officers, and Directors.* California Pizza Kitchen, Investor Relations, Corporate Governance, California Pizza Kitchen, Restaurant Support Center, 6053 W. Century Blvd., Suite 1100, Los Angeles, CA 90045, www.cpk.com (accessed March 25, 2008).

- Fellow salespeople and other colleagues are generally people oriented, gregarious, and enjoyable.

- Opportunities for travel exist, particularly in sales of airlines, cruise lines, travel agencies, and travel wholesalers.

- Opportunities for movement within the hospitality industry exist. Considerable career movement occurs within the industry. Salespeople move among the various industry members, such as from a hotel or resort to a cruise line or rental car firm.

- Management opportunities exist. Career growth to positions of sales manager is quite feasible. Career growth to vice presidency of sales or marketing is also possible.

It should be recognized that career promotion to GM within hotels and resorts from sales historically has not often occurred but is beginning to happen. These positions generally call for individuals with broader experience and training, including F&B, front desk, and other operational areas.

Neither the salesperson nor the company benefits by disguising true career objectives or the actual corporate culture. Experienced and astute sales managers seem to develop a sixth sense for determining whether a candidate's personality and background truly match the sales position. Once salespeople are selected and hired, they have to be trained.

Sales Force Training

Sales training is vital to success, yet unfortunately it remains a weak link within the hospitality industry. This is particularly problematic for recent graduates with little or no workplace experience. Fortunately, the situation is improving, and several hospitality companies now have training programs.

Sales training is not a one-time process but instead a career-long endeavor. Continuous training is part of the written philosophy of Singapore Airlines. This company believes that all employees must be trained and retrained continuously.

Types of Training Required

Members of a sales force require three types of training:

1. **Product/service training.** Technology creates continuous change within the hospitality industry. Reservation systems, equipment such as airplanes or cruise ships, and entire operational systems change. Service delivery systems, menus, branch locations, and other changes require regular and frequent training.

2. **Policies, procedures, and planning training.** As organizations increase in size and complexity, the need for formalized systems and procedures increases. Training is essential to ensure that all policies and procedures are understood.

   Effective salespeople continuously wink at some policies and procedures. This is generally done in an effort to satisfy customer needs and close the sale quickly. Unfortunately, a chronic failure to do things the "company way" leads to problems.

   Hospitality salespeople receive much criticism for their lack of attention to detail in the barrage of paperwork they must complete. Failure to complete paperwork correctly, on time, and in detail leads to costly errors, customer dissatisfaction, and ill will among other departments.

3. **Sales techniques training.** An age-old debate centers on the wisdom of attempting to teach techniques of selling. One camp firmly believes that salespeople are determined by genetics, personality, and motivation. The other side generally agrees that only a small percentage of individuals make effective salespeople but also contends their effectiveness can be enhanced by learning sales basics such as the following:

   - Prospecting
   - Obtaining the initial sales call (setting the appointment)

- Conducting the sales dialogue
  - Becoming acquainted
  - Asking questions and probing for prospects' needs
  - Listening to what the prospect says and doesn't say
  - Presenting benefits of product/service features to match prospects' needs
  - Overcoming objections
  - Further probing if necessary to determine needs
  - Closing the sale
- Follow-up
  - To continue sales dialogue if prospect did not buy
  - To say thank you for the order
  - To assure client that this was the correct thing to do
  - To look for opportunities to upsell or cross-sell
  - To ask for leads and testimonials
  - To ask for another appointment or ask for another sale when client is again ready to purchase

Although sales training is most effective when customized, general factors that contribute to the success or failure of a salesperson should be considered when developing a sales training program.

Six factors have been determined to contribute to sales failure. Each is relevant to salespeople within the hospitality industry.[32]

1. Poor listening skills[33]
2. Failure to concentrate on top priorities
3. Lack of sufficient effort
4. Inability to determine customer needs
5. Lack of planning for sales presentations
6. Inadequate product/service knowledge

Sales training is a responsibility of the sales manager. It has been suggested that hotel sales management should spend 50 percent of their time selling; 30 percent supervising and training staff; and the remaining 20 percent with paperwork, meetings, and reviewing marketing plans.[34]

Members of upper management often assist in training by presenting an overview of the company and its history, culture, and norms. This sends a clear message to the sales force and helps establish an effective learning attitude.

Sales managers often invite people from other departments, such as the chef or reservations manager, to attend selected sales meetings for the purpose of discussing product improvements. It is also important for salespeople to experience the company's service. Salespeople for a cruise line cannot effectively sell the excitement of sailing if they have never left dry land.

The hospitality industry has historically offered free or low-cost "fam trips" (familiarization trips) to travel agents and wholesalers. This may be considered as training of sales intermediaries. Other benefits, such as free flight privileges and expense accounts to entertain guests in the company's lounge and restaurants, also enhance product knowledge. These perks are often viewed with suspicion by employees and managers from other departments. It is essential that they be used judiciously.

Training Materials and Outside Training Assistance

Formal training may sometimes be necessary in which technical details must be memorized. The use of interactive video for this kind of training has proved effective. Some fast-food chains use such systems to help train operational employees.

Harrah's Cherokee Casino in North Carolina is connected with its other casinos through its Total Rewards program. Courtesy of PR NEWSWIRE/ AP Image.

Today, many companies are adding e-learning to their sales training programs. Most e-learning is Web based, but many companies now offer on-demand training for PDAs, cell phones, and even video iPods. Online and other e-learning approaches cut training costs and make training more efficient. One recent study estimates that companies spend forty cents of every sales training dollar on travel and lodging. Such costs can be greatly reduced through Web-based training. As a result, companies recently did 33 percent of their corporate training online, up from 24 percent a few years earlier.[35]

Online training may range from simple text-based product information to Internet-based sales exercises that build sales skills to sophisticated simulations that re-create the dynamics of real-life sales calls. Training programs must be carefully selected. Many sales managers err in purchasing an expensive training system of programmed learning from an outside vendor. Later these may be found to be too generic in content.

Organizations such as the Hotel/Motel Educational Association, CLIA (Cruise Lines International Association), the National Restaurant Association, universities such as Cornell University, and training institutes offer materials specifically designed for the hospitality industry.

Universities are now developing strategic relationships with companies and trade associations to train management and staff on an ongoing basis. A group of hospitality authors and researchers believes that "the main training partnership in the next century will be manifested by a closer alignment between the university, Hotel/Restaurant Management programs, and business partners. This alignment will plug into organizational needs, meaning fewer off-the-shelf programs."[36]

Ultimately, all training is perfected on the job. Some managers continue to believe that effective training consists solely of learning from one's trials and errors while selling. What is overlooked is that this is costly. For many, this sink-or-swim system creates unnecessary turnover and morale problems.

As the new salesperson learns through experience, it is critical for the sales manager to monitor progress and offer encouragement and suggestions for improving areas of weakness. Effective sales managers are effective teachers. Individuals who do not enjoy teaching or coaching may find that their own management careers are limited.

All teachers dread a moment of truth. That is the time when grades must be given. Granting an "A" is pleasurable and easy, but placing an "F" on someone's record requires soul searching. The same is true for a sales manager, who must eventually come to the conclusion that no amount of training will create a professional salesperson of an individual.

Once this decision has been reached after serious study and thought, the sales manager has no alternative other than to release the salesperson promptly. Those who rescind this decision in the face of emotion-laden pleas for a second chance only postpone the inevitable.

■■■ Managing the Sales Force

The research and study dedicated to this subject clearly indicate that successful sales management is not the result of following a formula.

Successful sales managers cannot be described by a narrow profile. Successful sales managers come in all sizes, shapes, colors, and backgrounds. Perhaps, if a universal truth exists, it is that long-run successful sales managers exhibit a strong affinity for their subordinates, are willing to learn, and are reasonably bright. Even these conclusions sometimes seem to be disputed by observing some sales managers who meet objectives and please upper management, yet seem weak in virtually every skill and talent normally accorded to successful sales managers.

The fact is that market conditions often have an inordinate influence over a sales manager's failure or success. An economic climate in which guests are begging for hotel rooms versus three years of deep economic recession with a surplus of hotel rooms can produce very different results.

Hospitality sales management is neither a precise science nor a formula-based work procedure. Nevertheless, certain functions or processes have historically been associated with the management of a professional sales force.

Selecting Sales Strategies

Sales successes within the hospitality industry are not the result of a hit-and-run sales mentality. Success depends on the development of excellent long-run relationships with clients or accounts. The 80/20 rule prevails within the hospitality industry. A B&B, a highway motel, or a discount airline may find no relevance, but major hotels and major airlines know well the phenomenon. This concept says that a majority of a firm's business comes from a minority of its customers. These are commonly referred to as key, national, or major accounts. Certain corporate clients and travel intermediaries, such as OTAs, generally serve as key accounts. These companies provide large numbers of customers.

Based on the concept of key customers, six general sales strategies must be recognized by members of the hospitality industry:

1. **Prevent erosion of key accounts.** It does little good to attract new customers if key customers are lost. Companies operating on this kind of treadmill inevitably have higher than average sales force turnover and experience employee morale problems. Determine reasons why key customers leave and initiate corrective steps. Initiate and carefully manage programs that treat key customers as royalty. A single sales/service person may be assigned to work with only a handful of key accounts. Unless these accounts are provided highly personal service, the risk of loss to a competitor is great.

    The CEO of a large hotel chain reportedly once told franchisees that they should view their properties as buckets with holes in the bottom. From these holes escape large numbers of customers. The message was that franchises must place even greater efforts into sales to attract new customers. Some who attended this meeting reported that the message had a depressing effect on the audience, who viewed themselves on a treadmill that regularly increased in speed. This was undoubtedly not the desired effect of the analogy. Instead, the message should have been that each of us has holes in our respective buckets, but it is our responsibility to close or lessen the size of these holes so we retain more of our customers.

    Harrah's Casinos introduced a loyalty card program known as "Total Rewards." This allowed each Harrah's casino to track the gaming and purchasing activities of its customers. Data collected from this system were fed into an information system called "WINet," which linked all Harrah's properties, allowing the company to collect company-wide customer information.

    This changed the corporate culture of Harrah's from an individual property focus to a chain-wide collaborative customer focus. The WINet system analyzes information such as gender, age, place of residence, and types of casino games played. Key customers and potential key customers are then identified, and promotional strategies are custom designed for them.

    Harrah's discovered that 30 percent of its customers generated 80 percent of company revenues. Use of this information resulted in a $100 million increase in revenue from key customers in the first two years.[37]

2. **Grow key accounts.** As Harrah's clearly demonstrated, key accounts usually offer more sales potential than is currently realized. Key accounts may split their businesses between several provider companies. A hotel property or a

hotel chain seldom obtains all or even a majority of a company's business. Increasing evidence indicates that companies are willing to reduce the number of hotel providers, and to give more of their business to a few hotels, if these companies meet their requirements for service and price.

Sometimes the sales force of a hotel becomes enamored with what appears to be a sales opportunity gold mine. Unfortunately, when this happens, traditional customers and traditional marketing channels that have consistently produced for the hotel are momentarily forgotten. This is the old and familiar phenomenon of "the grass is always greener on the other side of the fence."

The sales departments of many U.S. hotels thought they had discovered a "sure-fire" client that would fill their hotel rooms. Organizers of soccer's World Cup convinced hotels to reserve large quantities of rooms for thousands of anticipated fans. Some luxury hotels blocked off up to 1,000 room nights only to find that demand did not materialize, thus requiring them to release 50 to 80 percent of the reserved rooms.

Hyatt International Sales Vice President Craig Parsons later described previous demand predictions as ludicrous. "We lost a lot of rooms that will not be resold because they have been out of the inventory too long," said Parsons. "It's the busy summer season and we did not need to have these rooms out of inventory because we could have sold them anyway."[38]

In addition to negating probable sales, hotels blocking rooms may have infuriated good customers who were unable to book reservations and probably selected another hotel. It is possible that some of the guests may be difficult to recapture, particularly if they liked the competitor's hotel.

3. **Grow selected marginal accounts.**   Selected marginal accounts can become key accounts if given sufficient time and a consistent level of service. They are currently marginal accounts for a variety of reasons, such as the following:

- Experimenting or sampling your product or service. If they like it, they might provide substantially more business.

- Have received poor service in the past and therefore use your services only when necessary.

- Account manager changes have resulted in splitting the business between various hospitality firms.

- Comfortable with your service but competitors have acquired the bulk of their business through better follow-up.

4. **Eliminate selected marginal accounts.**   Unfortunately, some accounts result in net losses for a hospitality company. These negative-yield customers should be identified and eliminated whenever possible. It may be difficult to eliminate these customers due to an inability to identify them when the order of reservation is placed. A professional sales force has the responsibility to remove these customers from its list of prospects or active accounts, and refrain from future sales calls or sales promotions directed to them.

5. **Retain selected marginal accounts but provide lower-cost sales support.**   Many accounts represent infrequent purchases or low-yield business. These accounts cannot bear the cost of personalized sales calls or expensive promotions. A common method of dealing with these accounts is to assign them to an inside sales force. These salespeople don't make field calls but instead interact with customers via telephone, telemarketing, catalogs, direct mail, and fax machines.

6. **Obtain new business from selected prospects.**   The process of obtaining new accounts is costly and time consuming. Experienced salespeople know that it often requires five or more sales calls to obtain the business of a prospect. The cost of making a single sales call may be several hundred dollars when all costs are considered, such as travel expenses, salary, and benefits to the salesperson. The high cost of obtaining a new customer dictates that this person must have the potential to contribute significantly to profits. It is inefficient and nonproductive to pursue sales prospects who have little or no likelihood of ever providing significant returns to the company.

Sales Force Tactics: Principles of Personal Selling

We turn now to the purpose of a sales force: to sell. Personal selling is an ancient art. Effective salespersons have more than instinct. They are trained in tactics to achieve sales success. Selling today is a profession that involves mastering and applying a set of principles.

Today's companies spend hundreds of millions of dollars each year to train their salespeople in the art of selling. All the sales training approaches try to convert a salesperson from being a passive order taker to an active order getter.

In training salespeople to acquire signed orders (contracts), there are two basic approaches: a sales-oriented approach and a customer-oriented approach. The first trains the salesperson in high-pressure selling techniques, such as those often used in selling automobiles. The techniques include exaggerating the product's merits, criticizing competitive products, using a slick presentation, selling yourself, and offering some price concession to get the order on the spot. This form of selling assumes that customers are not likely to buy except under pressure, that they are influenced by a slick presentation and ingratiating manners, and that they will not be sorry after signing the order, or if they are, it doesn't matter.

The other approach trains salespeople in customer problem solving. The salesperson learns how to listen and question in order to identify customer needs and come up with good product solutions. Presentation skills are made secondary to customer-need analysis skills. The approach assumes that customers have latent needs that constitute company opportunities, that they appreciate constructive suggestions, and that they will be loyal to sales representatives who have their long-term interests at heart. The problem solver is a much more congruent concept for the salesperson under the marketing concept than the hard seller or order taker.

We examine briefly eight major aspects of personal selling.

Prospecting and Qualifying

The first step in the selling process is to identify prospects. Although the company will try to supply leads, sales representatives need skill in developing their own. Leads can be developed in the following ways:

- Through call-ins
- Having a booth at appropriate travel or trade shows
- Participating in international travel missions
- Asking current customers for the names of prospects
- Cultivating other referral sources, such as suppliers, dealers, noncompeting sales representatives, bankers, and trade association executives
- Through leads generated by the chain
- Joining organizations to which prospects belong
- Engaging in speaking and writing activities that will draw attention
- Examining data sources (newspapers, directories) in search of names
- Using the telephone and mail to find leads
- Dropping in unannounced on various offices (cold canvassing)
- Conducting a sales blitz

It is important not to overlook leads from internal sources. For example, working with the accounts payable department, a salesperson can find suppliers that may be sources of business. The reservations department should be trained to make inquiries of guests representing companies to find out if more business exists from those companies. Front-desk staff should talk with guests representing new companies and pass sales leads to the sales department. Prospecting internally and externally should be done daily. Once prospects have been identified, they need to be qualified.[39]

Sales representatives need skill in screening out poor leads. Prospects can be qualified by examining their financial ability, volume of business, special requirements, location, and likelihood of continuous business. The salesperson might phone or write to prospects before deciding whether to visit them.

Preapproach

The salesperson needs to learn as much as possible about the prospect company (what it needs, who is involved in the purchase decision) and its buyers (their personal characteristics and buying styles). The salesperson should set call objectives, which might be to qualify the prospect or gather information, or to make an immediate sale. Another task is to decide on the best approach, which might be a personal visit, a phone call, or a letter. Do not depend solely on e-mail as many e-mail messages are ignored. The best timing should be thought out because many prospects are busy at certain times.

Approach

The salesperson should know how to greet the buyer to get the relationship off to a good start. This involves the salesperson's appearance, the opening lines, and the follow-up remarks. The opening line should be positive, for example, "Mr. Smith, I am Alice Jones from the ABC Hotel Company. My company and I appreciate your willingness to see me. I will do my best to make this visit profitable and worthwhile for you and your company." This might be followed by key questions and active listening to understand the buyer and his or her needs.

Presentation and Demonstration

The salesperson now tells the product "story" to the buyer, following the AIDA formula of gaining *a*ttention, holding *i*nterest, arousing *d*esire, and obtaining *a*ction. The salesperson emphasizes customer benefits throughout, bringing in product features as evidence of these benefits. A benefit is any advantage, such as lower cost, less work, or more profit for the buyer. A feature is a product characteristic, such as weight or size. A common selling mistake is to dwell on product features (a product orientation) instead of customer benefits (a market orientation).

A need-satisfaction approach to selling starts with a search for the customer's real needs by encouraging the customer to do most of the talking. This approach calls for good listening and problem-solving skills. The salesperson takes on the role of a knowledgeable business consultant, hoping to help the customer save money or make more money.

Negotiation

Much of business-to-business selling involves negotiating skills. The two parties need to reach agreement on the price and other terms of sale. Salespersons need to win the order without making deep concessions that will hurt profitability.

Although price is the most frequently negotiated issue, other issues include quality of goods and services offered, purchase volume, and responsibility for financing, risk taking, and promotion. The number of negotiation issues is virtually unlimited.

Unfortunately, far too many hotel salespeople rely almost exclusively on price as their negotiating tool. Even worse, they often begin negotiating from an already discounted price rather than from rack rates. Negotiations should always begin with rack rates, and price concessions should be given only when absolutely essential. Numerous bargaining tools exist, such as upgrades, complimentary tickets for the ski lift or golf courses, first-class coffee breaks instead of coffee and soft drinks, airport pickup, and use of hotel services such as the fitness center. A hotel sales force might package these amenities into bundles of services and give them names such as the President's Package, the Connoisseur's Package, and the Executive Package.

Sales force members should be taught to negotiate using services or bundled services as the primary negotiating tool rather than price. Table 15–2 shows the

Marketing Highlight	Identifying and Qualifying Clients Pays Off for Cruise Line Salespeople

15–2

Cruise Line

The use of segmentation analysis to assist sales reps to become marketing consultants to travel agents.

Opportunity

Strong competition from specialty and "blue water" cruise products was eroding the passenger base of a major cruise line. Cabin revenue was slipping due to declining occupancy rates. In the past, the cruise line had successfully used direct mail for marketing promotions. But recent marketing returns, as measured by marketing dollars spent per cabin booking, showed this approach was no longer profitable. The cruise line needed a more effective way to identify and target its most profitable customers and prospects.

Implementation

First the cruise line needed to identify its best prospects. The cruise line turned to Claritas to segment and profile its customer database at the block group level. The profiling showed that the cruise line's best prospects were neighbors of past passengers. To identify these prospects by neighborhood, Claritas appended block group codes to each customer and prospect record.

The segmentation revealed that one segment of the customer database accounted for nearly half of the cruise line's past passengers for one of its summer cruise destinations. The travel behavior of this segment was analyzed for the summer cruise period. The analysis included indexing all cruise purchase components by this segment, including itinerary, booking period, cabin class, per diem, the selected offer redeemed, and specific buying patterns (e.g., travel agency bookings). This information was then integrated with the customer and prospect profiles.

The detailed customer profile was used to guide all aspects of the cruise line's marketing campaigns. The components of the profile determined the offer, the timing, and the message. The profile also identified the print publications, Internet travel sites, radio stations, and television shows the targeted segment preferred. These were the media channels through which the message was delivered. Last, the "most profitable customer" profile was matched against prospect lists to identify the most qualified lists.

The customer profile was also used to develop a "conversion index" for the cruise line's general collateral fulfillment. Each request for cruise line literature was scored against the conversion index to see how closely it matched the most profitable customer profile. Here the premise "birds of a feather flock together" comes into play. The requestor's address was profiled at the block group level. If this profile was a close match to the targeted customer profile, the request scored a high index. This indicated a strong prospect, and the expensive full-colored cruise line brochure was mailed. Requests whose profiles did not match the targeted customer profile scored a low index, and the prospect was mailed a less elaborate, low-cost flyer. This application of customer profiling enabled the cruise line to streamline its marketing budget, freeing up more resources for lead generation such as cooperative marketing activities with travel agents.

Analysis revealed that 96 percent of cruise passengers purchase tickets through a travel agent. Claritas developed detailed thematic maps targeting the areas where the cruise line's best prospects were concentrated. The cruise line's sales staff used the maps in their presentations to travel agents to educate them about the benefits of customer segmentation and target database marketing. By sharing the knowledge of customer segmentation, the sales reps served as marketing consultants to their travel agent partners, which significantly enhanced these important relationships.

Results

The application of customer segmentation and profiling was a success. Using the information provided by Claritas's customer segmentation analysis, the cruise line launched a special direct-mail promotion for one of its summer cruise destinations. Only those prospect households that fit the profile of their most profitable customers were targeted with the promotional offer. The result? Cabin occupancy rates jumped 15 percent and revenue increased by 20 percent. Follow-up analysis of the campaign indicated ROI over 40 percent.

Source: Case Study Cruise Line—Boosting with Segmentation, www.claritas.com/ (accessed March 19, 2008), pp. 1–3. Claritas is a Nielsen Company specializing in market segmentation research information. It identifies itself as "the world's leader in demographics."

possible difference in service package negotiations versus price negotiation. It is easy to see that the hotel benefits by offering a package of services rather than a price discount at all levels other than a 10 percent discount. Sales force members must understand the economic value of these kinds of tradeoffs before they enter into the negotiation process.

TABLE 15–2

Hotel Negotiation Cost Comparison: Offering a Service Package Versus Price

	50 Guests at 3 Nights Each	
	Cost/Guest	*Total Cost*
President's Package		
Airport pickup and delivery limousine service	$20	$1,000
Bottle of champagne in room	$25	$1,250
AV technician for meeting	2½ days at $50/hour × 20 hours	$1,000
		$3,250
Price Discounts	**Total Revenue Potential**	
Rack rate ($200/night; 50 guests at three nights each)	$3,000	
Price Cut (%)	*Revenue Lost ($)*	
10	3,000	
20	4,500	
30	6,750	
40	9,000	
50	11,250	

Sales people who find themselves in bargaining situations need certain traits and skills to be effective. The most important traits are preparation and planning skills, knowledge of subject matter being negotiated, ability to think clearly and rapidly under pressure and uncertainty, ability to express thoughts verbally, listening skills, judgment and general intelligence, integrity, ability to persuade others, and patience. These will help the sales person in knowing when and how to negotiate.[40]

WHEN TO NEGOTIATE   Consider the following circumstances in which negotiation in the hospitality industry is an appropriate procedure for concluding a sale:[41]

1.   When many factors bear not only on price but also on quality and service.

2.   When business risks cannot be accurately predetermined.

Negotiation is appropriate wherever a zone of agreement exists.[42] A zone of agreement exists when there are simultaneously overlapping acceptable outcomes for the parties.

FORMULATING A BARGAINING STRATEGY   Bargaining involves preparing a strategic plan before bargaining begins and making good tactical decisions during the bargaining sessions. A bargaining strategy can be defined as a commitment to an overall approach that has a good chance of achieving the negotiator's objectives. For example, some negotiators pursue a hard strategy with opponents, whereas others maintain that a soft strategy yields more favorable results.

The sales force of a hotel or resort is in a position to use negotiating skills nearly every day of their professional lives. Their negotiation process can be enhanced by understanding the negotiating strengths and weaknesses of the client, as shown in Table 15–3.

TABLE 15–3
Examples of Hotel Customer's Negotiation Strengths and Weaknesses

Strengths	Weaknesses
1. Provide many guests.	1. Provide few guests.
2. Come in low or shoulder seasons.	2. Come in prime season.
3. Stay low-occupancy nights.	3. Stay high-occupancy nights.
4. Bring quality guests.	4. Bring undesirable guests.
5. Provide cross-purchase potential.	5. Provide little or no cross-sale potential.
6. Purchase upscale rooms.	6. Purchase lowest priced rooms.

BARGAINING TACTICS DURING NEGOTIATIONS Negotiators use a variety of tactics when bargaining. Bargaining tactics can be defined as maneuvers to be made at specific points in the bargaining process. Threats, bluffs, last-chance offers, hard initial offers, and other tactics occur in bargaining.

Experts in negotiation have offered advice that is consistent with their strategy of principles negotiation. Their first piece of tactical advice concerns what should be done if the other party is more powerful. By identifying your alternatives if a settlement is not reached, it sets a standard against which any offer can be measured. It protects you from being pressured into accepting unfavorable terms from a more powerful opponent.[43]

Another tactic comes into play when the opposing party insists on arguing his or her position instead of his or her interests and attacks your proposals or person. Although the tendency is to push back hard when pushed, the better tactic is to deflect the attack from the person and direct it against the problem. Look at the interests that motivated the opposing party's position and invent options that can satisfy both parties' interests. Invite the opposing party's criticism and advice ("If you were in my position, what would you do?").

Another set of bargaining tactics involves opposition tactics that are intended to deceive, distort, or otherwise influence the bargaining. What tactic should be used when the other side uses a threat, or a take-it-or-leave-it tactic, or seats the other party on the side of the table with the sun in his or her eyes? A negotiation should recognize the tactic, raise the issue explicitly, and question the tactic's legitimacy and desirability—in other words, negotiate over it. Negotiating the use of the tactic follows the same principled negotiation procedure: Question the tactic, ask why the tactic is being used, or suggest alternative courses of action to pursue. If this fails, resort to your best alternative to a negotiated agreement and terminate the negotiation until the other side ceases to employ these tactics. Meeting these tactics by defending principles is more productive than counterattacking with tricky tactics.

Overcoming Objections

Customers almost always pose objections during the presentation or when asked for the order. Their resistance can be psychological or logical. Psychological resistance includes resistance to interference, preference for established hotel or airline, apathy, reluctance to giving up something, unpleasant associations about the other person, predetermined ideas, dislike of making decisions, and neurotic attitude toward money. Logical resistance might consist of objections to the price or certain product or company characteristics. To handle these objections, the salesperson maintains a position approach, asks the buyer to clarify the objection, denies the validity of the objection, or turns the objection into a reason for buying. The salesperson needs training in the broader skills of negotiation, of which handling objections is a part.

Closing

Now the salesperson attempts to close the sale. Some salespeople do not get to this stage or do not do it well. They lack confidence or feel uncomfortable about asking for the order or do not recognize the right psychological moment to close the sale. Salespersons need to know how to recognize closing signals from the buyer, including physical actions, statements or comments, and questions. Salespersons can use one of several closing techniques. They can ask for the order, recapitulate the points of agreement, offer to help the secretary write up the order, ask whether the buyers want A or B, get the buyer to make minor choices, or indicate what the buyer will lose if the order is not placed now. The salesperson might offer the buyer specific inducements.

Follow-Up/Maintenance

This last step is necessary if the salesperson wants to ensure customer satisfaction and repeat business. Immediately after closing, the salesperson should complete any necessary details on delivery time, purchase terms, and other matters. "Follow-up or foul-up" is a slogan of most successful salespeople. The salesperson should develop an account maintenance plan to make sure that the customer is not forgotten or lost.

Motivating a Professional Sales Force

Some sales representatives put forth their best effort without any special coaching from management. To them, selling is the most fascinating job in the world. They are ambitious and self-starters. But the majority of sales representatives require encouragement and special incentives to work at their best level. This is especially true of field selling, for the following reasons:

- *Nature of the job.* The selling job is one of frequent frustration. Sales representatives usually work alone, their hours are irregular, and they are often away from home. They confront aggressive, competing sales representatives; they have an inferior status relative to the buyer; they often do not have the authority to do what is necessary to win an account; they lose large orders that they have worked hard to obtain.

- *Human nature.* Most people operate below capacity in the absence of special incentives, such as financial gain or social recognition.

- *Personal problems.* Sales representatives are occasionally preoccupied with personal problems, such as sickness in the family, marital discord, or debt.

    Here is a basic model of motivating sales representatives:[44]

    motivation → effort → performance → rewards → satisfaction

    The model implies the following:

1. Sales managers must be able to convince salespeople that they can sell more by working harder or by being trained to work smarter.

2. Sales managers must be able to convince salespeople that the rewards for better performance are worth the extra effort.

Sales Force Compensation

To attract and retain sales representatives, the company has to develop an attractive compensation package. Sales representatives would like income regularity, extra reward for an above-average performance, and fair payment for experience and longevity. Management would like to achieve control, economy, and simplicity. Management objectives, such as economy, conflict with sales representatives' objectives, such as financial security.

The level of compensation must bear some relation to the going market price for the type of sales job and required abilities. If the market price for salespeople is well defined, the individual firm has little choice but to pay the going rate. The market price for salespeople, however, is seldom well defined. Data on the average take-home pay of competitors' sales representatives can be misleading because of significant variations in the average seniority and ability levels of the competitors' sales forces.

The company must next determine the components of compensation: a fixed amount, a variable amount, expenses, and fringe benefits. The fixed amount, which might be salary, is intended to satisfy the sales representatives' need for income stability. The variable amount, which might be commissions, bonuses, or profit sharing, is intended to stimulate and reward greater effort. Expense allowances enable the sales representatives to meet the expenses involved in travel, lodging, dining, and entertainment; fringe benefits such as paid vacation, sickness or accident benefits, pensions, and life insurance are intended to provide security and job satisfaction. Fixed and variable compensations give rise to three basic types of sales force compensation plans: straight salary, straight commissions, and combination salary and commission.

Many companies in the hospitality industry suffer from high sales force turnover. A variety of reasons have been given to explain this situation, such as burnout. A survey of college graduates preparing to enter the hospitality industry ranked salary as number 10 among variables relating to what they wanted in a job.[45] A different study of young managers who left hospitality careers demonstrated that money was indeed important. Pay-related issues were the second most common reason for leaving, following long hours and inconvenient scheduling as the primary reason. One respondent wrote, "I had poor pay, high stress, low praise and recognition, and worked 75 to 80 hours a week, all for the chance to be a GM in 10 or 15 years with the same job characteristics."[46]

The importance of monetary rewards to a hospitality sales force must not be minimized. These people are expected to maintain a large fashionable wardrobe, to work long hours, experience stress, and often give up family experiences for the sake of their career. Under these circumstances, monetary reward becomes very important.

Supplementary Motivators

Companies use additional motivators to stimulate sales force effort. Periodic sales meetings provide a social occasion, a break from routine, a chance to meet and talk with "company brass," and a chance to air feelings and to identify with a larger group. Sales meetings are an important communication and motivational tool.[47] They can also be used for training in subjects such as how to make effective presentations.[48] Thus, the sales meeting can and should assume increased importance to the sales force.

Companies also sponsor sales contests to spur the sales force to a special selling effort above what would normally be expected. The contest should present a reasonable opportunity for salespeople to win. If only a few salespersons can win or almost everyone can win, it will fail to spur additional effort. The sales contest period should not be announced in advance or else some salespersons will defer some sales to the beginning of the period; also, some may pad their sales during the period with customer promises to buy that do not materialize after the contest period ends.

Sales managers of hotels and resorts sometimes offer vacations at sister properties for winners of a sales contest. When the winners visit a sister property, they are introduced to the sales department and often learn new techniques. In turn, this information is transmitted to others when the winners return and give a report in the next sales meeting.

Evaluation and Control of a Professional Sales Force

Sales Quotas

Many companies set sales quotas prescribing what their sales representatives should sell during the year. Compensation is often tied to the degree of quota fulfillment. Sales quotas are developed from the annual marketing plan. The company first prepares a sales forecast. This forecast becomes the basis for planning production, workforce size, and financial requirements. Then management establishes sales quotas for its regions and territories, which typically add up to more than the sales forecast. Sales quotas are often set higher than the sales forecast in order to stretch sales managers and salespeople to perform at their best level.

The sales manager assigns the area's quota to each of the area's sales people. There are three schools of thought on quota setting. The high-quota school sets quotas that are higher than what most sales representatives will achieve but are attainable. Its adherents believe that high quotas spur extra effort. The modest-quota school sets quotas that a majority of the sales force can achieve. Its adherents feel that the sales force will accept the quotas as fair, attain them, and gain confidence. The variable-quota school thinks that individual differences among sales representatives warrant high quotas for some and modest quotas for others.

Developing Norms for Salespeople

New sales representatives should be given more than a territory, a compensation package, and training. They need supervision.

Companies vary in how closely they direct their sales representatives. Those who are paid mostly on commission generally receive less supervision. Those who are salaried and must cover definite accounts are likely to receive substantial supervision.

The number of calls that an average salesperson makes during a day has been decreasing. The downward trend is due to the increased use of technology. It is also due to difficulties in reaching prospects because of traffic congestion, busy prospect schedules, and other complexities of contemporary business.

Companies often decide how many calls to make a year on particular-sized accounts. Most companies classify customers into A, B, and C accounts, reflecting the sales volume, profit potential, and growth potential of the account. A accounts might receive nine calls a year; B, six calls; and C, three calls. The call norms depend on expected account profitability.

Regardless of how a sales force is structured, individual salespeople must classify their customer base. A salesperson responsible for channel intermediaries, such as tour operators and travel agents, quickly learns that not all are capable of producing the same sales volume/profit. This is equally true for a salesperson who has responsibility for the conference/meeting segment and for those responsible for national accounts.

Omni International Hotels emphasizes account planning with its sales force. A former president, Jon Canas, told a Harvard professor in a taped interview that not all prospects may be contacted in a particular year because they do not qualify as the best target customers. However, it is important to know the second- and third-tier prospects so that they can be contacted if a slowdown occurs within the top targeted groups.[49]

Companies often specify how much time their sales force should spend prospecting for new accounts. Companies set up prospecting standards for a number of reasons. If left alone, many sales representatives spend most of their time with current customers. Current customers are better known quantities. Sales representatives can depend on them for some business, whereas a prospect might never deliver any business. Unless sales representatives are rewarded for opening new accounts, they might avoid new account development.

Using Sales Time Efficiently

Sales representatives need to know how to use their time efficiently. One tool is the annual call schedule, showing which customers and prospects to call on in which months and which activities to carry out.

Actual face-to-face selling time can amount to as little as 25 percent of total working time.[50] Companies are constantly seeking ways to improve sales force productivity. Their methods take the form of training sales representatives in the use of "phone power," simplifying record-keeping forms, and using the computer to develop call and routing plans and to supply customer and competitive information.

Managing Trade Shows

Trade shows are commonly used as a means of generating sales leads, keeping in touch with commercial customers, and writing business. Members of the hospitality industry participate in many trade shows, ranging from local/regional ones to international travel missions sponsored by visitor destinations, travel associations, and government departments or ministries of tourism.

Unfortunately, the cost/return effectiveness of trade shows is often placed in peril or disregarded through lack of effective planning and control. The conclusions of a study of hospitality trade show exhibitors were that "it is likely that the true marketing potential of trade shows is not being realized. Commitments to more effective planning would enhance the productivity of trade shows for most companies."[51]

Six steps were suggested to improve trade show effectiveness:

1. Construct a mailing list of prospects using in-house information of the list of expected visitors from the trade show management company.

2. Identify potential leads and communicate with them before the show.

3. Promote the show with incentives that reflect the company's theme, products, and services.

4. Send letters to prospective buyers, inviting them to make a personal contact at the show or at an alternative location.

5. Keep good records of visitor contacts made during the show.

6. Follow up with qualified prospects after the show.

Sales force control and training are also needed to ensure success. The following are items a sales manager should implement before a trade show:

1. Review trade show objectives with the sales force before the show.

2. Designate a trade show captain responsible for managing sales activities.

3. Designate times when certain salespersons are expected to work the booth.

4. Prohibit smoking, drinking, eating, and bunching together in the trade booth.

5. Show sales force members how to deal with complaining/difficult visitors, greet customers/prospects (particularly key ones), develop prospects, identify nonprospects, and process and use leads, business cards, competitive data, and customer/prospect information acquired at the show.

Other Control Techniques

Management obtains information about its sales representatives in several ways. One important source is sales reports. Additional information comes through personal observation, customers' letters and complaints, customer surveys, and conversations with other sales representatives.

Sales reports are divided between activity plans and write-ups of activity results. The best example of the former is the salesperson's work plan, which sales representatives submit a week or month in advance.

The plan describes intended calls and routing. This report leads the sales force to plan and schedule their activities, informs management of their whereabouts, and provides a basis for comparing their plans and accomplishments. Sales representatives can be evaluated on their ability to "plan their work and work their plan."

Many hospitality companies require their sales representatives to develop an annual territory marketing plan in which they outline their program for developing new accounts and increasing business from existing accounts. This type of report casts sales representatives into the role of marketing managers and profit centers. Sales representatives write up their completed activities on call reports. Call reports inform sales management of the salesperson's activities, indicate the status of specific customer accounts, and provide useful information for subsequent calls. Sales representatives also submit expense reports, new business reports, lost business reports, and reports on local business and economic conditions.

These reports provide raw data from which sales managers can extract key indicators of sales performance. The key indicators are (1) average number of sales calls per salesperson per day, (2) average sales call time per contact, (3) average revenue per sales call, (4) average cost per sales call, (5) entertainment cost per sales call, (6) percentage of orders per hundred sales calls, (7) number of new customers per period, (8) number of lost customers per period, and (9) sales force cost as a percentage of total sales. These indicators answer several useful questions. Are sales representatives making too few calls per day? Are they spending too much time per call? Are they spending too much on entertainment? Are they closing enough orders per one hundred calls? Are they producing enough new customers and holding on to the old customers?

Formal Evaluation of Performance

The sales force's reports along with other observations supply the raw materials for evaluating members of the sales force. Formal evaluation procedures lead to at least three benefits. First, management has to communicate its standards for judging sales performance. Second, management needs to gather comprehensive information about each salesperson. Third, sales representatives know that they will have to sit down one morning with the sales managers and explain their performance or failure to achieve certain goals.

SALESPERSON-TO-SALESPERSON COMPARISONS   One type of evaluation is to compare and rank the sales performance of a company's sales representatives. Such comparisons, however, can be misleading. Relative sales performance is meaningful only if there are no variations in territory market potential, workload, competition, company promotional effort, and so on. Furthermore, current sales are not the only success indicator. Management should also be interested in how much each sales representative contributes to current net profits.

CUSTOMER SATISFACTION EVALUATION   A salesperson might be very effective in producing sales but not rate high with customers. An increasing number of companies are measuring customer satisfaction not only with their product and customer-support service but with their salespeople. Company salespeople who score high on satisfying their customers can be given special recognition, awards, or bonuses.

QUALITATIVE EVALUATION OF SALES REPRESENTATIVES   Evaluations can also assess the salesperson's knowledge of the company, products, customers, competitors, territory, and responsibilities. The sales manager should also review any problems in motivation or compliance. The sales manager should check that the sales representatives know and observe company policies. Each company must develop its own evaluation procedure. Whatever procedure is chosen, it must be fair to the salesperson and the company. If members of a sales force feel they are being judged against incorrect norms, they will quickly become dissatisfied.

Hospitality sales is a profession and must be treated as such. It is very much to the advantage of any hospitality company to develop a professional, loyal, and contented sales force. Measurement of a salesperson's value and contribution must not be left to the last minute or to inappropriate standards and measures. No aspect of sales management is more important than developing and using the correct appraisal system for members of a professional sales force.

Regardless of what evaluation system is used, it must be tied to performance. Sales performance and company performance are inherently married. Professor Bill Quain has said, "I believe it is getting harder and harder to find employees who have the drive to sell, the drive to create profits, and the drive to satisfy customers by filling more of their needs with ever improving products and services."[52]

■■■ KEY TERMS

Allocating. Sales representatives decide on which customers to allocate scarce products to.

Communicating. Sales representatives communicate information about the company's products and services.

Information gathering. Sales representatives conduct market research and intelligence work and fill in a call report.

Prospecting. The process of searching for new accounts.

Selling. Sales representatives know the art of salesmanship: approaching, presenting, answering objections, and closing sales.

Servicing. Sales representatives provide various services to the customers: consulting on their problems, rendering technical assistance, arranging financing, and expediting delivery.

Targeting. Sales representatives decide how to allocate their scarce time among prospects and customers.

■■■ CHAPTER REVIEW

I. **Management of Professional Sales**

II. **Nature of Hospitality Sales**
   A. **Competitive analysis and competitive sets**

III. **Sales Force Objectives**
   A. **Sales volume**
      1. **Sales volume by selected segments**
      2. **Sales volume and price/margin mix**
   B. **Upselling and second-chance selling.** Excellent profit opportunities exist for hospitality companies, particularly hotels and resorts, to upgrade price and profit margins by selling higher-priced products such as suites through upselling. A related concept is second-chance selling.
   C. **Market share or market penetration.** These are two important objectives.
   D. **Product-specific objectives.** Occasionally, a sales force is charged with the specific responsibility to improve sales volume for specific product lines.

IV. **Sales Force Structure and Size**
   A. **Territorial-structured sales force.** Each sales representative is assigned an exclusive territory in which to represent the company's full line.
      1. **Territorial size.** Territories are designed to provide either equal sales potential or equal workload.

      2. **Territorial shape.** Territories are formed by combining smaller units until they add up to a territory of a given sales potential or workload.
   B. **Market-segment structured sales force.** Company structures its sales force based on market segments.
   C. **Market-channel structured sales force.** The importance of marketing intermediaries, such as wholesalers, tour operators, travel agencies, and junket reps, to the hospitality industry has created sales force structures to serve different marketing channels.
   D. **Customer-structured sales force.** A sales force is organized by market segment, such as the association market and the corporate market or by specific key customers.
   E. **Combination-structured sales force.** A large hotel might have a catering/banquet sales force (product), a convention/meeting sales force (market segment), a tour wholesales sales force (marketing intermediary), and a national accounts sales force (customer).
   F. **Determining sales force size**
      1. Customers are grouped into size classes according to their annual sales volume.

2. The desired call frequencies are established for each class.

3. The number of accounts in each size class is multiplied by the corresponding call frequency to arrive at the total workload for the country in sales calls per year.

4. The average number of calls a sales representative can make per year is determined.

5. The number of sales representatives needed is determined by dividing the total annual calls required by the average annual calls made by a sales representative.

G. **Telephone sales**

V. Organizing the Sales Department

A. **Inside sales force.** The inside sales force includes technical support persons, sales assistants, and telemarketers.

B. **Field sales force.** The field sales force includes commissioned reps, salaried reps, and sales team.

C. **Team sales**

VI. Relationship Marketing and Strategic Alliances. The art of creating a closer working relationship and interdependence between the people in two organizations.

A. **Strategic alliances.** Alliances are relationships between independent parties that agree to cooperate but still retain separate identities.

B. **Why strategic alliances are necessary.** Globalization, complicated customer needs, large customers with multilocations, the need for technology, highly interdependent vendor/buyer relationship, intensified competition, and low profitability within the hospitality industry.

VII. Recruiting and Selecting Sales Representatives. The effective salesperson has two basic qualities: (1) empathy, the ability to feel as the customer does, and (2) ego drive, a strong personal need to make the sales.

A. **When to recruit.** There are three models: recruit and train salespeople in a batch process, recruit only as needed for replacement and growth, and

always recruit.

B. **Establish a profile of desired characteristics matching the corporate culture.**

C. **Matching career acquisitions with corporate objectives.**

D. **Training.** There are three types of training: product/service training; policies, procedures, and planning training; and sales techniques training.

E. **Directing sales representatives.** Responsibilities are developing norms for customer calls; developing norms for prospect calls; and using sales time effectively (travel, food and break, waiting, selling, administration).

VIII. Managing the Sales Force

A. **Selecting sales strategies.** The following are six general sales strategies:

1. Prevent erosion of key accounts

2. Grow key accounts

3. Grow selected marginal accounts

4. Eliminate selected marginal accounts

5. Retain selected marginal accounts, but provide lower-cost sales support

6. Obtain new business from selected prospects

B. **Sales force tactics: principles of personal selling.** These are prospecting and qualifying, preapproach, approach, presentation and demonstration, negotiation, overcoming objections, closing, and follow-up/maintenance.

1. **Basic model.** Motivation, effort, performance, rewards, satisfaction

2. **Sales quotas and supplementary motivator**

C. **Motivating a professional sales force**

1. Sales force competition

2. Supplementary motivators

D. **Evaluating sales representatives.** There are several means of formal evaluation of performance: sales-to-salesperson comparisons, current-to-past sales comparisons; customer satisfaction evaluation; and qualitative evaluation of sales representatives.

■■■ DISCUSSION QUESTIONS

1. Why should companies be concerned about key or national accounts?

2. What are the most common methods of structuring a sales force?

3. Discuss the importance of establishing sales objectives and the various kinds of sales force objectives common to the hospitality industry.

4. Many people feel they do not have the ability to be successful salespeople. What role does training play in helping someone develop selling ability?

5. Discuss the process of negotiation and how sales force members can use it effectively.

6. Good salespeople are familiar with their competitors' products as well as their own. What would you do if your company expected you to sell a product that you thought was inferior to the competition's? Why?

7. It has been said there are two parts to every sale: the part performed by the salesperson and the part performed for the salesperson by his or her organization. What should the company provide for the salesperson to help increase total sales? How does the sales manager's job differ from the sales rep's job?

8. A district sales manager voiced the following complaint at a sales meeting: "The average salesperson costs our company $40,000 in compensation and expenses. Why can't we buy a few less $40,000 full-page ads in *Time* magazine and use the money to hire more people? Surely one individual working for a year can sell more products than a one-page ad in one issue of *Time.*" Evaluate this argument.

■■■ EXPERIENTIAL EXERCISES

Do the following:

Conduct an interview with a salesperson for a hospitality or tourism organization. Ask the salesperson about the job. Find out what a typical day is like, and what they like and dislike about the job. Ask how they feel technology will affect the sales department in the future. You may of course ask other questions that are of interest to you. Write up your finding in a report.

■■■ INTERNET EXERCISE

Find a hotel Web site that has a section for meeting planners. Does this site appear to be taking the place of a salesperson or offering assistance to the sales department? Include the names of the sites you have visited in your response.

■■■ REFERENCES

1. Donna J. Owens, "To Offset Their Seasonality, Canada's Resorts Should Stretch Their Seasons by Appealing to Multiple Market Segments," *Cornell Hotel and Restaurant Administration Quarterly,* 35, no. 5 (1994): 29.

2. Ibid., p. 30.

3. Lisa C. Weiss, "Days Inns of America: To Give 1400 General Managers One Year Membership to Hospitality Sales and Marketing Associations International," *Business Travel News* (November 1993): 10.

4. Howard Feiertag, "Database Marketing Proves Helpful in Group Sales," *Hotel and Motel Management* (March 8, 1993): 14.

5. Jin-Young Kim and Linda Canina, "Competitive Sets for Lodging Properties" *Cornell Hospitality Quarterly,* 52, no. 1 (February 2011): 20–32.

6. Chekitan Dev, Kevin Zheng Zhou, Jim Brown, and Sanjeev Agarwal; "Customer Orientation or Competitor Orientation," *Cornell Hospitality Quarterly* (February 2009), 50, no. 1: 25.

7. Owens, "To Offset Their Seasonality."

8. William J. Quain and Stephen M. LeBruto, "Second-Chance Selling," *Cornell Hotel and Restaurant Administration Quarterly,* 35, no. 5 (1994): 81.

9. Peter Rainsford, "Selecting and Monitoring Hotel Management Companies," *Cornell Hotel and Restaurant Administration Quarterly,* 35, no. 3 (1994): 34.

10. Boca Raton Resort, http://www.bocaresort.com/PremierClub/PremierClubFeatures.aspx (accessed December 20, 2004); Michael P. Sim and Burritt M. Chase, "Enhancing Resort Profitability with Membership Programs," *Cornell Hotel and Restaurant Administration Quarterly,* 34, no. 8 (1993): 59–62.

11. "Cruise Lines, Boosting Bookings with Segmentation, Case Studies and Clients," www.claritas.com (August 2004).

12. Christopher Schulz, "Hotel and Travel Agents: The New Partnership," *Cornell Hotel and Restaurant Administration Quarterly,* 35, no. 2 (1994): 45.

13. Taketosh Yamazaki, "Tokyo Hotel Construction Push Roger On," *Tokyo Business Today,* 59, no. 3 (1991): 50–51.

14. William A. Kaven and Myrtle Allardyce, "Dalmahoy's Strategy for Success," *Cornell Hotel and Restaurant Administration Quarterly,* 35, no. 6 (1994): 86–89.

15. Alexandra Paraskevar, Ioannis Katsogridakis, Rob Law, and Dimitros Buhalis, "Search Engine Marketing: Transforming Search Engines into Hotel Distribution Channels," *Cornell Hospitality Quarterly,* 52, no. 2 (May 2011): 200.

16. "Intel to Handle Reservations for Omni," *Business Travel News* (November 22, 1993): 15.

17. Sheryl E. Kimes and Douglas C. Lord, "Wholesalers and Caribbean Resort Hotels," *Cornell Hotel and Restaurant Administration Quarterly,* 35, no. 5 (1994): 75.

18. Phillip R. Mogle, "Planner Under Siege," *Successful Meetings* (September 1990): 76.

19. Robert A. Meyer, "Understanding Telemarketing for Hotels," *Cornell Hotel and Restaurant Administration Quarterly,* 28, no. 2 (1987): 26.

20. Barbara Jean Ross, "Training: Key to Effective Reservations," *Cornell Hotel and Restaurant Administration Quarterly,* 31, no. 3 (1990): 71–79.

21. Ibid., p. 79.

22. See Neil Rackham, *SPIN Selling* (New York: McGraw-Hill, 1988); Frank V. Cespedes, Stephen X. Doyle, and Robert J. Freedman, "Teamwork for Today's Selling," *Harvard Business Review* (March/April 1989): 44–54, 58.

23. Fred Conner, "Resorts Makeup Means Sweet Smell of Success for Long-Term Client," *Cornell Hotel and Restaurant Administration Quarterly,* 35, no. 3 (1994): 9.

24. S. Dev Chekitan and Saul Klein, "Strategic Alliances in the Hotel Industry," *Cornell Hotel and Restaurant Administration Quarterly,* 34, no. 1 (1993): 43.

25. Bill Gillette, "HFS Carlson Strikes Strategic Alliance," *Hotel and Motel Marketing,* 208, no. 2 (1993): 1, 26.

26. Bill Gillette, "Hostmark Making Its Mark," *Hotel and Motel Management,* 207, no. 1 (1992): 3, 34.

27. George H. Lucas, Jr., A. Parasuraman, Robert A. Davis, and Ben M. Enis, "An Empirical Study of Salesforce Turnover," *Journal of Marketing* (July 1987): 34–59.

28. See Charles Garfield, *Peak Performers: The New Heroes of American Business* (New York: Avon Books, 1986; "What Makes a Supersalesperson?" *Sales and Marketing Management* (August 23, 1984): 86; "What Makes a Top Performer?" *Sales and Marketing Management* (May 1989); Timothy J. Trow, "The Secret of a Good Hire: Profiling," *Sales and Marketing Management* (May 1990): 44–55.

29. David Moyer and Herbert A. Greenberg, "What Makes a Good Salesman?" *Harvard Business Review* (July/August 1964): 119–125.

30. "Classified Post," *South China Morning Post,* 49, no. 193 (1993): 3.

31. K. Douglas Hoffman and John E. G. Bateson, *Essentials of Services Marketing* (Fort Worth, TX: Dryden Press, 1997), pp. 92–93.

32. Thomas N. Ingram, Charles H. J. Sobuepher, and Don Hutson, "Why Salespeople Fail," *Industrial Marketing Management,* 21, no. 3 (1992): 225–230.

33. Judi Brownell, "Listening: The Toughest Management Skills," *Cornell Hotel and Restaurant Administration Quarterly,* 27, no. 4 (1987): 64–71.

34. Howard Feiertag, "Sales Directors Build Productivity and Profitability," *Hotel and Motel Management,* 207, no. 19 (1992): 14.

35. David Chelan, "Revving Up E-Learning to Drive Sales," *EContent* (March 2006): 28–32. Also see "E-Learning Evolves into Mature Training Tool," *Call Center Magazine* (April 2007): 18; "E-Learning Evolve into Mature Training Tool," *T + D* (April 2006): 20; Rebecca Aronauer, "The Classroom vs. E-Learning," *Sales &*

Marketing Management (October 2006): 21; and Harry Sheff, "Agent Training Beyond the Classroom," *Call Center Magazine* (April 2007): 18.

36. Florence Berger, Mark D. Fulford, and Michelle Krazmien, "Human Resource Management in the 21st Century: Predicting Partnerships for Profit," *Hospitality Research Journals,* 17, no. 1 (1993): 90–91.

37. Vincent P. Magnini, Earl D. Honeycutt, Jr., and Sharon K. Hodge, "Data Mining for Hotel Firms: Use and Limitations," *Cornell Hotel and Restaurant Administration Quarterly,* 44, no. 2 (2003): 97.

38. "U.S. Hoteliers Fail to Net Enough World Cup Trade," *Travel Trade Gazette,* U.S. and Ireland (June 1, 1994): 32.

39. Howard Feiertag, "Different People Should Perform Sales and Marketing Jobs," *Hotel and Motel Management* (February 4, 2002): 24.

40. For additional reading, see Howard Raiffa, *The Art and Science of Negotiation* (Cambridge, MA: Harvard University Press, 1982); Samuel B. Bacharach and Edward J. Lawler, *Bargaining Power, Tactics, and Outcome* (San Francisco, CA: Jossey-Bass, 1981); Herb Cohen, *You Can Negotiate Anything* (New York: Bantam Books, 1980); Gerald I. Nierenberg, *The Art of Negotiating* (New York: Pocket Books, 1984).

41. Lamar Lee and Donald W. Dobler, *Purchasing and Materials Management* (New York: McGraw-Hill, 1977), pp. 146–147.

42. This discussion of zone of agreement is fully developed in Raiffa, *Art and Science of Negotiation.*

43. Roger Fisher and William Ury, *Getting to Yes: Negotiating Agreement Without Giving In* (Boston, MA: Houghton Mifflin, 1981).

44. See Gilbert A. Churchill, Jr., Neil A. Ford, and Orville C. Walker, Jr., *Sales Force Management: Planning, Implementation, and Control* (Homewood, IL: Richard D. Irwin, 1985).

45. See Ken W. McCleary and Pamela A. Weaver, "The Job Offer: What Today's Graduates Want," *Cornell Hotel and Restaurant Administration Quarterly,* 28, no. 4 (1988): 28–31.

46. David V. Pavesic and Robert A. Brymer, "Job Satisfaction: What's Happening to Young Managers," *Cornell Hotel and Restaurant Administration Quarterly,* 30, no. 4 (1990): 90–96.

47. Richard Cavalier, *Sales Meetings That Work* (Homewood, IL: Dow Jones-Irwin, 1983).

48. See Joyce I. Nies and Richard F. Tas, "How to Add Visual Impact to Your Presentations," *Cornell Hotel and Restaurant Administration Quarterly,* 32, no. 1 (1991): 46–51.

49. Dunfey Hotels Corporation, "An Interview with Jon Canas, President," video case number 9-833-502 (Boston, MA: Harvard Business School, 1996).

50. "Are Salespeople Gaining More Selling Time?" *Sales and Marketing Management* (July 1986): 29.

51. Ali A. Poorani, "Trade-Show Management: Budgeting and Planning for a Successful Event," *Cornell Hotel and Restaurant Administration Quarterly,* 37, no. 4 (1996): 77–84.

52. Bill Quain, "No One Ever Made Money by Discouraging Their Customers from Spending It," *Cornell Hotel and Restaurant Administration Quarterly,* 4, no. 5/6 (2003): 172.

Direct and Online Marketing: Building Customer Relationships

Objectives

After reading this chapter, you should be able to:

1. Define direct marketing and discuss its benefits to customers and companies.

2. Identify and discuss the major forms of direct marketing.

3. Explain how companies have responded to the Internet and other powerful new technologies with online marketing strategies.

4. Discuss how companies go about conducting online marketing to profitably deliver more value to customers.

5. Understand how databases can be used to develop direct-marketing campaigns.

Wiley Eiya, tribal chief of the Huli tribe in Papua New Guinea (PNG), is online as he presents his Web site on a laptop screen at the International Tourism Fair in Berlin. For countries such as PNG, which have a low tourism budget, the Internet allows access to tourists around the world. Even though the government has not made a major effort to promote tourism in PNG, individual tour operators can have a presence on the Internet. This presence can include pictures of the spectacular scenery and the people of the highlands. The Internet allows smaller travel organizations to have international coverage for a low cost. Tourists all over the world are discovering remote destinations through the Internet.

Papua New Guinea is a remote island off the northern coast of Australia. It has a population of a little over 5 million, with most of its people living in rural villages. With over 860 distinct tribal languages, PNG is home to more than a fourth of the world's languages. The land was inhabited 50,000 years ago. Agriculture dates back 7,000 years; its residents are credited with being the first farmers on earth. Europeans did not come to the country until the 1930s, and the tribes of the highlands had little contact with the outside world until the mid-twentieth century.

Travel writers Lipscomp, McKinnon, and Murray say this about PNG: "Few places in the world can match its famed waterways, fascinating village culture, abundant wildlife, smoking volcanoes, rainforest trekking, and offshore diving experiences."[1] The discovery of the highland tribes created an attraction for anthropologists and tourists interested in tribal culture. Its rich culture is only one of PNG's many tourist attractions. PNG is rapidly becoming known for diving that rivals the diving at the Great Barrier Reef. Another activity is white-water rafting in the mountain streams. Coastal and river cruising offer tourists the comfort of modern ships while they enjoy the rustic beauty of the country. It has many unique species of birds and mammals. Although the potential for tourism in PNG is great, the government continues to focus on other industries. Thus, the tourism potential is largely untapped. The numbers of tourists coming to the country has been increasing rapidly in recent years. Even though the Internet provides PNG with a great opportunity to build its tourism, the growth of tourism still has to be managed. A country such as PNG must make sure it has the infrastructure to support increased tourism, as well as policies in place to create sustainable tourism activities that do not destroy its culture and natural beauty. Thus, the Internet can be a two-edged sword. It can bring more tourists, but the destination must still be able to support the tourists when they arrive.[2]

▪▫▪ Direct Marketing

Many of the marketing and promotion tools that we've examined in previous chapters were developed in the context of mass marketing: targeting broad markets with standardized messages and offers distributed through intermediaries. Today, however, with the trend toward more narrowly targeted marketing, many companies are adopting direct marketing, as a primary marketing approach. Beyond brand and relationship marketing, direct marketers usually seek a direct, immediate, and measurable consumer response. Companies interact directly with their customers on their Web site, Facebook, Twitter, YouTube, and other online networks to build individual brand relationships, attract new customers, take orders and reservations, and provide customer service. In this section, we explore the exploding world of direct marketing and the related area of online marketing.

Direct marketing consists of connecting directly with carefully targeted individual consumers to both obtain an immediate response and cultivate lasting customer relationships. Direct marketers communicate directly with customers, often on a one-to-one, interactive basis. Using detailed customer databases, they tailor their marketing offers and communications to the needs of narrowly defined segments or even individual buyers.

Airlines, hotels, and others are building strong customer relationships through award programs. They are using their customer database to match their offers more carefully to individual customers. They are approaching a stage where offers are sent only to those customers and prospects most able, willing, and ready to buy the product. To the extent that they succeed, higher response rates to promotions will be gained.

Direct marketing is widely used in the hotel and travel industries. Continental Airlines sent its OnePass members a coupon for a $198 child's round-trip ticket (when accompanied by an adult) between any two cities that Continental serves in the contiguous United States. American Express offered its members in Houston a discount coupon to Birraporetti's restaurant. These promotions provide the buyer with a benefit and create sales and goodwill for Continental and American Express. In the case of American Express, it is also helping and creating goodwill with both its card members and one of its clients, Birraporetti's. Credit card companies often do joint direct-marketing campaigns with hotels and restaurants. Sometimes it is just a matter of asking what they can do for your organization.

Growth and Benefits of Direct Marketing

Direct marketing has become the fastest-growing form of marketing. According to the Direct Marketing Association (DMA), U.S. companies spent $163 billion on direct marketing in 2011, which now accounts for over half of the total advertising spending in the United States. These expenditures generated almost $2 trillion in sales, about 8.7 percent of total sales in the U.S. economy. The DMA estimates that direct-marketing share of advertising dollars will continue to grow through 2016. The DMA estimates a dollar of direct-marketing expenditures produces $12 in sales compared to $5.25 for general advertising.

Much of the direct-marketing growth is driven by online media. Leading the growth are mobile marketing, which had an annual growth of 50 percent in 2011, and social media which increased by over 20 percent.[3]

Whether employed as a complete business model or as a supplement to a broader integrated marketing mix, direct marketing brings many benefits to both buyers and sellers.

Benefits to Customers

For customers, direct marketing is convenient, easy, and private. Direct marketers never close their doors. From the comfort of their homes or offices, travelers can book airline flights and reserve hotel rooms on Web sites at any time of the day or night. Managers can learn about products and services without tying up time with salespeople.

TABLE 16–1
Gap Analysis of Loyalty Features

Feature	Performance (%)	Importance (%)	Gap
The hotel provides upgrades when available.	18.7	69.4	250.7
You can request a specific room.	4.9	44.7	239.8
If the hotel is likely to be sold out at a time you normally visit, someone from the hotel will call you to ask if you would like to make a reservation.	3.0	37.7	234.7
The hotel uses information from your prior stays to customize services for you.	24.3	57.7	233.4
The staff recognizes you when you arrive.	15.1	38.3	223.2
Employees communicate the attitude that your problems are important to them.	24.0	42.6	218.6

Source: John Bowen and Stowe Shoemaker, Conrad N. Hilton College, University of Houston.

Direct marketing gives buyers ready access to a wealth of products. For example, unrestrained by physical boundaries, direct marketers can offer an almost unlimited selection to consumers almost anywhere in the world. Customers in Australia can select and book a bed and breakfast inn in San Francisco. Direct-marketing channels also give buyers access to a wealth of comparative information about companies, products, and competitors. Web sites often provide more information in more useful forms than even the most helpful salesperson.

Companies also use direct marketing to access guests and gain information that will develop systems and products to better serve their guests. For example, luxury hotel guests were asked which hotel features would cause them to be more loyal to a hotel. A total of eighteen possible benefits developed from in-depth interviews were listed. The hotel customers were asked to rate each feature on a scale from 1, "would have no impact on loyalty," to 7, "would have a great impact on loyalty." In a separate area of the questionnaire, they were asked which of these features were offered currently at hotels to which they were loyal. If one considers what hotels are actually doing and compares this information with what customers would like hotels to do, one is easily able to see where hotels are either meeting the needs of guests or falling short. This is denoted as a gap (performance importance). Table 16–1 shows the gap for loyalty features.

The table shows there is tremendous opportunity to increase loyalty further. Of the eleven features tested, only one has a positive gap. Interestingly, the top two features where the largest gaps occur should be very easy and inexpensive for luxury hotels to implement. This type of analysis helps managers identify areas of opportunity for creating more customer-delivered value. In this case they see those attributes that create loyalty or value. They also see those areas that most hotels do not offer, giving them a chance to create a competitive advantage. Finally, they can cost out the price of providing the features. For example, giving guests unexpected periodic upgrades can be inexpensive if you are using unsold suites for this program. Gaining this information would not have been possible without a database that enabled the questionnaires to be sent out to selected frequent users of luxury hotels.[4]

Finally, direct marketing is interactive and immediate: Buyers can interact with sellers by phone or on the seller's Web site to create exactly the configuration of information, products, or services they desire, and then order them on the spot. Moreover, direct marketing gives consumers a greater measure of control. Consumers decide which catalogs they will browse and which Web sites they will visit.

Benefits to Sellers

For sellers, direct marketing is a powerful tool for building customer relationships. Using database marketing, today's marketers can target small groups or individual consumers and promote their offers through personalized communications. Because of the one-to-one nature of direct marketing, companies can interact with customers by phone or online, learn more about their needs, and tailor products

Royal Caribbean Cruise Lines keeps a customer database. By analyzing customer information, Royal Caribbean found its guests desired physical activities. Its new ships have rock-climbing walls, basketball courts, inline skating tracks, and ice rinks. Courtesy of Ron Buskirk/Alamy.

and services to specific customer tastes. In turn, customers can ask questions and volunteer feedback. Personalization could be as simple as recognizing certain restaurant customers' interest in fine wines and sending notices of food and wine pairing dinners to them. Hotels can also develop unique offers directed at individuals, such as offering a special weekend package in celebration of a guest's wedding anniversary, if they have this information in their database. McDonald's, Burger King, and other fast-food restaurants develop birthday clubs and send reminder notices to the child's parents before the birthday, offering their restaurant as a location for the child's birthday party. In the last two examples, timing, another advantage of direct mail, helped personalize the message. The manager can send the message before a person's birthday or anniversary or when a particular company will be planning its next sales meeting. The message will reach the client at the right moment.

Direct marketing also offers sellers a low-cost, efficient, speedy alternative for reaching their markets. Direct marketing has grown rapidly in business-to-business marketing, partly in response to the ever-increasing costs of marketing through the sales force. When personal sales calls cost an average of more than $350 per contact, they should be made only when necessary and to high-potential customers and prospects. Lower-cost-per-contact media—such as telemarketing, direct mall, and company Web sites—often prove more cost effective. A hotel sales director states, "I've always been a strong believer in direct-mail advertising. Direct-mail advertising plays a very important part in the success of a hotel's marketing program. It's an excellent balance to outside sales calls and telephone solicitation. It presents your product to a client without the expense of a personal sales call. In addition, you're able to solicit many more clients than you could solicit individually through direct mail."[5]

Direct marketing permits privacy because the direct marketer's offer and strategy are not visible to competitors. Continental Airlines sent an offer to its elite frequent flyers for up to $75 off tickets purchased within two weeks. By using direct marketing in this way, Continental can sell inventory at a discount without starting a price war because it is directed toward a select market and was not made through a public media, such as a newspaper. In periods of low demand, companies can use direct marketing to target known customers and produce quick results.

Another benefit of direct marketing is measurability. In Chapter 13 we quoted John Wanamaker: "I know half of my advertising is wasted, but I don't know which half." Direct marketing can be measured. If Wanamaker had used direct marketing, he would have known if he was wasting his money or making a good investment. A manager can track the response to a particular direct-marketing campaign and usually determine the revenue that it produced.

The time-share resort Eagles Nest located in southwest Florida was a newly opened property coming into the summer or trough season. The management of Eagles Nest wanted to introduce the property to residents within 300 miles and fill rooms in the slack period. A New York list broker provided fifteen lists of upscale residents within the 300-mile limit. It was decided to conduct a test market on no more than 20 percent of the total list. Following the test market, a rollout of the remaining 80 percent would be undertaken. A direct mailing was designed that included a letter describing Eagles Nest and offering a great introductory price and a second envelope. This envelope was closed with a seal that said, "Don't open this till you read the letter."

This creative use of reverse psychology apparently worked in much the same way as telling a small child to stay out of the cookie jar. Inside the sealed envelope were six certificates. Five were redeemable for discounts or gift offerings, such as a free drink. The sixth was a return postage-paid reservation card. The results of this campaign amazed everyone. Eagles Nest was able to measure the results of the campaign through the reservation requests it received. It canceled a rollout advertisement campaign it had planned because it had sufficient reservations from the test campaign.[6]

Direct-marketing efforts may be measured in three ways: (1) the number of inquiries generated, (2) the ratio of conversions or purchases realized from inquiries generated, and (3) communication impact.[7]

Direct-marketing tools are expanding today with the help of smartphones and e-mail. Computer-driven communication offers considerable promise as an advertising and sales vehicle. Many companies now communicate directly to key customers through e-mail.

Direct marketing can also offer greater flexibility. It allows marketers to make ongoing adjustments to prices and programs or make immediate, timely, and personal announcements and offers. For example, in its signature folksy manner, Southwest Airlines uses techie direct-marketing tools—including a widget (DING!) and a blog (Nuts about Southwest)—to inject itself directly into customers' everyday lives, at their invitation.[8]

DING! is an application that consumers can download to their computer desktops. Whenever exclusive discount fares are offered, the program emits the familiar in-flight seatbelt-light bell dinging sound. The deep discounts last only 6 to 12 hours and can be accessed only online by clicking on the application. Also available as a phone app, DING! lets Southwest Airlines bypass the reservations system and pass bargain fares directly to interested customers. Eventually, DING! may even allow Southwest Airlines to customize fare offers based on each customer's unique characteristics and travel preferences. In its first two years, the DING! application was downloaded by about 2 million consumers and generated more than $150 million in ticket sales.

Direct marketing is compatible and often works best when used with other elements of the promotional mix in a multiple-stage campaign. For example, the San Diego Convention and Visitors Bureau (CVB) placed an advertisement in *Travel Weekly,* offering a free "Travel Planner's Guide" to interested travel agents and meeting planners. This required the travel agent or meeting planner to give a direct response back to the San Diego CVB. Depending on the potential of business available from the agent or meeting planner, the CVB could simply mail the guide, or it could call and further qualify the contact and answer questions, and then for potential major sources of business it could follow up with a personal sales call.

This technique is known as **integrated direct marketing (IDM)**.[9] Consider the following sequence:

Paid ad with a response channel	→	Direct-mail mechanism	→	Outbound telemarketing	→	Face-to-face sales call

The paid ad creates product awareness and stimulates inquiries. The company then sends direct mail to those who inquire. Forty-eight to seventy-two hours following mail receipt, the company phones, seeking an order. Some prospects place an order; others might request a face-to-face sales call. Even if the prospect is not ready to buy, there is ongoing communication. This use of response compression, whereby multiple media are deployed within a tightly defined time frame, increases impact and awareness of the message. The underlying idea is to deploy select media with precise timing to generate greater incremental sales while offsetting incremental costs. A direct-mail piece alone may generate only a 2 percent response, but it is possible to generate responses of 12 percent or more using IDM.[10]

Finally, direct marketing gives sellers access to buyers that they could not reach through other channels. Internet marketing is a truly global medium that allows buyers and sellers to click from one country to another in seconds. A Web surfer from Paris or Istanbul traveling to Indiana can access a restaurant online in Indianapolis. Online direct marketing is an equalizer that independent restaurants, inns, and hotels have against the brands. Small marketers find they have ready access to global markets.

■■■ Customer Databases and Direct Marketing

Effective direct marketing begins with a good customer database. A **customer database** is an organized collection of comprehensive data about individual customers or prospects, including geographic, demographic, psychographic, and behavioral data. A good customer database can be a potent relationship-building tool. The database gives companies "a snapshot of how customers look and behave." Says one expert, "A company is no better than what it knows [about its customers]."[11]

In consumer marketing, the customer database might contain a customer's demographics (age, income, family members, birthdays), psychographics (activities, interests, and opinions), and buying behavior (buying preferences and the recency, frequency, and monetary value—RFM—of past purchases). In business-to-business marketing, the customer profile might contain the products and services the customer has bought; past volumes and prices; key contacts (and their ages, birthdays, hobbies, and favorite foods); competing suppliers; status of current contracts; estimated customer spending for the next few years; and assessments of competitive strengths and weaknesses in selling and servicing the account.

Some of these databases are huge. For example, casino operator Harrah's Entertainment has built a customer database containing 30 terabytes worth of customer information, roughly three times the number of printed characters in the Library of Congress.[12]

Database Uses

Companies use their databases in many ways. They use databases to locate good potential customers and to generate sales leads. They can mine their databases to learn about customers in detail and then fine-tune their market offerings and communications to the special preferences and behaviors of target segments or individuals. In all, a company's database can be an important tool for building stronger long-term customer relationships.

If a hotel has multiple databases, this can cause problems if they are not integrated. A **data warehouse** stores the information the company receives in a central repository of customer data.[13] Integrating all data collection systems into one central database created challenges. The consolidation that has occurred in the hotel industry has created the need for companies to build one centralized data warehouse for all their brands. Hilton Hotels has developed OnQ, a technology platform that will allow it to use information on its guests across all its brands.[14] Tim Harvey, Hilton's chief information officer, states, "The idea around OnQ is that we wanted to put employees on stage in front of customers to perform 'on cue,' giving them the information they need to deliver the most efficient service."[15]

Once the data are stored in a warehouse, companies use the

Aruba uses direct marketing to attract tourists. Courtesy of Paul Gatward © Dorling Kindersley.

16.2 Hilton
OnQ: This site
provides a pdf
of how OnQ has become a
comprehensive marketing tool,
http://www.hiltonfranchise.com/
Index.asp?S=2&P=51.

relational database to look at relationships in the data. For example, if a resort hotel was projecting a low occupancy for the weekend after next, managers could query the database, asking for all guests who came to the resort on a weekend and lived within 250 miles. This would produce a list of guests who enjoyed the resort on weekends and could drive to the resort. Thus, they would not have to worry about higher last-minute airfares. A restaurant could query the database for all persons who spent over $50 on a bottle of wine if it wanted to develop a potential list for a special event pairing wine and food. The development of relational data warehouses has created a powerful marketing tool to assist their direct-marketing effort.

In the example just cited, the manager formed the query for the database; her results might have been better if the computer developed the query. Data mining is the exploration and analysis of a database by automatic or semiautomatic means to discover patterns or rules.[16] It is the process of automating information discovery.[17] Data mining is used to predict which customers are most likely to respond to an offer, to segment a market, and to identify a company's most loyal customers. Data mining software uses a variety of methods, including regression analyses and neural networks, to find the best solution. One of the major benefits of data mining is that it is not limited to the relationships that the marketing manager may think exists. Rather, it explores all relationships with a variety of techniques. Data mining has increased the effectiveness and efficiency of direct marketing in the hospitality and travel industries.

We have all heard the expression "garbage in, garbage out." To be useful, the data stored in a database must be accurate. Errors are usually a result of data entry. It is important that everyone using the database understand the importance of accurate data. For example, a guest whose last name is Smith and is entered into the database as Smyth will now have two files. The resort will not know her real value because it is divided between the two files. If the resort sends direct mail, she could receive two pieces, one under both names. This shows her that the resort staff does not really know her because they think she is two separate people. To be effective, duplicate files have to be combined, and addresses must be accurate. A clean database starts with accurate entry. There are also software packages that can identify potential duplicate files, check addresses, and make corrections.

Sometimes employees use fields in the database for their own personal notes. Training the employees in the use and importance of the database will correct this problem. For example, a desk clerk typed under the guest's name in the address file, "This guy is a jerk." He wanted to alert the other employees that the guest had the potential of creating problems. What the clerk did not realize is the address was used for direct mail. You can imagine the response of the guest when he received a letter from the hotel addressed to him with "This guy is a jerk" under his name. Employee training to ensure that the database is clean is a critical and ongoing part of an effective database system.

Like many other marketing tools, database marketing requires a special investment. Companies must invest in computer hardware, database software, analytical programs, communication links, and skilled personnel. The database system must be user friendly and available to various marketing groups, including those in product and brand management, new-product development, advertising and promotion, direct mail, telemarketing, Web marketing, field sales, order fulfillment, and customer service. However, a well-managed database should lead to sales and customer-relationship gains that will more than cover its costs.

Finally, you should answer the question, "If you were a customer, why would you want to be in our database?" By answering this question, you find out whether your database has a strategic focus or is mainly used for tactical purposes.[18] Most marketers use their database tactically. For example, one of the most frequent uses of database marketing is in direct marketing. Direct-marketing campaigns often target recent customers, inviting them to return or offering incentives, as well as encouraging loyal customers to come during soft periods. There is nothing wrong with this use of database marketing; in fact, it often produces worthwhile results. However, if this is the only use of database marketing, much of the power of database marketing will be untapped.

To make a customer want to be on your database, it must provide the customer with benefits they would not receive if they were not on it. Database marketers must remember that only promotions relevant to the customer are benefits to the customer. A casino in Las Vegas sent a 2 for 1 buffet coupon to everyone on its database. The promotion was not relevant for the best players who could get comp meals in the casino's finest restaurant, but it was also an insult because it communicated to them that the casino did not know them.

Let us return to the original question: Why would a customer want to be on your database? Vail Associates, operators of skiing facilities, is an example of what can happen when you provide answers to this question. It knew its customers wanted a hassle-free experience, and Vail Associates wanted to maximize their time on the slopes. Vail Associates set about implementing a database system that would give its customers the experience they desired. If you rented skis at Vail Associates in the past, it has your information on file. Renting skis a second time then becomes a hassle-free experience. It wasn't always this way. Everyone was asked for his or her boot size, what type of skis his or her wanted, and a number of other questions. Guests often spent a good deal of time waiting in line, instead of skiing. Now, if you are staying in one of Vail Associates' lodges, it delivers the skis to the lodge, so skis are ready when the guests arrive. The guests avoid the lines and the questions! Its upscale dining rooms are usually booked on weekends; if a lodging customer usually dines in one of these restaurants, the reservationist is prompted to ask if the customer would like to make a restaurant reservation when he or she books his or her room to avoid disappointment later.

These are just a few of the ways Vail Associates uses its database system to provide a better experience for its customers. Harvard Business School has produced a video titled "Expanding Value: Building Loyalty," which describes Vail Associates' database marketing in detail. By using its database strategically, Vail Associates has created a competitive advantage. It is providing its customers with a better product, one that offers more benefits than the competitors' products.[19]

Several other examples of strategic databases are provided by Ritz-Carlton and Brennan's restaurant. Ritz-Carlton's database receives input from the frontline employees. They update the database based on information received from guests during the normal course of their work activities. For example, if a room service waiter finds out that a guest likes a certain type of mineral water, the mineral water is placed in the guest's refrigerator. The database is also used for service recovery. If a guest has encountered a problem, all departments in the hotel are notified, and everyone works to regain the guest's confidence and loyalty. Brennan's in Houston developed a database that included the customer's favorite table, captain, and wine. This information is used to provide the guest with a great experience. These companies, like Vail Associates, have used their database to create a competitive advantage. Companies that use a database to provide the guest with a better experience are gaining a major benefit. They are creating a competitive advantage based on

Casinos, such as Paris Las Vegas Resort and Casino, have developed effective loyalty programs to develop a strong relationship with their players. Courtesy of Dorling Kindersley © Paul Wilkinson.

the knowledge of their customers. They know what the customer likes and how to create messages that will be relevant to the customer. One of the uses of a database is to develop contact lists for direct marketing. No direct-marketing campaign can be successful if the list is poor. Thus, lists are a critical component of a successful direct-marketing campaign.[20] In conclusion, companies need to provide benefits to customers for being in their database.

■■■ Direct Marketing Builds Relationships

Direct marketing is an important tool in customer-relationship management (CRM) programs. Today, airlines, hotels, travel agents, restaurants, and rental car companies operate in very competitive markets. The major way to grow market share is to steal it from the competition. Direct marketing allows companies to develop a strong relationship with their customers, which helps prevent customers from switching to competitors. Hotel frequency programs offer their members special rates, upgrades based on availability, special amenities, their own floors, and often their own lounge with complimentary beverages. Airlines develop special offers for their frequent flyers. The general manager of a hotel often invites regular guests to an evening cocktail party. Managers recognize that spending money developing loyalty among current customers can be more effective than spending money trying to develop new guests. Studies have shown that it costs four to seven times as much to bring in a new customer as it does to maintain an existing one.

Once a manager has identified patrons who are likely to become loyal customers, he or she must identify ways of creating a relationship with these customers—a relationship that leads to customer loyalty. Relationship marketing involves creating, maintaining, and enhancing strong relationships with customers. The concept of relationship has expanded to include developing a relationship with all stakeholders who can help the company serve its customers. For example, employees and marketing intermediaries would fall into this group. Table 16–2 shows the differences between traditional marketing and relationship marketing.

Harrah's, an operator of casino resorts, provides an example of how companies can benefit from relationship marketing. Harrah's developed a loyalty program called Total Rewards. Before starting the program, its research revealed that its customers spent only about 36 percent of their gaming budget with Harrah's. Today that number has increased to 44 percent, meaning Harrah's is getting almost

TABLE 16–2

Relationship Marketing Compared with Traditional Marketing

Relationship Marketing	Traditional Marketing
Orientation to customer retention	Orientation to single sales
Continual customer contact	Episodic customer contact
Focus on customer value	Focus on product features
Long-term horizon	Short-term horizon
High customer service emphasis	Little emphasis on customer service
High commitment to meeting customer expectations	Limited commitment to meeting customer expectations
Quality concerns all staff members	Quality concerns only production staff

Note: Traditional marketing can also be considered transactional marketing, in which each sale is considered to be a discrete event.

Source: This table is based on ideas from F. Robert Dwyer, Paul Schurr, and Sejo Oh, "Developing Buyer–Seller Relationships," *Journal of Marketing,* 51 (April 1987): 11–27; and Adrian Payne, Martin Christopher, Helen Peck, and Moira Clark, *Relationship Marketing* (Oxford, UK: Butterworth-Heinemann, 1995).

25 percent more revenue from existing customers. This revenue came by getting customers to visit casinos near their home more frequently and trying to increase cross-market play by getting them to visit Harrah's casinos when they traveled. The increase in cross-market play has resulted in hundreds of millions of dollars in additional revenue for Harrah's. The object of any customer loyalty program is to change customer behavior. The programs are designed to get customers to shorten their purchase cycles, that is, to come back in two weeks instead of three or to purchase more when they do visit their restaurants or hotels. Harrah's Total Rewards is a great example of a loyalty program that has changed consumer behavior.[21]

Relationship marketing has a long-term orientation. The goal is to deliver long-term value to customers, and the measure of success is long-term customer satisfaction. Relationship marketing requires that all the company's departments work together with marketing as a team to serve the customer. It involves building relationships at many levels: economic, social, technical, and legal, resulting in high customer loyalty.

We can distinguish five different levels of relationships that can be formed with customers who have purchased a company's product, such as a meeting or a banquet:

1. **Basic.** The company sells the product but does not follow up in any way.

2. **Reactive.** The company sells the product and encourages the customer to call whenever he or she has any questions or problems.

3. **Accountable.** The company's representative phones the customer a short time after the booking to check with the customer and answer questions. During and after the event, the salesperson solicits from the customer any product improvement suggestions and any specific disappointments. This information helps the company improve its offering continuously.

4. **Proactive.** The salesperson or others in the company phone the customer from time to time with suggestions about improvements that have been made or creative suggestions for future events.

5. **Partnership.** The company works continuously with the customer and with other customers to discover ways to deliver better value.

What specific marketing tools can a company use to develop stronger customer bonding and satisfaction? It can adopt any of three customer value-binding approaches.[22] The first relies primarily on adding financial benefits to the customer relationship. For example, airlines offer frequent-flyer programs, hotels give room upgrades to their frequent guests, and restaurants have frequent-diner programs. Although these reward programs and other financial incentives build customer preference, they can be imitated easily by competition and thus may fail to differentiate the company's offer permanently. Frequency programs often use tiered programs to encourage guests' preference for one hotel brand. For example, Marriott has gold (fifteen nights), black (fifty nights), and platinum (seventy-five nights). Hilton has silver (ten nights), gold (thirty-six nights), and diamond (sixty nights). As guests move up into higher tiers, they gain more benefits.[23]

The second approach is to add social benefits, as well as financial benefits. Here company personnel work to increase their social bonds with customers by learning individual customers' needs and wants and then individualizing and personalizing their products and services. They turn their customers into clients: Customers may be nameless to the institution; clients cannot be nameless. Customers are served as part of the mass or as part of larger segments; clients are served on an individual basis. Customers are served by anyone who happens to be available; clients are served by the professional assigned to them.[24] For example, a server recognizes repeat guests and greets them by name. A salesperson develops a good relationship with his or her clients. Both these people have developed social bonds with their clients. This keeps the client coming back, but it also often means clients will follow that person when he or she changes jobs. Managers of hospitality and travel organizations want to make sure that their key clients have social bonds with multiple people in the organization. The general manager, front-desk manager, food and beverage manager, convention services manager, banquet manager, and restaurant manager should all know key clients. In fact, general managers should go on sales calls to key clients. If this is done, when the salesperson leaves, the client feels that he or she still knows key people in the hotel and is not dependent on the salesperson.

The third approach to building strong customer relationships is to add structural ties, as well as financial and social benefits. For example, airlines developed reservation systems for travel agents. Frequent guests have special phone lines they can call. Airlines have developed lounges for their first-class customers, and some send a limousine to deliver them to the airport. Sheraton developed flexible check-in and checkout time for its best customers. Hilton is using technology to provide a personalized welcome message on the guest's television. Structural changes are difficult to implement, but they are harder for competitors to match and create a competitive advantage until they are matched.

When it comes to relationship marketing, you don't want a relationship with every customer. In fact, there are some bad customers. A company should develop customer relationships selectively: Figure out which customers are worth cultivating because you can meet their needs more effectively than anyone else.[25] One of the purposes of customer frequency is to help companies track purchases so they know the characteristics of their customers and can classify them by their purchasing characteristics. Table 16–3 breaks customers into categories based on their frequency of purchase and their profitability. Those customers who are high on profitability and frequency deserve management attention. These are Marriott's platinum members and Hyatt's diamond members. The customers high on profitability but low on frequency sometimes can be developed in higher frequency customers. Some of these customers are spreading their business across several different providers of the same service. If we can make our company the preferred provider for this type of customer, then we can turn them into our best customers. For some of the high-frequency, low-profitability customers, there is a chance to motivate them to purchase by showing the value of additional purchases. For example, hotels can show a business traveler the advantage of staying on the concierge floor where there is a lounge to work in when he or she wants to take a break from working in his or her office. The concierge lounge also provides a quick and accessible breakfast, saving the guest time. Those guests who see the value in concierge floors are willing to pay the extra $30 a room. The guests who are in the low-frequency, low-profitability quadrant are often bargain hunters. They come when there is a promotion and avoid paying full price at all costs. It is very difficult to build a relationship with these price-sensitive customers. Knowing your customers helps you select the customers you want to develop a relationship with and to strengthen the relationship over time.

Benefits of Customer-Relationship Management

The benefits of CRM stem from building continued patronage of loyal customers, reduced marketing costs, decreased price sensitivity of loyal customers, and partnership activities of loyal customers. Loyal customers purchase from the business they are loyal to more often than nonloyal customers. They also purchase a broader variety of items. A manager loyal to a hotel brand is more likely to place his or her company's meetings with that hotel chain. Reduced marketing costs are the result of requiring fewer marketing dollars to maintain a customer than to create one and

TABLE 16–3

Types of Customers

	Low Frequency	High Frequency
High Profitability	Try to get these customers to come more often.	These are your best customers, reward them.
Low Profitability	These customers follow promotions. Make sure your promotions make money.	Some of these guests have the potential to become more profitable.

the creation of new customers through the positive word of mouth of loyal customers. When asked what leads them to new restaurants, the number-one response (48 percent) was that friends or relatives took them or recommended the restaurant. Thirty-three percent stated they like to try new restaurants; coupons were the highest mentioned promotional activity at 23 percent.[26] Loyal customers are less likely to switch because of price, and loyal customers make more purchases than do similar, nonloyal customers.[27] Partnership activities of hotel customers include strong word of mouth, business referrals, providing references, publicity, and serving on advisory boards. The combination of these attributes of loyal customers means that a small increase in loyal customers can result in a major increase in profitability. Riechheld and Sasser found that a 5 percent increase in customer retention resulted in a 25 to 125 percent increase in profits in nine service industry groups they studied.[28] As a result, the researchers claim that building a relationship with customers should be a strategic focus of most service firms.

Many products have reached the mature stage of the product life cycle. Competition is strong, and often there is little differentiation between products in the same product class. For example, general managers from Sheraton in Asia were shown pictures of hotel rooms from both their own chain and those of three competitors. Most managers could not give the brand identity of one room, even though they were given a list of eight brands from which to choose.[29] This exercise illustrates that it is very difficult to distinguish among competing hotel brands based on the physical attributes of a hotel's core product. Increased competition with little differentiation between core products is one of the factors that led to the development of relationship marketing in the 1990s. Relationship marketing enables companies to build loyalty with their customers.[30] Developing customers as partners is different from traditional marketing, which is more transaction based.

Beyond building a stronger relation with their partners in the supply chain, companies today must work to develop stronger bonds and loyalty with their ultimate customers. In the past, many companies took their customers for granted. Customers often did not have many alternative suppliers, the other suppliers were just as poor in quality and service, or the market was growing so fast that the company did not worry about fully satisfying its customers. A company could lose a hundred customers a week but gain another hundred customers and consider its sales to be satisfactory. Such a company, operating on a "leaky bucket" theory of business, believes there will always be enough customers to replace the defecting ones. However, this high customer churn involves higher costs than if a company retained all one hundred customers and acquired no new ones. Another problem is that the dissatisfied customers are spreading negative word of mouth. This makes it increasingly difficult to gain the one hundred new customers per week. In businesses that depend on local customers, such as a neighborhood restaurant, it soon becomes impossible to gain an equal amount of replacement customers. Building relationships with customers by creating value is part of relationship marketing.

▬▬▬ Traditional Forms of Direct Marketing

The traditional forms of direct marketing used in the hospitality industry are direct-mail marketing, telephone marketing, and kiosk marketing.

Direct-Mail Marketing

Direct-mail marketing involves sending an offer, announcement, reminder, or other item to a person at a particular address. Using highly selective mailing lists, direct marketers send out millions of mail pieces each year: letters, catalogs, ads, brochures, samples, DVDs, and other "salespeople with wings." Direct mail is by far the largest direct-marketing medium. The DMA reports that direct mail (including both catalog and noncatalog mail) drives more than almost a third of all U.S. direct-marketing sales.[31]

Direct mail is well suited to direct one-to-one communication. It permits high target market selectivity, can be personalized, is flexible, and allows easy measurement of results. Although direct mail costs more than mass media, such as television or magazines per 1,000 people reached, the people it reaches are much better prospects. Some analysts predict a decline in the use of traditional forms of direct mail in coming years, as marketers switch to newer digital forms, such as e-mail and mobile (cell phone) marketing. E-mail, mobile, and other newer forms of direct mail deliver direct messages at incredible speeds and lower costs compared to the post office's "snail mail" pace.

However, even though the new digital forms of direct mail are gaining popularity, the traditional form is still by far the most widely used. Mail marketing offers some distinct advantages over digital forms. It provides something tangible for people to hold and keep. E-mail is easily screened or trashed. "[With] spam filters and spam folders to keep our messaging away from consumers' inboxes," says one direct marketer, "sometimes you have to lick a few stamps."[32] Traditional direct mail can be used effectively in combination with other media, such as company Web sites.

Telephone Marketing

Telephone marketing involves using the telephone to sell directly to consumers and business customers. Telephone marketing now accounts for 19 percent of all direct marketing–driven sales. We're all familiar with telephone marketing directed toward consumers, but business-to-business marketers also use telephone marketing extensively, accounting for more than 55 percent of all telephone marketing sales.[33]

Properly designed and targeted telemarketing provides many benefits, including purchasing convenience and increased product and service information. However, the explosion in unsolicited outbound telephone marketing over the years annoyed many consumers, who objected to the almost daily "junk phone calls" that pull them away from the dinner table or fill the answering machine.

U.S. lawmakers responded with a National Do-Not-Call Registry, managed by the Federal Trade Commission (FTC). The legislation bans most telemarketing calls to registered phone numbers (although people can still receive calls from nonprofit groups, politicians, and companies with which they have recently done business). Delighted consumers have responded enthusiastically. To date, they have registered more than 191 million phone numbers at www.donotcall.com or by calling 888-382-1222. Businesses that break do-not-call laws can be fined up to $11,000 per violation. As a result, reports an FTC spokesperson, the program "has been exceptionally successful."[34]

Do-not-call legislation has hurt the telemarketing industry, but not all that much. Two major forms of telemarketing—inbound consumer telemarketing and outbound business-to-business telemarketing—remain strong and growing. Telemarketing also remains a major fund-raising tool for nonprofit groups. However, many telemarketers are shifting to alternative methods for capturing new customers and sales, from direct mail, direct-response TV, and live-chat Web technology to sweepstakes that prompt customers to call.

In fact, do-not-call appears to be helping most direct marketers more than it's hurting them. Many of these marketers are shifting their call-center activity from making cold calls on often resentful customers to managing existing customer relationships. They are developing "opt-in" calling systems, in which they provide useful information and offers to customers who have invited the company to contact them by phone or e-mail. These "sales tactics have [produced] results as good—or even better—than telemarketing," declares one analyst. "The opt-in model is proving [more] valuable for marketers [than] the old invasive one."[35]

Kiosk Marketing

As consumers become more and more comfortable with computer and digital technologies, many companies are placing information and ordering machines—called kiosks (in contrast to vending machines, which dispense actual products)—in stores, airports, and other locations. Kiosks are popping up everywhere these days, from self-service hotel and airline check-in devices to in-store ordering kiosks that let you order merchandise not carried in the store.

At JetBlue's terminal Five at New York's John F. Kennedy Airport, more than 200 screens throughout the terminal allow passengers to order food and beverages to be delivered to their gate. Business marketers also use kiosks. For example, at trade shows, kiosks are used to collect sales leads and to provide information on products. The kiosk system reads customer data from encoded registration badges and produces technical data sheets that can be printed at the kiosk or e-mailed to the customer. The system has resulted in up to a 400 percent increase in qualified sales leads.[36]

■■■ Digital Direct-Marketing Technologies

Today, thanks to a wealth of new digital technologies, direct marketers can reach and interact with consumers just about anywhere, at anytime, about almost anything. Here, we look into several exciting new digital direct-marketing technologies: e-mail, mobile phone marketing, podcasts and vodcasts, interactive TV (iTV) and online marketing domains. **Online marketing** refers to a company's efforts to market products and services and build customer relationships over the Internet.

E-Mail

Customer databases contain a field for an e-mail address. Thus, just as databases can generate mailing addresses, they can also create e-mailing lists. One advantage of e-mail is that it is quick and thus a good way to get rid of excess inventory. For example, Holland America sent out 250,000 e-mails on May 14 to try to fill up its spring and summer cruises.[37]

John Martin provides this checklist to make sure e-mails are effective:

- The greeting should be personalized and other persons being sent the same message should not be listed.

- The name of the company sending the message is identified. When an outside supplier is sending the e-mail, the supplier's name may be listed. In this case, it is important that the organization sponsoring the e-mail has its name listed before the supplier.

- The subject needs to be relevant to the reader.

Holland America used e-mail to fill up its spring and summer cruises. This is the Holland America's SS Zaandam in Komodo Island Bay, Indonesia. Courtesy of Phper/Dreamstime.

- E-mails need to be short. The best e-mails use no more than sixty-five characters per line. Some browsers break lines longer than this, creating a formatting problem.

- Text message is the preferred format because some browsers cannot accept enhanced HTML messages.[38]

Judd Goldfeder, president of the Customer Connection, claims 50 percent of e-mails sent to restaurant customers by his clients are opened. This is because these e-mails provide the customer with useful information; they are sent to customers who feel they have an affiliation to the restaurant; and there is an opt-out option for people who do not want to receive future e-mails.[39] Janet Logan, an e-mail marketing expert, has these suggestions for effective e-mail marketing. Make the e-mail event-driven and related to events that will be of interest to the person receiving the e-mail.[40] For example, a person who has expressed interest in a Caribbean cruise will receive an e-mail on a Caribbean cruise promotion or a guest who likes jazz receives information on a jazz brunch. She also suggests integrating e-mail with Web marketing, as when an inquiry about a skiing vacation in the Alps on the Web can trigger a request to send the inquirer information ski packages. E-mails can include Web links, allowing the receiver to go directly to a Web site to receive more information. Travel wholesalers often send travel agents messages about promotions with a link to their Web site. This reduces the size of the e-mail, and it allows agents to get the detailed information they will need to sell the travel package. E-mail marketing can be both low cost and effective. Red Lobster developed an e-mail program for members of its loyalty program, the Overboard Club. Red Lobster's goal was to focus on sweepstakes and members-only programs, such as gift cards and having live lobsters delivered to your home. Red Lobster wanted to avoid coupons because it believed couponing was not a good way to develop long-term relationships. Red Lobster sends out e-mails about once every four weeks, and the mailings are coordinated with the restaurant's promotions.[41]

Digital Alchemy, a service provider to the hospitality industry, has created a software program that captures e-mail address from guests making a reservation on a third party. It maintains the hotel's database and includes guest history and solicits guest comments via an electronic comment card during their stay. Using its service, the general manager gets negative comments sent to his or her smartphone, with the name, e-mail address, the room the guest stayed in, and when the guest checked out. It allows him or her to respond to the guest quickly, apologizing for the poor experience and providing an offer to bring the guest back to the hotel. The manager states, "A positive healing response counts more than a "rotten experience."[42] New smartphone technology coupled with advances in software and the Internet will ensure that e-mail will continue to be an important way to communicate with guests and prospective guests. Like any other form of direct marketing, the e-mail must be relevant to the sender. For example, Digital Alchemy can send a Golf Special to everyone in your database who lives within 200 miles, has stayed at your resort four times, played golf at least two times, and had an average daily rate of at least $195. It will also make sure your deals do not go out to people with existing reservations.[43]

But there's a dark side to the growing use of e-mail marketing. The explosion of **spam**—unsolicited, unwanted commercial e-mail messages that clog up e-mail-boxes—has produced consumer irritation and frustration. According to one research company, spam now accounts for almost 90 percent of all e-mail sent.[44] The result is that more and more e-mail goes unopened, and gaining permission to send someone an e-mail is becoming more important. E-mail marketers walk a fine line between adding value for consumers and being intrusive.

To address these concerns, most legitimate marketers now practice *permission-based e-mail marketing,* sending e-mail pitches only to customers who "opt in." Many companies use configurable e-mail systems that let customers choose what they want to get. Few customers object and many actually welcome such promotional messages.

Mobile Phone Marketing

With more than 285 million Americans now subscribing to wireless services, many marketers view mobile phones as the next big direct-marketing medium. Currently, 21 percent of cell phone subscribers use their phone to access the Web. Some 23 percent of cell phone users have seen advertising on their phones in the past 30 days, and about half of them responded to the ads.[45]

A recent study estimates that worldwide mobile ad spending will grow from the current $3.1 billion annually to $28.8 billion by 2013. By 2014 when there are predicted to be 100 million smartphone users in the United States, mobile Internet users will surpass the number of desktop users.[46] About 30 percent of marketers of all kinds are now integrating mobile phones into their direct marketing. Many marketers have created mobile Web sites, optimized for specific phones and mobile service providers. Others have created useful or entertaining apps to engage customers with their brands and help them shop. However, many companies have not embraced this new media. A study by EyeforTravel found that 61 percent of online travel companies did not have a mobile-friendly edition of their Web site and 71 percent did not have a mobile app.[47]

The majority of mobile messages come as text messages (SMS). SMS marketing is expected to generate $177 billion in global revenues by 2013, and it will account for 83 percent of all mobile messaging revenues through 2013. Mobile marketing is usually integrated with another media. For example, TAO nightclub in Las Vegas placed call-to-action signs in bathrooms, behind bars, and on its video displays. In addition to the in-club promotions, it used its Web site, e-mail, and print flyers. Its customers and potential customers were asked to text the word *TAO* to 25827 (CLUBS) to receive invitations to exclusive events. It now has over 6,000 in its text subscriber list and sends out an average of three messages per week. It claims the mobile marketing is more effective than any other media.[48]

Fresh Encounter Community Market in Findlay, Ohio, a grocery store featuring a deli with prepared meals, uses text messaging to help customers plan their meals.[49] Fresh Encounter Community Markets stores try to help shoppers resolve their daily dilemma: What to have for dinner? But this thirty-two-store chain has come up with a unique strategy: texting suggestions to the cell phones of shoppers who have opted into its Text-N-Save mobile advertising program. Last month, for example, Fresh Encounter sent text messages at 2 P.M. on a Thursday and Friday offering a deal on a whole rotisserie chicken to shoppers who came in after 5 P.M. on those days. "We asked them, 'What's for dinner?' and if they don't know, then how about this for $3.99?" says Fresh Encounter executive Eric Anderson. To cash in, on the specials, shoppers present their cell phone to the cashier, showing a PLU (price look-up) number in the text message. The redemption rates are "unbelievable," Anderson says—20 percent or more. Takers inevitably buy complementary items as well. When Fresh Encounter sends out a more urgent same-day offer, as in the chicken promotion, redemptions can exceed 30 percent.

Burger King and McDonald's are integrating mobile phones into their direct marketing. Cell phone promotions include everything from ring-tone giveaways,

McDonald's is now integrating mobile phones into its direct marketing. Courtesy of Bohemian Nomad Picturemakers/Corbis R. Morris/Corbis/Bettmann.

mobile games, and ad-supported content to text-in contests and sweepstakes. For example, McDonald's put a promotion code on 20 million Big Mac packages in a joint sweepstakes contest with the House of Blues, urging participants to enter to win prizes and to text in from concerts. Some 40 percent of contest entries came via text messaging, resulting in a 3 percent sales gain for McDonald's. More importantly, 24 percent of those entering via cell phones opted in to receive future promotions and messages.[50]

As with other forms of direct marketing, however, companies must use mobile marketing responsibly or risk angering already ad-weary consumers. "If you were interrupted every two minutes by advertising, not many people want that," says a mobile marketing expert. The key is to provide genuinely useful information and offers that will make consumers want to opt in or call in. One study found that 42 percent of cell phone users are open to e-mail advertising if it's relevant.[51] Quick Response (QR) codes and Microsoft tag are now commonly used to intergate print media with mobile media. The consumer can scan the code with his or her phone and get additional information and save the site for future use.

Podcasts and Vodcasts

Podcasting and vodcasting are on-the-go, on-demand technologies. With podcasting, consumers can download audio files (podcasts) or video files (vodcasts) via the Internet to a handheld device and then listen to or view them whenever and wherever they wish. These days, you can download podcasts or vodcasts on an exploding array of topics, everything from your favorite NPR show, a recent sitcom episode, or current sports features to the latest music video or Snickers commercial.

An estimated 25 percent of the U.S. population has listened to or viewed at least one podcast. A recent study predicts that the U.S. podcast audience will reach 38 million by 2013, up from 6 million in 2005.[52] As a result, this medium is drawing much attention from marketers. Companies are now integrating podcasts and vodcasts into their direct-marketing programs in the form of ad-supported podcasts, downloadable ads and informational features, and other promotions. For example, the Walt Disney World Resort offers weekly podcasts on a mix of topics, including behind-the-scenes tours, interviews, upcoming events, and news about new attractions.[53]

Interactive TV

Interactive TV lets viewers interact with television programming and advertising using their remote controls. In the past, iTV was slow to catch on. However, the technology now appears poised to take off as a direct-marketing medium. Research shows that the level of viewer engagement with iTV is much higher than with 30-second spots. A recent poll indicated that 66 percent of viewers would be "very interested" in interacting with commercials that piqued their interest. And broadcasting systems such as DIRECTV, EchoStar, and Time Warner are now offering iTV capabilities.[54]

Interactive TV gives marketers an opportunity to reach targeted audiences in an interactive, more involving way. During the ads, a bar at the bottom of the screen lets viewers use their remotes to choose additional content and offers, such as on-demand free product samples, brand channels, or video showcases. For example, in an early test last year, the Disney Travel Channel allowed subscribers to browse information about Disney theme parks and then request a call from an agent. The booking rate for people requesting a call was 25 percent.

Mobile phone marketing, podcasts and vodcasts, and iTV offer exciting direct-marketing opportunities. But marketers must be careful to use these new direct-marketing approaches wisely. As with other direct-marketing forms, marketers who use them risk backlash from consumers who may resent such marketing as an invasion of their privacy. Marketers must target their direct-marketing offers carefully, bringing real value to customers rather than making unwanted intrusions into their lives.

Online Marketing Domains

Figure 16–1 shows the four major online marketing domains. They include B2C (business to consumer), B2B (business to business), C2C (consumer to consumer), and C2B (consumer to business).

Business to Consumer (B2C)

The popular press has paid the most attention to **business-to-consumer (B2C) online marketing**—selling goods and services online to final consumers. Today's consumers can buy almost anything online—from clothing, kitchen gadgets, and air-

Figure 16-1
Online domains.

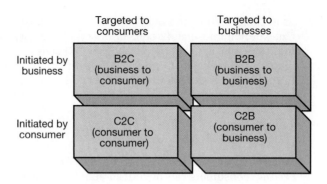

line tickets to computers and cars. Online consumer buying continues to grow at a healthy rate. Some 65 percent of American online users now use the Internet to shop. Current U.S. online retail sales of an estimated $279 billion will grow at a rate of 11 percent per year over the next five years, compared with a growth rate of 2.5 percent in total retail sales.[55]

Perhaps more importantly, the Internet now influences 42 percent of total retail sales—sales transacted online plus those carried out off-line but encouraged by online research. Some 97 percent of Web-goers now use the Internet to research products before making purchases. By one estimate, the Internet influences a staggering 50 percent of total retail sales.[56] Thus, smart marketers are employing integrated multichannel strategies that use the Web to drive sales to other marketing channels.

As more and more people find their way onto the Web, the population of online consumers is becoming more mainstream and diverse. The Web now offers marketers a palette of different kinds of consumers seeking different kinds of online experiences. However, Internet consumers still differ from traditional off-line consumers in their approaches to buying and in their responses to marketing. In the Internet exchange process, customers initiate and control the contact. Traditional marketing targets a somewhat passive audience. In contrast, online marketing targets people who actively select which Web sites they will visit and what marketing information they will receive about which products and under what conditions. Thus, the new world of online marketing requires new marketing approaches.

Business to Business (B2B)

Although the popular press has given the most attention to B2C Web sites, **business-to-business (B2B) online marketing** is also flourishing. B2B marketers use B2B Web sites, e-mail, online product catalogs, online trading networks, and other online resources to reach new business customers, serve current customers more effectively, and obtain buying efficiencies and better prices.

Most major B2B marketers now offer product information, customer purchasing, and customer support services online. For example, restaurants use their sites to sell merchandise such as gift cards and to take reservations. Dunkin' Donuts is known as much for its great coffee as it is for its donuts on the East Coast of the United States. In the past Dunkin' Donuts could distribute its coffee only through its stores. Now it has an Internet site that allows it to sell its coffee to customers who have moved from the East Coast and find themselves without a Dunkin' Donuts near them. Its site features coffee "subscriptions," allowing customers to receive two pounds of coffee delivered to their door monthly. Beyond simply selling their products and services online, companies can use the Internet to build stronger relationships.

Table 16–4 provides three basic principles of online marketing which apply to both B2C and B2B online marketing.

Consumer to Consumer (C2C)

Much **consumer-to-consumer (C2C) online marketing** and communication occurs on the Web between interested parties over a wide range of products and subjects. In some cases, the Internet provides an excellent means by which consumers can buy or exchange goods or information directly with one another.

TABLE 16–4

Three Basic Principles of Online Marketing

1. **Build and actively manage a customer database.**   In this era of scarce customers, when potential customers enter your Web site, try to capture the names and as much useful information as possible about potentially valuable prospects and customers. This can be done through contests that require an entry form, reservation forms, or signup forms for loyalty clubs. A rich customer database can provide the company with a strong competitive advantage. The company can search and rate different groups and individuals for their probability of responding to a given offer or highly tailored offers. A database permits a company's targeting to be superefficient.

2. **Develop a clear concept on how the company should take advantage of the Internet.**
   A company can develop a presence on the Internet in at least seven ways. The company can use the Internet to do research, provide information, run discussion forums, provide training, carry on online buying and selling (i.e., e-commerce), provide online auctioning or exchanging, and even deliver "bits" to customers.

   The company's Web page must be appealing, relevant, and current if it is to attract repeat visits. Companies should consider using state-of-the-art graphics, sound, and video. They should add weekly news or features (e.g., "coming next week: Chef Lambert's summer barbecue recipes"). The site can be developed to provide valuable help, such as links to a map showing the location of the hotel or restaurant. Virtual Vineyard provides product expertise and a personal connoisseur to recommend choice wines, and Chili's tells where its restaurants are located.

   The company must view its Web page critically and ask a number of questions: Why would someone want to surf our site? If I view the site using the equipment my customers use, does the site load quickly or is a customer likely to leave while he or she is waiting for graphics to load? What is interesting about our page? Why would someone want to return to our page? Why would someone want to advertise on our page?

3. **Be easily accessible and quick in responding to customer calls.**   Customers have high and rising expectations about how quickly and adequately they should receive answers to questions and complaints sent in by phone or e-mail. Make sure the Internet user can communicate directly with the company online. People like to be able to communicate with other people. One advantage of the Internet is that we can communicate automatically. The computer can be programmed to book reservations, select and confirm seat assignments on airlines, and send confirmations of reservations, changes in flight plans, and other information to the customer or perspective customer. However, when users have a question that the computer cannot answer or they have a problem they would like to discuss, they should be given a phone number to call or an option for a live chat over the computer and an automatic e-mail option. Too many sites have the goal of providing 100 percent electronic communication, and they do not include telephone contact information. When designing a Web site, one must not forget the customer and the importance of communicating with the customer in the method the customer desires. Often the preferred method for some communication is not electronic.

In other cases, C2C involves interchanges of information through Internet forums that appeal to specific special-interest groups. Such activities may be organized for commercial or noncommercial purposes. An example is Web logs, or *blogs,* online journals where people post their thoughts, usually on a narrowly defined topic. Blogs can be about anything. There are currently about 15 million active blogs read by 57 million people. Such numbers give blogs—especially those with large and devoted followings—substantial influence.[57]

As a marketing tool, blogs offer some advantages. They can offer a fresh, original, personal, and cheap way to reach today's fragmented audiences. However, the blogosphere is cluttered and difficult to control. "Blogs may help companies bond with consumers in exciting new ways, but they won't help them control the relationship," says a blog expert. Such Web journals remain largely a C2C medium. "That isn't to suggest companies can't influence the relationship or leverage blogs to engage a meaningful relationship," says the expert, "but the consumer will remain in control."[58]

Whether or not they actively participate in the blogosphere, companies should show up, monitor, and listen to them. For example, Starbucks draws the line at active participation in blogs but follows the consumer dialogue on the thirty or more online sites devoted to the brand. It then uses the customer insights it gains from blogs to adjust its marketing programs. For instance, it recently altered the remaining installation of a four-part podcast based on the negative blog feedback it gleaned on the first one.

In all, C2C means that online buyers don't just consume product information—increasingly, they create it. As a result, "word-of-Web" is joining word of mouth as an important buying influence.

Consumer to Business (C2B)

The final online marketing domain is **consumer-to-business (C2B) online marketing**. Thanks to the Internet, today's consumers are finding it easier to communicate with companies. Most companies now invite prospects and customers to send in suggestions and questions via company Web sites. Beyond this, rather than waiting for an invitation, consumers can search out sellers on the Web, learn about their offers, initiate purchases, and give feedback. Using the Web, consumers can even drive transactions with businesses, rather than the other way around. For example, using Priceline.com, would-be buyers can bid for airline tickets, hotel rooms, rental cars, cruises, and vacation packages, leaving the sellers to decide whether to accept their offers.

Consumers can also use Web sites such as PlanetFeedback.com to ask questions, offer suggestions, lodge complaints, or deliver compliments to companies. The site's aim is to help consumers "express their voice" and help companies "prime their ears." The site provides letter templates for consumers to use based on their moods and reasons for contacting the company. The site then forwards the letters to the customer-service manager at each company and helps obtain a response. "About 80 percent of the companies respond to complaints, some within an hour," says a PlanetFeedback spokesperson.[59]

■■■ Setting Up an Online Marketing Presence

In one way or another, most companies have now moved online. Almost one-half of hoteliers surveyed in 2011 indicated they had shifted funds from off-line marketing to online marketing, as they believe Internet marketing produces better results than offline marketing.[60] Companies conduct online marketing in any of the four ways, shown in Figure 16–2: creating a Web site, placing ads and promotions online, setting up or participating in online social networks, or using e-mail.

Creating a Web Site

For most companies, the first step in conducting online marketing is to create a Web site. However, beyond simply creating a Web site, marketers must design an attractive site and find ways to get consumers to visit the site, stay around, and come back often.

Figure 16-2
Setting up for online marketing.

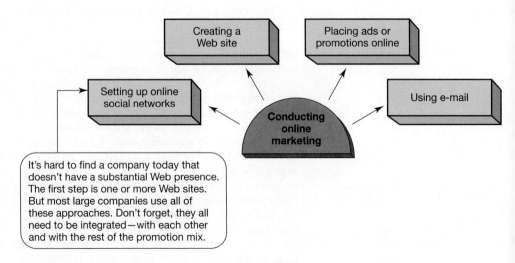

This tourist in Singapore can choose from a number of smartphone apps to help her find her way around Singapore and make her aware of the many options she will have while visiting the country. Courtesy of Dmitrijs Dmitrijevs/Fotolia.

Web sites vary greatly in purpose and content. The most basic type is a **corporate (or brand) Web site**. These sites are designed to build customer goodwill, collect customer feedback, and supplement other sales channels rather than sell the company's products directly. They typically offer a rich variety of information and other features in an effort to answer customer questions, build closer customer relationships, and generate excitement about the company or brand.

Other companies create a **marketing Web site**. These sites engage consumers in an interaction that will move them closer to a direct purchase or other marketing outcome. For example, creating a Web site is one thing; getting people to *visit* the site is another. To attract visitors, companies aggressively promote their Web sites in off-line print and broadcast advertising and through ads and links on other sites. But today's Web users are quick to abandon any Web site that doesn't measure up. The key is to create enough value and excitement to get consumers who come to the site to stick around and come back again. At the very least, a Web site should be easy to use, professional looking, and physically attractive. Ultimately, however, Web sites must also be *useful.* When it comes to Web browsing and shopping, most people prefer substance over style and function over flash. Thus, effective Web sites contain deep and useful information, interactive tools that help buyers find and evaluate products of interest, links to other related sites, changing promotional offers, and entertaining features that lend relevant excitement.

Placing Ads and Promotions Online

As consumers spend more and more time on the Internet, companies are shifting more of their marketing dollars to **online advertising** to build their brands or attract visitors to their Web sites. Online advertising has become a major medium. Total U.S. Internet advertising spending is expected to top $34 billion in 2014, making it the second-largest medium behind only TV but ahead of newspapers and magazines.[61] Here, we discuss forms of online advertising and promotion and their future.

The major forms of online advertising include search-related ads, display ads, and online classifieds. Online display ads might appear anywhere on an Internet user's screen and are often related to the information being viewed. For instance, while browsing vacation packages on Travelocity.com, you might encounter a display ad offering a free upgrade on a rental car from Enterprise Rent-A-Car. Or while visiting the Yahoo! Internet display ads have come a long way in recent years in terms of attracting and holding consumer attention. New *rich media* ads now incorporate animation, video, sound, and interactivity.

The largest form of online advertising is **search-related advertising** (or *contextual advertising*), which accounts for more than 47 percent of all online advertising spending.[62] In search advertising, text-based ads and links appear alongside search engine results on sites such as Google and Yahoo! For example, search Google for "Las Vegas Vacation." At the top and side of the resulting search list, you'll see inconspicuous ads for ten or more advertisers, ranging from the Venetian to New York. Nearly all of Google's $23.6 billion in revenues come from ad sales. Search is an always-on kind of medium. And in today's tight economy, the results are easily measured.

Groupon, Living Social, and other sites that offer daily deals provide to their community, creating the opportunity for hospitality organizations to provide online coupons. When using these coupons, managers should follow the guidelines we discussed earlier in Chapter 14. These sites typically ask a company to give 50 percent off in their offer. For example, a restaurant offers a Groupon for $25 that provides the purchaser with $50 of food at the restaurant. Groupon likes to get a 50–50 split of the Groupon price, in this case $12.50, leaving the restaurant with $12.50 for providing $50 worth of food. The restaurant will lose money on Groupon, and will make money only if the guest returns. To reduce this loss, try to negotiate a higher split with Groupon, such as 70 percent for the restaurant and exclude alcohol. The price of the Groupon is good even after the Groupon expires, so the customer could present the Groupon after it expired and receive $25 off his or her meal.[63]

Finally, an advantage of online marketing is the creation of buzz and viral marketing. **Buzz marketing** generates excitement, creates publicity, and communicates brand-relevant information through unexpected or outrageous means. **Viral marketing** is the Internet version of word-of-mouth marketing that encourages customers to pass along the message to others.

Creating or Participating in Online Social Networks

The results of a survey sponsored by the National Restaurant Association found that 69 percent of restaurant managers were using social media to promote their restaurants. This was the highest of any type of medium, followed by coupon booklets (58 percent), e-mail (56 percent), newspapers (45 percent), and online ads (45 percent).[64] Hotels are now hiring full-time social media managers. Like the position of revenue manager which sprang up in the last decade, this position is creating an opportunity for hospitality management students who want to specialize in marketing through social media.

A company's social media program should fit the goals it wants to achieve with its social media. Next it must develop a strategy it will use to achieve these goals. The company's presence in social media should also fit its brand image. For example the Jimmy Buffet's Margaritaville Café in Key West, Florida, would use different tactics than would the Four Seasons Hotel in Miami. In general, social media should be used to engage and listen to your customers. It is also an excellent vehicle for customer compliant resolution. A properly managed social media program will bring your customers together with a sense of community and loyalty.

Participating successfully in existing online social networks presents challenges. Web communities are largely user controlled. The company's goal is to make the brand a part of consumers' conversations and their lives. However, marketers can't simply muscle their way into consumers' online interactions—they need to earn the right to be there. "You're talking about conversations between groups of friends," says one analyst. "And in those conversations a brand has no right to be there, unless the conversation is already about that brand." Says another expert, "Being force-fed irrelevant content, or feeling tricked into taking in a brand is a major turn-off." Rather than intruding, marketers must learn to become a valued part of the online experience. A second challenge is to select the right channels; with new media appearing every month, a company must choose where to spend its time. If the company does not have a full-time social media manager, it should start with one or two social media. Fortunately, there are a number of social media analytical programs which allow managers to monitor responses across a number of sites, even if a company is not actively engaged in these sites.

One of the goals of a company's social media plan should be to engage its customers and create a conversation. Try to be unique and use engagement which fits your brand. For example, Adventures by Disney, a company which provides group tours for families, has an "Ask Our Mom" tab on its Facebook page. Moms who have traveled with Disney personally answer the question of mothers thinking about taking their family on a trip. Disney has engaged former travelers to answer the questions of future travelers. Many restaurants use foursquare, a location-based social media smartphone application. It is a great engagement tool for restaurants relying on local customers. For example, managers can create unique specials for customers who check-in five times during a month. Carnival Cruises asked its Facebook fans to comment on the favorite port they have experienced on a Carnival Cruise. Carnival received 479 likes and 700 comments. Most of them promoted Carnival Cruises.[65] *Travel and Leisure* magazine's best uses of social media by the travel industry can be a good way to get creative ideas on how to use social media to engage customers.[66]

Listening to what people are saying about a company is one of the benefits social media provides. Managers can find out what people are saying about their company as well as what they are saying about competitors. The following sites provide consumer reviews of your hotel or restaurant: TripAdvisor.com, HotelChatter.com, local.yahoo.com, CitySearch.com, yelp.com, ChowHound.com, OpenTable.com, and most of the online travel agencies such as Expedia.com. Listening to the conversation customers are having about one's company can provide valuable information—and free marketing intelligence. Companies like Loding Interactive and Envision provide Internet marketing and consultative Web site management services and offer a number of effective online tools and services to listen and even engage in the conversation with guests and potential guests online. In Chapter 5 we mentioned the importance of getting employees to feed back information on the company they heard from customers: the listening post concept. With social media we can monitor what customers are saying after they leave your business or travel destination. For example, one manager put TripAdvisor comments into a spreadsheet. This allowed the comments to be analyzed across segments and by rating. One of the findings was those who gave it the lowest rating were couples who stated this is not a luxury resort. In some media the resort advertised itself as a luxury resort, setting expectations it could not meet. Needless to say, the resort stopped marketing itself as a luxury resort.

Listening to your customers is good, but engaging in the conversation is better. It is often possible to participate in service recovery when someone posts a complaint. Managers I have talked to often avoid responding to negative comments. One manager stated that they know everyone at the resort is working hard to deliver good service and it makes them angry when someone posts a complaint. Others complain that they simply do not have time. This is why the position of social media manager is emerging. We should remember that social media amplifies the conversation. Whether the comment is good or bad, it will be communicated to hundreds, thousands, or perhaps hundreds of thousands of people. Ideally, one should respond to all comments, but those that are extremely good or negative deserve attention.

Holly Zoba, senior vice president of sales for the Hospitality Division of Signature Worldwide, provides this advice on how to respond online to a guest's comments. First remember others are viewing the comments, so be professional and avoid being defensive. When someone complains, apologize and show empathy for his or her situation. Don't use the response as a way to sell the hotel or restaurant's features. Respond to both negative and positive reviews; remember you want to engage in the conversation. Her final comment is to be proactive. If a guest says he or she had a great experience, ask him or her to go online and let others know about his or her experience.

A customer named Judy posted a comment on Jimmy John's (a popular sandwich shop) Facebook page. It seems Judy is a loyal customer; however, she writes that the last several times she came to Jimmy John's, her sandwich was not the way she ordered it and she is not sure if she will be back. The following is the response from Jimmy John's:

> I'm all over it Judy. Send me your address and phone number to facebook@jimmyjohns.com so I can gain your trust again.

The response was posted within 12 hours of the customer's post. It let Judy and other customers know Jimmy John's was interested in resolving customer problems. Finally, she took the conversation off-line. Rather than get into a public conversation with dissatisfied customers, managers should take them off-line and resolve the problem.

These are just a few of the commercial social media Web sites. Marketers must choose those that are best suited to their operation and resources. Courtesy of Dreamzdesi.../ Dreamstime.

16.3 TripAdvisor, look up a hotel you know and see the consumer ratings it received, http://www.tripadvisor.com/.

Affinia Hotels, with hotels in New York, Chicago, and Washington, D.C., was one of the first groups to link comments about its hotels from TripAdvisor to each hotel's home page. This includes all comments, both positive and negative. For a well-managed chain, this is a great marketing tactic. It spreads positive word of mouth and also provides feedback to the employees. Affinia's chief marketing officer, John Moser, states he plans to post video and audio testimonials to the Web site along with written comments provided by guests. Moser states, "My dream is to have a brand where customers and the hotels work hand in hand to create a better place to stay."[67] One reservation company is working on a method that will extract all positive comments and place them on the hotel's Web site. Although at first this may seem like a clever way to promote your product, it goes against the social media revolution which calls for transparency, integrity, authenticity, and trust. Social networks are about engagement and relationships. The most important attribute of a relationship is trust. If you lose the trust of your customers or employees, social media can destroy your personal reputation and your business.

Social media has moved marketing into a new era. Those that provide the customer with value and have a good product and consistently deliver that product will benefit from thousands of people seeing the positive word of mouth from their customers. Those that have a poor product and service delivery system will suffer. Before putting resources into a social media program, read what others are saying about you online and fix the problems guests are talking about online.

The Promise and Challenges of Online Marketing

Online marketing continues to offer both great promise and many challenges for the future. Its most ardent apostles still envision a time when the Internet and online marketing will replace magazines, newspapers, and even stores as sources for information and buying. Most marketers, however, hold a more realistic view. To be sure, online marketing will become a successful business model for some companies, and the Internet creates a good business model for retailers such as Travelocity and Orbitz. However, for most companies, online marketing will remain just one important approach to the marketplace that works alongside other approaches in a fully integrated marketing mix.

Despite the many challenges, companies large and small are quickly integrating online marketing into their marketing strategies and mixes. As it continues to grow, online marketing will prove to be a powerful direct-marketing tool for improving sales, communicating company and product information, delivering products and services, and building customer relationships more efficiently and effectively.

Legal and Ethical Issues

From a broader societal viewpoint, Internet marketing practices have raised a number of ethical and legal questions. In previous sections, we've touched on some of the negatives associated with the Internet, such as unwanted e-mail and the annoyance of pop-up ads.

Marketing Highlight How Hospitality Companies Use Social Media

16-1

Taco Bell had a class action lawsuit filed against it in January 2011, claiming its taco beef contained only 35 percent beef. Taco Bell used a blend of social media and traditional media to quickly respond to the suit.

Full-page newspaper ads were run saying, "Thank you for suing us." The ad went on to say, "Here's the truth about our seasoned meat." Taco Bell also responded with Facebook postings and a YouTube video. The president of Taco Bell told YouTube viewers that the company's taco mixture contained 88 percent as opposed to the 35 percent claimed in the suit.

Taco Bell fought hard by bringing the key words "taco," "bell," "lawsuit" on Yahoo!, Google, and Bing search engines ensuring that the company's official remarks would appear first during a search. The *Wall Street Journal* said, "The episode is a reminder of the power of social media in mounting an aggressive defense." Taco Bell's president, Greg Creed, said that "customer response on Facebook and Twitter were positive." Taco Bell was able to quickly restore the trust of its customers and the lawsuit was dropped.

RIU Hotels and Resorts in a collection of over one hundred properties concentrated around the Caribbean and Mediterranean Seas. At the beginning of 2010 it only had about 400 fans on its Facebook page. That was before it started a competition called the "Ultimate Fan." Guests were asked to send in their best photos and videos of the resorts and share their experiences at the resorts. At the end of the competition, more than 350 photos and 8 videos were uploaded. The fan base grew to 1,350. But that was just the start. After the competition, fans continued to post photos that were viewed by their friends and relatives. This created traffic for the Facebook page as well as drove customers to the resort. Today RIU has over 87,000 fans.

Eric's Restaurant in Houston uses foursquare to drive happy-hour business. Eric's offers reduced prices on its appetizers as a reward for those who check-in at Eric's on foursquare. The promotion drives people to the restaurant, as well as encourages their friends to stop by the restaurant. Most people do not want to go into a bar after work where they do not know anyone. By checking in on foursquare they can see who is at Eric's. Guests can draw their friends just by checking in on foursquare.

Gunstock Mountain Resort near Boston developed a promotional strategy to promote on-mountain specials to increase incremental revenue. Customers were asked to text JitterGram 1091 to receive up to four on-mountain specials a day. Signs were displayed around the ski slopes,

lifts, and lodges. Staff also told guests about the "Text to Save" club and encouraged them to sign up. Gunstock also used the database to text short-term promotions such as 2 for 1 ski tickets for tomorrow only. Since you had to receive the text to receive the promotion, the price was not lowered for everyone—just those redeeming the "JitterGram" promotion. The 2 for 1 promotion created almost $1,000 in incremental revenue with almost no incremental marketing expense.

The Ranch As director of social marketing for the LKCM Radio Group, Jared Darter believed that there were tremendous opportunities for the use of social marketing by radio stations. Jared was proud to demonstrate social marketing statistics for one of his stations 95.9 FM "The Ranch" which positioned itself as The Sound of Texas. The importance of Facebook in particular was demonstrated by nearly 50,000 "likes" registered for through Facebook. Jared Darter of LKCM Radio Group said that Facebook and Twitter were important parts of a package that the radio stations could offer advertisers such as restaurants, hotels, resorts, and conference centers. In the past radio stations mentioned the names of their advertisers on the air as well as played their ads. Now they could also plug them on social media. Jared worked with the station's salespeople to teach a friendly mention of a client's product, promotion, and special event on social media, where it was allowed, could be part of the advertising package they sold to the hotel or restaurant.

Instead of eliminating the need for creative promotions, social marketing intensified the need. This meant that the stations had to enhance partnerships with clients, such as entertainment venues, restaurants, or even resort hotels to ensure that they continuously offer fresh and engaging offers that could be tied into radio promotions and mentioned in social media. Jared said that social marketing worked best when it was part of "Integrated Communications" between various media and the ultimate customer or prospect.

Credit: Radio Group LKCM, 115 West 3rd St. Fort Worth, Texas 76102, Jared Darter, Engineering/IT/Programming.

Sources: Radio Group LKCM, 115 West 3rd St. Fort Worth,Texas 76102, Jared Darter, Engineering/IT/Programming; Jargon Julie, Emily Steel, and Joann Lublin, "Taco Bell Makes Spicy Retort to Suit," *Wall Street Journal,* Media Business (Monday, January 31, 2011): B5. Mobile Marketing: The New Frontier, HSMAI Foundation, September 9, 2009. "Social Media for Management Companies and Brands," HSMAI Foundation, June 15, 2010.

Online Privacy and Security

Online privacy is perhaps the number-one **e-commerce** concern. Most e-marketers have become skilled at collecting and analyzing detailed consumer information. Marketers can easily track Web site visitors, and many consumers who participate in Web site activities provide extensive personal information. This may leave consumers open to information abuse if companies make unauthorized use of the information in marketing their products or exchanging databases with other companies. Many consumers and policy makers worry that marketers have stepped over the line and are violating consumers' right to privacy.[68] A recent survey found that seven out of ten consumers are concerned about online privacy.

Many consumers also worry about *online security.* They fear that unscrupulous snoopers will eavesdrop on their online transactions or intercept their credit card numbers and make unauthorized purchases. In turn, companies doing business online fear that others will use the Internet to invade their computer systems for the purposes of commercial espionage or even sabotage. There appears to be an ongoing competition between the technology of Internet security systems and the sophistication of those seeking to break them.

In response to such online privacy and security concerns, the federal government is considering legislative actions to regulate how Web operators obtain and use consumer information. Congress is considering an online privacy bill that would require online service providers and commercial Web sites to get customers' permission before they disclose important personal information. That would include financial, medical, ethnic, religious, and political information, along with Social Security data and sexual orientation. The bill would also direct the FTC to enact rules imposing similar requirements on both online and off-line data collection. "I think this subject of privacy is a ticking time bomb because people do not want their personally identifiable medical and financial information spread all over every place," says one senator. "A doctor needs to know what ails you. But those ailments, your mortgage banker doesn't need to know that."

Of special concern are the privacy rights of children. In 1998, the FTC surveyed 212 Web sites directed toward children. It found that 89 percent of the sites collected personal information from children. However, 46 percent of them did not include any disclosure of their collection and use of such information. As a result, Congress passed the Children's Online Privacy Protection Act, which requires Web site operators targeting children to post privacy policies on their sites. They must also notify parents about the information they're gathering and obtain parental consent before collecting personal information from children under age 13.[69]

Many companies have responded to consumer privacy and security concerns with actions of their own. Companies such as Expedia have conducted voluntary audits of their privacy and security policies. It is important to protect the privacy and rights of consumers. Trust is one of the most important assets of a manager and a company.

■■■ KEY TERMS

Business-to-business (B2B) online marketing. Using B2B trading networks, auction sites, spot exchanges, online product catalogs, barter sites, and other online resources to reach new customers, serve current customers more effectively, and obtain buying effectiveness and better prices.

Business-to-consumer (B2C) online marketing. The online selling of goods and services to final consumers.

Buzz marketing. Generates excitement, creates publicity, and communicates brand-relevant information through unexpected or outrageous means.

Consumer-to-business (C2B) online marketing. Online and exchanges in which consumers search out sellers, learn about their offers, and initiate purchases, sometimes even driving transaction terms.

Consumer-to-consumer (C2C) online marketing. Online exchanges of goods and information between final consumers.

Corporate (or brand) Web site. Web sites that seek to build customer goodwill and to supplement other sales channels rather than to sell the company's product directly.

Customer database. An organized collection of comprehensive data about individual customers or prospects, including geographic, demographic, psychographic, and behavioral data.

Data warehouse. A central repository of an organization's customer information.

Direct-mail marketing. Direct marketing through single mailings that include letters, ads, samples, foldouts, and other "salespeople with wings" sent to prospects on mailing lists.

Direct marketing. Direct communications with carefully targeted individual consumers to obtain an immediate response and cultivate lasting customer relationships.

E-commerce. The general term for a buying and selling process that is supported by electronic means, primarily the Intranet.

Integrated direct marketing (IDM). Direct-marketing campaigns that use many vehicles and multiple stages to improve response rates and profits.

Marketing Web site. Web sites designed to engage consumers in an interaction that will move them closer to a purchase or other marketing outcome.

Online advertising. Advertising that appears while consumers are surfing the Web, including display ads, search-related ads, and online classifieds.

Online marketing. Company efforts to market products and services and build customer relationships over the Internet.

Spam. Unsolicited, unwanted commercial e-mail messages.

Search-related advertising (or contextual advertising). Text-based ads and links that appear alongside search engine results on sites such as Google and Yahoo!

Telephone marketing. Using the telephone to sell directly to customers.

Viral marketing. The Internet version of word-of-mouth marketing—Web sites, videos, e-mail messages, or other marketing events that are so infectious that customers will want to pass them along to friends.

■■■ CHAPTER REVIEW

I. **Direct Marketing** consists of direct connections with carefully targeted individual consumers to both obtain an immediate response and cultivate lasting customer relationships. Direct marketers communicate directly with customers, often on a one-to-one interactive basis.
  A. **Growth and benefits of direct marketing.** Direct marketing continues to become more Web oriented. The Internet now accounts for about 18 percent of direct marketing–driven sales.
    1. **Benefits to customers.** Direct marketing is convenient, easy, private, and open 24 hours. Companies can access customers and find out how to design products that will better fit their customer's needs. Direct marketing is interactive, allowing customers to customize their orders.
    2. **Benefits to sellers.** Direct marketing can build relationships through personalized communication. Direct marketing is low cost, efficient, and quick. Direct marketing is private and can be measured. Finally, direct marketing gives sellers access to buyers they could not reach through other channels.

II. **Customer Databases and Direct Marketing.** Effective direct marketing begins with a good customer database. A customer database is an organized collection of comprehensive data about individual customers or prospects, including geographic, demographic, psychographic, and behavioral data. A good customer database can be a potent relationship-building tool.
  A. **Database uses.** Companies use databases to locate good potential customers and to generate sales leads. They can mine their databases to learn about customers in detail and then fine-tune their market offerings and communications to the special preferences and behaviors of target segments or individuals. In all, a company's database can be an important tool for building stronger long-term customer relationships.
  B. **Data warehouse.** A data warehouse is used to combine direct databases a firm might have into one integrated database.
  C. **Relationships.** Companies use databases to find relationships in the data that will help them market better to their customers.
  D. **Databases should serve the customer.** A database should allow the company to better serve the customers by developing systems and providing products that will meet their needs.

III. **Direct Marketing Builds Relationships.** Direct marketing allows companies to develop a strong relationship with their customers, which helps prevent them from switching to competitors.
  A. **Relationship marketing has a long-term orientation.** The goal is to deliver long-term value to customers, and the measure of success is long-term customer satisfaction. Relationship marketing requires that all the company's departments work together with marketing as a team to serve the customer. It involves building relationships at many levels: economic, social, technical, and legal, resulting in high customer loyalty.
  B. **Building relationships.** Relationships can be built through financial benefits, social bonds, and changing the structure of how you do business to better fit the needs of your customers.
  C. **Benefits of customer-relationship management.** The benefits of customer-relationship management comes from building continued patronage of loyal customers, reduced marketing costs, decreased price sensitivity of loyal customers, and partnership activities of loyal customers.

IV. **Traditional Forms of Direct Marketing**
   A. **Direct-mail marketing** involves sending an offer, announcement, reminder, or other item to a person at a particular address. Using highly selective mailing lists, direct marketers send out millions of mail pieces each year: letters, catalogs, ads, brochures, samples, DVDs, and other "salespeople with wings." Direct mail is by far the largest direct-marketing medium.
   B. **Telephone marketing** involves using the telephone to sell directly to consumers and business customers. Telephone marketing now accounts for 22 percent of all direct marketing–driven sales.
   C. **Kiosk marketing.** As consumers become more and more comfortable with computer and digital technologies, many companies are placing information and ordering machines called kiosks (in contrast to vending machines, which dispense actual products) in stores, airports, and other locations.

V. **Digital Direct-Marketing Technologies**
   A. **E-mail.** Just as databases can develop mailing addresses, they can develop e-mail addresses. Given its targeting effectiveness and low costs, e-mail can be an outstanding marketing investment.
   B. **Mobile phones.** With more than 230 million Americans now subscribing to wireless services, many marketers view mobile phones as the next big direct-marketing medium. A growing number of consumers—especially younger ones—are using their cell phones as a "third screen" for text messaging, surfing the wireless Web, watching downloaded videos and shows, and checking e-mail.
   C. **Podcasting and vodcasting** are the latest on-the-go, on-demand technologies. The name podcast derives from Apple's ubiquitous iPod. With podcasting, consumers can download audio files (podcasts) or video files (vodcasts) via the Internet to an iPod or other handheld device and then listen to or view them whenever and wherever they wish.
   D. **Interactive TV (iTV)** lets viewers interact with television programming and advertising using their remote controls.
   E. **Online marketing domains**
      1. **B2C (business to consumer) e-commerce.** The online selling of goods and services to final consumers.
      2. **B2B (business to business) e-commerce.** B2B trading includes auction sites, spot exchanges, online product catalogs, barter sites, and other online resources to reach new customers, serve current customers more effectively, and obtain buying effectiveness and better prices.
      3. **C2B (consumer to business) e-commerce.** Online and exchanges in which consumers search out sellers, learn about their offers, and initiate purchases, sometimes even driving transaction terms.
      4. **C2C (consumer to consumer) e-commerce.** Online exchanges of goods and information between final consumers.

VI. **Setting Up an Online Presence**
   A. **Creating a Web site.** For most companies, the first step in conducting online marketing is to create a Web site. However, beyond simply creating a Web site, marketers must design an attractive site and find ways to get consumers to visit the site, stay around, and come back often.
   B. **Designing an effective Web site.** The seven Cs provide a framework for designing a Web site: context, the site's layout and design; content, the text, pictures, sound, and video that the Web site contains; community, the ways that the site enables user-to-user communication; customization, the site's ability to tailor itself to different users or to allow users to personalize the site; communication, the ways the site enables site-to-user, user-to-site, or two-way communication; connection, the degree that the site is linked to other sites; and commerce, the site's capabilities to enable commercial transactions.
   C. **Creating or participating in online social networks.** The popularity of the Internet has resulted in a rash of online social networks or Web communities. Countless independent and commercial Web sites have arisen that give consumers online places to congregate, socialize, and exchange views and information. Marketers can engage in online communities in two ways: They can participate in existing Web communities or they can set up their own.

VII. **Online Privacy and Security.** Marketers have a responsibility to protect the privacy of customer information and make sure personal information such as credit card numbers is secure.

■■■ DISCUSSION QUESTIONS

1. Discuss the benefits of direct marketing to both buyers and sellers.
2. Find an example of a good direct-marketing campaign. Why do you feel it was effective?
3. Define data warehouse and explain why it is a popular data management tool.
4. Discuss ways an Internet site can collect and use information from its visitors. For reference purposes you may frame the question so you are referring to the site of a hotel, restaurant, club, or a destination marketing organization.
5. Explain how online marketing and direct marketing are related.

■■■ EXPERIENTIAL EXERCISE

Do the following:

Sign up for a loyalty program for a hospitality or travel organization. What information did it request from you? Did the information seem useful? Is there information it should have asked for but did not? Did it ask you if it was all right if it sent you information? See if you receive any response from the company after signing up.

■■■ INTERNET EXERCISE

Go to two Web sites for the same type of hospitality or tourism organization. For example, go to two restaurants, two destination marketing organizations, and so forth. Evaluate the Web sites according to the "7 Cs" of effective Web site design.

■■■ REFERENCES

1. Adrina Lipscomb, Rowan McKinnon, and Jon Murray, *Papua New Guinea* (Hawthorn, Victoria: Lonely Planet, 1998).

2. National Statistical Office Papua New Guinea (accessed November 7, 2011), http://www.nso.gov.pg/statistical-data/tourism-statistics; Papua New Guinea Online, http://www.niugini.com/index.html (accessed December 24, 2004); Adrina Lipscomb, Rowan McKinnon, and Jon Murray, *Papua New Guinea* (Hawthorn, Victoria: Lonely Planet, 1998). Papua New Guinea, Introduction, Destinations, from http://www.lonelyplanet.com/destinations/autralasia/papua_new_guinea/index.htm (accessed December 21, 2001); Papua New Guinea Tourism, Tourism Overview, http://www.geocities.com/skyfdn/PNGtourismfacts.html (accessed December 19, 2001); Papua New Guinea Tourism Resources, Introduction, http://www.geocities.com/skyfdn/; Cruising in Papua New Guinea, Our Tourism Products, http://www.paradiselive.org.pg/cruises.html (accessed December 19, 2001); Cultural Excursions, http://www.west.net/~exotic/excursions.htm (accessed December 21, 2001); Papua New Guinea Travel Guide, Pacific Islands travel, accommodations information, http://www.pi-travel.co.nz/papua_new_guinea/scenic/p_content_scenic.html (accessed December 21, 2001).

3. "DMA Releases New 'Power of Direct' Report; DM-Driven Sales Growth Outpace Overall US Economic Growth," The Direct Marketing Association, October 2, 2011 (accessed November 26, 2011), http://www.newdma.org/news/dma-releases-new-power-direct-report-dm-driven-sales-growth-outpace-overall-us-economic-growth.

4. John Bowen and Stowe Shoemaker, "Relationship in the Luxury Hotel Segment: A Strategic Perspective" (Ithaca, NY: Cornell University, 1997). An overview of this research paper can be found in the February 1998 issue of the *Cornell Hotel and Restaurant Administration Quarterly.*

5. Susan Greco, "How to Reduce Your Cost of Sales," *Inc.* March 5, 2010), accessed at www.inc.com/guide/reducing-cost-of-sales.html#; James R. Abbey, *Hospitality Sales and Advertising* (East Lansing, MI: Educational Institute, 1989), p. 322.

6. "Eagles Nest," The Pete and Pierre Show, *Consumer Campaigns,* Hake Communications, Inc., 224 Seventh Street, Garden City, NY 11530.

7. Peter C. Yesawich, "Execution and Measurement of Programs," *Cornell Hotel and Restaurant Administration Quarterly,* 29, no. 4 (1989): 89.

8. Portions adapted from Mike Beirne, "A Wing—and a Ding," *Brandweek* (October 23, 2006): 22; and Jason Voight, "Southwest Keeps Fans from Straying," *Adweek* (August 20, 2007), accessed at www.adweek.com/aw/esearch/article_display.jsp?Vnu_content_id=1003627839. Other information from "Southwest Airlines Celebrates Anniversary of DING!" PR *Newswire* (February 28, 2008); Bob Garfield, "What's the Big Deal with Widgets?" *Advertising Age* (December 1, 2008): 1; www.blogsouthwest.com and "What Is DING!?" www.southwest.com/ding (accessed December 2010).

9. "Mauna Kea," The Pete and Pierre Show, *Consumer Campaigns,* Hake Communications, Inc., 224 Seventh Street, Garden City, NY 11530.

10. Ibid.

11. Alicia Orr Suman, "Ideas You Can Take to the Bank! 10 Big Things All Direct Marketers Should Be Doing Now," *Target Marketing* (February 2003): 31–33; Mary Ann Kleirzfelter, "Know Your Customer," *Target Marketing* (January 2005): 28–31; and Michele Fitzpatrick, "Socialize the Database Beyond Marketing," www.dmnews.com (accessed January 29, 2007).

12. Daniel Lyons, "Too Much Information," *Forbes* (December 13, 2004): 210; Mike Freeman, "Data Company Helps Wal-Mart, Casinos, Airlines Analyze Data," *Knight Ridder Business Tribune News* (February 24, 2006): 1; and John Foley, "Exclusive: Inside HP's Data Warehouse Gamble," *Information Week* (January 1–8, 2007): 30–35.

13. Martin Baier, Kurtis M. Ruf, and Goutam Chakraborty, *Contemporary Database Management* (Evanston, IL: Racom, 2002).

14. "Hilton Hotels Corp. Takes Lead With OnQ," *Hotels* (August 2003): 14.

15. Ibid.

16. Michael J. A. Berry and Gordon Linoff, *Data Mining Techniques* (New York: Wiley, 1997).

17. Robert Groth, *Data Mining* (Upper Saddle River, NJ: Prentice Hall, 1999).

18. See Rob Jackson and Paul Wang, *Strategic Database Marketing* (Chicago, IL: NTC Publishing Group. 1994).

19. *Making Loyalty the Mission* (Harvard Business School Video, 1995).

20. Edward L. Nash, *Direct Marketing* (New York: McGraw-Hill, 1986).

21. Phil Bligh and Doug Kurk, "Cashing In on Customer Loyalty," *CRM Magazine* (June 2004): 48+; and Matthew Haeberle, "Betting on Customer Loyalty: Harrah's Loyalty Program Is No Gamble—It's a Sure Thing," *Chain Store Age* (January 2004): 12A+.

22. Leonard L. Berry and A. Parasuraman, *Marketing Services: Competing Through Quality* (New York: Free Press, 1991), pp. 136–142.

23. Colleen Dejong, "Loyalty Marketing at a Glance; Hotel Programs," *Colloquy*, http://www.colloquy.com/cont_matrix.asp?industry=Hotel (accessed October 24, 2001).

24. James H. Donnelly, Jr., Leonard L. Berry, and Thomas W. Thompson, *Marketing Financial Services: A Strategic Vision* (Homewood, IL: Dow Jones–Irwin, 1985), p. 113.

25. Thomas E. Caruso, "Kotler: Future Marketers Will Focus on Customer Data Base to Compete Globally," *Marketing News* (June 8, 1992): 21.

26. Allison Perlik, "High Fidelity: Exclusive R&I Research Reveals What Draws Loyal Customers and What Drives Them Away," *Restaurants & Institutions* (February 15, 2003): 44+.

27. Frederick F. Reichheld and W. Earl Sasser, Jr., "Zero Defections: Quality Comes to Services," *Harvard Business Review,* 68 (1990): 105–111.

28. Ibid.

29. Philip Kotler, John T. Bowen, and James C. Makens, *Marketing for Hospitality and Tourism* (Upper Saddle River, NJ: Prentice Hall, 1996); "Hotel Values Profit from Service," *Hospitality* (February 2000): 32–34.

30. David Cravens, "Introduction to Special Issue," *Journal of the Academy of Marketing Science,* 23, no. 4 (1995): 235.

31. See DMA, *The Poiver of Direct Marketing, 2009–2010 Edition;* and "Mail Spend to Rise," *Deliver Magazine* (January 7, 2010), https://www.deUvermagazine.com/the-magazine/2010/01/07/mail-spend-to-rise; Direct Marketing Association, "The DMA 2007 Statistical Fact Book" (June 2007), p. 224.

32. Julie Liesse, "When Times Are Hard, Mail Works," *Advertising Age* (March 30, 2009): 14; and Sarah O'Leary, "Thanks to Spam, It's Not Junk Mail Anymore," *Huffington Post* (April 19, 2010), http://www. huffingtonpost.com/sarah-oleary/thanks-to-spam-its-not-ju_b_542024.html; For counterpoints, see Gavin O'Malley, "Direct-Mail Doomed, Long Live E-Mail," *MediaPost News* (May 20, 2009), accessed at www. mediapost.com/publications.

33. DMA, *The Power of Direct Marketing, 2009–2010 Edition.* Direct Marketing Association, "The DMA 2006 Statistical Fact Book" (June 2006), p. 250.

34. "Off the Hook," *Marketing Management* (January–February 2008): 5; Jeff Gelles, "Consumer 10.0: Calls Persist Despite List," *Philadelphia Inquirer* (January 24, 2010): D2; and www.donotcall.gov (accessed October 2010); Christopher S. Rugaber, "Do Not Call List Expanded 23% to 132M U.S. Phone Numbers in 2006, Federal Agency Says," *Associated Press* (April 5, 2007).

35. Teinowitz, "Do Not Call Does Not Hurt Direct Marketing," p. 3.

36. Stephanie Rosenbloom, "The New Touch-Face of Vending Machines," *New York Times* (May 25, 2010), accessed at www.nytimes.com/2010/05/26/business/26vending.html; "Interactive: Ad Age Names Finalists," *Advertising Age* (February 27, 1995): 12–14.

37. Richard Levey, "Cruising into the Mail Stream," *Direct* (June 2003): 9.

38. John Martin, "How to Use E-Mail Marketing to Increase Occupancy," *HSMAI Marketing Review* (Summer 2001): 27–29.

39. Tracking Customer Habits, *Nation's Restaurant News* (May 21, 2001): T6+.

40. Jant Logan, "Dialog Marketing Elevates E-Mail Effectiveness," *Customer Interaction Solutions,* http://prquest.umi.com/pdqweb?Did=000000091700542 (accessed December 30, 2001).

41. Beth Negus Viveiros, "Red Lobster to Upgrade Loyalty Program," *Direct* (July 2004): 10.

42. Carlo Wolff, "Cutting Through the Clutter," *Lodging Hospitality* (September 1, 2008): 46–48.

43. See http://portal.data2gold.com/.

44. Symantec, *The State of Spam and Phishing: Home of the Monthly Report—April 2010,* accessed at www. symantec.com/business/theme.jsp?themeid=state_of_spam.

45. Daniel B. Honigman, "On the Verge: Mobile Marketing Will Make Strides," *Marketing News* (January 15, 2008): 18–21; "Mobile Search Ads to Grow 130% by 2013," *TechWeb* (February 25, 2009); "Mobile Web Use Leaps. 34%," *Adweek* (September 30, 2009), www.adweek.com; Carol Flammer, "Cell Phones, Texting and Your Customers" (January 9, 2010), www. carolflammer.com/2010/01/cell-phones-text-messaging-marketing-to-consumers/; and "Wireless Quick Facts," http://www.ctia.org/advocacy/research/index-cfm/AID/10323 (accessed July 2010).

46. Max Starkov and Mariana Mechoso Safer, "It's Time for a Mid-Year Course Correction: The Results of the Annual Survey on Digital Marketing Are In, *HeBSdigital.*

com (July 26, 2011) accessed September 25, 2011, from hsamieconnect.org.

47. Gina Baillie, "Why the Travel Industry Needs to Wake Up to Mobile," *EyeforTravel* (July 7, 2011), accessed September 9, 2011, from hsamiecnnect.org.

48. Mobile Marketing: The New Frontier, HSMAI Foundation, September 9, 2009.

49. Adapted from Michael Garry, "Going Mobile," *Supermarket News* (January 12, 2009): 65.

50. For this and other examples, see Alice Z. Cuneo, "Marketers Get Serious About the Third Screen," *Advertising Age* (July 11, 2005): 6; and Louise Story, "Madison Avenue Calling," *New York Times,* www.nytimes.com (accessed January 20, 2007).

51. See Emily Burg, "Acceptance of Mobile Ads on the Rise," *MediaPost Publications* (March 16, 2007), accessed at www.mediapost.com/publications; Steve Miller and Mike Beirne, "The iPhone Effect," *Adweek.com* (April 28, 2008), www.adweek.com; Altmeyer, "Smart Phones, Social Networks to Boost Mobile Advertising," *Reuters.com* (June 29, 2009); and Richard Westlund, "Mobile on Fast Forward," *Brandweek* (March 15, 2010): M1–M5.

52. Arbitron/Edison Internet and Multimedia Study, "The Podcast Consumer Revealed 2009" (accessed at www.edisonresearch.com/home/archives/2009/05/the_podcast_consumer_2009.php); and "Marketing News' Digital Handbook," *Marketing News* (April 3, 2009): 9–18.

53. "Disney Online Podcasts," http://disney.go.com/music/podcasts/today/index.html (accessed December 2010); "HP Audio and Video Podcasts," www.hp.com/hpinfo/podcasts.html (accessed December 2010); and "Take These Shows on the Road," http://www.purina.com/downloads/Podcasts/Index.aspx (accessed December 2010).

54. Shahnaz Mahmud, 'Survey: Viewers Crave TV Ad Fusion,' *Adweek.com* (January 25, 2008), www.adweek.com; Andrew Hampp, "Addressable Ads Are Here; Who's Ready?" *Advertising Age* (April 13, 2009): 9; and Hampp, "Scorecard: Were We Wrong or Almost Right on LTV?" *Advertising Age* (April 12, 2010), http://adage.com/cabletvlO/article?article_id=143163.

55. See 'U.S. Web Retail Sales to Reach $249 Billion by '14—Study,' *Reuters* (March 8, 2010), accessed at www.reuters.com/article/idUSN0825407420100308; and "Retail and Travel Spending," *Advertising Age's Digital Marketing Facts 2010* section (February 22,2010).

56. Erick Schonfeld, "Forrester Forecast: Online Retail Sales Will Grow to $250 Billion by 2014," *Tech Crunch.com* (March 8, 2010), accessed at http://techcrunch.com/2010/03/08/forrester-forecast-online-retail-sales-will-grow-to-250-billion-by-2014/; and Anna Johnson, "Local Marketing: 97 Percent of Consumers Use Online Media for Local Shopping," *Kikabink Nexus* (March 17, 2010), accessed at www.kikabink.com/news/local-marketing-97-percent-of-consumers-use-online-media-for-local-shopping/.

57. Beth Snyder Bulik, "Who Blogs?" *Advertising Age* (June 4, 2007): 20.

58. Pete Blackshaw, "Irrational Exuberance? I Hope We're Not Guilty," *Barcode Blog,* www.barcodefactorycom/wordpress.?p=72 (accessed August 26, 2005).

59. Michelle Slatalla, "Toll-Free Apology Soothes Savage Beast," *New York Times* (February 12, 2004): G4; and information from www.planetfeedback.com/consumer (accessed November 2007).

60. Max Starkov and Mariana Mechoso Safer, "It's Time for a Mid-Year Course Correction: The Results of the Annual Survey on Digital Marketing Are In, *HeBSdigital.com* (July 26, 2011), accessed September 25, 2011, from hsamieconnect.org.

61. Lauren Goode, "Internet Is Set to Overtake Newspapers in Ad Revenue," *Digits News and Insights* (June 15, 2010), accessed August 4, 2012, from http://blogs.wsj.com/digits/2010/06/15/internet-is-set-to-overtake-newspapers-in-ad-revenue/.

62. Internet Advertising Bureau, *IAB Internet Advertising Revenue Report* (April 2012), accessed August 6, 2012, from http://www.iab.net/insights_research/industry_data_and_landscape/adrevenuereport.

63. See Should My Restaurant Use a Groupon Type Deal, *MCN Marketing* (March 28, 2012), accessed June 8, 2012, from http://www.mcngmarketing.com/should-my-restaurant-use-groupon-or-living-social/#.T9OHhHrl_zs.

64. Elissa Elan, "Operators Say Social Media Gets Marketing Message Out" (May 15, 2012), accessed June 9, 2012, from http://www.restaurant.org/nra_news_blog/2012/05/operators-say-social-media-gets-marketing-message-out.cfm.

65. Todd Wasser, "How Hotels and Travel Companies Are Nailing Social Media" (October 28, 2011), accessed June 10, 2012, from http://mashable.com/2011/10/28/hotels-travel-social-media/.

66. See "Best Use of a Social Media Platform" (accessed June 19, 2012), from http://www.travelandleisure.com/smittys.

67. Mike D'Antonio, "Affinia Hotels Brings Feedback Home," *1 to 1 Magazine* (July/August 2008): 13.

68. See Peter Han and Angus Maclaurin, "Do Consumers Really Care About Online Privacy?" *Marketing Management* (January–February 2002): 35–38.

69. See Jennifer DiSabatino, "FTC OKs Self-Regulation to Protect Children's Privacy," *Computerworld* (February 12, 2001): 32.

Managing Hospitality and Tourism Marketing

Destination Marketing

Objectives

After reading this chapter, you should be able to:

1. Discuss the benefits of tourism.
2. Explain tourism strategies and different options for creating and investing in tourism attractions.
3. Understand how to segment and identify visitor segments.
4. Explain how central tourist agencies are organized.

Best known as a professional football team within the National Football League (NFL), the Carolina Panthers is also an important member of the hospitality and tourism industry within Charlotte and the Carolinas. Indeed the name *Carolina Panthers* was chosen to demonstrate that this team serves two states.

The chapter opening photo shows the Panthers in Super Bowl XXXVIII which was played in Reliant Stadium. Reliant, like most other stadiums, is owned by a local government agency. The Panthers are unique, owner and former Baltimore Colts player Jerry Richardson, owns their 73,504-seat stadium in Charlotte, North Carolina. Private ownership permitted product line planning for the entire stadium. This enhanced the role of the Carolina Panthers as an important member of the Charlotte hospitality industry. Johnson & Wales University was enticed to move to Charlotte and become a neighbor of the Panthers.

The stadium was built in downtown Charlotte on property that had badly deteriorated and was in need of urban revitalization. Thus, the stadium became a tourist attraction for hundreds of thousands of visitors both during the season and outside the playing period. Huge lifelike statues of black panthers, with emerald green eyes, beautiful landscaping, nearby parking, and a Panthers pro shop serve as attractions for off-season visitors.

Although ticket sales represent the most important product, other product lines were carefully planned to increase revenue and enhance the excitement and image of the team. The stadium was planned to permit great views of the playing field from all seats from each of the three areas: lower level (less expensive), middle level (club level), and third level (luxury suites). Jerry Richardson's personal suite is not on the 50-yard line but directly behind the goalposts, a position often thought of as "cheap" seating.

Prior to opening the stadium, "Personal Seat Licenses" (PSLs) were sold to fans. All seats were sold out by opening day. A PSL is not a game ticket but instead allows fans to purchase tickets. The PSL may be sold or passed on to heirs. Originally PSLs sold for $1,500 to $3,000 but by 2007 had appreciated to $5,000 to $10,000.

Luxury boxes with plate-glass windows facing the playing field surround level three of the stadium. Suites include a mix of products from private corporate suites to shared suites in which tables for four are leased by individuals or companies. Suite 87, named for Mr. Richardson's Baltimore Colt number, has granite and marble tables, hardwood floors, and a humidor for the private stock of cigars for suite owners. A seat at a table in this suite costs $10,000 to buy plus $3,000 per year for tickets, meaning that a table of four would produce revenue of $52,000 plus food and beverage expenditures. Stadium smoking is allowed only in a well-ventilated smoking room or outside.

All suites receive first-class food and beverage attention, with food prepared by four full-time chefs in ultramodern stainless-steel kitchens in the stadium. The interior portion of level three was planned as six separate dual-purpose areas for pregame, after game, and halftime relaxation and on nongame days for use by sales meetings, reunions, and many other group functions such as high school proms. These six club areas have permanent bars for serving alcohol beverages, televisions and drop-down screens, stage areas for bands or presentations, and wait-staff service.

Each area is different, such as "The Locker Room" and the "Red Zone." These areas are covered with unique carpeting, such as a Panthers Claw carpet and a football cleat carpet. There is also an upscale Pro Shop in this area serving yet another product.

The subway area of the stadium is also rented for functions and has proven to be very popular for meetings. Again, food and beverage is served by a wait staff. Traditional concession areas exist on levels one and two, featuring sales of stadium foods such as hot dogs and soft drinks.

Signage is also a product line. Advertising rights are sold beginning with the name *Bank of America Stadium* and continuing with signage throughout the stadium, including LED screens that rotate with different sponsors during the game. Throughout the world, stadium signage is sold, but in many the amount exceeds good taste and creates confused and jumbled messages with advertising on each step, each stadium seat, and every available foot of the stadium visible to fans and television cameras. This is not the case with the Carolina Panthers.

Richardson knew that signage is an important product line but demanded that it be provided in a non-cluttered, sophisticated manner that would not offend fans and would also provide great exposure for advertisers. No field-level signage exists at this stadium. This means that available signage is relatively expensive.

The success of product lines is not accidental. A professional sales team is needed to ensure success. A five-person team is employed full time to sell the many Panthers products to corporate clients. Scott Auker is representative of those five salespeople. Scott loves the sport of football and played ball through college and briefly thereafter. He also served on the coaching staff for Washington State University, the University of Miami, and the University of California at Berkeley.

Scott also understands marketing and has responsibility for working with a portfolio of commercial sponsors. He custom-designs packages for clients and prospects to meet their needs. This might involve signage, a suite, use of club area space for sales meetings, and personal use such as weddings or anniversaries. Scott can arrange menus and professional entertainment such as a country-western band. The needs of clients continuously change as their companies introduce new products, build new distribution systems, enter new markets, and make other changes. Scott must understand the changing needs of these clients and create new packages for them while also looking for new clients. His experience with teams has proven invaluable because teamwork is required between various departments, such as catering, public relations, and sales. Occasionally a client might request holding a sales or motivation meeting in the team video room used by the Panthers during game days for strategy sessions, halftime review, and other coaching staff/player meetings. This means that Scott also works with the coaching staff and players because clients sometimes request a personal appearance by one or more of the players.

Careful attention to details in the planning and management of the complete product line of the Carolina Panthers created a unique hospitality and tourism attraction for Charlotte and the Carolinas.

Major-league sports teams such as the Carolina Panthers are an important tourism attraction. In this chapter we discuss a variety of tourism products, including medical tourism, agritourism, space tourism, purpose-driven, and even carp-tourism.

■■■ The Globalization of the Tourist Industry

The word **tourism** has many definitions. We use the British Tourist Authority's definition of tourism: "a stay of one or more nights away from home for holidays, visitors to friends or relatives, business conferences or any other purpose except such things as boarding education or semi-permanent employment."[1] This book

TABLE 17–1
The World's Top Tourism Destinations (International Tourist Arrivals)

Rank	Country	Arrivals in Millions
1	France	74.2
2	United States	54.9
3	Spain	52.2
4	China	50.9
5	Italy	43.2
6	United Kingdom	28.0
7	Turkey	25.5
8	Germany	24.2
9	Malaysia	23.6
10	Mexico	21.5

Source: Data 2009, The World Tourism Organization.

17.1 World Trade Organization, http://unwto.org/en: The World Tourism Organization sells much of its research. However, if you click the media button at the top of the page, you can get some interesting information.

uses the words *tourism* and *travel* interchangeably. Table 17–1 lists the international tourists arrivals at the top tourist destinations.

The world has become a global community, opening places unimaginable decades earlier: the wonders of Antarctica, the secrets of the Himalayas, the rain forests of the Amazon, the beauty of Tahiti, the Great Wall of China, the dramatic Victoria Falls, the origin of the Nile, and the wilds of the Scottish islands. Travel is a global business with an expanding market.

In 2005, Austria was number nine in tourist arrivals but by 2009 had been replaced by Malaysia. Mexico dropped to number 10 from its previous position as number 8. Turkey had not been listed among the top ten in 2005.

Today many industries of the world are dominated by relatively few competitors (oligopolies) who hold major market shares. It is often difficult or impossible for potential new competitors to enter those markets. Market entry in tourism is open, and new destinations can acquire the economic and social benefits of tourism.

Students reading this book today can enter the world tourism industry and plan strategies to help drive tourism growth for their nations, states, and cities. Successful destination planning and marketing can bring hundreds of millions and even billions of dollars in revenue to destinations. New supportive industries and jobs can be created and standards of living can be increased. At the same time, the interchange of cultures assists the quest for world peace. Destination marketing is a career worthy of college and university graduates.

Tourist destinations do not need spectacular attractions such as an Eiffel Tower, Grand Canyon, or Leaning Tower to participate in today's tourism. The modest city of Ruili in Yunnan, southwest China, is vying for the title of "Top Tourist City," a distinction awarded by the China National Tourism Administration. Ruili spent 10 million yuan to improve roads and actively promotes a water-sprinkling festival, its local jewelry manufacturing, local farms, and tropical scenes to attract foreign visitors from Thailand, India, Pakistan, and Myanmar, as well as domestic tourists.[2]

Regions such as Eastern Europe and countries such as China and India are rapidly developing. They are now generators of tourists, as well as destinations for tourists. In 2010, China gained US $200 billion from domestic tourism and US $46 billion from international tourism.[3] By 2020, China is

Tourism accounts for more than 50 percent of Bermuda's foreign exchange. Courtesy of Dorling Kindersley, Ltd.

expected to be the largest inbound and outbound market in the world. China has 2.5 million hotel rooms and in 15 to 20 years is expected to have 5 to 7 million more.

■■■ Importance of Tourism to a Destination's Economy

The Tourism Destination

Tourists travel to **destinations**, places with some form of actual or perceived boundary, such as the physical boundary of an island, political boundaries, or even market-created boundaries such as those of a travel wholesaler who defines a South Pacific tour solely as Australia and New Zealand. Central America consists of seven nations, but few, if any, national tourist offices or tour planners view it that way. A commonly packaged tour of Central America includes only two or three nations, such as Costa Rica, Guatemala, and Panama. Others are excluded for reasons of political instability or deficient **infrastructure**.

Although Australia and New Zealand are often packaged together for the North American visitor, Australia has worked hard for many years to make it a single destination rather than share the limited vacation time of visitors. In turn, destinations within Australia, such as the state of Western Australia, or cities such as Perth or Adelaide, believe they must develop a distinct destinations reputation to avoid being left out or used only as overnight stopovers.

The desire to become a recognized destination presents a difficult marketing challenge. Within eastern North Carolina, the town of New Bern has several interesting visitor attractions and events. The remainder of the county offers considerably less, yet visitor promotion funds are collected from a countywide hotel bed tax. Political pressure forced tourism officials to promote Craven County as a destination rather than just the town of New Bern. The promotion of a relatively unfamiliar town poses sufficient problems, but the promotion of a county greatly intensifies the challenge.

Macrodestinations such as the United States contain thousands of microdestinations, including regions, states, cities, towns, and even visitor destinations within a town. It is not unusual to find tourists who view their Hawaiian destination as the Hilton Hawaiian Village in Honolulu and may rarely, if ever, venture outside the perimeter. Thousands of visitors fly to Orlando and proceed directly to Disney World, where most or all of their vacation is spent. These tourists do not view Florida or Orlando as their destinations, but rather Disney World.

Benefits of Tourism

Tourism's most visible benefit is direct employment in hotels, restaurants, retail establishments, and transportation. A second but less visible benefit consists of support industries and professions (e.g., revenue management software companies and university tourism professors), many of which pay considerably more than the visible employment opportunities such as restaurant personnel. The third benefit of tourism is the **multiplier effect**, as tourist expenditures are recycled through the local economy. Governments use economic impact models to estimate overall employment gains in goods and services consumption resulting from tourism multipliers. Tourism's fourth benefit is state and local revenues derived from taxes on tourism.

Tourism helps shift the tax burden to nonresidents. For example, tourism accounts for more than half of Bermuda's foreign exchange and tax revenues. Bermuda's per head embarkation fee is one of the highest in the world, as are its import taxes on durables from cars to refrigerators. It is one of the few developed countries without an income tax. New York's cumulative bed tax on hotel rooms raises hundreds of millions of dollars in annual revenues. Dallas, Los Angeles, and Houston all have bed taxes in excess of 12 percent. Hawaii derives a heavy percent of its total state and county taxes from tourism. Taxation of travelers has become a popular, often hidden, tax, and includes airline ticket taxes, hotel taxes, and other user fees.[4]

Critics of such taxation contend that these schemes are taxation without representation and eventually lead to careless government spending or spending that has little relevance to promoting tourism and enhancing the travel experience. Hospitality and travel managers must make sure that bed taxes and other tourist-related taxes go back into promoting tourism and developing the infrastructure to support tourism. In turn, this supports a sub-industry of advertising, publicity, planning, and administration.

Tourism also yields a fifth benefit: It stimulates exports of locally made products. Estimates of visitor spending on gifts, clothing, and souvenirs are in the range of 15 to 20 percent of total expenditures. The degree to which these products are made or assembled in a destination affects the economic impact of the local economy.

Many tourist destinations provide government-supported market areas for the sale of locally produced handicrafts. This provides an income source to local producers and also creates an interesting and sought-after shopping experience for visitors.

Destinations may not welcome tourists uniformly. Due to location, climate, limited resources, size, and cultural heritage, some places have few economic choices other than to participate in tourism. Some engage in tourism with mixed emotions and, at times, ambivalence. For instance, Bali is concerned that tourism is destroying its culture, as farmland becomes resorts and new jobs unravel family values. "Bali and tourism is not a marriage of love," observed a Bali tourism official, clearly focusing on the dilemma of cultural breakdown.

This is becoming a serious issue in many parts of the United States, particularly the West. The people of Colorado voted against the use of tax revenues for use in tourism promotion. In many small communities, residents are increasingly opposed to the use of sales tax receipts for tourism promotion. Others have mounted opposition to large groups that bring thousands of visitors to the community, such as baseball tournaments, spring vacation students, or motorcycle events. The mixture of full-time residents versus owners of second homes is changing in many resort communities, with part-time residents becoming a greater percentage of the population. These people do not depend on the local economy for employment and often view masses of tourists as a negative factor in their enjoyment of the community.

"Tourism, long viewed as vile, repressive, and imperialistic by the Castro government, was out of necessity given center stage as the shining star upon which Cuba's hopes for a productive and economically sound future was pinned."[5] This reversal by the Castro government shows the importance of tourism, especially in island countries.

Management of the Tourist Destination

Responsibility for management of tourist destinations is generally shared by many diverse public and private organizations known as Destination Management Organizations. These include departments and ministries of tourism as well as chamber of commerce, hotel/motel associations, environmental organizations, and many more.

Bringing such groups together for planning and strategy purposes is often difficult. However, there is an area of common concern that has developed priority status in many communities following events such as 9/11 or the horrible tsunamis that struck Southeast Asia and later Japan.

Crisis planning and preparedness has come to the forefront in tourism management. The Pacific Area Travel Association (PATA) has developed a comprehensive Four-Phase Disaster Planning Model built on *Reduction, Readiness, Response,* and *Recovery.* Of these perhaps only Reduction needs further explanation.

Reduction refers to increasing crisis awareness through emphasizing and securing political awareness of the impact of a crisis to the tourism market.

A survey of crises in diverse communities showed that most respondents had experienced some form of emergency in the previous five years. Most common among them were the following:[6]

Crisis	Respondents (%)
Weather	75
Natural disaster	65
Crime	40

Crises are not the only negative factors that affect tourism destinations. Destinations that fail to maintain the necessary infrastructure or build inappropriate infrastructure face significant risks. Italy's Adriatic Sea coast has been devastated by the adverse publicity associated with the growth of brown algae that makes swimming nearly impossible. Growing pollution levels at the Grand Canyon and overcrowding in Yosemite Valley may significantly diminish the attractiveness of these great national parks. Some of East Africa's renowned game parks are being turned into dust bowls by tourists ferried around in four-wheel-drive vehicles.

Greece's national treasure, the formerly white marble Parthenon in Athens, stands as a pollution-stained symbol of environmental neglect. Thailand's beautiful beach resorts and temples have been severely damaged by pollution and poor sanitation.

"Destination marketing is an integral part of developing and retaining a particular location's popularity. Too often, however, tourism planners focus only on destination developments without paying attention to retaining and preserving the attributes that attracted travelers to the destination in the first place."[7]

Several locations have been identified as suffering from a lack of destination maintenance. These include Pattaya, Thailand; Bali, Indonesia; and Huatulco, Mexico. Many North American destinations are also experiencing visitor overuse, including the Sedona, Arizona, area. A professional observer of this area noted that destructive visitor behavior could destroy the base on which Sedona's tourism is built.[8]

A theory offered by futurist August St. John argues that a resort destination will experience a life cycle similar to the product life cycle and eventually go into decline, or the destruction stage, as St. John calls it.[9] Tourism managers must manage their products and make sure that during the growth stage the foundation is built for an infrastructure that will support future tourism demands. In some cases, sustaining tourism in the mature stage may mean limiting the amount of tourists to a number that the infrastructure can handle. Tourist development must balance the temptation to maximize tourist dollars with preservation of the natural tourist attractions and the quality of life for local residents. This is often a difficult task. Those tourist destinations that do not manage their product may have a short life. Tourist destinations that build solid infrastructures can look for increased business by expanding from a seasonal product to a multi-seasonal product or by expanding the geographic base of their product. For example, Aspen, Colorado, expanded from winter skiing to summer recreation, education, and culture. Quebec promotes summer and fall tourism and its winter carnival and skiing. West Virginia is popular in the summer and fall seasons, but it also aggressively promotes the spring and winter seasons.

The Shakespeare Festival in Stratford, Canada, began as a small regional event and became a North American event for the United States and Canada. Most musical and cultural festivals in Europe followed the same pattern, such as Salzburg, Edinburgh, and Spoleto. Europe's Festival of Arts provides a selection among fifty musical festivals from Norway to Spain, with several dozen dance competitions, major summer art exhibits, and theater from London's West End to Berlin's Festival Weeks. The entire European continent, including Eastern Europe, has exploded in summer-place competition for tourists.

Social/Cultural Effects of Tourism

Tourism growth affects the social/cultural basis of destinations in both positive and negative ways. Cuba offers an extreme example. After Castro opened Cuba's doors to tourism, an unexpected societal phenomenon occurred. The tourism boom

Tanzania is one of the most popular tourist destinations in Africa. In an effort to create sustainable tourism, tourists on safaris now carry cameras instead of guns.Courtesy of Richard Nowitz/National Geographic Image Collection.

resulted in the departure of highly trained professionals from their careers. Physicians, teachers, engineers, and others abandoned their professions to become waiters, bartenders, and bellhops. A teacher earning one hundred eighty pesos per month could easily earn that amount in a day in tourism. In addition, individuals with hard currency acquired from tips could shop in the "dollar store" where only foreign currency was accepted. These stores had no shortage of consumer products.

As regulations were relaxed in Cuba, thousands of Cuban citizens opened and operated a multitude of small ventures such as home restaurants and handcrafts.[10]

In many communities, women and young people are better suited for positions within the tourism industry. Men who are used for manual labor may find positions in landscaping, carpentry, or other fields, but individuals who are accustomed to working for themselves may find that work rules, required hours of work, and other requirements become constrictive.

Sustainable Tourism

"Tourism planners need to take into account the capacity of a location's environment to support all of the area's residents, not just tourists. Without such planning, a destination can be damaged to the point that travelers will stay away."[11] From a marketing standpoint, sustainable tourism can mean giving up current revenues from tourism by limiting capacity to ensure there will be demand for tourism in the future.

The Wave, a spectacular Jurassic-era Navajo sandstone formation near Big Water, Utah, is one of the most photographed rock formations in North America. It is also popular as a hiking destination that the Bureau of Land Management (BLM) limits daily visits to twenty people, who are selected by a random drawing of numbers.[12]

This may well be a view of things to come, as those responsible for natural and historical attractions throughout the world struggle to protect their properties yet serve increasing numbers of visitors.

Sustainable tourism is a concept of tourism management that anticipates and prevents problems that occur when carrying capacity is exceeded. Carrying capacity can be determined by an environmental impact assessment (EIA). An EIA typically follows these steps:

1. Inventory the social, political, physical, and economic environment.

2. Projects trends.

3. Sets goals and objectives.

4. Examines alternatives to reach goals.

5. Selects preferred alternatives.

6. Develops implementation strategy.

7. Implement strategy.

8. Evaluate outcome.

Ecotourism is one of the fastest-growing niche markets in the travel industry and generally viewed as representing sustainable tourism. In fact, this occurs only when government and private industry cooperate in planning and strict enforcement of regulations and laws. Costa Rica is commonly cited as a good example of ecotourism. By contrast, ecotourism in Nepal now resembles mass tourism. Two hundred mountain lodges have been built, with large areas cleared for timber, resulting in erosion. Excessive hiking has also resulted in erosion as well as trash and sewage problems, even on Mount Everest.[13]

Costa Rica attracts ecotourists from around the world.Courtesy of Steve Dunwell Photography/Getty Images, Inc.—Image Bank.

Modified Environments: Ecotourism Subsets

Today, members of the tourism industry such as resorts, ski lodges, golf courses, and city centers have developed habitats on their grounds that encourage wildlife. Peregrine falcons have learned to thrive in U.S. cities.[14]

Rather than provide neatly manicured lawns and plants that provide no food value to animals, some resorts are encouraging natural areas, nesting sites, and artificial reefs. Guests are usually thrilled to see wildlife on the grounds. Admittedly, problems can occur as deer populations explode or dangerous predators ranging from poisonous snakes to crocodiles and cougars find the grounds to their liking.

Industry and Community Cooperation

Many communities that directly depend on tourism fail to coordinate important sectors of the economy. Estes Park, Colorado, offers an example of such a community. Retirees and other residents are upset by tourism traffic. Residents want a rustic mountain getaway with modern conveniences, which are provided through tourism-based revenue. "A lodging-driven Chamber of Commerce results in an unconcerned attitude by retailers and restaurants that do not see themselves as part of the underpinning of the tourism industry, even though data point in the other direction."[15]

Communities with these divisions must expect to face continuous discord among important constituencies. Successful long-run tourism destinations require cooperation in planning among constituencies.

Carbon-Neutral Vacations

As the number of concerns about global warming increases, the demand for carbon-neutral vacations will also increase. Many adjustments lie ahead for hospitality providers and their guests. The challenge is already difficult at some luxurious resorts where energy-intensive amenities are plentiful. Prices at the King Pacific Lodge, a deluxe floating lodge on the remote British Columbia coast, start about $5,000 per head for three nights, including the float plane, spa treatment, and Cuban cigars. Even so, the lodge has said no to guests for requests determined to be environmentally unfriendly, such as one to hire three twin-engine boats to take a party of seven salmon fishing. The guest offered to pay extra for the fuel but was still denied because of concerns about the environment.[16]

Because leisure travel is emotional and discretionary, guests have come to expect amenities and services without questioning the environment. The following are guest privileges formerly taken for granted and now being questioned:

	Results (lbs of CO_2)
Using fresh towels each day	½
Jet ski (three hours)	730
Keeping hotel room cool (24 hours)	105
Eighteen holes of golf in a cart	3
Taking a Coke from minibar	2
45 minutes on treadmill	2
Two hours fishing trip in a boat	420 per passenger
45-minute helicopter ride	350 per passenger

The emphasis on CO_2 emissions will not be popular or acceptable to all guests. A Beverly Hills divorce lawyer who was a guest at King Pacific Lodge said this of such efforts, "It's putting a Band-Aid on a world-wide sore. It's great for liberal people—those who are antagonistic to the wealthy, who are able to afford to ride in a helicopter."

■■■ Tourism Strategies and Investments

Tourist competition is fierce amid a growing and constantly changing tourist market. In addition to strong tourist destinations, declining places upgrade and make new investments, and new places appear. Leavenworth, Washington, an old logging and mining town, experienced revival when it transformed itself into a Bavarian village. Winterset, Iowa, John Wayne's birthplace, is now visited by tourists. Seymour, Wisconsin, lays claim to being home of the first hamburger, hosting August Hamburger Days. Seymour organizers once cooked the world's largest hamburger, weighing 5,520 pounds.

Countless examples exist of destinations rediscovering their past, capitalizing on the birthplace of a famous person, an event, a battle, or other "hidden gems." Places rely on various monikers for identification: Sheboygan, Wisconsin, as City of Cheese, Choirs, Children, and Churches; Crystal City, Texas, as the Spinach Capital of the World; Lexington, Kentucky, as the Athens of the West; New Haven, Connecticut, as the City of Elms. Many places still bear nicknames of their economic heritage: Hartford, Connecticut, as Insurance City; Holyoke, Massachusetts, as Paper City; Westfield, New York, as Buggy Whip City; and Paterson, New Jersey, as Silk City. These destinations are not likely to become international tourist destinations, but they can be effective tourist products in the regional tourism market.

In Shandong Province of China, the city of Qufu was the hometown of Confucius, the ancient philosopher and educator. The local tourism department features the Confucian culture as a way of differentiating the city. In keeping with the principles of Confucius, the local tourism department and the police cooperate in a program to reprimand tour operators and others who engage in unethical business practices. This program includes a tourist complaint center and a training program in ethics for local hotel employees.[17]

With the current U.S. trend toward shorter but more frequent vacations, many places within 200 miles or so of major metropolitan areas have found new opportunities to access the tourist market. Local tourism and convention bureaus tout the theme, "Stay Close to Home." The Louisiana Office of Tourism spent $6 million to market a summer travel bargain program to a 500-mile market.

Cities create many tourist attractions. Darling Harbour in Sydney has developed as a major tourist attraction. It is the location of the Sydney Convention and Exhibition Centre and home to numerous restaurants, retail stores, and attractions, including the Sydney Aquarium, Australian National Maritime Museum, and an Imax theater. The district is also within walking distance of the Star Casino and

Marketing Highlight   Betting on a New Highway

17–1 During the Colorado gold rush of the nineteenth century, the twin cities of Central City and Black Hawk, Colorado, were boomtowns with great wealth and instant millionaires. Then it all ended, and the two became decaying ghost towns for nearly 100 years, with a handful of residents, old mining bars, and a few tourist shops.

Boom times returned in 1991 when the Colorado state legislature permitted casino gambling in the two towns located less than an hour west of Denver in the Rocky Mountains.

At first, casinos proved to be an incredible source of riches for Central City. Millions of dollars were spent by casino operators to renovate historical old buildings and to improve the town's infrastructure, including new water and sewage facilities. The Historic Preservation Fund received over $2.5 million from gaming revenues to use for a variety of projects.

A sure sign that the honeymoon between residents and casinos had ended occurred when the powerful Central City Historic Preservation Committee blocked permits for new casino construction in anything other than existing buildings. This meant that casinos would be small operations and find difficulty competing with those in Black Hawk. Parking also became a severe problem because buildings could not be torn down for parking and the mountain terrain offered few sites.

Meanwhile, the sister town of Black Hawk had other ideas and attitudes toward casinos. One observer offered the analogy of a brand new McDonald's competing against an old worn-out hamburger stand a mile away through traffic and without adequate parking. Black Hawk is positive about casinos, encourages expansion of buildings and parking, and is the first town on a narrow, winding road. Central City lies a mile farther up the road, with casinos that seem to lack the excitement of those in Black Hawk.

By 1996, Central City had witnessed the closing of twenty-one casinos and had only six remaining retail shops. In 1997, the city government's budget was $350,000 with eight city employees, down from an $8 million budget in 1991 with one hundred city employees.

Many casino operators believed it was possible and perhaps inevitable for casino gambling to cease in Central City. Casino gambling in Colorado is supported by repeat frequent gamblers from Denver and other front-range cities that represent about 90 percent of revenues. Many of these hard-core gamblers switched allegiances to casinos in Black Hawk, leaving Central City to low-spending tourists.

By 2003, Black Hawk had twenty-two casinos and Central City had only five. Something had to be done to prevent Central City from once again becoming a ghost town. The Central City Business and Improvement District raised $38.3 million from local businesses to build a four-lane highway from I–70 over a new 12-minute scenic drive with sunny exposures to melting snow and ice, direct to Central City. By contrast, Highway 119 to Black Hawk is a winding two-lane road known for its winter ice and summer congestion.

Black Hawk tried to block construction of the new highway, buying up old mining claims on the route and attempting to annex the land. These attempts failed and the highway, built in one year entirely with private funds, opened in November 2004.

"We call it the Highway of Opportunity," said city manager Lynnette Hailey of Central City. "It's our opportunity to bring people to Central City to experience our historic town."

Central City is betting on more than casinos to attract tourism dollars. The Tabor Opera House, meticulously restored rock walls throughout town, a museum, freshly painted Victorian-style homes, and antique stores are part of the planned attractions. City Manager Hailey said, "When gaming was approved, Central City had 350 historic properties and Black Hawk had a trailer park." Central City is betting that it can rejuvenate its casino trade and continue to adhere to the town's historic ordinances.

Opening day for the new highway brought smiles to Central City casino operators. "We've been slammed all day and we hope it holds," said Pam Kidwell of the Dostal Alley Casino. "Everyone takes the new road and it sure beats the heck out of coming through Black Hawk."

Doc Holliday Casino general manager Terry Houk said his business was double the normal on opening day. "The road that takes people to Black Hawk, they didn't even have to pay for," said Houk. "It was just there and paid with our tax dollars. Well, we've paid for our road."

Sources: Deborah Frazier, "Highway of Dreams," and David Montero, "Businesses Hoping for a Full House," *The Rocky Mountain News* (November 20, 2004): 2A, 20A. Copyright © James Makens. Reprinted with permission.

Sydney's Chinatown. It is easily accessible by monorail, water taxi, or train. By clustering a number of activities into one district, Darling Harbour gives tourists another reason to visit Sydney or stay an extra day to take in the attractions. In addition to attracting tourists, developments like Darling Harbour also provide benefits for local residents.

Within the Dallas metroplex a trail system is being developed to provide miles of open trails access to hikers and horseback riding along the Trinity River.

Tourist Events and Attractions

To attract tourists, destinations must respond to the travel basics of cost, convenience, and timeliness. Like other consumers, tourists weigh costs against the benefits of specific destinations and investment of time, effort, and resources against a reasonable return in education, experience, fun, relaxation, and memories. Convenience takes on various meanings in travel decisions: time involved in travel from airport to lodging, language barriers, cleanliness and sanitary concerns, access to interests (beaches, attractions, amenities), and special needs (elderly, disabled, children, dietary, medical care, fax and communication, auto rental). Timeliness embraces factors that introduce risk to travel, such as civil disturbances, political instability, currency fluctuations, safety, and sanitary conditions.

Events

Events and attractions are the two primary strategies used by tourist destinations to attract visitors. Events may be offered by nearly every community regardless of size. Pukwana, South Dakota, a town of only 287 people, features a Turkey Trot and a lawn mower race, and both have received national publicity.

Another South Dakota town hosts the annual Motorcycle Rally, which attracts hundreds of thousands of visitors to Sturgis, a town with a population of 6,442 people.

Organizations commonly responsible for tourism development and promotion are tourism authorities, tourism/visitor bureaus, Chambers of Commerce, convention and visitor bureaus, tourism ministries, and others. These organizations usually have responsibility for planning and organizing events designed to bring visitors to the community. In many cases, local organizations plan events designed for the enjoyment of community members. Oftentimes the events occur annually and take the form of a festival, such as a jazz festival or cherry blossom festival. Sponsors often expect financial assistance from tourism funds, but unfortunately these events may attract few if any outside visitors.

By law, government tourism funds generally must be spent on activities that will bring outside visitors and monies to the community. Local organizations may have worthy ideas for events to attract visitors and should be supported. If tax-based support is provided, the organization must adhere to guidelines. The organizations must have these characteristics:

- Adequate organization and experience to plan, organize, and market the event.

- A marketing plan, including a description of the target markets.

- A quantitative objective regarding number of expected visitors.

- A method to derive a count or estimate of the number of visitors who attended the event.

Events vary considerably in their complexity and contribution to a community's tourism base. In some cases, the organizers of an event may require payment to bring the event to a community. The organizer may also require changes/improvements in a community's infrastructure and services before agreeing to bring the event. These may include increased police presence, improvements to ballparks, swimming pools, or camping areas.

Professional event planners within tourism agencies commonly establish requirements concerning desirable events. Here are some examples:

- Event must attract a minimum number of visitors.

- Event must complement and enhance the cultural nature of the community.

Sydney, Australia's Darling Harbour is an example of a well-planned tourist center. Courtesy of r-o-x-o-r/Fotolia.

- Event should be replicable in future years, ideally on an annual basis.

- Workers from the community should be employed if part-time paid employees are needed.

- Events must not create destruction of private or public properties.

- As much as possible, events should use the services of local companies, such as food caterers.

- Events should provide guests for local hotels if hotel bed tax monies are used in their promotions.

- Events should allow/encourage participation by local residents.

Tourism planners should conduct a careful audit of the existing resources of their communities to determine opportunities for events. Rivers and ski slopes are obvious, but resources like a large vacant piece of land may be overlooked, yet this might lend itself to an event such as a balloon rodeo.

One of the biggest tourism draws in western Pennsylvania is Pymatuning Reservoir, where 400,000 visitors arrive each year to throw stale bread at carp. This has occurred by word of mouth. Thousands of carp swim in such tightly packed groups that ducks walk on top of them. The mayor of nearby Linesville said, "Carp-tourism keeps this town afloat. It supports several restaurants, a high-end gift shop and vendors of stale bread."[18]

Beyond their economic value, events help create an identity for a community. Urban newspapers and suburban weeklies often publish a list of events, festivals, and celebrations occurring within a day's driving distance. State and local tourism offices do the same, making sure that travel agents, restaurants, hotels, airports, and train and bus stations have event-based calendars for posting. Nearly every European country now has a 900 number you can call in the United States to get a listing of forthcoming events. Major U.S. cities have summer programs of scheduled events, and some, such as Milwaukee, have well-established year-round events. Milwaukee's June–September lakefront festivals (Festa Italiana, German Fest, Afro Fest, Polish Fest, and others) attract tourists regionally and nationally.

Wine festivals and wine trails and tours have been popular in Europe for generations. These are now occurring in the wine areas of Australia, New Zealand, and the United States. The Napa Valley of California has over 270 vineyards, each offering a unique visitor experience for the 5 million wine tourists annually.[19] Areas not previously known for wine production such as Texas, Missouri, Virginia, and North Carolina have established festivals and wine trails.

A study by the Washington State Wine Commission showed that 2 million visitors a year visit the 135 wineries in that state, generating $19 million in visitor income. The Australian Winemakers Association estimated that by 2025, wine tourism revenue would reach $1.1 billion.[20]

Event Marketing

Events that attract a desired market and harmoniously fit with a community's culture can provide beneficial results, particularly if the event regularly reoccurs over a period of years. Events that occur only once or that require substantial capital investment for a community may not offer sufficient economic returns. A common reply by event promoters is that the public relations value of the event outweighs cost considerations. This claim must be carefully and objectively analyzed before acceptance. Events must also be examined for the possible effect and cultural/societal impact they may have on the host community. "Destinations must choose their events to fit the needs of the locality, since each event draws on its own type of crowd."[21]

Sports Events

Many communities view sports events as attractive ways to bring visitors to their destinations. These events are often enjoyed by both visitors and residents.

Sports travel in the United States is estimated at $27 billion each year, with 75 million American adults traveling to attend a sports event as spectator or participant.[*]

BIKING AND MARATHON EVENTS Two very popular sports events are biking and marathons. A survey by the U.S. Department of Transportation estimated 57 million riders in 2002. Today that number has grown by millions as biking has grown greatly in popularity. An example is Ride The Rockies in which 4,000 people apply to ride 409 miles across Colorado. Riders come from all fifty states and many foreign nations. Host cities along the route benefit through travel expenditures from the riders as well as contributions from the sponsors to nonprofit charities in the host cities.[22]

The Walt Disney World Marathon covers a 26.2 mile course and attracts over 17,000 runners. This single event fills Disney World with 110,000 visitors during a normally slow part of the year. The success of this marathon prompted Disney to add a Princess Half Marathon for women. All Disney marathons sell out far in advance, despite comparatively high entry fees. "We literally take over Walt Disney World" said a spokesperson for Disney. "We overwhelm the property with runners."[23]

Attractions

Attractions may be natural, such as Niagara Falls or the Scottish Highlands, or manufactured, such as the shopping areas of Buckingham Palace, Hong Kong, or the Vatican.

Many nations have recognized the value of these natural attractions and have created national or state parks to protect them. However, the sheer numbers of visitors wishing to experience attractions threaten the ability of those in charge to protect them.

The long-run success of tourism will depend on manufactured attractions to satisfy the desire for travel. Historic attractions such as the pyramids of Egypt and Mexico are also at risk with increased visitor numbers. New attractions are continuously needed. This requires tourism investment.

Tourism investment ranges from relatively low-cost market entry for festivals or events to multimillion-dollar infrastructure costs of stadiums, transit systems, airports, and convention centers. Regardless of the cost, urban renewal planners seek to build tourism into the heart of their city's revitalization. Boston's Quincy Market, New York's Lincoln Center, and San Francisco's Fisherman's Wharf are examples. The ability to concentrate attractions, facilities, and services in a convenient, accessible location is essential to create a strong destination pull.

In centrally planned economies, governments control, plan, and direct tourist development. Tourism is necessary to earn hard currencies for trade and development and serves national purposes. Tourist expansion is highly dependent on public investments, which have proved to be woefully inadequate without private investment and market mechanisms to respond to changing consumer needs and wants. Many nations promote private investment through joint ventures, foreign ownership, and time sharing for individual investors. The Mexican Riviera (e.g., Puerto Vallarta, Cancun, and Istapa) is an example of public/private combinations of successful tourism investments, where state investment in infrastructure works with private investment in tourist amenities, from hotels, restaurants, and golf courses to shopping areas.

One of Hong Kong's attractions is its shopping. Courtesy of Chris Stowers © Dorling Kindersley.

[*]Eliza Ching-Yick Tse and Suk-Ching Ho, "Targeting Sports Teams," *Cornell Hotel & Restaurant Administrative Quarterly* (February 2006): 49–59.

Destination tourism in the United States depends on public/private partnerships or joint developing in planning, financing, and implementation. Public authority is required to clear, develop, and write down land costs and to make infrastructure investments. The destination must often subsidize or provide tax incentives for private investment in hotels, convention centers, transit, and parking. Restoration is often carried out by nonprofit development corporations from the National Historic Trust to the U.S. Park Service, with private investment promoted through various tax incentives. From airlines to hotels, the tourist industry provides dedicated tax revenues from fuel, leases, bed taxes, and sales taxes to support a long-term bonus for capital construction of tourist-related infrastructure and other public improvements. Such steps made it possible for New York City to add the South Street Seaport Museum, Javits Convention Center, and Ellis Island Immigration Museum to its tourist attraction portfolio.

Rejuvenating a Destination

Like a hotel or a restaurant, tourist destinations become dated, tacky, and undesirable for contemporary travelers. The Waikiki area on the island of Oahu fell victim to this. As of mid-2007, $2 billion had been spent to renovate Waikiki, with another $1 billion committed.[24]

A 93,000-square-foot retail and restaurant center was built in the heart of Waikiki Beach Walk. Zoning restrictions were removed and Outrigger Enterprises Group tore down five of its older hotels. Many other improvements were made, including the removal of T-shirt and souvenir shops on one street making it the upscale Rodeo Drive of Hawaii.

Even the beach was expanded by back-pumping 10,000 cubic yards of sand from offshore. To prevent Waikiki from becoming another noisy waterfront, banana boats, parasailing, speedboats, and jet skis were prohibited. Ed Fuller, president of Marriott International said, "The city made a major commitment to bring Waikiki back as a great destination."

Rejuvenating a destination requires the cooperation of various government entities and several sectors of private enterprise including heavy involvement by the hospitality industry.

Waterfront Attractions

Throughout much of the world, cities and towns have finally realized the tremendous value of their river, lake, and ocean waterfronts.[25] Many of these were used for warehouses, docks, power generation facilities, and heavy industry. These were ugly, dangerous, and often polluted areas. Now cities such as Los Angeles, Baltimore; Buenos Aires, Argentina; Hamburg, Germany, have discovered there is gold in redeveloping these areas for upscale housing, restaurants, hotels, shops, and even maritime commerce all within a relatively small area. HafenCity (Harbor City) of Hamburg is the largest urban development project in Europe. This area is not strictly a tourist attraction. "We want to join economic, social, cultural, and architectural forces in a way that translates into lasting urbanity," said Mr. Bruns-Berentelg, chief planner.

It should not be a surprise that people attract people. The concept of distinct tourist attractions is only a part of tourism planning. New York, London, Paris, and other cities are tourist attractions. The development of areas of cities such as waterfronts for multipurpose living is an extension of the natural attraction that cities have always held for travelers.

Destinations must make more than financial or hospitality investments to attract tourists. Places find that they must expand public services, specifically public safety, traffic and crowd control, emergency health, sanitation, and street cleaning. They must also promote tourism internally to their own citizens and business retailers, restaurants, financial institutions, public and private transit, lodging, police, and public servants. They must invest in recruiting, training, licensing, and monitoring tourist-related businesses and employees. Singapore's cab drivers are known for their professional training and service, which include English-language exams, safety programs, and location skills. Some places invest little in that area, even though airport cabs and public transit may be the first encounter points that visitors have with a destination and can be critical to tourist satisfaction.

The Burj Al Arab in Dubai is one of the world's most luxurious hotels. Courtesy of Kateshered/Dreamstime.

Dubai is a good example of a city that has developed a good infrastructure along with tourist attractions. The airport at Dubai is world class and offers excellent duty-free shopping. The highway system is well designed and maintained, making it easy to get from the airport to the resorts. The hotels realize the importance of service and customer satisfaction. Once at the hotel, the guest can select from a variety of activities, including water sports, tennis, golf, or sightseeing tours. Resorts spend a great deal of effort training their employees, who come from all over the world. The employee base also means that guests from almost any country will be able to find an employee speaking their language. Dubai set out on a strategy of using tourism to broaden its economic base and developed a plan to implement that strategy.

Two of the resorts in Dubai are the Burj Al Arab and the Jumeriah Beach Hotel. The Burj Al Arab is not only the world's tallest all-suites hotel but also one of the most luxurious. All of its 202 units are two-story suites. Guests staying at the Burj Al Arab have a choice of airport transportation: a Rolls-Royce limousine, or a helicopter. Each floor features a private reception, and there is a personal butler for each suite. The Jumeriah Beach Hotel has six hundred rooms and eighteen restaurants and features a reef a mile offshore for scuba divers. The hotel also features extensive meeting and conference facilities to attract international meetings.

Casinos as Attractions

States and municipalities typically look at jobs and tax revenues. Prior to the U.S. recession, commercial casinos employed 366,000 people and paid over $5 billion in direct gaming taxes. Many observers say this is not all good news. They say (1) casinos often take business from other entertainment such as theaters and sports bars, (2) new casinos need fewer employees due to video poker machines, (3) revenues taken from local residents often leave the area as profits for out-of-state corporations, (4) casinos may actually destroy some jobs, (5) casinos don't provide the kind of societal benefits as a biotech firm, a hospital, a university, or other enterprises, and (6) casinos foster societal problems such as pathological gambling.

Research has shown that casinos do not take business away from local restaurants and they do create jobs. However, just as many other businesses, a poorly planned casino can be a determent to the area, whereas a properly planned one can be beneficial to the region. To maximize its benefits, gaming should be incorporated into a strategic plan for the area. From a tourism perspective, gaming works best when it is part of several tourism attractions for the area, not the only tourism attraction for the area. Gaming destinations that include entertainment facilities featuring nationally known performers, golf courses, fine restaurants, hotel rooms, and meeting facilities can attract leisure tourists as well as meetings and conventions. In fact, gaming can be the source of funds to create tourist destinations.

The Greektown Casino project in Detroit shows how a casino can work with the community to create tourism. As part of the casino's effort to create a symbiotic relationship with area business, the casino owners put $200 million into refurbishing Trappers Alley, a historical area around the casino featuring restaurants and clubs, which encouraged businesses to invest their own funds to give their operations a facelift. Greektown also created an innovative loyalty program (players club) that allowed players to redeem their points in over twenty restaurants in the Trappers Alley area, generating revenue for local business owners. In this case, the casino served as the catalyst to revitalize a tourist area that had fallen on hard times.[26]

Other evidence indicates that casinos can be a positive influence on tourism. A National Gambling Impact Study Commission found that communities with casinos had 43 percent higher earnings in their hotel and lodging sectors than those that did not have casinos. The director of the Mississippi Coast Coliseum & Convention Center states a casino's entrance into a convention market "definitely has a lot more plusses for us than it does negatives." This convention center funded a $10 million facelift with tax increases brought in by hotels built to accommodate the additional tourists the casinos attracted to the region. Lisa Nossfer, director of sales and marketing for Vicksburg Convention and Visitors Bureau, said that casinos give conventioneers in her town something to do in the evening and have had a positive overall impact on the town's meeting and convention business by adding attractions in Vicksburg.[27] When casinos are focused on bringing in tourists as one of a number of amenities that tourists can enjoy, they have a positive effect on tourism.

Indian Gaming

Gambling (legalized gambling, mostly casinos) on 227 American Indian reservations has been described as "The Native American Success Story." The gambling operations and the businesses that support them are said to support 600,000 jobs. According to Ernest Stevens, chairman of the National Indian Gaming Association (NIGA), this has had a tremendous impact on reservation economies. Indian casino revenues have been estimated at $22.6 billion.[28]

Not all observers of Indian casinos believe they are healthy for the broader community. Critics say they exist despite the fact that state and neighboring communities do not recognize legalized casinos. Because these locations are often remote rural communities, they attract neighbors who are often bored, lonely, and not wealthy, who become addicted to gambling, thus creating financial hardships for their families.[29]

Stopover Tourism

Many visitor destinations are in fact only stopover destinations for travelers on their way elsewhere. Singapore has more than twice the number of annual visitors than its resident population, but visitors stay less than three days. Twenty-one percent are in transit or stopover guests.

Singapore's visitors shop, dine, and stay in world-class hotels. Sightseeing and entertainment represent only 3 percent of their expenditures. Despite short stays, Singapore ranks second in Asia and eleventh in the world in terms of tourism receipts.[30]

Kansas, Nebraska, Arkansas, Missouri, and many other states recognize the value of stopover visitors to their economies. Cities at the edge of large metroplex areas such as Lewisville, Texas, north of Dallas, also serve as stopover destinations. Many visitors prefer to stop outside a metroplex at a convenient roadside motel rather than attempt to find lodging in the city center.

■■■ Segmenting and Monitoring the Tourist Market

The decision to spend one's disposable income on travel versus furniture, a boat, or other purchase alternatives involves important psychological determinants. Table 17–2 lists some of the major psychological determinants of demand for tourism. These determinants can be used as segmentation variables. Demographics and lifestyles are also important segmentation variables.

The growing percentage of retirees in many nations has vastly expanded the tourism business. An increasing percentage of two-career couples has resulted in a trend toward shorter, more frequent vacations. Longer vacations (ten or more nights) have been declining for years in the United States; shorter vacations (three nights, including weekends) have become increasingly popular. Hotels and airlines have accommodated these trends with low-cost weekend excursion packages. Business travel now includes mixed business and leisure. To capture the trend toward shorter vacations within driving distance of home, new local and regional tourist attractions have been growing, as have family-oriented resorts.

TABLE 17–2
Psychological Determinants of Demand

Prestige. A level of prestige has always been attached to travelers, particularly long-distance travelers. Marco Polo gained historical fame through travel, as did the heroes of Greek and Roman mythology, such as Ulysses. Travel to Aspen, the Riviera, Switzerland, and many other destinations provides the traveler with a level of prestige, if only in the mind of the traveler.

Escape. The desire to escape momentarily from the day-to-day rhythm of one's life is a basic human need. Travel marketers have long recognized this need, as reflected by glamorous advertisements in which the word *escape* is often mentioned.

Sexual opportunity. This has both a positive and an ugly side. Travel has long been viewed as a means to meet attractive people. This has been part of the heritage of transatlantic ocean travel, the Orient Express, and riverboat travel. Unfortunately, the existence of sex tours to certain Asian nations and the preponderance of houses of prostitution in some destination areas provide examples of a darker side.

Education. Travel in and of itself has historically been viewed as broadening. Many deeper psychological reasons for travel are masked by the rationale that educational benefits outweigh the cost, risks, and stress.

Social interaction. The opportunity to meet and interact with people previously unknown is a powerful motivator. Destination resorts and cruise lines commonly appeal to this need.

Family bonding. Family reunions have become an important market segment for many in the travel industry. In an era of intense pressure on the family, such as two careers, there is a strong need to refocus priorities and bond as a family. Unfortunately, the types of vacations selected by families do not always lead to bonding. If adults participate all day in activities such as diving, skiing, or golf, young children may be relegated to organized kids' programs and experience little bonding with parents.

Relaxation. Observers of human and animal conduct sometimes state that the human being is either alone or among a limited number of species that continue to play into adulthood. Destination resorts and cruise ships best exemplify need fulfillment for play. It is small wonder that cruise line travel has become a "destination" in direct competition with land-bound places.

Self-discovery. For many, travel offers the opportunity to "find oneself." Witness the action of many people following a dramatic event in their lives, such as a divorce or the death of a family member. Throughout recorded history, people have sought self-discovery by "visiting the mountain," "finding solace in the desert," and "losing oneself." Many cultures, including so-called primitive ones, have encouraged or even forced their youth to travel alone to find self-discovery. Youth hotels throughout the world serve a group of travelers, many of whom are seeking self-discovery. Temporary employment opportunities at resorts are often filled by those taking time off to learn more about who they are and wish to be. The concept of "holistic vacations" has been developed for people seeking self-discovery.

Sources: Peter Hawes, "Holistic Vacations," *Hemisphere* (March 1995): 85–87; A. J. Crompton, "Motivations for Pleasure Vacations," *Annals of Tourism Research,* 6 (1974): 408–424; A. Mathieson and G. Wall, *Tourism: Economics, Physical and Social Impacts* (Harlow, Essex, UK: Longman, 1982).

Foreign visitor travel has become an increasingly important segment of the North American travel industry. Since the decline of the U.S. and Canadian dollars, foreign tourism has grown. British Isles visitors seek out New York, Florida, and Playa del Carmen, while continental visitors have a strong fascination for the U.S. West, particularly California. Hawaii targets Japan because of its high gross national product and spending, and because 50 percent of all Japanese visitors to the U.S. mainland spend part of their trip in Hawaii. The Japanese repeat market outspends visitors from the U.S. mainland by a 4:1 margin.

Accommodating changing lifestyles and needs is a dynamic challenge for the tourism industry in light of demographic trends and income shifts. Where baby boomers once opted for status destinations and elaborate accommodations, many now opt for all-inclusive resorts and package tours that promise comfort, consistency, and cost effectiveness. Tourism planners must consider how many tourists are desired, which segments to attract, and how to balance tourism with other industries. Choices

The strong euro has made Playa del Carmen, Mexico, an attractive and inexpensive destination for European tourists. Courtesy of Dan Bannister/Dorling Kindersley.

will be constrained by the destinations' climate, natural topography, resources, history, culture, and facilities. Like other enterprises, tourist marketers must know the actual and potential customers and their needs and wants, determine which target markets to serve, and decide on appropriate products, services, and programs.

Charleston, South Carolina, has several times won the South Carolina Governor's Cup for Travel and Tourism, been named the "most mannerly" city in the United States ten times, and has been a top-ten travel destination by *Conde Nast* magazine readers eleven times. It has also won awards from *National Geographic*, *Brides* magazine, and *Travel & Leisure* magazine.

Another South Carolina travel destination, Myrtle Beach, attracts many more tourists, but Charleston remains "the Award Winner Jewel in South Carolina's Destination Crown."[31]

How does Charleston prevail as a top destination? The answer is that it does its best to preserve and retain what has historically attracted people to Charleston: history, charming architecture, pleasant and mannerly people, helpfulness, gardens, quaintness, and excellent cuisine.

These winning attributes could quickly disappear if discount shopping areas replaced old homes or if a multimillion-dollar theme park was built in the heart of the city. Vigilance is essential to preserve and further the genuine differentiating factors of a destination. These can disappear in a short period of time to the detriment of residents and visitors.

Not every tourist is interested in a particular destination. A destination would waste its money trying to attract everyone who travels. Instead of a shotgun approach, destinations must take a rifle approach and sharply define target markets. Many visitors to Myrtle Beach would find Charleston stuffy and boring. Attempts to attract those individuals would result in mutual dissatisfaction.

Agritourism

In an era in which most people in industrialized nations are urban or suburban dwellers, farm and ranch tourism has become increasingly important. This is particularly true in many European nations, North America, and Australia/New Zealand.

A study by Colorado State University provides evidence of the importance of **agritourism**. "Summer and fall had the highest agritourism visitation rates," said Dawn Thilmany, professor in Colorado State's Department of Agriculture and Resource Economics, who led the study.

In a state known for its skiing, agricultural activities have shown the potential to provide a real boost to Colorado's tourism efforts outside of winter months.

Thilmany said, "Increased visitations during these times help fill the underutilized capacity of lodging and service industries." More than 20 percent of those surveyed took more than three agritourism trips each year, offering great potential for farm and ranch enterprises considering agritourism activities, according to the report.

Tourists from outside Colorado reported spending an average of $860 per trip; in-state tourists reported spending an average of $368, according to the report. Both in-state and out-of-state tourists said they would spend more during their next trip to Colorado ($450 for state residents; $1,023 for out-of-state tourists). Among the more frequent agritourism travelers, about 56 percent were Colorado residents.[32]

"We found there is sufficient interest in agritourism in Colorado to warrant active joint planning by communities and the agritourism enterprises they support," Thilmany said, offering as an example a joint-marketing plan of Grand Junction's wine country. "Many regions of Colorado already see significant amounts of visitors to farm and ranch-based diversions. Through coordinated marketing efforts, these regions can continue to capitalize on agritourism activities."

Space Tourism

In April 2001, Dennis Tito became the first space tourist when he paid $20 million to fly on the Soyuz taxi mission to the International Space Station. In October 2008, Richard Garrett paid $30 million to fly on a Soyuz mission and become the sixth space tourist. As a result of the Russians willingness to allow space tourists on their missions, there is now a travel agency, Space Adventures, specializing in space tourism.[33]

A number of private companies have been formed to provide trips into space for tourists. The founder of Virgin Atlantic Airline, Sir Richard Branson, has formed Virgin Galactic, with test flights scheduled soon. Commercial space travel for up-scale tourists is planned from Las Cruces Spaceport America in New Mexico. Additional sites will be in the United Kingdom, Australia, and Sweden.

Space travelers will have to undergo elite cosmonaut training. They will be in a vehicle named SS2, which will climb to 50,000 feet altitude under a mother ship Space Ship Two. After release, the SS2 will free fall for a few seconds, fire its rockets, and accelerate into a vertical trajectory climbing to an altitude of 360,800 feet. Those aboard the SS2 will enjoy a 1,000-mile horizon of the earth in zero gravity. The entire flight will last about two and a half hours.[34]

NASA is preparing for moon tourism, including developing plans to prevent looting of the six areas where manned space missions landed on the moon between 1969 and 1972. Under its guidelines, people can walk only within 246 feet of the first site where Neil Armstrong first walked on the moon. NASA's concern over protecting the sites was prompted by Google's $30 million prize for the first privately funded team to land a robot on the moon. It appears that NASA feels that people will soon follow robots on the moon. It wants to make sure that tourists don't trample on the footprint of Armstrong's "one small step for man."[35]

Multiday Hiking and Religious Pilgrimages

Many potential tourists are tired of traditional tourism opportunities, such as a beach resort. A huge and growing market exists for multiday trekking (hiking). In some cases, hiking has a religious basis, such as in pilgrimages to significant religious sites such as the Camino de Santiago de Campostela in northern Spain. This trip may be accomplished by foot, horseback, or bicycle and may be as long as a month or just a few days. In 1990, the Cathedral in Santiago registered 4,918 hikers (pilgrims), but today over 100,000 people are recorded each year and that is probably an underestimate.

Christian sites are by no means the only ones that are visited. Millions of pilgrims visit Hindu, Buddhist, Islamic, and other religious sites. Although most visitors arrive by some form of modern transport, many prefer to walk.

In western Japan, a walking pilgrimage to thirty-three sacred sites and the 1,300-km pilgrimage to the eighty-eight holy sites of Shikoku Island are experienced by hundreds of thousands of hiking pilgrims. Most devotees on these pilgrimages carry a staff bearing the words, "We too walk together." Many of those on the Camino de Santiago carry a staff bearing a seashell.

Perhaps the most publicized pilgrimages are those of the Islamic faith such as that of Hajj, a pilgrimage to Mecca in which millions of Muslims participate, including 10,000 Americans in 2006. The Shrine of Iman Reza in Iran attracts over 12 million visitors each year. Visitors to these shrines arrive via many forms of travel.

Trails are available for special-interest hikers with cultural, scientific, religious, or gastronomical interests such as wine tours. Some trails such as the Milford in New Zealand are so popular that visitor numbers are restricted.

A North Sea Trail is being developed in Europe, which crosses six countries and extends for 3,000 miles and was funded by the European Union with nearly $15 million. The EU already had eleven long-distance paths from Lapland to Gibraltar and Cyprus.

The 2,175-mile-long Appalachian Trail on the East Coast of the United States from Maine to Georgia has long been popular. Extended hikes such as this are supported by tourism organizations throughout the world as they disperse visitors, lessen the negative aspects of tourism, and provide economic support to rural communities.

Hundreds of cultural routes with tourism potential exist throughout the world, such as The Silk Road that started at the Chinese imperial city of Xian and extended across the Taklimakan desert to the Mediterranean. Long and arduous treks such as this will be completed in entirety by very few tourists, but many are likely to hike portions of the trail.[36]

Volunteer Vacationing

This form of tourism is also called purpose-driven tourism. Thousands of individuals increasingly choose to spend their vacation period assisting others, particularly in underdeveloped nations.

Many churches and synagogues sponsor work vacations for volunteers to work in communities, particularly rural ones in Latin America, Africa, and parts of Asia. These individuals repair or build facilities, work in orphanages, teach children sports or games, and assist in many other ways.

Nonaffiliated individuals also volunteer through groups such as Globe Aware. One reason for this type of travel was expressed by Mary Ellen Connolly of Chelsea, Quebec, who said, "I'm so sick of going to typical tourist attractions and doing the same old tourist thing." Connolly said she wanted to "give back" and saw the trip as a way to experience a country on a deeper level.[37]

This type of tourism may carry risk such as health and accident problems and it is generally advisable to participate through a recognized and experienced organization. These organizations also frequently have access to less expensive travel.

Medical Tourism

Medical tourism is one of the fastest-growing and most lucrative segments of tourism, as people travel internationally to gain access to less expensive medical care. In 2003 there were 350,000 medical tourists, by 2010 that number grew to 6 million, and by 2017 the number is expected to grow to 16 million. Medical tourism is expected to bring $2 billion in foreign currency to India in 2012.

The growth in medical tourism is driven by four main factors: low cost, long waiting lines in national health-care services, accessibility to procedures and treatments, and opportunity for a vacation and privacy. Cost is the main driver. For people with no or inadequate insurance, low-cost health care at an international destination may be the only viable solution for health care. In an effort to stay young, baby boomers are seeking cosmetic surgery and dental work. These elective procedures are often not covered by insurance, creating a booming business for these procedures in Mexico, Central America, Asia, and Eastern Europe. In countries with national health care, such as Australia, Canada, and England, people needing elective surgery are often put on a waiting list. To some of those on the waiting list, a low-cost procedure overseas is often preferred to putting up with the malady for months. International health care also provides access to experimental procedures or treatments that are prohibited by law in one's home country. This includes experimental cancer treatments and treatments using stem cells. The privacy of having cosmetic surgery done overseas, recovering on the beach, and coming home healed and looking 10 years younger is a great alternative to hiding out at home while the scars are healing.

Medical tourism is being blended with the opportunity for a vacation. Some insurance companies in North America are offering their customers, who qualify for health care, the option to have it done at an international location. As an incentive, they will waive the deductable and co-pay, as well as provide airfare and lodging during and after treatment. They sell both the cost savings and the opportunity for a free vacation to their client. The insurance company still comes out over the cost of having the surgery done in the United States. The biggest concern for the patient is the quality of the health care. Countries that want to capture the medical tourism market need to develop standards and accrediting procedures to create a perception of quality and build trust among medical tourists.[38]

e **17.2** Medical Tourism, http://www.medicaltourism.com/: Explore this Web site to get an idea of the options for a medical tourist.

Genealogical Tourism

The interest in knowing more about one's ancestors has grown substantially in recent years.[39] Many people plan vacations to visit genealogical research sites.

The Allen County Public Library in Fort Wayne, Indiana, hosts 400,000 visitors annually. The Church of Jesus Christ of Later Day Saints in Utah has become a "must visit" site for 700,000 annual visitors. This is the world's largest depository of family records.

Other nations that received large numbers of immigrants from Europe such as Australia, New Zealand, Argentina, and Canada have growing numbers of genealogical tourists.

Identifying Target Markets

A destination can identify its natural target markets in two ways. One is to collect information about its current visitors. Where do they come from? Why do they come? What are their demographic characteristics? How satisfied are they? How many are repeat visitors? How much do they spend? By examining these and other questions, planners can determine which visitors should be targeted.

The second approach is to audit the destination's events and attractions and select segments that might logically have an interest in them. We cannot assume that current visitors reflect all the potentially interested groups. For example, if Kenya promoted only safaris, it would miss groups interested in native culture, flora, or bird species.

Tourist segments are attracted by different features. The local tourist board or council could benefit by asking questions keyed to segmentation variables. These variables, including attractions sought, market areas or locations, customer characteristics, and/or benefits sought, can help define the best target markets.

After a destination identifies its natural target markets, tourism planners should conduct research to determine where these tourists are found. Which countries contain a large number of citizens who have the means and motivation to enjoy the particular place? For example, Aruba attracts mainly sun-and-fun tourists. The United States, Canada, and certain European countries are good sources. Eastern Europeans have been ruled out because they lack the purchasing power, but this is changing. Australians are ruled out because they have their own nearby sun-and-fun destinations, even though they are frequent travelers. This analysis can uncover many or few natural target markets. If many are identified, the relative potential profit from each should be evaluated. The potential profit of a target tourist segment is the difference between the amount that the tourist segment is likely to spend and the cost of attracting and serving this segment. The promotional cost depends on the budget. The serving cost depends on the infrastructure requirements. Ultimately, potential tourist segments should be ranked and selected in order of their profitability.

Ireland is trying to capture a high-income, culture-seeking tourist. It is promoting its literary giants which include Oliver Goldsmith, shown in this statue on the main green at Trinity College in Dublin. Courtesy of Sepavo/Dreamstime.

If the analysis identifies too few natural tourist segments, investments may be needed in infrastructure and visitor events and attractions. The payoff from these investments may come years later, but this lag is often necessary if the destination is to become an active participant in an increasingly competitive marketplace.

The Irish Tourist Board observed that many young European tourists visited the Emerald Isle to enjoy its natural, unspoiled beauty as backpackers and campers, but they spent little money. A serious question for Ireland was whether its tourism scorecard should be based on the number of tourists attracted (the prevailing standard) or their spending level. A consensus emerged that Ireland should try to attract a relatively small market of high-income tourists who stay longer, spend more, and are culturally and environmentally compatible.

Toward this end, the Irish Tourist Board now touts not only Ireland's mountains, water, and ancient buildings, but also its literary giants, such as Oscar Wilde, George Bernard Shaw, and James Joyce. The board wants to attract high-income, culture-seeking tourists to Dublin, where the sparkling Irish speech and wit can be experienced.

Whatever tourist segment a destination seeks, it needs to be very specific. A ski area attracts skiers. Natural reefs attract snorkelers and divers. Arts and crafts attract the art crowd, and gambling attracts gaming tourists. Yet even with such givens, potential visitors must be segmented by additional characteristics. Sun Valley, Aspen, Vail, and Alta appeal to upper-income and professional skiers, and Keystone, Winter Park, Copper Mountain, and Telluride attract the family market. Tahoe and Squaw Valley draw the skiing and gaming markets. Monte Carlo appeals to an international gaming segment, whereas Deauville, France, promotes a more regional gaming market near Paris.

Tourism marketers know that even though an area may attract an activity-specific segment, there is great potential in providing reasons for others to come. For instance, a ski family or group often contains individuals who do not wish to ski. Why then should they come? If the answer is "we offer only a single activity," the group may decide to go somewhere else that offers broader vacation opportunities.

Las Vegas discovered that shopping, dining, and entertainment could attract nongamblers and also serve as secondary activities for all but the most dedicated gamblers. The Forum shopping mall at Caesars in Las Vegas provides continuous entertainment and a great variety of restaurants, making the retail sales areas some of the most costly and desirable to rent in North America. Today, the top attraction in Las Vegas is shopping and entertainment, not gambling.

Self-Contained Attraction and Event Destinations

The historical concept of travel has been to go someplace for a purpose. It can be argued that for many contemporary pleasure travelers, the real destination is the vehicle of travel, such as a cruise ship, river paddle ship, or a special railroad such as the Orient Express. The fact that this vehicle travels to various ports may be secondary in the minds of the travelers. The pure pleasure of moving about in this special mode of travel is the primary travel purpose. Upon reaching in-transit ports, not all passengers choose to leave a cruise ship.

These "moving destinations" offer a variety of events for passengers, and dining is particularly important. Games, gambling, theater, musicals, participatory murder mysteries, seminars, dances, and a host of other on-board events enhance the pleasure of moving destinations.

As industrialized societies experience enlarged numbers of senior citizens, these relatively passive moving destinations are likely to receive increased demand.

Classification of Visitor Segments

Several classifications have been used to describe different visitor destination segments. The most commonly used classifications are based on whether the tourist travels with a group or independently. The common terms are group-inclusive tour (GIT) and independent traveler (IT). National tourism offices, international airlines, and others involved in international travel frequently use these designations.

Here are some classifications describing tourists by their degree of institutionalization and their impact on the destinations:

- *Organized mass tourists.* This corresponds to the GIT. These people have little or no influence over their travel experience other than to purchase one package or another. They commonly travel in a group, view the destination through the windows of a tour bus, and remain in preselected hotels. Shopping in the local market often provides their only contact with the native population.

- *Individual mass tourists.* These people are similar to the previous category but have somewhat more control over their itinerary. For instance, they may rent a car to visit attractions.

- *Explorers.* These people fall in the IT classification. They plan their own itineraries and make their own reservations. They tend to be very sociable people who enjoy interacting with people at the destination.

- *Drifters.* These people, the backpacker group, seldom, if ever, are found in a traditional hotel. They may stay at youth hostels with friends or camp out. They tend to mix with lower socioeconomic native groups and are commonly found riding third-class rail or bus. Most tend to be young.

- *Visiting friends and relatives.* VFR, as the name suggests, are people who stay in the homes of friends or relatives. For this reason, they are often discounted as important tourists. This is incorrect. They may not spend money on lodging, but they do spend on dining, attending attractions/events, and shopping.

- *Business travelers.* This often encompasses any form of business, including conventions, trade shows, and job seeking.

- *Pleasure travel.* This too is a very wide and all-encompassing classification. It may be of limited use without further segmentation.

- *Business and pleasure travelers.* Many convention and business travelers plan to incorporate a period of relaxation prior to or after their business.

- *Tag-along visitors.* Members of the family are common "tag-along" visitors. The presence of tag-along children has created a sub-industry of child care and entertainment.

- *Grief travel.* Airlines offer special fares for family and friends attending funeral services. This segment will increase in importance as society ages.

- *Education and religious travel.* This broad category includes students, those on a pilgrimage, missionaries, and a host of others. It may be of limited use in tourism planning unless further segmented.

- *Pass-through tourists.* These are extremely important visitors to states such as Kansas and Nebraska and to cities in Texas that serve as convenient rest or overnight stopping areas.

Another well-known tourist classification system is *Plog's categorization* (Figure 17–1).[40] These designations are similar to the groups mentioned previously but range from psychocentric to allocentric. Plog observed that destinations are first discovered by **allocentrics** (backpackers or explorers). As the natives discover the economic benefits of tourism, services and infrastructure are developed. When this occurs, allocentrics are turned off and find another unspoiled destination. The nature of visitors now changes, with each new group somewhat less adventurous than the preceding group, perhaps older, and certainly more demanding of creative comforts and service. Finally, a destination becomes so familiar that the least adventurous group of **psychocentrics** finds it acceptable.

Figure 17–1
Plog's categorization of destinations. The height of the curve indicates the number of travelers in each category. Reprinted by permission of Elsevier Science, Inc., "Why Destinations Rise and Fall in Popularity," by Stanley C. Plog, *Cornell Hotel and Restaurant Administration Quarterly,* 14, no. 4, p. 58, ©1974 by Cornell University.

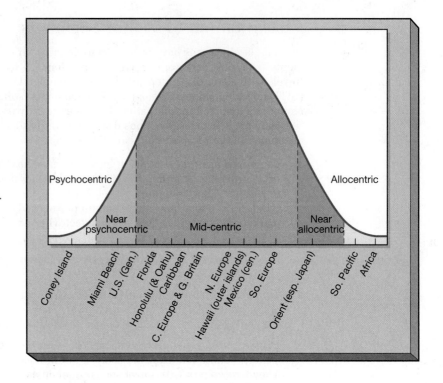

A study of travelers' behaviors and preferences demonstrated that Costa Rica position is evolving from being a destination for near allocentric to one that attracts mid-centrics. The researchers concluded that Costa Rica had indeed built its infrastructure to the point that adventurers are put off and mid-centrics are attracted, just as Plog's model predicted.

Knowing this, other nations in Central America, Honduras, Belize, and Nicaragua, are pursuing the adventures market. Therefore, preservation of the natural environment in those nations is essential, including the need to set aside particular areas for special protection.

The researchers also noted that parts of Asia, China, Cambodia, Thailand, and Vietnam are rushing into a phase of development that is poorly planned based on the Plog Analysis.[41]

Monitoring the Tourist Markets

Tourist markets are dynamic, and a marketing information system is part of any well-run tourist organization. Destinations need to closely monitor the relative popularity of their various attractions by determining the number and type of tourists attracted to each. The popularity of the Metropolitan Museum of Art, Big Ben, or the Coliseum can suddenly or gradually change. Marketing information systems help identify and predict environmental trends that are responsible for these changes. Information should be collected on changes, emerging markets, and potential target markets.

The Las Vegas Convention and Visitors Authority (LVCVA) conducts an annual tourist profile. Information for this profile is collected through ongoing customer surveys. Survey results indicate that the majority of visitors spend less than four hours a day gambling. The visitors are coming for entertainment and the non-gaming amenities of the mega-resorts. This information helped to attract a number of new restaurants, such as Spago, Wolfgang Puck's, Cafe Coyote, and Planet Hollywood. Las Vegas has developed a reputation as a restaurant town. This further enhances its image as a diverse destination rather than just a gaming venue.

One job of a tourist organization is to increase the accessibility of a destination. The LVCVA uses information from its survey to identify emerging markets that can support direct airline flights. Armed with current travel patterns and projected travel patterns based on its surveys, the LVCVA makes presentations to airlines, trying to convince them to start new routes, which will be profitable for the airlines and provide another region of the country with direct air service to Las Vegas. The accessibility of Las Vegas by frequently scheduled and relatively inexpensive airfare is in part responsible for it being one of the top convention centers in the United States. This did not happen by accident; it happened as a result of efforts by the LVCVA.

The Steamboat Springs, Colorado, Chamber Resort Association, and other resorts' visitor bureaus also work with airlines to ensure air accessibility to their cities. However, because these areas have a small population base and experience varying snowfall levels, airlines are reluctant to include them in their schedule without a financial guarantee. This means the visitor bureau must assume an active role to ensure that funding is available for the airline guarantees should this be necessary.

The Wales Tourist Bureau used market research to identify a target market for the Swansea Marina. Using research, it identified persons in the West Midlands of England who had a similar socioeconomic profile to their existing users. These potential customers were reached through well-targeted advertising campaigns. The small size of the potential market for the Swansea Marina means that mass communication media would not be cost effective. Rather than waste advertising dollars covering a broad market, information from the Wales Tourist Bureau was used to target the market effectively for the marina.[42]

Tourist organizations need information to stay competitive. Tourist products must change to meet the needs of the changing market. Emerging markets must be identified and served. New markets that can be served by the existing tourist product must be identified. Tourist organizations trying to accomplish these tasks without good information are at a disadvantage.

Marketing Highlight   Tourism Rebound—After the London Riots

17–2 The cover of the August 2011 issue of Private Eye, a fortnightly satirical magazine, shows cars ablaze in a London street as marauding rioters look on. The riots in early August coincided inconveniently with the city's first rehearsals for next year's Olympic games, prompting the magazine's cover caption: "This is the worst opening ceremony ever." Now that the broken glass has been swept up in the affected areas and the insurance claims have been filed, London is taking stock of the damage to its international reputation. Will its brand recover quickly, or might the riots have done long-term harm to the capital's attractiveness to foreigners?

These words from *The Economist* magazine following the August 2011 London riots were on the minds of the U.K. tourism industry. The riots with looting, fire, heavy losses to property owners, and even deaths had been transmitted to the world through all existing communication sources.

One specialist in urban image building, Simon Anholt, told *The Economist*, "Urban brands are built up over many years and don't swing around so quickly." He went on to say that if tourists and investors were put off by sporadic natural and unnatural disasters then the fortunes of New York, London and Tokyo would be a lot more erratic than they have proved to be."

Many cites have experienced riots such as the one in Vancouver, B.C. Canada, in June 2011 following a hockey game, but in the presence of continuing worldwide problems, people tend to quickly forget an incident like this one. Following the London riots, the European Tour Operators Association experienced only 330 cancellations, or 0.2 percent of all bookings.

Visit Britain, whose purpose is to promote tourism to the United Kingdom, launched a $164 million campaign to attract visitors in 2012. A spokesman for this group said, "We've had our fair share of setbacks and volcanic ash from Iceland but all have had only temporary setbacks."

The message seems to be that strong tourist destinations are likely to bounce back after disasters and remain desirable destinations. Obviously, the traveling public expects the host nations to repair damaged areas and to confront the offenders with justice.

In London, the public formed "broom armies" to clear away the debris. These images were also sent worldwide via television and other media. The criminal justice system in the United Kingdom also quickly responded. Some courts operated through the night to process cases with overwhelming support from the British public.

Sources: "Bouncing Back" *The Economist* (August 27, 2011): 49; Ibid; "Judge Dreads, London After the Riots, Part 2," *The Economist* (August 27, 2011): 49.

Loyalty of Tourism Destination Visitors

Outbound markets have been found to be loyal to tourism destinations in mass but not as individuals. Destinations replenish their stock of visitors from prospect markets with similar psychodemographic profiles to actual visitors.[43]

An interesting phenomenon known as cycling has been observed in visitor markets. Masses of tourists may decide to visit Country A this year, Country B next year, and then recycle to Country A for the third year. This does not imply that the composition of the mass of tourists is the same each year. Reasons for this are not well understood.[44]

Short-Haul Versus Long-Haul Tourists

Tourists who travel short distances tend to stay for short durations. They also show preferences for package tours.

Long-haul tourists tend to engage in longer duration, multi-destination trips and seek to fulfill multipurposes, such as city sightseeing, country hikes, attending several cultural events, and participating in events.

Another interesting phenomenon is the existence of the Effective Tourist Exclusion Zone (ETEZ). This is a physical and psychological transition zone between short-haul and long-haul travel. Travelers often overlook this zone as a visitor destination. Destination tourism marketers should be aware of this, particularly if their respective destination is an ETEZ.

■■■ Communicating with the Tourist Market

Competition for Visitors Involves Image Making

Destination images are heavily influenced by pictorial creations used in movies or television, by music, and, in some cases, by popular entertainers and celebrities.

State media investment to attract tourists has grown rapidly. States such as Texas and Alaska have more than quadrupled their tourism media budgets. Nations and states invade and advertise in each other's markets. For instance, Illinois targets New York, California, Texas, and Japan. It produces multilingual travel guides, DVDs, and radio segments.

Destinations have formed partnerships with travel, recreational, and communication businesses on joint marketing efforts. They advertise in national magazines and travel publications and work with business-travel promotions to link the growing business-leisure segment of the traveling public, and they target travel agencies. Many states have located welcome centers along major interstate highways that include unstaffed two-way video systems to answer questions from a central location or otherwise assist travelers. States also target their own residents with brochures, maps, and a calendar of events.

Finally, effective destination imaging requires congruence between advertising and the destination. Glossy photographs of sunsets, beaches, buildings, and events need to have some relationship to what tourists actually experience; otherwise, destinations run the risk of losing tourist goodwill and generating bad word of mouth.

Many tourist destinations have discovered that it is important to show residents interacting with tourists in their advertisements. Thousands of mountain slopes and beaches exist in the world and most look alike in photos. Very few tourists seek a completely secluded vacation site. People are social creatures by nature and consciously or unconsciously seek the company of fellow humans.

Curiosity is another common human trait. We wish to see how others live and to intermingle with them if for only brief periods before retreating to a five-star hotel. A classic success story of reversing a serious decline in tourism occurred in Jamaica. The decline had occurred under a government that seemingly expressed anti–North American viewpoints. Unfortunately, crime increased, visitors were abused, and tourism fell. A new government was installed with different attitudes, and the Jamaica Tourist Board was determined to rebuild its tourism base. A U.S. advertising agency was hired to develop an advertising campaign.

This campaign emphasized local people welcoming visitors. The theme was "Come Back to Jamaica, Come Back to the Way Things Used to Be." Television ads were designed for passive and active tourist segments, including families and honeymooners. Tourism once again rebounded, and credit must be given to the Jamaica Tourist Board.

Effectiveness of Current Advertising/Promotion

The success of yesterday's advertising/promotion as a model for today is increasingly being questioned. The results of research on the subject of effectiveness of state expenditures to promote tourism are certain to be controversial.

The researchers concluded in the *Journal of Travel Research* that "our results suggest that states with lower levels of tourism activity can enjoy small benefits from increased spending while states with higher levels of tourism would benefit from decreased spending."[45]

Another study concerning the effectiveness of advertising suggested that "there was no significant difference between the control group that was not exposed to anything and the group that saw the advertisement as far as attitude formation and interest in visiting a destination were concerned."[46]

The two studies referred to may be in the vanguard of demonstrating the need for new marketing strategies to effectively market visitor destinations. Society has changed. Traditional media such as television, newspaper and magazine ads, and AM/FM radio may not be utilized by target markets, particularly younger ones. Recognizing this, the authors of one of the studies previously mentioned suggestions provided on how to improve destination tourism marketing.

A. If Web sites work for you, use ad money to drive people to your Web site.

B. Create great Web sites. Don't skimp on funds and professionalism.

C. If you use ads, test them first, scale them down, and see what happens (i.e., perhaps large ads are not needed).

D. Use focus groups and personal interviews.

E. Make sure details are in the Web site. Test it using mystery shoppers.

F. Take charge of your Web site. Track which parts of your Web site get hits.

UNESCO World Heritage Sites

17.3 World Heritage Sites, http://whc.unesco.org/en/list: Look at this list to find the World Heritage Sites in your country, province, parish, and/or state.

Regardless of one's opinion about the United Nations, the designation of World Heritage Sites by The United Nations Educational, Scientific, and Cultural Organization (UNESCO) is important to world tourism and very important to selected sites. This program designates and thereby hopes to help conserve sites of outstanding cultural or natural importance to the common heritage of humanity. In 2011, a total of 936 such sites were listed: 725 cultural, 183 natural, and 28 mixed. Each site belongs to the country in which it is located, but it is considered to be of international interest to preserve and protect these sites.[47]

Tourism authorities view inclusion on this list as very important. In 2008, Dresden, Germany, wanted to build a 2,100-foot-long bridge called Waldschlosschen Bridge over a picturesque river. UNESCO threatened to take Dresden off the list if it built the bridge.

Developing Packages of Attractions and Amenities

An effective way of communicating with potential travelers is by offering packages. Tourist organizations must develop a package of attractions and amenities. Travelers make comparisons about the relative advantages and disadvantages of competing destinations. Destinations must provide easy access to attractions by bus, boats, carriages, and planes. They need to distribute brochures, audiotapes, and videotapes to travel agents and individual prospects. City bus companies might

The Hwaseong Fortress in Seoul, Korea, is a UNESCO cultural World Heritage Site. Courtesy of Hendrik H/Shutterstock.

prepare half-day, full-day, and evening tours to highlight the destination's major attractions. Concentrating attractions, services, and facilities in a small area creates excitement, adventure, and crowds.

Destinations constantly discover hidden assets that have vast tourist potential. Illinois, for example, has more public and semipublic golf courses per population than any other state except Florida. It now promotes golf tours. Japanese tours responded to a package of golf and Chicago shopping. Pennsylvania has reclaimed old coal mining areas with championship golf courses, expanding its recreational facilities to promote tourism.

Victoria, Canada, "The City of Gardens," is home to The Butchart Gardens, a fifty-five-acre abandoned quarry that was transformed into a beautiful living garden of flowers. The Butchart Garden has become synonymous with Victoria's tourist industry, featuring special events, dining, and gift shopping. When combined with other activities such as golf, shopping, dining, and museums, many packages can be developed for different visitor segments.

The Koshare Indian Museum at La Junta, Colorado, is an example of a cultural tourist attraction. The museum houses one of the largest collections of North American art and artifacts in the world and a library on Native American history. Native American dances are preserved by teaching them to the young men of the community, who perform throughout the nation as the Koshare Indian Dancers.

A destination may promote one, a few, or many of its attractions. Chicago's marketing theme "Chicago's Got It" featured pictures of its famous architecture, lakefront, symphony, world's tallest building, financial exchanges, and Wrigley Field (home of the Chicago Cubs) to suggest that the city had everything: business, culture, entertainment, recreation, and sports. In contrast, San Francisco played off its well-developed image as seductive and mysterious: a photo of a foggy, softly lit Golden Gate Bridge with the copy, "In the Beginning, God Created Heaven and Earth. San Francisco Took a Little Longer."

Attractions alone do not attract visitors. Most places seek to deepen the travel experience by providing greater value and making the experience more significant and rewarding. Such appeals are couched in history, culture, and people. New York City is a case in point. About one in four of the city's visitors is a foreign tourist. Consequently, city officials must make New York "foreign friendly" by creating tours that emphasize nationality interests, designing brochures in a variety of languages, and providing hassle-free currency exchanges.

Competition among destinations extends to restaurants, facilities, sports, cultural amenities, and entertainment. Which place has the most four-star hotels, best culinary fare, most museums and theaters, best wine and drink, best chefs, or best native, cultural, or ethnic flair? Campaigns are carried out in specialty publications. Testimonials and rankings are found in travel brochures, advertising, and travel guides.

Despite the best offers of a destination to portray a positive image through public relations and advertising, image building is affected by reports of disturbing societal problems, including human rights abuse.

Charges of human rights abuse from Western governments directly affect tourism development and growth. The government of Myanmar viewed its people as "contributing labor" to the development of the tourism-related infrastructure. International human rights observers viewed this development as forced labor. The United Kingdom–based Tourism Concern reported that the Myanmar State Law Order Restoration Council (SLORC) is "implementing projects earmarked for tourism through the use of forced labor and the displacement of people."[48] Tourism Concern reported that chained prison gangs and conscripted families had been used to build roads and prepare tourism sites. According to the reports, army members went from house to house taking people for forced labor.

The SLORC denied these reports and stated that people were contributing their voluntary labor happily. Whatever the truth, reports of human rights abuse, crime, disease, and other societal problems have a negative effect on tourism and may persist long after the problem is corrected.

Making a destination tourist friendly is the task of a central tourist agency, which may be public, quasi-public, nonprofit, or private. These agencies are referred to as **national tourist organizations (NTOs)**. Outside the United States, this agency is often run by the central government, state, or province, together with local government officials. The European Travel Commission, a twenty-four-nation group bent on luring U.S. visitors to Europe, coordinates promotional activity in the United States.

■■■ Organizing and Managing Tourism Marketing

National Tourism Organizations

Countries and states usually have government or quasi-government agencies that market destination tourism. On the national level, these are referred to as NTOs. An NTO has two marketing tasks: (1) The NTO can formulate and develop the tourist product or products of the destination and (2) it can promote them in appropriate markets. It can base its approach to development and promotion on market research and thus achieve a close match between the products and the markets. In doing this, the tourist organization is acting on behalf of the whole destination and is complementary to the development and promotion activities of individual tourist providers. Even though direct travel spending in the United States generates over $800 billion, the country does not have a federally funded NTO. The Travel Industry Association (TIA) serves many of the same functions for the United States as an NTO. It produces the official U.S. travel and tourism Web site, www.DiscoverAmerica.com, and does receive some support from the government for the development and maintenance of the Web site.[49]

The NTO is responsible for the following functions:

- *Flow of research data.* The NTO coordinates tourism research for the area. Information on origin of visitors, length of stay, type of accommodation used, and expenditures on different tourism products are collected and disseminated to members of the organization. This information helps the NTO evaluate trends and develop marketing strategy. It also provides valuable information to hospitality and travel businesses.

- *Representation in markets.* The NTO often has offices in major markets. These promote the country within the market. The promotion comes in the form of advertising with response mechanisms, such as advertisements in travel magazines featuring a toll-free number to call for additional information. Respondents receive a tour manual. The offices answer questions from prospective visitors and facilitate the development of distribution linkages. They also serve as important sources of information about trends in the market.

- *Organization of workshops and trade shows.* The NTO facilitates the interaction of tourism with members of the distribution channels, such as travel agents and wholesalers. In addition to developing workshops, the NTO purchases space at major travel shows and invites travel industry members to participate in the booth, by either displaying material or having a physical presence. This saves the member the cost of purchasing an individual booth.

- *Familiarization trips (Fam trips).* The NTO develops **familiarization trips** for key members of the distribution channel and travel writers. A fam trip is a low-cost or no-cost trip sponsored by a travel destination including hotels, cruise lines, and resorts for travel agents or others who can send business to the travel destination.

- *Participation in joint marketing schemes.* Some NTOs provide cooperative advertising support to help members promote to selected markets. The British Tourist Authority, for example, helps support British Airways advertising in the United States. It is hoped these advertisements will develop additional tourists for Britain, thus helping the British hospitality and travel industry.

- *Support for new or small businesses.* NTOs may provide support for new products and small businesses that are important to the overall tourism of the area. For example, rural tourism, regional festivals, and bed and breakfast (B&B) accommodations are often promoted by NTOs.

- *Consumer assistance and protection.* NTOs assist the consumer by providing product information. For example, in some countries there are classification schemes for lodging accommodations. These are designed to educate travelers concerning types of available lodging. Sometimes NTOs influence the design of lodging brochures and menus appropriate for a particular market segment.

- *General education.* NTOs conduct conferences and courses to educate travel industry providers from their nation to understand the needs of foreign markets.

Like other organizations, NTOs must develop a mission statement, goals, and a strategy. The following guidelines were developed to assist in formulating a mission statement:

1. The past experiences in the region with regard to tourism must be considered, including the salient characteristics and history of the region, the regional tourism organization(s), and the tourism business units.

2. The regional tourism organization must be prepared to adapt the region's mission in response to the characteristics of the regional tourism environment. For example, there is increasing concern for the protection of the ecological environment. This should be incorporated into a regional mission statement.

3. The region's tourism resources make certain missions possible and others not. Northern Canada, for example, is unlikely to become the surfing Mecca of North America.

4. The preferences of the region's major tourism publics, such as regional tourism organizations, tourism business units, local governments, and community organizations, must be considered. A successful mission statement will attempt to incorporate the priorities and expectations of the major publics in the region.

5. The mission must be based on the region's distinctive competencies. A concerted effort must be made to concentrate on the region's strengths. If, for example, a region's major tourism resource is its cultural heritage, this should receive primary emphasis in the mission statement.

Goals provide direction to the organization. The following are typical tourism goals:

- *Economic:* To optimize the contribution of tourism and recreation to economic prosperity, full employment, and regional economic development.

- *Consumer:* To make the opportunity for and the benefits of travel and recreation universally acceptable to residents and visitors and to contribute to the personal growth and education of the population and encourage their appreciation of the geography, history, and ethnic diversity of the region.

- *Environmental and natural resources:* To protect and preserve the historic and cultural foundations of the region as a living part of community life and development and to ensure future generations an opportunity to enjoy the rich heritage of the region, as well as to ensure the compatibility of tourism, recreational, and activity policies with other regional and national interests in energy development and conservation, environmental protection, and judicious use of natural resources.

- *Government operations:* To harmonize to the maximum extent possible all government-related activities supporting tourism and recreation; to support the needs of the general public and the public and private sectors of industries involved with tourism and recreation; and to take a leadership role with all those concerned with tourism, recreation, and cultural heritage conservation.

The underlying objective of national strategy formulation is to translate current conditions in the region into desired situations. For example, a federal government with the goal of increasing the economic benefits of tourism to a specific subregion may select a strategy to increase visitation to that area. A country that is highly dependent on one specific geographic market for its demand may adopt a strategy of diversification. For example, Mexico, known for its sun and sea destinations, has developed historical sites to attract a different segment of tourists.

Destinations marketers who are able to influence site selection of groups such as associations can expect invaluable visitors' income for the community. To have a chance of being selected as a meeting site, a destination must be included in the initial decision process. Careful study and research is needed of those responsible for site selection. Research of targeted associations and understanding who the real decision makers are within the providence of the site selection committee is needed.[50]

Regional Tourist Organizations: State Associations and Convention and Tourist Bureaus

Many state or provinces have their own tourist organizations. Queensland in Australia has created Tourism Queensland, statutory authority of the Queensland government. State tourist organizations (STOs) perform many of the same functions of an NTO, only on a regional level. They also work with the NTOs, to obtain funds and effectively employ resources in their area. Tourism Queensland, working with other tourism organizations, has developed a 10-year strategic plan for the state.[51] New York State's STO developed the *I Love New York* campaign. Like many STOs, New York divided the state into regions that have a common theme for tourists. For example, some of the names of the regions are New York City, The Catskills, Greater Niagara, and the Thousand-Islands-Seaway Region.[52] The owner and manager of hospitality organizations such as a hotel, restaurant, or attractions that entice tourists should work with STOs to see how they can promote their business.

City, county, or area convention and visitors' bureaus (CVB) promote tourism on the local level. Because they promote a specific destination, they are often referred as a **destination marketing organization (DMO)**. A major focus of DMOs is to bring meetings and conventions to the local convention facilities and hotels with meeting space. The convention facilities are often owned by the local government and sometimes built knowing they would not make money off the rental of the facility. The dollars the tourists bring to the city and the sales taxes and hotel occupancy taxes would cover the loss on the convention center. Sometimes the DMO and the convention center management are two separate organizations, which calls for close communication between the two organizations.

Hotels, restaurants with banquet space, and restaurants near convention hotels should work closely with their CVB to make sure they get their fair share of the convention business. The local hotel association and restaurant association usually have board positions on the CVB's board to make sure their interests are represented.[53]

Sardinia is one of the twenty regions in Italy. It is known for its beautiful beaches. However, it is expanding its markets and now promoting its interior to hikers and persons on bicycle tours. It has also become a popular spot for Europeans who want to relax in the country. Courtesy of jiri jura/Shutterstock.

CVBs often work with airlines serving their area and create travel missions to visit markets, domestic and international, that represent opportunities for all tourist industry members within a destination to work together. Large enterprises such as a ski resort or a large attraction such as the Biltmore house in Asheville, North Carolina, may provide a booth with representatives, whereas small members such as a B&B may be able to only provide brochures and support the sponsoring tourist promotion organizations.

Travel missions are commonly organized by government or quasi-government tourism promotion bureaus. Travel missions fall into two general categories:

1. Exploratory missions, where the primary objective is to explore new business opportunities and to develop new markets.

2. Travel sales missions where participants intend to make direct business contacts and close sales.

Reasons for sponsoring travel missions by the N.C. Division of Tourism, Film, and Sports Division follow:

1. Travel missions are cost effective because they spread costs over many participants.

2. Missions attract greater numbers of participants than would be possible under other promotional formats.

3. Travel missions to secondary markets serve as a relatively inexpensive marketing research tool.

4. Sales and profits can be directly traced to the missions.

5. Cross-selling usually always occurs. For instance, during North Carolina's missions, resorts and hotels sell the benefits of theme parks. Golf operators refer clients to ocean-side resorts.

6. Meeting planners seem to be encouraged by the spirit of a team selling the entire destination. The intermediaries bear hundreds of pitches but are notably impressed by the cooperative enthusiasm of a travel mission.

7. Whether on a travel mission or not, promoting a visitor destination is always a team effort.

■■■ KEY TERMS

Agritourism. Agriculture-based tourism that includes farms, ranches, and wineries. It provides rural areas with a means to attract tourists.

Allocentrics. Persons with a need for new experiences, such as backpackers and explorers.

Destination marketing organization (DMO). A group that promotes a specific destination. Often a local convention and visitors' bureau (CVB) serve as the DMO.

Destinations. Places with some form of actual or perceived boundary, such as the physical boundary of an island, political boundaries, or even market-created boundaries.

Familiarization trip (Fam trip). A trip where travel agents or others who can send business to a tourist destination attraction, cruise, or hotel are invited to visit at a low cost or no cost.

Infrastructure. The system according to which a company, organization, or other body is organized at the most basic level.

Macrodestinations. Destinations such as the United States that contain thousands of microdestinations, including regions, states, cities, towns, and visitor destinations within a town.

Medical tourism. One of the fastest-growing and most lucrative tourism markets. Tourists spend a large amount on medical treatment, stay in top hotels, and often travel around the country after their surgery.

Multiplier effect. Tourist expenditures that are recycled through the local economy, being spent and spent again.

National tourist organizations (NTOs). A national government or quasi-government agency that markets destination tourism.

Psychocentrics. Persons who do not desire change when they travel. They like to visit nonthreatening places and stay in familiar surroundings.

Tourism. A stay of one or more nights away from home for holidays, visits to friends or relatives, business conferences, or any other purpose, except such things as boarding, education, or semipermanent employment.

■■■ CHAPTER REVIEW

I. Globalization of the Tourist Industry. Definition of tourism: "a stay of one or more nights away from home for holidays, visits to friends or relatives, business conferences, or any other purpose except such things as boarding, education, or semi-permanent employment."

II. Importance of Tourism to a Destination's Economy
  A. Tourism destination
    1. **Destinations** are places with some form of actual or perceived boundary.
    2. **Macrodestinations** such as the United States contain thousands of microdestinations, including regions, states, cities, towns, and visitor destinations within a town.
  B. Benefits of tourism
    1. **Employment.**
    2. **Supports industries and professions.**
    3. **Multiplier effect.** Tourism expenditures are recycled through the economy.
    4. **Source of state and local taxes.**
    5. **Stimulates exports of place-made products.**
  C. Management of the tourism destination
    1. **Destinations must maintain the infrastructure.** Destinations that fail to maintain the necessary infrastructure or build inappropriate infrastructure run significant risks.
    2. **Sustainable tourism.** A destination's attractiveness can be diminished by violence, political instability, natural catastrophe, adverse environmental factors, and overcrowding.
  D. Sustainable tourism
    1. **Modified environments and ecotourism subsets**
    2. **Industry and community cooperation**
    3. **Carbon-neutral Vacations**

III. Tourism Strategies and Investments
  A. Tourism events and attractions
    1. **Events** that attract a desired market and harmoniously fit with a community's culture can provide beneficial results, particularly if the event regularly reoccurs over a period of years.
    2. **Attractions** may be natural, such as Niagara Falls or the Scottish Highlands or a beach. They can also be manufactured, such as the shopping areas of Buckingham Palace, Hong Kong, the Vatican, or a casino resort.
    3. **A decision framework:** event planning
  B. Sports events
    1. **Biking and marathon events**
  C. Attractions
    1. **Rejuvenating a destination**
    2. **Waterfront attractions**
    3. **Casinos as attractions**
    4. **Indian gaming**
    5. **Stopover tourism.** Many visitor destinations are in fact only stopover destinations for travelers on their way elsewhere.

IV. Segmenting and Monitoring the Tourist Market. Tourism planners must consider how many tourists are desired, which segments to attract, and how to balance tourism with other industries.
  A. Agritourism. Agriculture-based tourism that includes farms, ranches, and wineries. It provides rural areas with a means to attract tourists.
  B. Space tourism. As private companies provide vehicles to send tourists into space, this form of tourism will develop. In the near term, it will just be for the very rich.
  C. Multiday hiking and religious pilgrimages
  D. Volunteer vacationing. Families and individuals take trips to less developed areas to help the people in the area and gain an understanding of their culture. The tourists perform tasks such as building housing, schools, and churches.
  E. Medical tourism is one of the fastest-growing and most lucrative tourism markets. Tourists spend a large amount on medical treatment, stay in top hotels, and often travel around the country after their surgery. The aging baby boomers and the growing cost of health care will ensure the growth of medical tourism in the future.
  F. Genealogical tourism.
  G. Identifying target markets
    1. **Collect information about its current visitors.**
    2. **Audit the destination's attractions and select segments that might logically have an interest in them**
  H. Self-contained attraction and event destination.
  I. Classification of visitor segments
    1. **Group-inclusive tour (GIT)**
    2. **Independent traveler (IT; formerly FIT)**
  J. Monitoring the tourist markets. Tourist markets are dynamic and a marketing information system is part of any well-run tourist organization.

V. Communicating with the Tourist Market
  A. Competition for visitors requires image making.
  B. Developing packages of attractions and amenities is an effective way of communicating with potential travelers.
    1. Attractions alone do not attract visitors. Most places seek to deepen the travel experience by providing greater value and making the experience more significant and rewarding.
    2. Competition among destinations extends to restaurants, facilities, sports, cultural amenities, and entertainment.
  C. UNESCO World Heritage Sites
  D. Developing packages of attractions and amenities

VI. Organizing and Managing Tourism Marketing. Making a destination tourist friendly is the task of a central tourist agency, which may be public, quasi-public, nonprofit, or private. These agencies are referred to as national tourist organizations (NTOs), state tourist organizations (STOs), convention and visitors' bureaus (CVBs), or destination management organizations.

■■■ DISCUSSION QUESTIONS

1. How does a tourism destination determine what to promote and to whom it should be promoted?

2. What benefits does tourism bring to your area?

3. Choose one of the psychological determinants of demand listed in Table 17–2 and describe a tourism product that is based on the determinant you have chosen.

4. Choose what you believe to be a good tourism promotion for a city, region, state, or country and explain why you think it is a good promotion. In your critique, discuss the media used, target audience, and benefits the destination offers.

■■■ EXPERIENTIAL EXERCISE

Do the following:

Choose an event (festival, concert, play, etc.) in your area that draws tourists. Look into how the event is promoted and the benefits it brings to the community. Is this event effectively promoted? If yes, why? If no, how could it be improved?

■■■ INTERNET EXERCISE

Find two different sites of tourism marketing organizations, national, state, or convention and visitors' bureaus. Evaluate how effective you feel these Web sites are in promoting the destination. Explain your answer.

■■■ REFERENCES

1. Chris Ryan, "The Determinate of Demand for Tourism," in *Recreational Tourism: A Social Science Perspective* (London: Routledge, 1991), p. 5.

2. "Ruili Strives to Become a Top Tourist City," *Travel China,* 9, no. 13 (1997): 9; *Tourism Highlights,* 1999, 2–17.

3. Laura Wood, "Research and Markets: China Tourism Industry Report, 2011—Tourism in China Emerges out of the Economic Crisis in 2010," *Business Wire* (Dublin), August 19, 2011, accessed August 4, 2012, from http://www.businesswire.com/news/home/20110818006045/en/Research-Markets-China-Tourism-Industry-Report-2011.

4. Changfeng Chen, "Rising Chinese Overseas Travel Market and Potential for the United States," in *Advances in Hospitality and Tourism Research,* eds. K. S. Chon and Connie C. B. Mok (Houston, TX: Conrad N. Hilton College, 1998), pp. 468–478.

5. Sergei Khrushckev, Tony L. Henthorne, and Michael S. Latour, "Cuba at the Crossroads," *Cornell Hospitality Quarterly* (November 2007): 402–414.

6. Brijesh Thapa, Kyriaki Kaplanedou, Ignatius Cahyanto, and Elaine McLaughlin, "Crisis Planning and Preparedness in the U.S. Tourism Industry," *Cornell Hospitality Quarterly,* 52, no 3 (August 11, 2010): 312–318.

7. Jim Bergstorm, Lawrence Yu, and Edgar Medweth, "Destination Maintenance: Why Sedona Needs Schnebly Hill," *Cornell Hotel and Restaurant Administration Quarterly,* 35, no. 4 (1994): 32.

8. Ibid., pp. 33, 37.

9. Andrew Nemethy, "Resorts Go Up and Down," *Snow County* (November 1990): 31–32.

10. Sergie Khrushchev, Tony L. Henthorne, and Michael S. Latour, "Cuba at the Crossroads," *Cornell Hospitality Quarterly* (November 2007): 402–414.

11. Edward Manning and T. D. Dougherty, "Sustainable Tourism," *Cornell Hotel and Restaurant Administration Quarterly,* 36, no. 2 (1995): 29.

12. Hugo Martin, "Utah's Wave Is a Rock Star Without a Crowd," *The Denver Post* (January 6, 2008): 1T, 6T.

13. Rex S. Toh, Habibullah Kahn, and Karen Kim, "Singapore Tourist Industry: How Its Strengths Offset Economic, Social and Environmental Challenges," *Cornell Hotel and Restaurant Administration Quarterly,* 42, no. 1 (2001): 46.

14. David Bruce Weaver, "Eco-Tourism as Mass Tourism: Contradiction or Reality?" *Cornell Hotel and Restaurant Administration Quarterly,* 42, no. 2 (2001): 112.

15. Susan Gregory and Kathy Koithan-Louderback, "Marketing a Resort Community," *Cornell Hotel and Restaurant Quarterly,* 38, no. 6 (1997): 54.

16. Jeffrey Ball, "The Carbon Neutral Vacation," *Wall Street Journal* (July 28–29, 2007): P1, P4, P5.

17. "Qufu Stresses Confucian Culture and Tourism Market Order," *Travel China,* 9, no. 13 (1997).

18. James R. Hagerty, "Loaves and Fish: Piscine Gluttony in Pennsylvania," *Wall Street Journal* (June 16–17, 2007): A1, A2.

19. Martin A. O'Neill and Adrian Palmer, "Wine Production and Tourism: Adding Service to a Perfect Partnership," *Cornell Hotel and Restaurant Administration Quarterly,* 45, no. 3 (2004): 271.

20. Ibid.

21. Juergen Gnoth and Syed Aziz Anwar, "New Zealand Bets on Event Tourism," *Cornell Hotel and Restaurant Administration Quarterly,* 41, no. 4 (2000): 80.

22. Wargin, Susan, "Update," accessed July 10, 2011, from www.9news.com

23. An Earful of Cheer, Disney Does Marathons the Only Way It Knows How, *Hemispheres Magazine.com* (May 2011).

24. Norman Skiareivitz, Copley News Service, "Going Places: Waikiki $2 Billion Makeover," *Steamboat Pilot & Today* (November 4, 2007): 1D, 2D.

25. Deborah Steinborn, "On the Waterfront," *Wall Street Journal* (June 11, 2007): R11.

26. http://www.greektowncasino.com/Gaming/ClubGreektown/ (accessed October 11, 2008); R. Ankeny, "Greektown Casino: We'll Bring Neighborhood Firms to Table," *Crain's Detroit Business,* 15, no. 33 (1999): 3–4 (retrieved June 13, 2004, from EBSCOhost online article search engine); T. Lam, "Home Court Advantage: Greektown Casino Owners Are Betting on Metro Detroiters' Affection for the Neighborhood," *Detroit /Windsor Casino Guide* (November 10, 2000), as originally printed in the Detroit Free Press, http://www.freep.com/casinoguide/greektown/greek.htm (accessed June 14, 2004).

27. "How Do Casinos Affect Your Business?" *Amusement Business,* 108, no. 7 (1996): 3–4; National Gambling Impact Study Commission, June 1999; NGISC Final Report, American Gaming Association,www.unt.edu, http://govinfo.library.unt.edu/ngisc/reports/fullrpt.html (accessed June 12, 2004); B. Gillette, "New Casino Facilities Boost Business Elsewhere on Coast," *Mississippi Business Journal,* 21, no. 30 (1999): 18–19; S. Ray, "Gaming Makes Big Winners out of Tradeshows," *Amusement Business,* 107, no. 21 (1995):18–19.

28. www.fortune.com/sections, Special Advertising Feature, "Indian Gaming, The Native American Success Story," 2007.

29. Mark Whitehouse, "Bad Odds," *Wall Street Journal* (June 11, 2007): R5.

30. Rex S. Toh, Habibullah Kahn, and Karen Lim, "Singapore's Tourism Industry: How Its Strength Offsets Economic, Social and Environmental Challenges," *Cornell Hotel and Restaurant Administrative Quarterly,* 42, no. 1 (2001): 42, 48.

31. Tom Crosby, "Kiawah Island Joins Charleston as Major South Carolina Destination," *Go Magazine* (March/April 2004): 29.

32. "Colorado's Agritourism Market Climbing Says New CSU Report," College of Agricultural Sciences, *AG Family* (Fall 2007), Colorado State University, p. 4.

33. *Houston Chronicle,* http://www.chron.com/disp/story.mpl/front/6052360.html (accessed October 11, 2008).

34. See www.virgingalactic.com.

35. Dan Vergano, "NASA Prepares for Moon Tourism," *USA Today* (November 10, 2011): 1

36. *Centennial Journal* (May 2007): 11C, 12C.

37. Gene Sloan, "Double Duty," *USA Today* (December 7, 2007): 1D, 2D.

38. Michael D. Horowitz and Jeffrey A. Rosenweig, "Medical Tourism—Health Care in the Global Economy," *Physician Executive,* 33, no. 6 (2007), 24–30; "Healthcare Cost," *Healthcare Financial Management,* 62, no. 9 (2008): 12.

39. Carla Almeida Santos and Grace Yan, "Genealogical Tourism: A Phenomenological Examination," *Journal of Travel Research,* 49, no. 1 (February 2011).

40. Stanley C. Plog, "Why Destinations Rise and Fall in Popularity," *Cornell Hotel and Restaurant Quarterly,* 14, no. 4 (1984): 55–59.

41. Zhaoping Liu, Judy A. Siguaw, and Cathy A. Enz, "Using Tourist Travel Habits and Preferences to Assess Strategic Destination Positioning," *Cornell Hospitality Quarterly* 49, no. 3 (August 2008): 258–280.

42. Richard Prentice, "Market Targeting," in *Tourism Marketing and Management Handbook,* eds. Stephen F. Witt and Luiz Moutinho (Upper Saddle River, NJ: Prentice-Hall, 1989), pp. 247–252.

43. Bob McKercher and Basak Denizci Guillet, "Are Tourists or Market Destinations Loyal?" *Journal of Travel Research,* 50, no 2 (March 2011): 128–129.

44. Ibid.

45. John Deskins and Matthew Seevers, "Are State Expenditures to Promote Tourism Effective?" *Journal of Travel Research,* 50, no. 2 (March 2011): 167.

46. Marsha Coleman and Kenneth F. Backman, "Walking in Memphis: Testing One DMO's Marketing Strategy to Millennials," *Journal of Travel Research,* 49, no. 1 (February 2010).

47. World Heritage Centre, World Heritage List, accessed October 25, 2011, from http://whc.unesco.org/en/list/; Nicholas Kulish, "Proposed to Better Unite City Leaves Dresden Divided," *New York Times International* (January 5, 2008): A3.

48. J. S. Perry Hobson and Roberta Leung, "Hotel Development in Myanmar," *Cornell Hotel and Restaurant Administration Quarterly,* 38, no. 1 (1997): 60–71. See also F. Doherty, "Come Ye Back to Mandalay," *Tourism in Focus,* 15 (Spring 1995): 8.

49. http://www.tia.org/index.html (accessed October 11, 2008); "Travel and Tourism Works for America," published by the Travel Industry Association, January 2008.

50. Chris Ryan, *Recreational Tourism: A Social Science Perspective* (New York: Routledge, 1991), pp. 5–34; A. J. Burkhart and S. Medlik, *Tourism: Past, Present, and Future* (London: Heinemann, 1981), p. 256; T. C. Victor Middleton, *Marketing in Travel and Tourism* (Oxford, UK: Butterworth-Heinemann, 1994); Ernie Heath and Geoffrey Wall, *Marketing Tourism Destination* (New York: Wiley, 1992), p. 65; R. C. Mills and A. M. Morrison, *The Tourism System: An Introductory Text* (Upper Saddle River, NJ: Prentice Hall, 1985), p. 248; S. Crystal, "What Is the Meeting Industry Worth?" *Meeting News,* 17, no. 7 (1993): 1, 11.

51. http://www.tq.com.au/ (accessed October 11, 2008).

52. http://www.iloveny.com/home.aspx (accessed October 11, 2008).

53. "Best Practices Convention Center Sales and Convention Center Operations," A report from the Joint Study Committee, Destination Marketing Association International, and International Association of Assembly Managers, August 25, 2007.

Courtesy of Thomas Barrat.

Next Year's Marketing Plan

18

Objectives

After reading this chapter, you should be able to:

1. Understand why it is important to have a marketing plan and be able to explain the purpose of a marketing plan.

2. Prepare a marketing plan following the process described in this chapter.

Hospitality companies know that planning and research go hand in glove. This is particularly true of companies such as Preferred Hotels & Resorts Worldwide that serve the affluent guest, as described by Peter Cass, president and CEO. Pictured above is the Post Ranch Inn in California which is built on a cliff 1200 feet above the Pacific Ocean, a member of Preferred's Boutique collection.

The rationale is that the experience of the truly discerning traveler is shaped by the "little things," beyond guaranteeing merely a clean, comfortable room and a desirable package of amenities. In-depth guest input will also be used to shape the criteria that go into defining the on-property guest experience. Through a proprietary customer satisfaction program currently under development, Preferred Hotels and Resorts will refine still further fine points of detail that create a truly memorable and complete "luxury experience."

For example, at the Rittenhouse Hotel in Philadelphia, frequent guests are greeted nightly with an expensive pearl on their pillow instead of the usual chocolate. At Halekulani in Honolulu, named the number-one hotel in the world by *Gourmet* magazine, guests are escorted to their rooms for swift, private check-in and receive a welcoming box of chocolates made by their in-house chocolatier soon afterward.

Although "comment cards" and guest preference sheets remain commonplace at many luxury hotels, no other worldwide lodging brand has built into its core mission the complete and total fulfillment of the guests' individual tastes, requirements, and predilections.

We have found that complete attention to detail—a total commitment to guest satisfaction that saves a guest time, energy, and efforts, provides completely personalized and individual service, and creates the experience of "intellectual surprise" for its consumers—is what drives repeat business among the affluent.

To better understand its affluent consumer, Preferred Hotels & Resorts launched a market research effort that "drills down" to the deepest level of guest preference and expectation. Using a prospect identification and lifestyle data collection system, detailed and segmented data are gathered not only about the preferences of luxury travelers but also about unperceived "micromarkets" that make up the luxury travel segment.

At the individual property level, the expectation is that property managers will soon be able to learn not only what kind of room guests prefer when they travel on business, but also what their favorite leisure activities are, what kind of wine they like to drink—even their favorite reading material. At the macrolevel, Preferred targets programs, promotions, and partnerships tailored to the micromarket segments that make up its customer base. Examples are West Coast lawyers who golf or company CEOs who travel with children. Data collected from drilling down into the guest experience enable Preferred to provide the ultimate in guest service. Unique data can also be for partners who seek unique channels and distribution mechanisms in marketing to the affluent.

Initial Applications of the Research: "Experiential" Associations and New Marketing Programs

Although affluent guests value individuality and attention to detail, Preferred has begun to identify certain distinct attributes or expectations that define the affluent as a group. More than anything else, affluents tend to flock together around common symbols, expectations, and experiences. In a word, they associate themselves into groups. Membership in the group, in turn, comes to define participation in the affluent experience.

Association is built into the concept of the affluent experience so that Preferred's creation of programs that target the affluent can be understood as a universal affinity program for the discerning consumer. It is the ultimate "affinity program for the affluent."

Preferred has taken the affinity concept a step further by identifying an interlinked series of value and quality associations that respond to the affluent client's desire for unique, memorable experiences and superior service, and by using that information to provide experiences that cater directly and uniquely to that desire.

Seabourn/Windstar

An example of the research in action is a partnership between Preferred and Seabourn/Windstar Cruises. The linkage is the desire of guests who stay at exclusive Preferred hotel properties also to take expensive cruises on these two cruise lines, among the world's finest. The customer reward is the ability to translate stays at Preferred hotels into free nights on these cruises. This allows Preferred and Seabourn/Windstar to share guest histories and databases that reveal a guest's preferences and thus guarantees the ability to service the guest "to a T" with the expectation of creating return business.

Golf the Preferred Way

Another example of the application of the lifestyle marketing approach is "Preferred Golf," a partnership with Wide World of Golf, a worldwide marketer of upscale golf services. Preferred Golf provides Preferred guests with access to the world's finest golf courses by means of staying at a Preferred hotel or resort.

Engaging New Partners: Travel Agents and the Lifestyle Client Building Program

Lifestyle marketing programs that target the affluent have applications that extend far beyond merely "selling room nights."

For example, through programs such as Wide World of Golf and the cruise redemption program, Preferred properties and travel agents can work together to sell complete "experiential packages" for the affluent traveler. Travel agents enter Preferred's luxury marketing "loop" as partners and build relationships with discerning travelers. This goes well beyond the usual booking of air travel and hotels on the basis of price and availability. Client building is achieved through educational seminars, training programs, and special package promotions. Agents are encouraged to position themselves as key components of Preferred's affluent marketing channel.[1]

Success in the marketplace is not guaranteed by understanding marketing concepts and strategies. Successful marketing requires planning and careful execution. It is easy to become so involved in the day-to-day problems of running a marketing department that little or no time is devoted to planning. When this occurs, the marketing department is probably operating without purpose and is being reactive rather than proactive. Even experienced managers sometimes fail to see that this is occurring until it is too late. This may be one of the root causes for high turnover within hospitality, marketing, and sales departments.

▪▪▪ Purpose of a Marketing Plan

A marketing plan serves several purposes within any hospitality company:

- Provides a road map for all marketing activities of the firm for the next year.

- Ensures that marketing activities are in agreement with the corporate strategic plan.

- Forces marketing managers to review and think through objectively all steps in the marketing process.

- Assists in the budgeting process to match resources with marketing objectives.

- Creates a process to monitor actual against expected results.

The development of a marketing plan is a rigorous process and cannot be accomplished in a few hours. Instead, it is best to set aside one or more days to develop next year's plan. Many marketing managers find it best to leave the office along with their staff and all necessary data while writing the plan. Constant interruptions that occur in the office are detrimental to the planning process.

To be effective, a new marketing plan must be written each year. Marketing plans written for periods longer than a year are generally not effective. At the same time, the annual marketing plan must be written against a longer-term strategic plan that states what the company hopes to achieve, say, three to five years down the road.

Many managers believe that the process of writing a plan is invaluable because it forces those writing it to question, think, and strategize. A plan should be developed with the input and assistance of key members of the marketing department. The discussion and thought process required to produce a plan is stimulating and very helpful in team building. It is also an excellent training device for younger staff members who wish to be managers.

Marketing plans are not created in a vacuum. To develop successful strategies and action programs, marketers need up-to-date information about the environment, the competition, and the market segments to be served. Often, analysis of internal data is the starting point for assessing the current marketing situation, supplemented by marketing intelligence and research investigating the overall market, the competition, key issues, and threats and opportunities. As the plan is put into effect, marketers use a variety of research techniques to measure progress toward objectives and identify areas for improvement if results fall short of projections.

Finally, marketing research helps marketers learn more about their customers' requirements, expectations, perceptions, and satisfaction levels. This deeper understanding provides a foundation for building competitive advantage through well-informed segmenting, targeting, differentiating, and positioning decisions. Thus, the marketing plan should outline what marketing research will be conducted and how the findings will be applied.

A market estimated at $630 billion globally remains unfamiliar to many hospitality and tourism planners. This is the global Muslim market. The KFC chain has conducted a trial of halal food in eight of its British restaurants. European supermarket chains such as Tesco, Sainsbury, and Casino now carry a line of halal food.

Muslims spend a heavy percentage of their income on food. In part this is due to their custom of communal feasting. It has been estimated that French Muslims spend a quarter of their income on food as compared to 12 to 14 percent for non-Muslims. In particular, meat represents a heavy percentage of the Muslim food budget. The slaughtering of all lamb and goat meat in Australia for export is now done in accordance with halal custom. Halal meat from Australia represents $570 million per year.

Hospitality and tourism marketers need to acquaint themselves with this growing market and provide management with ideas as to how to attract and satisfy these customers.[2]

The marketing plan shows how the company will establish and maintain profitable customer relationships. In the process, however, it also shapes a number of internal and external relationships. First, it affects how marketing personnel work with each other and with other departments to deliver value and satisfy customers. Second, it affects how the company works with suppliers, distributors, and strategic alliance partners to achieve the objectives listed in the plan. Third, it influences the company's dealings with other stakeholders, including government regulators, the media, and the community at large. All of these relationships are important to the organization's success, so they should be considered when a marketing plan is being developed.

Unlike a business plan, which offers a broad overview of the entire organization's mission, objectives, strategy, and resource allocation, a marketing plan has a more limited scope. It serves to document how the organization's strategic objectives will be achieved through specific marketing strategies and tactics, with the customer as the starting point. It is also linked to the plans of other departments within the organization. Suppose a marketing plan calls for selling 200,000 units annually. The production department must gear up to make that many units, the finance department must arrange funding to cover the expenses, the human resources department must be ready to hire and train staff, and so on. Without the appropriate level of organizational support and resources, no marketing plan can succeed.

Although the exact length and layout varies from company to company, a marketing plan usually contains the sections described in this chapter. To guide implementation effectively, every part of the plan must be described in considerable detail. Sometimes a company posts its marketing plan on an internal Web site, which allows managers and employees in different locations to consult specific sections and collaborate on additions or changes. We now discuss the following sections of a marketing plan in detail.

   I. Executive Summary

  II. Corporate Connection

 III. Environmental Analysis and Forecasting

  IV. Segmentation and Targeting

   V. Next Year's Objectives and Quotas

  VI. Action Plans: Strategies and Tactics

 VII. Resources Needed to Support Strategies and Meet Objectives

VIII. Marketing Control

  IX. Presenting and Selling the Plan

   X. Preparing for the Future

We examine the role played by each section of the marketing plan.

▪▪▪ Section I: Executive Summary

The **executive summary** and a few charts or graphs from the body of the plan may be the only parts ever read by top management. Consequently, it is of great importance to write this section carefully, with top management in mind.

A few tips may assist in writing the executive summary:

- Write it for top executives.

- Limit the number of pages to between two and four.

- Use short sentences and short paragraphs. Avoid using words that are unlikely to be understood.

- Organize the summary as follows: Describe next year's objectives in quantitative terms; briefly describe marketing strategies to meet goals and objectives, including a description of target markets; describe expected results by quarter; identify the dollar costs necessary, as well as key resources needed.

- Read and reread the executive summary several times. Never write it once and then place it in the plan. Modify and change the summary until it flows well, is easily read, and conveys the central message of the marketing plan.

■■■ Section II: Corporate Connection

Relationship to Other Plans

A marketing plan is not a stand-alone tool. Instead, it must support other plans, such as the firm's strategic plan. Whenever possible, the marketing manager should participate in or provide input to the development of a strategic plan. If this is not practical, it remains imperative to understand the contents of the strategic plan prior to development of next year's marketing plan.

A marketing plan supports the company's strategic plan in several ways. Next year's marketing strategies and tactics must support strategic decisions such as the following:

- Corporate goals with respect to profit, growth, and so on

- Desired market share

- Positioning of the company or of its product lines

- Vertical or horizontal integration

- Strategic alliances

- Product-line breadth and depth

- Customer-relationship management (CRM)

Marketing-Related Plans

In large corporations, marketing-related plans are sometimes developed by people who do not report to marketing. This is usually the result of (1) originally establishing these departments independent of marketing, (2) political maneuvering in which a nonmarketing executive desired control of these areas, and (3) the failure of top management to understand the need to unify marketing-related activities.

Marketing-related areas in which plans are sometimes written independently of marketing include the following:

- Sales

- Advertising and promotion

- Public relations and publicity

- Marketing research

- Pricing

- Customer service

If these plans are developed independently of a marketing plan with no consideration as to how they tie together, the result is often chaotic, counterproductive, and a source for continuous infighting among marketing-related areas.

When the organizational design of a company fails to place major marketing activities under the marketing umbrella, the task of writing and implementing a marketing plan is made more complex. Under these conditions, it behooves the marketing manager to invite the managers of other marketing-related areas to participate in the marketing plan development process. This action should then be reciprocated.

The director of sales works with her sales managers on the marketing plan.Courtesy of Steve Gorton © Dorling Kindersley.

The activities of marketing and many other departments within a company are closely intertwined. Operations and finance are two areas that affect and in turn are affected by marketing. If guest experiences are diminished because of problem areas in operations, marketing will be adversely affected. Similarly, if financial projections are unrealistic for certain months or for various product lines, marketing will be called to task.

It is unrealistic to expect perfect harmony between marketing and other departments. It is by no means unrealistic to suggest that relations can usually be greatly improved and that a critical place to begin is by interchanging data, suggestions, and other assistance when department plans are being developed.

Corporate Direction

A good marketing plan begins with the fact that the only purpose of marketing is to support the enterprise. It is good politics and good sense to begin next year's plan by recognizing and restating these corporate elements. Let top management know that the following helped guide the development of next year's plan:

- Mission statement
- Corporate philosophy
- Corporate goals

Hospitality companies are highly sensitive to changes in their social, political, and economic environments. A manufacturer of food or toiletries may not immediately feel the impact of these changes, but airlines, hotels, auto rental firms, and cruise lines witness an instant reaction.

■■■ Section III: Environmental Analysis and Forecasting

After the terrorist attacks of September 11, 2001, hospitality firms felt the impact. Pleasure travel instantly evaporated as fear of terrorism gripped Americans. Unfortunately, some companies responded without clearly thinking. Several hotel chains quickly offered substantial discounts to guests. This did nothing to increase demand but instead simply gave discounts to people who had to travel for business and would have paid a higher rate. A marketing plan is not a political or economic treatise, and hospitality marketers are not expected to be experts in these fields. They are expected to be aware of major **environmental factors** likely to affect the industry and the company, to consider their possible impact on marketing, and to respond quickly and intelligently to new events and trends.

Positioning Statement

A marketing plan should provide a positioning statement of how the enterprise intends to differentiate—position itself—in the marketplace. This provides essential guidance to the rest of the plan.

Major airlines such as American Airlines have traditionally positioned themselves as hub-and-spoke carriers serving multimarket segments and as market share companies. Other airlines have positioned themselves as low-price niche carriers, such as Southwest, serving point-to-point markets.

Small resort hotels usually position themselves as providers of vacation/holiday service for individuals, couples, and small groups. Larger resort hotels position themselves as serving this market but also serving the corporate seminar, meeting, and conference market.

A limousine service positions itself differently from a taxi cab business. A tour bus business positions itself differently from a sightseeing bus business.

All members of the marketing and sales departments and their service suppliers such as ad agencies, public relations firms, marketing research firms, and others must know the desired positioning of the enterprise. Otherwise, their efforts may result in a confused array of strategies, tactics, and results that may not serve the company well.

Tourist/visitor destinations usually have a more difficult task selecting a single unifying positioning statement due usually to political pressures and end up trying to be all things to all people. It is little wonder that their advertising and sales tactics mimic others.

Major Environmental Factors

Hospitality organizations need to anticipate the influence of these broad environmental factors on their business.

Social

Consider the possible impact of major social factors, such as crime and changing demographics. These factors vary in their intensity and their geographic incidence. Social factors relevant to Los Angeles, California, or Sydney, Australia, may have little relevance to Rapid City, South Dakota.

Social conditions sometimes change rapidly to the benefit of alert marketers. The hotel market within India had long been considered as uninteresting by many hotel chains. In the 1990s, India's social and economic structure suddenly became conducive to midpriced hotel development.

In the mid-1990s, India had only 2,000 international standard midpriced hotel rooms in a nation of 900 million people, compared with 3.5 million midpriced rooms in the United States. The sudden emergence of a potentially gigantic market attracted many chains, including Holiday Inn Worldwide, Choice Hotels, Carlson Hotels Worldwide, Southern Pacific Hotels (Australia), and Oberoi Hotels and Resorts (India).

Political

Legislation affecting taxation, pension benefits, and casino gambling are only a few examples of political decisions likely to affect marketing directly. International politics is increasingly important to corporate hospitality marketing plans. The opening of Vietnam to investors and tourists after years of being off limits provides risk as well as potential rewards for the hospitality industry.[3]

Economic

Changes in economic variables such as employment and interest rates should be recognized. The hospitality industry, especially the lodging and cruising sectors, is highly sensitive to business-cycle movements.

Economic Drivers of Growth

Economic drivers of growth have the ability to rapidly affect change. Marketers must be aware of these drivers before, during, and after entry into a market. An example is the Aerotropolis, which has been seriously considered for many communities, including Honduras in Central America.

The Aerotropolis

The term *aerotropolis* was developed by Professor John D. Kasarda of the University of North Carolina. An aerotropolis is a transportation and urban development concept built around an airport. An aerotropolis is designed to serve as a powerful economic development force. These centers are built to facilitate the rapid movement of freight and passengers, such as Schiphol Airport in the Netherlands. A huge market for flowers and plants, Bloemenveiling Aalsmer of Amsterdam exists

18.1
Aerotropolis, http://
www.aerotropolis.
com/: Visit aerotropolis to find
out more about the concept.

in tiny Netherlands as the largest and most important market in Europe. This is due in heavy part to the existence of Schiphol Airport.

Many aerotropolis centers are being built in China, Korea, and other nations where they serve as centers for tourism, transportation, and international business. Hotels, restaurants, and entertainment centers are critical participants in a successful aerotropolis.[4]

Competitive Analysis

It is common practice for hospitality companies to conduct a **competitive analysis**. In some cases, this analysis deals primarily with the observable physical properties of a competitor. For example:

Our Hotel	Their Hotel
500 rooms	600 rooms
One ballroom	Two ballrooms
Executive center	No executive center

An analysis solely of physical differences usually misses major competitive advantages or disadvantages. It is doubtful that most guests know or care about the room count of competitive hotels. They do recognize differences in service level, cleanliness, staff knowledge, and the responsiveness of the sales department. A competitive analysis must extend beyond inventory comparisons. True competitive advantages are factors that are recognized by guests and influence their purchase decisions. A creative and alert marketing manager recognizes competitive variables that are truly of importance to the customers and are controllable. Such a manager develops strategies and tactics to improve areas of weakness and enhance already strong points.

There is an explosion of branded hotels in China. The Holiday Inn in Chengdu is one of a growing number of international hotels. Courtesy of Steve Gorton/Dorling Kindersley

Based strictly on a comparison of physical attributes, many hospitality firms should not exist. Bed and breakfast (B&B) establishments are usually old homes without a swimming pool and may have shared bathrooms, yet they fill a competitive niche. Hertz and Avis may compete head-to-head, offering clean, late-model cars, but Rent-a-Wreck auto rental company successfully offers automobiles that many people would be ashamed to be seen driving.

The single best way to conduct a competitive analysis is to involve members of the marketing sales department, such as the sales force. These people often have difficulty discussing environmental variables such as interest rates, but they can talk knowledgeably for hours about the competition and guest preferences.

Market Trends

Market trends are a reflection of environmental competitive variables. Market trend information for the hospitality industry is often available from outside organizations free of charge. Common sources include chambers of commerce, visitors' bureaus, universities, government agencies, banks, trade associations, and commercial organizations such as firms of certified public accountants or consultants who carry public information for publicity purposes.

Useful market trend information for writing a hospitality marketing plan includes the following:

- *Visitor trends:* Origination areas, stopover sites, visitor demographics, spending habits, length of stay, and so on.

- *Competitive trends:* Numbers, location, type of products offered (e.g., all-suite hotels), occupancy levels, average rates, and so on.

- *Related industry trends:* Interdependence of the members of the hospitality industry with airline flights, convention center bookings, new airport construction, and new highways. It is important to study trends for supporting or related industry.

Caterers of in-flight meals were dramatically affected by the trend among U.S. airlines to eliminate or reduce onboard meal service. Companies such as Dobbs International Services, which provided full-course meals, had to find new markets and new products. Caterair International Corporation diversified into the repair of airplane audio headsets, and Sky Chefs explored the private-label business and food preparation for prisons, schools, and hospitals. Randall C. Boyd, senior vice president of marketing and customer service for Sky Chefs, said, "We are good sandwich makers, salad makers, and pasta makers. Whether a prisoner or a college student is eating our sandwich, we don't care."[5]

Select only those trends that are useful in developing the plan. It is of no value to fill a plan with pages of information that have little or no direct relevancy.

Ritz-Carlton's World Concierge Program

It is not always easy to determine whether a service offered by another hotel represents the beginning of an industry trend or just an interesting experiment. This would seem to be the case with Ritz-Carlton's World Concierge Foursquare service.

Ritz-Carlton is a highly respected hotel chain, and therefore this service is being watched closely by others in the hotel industry.

The concept is to reach known customers and noncustomers by utilizing the knowledge of concierges in the seventy-five Ritz-Carlton properties to provide travelers with tips about the markets these seventy-five concierges serve. "As an organization, we are always seeking opportunities to evolve the communications landscape for our brand," said Chris Gabaldon, Chief marketing officer at Ritz-Carlton Hotels. "Over the years, we have launched brand channels on Facebook, Twitter, and YouTube. Foursqare is a rapidly growing social medium at this time that is populated by many Ritz-Carlton fans and loyalists, so it makes sense for us to be there. Both Facebook and Twitter have been successful platforms for us to engage at a deeper level with our guests. This is an extension of that process." "We don't tend to make decisions based on peer pressure," continued Mr. Gabaldon, "instead, we opted to extend our services not only to guests who know us well and expect content of value but also to the travelling public at large. This tailor-made approach is a wonderful way to showcase who we are as a brand and as destination and travel experts."[6]

Perhaps so, but will Ritz-Carlton witness these benefits in its seventy-five hotels in RevPAR and occupancy?

Market Potential

Estimates of **market potential** often seem to be ignored by those who write hospitality marketing plans. Marketing managers in hotels sometimes feel that the concept has no application to them. "We view all travelers as potential guests" is a frequently heard comment. Others reply that the concept is theoretical for the hospitality industry and applies primarily to consumer-packaged goods.

These opinions are incorrect! Although it is true that measurement of true market potential is impossible, estimates can and should be made. The hospitality industry is notorious for ignoring or misinterpreting market potential estimates, thus leading to overbuilding, overcapacity, price cutting, and frantic advertising and promotion in an attempt to fill rooms or fill seats.

Market potential should be viewed as the total available demand for a hospitality product within a particular geographic market at a given price. It is important not to mix different hospitality products into an estimate of market potential.

It is common to hear individuals speak of the market for hotel rooms in a region as a number of room nights. For purposes of writing a marketing plan, such figures are interesting but do not indicate market potential for your products. Most markets consist of a mix of hotel properties, ranging from luxury to budget, with specialty lodging such as all-suites, condominium hotels, and B&Bs.

Each type of property faces its own peculiar market potential, except for times when a special event fills every bed in town. Estimates of market potential normally begin by examining the market for all hotels but should then shift to specific markets for your hotel and directly competitive properties, often referred to as a competitive set. To be precise, market potential estimates should be shown as demand estimates at various price points; however, this is generally unnecessary for most marketing plans. The average marketing manager for a property such as a hotel finds it impossible to make good quantitative estimates of market potential in room nights or dollars. These people lack marketing research support, and most were not trained in quantitative analysis. Therefore, market potential estimates are often expressed in "guesstimates," such as "The market seems to be growing or declining by about 5 percent a year."

Warning! Even though precise estimates may be beyond the abilities of many hospitality marketing managers, it is essential to go through the thought process of examining market potential. Never assume that market potential is static or unimportant to marketing success.

By engaging in the process of trying to guesstimate or estimate market potential, those who develop marketing plans become aware of potentially important market conditions and can then adjust marketing strategies appropriately. Remember, the process of developing a marketing plan is not a precise discipline such as engineering or chemistry. The exercise of writing a plan is usually as important to marketing success as the plan itself.

Estimated marketing potential has led U.S. ski resort developers to Asia. The world's highest and snowiest mountains remain virtually untapped for snow reports. Developers estimate that 3 percent of the Chinese population might be potential skiers. This means 43.3 million people. Within India the great-grandson of Henry Ford and other Americans are planning the Himalayan Ski Village in the Indian state of Himachal Pradesh.

John Sims, managing director of the project, estimated a market potential of 100 million people with sufficient disposable income. Professor Simon Hudson of the University of Calgary said there are 70 million skiers and snowboarders worldwide and that if 3 percent of India's population took up skiing that would be a 36.6 million person market.[7]

Although these estimates of market potential are not very sophisticated, they represent the kind of potential that excite entrepreneurs and investors.

Marketing Research

The need for marketing intelligence is ongoing. Much of the information acquired by marketing research in a current calendar or fiscal year serves as the basis for developing next year's marketing plan. Marketing research needs vary considerably by type and size of the hospitality company. Companies such as Hertz or Hilton Hotels have corporate marketing research departments. An individual hotel property or car rental location may have a need for additional marketing information. In these cases, the individual property or location is generally responsible for acquiring these data.

Marketing research needs can usually be divided into macromarket and micromarket information. Macromarket information includes, but is not restricted to, the following:

- Industry trends

- Socioeconomic and political trends

Marketing Highlight

The Indigo Pearl Resort: Facebook Strategy and Planning the Indigo Pearl

18–1 The Indigo Pearl Resort is an independent, luxury design property located in Phuket, Thailand. Michael Nurbatlain joined the resort as a sales manager, but this role quickly expanded to include managing digital marketing, e-commerce, and social media.[8]

Indigo Pearl Resort had witnessed a clear shift in its market mix: growing from a heavy reliance on tour operators to direct bookings and online channels. Michael Nurbatlain and the team at Indigo Pearl led this growth by developing a presence in a variety of channels, with Facebook emerging as one of the biggest successes. In just one year, Michael grew the resort's Facebook fan page to more than 8,000 followers. "While Twitter is beginning to gain popularity here in Asia, Facebook has nearly complete market adoption with our customers," said Michael.

It's all about planning. "Have a solid plan when it comes to Facebook, and create an editorial calendar. Be very strict about creating and following deadlines." Too many people just wake up in the morning and try to create content on the fly. "If there is no solid plan for 3–12 months, it's difficult to consistently deliver good quality results."

Facebook Contents: The Key to Growth

"Last year we wanted to give something to our Facebook fans," said Michael. "At the time, we had about 3,000 fans, and decided to create a photo contest around what symbolizes Indigo Pearl."

Fans were asked to post pictures, and then vote on their favorites. But Facebook contacted them, saying the contest setup violated terms and conditions. This forced them to set up an independent voting scheme allowing their fans to vote, which worked even better in the end. The contest generated great interaction among existing fans, strengthening their online community. Additionally, the contest generated a couple of hundred new fans—which was considered a great success at that time.

Latest Facebook Contest: Ultimate Holiday Package

This year's idea was to set up a new system. Rather than just asking fans to submit pictures, Indigo Pearl Resort wanted to add another layer of involvement. Michael and Indigo Pearl Resort asked fans to design their dream three-day holiday package. What would they like to do in Phuket? The resort was not very strict with the guidelines, so that if someone wrote some poetry about the perfect holiday, for example, it was still accepted as an entry.

"I imagined Mercedes running a promotion around designing your dream car," said Michael. "Although I'm a big fan of cars, I wouldn't know what horsepower to put in or the details of the engine. While our guests travel a lot, they are not hoteliers, so it would be somewhat difficult for them to come up with a breakdown package of all the amenities, so we left it very open."

"We didn't buy any Facebook ads or spend much time promoting the content." Michael worked a bit with the local media to get mentioned on their Web sites and sent out some tweets to promote it. But no other public relations or press releases were used. Everything was done through Facebook.

"Within days we had 10–15 entries and then we started to get a snowball effect. We asked fans to send in their pictures, screened them and placed the photos in the album called Ultimate Family Package. Once the photo was approved, the contest participants could ask their friends and family to vote on the entry."

"This is what created a VIRAL MARKETING effect for the resort. One photo had over 1,000 likes. It surpassed our expectations and we could hardly believe it."

Lessons Learned

1. Always respond and interact with your online community. Don't get arrogant and forget to thank fans. You should thank every single person who contributes to your Facebook or Twitter account—whether you have 5 friends or 5,000 followers. Each fan is an immense asset to you.

2. Have more than one prize. Last year the prize was a seven-day stay in a quite resort. But if one person in the contest has 1,000 votes for his or her entry, other people could be discouraged from participating. This year, having two good prizes encouraged more people to enter the contest.

3. Photos are the lifeblood of Facebook. As Guy Kawasaki says, Facebook is a pictures economy. "Often I just put a picture of our sunset or property, and it gets me a few hundred Likes and 30–50 comments. A few times I've spent hours creating a huge post, and it doesn't get nearly the same levels of feedback as that beach picture gets. Sometimes the easy route gets the best."

4. Avoid constantly bombarding fans with Facebook promotions. For every twenty posts, put only one promotional post if you must include sales messages.

5. Act as an online concierge on Facebook and Twitter, helping people by providing answers and suggestions.

6. Try to reflect the hotel's personality without being too flamboyant.

- Competitive information

- Industry-wide customer data

  Micromarket information includes, but is not restricted to, the following:

- Guest information

- Product/service information

- New-product analysis and testing

- Intermediary buyer data

- Pricing studies

- Key account information

- Advertising/promotion effectiveness

A time-proven method of collecting marketing information is to personally visit the company's properties, distributors who serve the company, employees, customers, franchisees, and others knowledgeable about the company.

After assuming the position of CEO of CiCi Pizza in 2009, Mr. Mike Shumsky visited many of the company's 650 restaurants, of which only sixteen were company owned. Following this trip he said, "I came, I listened, I got your ideas. I came back and told you what we were going to do about them. Now I'm coming back and saying here's what you need to do to make me happy. You have to be one brand."[9]

One of the promising areas of marketing research has been called yield marketing by executives from two advertising agencies serving the hospitality industry. These advertising executives envision a linking of customer responses with a hotel's advertising and promotional efforts. This will be accomplished by linking sales, marketing, and reservations systems with property management systems through the use of small but powerful computers. This would enable a hotel to make accurate, quick measurements of the effectiveness and efficiency of past marketing investments and permit them to make better estimates of the value of future investments.[10]

Harrah's Entertainment, Inc. (Harrah's), has proven to the worldwide hospitality industry that CRM combined with technology and management support can provide impressive financial results while extending a close relationship with one's customers (See Chapter 5). Under the leadership of Gary Loveman, a former Harvard professor, this casino company developed Harrah's Winner Information Network.

"To generate the necessary data, Harrah's had to make a substantial investment in information technology. It had to capture data from customer touch points, integrate it around the customer, and store it for later analysis. In order to understand customers' preferences, Harrah's had to mine the data, run experiments using different marketing interventions (i.e. special offerings), and learn what best met customers' needs at the various casinos."[11]

Harrah's left little to chance. It invested more than $100 million in computers and software to develop what is widely regarded as the industry's most sophisticated "frequent bettor" program. With the Total Rewards program, which contains the world's largest database of casino customers, it has been able to create sustainable loyalty, a dominant competitive advantage, and insulate the business from local market volatility.

Harrah's innovative idea was to grow by getting more business from its existing customer base. This approach was in contrast to the prevalent strategy of building ever more elaborate and splashy new casinos. Gary W. Loveman refers to its success as "the triumph of software over hardware in gaming."

The Total Rewards program increased traffic in Harrah's casinos, and marketing programs driven by data from the warehouse increased retention. Keeping customers goes right to the bottom line. An increase in retention of just 1 percent is worth $2 million in net profit annually.[12]

The success of Harrah's has clearly demonstrated that new strategies and tactics are essential for all members of the hospitality industry. Technology, CRM,

e **18.2** Indigo Pearl Phuket, http://www.indigo-pearl.com/: After viewing the Web site you will see why the Indigo Pearl is able to attract the upscale independent traveler.

and social marketing pose dramatic opportunities to marketers. Traditional support areas such as marketing research and advertising must support management with existing new concepts and quantitative answers or perish. It is no longer sufficient to be content with customer surveys, in-room questionnaires, and advertising research measuring such nebulous intangibles as "share of mind."

■■■ Section IV: Segmentation and Targeting

Segmentation Analysis

The heart of any marketing plan is careful analysis of available market segments and the selection of appropriate target markets. Not all market segments are appropriate for a hospitality company. The selection of segments is the result of (1) understanding what the company is and what it wishes to be and (2) studying available segments and determining if they fit the capabilities and desires of the company to obtain and secure them.

A common mistake within the hospitality industry is the selection of inappropriate segments. Marketing managers commonly err by allowing or encouraging the acquisition of low-yield segments in an effort to maintain occupancy. At the opposite extreme, companies sometimes feel they are serving "low-class" customers and attempt to attract quite different segments. If this is done in the absence of genuine product/service changes, the chances for success are slim to nonexistent.

In the case of a hotel, "A marketing plan tells you who is using your hotel and where you can look to expand your business."[13] The Los Angeles Biltmore Hotel had been the center of Los Angeles society for many years, but the property began to deteriorate and was sold. The new owners faced the task of restoring life to the hotel. One of the first discoveries by the new owners was that the Biltmore's marketing plan was confused. Some people believed that the hotel catered only to groups and tours, whereas others felt the hotel did not want their business and marketed only to commercial and transient guests. The guest mix was found to be 28 percent commercial, 40 percent groups, and 32 percent leisure. The new management decided that a more appropriate mix was 40 percent commercial, 50 percent groups, and 10 percent leisure. With this directive in mind, the hotel was able to establish a new marketing plan that included repositioning the hotel, changing food and beverage operations, and changing prices.[14]

Analysis of Internal Data	Analysis of External Data
Guest registrations	Published industry information
Credit card receipts	Marketing research
Customer surveys	Guesstimates after talking with competitors, vendors, and others in the industry
Customer database	

When developing a marketing plan, marketers must look to both internal and external data sources for information concerning market segments.

Market-Segment-Profitability Analysis (MSPA)

Information that identifies each of a company's existing customer segments by revenue, cost, and profitability is extremely valuable but information about guests by segment is often not gathered or not analyzed. "Hotel marketers usually focus on customer segments. On the other hand, accountants record and report the operational results by department, not market segments."[15]

Market segment profitability data are even less likely to be available for most restaurants and are virtually nonexistent for tourism marketers such as those with most convention and visitor bureaus.

Targeting

No area of the marketing plan surpasses the selection of target markets in importance. If inappropriate markets are selected, marketing resources will be wasted. A high level of expenditures for advertising or sales promotion cannot compensate for misdirected marketing efforts.

Like the previous example of the Los Angeles Biltmore Hotel, targeting begins by defining the mix of desired guests. Commonly used broad groupings for guests are listed in the following table:

Business	*Versus*	*Pleasure*
Individual guests		IT (individuals who make their own reservations)
Conventions		
Seminars/ conferences		GIT (group-inclusive tours)

The selection of a customer/guest mix must support the positioning strategy of the company. The mix should also support revenue management. This is not always the case. It is altogether too common for marketing/sales to plan and operate without consulting or working with the revenue or yield-management department.

Target markets are selected from the list of available segments. These include segments currently served by the company and newly recognized markets. The selection of target markets is a primary responsibility of marketing management. This requires careful consideration of the variables already discussed in the development of the marketing plan. Far too many marketing managers in the hospitality industry simply select last year's target markets. Although it is normally true that the majority of target markets remain the same, new ones appear and the order of importance can change between years.

Many Asian and Australian hotel managers discovered that their key segments in terms of spending and room nights were no longer American or European guests. Guests from Asian nations surpassed in importance those from Western nations.

Women travelers represent a solid and growing percentage of travelers. Observation of hotel advertisements shows that hotel marketers realize the importance of this segment.

A study of gender-based lodging preferences showed that "there were several significant differences between male and female business travelers in their hotel selection and use criteria."[16] For instance, women considered security, room service, and low price to be more important, whereas men were more concerned about the availability of suite rooms with separate bed and office spaces.

Marketing planners need to stay abreast of such preferences, relay them to other departments within the hotel, and use this information in the selection of market segments.

An interesting market is couples expecting their first baby. These are people who delayed having children until their mid-thirties and want a "last hurrah" together before the infant arrives. The Bodega Bay Lodge and Spa in California offers a one-night babymoon package. Guest preferences change from champagne and a heated spa to bottled water and a gentle massage.[17]

■■■ Section V: Next Year's Objectives and Quotas

Objectives

The establishment of objectives provides direction for the rest of the marketing plan. The purpose of marketing strategies and tactics is to support objectives. The marketing budget must be sufficient to ensure adequate resources to achieve objectives and to meet **timetables** that describe the time period in which expected sales results will occur.

Occasionally, there is confusion as to what constitutes an objective. Statements such as "To be the best in our industry" or "To provide excellent guest service" are accepted as objectives. That is always an error because these types of statements are slogans or mottos. They are not objectives. The following are examples of objectives:

- Quantitative (expressed in monetary terms [dollars, pesos] or unit measurements such as room nights, passenger miles, number of cars to rent, or occupancy)

- Time specific (one year, six months)

- Profit/margin specific (e.g., an average margin of 22 percent)

The process of establishing objectives is not an easy task and should not be accomplished by simply adding a random percentage to last year's objectives.

Objectives should be established after carefully considering the areas already discussed:

- Corporate goals

- Corporate resources

- Environmental factors

- Competition

- Market trends

- Market potential

- Available market segments and possible target markets

To ensure profitability and remain competitive in today's marketplace, it has become necessary to establish several sub-objectives. For instance, a hotel with 1,000 rooms undoubtedly will have two broad objectives: average occupancy and average room rate. By themselves, these objectives do not serve as sufficient guides for developing marketing strategies. A set of sub-objectives is needed, as shown in Table 18–1.

Other sub-objectives may also be established by the marketing department. Again, these should support corporate goals and next year's primary objectives. They should never stand alone as objectives, unrelated to the primary function of the marketing department.

Each marketing support area needs to be guided by a set of sub-objectives. This includes areas such as advertising, promotion, public relations, marketing research, and, of course, sales.

Establishing measurable quantitative objectives for these areas is not an easy task, but increasingly, top management is requiring that such be done. Advertising and promotion are areas in which measurement of results is particularly difficult. Management would like to know what the dollar return was for advertising or how much market share or occupancy increased as a result of advertising/promotion. With few exceptions, such as direct advertising, current measurement techniques do not permit accurate measurements of this type. Consequently, objectives for advertising, such as share of mind and awareness level, are commonly used. These are not suitable substitutes.

Rating System Objectives

Some hotels are obsessed with ratings such as those by AAA, Mobile, or Michelin. The management of these hotels may drive corporate behavior, including marketing/sales, to help the hotel achieve another star or diamond or other symbol rating.

Because Internet distribution, companies, and user customers rely on ratings, it is quite possible that many additional hotels will set objectives to attain higher ratings.

TABLE 18-1

Examples of Objectives Common to the Hotel Industry

Objectives	Average Occupancy	Average Room Rate
Sub-objectives	Occupancy per period of time	Average rate per period of time and by type of room
	Seasonal: prime, shoulder, trough	
	Monthly	
	Weekly	
	Daily	
	Weekend	
	Midweek	
	Types of Sleeping Rooms	**By Time**
	Suites	Seasonal
	Poolside	Monthly
	Regular room	Weekly
		Daily
		Weekend
	Occupancy by type of sleeping room	*Note:* Yield objectives are used by many members of the hospitality industry, such as hotels, rental cars, cruise lines, airlines, and passenger rail.
	Suites	
	Pool side	
	Cabaña	
	Cottage	
	Regular sleeping rooms	
	Occupancy per type of function room	
	Ballroom	
	Seminar room	
	Executive conference room	

Objectives	Annual Sales by	Annual Sales by: Units Dollars
	Time period	
	Seasonal	
	Monthly	
	Weekly	
	Daily	
	Weekend	
	Department	
	Group sales	
	Incentive sales	
	Sales territory	
	Eastern United States	
	Western United States	
	Salesperson	
	Joe	
	Sally	
	June	
	Fred	

Quotas

No word creates more fear within the sales/marketing department than **quotas**. Yet, without quotas, the probability of accomplishing objectives is slim at best. To be effective, quotas must be

- based on next year's objectives;

- individualized;

- realistic and obtainable;

- broken down to small units, such as each salesperson's quota per week;

- understandable and measurable (e.g., quota = $10,000 sales for product line x in week 5). An example of a quota that is not understandable or measurable is "to obtain 10 percent increase of market share early in the year."

Communicating the Plan

A sophisticated and brilliantly developed plan is of no use if it is not understood, believed, or used. "A marketing plan should not be just a call to action or a bench-mark by which to judge the efficiency and effectiveness of decisions. The plan should also serve as a method for communicating marketing strategy to those people whose duty it is to implement or authorize the company's marketing strategies."[18] Several groups may serve as an audience for a marketing plan.

Top Management

This group must be convinced that the plan will accomplish the stated goals and objectives. Top management demonstrates acceptance or denial by its level of monetary support.

Marketing managers should strive for more than budgeting support. If top management buys in and demonstrates visible support, morale within the marketing department will increase, and other departments will be willing to lend support. To the contrary, the company grapevine quickly knows if marketing is only weakly supported by top management. Support from others will be weak at best if there is a perception that management is not solidly behind marketing.

Board of Directors or Group of Investors

Occasionally, a board of directors or an investor's group may ask to be apprised of next year's marketing plan. This group generally does not seek details but instead wants to know the answers to these questions:

- Does the plan support corporate goals?

- What are the dollars and unit objectives?

- What are the major strategies to achieve these objectives?

- What is the cost?

- When can we expect to see results?

- Does the plan support revenue management objectives?

Subordinates

Members of the marketing and sales departments must understand and support the marketing plan. It is important to develop a group mentality that the marketing plan for next year is a realistic and important road map. Unfortunately, far too many people in hospitality companies believe that the development of a marketing plan is a waste of time because no one will ever pay it any heed.

The InterContinental Playa Bonita Resort and Spa is part of Bern Hotels and Resorts. Bern operates hotels throughout Panama (see case 34). It is important that each hotel has a marketing plan that fits with the corporate plan. Courtesy of Bern Hotels and Resorts.

Vendors

It is important to transmit some aspects of the marketing plan to selected vendors. This is particularly true as strategic alliances develop. Vendors such as advertising agencies, marketing research firms, computer software providers, public relations firms, and consultants need to know and understand the marketing plan. It may be advisable to include these people in the plan's development. Supply chain management is not generally a responsibility assigned to marketing, but there are strategic alliances between hospitality companies and suppliers that affect the pricing customer service and other marketing functions. It is in the best interests of marketing to cooperate closely with those responsible for supply chain management. Advances in this management tool could and probably will affect what marketing will do. Such changes may need to be recognized in the marketing plan.

Supply chain management has been successfully used by manufacturers and by large retail chains for many years. The result has been cost savings and increased efficiencies of operators. Now, the restaurant industry is employing supply chain management.

Starbucks decided to use this tool to team with other hospitality companies and purchase basic items such as sugar and milk. Darden Restaurants, owner of Red Lobster and Olive Garden restaurants, is using supply chain management to purchase only the quantities it needs at specific times.

The need for this management tool is the result of worldwide price increases in agricultural commodities. Commodity price increases are the result of increased worldwide demand for food. Unless worldwide production increases sufficiently to meet this demand, restaurants will need to continuously seek new approaches to acquiring foodstuffs in a cost-effective and efficient manner.

Some restaurants (individual and chain) have decided to buy directly from producers. However, farmers are often not prepared to harvest, package, and prepare their crops for direct use by restaurants. The future marketplace for agriculture products could look quite different from the existing market in which producers view their crops as commodities not table-ready products.[19]

Other Departments

Other departments, such as yield or revenue management, housekeeping, front desk, customer service, and maintenance, will be affected by next year's plan. They have a right to know key elements of the plan.

It is common for marketing managers to be asked to outline the marketing plan briefly and answer questions in a monthly manager's meeting. If a forum such as this does not exist, marketing managers should initiate a review of next year's marketing plan with other department heads after obtaining clearance from the general manager or president.

■■■ Section VI: Action Plans: Strategies and Tactics

Marketing strategies are designed as the vehicle to achieve marketing objectives. In turn, marketing tactics are tools that support strategies. Far too often, strategies and tactics have little relationship to objectives. This is always an error and is commonly the result of the following:

- Desire to maintain status quo. Strategies and tactics do not change because they are perceived to be working even though solid proof of their effectiveness seldom exists.

- Lazy, incompetent, or unsure management. These people do not wish to risk their positions through new strategies and tactics.

- Failure to engage in marketing planning or to view the processes as serious and meaningful to decision making.

- Undue heavy influence of outside vendors, such as advertising agencies, which do not wish to change direction or try new media.

- Failure to understand the relationship between objectives, strategies, and tactics.

- Myopic thinking that things are going well and one does not fix something that is not broken. Unfortunately, in the fast-paced, competitive hospitality industry, by the time the product is demonstrably broken, it is beyond repair.

Marketing strategies and tactics employ advertising and promotion, sales and distribution, pricing and product. Each must be custom designed to meet the specific needs of a company. It is unwise to follow ratios or industry averages concerning expenditures for advertising, new-product development, or other strategy areas.

Strategies and tactics must always be custom made to fit the needs and culture of a company and to allow it to meet or exceed objectives. A study of marketing strategies and tactics employed by restaurants was conducted. It was found that many restaurants employ weak strategies, including following the leader, rather than developing individualized, unique strategies and tactics. The authors concluded, "Firms that seem to exhibit no strategy cannot expect to enjoy long-run successful performance. They may enjoy excellent returns for a number of years, but at some point their lack of strategy will cause the business to fail. When they begin to experience the consequences of this lack of strategic direction, it may well be too late to mount an effective alternative, especially if they operate a larger number of units."[20]

Nonqualified Audience: Cluster Marketing

In recent years, some hotel companies have formed cluster marketing groups. These consist of different properties managed by the same management company within a common market area; however, each may represent a separate flag and have different ownership.

In extreme cases, a cluster marketing manager is appointed and each of the different properties is expected to submit otherwise confidential data such as leads and pending contracts to a common pool. This is highly questionable marketing behavior and may place the hotels' marketing/sales departments in a position of violating fiduciary and professional responsibilities to their hotels.

Marketing and sales plans are not to be shared with competitors. Before honoring a request by a cluster marketing group to share any confidential data, the management company must receive a written, dated, and signed statement from the general manager granting permission to do so.

Sales Strategies

The sales force must develop and use sales strategies to support objectives. Examples of sales strategies follow:

1. Prevent erosion of key accounts.

2. Grow key accounts.

3. Grow selected marginal accounts.

4. Eliminate selected marginal accounts.

5. Retain selected marginal accounts but provide lower-cost sales support.

6. Obtain new business from selected prospects.

A description of sales strategies should start with these six general strategies and indicate how the sales department is going to implement each one. The general strategy is supported by specific sales tactics, such as the following:

Outside the Company (Examples)

- Sales blitz of all or targeted accounts and projects

- Telephone, direct mail, and personal sales calls to selected decision makers and decision influencers

- Trade booths at selected travel shows

- Sales calls and working with travel intermediaries: tour wholesalers, travel agencies, incentive bonuses, and international sales reps

- Luncheon for key customers, prospects, or decision influencers

- Travel missions and other tactics

Inside the Company (Examples)

- Training of sales staff

- Involvement and support of nonsales personnel

- Motivational and control programs

- Involvement and support of management

Distribution Strategies

The selection of appropriate channels of distribution is basic to the development of successful sales strategies. Hospitality companies must be ever alert to changing distribution channels and the need for change.

Internet reservation systems and the reduced number of travel agents are two important changes in the distribution system. It is critical for a marketing plan to identify each of the major distribution channels that is expected to produce sales and to forecast by week, month, and quarter the expected volume of sales each will provide.

Distribution systems do not provide equal sales volumes and, just as important, they do not provide equal profit margins.

Hospitality managers will increasingly be tempted to accept ever greater sales volumes from independent company Internet sales, such as Expedia, Travelocity, Priceline.com, and Hotels.com. This will almost assuredly erode profit margins.

In the absence of establishing sales and profit goals and sales limits for some distribution channels, hospitality managers may one day awaken to see a particular channel or company dominating their sales volume. Undoubtedly, other channels exist and should be added to a marketing plan if they are important to a company. (See Chapter 13 for a discussion on distribution channels.)

Advertising and Promotion Strategies

Advertising and promotion strategies should be established by people within the company responsible for these strategies, such as the director of advertising, the sales manager, or the marketing manager. It is critical for this person to work with supporting groups, such as an advertising agency, sales promotion firm, specialty advertising agencies, and consultants directly involved in the establishment and performance of advertising and promotion strategies.

It is inadvisable to give outside firms the sole authority for deriving and implementing these strategies. History has shown that when this occurs, the supporting group, such as an advertising agency, may produce brilliant copy and illustrations placed in well-respected media, only to find that the company fails totally to meet objectives. The reason is that outside groups may not view objectives the same way as the client. Many advertising agencies have won distinguished honors for ads that did little or nothing to increase sales or market share for the client. Outside professionals correctly view their client as the company or the company's management, not the end consumer. Unfortunately, this view leads to pleasing the managers who hired them rather than achieving corporate or marketing objectives. Theoretically, corporate and marketing objectives and those of the manager should be synchronized. In fact, often a wide gap exists between the two. In some cases, outside professionals disdain client corporate or marketing objectives and view these as a detriment or obstacle to the creative process. The ideal is for corporate managers responsible for advertising/promotion to work as a team with selected outside professionals to derive strategies and tactics that satisfy objectives in a timely and cost-effective manner.

When this is accomplished, the team will develop an advertising/promotion mix of vehicles that includes tactics selected to achieve objectives, not simply to provide commissions, make life easy for the professionals, or produce a bland program that probably won't be criticized by management but may accomplish little.

Those who create advertising/promotion strategies have the following responsibilities:

- Select a blend or mix of media that may include commissionable mass media, direct mail, trade shows, billboards, specialty advertising, social media (Facebook and others).

- Select or approve the message. This includes graphics, color, size, copy, and other format decisions.

- Design a media schedule showing when each medium, including noncommissionable media, will be used.

- Design a schedule of events, such as public relations events and familiarization (FAM) trips for travel writers.

- Carefully transmit this information to management.

- Supervise the development and implementation of advertising/promotion programs, with particular care given to timetables and budget constraints.

- Assume responsibility for the outcome. Increasingly, top management is requiring those in charge of advertising/promotion to prove effectiveness and to stand behind results.

Unfortunately, despite decades of marketing teaching and thousands of articles on the subject, many managers in the hospitality industry continue to equate marketing with advertising. They fail to realize that advertising is simply one part of marketing. The authors of the restaurant strategy referred to earlier concluded: "Many firms [restaurants] have attempted to hold market share by increasing advertising expenditures. Advertising alone will not ensure success."[21]

Another area of the advertising/promotion mix that needs consideration in a marketing plan is cooperative advertising/promotion. This requires teamwork and a place in the budget. For example, in the case of a resort, cooperative opportunities exist between the following entities:

- Resort and resort community (e.g., all resorts, restaurants, and attractions in Provincetown, Cape Cod, Massachusetts)

- Resort and tourism promotion groups (e.g., state tourism department or local Chamber of Commerce)

- Resort and suppliers (e.g., Citrus Board or Columbia Coffee)

- Resort and transportation companies (e.g., airlines, motor coach, cruise lines)

- Resort and sister hotels or resorts

An example of cooperative advertising/promotion opportunities is offered by hotels in Mexico. After an examination of the brochures of ten hotel chains in Mexico, it was found that most made minimal or no reference to other Mexican hotels operated by the chain. Club Med made good use of this marketing tool. Club Med not only had a Mexican brochure for all its properties but also had a special supplemental brochure for its properties near prestigious archaeological sites.[22]

Destination marketing organizations provide information for tourists and offer a way for hotels, tour guides, and restaurants to promote their service. This information booth is in Miraflores district of Lima, Peru. Courtesy of Ildipapp/Dreamstime.

Pricing Strategies

Pricing remains a function of marketing. Marketing managers must maintain control of this area; they must interface with internal pricing departments. Marketing and sales departments will continuously be in conflict with pricing if pricing strategies are not understood and considered in marketing and sales plans. Today pricing is more critical than ever before due largely to the role of online travel agencies (OTAs).

For instance, sales has responsibility for working with intermediaries such as tour wholesalers and with key customers. Both these customers will ask for price discounts. Commitments for large blocks of rooms, airline seats, autos, or ship berths will inevitably create problems with revenue or yield-management departments. Marketing and sales plans cannot be effective if they are developed without sales forecasts and revenue projections by major market segments. If forecasts and revenue projections are made without the input of the revenue or yield-management departments, conflict will occur.

Review again the objectives and sub-objectives presented in Table 18–1. These call for average room rate objectives for each product class by season of the year. Using the concepts and practices of yield management, pricing objectives may be considerably enhanced to include weekly objectives and objectives by subsegments. Marriott Hotels uses a strategy known as rational pricing. This calls for *fencing*, placing restrictions on customer segments selected due to their perceived level of price elasticity. Fencing restrictions will immediately affect marketing and sales plans. Marketing managers are also advised to work with the reservations department during the planning process. Reservations often have considerable latitude to adjust prices and may account for a significant percentage of sales.

Pricing objectives and strategies affect every facet of marketing and sales. Sales promotions and advertising must support pricing decisions. The selection of appropriate target markets and the emphasis to be given each again depend on pricing.

Marketing and sales managers who view themselves at war with pricing managers are probably doomed to eventual failure. The top managers in most hospitality companies realize that a 10 percent upward adjustment in rates can produce favorable profit results in excess of cost cutting or traditional marketing and sales strategies to increase the number of guests. Today, however, the emphasis is on price butting due heavily to the strength of OTAs.

Pricing strategies are of great importance to chain restaurants and need to be reviewed constantly. As an example, food-service quality is the predominant influence on guest ratings for family, steakhouse, and casual dining restaurants. Family price appeal enhances a guest's rating for a family restaurant chain but not necessarily for a steakhouse or casual dining.[23]

A marketer who has gained experience in a family restaurant chain might make erroneous pricing decisions when hired by a steakhouse or casual dining chain. Despite the fact that restaurant chains may seem alike, different pricing strategies may need to be developed for each.

Product Strategies

Marketing has an important role to play in the improvement of existing products and the development of new ones. In some hospitality firms, marketing is expected to be heavily involved in the process; in others, marketing assumes only an advisory role; and sadly, in others, marketing is excluded from the process.

Marketing professionals can exert considerable input and strategic direction when planning basic product changes as dramatic as those occurring within the resort industry. Marketing can also help greatly to enhance revenue from product changes as additions to the current product line. Hundreds or thousands of new product opportunities exist in most hospitality companies. The Alexis Park Resort in Las Vegas invented "Cocktail Cruises," which is essentially a motorized cart driven by an employee who offers poolside guests drinks so they can stay by the pool.[24] The Opryland Hotel in Nashville uses a similar concept to sell hotel logo souvenir merchandise. "Whenever there is more to be sold than your customers are buying, profit potential is not being realized. Revenue boosting opportunities abound for the creative operator who is willing to offer facilities, services, and events that will attract customers and to train customer-contact employees to stimulate add-on sales and sales upgrades."[25]

The process of making product line changes requires the input and advice of many individuals and departments. Marketing may identify a need, such as the "neighborhood bakery" concept, for use in fast-food chains, but this product concept directly affects production, finance, and human resources. When McDonald's, Burger King, and Wendy's experimented with fresh biscuits or croissants, they discovered that these products prepared from scratch or frozen dough required additional working space, equipment, and employee training.[26]

Unfortunately, most hotel marketing plans do not list or break down product categories in a marketing plan other than by type of room, catering/banquets, food and beverage, and perhaps a catch-all "other" products category. One reason for this is that many management contracts between owners and management companies place little, if any, emphasis on products other than rooms and food and beverage. Therefore, management pays little attention to lesser product categories. The result is that many marketing plans do not consider cross-selling and upselling opportunities using existing products, to say nothing of new product opportunities.

■■■ Section VII: Resources Needed to Support Strategies and Meet Objectives

Marketing plans must be written with available resources, or those likely to become available, in mind. A common error in writing a marketing plan is to develop strategies that are probably highly workable but for which there is insufficient support.

Another error is to assume that top management will not provide additional support regardless of the brilliance of the plan. Marketing plans can and must be sold to top management. A balance between mythical over-the-top plans and total acquiescence to perceived inflexibility of management is needed in any solid marketing plan.

Personnel

Generally, the most costly and difficult resource needed to ensure success with marketing/sales strategies is personnel. Management commonly views the addition of personnel as unnecessary, impractical, or unwise, given current budgetary restrictions.

Obviously, sometimes the addition of salespeople, secretaries, analysts, and others is absolutely essential. Be prepared to justify this request, and remember that many people, particularly salespeople, are not instantly productive. Training and recruiting costs must be considered with this resource request, as well as the time required by members of management to interview and work with these people.

The influence of the corporate culture cannot be overlooked in this process. Imagine a company such as the Ritz-Carlton with the philosophy "We are ladies and gentlemen serving ladies and gentlemen." Fulfillment of this pledge with appropriate new personnel is demanding and may be time consuming.[27]

A marketing plan may need to specify the type of person required for a position if it is not described elsewhere, such as in company policies and procedures. Some hospitality companies operate under the philosophy that "we are always hiring excellent people." Marketing managers must plan personnel needs ahead for seasonal cost differences, such as a month with heavy trade show expenses or several weeks when brochures will be mailed to key customers and prospects. Budgets should reflect careful planning of resource use, such as temporary help on a week-by-week basis. A carefully constructed budget is simply a reflection of a well-thought-out marketing plan.

Other Monetary Support

Monetary support not accounted for by salary, wages, and benefits must be considered carefully and included. This includes travel expenses; motivational costs, such as a trip to Las Vegas; and other monetary needs.

Research, Consulting, and Training

Hospitality companies often have need for outside professionals to assist with marketing research, such as focus groups; training, such as sales training; or consulting to provide objective outside appraisals and advice.

Miscellaneous Costs

This area should not be a source of slush funds. Many expenses, such as subscriptions to professional books and journals, may be included here.

Budgets

In larger organizations, corporate policies and procedures may direct marketing managers as to categories of expenses and items that may be included. Marketing managers of smaller companies may need to develop their own list and to use it each year as a guide to ensure that all essential resources are included.

Budgets should be established to reflect projected costs weekly, monthly, quarterly, and annually. This is not simply to make life easier for the finance/account area personnel next year.

■■■ Section VIII: Marketing Control

This discussion of marketing control presupposes that the sales plan is part of the marketing plan. This is not always the case; some hospitality organizations separate the two functions.

The essentials for writing a sales plan follow the same general procedure as those described for a marketing plan. A sales plan does not need all the aspects of a marketing plan, such as advertising or marketing research, because these may be furnished by support departments. A sales plan should pay particular attention to the sales force and its objectives and to strategies to ensure that sales quotas are met and possibly exceeded.

Sales Objectives

Sales objectives must be established for each sales area, division, region, salesperson, and time period. The broad sales objectives discussed previously serve as the basis for establishing individual objectives. The sum of all sales objectives or quotas for members of the sales force must equal or exceed annual objectives.

One method of establishing annual sales objectives for the company is to begin with sales planning among members of the sales force. Each member should be expected to develop a list of all sales accounts currently served by that person, plus prospects for the coming year. From this, an estimate of potential sales by account and prospect will provide a means of forecasting next year's sales.

Management, beginning with the sales manager and ending with the general manager or other member of top management, then has the responsibility for critically examining these forecasts. Management seldom accepts the forecasts of the sales force without amending them, usually upward. This is known as bottom-up, top-down planning.

Management amends sales force forecasts for these reasons:

1. Sales force members often wish to protect themselves and give lower sales estimates than are actually possible.

2. The company has certain sales objectives that it expects based on the needs of the company.

3. Management may have access to marketing research information not available to the sales force.

4. Management may have a history of dealing with the sales force and realize that forecasts are generally too high or too low by x percent.

5. Management may be willing to provide the marketing/sales department with additional resources that are unknown to members of the sales force.

Table 18–2 shows a typical hotel sales forecast for a salesperson. Sales managers have the responsibility to work closely with their salespeople to ensure that sales forecasts are accurate. They must then provide a composite sales forecast for their department and present it to management.

Sales Forecast and Quotas

Eventually, all members of the sales force must be presented with sales quotas. Annual sales quotas should then be broken down into monthly and quarterly sales. Many sales managers and experienced salespeople break monthly quotas into weekly figures.

Sales managers have the responsibility for working with their salespeople to ensure that quotas are met or surpassed. It is important to evaluate sales results continually and develop corrective tactics if it appears that actual sales will not meet forecasts or quotas. Sales managers and salespeople who wait several months before evaluating actual sales against forecasts usually find it is too late to take corrective action.

TABLE 18-2
Example of a Sales Forecast for a Hotel Salesperson

Salesperson: Janet Chin	SALES CURRENT YEAR			SALES PROJECTED NEXT YEAR		
	Room Nights	Revenue	Avg. Rate	Room Nights	Revenue	Avg. Rate
Major commercial accounts (key accounts)						
1.						
2.						
3.						
4.						
Other commercial accounts						
1.						
2.						
3.						
4.						
Major intermediary accounts						
1.						
2.						
3.						
4.						
Other intermediary accounts						
1.						
2.						
3.						
4.						
Airline accounts						
1.						
2.						
3.						
4.						
Other accounts						
1.						
2.						
3.						
4.						
Prospects for next year						
1.						
2.						
3.						
4.						
Total accounts/prospects	Total current year			Totals projected next year		

Expenditures Against Budget

It is also important for marketing/sales managers to monitor actual expenditures continually against budgeted figures. This, too, must be done on a regular basis. As described in the Red Robin case, this chain now establishes budgets each quarter.

Periodic Evaluation of All Marketing Objectives

The role of marketing and sales managers is sometimes compared to that of an adult babysitter. A frequent comment made by people in these positions is that they spend a great deal of time simply making sure that people under their direction perform tasks in a timely fashion. There is much truth in this comment because a critical role of marketing/sales managers is to ensure that all objectives are met or exceeded on time.

Managers responsible for functions such as advertising, promotions, and marketing research also have a responsibility to ensure that all tasks are performed on time. If a summer brochure is printed three weeks after the due date, chances are very good that the sales force may miss the opportunity to send or deliver this advertising medium to prospects and key accounts during the time that they make travel decisions. In turn, the sales force may fail to make summer sales quotas. All marketing/sales tasks are important. If this is not true, the task and the position should be eliminated.

Marketing Activity Timetable

One method commonly used by marketing/sales managers to ensure that tasks are completed on time is the use of a marketing activity timetable. This simple device lists major activities, the dates they must be completed, the person responsible, and a space for checking whether the task has been accomplished.

Readjustments to Marketing Plan

Human beings are incapable of devising a perfect marketing plan. Market conditions change, disasters occur, and many other reasons create a need to refine marketing plans. Generally, refinements should be made in the area of tactics, budgets, and timing of events rather than in major objectives or strategies. Changes in tactics normally do not require top management approval and are viewed as the normal responsibility of marketing/sales managers.

■■■ Section IX: Presenting and Selling the Plan

Changes in major objectives such as annual sales volume and in major strategies always require approval by top management. Marketing/sales managers are advised to refrain from considering changes in major objectives and strategies unless absolutely necessary. Top management will almost certainly view the necessity for change as a reflection of poor management by marketing/sales managers unless the cause was a disaster, such as a major fire in a hotel.

Never assume that a marketing plan is so logical that it will sell itself. A marketing plan must be sold to many people, including the following:

- *Members of marketing/sales department.* Many people within the marketing/ sales areas do not believe in planning. They view the process of developing, writing, defending, and using a written plan to be a waste of time. Comments are frequently heard such as, "If management would just let us do our job and quit all this planning, the company would do better." This common sentiment may exist due to poor experience with prior planning, fear of the process, or genuine ignorance about the benefits. Marketing/sales managers need the support of subordinates in the planning process. It is best to sell the benefits of the process rather than to force acquiescence.

- *Vendors/ad agencies and others.* Outside organizations, such as advertising and marketing research agencies, need to be involved in the planning process. They must be made aware that their participation in the marketing planning process is an expected part of their responsibilities as team members.

- *Top management.* Top management must approve the annual marketing plan. It is seldom sufficient to write a lengthy plan, send it through company mail or e-mail to top management, and expect an enthusiastic endorsement. Marketing/sales managers must sell the plan to members of management through meetings, such as friendly luncheons and formalized presentations. Key members of the staff may be expected to participate in formal presentations. These appearances should always be treated with the same careful planning and professionalism that would be expected if a sales presentation were made to a key prospect for $2 million worth of business. Use professional presentation materials when appropriate, such as PowerPoint presentations, overheads, and bound copies of the annual plan. Prepare selected charts, graphs, and tables that are easy to understand and quickly reinforce key points.

■■■ Section X: Preparing for the Future

The process of marketing planning is a continuum. The task is never ending. Marketing/sales managers must always be planning. In reality, the development of next year's marketing plan begins the day this year's plan is approved.

Data Collection and Analysis

Marketing plan development depends on the availability of reliable information. This task can always be improved. The process of data collection and analysis from internal and external sources continues each day. Marketing/sales managers must always be alert for methods to improve the process.

Marketing Planning as a Tool for Growth

A good marketing plan will assist your company and department to prosper and grow. What is not so obvious to many is that a good plan will also enable people to prosper and grow. This occurs in several ways:

- The participatory planning process allows people to understand the management process.

- People learn to become team players during the process.

- People learn to establish objectives and set timetables to ensure they are met.

- The process of establishing realistic strategies and tactics to meet objectives is learned.

- People who approach the planning process with a receptive mind and employ the marketing plan usually find it enhances their professional career.

Many hospitality companies have developed a planning culture in which there is a respect for planning as a positive process. This is a reflection of a corporate culture and top management support. Changes in top management sometimes mean that support for marketing planning will decrease or in some instances planning will be discouraged. A strong corporate culture that emphasizes and encourages planning within all levels of the company will be rewarded. Sometimes management becomes discouraged by the process, particularly when market conditions worsen as a new competitor threatens market share. It is at times like this that a corporate culture of planning provides stability and assurance of purpose and direction.

An example of the need for planning in poor economic times, rather than resorting to reactive "just-do-something" tactics, is offered by the California Country Club (CCC) of Los Angeles. This club, like many others in southern California, had a waiting list of potential members, but suddenly the waiting list changed to members wanting to leave the club.

Instead of panicking and grasping for an immediate marketing cure-all, the management of CCC pursued a process of market planning, starting with an analysis of

e

18.3 The Los Angeles Country Club, https://www .thelacc.org/: This is one of the most exclusive clubs in the country. The country clubs in a major city that are the number one or two in the region do well because of the position they have been able to achieve and maintain.

the market and competitors. The planning process allowed CCC to recognize marketing opportunities, such as pricing strategies, including the elimination of golf-only fees. The need for a customer-directed policy of "just say yes" was also discovered and implemented. These and other changes represented a complete turnover from previous policies and procedures, thus allowing the club to increase market share and revenue.[28]

A study of the process used by hotels to develop marketing plans has shown that "the most important features in the development of a marketing plan appear to be management participation and commitment at all levels, sufficient time for development, specific training in developing a marketing plan, and tying incentives to the achievements of goals and objectives."[29]

In good times or bad, consistency in marketing planning pays good dividends for any hospitality company and its employees.[30]

■■■ KEY TERMS

Competitive analysis. An analysis of the primary strengths and weaknesses, objectives, strategies, and other information relative to competitors.

Environmental factors. Social, political, and economic factors that affect a firm and its marketing program.

Executive summary. A short summary of the marketing plan to quickly inform top executives.

Market potential. The total estimated dollars or unit value of a defined market for a defined product, including competitive products.

Market trends. External trends of many types that are likely to affect the marketing in which a corporation operates.

Quotas. Quantitative and time-specific accomplishment measurements established for members of a sales force.

Timetable. Specific dates to accomplish strategies and tactics.

■■■ CHAPTER REVIEW

I. Purpose of a Marketing Plan
  A. Serves as a road map for all marketing activities of the firm for the next year.
  B. Ensures that marketing activities are in agreement with the corporate strategic plan.
  C. Forces marketing managers to review and think objectively through all steps in the marketing process.
  D. Assists in the budgeting process to match resources with marketing objectives.

II. Tips for Writing the Executive Summary
  A. Write it for top executives.
  B. Limit the number of pages to between two and four.
  C. Use short sentences and short paragraphs.
  D. Organize the summary as follows: Describe next year's objectives in quantitative terms; briefly describe marketing strategies to meet goals and objectives; identify the dollar costs necessary as well as key resources needed.
  E. Read and reread before final submit.

III. Corporate Connection
  A. Relationships to other plans
    1. Corporate goals: profit, growth, and others
    2. Desired market share
    3. Positioning of the enterprise or of product lines
    4. Vertical or horizontal integration
    5. Strategic alliances
    6. Product-line breadth and depth

  B. Marketing-related plans also include the following:
    1. Sales
    2. Advertising and promotion
    3. Marketing research
    4. Pricing
    5. Customer services
  C. Corporate direction
    1. Mission statement
    2. Corporate philosophy
    3. Corporate goals

IV. Environmental Analysis and Forecasting
  A. Positioning statement (although it should be its own Roman numeral)
  B. Analysis of major environmental factors
    1. Social
    2. Political
    3. Economic
  C. Economic drivers of growth
    1. The aerotropolis
  D. Competitive analysis
    1. List the major existing competitors confronting your firm next year.
    2. List new competitors.
    3. Describe the major competitive strengths and weaknesses of each competitor.
  E. Marketing trends: Monitor visitor trends, competitive trends, related industry trends.
  F. Market potential
    1. Market potential should be viewed as the total available demand for a firm's product

within a particular geographic market at a given price. It is important not to mix different products into an estimate of market potential.

2. Provide an estimate or guesstimate of market potential for each major product line in monetary terms such as dollars and in units such as room nights or passengers.

G. Marketing research

1. **Macromarket information:** Industry trends, socioeconomic and political trends, competitive information, industry-wide customer data.

2. **Micromarket information:** Guest information, product/service information, new-product analysis and testing, intermediary buyer data, pricing studies, key account information, and advertising/promotion effectiveness.

V. Segmentation and Targeting. The selection of segments is the result of the following:

A. Understanding who the company is and what it wishes to be.

B. Studying available segments and determining if they fit the capabilities and desires of the company to obtain and secure them.

VI. Next Year's Objectives and Quotas

A. Objectives

1. **Quantitative objectives:** Expressed in monetary terms, expressed in unit measurements, time specific and profit/margin specific.

2. **Other objectives:** Corporate goals, corporate resources, environmental factors, competitions, market trends, market potential, and available market segments, and possible target markets.

3. **Actions**

   a. List primary marketing/sales objectives for next year.

   b. List sub-objectives for next year.

   c. Break down objective by quarter, month, and week.

   d. List other specific sub-objectives by marketing support area, such as advertising/promotion objectives.

B. Rating system objectives

C. Quotas

1. Based on next year's objectives
2. Individualized
3. Realistic and obtainable
4. Broken down to small units, such as each salesperson's quota per week
5. Understandable/measurable

D. Communicating the plan

E. Top management

F. Board of directors or group of investors

G. Subordinates

H. Vendors

I. Other

J. Action quotas. Break down and list quotas for sales departments, sales territories, all sales intermediaries, each sales intermediary, and each salesperson.

VII. Action Plans: Strategies and Tactics

A. Cluster marketing

B. Sales strategies

1. Prevent erosion of key accounts
2. Grow key accounts
3. Grow selected marginal accounts
4. Eliminate selected marginal accounts
5. Retain selected marginal accounts but provide lower-cost sales support
6. Obtain new business from selected prospects
7. Distribution strategies

C. Advertising/promotion strategies

1. Select a blend or mix or media.
2. Select or approve the message.
3. Design a media schedule showing when each medium, including noncommissionable media, will be used.
4. Design a schedule of events.
5. Carefully transmit this information to management.
6. Supervise the development and implementation of advertising/promotion programs, with particular care given to timetables and budget constraints.
7. Ensure responsibility for the outcome.

D. Pricing strategy

1. Carefully review pricing objective with departments responsible for pricing, planning, and implementation.
2. Refine pricing objectives to reflect sales and revenue forecasts.
3. Describe pricing strategies to be used throughout the year.
4. Make certain that price, sales, and promotion/advertising objectives are synchronized and working in support of corporate objectives.

E. Product strategies

1. Describe the involvement of the marketing department in major strategic product development.
2. Describe the role of marketing in new-product acquisition or product development.
3. Describe ongoing or planned product development programs for which marketing has responsibility.

VIII. Resources Needed to Support Strategies and Meet Objectives

A. Study and then list the need for new marketing/sales personnel, including temporary help during the next year.

B. Study and list the type and amount of equipment and space that will be needed to support marketing/sales.

C. Study and list the amount of monetary support needed next year.

D. Study and list the amount and type of other costs necessary next year.

E. Study and list the amount of outside research, consulting, and training assistance needed.

F. Prepare a marketing budget for approval by top management.

IX. Marketing Control
- **A.** Sales force members often wish to protect themselves and give lower sales estimates than are actually possible.
- **B.** The company has certain sales objectives it expects based on the needs of the company.
- **C.** Management may have access to marketing research information not viewed by the sales force.
- **D.** Management may have a history of dealing with the sales force and realizes that forecasts are generally too high or too low by x percent.
- **E.** Management may be willing to provide the marketing/sales department with additional resources.

X. Presenting and Selling the Plan
- **A.** Members of marketing/sales departments
- **B.** Vendor/ad agencies and others
- **C.** Top management

XI. Preparing for the Future
- **A.** The participatory planning process allows people to understand the management process.
- **B.** People learn to become team players during the process.
- **C.** People learn to establish objectives and set timetables to ensure they are met.
- **D.** People learn the process of establishing realistic strategies and tactics to meet objectives.
- **E.** People who approach the planning process with a receptive mind and employ the marketing plan will usually find it enhances their professional career.

■■■ DISCUSSION QUESTIONS

1. What is the purpose of a marketing plan?
2. What is the relevancy of environmental factors to an annual marketing plan?
3. Why is the determination of market potential so important?
4. How should market segments and targets be described in a marketing plan?
5. Should marketing objectives be described in quantitative terms? Why or why not?
6. What is the relationship, if any, between marketing strategies and marketing objectives?
7. Is marketing control really necessary in a marketing plan, or is it an optional managerial exercise?

■■■ EXPERIENTIAL EXERCISE

Do the following:

Meet with a director of sales of a hotel, a general manager of a hotel, or the director of a tourism marketing organization and ask him or her to go over the organization's marketing plan with you. Have him or her explain the process he or she uses to develop a marketing plan.

■■■ INTERNET EXERCISE

Choose a hospitality or tourism organization in your area. On the Internet find information that would be useful to you if you were developing a marketing plan for the organization. Explain how you would use this information.

■■■ REFERENCES

1. Condensed with permission from Peter Cass, "Luxury Lifestyle Marketing: New Frontier," *Hospitality Business Review*, 2, no. 3 (Fall 1999): 27–30.
2. Halal Food, Cut-Throat Competition, *The Economist* (September 19, 2009): 77.
3. Perry J. S. Hobson, Henry C. S. Vincent, and Kye-Sung Chon, "Vietnam's Tourism Industry: Can It Be Kept Afloat?" *Cornell Hotel and Restaurant Administration Quarterly*, 35, no. 5 (1994): 42–49.
4. John D. Kasarda and Greg Lindsay, *Aerotropolis: The Way We'll Live Next,* 2011, ISBN 978-03741001193.
5. Richard Gibson, "Flight Caterers Widen Horizons Beyond Airlines," *Wall Street Journal* (January 16, 1995): B1, B8.
6. Rachel Lamb, Ritz-Carlton Highlights Brand Values with Foursquare-backed World Concierge, June 28, 2011, pg. 1, www.luxurydaily.com
7. David O. Williams, "Ski Execs Target Asian Markets," *Rocky Mountain News* (January 4, 2008): 5.
8. Josiah Mackenzie, Michael Nurbatlian's Photo Contest Gained 2000+ New Faces in Two Weeks for Indigo Pearl Resort, Hotel Marketing Strategies-Technology

for Better Guest Experiences, July 17, 2011, www.ho-telmarketingstrategies.com

9. Chad Eric Watt, CiCi's Higher Returns from Revamped Stores, *Dallas Business Journal,* 33, no. 46 (July 2–8, 2010).

10. Peter Warren and Neil W. Ostergren, "Marketing Your Hotel, Challenger of the 90's," *Cornell Hotel and Restaurant Administration Quarterly,* 31, no. 1 (1990): 58.

11. Hugh J. Watson and Linda Volonino, Case Study: Harrah's High Payoff from Customer Information, www.terry.uga

12. Ibid.

13. Carl K. Link, "Developing a Marketing Plan: Lessons from the Inn at Plum Creek," *Cornell Hotel and Restaurant Administration Quarterly,* 34, no. 5 (1993): 35.

14. L. K. Prevette and Joseph Giudice, "Anatomy of a Turna-round: The Los Angeles Biltmore," *Cornell Hotel and Restaurant Administration Quarterly,* 30, no. 3 (1989): 32.

15. Karady Islam and Woo Gon Kim, "Comparing Market Segment Profitability Analysis with Department Profit-ability Analysis and Hotel Marketing-Decision Tools," *Cornell Hotel & Restaurant Administration Quarterly,* 47, no. 2 (2006): 155–173.

16. Ron Leiber, "A New Parenting Ritual: The Last Hur-rah," *Wall Street Journal* (July 7, 2004): D1.

17. Ibid.

18. Francis Buttle, "The Marketing Strategy Worksheet: A Practical Tool," *Cornell Hotel and Restaurant Adminis-tration Quarterly,* 33, no. 3 (1992): 57.

19. Julie Jargon, "Eateries' New Way to Shop," *Wall Street Journal,* Corporate News (April 1, 2011): B5.

20. Joseph J. West and Michael D. Olsen, "Grand Strat-egy: Making Your Restaurant a Winner," *Cornell Hotel and Restaurant Administration Quarterly,* 31, no. 2 (1990): 77.

21. West and Olsen, "Grand Strategy."

22. Hanam Ayala, "Mexican Resorts: A Blueprint with an Expiration Date," *Cornell Hotel and Restaurant Admin-istration Quarterly,* 34, no. 3 (1993): 40.

23. Michael S. Morgan, "Benefit Dimensions of a Midscale Restaurant Chain," *Cornell Hotel and Restaurant Ad-ministration Quarterly,* 34, no. 2 (1993): 44–45.

24. Carl K. Link, "Internal Merchandising: Creating Rev-enue Opportunities," *Cornell Hotel and Restaurant Ad-ministration Quarterly,* 30, no. 3 (1989): 56.

25. Ibid., p. 57.

26. Regina Robichald and Mahmood A. Khan, "Respond-ing to Market Changes: The Fast Food Experience," *Cornell Hotel and Restaurant Administration Quarterly,* 29, no. 3 (1988): 47.

27. William E. Kent, "Putting Up the Ritz: Using Culture to Open a Hotel," *Cornell Hotel and Restaurant Adminis-tration Quarterly,* 31, no. 3 (1990): 16–24.

28. Jeffrey L. Pellissier, "Remarketing: One Club's Re-sponse to a Changing Market," *Cornell Hotel and Res-taurant Administration Quarterly,* 34, no. 4 (1993): 53–58.

29. S. Dev Chekitan, "Marketing Practices at Hotel Chains," *Cornell Hotel and Restaurant Administration Quarterly,* 31, no. 3 (1990): 54–63.

30. For more on developing a marketing plan, see James C. Makens, *The Marketing Plan Workbook* (Upper Saddle River, NJ: Prentice-Hall, 1985); and *Hotel Sales and Marketing Plan Workbook* (Winston-Salem, NC: Marion-Clarence, 1990).

The Five-Gap Model of Service Quality

A widely used model of service quality is known as the five-gap model (Figure A-1). This model defines service quality as meeting customer expectations. In the words of those who developed the model, "Knowing what customers expect is the first and possibly the most critical step in delivering service quality. Stated simply, providing service that customers perceive as excellent requires that a firm know what customers expect." This model is closely linked to marketing because it is customer based. The model has five gaps.

■■■ Gap 1: Consumer Expectations versus Management Perception

Hospitality executives may fail to understand what consumers expect in a service and which features are needed to deliver high-quality service. When management does not understand what its customers want, a gap 1 exists. For example, a manager may develop a system to ensure that all guests wait no longer than 15 minutes to check in. However, if guests start getting upset after 10 minutes, this system will cause dissatisfaction. Talking to guests before developing the check-in system would enable the manager to learn that the critical time is 10 minutes, not 15 minutes. Marriott Hotels observed that guests were not using the complimentary bath crystals provided as a bathroom amenity. They discontinued the bath crystals in favor of cable television, a more important benefit to most guests than bath crystals. Originally, management believed bath crystals would be considered a benefit. However, after observing its guests, management found that guest satisfaction could be increased by offering a different service.

Many firms conduct initial studies to find out what their market wants, but later they become internally focused and oblivious to the fact that customers' needs have changed. If customer needs change but the product does not, the marketing mix becomes less attractive to the target market, and gap 1 has increased. Managers should walk around their operations, talk with customers, and encourage feedback. Management can also gain information on customers from marketing information systems.

Figure A–1
Conceptual model of service
quality: the gap analysis
model.
Source: A. Parasuraman,
Valarie Zeithaml, and
Leonard L. Berry, "A
Conceptual Model of Service
Quality and Its Implication
for Future Research," *Journal
of Marketing, Fall* 1985, 44.
Reprinted with permission
of the American Marketing
Association.

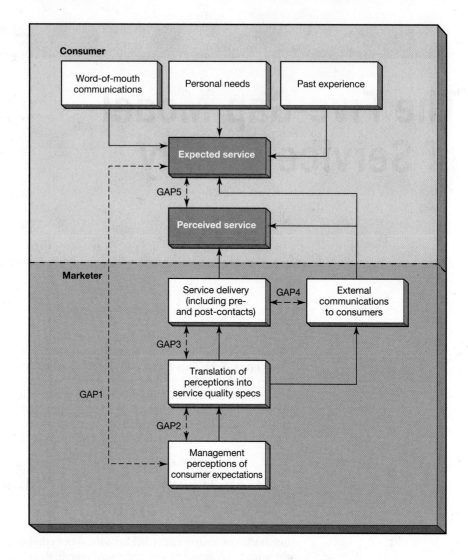

■■■ Gap 2: Management Perception versus Service Quality Specifications

Gap 2 occurs when managers know what their customers want but are unable or unwilling to develop systems that will deliver it. Several reasons have been given for gap 2: (1) inadequate commitment to service quality, (2) lack of perception of feasibility, (3) inadequate task standardization, and (4) absence of goal setting.

Some companies look for short-term profits and are unwilling to invest in people or equipment. This almost inevitably causes service quality problems. Hotel owners who are reluctant to provide enough operating capital can be a cause of gap 2 errors. For example, the hotel owner who budgets for just enough linen to get by may discover that the linen inventory quickly drops below critical levels as linen is stolen and destroyed. A visitor experienced this in Ft. Lauderdale, Florida. The guest returned from a walk on the beach to a freshly cleaned room, started to get ready to take a shower, and noticed there were no towels in the room. The guest called housekeeping and explained that he had to take a shower to get ready for a business appointment and there were no towels in the room. Housekeeping apologized, saying they were short on towels. In about 15 minutes, a housekeeper arrived with towels, causing the guest to arrive late for the appointment. Incidents such as this detract from a positive guest experience, create unnecessary tasks, and decrease employee morale. In this case, hotel management knew that the linen inventory was low, but the owner either did not want to invest in linen or did not have the money to supply the hotel properly.

Sometimes managers feel that improving an existing problem is not feasible. For example, most business guests want to check out after breakfast. They are usually in a hurry to get started with the day's business. Many hotel managers understand this but accept a 10- to 20-minute wait as the best they can do because they are unwilling to hire extra employees to help during the rush period. Bill Marriott Jr. felt that the problem was important enough to develop a system to solve it and invented express checkouts. Guests receive their bills the evening before. If the bills are accurate, the guests simply drop them off with their keys at the front desk. Today, most hotel chains use some type of express checkout system. Some hotels make use of technology and allow the guest to check the accuracy of bills on their television screens and check out using in-room television equipment. The express checkout system was developed by a person who viewed reducing checkout queues as a challenge rather than a problem that was an inherent part of the system. Bill Marriott eliminated this gap 2 error. He demonstrated that capital is not the only cure for a gap 2 problem. Innovative thinking can also eliminate gap 2 problems. Sometimes we need to look for unconventional solutions to the problem. Translating customer needs into service specifications is critical to service quality.

Finally, goals must be accepted by employees. Management must show its support through measurement of results, communication, and rewarding employees for superior service.

■■■ Gap 3: Service Quality Specifications versus Service Delivery

Gap 3 is referred to as the service-performance gap. Gap 3 occurs when management understands what needs to be delivered and appropriate specifications have been developed but employees are unable or unwilling to deliver the service. Gap 3 errors occur during moments of truth, when the employee and the customer interact. Employees are expected to act cheerfully and solve the guests' problems. When they do not, guests may perceive a problem with functional quality. Often Gap 3 errors occur when management assumes that the employees are delivering excellent service and do not pay attention to detail. It is important for management to inspect service delivery to let employees know it appreciates the job they are doing.

Gap 3 errors can be minimized through internal marketing programs. Management of the human resources functions (hiring, training, monitoring working conditions, and developing reward systems) is important in reducing gap 3 errors. Gap 3 errors are also the result of customer-contact employees being overworked. This can occur when a business is understaffed or an employee is required to work a second shift for an employee who called in sick. Under these conditions employees become tired and stressed. They lose their enthusiasm for the job and become less willing to solve customer problems. This lack of customer orientation leads to gap 3 errors.

■■■ Gap 4: Service Delivery versus External Communications

Gap 4 is created when the firm promises more in its external communications than it can deliver. Earlier in this book we mentioned the advertising campaign put on by the government of Bermuda, inviting travelers to enjoy the attractions of the island during its uncrowded low season. Visitors were disappointed when they discovered that many attractions were closed during the off season. Marketers must make sure that operations can deliver what they promise.

During the last week of ski season, skiers were surprised to find that only half the runs on one side of the mountain had been groomed. This was particularly annoying and even dangerous because the half-grooming occurred on intermediate runs where less-than-expert skiers might suddenly encounter bad conditions. The runs had been perfectly groomed all season until that final week. Late-season arrivals undoubtedly felt they had been slighted.

The Regent of Fiji encountered a severe problem when a military takeover occurred and discouraged tourism. A consultant, Chuck Gee, dean of the School of Travel Industry Management at the University of Hawaii, was hired to advise the hotel during this crisis. Chuck's advice was "Do nothing different. Do not reduce your staff, your lighting, your food quality, or your service." When asked why, Chuck's answer was that the Regent had positioned itself as a luxury resort and must continue to offer that level of service even if only one guest appeared. He further explained that the Regent knew there were risks when it entered this market and must now be prepared to accept them and pay the price to continue as an upscale resort.

Lack of consistency can also cause gap 4 problems. Hotel policies were discussed during a marketing seminar. After the seminar a manager from La Quinta told of a problem with a guest when the cashier refused to cash a personal check. The check was over the limit that La Quinta had set for personal checks. However, the guest had cashed a check for the same amount during a previous stay at a La Quinta Inn. The first desk clerk had given the implicit message that it was all right to cash personal checks for that amount. The clerk may have known the guest, had enough cash, and felt the guest should receive a favor. This clerk did not realize that problems were being developed for the next La Quinta. Customers expect chains to have similar products and policies. Inconsistency results in gap 4 errors.

■■■ Gap 5: Expected Service versus Perceived Service

Gap 5 is a function of the others. As any of the other gaps increase in size, gap 5 also increases. It represents the difference between expected quality and perceived quality. The expected quality is what the guest expects to receive from the company. The perceived service is what the guest perceives he or she received from the company. If the guest receives less than he or she expected, the guest is dissatisfied.

The five-gap service model provides insights into the delivery of quality service. By studying this model, we can develop an understanding of the potential problem areas related to service quality. This insight will help to close any gaps that may exist in our operations.

Gap 1 is reduced when managers talk to customers. Courtesy of United Airlines. Source: A. Parasuraman, Valarie Zeithaml, and Leonard L. Berry, "A Conceptual Model of Service Quality and Its Implication for Future Research," *Journal of Marketing,* Fall 1985, 44. Reprinted with permission of the American Marketing Association. Updated 11/15/2001.

Forecasting Market Demand

■■■ Defining the Market

Market demand measurement calls for a clear understanding of the market involved. The term *market* has acquired many meanings over the years. In its original meaning, a market was a physical place where buyers and sellers gathered to exchange goods and services. Medieval towns had market squares where sellers brought their goods and buyers shopped for them. In today's cities, buying and selling occurs in what are called shopping areas rather than markets.

To an economist, the term *market* describes all the buyers and sellers who transact over some good or service. Thus, the limited-service hotel market consists of all the consumers who use limited-service hotels and the companies who supply limited-service hotel rooms. The economist is interested in the structure, conduct, and performance of each market.

To a marketer, a market is the set of all actual and potential buyers of a product or service. A market is the set of buyers, and the industry is the set of sellers. The size of the market hinges on the number of buyers who might exist for a particular market offer. Potential buyers for something have three characteristics: interest, income, and access.

Consider the market for Carnival Cruises. To assess its market, Carnival must first estimate the number of customers who have a potential interest in going on a cruise. To do this, the company could conduct a random sampling of consumers and ask the following question: "Do you have an interest in taking a cruise?" If one person out of ten says *yes,* Carnival can assume that 10 percent of the total number of consumers is the potential market for cruises. The potential market is the set of consumers that professes some level of interest in a particular product or service.

Consumer interest alone is not enough to define the cruise market. Potential consumers must have enough income to afford the product. They must be able to answer *yes* to the following question: "Can you afford to purchase a cruise?" The higher the price, the fewer the number of people who can answer *yes* to this question. Thus, market size depends on both interest and income.

Access barriers further reduce the cruise market size. If Carnival markets its cruises in remote areas not served by travel agents, the number of potential customers in these areas is limited. The available market is the set of consumers that has interest, income, and access to the product.

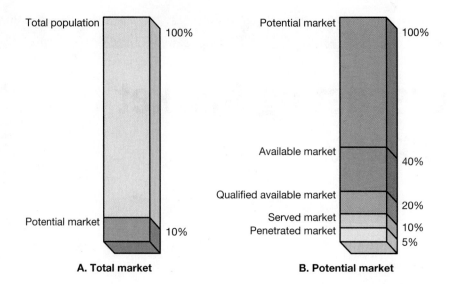

For some market offers, Carnival might have to restrict sales to certain groups. A particular state might not allow the signing of a contractual agreement by anyone under the age of 21. The remaining adults make up the qualified available market: the set of consumers that has interest, income, access, and qualifications for the product.

Carnival now has the choice of going after the whole qualified available market or concentrating on select segments. Carnival's served market is the part of the qualified available market that it decides to pursue. For example, Carnival may decide to concentrate its marketing efforts on the East Coast, the Chicago area, and the Southwest. These areas become its served market. Carnival and its competitors will end up selling a certain number of cruises in their served market. The penetrated market is the set of consumers that has bought cruises.

Figure B-1 brings these market concepts together with some hypothetical numbers. The bar on the left of the figure shows the ratio of the potential market—all those who are interested—to the total market. Here the potential market is 10 percent. The bar on the right shows several possible breakdowns of the potential market. The available market—those who have interest, income, and access—is 40 percent of the potential market. The qualified available market—those who can meet the legal requirements—is 50 percent of the total available market (or 20 percent of the potential market). Carnival concentrates its efforts on 50 percent of the qualified available market—the served market, which is 10 percent of the potential market. Finally, Carnival and its competitors already have penetrated 50 percent of the served market (or 5 percent of the potential market).

These market definitions are a useful tool for marketing planning. Carnival's management can take a number of actions if it is not satisfied with current sales. It can lobby to get the age for signing a legal contract lowered. It can expand its markets in North America or in other areas of the world. Carnival can lower its prices to expand the size of the potential market. It can try to attract more buyers from its served market through stronger promotion or distribution efforts to target current customers. Or it can try to expand the potential market by increasing advertising to convert uninterested consumers into interested consumers. This is what Carnival did when it created the "Fun Ships."

■■■ Market Areas for Restaurants

In the restaurant industry, it is common to describe market areas geographically and call them *trade areas,* which vary by type of restaurant and area description. For example, in rural areas it is common for people to make a 100-mile round trip to dine at a favorite restaurant. In contrast, 90 percent of the customers of a fast-food restaurant in a residential area of a major city live within 3 miles of the restaurant. People are not willing to spend a great deal of time getting a fast-food meal. But if they eat at a specialty restaurant such as a Hard Rock Café, they are willing to drive across town. Thus, Hard Rock Café's trade area may encompass a 15-mile radius. A McDonald's in the same town may define its trade area as a 3-mile radius.

John Melaniphy, a restaurant site location expert, describes the trade area of a restaurant as an area that provides 85 percent of the restaurant's business. Restaurants that serve out-of-town guests can examine customers' zip codes and find out where their guests are staying while they are visiting the city. He gives other factors that influence the trade area of a restaurant. Topography defines trade areas. Rivers, lakes, or mountains may set boundaries. Psychological barriers can also exist. For example, expressways, airports, and industrial parks may create barriers. Demographic differences in neighborhoods can also create psychological barriers. For example, residents of a lower-class neighborhood may feel more comfortable eating in their own neighborhood than eating in a restaurant in an upper-middle-class neighborhood, even though both restaurants are the same distance from their houses and have the same average check.

Competition has a big impact on the trade area. Sometimes competition from the same chain may define a trade area. For example, in a city that has eight McDonald's, an adjacent McDonald's may set the boundaries of the trade area for another.

Traffic flows and road patterns also help define trade areas. Accessibility is an important consideration: The better the access, the more extensive the trade area. People also become accustomed to traveling in certain directions and are more likely to travel 4 miles to a restaurant that they pass every day going to work than 4 miles in a direction that they travel infrequently. Thus, a knowledge of normal traveling routes to major employment and shopping areas is useful in determining a trade area.

◼▦▦ Measuring Current Market Demand

We now turn to some practical methods for estimating current market demand. Marketers want to estimate three different aspects of current market demand: total market demand, area market demand, and actual sales and market shares.

Estimating Total Market Demand

The total market demand for a product or service is the total volume that would be bought by a defined consumer group in a defined geographic area in a defined time period in a defined marketing environment under a defined level and mix of industry marketing effort.

Total market demand is not a fixed number but a function of the stated conditions. One of these conditions, for example, is the level and mix of industry marketing effort. Another is the state of the environment. Part A of Figure B-2 shows the relationship between total market demand and these conditions. The horizontal axis shows different possible levels of industry marketing expenditure in a given period. The vertical axis shows the resulting demand level. The curve represents the estimated level of market demand for varying levels of industry marketing expenditure. Some base sales (called the market minimum) would take place without any marketing expenditures. Greater marketing expenditures would yield higher levels of demand, first at an increasing rate and then at a decreasing rate. Marketing expenditures above a certain level would not cause much more demand, suggesting an upper limit to market demand called the *market potential*. The industry market forecast shows the level of market demand corresponding to the planned level of industry marketing expenditure in the given environment.

The distance between the market minimum and the market potential shows the overall sensitivity of demand to marketing efforts. We can think of two extreme types of markets, the expandable and the nonexpandable. An expandable market,

Figure B-2
Market demand.

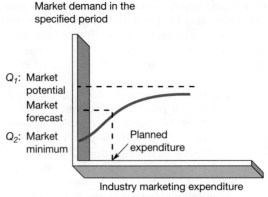

A. Market demand as a function of industry marketing expenditure (assumes a marketing environment of prosperity)

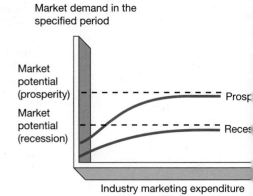

B. Market demand as a function of industry marketing expenditures (under prosperity recession)

such as the market for air travel, is one whose size is affected by the level of industry marketing expenditures. In terms of Figure B–2, in an expandable market, the distance between $Q1$ and $Q2$ would be fairly large. A nonexpandable market, such as the market for opera, is one whose size is not much affected by the level of marketing expenditures; the distance between $Q1$ and $Q2$ would be fairly small. Organizations selling in a nonexpandable market can take primary demand—total demand for all brands of a given product or service—as a given. They concentrate their marketing resources on building selective demand—demand for their brand of the product or service.

Given a different marketing environment, we must estimate a new demand curve. Figure B–2 shows the relationship of market demand to the environment. A given level of marketing expenditure will always result in more demand during prosperity than it would during a recession. Marketers should carefully define the situation for which they are estimating market demand.

Estimating Area Market Demand

Companies face the problem of selecting the best sales territories and allocating their marketing budget optimally among these territories. Therefore, they need to estimate the market potential of different cities, states, and even national markets. Two major methods are available: the market-buildup method and the market-factor index method. The market-buildup method calls for identifying all the potential buyers in each market and estimating their potential purchases. The market-factor index method is used in the fast-food industry. A common method for calculating area market potential is to identify market factors that correlate with market potential and combine them into a weighted index.

Many companies compute additional area demand measures. Marketers now can refine state-by-state and city-by-city measures down to census tracts or zip code centers. Census tracts are small areas about the size of a neighborhood, and zip code centers (designed by the U.S. Postal Service) are larger areas, often the size of small towns. Information on population size, family income, and other characteristics is available for each type of unit. Marketers can use these data for estimating demand in neighborhoods or other smaller geographic units within large cities.

Estimating Actual Sales and Market Shares

In addition to estimating total and area demand, a company will want to know the actual industry sales in its market. Thus, it must identify its competitors and estimate their sales. The industry's trade association often collects and publishes total industry sales, although it does not list individual company sales separately. In this way, each company can evaluate its performance against the industry as a whole. Suppose that the company's sales are increasing at a rate of 5 percent a year and industry sales are increasing at 10 percent. This company is actually losing its relative standing in the industry.

■▪▪ Forecasting Future Demand

Forecasting is the art of estimating future demand by anticipating what buyers are likely to do under a given set of conditions. For example, an association wants to book 100 rooms for three nights in a 250-room hotel next year. They will pay $95 per room per night. The current rate structure of the hotel is as follows: rack rate $150, corporate rate $125, and average rate $105. Should the manager take the 300 room-nights at a low rate, or does the manager turn down this request for $28,500 worth of business? Without forecasting, it is difficult to answer this question. Forecasts help managers maximize their profits.

Most markets do not have a stable industry or company demand, so good forecasting becomes a key factor in company success. Poor forecasting can lead to overstaffing and excess inventories or understaffing and running out of products. The more unstable the demand, the more the company needs accurate forecasts and elaborate forecasting procedures.

Forecasting Methods

Many firms base their forecasts on past sales. They assume that the causes of past sales can be uncovered through statistical analysis and that analysts can use the causal relations to predict future sales. One popular method, time-series analysis, consists of breaking down the original sales into four components—trend, cycle, season, and erratic components—and then recombining these components to produce the sales forecast. *Trend* is the long-term underlying pattern of growth or decline in sales resulting from basic changes in population, capital formation, and technology. It is found by fitting a straight line through past sales.

Cycle captures the medium-term wave movement of sales resulting from changes in general, economic, and competitive activity. The cyclical component can be useful for medium-range forecasting. Cyclical swings, however, are difficult to predict because they do not occur at regular intervals.

Season refers to a consistent pattern of weekly, monthly, or quarterly sales movements within the year. In the hospitality industry, we usually think of seasonal changes on a yearly basis, but weekly and hourly sales changes are important. The seasonal component can be related to weather factors, holidays, and trade customs. The seasonal pattern provides a norm for forecasting short-range sales. Yield management depends on forecasting demand by day, by flight or cruise, and by hour of the day. Historical sales patterns are carefully analyzed, such as examining sales for Tuesdays of the second week of September or total passengers and the mix of passengers on flight 482 each Wednesday afternoon at 3:30. Forecasting in the airline industry is further complicated by the presence of interconnecting stops. Large hospitality companies, such as hotel chains, and car rental firms, such as Hertz, depend on sophisticated software to analyze huge volumes of data.

Finally, *erratic events* include strikes, snowstorms, earthquakes, riots, fires, and other disturbances. These components, by definition, are unpredictable and should be removed from past data to reveal the more normal behavior of sales. Most of these events cannot be accurately forecasted, but a few, such as snowstorms and strikes, lend themselves to short-run forecasting. Hotel managers in Washington, D.C., know that if a major snowstorm is predicted for the city, room demand will increase. Visitors will be unable to leave the city and will want to retain their rooms. Office workers may be unable to return home and will also want a room. Managers who have a knowledge of the past behavior of demand when erratic events occurred can factor this into their thinking in times of crisis management.

The first step in managing demand is understanding the factors that affect the demand of the firm's market segments. The payday of a major employer may drive area customer demand. For example, in north Dallas the Friday and Saturday nights after a payday at Texas Instruments are much busier than non-payday weekends. There also may be seasonal variations. The Boulders, a resort in Arizona, charges more than $500 a room in season, yet it closes in July and August because of a lack of demand for rooms at less than half this price. Holiday periods have a positive influence on demand at most resorts. Business travel drops off between mid-December and mid-January, during the summer period, and over weekends. Although there is fluctuation in demand, much of the fluctuation can be explained. Managers must understand the factors that drive demand and build it into their forecasts.

Suppose that a 250-room hotel had an occupancy of 76 percent, selling 69,350 room-nights during the year at an average rate of $80. During the last seven years, the number of room-nights sold and average rate have both increased by 5 percent. The hotel has undergone two expansions to keep up with the growth. This information suggests that next year the hotel will sell 72,818 room-nights (69,350 × 1.05) at an average rate of $84 (1.05 × $80). The manager first has to determine whether the hotel has the capacity to handle the increase. If the hotel sold out to business travelers from Tuesday to Thursday during February through May and September through October, it is unrealistic to expect that the growth will continue at a 5 percent rate because it will be constrained by capacity. The only opportunity to increase occupancy is during the low-demand periods.

Let us assume that a recession is expected next year. As a result, the number of room-nights is expected to drop by 10 percent, and the average rate is expected to decrease by 15 percent as competitors cut their rates to attract customers. If the manager did not factor in the recession and projected based solely on past information, the occupancy and average room rate would be greatly overstated. Taking the recession into consideration, the forecast will call for a lower occupancy at a greatly reduced room rate.

When a forecast calls for a decrease in sales, it is important to document the reasons for the decrease. This is especially true of regional recessions. A regional economy with a heavy dependence on one industry can suffer a regional recession when that industry declines while the rest of the country enjoys prosperity. When the hotel management sends its forecast showing a decline in sales to the home office, it will be rejected unless it is well supported. In many cases when a director of sales has presented a marketing plan calling for a decrease in sales without supporting documents to defend the projected decrease, corporate management required the director of sales to increase the forecast. In this scenario, the hotel fails to meet the revised forecast, and the director of sales is fired for not meeting the sales goal. Managers must forecast accurately and provide information to support their forecasts.

Statistical Demand Analysis

Time-series analysis views past and future sales as a function of time rather than as a function of any real demand factors. But many factors affect the sales of any product. Statistical demand analysis is a set of statistical procedures used to discover the most important real factors affecting sales and their relative influence. The factors most commonly analyzed are prices, income, population, and promotion.

Statistical demand analysis consists of expressing sales (Q) as a dependent variable and trying to explain sales as a function of several independent demand variables X1, X2, ... Xn. That is,

$$Q = f(X_1, X_2, \ldots X_n)$$

Using a technique called multiple-regression analysis, various equation forms can be statistically fitted to the data in the search for the best predicting factors and equation. For example, a restaurant near Marquette University in Milwaukee,

Wisconsin, found that its sales were explained by whether Marquette University was in session and the preceding week's sales:

$$Q = 2614.3 + 1610.7X_1 + 0.2605X_2.$$

where X1 is a dummy variable indicating whether Marquette was in session, with 1 given when it was in session and 0 used when it was not in session, and X2 is last week's sales. For example, if Marquette had just finished a term and management wanted to predict sales for next week when last week's sales were $6,000, forecast sales for next week would be as follows:

$$
\begin{aligned}
Q &= 2614.3 + 1610.7X_1 + 0.2605X_2 \\
&= 2614.3 + 1610.7(0) + 0.2605(6000) \\
&= 2614.3 + 0 + 1563 \\
&= \$4177.30
\end{aligned}
$$

The manager could also expect a gradual decline in sales (because the preceding week's sales will be falling) as activity around the campus slows down. For example, if the restaurant achieved the forecasted sales of $4,177.30, the next week's projected sales would be $3,702.49. The decline is due to the drop in the previous week's sales from $6,000 to $4,177.30. Sales for the restaurant when the university is not in session will level off at $3,535 in the sixth week of the break.

Two precautions apply to the use of regression in forecasting. First, the equation just stated will not be sensitive to extraordinary events. For example, on parents' weekend the restaurant may generate very high sales. The equation does not include parents' weekend as a variable; therefore, it is unable to project sales accurately for this event. The sales for the week after parents' weekend will be overstated because the figure for the previous week will be extraordinarily high. Second, it is dangerous to forecast outside the range of the different variables used to build the forecast. For example, if a manager examines the relationship between advertising and room sales, the manager may find that room sales increase $5 for every dollar spent on advertising. If the hotel advertising expenditures had ranged from $75,000 to $150,000, we could not necessarily expect this relationship to hold up for advertising expenditures of $250,000 because this level of advertising has not been tested.

The precautions cited earlier illustrate two types of errors caused by the misuse of regression analysis. Statistical demand analysis can be very complex, and the marketer must take care in designing, conducting, and interrupting such analysis. Yet constantly improving computer technology has made statistical demand analysis an increasingly popular approach to forecasting.

Two other forecasting techniques used in the hospitality industry are moving average and exponential smoothing. A moving average is the average of a set number of previous periods (n); this average is used to predict sales for the next period. For example, if a restaurant had sales of $12,000, $12,500, $13,000, and $12,500 over the last four weeks, using a four-week moving average, the sales forecast for the next week would be $12,500.

$$\frac{\$12,000 + \$12,500 + \$13,000 + \$12,500}{4} = \$12,500$$

A limitation of moving averages is that the latest period used in the average has the same weight as the current period. Exponential smoothing is a simple but useful mathematical technique, which allows recent periods to be weighted.

The forecasting techniques presented in this chapter represent a few of the techniques that managers use. It is not within the scope of this book to provide a detailed explanation of all forecasting techniques. We simply want to illustrate that tools are available to assist managers with their forecasts.

Case Studies

■■■ Case 1 The Sleep Well Motel

Will Shelton was evaluating information received from the owner of a motel that was for sale in Fort Morgan, Colorado. Will had answered an ad in the *Wall Street Journal* under the heading "Business for Sale." To Will's surprise, he received a call directly from Hank Bennington, the owner of the Sleep Well Motel of Fort Morgan, Colorado.

During the conversation, Mr. Bennington described his motel and his reason for wanting to sell. He also described the many advantages of living in Colorado and promised to send Will more information on his company. The next day an overnight package of information arrived at Will's home.

Background on Will Shelton

At forty-four years of age, Will felt that he had climbed the corporate ladder about as high as he could go. He also had doubts about remaining in a large corporation the rest of his working life. The present position Will held was director of marketing research for a large electronics corporation located in Houston, Texas. Despite the title, Will felt his position was not satisfying. "Marketing research in an industrial company just isn't very exciting or personally rewarding; in fact, it's downright dull." This statement pretty well summarized Will's feelings. Although Will had been trained as an engineer, he discovered that engineering wasn't his primary interest and began to move into marketing. When the position of marketing research director opened in his company, Will applied and was elated when he learned he had received the position. In reviewing this move, Will stated that he believed the fact he had recently completed an MBA during part-time studies had helped him to obtain the position.

In his earlier years, Will had studied and worked in New Mexico. He had learned to ski and also enjoyed hunting and fishing in that state. Will felt the people in that part of the United States were somehow more genuine and that life was better in many ways than his present life in Houston. As a result, when he read about a motel for sale in Colorado, Will had an automatic interest.

Background on the Sleep Well Motel

As Will began to pull his thoughts together, he reviewed what he had already learned about the Sleep Well Motel. This information had been gained through a telephone conversation with Mr. Bennington plus sales literature and a brief historical sketch that had been included with data sent by Mr. Bennington.

The motel had eighty rooms and had been affiliated with a chain several years ago but was no longer associated with this company. The property was located off U.S. Highway 76, which carried traffic between Denver and Nebraska. Mr. Bennington did not have data concerning the profile characteristics of his customers but told Will that his customers were commercial travelers such as repair crews, independent sales reps, middle-aged retired couples, and young budget-minded travelers. The motel did not have an attached restaurant, but there was a café about two blocks away. There was also a laundromat nearby that was frequently used by his guests. The property was seventeen years old and was described as clean and comfortable but in need of "cosmetics" and new carpeting. Mr. Bennington said he had a dependable night clerk but served as the manager/front desk clerk himself during the day. He said that dependable maid service was a problem for all the motels in the area, and his was no exception.

Reason for Selling

In the telephone conversation, Mr. Bennington stated he had recently lost his wife in a tragic car accident. Since that time he had been unable to concentrate on the business and now wanted to return to his home state of Illinois to be near his son's family. In addition, Mr. Bennington said he wanted to be perfectly candid. He said that after the car accident he failed to keep as close a watch on the business as he should have. Mr. Bennington admitted that he felt ill at ease in the field of marketing and felt the company would need strong direction in that area. He went on to say that Will should be a "natural" to manage this type of business.

After skimming the material, Will became increasingly enthusiastic about the possibility of owning and managing this motel. He knew there were many additional questions he would need to ask in his next phone conversation. At the moment, the most exciting part was the possibility of living in Colorado and being his own boss. Will knew he would have to develop a list of penetrating questions to ask Mr. Bennington and also knew he needed to study the financial sheets in detail. That could come later. For the moment, Will was picturing himself on the slopes of Colorado's beautiful mountains gracefully skimming down the snow.

This case was written by Professor Cathy H. C. Hsu, Hong Kong Polytechnic University. Reproduced with permission.

▪▪▪ DISCUSSION QUESTIONS

1. Discuss the pros and cons of Will Shelton owning and operating the Sleep Well Motel.

2. Do you believe that Will's marketing/marketing research background will be of great assistance to him in running this motel?

3. Why do you suppose Mr. Bennington said that Will's marketing background would be a real benefit?

4. What kinds of marketing/sales tactics are best suited for a motel such as the Sleep Well Motel?

▪▪▪ Case 2 Cafeteria I.C.E.

The cafeteria for employees of I.C.E. (the national electric company of Costa Rica: Instituto Costarricense de Electricidad) was experiencing difficulties, and top management felt compelled to see what corrective actions could be taken. Responsibility for correcting the problems had been assigned to Antonio F. Caas Mora, assistant manager for telecommunications.

The problems were two types. First, no one was satisfied with the time required for lunch. The time often extended beyond the allocated half hour, resulting in loss of productivity. The second, related, problem was how to change the lunchtime eating habits of the employees. The majority of employees used the main serving line, where they purchased a heavy traditional Latin meal. This required a considerable amount of time and also made the employees sleepy after eating. As a result, afternoon productivity among office personnel declined.

Background on I.C.E. and the Cafeteria

I.C.E. was the largest electric utility and the only telephone company in the nation of Costa Rica. It was owned and operated by the government of Costa Rica. Although I.C.E. had field office locations throughout Costa Rica, the central administrative offices were located in the city of San José in a modern fifteen-story building. A total of 4,486 persons were employed by I.C.E., and 1,453 of these worked in the central office building. This group used the cafeteria facilities.

The cafeteria had been in operation for five years. It was under the management of an employee cooperative. This cooperative was managed by an elected board of directors consisting of employees of I.C.E. The board of directors of the cooperative hired a full-time manager who had direct responsibility for the cafeteria operation.

Description of Employees

Employees who worked in the I.C.E. building and used the cafeteria were primarily white-collar personnel. A minority of blue-collar employees such as maintenance personnel used the cafeteria. Employees who worked in the I.C.E. building consisted primarily of administrators, staff specialists, engineers, clerical personnel, secretaries, and receptionists.

The Menu and Eating Habits

The cafeteria consisted of two serving lines; the main serving line was the most popular with the employees and was the one with the long waiting lines. This line served what was known as the *casado,* a typical Latin meal. The menu changed each day. A typical meal consisted of a meat dish such as a small steak, sausage, or liver. This was accompanied with rice, beans, and a vegetable such as corn or, more commonly, potatoes.

The meals served in the main serving line reflected the cultural habits of Costa Ricans with traditional food. The noontime meal historically had been eaten with the family and required two or three hours, including family conversation and sometimes a short nap. This custom was the basis for closing stores during midday. It was still the custom in many parts of Latin America for all types of businesses to close until 2 or 3 P.M. The traditional long lunch hour meant that employees would arrive for work early in the morning, take a long lunch break, return for work, and stay late in the evening until 6 or 6:30 P.M. The management of I.C.E. had decided to break with this tradition to allow as smooth a workday as possible without the interruption of a long lunch break. The I.C.E. system closely paralleled that found in the United States.

There was evidence of change in eating habits in San José. Several U.S.-style restaurants had entered the market and did a brisk business at lunch with hamburgers, pizza, and other quick foods. McDonald's, Hardee's, and Pizza Hut were popular noontime restaurants, especially with younger people. After witnessing the success of restaurants such as McDonald's, the board of directors of the cooperative decided to open a sandwich line in the cafeteria. This was separate from the main serving line. It consisted of a long counter. Plastic food trays were placed on the counter and filled with stacks of unwrapped cold sandwiches such as cheese or ham and cheese. Other trays contained slices of fruit such as papaya or watermelon and cake. Coffee, milk, and carbonated beverages were available from dispensers located on the counter.

Two cash registers were located at the end of the main serving line, and one at the end of the sandwich line. Information was not recorded concerning the number of employees who used each line or the average expenditure per person in the sandwich line. However, it was felt that the average lunch expenditure per employee would probably be about two thirds of the per person expenditure in the main serving line.

Working Hours and Office Rules

The office hours at I.C.E. extended from 7:30 A.M. to 3:30 P.M., with half an hour for lunch. Employees were expected to arrive on time. This meant that some employees had to rise as early as 5:30 A.M., and few could rise later than 6:30 A.M.

Coffee breaks were not officially permitted, and there were no vending machines in the building. The policy of no coffee breaks had been instituted because many employees spilled coffee or other liquids on reports. It was also felt that a coffee break was unnecessary because half an hour was given for lunch. Workers would occasionally bring a cake or cookies from home and share them with employees in their work area, even though this was officially frowned upon.

A system had been devised to prevent all employees from crowding into the cafeteria at one time. The doors of the cafeteria were locked until 11 A.M., at which time employees began to arrive on a set schedule by floors. The line closed promptly at 1:30 P.M.

Survey Results

Before attempting to make changes to correct the situation in the cafeteria, management felt it would be wise to conduct a survey among the employees. This was done through the use of a written questionnaire, which was given to all persons using the cafeteria on a selected day. The results of this questionnaire follow.

Opinions Concerning Selected Factors (%)

	OPINION				
FACTOR	VERY GOOD	GOOD	AVERAGE	BAD	NO OPINION
Quality	0.63	16.46	44.78	23.42	14.71
Variety	4.59	35.28	28.96	18.67	12.50
Cleanliness	1.74	18.67	36.55	29.75	13.24
Courtesy	5.38	27.37	39.24	25.16	2.85
Convenience	8.07	30.70	34.65	23.26	3.32
Quality of cooking	8.39	35.28	33.70	18.83	3.80
Quantity	3.16	28.48	39.72	20.41	8.23

Opinions Concerning Type of Food Served (%)

	OPINION				
FOOD	VERY GOOD	GOOD	AVERAGE	BAD	NO OPINION
Chicken w/rice	8.86	43.04	29.59	7.59	10.92
Shrimp w/rice	1.11	12.34	33.23	31.64	21.68
Meatballs	2.37	12.97	31.33	31.65	21.68
Sea bass	10.28	37.18	25.63	8.86	18.04
Breaded steak	4.11	22.47	34.02	18.04	21.36
Flank steak in sauce	3.64	24.68	30.85	15.82	25.06
Tongue in sauce	5.54	26.58	26.42	17.41	24.05
Chicken in sauce	3.32	23.10	29.43	16.30	27.85
Fried chicken	2.37	23.89	30.70	12.97	30.06
Pork chop	3.32	19.15	29.43	21.99	26.11
Spaghetti w/meat	1.90	13.77	29.11	33.07	22.15
Spaghetti w/tuna	2.37	10.92	26.42	34.18	26.11
Chickpeas w/tripe	3.64	17.56	28.80	28.01	21.99
Chop suey	1.90	14.40	24.05	38.76	20.89

Opinions Concerning Diet
and Type of Meal (%)

	YES	NO	NO OPINION
Do you believe the diet is well balanced?	17.88	75.63	6.49
Do you feel that the special plate of the day should be eliminated?	27.69	66.61	5.70
Do you believe the *casado* should be eliminated?	26.42	68.04	5.54
Do you believe a lighter meal should be served?	36.23	14.40	49.37

Light Meal
Preferences[a] (%)

	YES	NO
Hot dogs	44.46	55.54
Hamburgers	30.85	69.15
Chicken	42.41	57.54
Pastry	36.55	63.45
Fruit	18.99	81.01
Sandwiches	49.53	50.47
Desserts	31.80	68.20
Soup	18.35	81.65
Salads	23.10	76.90
Fruit salads	33.86	66.14
Other	10.28	89.72

[a]If a light meal was served. This was answered by all respondents.

Answers Concerning Eating
Habits (%)

	YES	NO	NO ANSWER
Do you follow a special diet?	14.72	76.58	8.70
Do you usually bring your lunch?	10.76	81.33	7.91

Average Time Taken to Eat
Lunch (%)

20–30 minutes	18.83
30–45 minutes	61.87
45–60 minutes	12.50
Over 60 minutes	0.79
No answer	6.01

Observations Concerning Seating in Cafeteria

A series of observations were made in the cafeteria on typical days. The cafeteria held fifty-eight tables with four chairs each, for a total of 232 places. The utilization of this space on the days observed is shown in the tables that follow.

Use of Available Seating
Capacity

TIME	AVAILABLE SEATS	PERSONS IN WAITING LINE	THEORETICAL SURPLUS OR SHORTAGE OF SEATS
Wednesday, August 16			
11:45	45	80	235
12:25	16	90	274
12:30	48	90	274
1:05	68	40	128
1:20	88	27	161
Thursday, August 17			
11:15	44	16	128
11:42	68	38	130
11:56	39	43	24
12:00	44	55	211
12:10	80	53	127
12:15	56	37	119
12:30	56	52	24
12:40	56	47	19
12:55	26	46	220
1:15	56	3	153

Tables Occupied by One or
Two People

	TABLES OCCUPIED BY ONE	TABLES OCCUPIED BY TWO	TOTAL
Wednesday, August 16			
11:42	12	22	34
11:56	6	26	32
12:00	6	38	44
12:10	3	30	33
12:15	15	18	33
12:30	6	26	32
12:55	15	20	35
1:15	6	14	20

Rate of Flow Through Serving Line

Main line. After two days of observation, it was found that the average time
required for a person to pass through the main serving line from the moment a
person picked up a tray until leaving the cash register was slightly in excess of
three minutes, with a range of two to four minutes. There was never a break in
this line from the moment the cafeteria opened at 11 A.M. until it closed at 1:30.
The line moved steadily, yet a waiting line would form between 12:00 and
12:45, which at times extended well into the hallway in front of the elevator
and caused waiting times of 20 minutes before reaching the actual food line.

Sandwich line. The amount of time required per person to pass through the
sandwich line ranged from 0.5 to 4 minutes. The average time for persons
who used the sandwich line but did not use a sandwich grill to cook cold

sandwiches was 2.10 minutes. The amount of time required in this line when someone used the sandwich grill located beyond the cash register ranged between 3 and 8 minutes, with an average time of 4.5 minutes. At times as many as eight or ten persons would be waiting to use the sandwich grill.

■■■ DISCUSSION QUESTIONS

1. Can the use of marketing concepts/strategies be of use in solving the problem with Cafeteria I.C.E.?

2. What effect can an individual organization such as I.C.E. have on changing ingrained cultural habits such as those of noontime dining?

3. What would you suggest be done to increase patronage of the sandwich and fruit line?

■■■ Case 3 Southwest Airlines

Southwest Airlines entered the airline industry in 1971 with little money but lots of personality. Marketing itself as the LUV airline, the company featured a bright red heart as its first logo and relied on outrageous antics to generate word of mouth and new business. Flight attendants in red-orange hot pants served Love Bites (peanuts) and Love Potions (drinks).

As Southwest grew, its advertising showcased its focus on low fares, frequent flights, on-time arrivals, top safety record, and how bags fly free. Throughout all its communication efforts, Southwest uses humor to poke fun at itself and convey its warm, friendly personality. One TV spot showed a small bag of peanuts with the words, "This is what our meals look like at Southwest Airlines... It's also what our fares look like." Its ongoing "Wanna Get Away?" campaign uses embarrassing situations to hit a funny bone with consumers. And its tagline: "Ding! You are now free to move around the country" is a self-parody of its in-flight announcements. This lighthearted attitude carries over to the entertaining on-board announcements, crews that burst into song in the terminal, and several personalized aircrafts, including three painted as flying killer whales, "Lone Star One" painted like the Texas flag, and "Slam Dunk One," symbolizing the airline's partnership with the NBA.

Southwest's business model is based on streamlining its operations, which results in low fares and satisfied consumers. The airline takes several steps to save money and passes the savings to customers through low fares. It flies over 3,100 short, "point-to-point" trips in a day—shuttling more passengers per plane than any other airline. Each aircraft makes an average of 6.25 flights a day, or almost 12 hours each day. Southwest can accomplish such a feat because it avoids the traditional hub-and-spoke system and has extremely fast turnaround service. In its early years, it turned planes around in less than 10 minutes. Today, its turnaround averages 20 to 30 minutes—still the best in the industry and half the industry average. Southwest's unique boarding process helps. Instead of assigned seating, passengers are assigned to one of three groups (A, B, C) and a number when they check in. The number refers to where they stand in line at the gate. Group A boards first, and once on board, passengers may sit anywhere they like.

Southwest grows by entering new markets other airlines overprice and underserve. The company believes it can bring fares down by one-third to one-half whenever it enters a new market, and it expands every market it serves by making flying affordable to people who could not afford it before. Southwest currently serves sixty-eight cities in thirty-five states, usually secondary cities with smaller airports that have lower gate fees and less congestion—another factor that leads to faster turnaround and lower fares.

Another unique cost savings strategy is Southwest's decision to operate Boeing 737s for all its flights. This simplifies the training process for pilots, flight attendants, and mechanics and management can substitute aircraft, reschedule flight crews, or transfer mechanics quickly.

Jet fuel is an airline's biggest expense. According to the industry's trade group, Air Transport Association, jet fuel now accounts for 40 percent of an airplane ticket versus 15 percent just eight years ago. Southwest's biggest cost savings technique and competitive advantage has long been its program to hedge fuel prices by purchasing options years in advance. Many of its long-term contracts allow the airline to purchase fuel at $51 per barrel, a significant savings especially during the oil shocks of the 2000s that drove oil past $100 per barrel. Analysts estimate that Southwest has saved more than $2 billion with fuel hedging.

Because lighter planes use less fuel, Southwest makes its planes lighter by, for instance, power-washing their jet engines to remove dirt each night. It carries less water for bathrooms and has replaced its seats with lighter models. Southwest consumes approximately 1.5 billion gallons of jet fuel each year so every minor change adds up. The airline estimates that these changes saved $1.6 million in fuel costs over just three months.

Southwest has pioneered services and programs such as same-day freight service, senior discounts, Fun Fares, and Ticketless Travel. It was the first airline with a Web site, the first to deliver live updates on ticket deals, and the first to post a blog. Despite its reputation for low fares and no-frills service, Southwest wins the hearts of customers. It consistently ranks at the top of lists of customer service for airlines and receives the lowest ratio of complaints per passenger.

Southwest has been ranked by *Fortune* magazine as the United States' most admired airline since 1997, the fifth-most admired corporation in 2007, and one of the top five best places to work. Its financial results also shine: The company has been profitable for 37 straight years. It has been the only airline to report profits every quarter since September 11, 2001, and one of the few with no layoffs amid a travel slump created by the slow economy and the threat of terrorism.

Although the hot pants are long gone, the LUVing spirit remains at the heart of Southwest. The company's stock symbol on the NYSE is LUV, and red hearts can be found across the company. These symbols embody the Southwest spirit of employees "caring about themselves, each other, and Southwest's customers." "Our fares can be matched; our airplanes and routes can be copied. But we pride ourselves on our customer service," said Sherry Phelps, director of corporate employment. That's why Southwest looks for and hires people who generate enthusiasm. In fact, having a sense of humor is a selection criterion it uses for hiring. As one employee explained, "We can train you to do any job, but we can't give you the right spirit." And the feeling is reciprocated. When Southwest needed to close reservation centers in three cities in 2004, it didn't fire a single employee but rather paid for relocation and commuting expenses.

■■■ **DISCUSSION QUESTIONS**

Chapter 3

1. Southwest has mastered the low-price model and has the financial results to prove it. Why don't the other airlines copy Southwest's model?

2. What risks does Southwest face? Can it continue to thrive as a low-cost airline when tough economic times hit?

Chapter 7

3. What product benefits does Southwest have that would attract a company to recommend that its employee's fly Southwest Airlines?

Chapter 9

4. Explain how Southwest airlines used product design to create a competitive advantage.

Sources: Barney Gimbel, "Southwest's New Flight Plan," *Fortune* (May 16, 2005): pp. 93–98; Melanie Trottman, "Destination: Philadelphia." *Wall Street Journal* (May 4, 2004); Andy Serwer, "Southwest Airlines: The Hottest Thing in the Sky," *Fortune* (March 8, 2004); Colleen Barrett, "Fasten Your Seat Belts," *Adweek* (January 26, 2004): p. 17; Jeff Bailey, "Southwest Airlines Gains Advantage by Hedging on Long-Term Oil Contracts," *New York Times* (November 28, 2007); Michelle Maynard, "To Save Fuel, Airlines Find No Speck Too Small," *New York Times* (June 11, 2008); Daniel B. Honigan, "Fred Taylor Leads Southwest Airlines' Customers to New Heights of Customer Satisfaction," *Marketing News* (May 1, 2008): pp. 24–26; Matthew Malone, "In for a Landing," *Conde Nast Portfolio* (August 2008): pp. 91–93; www.southwest.com.

■■■ Case 4 The Excelsior Hotel

A most significant competitive threat was about to affect the four-star Excelsior Hotel. A new luxury hotel was under construction directly across the street. The staff was concerned there might not be enough business to support two upscale hotels in the same market.

Hotel History

The 305-room Excelsior had operated in the city for 10 years. During these years, it had served as the only upscale hotel in the city. It had an excellent location downtown between a 600-space parking deck and the Convention Center. The hotel featured an indoor swimming pool, a Jacuzzi, two restaurants, a cocktail lounge, and several unique amenities. Many of the rooms had balconies overlooking the garden-level dining area and Greenhouse Café. Each floor was accessed by three glass-enclosed elevators. Other major attributes of the hotel were the ice skating rink located under the hotel and tunnel connecting the hotel with the Convention Center.

The Excelsior was managed by a management group but was owned by the Concept Corp., a real estate and investment company. An interview with the general manager of the Excelsior revealed the following:

- *What are your goals for the hotel?* "Locally, for the next year, we would just like to be competitive productwise. Our long-term goal is to be one of the leading hotels in our state."

- *How do you perceive the increasing competitive pressure?* "It has been tremendous. The increase in hotel rooms over the last five years within our competitive market has been unbelievable. The Stouffer will open up on July 1, and a new Sheraton will open up later this year. Radissons are going up left and right. A lot of smaller hotel chains are putting up budget hotels. Right now I would say we are overbuilt until the city gets its convention center expanded so that we can attract larger groups. There is not enough corporate business to go around to supply all of us with a decent occupancy."

- *What actions does the Excelsior plan to take within the increasingly competitive environment?* "To be competitive, you have to have the product. Once again, that's our first step. We want to bring our overall product of service back up to a competitive level, meaning that we have to renovate and make some other adjustments decor-wise—new rooms, new furniture, and some other things. Those are tangible things."

- *Describe the relationship between the management and the hotel owners.* "We are a management company. We don't own a nickel here. Our ownership is another company. They have a little different philosophy on how to make money and to provide quality service to the guests. They don't have the same idea regarding bottom-line profits and quality rendered to the guests. Obviously, you have to realize the relation between profit and quality service to the guest. If you put in "turn-down" service, it is costing you money. If you give your employees benefits, it costs you money. Anything you do other than supplying them with one towel and a clean room costs you money. It means that the profit level between what we feel is obtainable provided that we give the guests great service and what our ownership thinks we should make as a hotel is different. They feel we should make a lot more money."

The general manager was perplexed as to what direction the hotel should take. The building is in need of renovation to maintain its attractiveness and "image." There is pressure from the owners to offer less and make more, which is inconsistent with long-standing image. The biggest threat, though, is coming from the increased competition for the lucrative group business from newer hotels and convention centers. However, the city was beginning to enter a "renaissance" period with the planned expansion of the Convention Center, the completion of the Super Block area, and a push for retail stores and businesses to relocate downtown.

■■■ DISCUSSION QUESTIONS

1. Why should a conflict exist between the philosophies of the hotel Excelsior's management group and its owner, the Concept Corp.?

2. What steps in addition to renovation should the Excelsior be taking to prepare for increased competition?

■■■ Case 5 The Honolulu Armed Services YMCA

The board of management of the Armed Services YMCA of Honolulu, Hawaii, was considering the possibility of converting the top two floors of the building into a commercial hotel. The location of the building within the downtown business area near the state capital seemed perfect to satisfy the lodging needs of budget-minded business travelers plus the military and their dependents, known as the temporary living allowance (TLA) market. Costs involved in operating the building as a YMCA were increasing rapidly, but revenue was not keeping pace. The concept of converting only the top two floors to moderate-priced hotel rooms was to allow the YMCA to continue to operate the traditional areas such as the gym while the conversion process was ongoing. If the rooms on the top two floors proved to be popular, the remaining floors could gradually be converted until the entire building became a moderate-priced hotel.

Description of the Building

Built in 1927, the architectural design of the building was neocolonial, incorporating the mode of Mediterranean culture. It stood five stories high and embodied several outdoor patios or lanais within its structure. Zoning restrictions and the construction of the building prevented the consideration of adding additional stories. The building was built in the form of a rectangular horseshoe and contained approximately 83,000 square feet. It had been solidly constructed of reinforced concrete and showed a few cracks but no major structural problems.

The wooden windowsills and frame suffered from dry rot and termites. It was felt that the tile roof might need to be replaced or repaired substantially in the next few years. The original plumbing remained throughout the building. Part of the wiring had been modernized, but a large portion of the original wiring still remained. Hot water was provided by large boilers, which continued to function but required frequent maintenance. A parking lot in the foreground that could accommodate approximately seventy cars separated the YMCA building from Hotel Street. A privately owned taxi company had leased a portion of this parking lot for its own use. This cluttering aspect coupled with the trees in front of the building created a visibility problem for the premises.

The front section of the first floor facing Hotel Street consisted of a lobby, the front desk, a coffee shop and kitchen, a barbershop, and four office lease spaces. The front desk was a traditional YMCA-type semienclosed area. It was situated near the elevator and allowed the desk clerk good visibility of most of the activity in the ground-floor lobby area. The lobby was an open tiled area; it did not contain any traditional lobby furniture. Adjacent to it was a small area that contained beverage-dispensing machines.

Upon entering the lobby from the outside, the coffee shop was located to the left. It offered a traditional breakfast and lunch menu, and customer traffic was slow. Approximately half the seating area had been sectioned off by means of a rope with a closed sign attached to discourage patrons from sitting in the back area. The coffee shop offered counter and booth service and was patronized primarily by YMCA residents and by some nearby office workers who occasionally dropped in for coffee. The kitchen area was old and in need of remodeling.

The barbershop was a conventional men's barbershop and was distinguishable by a small, traditional, red-and-white-striped barber pole. About 90 percent of the customers were walk-ins. Several areas on the first floor had been converted to office space and leased out to tenants. This included the public men's room on the first floor next to the barbershop. The back section of the first floor included facilities traditionally associated with a "Y": a large gymnasium (4,816 square feet), two saunas, an exercise room, a swimming pool, men's and women's locker rooms, and shower areas. The entire second floor had been converted into offices, including space for the YMCA offices or to office space. The second floor also contained the original ceramic-like flooring and was quite impressive. The remaining area on the second floor served as airspace above the first-floor gymnasium with a running track around the edge.

The third floor consisted of two wings and a front section facing Hotel Street. The front section was utilized as a day-care center and living quarters for welfare mothers and was deliberately partitioned to prevent passage by male residents. The east wing included a recreational room with pinball machines, a TV viewing area, a lounge, program room, and laundry facilities, along with office space for the resident manager, executive director, and staff. The west wing was devoted to thirty-two individual rooms for residents with a communal shower and toilet area.

The fourth and fifth floors also consisted of two wings connected by the front section. This rectangular horseshoe arrangement was typical of buildings built in that era. The center portion of the building above the ground-floor swimming pool was open air. The entire space on the fourth and fifth floors was devoted to individual rooms with a communal shower–toilet area in each wing. Altogether, the building contained 244 individual units for residents: 32 on the third floor, 93 on the fourth, and 119 on the fifth. These were approximately 8 by 10 feet in dimension (or 75 square feet) and did not offer air conditioning, running water, or toilet facilities. During the summer months, the top floors were rather uncomfortable. Rental rates were $120 a week or $360 per month.

Approximately 99 percent of all persons utilizing the Physical Fitness Center, including the swimming pool and gym, were civilians. Only 30 percent of the YMCA residents were members of the military. The remaining resident mix consisted of a variety of transients, including young, low-budget backpacker tourists; older seasonal tourists whose primary source of income was Social Security; single men who were seeking employment in Hawaii; and others who exhibited drug- or alcohol-related problems. A few residents remained for months at a time, but most remained for less than two weeks.

The mix of tenants and residents in the building necessitated the employment of a full-time security officer and the use of surveillance TV cameras at critical spots within the building, such as doors leading to the female quarters. Unfortunately, the problems faced by many of the residents had led to several suicides or attempted suicides in the past years, including cases where residents leaped from their rooms.

Description of the Armed Services YMCA Organization

The Armed Services YMCA, a nonprofit organization, served as a department of the National Board of YMCAs throughout the United States. Its central mission was viewed as providing temporary lodging, recreation, and education for members of the U.S. military and their dependents. Special attention was directed to the military of junior ranks; nevertheless, all ranks were welcome. In total there were twenty-three branches of the Armed Services YMCA throughout the United States, with headquarters in New York City. There were also two branches in the Canal Zone and one branch located in Scotland.

The Honolulu Armed Services YMCA was the only branch established in Hawaii. There were three other YMCAs in Honolulu, but none of these belonged to the Armed Services Department, nor did they share the same stated objectives. Although the primary mission of the Armed Services "Y" was to meet the needs of the military, in recent years it had taken on a broader responsibility of serving the community at large, as long as those activities did not interfere with the central mission of serving the military.

■■■ DISCUSSION QUESTIONS

1. What do you think of the concept of converting the top two floors of the YMCA to a budget hotel and then gradually converting the rest?

2. Discuss the client mix that evolved in the YMCA and what effect this will have on any plans for hotel conversion.

3. Discuss possible strategic options for the YMCA.

4. Will conversion of the current building assist the Honolulu Armed Services YMCA to meet its mission?

■■■ Case 6 JetBlue: Delighting Customers Through Happy Jetting

In 2007, JetBlue was a thriving young airline with a strong reputation for outstanding service. In fact, the low-fare airline referred to itself as a customer service company that just happened to fly planes. But on Valentine's Day 2007, JetBlue was hit by the perfect storm—literally—of events that led to an operational meltdown. One of the most severe storms of the decade covered JetBlue's main hub at New York's John F. Kennedy International Airport with a thick layer of snow and ice. Small JetBlue did not have the infrastructure to deal with such a crisis. The severity of the storm, coupled with a series of poor management decisions, left JetBlue passengers stranded in planes on the runway for up to 11 hours. Worse still, the ripple effect of the storm created major JetBlue flight disruptions for six more days.

Understandably, customers were livid. JetBlue's efforts to clean up the mess following the six-day Valentine's Day nightmare cost over $30 million dollars in overtime, flight refunds, vouchers for future travel, and other expenses. But the blow to the company's previously stellar customer-service reputation stung far more than the financial fallout. JetBlue became the butt of jokes by late night talk show hosts. Some industry observers even predicted that this would be the end of the seven-year-old airline.

But just three years later, the company is not only still flying, it is growing, profitable, and hotter than ever. During the recent economic downturn, even as most competing airlines were cutting routes, retiring aircraft, laying off employees, and losing money, JetBlue was adding planes, expanding into new cities, hiring thousands of new employees, and turning profits. Even more, JetBlue's customers adore the airline. For the fifth consecutive year (even including 2007), JetBlue has had the highest J.D. Power and Associates customer satisfaction score for the entire airline industry. Not only did JetBlue recover quickly from the Valentine's Day hiccup, it's now stronger than ever.

Truly Customer Focused

What's the secret to JetBlue's success? Quite simply, it's an obsession with making sure that every customer experience lives up to the company slogan, "Happy Jetting." Lots of companies say they focus on customers. But at JetBlue, customer well-being is ingrained in the culture.

From the beginning, JetBlue set out to provide features that would delight customers. For example, most air travelers expect to be squashed when flying coach. But JetBlue has configured its seats with three more inches of legroom than the average airline seat. That may not sound like much. But those three inches allow six-foot three-inch Arianne Cohen, author of *The Tall Book: A Celebration of Life from on High,* to stretch out and even cross her legs. If that's not enough, for as little as $10 per flight, travelers can reserve one of JetBlue's "Even More Legroom" seats, which offer even more space and a flatter recline position. Add the fact that every JetBlue seat is well padded and covered in leather, and you already have an air travel experience that rivals first-class accommodations (something JetBlue doesn't offer).

Food and beverage is another perk that JetBlue customers enjoy. The airline doesn't serve meals, but it offers the best selection of free beverages and snacks to be found at 30,000 feet. In addition to the standard soft drinks, juices, and salty snacks, JetBlue flyers enjoy Terra Blues chips, Immaculate Baking's Chocobillys cookies, and Dunkin' Donuts coffee. But it isn't just the selection; it's the fact that customers don't feel like they have to beg for a nibble. One customer describes snacking on JetBlue as an "open bar for snacks. They are constantly walking around offering it. I never feel thirsty. I never feel hungry. It's not 'Here, have a little sip,' and 'Good-bye, that's all you get.' "

Airlines often can't control flight delays, especially at busy airports like JFK. So JetBlue wants to be sure that customers will be entertained even in the event of a delay. That's why every seat has its own LCD entertainment system. Customers can watch any of 36 channels on DirectTV or listen to 100+ channels on Sirius XM Radio, free of charge. If that isn't enough, six bucks will buy a movie or your favorite television show. JetBlue rounds out the amenities with free Wi-Fi in terminals and free sending and receiving of e-mails and instant messages in the air.

Even JetBlue's main terminal, the new state-of-the-art T-5 terminal at JFK, is not the usual airline experience. With more security lanes than any terminal in the United States, travelers scurry right through. High end dining (tapas, lobster tempura, and Kobe sliders, just to name a few options) can be found among the terminal's twenty-two restaurants. And its twenty-five retail stores are characteristic of the latest mall offerings. A children's play zone, comfortable lounge areas, work spaces, and piped in music from Sirius XM Radio make travelers hesitant to leave.

More Than Amenities

Although the tangible amenities that JetBlue offers are likely to delight most travelers, CEO David Barger recognizes that these things are not nearly enough to provide a sustainable competitive advantage. "The hard product—airplanes, leather seats, satellite TVs, bricks and mortar—as long as you have a checkbook, they can be replicated," Barger tells a group of new hires in training. "It's the culture that can't be replicated. It's how we treat each other. Do we trust each other? Can we push back on each other? The human side of the equation is the most important part of what we're doing."

It's that culture that gives JetBlue customer service unlike that of any other airline. Taking care of customers starts as early as a customer's first encounter with a JetBlue call center. Many callers feel like they are talking to the lady next door. That's because, in all likelihood, they are. JetBlue's founder pioneered a reservation system that employs part-time reps working from home. Mary Driffill is one of 700 at-home reservations agents in Salt Lake City alone. She logs on to her computer and receives calls in her four-year-old daughter's bedroom, under the watchful eye of Raggedy Ann, Potbelly Bear, and Chewy, the family Pomeranian-Chihuahua mix. "It's the best job I've ever had," says Driffill. "Every day I talk to people who love the company as much as I do. That reminds me I'm part of this."

JetBlue employees are well acquainted with the company's core values: safety, integrity, caring, passion, and fun. If that sounds like an awful lot of warm fuzzies, it's intentional. But JetBlue hires the types of employees that fit these values. The values then provide the basis for what Robin Hayes, JetBlue's chief commercial officer, calls the company's S.O.C.I.A.L. currency program. In JetBlue's words:

> *Standing for something.* JetBlue was formed with the idea of bringing humanity back to travel, and our engagement with our customers is central to that mission.
>
> *Operationalizing the brand.* Whether it be in the airport, on the planes, on the phones, or online, the connection with our customers is a key factor in how we do business.
>
> *Conversing with customers, broadly.* To be properly in touch with the community, it requires the ability to understand and react to the collective conversation that occurs.
>
> *Involving, immersing employees.* Social media involvement requires understanding and involvement from all aspects and departments of the company.
>
> *Advocating the brand.* For JetBlue, we understand the ability to market to a social community is dependent on our customers' willingness to hear and spread those marketing messages.
>
> *Listening.* Waiving the carry-on bike fee . . . shows we quickly identify and adapt new policies based on feedback we receive through social media channels. It demonstrates our ability to listen and react holistically.

When you Love your Customers, They Love you Back

Customers who spread positive word of mouth are called many names—true friends, angels, apostles, evangelists. The religious overtones of such labels come from the idea that loyal customers are like true believers who share the good word like a missionary would. JetBlue has an unusually high ratio of such customers. Most airline customers are loyal because they have frequent flyer points. If not for those points, most couldn't care less with whom they fly. For most, flying is a generally unpleasant experience regardless of who operates the plane.

However, JetBlue customers are so enthralled with what the airline has to offer that they look forward to flying. And they want to keep in touch with the brand even when they aren't flying. JetBlue has 1.1 million followers on Twitter, more than any other company except Whole Foods Market and Zappos.com, two other customer service legends. Twitter even features JetBlue as a case study on smart corporate twittering. More broadly, by the metric of social currency (a fancy term for networks of customers spreading by word of mouth), JetBlue is the strongest U.S. brand, outperforming even Apple.

JetBlue's strong word of mouth has been fueled by the company's ability to delight customers. People love to talk about JetBlue because the experience is so unexpected. Most airline travel has a particular pattern: small seats, bad entertainment, and little (if any) food. JetBlue breaks this pattern. Leather seats, your own entertainment system with dozens of channels, and at least some choice of food. People can't stop talking about the experience because they have to express their surprise, especially given the "value" price. They are so used to airline travel being poor, late, or uncomfortable these days that cases where a company seems to care and provide good service seems noteworthy. Satisfaction itself is unexpected.

In 10 short years, JetBlue has proven that an airline can deliver low fares, excellent service, and steady profits. It has shown that even in the airline business, a powerful brand can be built. Few other airlines have been able to write this story. If you're thinking Southwest Airlines, you'd be on target. In fact, JetBlue's founders modeled the airline after Southwest. JetBlue has often been called, "the Southwest of the Northeast." JetBlue's onboard crews even greet customers onboard with jokes, songs, and humorous versions of the safety routine, something Southwest has been known for since the 1970s. But where Southwest has made customers happy with no frills, JetBlue is arguably doing it all, including the frills.

Until last year, Southwest and JetBlue steered clear of each other. But then both airlines added a Boston-Baltimore route. Boston is a JetBlue stronghold; Baltimore is Southwest's biggest market. But with JetBlue's younger workforce and newer, more fuel-efficient planes, its cost per available seat mile is 8.88 cents, whereas it's 9.76 cents for Southwest. That has allowed JetBlue to do something that no other airline has done to Southwest; undercut it on price with $39 tickets that are $20 cheaper than Southwest's lowest fare. It's not clear yet how the battle of the low-fare, high-service airlines will play out. But it may well turn out that as JetBlue and Southwest cross paths on more routes, the losers will be the other airlines.

■■■ DISCUSSION QUESTIONS

Chapter 1

1. Give examples of needs, wants, and demands that JetBlue customers demonstrate, differentiating these three concepts. What are the implications of each for JetBlue's practices?

2. Describe in detail all the facets of JetBlue's product. What is being exchanged in a JetBlue transaction?

3. What value does JetBlue create for its customers?

4. Is JetBlue likely to continue being successful in building customer relationships? Why or why not?

Chapter 2

1. Explain how JetBlue has created a service culture.

2. Do you think JetBlue would be a good company to work for? Explain your answer.

Sources: Stuart Elliott, "JetBlue Asks Its Fliers to Keep Spreading the Word," *New York Times* (May 10, 2010): p. B7; Marc Gunther, "Nothing Blue about JetBlue," *Fortune* (September 14, 2009): p. 114; Chuck Salter, "Calling JetBlue," *Fast Company* (May 1, 2004), accessed at www. fastcompany.com/magazine/82/jetblue_agents.html; Kevin Randall, "Red, Hot, and Blue: The Hottest American Brand Is Not Apple," *Fast Company* (June 3, 2010), accessed at www .fastcompany.com/1656066/apple-jetblue-social-currency-twitter.

∎∎∎ Case 7 Pepsi: Can a Soda Really Make the World a Better Place?

This year, PepsiCo did something that shocked the advertising world. After 23 straight years of running ads for its flagship brand on the Super Bowl, it announced that the number-two soft drink maker would be absent from the Big Game. But in the weeks leading up to Super Bowl XLIV, Pepsi was still the second-most discussed advertiser associated with the event. It wasn't so much what Pepsi wasn't doing that created such a stir as much as what it was doing.

Rather than continuing with the same old messages of the past, focusing on the youthful nature of the Pepsi Generation, and using the same old mass-media channels, Pepsi is taking a major gamble by breaking new ground with its advertising program. Its latest campaign, called Pepsi Refresh, represents a major departure from its old promotion efforts in two ways: (1) The message centers on a theme of social responsibility and (2) the message is being delivered with a fat dose of social media.

At the center of the campaign is the Pepsi Refresh Project. PepsiCo has committed to award $20 million in grants ranging from $5,000 to $250,000 to organizations and individuals with ideas that will make the world a better place. The refresheverything.com Web site greets visitors with the headline, "What do you care about?" PepsiCo accepts up to 1,000 proposals each month in each of six different areas: health, arts and culture, food and shelter, the planet, neighborhoods, and education. Then crowd-sourcing takes over, as consumers vote for their favorites. Pepsi awards the grants each month. One-third of the way through its one-year run, the company had funded more than 100 projects, giving approximately $5 million back to local communities. The company stated that the project was right on target to award the full $20 million by the end of the yearlong effort.

Integrating Digital Throughout the Promotional Mix

The Pepsi Refresh campaign has been a groundbreaking effort, in part because of its heavy use of social media. PepsiCo is capitalizing on a growing trend in a way that no other major brand has done so far. The company is quick to point out that Pepsi Refresh is not a social media add-on like almost others, where an ad simply directs people to a Web site for reasons that may or may not be relevant to the message. Nor is it a social media campaign as such, where the entire campaign takes place through social media. Rather, social media are the glue that holds together a truly integrated marketing communications effort. "It's not about digital as its own channel anymore," says Bonin Bough, director of digital and social media for PepsiCo. "It's how do we infuse digital across all of our marketing programs?"

For starters, although PepsiCo bypassed the Super Bowl, it is not ditching broadcast media. To the contrary, Pepsi is running spot ads on the main networks as well as thirty different cable channels. The ads initially informed people about the Pepsi Refresh campaign, directing them to the refresheverything.com site. But shortly after the first grants were awarded, ads began highlighting projects that had been funded. Traditional media efforts extend to ten print publications as well. And PR plays a role through agreements such as the one with NBC Universal for paid pitches on the "Today" show.

But this campaign underscores a shift in how PepsiCo is spending its advertising dollars. According to CEO Indra Nooyi, the world's number-two soft drink seller is shifting as much as one-third of its marketing budget to interactive and social media. This move involves not only the Pepsi brand but also Mountain Dew, Doritos, Sobe, and PepsiCo's other brands. Certainly, PepsiCo is not alone in the trend toward digital and social media marketing. But analysts point out that its approach, moving away from high-profile spots in favor of heavy spending on a digitally focused social responsibility campaign, is both compelling and risky. "I applaud Pepsi for embracing social media and technology," said Marc Lucas, an advertising executive. "On the flip side, I think it's very bold to not be in a place where you know you're going to have an audience."

The refresheverything.com Web site is just one component of the brand's on-line efforts. PepsiCo is spreading the message through the big networks, such as Facebook and Twitter, and even partnering with them for advertising opportunities. For example, Pepsi Refresh held the lead ad position on Facebook during the Super Bowl. Pepsi has also partnered with Hulu to sponsor its first original series, the reality show *If I Can Dream.* "It amplifies an advertising campaign by making it something people talk about, more of a social conversation," said Jean-Paul Colaco, senior vice president for advertising at Hulu. PepsiCo even partnered with *Spin* magazine, music festival South by Southwest and two Indie bands in a Web-based contest where music lovers could vote for their favorite. Metric beat out Broken Social Scene for a $ 100,000 grant that it gave to the Women's Funding Network.

As another component of the integrated campaign, the company has not shied away from using celebrity endorsers. Through clever network spot ads that place celebrities inside a life-sized, three-dimensional laptop made of tag board, Kevin Bacon appeals to people to vote for his cause, SixDegrees.org. He is quick to point out that this has nothing to do with the cult trivia game, Six Degrees of Kevin Bacon. Rather, he proposes using a $250,000 grant to hand out "good cards" that people can use to donate to any of more than a million different charities. But Bacon goes on to explain that the power of Six Degrees comes from the social networks of good card recipients. They buy more good cards and pass them on to others, and as social networking works its magic, that $250,000 grows into millions.

Among various other celebrities, Pepsi has also recruited Demi Moore; NFL players Mark Sanchez, DeMarcus Ware, and Drew Brees; and NASCAR veterans Jeff Gordon, Dale Earnhardt Jr., and Jimmie Johnson to apply for grants and act as spokespersons for the project. These celebrities are vying for votes to award grants to such organizations as the Girls Education and Mentoring Service, the American Cancer Society, and the Brain Aneurysm Foundation.

PepsiCo is also getting its message out to consumers at the point of purchase. Cans, bottles, and multipacks feature updated graphics that minimize an all low-ercase Pepsi logo written vertically and highlights a new Pepsi brand mark: a large circle with swaths of red, white, and blue. That symbol replaces any "o"in Pepsi's packaging and promotional materials. Thus, both "Do Some Good" and "Doing Good 101" each carry four of the new Pepsi circles. To draw people into retailer outlets to see the point-of-purchase (POP) materials and hopefully buy its soft drinks, Pepsi has partnered with foursquare, the social network that connects people through GPS in real time. Foursquare members are directed to Pepsi retailers and given offers as an incentive for them to visit.

Doing Well by Doing Good

Despite the growth of cause-related marketing, PepsiCo's effort is perhaps the first example of a major brand making social responsibility the main theme of its campaign, rather than an add-on. This does not downplay the efforts of companies like Target, which has given $273 million to local schools since 1997 through its Red Card program. But PepsiCo's effort is built around a theme that drives the concept of "doing good" as much as it drives the brand. Coca-Cola's response to Pepsi Refresh, donating a dollar to Boys and Girls Clubs of America each time a visitor to Coke's Facebook page shares a virtual Coke gift, illustrates how most advertiser's cause-related marketing efforts are peripheral to other advertising activities.

Nooyi brings the centrality of Pepsi's socially responsible message into perspective. The Pepsi Refresh Project is a platform, but at the end of the day, what we are doing is awarding the grants, we are enabling connections. It's having a catalytic effect on people who are actually embracing these organizations. So, we're not only benefiting the person who received the grant, we're benefiting the people who are the recipients of the outcome of that idea. With schools, for instance, it's not just one classroom that's benefited. It's all the kids who will be able to go to that classroom. And there have been people who have worked so hard to get this money that others have stepped in and matched the money they receive.

Projects funded thus far are too numerous to list. But they include more than high-profile efforts like the celebrity campaigns. Many awards are being given to everyday people just trying to improve their own little corners of the world. Calvin Cannon received $5,000 for Clothe the N.A.K.E.D. Prom Date. He enabled low-income high school students in Shelbyville, Tennessee, to attend their senior prom in style by paying for their tuxedo rentals for the prom. Jeanne Acutanza from Kirkland, Washington, got $5,000 for her children's school so that it could manage a sustainable garden and give the harvest to local food banks. And the Associates of Redlands Bowl received $25,000 to support performing arts in the community of Redlands, California. "I'm proud of every idea we're supporting, but it's the simplicity of [these ideas that is] so innovative," says Nooyi. "You would never have thought that one simple thing could bring about a big change in the community."

In Search of the Holy Grail

All this cutting-edge promotion and the effort to change the world are wonderful. But at the end of the day, PepsiCo has to sell soft drinks. After all, it is the fiftieth largest publicly held corporation in the *Fortune* 500. Pepsi is also the 23rd most valuable brand in the world according to Interbrand. If this experiment fails to support sales of its core brand, PepsiCo will no doubt abandon its innovative promotion efforts and return to its old ways. As one social marketer states, "This is big, new, getting a lot of attention. It's impactful; it's innovative. What the industry is talking about now is, is this a gamble that was worth taking, in terms of a lift in sales? That's the holy grail."

But PepsiCo remains extremely optimistic. In the first few months of the campaign, the number of Facebook fans doubled. The company formerly got a Twitter tweet every five minutes or so. Now, it receives more tweets per minute than a person can read. But just what is the value of a Facebook or a Twitter fan? Although many advocates of social networking say questions like that are irrelevant, budget-strapped chief marketing officers want to see return on investment. That's why Bough and his team have developed a scorecard that ties different elements of the Pepsi Refresh campaign back to the health of the brand. Using standard research methods, PepsiCo will be measuring whether or not this campaign merits the expense.

Pass or fail, many observers inside and outside PepsiCo will learn much from this first-of-its-kind social media and social responsibility campaign. Ana Maria Irazabal, director of marketing for PepsiCo, wants this campaign to become the model of the future. "We want people to be aware that every time you drink a Pepsi you are actually supporting the Pepsi Refresh Project and ideas that are going to move this country forward. We may be the first to do something like this, but hopefully, we're not the last."

■■■ QUESTIONS FOR DISCUSSION

1. Consider PepsiCo's advertising throughout its history. (For a list of Pepsi slogans over the years, visit http://en.wikipedia.org/wiki/Pepsi#Slogans.) Identify as many commonalities as possible across its various ad campaigns. How is this campaign consistent with PepsiCo's brand image?

2. List all the promotional mix elements used in the Pepsi Refresh campaign. What grade would you give PepsiCo on integrating these elements into an integration marketing communications campaign?

3. Describe PepsiCo's target audience. Is the Pepsi Refresh campaign consistent with that audience?

4. As completely as possible, analyze the campaign according to the steps listed in the chapter for developing effective marketing communication.

5. Will the Pepsi Refresh campaign be successful? Why or why not?

Sources: Natalie Zmuda, "Pass or Fail, Pepsi's Refresh Will Be Case for Marketing Textbooks," *Advertising Age* (February 8, 2010): p. 1; Stuart Elliott, "Pepsi Invites the Public to Do Good," *New York Times* (January 31, 2010): p. B6; Elaine Wong, "Pepsi Community Effort Finds Fans on Social Nets," *Brandweek* (June 8, 2010), accessed at www.brandweek.com.

■■■ Case 8 Enterprise Rent-A-Car: Measuring Service Quality

Surveying Customers

Kevin Kirkman wheeled his shiny blue BMW coupe into his driveway, put the gearshift into park, set the parking brake, and got out to check his mailbox as he did every day when he returned home. As he flipped through the deluge of catalogs and credit card offers, he noticed a letter from Enterprise Rent-A-Car. He wondered why Enterprise would be writing him.

The Wreck

Then he remembered. Earlier that month, Kevin had been involved in a wreck. As he was driving to work one rainy morning, another car had been unable to stop on the slick pavement and had plowed into his car as he waited at a stoplight. Thankfully, neither he nor the other driver was hurt, but both cars had sustained considerable damage. In fact, he was not able to drive his car.

Kevin had used his cell phone to call the police, and while he was waiting for the officers to come, he had called his auto insurance agent. The agent had assured Kevin that his policy included coverage to pay for a rental car while he was having his car repaired. He told Kevin to have the car towed to a nearby auto repair shop and gave him the telephone number for the Enterprise Rent-A-Car office that served his area. The agent noted that his company recommended using Enterprise for replacement rentals and that Kevin's policy would cover up to $20 per day of the rental fee.

Once Kevin had checked his car in at the body shop and made the necessary arrangements, he telephoned the Enterprise office. Within 10 minutes, an Enterprise employee had driven to the repair shop and picked him up. They drove back to the Enterprise office, where Kevin completed the paperwork and rented a Ford Taurus. He drove the rental car for 12 days before the repair shop completed work on his car.

"Don't know why Enterprise would be writing me," Kevin thought. "The insurance company paid the $20 per day, and I paid the extra because the Taurus cost more than that. Wonder what the problem could be?"

Tracking Satisfaction

Kevin tossed the mail on the passenger's seat and drove up the driveway. Once inside his house, he opened the Enterprise letter to find that it was a survey to determine how satisfied he was with his rental. The survey itself was only one page long and consisted of thirteen questions (see Exhibit 1).

Enterprise's executives believed that the company had become the largest rent-a-car company in the United States (in terms of number of cars, rental locations, and revenue) because of its laser-like focus on customer satisfaction and because of its concentration on serving the home-city replacement market. It aimed to serve customers like Kevin who were involved in wrecks and suddenly found themselves without a car. While the more well-known companies like Hertz and Avis battled for business in the cutthroat airport market, Enterprise quietly built its business by cultivating insurance agents and body-shop managers as referral agents so that when one of their clients or customers needed a replacement vehicle, they would recommend Enterprise. Although such replacement rentals accounted for about 80 percent of the company's business, it also served the discretionary market

SERVICE QUALITY SURVEY

Please mark the box that best reflects your response to each question.

	Completely Satisfied	Somewhat Satisfied	Neither Satisfied Nor Dissatisfied	Somewhat Dissatisfied	Completely Dissatisfied
1. Overall, how satisfied were you with your recent car rental from Enterprise on January 1, 2000?	☐	☐	☐	☐	☐

2. What, if anything, could Enterprise have done better? (*Please be specific*) _____

_____

3a. Did you experience any problems during the rental process?	Yes ☐ No ☐	3b. If you mentioned any problems to Enterprise, did they resolve them to your satisfaction?	Yes ☐ No ☐ Did not mention ☐

	Excellent	Good	Fair	Poor	N/A
4. If you personally called Enterprise to reserve a vehicle, how would you rate the telephone reservation process?	☐	☐	☐	☐	☐

	Both at start and end of rental	Just at start of rental	Just at end of rental	Neither time
5. Did you go to the Enterprise office	☐	☐	☐	☐
6. Did an Enterprise employee give you a ride to help with your transportation needs	☐	☐	☐	☐

7. After you arrived at the Enterprise office, how long did it take you to:	Less than 5 minutes	5–10 minutes	11–15 minutes	16–20 minutes	21–30 minutes	More than 30 minutes	N/A
♦ pick up your rental car?	☐	☐	☐	☐	☐	☐	☐
♦ return your rental car?	☐	☐	☐	☐	☐	☐	☐

8. How would you rate the ...	Excellent	Good	Fair	Poor	N/A
♦ timeliness with which you were either picked up at the start of the rental or dropped off afterwards?	☐	☐	☐	☐	☐
♦ timeliness with which the rental car was either brought to your location and left with you or picked up from your location afterwards?	☐	☐	☐	☐	☐
♦ Enterprise employee who handled your paperwork ...					
at the START of the rental?	☐	☐	☐	☐	☐
at the END of the rental?	☐	☐	☐	☐	☐
♦ mechanical condition of the car?	☐	☐	☐	☐	☐
♦ cleanliness of the car interior/exterior?	☐	☐	☐	☐	☐

	Yes	No	N/A
9. If you asked for a specific type or size of vehicle, was Enterprise able to meet your needs?	☐	☐	☐

10. For what reason did you rent this car?	Car repairs due to accident	All other car repairs/ maintenance	Car was stolen	Business	Leisure/ vacation	Some other reason
	☐	☐	☐	☐	☐	☐

11. The next time you need to pick up a rental car in the city or area in which you live, how likely are you to call Enterprise?	Definitely will call	Probably will call	Might or might not call	Probably will not call	Definitely will not call
	☐	☐	☐	☐	☐

12. Approximately how many times in total have you rented from Enterprise (including this rental)?	Once—this was first time	2 times	3–5 times	6–10 times	11 or more times
	☐	☐	☐	☐	☐

13. Considering <u>all rental companies</u>, approximately how many times <u>within the past year</u> have you rented a car in the city or area in which you live (including this rental)?	0 times	1 time	2 times	3–5 times	6–10 times	11 or more times
	☐	☐	☐	☐	☐	☐

Exhibit 1

(leisure/vacation rentals), and the business market (renting cars to businesses for their short-term needs). It had also begun to provide on-site and off-site service at some airports.

Throughout its history, Enterprise had followed founder Jack Taylor's advice. Taylor believed that if the company took care of its customers and employees first, profits would follow. So the company was careful to track customer satisfaction.

About one in twenty randomly selected customers received a letter like Kevin's. An independent company mailed the letter and a postage-paid return envelope to the selected customers. Customers who completed the survey used the envelope to return it to the independent company. That company compiled the results and provided them to Enterprise.

Continuous Improvement

Meanwhile, back at Enterprise's St. Louis headquarters, the company's top managers were interested in taking the next steps in their customer satisfaction program. Enterprise had used the percentage of customers who were completely satisfied to develop its Enterprise Service Quality index (ESQi). It used the survey results to calculate an overall average ESQi score for the company and a score for each individual branch. The company's branch managers believed in and supported the process.

However, top management believed that to really "walk the walk" on customer satisfaction, it needed to make the ESQi a key factor in the promotion process. The company wanted to take the ESQi for the branch or branches a manager supervised into consideration when it evaluated that manager for a promotion. Top management believed that such a process would ensure that its managers and all its employees would focus on satisfying Enterprise's customers.

However, the top managers realized they had two problems in taking the next step. First, they wanted a better survey response rate. Although the company got a 25 percent response rate, which was good for this type of survey, it was concerned that it might still be missing important information. Second, it could take up to two months to get results back, and Enterprise believed it needed a process that would get the customer satisfaction information more quickly, at least monthly, so its branch managers could identify and take action on customer service problems quickly and efficiently.

Enterprise's managers wondered how they could improve the customer-satisfaction-tracking process.

■■■ DISCUSSION QUESTIONS

1. Analyze Enterprise's Service Quality Survey (Exhibit 1). What information is it trying to gather?

2. What are its research objectives?

3. What decisions has Enterprise made with regard to primary data collection: research approach, contact method, sampling plan, and research instruments?

Note: Officials at Enterprise Rent-A-Car contributed to and supported the development of this case.

■■■ Case 9 The Hunt Room: Change the Concept or Just the Decor?

The Rolling Hills Country Club is an established club in a major eastern city. Jimmy Johnson, the general manager of the club, had just convened the regular weekly meeting of the executive committee. The first item on the agenda was The Hunt Room.

Hans Krueger, the food and beverage manager, claims that sales have been declining for the last five years. He states the overall concept of the room is excellent. There have been some minor upgrades (replacing the chairs and the carpet), but no major renovation has taken place since 1990. He feels it is time for a major renovation. He claims that the food, service, and pricing are fine, but the atmosphere has grown tired. He claims that the comment cards returned by the guests have been highly favorable. Mr. Krueger has submitted plans for a $500,000 renovation package. His package calls for an updating of the same concept.

Alice Whitaker, the catering manager, claims the concept is no longer viable. She states that patronage of the restaurant has dropped. She says the people who use The Hunt Room may still enjoy it, but a very small percentage of the members use the room. Jimmy Johnson is concerned that if the changes to the room are major he may lose the room's current customers and not be able to replace them with members drawn to the new concept. He is tending to side with Hans, viewing minor changes to the concept as a safe alternative.

The club has three restaurants: The Venetian Room, The Hunt Room, and The Terrace Room. The Venetian Room is the main dining room. It is a light, open room that overlooks the golf course. Its menu is eclectic and includes a selection of European, American, and Asian cuisine. The average check in the Venetian room is $22 for lunch and $45 for dinner. The Hunt Room is the casual dining room. It has rich wood paneling, red leather chairs, and features paintings of hunting scenes on the walls. The Hunt Room's menu features beef, quail, and several seafood items. The average check is $40 for dinner. The Hunt Room closed for lunch in 2007, due to declining lunch sales. The Terrace Room is an informal room with the same menu for lunch and dinner. The menu is similar to one that might be found in a family-oriented restaurant. It is on the ground floor and features a patio that is popular with members using the swimming pool, who want more than the snack bar offers. The average check is $10 for breakfast, $14 for lunch, and $20 for dinner. Dinner business is very slow, except for the summer. In fact, Johnson is thinking of closing this room for dinner.

Referring to The Hunt Room, Alice Whitaker claims the club's members no longer want a heavy beef menu. She has also observed what she feels is a trend: Members are seeking new dining experiences. They want excitement in the menus and would enjoy a room with a casual atmosphere. Additionally, she claims that the restaurant prices have gradually crept up, and the restaurant is no longer considered casual dining. Those guests who want a casual meal usually end up in The Terrace Room or in a local restaurant. Ms. Whitaker feels the local restaurants offer better value for the money.

Mr. Krueger responded by stating that the restaurant offers a much better value than it did when it opened. He claims that beef prices have risen by 140 percent since 2000, but he has absorbed some of these increases and menu prices have only increased by 100 percent. He further stated that he was not in competition with every restaurant in town—the club has prestige and members come here because it is their club. Krueger claims the club gives good value compared with the fine dining restaurants in town.

Jimmy Johnson did not want the discussion to escalate into an argument. He therefore tabled the discussion on The Hunt Room until more information could be obtained. He was also proceeding very carefully. He has only been at the club for two years. He has been able to maintain the status quo of the club but has not made any significant changes. The club's membership wait list has continued its downward trend. The club had an average wait of four years in 2005; today the wait is 18 months. Food and beverage sales have remained flat over the last three years, despite an average menu increase of 4 percent per annum. Jimmy feels he has "stabilized the club," but he has not been able to show increases in sales. He feels the turnaround has come, but he also knows some board members are growing impatient. Thus, he feels a mistake with the new concept for The Hunt Room could cost him his job. He also knows many of the older board members enjoy The Hunt Room.

Another problem with the club is that the membership is aging. Most of the young members are sons or daughters of members. The club does not seem to attract members under forty. This makes it hard for Johnson to make changes because many of the older members do not want change, and the younger members who came to the club with their parents have grown used to it. They seem to like the club the way it is, yet they do not use the food and beverage facilities. Most of the younger members use the golf course and drop their children off at the pool. For the most part, their food and beverage sales are limited to the snack bars at the golf course and swimming pool.

Johnson ponders his options: Do nothing, or try to keep things from declining. He knows preventing further declines is a significant accomplishment. However, he feels the board is looking for increases. If he makes a mistake with The Hunt Room, he will quickly lose his job. If he does nothing, he may be able to hang on for several more years but if he does not turn sales around, eventually he will lose his job.

Note: This is based on a real case; however, the names have been changed.

■■■ DISCUSSION QUESTIONS

1. If you were the general manager, what process would you go through to determine a new concept for The Hunt Room?

2. What information would you seek? Where would you find this information?

3. What makes restaurant concepts grow out of favor? How often should a room be reconcepted?

4. Should club restaurants compete with local restaurants?

5. Brainstorm to come up with possible concepts for The Hunt Room. You should include decor and menu ideas.

■■■ Case 10 The Australian Tourist Commission

The Australian Tourist Commission (ATC) was planning a marketing research study within the United States. The plan had originated in the home office in Melbourne and was sent to regional offices for comment before soliciting bids. These regional offices were located in London, Frankfurt, New York, Los Angeles, Tokyo, and Auckland. Visitor traffic to Australia from the United States had grown at a slower rate than other major market areas. It was apparent that marketing strategies were needed to increase the number of American visitors to Australia. Before developing a new marketing plan, it was felt that a study should be conducted within the United States to identify target markets.

Research Objectives

Objectives had been identified for the study:

1. To identify and quantify groups in the U.S. population with the highest potential for holidaying in Australia.

2. To investigate in detail the factors that determine holiday destination choice among the high-potential groups.

3. To provide information indicating the types of holiday products, taking into account time and cost factors, which would satisfy the holiday needs of the high-potential groups.

4. To investigate the awareness of and preferences for alternative destinations.

5. To provide information to guide publicity agencies as to the type of creative approaches that will appeal to and motivate the high-potential groups.

6. To provide a guide to media patterns that will enable efficient communication to the high-potential groups.

7. To identify the best distribution modes for holiday products aimed at the high-potential groups (e.g., airlines, travel agents, bank travel departments).

8. To investigate the role of the travel trade and its importance in determining holiday destination choice.

9. To determine past and intended future holiday behavior among the high-potential groups and to describe them in socioeconomic terms. Detailed information must be collected on the destinations visited on past trips and the sequence of these visits.

In addition to the objectives, the ATC felt that the study should be designed with the following purposes in mind:

- To enable the development of a comprehensive understanding of the destination selection process—essential if Australia is to be marketed more successfully in the United States.

- To enable the design of products of greatest appeal to the high-potential groups, in terms of cost, length of holiday, preferred standard of accommodation, and domestic transportation.

- To enable Australia to be promoted in a way that will capitalize on its perceived strengths, overcome its perceived weaknesses, and compete more effectively with the strengths and weaknesses of competing long-haul destinations.

- To provide an adequate measurement of the extent of awareness of and interest in various Australian features (e.g., the Barrier Reef, the outback, Sydney Harbor).

- To provide detailed knowledge of the holiday planning process, including the time involved and the sources of information used.

- To enable more efficient communication and distribution of available products to the high-potential groups.

Proposed Methodology

It was the opinion of the ATC that the study should be divided into two stages. The first would be of a "qualitative" nature for the purpose of developing personality and attitudinal questions that would then be used in the second quantitative phase. The general opinion was that face-to-face interviews of 30 to 35 minutes each would be needed for both parts of the study. The use of telephone interviews was considered but rejected because it was feared that they could not provide the depth of answers needed, particularly as "tradeoff" questions were being asked.

Due to the high cost of field research in the United States, it seemed imperative to minimize the sample size. Consequently, a total of a thousand face-to-face interviews during the primary research were considered to be sufficient to provide good precision for estimates from the total sample and from the various subgroups.

The ATC felt that respondents should be selected on the basis of four criteria: (1) past travel experience, (2) future travel intentions, (3) travel desire, and (4) interest in Australia. Those who should be interviewed would include people who had never traveled and had no intention or desire to travel. The term *travel* was defined as long-haul international travel for pleasure purposes, excluding Mexico, Canada, and the Caribbean. In addition, people with immediate family living in Australia were to be excluded.

In the interests of efficiency, it was felt that the sample should overrepresent key markets; hence a screening process was to be used in the interviews. The screening questions were to be administered in sequential fashion, with the first criterion being "past travel experience." The sample structure emphasized those with extensive travel experience, as research indicated that this was a prime market for Australia. The recommended structure was as follows:

- Past travelers: Traveled in the last five years to a long-haul destination for pleasure, with or without a stated intention to travel.
  $N = 600$ broken down as:
  a. At least 200 "experienced travelers"
  b. At least 200 with "stated travel intention"
  c. At least 200 with "interest in Australia"

- Potential travelers: Stated intention to travel in the next three years to a long-haul destination for pleasure, without past travel experience.
  $N = 300$ broken down as:
  a. At least 100 whose primary intended destination is not UK/Europe
  b. At least 200 with "interest in Australia"

- Non/latent travelers:
  a. $N = 100$ comprising persons with no past travel experience and no stated intention to travel, but who:
  b. Have an expressed desire to travel (to a long-haul destination for pleasure purposes)
  c. Express an interest in visiting Australia

Although a random sampling technique was desired, the sample was to be heavily biased toward upper-income groups and not representative of the general mix of the U.S. population. Further sampling restrictions that were felt to be necessary included the following:

1. No interviews from persons who lived in rural areas or small urban centers.

2. Undersampling from the East Coast, with the exception of New York.

3. Undersampling from the southern states, with the exception of Florida.

4. Oversampling from California, Hawaii, New York, Texas, and Florida. The reason for this was an observation of incidence patterns based on data generated from past international visitor surveys by the ATC.

5. Use of a form of multistage sampling in which cities would be the primary unit. For reasons of cost, no more than twenty cities should be selected. This selection of cities should not be "purposive"; however, it should be a random selection of cities within the constraints specified next.

Responses

100	New York
50	Florida
50	Texas
150	California
100	Hawaii
50	New England
150	Eastern North Central
50	Western North Central
100	Other South Atlantic
50	Other Western South Central and Eastern South Central
100	Mountain
50	Pacific
1,000	

One of the reasons for the suggested sampling procedure was that the ATC had data on a large sample from the United States known as Travel Pulse, plus data from an earlier ATC study known as the International Visitors Survey. It was felt that the new study should provide data that would be cross-comparable with the results from the previous studies.

U.S. Arrivals in Australia by Purpose of Visit (%)

Holiday	43
Visiting relatives	15
Business	23
Other	19
Total	100

Age of International Visitors to Australia (%)

0–4	8.3
15–24	14.5
25–34	20.4
35–49	23.5
50–64	22.3
65+	11.0

Occupations of International Visitors to Australia (%)

Professional (excluding teachers)	13.1
Teachers	3.5
Administrative workers	15.9
Clerical and sales workers	9.8
Service workers (including armed services)	3.9
Other	11.1
Inadequately described	5.8
Total (working persons)	63.1
Children (0–14 years)	8.3
Students (15 years and over)	4.8
Home duties	14.8
Independent means, pensioners, etc.	9.0
Total (nonworking persons)	36.9
Total	100.0

Seasonality of foreign Arrivals to Australia Ranked by Number of Monthly Arrivals

	OCEANIA	AFRICA	AMERICAS	ASIA	EUROPE
January	7	6	5	5	3
February	6	4	3	4	12
March	4	2	4	3	10
April	3	8	7	8	4
May	9	9	11	11	5
June	11	12	12	12	9
July	2	7	10	7	6
August	12	11	8	10	2
September	5	10	9	9	8
October	10	5	6	6	7
November	8	1	1	1	11
December	1	3	2	2	1

Top-Ten Origin Countries of Visitors to Australia (%)

New Zealand	28.9
U.K. and Ireland	14.6
United States	13.5
Japan	5.5
Papua New Guinea	4.4
Canada	3.2
Germany	2.7
Netherlands	1.9
Malaysia	1.8
Hong Kong	1.8

Regional Travel Patterns Within the United States (Holiday Visitors per 100,000 Population)

East South Central	3.77	Rhode Island	5.7
Kentucky	3.9	Connecticut	11.8
Tennessee	4.6	Mid Atlantic	10.56
Alabama	3.6	New York	13.3
Mississippi	2.4	New Jersey	10.5
West South Central	9.06	Pennsylvania	6.4
Arkansas	7.4	East North Central	10.57
Louisiana	3.4	Ohio	10.7
Oklahoma	12.6	Indiana	8.6
Texas	10.4	Illinois	13.3
Mountain	29.13	Michigan	9.7
Montana	28.4	Wisconsin	7.3
Idaho	25.1	West North Central	14.67
Wyoming	10.8	Minnesota	18.3
Colorado	28.1	Iowa	14.6
New Mexico	22.8	Missouri	14.5
Arizona	26.2	North Dakota	8.7
Utah	18.6	South Dakota	13.4
Nevada	54.8	Nebraska	10.9
Pacific	43.91	Kansas	13.5
Washington	33.0	South Atlantic	11.12
Oregon	29.9	Delaware	6.6
California	42.5	Maryland	10.0
Alaska	88.7	District of Columbia	52.0
Hawaii	148.5	Virginia	7.3
New England	9.06	West Virginia	3.1
Maine	5.4	North Carolina	4.2
New Hampshire	2.4	South Carolina	4.8
Vermont	8.1	Georgia	5.5
Massachusetts	9.7	Florida	23.7

■■■ DISCUSSION QUESTIONS

1. What is your opinion of the research objectives and purposes for the study?
2. What is your opinion of the proposed methodology?
3. Why do you suppose that travel to Australia from the United States was lower than desired? In answering this question, consider the cost of travel, time required, and other factors.
4. In your opinion, will information from the survey permit the ATC to address the issues raised in Question 3?

■■■ Case 11 Mayo Clinic

Mayo Clinic is the first and largest integrated not-for-profit medical group practice in the world. William and Charles Mayo founded the clinic over 100 years ago as a small outpatient facility and pioneered the concept of a medical group practice—a model that is widely used today.

Mayo Clinic provides exceptional medical care and leads the United States in many specialties such as cancer, heart disease, respiratory disorders, and urology. It consistently ranks at the top of *U.S. News & World Report's* Best Hospitals list and enjoys 85 percent brand recognition among U.S. adults. It has reached this level of success by taking a different approach from most clinics and hospitals and putting a relentless focus on the patient's experience. The clinic's two interrelated core values trace back to its founders and are at the heart of all the organization does: placing the patient's interests above all others and practicing teamwork.

Every aspect of the patient's experience is considered at Mayo Clinic's three campuses in Rochester (MN), Scottsdale (AZ), and Jacksonville (FL). The moment a patient walks into one of Mayo Clinic's facilities, he or she feels the difference. New patients are welcomed by professional greeters who walk them through the administrative processes. Returning patients are greeted by name and with a warm smile. The buildings have been designed so that, in the words of the architect of one, "patients feel a little better before they see their doctors." The twenty-one-story Gonda Building in Rochester has spectacular wide-open spaces with the capability of adding ten more floors. Fine art hangs on the walls, and doctor's offices are designed to feel cozy and comforting rather than sterile and impersonal.

The lobby of the Mayo Clinic hospital in Scottsdale has an indoor waterfall and a wall of windows overlooking mountains. In pediatric exam rooms, resuscitation equipment is hidden behind a large cheery picture. Hospital rooms feature microwave ovens and chairs that really do convert to beds because, as one staff member explained, "People don't come to the hospital alone." The newest emergency medical helicopter was customized to incorporate high-tech medical equipment and is one of the most advanced aircraft in the world.

The other significant difference in serving patients is Mayo Clinic's concept of teamwork. A patient can come to Mayo Clinic with or without a physician's referral. At that time, the patient's team is assembled, which can include the primary physician, surgeons, radiation oncologists, radiologists, nurses, residents, or other specialists with the appropriate skill, experience, and knowledge.

Teams of medical professionals work together to diagnose patients' medical problems, including debating test results for hours to determine the most accurate diagnosis and best treatments. Once a team consensus has been reached, the leader meets with the patient and discusses his or her options. Throughout the process, patients are encouraged to take part in the discussion. If surgery is necessary, the procedure is often scheduled to take place within 24 hours, a dramatic difference from the long wait patients experience at many hospitals. Mayo Clinic's doctors understand that those who seek their care want action as soon as possible.

Mayo's doctors are put on salary instead of being paid by the number of patients seen or tests ordered. As a result, patients receive more individualized attention and care, and physicians work together instead of against each other. As one pediatrician at Mayo explained, "We're very comfortable with calling colleagues for what I call 'curbside consulting.' I don't have to make a decision about splitting a fee or owing someone something. It's never a case of quid pro quo."

Mayo Clinic is a not-for-profit, so all its operating income is invested back into the clinic's research and education programs. Breakthrough research is quickly implemented into the quality care of the patients. Mayo Clinic offers educational programs through its five schools, and many of its physicians come up through these programs with Mayo's philosophies engrained in their heads, including Mayo's motto: "The best interest of the patient is the only interest to be considered."

President Obama often cites Mayo Clinic as a key example in health-care reform. Mayo Clinic has been recognized by third parties for decades for its independent thinking, outstanding service and performance, and core focus on patient care and satisfaction.

■■■ QUESTIONS

1. Explain why Mayo Clinic is so good at customer service. Why has it been so successful practicing medicine differently from other hospitals?

2. How has the Mayo Clinic used tangible elements of the service product to enhance its service delivery?

Sources: Avery Comarow, "Americas Best Hospitals," *U.S. News & World Report* (July 15, 2009); Chen May Yee, "Mayo Clinic Reports 2007 Revenue Grew 10%," *Star Tribune* (March 17, 2008); Leonard L. Berry and Kent D. Seltman, *Management Lessons from Mayo Clinic* (New York; McGraw-Hill, 2008); Leonard L. Berry, "Leadership Lessons from Mayo Clinic," *Organizational Dynamics* 33 (August 2004): 228–42; Leonard L. Berry and Neeli Bendapudi, "Clueing in Customers," *Harvard Business Review* (February 2003): pp. 100–106; John La Forgia, Kent Seltman, and Scott Swanson, "Mayo Clinic: Sustaining a Legacy Brand and Leveraging Its Equity in the 21st-century Market," Presentation at the Marketing Science Institute's Conference on Brand Orchestration, Orlando, FL, December 4–5, 2003; Paul Roberts, "The Agenda—Total Teamwork," *Fast Company* (March 31, 1999).

■■■ Case 12 Gomez Executive Bus Service

After three months of operation, it was apparent that something needed to be done to increase the use of Gomez Executive Bus Service. The bus service was established to provide a new type of service between the two principal cities of Honduras (Tegucigalpa and San Pedro Sula). This service consisted of two nonstop trips each way. The trip was completed in three-and-one-half hours. Buses left from the Hotel Maya in Tegucigalpa and the Hotel Sula in San Pedro Sula. Trips began at 6 A.M. and 6 P.M. from both cities and arrived in the other at 9:30 A.M. and 9:30 P.M.

The Hotels Maya and Sula were considered to be the best hotels in each of the respective cities. They catered to business travelers, foreign tourists, and convention trade. Many of the guests lived in the United States, Europe, and Japan.

The buses were made by Mercedes-Benz and considered to be the most comfortable and luxurious available anywhere with room for thirty-six passengers and a bar in the rear. A pair of uniformed and attractive young hostesses accompanied the passengers. During the trip, passengers were served their choice of free alcoholic beverages, soft drinks, coffee, tea, and sandwiches. Because the bus left from the best hotels in town, there was no reason for passengers ever to be exposed to long waiting periods in crowded bus terminals or to wait in long lines to purchase tickets. They could instead purchase tickets at a counter in the hotel lobby. Tickets were sold on a commission basis by a company that also sold sightseeing excursion trips. In the Hotel Maya, the service was advertised by the use of a hand-drawn sign about the size of ordinary notebook paper. The sign read:

BUS

EJECUTIVO

GOMEZ

SALE A SAN PEDRO SULA

6 A.M.

6 P.M.

Despite the fact that each bus had a capacity for thirty-six passengers, an average of only seven or eight were taking each trip. This was less than the number required to break even, which had been estimated at twelve.

Tegucigalpa, the capital of Honduras, had a population of approximately 300,000. San Pedro Sula, with 160,000 people, was known as the industrial center of Honduras. The highway between the two cities was in good condition. The countryside consisted of beautiful mountains and a few valleys.

Advertising

Prior to the beginning of the service and shortly thereafter, a series of newspaper advertisements was used in the two cities. These were later discontinued and television advertisements were used but were not scheduled for any particular program. The theme of the ads was directed to people who drove their cars between the two cities. Although a grand opening was never held, a total of fifty free tickets were sent to members of the press. It was not known if any of these tickets had been used, but as far as anyone could see, there had been no free publicity in any of the media. A free ticket was also sent to the Minister of Tourism, but no reply was received. A total of 400 letters were also sent to companies within San Pedro Sula and Tegucigalpa.

The typical customer who had been using the executive bus service came from the Honduran upper classes. There seemed to have been quite a bit of repeat business. The primary problem, according to Sr. Gomez, owner and manager, was a lack of advertising and publicity.

None of the passengers were tourists. It was felt that very few tourists came to Honduras simply to wander about as they do in Mexico and Europe. Most seemed to have a planned itinerary and prepurchased tickets for airline travel. The aid of an ad agency in helping to plan strategy had been dismissed because it was felt that no agency existed in Honduras that was sufficiently knowledgeable about marketing to assist in this project.

Pricing and Competition

To obtain permission for a new bus service from the Honduran government, Gomez was required to charge twice the regular fare charged by existing bus lines on this route. Four companies offered regular bus service between the two cities. These were San Juan, El Sol, Colombo, and Gomez. Each had its own bus terminal and ticket office.

- *El Sol.* The company El Sol offered bus service every two hours between the two cities. This service was generally considered good but not luxury class. Buses were not air conditioned; nor was there service on board. There were also stops at small towns along the way. This company owned a small hotel in Tegucigalpa and would deliver and pick up customers directly from this hotel.

- *Colombo.* The service on this bus was nonstop and was considered to be very good, but buses were not air conditioned nor was there on-board service. Colombo owned a middle-class hotel in Tegucigalpa and picked up and delivered customers from this hotel.

- *San Juan.* This company offered service with stops between the two cities and ran every two hours. Service was generally considered average.

Airline Service

Commercial airline travel between the two cities was provided by SAHSA airlines. This airline was 40 percent owned by the ex-president of Honduras. The cost of single-class round-trip travel on SAHSA was five times the price of travel by the Gomez Executive Bus Service. The flight normally took 25 minutes, but Sr. Gomez felt that it was really a two-hour trip counting waiting time and trips to and from the airport. Flights were sometimes overbooked and canceled due to mechanical or weather problems.

It was also believed that a certain number of people were afraid to fly due to the difficult airport at Tegucigalpa. This airport had a short runway, which literally ended on the edge of a mountain. There was no train service between the two cities, so the only other competitive means of travel was private auto. The distance between the two cities was 265 kilometers.

Although statistics were not available, it appeared that most of the customers of the Gomez Executive Bus Service paid for the ticket with their own funds. By contrast, it was felt that a great number of those who flew SAHSA did so with tickets purchased by their employers. It appeared as though SAHSA had chosen to ignore them because the new bus service was not considered a threat by the management of SAHSA. Sr. Gomez believed that SAHSA was wrong and that he just needed time and the right marketing formula to experience success.

■■■ **DISCUSSION QUESTIONS**

1. What markets was Gomez Executive Bus Service trying to reach?

2. From a consumer behavior standpoint, why do you think tourists were not using the bus service? How could this be corrected?

3. Why do you think this service might not appeal to local business executives?

■■■ **Case 13 Hawaiian Sights**

After nine months in operation, Hawaiian Sights was struggling to solicit support from tour operators. Despite earlier comments from many that this type of tour was needed and should sell without any problems, sales success had been elusive.

As a walking tour, Hawaiian Sights covered the least explored areas of "Olde Honolulu" ordinarily bypassed by tour buses: (1) the Civic and Historical Center, (2) downtown Honolulu, and (3) Chinatown. The tour allowed tourists to mingle and make friends with Hawaii's "real" people—away from Waikiki—and was viewed as an oral historical excursion.

Tours began with an escort/guide meeting clients at a predetermined location in Waikiki. The group would board the city bus and disembark (20 minutes later) in front of the state capital building. The narration continued for the next four hours. The group spent one hour for lunch and shopping on Fort Street Mall and returned to Waikiki on the city bus. The idea for Hawaiian Sights occurred to Evelyn Wako when she noticed that conventional city tours ignored the most important part of Hawaii: its people. The majority of tourists rode through Honolulu, viewing the city through bus windows. Evelyn felt that if tourists really wanted to learn about Hawaii, they had to get off those buses. Evelyn knew that walking tours were successful in Europe, so why not Hawaii?

The concept of a tour that forced customers to take the city bus and to walk was so different that operators of travel desks and travel agencies gave Hawaiian Sights little encouragement or cooperation. They also said that the original commission structure of 20 percent on a $20 (retail price) item did not produce enough revenue to interest them. Lunch was not included, but clients could eat at any of the restaurants or food concessions around the Fort Street Mall area. Tourists were encouraged to eat with the "natives" on benches in the tree-shaded mall. They could get to meet Hawaiians, observe life in Hawaii, feed the birds, or just be alone to shop in stores that were less expensive than those in Waikiki.

During each tour the escorts would board city buses with their groups at the Historical Center. Prior to boarding, the group was given a short briefing as to what would transpire. They were informed that more than 70 percent of Hawaii's population was "non-Caucasian." The tourists observed how the bus would change from a touristy one into a local bus the farther it moved away from Waikiki.

The unusual nature of Hawaiian Sights enabled it to be included in the tour brochures of several tour operators and two airlines. With sales lower than expected, Evelyn was searching for ways to advertise her tours. She felt that one way might be to distribute brochures to tourists on the street. She was thinking of hiring girls dressed in grass skirts to act as salesgirls. This was sure to bring some negative reaction from certain segments of the Hawaiian population. Evelyn knew that the hotel travel desks remained a key sales tool. Operators of one desk were negative from the beginning. They felt that their clientele were too upscale to ride the city bus.

Tourists who had taken the Hawaiian Sights walking tour rated it far superior to conventional bus tours. Hawaiian Sights offered a "satisfaction guaranteed or money back" guarantee, and so far no customer had expressed dissatisfaction. Despite this, Evelyn had not yet found a way to attract sufficient numbers of tourists to make the new business profitable.

▪▪▪ DISCUSSION QUESTIONS

1. Do you believe that Hawaiian Sights would appeal to most tourists who visit Hawaii? If not, why not?

2. What is the probable profile of the market segment for Hawaiian Sights?

3. What promotional techniques could Evelyn use to sell this tour to tourists? To the tour operators? To the clerks at the travel desks?

4. Why do you think the travel desks and travel operators have been unenthusiastic concerning Hawaiian Sights?

5. What do you think of Evelyn's idea to hire girls and dress them in hula skirts to distribute brochures on the sidewalks of Waikiki to passing tourists?

▪▪▪ Case 14 Grand Targhee

In the competitive world of ski resorts, the race for profitability is always an uphill battle. But Grand Targhee Resort is carving out an innovative path to success that counters conventional wisdom and rethinks strategies popular with larger resorts. Personalized service gave Targhee the lift it needed.

At first glance, Wyoming's Grand Targhee Ski & Summer Resort would seem to have less chance of survival than a ball of its signature talcum-powder snow on a hot summer's day. The crucial element for a successful destination ski resort, according to conventional wisdom, is land. The skiers and snowboarders demand a return on their hefty investment in a roundtrip airline ticket, accommodations, and skyrocketing lift fees in the form of an enormous and varied terrain crisscrossed by numerous high-speed lifts. Off the mountain, it's no longer enough to throw up a couple of pseudo-chalets housing a lodge, a rental shop, and a cafeteria. Today, visitors expect a base village crammed with spiffy shops, luxury hotels, and high-octane restaurants—a destination in itself.

Based on those parameters, Targhee wouldn't appear to have what it takes. Located on the western side of the Grand Tetons about 30 miles from tiny Jackson Hole, Targhee grabs the edge on size—3,000 acres compared to Jackson Hole's 2,500—but accesses it with just four fill-size lifts and a snow card, compared to Jackson Hole's eight lifts, a gondola, and a tram. Similarly, visitors who white-knuckle their way up the long and hairpin approach road to Targhee find a handful of low-slung lodges, shops, and restaurants grouped around a plaza that can be explored thoroughly in 15 minutes, whereas Jackson Hole's crowded base village recently slotted in a Four Seasons hotel, and the town of Jackson is an easy twelve miles away.

Land usage in the base area is traditionally the key to a destination ski area's bottom line. "Real estate has become a huge part of the business plans for all the major ski operations," says Mary McKhann, editor of *The Snow Industry Letter*, a trade publication covering the ski and snowboard industry. That real estate generates hefty rents from shops and restaurants and sizable amounts of income from sales of high-priced single-family homes, townhouse condominiums, and interval ownership (the latest euphemism for time-shares). "It is extremely difficult just making it on lift tickets alone, without having the real estate and a village," says McKhann.

Targhee's pristine terrain is located in the Targhee National Forest and is subject to strict regulations regarding the usage of public land. It took six years to get permission to build a new lift on Peaked Mountain; further expansion of either the slope system or the base area is unlikely in the near future.

Yet 80 percent of the skiers who have tasted Targhee's powder come back for seconds. Although that figure might not seem notable compared to an average return rate of 77 percent for destination skiers at seventy-nine major areas nationwide, many of those areas are within just an hour or two of a significant urban center. Targhee's nearest city is Idaho Falls, Idaho, 80 miles away.

What Is Targhee's Secret?

Because Targhee literally could not expand into new territory, it was forced to take another look at what it already had. In doing so, it found that it was sitting on a mother lode of resources just waiting to be discovered. The light went on for Larry

Williamson seven summers ago. At the time, Targhee's horseback riding concession was run by an outside outfitter that strictly scheduled everything: One-hour rides left at 9:00 A.M., 10:30 A.M., and 1:00 P.M., and two-hour rides went out at 10:00 A.M. and 1:30 P.M. "We couldn't get them to accept the idea that if its 9:30 and you've got guests waiting and two wranglers and fifteen horses sitting down there, why wait half an hour to go on a ride?" Williamson recalls.

Targhee took over the riding program, and Williamson quickly realized that guests didn't want riding lessons per se; they wanted to enjoy being on a horse. The program was changed to accommodate their wishes. The result: "We went from $24,000 to more than $45,000 in one three-month season with no change in marketing, except that when you come in, we'll put you on a horse as soon as possible." Today, the horse concession is pushing $84,000 in revenues.

The next task is to figure out how to satisfy the customer when the snow fell. As a former ski instructor, Williamson knew that the ski school experience could make or break a guest's visit. A University of Idaho survey found that virtually 100 percent of the people who had taken lessons at Targhee's ski school planned on returning, whereas less than half who had not taken lessons were willing to come back. "The obvious answer was that if you're in ski school, you develop a friendship and become part of Targhee," says Williamson.

But there was a less obvious and even more compelling aspect to the lessons. Many ski schools judge their success on how much the student improves. One problem with that method is that success is defined by the instructor's parameters, rather than the guests' preferences.

Williamson came up with a different winning formula. "It really wasn't about how much the guest improved," he concluded. "It was more about how much fun the guest had. People don't like to pay for classes on vacation unless it's something fun. Fun became my focus for the industry."

A key element in Williamson's idea about fun is Mark Hanson, the snow sports school director. Hanson had run the children's program at Targhee for five years before becoming overall director. He knew the secret of a superb program: "If little kids don't have fun, mom's not going to bring them back again. And if they do have fun, mom isn't going to be able to keep them from coming back."

In transferring the successful elements of the kids' program to the adult lessons, Hanson had to take into account the fact that about 80 percent of Targhee's adult clientele is either level II or III skiers, compared to 60 percent at most other resorts. Such advanced skiers are not nearly as inclined to take a lesson as beginners. "We teach, on a percentage basis, far fewer lessons than Vail, so it became a particular challenge to get those advanced skiers into lessons," Williamson says. "Their attraction to powder is part of the answer. Customized options are another. Finding out what people want to accomplish became a priority. Rather than worrying about what they do with their bodies, get them doing things that help develop confidence."

Hanson examined Targhee's liabilities and realized that they could help the company differentiate itself and even provide opportunities. Targhee welcomes about a tenth of those who throng the slopes at Steamboat Springs, a Colorado resort with comparable acreage. But rather than sulk about empty slopes, Hanson says, "The lack of exorbitant volume becomes an advantage. We can be more personal with folks. We can say, 'It's just you and me now, so let's go play and do what you want.' "

Thanks to the small volume, Targhee's snow sports school can afford to be more flexible. At Big Sky, Montana, four hours to the north, semiprivate intermediate lessons go out in the afternoon only; if the snow has turned to slush by 2 P.M., that's tough luck. With so few crowds at Targhee, lessons billed as "group" frequently have attendance that would be more accurately labeled "semiprivate."

But it's the private lessons that best demonstrate Hanson's determination to bend over backward to achieve customer satisfaction. "You can go on a private lesson any time or any day," says public relations director Susie Barnett Bushong. "If you decide you don't want to learn a technical skill, that you just want the instructor to show you secret powder stashes, that's fine. And if you aren't happy with your lessons, you can come back the next day and get a free one."

As the program changed from the standpoint of value and product, the pay strategy changed too. Instead of being paid merely for the cost of their labor, Targhee instructors have a hefty incentive to ensure customer satisfaction through repeat business. "Instructors make much more money from returning mountain tours or returning private lessons than from lessons just assigned to them," Williamson says.

Although an expected amenity, a ski school is often something of a loss leader. Whereas larger areas amortize the various expenses involved in building up and staffing a school through other revenues, Targhee is too small to afford that kind of luxury. Hence the push to sell private and semiprivate lessons. "Financially, they're a win for us because they generate more revenue, they're a win for the instructors because they can make more money, and they're a win for the guests because they're getting what they want," says Hanson.

Hanson spends a lot of time ensuring he's got the right staff. "They have to be pros at working with people," he says. Again, Targhee's size is an advantage. "We might hire 10 or 12 people every year, whereas some resorts hire 200 each season," he says. "That smaller need allows me to be choosy."

It also enables him to keep a close eye on his staff; no supervisor is in charge of more than fifteen instructors. Hanson monitors requests for private and semiprivate lessons and checks responses to guest surveys. "I don't do any formal spying, but I spend a lot of time on the hill myself," he allows. "I can say, 'Hey, I noticed you were doing this. Why?'"

Hanson's attentions have paid off. Grand Targhee's ski school brings in only 4.5 percent of revenue, compared to a national average of 7.5 percent. But in terms of EBITDA (earnings before interest, taxes, depreciation, and amortization), the school contributes a whopping 30.1 percent, whereas the national average is a little more than half that amount.

Targhee also bucks the industry trend by fervently pursuing the local market. "All the research will tell you that the destination guest spends more money, but to be successful, we can't afford to concentrate on that one aspect of our market," says Hanson. To broaden its share of the regional market, Targhee has adopted an all-encompassing approach, sponsoring ski programs in elementary, middle, and high schools, partnering with ski clubs in nearby Idaho Falls and at the University of Idaho at the other end of the state, and organizing programs aimed at niche audiences as narrow as, say, women from southeastern Idaho. Not surprisingly, discounted lessons and instructional weekends are a big part of the perks of membership in those ski clubs. "We get a lot of the same people who come to every instructional they can, and they generate more business for us by telling their friends," says Hanson.

Targhee's drive for customer satisfaction and repeat business pervades every aspect of its efforts, from the parking lot attendants to the ski patrol. Each department is graded on its performance, with guest satisfaction accounting for a large portion of the rating. Five years ago, the ski patrol had a 44 percent performance rating. Then patrol staff members started to have lunch with guests, give demonstrations with their avalanche dog, and make themselves more visible. Last year, their score hit 88 percent.

Similarly, the parking lot attendants had barely eked out a 40 percent rating. They decided that guests wanted to see them working efficiently, so they donned bright orange vests, worked out a series of hand signals, were friendlier, and boosted their rating up to the 90s. Says Williamson, "The whites of the teeth are the number-one factor."

Williamson knows that Targhee will never be able to compete directly with places like Vail or Jackson Hole. It will never have the same number of chair lifts or the swanky base village that can be subsidized by real estate sales and rentals. "We try to focus not on competing with other resorts but on those features that make Targhee unique," he says. By mining those already existing assets, Williamson's team has figured out a way to turn Targhee's famous effervescent powder into cold, hard cash.

■■■ DISCUSSION QUESTIONS

Chapter 2

1. How did the management of Grand Targhee create a service culture?

2. How does fun relate to establishing a service culture?

3. What product did Grand Targhee focus on to create interaction between the guests and employees? Why was this product successful?

Chapter 10

1. Find evidence from the case to show that Grand Targhee practiced good internal marketing concepts.

■■■ Case 15 Coconut Plantation Resort

The management of Blackfield Hawaii Corporation was faced with a decision concerning the most appropriate type of restaurant for its resort development. The new restaurant must complement the existing resort. Additionally, it should not replicate similar types in the immediate resort area. The new restaurant was planned as a freestanding 150- to 200-seat unit between beach-front hotels, condominium units, and the main highway. There was a divergence of opinion concerning what type of restaurant it should be. Suggestions that had been offered to Bob Cooper, vice president for corporate development, included a moderately priced family restaurant with all three meals, a deluxe tablecloth restaurant, a fast-food restaurant, a lunch and dinner steak and chops restaurant, and a specialty restaurant such as an Italian restaurant.

Description of Coconut Plantation Resort

Coconut Plantation Resort was located on the eastern coast of the island of Kauai, off Highway 56, less than two miles from the largest town, Kapaa, and approximately eight miles from Lihue. The Blackfield Hawaii Corporation, a land development company, specialized in developing commercial and residential properties. The company did not wish to become involved in the operational end of the business but preferred to develop properties for others to lease and operate.

The resort complex covered ninety acres of prime resort land with beach frontage. Hotels had been built on fifty acres. These included:

Holiday Inn	311 units
Kauai Beach Boy	243 units
Islander Inn	200 units

The remaining land was designated for condominiums, a shopping center known as the Market Place, two additional hotels, and the independent freestanding restaurant under question.

The condominiums and hotels were planned to have the following numbers of units:

- Hotels
  Travelodge (350–400)
  Hawaiian Pacific Resort (297)

- Condominiums
  Condominium Development (1,180)
  (50% one-bedroom; 50% two-bedroom)
  Condominium Development 2 (160)
  (100% one-bedroom)

The Market Place shopping center had been fully completed and was in operation. It offered a variety of retail stores featuring Polynesian fashions, jewelry, scrimshaw (carved ivory), art goods, a twin-screen movie theater, various food outlets, and many other shops that appealed to tourists.

Restaurants Within Coconut Plantation Resort

Several restaurants existed within Coconut Plantation Resort. These were located within the hotels and within or adjacent to the Market Place. Each of the three existing hotels had a restaurant, and each of the two new hotels would also contain restaurants. Restaurants located in or near the Market Place appeared to be well established and included:

- Fast food
  Ice cream parlor
  Mexican outlet
  Chinese outlet
  Hamburger outlet

- Other
  Steaks, fish, chops
  Buzz's Steakhouse
  The Spindrifter
  J.J.'s Boiler Room

With the exception of the fast-food establishments and J.J.'s Boiler Room, all of the hotel restaurants and independent restaurants served three meals a day. Demand for breakfast had apparently reached market saturation. Buzz's Steakhouse was phasing out its breakfast service, and others, such as Holiday Inn and Spindrifter, had stretched their breakfast menu to span a brunch period. The Holiday Inn had recently initiated a special noontime buffet for Japanese tour groups.

All the restaurants operated on a limited-menu concept and featured steaks, chops, limited seafood, and a few other specialty items. There appeared to be little genuine diversification or originality in food service among the table service restaurants in Coconut Plantation Resort. All of the operations except the Kauai Beach Boy were chain based, where limited menus were a key to standardization and efficiency.

Description of Kauai

As the northernmost island in the chain of Hawaiian islands, the island of Kauai is situated about 20 air minutes from Honolulu. Known as the "Garden Island" due to its lush foliage and beautiful tropical setting, the island offered an almost ideal climate, with average temperatures near the coast of 71°F in February and March and 79°F in August and September. Rainfall varied widely depending on location, but the summit of Waialeale was the wettest spot in the United States, with a recorded rainfall of 486 inches a year. Twenty miles away, Kekaha on the southern coast had an average rainfall of 20 inches per year. The normal annual rainfall in Lihue was about 40 inches per year. Most of this occurred between October and April, with January as the wettest month.

The island of Kauai constituted a county with a total resident population of about 35,000. The largest towns on Kauai were Kapaa, with approximately 3,600 residents, and Lihue, with about 3,100. The ethnic makeup of the resident population was Japanese, 27.5 percent; Filipino, 19.1 percent; Caucasian, 20.0 percent; Hawaiian and part Hawaiian, 18.4 percent; Chinese, 0.3 percent; mixed, 13.2 percent; and other, 1.1 percent.

Tourism on Kauai

Kauai was usually considered as the last island to be visited by tourists. Tour groups commonly arranged for it to be last, due to its unique beauty and Polynesian atmosphere. The island was also a popular weekend or short-holiday vacation site for residents of Honolulu. A mix of group (GIT) and nongroup travelers visited Kauai, but a majority (55 percent) were represented by independent travelers (ITs). These persons did not travel in a large group with a set itinerary and a prepurchased package of services.

Each of the resort hotels had at least one table-service restaurant. These served three meals a day. The variety and quality of food and service tended to resemble those of the hotels in Coconut Plantation Resort. A Polynesian decor was common throughout these resorts. Although it was not unusual to find a different specialty dish associated with each restaurant, in general the menus were quite similar.

The nearest resort to Coconut Plantation Resort was the 416-room Coco Palms Resort, which was located less than two miles south. The Coco Palms was built in a grove of 100-year-old coconut palms on the grounds where Kauai's ancient kings held court. The decor of the Coco Palms was Polynesian, with thatched-roof cottages, flaming torches, drums, canoes, and other decor typical of the South Pacific. A restaurant known as Coconut Palace was located at the Coco Palms. This restaurant was frequently mentioned by travel writers, who referred to it as an "award-winning restaurant." It featured Polynesian specialties such as *kupa hei maka* (green papaya soup).

Purchasing Habits of Condominium Users

The possible effect of condominium occupants on a new restaurant was felt to be a factor for consideration. A study had been conducted by the School of Travel Industry Management at the University of Hawaii and demonstrated that occupants of condominiums spent less in restaurants than was spent by occupants of hotels. It also showed that the amount spent in restaurants by this group declined as the length of stay increased. The restaurant eating habits of condominium occupants was restricted primarily to the main meal of the day.

■■■ DISCUSSION QUESTIONS

1. What additional information, if any, is needed before selecting the type of restaurant to build?

2. What are the probable market targets for this restaurant?

3. What marketing strategy should be employed prior to opening?

■■■ Case 16 The Bleeding Heart Restaurant: The Finest French Restaurant in London

Unique Positioning of a Top-20 Restaurant

The Bleeding Heart Restaurant and Bistro has been a favorite with Londoners (UK) for 30 years. The perennially popular restaurant and Bistro was started in 1983 by Robert and Robyn Wilson, two former journalists, as a tiny basement wine bar in a deserted and derelict cellar that had once been the warehouse of a Victorian clock manufacturer. Despite warnings from fellow members of London's wine trade that a bar so hidden could never succeed, The Bleeding Heart prospered from the start. Today it serves over a thousand guests per day.

History

Bleeding Heart Yard
The long-established and extremely popular Bleeding Heart restaurant offers superb French food in historical surroundings. The restaurant takes its name from the yard where it is located which, according to the history books, was named after an eleventh-century beauty, Lady Elizabeth Hatton, who was found murdered there.

The Legend

Lady Elizabeth Hatton was the toast of eleventh-century London society. The widowed daughter-in-law of the famous merchant Sir Christopher Hatton (one-time consort of Queen Elizabeth I), Lady Elizabeth was young, beautiful, and very wealthy. Her suitors were many and varied, and they included a leading London bishop and a prominent European ambassador. Invitations to her soirees in Hatton Garden were much sought after.

Her annual Winter Ball, on January 26, 1626, was one of the highlights of the London social season. Halfway through the evening's festivities, the doors to Lady Hatton's grand ballroom were flung open. In strode a swarthy gentleman, slightly hunched of shoulder, with a clawed right hand. He took her by the hand, danced her once around the room and out through the double doors into the garden. A buzz of gossip arose. Would Lady Elizabeth and the European ambassador (for it was he) kiss and make up, or would she return alone? Neither was to be. The next morning her body was found in the cobblestone courtyard—torn limb from limb, with her heart still pumping blood onto the cobblestones. And from henceforth, the yard was to be known as The Bleeding Heart Yard.

Charles Dickens and The Bleeding Heart

Charles Dickens knew Bleeding Heart well. In *Little Dorrit* he wrote of folks in the yard, saying, "The more practical of the Yard's inmates abided by the tradition of the murder." But he went on to document another Bleeding Heart story: "The gentler and more imaginative inhabitants, including the whole of the tender sex, were loyal to the legend of a young lady imprisoned in her own chamber by a cruel father for remaining true to her own true lover—but it was objected to by the murderous party that this was the invention of a spinster and romantic, still lodging in the Yard."

Today The Bleeding Heart has grown well beyond that tiny basement wine bar but has preserved and enhanced the architectural, cultural, and historic value of its unique location while serving a multisegment market.

The Tavern has guarded the entrance to Bleeding Heart Yard since 1746 with a history of conviviality encapsulated in its then boast of "drunk for a penny and dead drunk for two pence." Today the Tavern offers a traditional neighborhood bar with real ale and a light lunchtime menu for those pressed for time.

Downstairs the Tavern Dining Room with its jolly farmyard illustrations features an open rotisserie and grill and provides a warm and comforting setting in which to enjoy free-range organic British meat, game, and poultry along with an excellent-value wine list.

The Tavern is also open for breakfast, with freshly squeezed orange juice, home-baked croissants, and "The Full English" with tasty Suffolk Bacon.

Early Days

In the early days, The Bleeding Heart's proximity to the headquarters of many of the national dailies—*The Times, The Mirror,* and *The Guardian*—coupled with the media connections (and the media's partiality to a decent bottle of wine) meant that from its inception the wine bar attracted a number of leading journalists and, in their wake, the public relations industry.

The Barristers Chambers of Gray's Inn were also but a corkscrew's throw away, and The Bleeding Heart became a popular lunch spot for this learned group to discuss their briefs over a decent bottle of claret and a platter of charcuterie or cheese.

The increasingly upscale clientele began to demand a more sophisticated menu than the simple wine bar fare originally offered. In response, the bar expanded its horizons into an adjoining basement and its kitchens to include a white tablecloth restaurant with more sophisticated, although still classically French, cuisine.

From that forty-seat bar, The Bleeding Heart expanded, above and around the ancient cobblestoned courtyard to encompass a formal fine-dining restaurant seating 160 with a 30-seat terrace, a 60-seat bistro with its own 40-seat terrace, a 70-seat tavern and bar, and two private dining rooms: The Parlor and The Wine Cellar. Adjoining Bleeding Heart Yard in Ely Place is the stunning medieval function room, The Crypt, and its intimate Crypt Café. The twelfth-century crypt, which seats 120, was the venue for the celebration following the wedding of Henry VIII and Catherine of Aragon.

Marketing

Opening day was December 1, 1983. The Wilsons deployed two French waitresses to hand out "How to Find Us" maps at the local underground station (subway). There was no advertising because there was no budget. As a launch tool, the leaflets were not an instant success; on that first day the restaurant earned only £39.37. However, within a week, word started to spread and turnover tripled. The week-long distribution of those leaflets was Bleeding Heart's only external promotion since it opened in 1983.

Word of mouth was relied on to reach the right sort of customer. It worked, building a loyal and homogeneous clientele who believe that they have, by finding the tucked-away little Yard and the bustling bistro beneath it, made a personal discovery. The restaurant was a "best kept secret," a secret that, fortunately, lots of people were in on. The USP (Unique Selling Proposition) was their unique location.

Shortly after opening, Bleeding Heart was described by a New York reviewer as "bleeding hard to find but worth it." A London cab driver commented to a lost diner that the reason it was called Bleeding Heart was that it was Bleeding Hard to find. Robert and Robyn used the mantra that you had to discover Bleeding Heart rather than read an advertisement about it. They also worked hard building a database of regular customers, mainly by running monthly prize drawings to garner business cards, which, in those pre-e-mail days, had postal addresses and telephone numbers. It was a labor-intensive task, but they built a customer base of some 5,000 with a shorter list of 500 of those with a special interest in wine.

To the short list they promoted their regular wine and food evenings and any wine-related events such as the New Beaujolais Breakfast. Magnum Night was launched offering a special half-price deal on Friday evenings (the quietest night) for magnums of champagne. The Seagram Company had discovered a large stock of magnums of Heidsieck champagne in Ireland, which they were keen to offload at a very attractive price.

Despite the fact there was no promotion; Magnum Night became a rapid and astonishingly successful draw card. The hours it was available were cut from 5:30 until 7:00 P.M. only to discover that queues were forming in the yard. On one occasion, a journalist from the BBC phoned offering to pay in advance by credit card lest he miss the 7:00 P.M. cutoff.

However, there was a downside to this promotion. Regular evening diners (long-term bread-and-butter customers) couldn't get in the door past the queues of Johnny-come-lately champagne quaffers, and with much regret, especially from the champagne drinkers; the promotion was stopped after a year. In its place the Magnum Club was created based on the premise that wine tastes better in bigger bottles. Regular customers were invited to join. Initially members were offered a discount on champagne. Then the offer expanded to include invitations to wine tastings and wine making dinners. The Club is still going strong and membership is free but by invitation only, and it is much sought after.

Today, the Wilsons still do no advertising for Bleeding Heart Restaurant, Bistro, or Tavern, but they have begun carefully targeted promotions for special functions in special publications aimed at the corporate event market and the wedding sector. These are always tied to associated editorial features.

Talking to regular customers has become much easier with e-mail, but the Wilsons are hypercautious about invading their e-space. Mailings are used only for major events such as the summer opening of the outdoor terrace when regular customers are given a complimentary glass of rosé wine to celebrate the sunshine.

The Wilsons believe that keeping a low profile has worked in an increasingly crowded marketplace. In 2008, despite the economic slowdown in the financial sector, turnover was still increasing. During this difficult economic period, the

London Evening Standard newspaper wrote a feature about restaurants feeling the pinch of the recession. Bleeding Heart was one of the few restaurants to be lauded as "fully booked."

Media Comments

"Fantastic venue. Congratulations for making our event the outstanding success it was."

—Chicago Mercantile Exchange

"The Crypt looked wonderful by candlelight, and everyone commented on what a superb location it was. Your staff were professional in every way."—Transworld Publishers

"Serious contender after the stunning extension of the basement dining room below the unassuming pub facade, listing classics such as Roast Ale-fed Pork from Suffolk and Poached Haddock on Mash with Hollandaise. It matches its sibling's (the Bleeding Heart Restaurant and Bistro) cozy ambiance and skillful service."

—The Times 20 Top British Restaurants

"Great for business lunches."

—Wall Street Journal

"Takes the 'gastropub' to a new level of comfort and style."

—Business News

"Tucked-away location in a Holborn yard adds to the cozy and rustic charm of this brasserie (which has a special and intimate feeling despite the number of suits). A wide array of good, honest French dishes is backed up by a fantastic wine list."

—Harden's London Restaurant Guide

Awards

During its first six months, the tiny wine bar/bistro was voted one of London's Top Ten Wine Bars by *Time Out Magazine* and has continued to win plaudits from national and international press ever since, including "London's most romantic restaurant" from *The Times,* "Best Venue in Europe" from the *Guardian,* and "Best Private Dining."

The *Zagat Guide* put it in the top three restaurants in London for a business lunch. *Hardens,* the most authoritative London restaurant guide, and *Square Meal,* the city of London's eating-out bible, both rate it number one for business. Since its inception, Bleeding Heart has always been known for its extensive and well-priced wine list. The Wilsons have been frequent winners of an annual Award of Excellence for "One of the Best Wine Lists in the World" from *Wine Spectator* magazine.

■■■ DISCUSSION QUESTIONS

Chapter 13

1. Explain the elements of the promotional mix that The Bleeding Heart Restaurant used.

2. Why do you think The Bleeding Heart was so successful with such a small budget for promotion?

Chapter 14

1. If you were hired as a public relations firm for The Bleeding Heart, how would you plan its public relations campaign?

2. There are a number of favorable mentions in popular media about the restaurant. How do you think it was able to get these mentions in the media?

Chapter 16

1. The Bleeding Heart has not changed its promotional strategy since it opened. If you purchased The Bleeding Heart, would you use social media? If you would, explain how you will use it. If not, explain why not.

■■■ Case 17 The Grand Canyon Railway

One interesting feature of the southwestern United States is the area known as the "Four Corners," the only place in the United States where four states meet at one point. Within the 130,000 square miles of the Colorado Plateau in this region lie many wonders of nature. The plateau contains eight national parks and twenty national monuments, as well as numerous other nationally designated areas and huge tracts of national forests. This wealth of natural features and the cultures of the various Native American tribes in the region have made the area an important destination for tourists, especially those interested in natural history and culture.

The crown jewel for this region is generally considered to be the Grand Canyon, one of the seven natural wonders of the world. This wonder of nature is 190 miles long, a mile deep, and between 4 and 18 miles wide. The Grand Canyon covers 1,900 square miles of the Colorado Plateau and is home to 1,000 species of plants, 250 species of birds, and 70 species of animals. A number of Native American tribes are found in the region of the Grand Canyon, including the Hualapai, Hopi, Navajo, and Havasupai (who live on the floor of a side canyon).

The principal attraction to visitors is the sheer size and beauty of the canyon itself. The walls of the Grand Canyon are made up of many layers of rock, with widely varying textures, colors, and hues. This panorama of nature changes by the season, weather, and time of day. Generally, the morning and late afternoon offer the most striking views for visitors to the canyon. The South Rim in Grand Canyon National Park (Grand Canyon NP) is open year round, whereas the North Rim (also in the park) is closed in winter. In the summer months, Grand Canyon NP becomes quite crowded with visitors and motor vehicles. Consideration is being given by the National Park Service to ban vehicles from the park and move visitors around the park by shuttle buses.

Williams, Arizona, serves as one important "jumping-off" point for visitors traveling to Grand Canyon NP, with the South Rim of the canyon only 59 miles north of the town. Williams is closely identified with travel to the canyon and has even registered the trademark "The Gateway to the Grand Canyon," which no others may use. At an elevation of 6,800 feet, Williams, by itself, has many attractions in the town and surrounding area such as lakes for swimming and fishing, horseback riding, and a downtown listed on the National Register of Historic Places. The surrounding Kaibab National Forest in the vicinity of Williams offers opportunities for camping, fishing, and hiking for both visitors and residents alike.

The town has for many years been an important transportation hub for both rail and highway. Williams is closely identified with Route 66, also known as the "Mother Road," that connected Chicago, Illinois, and Santa Monica, California, long before the interstate highway system was developed. Williams has the last stretch of the original Route 66 bypassed by the interstate system (in this case, I-40). Even before highways became highly developed, Williams has served as a railroad terminal (since 1882) for the forerunners of the Atchison, Topeka, & the Santa Fe Railroad (Santa Fe); the latter continues to serve the town today with freight-only service.

The most popular way for visitors to get from either Williams or Flagstaff (32 miles to the east) to Grand Canyon NP is by motor vehicle, although the pending restrictions on vehicles might be expected to change this somewhat. An attractive alternative for some visitors is to travel between Williams and the Grand Canyon by rail. The Grand Canyon Railway (GCRy) offers this option with one round-trip per day. This rail service, which operates purely as a tourist railroad, began operations in September 1989 and has provided daily service since that day (except for December 24 and 25).

Historically, rail service on this line began much earlier, but passenger service was abandoned in the 1960s due to economic pressures from the automobile. Freight service from the Santa Fe was abandoned in 1974, with no work performed on the track between Williams and the Grand Canyon until 1989. The work to get the GCRy running was monumental because all engines and passenger cars had to be acquired and completely rebuilt. In addition, the depot at Williams and the adjoining Fray Marcos Hotel were in need of substantial refurbishing. In the depot, operating offices, ticket offices, a waiting room, and souvenir shop are found. All of this work was accomplished in a span of seven months to be ready for the September 1989 opening.

Today, the GCRy provides an interesting and nostalgic way for visitors to travel to the canyon. During the summer months, daily round-trip rail service is provided by steam locomotive, and in the winter diesel locomotives are used due to the severity of weather conditions. For all service, passengers travel in railcars that date from 1923 and are reconditioned to approximate that time period. Departure from Williams is at 9:30 A.M. and arrival at Grand Canyon NP is at 11:45 A.M., in the center of the park's historic district at the 1910 Grand Canyon Depot. The train departs from the Grand Canyon at 3:15 P.M. and arrives back in Williams at 5:30 P.M. No smoking is allowed on the train in any of the railcars.

Reservations and information are available at www.thetrain.com. Different classes of service are offered to travelers, depending on the fare paid and the car in which a passenger rides. The coach service is priced at $70 per adult and $40 per child. Snacks and soft drinks are available for purchase. First Class, which includes the availability of alcoholic beverages and complimentary coffee and pastries in the morning, is priced at $140 for adults and $110 for children. The next two classes are for adults only; an observation dome which includes refreshments for $170, and a Luxury Parlor that recreates a luxury train experience for $190.

For all classes, the entrance fee to Grand Canyon NP is an additional charge. Other services are also available from the GCRy for additional charges. A buffet breakfast is served in the Grand Depot Cafe. The Grand Canyon Railway Hotel offers rooms starting at $169. Packages are available that include room and train tickets at a discounted price. Packages that include a night at the GCR Hotel, round trip train tickets, one night at the Maswick Lodge, motor coach tour of the rim and a breakfast and dinner are $575 per couple, with children an additional $70.

During the ride from/to Williams many natural and manufactured venues can be seen. There is formal narration for some of these venues and a printed guide is available for purchase, which describes these sights and provides a history of the GCRy. Interestingly, only a very limited view of the Grand Canyon is available from the train just as it arrives at and departs from the park. In Coach Class, each railcar has an attendant who serves beverages (Coke and Diet Coke), goes around with snacks for sale, and engages in conversations with the passengers. During the summer, many of these attendants are college students on break from their studies.

The Grand Canyon Railway uses costumed performers in a number of different ways to simulate an earlier time period. Before the train departs from Williams, performers stage an "Old West" gunfight, just as was found some one hundred years ago. Performers also move among the railcars, often singing songs of the "Old West," during the trip to the Grand Canyon. Passengers are encouraged to sing along with the performers. All of the performers are costumed in the type of dress found at the "turn-of-the-century."

On the return trip, the activities are slightly different. A group of performers stage a train robbery, just as was found during earlier times in the southwestern United States. Passengers are included in portions of the action, but none are actually robbed. Eventually, the sheriff captures the train robbers and takes them away to be put in jail. Passengers, especially younger children, enjoy this activity, which makes the trip back to Williams seem much shorter than it actually is. The other activity that some engage in is to take a nap because many are tired due to their activities at the high altitude and in the low humidity of the Colorado Plateau.

A recent survey conducted by the GCRy found that many passengers rate their train trip experience as excellent. Perhaps just as important, these passengers say that they would recommend the GCRy trip to friends. Additionally, the most satisfied passengers were likely to return again. Passenger satisfaction derives from the varied experiences received during the round-trip ride and the Grand Canyon itself, with the latter experience not under control of the GCRy but rather the National Park Service.

This case was prepared by Dr. Fredrick M. Collison and is intended for classroom use. The situations portrayed here do not imply either effective or ineffective management on the part of the Grand Canyon Railway. The case was written based on published materials of the railroad, the National Park Service, the *Williams-Grand Canyon News,* and the author's personal experience. Updated November 21, 2011. *Source:* www.thetrain.com.

■■■ DISCUSSION QUESTIONS

1. What are the components of the product offered by the GCRy and received by the passengers?

2. How appropriate are the components of the product that you mentioned in Question 1?

3. In what ways does the GCRy contribute to the marketing to travelers of Williams, Grand Canyon NP, and the surrounding Colorado Plateau?

4. Would you take this train ride? Why or why not?

■■■ Case 18 Starbucks: Just Who Is the Starbucks Customer?

By now, you should be familiar with the Starbucks story. After a trip to Italy in the early 1980s, Howard Schultz was inspired to transform Starbucks—then just a handful of coffee shops in Seattle—into a chain of European-style coffeehouses. His vision wasn't based on selling only gourmet coffees, espressos, and lattes, however. He wanted to provide customers with what he called a "third place"— a place away from home and work. As CEO of Starbucks, Schultz developed what became known as the *Starbucks Experience,* built around great coffee, personal service, and an inviting ambiance.

What Goes up . . .

It wasn't long before Starbucks became a household word—a powerhouse premium brand in a category that previously consisted of only cheaper commodity products. In 20 years' time, Schultz grew the company to almost 17,000 stores in dozens of countries. From 1995 to 2005, Starbucks added U.S. stores at an annual rate of 27 percent, far faster than the 17 percent annual growth of McDonald's in its heyday. At one point, Starbucks opened over 3,300 locations in a single year—an average of 9 per day. In one stretch of crowded Manhattan, a person could get his or her caffeine fix at any of five Starbucks outlets in less than a block and a half. In fact, cramming so many stores so close together caused one satirical publication to run this headline: "A New Starbucks Opens in the Restroom of Existing Starbucks."

For many years, new store growth was what kept Starbucks percolating. As it grew, company sales and profits rose like steam from a mug of hot Java. Growth routinely averaged 20 percent or more each year. And Starbucks made investors happy with a 25 percent annual increase in the value of its stock for more than a decade. Schultz confidently predicted that there was no end in sight for the Starbucks boom. Just a few years ago, he announced his intentions to open 10,000 new stores in just four years and then push Starbucks to 40,000 stores.

But not long after Schultz shocked Wall Street and the industry with his projections, Starbucks' steam engine of growth started to slow. Then it started running in reverse. By the end of 2008, the 20 percent annual growth had dropped to 10 percent, with existing-store sales *decreasing* by 3 percent. Total company profits dropped by a scalding 53 percent for the year. And for a second year in a row, Starbucks' stock value dropped by 50 percent to around $10 a share.

The weakened economy certainly played a role. But for years, many industry observers had worried that the company was growing too fast. Revenue and traffic at Starbucks began slowing more than a year before anyone uttered the word *recession*. In a sign of recognizing a problem, Schultz cut back on the number of new store openings. Then he did what had previously seemed unthinkable. In 2008, he announced store closures—first 600, then 300 more. In fact, as Starbucks trimmed its 2009 forecast for new store openings to 310, it projected a *decrease* in its number of outlets for the first time ever.

The Evolution of the Starbucks Customer

There was no shortage of armchair CEOs willing to give their opinions as to what had gone wrong that led to Starbucks' fall from perpetual growth. One issue often mentioned was that Starbucks had developed an identity crisis with respect to its target customer. In its early years, the Starbucks customer profile was clearly defined. The typical customer was wealthier, better educated, and more professional than the average American. The customer was far more likely to be female than male, predominately Caucasian, and between the ages of 24 and 44. It was this customer who fell in love with the *Starbucks Experience.* She was very loyal, often visiting a store every day or even more than once a day. She loved the fact that the barista greeted her by name when she came in and chatted with her while making her custom coffee drink, not caring if it took a while. She lounged on the comfy furniture, enjoying the perfect mix of music that always seemed to fit her mood. She met friends or just hung out by herself reading a good book.

But the more Starbucks grew, the more the *Starbucks Experience* began to change. With more stores, the place wasn't quite so special. As each location filled with more customers, baristas had more names to put with faces. As the menu expanded with more options, the number of combinations for coffee drinks grew into the hundreds, leaving baristas less time to chat with customers. As the atmosphere in each store turned to "hustle and bustle," it became a less attractive place to hang out.

With all these changes, Starbucks progressively appealed less to the traditional customer and more to a new customer. This customer shift was inevitable; there simply were not enough traditional customers around to fuel the kind of growth that Schultz sought. The new breed of customer was less affluent, less educated, and less professional. Not only was Starbucks drawing in different customers in places where stores already existed, but it was also putting stores in different neighborhoods, cities, and countries.

As the customer profile evolved, the *Starbucks Experience* grew to mean something different. To the new breed of customer, it meant good coffee on the run. It was a place to meet and then move on. The more accessible Starbucks was the better. Speed of service was more important than a barista who wanted to talk current events. This new customer came in much less frequently than the traditional customer, as seldom as once a month. As a sign of just how much this shift in customer was affecting its business, by 2007, 80 percent of all Starbucks coffee purchased was consumed outside the store.

Soul Searching

When Starbucks' growth first started tapering off, the executives took notice. In a now famous memo to management, Schultz lamented that "in order to achieve the growth, development, and scale necessary to go from less than 1,000 stores to 15,000 stores and beyond, [Starbucks had made decisions that may] have led to the watering down of the Starbucks experience. Stores no longer have the soul of the past and reflect a chain of stores versus the warm feeling of a neighborhood store."

Starbucks management believed that efforts to recapture that soul would get the company back on track. At first, however, Starbucks was caught between the conflicting goals of reestablishing its image as the provider of a holistic experience and offering better value to the cash-strapped consumer. Starbucks set out to put some water on the fire and get some of its customers back. It added labor hours and time-saving automated machines to stores. It focused on the quality of its coffee with a Coffee Master training program for its baristas and a new line of ultra-premium whole-bean coffees. It even tried free Wi-Fi service and sold its own music.

But none of these actions seemed to address the core problem: Although Starbucks still charged a premium price, it was no longer a special place. As the recession tightened its grip and more people cut back on discretionary purchases, the problem grew worse. Compounding the problem was an increase in competition. For years, if you wanted a latte, Starbucks was about the only option. Not only were Dunkin' Donuts and McDonald's selling premium coffee drinks to the masses, but just about every mini-mart in the country boasted about the quality of its coffee. All of these competitors had prices considerably lower than those of Starbucks, which made the most well-known coffee bar much less justifiable to the "grab and go" crowd. As much as Schultz denied being in direct competition with the lower-status coffee pourers, many critics seemed to be thinking the same thing: Starbucks had shifted from a warm and intimate coffeehouse to little more than a filling station, battling fast-food outlets for some of the same customer dollars.

"Value" to the Rescue?

Throughout 2009, Schultz continued to direct activities aimed at increasing growth. Starbucks launched a campaign designed to educate consumers that Starbucks really wasn't as expensive as they thought it was. That was followed by something Schultz held back for as long as possible: price reductions. "Breakfast pairings"—coffee cake, oatmeal, and an egg sandwich—soon followed.

All these tactics helped. By the end of 2009, Starbucks was regaining ground. With same-store sales up 4 percent and profits up 24 percent for the year, Starbucks' stock price doubled versus the previous year. But Schultz made it clear that he was just getting started. "What a difference a year makes. We're going to radically reframe Starbucks growth strategy." He outlined a three-pronged growth strategy to illustrate that Starbucks might have a grip on defining segments of coffee customers after all. In searching for Starbucks' roots and re-creating the Starbucks store experience, Schultz also aimed to reach customers outside the store.

The first prong of the new strategy centered on Via, Starbucks instant coffee. It is available in single-serve packets at all Starbucks stores and in grocery stores at $1 each or $9.95 for 12 packs. Via lets Starbucks promote a genuine cup of Starbucks coffee for under a buck. Promotions for the new instant have made it clear that Starbucks isn't moving downscale; instant coffee is moving upscale. At a New York taste testing, Schultz told a group of analysts, journalists, and retailers that he was ready for the critics who say, "This is desperate, this is a Hail Mary pass, this is off-brand for Starbucks. We are going to reinvent the category. This is not your mother's instant coffee."

Via is off to a good start, having surpassed company expectations. In fact, Via accounted for more than half of the 4 percent increase in Starbucks' 2009 same-store sales. According to Annie Young-Scrivner, global chief marketing officer for Starbucks, half of all Via serving occasions are at home, 25 percent are in the office, and 25 percent are "on the go." Many Via customers aren't just out for a cheap coffee fix. (You can mix up a cup of Folger's for about 25 cents.) They are people who want premium coffee but are in situations where they don't have access to a store or brewing their own. An ad campaign supporting Via is the first concerted advertising push aimed at grocery customers, who are now accessible through 37,000 retail locations.

The second prong of Starbucks strategy also focuses on the grocery business but through ground-flavored coffees. According to NPD Group, four out of five cups of coffee are consumed at home. Starbucks has a very small share of that market. Via will certainly help. But aiming more directly at the "brew it at home" customer, Starbucks is partnering with Kraft to launch flavored coffees you can brew yourself. Sixty percent of bagged coffee buyers are either drinking flavored coffee or adding flavored creamer. Seventy-five percent of those customers said they would buy a flavored product at the grocery store if Starbucks made one. So after more than two years of testing, this substantial segment of grocery-store buying customers can now get Starbucks Natural Fusion Flavored Coffees.

Fusions in Vanilla, Caramel, and Cinnamon

The third prong of *Starbucks strategy is its ace in the hole*—Seattle's Best Coffee. Starbucks purchased the brand back in 2003 but is just now doing something with it. Rebranding efforts have given Seattle's Best a new look and tagline, "Great Coffee Everywhere." As with Via and Natural Fusions, and now with Seattle's Best, Starbucks is going after customers who don't normally buy Starbucks coffee. It is placing Seattle's Best where Starbuck's customers aren't—in vending machines, coffee carts, fast-food restaurants (Burger King and Subway, among others), theatres, and convenience stores. These are places that Starbucks has avoided for fear of eroding its upscale image. With prices ranging from $1 to just over $2, Seattle's Best also reaches customers who perceive Starbucks as too expensive. Gap has Old Navy. BMW has Mini. Now, Seattle's Best allows Starbucks to go head-to-head with competitors like McDonald's without putting the Starbucks name in the same sentence as downscale competitors.

Michelle Gass, Seattle's Best president, clearly defines the difference versus Starbucks: "Starbucks is a destination coffee experience and an active choice made by the customer. Seattle's Best will instead be brought to the consumer when they make other retail choices." Gass is going to make sure that she has as many of those other retail choices covered as possible. She is taking the brand from 3,000 points of distribution in 2009 to more than 30,000 by the end of 2010.

The three-pronged strategy provides three good reasons to believe that Starbucks growth story will return, even without opening nine stores per day. As icing on the coffee cake, only one-fifth of Starbucks' sales come from outside the United States. The company sees huge potential growth abroad. But perhaps the greatest strength in Starbucks' new strategy is that it will allow the company to go after new customer segments while also restoring the essence of the *Starbucks Experience.*

QUESTIONS FOR DISCUSSION

1. Using the full spectrum of segmentation variables, describe how Starbucks initially segmented and targeted the coffee market.

2. What changed first—the Starbucks customer or the *Starbucks Experience?* Explain your response by discussing the principles of market targeting.

3. Based on the segmentation variables, how is Starbucks now segmenting and targeting the coffee market?

Sources: Beth Kowitt, "Can Starbucks Still Be Seattle's Best If It Grows by Hyping Seattle's Best?" *Fortune* (May 25, 2010), accessed at http://moneycnn.com/2010/05/25/news/companies/starbucks_seattles_best.fortune/index.htm; Emily Bryson York, "Why You Are Not Drinking Nearly Enough Starbucks," *Advertising Age* (May 17, 2010): p. 1; Dan Mitchell, "Starbucks Faces Existential Crisis in Downturn," *Washington Post* (March 22, 2009): p. G01; Bruce Horovitz, "Starbucks Perks Up with First Dividend," *USA Today* (March 25, 2010): p. 1B.

■■■ Case 19 Pricing Almost Destroys and Then Saves a Local Restaurant

"As I pulled into the gravel parking lot I knew immediately that the Mexicatessan was a warm, friendly Mexican restaurant. There was nothing new here, and I don't mean that in a negative way. Nothing looked new but it all looked comfortable, well worn with the passage of time. The front entrance is laden with business cards stapled over the last 30 years. A World War II photo of the owner adorns one wall and Mexican motifs line the walls and ceiling right next to the window air conditioners. Somehow this all looked familiar, although I knew I had never been to the Mexicatessan before."

This is how Sally Bernstein, the restaurant reviewer for the *Houston Post,* described the Mexicatessan in an article celebrating the restaurant's thirtieth birthday. Mr. and Mrs. Herrera established the Mexicatessan in 1957. The restaurant, located in a lower-middle-class neighborhood, attracts both locals and Houston's rich and famous. In the early 1980s, the restaurant's profitability started to drop. Herrera worked long, hard hours producing a high-quality product that his customers enjoyed, but he received very little reward for his time and investment. He had a good product, a good location, and a strong following. The problem was pricing. The prices at the Mexicatessan were far below those of the competition. Herrera wanted to offer good value, and he felt that he had to keep his prices below the chains. He used price to gain a competitive advantage against the chain's expensive buildings and their large regional advertising budgets.

Instead of attracting and maintaining loyal customers, the Mexicatessan's low prices almost destroyed the business. The prices were not high enough to produce sufficient cash flow to keep the restaurant in good repair. Herrera was unable to receive financial reward for his efforts. After several years of struggling, the owner commissioned a research project to see how he could increase his cash flow. The research suggested that his prices were 50 percent less than those of the competition, even though his customers thought the food quality was better. Herrera decided to increase his prices so they were only 10 percent less than the competition. He felt this price difference and his food quality would offset the competitive advantages of the chains. He set out to achieve his strategy through a series of planned price increases. Because achieving his target would mean price increases of 70 percent or more on some items, the first price increase was about 25 percent, with subsequent price increases gradually moving him to his desired pricing levels. Over a three-year period from 1982 to 1985, the menu prices increased by 40 to 70 percent. This was a bold move at a time when Houston was in the middle of a decade-long recession.

After the price increases, the Mexicatessan's revenues increased at a higher percentage than the price increases, indicating there was little resistance to the price increases. Herrera's customers still thought they were getting good value. The price increases allowed him to put a new roof on the building, hire additional staff, decorate the restaurant's interior, and receive a good return on his investment. This case study demonstrates the importance of price. Operations that charge too little often do not have money to maintain the business, although they have many customers and appear prosperous.

Herrera was lucky. It is easier to move up the price of a product that is underpriced than it is to lower the price of an overpriced product. Companies that overcharge create a negative attitude among those who have tried their products. Even when prices are lowered, customer attitudes may remain unchanged. Pricing must be a carefully planned management process.

■■■ DISCUSSION QUESTIONS

1. Why was Mr. Herrera reluctant to raise his prices? How did these low prices almost destroy the business?

2. Using this case as an example, explain how the concepts of demand, price, and profits are interrelated.

■■■ Case 20 Apollo Hotel

After just 10 months of operation, Ryan Sawyer was proud of what he had accomplished managing the Apollo Hotel, but he knew that much work remained.

The Apollo was owned by The Williams Cosmetic Company and was located in Kentucky. The hotel had originally been built to serve as housing for students who attended The Williams Cosmetology School and was converted to an eighty-two-room hotel in September 2002 to serve the general public.

In addition to the hotel, the complex contained a manufacturing plant for personal care products and the corporate headquarters of The Williams Cosmetic Company.

The Williams Cosmetic Company discontinued the operation of a cosmetology school and decided to concentrate on the manufacture and sale of cosmetics. The hotel was opened to use the existing building.

When the hotel opened, there were very few guests, almost no staff, and a limited budget. The hotel had no brochure, Web site, or even a listing in the yellow pages. Although Ryan had no previous hospitality industry experience, he was told to build the business and turn it into a profitable operation.

Ryan held a bachelor's degree in economics/business management from Colorado State University. He had worked with a large regional bank and with JCPenney Company.

Marketing Strategy

Ryan decided that the hotel should be marketed to a wide spectrum of guests. Over the years Mr. and Mrs. Williams had met many people through their church and community work. These contacts proved useful in promoting the hotel.

The Convention and Visitors Bureau also proved to be helpful and referred many guests. Ryan contacted the Little League and secured contracts for teams to stay in the hotel by offering free lodging to referees on a double occupancy per room basis.

To entice guests during the season, Ryan decided to offer three nights for the price of two if guests would make reservations two months prior to arrival and pay in advance. This proved to be moderately effective.

A large electric utility company was offered very good rates to encourage their crews to stay at the hotel. This resulted in many nights of occupancy.

U.S. military personnel were also encouraged to stay at the hotel through very good rates. Ryan believed that with only eighty-two rooms, the best opportunity to fill beds was to contact organizations rather than attempt to market to individual travelers.

The hotel seemed to be gaining a reputation as "value lodging" and had experienced 58 percent occupancy on average for the last four months.

Ryan observed that the company's cosmetic items were not used or sold in the hotel even though they were manufactured on the grounds. This was corrected by placing Williams amenity products in the rooms and opening a gift shop in the hotel, which sold the company's personal care products as well as other traditional gift shop items.

Personnel

As a small, privately owned hotel not operating as a flag property, the management of Apollo could explore different operational strategies. As an example, front-desk employees were paid a commission on business that they brought to the hotel. This encouraged front-desk people to continuously be aware of sales opportunities when someone called or dropped in. It also encouraged them to "sell" the hotel to their friends and to organizations they knew such as churches, schools, and clubs. Ryan said that with commissions, front-desk employees averaged more income than their counterparts in other area hotels.

Ryan believed that his primary responsibility was to "keep the lights on" by marketing the hotel and that operational decisions should be left to those responsible for the operational areas. He held the belief that most people who desired personal growth and responsibility could learn the operational tasks and would find ways to do the job better without top-down micromanagement. He also believed that all employees should be cross-trained and willing temporarily to accept responsibilities outside the primary department. The maintenance man had once been asked to wear a suit and serve as bellboy during a heavy occupancy period. This seemed to work well.

All new employees were expected to learn how to clean rooms and make beds so they could help with that important area in crunch times. The number-one criterion for employment with Apollo was, "Are you willing to learn and willing to work?"

Employees were also expected to constantly improve their professionalism. When decisions were needed by management, department heads were expected to type up their proposal and present it in a professional manner. This forced the department heads to think through the proposal, take it seriously, and be prepared to defend it.

Openness to New Ideas

Ryan said he was open to new ideas from employees and others concerning ways to improve occupancy and operations at the hotel.

DISCUSSION QUESTIONS

Chapter 9

1. What recommendations would you offer to Ryan to:
   a. Increase occupancy
   b. Improve REVPAR
   c. Improve operations

Chapter 10

2. What would you do to further increase the level of personal responsibility that Ryan developed among employees?

3. Do you believe that employees should be cross-trained to do many tasks in a hotel? Does this alienate applicants who might otherwise be good employees?

Chapter 13

4. Should Ryan hire an ad agency to help position and market the hotel?

■■■ Case 21 Chuck E. Cheese CEC Entertainment: "Where a Kid Can Be a Kid"

Chuck E. Cheese is going to Latin America. Binvenidos! Mike Magusiak, president and CEO, announced that the company's management and board of directors strongly supported a strategy of developing new entertainment centers in Latin America.

Several factors were considered in this decision.

- The demographics of Latin America demonstrate a heavy percentage of kids. CEC understands this market segment and has a proven track record in its 540 entertainment units which annually entertain 40 million kids.

- According to information provided by CEC Entertainment, Chuck E. Cheese is more popular with kids than Mickey Mouse and Ronald McDonald.

- The mission of Chuck E. Cheese is to bring families together in a wholesome environment for fun, games, and food. This mission fits well with the culture and demographics of Latin America.

- A writer for the publication *Real Money* said, "Parents are constantly scratching their heads to understand how to entertain kids. After a few trips to a stuffy restaurant with a couple young kids who end up crawling around the floor under your table or worse, running around the restaurant earning you dirty looks from other patrons, you won't be likely to return anytime soon. Likewise when you find a comfortable place where the kids are happy, the parents will be happy and will gladly spend their money. Kids love Chuck E. Cheese. It's like going to a state fair indoors and they serve pizza. What's not to like? You run around and you spend money on arcade games. The food is basic—pizza and wings—but sufficient to satisfy the kids."[1]

- Despite language differences, Latin America is culturally similar to the U.S. Millions of Latin Americans visit the United States each year and many of them head for Disney World, Disneyland, and other entertainment providers.

- Latin Americans are family focused. Parents and grandparents can be expected to visit a Chuck E. Cheese restaurant with children. Repeat visitations are almost guaranteed to occur.

- Many sophisticated investors live in Latin America. In most cases, these people speak English and many studied or worked in the United States.

Chuck E. Cheese has over 30 years of operating success and offers attractive unit profitability. According to Mike Maguisak, the operating margins of 13 percent at Chuck E. Cheese surpass most other chain restaurants.

- Mexico and Central America are only a few hours from major U.S. cities such as Houston, Miami, Los Angeles, and others. This facilitates management support for new restaurants. Although countries such as Chile, Argentina, and Brazil are further away, they are well served by U.S. and international air carriers.

- Latin Americans are a friendly and hospitable people who enjoy working with customers, particularly children.

- Unlike some food dishes which suffer from recipe changes, the menu items of Chuck E. Cheese such as pizza, salads, oven roasted sandwiches, buffalo wings and desserts can easily be modified to meet local food tastes and preferences.

- Little or no direct competition against the Chuck E. Cheese concept exists in most Latin American cities.

- All the food ingredients needed for a Chuck E. Cheese operation are readily available throughout Latin America.

[1]Jackson, Eric, "Forget Kids, Investors Can Go for Chuck E. Cheese, *Breakout Performance*, Thursday, March 4, 2010, accessed November 22, 2011, http://breakoutperformance. blogspot.com/2010/03/forget-kids-investors-can-go-for-chuck.html.

- CEC Entertainment has experience with entertainment centers in Canada, Puerto Rico, Saudi Arabia, Dubai, Guam, and three units in Chile and Guatemala. It was felt that this experience would prove invaluable to the success of multiunit operations in Latin America.

- *Merchandise Sales Opportunities.* Observations of Latin American markets demonstrated that young people are highly attracted to merchandise with logos of consumer products and services. This should provide CEC units within Latin America with excellent opportunities for increased revenue per customer.

- *Fiestas, Birthdays, and Other Celebrations.* Latin Americans have to celebrate birthdays and other special times with the family. Chuck E. Cheese provides over 2 million birthday parties each year.

- Latin American customers, like those in the United States and Canada, are increasingly active in the use of computers. Chuck E. Cheese has experience with online management/marketing and has a database of over 3 million members who receive e-mail updates and specials.

Mike expressed strong optimism that the decision to concentrate international growth in Latin America would eventually provide increased employment opportunities for employees, particularly those fluent in Spanish and Portuguese.

New ideas and concepts might be learned from successful Latin American operations. These might be incorporated into Chuck E. Cheese units elsewhere to the increased entertainment pleasure of kids and thus to profit potential for CEC Entertainment.

■■■ DISCUSSION QUESTIONS

Chapter 8

1. Many of the preceding facts suggest that family segment in Latin American will be attracted to Chuck E. Cheese, just as families in the United States are attracted to the entertainment complex. What are the arguments used in the case to defend this argument?

2. What questions do you have that you would want answered before you expanded into Latin America.

Chapter 6

1. Explain from a consumer behavior standpoint why Chuck E. Cheese appears to be a good fit for Latin America.

2. How do you think consumer behavior in Latin America may differ from consumer behavior in the United States?

■■■ Case 22 World View Travel, Inc.

The president and the general manager of World View Travel were discussing the possible need for new strategies to meet increased competition and to take advantage of a market they both regarded as unsaturated.

History of the Company

World View Travel was located in a southwestern U.S. city of 150,000 people and was owned by Rene Townsend and her husband, Bob. Although Bob was a full partner, he continued to work full time in his career as a pathologist and did not participate in active management of the company. Rene served as president and shared management responsibilities with Sylvia Franklin, the general manager.

After 10 years of operation, World View had become the largest travel agency in town. Prior to establishing World View, Rene had worked two years for a competitive travel agency. At that time only two travel agencies existed in town, with eight or nine employees each. The growth of World View had been fairly constant and some in the industry regarded it as extraordinary. In the first year of operation, World View recorded over $1 million in billings. Growth occurred each subsequent year, despite the existence of two recessions in the 10 years.

City Location

The southwestern city in which World View was located consisted of approximately 150,000 residents with approximately 30 percent classified as minority. The largest part of the minority population was Mexican Americans. Blacks represented approximately a fourth of the minority group.

The city was heavily represented by a middle class, and although there were lower-income areas, there were surprisingly few areas that could be regarded as slums. This was due to a combination of a good industrial base, good public administration, and a civic pride among the residents. There were four major employers in the area and many smaller ones. The city was corporate headquarters for a company listed on the New York Stock Exchange and one listed on the American Exchange. These were involved in electronics and pharmaceuticals.

The predominant industries in the city were banking-finance, insurance, pharmaceuticals, and electronics. The city also boasted a large medical complex that attracted many patients from outside the area and two universities. The city was located on a major interstate highway and was served by three major airlines and two commuter airlines. Two national hotel chains operated downtown properties, and several chains operated motels along the interstate highway.

Competition

Eleven travel agencies existed in the city. One of these was an in-house agency for the largest employer in town. Consequently, very little direct business was generated by this company for any of the ten independent agencies. All the agencies offered a mixture of services and were not particularly distinguishable in terms of product offering or market segments served. The largest increase in numbers of travel agencies had occurred three or four years earlier and there currently seemed to be relative stability in the industry. There were no rumors of new firms opening in town or major expansion by competitors.

Description of World View Travel

After establishing World View Travel, Rene personally called on companies in the area and asked for their travel business. This approach proved to be so successful that after only three years of operation, her agency was as large as that of any competitor. Most of the calls were made to people who Rene or her husband knew through prior business or social settings. Rene admitted to having distaste for "cold calls" to organizations and firms unknown to her and preferred to call persons with whom a prior contact of some kind had been established. In several cases these were referrals by friends or satisfied clients. Time after time she was told by the prospect that this was the first time the owner or manager of a travel agency had ever asked for their business.

Location

The location of World View was not conducive to walk-in. World View leased space in a new office building located on a side street in a light industrial park. The street was not a thoroughfare and dead ended in a cul-de-sac. A sign in front identified World View Travel but was not large or particularly distinct from the signs of neighboring businesses.

Client Mix

The mix of billings for World View was approximately 56 percent commercial and 44 percent group and individual. Of the commercial accounts, six clients had billings of $500,000 or more. These were the larger companies in town. World View did most of the travel business for the second-largest employer in town. However, Rene said that this business was not evenly distributed among all departments within the company. She was certain there were two or three major departments within the client company that did not deal with World View.

The rest of the commercial business came from a mixture of small- and medium-size companies. Rene emphasized that she had purposely tried to have a large mix of commercial clients. She stated that it was likely that on a time-per-client basis, the sales productivity and earnings were less for small clients than for large ones and felt that from a standpoint of the bottom line, her agency would probably be better off with fewer of the smaller commercial clients and more of the larger ones. For instance, "We probably could get every bit of the business of the second-largest employer in town. However, that frightens us since we would then have too many of our eggs in one basket. At this point, we feel we're better off with a larger number of corporate clients, even if some are relatively unproductive."

Revenue comparisons between international and domestic billings revealed that revenue from all international billings contributed 15 percent while domestic contributed 85 percent. Nearly all the services performed by World View could be considered as outbound. A small percentage consisted of making local reservations for corporate clients and helping with inbound groups such as sales meetings and seminars in which corporate clients brought visitors to the local area.

In reviewing the current customer and product mix, Rene commented that she felt commercial business would be significantly more important in the future. The failure of other agencies to gain reputations as strong corporate service firms meant that World View could strengthen its relationship with the area's major employers, resulting in more travel billings. Rene also expressed interest in moving toward the meeting and convention planning business on both an inbound and an outbound basis. She believed that corporate clients were receptive to professional outside assistance in this area and that in the future professional fees could be charged for this service. If a decision was made to expand in this area, changes or additions to the number of sales personnel would be needed.

Advertising and Promotion

Advertising was not regarded as an activity that deserved a heavy budget appropriation. Rene confined advertising to the Yellow Pages telephone directory. Advertisements were purchased in high school annuals and theater programs, but these were regarded as contributions in terms of their effect on sales. A limited number of baggage tags and flight bags were purchased that had the name World View, but these were limited in quantity and given only to selected clients. Rene felt that the best advertising was word-of-mouth referrals based on professional service for clients.

A special corporate relations program existed, which seemed to have been very successful. This consisted of the following factors:

1. A free $100,000 automatic free flight insurance policy for corporate clients who flew on tickets issued by World View.

2. A corporate-rate hotel program. A handbook of nearly 350 pages was given to all corporate clients. This contained names of hotels and the best corporate rates available to them.

3. An emergency 800 number that could be used in case of a travel problem anywhere in the United States.

4. A special training program for executive secretaries to acquaint them with the basics of business travel. This seminar was conducted at the offices of World View and had been popular with executive secretaries.

5. A regular newsletter that was sent to clients.

6. The addition of a special staff person to recheck all fares to ensure the lowest cost to the client.

7. A computer-generated statistical capability to assist major clients in analyzing their travel expenditures and trends.

The Future

The past 10 years had been rewarding ones for World View. Rene and Bob were confident that their travel agency was as well equipped to meet future opportunities and challenges as any in town. Rene spoke very encouragingly of the future.

She felt that the most difficult years were behind and that the future offered excellent opportunities for growth. Rene summarized her feelings by saying, "World View Travel may look quite different ten or even five years from now, but we intend to remain the leading travel agency in this area. In fact, there is no reason we have to confine our plans to this area. We proved we were capable of success in this market and there is no reason we can't think in broader terms. We have the organization, the know-how, and the desire to grow; it's just a matter of setting our objectives, deciding on a strategy, and getting on with the task."

■■■ DISCUSSION QUESTIONS

1. How would you describe World View Travel? What kind of agency is it?

2. What kind of an image do you feel this agency has?

3. What do you consider to be the primary strengths and weaknesses of this agency?

4. What are the primary target markets for World View in the next year? The next five years?

5. Which of the four marketing "Ps" (product/package, price, place, promotion) have contributed directly to the success of World View?

6. Which of the following general strategies should World View employ: sell out, retrench, do nothing/status quo, or planned growth?

7. If you believe World View Travel should adopt a marketing plan for continued growth, which strategy or strategies should the agency employ? Use the below chart to answer Question 7.

■■■ Case 23 Red Rooster Fast-Food Chain

Frank Romano, managing director of Australian Fast Foods, was a key member of the team that in May 2002 brought the head office of the national Red Rooster fast-food chicken networks back home to Perth. The genesis of the group was the Western Australian capital city, under the tutelage of Peter Kailis. It progressively grew interstate and was eventually sold to giant national retailer Coles-Myer.

	YES	NO
A. Product		
1. Product line extension (use same product mix but go after new market segments)?		
Why?		
2. Product offering expansion?		
Examples:		
New product		
Examples:		
Will we need to find new market segments?		
If so, what are they?		
B. Place		
1. A centralized strategy?		
Why?		
2. A decentralized strategy?		
Why?		
C. Promotion		
Paid advertising:		
To reinforce corporate image?		
To sell products?		
If yes, what kinds?		

The overlay of a corporate management structure proved to be incompatible with the essential culture and nature of the original company and the industry. Mass-market strategies that drive the supermarket sector and were delivered by centralized head office executives proved to be inappropriate to a dynamic network of small retail operations, which were greatly influenced by local weather conditions and trading circumstances.

Frank Romano is sensitive to and insistent on "fresh" being a concept and promise of the core product. It requires hands-on, one-on-one quality control monitoring, ordering, and preparation by a conspicuous, active store manager and team members. Profit margins in the industry are wafer thin. Therefore, delegation of authority and responsibility to store level is literally a non-negotiable imperative. Thus, the issue within Red Rooster was one of management style.

Under Australian Fast Foods, the total focus of all executives is on the day-to-day running of the business, complemented with good online, real-time systems that keep people informed, up-to-date, and enable prompt responses to changing circumstances and demands. The company plans to be a paperless operator in the near future.

Frank does not claim possession of a secret recipe of herbs and spices. Instead, the company's management philosophy and practices serve as the foundation for success. In December 2003, the two distinctly branded networks of Red Rooster (335 outlets) and Chicken Treat (63) totaled 398, and rising. Eleven new Red Rooster stores were opened in the 2003 calendar year.

There is a predominance of company-owned and managed outlets, with twelve Chicken Treat franchises and fifty-eight franchised Red Rooster operators.

Frank contends the key marketing lesson to be learned from his company is the importance of employing the right people to provide good service and quality, at the best affordable price. His chicken product, which has lower fat content because of the cooking method, has always provided a competitive edge. Barbecued chicken was the traditional available healthy choice for Australian fast-food customers.

New competitors and new menus have created challenges. McDonald's has introduced salads, the Subway chain has been quickly accepted, and the chain Nando's provides a healthy, tempting alternative. The Domino's Pizza Group plans to offer low-fat cheeses in its product range. KFC has also been innovative, with new fillet burgers and wraps, which in the overall marketplace are not considered passé!

Frank Romano and his team at Australian Fast Foods have been quick to respond. Fresh subs were rolled over in December 2002. A new salad selection was launched on January 1, 2004, and a new healthier chicken was released later that year. Product differentiation remains a key fundamental in the chain's competitive strategy.

These initiatives will complement store decor refurbishments and a fresh positioning, marketing, and advertising strategy.

Attention will be given to New South Wales and Queensland where the company was least represented under the ownership of Coles-Myer, because of what is considered the previous owner's poor distribution strategy. No new Red Rooster store was opened in Queensland for two years.

Frank respects the importance of the supply chain. There are a limited number of suppliers in frozen food, chicken, beverage, and packaging. Significantly, in 25 years there have not been changes in the major suppliers.

Frank feels that his company has always been well treated by supply entities. Relationships are direct, one-on-one, and Frank oversees negotiations. His open-book policy reflects acceptance of price rises in circumstances where there is transparency on all relevant facts and factors.

The price-sensitive, competitive nature of the fast-food sector demands confidentiality and flexibility. Strategic avenues exist and evolve, enabling some degree of annual planning and scheduling. However, to retain a confidential and a competitive edge, suppliers are not directly involved in the early stages of the chain's marketing activities.

Frank and his executive team plan their own media strategies with placements through an external media-buying group. This is part of the hands-on management philosophy and the need to localize tactics and resource deployment. The company's research and development department was recently relocated from Melbourne to the head office in Perth.

The Future

Significant growth is forecast for the next two years, with a target of 132 store openings, including entry into New Zealand. Unlike the Coles-Myer approach, the focus will be on the core chicken product range.

Collectively these will be the drivers for a projected market share increase from around 12 percent to between 16 and 18 percent of the fast-food marketplace by the conclusion of 2005.

About the Author

Barry Urquhart is the managing director of Marketing Focus, in Perth, Australia. Barry is an internationally recognized conference keynote speaker, a facilitator of strategic planning workshops, and a marketing business coach.

Barry is author of six top-selling books, including the two largest-selling publications on service excellence in Australia.

Barry's latest keynote presentation is "The Business Lessons of the Iraq War." e-mail: urquhart@marketinfocus.net.au. Web: www.marketingfocus.net.au.

▪▪▪ DISCUSSION QUESTIONS

1. The fast-food industry is changing rapidly. What significant changes do you envision for this industry in the area in which you live during the next five years?

2. Why do you believe the fast-food chain Red Rooster was unable to thrive and grow when it was part of a large national retail chain?

3. What are the dominant management/marketing factors that permit success within the fast-food business?

4. Can a large retail chain such as Coles-Myer, Safeway, Wal-Mart, and others effectively compete in the fast-food business? If so, what do you believe they must do?

▪▪▪ Case 24 Tropicana Fishing Lodge

How does a fishing lodge fit into our operations as a major producer of bananas? This was the question that faced the Costa Rican division of an international banana company.

Location and Description of Tropicana

Tropicana was a fishing lodge located on the Caribbean coast of Costa Rica. It was situated on the banks of the River Pastura. It could be reached by light plane because there was a paved landing strip on the nearby properties of Del Monte. It could also be reached by means of a mountain highway from San José. This road was 98 percent paved and required approximately three to three-and-a-half hours of travel. Fog could be a problem on this road and could impede travel. A small dock had been built to accommodate loading and unloading the boats. A series of steps, including rather steep steel ones with a rope handhold, led to the grassy bank above.

Immediately behind the lodge was a banana plantation. A cement sidewalk separated the plantation from the lodge and homes. The grounds surrounding the lodge were well kept and quite attractive. The beauty was not dramatic or awe inspiring but was instead peaceful and relaxing. Jungle growth could be seen on the opposite bank of the river, and monkeys could be heard howling in the forest.

The lodge was built in the fashion of a jungle building—it was not constructed on the ground but on wooden stilts. This allowed ventilation and helped prevent rotting. It also helped discourage insects and small animals from entering. The lodge was small but would accommodate twenty-two guests. Guest rooms were contained in a separate cabin that formed an "L" to the main lodge. The rooms were clean and well maintained. Each room had a bathroom with a shower and other bathroom fixtures. Beds were of the single-bed or bunk-bed style. There was no air conditioning in the rooms, but the evening breeze was pleasant. A light blanket was sometimes necessary.

Recreational Facilities

Fishing for tarpon and snook was the primary entertainment offered by Tropicana. This occurred in the intercoastal canal, which runs from Limón to the Nicaraguan border. It was also done in lagoons and the mouths of rivers. The river in front of Tropicana offered little opportunity for fishing; it was necessary to go downstream 30 to 40 minutes by boat to reach fishing sites.

Three principal areas were noted for tarpon and snook. One was in a lagoon 40 minutes downstream and to the south of Tropicana. Another was downstream and north of Tropicana near the village of Parisminas. This was 45 minutes to an hour away and near a competitor's lodge. The third was much farther north, in the area of Toruguero. This was roughly one-and-a-half hours away.

The scenery in the intercoastal canal and along the jungle rivers was beautiful. One could see a variety of bird life, including many rare species. Monkeys could be heard and sometimes seen in the trees. Both Walt Disney and Jacques Cousteau had made movies featuring the region. Crocodiles were difficult to see. Deer, marguary, jaguar, and many small animals also lived there but were rarely seen. Botanists and other nature lovers could find hours of enjoyment in the variety of trees, flowers, orchids, and other plant life, including a perfume tree that filled the air with a beautiful aroma in the evening.

There was little or no opportunity to exploit commercial hunting in the area. The area was not known for ducks or geese, and the deer were quite small. In addition, much of the area was gradually being turned into national parks, and wildlife would be protected. Swimming or water skiing in the lagoons and intercoastal waterway would be dangerous due to submerged logs. There was also the possibility of sharks. The Caribbean coast represented miles of uninhabited dark sandy beach. It had palm trees and was attractive but was not developed. Moreover, it was very difficult to reach the beach from Tropicana. The surf at the mouth of the river was too strong to permit entry into the sea with the flat-bottom boats and motors. Thus the boats could not be used for ocean fishing.

Any large-scale building projects such as a lodge, modern tennis courts, or a golf course would require land. This would almost certainly have to come from land that was profitably planted in bananas.

Fishing Season

Although Tropicana remained open all year, guests were advised that fishing was impossible from November 1 to January 15. This was the time of year when the heaviest rains occurred. The longest periods of dry weather were from the latter part of January through most of May and then again from August through October. The best time for snook fishing occurred in late August until November 1. A schedule of the best fishing months versus the traditional months of high occupancy at Tropicana follows. This schedule presented certain difficulties in promoting Tropicana as a year-round lodge. During the months of May through August, Tropicana had to compete with vacation areas in the United States. September and October represented excellent months for fishing but relatively weak ones for occupancy due to the fact that school was open in the United States. In addition, these were fall months in the United States, with nice weather conditions there. November and December were winter months in the United States and could be promoted as vacation months, but fishing was impossible during that time. Increased promotion would be necessary to reduce the dependency on three to five months of natural draw. November, December, and half of January would remain poor months due to weather and fishing conditions. Thus Tropicana would face, at a maximum, nine favorable months.

MONTH	FISHING CONDITIONS	FIVE HIGHEST MONTHS OF OCCUPANCY AT TROPICANA (APPROXIMATELY 80% OF TOTAL OCCUPANCY)
January	Good	
February	Excellent	1
March	Fair	2
April	Fair	3
May	Excellent	
June	Excellent	
July	Good	
August	Good	
September	Excellent	4
October	Excellent	5
November	Poor	
December	Poor	

Value of Lodge

It was difficult to estimate the market value of the lodge, but Eric estimated that it would probably be valued somewhere between $250,000 and $500,000 (U.S.). A difficulty in appraising the lodge was that its success was tied directly to the banana company, which owned and operated the source of electrical power for the lodge. A buyer might find this factor of concern. However, a generator and an independent well would not be difficult to acquire.

Competitors

- *Azul Grande.* The fishing lodge of Azul Grande was the primary competitor and could accommodate twenty-four guests. This lodge was located in the fishing village of Parisminas and could be reached only by private airplane or boat. It was not as attractive as Tropicana. It was surrounded by poor fishing shacks and older in appearance than Tropicana. However, it was clean and well maintained. A monkey in the front yard greeted all visitors. Clients for this lodge were almost exclusively from the United States. The owners advertised in select outdoor magazines. The owner also appeared on TV talk shows when he was in the United States. Bookings in the United States were handled through an exclusive agent in Chicago who worked on a commission basis.

- *Isla Del Sol.* This fishing lodge was located at the mouth of the San Juan River, which forms a border for Nicaragua and Costa Rica. The manager/owner was a Mr. Laurie from Detroit. This lodge was experiencing difficulty in breaking even and was open six months or less each year.

- *Casa Fantastica.* This fishing lodge was also located at the mouth of the San Juan River and open six months or less each year. There was no information concerning the success of this lodge, but it was apparent that the management was fairly aggressive, as witnessed by advertisements from the outdoor magazine *The Salt Water Sportsman.*

Rates

Rates for competitive fishing lodges on the Caribbean coast ranged from $2,000 to $3,500 per person per week. Tropicana and other lodges did not encourage guests to come for periods of less than five days. This was due to the cost of transportation.

It also provided a guest with more opportunities to catch fish. Guests who stayed for shorter periods of time sometimes arrived when fishing was poor and returned to spread stories of poor fishing. All lodges provided competitive services, although Tropicana provided even more individualized attention to guests and was willing to spend more time and money to transport guests to good fishing sites.

Promotion and Client Profile: Las Perla

Promotion for Tropicana was handled primarily through ads in the English-print newspapers in San José. Word-of-mouth advertising seemed to be the primary means by which people heard of the lodge. A review of the guest book indicated that the majority of guests had been from the United States; the second largest group were Costa Ricans.

■■■ DISCUSSION QUESTIONS

Chapter 12

1. What distribution channels would you use for the Tropicana Fishing Lodge?

2. How are distribution and segmentation related?

Chapter 13

3. What promotional strategies/tactics would you suggest for Tropicana?

4. Discuss the differences in management and marketing between a commercial fishing or hunting lodge and a commercial hotel.

5. Could the marketing of diverse hunting/fishing lodges be conducted effectively by an independent group responsible for multiple properties?

■■■ Case 25 Boulder Creek

One of the most difficult marketing tasks in any industry is to reposition a declining product, attract new market segments, and achieve market success. Yet that is exactly what Andrea Lewis did with a former Econo Lodge in a nonhighway location in Boulder, Colorado.

"This was the hardest thing I had ever done," said Andrea. "My husband, Burt and I, purchased the property in 1999 but Burt was busy with real estate in Chicago and left most of the responsibility to me."

Andrea knew nothing about hotels but found that her training and experience supervising twenty-six salespeople in nineteen states as manager of corporate sales for Tiffany & Company was invaluable. Andrea had just been offered a promotion with Tiffany's when Burt called to say they were purchasing an ignored Econo Lodge in Boulder that had great potential. "I need you to quit your job, move to Boulder, and remake this hotel," said Burt. Andrea had recently experienced the death of two young friends and said to herself, "I love Boulder, and I love Colorado. This will be a challenge, but life is short, so let's do it."

Life at Tiffany's was a dream compared to the task that confronted Andrea. The property contained a hundred-year-old home suffering from geriatrics, a motel complex that had been built in stages with little or no curbside appeal, a lack of landscaping, a rutted parking lot, and a lack of physical amenities such as a swimming pool and exercise room. Located in a student residential area, the property did not easily lend itself to drive-by stopovers.

Employee quality and attitudes matched the property. Several employees were drug dealers or addicts, and an attitude of ignoring the guest prevailed. The management and staff seemed more interested in naked pool parties than guest interaction. One unusual guest service offered at the front desk was a tattoo on the ankle with real tattoo machines. Maintenance and housekeeping were not prepared to provide anything more than a barely acceptable level of guest satisfaction.

"The staff we inherited could not embrace customer service and consistently attracted low-life guests," said Andrea. It was not surprising that the front office was protected by bulletproof glass.

Management practices had discouraged customers from their nearest neighbors, The University of Colorado and Naropa University, a Buddhist institution. The hotel's policy had been, "No we won't direct bill even the most upstanding and desirable commercial clients, including Colorado University."

Turnaround

Within three years, this property changed from despair to being the winner of the gold award and a nomination for Platinum as the only Quality Inn in the United States. Repeat business at Boulder Creek was high and in a period of low hotel occupancy for the industry, Boulder Creek achieved a 78 percent average occupancy compared to 50 percent for Boulder hotels. Simultaneously, the Boulder Creek enjoyed an average daily rate (ADR) of $70, high for its category in 2002.

How did this remarkable turnaround occur?

Flag Change

Burt and Andrea believed that dramatic change was not possible under the Econo Lodge name but felt there was an advantage in remaining within the family of Choice Hotels International. They realized that the brand Quality Inn and Suites had not been used in the Boulder market. Andrea developed a presentation for the management of Choice Hotels that demonstrated the dramatic changes she planned and was granted the right as the first and only Econo Lodge to change to a Quality Inn.

Physical Property

The city of Boulder has very strict building codes and building permits are difficult to acquire. Knowing this, Andrea hired a respected architect with knowledge of the city and the elected officials. Andrea and the architect decided that the century-old home should be preserved and enhanced as a historic building and given multiple uses as front desk, business center, management offices, breakfast room, and two guest rooms upstairs.

A fireplace of colored river rock serves as a focal point near the front desk. The work of Colorado western artists was selected to furnish the historic home and the guest rooms. Curbside appeal was greatly enhanced by improving visibility, particularly of the historic home as a focal point. Landscaping with native wildflowers and rocks serves as the area of support for an attractive sign announcing the brands Quality Inn and Suites and Boulder Creek.

The forty guest rooms and six suites were remodeled with "casually upscale lodge furnishings." Each room has many of the features expected in an upscale hotel such as Hyatt or Westin.

- Private voice mail with off-site access

- Two-line data port speaker phones

- Internet access

- Twenty-five-inch color TV, microwave, refrigerator

- Coffee maker, coffee, iron, full-size ironing board, hair dryer

- Massage shower head

Andrea sought local artisans to make Western-style lamps, furniture, and bedspreads.

A fitness center was built and furnished with new state-of-the-art equipment. An inside sauna and a hot tub were built near a refurbished indoor swimming pool and a coin-operated laundry for guest use only.

The breakfast bar offers an assortment far beyond the typical cold cereal and doughnuts of many hotels. Free daily breakfast at Boulder Creek is a deluxe hot breakfast buffet of eggs, sausage, waffles, cereal, bakery goods, fruit, yogurt, and three types of juice, tea, or coffee.

Samantha

Samantha, a soft-coated Wheaton Terrier, is Andrea's personal pet and friend of the staff and guests. When Boulder Creek opened, pets were not accepted. This proved to be a bit awkward as Samantha found the space immediately beneath the No Pets Allowed sign perfect for naps. Several guest rooms are now reserved for guests with pets. Other rooms remain pet free because some guests have allergies to pets.

New Staff

Because retraining staff and changing old attitudes proved much more difficult than changing the physical structure, the entire original staff was fired.

Andrea originally went to an organization called the Boulder Workplace, which placed her in touch with individuals 50 years and older seeking employment. A manager lacked hotel experience but held a degree in operations management and exhibited the correct people skills and positive attitude.

Andrea personally took charge of employee training using a philosophy that if you treat your employees as gold, they will in turn treat you as gold. Although Andrea held an MBA from Vassar, she credited her training at Tiffany's and earlier at Estee Lauder with instilling the concept of "Excellence."

A constant theme of Andrea's that is taught to all employees is "Customer Service Doesn't Get a Day Off." Many of the first hires had to be taught computer skills, but recent hires generally bring these skills to the job.

Marketing/Sales

Unlike some hotels where the guest is expected to step around ladders and paint cans, Andrea refused to open until the hotel was ready. "Sure we needed the cash flow, but it was critical that the guests enjoy a finished product." Many people wanted to come even during remodeling, but were told, "You can't come here now, wait until we are ready; we do not want to disappoint you." Guests waited and were pleased that they did. Andrea said there is something in all of us that says, "If I can't have something, that is exactly what I want."

An initial budget of $60,000 was established for marketing/public relations expenses. Andrea personally visited target organizations in Boulder prior to the grand opening on May 9, 2000. She felt that selected organizations could provide guests who would recognize and appreciate quality lodging. Those seeking only a "cheap sleep" were not viewed as target guests.

The University of Colorado and Naropa University had visiting professors, parents, and many others who visit during the year. Successful corporations, particularly those in technology, could provide many business travelers.

Direct billing was welcomed and individuals from these target organizations who might influence visitor hotel selection were personally given tours of the property. A list of potential guests and gatekeepers was developed and used for extending invitations to launch parties, swim parties, cocktail parties, and other planned events.

Travel writers were invited and given red carpet treatment as well as an honest and interesting story about the development of Boulder Creek. This resulted in many articles written in newspapers and magazines. Many free nights were given to individuals who could influence future business.

Andrea also targeted supportive hospitality businesses in which there might be a possibility of quid pro quo ("You scratch my back; I'll scratch yours"). Packages that supported local businesses such as restaurants were developed. Andrea felt that these built support among "local partners" and also provided the hotel guests with something above and beyond what they expect.

Now after building the business and understanding what is required to market the property successfully, Andrea said she was ready to hire a salesperson to ensure the continuation and growth of business.

Going Green

A majority of Boulder Creek's guests have some affiliation with one of the local universities. These guests ask for services that are regarded as healthy and environmentally friendly. A policy of no smoking was expected, but a recent request had caused Andrea to think creatively. The hotel offered quality amenities in each room such as shampoo, soap, and lotion. Lately many guests had stated these were not environmentally friendly and that amenities should be offered in a liquid dispenser.

Andrea was considering how to comply with this request without resorting to the common institutional look of dispensers and without offending guests who preferred the traditional mini-bottle amenities.

Keeping It Fresh and Different

Andrea knew that her key to future success would depend on keeping the property fresh, upscale, and different. This meant examining details.

Each room featured Boulder Creek's own custom coffee blend created by Wolfgang Puck. Cordless phones in each room permitted guests to walk and talk rather than being tied to a phone by the bed. An outside dog run had been discussed but was not currently possible due to lack of space. Backup bedspreads were also used when a dog had been in the room.

Andrea felt that new windows were needed and would result in considerable energy savings. However, the swimming pool needed freshening. Should she spend the money on windows that would probably not be recognized by the guest or in the pool? This was typical of the type of decision Andrea faced.

Expansion

Andrea and Burt felt comfortable that they understood the Boulder market and had recently purchased another older property in Boulder. This would again require the hands-on skills of Andrea.

Beyond that was Fort Collins with Colorado State University, Greeley with Northern Colorado University, and other Colorado cities. The question of flag affiliation also affected the future. Should Boulder Creek remain a Quality Inn? Only about 10 percent of actual guest reservations came from the parent company, but there was value in the flag. Andrea and Burt felt they could do well as an independent, but then someone else would acquire the Quality Inn brand in the area and benefit from their hard work.

Boulder had been good to Andrea, and many townspeople regularly commented about how much they appreciated what Boulder Creek had done for the neighborhood and the town. The planning and work of Andrea and Burt had paid off, but both realized that they could not relax and would need to remain constantly alert and open to new ideas and concepts.

■■■ DISCUSSION QUESTIONS

1. Andrea and Burt repositioned Boulder Creek. Explain who the market was before repositioning and who their target market is now.

2. How did they change the marketing mix to fit their new target market?

3. Would you retain the Quality Inn flag? Explain your decision.

■■■ Case 26 Lucky Larry's

Effective database marketing combined with key customer programs are the ingredients for success at Lucky Larry's Casino. How else could you effectively market the last casino on a twisting mountain road lined with casinos in the gambling towns of Black Hawk and Central City? With limited parking and limited casino space, Lucky Larry's faces heavy competitive pressure. The general manager, Roger Worth, described the overall problems as location and restrictions on all casinos in Central City that do not permit expansion beyond the constraints of existing historical buildings in which they are housed.

The twin cities of Black Hawk and Central City initiated casino gambling in 1991, but by 1997 Black Hawk was rated as the number-one casino city in Colorado, whereas Central City had dropped to third place. Twenty-five casinos had ceased operation in Central City and more seemed likely to close, whereas those in Black Hawk grew larger and more attractive to casino-gambling customers.

Like other casinos, Lucky Larry's depended on high spending and frequent gamblers. Lucky Larry's had tried table games, but a $5 maximum bet law in Colorado made them unprofitable. Slot machines and video poker games now represent the only casino offerings.

During the gold rush days of the nineteenth century, Lucky Larry's had served as a hotel, bar, and restaurant. Unfortunately, hard-core gamblers showed little interest in history, and history buffs showed little interest in gambling. The perception among dedicated slot players was that crowded casinos with lots of action must be good payout casinos as opposed to smaller, quieter ones such as the Teller House.

Roger knew that he must retain and build its group of key customers. A sophisticated database marketing program was managed by Kay Palace, who collected player data electronically by means of a plastic Lucky Larry's Casino Club Card from players who inserted the card into a box attached to the slot or poker machine. Players were encouraged to join the club and use the card to accumulate points, which could be redeemed for cash or gifts and also allowed them to participate in club activities. Use of the card permitted Lucky Larry's to accumulate usage data about each player and cross-tabulate it against demographic data, including address, zip code, date of birth, and length of club membership. Usage information included type of game preferred, average amount bet per visit, total amount bet since becoming a member, total win/loss, last date of play, and total membership points earned.

Kay said that this information was invaluable in designing promotional programs for key customers but had proven to be of limited use in attracting new players. "The fact that a frequent player lives in a certain zip code or is a certain age does not mean that neighbors of the same age will also be avid slot players," said Kay. She added that the database had proven effective in developing programs aimed at combating key player defection, as these people could be identified easily. Unlike some casinos, Lucky Larry's did not rely as heavily on media aimed at a general market or on enticement coupons. Instead, Lucky Larry's preferred to develop programs for known heavy gamblers. One of Kay's responsibilities was to measure the impact of each promotional program. As an example, this information revealed that newsletters were a more effective medium than tabloid-type publications sent to known gamblers.

Everyone at Lucky Larry's, from management to the floor personnel, understands that success depends on continuously pleasing those hard-core gamblers and enticing them to return. Theme programs such as a cruise theme found employees dressed in tropical attire and offering tropical drinks to patrons.

Slot machine tournaments were designed for key players to build enthusiasm and differentiate Lucky Larry's. Players were ranked by Lucky Larry's based on their amount of play. A VIP club was designed for "A"-level players who were occasionally given premiums such as a 99 percent silver commemorative Lucky Larry's Coin. New programs offering player excitement were continuously developed by the marketing/sales department. Ideas were welcome from any employee.

Source: ©James Makens; used with permission.

■■■ DISCUSSION QUESTIONS

1. Explain how creating and using a database creates a competitive advantage.

2. How did Lucky Larry's use its database to create customer loyalty?

3. Was the database marketing at Lucky Larry's part of an integrated marketing program? Explain your answer.

■■■ Case 27 International Travel Agency

The president of International Travel Agency was concerned about the performance of the sales force. It was felt that members of the sales force did not really use their sales opportunities but instead thought only about selling a ticket to a customer from point A to point B. The sales force did not seem to have an interest in maximizing sales and profits by aggressively selling the entire product mix.

In total, the agency had a sales force of eight. Three members of the sales force were referred to as executive sales consultants. These people called on commercial accounts and were expected to spend more of their time outside the office. The remaining five persons were referred to as travel counselors and worked entirely within the agency.

None of the travel counselors who worked within the agency were assigned a quota. The executive sales consultants, who worked outside the office, were assigned a sales quota. Failure to meet a quota would be discussed with the salesperson, but no other action was usually taken unless this failure continued for several months. If serious and persistent deficiencies existed, the salesperson could be subject to discharge.

The agency provided nine to twelve familiarization (fam) trips for members of the sales force each year. This meant that each salesperson could experience at least one trip per year, and they were assigned on a rotating basis. These trips did not reduce time from the salesperson's guaranteed number of days of annual vacation. The purpose of a fam trip was to acquaint travel agents with destination areas and the services of airlines, hotels, restaurants, and so on.

The president felt that the agency could maximize profits by selling more travel services to clients and that the sales force was concerned only about selling tickets. An analysis of the product mix of International Travel revealed that approximately 85 percent was accounted for by airline tickets. The remaining 15 percent consisted of allied travel services, including hotels, rental cars, and entertainment. Of these, the majority consisted of hotel reservations. Less than 1 percent was accounted for by the sale of traveler's checks. One of the members of management offered the analogy of a businessman entering a clothing store. If a customer purchases a suit, the salesclerk asks if the customer might need a new shirt or tie to go with the suit. Travel agents are no different. They write a ticket from Chicago to Hong Kong or London for a client and never bother to ask if the client needs hotel accommodations, rental cars, traveler's checks, or other services that an agency handles.

The president of International Travel had tried to encourage the sales force to sell other services but felt that they seemed uninterested in taking the time and effort required. The president believed that maximizing sales of the complete product mix would lead to maximum profits and that something must be done to encourage cross-selling.

■■■ DISCUSSION QUESTIONS

1. What can be done to encourage the sales force to engage in more cross-selling?

2. Does the current fam trip program serve as a motivational tool for the sales force?

3. Discuss what is needed in terms of sales incentives and sales controls to achieve the objectives of the International Travel Agency.

■■■ Case 28 Superior Hotels

Jan Trible, president of Superior Hotels, was concerned with the future expansion of the company. Superior Hotels had built a strong reputation in the management of time-share resorts in Florida. The company had recently acquired a consulting contract for a ski resort in the Rocky Mountains, which would mark its entrance into a new area of resort management. Now there was serious discussion concerning the advisability of entering the commercial hotel segment of the hotel industry within cities of 100,000 to 200,000 in population.

Management of Time-Share Resorts

The management style of Superior Hotels was exemplified in the management of the company's time-share resorts. Superior managed five time-share resorts, with a total of 240 units. The company maintained a policy of not accepting management contracts for time-share projects that were in trouble. The company philosophy maintained that most of these had been ill planned and probably had little likelihood of long-range success. Jan personally believed that a major shakeup in the time-share industry was coming and that many existing projects would fail.

The Superior Hotel policy was to begin working with the developers of a time-share resort at the beginning of the project. It was felt that developers have a short-run viewpoint, but a management company must think of the long run. The policy was to become involved in the entire planning process of the project, including blueprints and interior decorations. If a developer refused to cooperate, Superior would remove itself from future management. Management believed that a time-share project differed considerably from a conventional hotel or resort development.

1. A time-share project has hundreds or thousands of owners. A conventional hotel or resort has one or a few.

2. Time-share projects receive high-intensity use, with 95 percent occupancy being normal. Furniture, carpeting, and other furnishings can wear out in a third of the time. Therefore, rules of thumb developed for hotels would often not apply in time-share.

3. The guest assumes a proprietary interest in a time-share. Guests are extremely critical because they view the units as theirs and complain about things that a hotel guest would accept.

4. A great deal of hype goes into the sales of a time-share unit, and guests arrive with extreme expectations. Superior has to bring reality into the dreams that the sales department creates.

5. The long-run success of a time-share unit depends on attracting the same guests each year for as long as 20 years or more. If guests became dissatisfied and enough guests decided to drop their ownership, resales can be very difficult and the entire project can be in jeopardy.

Several management practices had been developed by Superior to deal with these complexities.

Owner Feedback

Owner comment sheets were distributed to each owner/guest during each visit. Jan took pride in the fact that she read each one personally. These sheets covered a variety of areas, from general appearance of the unit to any evidence of insects and rodents. If the comments were particularly bad, a member of management, including Jan, would personally contact the owner and report on the steps that had been taken to correct the problem.

Feedback was also received in "owner coffees." These weekly meetings with owners included attendance by one or more members of management. These could include the resort owner, the head of housekeeping, the director of internal management, and others. A quarterly newsletter was published by Superior and sent to all owners. In addition to information of a general nature such as changes in air fares to the resort, the newsletter was personalized to the extent that it reminded all owners of their vacation week.

Recreation Management

Superior Hotels believed that even the most beautiful and best-maintained resort could eventually become boring. To ensure that guests would find something new each year, a recreation program was established with a full-time professional in charge. Programs were designed for all ages. These employed some of the successful concepts of Club Med.

Supervised programs for children allowed parents a freedom they could not enjoy at most resorts. Hot dog parties, beach parties, tennis competitions, seashell classes, and many other programs offered a variety of recreational and educational pursuits. Each recreational program was monitored as to attendance and guest satisfaction, and weak ones were eliminated. A dominant feature of all the programs was the opportunity for interaction among guests. Jan believed that a guest at the average resort could spend a week and never develop new friendships. Ideally, the recreation programs encouraged friendships to develop.

Housekeeping and Maintenance

The turnover of a majority of the guests one day and the mass arrival of an equal number the next provides special housekeeping and maintenance problems for time-share projects. A full-time maintenance crew was employed, and a large inventory of replacement furnishings was carried. If a TV set or electric range had a problem, it was replaced immediately rather than sending a repair technician. With only one vacation week, Jan felt that a guest did not want to share it with a repair person. Housekeeping was performed for the time-share resorts under contract with an independent housekeeping company. Housekeeping managers were responsible for examining each room personally and ensuring that corrections immediately followed discovery of a problem.

The Superior Hotel Image and Philosophy

"All Superior properties must be first class; there is no room in this corporation for mundane or second-class properties." This statement by Jan summed up the company's philosophy. The philosophy concerning quality had led management to change its policy concerning the new properties it would manage. The company recently initiated a policy of holding an equity position in all future properties. This decision was made for two reasons. First, an ownership position would allow Superior to have a stronger voice in the development and management of properties and would help ensure quality. Second, Superior Hotels had no interest in "bringing up" properties to a desired quality and performance level only to find that the managers had decided not to renew the management contract.

Corporate Objectives

The management and ownership of Superior Hotels desired for the company to be recognized as a strong national resort and commercial hotel management company within 10 years. It was felt that resort properties offered limited growth opportunities because the most desirable locations had been developed by others.

The best strategy for the next five years seemed to lie in the development of first-class commercial properties within Sunbelt cities of 100,000 to 200,000 people. It was felt that the development of three new properties per year in this market was realistic. Sunbelt cities were believed to offer the best potential for growth because of the scarcity of 150- to 200-room high-quality hotels. These second-tier cities remained important industrial and agricultural centers and did not usually offer truly first-class hotel accommodations. In many cases a respected medical complex had been developed in these cities, and it was felt that this factor alone would serve as a magnet for visitors.

■■■ DISCUSSION QUESTIONS

1. What are the core competencies of Superior Hotels? Management of resorts? Management of time-share resorts? Management of ski resorts? Management of commercial hotels? Other?

2. Do you believe that Superior Hotels should be entering diverse markets such as ski resorts and commercial hotels?

3. Do you believe that Superior Hotels can effectively market and manage a wide diversity of properties?

4. What would you advise Jan Trible to do?

■■■ Case 29 The Cameron Trading Post & Lodge

Travelers who venture 52 miles north of Flagstaff, Arizona, on Highway 89 are surprised and delighted when they stop at the Cameron Trading Post along the Little Colorado River Canyon. In reality, Cameron Trading Post represents most of the commercial activity in the town of Cameron. A decommissioned swayback suspension bridge built in 1911 sits next to the property.

Cameron began as a trading post where Hopi and Navajo residents bartered wool, blankets, and livestock for flour, sugar, canned goods, and household products. A trip to the post would take days of travel by horse-drawn wagon. Customers were always treated as family and fed and housed at the trading post. Traders at Cameron were trusted by the local people because they understood local dialects and customers and explained the confusing American legal and social system.

Today the trading post is owned by the employees and Joe Atkinson, a direct descendent of the original owners. It serves as a stopping point for travelers headed to the Grand Canyon, Lake Powell, The Painted Desert, and Utah.

The Cameron Trading Post and Lodge represent an example of:

Quality

Customer service

Respect for Native American culture

Excellent merchandising

Fair treatment & training of employees

Employee empowerment

Continuous product innovation

Cameron Trading Post may also represent a warning for the entire hospitality industry concerning the delicate balance between natural resource use, particularly water, and commercial growth.

The strength behind Cameron Trading Post is Joe Atkinson, a product and heir of Western pioneers and their attitudes—not the Hollywood version.

Joe's family came to Arizona and New Mexico as Indian traders. One was killed by Paiutes, Navajos, or outlaws in the 1840s as he carried trading goods by horse and mule to his customers.

Joe was born to the business at the Three Hogans Trading Post in Arizona. His uncles, CD and Hubert Richardson, moved to Arizona from Cleburne, Texas, and established a trading post at Cameron in 1916. In 1964, it was leased to Chevron Oil Company and later to the Harvey Corporation, a hospitality company pioneer who had built a successful western hotel, restaurant, and gift shop chain in cooperation with the Santa Fe Railroad.

In 1977, Joe gained control of the Cameron Trading Post as well as Indian jewelry stores in Gallup, Santa Fe, Albuquerque, and Phoenix.

Joe didn't have the advantage of a college education but became an acknowledged expert in Indian jewelry and art and also learned to fly his own twin-engine Cessna. Joe discovered cigars at age four and until recently he and a good cigar were inseparable. That was the second time he had to give up cigars. The first was when he started grade school and the principal would not permit a cigar-smoking first grader.

The Cameron Trading Post serves as a source of southwestern art, souvenirs, and curios. The store features quality hand-crafted traditional patterns on weaving, baskets, pottery, jewelry, and carvings. A free gallery of American Southwest Indian art is situated in a historic building of sandstone and log on the property.

Visitors dine in an atmosphere of antique luxury. A huge stone fireplace and beautiful local art provide a southwestern setting for breakfast, lunch, and dinner. The menu features American and Mexican foods as well as a signature "Navajo taco."

The sixty-six-room lodge follows the upscale Southwest theme with exquisite furnishings and impeccable maintenance. Prices are moderate, yet 100 percent occupancy occurs only twenty-five to thirty nights a year.

ROOM RATES

January–February	$59–$129 + tax
March–April	$79–$159 + tax
May–October	$99–$179 + tax
November–December	$69–$159 + tax

Additionally, the property contains RV sites with full hookup, electricity, sewage, and water.

RV RATES

Nightly	$25 + tax
Monthly	$350 + tax

Joe said that marketing by Cameron Trading Post is almost nonexistent other than information in the AAA guide book and a few signs. The Southwest has experienced a prolonged drought and the property has been strictly limited to 24 million gallons per year, which it pulls from the Little Colorado River. With current use at 22.5 million gallons, Joe said the management was forced to consider customer tradeoffs. Lodge customers use more water than restaurant guests or stop-by shoppers, yet hotel guests provide cross-sales in the restaurant and in the gift shop.

Prior to 9/11, the property hosted forty-five tour buses per day. Forty percent of these were European tourists; the remainder were U.S. and Canadian retirees. The management originally felt that these guests would appreciate a cafeteria line because the stop time was only 30 to 40 minutes. Instead, the guests, particularly the Europeans, wanted sit-down service.

Once this was known, the management and staff found a system to serve all guests hot meals of their choice in 25 minutes. Joe expressed pride in the willingness of his employees to provide such service.

In 2004, bus tours had reached eighteen per day, and further gains were expected unless another terrorist attack or unforeseen problem occurred in the United States. The European travelers from Germany, Italy, and France were particularly excited by the Indian products and gallery and the fact that 90 percent or more of the employees are Native American, largely of the Hopi and Navajo cultures.

The Alumni Club of Stanford University also discovered Cameron. Members of this group annually stayed in the RV camp or the lodge and brought their own chef who prepared open-air meals in the garden.

Collector's Auction

Although Joe downplayed his company's marketing activity, he said that tremendous success had been achieved with a collector's auction of Southwest Indian Art, first held in 1985 with only fifteen to eighteen people in attendance. By 1999, over 300 people attended filling rooms, RV sites, and the restaurant and gift shop. Eventually this was discontinued as the availability of antique Indian art diminished. The front cover of the final auction catalog featured four-year-old Joe sitting in a wooden rocking chair with cigar in hand.

Joe admitted that other promotional events could be organized to help increase occupancy in off-seasons. Typical occupancy percentages follow:

Summer	85%
Winter	30%
Fall/Spring	60–70%

U.S. vacation patterns account for the summer peak, but the best months for cool weather in northern Arizona occurs in the trough seasons.

Management Style

Joe personally takes charge of selecting room furnishings, gallery displays, and overseeing future expansion ideas such as the possible construction of Navajo-style Hogans along the rim of the canyon to serve as unique guest rooms.

Mike Davis, general manager, is charged with daily operations, including the critical task of merchandise buying. Mike came from a strong retail background and Joe said he largely takes a hands-off approach yet consults with Mike.

Very little turnover exists among employees, and many retire with a retirement package that is quite good for the area. Joe said the following of his employees:

- They are dedicated to Cameron.

- They offer great input for improving operations.

- They want to learn and improve.

- They are customer friendly and provide good service.

- They are not afraid to say "that's a dumb idea."

- They are cross-trained to work in different areas and willingly do so.

- They look on themselves and management as an extended family.

Joe and his management group realize the many advantages of the Native American workforce, the history of Cameron, and emphasis on quality that has been established. However, they know that the task of balancing customers and product offerings with the natural resource base will grow even more pressing in the future.

At present, merchandise sales represent the largest source of income with food and beverage second, followed by lodging. Joe believes it is important to have a mix of the three product areas and to resist any temptation to overemphasize merchandise. His goal is to maintain the cultural and historical foundation of the Cameron Trading Post and Lodge and provide a secure employment base for the 110 full-time employees who would otherwise be forced to drive or move to Flagstaff or Phoenix to support their families, thus disrupting their centuries' old cultural and societal heritage.

Updated November 21, 2011; http://www.camerontradingpost.com/

■■■ DISCUSSION QUESTIONS

1. Discuss the tradeoff issues that Joe and his management team face concerning marketing, growth, natural resources, and the posts' traditional employment base.

2. What would you recommend to the management of Cameron Trading Post and Lodge?

3. What other sensitive resource issues are hospitality companies likely to face in the next five to ten years? In the United States? In other countries?

4. What is the proper role for marketing in resource management?

5. What should Cameron Trading Post and Lodge do about the relatively low occupancy during the nonpeak seasons?

■■■ Case 30 Elk Mountain Hotel

History of Elk Mountain Hotel

When Peter Thieriot first saw Elk Mountain Hotel, it looked like the proverbial money pit, an endless hole into which renovation funds could be thrown. Peter's lawyers strongly advised him to walk away and forget any thought of buying and remodeling this 1905 hotel in Elk Mountain, Wyoming.

Yet its history, its tranquil location in a beautiful grove of cottonwoods, the Old West appearance of the town of Elk Mountain, and the natural charm of the hotel and its proximity to Peter's buffalo ranch served as a magnet, and in 2000 Peter became owner and renovator of Elk Mountain Hotel.

The Garden Spot Pavilion had sat on the grounds of the hotel for decades and attracted big names such as Louis Armstrong, Tex Beneke, Tommy Dorsey, and Les Brown, all popular with crowds in the 1940s and 1950s. Old-timers said, "You didn't have to know how to dance at the Pavilion, the floor would do it for you." Sure enough, the floor moved to the rhythm of the band and the crowd.

Peter Thieriot Renovates Elk Mountain Hotel

Wyoming winters and time took the Pavilion, but Peter believes he can bring it back with modern construction and a special spring floor so once again "you won't need to know dancing to dance real good."

"We stripped the hotel and then built it back again room by room" said Trey Webb, the front-desk clerk and head waiter. Nine layers of wallpaper were removed from the dining room, but a large enough chunk of each remained to frame them and place them in the dining room.

Trey exemplifies the spirit and drive of Wyoming people that helped draw Peter to Elk Mountain from San Francisco. Trey, a high school senior, is headed to the University of Wyoming on a rodeo scholarship to study biology and eventually become a doctor. An expert in "bull dogging and calf roping," Trey knows horses and he knows people. He and other high school kids from the area find part-time employment at the hotel. Their native "Western personalities" and desire to help others makes them popular with guests. They also display a genuine affection for the hotel and pride in its renaissance.

It's easy for employees and guests to love the place because the restoration built warmth and coziness into the twelve guest rooms, the parlor, and the dining room. Peter developed an attic on the third floor into a conference room to host meetings of sixteen people around a table with ample wall space for flip-chart pages temporarily held with masking tape, so common to meetings of this size.

Prior to renovations, the hotel served as a watering hole for a sometimes rough bunch of characters from the Medicine Bow area. Ten years before Peter bought the hotel, two of the rowdies took their argument to the hotel's parking lot where they settled it the old-fashioned way with six-shooters. Fortunately, neither of those would-be Wyatt Earps could aim straight, and the sheriff arrived before lead could accidentally find its mark.

Rowdies have been replaced by less colorful, middle-aged professional couples. "A few of the old customers returned looking for a beer and some action after renovations but when they spotted the wine and cheese, the Lexus and Lincoln cars in the parking lot, and heard English spoken without cussin' every other word, they promptly left and never returned," said Peter.

"Half this country loves what we did to this hotel and the other half has a different opinion." That was confirmed by a ranch family in McFadden 30 miles east who placed themselves squarely in the "love" section. Their opinion was that the renovated hotel added much to the community.

There is no fear that guests accustomed to fine dining when traveling and dining out at home will have to settle for less at Elk Mountain Hotel. The menu was designed to "combine a touch of flair, a hint of the Old West, and a big pinch of professionalism." With buffalo and caribou on the menu, there is more than a hint of the Old West. With a good selection of California and imported wines, seafood-based appetizers, and desserts such as crème brulée, compliments, not complaints, are most often heard.

The unanimous opinion of guests is that the hotel was renovated with style. The area on which the hotel sits had once been a stagecoach station for the Overland Trail. Although that building is gone, the Victorian style of the original 1905 building has been enhanced. The original embossed tin ceilings were cleaned and repainted, and the exterior asbestos shingles that used to hide the natural beauty were removed to expose the original cedar lap siding. Peter knew the hotel could be restored to this level of quality.

Susan and Arthur Havers Purchase the Hotel

Arthur and Susan Prescott Havers purchased the hotel in 2007. Susan was a marketing consultant in San Francisco, but had a culinary background. She had owned and managed a restaurant and catering company in Belgium and earned a Grand Diplome from Le Cordon Bleu in Paris. Arthur was vice president of international development for E-Trade. It was their dream to open a business together, and although they had this dream for many years they were not able to find the right project. While searching the Internet, Arthur came across the Elk Mountain Hotel. The historic hotel aroused their curiosity. Although the hotel was not for sale they contacted Peter, who also had a residence in San Francisco, to see if he would be interested in selling it. In February of 2006, they went to Elk Mountain to see the hotel and the region. They found the people to be friendly, with a sense of humor. In addition to the people they enjoyed the wide open spaces. A year later the Havers were owners of Elk Mountain Hotel.

Susan's culinary background enabled the restaurant to be turned into a "hidden gem" and customers who discovered it, encouraged people driving across I-80 to take the four-mile drive off the Interstate highway to Elk Mountain Hotel. The Havers used their marketing and culinary skills to create special dinners that pair food with wine, beer, or whiskey. They also created special events such as the Paranormal Dinner Party. According to the hotel's Web site, "The event is limited to a maximum of 5 couples. They will be the only guests in the hotel and should be prepared to stay up till 1 A.M. helping track down shadows and bumps in the night. Package price is $250 per couple inclusive of room & dinner but excludes taxes and gratuities." Employees of the hotel swear it has a friendly ghost, and perhaps the guests at the dinner will find it.

Friendly or not, ghosts don't pay bills. That requires live paying guests, and getting more of those, particularly in the low season, requires marketing. Positive word of mouth can't be beat, but it takes marketing to get enough of those mouths talking.

Peter Thieriot had the vision to renovate the Elk Mountain Resort; the Havers used marketing skills and Susan's culinary skills to turn the hotel into a destination. However a town of 200 people cannot create the demand necessary to support. Elk Mountain needs to be a destination for people in nearby towns and a place for organizations to hold events and retreats.

Updated November 2011 Sources accessed 11/20/21011; "Elk Mountain, Wyoming," *MuniNetGuide,* http://www.muninetguide.com/states/wyoming/elk-mountain/; Jackie Borchardt, "Elk Mountain Hotel offers serenity, escape," *trib.com* (March 27, 2011), http://trib.com/business/article_46602367-c87f-5f72-857b-3867c8734ae2.html; "Historic Elk Mountain Hotel Finding an International fFavor," *Rawlins Daily Times*, undated http://www.elkmountain-hotel.com/attachments/RawlinsDaily.pdf; Elk Mountain Hotel Web site; www.elkmountainhotel.com.

■■■ DISCUSSION QUESTIONS

Chapter 8 or Chapter 18

Examine a map of the state of Wyoming and its neighboring states.

1. What percentage of lodging business would you expect from Wyoming residents in the three seasonal periods: peak, summer; shoulder, late fall and early spring; trough, winter? Which Wyoming towns are target markets?

2. From what markets would the remaining occupancy come?

3. What market targets would you select in terms of demographics and lifestyle?

Chapter 14

4. Develop a publicity/public relations campaign appropriate for Elk Mountain Hotel. Include cost estimates. Remember that free publicity costs something, such as room and board for travel writers.

5. Develop a series of creative packages that might be used to increase occupancy in shoulder and trough periods.

6. The Havers have linked their site to Tripadvisor, and have posted photos on Flickr. Arthur stated if it was not for the Internet, they would have not survived. How does the Internet help a small hotel like Elk Mountain Hotel?

7. After visiting the hotel's Web site what suggestions would you have for additional uses of the Internet to market the hotel.

■■■ Case 31 IRTRA—Recreational Park XETULUL

Amazing, unbelievable, fantastic! These are words commonly used to describe XE-TULUL, a Guatemalan recreational park developed and operated for private-sector workers by their employers. This park is located in the province of Quezaltenango (pronounced "kay-sot-in-al-go") near the town of San Martin on the Pacific Coast Highway about 50 miles south of the Mexican border and 100 miles from the capital city of Guatemala City. The park is owned and operated by IRTRA, the Institute of Recreation for Workers of Private Companies in Guatemala, and opened in June 2002.

The XETULUL park instantly reminds one of Disney World with hotels, restaurants, individual cabanas, and three theme parks: an aquatic park with wave pool, superslides, and swimming pools; a sports park under construction; and a theme park. The theme park combines beautiful buildings that replicate historic sites of Europe and the Americas. Gift shops feature quality Guatemalan and imported products including clothing, cosmetics, footwear, and gifts. Restaurants are sparkling clean and feature Guatemalan, U.S., and European menus. Cafeterias, sit-down restaurants, and snack areas are open to serve 12,000 visitors per day.

A variety of rides include roller coasters, bumper cars, a train, and water rides including replicas of Venetian gondolas and a waterfall drop.

The park was developed in a former coffee plantation and tropical forest. Huge trees, grass, and shrubs provide shade for tropical birds and animals that share the park with human visitors.

Most Guatemalan workers might never be able to visit the recreational/theme parks of the United States or Europe, but they can enjoy an affordable and unique Guatemalan version.

None of this would be unusual if one of the traditional theme park operators such as Six Flags or Disney owned the park, but instead a unique organization known as IRTRA is the owner/operator. IRTRA was established by the private industry of Guatemala to provide affordable recreation for employees and their families as well as owners and managers of the companies.

The Chamber of Commerce, the Association of Agriculturalists, and the Association of Industry in Guatemala petitioned the Guatemalan Congress to pass a law permitting the establishment of IRTRA the right to fund it with tax-exempt monies. Thus, the theme park was built and continues to be supported totally by monies from Guatemalan private industry. A small fee is charged for entrance to the park but is purposely kept low. Other costs such as meals and beverages are reasonably priced.

The vision and mission statements of IRTRA include the following:

- To develop a recreation opportunity for Guatemalan workers and employees at international standards.

- To create parks and gardens using the latest technology for the benefit of Guatemalan workers and employees.

- To provide employees opportunities with educational/training to improve their professional and personal lives.

- To assist in the development of Guatemala.

- To create recreational parks that are designed according to the latest technology and operated by the most competent individuals.

- To preserve the ecology of our places of recreation.

Although IRTRA is a secular organization, it has a creed that expresses a faith in God, a belief in serving one's fellows, a belief in work based on courtesy and cleanliness, a belief in working with nature rather than against it, and a belief in the need to inspire and motivate others to achieve happiness.

Personnel

The executive staff of XETULUL includes full-time salaried managers and a staff of medical doctors and nurses. The general manager of lodging, Randolph Brenner, earned an MBA from INCAE, the prestigious Central American affiliate of the Harvard Business School.

The entire staff, including groundskeepers, waiters, front-desk personnel, cashiers, ride operators, gift shop salespeople, and many more, are Guatemalans. Because many lack extensive formal education and cultural experience outside small villages or farms, extensive training programs exist on the grounds of XETULUL. Personnel are instructed in basic skills such as hygiene, guest interaction, handling complaints, and proper dress. Several are given instruction in the use of computers, cash registers, and the operation and maintenance of rides and other machinery.

These skills have allowed many employees to find employment in other sectors of Guatemalan society. The prevailing attitudes among the 1,500 employees of XETULUL are friendliness, helpfulness, and a willingness to listen to guests.

Results

The development of XETULUL created a tourist industry outside the park consisting of hotels, restaurants, retail stores, and auto service.

Since opening, the park has received more than 3.7 million visitors. Although most of these were from Guatemala, a growing percentage comes from other Central American countries and Mexico, with a small percentage from Europe and the United States/Canada. Annually, 1.2 million visitors enjoy the park.

Perhaps the most impressive results are in the mix of guests. The great majority are skilled and unskilled Guatemalan workers, but a large number of mid- and upper-management, including owners of Guatemalan enterprises, mix freely with their employees.

Pricing and Attractions

Lodging within the park is reasonable and of four-star caliber. Restaurants are open from 7 A.M. until 10 P.M., and the swimming pool is available from 9 A.M. to 9 P.M. Special honeymoon packages are available such as the three-night junior suite package for Q1,685 (approximately $210 U.S.), which includes lodging, meals, a bottle of champagne, and a basket of fruit in the room.

Many special attractions are offered to guests such as weekend dancing and fireworks displays on holidays.

■■■ DISCUSSION QUESTIONS

1. The park was started and continues to be maintained through a contribution from private industries, whose workers and managers can use the park. What benefit does this create for the company?

2. XETULUL not only attracted workers from the companies associated with it, it also created a tourism attraction. What benefits of the park that enabled it to become a regional attraction?

■■■ Case 32 The Witchery by the Castle

Andrew Lloyd Webber commented, "It's the prettiest restaurant ever." "Number Four in the 50 Best Places in the World for Honeymooners" is The Witchery by the Castle in Edinburgh, Scotland, which is consistently recognized as one of the world's great places to dine and stay. It has won numerous awards, such as the prestigious AA Wine Award for Scotland and the Scottish Tourist Board's Thistle Award. The *Sunday Times* rated the luxurious suites at the Witchery as "among the most sought-after romantic hideaways in Scotland," and the *Sunday Herald* described them as a "Jewel Box Setting."

Located at the top of the Royal Mile, close to the gates of Edinburgh Castle, the Witchery sits in the heart of Edinburgh's historic old town. A gilded heraldic metal sign marks the entrance. A short walk away are the Scottish Parliament, the Museum of Scotland, St. Giles, and the National Galleries. The Edinburgh Airport is only eight miles away, and Waverly Rail Station is just a few hundred yards away.

The Witchery was originally built for an Edinburgh merchant in 1595. Edinburgh, like Salem, Massachusetts, went through a period of "witch accusations" and persecutions, which occurred at the site of the current witchery.

By 1979, the building that now houses the Witchery was in total disrepair. James Thomson, an Edinburgh native, saw opportunity beyond the decay in a neglected part of Edinburgh. James began his career as a young man with a Saturday job in Crawford's tearooms and gained an appreciation for history at George Heriot's School. Years later, James became Scotland's youngest hospitality licensee as creator and owner of the Witchery.

Today, witches are a historic oddity, replaced by suites and a restaurant serving some of the finest cuisine in the United Kingdom in a candle-lit ambience in which the only electric light identifies the fire exit.

In 1979, the success of the Witchery led James to open a second restaurant, Secret Garden, in a derelict schoolyard adjacent to the Witchery. James could see opportunity in what others regarded as trash and incorporated a wealth of salvaged building materials into the Secret Garden, including a sixteenth-century doorway from the Duke of Gordon's ceiling, to build the Secret Garden restaurant, named by one reviewer as the "most civilized dining room in Scotland."

Now bookings at the Witchery and the Secret Garden are made weeks in advance because both have become the most popular destination restaurants in Edinburgh and remain fully booked. Annually they serve over 200,000 guests.

Above the Witchery restaurant, atop a winding staircase, are two magical and opulent suites, The Old Rectory and The Inner Sanctum, packed with antiques and enough atmosphere to have pleased Cleopatra and Antony, royalty, or movie stars. Named as one of the UK's top-ten romantic destinations, these suites stay booked throughout the year at a room rate of £250 per night, including a bottle of champagne, chocolates, a continental breakfast, and a newspaper (who wants to read?).

The success of the original suites led James to develop five more as the "world's greatest places to stay." The Library, Vestry, Guardsroom, and Armory all boast their own individuality. All were designed as perfect romantic hideaways with masses of antiques, opulently draped beds, rich textiles, and huge roll-top baths built for two. These are located in a lavishly restored seventeenth-century building just a few steps from the Witchery in Edinburgh's historic Castlehill. If possible, these suites are even more theatrical and opulent than the original two.

The gothic library suite overlooks the historic Royal Mile and includes masses of antique books, paisley-covered walls, and a book-lined bathroom with an open fire.

The Armory is discreetly located, overlooking a small private courtyard. This huge and glamorous suite is hung with dramatic tapestries and features an oak-paneled bathroom. The Guardroom is exceptionally spacious overlooking the historic old-town rooftops and a romantic bedroom paneled with antique leather.

Fully booked restaurants and suites did not occur without reason. The Witchery developed a worldwide reputation for sensational food in the most indulgent setting. The very best of Scotland's produce, such as Angus beef, lamb, game, and seafood, are served. Scottish lobster and Loch Fyne oysters are regularly featured alongside Witchery classic dishes such as hot smoked salmon with leeks and hollandaise or Angus beef fillet with smoked garlic broth.

The Witchery also developed a reputation for its wines, gaining a prestigious *Wine Spectator* Award for Excellence and many other awards for its cellar.

Its comprehensive list of almost a thousand wines covers all of the great wine-producing areas, varieties, prices, and styles with a special selection of seventeen available by the glass. A skilled and enthusiastic wine team, supported by a respected sommelier, constantly taste, source, and buy wines to add to the already extensive cellar. Their extensive knowledge is available to guests in the restaurant.

As well as a large selection of old-world classics from Burgundy and Bordeaux, there are extensive selections from New World producers such as Australia, Chile, and New Zealand and a comprehensive Spanish and Italian list. Champagne is a Witchery specialty with selections from Pommery to the deluxe cuvées of Krug, Roederer Christa, and Dom Perignon.

An extensive range of malt whiskey, armagnacs, and liqueurs are also available. Mineral water is locally produced by Findlay's in East Lothian, Scotland.

Obviously, much of the success of the Witchery, Secret Garden, and the suites may be attributed to their historic location, the ambience, the quality of the products, and the excitement and theater built into each.

James knows that these factors need to be continuously supported to ensure success. He is well aware of the tendency of hospitality guests to seek new dining and lodging experiences. He also recognizes the importance of word of mouth to deliver new guests. He believes that the product must be supported by staff loyalty and excellence, community involvement, personal leadership, and an appropriate use of technology.

Staff Development

Following attendance at the Disney Institute in Florida, James instituted a new mind-set in the company, encouraging staff to constantly seek to exceed guests' already high expectations. Staff members are empowered to deal with any guest request and are personally responsible for delivering each guest's total satisfaction. James encourages his team to develop rewarding long-term careers within his company, so staff turnover is significantly below the industry norm, and many of his staff have been with him long term. A large proportion have returned to work with him again after gaining experience with other organizations at home and abroad.

Community and Industry Involvement

James believes the hospitality industry offers exciting careers, and he encourages young people to enter. James supports and funds a number of educational initiatives at primary, secondary, and higher education levels, including supporting students in local high schools with cooking competitions, training with restaurant chefs, and work experience within his restaurants. Recently he was delighted to see a student reach the Scottish final of the *Future Chef of the Year.*

In 1999, he endowed the *James Thomson Award for Outstanding Customer Service,* which annually recognizes and financially assists a student who has shown outstanding commitment to excellence in customer service during his or her studies at Edinburgh's Telford College. He continues to be a significant sponsor of an annual exchange trip between Edinburgh students and the François Rabelais College in Lyon, France, giving up to twenty students and lecturers hands-on experience in Michelin-starred restaurants in France's culinary capital.

A strong believer in rewarding and recognizing the very best led James to sponsor the Scottish tourism "Oscars," the Visit Scotland Thistle Awards, the Caterer.com Best Tourism Website Award, and the recent Caterer.com Web Awards. Frequently asked to lend his expertise to others in the industry, he has judged the Caterer Hospitality Week Innovations Awards over recent years as well as being a regular judge for the Thistle Awards.

As an industry leader, James frequently speaks publicly to promote tourism and hospitality issues, and his restaurants maintain a high media profile in Scotland worldwide. He has written a food column in *The Herald* newspaper and speaks at industry events. Making his restaurants and suites available to the media has promoted a positive quality image of Scottish hospitality in dozens of publications, including *Vogue, Hello, Elle, Cosmopolitan,* and the *New York Times* as well as on television around the world.

James believes that he has an obligation to assist in the growth of tourism to Scotland and especially to Edinburgh. Aware that visitors to Edinburgh were looking for more information about the historic but neglected Old Town, James supported the creation of the Caddies and Witchery Tours, the city's first customer walking tours. Tours leave from outside the Witchery every evening and have become a memorable part of the visitor experience for thousands of visitors to Edinburgh.

James works closely with several public and private-sector organizations, including the Scottish Enterprise Innovation Group, the Scottish Borders Tourist Board, and the National Museums of Scotland to improve the standards of Scotland's hospitality products. An enthusiast for Disney's approach to customer care, James has encouraged a range of tourism businesses to learn from the best, including leading study tours to the Disney Institute in Florida. He often speaks on the lessons that can be learned from Disney. In 2002, in conjunction with other partners, he launched Castlehill Christmas, a joint initiative to bring business to local tourism enterprises at what was a traditionally quiet time of the year with a dramatic architectural lighting display and a program of events focused on Castlehill. James is a key member of the finance committee, raising over £300,000 in sponsorship to bring the prestigious Meeting Planners International Conference to Edinburgh in 2004, an international event with huge benefits for the city and Scotland.

Supporting the wider community, especially in Edinburgh's historic Old Town, has a place too. James acts as a trustee of the Old Town Charitable Trust, a member of the Board of the Queen's Hall, and support of the advisory group of the local homelessness initiative, the Edinburgh Streetwork Project. He also supports an under-10 football team. The Witchery supports a local community football team and the National Judo Academy. The innovative Just for Starters program that James pioneered as a collaborative venture brought a number of people with difficult backgrounds into the industry by harnessing the resources of a number of public and private-sector organizations, including the police and army, to support, educate, and mentor them in the transition from homelessness to employment.

As sole shareholder, James is able to commit a significant proportion of the company's profits back to the community through ongoing support of charities including the Hospitality Industry Trust, Crusaid Shelter, The Army Benevolent Fund, St. Columbia's Hospice, Save the Children, and the Royal Lyceum Theatre. Regular donations of dining or accommodation vouchers from the restaurants are also given to organizations to use for their own fundraising purposes.

Technology

James's basic concept of giving the diner a magical dining experience where each of the elements of food, wine, service, location, and decor all combine to create a magical dining experience was innovative when he established the Witchery, and constant innovation has been a hallmark ever since. He was ahead of other restaurants, installing specialist EPOS systems to process diners' orders and bills discreetly. James established a state-of-the-art mini call center to allow all guest enquiries for his restaurants to be dealt with centrally by a highly skilled team using specially developed reservation software. For guests looking to book online, he was an early investor in Web sites that have given the restaurants and suites a 24-hour worldwide presence with an average of a thousand hits each day. His restaurants were among the first in the UK to offer real-time table reservations online using his reservations database. James believes that hospitality firms can use the latest technology to provide a truly old-fashioned level of service. He credits much of his success to community and employee support. For James, marketing is far more than advertising or brochure development. He has demonstrated the importance of personal involvement by owners/managers in the community and the industry and strong product differentiation.

■■■ DISCUSSION QUESTIONS

Chapter 4

1. From the preceding discussion, analyze the strengths and weaknesses of The Witchery.

Chapter 14

2. Discuss The Witchery's public relations efforts. Offer any suggestions you have for how The Witchery could gain publicity outside of Scotland.

∎∎∎ Case 33 Enterprise Rent-A-Car: Selling the Dream

In the Fast Lane

Early on a bright August 2002 morning, Anne Cain pulled her Pontiac Grand Prix into a parking place at the Sacramento, California, International Airport. Anne, an area manager for Enterprise Rent-A-Car, walked briskly into the airport's consolidated car-rental center. She smiled as she walked past competitors' rental counters toward the green-and-white Enterprise location. Most Enterprise locations were in neighborhood facilities, but several years ago the company had begun to move into the airport market and now had a number of on-airport locations like hers. She liked being able to see the competition and watch them work. She believed it kept her on her toes and was always looking for ways to satisfy Enterprise's customers better than the other companies.

Anne also smiled because she realized how far she had come—and how fast. She had grown up in Turlock, California, and graduated from California State University at Stanislaus with a major in English and a minor in psychology. Anne had put herself through school, sometimes working several jobs at a time. One job had been with an insurance company, and in that role she had met Enterprise employees who often called on the insurance company to encourage it to use Enterprise's cars for its customers who needed replacement rentals. She did not know much about Enterprise, but she saw that the employees were sharp, well trained, and clearly liked their jobs. One had suggested that she consider interviewing with Enterprise when she graduated. "Me? I'm an English major. And, a rental car company?" she remembered thinking. But she had gone for the interview, liked what she heard, and a week later decided to take the job.

Enterprise had told Anne that it would give her all the training and tools she would need to be successful and that she would be able to chart her own career. She completed the manager training program in 10 months, served as an assistant manager in a branch for 10 months, and then earned promotion to branch manager. In four years, she had become an area manager, responsible for six branches, thirty full-time employees, millions of dollars in annual revenue, and millions of dollars' worth of rental vehicles. Her pay when she started had been about equal to her classmates who had taken other jobs, but since then it had doubled and tripled based on Enterprise's philosophy of sharing branch and area profits with employees. Now, Enterprise had asked her to be the area manager with responsibility for establishing and running the new airport location.

Anne sat down at her desk and began to review her work plans for the day. She paused and smiled again as she thought about her success. Her job really was a dream come true. Where else could someone her age have so much responsibility, so much fun at work, such high earnings, and such a feeling of empowerment?

Company and Industry Background

Anne's good fortune mirrored that of Enterprise itself. The company's founder, Jack Taylor, had started Enterprise as a leasing company in 1957 and then entered the rental car business in 1962 with a single location and seventeen cars in St. Louis, Missouri. Since then, Enterprise had grown dramatically to become largest rental car company in the United States. By 2002, Enterprise had 5,000 offices in five countries, including 400 offices in Canada, the United Kingdom, Germany, and Ireland. Worldwide sales had reached nearly $7 billion. The company had more than 600,000 vehicles in its fleet and 50,000 employees.

Auto Rental News, an industry trade publication, estimated that the entire U.S. rental car market, including the local (home) market and the airport market, was about $18.7 billion in 2001 revenues. *Auto Rental News* divided the local market into replacement rentals, business rentals, service/maintenance rentals, and leisure rentals. It divided the airport market into business and leisure segments.

A Winning Strategy

Analysts attributed Enterprise's success to several factors. First, cars had become a more important part in people's lives. They just couldn't do without their cars, even for a day or two. And, as less and less families included a stay-at-home spouse, there was often no one in the family who could pick people up when they had car problems. Tied in to this, the courts ruled in the 1970s that insurance companies had to offer replacement coverage so that insured motorists would be covered for a replacement rental car if they lost the use of their car.

Beyond theses environmental factors, the company's success resulted from its focus on one segment of the rental car market. Instead of following Hertz, Avis, and other rental car companies by setting up branches at airports to serve national travelers, Enterprise built an extensive network of neighborhood locations serving the "home-city" market, people who needed rental cars as replacements when their cars were wrecked or in the shop being repaired. Because these customers often needed a ride from a body shop or repair garage and had no easy way to get to a rental office, Enterprise offered to pick them up.

However, Enterprise's first customer in the replacement market was often the referral source—the insurance agent or auto body shop employee who recommended Enterprise to the stranded customer. Few of Enterprise's customers got up in the morning thinking they'd need to rent a car, but then they were involved in a wreck. So employees visited the referral sources frequently, often taking them doughnuts or pizza as a way of thanking them for their business. The company also developed an online product that allowed insurance companies to reserve and pay for replacement rentals online. Some analysts estimated that the company served the majority of the insurance replacement market, partly because its rental rates in the replacement market tended to be lower than rates for comparable rentals at airport-based companies—some analysts estimated up to 20 percent lower. A focus on efficient operations helped it keep rates lower.

Enterprise also began to serve a second home-city market segment, the "discretionary" or "leisure/vacation" segment. Many people found that their car just wouldn't do for all occasions. Friends or relatives might visit and need a car, or the family might decide to take a vacation and believe that the family car was really not as dependable as they would like. More and more people were renting for trips just to keep the extra miles off the family car. Finally, Enterprise was also developing the local corporate market. Many small businesses and some large ones had found that it was less expensive and easier for them to rent their fleets from Enterprise rather than trying to maintain their own fleets. Some businesses preferred that their employees rent a car for business trips rather than drive their own and get reimbursed.

Enterprise's success in the home-city market attracted competition. Although it had the largest share of that market, a handful of major regional competitors, when combined, captured a large market share. The airport-rental companies, such as Hertz, Avis, Budget, Thrifty, and Alamo, got only a small portion of the home-city business. Hertz, a wholly owned subsidiary of Ford Motor Company, had started "Hertz Local Edition," which had neighborhood locations that operated in a fashion similar to Enterprise's locations, including offering the pickup service. Also, there was a wide range of smaller, regionally based rental companies that served the remainder of the market.

Enterprise grew very quietly, depending on its referral sources and word-of-mouth promotion. It wasn't until 1989 that the company did its first national advertising. At that time, marketing research indicated that if you showed people a list of company names and asked them to identify the rental car companies, only about 20 percent knew Enterprise. The company started advertising nationally, but still kept its ads low key. By 1997, it had more than quadrupled its annual advertising and promotion spending, using the theme "Pick Enterprise. We'll pick you up." By 2001, the company's research showed that 80 percent of consumers were aware of the company and 60 percent associated the brand with the "pick-you-up" attribute. In late 2001, *Advertising Age* reported that Enterprise had initiated a $30 million ad campaign encouraging drivers to rent its cars, trucks, and vans for special purposes, like carrying building materials or the neighborhood softball team. AdAge.com reported that in 2000 the average auto rental/leasing company spent about 2.6 percent of sales on advertising.

The Importance of Culture

Company founder Jack Taylor's philosophy drove the company's strategy. Taylor believed that the employees' and the company's first job was to serve the customer. From the beginning, Taylor urged his employees to do whatever they had to do to make the customer happy.

Taylor believed that to satisfy customers, a company had to have satisfied, challenged employees who worked as a team. So he set up the company so that all of Enterprise's branch employees, from assistant manager on up, earned a substantial portion of their pay based on branch profitability. In addition, the company had a profit-sharing plan for all employees. Enterprise hired primarily college-educated employees and promoted from within. Ninety-nine percent of its senior managers started as management trainees at the branch level, so they understood the customer-oriented culture. As important, they understood their local markets and the needs of customers in those markets. Thus, Enterprise was really a collection of small, independent businesses, with the corporation providing capital and logistical support.

Finally, Taylor believed that if the company took care of its customers and employees, profits would follow. And sure enough, Enterprise had consistently been profitable in an industry where many firms had not. In 2001, Enterprise was the only one of the top-seven rental companies to report an increase in revenue over 2000.

In fact, in late 2001, ANC Rental Corporation, owner of the Alamo and National brands, filed for Chapter 11 bankruptcy protection. Then, in July 2002, Budget Group filed for bankruptcy protection, and Cendent Corporation, the owner of Avis, purchased the company. This created the nation's second largest car-rental company, behind Enterprise. The September 11, 2001, terrorist attack badly hurt the pure-airport rental car companies due to reduced business and leisure travel.

What's Next?

The question is, how can Enterprise continue to grow and prosper in the face of growing competition and market uncertainty?

First, Enterprise must continue to attract and retain college-educated employees. The company needs to hire more than 5,000 management trainees a year, making it one of the largest recruiters of college graduates. Yet many college grads, like Anne Cain, may know little or nothing about Enterprise and may have negative feelings about working for a rental car company. Furthermore, Enterprise is committed to having a diverse workforce that reflects the racial and ethnic makeup of its local markets. The company's workforce is about 20 percent African American and 30 percent minority. How can Enterprise continue to recruit college graduates, especially members of racial and ethnic minorities and women?

Second, Enterprise must continue to examine its marketing strategy. Despite its focus on the local market, it also began to venture into the airport market in the late 1990s as its customers asked it to take its brand of customer service and value pricing to that market. The company responded by opening some on-airport locations. These operations served the local market as well as targeted the "infrequent" air travelers and budget-conscious business travelers who would appreciate its personal service and lower rates. By 2002, Enterprise served more than 100 of the top 150 U.S. airports and had plans to add 22 more. J. D. Power and Associates found that Enterprise had the number-one customer-satisfaction rating among airport customers for four years in a row.

As Enterprise considers its growth options, it must decide which markets it should target. How should it position itself in those markets? Are there new services it could offer that would make sense given its current strategy? How can it do a better job of increasing Enterprise's awareness among targeted customers? And how should it respond as new competitors, including the airport-based firms like Hertz, attack the home-city and leisure travel markets?

Perhaps the most important question is, how can Enterprise continue to grow without losing its focus and without losing the corporate culture that has been so important in helping it and its employees, like Anne Cain, realize their dreams?

Sources: Enterprise Rent-A-Car supported development of this case. *Auto Rental News* also provided information. Also see Kortney Stringer, "Industry Turmoil Sparks a New Car-Rental Game," *Wall Street Journal* (July 31, 2002): Dl; Kortney Stringer, "Budget Group's Bankruptcy Filing Could Lead to Sale to Competitor," *Wall Street Journal* (July 30, 2002): D5; Eric Berkman, "How to Stay Ahead of the Curve," *CIO* (February 1, 2002): 72; Luisa Kroll, "Hard Drive," *Forbes* (November 26, 2001): 160; Jean Halliday, "Enterprising Angle: New Auto-Rental Effort Plays to Everyday Renters," *Advertising Age* (September 10, 2001): 4; and www.enterprise.com.

■■■ DISCUSSION QUESTIONS

Chapters 4 or 18

1. Who are Enterprise's competitors, and what is the nature of competition in its markets?

2. What marketing recommendations would you make to Enterprise to help it improve its recruiting?

3. What marketing recommendations would you make to Enterprise to improve its marketing strategy?

Chapter 7

4. Explain the different organizational markets that Enterprise could go after and how it would approach these markets.

Chapter 15

5. If you were manager of a non-airport location how would use personnel selling to increase your sales?

6. Why is it important that a sales person feel that his product is a good value?

■■■ Case 34 Bern Hotels and Resorts Panama

Strategic planning for the leading hotel and resort group in Panama had always been important but twelve new hotels were scheduled to enter their market adding 4,304 additional rooms by 2017. The two new upcoming Westin projects belonged to Bern Hotels and Resorts but the remainder were direct competitors (see Table 1).

Many first-time visitors to Panama are surprised and impressed to witness skyscrapers, multi-lane highways, a modern airport and condos, apartments and homes equal to those in the United States and Europe. Economic growth of the country during the late 1990s had been upwards to 10 percent and this had fueled the boom in hotel development. The short to medium term concern was that hotel supply was quickly going to outpace demand unless the country was able to promote and attract more visitors; a job for both the public and private sectors.

Mr. Glen Champion, vice president of Bern Hotels and Resorts (BHR), had responsibility for strategic planning and direction to insure that their current operating group of hotels would continue to be strong in an increasingly competitive environment. This group included two Intercontinental Hotels, one Holiday Inn and one Crowne Plaza, owned and operated under franchise agreements with IHG hotels as well as the Le Meridian Panama hotel under a franchise with Starwood hotels. The group also had the Gamboa Rainforest Resort in the jungle alongside the Panama Canal as well as a number of other tourism related service businesses that were directly or indirectly affected by the hotel business. Further. franchise agreements had been signed with Starwood to open two Westin hotels, The Westin Playa Bonita resort in 2011 and The Westin Panama City, Panama in 2012.

Glen said that enhanced marketing/sales strategies and tactics might be needed but that they would need to support rather than replace the company's basic goals which had proven to be the mission for the company's success. These were:

• To provide excellent service to guests.

• To provide continuous training and motivation to all employees, including empowerment whenever possible.

TABLE 1
Hotel Additions Proposed For Panama

NAME OF HOTEL PROJECT	LOCATION	ROOMS	2011	2012	2013	2014	2015	2016	2017
Under Construction									
Hilton Panama	Balboa		353	351	351	351	351	351	351
DoubleTree by Hilton	Via Espana	156	78	156	156	156	156	156	156
Panamera, a Waldorf Astoria Hotel	Calle 47		130	130	130	130	130	130	130
Trump Ocean Club	Punta Pacifica	369	185	369	369	369	369	369	369
Westin Plaza Bonita	Playa Bonita	611	102	611	611	611	611	611	611
Westin	Costa del Este	198		34	198	198	198	198	198
Hyatt Place	Fin. District	167			84	167	167	167	167
Bristol addition	Fin. District	62		62	62	62	62	62	62
Aloft by Starwood	Convention Ctr	312			150	234	312	312	312
Renaissance	Fin. District	300				300	300	300	300
Megapolis—Decameron Ritz Carlton	Balboa	300	300	150	300	300	300	300	300
Subtotal		3,176	364	1863	2,411	2,878	3,176	3,176	3,176
Annual Additions			364	1,498	548	467	298	0	0
Medium—High Probability (>50%)									
Hilton Garden Inn	Behind the El Panama	176			176	176	176	176	176
Planet Hollywood	Fin. District	309				155	309	309	309
Crowne Plaza—CBT Tocumen Airport	Tocumen	176			176	176	176	176	176
Hyatt Place	Costa del Este	167				84	167	167	167
Embassy Suites by Hilton	Calle 50	300				300	300	300	300
Subtotal		1,128	0	0	352	891	1,128	1,128	1,128
Annual Additions			0	0	352	539	238	0	0
Total Additional Rooms—UC			364	1,863	2,411	2,878	3,176	3,176	3,176
Total Additional Rooms w/50% Probability			0	0	352	891	1,128	1,128	1,128
Grand Total Additional Rooms UC and Probable			364	1,863	2,763	3,769	4,304	4,304	4,304
Annual Additions			364	1,498	900	1,006	536	--	--

- To control expenses and permit continuous improvement through solid financial returns.

Key to supporting as well as building upon the mission that these three goals represented for the company were strategic marketing actions and efforts. A long-term strategy began with the conceptualization of products and services offered. The sales and marketing efforts which followed up with proper systems and analysis since ongoing adjustments were crucial to the success of a multiunit growth company such as BHR. An overview of this follows:

Strategic Plan—Reinforcing the Marketing Efforts

1. **Protect the Product and Service** by offering and delivering consistently high-quality operations in all the businesses, performing renovations on some of the older properties and refreshing spaces in others. Renew service training in all properties with stronger BHR backbone, ongoing training, and staff certification using The Panama International Hotel School as a driving platform.

2. **Marketing the Brands** and capitalizing on brand distinct initiatives to differentiate properties. Maximize the resources of the brand affiliations with the international chains as much as possible and promote our own internal initiatives consistently, that is, Corporate Marketing Plan, loyalty programs, online Web-based marketing, industry alliances, social media, public relations initiatives, print, television, and other media.

3. **Revenue Management Effectively Performed** working in tune with reservations call centers, sales teams, and hotel front office teams to maximize the yield on the ever-changing demand in the market. Continuously analyze channels regarding sources of business per region. Insure that our products and services are found on the different reservation systems with accurate information and are easy to purchase. Insure that market analysis information is provided to the sales force to make its efforts more effective and focused.

4. **Sales and Prospecting Through Coordinated National and International Sales Teams.** Insure proper market segmentation follow-up using all internal and external teams and resources to cover all potential areas such as regular trade fair ad exhibition participation to drive sales and improve exposure. Individual properties site inspection and in-house prospecting. Emphasize individual brand and BHR loyalty programs for demand generation. Insure proper systems control and prospecting for repeat or similar demand generation. Utilize third-party database communication of promotions and targeted mailings.

5. **Vertical Integration.** A unique business model had been adopted by the Bern Group based on vertical integration and the development of corporate-owned and operated supporting companies such as "Sensory Spas by Clarins," a deluxe spa service, retail stores within the hotels, The Panama International Hotel School, GT incentives aimed at corporate incentive group travel, Ocean Business Center, a turnkey short-term office solution and Gamboa Tours, originally designed to offer jungle tours but now offering many tour packages. The company had grown and developed many synergies for handling back of the house operational tasks that were supported by a lean corporate structure of human development, financial control, systems, and sales and marketing.

   The Panama International Hotel School, a division of Bern Hotels and Resorts, was open to multinational qualified students who were free to seek employment wherever they wished following graduation. However, Glen said he hoped to hire as many as possible for employment in the Bern group. This organizational structure of Bern was not present in other hotels within Bern's competitive set. This competitive set agreed to share some data on a daily basis, including:

   - Occupancy—previous night
   - Average daily rate—ADR

6. **Medical Tourism Market Segment.** The Bern management feared that the first response by the Panama hotel community to added competition would

be to cut rates. To reduce this risk to Bern properties, Glen and the marketing staff had been working on new strategies such as the development of different segments such as the Caribbean medical market. The Caribbean represented a market of 5 million people with few local secondary care opportunities. This market was accustomed to travel elsewhere for medical treatment such as hip replacement, serious cardiovascular problems, dermatology, and other needs. Glen had been working with a team of Panama medical doctors to evaluate this as a new or expanded market.

It was well known that the Venezuelan market liked to visit Panama and many had purchased property there. However, under the existing administration, it was difficult to transmit funds from Venezuela.

7. **Sales Force Structure.** The structure of the sales force had been changed to make it more efficient and to better combat the new competition. Previously, the sales force had been divided into national and international. Each salesperson had been expected to call on accounts and then perform all the paperwork and follow-up associated with each account.

The new organization was divided into Outside—Pro Active salespeople and Inside—Reactive sales support staff. The later were expected to relieve the Pro Active sales force of most or all of the required paperwork thus leaving them with more time to make additional sales calls and to perform essential public relations activities associated with their positions.

8. **Sales Force Career Portfolios.** All Bern employees and especially those in the sales force were required to develop and maintain an actual career portfolio. Members of the sales force were encouraged to keep learning new sales skills and to apply them in the field. Evidence of attendance at sales training sessions and other self-help programs were placed in their BHR career portfolios and were examined during performance review.

9. **Cross-Selling.** Glen felt that improved cross-selling opportunities surely existed between the hotels and the various enterprises owned and operated by Bern such as Royal Card, Panama Rental Solutions, and Gamboa Tours.

As Glen reviewed the company's policies and strategies, he believed that Bern Hotels and Resorts was well positioned in the Panama market to meet the threat of increased competition, yet he was well aware of the importance to remain open to new ideas. For this reason Glen made it a point to attend several seminars and conferences in the United States and Europe which were sponsored by major universities and professional associations. These were not restricted to the hospitality and tourism industries as Glen felt that many ideas and concepts developed for other industries had relevance for the many properties under his direct leadership.

Note: Mr Glen Champion has indicated that he would welcome suggestions and new ideas from readers of this book. He may be reached at gchampion@ bernhotelspanama.com

■■■ DISCUSSION QUESTIONS

Chapter 3

1. From information you receive on the Internet (http://www.empresasbern.com/; http://www.bernhotelspan-ama.com/) do a SWOT analysis of Bern Hotels.

2. From your SWOT analysis how would you prioritize the nine items of the strategic plan?

Chapter 12

3. Bern Hotels and Resorts Panama is a collection of branded and nonbranded properties. How would you develop a distribution system that would promote this group of hotels? Look at using multiple channels; some might be hotel specific, while others could be used for all their brands.

Glossary

Administered VMS. A vertical marketing system that coordinates successive stages of production and distribution, not through common ownership or contractual ties, but through the size and power of one of the parties.

Advertising. Any paid form of nonpersonal presentation and promotion of ideas, goods, or services by an identified sponsor.

Agent. A wholesaler who represents buyers or sellers on a more permanent basis, performs only a few functions, and does not take title to goods.

Agritourism. Agriculture-based tourism that includes farms, ranches, and wineries. It provides rural areas with a means to attract tourists.

Alliances. Alliances are developed to allow two organizations to benefit from each other's strengths.

Allocating. Sales representatives decide on which customers to allocate scarce products to.

Allocentrics. Persons with a need for new experiences, such as backpackers and explorers.

Ansoff product–market expansion grid. A matrix developed by cell, plotting new products and existing products with new products and existing products. The grid provides strategic insights into growth opportunities.

Aspirational group. A group to which a person wishes to belong.

Atmosphere. Designed environments that create or reinforce a buyer's leanings toward consumption of a product.

Attitude. A person's enduring favorable or unfavorable cognitive evaluations, emotional feelings, and action tendencies toward some object or idea.

Augmented products. Additional consumer services and benefits built around the core and actual products.

Aural. The dimension of atmosphere relating to volume and pitch.

Baby boomers. The 78 million people born between 1946 and 1964.

Backward integration. A growth strategy by which companies acquire businesses supplying them with products or services (e.g., a restaurant chain purchasing a bakery).

Behavioral segmentation. Dividing a market into groups based on consumers' knowledge, attitude, use, or response to a product.

Belief. A descriptive thought that a person holds about something.

Brand. A name, term, sign, symbol, design, or a combination of these elements that is intended to identify the goods or services of a seller and differentiate them from competitors.

Brand equity. The added value endowed on products and services. It may be reflected in the way consumers think, feel, and act with respect to the brand, as well as in the prices, market share, and profitability the brand commands for the firm.

Brand image. The set of beliefs consumers hold about a particular brand.

Brand promise. The marketer's vision of what the brand must be and do for consumers.

Branding. The process of endowing products and services with the power of a brand. It's all about creating differences between products.

Broker. A wholesaler who does not take title to goods and whose function is to bring buyers and sellers together and assist in negotiations.

Business-to-business (B2B) online marketing. Using B2B trading networks, auction sites, spot exchanges, online product catalogs, barter sites, and other online resources to reach new customers, serve current customers more effectively, and obtain buying effectiveness and better prices.

Business-to-consumer (B2C) online marketing. The online selling of goods and services to final consumers.

Buying center. All those individuals and groups who participate in the purchasing and decision-making process and who share common goals and the risks arising from the decisions.

Buzz marketing. Cultivating opinion leaders and getting them to spread information about a product to others in their community.

Cast members. A term used for employees. It implies that employees are part of a team that is performing for their guests.

Causal research. Marketing research to test hypotheses about cause-and-effect relationships.

Channel conflict. Disagreement among marketing channel members on goals and roles—who should do what and for what rewards.

Channel level. A level of middleman that performs some work in bringing the product and its ownership closer to the final buyer.

Cognitive dissonance. Buyer discomfort caused by postpurchase conflict.

Communicating. Sales representatives communicate information about the company's products and services.

Competitive advantage. An advantage over competitors gained by offering consumers greater value either through lower prices or by providing more benefits that justify higher prices.

Competitive analysis. An analysis of the primary strengths and weaknesses, objectives, strategies, and other information relative to competitors.

Competitors' strategies. When competitors use segmentation, undifferentiated marketing can be suicidal. Conversely, when competitors use undifferentiated marketing, a firm can gain an advantage by using differentiated or concentrated marketing.

Concentric diversification strategy. A growth strategy whereby a company seeks new products that have technological or marketing synergies with existing product lines.

Confused positioning. Leaving buyers with a confused image of a company.

Conglomerate diversification strategy. A product growth strategy in which a company seeks new businesses that have no relationship to the company's current product line or markets.

Consumer-to-business (C2B) online marketing. Online and exchanges in which consumers search out sellers, learn about their offers, and initiate purchases, sometimes even driving transaction terms.

Consumer-to-consumer (C2C) online marketing. Online exchanges of goods and information between final consumers.

Consumption phase. Takes place when the customer consumes the service.

Contests, sweepstakes, and games. Give consumers a chance to win something, such as cash or a trip.

Continuity. Scheduling ads evenly within a given period.

Contractual VMS. A vertical marketing system in which independent firms at different levels of production and distribution join together through contracts to obtain more economies or sales impact than they could achieve alone.

Convention. A specialty market requiring extensive meeting facilities. It is usually the annual meeting of an association and includes general sessions, committee meetings, and special-interest sessions.

Copy testing. A process performed before or after an ad is printed or broadcast.

Core product. Answers the question of what the buyer is really buying. Every product is a package of problem-solving services.

Corporate (or brand) Web site. Web sites that seek to build customer goodwill and to supplement other sales channels rather than to sell the company's product directly.

Corporate communications. This activity covers internal and external communications and promotes understanding of an organization.

Corporate meeting. A meeting held by a corporation for its employees.

Corporate mission statement. A guide to provide all the publics of a company with a shared sense of purpose, direction, and opportunity, allowing all to work independently, yet collectively, toward the organization's goals.

Corporate VMS. A vertical marketing system that combines successive stages of production and distribution under single ownership. Channel leadership is established through common ownership.

Cost-plus pricing. Adding a standard markup to the cost of the product.

Counseling. Involves advising management about public issues and company positions and image.

Coupons. Certificates that offer buyers savings when they purchase specified products.

Cross-selling. The company's other products that are sold to the guest.

Cross-training. Training employees to do two or more jobs within the organization.

Crowdsourcing. Is an open-innovation new-product idea program.

Culture. The set of basic values, perceptions, wants, and behaviors learned by a member of society from family and other important institutions.

Customer database. An organized collection of comprehensive data about individual customers or prospects, including geographic, demographic, psychographic, and behavioral data.

Customer equity. The discounted lifetime values of all the company's current and potential customers.

Customer expectations. Expectations based on past buying experiences, the opinions of friends, and market information.

Customer relationship management (CRM). It involves managing detailed information about individual customers and carefully managing customer "touch points" in order to maximize customer loyalty.

Customer touch point. Any occasion on which a customer encounters the brand and product—from actual experience to personal or mass communications to casual observation.

Customer value. The difference between the benefits that the customer gains from owning and/or using a product and the costs of obtaining the product.

Data warehouse. A central repository of an organization's customer information.

Decline. The period when sales fall off quickly and profits drop.

Degree of product homogeneity. Undifferentiated marketing is more suited for homogeneous products. Products that can vary in design, such as restaurants and hotels, are more suited to differentiation or concentration.

Demands. Human wants that are backed by buying power.

Demographic segmentation. Dividing the market into groups based on demographic variables such as age, gender, family size, family life cycle, income, occupation, education, religion, race, and nationality.

Demography. The study of human populations in terms of size, density, location, age, sex, race, occupation, and other statistics.

Derived demand. Organizational demand that ultimately comes from (derives from) the demand for consumer goods.

Descriptive research. Marketing research to better describe marketing problems, situations, or markets, such as the market potential for a product or the demographics and attitudes of consumers.

Destination marketing organization (DMO). A group that promotes a specific destination. Often a local convention and visitors' bureau (CVB) serves as the DMO.

Destinations. Places with some form of actual or perceived boundary, such as the physical boundary of an island, political boundaries, or even market-created boundaries.

Detachment phase. When the customer is through using the product and departs.

Direct marketing. Direct communications with carefully targeted individual consumers to both obtain an immediate response and cultivate lasting customer relationships.

Direct marketing channel. A marketing channel that has no intermediary levels.

Direct-mail marketing. Direct marketing through single mailings that include letters, ads, samples, foldouts, and other "salespeople with wings" sent to prospects on mailing lists.

Direct rating.   The advertiser exposes a consumer panel to alternative ads and asks them to rate the ads.

Discriminatory pricing.   Refers to segmentation of the market and pricing differences based on price elasticity characteristics of the segments.

Disintermediation.   The elimination of intermediaries.

Drop.   The action taken toward a product that may cause harm or customer dissatisfaction.

Echo boomers.   *See* Millennials. Born between 1977 and 1994, these children of the baby boomers now number 72 million, dwarfing the Gen Xers and almost equal in size to the baby-boomer segment. Also known as Generation Y.

E-commerce.   The general term for a buying and selling process that is supported by electronic means, primarily the Intranet.

Economic environment.   The economic environment consists of factors that affect consumer purchasing power and spending patterns. Markets require both power and people. Purchasing power depends on current income, price, saving, and credit; marketers must be aware of major economic trends in income and changing consumer spending patterns.

Emotional labor.   The necessary involvement of the service provider's emotions in the delivery of the service.

Empowerment.   When a firm empowers employees, it moves the authority and responsibility to make decisions to the line employees from the supervisor.

Environmental factors.   Social, political, and economic factors that affect a firm and its marketing program.

Environmental management perspective.   A management perspective in which a firm takes aggressive actions to affect the publics and forces in its marketing environment rather than simply watching and reacting to it.

Environmentalsustainability.   A management approach that involves developing strategies that both sustain the environment and produce profits for the company.

Ethnographic research.   Trained observers interact with and/or observe consumers in their natural habitat.

Events.   Occurrences staged to communicate messages to target audiences, such as news conferences or grand openings.

Exchange.   The act of obtaining a desired object from someone by offering something in return.

Executive summary.   A short summary of the marketing plan to quickly inform top executives.

Experimental research.   The gathering of primary data by selecting matched groups of subjects, giving them different treatments, controlling related factors, and checking for differences in group responses.

Exploratory research.   Marketing research to gather preliminary information that will help to better define problems and suggest hypotheses.

Facilitating products.   Those services or goods that must be present for the guest to use the core product.

Familiarization trip (Fam trip).   A trip where travel agents or others who can send business to a tourist destination attraction, cruise, or hotel are invited to visit at a low cost or no cost.

Family life cycle.   The stages through which families might pass as they mature.

Financial intermediaries.   Banks, credit companies, insurance companies, and other businesses that help finance transactions or insure against the risks associated with the buying and selling of goods.

Fixed costs.   Costs that do not vary with production or sales level.

Forward integration.   A growth strategy by which companies acquire businesses that are closer to the ultimate consumer, such as a hotel acquiring a chain of travel agents.

Franchise.   A contractual vertical marketing system in which a channel member called a franchiser links several stages in the production distribution process.

Gender segmentation.   Dividing a market on the basis of gender.

General need description.   The stage in the industrial buying process in which a company describes the general characteristics and quantity of a needed item.

Generation X.   A generation of 45 million people born between 1965 and 1976; named Generation X because they lie in the shadow of the boomers and lack obvious distinguishing characteristics; other names include "baby busters," "shadow generation," or "yiffies"—young, individualistic, freedom-minded few.

Generation Y.   *See* Millennials.

Geographic segmentation.   Dividing a market into different geographic units such as nations, states, regions, counties, cities, or neighborhoods.

Going-rate pricing.   Setting price based largely on following competitors' prices rather than on company costs or demand.

Group.   Two or more people who interact to accomplish individual or mutual goals.

Growth.   The product life-cycle stage when a new product's sales start climbing quickly.

Horizontal conflict.   Conflict between firms at the same level.

Horizontal diversification strategy.   A product growth strategy whereby a company looks for new products that could appeal to current customers, which are technologically unrelated to its current line.

Horizontal integration.   A growth strategy by which companies acquire competitors.

Horizontal marketing systems (HMS).   Two or more companies at one level join to follow new marketing opportunities. Companies can combine their capital, production capabilities, or marketing resources to accomplish more than one company working alone.

Hospitality industry.   Made up of those businesses that offer one or more of the following: accommodation, prepared food and beverage service, and/or entertainment.

Human need.   A state of felt deprivation in a person.

Human want.   The form that a human need takes when shaped by culture and individual personality.

Incentive travel.   A reward that participants receive for achieving or exceeding a goal.

Income segmentation.   Dividing a market into different income groups.

Information gathering.   Sales representatives conduct market research and intelligence work and fill in a call report.

Informative advertising. Advertising used to inform consumers about a new product or feature to build primary demand.

Infrastructure. The system according to which a company, organization, or other body is organized at the most basic level.

Intangibility. A major characteristic of services; they cannot be seen, tasted, felt, heard, or smelled before they are bought.

Integrated direct marketing (IDM). Direct-marketing campaigns that use many vehicles and multiple stages to improve response rates and profits.

Integrated marketing communications. Under this concept the company carefully integrates its many communications channels to deliver a clear, consistent, and compelling message about the organization and its brands.

Interactive marketing. Marketing by a service firm that recognizes perceived service quality depends heavily on the quality of the buyer–seller interaction.

Internal data. Internal data consist of electronic databases and nonelectronic information and records of consumer and market information obtained from within the company.

Internal marketing. Marketing by a service firm to train effectively and motivate its customer-contact employees and all the supporting service people to work as a team to provide customer satisfaction.

Introduction. The product life-cycle stage when a new product is first distributed and made available for purchase.

Joining stage. The product life-cycle stage when the customer makes the initial inquiry contact.

Junket reps. Serve the casino industry as intermediaries for premium players.

Laboratory test. This test uses equipment to measure consumers' physiological reactions to an ad: heartbeat, blood pressure, pupil dilation, and perspiration.

Learning. Changes in a person's behavior arising from experience.

Lifestyle. A person's pattern of living as expressed in his or her activities, interests, and opinions.

Lifetime value (LTV). The lifetime value of a customer is the stream of profits a customer will create over the life of his or her relationship to a business.

Lobbying. Dealing with legislators and government officials to promote or defeat legislation and regulation.

Macrodestinations. Destinations such as the United States that contain thousands of microdestinations, including regions, states, cities, towns, and visitor destinations within a town.

Macroenvironment. The larger societal forces that affect the whole microenvironment: competitive, demographic, economic, natural, technological, political, and cultural forces.

Macroenvironmental forces. Demographic, economic, technological, political, legal, social, and cultural factors.

Market. A set of actual and potential buyers of a product.

Market development strategy. Finding and developing new markets for your current products.

Market homogeneity. If buyers have the same tastes, buy a product in the same amounts, and react the same way to marketing efforts, undifferentiated marketing is appropriate.

Market positioning. Formulating competitive positioning for a product and a detailed marketing mix.

Market potential. The total estimated dollars or unit value of a defined market for a defined product, including competitive products.

Market segmentation. The process of dividing a market into distinct groups of buyers who have different needs, characteristics, or behavior and who might require separate products or marketing programs.

Market targeting. Evaluating each market segment's attractiveness and selecting one or more segments to enter.

Market trends. External trends of many types that are likely to affect the marketing in which a corporation operates.

Marketing. The art and science of finding, retaining, and growing profitable customers.

Marketing concept. The marketing management philosophy that holds that achieving organizational goals depends on determining the needs and wants of target markets and delivering desired satisfactions more effectively and efficiently than competitors.

Marketing dashboards. Are like the instrument panel in a car or plane, visually displaying real-time indicators to ensure proper functioning.

Marketing environment. The actors and forces outside marketing that affect marketing management's ability to develop and maintain successful transactions with its target customers.

Marketing information system (MIS). A structure of people, equipment, and procedures to gather, sort, analyze, evaluate, and distribute needed, timely, and accurate information to marketing decision makers. The MIS begins and ends with marketing managers, but managers throughout the organization should be involved in the MIS. First, the MIS interacts with managers to assess their information needs. Next, it develops needed information from internal company records, marketing intelligence activities, and the marketing research process. Information analysts process information to make it more useful. Finally, the MIS distributes information to managers in the right form and at the right time to help in marketing planning, implementation, and control.

Marketing intelligence. Everyday information about developments in the marketing environment that help managers prepare and adjust marketing plans.

Marketing intermediaries. Firms that help the company to promote, sell, and distribute its goods to final buyers; they include middlemen, physical distribution firms, marketing service agencies, and financial intermediaries.

Marketing management. The art and science of choosing target markets and building profitable relationships with them.

Marketing manager. A person who is involved in marketing analysis, planning, implementation, and control activities.

Marketing mix. Elements include product, price, promotion, and distribution. Sometimes distribution is called place and the marketing situation facing a company.

Marketing opportunity. An area of need in which a company can perform profitably.

Marketing research. The systematic design, collection, analysis, and reporting of data and findings relevant to a specific marketing situation facing a company.

Marketing services agencies. Marketing research firms, advertising agencies, media firms, marketing consulting firms, and other service providers that help a company to target and promote its products to the right markets.

Marketing strategy.   The marketing logic by which the company hopes to create this customer value and achieve these profitable relationships.

Marketing Web site.   Web sites designed to engage consumers in an interaction that will move them closer to a purchase or other marketing outcome.

Maturity.   The stage in a product life cycle when sales growth slows or levels off.

Media.   Nonpersonal communications channels, including print media (newspapers, magazines, direct mail), broadcast media (radio, television), and display media (billboards, signs, posters).

Medical tourism.   One of the fastest-growing and most lucrative tourism markets. Tourists spend a large amount on medical treatment, stay in top hotels, and often travel around the country after their surgery.

Membership groups.   Groups that have a direct influence on a person's behavior and to which a person belongs.

Microenvironment.   The forces close to a company that affect its ability to serve its customers: the company, market channel firms, customer markets, competitors, and the public.

Microenvironmental forces.   Customers, competitors, distribution channels, and suppliers.

Millennials (also called Generation Y or the echo boomers).   Born between 1977 and 2000, these children of the baby boomers number 83 million, dwarfing the Gen Xers and larger even than the baby-boomer segment. This group includes several age cohorts: tweens (ages 8 to 12), teens (13 to 18), and young adults (the twentysomethings).

Moment of truth.   Occurs when an employee and a customer have contact.

Motivational houses.   Provide incentive travel offered to employees or distributors as a reward for their efforts.

Motive (or drive).   A need that is sufficiently pressing to direct a person to seek satisfaction of that need.

Multichannel marketing.   Multichannel distribution, as when a single firm sets up two or more marketing channels to reach one or more customer segments.

Multiplier effect.   Tourist expenditures that are recycled through the local economy, being spent and spent again.

Mystery shoppers.   Hospitality companies often hire disguised or mystery shoppers to pose as customers and report back on their experience.

National tourist organizations (NTOs).   A national government or quasi-government agency that markets destination tourism.

Observational research.   The gathering of primary data by observing relevant people, actions, and situations.

Olfactory.   The dimension of atmosphere relating to scent and freshness.

Online advertising.   Advertising that appears while consumers are surfing the Web, including display ads, search-related ads, and online classifieds.

Online marketing.   Company efforts to market products and services and build customer relationships over the Internet.

Online social networks.   Online social communities—blogs, social networking, Web sites, or even virtual worlds—where people socialize or exchange information and opinions.

Online travel agency (OTA).   A travel agency that conducts business through the Internet with no physical locations or stores.

Opinion leaders.   People within a reference group who, because of special skills, knowledge, personality, or other characteristics, exert influence on others.

Order-routine specification.   The stage of the industrial buying process in which a buyer writes the final order with the chosen supplier(s), listing the technical specifications, quantity needed, expected time of delivery, return policies, warranties, and so on.

Organization image.   The way a person or group views an organization.

Organizational buying process.   The decision-making process by which formal organizations establish the need for purchased products and services and identify, evaluate, and choose among alternative brands and suppliers.

Organizational culture.   The pattern of shared values and beliefs that gives members of an organization meaning and provides them with the rules for behavior in that organization.

Overpositioning.   Giving buyers a too-narrow picture of the company.

Patronage rewards.   Cash or other awards for regular use of a company's products or services.

Performance review.   The stage of an industrial buying process in which a buyer rates its satisfaction with suppliers, deciding whether to continue, modify, or drop the relationship.

Perishability.   A major characteristic of services; they cannot be stored for later use.

Personal selling.   Personal presentation by the firm's sales force to make sales and build customer relationships.

Personality.   A person's distinguishing psychological characteristics that lead to relatively consistent and lasting responses to his or her environment.

Phase-out.   The ideal method of removing an unpopular or unprofitable product; it enables a product to be removed in an orderly fashion.

Physical evidence.   Tangible clues such as promotional material, employees of the firm, and the physical environment of the firm. Physical evidence is used by a service firm to make its product more tangible to customers.

Point-of-purchase (POP) promotions.   Includes displays and demonstrations that take place at the time of sale.

Political environment.   Laws, government agencies, and pressure groups that influence and limit the activities of various organizations and individuals in society.

Portfolio tests.   Consumers view or listen to a portfolio of advertisements, taking as much time as they need.

Premiums.   Goods offered either free or at low cost as an incentive to buy a product.

Press relations.   Placing newsworthy information into the news media to attract attention.

Press release.   Information released to the media about certain new products or services.

Price.   The amount of money charged for a product or service, or the sum of the values that consumers exchange for the benefits of having or using the product or service.

Primary data.   Information collected for the specific purpose at hand.

Problem recognition. The stage of the industrial buying process in which someone in a company recognizes a problem or need that can be met by acquiring a good or a service.

Product concept. A detailed version of a product idea stated in meaningful consumer terms.

Product idea. Envisioning a possible product that company managers might offer to the market.

Product image. The way that consumers picture an actual or potential product.

Product publicity. Various efforts to publicize specific products.

Product specification. The stage of an industrial buying process in which the buying organization decides on and specifies the best technical product characteristics for a needed item.

Production concept. Holds that customers will favor products that are available and highly affordable, and therefore management should focus on production and distribution efficiency.

Promotion mix. The specific mix of advertising, personal selling, sales promotion, and public relations a company uses to pursue its advertising and marketing objectives.

Prospecting. The process of searching for new accounts.

Psychocentrics. Persons who do not desire change when they travel. They like to visit nonthreatening places and stay in familiar surroundings.

Psychographic segmentation. Dividing a market into different groups based on social class, lifestyle, or personality characteristics.

Public. Any group that has an actual or potential interest in or impact on an organization's ability to achieve its objectives.

Public relations. The process by which a positive image and customer preference are created through third-party endorsement.

Pulsing. Scheduling ads unevenly over a given period.

Purpose of a business. To create and maintain satisfied, profitable customers.

Quotas. Quantitative and time-specific accomplishment measurements established for members of a sales force.

Recall tests. The advertiser asks people who have been exposed to magazines or television programs to recall everything they can about the advertisers and products that they saw.

Recognition tests. The researcher asks readers of, for instance, a given issue of a magazine to point out what they have seen.

Reference groups. Groups that have a direct (face-to-face) or indirect influence on a person's attitude or behavior.

Relationship marketing. Involves creating, maintaining, and enhancing strong relationships with customers and other stakeholders.

Reminder advertising. Advertising used to keep consumers thinking about a product.

Retailer. Business whose sales come primarily from retailing.

Return on marketing investment (or marketing ROI). The net return from a marketing investment divided by the costs of the marketing investment. It measures the profits generated by investments in marketing activities.

Revenue management. A pricing method using price as a means of matching demand with capacity.

Role. The activities that a person is expected to perform according to the persons around him or her.

Run-out. Removing a product after existing stock has been depleted; used when sales for an item are low and costs exceed revenues, such as the case of a restaurant serving a crabmeat cocktail with sales of only one or two items per week.

Sales promotion. Consists of short-term incentives to encourage the purchase or sale of a product or service.

Sample. (1) A segment of a population selected for marketing research to represent the population as a whole; (2) offer of a trial amount of a product to consumers.

Samples. Offers of a trial amount of a product.

Search-related ads (or contextual advertising). Text-based ads and links that appear alongside search engine results on sites such as Google and Yahoo!

Secondary data. Information that already exists somewhere, having been collected for another purpose.

Self-concept. Self-image, the complex mental pictures people have of themselves.

Selling. Sales representatives know the art of salesmanship: approaching, presenting, answering objections, and closing sales.

Selling concept. The idea that consumers will not buy enough of an organization's products unless the organization undertakes a large selling and promotion effort.

Service culture. A system of values and beliefs in an organization that reinforces the idea that providing the customer with quality service is the principal concern of the business.

Service profit chain. A model that shows the relationships between employee satisfaction, customer satisfaction, customer retention, value creation, and profitability.

Servicing. Sales representatives provide various services to the customers: consulting on their problems, rendering technical assistance, arranging financing, and expediting delivery.

SMERF. SMERF stands for social, military, educational, religious, and fraternal organizations. This group of specialty markets has a common price-sensitive thread.

Social classes. Relatively permanent and order divisions in a society whose members share similar values, interests, and behaviors.

Societal marketing concept. The idea that an organization should determine the needs, wants, and interests of target markets and deliver the desired satisfactions more effectively and efficiently than competitors in a way that maintains or improves the consumer's and society's well-being.

Spam. Unsolicited, unwanted commercial e-mail messages.

Specific product attributes. Price and product features can be used to position a product.

Strategic alliances. Relationships between independent parties that agree to cooperate but still retain separate identities.

Strategic business units (SBUs). A single business or collection of related businesses that can be planned separately from the rest of the company.

Strategic planning. The process of developing and maintaining a strategic fit between the organization's goals and capabilities and its changing marketing opportunities.

Subculture. A group of people with shared value systems based on common life experiences and situations.

Supplier search. The stage of the industrial buying process in which a buyer tries to find the best vendor.

Supplier selection. The stage of the industrial buying process in which a buyer receives proposals and selects a supplier or suppliers.

Suppliers. Firms and individuals that provide the resources needed by a company and its competitors to produce goods and services.

Supply Chain. Upstream and downstream partners. Upstream from the company is a set of firms that supply raw materials, components, parts, information, finances, and expertise needed to create a product. Downstream marketing channel partners, such as wholesalers and retailers, form a vital connection between the firm and its customers.

Supporting products. Extra products offered to add value to the core product and to help differentiate it from the competition.

Survey research. The gathering of primary data by asking people questions about their knowledge, attitudes, preferences, and buying behavior.

Survival. A technique used when a company's or business unit's sales slump, creating a loss that threatens its existence. Because the capacity of a hotel or restaurant is fixed, survival often involves cutting prices to increase demand and cash flow. This can disrupt the market until the firm goes out of business or the economy improves.

SWOT analysis. Evaluates the company's overall strengths (S), weaknesses (W), opportunities (O), and threats (T).

Tactile. The dimension of atmosphere relating to softness, smoothness, and temperature.

Targeting. Sales representatives decide how to allocate their scarce time among prospects and customers.

Telephone marketing. Using the telephone to sell directly to customers.

Timetable. Specific dates to accomplish strategies and tactics.

Total costs. Costs that are the sum of the fixed and variable costs for any given level of production.

Tourism. A stay of one or more nights away from home for holidays, visits to friends or relatives, business conferences, or any other purpose, except such things as boarding, education, or semipermanent employment.

Transaction. Consists of a trade of values between two parties; marketing's unit of measurement.

Underpositioning. Failing ever to position the company at all.

Upselling. Training sales and reservation employees to offer continuously a higher-priced product that will better meet the customers' needs, rather than settling for the lowest price.

Value-based pricing. Uses the buyer's perceptions of value, not the seller's cost, as the key to pricing.

Value proposition. The full positioning of a brand—the full mix of benefits upon which it is positioned.

Variability. A major characteristic of services; their quality may vary greatly, depending on who provides them and when, where, and how they are provided.

Variable costs. Costs that vary directly with the level of production.

Vertical conflict. Conflict between different levels of the same channel.

Vertical marketing systems (VMS). Distribution channel structures in which producers, wholesalers, and retailers act as a unified system: Either one channel member owns the others, or has contracts with them, or has so much power that they all cooperate.

Viral marketing. The Internet version of word-of-mouth marketing—Web sites, videos, e-mail messages, or other marketing events that are so infectious that customers will want to pass them along to friends.

Visual. The dimension of atmosphere relating to color, brightness, size, and shape.

Wholesaler. Firms engaged primarily in wholesaling activity.

Index